Dictionary of EARLY ENGLISH

by

JOSEPH T. SHIPLEY

About the Book

Words likely to be met in literary reading. Chaucer, Spenser, Shakespeare, the Tudor pamphlets and translations, are richly represented in words and illustrative quotations. The late 18th and early 19th century revival has been culled: Chatterton, Ossian; Percy's *Reliques* and Child's *Ballads;* Scott, in his effort to bring picturesque words back into use. In addition, anthologies, for the general reader or the student, have been examined, and works they include combed for forgotten words.

Words that belong to the history of early England, describing or illuminating social conditions, political (e.g. feudal) divisions or distinctions, and all the ways of living, of thinking and feeling, in earlier times. Anxiety, for example, is indicated, not in the 99 *phobias* listed in a psychiatric glossary of the 1950's but in the 120 methods (see *aeromancy*) of determining the future.

Words that in various ways have special interest, as in meaning, background, or associated folklore. Included in this group are various imaginary beings, and a number of magic or medicinal plants.

Words that are not in the general vocabulary today, but might be usefully and pleasantly revived.

LITTLEFIELD, ADAMS & CO.
PATERSON, NEW JERSEY

DICTIONARY OF
EARLY ENGLISH

by

JOSEPH T. SHIPLEY

With a Preface by

MARK VAN DOREN

1963

LITTLEFIELD, ADAMS & CO.
PATERSON, NEW JERSEY

1963 Edition

By LITTLEFIELD, ADAMS & CO.

Printed in the United States of America

To

BURKE *and* THORNE
NICOLE *and* LINDA

PREFACE

Mr. Shipley's *Dictionary* has been a delight to me, and I can imagine no reader, erudite or otherwise, to whom it will be anything less than that. I claim no erudition in my own case; I am not a student of the English language —of its history, at any rate—nor am I, to tell the truth, a scholar of any sort. But this does not prevent me from taking a lively and perpetual interest in the words men use and have used. There is a sense in which man lives by words more than he does by bread; neither is enough for life alone, but whereas all animals must eat in order to keep on being themselves, only man must talk to this same end. And Mr. Shipley shows him, in so far as he talks English, as having pleased himself, generation after generation, by more words than we might suppose would ever be remembered, let alone written or spoken in their time.

Among these there are monsters like *floccinaucinihilipilification* and *honorificabilitudinitatibus* which amuse us rather than enlighten us concerning the way our forebears thought. Mr. Shipley is rightly more interested in a host of terms, gathered by him out of a thousand years, from which we can learn fascinating things about the folklore, the medicine, the psychology, the philosophy, the art, the cookery, the morals, and the entertainments of ages that long since went to sleep and for the most part have ceased even to dream. Yet some of them do dream, and to the extent that we can participate in the experience we may find ourselves edified; for it is not alone in our generation that men have been sensible, acute, and wise. Mr. Shipley is nowhere more interesting than he is in those unobtrusive notes or side-remarks which span like an electrician's arc the distance between dead and living days, and make us wish that we had not thrown away certain words for which we still have the things. "Everyman's wife, in America, is noted for her *emacity*." *Absalonism,* he suggests, might still "serve the psychoanalysts." *Accidie* has been a genuine loss for something we shall have always with us; so has *atonement* in its original meaning; and so perhaps has *glother*—I should love to be able to say to someone, "Don't glother me," and be sure that he understood.

But every reader will find his own examples in this copious work which will so richly repay the investment of long evenings devoted to it; and these evenings need not be merely winter ones; they could be *aestival* as well.

Mark Van Doren

INTRODUCTION

"Forgotten" Words

If a word were completely forgotten, I could not list it here. One man's oblivion, moreover, may be another's crowded store.

Gathered in this DICTIONARY are, in the main, words that have dropped from general use. Many of them are Anglo-Saxon words that have been replaced by other terms, or that describe ways of living that have passed. Others are learned introductions into our tongue, fashioned from Latin or Greek forms, that failed to take long root. In many cases, words came into the language in various forms, only some of which—not always the simplest; see *couth*—may have won survival.

Language is in a constant process of change, of growth here and decay there; although, since recorded writing, no word has wholly died. Some words, indeed, have been so transformed as to mean their own opposite (see *avaunt*). In this DICTIONARY are a few still current words, included because of their old associations, or because of older meanings lapsed from use.

The Basis of Selection

From the vast number of words used in the English past, selection has been guided by the following principles. There have been included:

(1) Words that are likely to be met in literary reading. Chaucer, Spenser, Shakespeare, the Tudor pamphlets and translations, are richly represented in words and illustrative quotations. The late 18th and early 19th century revival has been culled: Chatterton, Ossian; Percy's *Reliques* and Child's *Ballads;* Scott, in his efforts to bring picturesque words back into use. In addition, anthologies, for the general reader or the student, have been examined, and works they include combed for forgotten words.

(2) Words that belong to the history of early England, describing or illuminating social conditions, political (e.g., feudal) divisions or distinctions, and all the ways of living, of thinking and feeling, in earlier times. Anxiety, for example, is indicated, not in the 99 *phobias* listed in a psychiatric glossary of the 1950's but in the 120 methods (see *aeromancy*) of discovering if not influencing the future.

Incidentally, research for this volume has made it quite clear that once upon a time (as all good stories start!) the English were superb cooks. Cardinal

Wolsey had 22 specialists in his private kitchen. Some of the early dishes, recipes of which are given in this volume, water the anticipant mouth. Judging by the dates, it was when the Stuarts returned from their exile in Paris that French menus became the London fashion, so that gradually the native cooking fell into desuetude.—In such ways, the forgotten words send flashes of light upon the olden culture.

(3) Words that in various ways have special interest, as in meaning, background, or associated folklore. Included in this group are various imaginary beings, and a number of magic or medicinal plants.

(4) Words that are not in the general vocabulary today, but might be pleasantly and usefully revived.

The Times' Emphases

Among the many contributions to our English speech, a few tendencies seem notable for our purpose, currents in the two main rivers, Germanic and Romanic-Greek, that have fed the English ocean. From the Norman Conquest (1066) to the 16th century, there was a continuous process of commixion of the Anglo-Saxon tongue and the Norman French, with a seeping in of Latin terms from the law court, and Latin and Greek from the church. The best known example of this amalgamation is in Scott's *Ivanhoe,* where the jester and the swineherd present the point that, when domestic animals have to be cared for and tended, they are the defeated but stalwart Saxon *pig, bull, calf,* or *sheep,* but when they are dressed and served to be eaten, they are the triumphant but tender Norman *pork, beef, veal,* or *mutton.*

This observation, however, was rather Scott's than the jester's; it manifests a consciousness largely lacking in the language growth of those five hundred years. It was in the late 16th century that a conscious concern with words developed widely, never to slacken since. Holinshed in his *Chronicles* (1577) said that Anglo-Saxon was "an hard and rough kind of speech, Godwotte, when our nation was brought first into acquaintance withall." The many monosyllables in the current speech, mainly Anglo-Saxon, were attacked, and a wide-ranging quest of variety was begun, that produced the Elizabethan profusion.

Reaction against newfangled words, inkhorn terms, against phrases borrowed like fashions in dress from Italy, France, and Spain, set in with the surge of national spirit that hailed the defeat (1588) of the Invincible Armada. For the first sixty years of the 17th century, there was a remarkable interest in Anglo-Saxon. An Anglo-Saxon lectureship was established at Cambridge University; a dictionary of the Anglo-Saxon tongue was compiled. Enthusiasts went so far as to declare that the parent of Anglo-Saxon, German, was the oldest and best of all tongues—the original language, indeed, of the Bible.

As the Germans (Cambrians) were not among the builders of the Tower of Babel, their speech in its purity had survived. This boast of preeminence of tongue, in Richard Hawkins' *A Discourse of the Natural Excellences of England* (1685), was expanded to a more general claim: "The English descend from those people of Germany which are called Saxons. These by good authors were esteemed the strongest and valiantest of its nations . . . In a word, they were dreaded for their arms, and commended for their extraordinary chastity: so that the English derive from a most noble and pure fountain, being the offspring of so valiant and so chaste a people."

The courtiers and writers exiled with the Stuarts had other thoughts. Back across the Channel in 1660 came more than Parisian cooking, came also a scorn for the rough though chaste "German" speech of the Puritans, and a taste for the fluent French. James Howell in 1662 declared, of the English tongue, that the French "hath not only enriched but civilized and smoothed her with many thousands of words derived from the Latin."

Some scholars emphasized the idea that in truth all the modern tongues were mutable, were ephemeral, that permanence was to be found only in Hebrew, Latin, and Greek. This was no new notion; while Chaucer in the 14th century was shaping modern English, Gower, to ensure survival, wrote three long poems each in a different tongue. In the 17th century not only church ritual but international correspondence was still carried on in Latin. About 1650, Edmund Waller wrote:

> But who can hope his lines should long
> Last in a daily changing tongue?
> While they are new, envy prevails,
> And as that dies, our language fails.
> Poets that lasting marble seek
> Must carve in Latin or in Greek.

While such opinions did not loose a flood of works in the classical languages —Milton wrote Latin poems, but his major works speak to his countrymen in their own tongue—for a century there were many borrowings from Greek and Latin, the classical words being given English forms. Writers sprinkled Latinisms in their works, as offering alms to oblivion. Macaulay's schoolboy knows how Johnson corrected his lapse into Anglo-Saxon: "It has not wit enough to keep it sweet . . . Hrmph . . . It has not vitality sufficient to preserve it from putrefaction."

Hence it is that many words of Anglo-Saxon origin lapsed from use in the 16th and 17th centuries; while many from Latin and Greek, in those centuries first used, lapsed in the 18th or early 19th century. Not within the scope of this volume, of course, are the many more, along either stream of history, that remain a vital part of our living speech and that, in the joining of their turbulent flow, make English the richest language of all time.

The Period Covered

The centuries covered by this DICTIONARY are, roughly, the 8th to the 18th. Where a word's use was limited, the period is usually indicated in the discussion. Dates of books quoted are, in some cases, approximate; the purpose is to indicate the period during which the word was used.

The Spelling

In the early, more flexible times, many variations of spelling developed; major ones are included. Thus *dole, dool, dule* appear in the general listing; under the main entry, *dole,* thirteen variants are given. In the illustrative quotations, spelling has been shaped to the reader's convenience: the old form of the word under discussion has been retained; with other words, the old spelling is usually retained if the sense is clear. The aim has been to focus attention on the word in hand.

A capital within a quotation usually indicates the beginning of a new line of verse.

Acknowledgments

The indebtedness of a lexicographer extends to all his predecessors. In addition to the literary works of the authors named above, I have had recourse to the more technical volumes listed below, and my thanks go to the many that have lighted and lightened my way. "Forgotten" words have cropped up, also, in many an odd corner of my reading, and friends have frequently asked me whether one of their favorites is in. Beyond all such aid must be listed hers whom I cannot and would not forget, bully in word-play, but ever concerned, the golden thread in the pattern of my days.

WORKS IN MY LIBRARY

An Universal Etymological English Dictionary, **by N. Bailey. London. First Edition, 1721; my copy, 1751.**

A Glossary and Etymological Dictionary, **by W. Toone. London, 1834.**

English Etymologies, **by H. Fox Talbot. London, 1847.**

A Dictionary of the First, or Oldest Words in the English Language, **by the late Herbert Coleridge. London, 1863.**

Dictionary of Obsolete and Provincial English, **by Thos. Wright. London, (2 vols.) 1869.**

A Dictionary of the Old English Language, by Francis Henry Stratmann. Krefeld, 1878.

A Glossary . . . in the works of English authors, particularly Shakespeare and his contemporaries, by Robert Nares, with additions by Halliwell and Wright. London (2 vols.), 1882.

Renaissance Dictionaries, by De Witt T. Starnes. Austin, 1954.

A Shakespeare Glossary, by C. T. Onions. Oxford, 1941.

Shakespeare's Bawdy, by Eric Partridge. New York, 1948.

Two dozen dictionaries and glossaries of cant, slang, and specialized vocabularies. An excellent general volume is the *Dictionary of Slang and Unconventional English,* by Eric Partridge. New York, 1908.

The Oxford English Dictionary (13 vols.). Referred to in the text as the O. E. D.—being a revision of the *New English Dictionary on Historical Principles.* The most comprehensive dictionary of the kind in any language, especially rich in illustrative quotations; to it, all succeeding lexicographers, myself included, owe an inestimable debt.

OTHER WORKS FOUND USEFUL

The Dictionary of Thomas Eliot knyght. 1538.

An Alvearie or triple dictionarie . . . by John Baret. 1573.

Bibliotheca Scholastica, by John Rider. 1589.

A Worlde of Wordes, by John Florio. 1598 (enlarged 1611).

A Dictionarie of the French and English Tongues, by Cotgrave. 1611.

Glossographia, by Thos. Blount. 1656.

A Collection of English Words Not Generally Used, by John Ray. 1674.

Dictionary . . . by E. Coles. 1676.

B.E.'s Dictionary of the Canting Crew. 1700.

Vocabularium Anglo-Saxonicum, by Thos. Benson. 1701.

Grose's Dictionary of the Vulgar Tongue. 1785.

Welsh and English Dictionary, by W. Owen. 1793.

A Dictionary of the Anglo-Saxon Language, by J. Bosworth. 1838.

A Dictionary of Archaic and Provincial Words, by J. O. Halliwell. 1850.

Slang and Its Analogues, by Farmer and Henley (7 vols.). 1904.

J. T. S.

A

aadorn. An afternoon repast; afternoon. Also *aandorn; arndern* is evening. Used to the 13th century.

aande. Breath. Not uncommon in the 15th century, as in Hampole: *Hys mynde es schort when he oght thynkes, Hys nese* [nose] *oft droppes, hys aande stynkes.*

aas. An early form of *ace, aces.*

abacinate. To blind by holding red hot metal close to the eyes. Latin *ab,* off + *bacinus,* basin. Hence *abacination;* a mild medieval torture.

abactor. One who steals cattle in herds. From Latin *ab,* away + *agere,* to drive. Hence, *abaction,* cattle-stealing. Hammond in his commentary ON PSALMS (1659) speaks of *abactors, whose breaking in . . . is attended with the cattles passing through or going out.* Lamb, in a letter of 1829, refers to an *abactor's wife.* There is no English verb *to abact,* but N. Bailey's ETYMOLOGICAL DICTIONARY of 1751 includes *abacted,* drawn away by stealth or violence.

abafelled. Treated scornfully; an early form (and sense) of *baffled.*

abalienate. To estrange; to make mad. From Latin *ab-,* away + *alienare,* to estrange, to give to another; *alienus,* belonging to another. John Gaule in PYSMANTIA THE MAG-ASTRO-MANCER (1651) says: *Extasies of prophets did not so abalienate their minds as that they apprehended not what they did.* S. Clark in his LIVES (1683) states: *Neither difference of opinion, nor distance of place, nor seldomness of converse, nor any worldly respect, did cause the least abalienation.* Note that one meaning of *alienation* (from 1450 on) is also loss of mental faculties; Lord Brougham on THE BRITISH CONSTITUTION (1862) speaks of *a state of mental alienation.*

abarcy. A state of always desiring more. In the 1731 edition of his ETYMOLOGICAL DICTIONARY, N. Bailey traces this to a medieval Latin word *abartia,* insatiableness. The word, in both languages, seems to be the lexicographer's invention. The present lexicographer, in a 1953 letter to THEATRE ARTS, invented the word *euciliast,* a deliberately pompous term (*eu,* good + *cilia,* hairs + *-ast,* an eager one) for a person interested in hirsute adornment. In similar vein, H. L. Mencken offered the word *ecdysiast* as an elevated term for the burlesque 'strip-teaser.' This has, however, counterpart in other creatures; *ecdysis* (from Greek *ec-, ex-,* out, off + *dyein,* to put) is the scientific term for the shedding of its shell by the crayfish, and for other such slough.

abarnare. To report or disclose a secret crime. The word seems another invention of the fertile N. Bailey in his ETYMOLOGICAL DICTIONARY (1751).

abastardize. To render illegitimate or base. Daniel in THE QUEEN'S ARCADIA (1605) wrote: *Being ourselves Corrupted* *and abastardized thus, Thinke all lookes ill, that doth not looke like us.* Also *to abastard.*

abastick. Insatiable. *Cp. abarcy.*

abate. In the 13th century (Robert of Gloucester's CHRONICLE) *abate* meant not to lessen, but to put an end to, to cease.

abawe. To astonish, confound. Also *abaue; abave.* Also, to bow, *cp. abow.* Chaucer, in THE ROMAUNT OF THE ROSE (1366) has: *For soche another, as I gesse, Aforne ne was, ne more vermaile; I was abawed for merveile.*

abb. The woof or weft in something woven. Also *awebb, oweb;* Old English *awefan; a,* up + *wefan,* to weave.

abbey-lubber. A lazy monk; a fat sluggard, a porridge-belly. A term used in scorn by the anti-Catholics of the 16th and 17th centuries. Thus Cotgrave in 1611 defined *archimarmitonerastique: an abbey-lubber, or arch-frequenter of the cloyster beefe-pot.* THE BURNYNGE OF PAULES CHURCH (1563) said it was a *commen proverbe to call him an abbey-lubber, that was idle, wel fed, a long lewd lither loiterer, that might worke and would not.*

abbord. See *abord.*

abditorium. A secret place, especially for hiding things. Also *abditory.* From the Latin *abdere, abditum,* from *ab,* away + *dare,* to put. The word is used of a chest in which religious relics are kept, or money—but also, by Dr. Robinson in EUDOXA (1658) to say: *In the center of the kernel of grain, as the safest abditory, is the source of germination.* Hence also *abditive,* remote, hidden.

abdominous. Paunch-bellied; unwieldy. This is, of course, *abdomen* + *ous,* full of. The origin of *abdomen* is unknown; it may be related to *abdere,* to put away, or to *adipem, adipomem,* fat. Cleveland in the DIALOGUE OF TWO ZEALOTS (1651) says: *It's so abdominous, the Trojan Horse was not so fully lined.* H. M. Stanley, whose most famous words are "Dr. Livingstone, I presume?", spoke in THE DARK CONTINENT (1878) of a native *surrounded by fat wives and abdominous brats.* Several members of the New York sophisticates' Three-hours-for-lunch Club were, as might be expected, *abdominous.*

abece. A B C; the alphabet, or an alphabet-book. In Robert of Gloucester's CHRONICLE, 13th century: *He was more than ten yer old ar he couthe ys abece. Cp. abecedary; absey-book.*

abecedary. An alphabet book; a primer. Used from the 15th to the 18th century; also *abscedary, absedary. ABCDary;* accent on the *see.* Also used as an adjective, relating to the alphabet; needing the alphabet, illiterate. Also *abecedarie; abecedario* (plural *abecedarii*), a teacher, or a learner, of the ABC's. *Cp. abece; absey-book.* Florio in his translation (1603) of Montaigne said: *There is a kind of abecedarie ignorance preceding science; another, doctorall, following science.*

abeche. To feed; to satisfy. From Old French *abeschier; a,* to, with + *bec,* beak: the early references were to birds. Gower in CONFESSIO AMANTIS (1393) has: *Yit schulde I sum delle been abeched, And for the tyme wel refreched.*

abelde. Become bold. In the romance of KYNG ALYSAUNDER, 13th century.

abequitate. To ride away. Latin *ab,* away + *equus,* horse. In 17th century dictionaries.

abie. See *abye.*

abigail. A waiting-woman. In the BIBLE

(First Book of Samuel, XXV. 24-31) Abigail of Carmel throws herself at the feet of King David, calling herself "thine handmaid . . . I pray thee, forgive the trespass of thine handmaid . . . thine handmaid"—until he marries her. In Beaumont and Fletcher's play The Scornful Lady (1610) the "waiting gentlewoman" is named Abigail; from the popularity of the play, the name became the common term for a maid-servant. Smollett in Humphrey Clinker (1771) speaks of *an antiquated abigail, dressed in her lady's cast clothes.* Congreve in The Old Bachelor (1693) indicates another role she often played: *Thou art some forsaken abigail we have dallied with heretofore.*

abject. As a noun, a servile person; one cast off, an outcast. Latin *abicere,* to cast off; *ab,* away + *iacere, iactum* (in compounds *iectum,* whence also *conjecture* and many an *object*). Shakespeare in Richard III (1592) speaks of *the Queen's abjects;* Shelley in Prometheus Unbound (1818): *The subject of a tyrant's will Became, worse fate! the abject of his own.*

ablactation. Weaning of a child from the mother. From the Latin *ab,* from + *lactare,* to suckle, from *lac, lactis,* milk —the *galactic* universe is the Milky Way. *Ablaction* is also used of a type of grafting trees in which the "mother" tree is so close to the new stock that they may be at first joined, then gradually separated. Hence *ablactate,* to wean; *ablacted,* weaned.

ablaqueate, ablaqueation. This is a term drawn from Roman husbandry: Latin *ab,* from + *laqueatum,* entangled, from *laqueus,* a noose. It meant at first loosening hard soil around the roots of trees, so that their fibres might spread. Later, it meant (Bailey's Dictionary, 1751) to lay bare "the bottom of the trunks and roots of trees, that so being exposed to the sun and air, etc. they may bear fruit the better."

ablegate. To send abroad; to send far off, as used to be done with a son in disgrace. Latin *ab,* away + *legare, legatum,* to send on a message, whence *legate.* An *ablegate* is (still) a messenger of the pope, that brings his insignia to a newly appointed cardinal. Hence *ablegation,* despatch, dismissal. Used in the 17th century.

ablende. To make blind. In Robert of Gloucester's Chronicle, 13th century.

ablepsy. Blindness. Greek *a,* not + *blepso,* I see. Also figuratively, as in Urquhart's The Jewel (1652): *Who doubteth, that is not blinded with the ablepsie of an implicite zeal?*

abligate. To bind away from; to tie up so as to keep away. Latin *ab,* from + *ligare, ligatum,* to bind, whence *ligature.* An 18th century dictionary word (Bailey; Johnson). Also *abligation.*

abligurition. Squandering, spending lavishly, on food and drink. Latin *ab,* away + *ligurire,* to eat delicately, to enjoy dainties; *lingere,* to lick; *lingua,* the tongue. Some 17th century dictionaries give the form *abligury, abligurie,* spending in belly-cheer.

abluted. Washed away; washed clean. Latin *ab,* away + *luere, lutum,* to wash. *Abluvion,* that which is washed away. *Ablution,* the act or process of washing clean: in alchemy first, the purification of bodies with suitable liquids; Chaucer in The Canon's Yeoman's Prologue (1386) speaks of *oyles ablucioun, and metal fusible.* Then, washing the body as a religious rite (16th century); thence (mid-18th century) the washing of one's person. When George Gissing, the Grub Street writer (1857-1903) found it necessary to use the British Museum Library as his washroom, he came one morning to discover the sign, *For casual ablutions only.* Although the positive form seems not to have been used in English, that which cannot be washed clean, or washed away, is *inablutible.*

abodement. A foreboding, especially of ill. Also to *abode,* to presage, to be ominous; an *abode* was also (17th century) a prediction. Shakespeare has both noun and verb in HENRY VI, PART THREE (1590): *The owle shrieked at thy birth, an evill signe, The night-crow cryde, aboding locklesse time . . . Tush man, aboadments must not now affright us.*

aboht. A 13th century form of *bought.*

abolete. Obsolete. Latin *abolere, aboletum,* to abolish; *ab,* away + the root *ob, or,* to grow, whence also *origin; abortive; adolescent; proletarian.* Skelton in WHY COME YE NOT TO COURTE? (1522) spoke of those that *dare use this experiens To practyse such abolete sciens.* I wonder when our sciens will seem abolete.

abone. (1) To make good or seasonable; to ripen. (2) an early form of above. (3) well. The 14th century SIR GAWAYNE spoke of *a good swerde, what wolde byte abone.*

abord. To approach; enter, take footing upon; to accost; to challenge. Also *abourd, abbord, abboard;* later *aboard;* French *aborder,* from *à bord,* to the side of. It was also used as a noun, manner or avenue of approach, as in Lassels' VOYAGE TO ITALY (1670), of Genoa: *I never saw a more stately abord to any city then to this. abordage,* an attack on a ship by boarding it. *abordering,* neighboring. Greville in THE LIFE OF THE RENOWNED SIR PHILIP SIDNEY (1652) calls Sidney *born in too strong a fortification of nature for the less worthy to abbord, either with question, familiarity, or scorn.*

abow. To make bend; to bow. *Cp. abawe.* He *abueth;* past tense forms, *abuyde, abouynde.* In Robert of Gloucester's CHRONICLE, 13th century.

abowes. Patron saints. French *avoués,* sworn ones, devotés. Used in Robert of Gloucester's CHRONICLE, 13th century.

abrade. See *abrase.*

abraham. A tawny or brown color; applied to human hair. Also *abram.* Perhaps a corruption of auburn, which was sometimes spelled *abron.* But Shakespeare, who uses the term in CORIOLANUS (1607): *Our heads are some brown, some black, some abram, some bald,* in THE MERRY WIVES OF WINDSOR tells us Slender has a *Cain colored beard;* and many writers speak of *Judas-hair.* In the old tapestries Judas' hair was red; Cain's, yellow; Abraham's, brown. The 1685 edition of CORIOLANUS altered *abram* to *auburn.* An *Abraham man, Abram man,* was a vagabond, especially after the closing of the monasteries, as Amdelay said in THE FRATERNITYE OF VACABONDES (1565), *that walketh bare armed and bare legged, and fayneth him selfe mad.*

abraid. To wrench or pull out, to draw (a sword); to start, as out of sleep; to startle, arouse; to burst into speech or sudden cry. Chaucer in THE SQUIRE'S TALE (1386) says *she gan of swoun abreyde.* Lydgate uses the word in these senses (it is from Old English *a,* back + *bregdan,* to twist), but he adds another meaning, to consort with, to frequent, as in his translation (1430) of Bochas' FALL OF PRINCES: *To thy flatterers I never did abrayde. See abray.*

abraxas. This meaningless word was used in cabalistic writings as a charm. It was also engraved on rings and gems worn as a talisman; hence Warburton in 1738 speaks of *gems called abraxas.*

abray. An error by Spenser for *abraid, q. v.* Spenser took the form *abraid, abrayde,* as though it were the past tense of *abray.* He uses the verb four times, e.g. THE FAËRIE QUEENE (1596): *the brave maid would not for courtesy Out of his quiet slumber him abrade.*

abrodietical. This word appears in 17th century dictionaries, from the Greek *abrodiaitos,* as meaning eating daintily, or a person of delicate ways. No instance of its use has been found.

abrook. To endure; replaced by *brook.* Shakespeare in HENRY VI, PART TWO (1590) says: *Sweet Nell, ill can thy noble mind abrooke the abject people, gazing on thy face.*

abrase. To rub or wear off. Also to *abrade,* Latin *ab,* off + *radere, rasum,* to smooth, scrape, shave. Also *abraded, abrased, abrase,* with all marks rubbed off; blank, clear. Jonson in CYNTHIA'S REVELS (1600) remembers the Latin *tabula rasa: The fourth, in white, is Apheleia, a nymph as pure and simple as the soul, or as an abrase table, and is therefore called Simplicity.*

abruption. A breaking off, as in one's utterance. Latin *ab,* off + *rumpere, ruptum,* to break; whence *abrupt, corruption, eruption, rupture.* Thus Shakespeare, in TROILUS AND CRESSIDA (1606): *Troilus: O Cressida, how often have I wished me thus! Cressida: Wisht my Lord? the gods grant—O my Lord, Troilus: What should they grant? What makes this pretty abruption?*

absalonism. The practice of rebellion against a father, from the ways of the son of David, in the BIBLE. Listed in Bailey's DICTIONARY (1751), this word never came into use, but might well serve the psychoanalysts.

absconce. To hide. Used in the 16th century. Latin *abscondere, absconditus; absconsus,* to hide; *ab,* away + *con,* together + *dare,* to put. This is an early form of *abscond,* which in the 17th century meant to hide; then, to hide oneself (as when one seeks to elude the law). Hence *abscond, absconded,* hidden; D'Urfey in PILLS TO PURGE MELANCHOLY (1719) is *pleased with the thought that he should sit abscond and see them.* Also *abscondence, abscondment,* concealment, seclusion. In monasteries and churches, an *absconce* was a dark lantern.

absentaneous. This word, which never grew into use, is found in 18th century dictionaries. Fashioned by analogy with *instantaneous,* etc., it refers to something done in absence, or while one is absent.

absey-book. An a-b-c-book, a hornbook. See *abece.* Shakespeare has in KING JOHN (1596): *And then comes answer like an absey-book.*

absinthe. See *wormwood.*

absist. To desist, withdraw. Latin *ab,* from + *sistere,* to stand, reduplicative of *stare, statum,* to be erect, whence *status, destiny, obstinate.* The agent-verb was *statuere,* to make stand, to set up, whence *statue, statute, obstinate, obstacle, restitution, destitute; resistance; assist, desist.* The first meaning of *to assist* was to be present at, which *assister* still means in French. Raleigh in A HISTORY OF THE WORLD (1614) wrote: *They promised to absist from their purpose of making a war.*

absoil. See *assoil.*

absonism. The practice of being discordant in the use of language, incongruous, absurd—or an instance of such incongruity. From the Latin *ab,* away + *sonus,* sound + *ism,* this term was used only by Thomas Nashe, in STRANGE NEWS (1592): *Everie third line hath some of this over-rackt absonisme.* The adjective *absonous,* incongruous, unreasonable, was more frequently used through the 17th century, though even the still current *absonant* was employed in the same sense. (All have the accent on the first syllable.)

abster. To deter. Latin *ab(s),* from + *terrere,* to frighten. Becon in A PLEASANTE NEWE NOSEGAY (1542) wrote that *unfeigned humility . . . also absterreth and frayeth us from all arrogancy, pride, and elation of mind.*

abuccinate. To trumpet abroad, to proclaim. This word, from Latin *bucina,* a trumpet, occurs only once in the language, in T. Newton's essay (1569) on CICERO: *But all men cannot be Scipiones or Maximi, to abuccinate and recount what Cities they have sacked.* Modern publicity serves the same purpose. See *ebuccinate.* Latin *bucina* may be from *bovicina,* from *bos, bovis,* bull (from the bull's horn used as a trumpet) + the root *can,* to sound, to sing; but note also that *bucca* means the cheek, as the wall of the mouth. The mouth-piece of a helmet, in Latin, was *buccula;* and *bucca* itself is used, as a figure of speech, for a trumpeter.

abusion. Misuse; deceit; violation of law or right. The old (14th through 16th century) noun of the verb *abuse,* from Latin *ab,* away + *uti, usus,* use. A very common word, often used by Chaucer, Caxton, Occlere, Penn, Spenser, e.g., in THE FAËRIE QUEENE (1596): *Foolish delights and fond abusions, Which do that sense besiege with fond illusions.*

abuyde. See *abow.*

aby. See *abye.*

abydocomist. Stating that the inhabitants of *Abydos* were known for their slanderous tongues, Bailey in his DICTIONARY (1751) defines the *abydocomist* as a sycophant who boasts of his successes achieved by flattery and falsehood. Do you know such a fellow?

abye. This was an early alternate form of *buy;* having the prefix *a,* it meant to buy from or buy back. In the sense of pay for, it came to be used, figuratively, to pay the penalty for. It died out of the language about 1600; the latest recorded use was in Beaumont and Fletcher's THE KNIGHT OF THE BURNING PESTLE (1613): *Foolhardy knight, full soon thou shalt aby this fond reproach; thy body will I bang.* Then the word was revived by Sir Walter Scott, in the LORD OF THE ISLES (1815): *By Heaven . . . they shall abye it!* and used by others since, as Bancroft in his HISTORY OF THE UNITED STATES (1876): *Dearly did the Cherokees aby their rising.* Also (13th century) *abie, abigge;* past tense *aboughte.* In the early uses, from paying the penalty the word *abye* came also to mean to suffer, to endure; and in the sense of endure it came also to mean to last—in which meaning *abye* was confused with *abide.* Thus Spenser, who uses the word twenty times in THE FAËRIE QUEENE (1596) observes that *nought that wanteth rest can long aby.*

ac. But. Common from the 10th to the 15th century. Also *ak, oc, ok, ah, ach,* and the like. When Orfeo (*cp. levedi*) found his wife stricken, *He asked conseil at ech man, Ac no man him help no can.* For another instance of its use, see *ferly.*

academe. See *deme.*

Acadina. Used in the expression *to sink in Acadina.* Acadina was a fountain in Sicily wherein a false oath written on a tablet would sink. The lie lay heavy on the board. The word is listed in Bailey's DICTIONARY (1751).

acate. Originally this meant purchasing, then a thing purchased. It is from Norman *achater* (French *acheter,* to buy). In the plural, *acates,* things purchased, it was used of all provisions not baked and brewed at home; hence, delicacies. In this sense it was shortened (about 1450) to *cates.* The purchaser, then provider and preparer of *cates,* delicacies, was an *acater,* later *caterer.* Variant forms were *achate* (used by Chaucer and Spenser); hence *achater, achatour, achatry (acatery),* the room of the *achatour.* Ben Jonson in THE SAD SHEPHERD (1637) speaks of *all choice that plenty can send in: bread, wine, acates, fowl, feather, fish or fin.* In THE DEVIL IS AN ASS (1637), Jonson has: *He is my wardrobe man, my acater, cook, butler and steward.*

acatharsy. Filth, impurity; lack of purging. Greek *a,* not + *katharsios,* purging; *kathairein,* to cleanse; hence also the tragic *catharsis* (described by Aristotle as the consequence of tragedy, which through the arousal of pity and horror effects their purging) and the physical *cathartics.*

accend. To kindle, to set on fire. From the Latin *ad,* to + *cendere,* to light, from *candere,* to glow—whence also *candid* and *candidate,* one (originally) garbed in white as a sign he was seeking office. Trevisa about 1440 speaks of a stone called asbestos, "which accended once is never extinct." The noun is *accension;* Shelvocke in his treatise on ARTILLERY (1729) speaks of *the great quantity of windy exhalation, produced by the accension of the salpeter.* The verb may be used figuratively, as in Twyne's ÆNEID (1573): *The valiant brothers band with grief accensed in ire.* In this use, *accensed* has been supplanted by *incensed.*

acceptilation. A term in Roman law: canceling a debt by a receipt from the creditor—who has not been paid. Latin *accepti lationem,* accounting (a thing) as received. Hence, *to acceptilate,* to discharge a debt in this fashion. Used also as a religious term (16th and 17th centuries) applied to Christ's forgiveness. *Our justification which comes by Christ,* said Jeremy Taylor in his ANSWER TO THE BISHOP OF ROCHESTER (1656), *is by imputation and acceptilation, by grace and favour.*

accidie. This is the English form of the Latin *acedia,* sloth—the fourth cardinal sin, from Greek *a,* not + *kedos,* care: the state of not caring. Also *acyde, accydye, acedy* (17th century), torpor. It was thought of, by the ecclesiastics, especially as an indisposition to devotion. The word was quite common, from the ANCREN RIWLE (1230)—used by Chaucer, Gower, Caxton—to the middle of the 16th century. Bailey in his 1731 DICTIONARY lists *accidious,* slothful; he omits it from the 1751 edition, presumably because he found no instance of its use. Neither has anyone else. The origin of the word *accidie* was forgotten for several centuries, during which it was supposed to be derived from *acid,* sour, hence repulsive, or from *accidere,* to happen as by a spell, an *access.* Chaucer, who uses the word eighteen times just in THE PARSON'S TALE (1386), calls it this *roten-herted sinne,* and warns that one needs *great corage against accidie.*

accite. To summon, to quote; an early form of *cite.* Also to arouse, an alternate form of *excite.* Used by Chapman, Donne, Jonson, Milton; Shakespeare uses it in both senses: in TITUS ANDRONICUS: *He by the Senate is accited home from weary wars;* In HENRY IV, PART TWO (1597): *And what accites your most worshipful thought to think so?*

accoup. See *acoup.*

accoutre. To dress, equip. Also *acoutre, accoustre;* French *à* to + *coustre,* the church vestry keeper, one of whose function was to robe the clergyman. Used mainly in the participial form; Shakespeare in JULIUS CAESAR (1601) has Cassius boast: *Upon the word, accoutred as I was, I plunged in.* Hence *accoutrement* (mainly in the plural), apparel, equipment; especially of a soldier, except his arms and dress. Shakespeare in THE MERRY WIVES OF WINDSOR: *Not onely in the simple office of love, but in all the accustrement, complement, and ceremony of it.*

accoy. To calm, appease; to soothe; coax; tame, daunt. Old French *à* to + *coi,* calm; Latin *quietum,* whence also *quietude.* Spenser in THE FAËRIE QUEENE (1596) tells: *I received was, And oft imbrast . . . And with kind words accoyd.*

acedy. See *accidie.*

aceldama. A field of bloodshed; a scene of slaughter. Pronounced with a *k* sound, accent on the *dah;* Aramaic *okel damo,* the field of blood; the field near Jerusalem bought with the blood money given to Judas Iscariot, and in which (THE BIBLE: Acts 1) "falling headlong, he burst asunder in the midst, and all his bowels gushed out." Young in NIGHT THOUGHTS (1742) spoke of *earth's aceldama;* De Quincey said that THE CAESARS (1859) *all brought their tributes of beauty or deformity to these vast aceldamas of Rome.* Gilbert in PATIENCE (1881) has the poem *"Heart Foam": Oh to be wafted away From the black aceldama of sorrow, Where the dust of an earthy today Is the earth of a dusty tomorrow.*

acele. To seal. Also *asele.* In Robert of Gloucester's CHRONICLE, 13th century.

acephalist. One that acknowledges no superior. Greek *a,* not + *kephale,* head. Hence *acephal, acephalan, acephalous,* recognizing no head; headless; a headless animal or man. The *acephali* were a race of men without heads, as the *cynocephali* were men with heads like those of dogs. Also *acephalisis, akephalisis* (accent on the *phal*), headlessness; refusal to recognize a head or leader; applied (17th century) to the condition of a country without a head.

acerb. Bitter. Latin *acerbus,* harsh to the taste, surviving in *acerbity.* Shakespeare has, in the First Folio OTHELLO (1604): *The food that to him now is luscious as locusts shall be to him shortly acerb as coloquintida.*

acerophobia. See *aeromancy.*

acersecomic. One whose hair has never been cut. Also an adjective; Greek *akersekomes,* with unshorn hair. In 17th century dictionaries.

achape. See *chape.*

achate. See *acate.* (Modern French *acheter,* to buy.)

achesoun. See *anchesoun.*

acme. The period of full growth, the full bloom of life. So used especially in the 17th century. Jonson in the Prologue to THE STAPLE OF NEWS (1624) says: *He must be one that can instruct your youth And keepe your acme in the state of truth.*

acolaust. A riotous liver. Greek *a,* not + *kolastos,* chastened. Applied to the prodigal, in the Biblical parable, by T. Adams in his EXPOSITION (1633) of THE SECOND GENERAL EPISTLE OF PETER. Hence *acolaustic,* preferably *acolastic,* unbridled, licentious, lascivious.

acomelyd. Enervated with cold. In the PROMPTORIUM PARVULORUM (1440).

aconite. A plant, wolf's-bane; an extract from this plant, used as a poison; hence, a deadly poison. Shakespeare uses *aconitum* in HENRY IV PART TWO (1597); Dekker, in a note to NEWES FROM HELL (1606): *Ingenious, fluent, facetious T. Nash, from whose abundant pen hony flow'd to thy friends, and mortall aconite to thy enemies.* Hence (Urquhart, 1642) *aconital,* poisonous.

acopede. A variant form of the past tense of *aculp, q.v.* Used in Robert of Gloucester's CHRONICLE, 13th century.

acore. To make sorry; to grieve. Hence *acorye,* chastened, punished. In Robert of Gloucester's CHRONICLE, 13th century.

acoup. To accuse. By way of the French *acoulper,* from Latin *ad,* to + *culpare,* blame—whence English *culpable,* etc. Langland in PIERS PLOWMAN (1377) uses *till conscience acouped him;* Blount (1717) and Bailey (1731) in their dictionaries quote this as *his conscience accouped him.*

acoynte. An early form (in the METRICAL CHRONICLE of Robert of Gloucester; 1297) of *acqueynt, acquainted.* Gower also used *acqueynt* for quenched: *so that me thynketh, my thurst shall never be acqueynt.*

acquist. The act of acquiring; that which has been acquired. Used by Milton at the end of SAMSON AGONISTES (1671): *His servants he with new acquist Of true experience from this great event With peace and consolation hath dismist.* Also *acquest,* which is commonly used for the thing acquired, *acquist* being used for the action of acquiring.

acrasia. Intemperance. Used nine times by Spenser who in THE FAËRIE QUEENE (1596) personifies *Acrasy* as the Enchantress of intemperance. Late Latin *acrasia* probably fuses and confuses Greek *akrasia* (second *a* long), meaning in a badly mixed state and *akrasia* (second *a* short), incontinence, lack of power.

acratism. A cordial, a drink before meals, as an appetizer. Accent on the first syllable. Greek *akratos,* neat (wine); *akratisma,* breakfast.

acrilogy. Bitter speaking; the use of sharp words, as in reproof or scorn. Latin *acer, acris,* sharp; Greek *logos,* word. Used in the 17th century.

acrisy. Lack of judgment. Also, from medieval Latin *acrisia,* a state of disease "in which no right judgment can be made of it, or of the patient, whether he will recover or no." So Bailey's DICTIONARY (1731); the few known uses of the word employ the Latin form. It is from Greek *a,* not + *crisis,* a judging, a quarrel, related to *crites,* a judge, *criterion,* and *critikos, critic.* Many a reputed critic suffers from *acrisy.*

acrity. Keenness, sharpness. Latin *acris,* keen; also *alacrity.* But *acritude* (*acridity* as well) is limited to sharpness of taste, pungency.

acroamatic. Relating to hearing; hence (with relation to Aristotle's *acroama,* private lectures, *esoteric* doctrines for his initiate disciples, as opposed to the *exoteric* doctrines of his public lectures), privately communicated by word of mouth; esoteric; secret. Also *acroamatical, acroatic.* An *acroasis* (plural *acroases*) a discourse or poem spoken or read aloud.

acroke. Crooked, awry. Used by Chaucer.

acrospire. The first sprout or curling shoot of a plant in spring. Greek *akros,* tip, peak + *speira,* curling shoot; *speirein,* to sow. Also *acrospyre, ackerspyre, akerspire; ackersprit.* Used also of corn, and barley germinating before it is malted; gathered potatoes that sprout prematurely are *ackerspritted.* Used from the 17th century. Also as a verb, to *acrospire,* to shoot up the first sprout.

active citizen. A louse. A late 18th and early 19th century phrase, listed in LEXICON BALATRONICUM: A DICTIONARY OF BUCKISH SLANG, UNIVERSITY WIT, AND PICKPOCKET ELOQUENCE (1811).

acton. A quilted cotton (later, a leather) jacket worn under a suit of mail. In later use, a plated jacket worn instead of heavy armor. Used from the 12th to the 16th century. Roundabout from Arabic *al qutn,* the cotton. The French form, in the 15th century, developed an *h (hocqueton),* whence English *hequeton, haketon, hacton.* The word occurs in the 13th century romance of KYNG ALYSAUNDER; Chaucer in THE RIME OF SIR THOPAS (1386) states: *And next his schert an aketoun, And over that an haberjoun.*

acuation. See *acuminate.*

acue. On his rump. French, *au cul.* From the 13th century (THE LIFE OF ST. MARGARET).

aculp. To accuse. A 13th century form. *Cp. acopede.* Literally, to put guilt upon; Latin *culpa,* fault, guilt, whence *culpable, culprit.*

acuminate. To sharpen, bring to a point. Also as an adjective, pointed. Also, intellectually sharpened; keen in discernment, concentrated in attention. Hence, *acumination;* also *acuminous,* marked by *acumen,* as in Bolton's Address to the Reader in FLORUS (1618); *whose writings are altogether as luminous as acuminous.* Used both literally: Whewell, HISTORY OF THE INDUCTIVE SCIENCES (1837) : *Truncation, acuation, and acumination, or replacement by a plane, an edge, a point, respectively*—and figuratively: CORNHILL MAGAZINE (December 1879); *The acumination consisting mainly in a more frequent and sarcastic repetition of the unfortunate Mr. Disraeli's titles and distinctions.* The diminutive form has also been used: *acuminulate,* tapering; somewhat pointed.

acupunctuate. To prick with a needle or pin; also *acupuncture.* The noun was represented (17th to 19th century) by *acupunctuation, acupunchuration, acupunchure;* it was applied, specifically, to the thrusting of needles into the body for remedial purposes, as for gout in 17th century England—though M. Collins observed (1875) that the bees were *stinging* *with unusual sharpness of acupuncture.* The verb was also used figuratively, as when MACMILLAN'S MAGAZINE of January, 1865, commented on *that exquisite sweet malice wherewith French ladies so much delight to acupunctuate their English sisters.*

acydenandys. See *asiden.* This form occurs in the lexicon PROMPTORIUM PARVULORUM (1440).

acyrology. Incorrect use of language. Greek *a,* not + *kyros,* authority + *logos,* speech. Hence *acyrological.* Used from the 17th century. Lady Rosina Bulwer-Lytton in CHEVELY; OR, THE MAN OF HONOUR (1839) wrote: *His work . . . was meant to be . . . a condensation of all the 'logics' and all the 'ologys'; but, unfortunately, tautology and acryology were the only ones thoroughly exemplified.*

ad. A fire; especially, a funeral pyre or blazing pile. Also *od.* Gothic root *aids;* Greek *aithos,* burning heat. Used from the 9th to the 13th century.

adaction. Driving in violently or by force. Also adact, to drive or force (to a course of action). Latin *ad,* to + *agere, actum,* to drive, to act. Fotherby in ATHEOMASTIX (1622) said: *God himselfe once compelled the wicked Egyptians, by flyes, and frogs . . . to confesse the power of his divine Majestie; not vouchsafing to adact them by any other of his creatures.*

Adam. The first man; hence, the basic or unregenerate traits in a person: *the old Adam;* Shakespeare in HENRY V (1599) has *the offending Adam.* Also (*buff* was used for the bare skin; the bailiff's officer of Elizabethan times wore buff) in THE COMEDY OF ERRORS, *the Old Adam,* the bailiff's office. In MUCH ADO ABOUT NOTHING: *Hang me in a bottle like a cat and shoot at me, and he that hits me, let him be clapped on the shoulder and called Adam—Adam,* expert, from the famous archer, Adam Bell. Hence the emendation in ROMEO AND JULIET: *Young Adam Cupid, he that shot so trim When King Cophetua loved the beggar maid;* the early editions have *Abraham Cupid,* which has not been explained.

adamant. This is still used to mean a material, especially stone, of surpassing hardness, its first sense, from Greek *adamas, adamanta,* invincible; *a,* not + *damao,* I tame. By way of Late Latin *diamas* came English *diamond.* The word was mistaken, in Medieval Latin, as coming from *adamantem,* having a liking for; *ad,* to, for + *amantem,* present participle of *amo, amare, amatum,* to love. Hence—up to the 17th century—*adamant* was often used to mean a magnet. Thus Dreyton in THE TRAGICALL LEGEND . . . (1596) wrote: *My lookes so powerfull adamants to love.* Lyly in EUPHUES (1579) confounds the two senses in one image; Shakespeare does likewise in A MIDSUMMER NIGHT'S DREAM (1590): *You draw me, you hardhearted adamant, But yet you draw not iron, for my heart Is true as steele.* Minsheu's THE GUIDE INTO TONGUES (1617) lists *adamate,* to love dearly.

adaw. (1) To wake up; recover consciousness; to rouse. Old English *a,* to + *daw; dayian,* to *dawn,* become *day.* Used by Chaucer, as in TROILUS AND CRISEYDE (1374): *He gan his breeth to drawe, And of his swoun soone aftir that adawe.* (2) *adawe,* out of life. Old English *o dawe, of dayum,* from days, from life. Used from the 13th to the 16th century, usually in the expression *to bring (do) adawe,* to put out of life, to kill. The expression *they did him adawe* led some in the 16th century to assume that *adawe* was a verb, formed from *awe;* hence (in Tottel's MISCELLANY; 1557, and into the 17th century). (3) *to adaw,* to daunt, to subdue. Spenser uses this form several times, as in THE FAËRIE QUEENE (1596): *Therewith her wrathful courage gan appell, and haughty spirits meekly to adaw.*

addle. This is two words, one quite common from the 10th to the 19th century, the other in northern England since 1200. (1) *Addle* akin to German *adel,* mire, originally meant stinking urine, or other miry filth. As late as Burns (1789) we find *Then lug out your ladle Deal brimstone like adle.* This early became an adjective in *addle egg,* corresponding to Latin *ovum urinum,* a rotten egg. Since that egg would not hatch, many wordplays linked *addle* and *idle;* Thus Shakespeare in TROILUS AND CRESSIDA (1606): *If you love an addle egg as well as you love an idle head, you would eat chickens i' the shell.* Thus *addle* came to mean idle, vain, or muddled, and developed such compounds as *addle-brain, addle-head, addle-pate.* Then the adjective (in the 17th century) appeared as *addled,* from which by back-formation came the verb *to addle* (like *to sour, to wet,* etc.). Charles Dickens complains, in a letter of 1841: *I have addled my head with writing all day.* (2) From the Old Norse *öthla,* to acquire, comes a form *addle* meaning to earn or (of crops) to produce. A 1680 trial at York records the words: *He would give me more than I could addle in seven years.* Tusser, in his HUSBANDRY (1580) wisely warns: *Where ivy embraces the tree very sore, kill ivy, or tree will addle no more. Addlings* are wages, but *addling* is muddling of the wits.

adelantado. A Spanish grandee; a governor of a province; a commander. Spanish *adelantar,* to promote, advance; *ad,* to + *el,* the + *ante,* fore. Common in early 17th century pamphleteers and playwrights: Nashe; Jonson; Massinger and Dekker in THE VIRGIN MARTIR (1622): *Invincible adelantado over the armado of pimpled faces.*

adhibit. To let in; to apply; to employ. From Latin *adhibere,* from *ad,* to + *habere,* to hold; whence, with different prefixes, the more familiar spirituous *prohibition* and the psychic *inhibition.* This word was used from the 16th into the 19th century; thus an advertisement in Scott's OLD MORTALITY, in 1862, said: *The subscribers to the Shilling Edition of the Waverley Novels . . . will receive a set of adhesive labels, which may be adhibited to the back of the volumes.* The noun *adhibition* was used, literally, in various fields, as with (1838) *the adhibition of the Seal of the body corporate;* or as in Leigh Hunt's LONDON JOURNAL (1835): *An apple pie was improved by the adhibition of a quince.* (Good cooks take notice!) See *assation.*

adiaphory. Indifference. Accent on the *aff.* Also *adiaphoricy;* Greek *a,* not + *diaphoros,* differing; *dia,* apart + *pherein,* to bear. The form *adiaphorism* was used especially of religious indifferentism. Hence *adiaphorist, adiaphorite,* one that is indifferent (as of religious matters, or among the creeds); also *adiaphoral, adiaphorous, adiaphoristic.* An *adiaphoron* is a matter of indifference; specifically, a practice or belief for which there is no church decision, which is therefore left to the will of the individual. J. Smith (SELECTED DISCOURSES; 1652) said: *These we may safely reckon, I think, amongst our adiaphora in morality, as being in themselves neither good nor evil.*

adible. Accessible. Used from the 16th century; Latin *adire, aditum,* to go to; *ad,* to + *ire, itum,* to go;; whence also *reiterate, itinerary,* and (from the 17th century) *adit,* an approach, entrance. Tennyson in THE PRINCESS (1847) promises: *Yourself and yours shall have free adit.*

adipate. To eat fat; to eat so as to grow fat. A 17th century dictionary word that describes the procedure of one that should diet. Latin *adeps, adipem,* fat; whence also *adipal, adipous,* and the current *adipose* (Latin *-osus,* full of). Also *adiposity, adiposeness.*

adipsy. Lack of thirst. Greek *a,* not + *dipsa,* thirst. Also *adipsia.* An *adipson* (17th century) is a drink that allays thirst, sometimes prescribed for a fever, more often imbibed in a bar. *Adipsic, adipsous,* quenching thirst. The converse of adipsy produces the dipsomaniac.

adlubescence. Delight. From Latin *ad,* to + *lubescare,* to be pleasing; *libet* or *lubet,* it is pleasing; *libido,* pleasure, desire—whence the Freudian *libido.* Andrew Marvell, in THE REHEARSAL TRANSPOSED (1673), speaks of *Such an expansion of heart, such an adlubescence of mind . . . that he could scarce refrain from kissing it.* Samuel Johnson copies from Bailey's 1731 DICTIONARY the form *allubescency,* willingness, content; it exists only in the lexicographers' listings.

admirative. Relating to or characterized by wonder. Hence, an early term for the exclamation point (!). Latin *ad,* at + *mirari,* to wonder. The phrase *note of admiration* was also used to mean the exclamation point, by Swift (1719) and earlier by Shakespeare in THE WINTER'S TALE (1611): *The changes I perceived in the King and Camillo, were very notes of admiration.*

admonish. See *comminate.* Also *admonest;* Caxton in POLYCRONICON (1482) said that *Those thynges whiche our progenytours by the taste of bytternes and experyment of grete jeopardyes have enseygned, admonested, and enformed us excluded fro such peryllys, to know what is prouffytable to oure lyf. Enseygned* means given a sign of, pointed out.

adnate. See *agnate.*

adnichil, adnitchil. Occurring only in 17th century dictionaries, this is derived from an old French *adnichiller,* modern *annihiler,* whence *annihilate.* It is described as an old law term, meaning to annul, make void. The word seems to have been adnichiled before it was used.

adnomination. An early form of *agnomination, q.v.* Note however that *adnominal* is also a grammatical term, meaning attached to a noun, relating to an adnoun (*adnomen, adname*: which is an adjective used with a noun).

adnoun. An adjective "added to" a noun. Occasionally *adnoun* is used for an "adjective" employed as a substantive, as: The *good* are outnumbered. *Cp. adnomination.*

adonize. To adorn (of a man); to make an *Adonis* of. The word (accent on the *ad*) is from *Adonis,* the young man whose beauty attracted Venus; hence, an *Adonis,* a dandy.

adosculation. Impregnation by external contact, without intromission. Latin *ad,* to + *osculari, osculatum,* to kiss; *osculum,* diminutive of *os, orem,* mouth. *Divers kinds of birds and fishes,* said the CHAMBERS CYCLOPEDIA (1753) *are also impregnated by adosculation.* One wonders what is implied in that *also!*

adown. Down. The earlier form, *adown* (*adun, adoun, adown,* etc.) is from Old English *of dune,* off the hill. As early as

1200 *adown* was shortened to *down,* which supplemented but never quite supplanted the earlier form, still used by poets. Chaucer, in THE KNIGHT'S TALE (1386): *On their bare knees adoun they falle;* Scott, in MARMION (1808): *His gorgeous collar hung adown;* Hawthorn, in AMERICAN NOTE-BOOKS (1868): *There is a beautiful view from the mansion, adown the Kennebec;* Morris, in THE EARTHLY PARADISE (1870) *Till the wretch falls adown with whirling brain.* CHAUCER'S DREAM (1500) shows the transition: *There were a few wells Came running fro the cliffs adowne, That made a deadly sleeping soune, And runnen downe right by a cave That was under a rocky grave.* Also see *drury. Cp. bove,* which has added, instead of losing, the *a.*

adreint. Drowned. Past participle of *adrenchen,* to drown; past tense, *he adrente.* Also *adrench;* past participle *adraynt, adreynt.* The verb was an alternative form (in all senses) of *adrink,* meaning also to give to drink; as in the AYENBITE OF INWIT (1340): *And hire adraynkth and maketh dronke of holy love.* The ANCREN RIWLE (1230) said: *Ther adreinte Pharao.* Lydgate's PYLGRYMAGE OF THE SOWLE (1413) pictures one *adrenchyng hym self, as it were, in wordly vanyte.*

adrench. See *adreint.* Earlier *adrenchen.*

adrink. To swallow too much water; that is, to drown. Let that be a warning to you! Past forms are *adranc, adronke, adrunken.* See *adreint.*

adrogation. Taking, as a member of one's family, of a person of legal majority, of one that is his own master. Especially in Roman law; *adoption* means the taking into one's family of a minor. Hence *adrogator; to adrogate.* Latin *ad,* to + *rogare, rogatum,* to ask, whence also *arrogate,* which now means to take without asking. *Adopt* is from Latin *ad,* to + *optare,* to choose; *opere,* to wish.

adscititious. Originally meaning added from outside, supplementary, this word was used in the 18th century (Bailey's DICTIONARY, 1751) to signify counterfeit, false. Also *ascititious.* It is from Latin *ad,* to + *sciscere,* to acknowledge, the inceptive form of *scire,* to know. It is still occasionally employed in the original sense, which Bacon exemplifies in the NOVUM ORGANUM (1620), referring to "perpetual and proper" motions on the one hand, and on the other motions that are *adscititious.*

adure. To scorch; to burn up; to calcine. Latin *ad,* to + *urere, ustum,* to burn, whence also *combustion. Adure* was used from the 15th century. In the 16th and 17th the less common verb *to adust* was used, to scorch, to dry up with heat; Milton in PARADISE LOST (1667) has *Sulphurous and nitrous foame . . . Concocted and adusted they reduced To blackest grain.* More common was the adjective *adust (adusted),* burnt up, parched; browned, sunburnt; dried out —especially of the four humours in the body (see *humour*), resulting in a state that alarmed Medieval and Renaissance physicians. The word was also used figuratively; Nabbe in his MICROCOSM (1637) exclaimed: *Provoke me no more; I am adust with rage.* Note that *adust* may also be an alternate form for *dusty;* George Eliot in ROMOLA (1863) says: *He was tired and adust with long riding.* Also *adustion,* burning, fiery; *adustible,* capable of being burnt. John Bale in his APOLOGY AGAINST A RANKE PAPYST (1550) declares: *What your adusted conscyence thynketh of it I can not tell.*

adust. See *adure.*

advertence. Notice, attention, consideration. Via the French from Latin *ad,* to + *vertere,* to turn. Chaucer in TROYLUS AND CRISEYDE (1370) has the query: *What fel experience Hath fro me reft, alas, thine advertence?* (The accent, nonetheless, is on the second syllable.) THE LADY'S CALLING of 1673 admonishes that *a serious advertence to the divine presence is the most certain curb to all disorderly appetites.* The habit or quality of being attentive is *advertency;* thus Dryden in THE LIFE OF PLUTARCH (1683) states that *through want of advertency he has been often guilty of that error.* We still must frequently admit that an act was *inadvertent.*

advertisement. The act of turning the mind toward, noticing; heed. Also, the act of calling attention to; hence, a notice, a public notice, as by the town-crier; thence (from the 18th century) the current use. Accent always on the second syllable. Latin *ad,* to + *vertere, versum,* whence *verse, obverse, reverse,* and more *diversions.* Shakespeare uses it in the sense of information, in HENRY IV, PART ONE (1597); in other senses in PART ONE, in ALL'S WELL THAT ENDS WELL, and in MUCH ADO ABOUT NOTHING: *My griefs cry lowder than advertisement.*

advesperate. From Latin *ad,* to + *vesper,* evening: *advesperascere, advesperatum,* to draw toward evening; this word means to grow toward night. It exists in 17th and 18th century dictionaries.

advision. See *avision.*

advoutress. An early variant of *adulteress; cp. advowtrie.*

advowtrie. An early variant (as in Chaucer), of *adultery.* Also *advouter, advowter, advowterer; advowteress, advoutress; advowterie, advowtry, avowtry. Cp. spousebreach.*

adwole. Mistaken, in error. *Cp. dwale.* Used in the 13th century (THE OWL AND THE NIGHTINGALE).

ae-. In words from Latin and Greek, an original *ae* has frequently been shortened to *e.* As late as March 1847, we could read in THE LONDON QUARTERLY REVIEW, of Johnson's edition of Shakespeare's plays: *His great general powers enabled him to paraphrase into perspicuity many an involved and aenigmatical line—to stamp with a more legible impress many a noble specimen of worn or corroded coinage.*

aegritude. See *egritude.*

aeipathy. A long-felt passion. From Greek *aiei, aei,* always + *pathos,* feeling, this word, pronounced *I-ip'-athy,* captures the lovelorn.

aeolist. A pretender to inspiration; a wind-bag. From Latin *Æolus,* the god of the winds. One use is recorded, by Swift in the TALE OF A TUB (1704): *The learned aeolists maintain the original cause of all things to be wind.* Hence *aeolistic,* long-winded.

aequiparate. See *equiparate.*

aeromancy. Divination—foretelling events, predicting the future—by appearances in the air. The depths of the desire to know what is coming, or what is the best course to pursue to bring about a wished-for end, are indicated by the great number of types of divination practiced in times not long gone by. These include: *aichomancy,* by sharp points. *alectromancy,* by a cock's picking up grains. *aleuromancy,* by dough. *alphitomancy,* barley meal. *amathomancy,* dust. *anthomancy,* flowers (She loves me, she loves me not!) *anthropomancy,* human entrails; *anthroposcopy,* observation of personal characteristics; *auspicy, haruspicy,* appearance of things being sacrificed; *heiromancy,* entrails of sacrificed animals; *extispice,* entrails plucked from a fowl. *armomancy,* shoulders of beasts. *austromancy,* winds. *axinomancy,* a balanced hatchet. *belomancy,* arrows. *bibliomancy,* the Bible; *sortes Virgilianae,* opening at random to a page of Virgil's works; *stichomancy,* a verse, a passage in a book; *foliomancy,* leaves (of a book; later, tea leaves). *brontomancy,* thunder. *capnomancy,* altar smoke. *catotromancy,* mirrors. *ceromancy,* melted wax on water. *chaomancy,* clouds. *chiromancy,* palm reading. *cleromancy,* dice. *conchomancy,* shells. *coscinomancy,* a sieve. *cristallomancy, crystallomancy,* images in a crystal ball; *spheromancy,* a crystal sphere. *crithomancy,* cake dough, barley. *cryptomancy,* by unrevealed means. *dactyliomancy,* a suspended ring; *dactylomancy,* finger rings. *daphnomancy,* a laurel tree, or branch therefrom. *demonomancy,* with the help of demons; *necyomancy, necyomanty,* calling up the devil or other damned spirits. *dririmancy,* dripping blood. *gastromancy* (1) rumbles of the belly—a sort of "fatiloquency," said Rabelais (1533), long practiced in Ferrara (2) ventriloquism (3) a child looking into the "belly" of a glass bottle of water. *geloscopy,* observing the manner of laughing. *geomancy,* digging. *graphomancy,* handwriting. *gyromancy,* spinning in a circle. *halomancy,* salt. *hariolation,* soothsaying. *hydromancy, ydromancy,* water (in many ways). *hyomancy,* the tongue bone; as the tongue wags. *ichthyomancy,* the next fish caught. *iconomancy,* images. *keraunoscopy,* thunder and lightning. *lampadomancy,* candles; what burns (and how it burns or the wick floats about) in a lamp; *libanomancy,* burning of incense (so the Fates are not incensed); *lecanomancy,* a bowl of water reflecting candle flames—a practice still current in some Slavic lands, especially at Christmastide. THE PSYCHOANALYTIC REVIEW in 1913 reported that testing with free association shows "the divinations are merely the results of the medium's own complexes." *lithomancy,* (precious) stones; *psephomancy,* heaped pebbles; *pessomancy,* tossed pebbles. *logomancy,* words. *macromancy,* the largest thing near; *micromancy,* the smallest thing near. *maculomancy,* spots. *mathemancy,* quantity. *mazomancy,* a suckling babe. *meconomancy,* sleep, induced by drugs; poppies. *meteoroscopy, meteoromancy,* shooting stars. *mineramancy,* found minerals. *molybdomancy,* motions and forms in molten lead. *myomancy,* mice. *necromancy* (Greek *nekros,* corpse; Latin *nigrem,* black), communicating with the dead; *sciomancy,* shadows, or the shades of the dead. *necromancy* is also the general term for illicit divination, black magic; also *nygromauncy, negromancy, nycromancy, necromancy, necromonseys. nephromancy,* the kidneys. *odontomancy,* the teeth, *oenomancy, oinomancy,* wine. *omoplatoscopy, scapulimancy,* the cracks in a shoulder-blade when the bone is placed on a fire. See *omphalomancy*: by the navel. *oneiromancy,* dreams. *onomancy, onomatechny,* the letters of one's name. *onychomancy,* nails reflecting the sun. *ooscopy,* inspection of eggs. *ophiomancy,* serpents, *orniscopy,* birds; *ornithomancy,* the flight of birds. *oryctomancy,* things dug up. *ossomancy,* bones. *ouranomancy, uranomancy,* the heavens. *pegomancy,* fountains. *physiognomancy, phyznomancy, fiznomancy,* the countenance; *metoscopy,* the face. *pneumancy,* blowing; a vestigium of this is the blowing out of candles on a festival cake. *pseudomancy,* with intent to deceive, as when the witches promise Macbeth he'll be safe till Birnam Wood shall come to Dunsinane—which would leave more than a dunce inane. *psychomancy,* spirits. *pyromancy,* flames; *ceneromancy,* ashes; *tephramancy,* tracings in ashes. *retromancy,* things seen looking over one's shoulder. *rhabdomancy,* a rod or wand. *scatomancy,* feces, dung. *selenomancy,* the moon. *sideromancy,* hot metal. *sortilege, sortilegy,* casting lots, *spasmatomancy,* bodily twitchings. *stercomancy,* seeds in dung. *sycomancy,* figs. *teratoscopy,* prodigies, natural marvels. *theomagic, theomancy,* oracles, or calling on the god. *theriomancy,* by the movements of wild animals. *topomancy,* the shape of the terrain. *trochomancy,* wheel tracks. *tyromancy,* the coagulation of cheese. *urimancy,* urine. *xenomancy,* the first stranger that appears. *zygomancy,* weights. *Astrology* has many terms, including *astromancy,* the position of the stars; *genethliacs,* the stars at birth. *alchocoden,* the planet that reigns over a nativity; *cp. apotelesm.*

Persons today may be less gullible as to the prophets and soothsayers and mantics in general; less hopeful of foretelling the future, they are more manifold in their fears of what is to come. The OXFORD PSYCHIATRIC DICTIONARY lists 264 words for specific dreads, from *acerophobia,* fear of sourness (to many, the world has turned sour) to *zoophobia,* fear of animals. While it lists *ponophobia,* dread of work, it does not list *logophobia,* dread of words. The topic is capped with *moromancy,* foolish divination, a 17th century term that covers them all.

aerwene. Desperate. The Old English prefix *ae-, aer-* is a privative, like the current suffix *-less.* An old word for hope is *wen.* Layamon, in BRUT (1205) used *aerwene* to mean without hope.

aerwitte. Witless, foolish. Used in Layamon's BRUT (1205). For etymology, see *aerwene.*

aestivate. To spend the summer. Latin *aestus* means heat; hence English *aestival,* relating to summer. In zoology, *aestivate* is used as the converse of *hibernate,* spending the season in torpor or suspended animation. Often used figuratively, as in the PALL MALL GAZETTE of December 11, 1870: *With what we are pleased to call the cold weather Calcutta rouses herself from her aestivation of seven long months.* There are other forms than the verb and the noun—with other meanings: *aestive, estive,* hot; *aestuant,* heaving with heat. By extension, the sense of boiling suggesting turbulent tides, we find *aestuary,* a vapor bath; *aestuate,* to heave, to surge like the tide, to boil; *aestuous,* agitated, heaving. Chapman in his translation of the ODYSSEY (1615) says that *the seas retain Not only their outrageous aesture there.* It is by calmer seas that city folk delight to aestivate.

aesture. Boiling; rage. See *aestivate.*

aetites. Pronounced in three syllables, this is the English form of a Greek word that means of the eagle. *aetites* is the eagle-stone, so-called from its being found (according to the fable) in the eagle's nest. Lyly in EUPHUES (1579) called it *the precious stone aetites;* Bacon in SYLVA (1626) mentions the peculiarity that gave it distinction: *the aetites or eagle's stone, which hath a little stone within it.* This effect is produced, according to CHAMBERS' CYCLOPEDIA (1753) through the fact that it "consists of several crusts, which have in them a cavity with matter in it, loose and moveable." Such a stone naturally had powers attributed to it; as late as 1862 the London READER (July 8) said that *the aetites possessed the singular property . . . of detecting theft.* The word, despite its plural form, is also singular.

aeviternal; aeviternity. The emphatic (and original) forms of *eternal* and *eternity,* from Latin *aevum,* age + the adjective suffix. Thus T. Stanley in the HISTORY OF PHILOSOPHY (1660) mentions the *Gods placed in the highest regions of aether, aeviternal.*

afait. This is an early form of *affect,* via Old French *afaiter* from Latin *affectare,* frequentative of *afficere, affectum; ad,* to + *facere,* to make, to do. It meant to influence; to shape, mould, adapt to a purpose; to fit out, dress; to train (hawks and hounds), hence, to tame; to subdue. Also *affayte, afaytye, affaite; afaite.* Hence *afaitement,* training; proper behavior; breeding. Robert of Gloucester's CHRONICLE (1297) said: *To Yolond he gan wende Var to afayty that lond, and to wynne ech ende.* Langland in PIERS PLOWMAN (1362) wrote: *It afaiteth the flesh From folies ful manye.*

afear. See *affeer.* Also *afere, afered, afeir.*

afeng. To take up, receive. The past tense was *afong.* Used in the 13th century (Robert of Gloucester's CHRONICLE).

aferd. Busied, charged with a matter to be executed. A variant form of *affaired,* used in the 13th century (the romance of KYNG ALYSAUNDER).

affect. (The surviving sense, to influence, came from the simple Latin *afficere,* to do to, to attach to; *ad,* to + *facere,* to make, to do. Other senses came from the reflexive form, *se facere ad,* to apply oneself to, to aim at. Hence:) To aim at, aspire to; to be drawn toward, to have affection for; to do (wear, go) often; to show a liking for; to put on, to pretend. Shakespeare, in HENRY IV, PART TWO (1593): *Have I affected wealth, or honour?* (TWELFTH NIGHT): *Maria told me once, she did affect me.* (LEAR): *Who having beene prais'd for bluntnesse, doth affect A saucy roughnes.* Also, to prefer. Marlowe in HERO AND LEANDER (finished by Chapman; 1598) states that life (fate) chooses for us: *And one especiallie do we affect Of two gold ingots like in each respect. The reason no man knows; let it suffice What we behold is censur'd by our eies. Where both deliberat, the love is slight; who ever loved, that loved not at first sight?*

affectuosity. The vehemence of passion; great affection. More common (15th to 17th century) were the adjective forms, *affectious, affectuous, affectual,* earnest, eager; tender, loving affectionate; rousing the emotions; (more rarely) influential, successful—perhaps by error for *affectuous.* In NERO (1607) we read: *Therefore my deare, deare wife, and dearest sonnes, Let me ingirt you with my last embrace: And in your cheekes impress a fare-well kisse, Kisse of true kindness and affectious love.*

affeer. To set a price. Also *affear, affere, affeir, affure.* In law courts, to settle the amount of an amercement; to reduce to a fair price. From Old French *afeurer,* from Late Latin *afforare,* from *ad,* to + *forum,* market. The word was a legal term from about 1450; Blackstone's COMMENTARIES (1768) says that the precise sum of an amercement (q.v.) is usually set by *afeerors, or jurors sworn to affeere, that is tax and moderate, the general amercement according to the particular circumstances of the offence and the offender.* From the meaning, to settle, *affeer* was used figuratively in the sense of to confirm, as by Shakespeare in MACBETH (1605): *Wear thou thy wrongs, the title is affeard.*

In the north of England and in Scotland, from about 1350 (in Barbour's BRUCE, 1375) to about 1600, quite another word, from Old French *affeirir,* to pertain, from Latin *ad,* to + *ferire,* to strike, to affect, also took the form *affere, affeir.* Thus Lyndesay in his DREME (1552) wrote *Some swift, some slow, as to their kind affeirs* (pertains). They *did him great honour,* said MERLIN (1450) *as affiered to so high a man.*

These words are not to be confused with *afear,* meaning in fear, *afere, afered, afeir,* as in Chaucer's MONK'S TALE (1386): *Ever he is afere to do amiss.*

John Shakespeare, father of William, was elected in 1559 one of the *affeerors* of Stratford.

affie. A variant of *affy, q.v.*

affine. A relation by marriage; more loosely, a relative. *Affined* related; also *affinal,* in relation to, derived from the same source. Latin *ad,* to + *finem,* end, border. In a letter of Henry VII (1509) we read: *His cousyn and affyne the king of Spayne.* Hence, also *affined,* related; bound by some tie. Thus Shakespeare in OTHELLO (1604) bids: *Be judge yourself, Whether I in any just terme am afin'd To love the Moor.*

afflate. To blow upon. Latin *ad,* to + *flare, flatum,* to blow, whence also *inflated* and *flatulence.* Hence *afflation,* a blowing or breathing upon; *afflatus,* breathing. Latin *afflatus serpentis,* hissing. Since among many peoples the snake was an agent of supernatural communication—the pythoness of Greek oracle, the serpent of the Garden of Eden, and other worms—*afflation, afflatus* came also (first in the Latin forms) to mean the imparting of supernatural knowledge, or of a creative impulse: inspiration, *the divine afflatus.* Also *afflatitious* (17th century), *afflated* (19th century), inspired. Thackeray in THE ROUNDABOUT PAPERS (1862) remarks: *We spake anon of the inflated style of some writers. What also if there is an afflated style—when a writer is like a pythoness?* Cary in his translation (1814) of Dante's PARADISO wrote: *Diversely Partaking of sweet life as more or less Afflation of eternal bliss pervades them.*

affodill. See *daffadowndilly.* Also *affadille, affodell,* and more. Applied to the king's spear, or *asphodel,* and to the *daffodil,* a species of narcissus.

affrication. The Latin verb *fricare,* to rub, had two forms for the past: *fricatum* and *frictum.* From the second comes the common English word *friction;* from *ad,* to, upon + *fricatum* come *affrication* and *affricate.* Both exist mainly in late 17th and early 18th century dictionaries (Blount 1656; Bailey 1751), but Francis Hauksbee, in his PHYSICO-MECHANICAL EXPERIMENTS (1709) speaks of the *affrication* of a glass tube.

affrend. To reconcile. A variant of *affriend.* Apparently used only in the past, as by Spenser in THE FAËRIE QUEENE (1596): *She saw that cruell war so ended, And deadly foes so faithfully affrended.*

affy. To trust; to entrust; to confide in; to assure, to secure by solemn promise; hence (since the 16th century) to *affiance,* to betroth, whence also (though by a second trip from France) *fiancée.* Early forms were *affie, afye, afyghe.* Via Old French *afier;* Latin *ad,* to + *fidare; fidus,* trusty, *fides,* faith. Shakespeare in HENRY VI, PART TWO (1593) exclaims: *And wedded be thou to the hags of hell For daring to affye a mighty lord Unto the daughter of a worthlesse king.*

afgod. An idol; a false god. Old English *af,* off + *God.* THE GENTLEMEN'S MAGAZINE in 1793 stated: *The figure on the stone was not intended to represent a griffen, but an afgod. The afgod was an image like a dragon placed at the feet of Woden.*

afoled. Made a fool of. Used in the 13th century (THE OWL AND THE NIGHTINGALE).

afrete. To devour. Old English *of,* away + *fretan,* to gnaw. Also *afretie, afretye.* A political song of the 13th century expresses the pious hope: *The devel them afretye!*

afterblismed. Pregnant. Anglo-Saxon *blosma,* a bud, *blossom.* In a 13th century translation of the 77TH PSALM.

afterclap. An unexpected blow after one has ceased to be on guard, a further disaster when it seems life can bring no more, a misfortune that 'caps the climax.' Used from the 15th century. Butler in HUDIBRAS (1663) knows the unrelenting drive: *What plaguy mischiefs and mishaps Do dog him still with afterclaps.*

afterdeal. A disadvantage. Caxton's translation of REYNART THE FOXE (1481) stated: *Isegryn was woe begon, and thought he was at an afterdele.* Malory, in THE HISTORY OF KING ARTHUR (1634), reported: *The battle was great, and oftentimes that one party was at a fordele, and anon at an afterdele, which endured long.*

afterspring. Posterity; *offspring.* Golding in his translation (1583) of Calvin on DEUTERONOMY has: *If He should destroy the whole world and leave no afterspring to call upon Him.*

afterwending. Following. Used in the 13th century (romance of KYNG ALYSAUNDER).

afterwit. (1) Knowledge arrived at in later years. (2) Second thought, reconsideration. Both of these were 17th century uses. (3) Wisdom that comes too late. G. Whitney (1586): *Afterwits are like a shower of rayne Which moistes the soile when witherd is the graine.* The French call *l'esprit d'escalier,* staircase wit, the clever remark one thinks of on the way home. (4) By extension, recognition of one's former follies, 'coming to one's senses.' Hence *afterwitted,* lacking forethought; wise when too late.

again-bite. See *agenbite.*

againchar. See *chare.*

againsay. To refuse; to reverse (a verdict); to contradict. Literally, to speak *against.* Hence *againsaw, againsaying,* contradiction. Used since the 13th century; later shortened to *gainsay.*

agambo. An early variant of *akimbo.*

agamy. Non-recognition, or non-existence, of the marriage tie. From Greek *a,* not + *gamos,* marriage. (The accent is on the first syllable.) The word had some popularity around the beginning of the 19th century, when rebellious romantics preferred *agamy* to *bigamy,* and certainly to *monogamy.* The adjective *agamous* was more frequent, and has survived as a biological term meaning without (distinguishable) sexual organs.

An *agamist* is one opposed to the institution of matrimony.

aganippe. A source of inspiration; poetic power. *Aganippe* was a fountain on Mount Helicon, sacred to the Muses. THE LIFE OF ANTONY À WOOD (1695) said: *Such towering ebullitions do not exuberate in my aganippe.*

agape. In two syllables, this means *on the gape,* in a state of wonder. Milton in PARADISE LOST 1667) mentions a rich retinue that *Dazzles the crowd, and sets them all agape;* Tennyson in MAUD (1855) pictures *a rabbit mouth that is ever agape.* In three syllables, from Greek *agape,* brotherly love, the word was used of a love-feast of the early Christians, at first in connection with the Lord's Supper. *In the primitive days,* as Chambers observes in his CYCLOPEDIA (1727), *the agapes were held without scandal or offence.* That they later became more licentious is evident from Bailey's definition (1736) of *agapet:* a man that hunts after women.

agar. A sea-monster. So-called in early dictionaries, and so felt to be in Tudor times: later identified with the *eager,* a tidal bore, also *eagre, q.v.* The bores (unusually high tidal waves) were found especially in the estuaries of the Humber, Trent and Severn. Lyly in GALLATHEA (1592) said of Neptune: *He sendeth a monster called the agar, against whose coming the waters roare, the fowles flie away, and the cattel in the field for terrow shunne the bankes.* Sprigge in 1647 neatly defined *eager, a sudden surprisal of the tide.*

agaric. From Greek *agaricon,* which Dioscoribes said was named from *Agaria,* a place in Sarmatia, comes this word *agaric,* the tree fungus used for tinder. It is still a botanical term for a genus of mushroom. In Renaissance pharmaceutics, the "female agarick" was widely used as a cathartic; another type of tree fungus, the "male agarick," was used as a styptic to coagulate blood. The Fairy Agaric was frequently found in the circles of grass called Fairy Rings. From such associations, the word moved into poetry. Note that Shelley accents the second syllable, in THE SENSITIVE PLANT (1820): *And agarics and fungi, with mildew and mould;* while Tennyson accents the first, in GARTH (1859): *As one That smells a foul-flesh'd agaric in the holt.*

agast. To terrify. From the 13th through the 16th century; by 1700 the participle *agasted,* struck with terror, had been replaced by *aghast.* The *h* came in under the influence of the word (and the idea) *ghost.* Spenser in THE FAËRIE QUEENE (1596) has: *Or other griesly thing, that him aghast. Cp. gast.*

agate. A tiny person—in reference to the small figures cut in the precious stone, *agate,* set in rings and used as seals. Shakespeare has Falstaff say to his new page (HENRY IV, PART TWO; 1598): *Thou whoreson mandrake, thou are fitter to be worn in my cap than to wait at my heels. I was never manned with an agate till now.* Note the verb *to man,* to equip with a serving-man.

agathodemon. See *eudemonic.*

agathokakological. See *eudemonic.*

agathopoietic. Tending, or intended, to do good. Greek *agathos,* good + *poiein,* to make, do.

agelast. This three-syllable word is from Greek *a,* not + *gelastes,* a laugher: one who never laughs. George Meredith in the London TIMES of February 5, 1877, wrote of *men whom Rabelais would have called agelasts.* The form *agelastic* is also found (in Bailey's DICTIONARY, 1731) with the same meaning; or, as an adjective, never laughing; sullen, sad.

agemate. A person of the same age. Stanyhurst in the AENEIS (1583) has: *Whilst I beheld Priamus thus gasping, my sire his agemate.* Even the staid O.E.D. ventures the opinion: "This word is worth reviving." That is especially true in this era of increased longevity.

agenbite. Remorse. Also *ayenbite;* actually *again-bite, again* here meaning back, on oneself, *against.* See *commorant.* The AYENBITE OF INWIT, Remorse of Conscience, is a translation (about 1340) by Dan Michel of Northgate, Canterbury, of a French moral treatise.

agerasia. Eternal youth; a green old age; aging without the signs of years. Also *agerasy.* From Greek *a,* not + *geras,* old age. Leo H. Grindon, on LIFE; ITS NATURE, VARIETIES AND PHENOMENA (1856) cogently remarks: *Agerasia belongs only to the soul.*

agesse. To expect. The *a* is intensive, the verb (hard g) became *guess.* The 13th century KING HORN has: *He sede he wolde agesse To arive in westernesse.*

aggerate. To heap up. Latin *aggerare, aggeratum,* to pile; *agger,* a heap, whence also *exaggerate.* Foxe plays on the two words in THE BOOK OF MARTYRS (1587): *aggerating and exaggerating the fault to the uttermost.* Hence *aggeration,* raising a heap; *aggerose,* formed in heaps; full of heaps. To *aggerate a tree,* to heap earth or dung about it. The term *aggeration* is used in archaeology to mean the making of a mound, as a method of raising the menhir, the giant standing stone of certain ancient peoples, as at Stonehenge, England—though many agree with what Southey wrote in a letter of 1832: *I think the stones are more likely to have been raised by mechanical means than by the rude process of aggeration.*

aghast. See *agast.*

agilt. An early spelling (also *agulte, aguylt, agelte*) of the verb *aguilt, q.v.*

aginator. A retail dealer. *To aginate,* to retail small wares, Latin *aginare, aginatum,* to trade; *agina,* the tongue of a balance. In 17th century dictionaries.

agio. A percentage charged for exchanging currency. Italian *agio, aggio,* ease, convenience. By extension, money-changing; also *agiotage,* which was extended in the 19th century to mean speculation, stock-jobbing. Disraeli in ENDYMION (1880) says: *What they mean by peace is agiotage, shares at a premium, and bubble companies.*

agist. To take cattle in, for pasture, at a price. *To agist* cattle; also, *to agist the forest,* to pasture cattle in the forest. Perhaps from French *à giste,* for pasture, perhaps from *adgistare* (a Late Latin form after the French); Latin *jacitare,* frequentative of *iacere,* to lie. Hence *agistage, agistation, agistment,* the process of agisting, of pasturing or of opening the forest for pasturage. The *agistor* was the King's officer who kept charge of cattle *agisted* in the royal forests, or kept the accounts of the *agistment.*

aglet. The metal tip (earlier called *point*) of a lace, intended for easier threading through the eyelets, but later made in various shapes as an ornament on the lace-ends. Hence, an ornament attached to a lace or fringe, a metallic stud or spangle on a dress. By extension, a fragment of flesh hanging by the skin; hence, a scrap, a shred. In current use, *aiguilette,* the point or cord over the shoulder in certain uniforms. Also *aiglet, aglotte, aigulet,* via French *aiguilette,* diminutive of *aiguille,* needle; Late Latin *acicula,* diminutive of *acus,* needle, *acuere, acutus,* to sharpen, whence also *acute.* At the Progress of Queen Elizabeth I in 1564, when Lord Leicester was made a Knight of the Garter, the robe of the Garter King at Arms had on the sleeves *38 paire of gold aglets.* Spenser in THE FAËRIE QUEENE (1596) mentions *a silken camus . . . Which all above besprinckled was throughout With golden aygulets that glistred bright, Like twinckling starres.* An *aglet-baby* was either a tag shaped like a baby, or a doll or baby adorned with *aglets;* Shakespeare in THE TAMING OF THE SHREW (1596) says: *Give him gold enough, and marry him to a puppet or an aglet-babie, or an old trot with ne'er a tooth in her head.*

agnail. This word was corrupted to *hang-nail,* which has supplanted it. The change was established in Bailey's DICTIONARY (1742), where *agnail* is defined as "a sore slip of skin at the root of a nail." From 900 to 1700 *agnail* meant a corn on the foot. It is from *ang,* compressed, painful (Gothic *aggurus,* whence *anguish*) + *nail.* The word *nail* at first did not refer to a fingernail or toenail, but to a nail one hammered; by extension, the word was applied to a round-headed excrescence in the flesh, like a wart (originally a *wer-nail, wer* meaning man, as in *werwolf:* a *wernail* or *warnel* was a wart). Thus *agnail* meant first a corn, then a *whitlow* (from *white* + *flaw?;* a pus-producing inflammation near or under the nail), then a hangnail. The term *hang* seems appropriate to the hanging shreds of flesh, but originally the *h* was just the cockney addition to the sound of the word.

agname. A name in addition to one's formal appellation, a nickname. Latin *agnomen, ag, ad,* to + *nomen,* name, whence also *agnomen.* In Roman use, *agnomen* referred to a third or fourth name added because of some special event, as *Publius Cornelius Scipio* was called *Africanus,* as we learn in the first act of Shakespeare's play that *Gaius Marcius,* victor at Corioli (493 B.C.) was called *Coriolanus.* In English, Scott in WAVERLY (1814) speaks of *small pale features, from which he derived his agnomen of Bean;* Urquhart in THE JEWEL (1652) mentioned *Colonel Alexander Hamilton. agnamed dear Sandy.*

agnate. A descendant wholly on the male side. *Agnation* is relationship through the male line, through male links alone, as in the Salic law. The Salic law was established by Clovis (died 511); Edward III of England claimed the French throne by virtue of the Salic law (referred to in Shakespeare's Henry V) and thus started the Hundred Years War. When Victoria became Queen of England in 1837, the Salic law kept her from the throne of Hanover. The Justinian Code (529-565), however, modified the regulations, so that *agnation* and *agnate* came to include descendants in the male line even though female links have intervened. *Agnate* is also used as an adjective, although both words have now purely historical associations. *Agnate* and *agnation* are from Latin *adgnatum,* from *ad,* to + *gnasci,* to be born, of the stem *gen-,* to beget, *generate.* From the same source come the forms *adnate* and *adnation,* which are still used in botany and physics; but *adnate* was used in the 17th century in the sense of acquired, as opposed to native, thus in Theophilus Gales' THE COURT OF THE GENTILES (1677): *There is an adnate or acquired hardness by custom in sin.*

agnification. Representing persons as sheep. From Latin *agnus,* lamb + *fication,* the act of making, from *facere,* to make. When God's minister is called a pastor (shepherd) it is natural that his "flock" be pictured as sheep. The image appears throughout medieval church literature and painting. Also, of course, Jesus as *agnus Dei,* the lamb of God.

agnit. An early form of recognize, from the 16th through the 18th century. Also *agnize, agnition.* Motteux, in his translation of Rabelais (1708), says that *the silence of the Egyptians was agnited as an expressive manner of Divine adoration.* Cary, in his translation (1814) of Dante's INFERNO, has: *I was agnized of one, who by the skirt Caught me.* Richard Cromwell's succession as Protector of the Commonwealth of England was established more firmly, it was thought, by changing *recognizing* to *agnizing,* "that so his right might appear to be founded upon the consent of the people represented in this assembly." Neither the succession nor the word proved firm.

agnomination. (1) The giving of a surname; also *adnomination, q.v.; annomination.* (2) A word-play, pun; allusion of one word to another. On hearing that in THE SECOND SHEPHERD'S PLAY a stolen lamb was hidden in the cradle that awaited the about-to-be-born Jesus, a schoolboy—not knowing how many layers of thought were in the agnomination—commented: "Mary had a litle lamb." *Cp. agnification.* (3) Alliteration. Camden (REMAINS, 1605) remarked that *the English and the Welsh delighted much in licking the letter and clapping together agnominations.*

agnosy. Ignorance. Greek *a,* not + *gno-,* to know (akin to *gnaw:* "Chew upon this"). *Agnostic* is a common word: *agnosy,* not in the O.E.D., has the accent on the first syllable.

agonal. A book of martyrs, or of stories of heroes that sacrificed their lives. Also *agonel.* Shortened from Latin *liber agonalis,* book of agonies.

agonyclite. From Greek *a,* not + *gony,* knee + *clitos,* bending, this word marks one of the 7th century heretics that would not kneel but prayed standing. By extension, one that refuses to bow to authority.

agoreblood. Adrip with clotting blood. Plutarch's LIVES in the North translation (1580) mentions *the floods and rivers running all agore-blood, by reason of the great slaughter.*

agrest. Rustic, rude. From Latin *agrestis,* of the open country, from *agrum,* field. Caxton in Ovid's METAMORPHOSES (1480) uses it as a noun, the *agrests* that enjoy the countryside. *Agresty* appears in 18th century dictionaries, meaning rusticity. More frequent from the 17th through the 19th century is *agrestic;* Disraeli mentions in ENDYMION (1880) *a delightful ramble to some spot of agrestic charm.*

agrill. To annoy. Used in the 13th (THE OWL AND THE NIGHTINGALE) and the 14th centuries.

agrise. To shudder, to be full of terror; to dread, abhor; to terrify. From *a-,* an intensive prefix + *gris,* horror, as in *grisly.* See *grise.* A common word, found in the Laws of Cnut (1000) and up to

1650, in many spellings. Thus Chaucer in The Legend of Good Women (1385) *And in his heart he suddenly agroos, and pale he waxed;* Spenser uses the word several times in The Faërie Queene (1596) e.g., *whom when she saw . . . Like ghost late risen from his grave agryz'd, She knew him not.* Past tense forms include *agras, agros, agroos; agresyd, agryzd.* For another instance of its use, see *garboil.*

agrodolce. See *aigredoux.*

agrote. To cram, to cloy. This verb, of unknown origin, is found from about 1350 to 1450, only in the past participle form, *agroted,* surfeitéd, as in Chaucer's Legend of Good Women (1385): *I am agrotyed here beforn to write of them that been on love forsworn.* This also appears in the form *agroten: agroten (agrotonyd) with meat or drink.*

agrypnia. Sleeplessness. Greek *a,* not + *grypnia,* drowsiness, sleeping. Hence *agrypnode,* sleep preventing; *agrypnotic,* something administered to keep one awake. [The form, from Greek *agrypnetikos,* should be *agrypnetic;* the word was fashioned, in the mid 9th century, after *hypnotic.*]

aguilt. To offend, to sin against. From Old English *a-,* with intensive force + *gyltan,* to sin; *gieldan,* to pay for, to requite. Sometimes used with *against,* sometimes directly as in Chaucer's Parson's Tale (1386): *He hath agultid his God and defoulid his soule.*

aguise. To adorn; to dress. Used several times by Spenser, as in Mother Hubberd's Tale and in The Faërie Queene (1596): *Sometimes her head she fondly would aguize With gaudy girlonds.*

aha. A variant of *haha, q.v.* Not to be confused with the exclamation *Aha!,* which runs from Chaucer and the villains of melodrama, a combination of the two interjections *Ah!* and *Ha!*

aheave. To lift up *(heave);* hence, to rear, to educate. Also *aheve, ahebban.* Used from the 10th to the 14th century; Layamon in 1205 recorded: *Cador his sweard ahof.*

ahof. An old past tense of *aheave, q.v.*

ahte. (1) Possessions, property. (2) ought. (3) aught. (4) eight.

ahwene. See *awhene.'*

aichomancy. See *aeromancy.*

aiel. A grandfather; forefather, ancestor. Old French *aiel, aieul;* Late Latin *aviolus,* diminutive of *avus,* grandfather. Chaucer in The Knight's Tale (1386) has: *I am thyn aiel, redy at thy wille.*

aigredoux. Sweet and sour. Also *aigredouce, agerdows.* Skelton in A Garland of Laurel (1523) said *He wrote an epitaph for his grave stone With wordes devoute and sentence agerdows.* The 19th century used an Italian form; Ford in Handbook For Spain (1845) said: *In Spain, as Sappho says, love is . . . an alternation of the agrodolce.* The term is also applied to food, as described in Badham's Halieutics (1854)—*a blending of sweets and sours, and is made by stewing in a rich gravy prunes, Corinth currants, almonds, pine-kernels, raisins, vinegar, and wine.*

aimcrier. One that indicates the mark. By extension, an encourager, applauder; one that helps with words alone. Markham in England's Arcadia (1638) said: *Her own creatures, like aimcriers, beheld her mischance with nothing but lip-pity.*

airling. A young, thoughtless person; a coxcomb. Also *earling.* Jonson in Cati-

LINE (1611) says: *Some more there be, slight airlings, will be won With dogs and horses.*

airstone. A meteorite. A letter of 1608 said: *They talk of divers prodigies, as well in these parts as in Holland, but especially airstones.*

aischrology. Shameful discourse. Greek *aischros,* disgracing, shameful; also, ugly (opposed to *kalos,* beautiful, whence *callisthenics, calligraphy;* see *callipygian*). *Aischrology* is not in O.E.D., but for an illlustration of its use, see *morology.*

ait. See *eyot.*

ajar. See *chare.*

ajax. An outhouse; a privy; a room for a close-stool, *q.v.* The word is a pun on the name of the ancient hero, which in Tudor times was pronounced *a jakes.* A *jakes* (q.v.) was a toilet. Sir John Harington is credited with the invention of the overhead water closet for flushing; for his punning discussion of it, THE METAMORPHOSIS OF AJAX (1596), Queen Elizabeth I kept him in disgrace. Camden in his REMAINS (1625) told that one *Solomon, a Jew, fell into a jakes at Tewkesbury on a Saturday.* Shakespeare used the word earlier, in LOVE'S LABOUR'S LOST (1588): *Your lion that holds his pollax sitting on a close stoole, will be given to Ajax.* Camden, speaking of *pet* (French for an anal expulsion of wind) said: *Inquire, if you know it not, of Cloacina's chaplains, or such as are well read in Ajax.* The subtitle of Harington's work was A CLOACINEAN SATIRE; *Cloacina* was the goddess of disposal; Latin *cloaca,* sewer; *cluere,* to purge. In English, *cloaca* has been used for a privy; figuratively, for a receptacle of moral filth. Adjectives formed from it were *cloacal* (current as a scientific term), *cloacaline, cloacean, cloacinal, cloacinean;* Meredith in THE EGOIST (1879) says: *We, sir, dedicate genius to the cloacaline floods.* The cloaca makes a sorry end for—next to Achilles—the bravest of all the Greek heroes, Ajax. Jonson shows the rhyme in his poem ON THE FAMOUS VOYAGE: *And I could wish for their eterniz'd sakes My muse had plough'd with his that sung Ajax.*

akerspire. See *acrospire.*

alabandical. Barbarous, sottish, stupid. A good word though hitherto found only in dictionaries of the 17th and 18th centuries. Pliny (who died A.D. 79 through trying too closely to observe an eruption of Vesuvius) speaks of *Alabanda,* a city in Caria, as a barbarous place. In Medieval Latin the word took on meaning from Old Teutonic *alilandisc,* foreign, outlandish.

alacriate. To speed up; brighten; to fill with *alacrity.* Also *alacrify.* Latin *alacris,* brisk, lively. Hence *alacrative,* pertaining, or tending, to alacrity; speeding up; sprightly; also *alacrious.* Warner in ALBION'S ENGLAND (1602) spoke of *his alacrious intertainments, and upright government.*

aladdinize. To transform as if at a rub of Aladdin's magic lamp, described in the ARABIAN NIGHTS.

alamort. A form of the French *à la mort,* to the death; mortally sick, dispirited. Common from 1550 to 1800. Also *all amort, amort.* Thus Shakespeare in THE TAMING OF THE SHREW (1596): *What sweeting, all-amort?;* Dryden in THE WIFE OF BATH'S TALE (1700): *Mirth there was none, the man was a-la-mort;* Keats in THE EVE OF ST. AGNES (1820): *She sighs . . . all amort.*

alan. A large hunting dog, a wolf-hound. Also *alant, alaunt.* Chaucer in THE KNIGHT'S TALE (1386) says: *Aboute his chaar ther wenten white alauntz.* Used into the 18th century; Bailey in his DICTIONARY calls the dog *aland;* revived by Scott in THE TALISMAN (1825) as the wolf-greyhound.

alange. Wearisome, dreary; lonely—and by confusion with *elelende* (see *alabandical*), strange, foreign. Also *alenge.* In ARTHUR AND MERLIN (1330) we read *In time of winter alange it is.* The same work uses the word as a verb: *Rain alangeth the country;* this is the only such use. The adjective is found in Occleve and Chaucer. It also takes the form *elenge,* which Chaucer accents to rhyme with challenge. As late as 1858 MURRAY'S HANDBOOK TO KENT claimed that *the fairies . . . may still be heard in the more elenge places of the Downs.* A noun meaning loneliness was also formed; in THE ROMANCE OF THE ROSE (1400): *She had a . . . scrippe of faint distresse, that full was of elengenesse;* in a letter of 1536 King Henry VIII wrote to his Queen of the hour, of *the great ellingness that I find here since your departure.*

alapat. To strike. Medieval Latin *alapare, alapatum; alapa,* a slap. Melton in SIXE-FOLD POLITICIAN (1609) warned *not with a wand to alapat and strike them.* An *alapite,* in Old French, was a clown that took a beating to amuse the public, what we might call a *slapstick artist.*

alaski. To release, free. Via Old French *à* + *laskier* (modern French *lâcher*); Late Latin *lascare;* Latin *laxare,* whence also *relax; laxative;* Latin *laxus,* loose. Layamon (1250) wrote *Ich wole . . . alaski him of care.*

alastor. An avenging spirit, a nemesis. Greek *a,* not + *last-; lathein,* to forget. Taylor in THE MONTHLY MAGAZINE in 1810 wrote of *Imps, alastors, and every other class of cacodemons.* Shelley's first important poem (1816) was *Alastor, or The Spirit of Solitude.*

alate. Three words have used this form. (1) *alate,* lately. *A* of + *late.* Greene in a poem of 1590 wrote: *Where chilling frost alate did nip, There flasheth now a fire.* Mrs. Browning used the word in a poem of 1842. (2) *alate,* to suckle. Latin *adlactare,* to give milk to; *ad,* to + *lactum,* milk, whence also the *galactic* universe. (3) *alate,* winged. This meaning demands the accent on the first syllable; the word is used of leaves, insects and the like, as in the observation of G. Buckton (1876) of the aphis: *The alate females are never so plentiful as the apterous.*

alatrate. To bark, bark at. More properly *allatrate;* Latin *allatrare, allatratum,* from *ad,* at + *latrare,* to bark. Stubbes in THE ANATOMY OF ABUSES (1583) said: *Let Cerberus, the dog of hel, alatrate what he list to the contrary.*

albification. The process or art of making white. The verb, *to albify* is used by Nicholas Breton in his lines for Sir Philip Sidney's OURANIA (1606): *As a red brick by waters albified.* The noun was used chiefly as a term in alchemy; Chaucer in THE CANON YEOMAN'S TALE (1386) speaks of *watres albificacioun. To albify* might well be used figuratively, as now *to whitewash.*

albricias. In the days when the bearer of ill tidings might be whipped or put to death, *albricias* (still current in Spanish) meant a reward given one that brought good news.

alcahest. A variant of *alkahest, q.v.*

alcatote. A simpleton, silly fellow. Ford in his FANCIES (1638) confessed: *I am . . . an oaf, a simple alcatote, an innocent.*

alchemusy. A reflector to catch the sun's rays, for prophesying; forecasting by the use of this. *Cp. aeromancy.* Golding in his translation (1587) of P. de Mornay's WOORKE CONCERNING THE TREWNESSE OF THE CHRISTIAN RELIGION wrote: *Afterward he (who would prophecy) must gather together the beames of the skie into a mirror, which they call alchemusic, made according to the rules of catoptrick.*

alchocoden. See *aeromancy.*

alday. Every day; all the day. Chaucer prefers this form to the later *all day.*

alder-. In combinations, this is a variant of *aller,* the old genitive plural of *all.* Thus *alderbest* means best of all. Chaucer uses this prefix with many words, among them: *alderfairest, alderfastest, alderfirst, alderlast, alderleast, aldermost, aldernext* (nearest of all), *alderliefest* (best loved of all), *alderwisest, alderworst. Alderman* is from a different source: the *aldor* or *elder* was oldest and therefore most respected, therefore leader of the family (as in China until 1948) or of the clan. The *alderman* is the political successor of the *aldor.* Humorous words have sprung from this: *aldermanity,* behavior proper to an *alderman* (coined after *humanity*); *aldermanikin,* a petty office-holder. Shakespeare in HENRY VI, PART TWO (1590) has Queen Margaret pay respect to *mine alderliefest sovereign.*

aleatory. Dependent on the throw of a die, hence, hanging upon uncertain contingencies. From Latin *aleatorius,* from *aleator,* dice player, from *alea,* die. As Caesar crossed the Rubicon—which committed him to the march on Rome—he said *Alea jacta est,* The die is cast. Urquhart, in his translation (1693) of Rabelais, speaks of the *aleatory way of deciding law debates.*

aleberry. Ale boiled with spice and sugar and sops of bread. Also *albry, alebrue, alemeat.* The word is from ale + Old English *briw,* pottage; this shifted to *alebre, alebrey,* and then by folk-etymology to *aleberry.* It was a popular concoction of the 15th and 16th centuries. By a similar folk-fancy, *bread brewed* in hot water and spiced or sweetened was called *breadberry.*

alec. A herring; also, a sauce of or with small herrings, anchovies and the like. Used from the 16th century. Hence, *alecize, halecize,* to dress with such a sauce.

alecie. Intoxication; wandering of wits, under the influence of *ale* (as *lunacy* means the state of being under the influence of *luna,* the moon). Also *alecy.* Lyly in MOTHER BOMBIE (1594) said: *If he had arrested a mare instead of a horse, it had beene a slight oversight, but to arrest a man, that hath no likenesse of a horse, is flat lunasie, or alecie.*

aleconner. An inspector of ale—also of bread, beere, etc. sold within his jurisdiction. From the 13th century; also *alekonner, alecunner.* Johnson in 1755 observed: "Four of them are chosen annually by the common-hall of the city; and whatever might be their use formerly, their places are now regarded only as sinecures for decayed citizens." The ENCYCLOPEDIA BRITANNICA nevertheless recorded in 1876: *In London four aleconners are still chosen annually by the liverymen in common hall assembled on Midsummer Day (cp. midsummer men).*

The British Information Office tells me they serve today.

alectorian. A stone (said John de Trevisa in his translation (1398) of Bartholomews' DE PROPRIETATIBUS RERUM) *that is founde in the mawes of capons and is lyke to dymme cristall.* It had the valuable property of rendering one invisible. The word is from Greek *alector,* cock; the story is cock and bull.

alectromancy. See *aeromancy.* Also *alectoromancy* and *alectryomancy.*

alectryomachy. Cock-fighting. A common sport, for centuries, in various parts of the world. The English also enjoyed bear-baiting; the Chinese wagered large sums on cricket fights. The word is from Greek *alectryon,* cock + *machia,* fighting; the accent falls on the *om.* A good fighting cock is still worth over $1000 in Spanish-speaking countries, where alectryomachy rivals bull-fighting. The word *alectryomachy,* however, seems confined to 17th and 18th century dictionaries.

alecy. See *alecie.*

aleger. (1) Ale-vinegar: *alegar is to ale what vinegar is to wine* (1881 glossary). Also *aleager, alegre; ale + eager;* French *aigre,* sharp, sour. Used from the 16th century; Carlyle in THE FRENCH REVOLUTION (1837) inquires: *Whose small soul, transparent wholesome-looking as small ale, could by no chance ferment into virulent alegar?* (2) lively, cheerful. Via Old French from Latin *alacrem,* whence also *alacrity;* Italian *allegro.* Bacon in SYLVA (1626) noted that *the root, and leafe betell; the leafe tobacco; and the teare of poppy . . . doe all condense the spirits, and make them strong, and aleger.* (Both words are pronounced in three syllables; the first is accented on the long *a;* the second, with short *a,* is accented on the *ledge.*)

aleiptic. Relating to physical training. A 17th century word that somehow our modern educators have missed. From Greek *aleiptikos, aleiptes,* a gymnastic trainer, a rubber; *aleiphein,* to anoint.

ale-knight. A tippler (used in scorn). Guilpin, in SKIALETHEIA, OR A SHADOWE OF TRUTH IN CERTAINE EPIGRAMS (1598) said: *There brauls an aleknight for his fat-grown score.*

alembic. An early type of apparatus, used for distilling, especially by the alchemists. From 1500 to 1700 almost completely supplanted by the shorter form *limbec, q.v.;* then the full form reappeared, often in figurative use, as when Scott in WAVERLY (1814) speaks of *the cool and procrastinating alembic of Dyer's Weekly Letter,* or Walpole in a letter of 1749, *the important mysteries that have been alembicked out of a trifle.*

alembroth. A universal solvent. Long sought by the alchemists, this self-contradictory substance was often hailed but never held.—What could hold it? Thus *sal alembroth* was the double chloride of mercury and ammonium, also called the salt of wisdom.

alenge. See *alance.*

aleuromancy. See *aeromancy.*

alexicacon. A preservative against, or remedy for, evil. A panacea sought in the 17th and 18th centuries. The word is from Greek *alexein,* to keep off + *kakon,* evil. We need an alexicacon for current cacophony via the air waves. A dose against poison was called an *alexipharmic;* something to ward off contagion was an *alexiteric* or *alexitery.* The PHILOSOPHICAL TRANSACTIONS OF THE ROYAL SOCIETY for 1671 declare that *the heart or liver of a viper is one of the greatest alexitery's in the world.* The name *Alexander,* by the way, means protector of men.

alexipharmac. An antidote to poison. Also *alexipharmic;* see *alexicacon.* Greek *pharmakon,* poison; hence *pharmacy,* where remedies against poison were available. For an illustration of its use, see *theriac.*

alfavourite. A 17th century hairdress, for ladies; probably from France. THE LADIES DICTIONARY (1694) listed: *alfavourites, a sort of modish locks hang dangling on the temples.*

alfin. A 15th and 16 century word for the bishop, in the game of chess. Also *alphin, alphyne, alfyn, aufyn, awfyn.* Via the Romance tongues from Arabic *al-fil* (Sanskrit *pilu*), the elephant. Rowbotham in his ARCHAEOLOGY (1562) said: *The bishoppes some name alphins, some fooles, and some name them princes; other some call them archers.* The second book on the first English printing press, translated (1475) by the printer, Caxton, THE GAME AND PLAY OF THE CHESSE, said that *the alphyns ought to be made and formed in manner of judges, sitting in a chair, with a book open before their eyes.* By extention, *alfin,* a person of limited powers, a fool; The MORTE D'ARTHUR (1440) exclaimed: *Myche wondyre have I, that syche an alfyne as thow dare speke sych wordez!* Wright (1869) defines this as *a lubberly fellow* and suggests it is a form of *elfin, elvish.*

alfridary. According to astrology, a temporary power the planets have over the life of a person, each presiding over his destiny for seven years. From the Arabic, *al,* the + *fariydah,* a fixed part. *Cp. almuten.*

algate. In Old English, this was *alle gate,* every way; its meaning grew in many ways, and it was a very common word into the 17th century. Also *algates.* It still survives, meaning everywhere, in northern dialects, along with the forms *any gate, na-gate, sumgate.* Among the meanings are: (1) Always, continually. Used by Wyclif; Staynhurst (AENEIS; 1583); Holinshed in the CHRONICLES (1587): *These strangers in Ireland would algate now be also called and accompted Normans.* (2) In any way, by any means. Lydgate; Gabriel Harvey in THREE WITTY LETTERS (1580): *Seeing you gentlewomen will allgates have it so.* (3) At all events, in any case. Chaucer; Lydgate; Douglas (AENEIS; 1513): *Since algatis I must die.* (4) Altogether. Chaucer (THE SQUIRE'S TALE; 1386): *Which is unknown algates unto me;* Spenser.

algor. Cold; specifically, the chill that marks the onset of fever. Latin *algor; algere,* to be cold. Also *algidity, algidness,* in 17th and 18th century dictionaries. More frequent (especially in science and medicine, 17th century) were the adjectives: *algid,* cold; *algific, algifical,* causing cold, making one chill; *algose,* very cold. Burton in his picture of DAHOME (1864) spoke of *the algid breath of the desert wind.*

algorism. The Arabic system of numbering; hence, arithmetic. Hence *algorism-stones,* counters; *cypher in algorism,* the figure 0; hence, a dummy, a nobody. An *algorist* was one skilful in figuring. From the Arabic surname of Abu Ja' far Mohammed Ben Musa, the translation of whose early 9th century treatise on algebra brought Arabic numerals into wide use in Europe. A native of *Khwarazm,* he was called *al-Khowarazmi;* this gave his figures, in English, such names as *augrim, awgrym, algram, agrim, agrum, algrim, algarisme, algorithm, algarosme.* Chaucer in THE MILLER'S TALE (1386) says: *His augrym stoones leyen faire apart.*

alicant. A wine of mulberries, made at *Alicante,* Spain. Also *alegant, aligaunt, allegant, alycaunt, alligaunte, aligant,* and the like. Fletcher, in THE CHANCES (1620) said: *You brats, got* [begotten] *out of alicant.* TIMON (1585) depicts a wondrous land: *Thirtie rivers more With aligaunte; thirtie hills of sugar; Ale flowed from the rockes, wine from the trees Which we call muscadine. Alicant* was a popular drink; its deep red color was attractive; many a courtier wore a *doublet of allicant.* Shakespeare may have had this in mind when Mistress Quickly tells Falstaff (in THE MERRY WIVES OF WINDSOR; 1598) that he has brought Mistress Ford *into such a canaries as 'tis wonderful,* when knights and lords wooing her have failed, despite *gift after gift; smelling so sweetly—all musk—and so rushling, I warrant you, in silk and gold; and in such alligant terms; and in such wine and sugar of the best and the fairest, that would have won any woman's heart.* Mistress Quickly uses elegant, if not alicant, terms.

alienation. See *abalienate.*

alife. Dearly. Especially in the expression *to love alife;* Shakespeare in THE WINTER'S TALE (1610) has: *I love a ballad in print alife.* Some editions print this *o' life,* as though it meant *as one's life;* but it is probably an adverbial form from *lief,* dear, which survives in the expression *I'd just as lief.*

aligaunt. See *alicant.*

alkahest. The universal solvent sought by the alchemists. Also *alcakest, alchahest; cp. alembroth; alexicacon.* The word *alkahest* was created by Paracelsus (*cp. bombast*), as though from an Arabic form; a number of English words begin with Arabic *al,* the. Hence *alkahestic, alkahestical.* It has also been suggested, however, that *alkahest* is (1705) *from the German word Al-gehest, which signifies all spirit.* There remains the old query: if the universal solvent be found, what container will hold it? The word has also been used figuratively, as of love; Carlyle (MISCELLANEOUS ESSAYS; 1832) said *Quite another alcahest is needed.* Alger in THE SOLITUDES OF NATURE AND OF MAN (1866) spoke neatly of *an intellectual alkahest, melting the universe into an idea.*

alkanet. A plant, whose root yields a bright red dye. Also *alcanna* and, in the East, *henna; orcanet, orchanet;* a kind of bugloss, *q.v.;* also used in cookery, and esteemed as a cordial.

alker. A kind of custard. A recipe of 1381 might still prove good to follow: *For to make rys alker. Take figys, and raysons, and do awey the kernelis, and a god party of applys, and do awey the paryng of the applis and the kernelis, and bray hem wel in a morter; and temper hem up with almande mylk, and menge hem with flowr of rys, that yt be wel chariaunt, and strew therupon powder of galyngale, and serve yt forth.*

alkermes. A confection or cordial, made with the *kermes* 'berry.' Arabic *al,* the + *girmiz,* kermes—only the 'berry' turned out to be an insect, the scarlet grain (female of *coccus ilicis*). Alkermes was also used to mean the 'berry' of which the concoctions were made. Accent on the *kur.* Captain John Smith, in his account of his VOYAGE TO VIRGINIA (1624) stated that the *fruits are of many sorts and kinds, as alkermes, currans, mulberries* . . . Bacon in THE ADVANCEMENT OF LEARNING (1605) lists *Venice treacle, mithridate, diascordium, the confection of alkermes.*

alkin. Of every kind, all kinds of. A 12th to 16th century form; also *alra cynna, alle kunnes, alkyns, alken. Wors than they,* said Lyndesay in a COMPLAYNT of 1552, *in alkin thyng.*

allatrate. See *alatrate.*

allect. To allure. After the Latin *allectare,* frequentative form of *allicere,* from *ad,* to + *lacere,* to entice, *laqueus,* a noose, a snare. Sir Thomas More in HERESYES (1528): *To allect the people by preaching. Allectation,* found only in old dictionaries, and the once-used (1640) *allection* were formed from *allect,* to mean an alluring, enticement. *Allective,* as adjective and noun, was more frequent in the 16th and 17th centuries; Elyot in THE GOVERNOUR (1531): *There is no better alective to noble wits;* Gabriel Harvey in PIERCES SUPEREROGATION (1592): *Her beautiful and allective style as ingenious as elegant.* THE REMEDY OF LOVE (1532) speaks of *most allective bait,* which has its place and allective power in our time. The same meaning appears with the forms *alliciate* and *allicit.* See *illect.*

alliciate, allicit. See *allect.*

allide. See *allision.*

alligate. To tie or bind. From Latin *ad,* to + *ligare,* to bind. More common was the noun, *alligation,* the act of attaching, or the state of being attached or bound. Phillips (1706) and Bailey (1731) in their dictionaries list *alligator,* a binder (as of vines to the stakes up which they are to grow). The reptile *alligator* is from Spanish *al lazardo,* the lizard, applied to the large American saurians. *Allegation* and *allegator* (one that *alleges* or asserts) are via Norman *alegier* from Latin *exlitigare,* to clear at law, modified by confusion with Latin *allegare,* from *ad,* to + *legare,* to designate. There is another obsolete *allege,* to lighten a burden, to *allay,* via Old French *aleger* from Latin *alleviare* (whence also *alleviate*), from *ad,* to + *levis,* light. THE ROMANCE OF THE ROSE (1400) says: *I would this thought would come ageyne, For it alleggith well my peyne.* These words should not be confusedly alligated.

alling. Altogether, wholly; quite; indeed. Also *allings; allunga, allinge, allynge, allyng.* Used from the 9th into the 15th century. Maundeville wrote in 1366: *It is not allynges of suche savour.*

allision. The action of dashing against or striking upon. Latin *al, ad,* to + *laedere, laesum,* to dash, strike violently, whence the frequent *collision.* Thus also, *to allide.* Donne, in a sermon of 1631, held the old view *that the allision of those clouds have brought forth a thunder.*

allodium. An estate held in full and free ownership, without any service or recognition of an overlord; as opposed to *feudum, feud.* Also *alodium, allody, alody, allod, alod.* From *all* + *od,* property, estate. An early Teutonic term; the forms ending *ium* are Latinized, and in the DOMESDAY BOOK (1086).

allograph. A writing (as a signature) of one person for another. Greek *allos,* other + *graph,* writing. The opposite of *autograph;* Greek *auto,* self. Among words in English formed with *allos* may be mentioned: *allogeneity,* difference in nature; *allogeneous,* the opposite of *homogene-*

ous. allonym, an assumed name; a book bearing a name as the author's, not that of the author; *allonymous,* falsely attributed. *allotheism,* worship of other or strange gods. *allotropy* (accent on the *lot;* current in scientific use), the variation of physical properties without change of substance—first noticed (by Berzelius) of charcoal and diamond.

allophyle. This is a formal term for an alien; hence, sometimes, with a measure of scorn, a Philistine. It is from Greek *allos,* other + *phyle,* tribe. It is mainly a 19th century term. J. Pritchard, in BLACKWOOD'S MAGAZINE of 1844, speaks of the allophylian nations.

alloquial From Latin *ad,* to + *loquor,* to talk, *alloquial* refers to the style of speech used in talking *to*—addressing—others. It is thus contrasted with the *colloquial* style, used in talking *with* others; conversational.

allubescency. See *adlubescence.*

allycholly. Misused for *mallycholly,* a corrupt form of *melancholy* (Greek *melan,* black + *choler,* bile). Dame Quickly in Shakespeare's THE MERRY WIVES OF WINDSOR (1598) says: *She is given too much to allicholy and musing;* in his THE TWO GENTLEMEN OF VERONA the Host says to Julia (disguised as a boy): *Now, my young guest, methinks you're allycholly. I pray you, why is it?* Julia responds: *Marry, mine host, because I cannot be merry.* To cheer her, he has sung the charming song *Who is Silvia?*

almagest. Originally, the great astronomical treatise of Ptolemy, of Alexandria, 2d century; later applied to any important book of astrology or alchemy. Thus Chaucer in THE MILLER'S TALE (1386) has: *His almageste and bokes gret and smale.* The word is the title of the Arabic translation of Ptolemy's work; it adds the Arabic *al,* the, to Greek *megiste,* greatest. Scott revived the word in THE LAY OF THE LAST MINSTREL (1805): *on cross, and character, and talisman, And almagest, and altar, nothing bright.* We have had many almagests, but only the stars remain bright.

almain. A dance; also, the music therefor. References in the 17th century and later speak of a slow tempo, and grave or solemn measures, but many references indicate a livelier dance, also called the *almain-leap.* Thus Jonson in THE DEVIL IS AN ASS pictures a man *take his almain-leap into a custard.* Also *almaun, alman, almane, aleman, almond.* The word literally meant German (French *aleman, allemand*); *Almany,* Germany, and an *Aleman* was a German. *almain-quarrel,* a dispute over nothing, an unnecessary argument. *almain-rivets,* a flexible type of light armor, first worn in Germany.

almariole. See *ambry.* An *l,* in combinations, often replaced an *r.*

almifluent. Benovolent, bounteous. Latin *almus,* kindly (as in *alma mater*) + *fluentem,* flowing. Used in the 15th century.

almoner. An official, in a monastery, or the household of a noble, whose function it was to distribute *alms.* The word was naturally popular; it took many forms, including *almner, aumoner, almoseir, almousser, almaser; almosner, almoisner, almosyner; almener, almonar, almoigner, aumere, amonerer.* These are all roundabout from Latin *eleemosynarius,* relating to alms; Greek *eleos,* compassion. *Almoner* was also the purse such a person carried; by extension, a bag, a purse. Other forms for *alms* were *almose, almus,* *almous.* The *almonry* (see *ambry*) was the place where the alms were distributed; also *almosery.* Cavendish in THE LYFFE AND DEATH OF CARDYNAL WOOLSEY (1557) wrote: *Now let us retorne agayn unto the almosyner, whose hed was full of subtyll wytt and pollecy.*

almuten. The prevailing planet in a horoscope. *Cp. alfridary.* Originally, the *horoscope* meant the point of the ecliptic just rising at the time of a person's birth; hence, the "house" then at that position; hence, one's future as forecast by the stars. The heavens were divided into 12 houses or sections of 30° each: life, riches, brethren, parents, children, health, marriage, death, religion, dignities, friends, enemies. The planet in the eighth house (at the time of one's birth) is called the *anareta* (accent on the *nar;* Greek *anairetes,* destroyer). The *apheta* is the giver of life, which must counteract the *anareta;* it stems from Greek *aphetes; aph,* off + *hienai,* to send, the starter in the chariot race, hence, the one that starts a human on his life's journey. The twelve signs of the *zodiac* (Greek *zodion,* diminutive of *zoon,* animal; so called from their various names), which successively occupy the twelve houses, are Aries, Taurus, Gemini, Cancer, Leo, Virgo, Libra, Scorpio, Sagittarius, Capricornus, Aquarius, Pisces. The Chinese named them more humbly: rat, ox, tiger, hare, dragon, serpent, horse, sheep, monkey, hen, dog, pig. The fault, dear Brutus, is not in our stars . . . but the word *disaster* means that the star (*aster*) has not been shining. While *almuten* is the usual form, *almute,* with plural *almutes,* also occurs.

alod. See *allodium.*

alogy. Absurdity. From Greek *alogia,* from *a,* not + *logos,* reason. Sir Thomas Browne in PSEUDODOXIA EPIDEMICA (1646) an inquiry into common errors, remarks that the error *and alogy in this opinion is worse than in the last.* An *allogism, alogism* is an instance of *alogy,* being an *alogical* or illogical statement. The poet Swinburne uses the Greek form as a suffix, in the title of his parodies: *Heptalogia, or Seven Against Sense.*

a lostell. Disperse! A command for a crowd to go to their homes, or soldiers to their quarters; used also by heralds to the finished fighters at a tournament. From Old French *à l'ostel* (whence English *hostel*), to your quarters. *The Kyng,* said Hall's CHRONICLES (1548) caused *the heraldes to cry a lostell, and every man to departe.* Old *ostel, hostel,* became *hotel,* and gave Sarah Bernhardt her one pun. When she became famous, the public wished to know whether she was married to the man she was living with. No one dared ask, but one reporter ventured to inquire: "Where were you married, Madame Bernhardt?" Knowing his intent, the actress mischievously replied: Naturellement, *à l'autel!* (*Naturally, at the altar*—altar, in French, having the same sound as *hotel*). *Cp. hostelity.*

alow. (1) To lower, lessen. Also *allow.* Used in the 16th century, as in Wyatt's PSALMS (1541): *Whereby he . . . gynneth to alowe his payne and penitence.* (2) Ablaze, in flame. Used in the 13th century; revived by Scott in THE HEART OF MIDLOTHIAN (1818): *To speak to him about that . . . wad be to set the kiln alow.* From *a,* in, on + *low,* flame. *Low* (*logh, lawe, lou;* Aryan root *lauk,* akin to *light*) was a common word for flame or blaze into the 16th century, much later in Scotland. Burns in his VISION (1785) says: *By my ingle lowe I saw . . . a tight, outlandish hizzie.* Kipling used the word in

BARRACK-ROOM BALLADS (1892). *In a low,* on fire. *To take a low,* to catch fire, literally or figuratively.

alp. In addition to the mountains (which are probably from Latin *albus,* white, whence also *perfidious Albion:* the white cliffs of Dover) *alp (alpe, awbe, olph)* meant (1) a bullfinch; 15th to 17th century; (2) an elephant; *elp.* Hence *alpes-bone,* ivory; 13th century; (3) a bogie, nightmare; BLACKWOOD'S EDINBURGH MAGAZINE of 1836 mentioned *those alps and goblins, those nixies and wood-nymphs.*

alphin. See *alfin.*

alphitomancy. See *aeromancy.*

Alsatia. See *bonaroba.*

alsauf. Without fail. Literally, *all safe.* The CHRONICLE of Robert of Gloucester (1297) recorded: *The kyng . . . bed hym alsauf to hym to Gloucestre wende.*

als ob. See *ob.*

altam. A variant form of *autem (mort), q.v.*

altiloquence. Pompous discourse. In the 18th century dictionaries. A criticism of 1808 spoke of *elegant archaisms . . . containing an altisonant altiloquence. Altiloquent* and *altisonant* are synonyms; *altiloquious* means talking much and loud. There is more merit in *altitonant* speech; the word is applied to the gods "thundering from on high." Thus Cowley in THE GUARDIAN (1641): *Hear, thou altitonant Jove, and Muses three.*

altitonant. See *altiloquence.*

alveary. A company of busy workers; a monumental work, such as an encyclopedia. (From Latin *alvearium,* a range of beehives; *alveus,* a hollow vessel, hence a beehive. Also Latin *alvus,* womb; hence English *alvary,* womb, lap, as in Barnfield's CASSANDRA, 1595: *From his soft bosom, th' alvary of bliss.*) Baret, in 1580, used the word *alveary* of an interlingual dictionary (English, Latin, French, and Greek), *which, for the apt similitude between the good scholars and diligent bees in gathering their wax and honey into their hive, I called then their alvearie.* For another quotation from Baret, see *prick (11).* By an equal similitude, anatomists call the hollow of the ear, where wax accumulates, the *alveary.*

amabyr. See *amober.*

amand. To send away, dismiss. Latin *a, ab,* off + *mandare,* to order. R. Carpenter in THE PRAGMATICAL JESUIT NEW-LEVEN'D (1665) wrote: *I will amand . . . thee to some vast and horrid desert.* Hence *amandation,* dismissal; the act of sending on an errand.

amanse. To curse, to excommunicate. Old English *a,* away + *mansum,* familiar; literally, to put out of familiarity. *Cp. manse.* Used until the 14th century (Bede, 9th century; THE OWL AND THE NIGHTINGALE, 13th). Hence, *amansed, amansumod,* anathematized, excommunicated; *amansing,* curse, excommunication.

amarant. The *amaranthus* (as though from Greek *a,* not + *mar,* mortal + *anthos,* flower) was a legendary flower that never faded; then the word was used figuratively. Drummond of Hawthornden speaks (1630) of *th' immortal amaranthus;* Milton uses this form in LYCIDAS (1637), but in PARADISE LOST (1667) he exclaims: *Immortal amaranth! a flower which once In Paradise, fast by the tree of life Began to bloom.* Southey in the QUARTERLY REVIEW of 1815 says: *His laurels are entwined with the amaranths of righteousness.*

Amaranth is still used in botany, of a flower; also, of its purple color. See *asphodel.* There is also an adjective *amarant(h)ine,* meaning immortal, unfading. Cowper in HOPE (1781) declares that *hope Plucks amaranthine joys from bowers of bliss.* May yours be likewise!

amaritude. Bitterness. From Latin *amaritude,* from *amarus,* bitter. Used from about 1450 to 1700, as in Speed's HISTORY OF GREAT BRITAIN (1611): *with much more bleeding amaritude of spirit.* The adjective *amarous* (accented on the second syllable), bitter, hard to be appeased, though found only in dictionaries, is a useful word; it must not be confused with *amorous,* in love, from Latin *amor,* love—though this state often leads to the other.

amate. (1) To dismay, dishearten, daunt. Common in the 16th century; from Old French *à,* to + *mater; mat,* downcast. Revived by Keats (1821): *A half-blown flow'ret which cold blasts amate.* (2) *amate,* to match, equal, be a *mate* to. Spenser in THE FAËRIE QUEENE (1596) has *Many a jolly paramoure, The which them did in modest wise amate.* Note that while *amating* meant dismaying, daunting, *amation* is listed in 17th century dictionaries as meaning wanton love. Latin *amor,* love; *amare, amatum,* to love (only fortuitously related to *amare,* bitter, *cp. amaritude*). Thus *amatorian, amatorious,* older forms of *amatory,* loving, pertaining to love. In the 17th century, *amatory* was also used to mean a love-potion. An *amatorculist* was a man that trifled with women's affections, a Don Juan, a 'general lover.' Also *amorevolous* (17th century), loving tender, affectionate. Thomas Heywood in THE HIERARCHIE OF THE BLESSED ANGELLS (1635) listed *magicke vanities, exorcisms, incantations, amatories.*

amathomancy. See *aeromancy.*

amatorculist. See *amate.*

ambage. Circumlocution, equivocation. Usually used in the plural, *ambages,* from Latin *amb-,* about + *agere,* to drive. *Ambage* was used in the Renaissance as a term in rhetoric, periphrasis, or roundabout discourse. It may be used literally, of winding paths; or figuratively of indirect ways and delaying practices. Bacon in THE ADVANCEMENT OF LEARNING (1605) gave the formula: *by ambages of diets, bathings, anointings, etc., prolong life.* Sir Francis Palgrave, in THE HISTORY OF NORMANDY AND OF ENGLAND (1857) cut through the ambagious obscurity: *He commenced by a few politic ambages, or —to speak more plainly—lies.* Hence *ambagical, ambaginous, ambagious, ambagitory,* roundabout; winding; circumlocutory. Thus *ambagiosity.* Scott in WAVERLEY (1814) wrote: *Partaking of what scholars call the periphrastic and ambagitory, and the vulgar the circumbendibus.*

ambesas. Two aces, the lowest throw at dice. Latin *ambo, q.v.* Hence, *to cast an ambesas,* to have bad luck. Used 10th to 14th century, as in THE LIFE OF BEKET, 13th century. Also *ambezas; ambsace, ambes aas, aumsase, almsace, amsace, ame's ace,* and the like. Shakespeare in ALL'S WELL THAT ENDS WELL (1601) has: *I had rather be in this choice than throw ames-ace for my life.* Lowell in AMONG MY BOOKS (1870) speaks of *a lucky throw of words which may come up the sices of hardy metaphor or the ambsace of conceit.*

ambidextrous. The earlier form, both as an adjective and as a noun (the person), is *ambidexter* (in the 17th century usually *ambodexter*) from Latin *ambo,* both + *dexter,* right-hand. And those that know the meaning "able to use both hands alike" may be surprised that the first English use of the word (1532) signified double-dealing; or, in the law courts, a juror that took bribes from both sides. Thus De Foe in 1731 spoke of *those ambodexters in religion, who can anything dispute, yet anything can do.*

ambient. As a noun. The atmosphere; an encompassing circle or sphere; by extension, a 'hanger around,' a suitor or aspirant. Bishop Hall in CONFIRMATION (1649) asked: *What fair-like confluences have we there seen of zealous ambients?* Latin *amb-*, on both sides, around + *ientem,* present participle of *ire,* to go. The noun is a special use of the adjective, *ambient,* turning round; surrounding.

ambigu. An entertainment where the various courses are served together, the viands and the desserts at the same time. The term was used during the 17th and 18th centuries; the practice continues at parties and picnics.

ambilevous. See *ambo.* Accented on the *lee.*

ambiloquent. Double-tongued, competent in "double talk." From Latin *ambi-*, both + *loquor,* to talk. The great number of those that can—and do—take either side of an argument makes this a good word to revive. It is accented on the second syllable.

ambo. The pulpit or reading desk in early Christian churches; usually a raised oblong enclosure with steps at both ends. Also *ambon;* plural *ambos* or (three syllables) *ambones.* Greek *ambon,* a rising; *anaba-*, go up. Milton in 1641 exclaimed: *The admirers of antiquity have been beating their brains about their ambones.* Note that Latin *ambo* (as in the quotation *Arcades ambo,* Arcadians both) meaning both, is a frequent prefix in English (*ambosexous,* hermaphrodite) in the form *ambi-*, as in *ambiguous; ambiloquent; ambidextrous* and its opposite *ambilevous,* doubly lefthanded, also *ambisinistrous, ambilaevous;* hence, uncommonly awkward.

ambry. A place for keeping things; a cupboard; especially, a place for keeping food. Thus an *ambry of hair* was a meatsafe lined with haircloth. Also *aumbry;* from Latin *armarium,* a place for keeping *arms* and *armor,* then clothing, etc. (The sound *b* frequently slips into words, e.g., Latin *numerus,* English *number.*) *Ambry* was a common English word, with a dozen spellings, from the 14th to the mid-19th century. Through the 17th and 18th century, *ambry* was sometimes used as a short form of *almonry,* the place in a church or palace from which *alms* were distributed. *Cp. almoner.* Stanyhurst in his AENEIS (1583) uses *ambry* of the Trojan horse into which the Greeks "rammed a number of hardy tough knights." The word was also used figuratively; Earl Rivers in THE DICTES OF THE PHILOSOPHERS (1477) says *The tongue is the door of the almerye of sapience.* Langland in PIERS PLOWMAN (1393) points out that *avarice hath almaries and yre-bounden* [ironbound] *cofres.* The *ambry* appeared also as *almary;* a little closet was an *almariole.*

ambsace. See *ambesas.*

amel. An early form of *enamel.* Used from the 14th century; also *ammel, aumayl, amall; anmaile* and *esmayle* were also used in the 16th century, before they were superseded by *enamel.* The forms are via Old French *esmail* from a Teutonic root *smalti,* to smelt. The word was often applied figuratively; Phineas Fletcher in THE PURPLE ISLAND (1633) mentioned *Heav'ns richest diamonds, set in ammel white.*

amerce. To fine. Also *amercement,* a penalty, fine. From the French phrase *à merci,* at the mercy of. To be *amerced* was to be at some one's mercy as to the penalty one must pay; to *amerce* was to set an arbitrary penalty. (Often this was lighter than could have been exacted.) Chaucer uses various forms, as in THE PARSON'S TALE (1386): *Else take they of their bondman amerciament which might more reasonably be cleped extortions than amerciments.* Grote, in his HISTORY OF GREECE (1849) speaks of *the defeat, the humiliation, and the amercement of the Carthaginians.* The words are now mainly legal or historical, though it has been asked, in recent humorous verse: *May a miss amerce a mister if he missed her for a kiss?* See also *affeer.*

ames-ace. See *ambesas.*

amess. See *amice.*

amethodist. A person that follows no rational procedure; applied often to a quack doctor. Used in the 17th century; Whitlock in ZOOTOMIA, OR OBSERVATIONS ON THE PRESENT MANNERS OF THE ENGLISH (1654) observed: *It cannot be lookt for, that these empirical amethodists should understand the order of art, or the art of order.*

amfractuous. See *anfractuous.*

amice. Two words fused in this one—which also took other forms: *amess, amict, amit, ammas, ames, amysse, ammesse,* and more. One form came, perhaps, from Arabic *al,* the + German *mutse,* cap. The other came from Latin *amictus,* something thrown around; *amicere, amictus,* to throw or wrap around; *amb,* about + *iacere (iaciere),* to throw. The first meaning, from the Latin, was a scarf, a kerchief, or other loose wrap; then, in church use, an oblong of white linen for the head and neck, later the neck and shoulders. In religious costume symbolism this was taken as the 'helmet of salvation'; although this was disputed by protestant Tindale, who in his ANSWER TO SIR THOMAS MORE'S DIALOGUE (1530) said: *The amice on the head is the kerchief that Christ was blindfolded with . . . now it may well signify that he that putteth it on is blinded, and hath professed to lead us after him in darkness.* From the other source, *amice* was a part of the religious costume (originally a cap) lined with gray fur; later, a hood or a cape with a hood. Marriott in his study of church costume, VESTIARIUM CHRISTIANUM (1868) tries to keep the two apart: *Of similar origin is the amess, often confused with the amice.* Sometimes the word *amice* was used of the fur with which the garment was lined (marten or gray squirrel). Since the 17th century, if a distinction is drawn, the fur-lined article is called a *gray amice.* This was used figuratively by Milton in PARADISE REGAINED (1671): *Morning fair Came forth with pilgrim steps in amice gray.* For a use by Francis Thompson, see *thurifer.*

amicitial. Relating to friendship; friendly. Also *amicous.* Used in the 17th century. Latin *amicitia,* friendship; *amicus,* friend; *amare, amatum,* to love. These forms were superseded by *amical* and *amicable;* the latter, however, is a late variation of *amiable;* similarly, *appliable* existed before *applicable.*

amiss. As a noun. An error; an evil deed. Shakespeare in HAMLET (1602) says:

Each toy seemes prologue to some great amisse. For another instance, see *cantharides.*

amit. See *amice.*

amiture. The O.E.D. defines this as clothing, dress; as from Latin *amicire, amictum,* to cover, from *amb-,* about + *iacere,* to throw, whence also English *amict,* also *amice, q.v.; amit,* a kerchief, a cloth for enveloping the head, or covering the neck and shoulders. Thus in KYNG ALYSAUNDER (13th century) we find: *Yursturday thow come in amiture.* Herbert Coleridge, however, referring to the same passage in his DICTIONARY OF THE OLDEST WORDS IN THE ENGLISH LANGUAGE (1863), defines *amiture* as friendship (as from Latin *amicus,* friend, whence also *amity.* Both meanings fit the use of the word in English.

ammove. To move away. Supplanted by *remove,* which literally meant to move back. *Ammove* was not found by the compilers of the O.E.D. It occurs in a municipal order in York (1476), calling four players in the mystery cycle to *examen all the players and plays and pageants. And all such as they shall find sufficient in person and connyng, to the honour of the city, and worship of the said crafts, to admit; and all other insufficient persons, either in connyng, voice or person to discharge, ammove and avoid. Connyng* was sometimes an old form of *cunning,* which then meant skilful, but here it is the noun from the verb to *con,* to learn (by repetition).

amnicolist. See *amnigenous.*

amnigenous. From Latin *amnis,* river + *genus,* born, this word signifying born by a river, like Moses, Shakespeare and me, or born on a river, was copied in Johnson's DICTIONARY from Bailey's (1731). It is a good but apparently unused word. Also *amnicolist,* one that dwells by a river. Both are accented on the second syllable.

amober. The maiden-fee, formerly payable to a lord (in Wales) on the marriage of a maid of his manor. From Welsh *am* + *wobr, gwobr,* reward. The lord had the right *primae noctis,* of the first night, when virgins of his household were married; if the husband wished to have that privilege, he had to buy his bride's virginity with the *amober.* Another spelling of the word for this practice, or for the fee, is *amabyr.*

amoebaean. Alternately answering; of verse in which two speak alternately. Also *amoebean,* accent on the *be.* Greek *amoibaios,* interchanging; *amoibe,* change, whence the volatile *amoeba.* THE SATURDAY REVIEW of 25 May, 1861, spoke of *that amoebean exchange of witticisms between the Bench and the Bar.* THE CORNHILL MAGAZINE of January 1883 said that Spring and Winter *sing an amoebean ode.*

amoret. This word has a number of lovely senses, from French *amourette,* diminutive of *amour,* love; Latin *amorem.* (1) A sweetheart, a girl in love. (2) A paramour, a mistress. (3) A love-knot or other amorous decoration. (4) A love-song or sonnet. (5) Loving glance or dalliance; allurement, love-play. The Italian form (masculine) *amoretto,* similarly has several meanings as an English word: (1) A lover. (2) A love song. Spenser entitled his sonnets (1596) AMORETTI. (3) A game or play of love. (4) A Cupid, in statue or painting. For this, the word *amorino* was also used. Other forgotten words drawn from Latin *amorem,* both of the 17th century, are *amorevolous* (via Italian from *amorem* + *volo,* I want), loving; and *amoring,* love-making. Also *amorist,* a specialist in love-making, like jolly Dan who's determined to know a lass of every land. Sidney, in a Sonnet of 1581, exclaims: *Faint amorist! What, dost thou think To taste love's honey and not drink One dram of gall?* Like all Gaul, the realm of the amorist is divided into three parts: anticipation, exploration, disillusion. *Amoret* was spelled *amorit* in Lodge's ROSALYNDE (1590), from which Shakespeare drew the plot of AS YOU LIKE IT. Thus Rosalynde's eyes were *sparkling favour and disdaine, courteous and yet coy, as if in them Venus had placed all her amorits, and Diana all her chastity.*

amorevolus. See *amate; amoret.*

amoroso. A lover. This is the Italian word, used in English in the 17th and early 18th centuries. (In the 15th century, *amorous* was used as a noun, a lover.) A RICH CABINET FURNISHED WITH VARIETIE OF EXCELLENT DISCRIPTIONS (1616) recounted that *Nobody many times maketh the good man cuckold, for though his wife's amoroso have beene at home all day, yet if hee aske who hath beene there, she answereth suddenly, nobody, who should be here, I say againe, sweete hart, nobody.* In opposite vein Polyphemus the Cyclops was misunderstood, when his fellow Cyclopes asked who had blinded him; they took his answer, 'No-man,' to imply that it was one of the gods. (As a matter of fact, the gods had dropped out of the picture: when asked his name *Odysseus* sloughed the *Zeus,* replying *Odys,* which means no man.)

amort. See *alamort.*

amphisbaena. A serpent with a head at each end. From Greek *amphis,* both ways + *bainein,* to go. Poets have favored the ancient creature: Milton (see *ellops*); Pope, in THE DUNCIAD (1728): *Thus amphisbaena (I have read) At either end assails: None knows which leads, or which is led, For both heads are but tails;* Tennyson more seriously in QUEEN MARY (1878): *For heretic and traitor are all one: Two vipers of one breed—an amphisbaena, Each end a sting.* The figurative use still has its uses.

amphiscii. The dwellers in the torrid zone, whose shadows fall northward or southward according to the season and the sun. Also *amphiscians.* From Greek *amphi,* on both sides + *skia,* shadow. One of them is an *amphiscius, amphiscian.*

amygdaline. This pleasant but ever neglected word means relating to the almond, which from the 10th to the 13th century was also called an *amygdal.* Greek *amygdale,* almond; also (from its shape) a tonsil. Hence *amygdalate,* made of almonds; also as a noun, almond-milk, which, heated, makes a delicious dessert-broth in China. *Amygdaliceous, amygdalaceous, amygdalicious,* relating to the almond. *Amygdaliferous,* almond-bearing; *amygdaloid,* almond-shaped, also a rock with mineral nodes (agate, etc.) the shape of almonds, *Amygdalitis,* however, is tonsillitis. It would be pleasant to rest, of a late Spring twilight, within an amygdaline grove.

anabiotic. A restorative; a tonic, a stimulant. Greek *ana,* again + *biotikos,* pertaining to life. *Anabiosis,* recovery; return to life after death (as Lazarus) or seeming death. Greek *anabioein,* to come to life again.

anacampserote. An herb that restores departed love. From Greek *ana,* again + *camptein,* to bend + *erot-,* love. Motteux says, in his translation (1708) of

Rabelais: *Let's taste some of these anacampserotes that hang over our heads.* He was not referring to the mistletoe. Anacampserotes now are harder to find than four-leaf clovers.

anacamptic. Producing or undergoing reflection, as a ball or sound from a wall, and light from a surface. From Greek *ana,* back + *camptein,* to bend. Echoes, said the 18th century physicists, are sounds produced *anacamptically. Anacamptics* is the branch of acoustics or optics that deals with reflection, *anacampsis.* I once saw a deer, on a frozen lake, turn and advance toward the hunter because the far-off anacamptic forest echoed the shot.

anachorism. Something out of place in a reference to a land, as lions in Bohemia, or a seaport in Switzerland; also, the fact of such a misplaced reference, in a literary work. Greek *ana,* back + *chorion,* country, place. Lowell in THE BIGLOW PAPERS (1862) spoke of opinions that were *anachronisms and anachorisms, foreign both to the age and to the country. Anachronism,* Greek *chronos,* time: as a wrist watch on Julius Caesar.

anachronism. See *anachorism.* Also (17th century) *anachronicism.*

anadem. A wreath, a garland, a circlet of flowers for the hair. Greek *ana,* together, up + *deein,* to bind; Greek *diadeein,* to bind around, gave us English *diadem.* Used from the 17th century. Shelley in ADONAIS (1821) has: *Another clipt her profuse locks, and threw The wreath upon him, like an anadem.* In the 17th century the form *anadesm* was used for a surgeon's bandage.

analeptic. Strengthening, restorative. Also *analeptical.* Used since the 17th century, mainly in medicine. In sundialling and astronomical calculation, the form *analemma* was used; first it meant the pedestal of the sundial, then the dial; also, an astrolabe. Greek *analemma,* a support; *analeptikos,* restorative; *ana,* up, back + *lambanein,* to take. THE EDINBURGH REVIEW in 1805 noted that *sage is analeptic.*

anapes. From Naples; originally (15th century) of cloth, *fustian a napes, fustian o' (of) Naples.* The term later became corrupted; Middleton (WORKS; 1627) complained: *One of my neighbors . . . set afire my fustian and apes breeches.* Having lost its meaning, it lost its usefulness.

anaphroditous. Without sexual desire; accent on the *die.* Greek *an,* not + *Aphroditos,* love. Hence *anaphroditic,* "developed without concourse of sexes," as the O.E.D. phrases it; and the current *anaphrodisiac, antaphrodisiac,* something that lessens or removes sexual desire.

anaplerosis. The making up of a deficiency. Hence *anaplerotic,* that which makes up a deficiency (current in medicine, of deficiencies in tissue, as with an ulcer); *anaplerotical.* Greek *ana,* again + *pleroun,* to make full, *pleres,* full, whence English *pleroma,* plenitude, used in religion to mean the spiritual universe as filled with the totality of the divine powers and emanations. Thus Lightfoot in his COMMENTARY ON COLOSSIANS (II, 9: 1875) observed: *The ideal church is the pleroma of Christ, and the militant church must strive to become the pleroma.* Used since the 17th century; Henry More in APOCALYPSIS APOCALYPSEOS (1680) wrote *respecting the voices of the three angels, and anapleroses of them.*

anareta. See *almuten.*

anagrif. According to the laws of the Longobards, this otherwise unused word meant rape. Also *anagriph.* Bailey (1751) defines it as the lying with an unmarried woman.

anamnesis. Recollection; memory. From Greek *ana,* back + *mna-,* call to mind, from *menos,* mind: *anamimenokein,* to remember. In rhetoric, a figure of speech: the dwelling upon past joys or sorrows. In medicine: (1) the story the patient tells of his illness, as in *diagnosis from anamnesis* (1876); (2) in *anamnestic symptoms,* phenomena recurring and remembered, by which the present condition is clarified (1879). *Anamnetics* are medicines, or exercises, to aid the memory. In religion, the doctrine (from Plato) that the soul had an earlier existence in a purer state, where its basic ideas came to it. *Anamnesis* is not to be confused with *amnesia,* loss of memory: *a-,* back, away + *mna-.*

ananym. A name written backward: *Revel; Serutan.* Etymologically the form should be *anonym,* from Greek *ana-,* back + *onoma,* name; but *anonym* is used with quite other meaning. A man may, however, use an *ananym* seeking to remain *anonymous.*

anatocism. Compound interest. Term used in the 17th and 18th centuries for the "yearly revenue of usury, and taking usury for usury." From Greek *ana-,* back, again + *tokos,* interest. (Literally this *tokos* meant something produced, from *tiktein, tektein,* whence all our *technologies* and *techniques,* not to mention (*puro-, pyro-,* fire) our *pyrotechnics.* Or consult any bank. (The accent falls on the second syllable.)

anatomy. From the 16th century: a skeleton; a skeleton with the skin on; a mummy; a withered lifeless form; a 'walking skeleton,' a person all skin and bone. In these senses, often *atomy, q.v.* Shakespeare uses the word in several senses. It was also used figuratively, as in PAPPE WITH A HATCHET (1589) *So like the verie anatomie of mischiefe, that one might see through all the ribbes of his conscience.* Shelley in EPIPSYCHIDION (1821) pictures *Incarnate April, warning . . . Frost the anatomy Into his summer grave.*

anchesoun. Occasion, reason, motive, cause. Later and more commonly *encheason;* also *ancheisun, ancheysone,* and the like. Earlier *achesoun;* via Old French from Latin *occasionem,* occasion. The *ancheysoun* forms were used in the ANCREN RIWLE (1230) and the AYENBITE OF INWIT (REMORSE OF CONSCIENCE; 1340).

anchor. An early variant of *anchoret, anchoress;* used from the 10th century. Hence *anchorhouse, anchorage, anchoridge,* an anchoret's cell, a monastery or nunnery. The word took many forms, including *ancra, anker, ankyr;* the plural is well known from the book (1230) ANCREN RIWLE, Rule of Nuns. The longer forms superseded *anchor* after Shakespeare, who has the Player Queen in HAMLET (1602) exclaim: *To desperation turn my trust and hope, An anchor's cheer in prison be my scope.*

anchoret. See *eremite.* Also *anchorite, anachorete.*

ancile. The sacred shield of the Romans. Like the Stone of Scone, it was said to have fallen from heaven, and upon its possession hung the power of the city. The Trojans had, similarly dropped from heaven, an image of the goddess Pallas, called the *palladium,* on which their safety hung. It is reputed to have been borne (like Anchises) from the city doomed by more potent signs, and ultimately brought to Rome. Gower in the CONFESSIO AMANTIS (1390) reports that *the priest Thoas . . . Hath suffered Anthenor to come And the palladion to steal.* Thence the word *palladium* has been used of anything on which the safety of a nation or whatnot may be said to depend. Thus, for England: Hume in 1761 remarked: *This stone was carefully preserved at Scone as the true palladium of their monarchy;* Blackstone in 1769 stated that *the liberties of England cannot but subsist, so long as this palladium* [trial by jury] *remains sacred and inviolate;* and McCulloch in 1845 declared that *the Habeas Corpus act (is) denominated the palladium of an Englishman's liberty.* It's good to have one! The element *palladium* was named in 1803, from the goddess, but via the newly discovered asteroid named *Pallas;* likewise named from gods via stars are *plutonium* and *cerium. Cp. Palladian.*

ancilla. A maidservant. Directly from Latin *ancilla,* diminutive of early Latin *anca,* servant. A word in the 19th century world of fashion; M. Collins in THE INN OF STRANGE MEETINGS (1871) says: *The pert ancilla flutters foolish feet.* Similarly affected in the 19th century was the adjective, *ancillary,* as used by Thackeray and others, e.g. Charles D. Badham in PROSE HALIEUTICS (1854): *Ancillary reformation has not yet begun to be thought of; cats are no more detrimental to mice . . . than these smashing wenches to . . . Sèvres teacups.* Much earlier, these words had legitimate use. In CHAUCER'S ABC (1365) we find: *From his ancille he made the mistress of heaven and earth;* and *ancelle to the lord* was a frequent phrase, in both lay and religious reference. The adjective is still used, in the sense of subservient or subordinate, as *a teacher's ancillary licence.* The word has recently been revivified (1954) as the title of Moses Hadas' learned volume, ANCILLA to CLASSICAL READING.

ancipitous. Doubtful. From Latin *an, am, ambi,* both (as in *ambiguous, ambidextrous*) + *capit-,* head. A 17th century term, used in astrology when a planet hung hesitant over one's birth, whether to tip toward evil or toward good. The form *ancipitate* is used literally of two-headed things; the form *ancipital* means having two sharp edges, like certain blades of steel or grass.

anconal. Relating to the *ancon,* the elbow. Also *anconeal, anconeous.* Hence *anconoid,* elbow-like. Greek *ankon,* a nook, a bend; the elbow.

ancren. See *anchor.*

and. Sometimes used to mean if; in this sense, more often *an.* For an illustration of this use, see the Shakespeare quotation for *very.*

anecdotographer. Obviously, one who writes down *anecdotes.* The word, used but once, by F. Spence in 1686, belongs to our era of the gossip-columnist. *Anecdotes,* by the way, originally meant secret and unpublished details of history. The word is from Greek *an,* not + *ekdotos,* published, from *ek (ex)-* out + *didonai,* to give. Procopius called by the term *Anecdota* his "unpublished memoirs" of the private life of the court of Emperor Justinian; from this use, the term was applied to brief personal episodes, the tidbits of the *anecdotographer.*

anele. To anoint; to administer the last anointing, the 'supreme unction,' to the dying [*Unction;* Latin *ungere, unctum,* to anoint; whence also *unctuous, unguent.*] *Anele* (also *aneyle, anneal, aneal, aneil, enele*) is from *an,* on + *elien,* to oil; Old English *ele, oele,* oil; Latin *oleum,* whence also *petroleum* (rock oil). See *unaneled.*

anend. At the end; to the end, straight through; on end, upright. Shakespeare uses the word in the first and the third senses; the third in HENRY VI, PART TWO (1593) *Mine hair be fixed anend, like one distract.* Richardson shows the second sense in CLARISSA HARLOWE (1748) of a man who *would ride a hundred miles anend to enjoy it.* The use lasted to Coleridge, and well into the 19th century.

anenst. Over against, against, towards. Also *anempst, aneynst;* these are variants, in form and meaning of *anent, q.v.* Thomas Heyword in TROIA BRITANICA (1609) wrote: *Foure times the brazen horse, entring, stuck fast Anenst the ruin'd guirdle of the towne.*

anent. Originally this meant on even ground with (Old English *on efen, on emn*); by 1200 it had acquired the final *t.* From the original sense it came to mean in company with, in the sight of; then it was applied to position beside or facing something—therefore (its latest sense) "regarding," in respect to. *Cp. anenst.* In Wycliff's BIBLE, MARK (1382) we read that *all things ben possible anemptis God.* Scott in THE ABBOTT (1820) writes: *Nor is it worth while to vex oneself anent what cannot be mended.*

anerithmoscope. A magic lantern to display any number of successively shown pictorial advertisements, changed electrically. Greek *anerithmos,* countless; *an,* not + *arithmos,* number + *skopos,* observing (whence also many other words with *scope*). A primitive (19th century) anticipatory form of television.

anether. To lower; humiliate. *Nether* is still used, in the literal sense of *neath,* low (whence *underneath*); *nether,* lower, as: *The can-can exposed upper reaches of her nether extremities.*

anfractuous. Winding, involved, circuitous. The Latin *anfractus,* a breaking round, a bending, from *an-, amb-,* about + *frangere, fractus,* to break, led to several English forms. *Anfractuosity,* circuitousness, was usually used in the plural, to mean winding crevices or passages. A winding route (as in Coryat's CRUDITIES, 1611) was an *anfract,* or an *anfracture.* Sometimes the forms are spelled with an *m, amfractuous,* as in Bailey's DICTIONARY (1751). Urquhart in THE DISCOVERY OF A MOST EXQUISITE JEWEL (1652) revels in *the sweet labryinth and mellifluent anfractuosities of a lascivious delectation.* Henry More, in DIVINE DIALOGUES (1667) prefers to ponder: *So intricate, so anfractuous, so unsearchable are the ways of Providence.* Boswell (1780) tells us that Johnson once remarked: *Sir, among the anfractuosities of the human mind I know not if it may not be one, that there is a superstitious reluctance to sit for a picture.* In anatomy, scientists still speak of the *anfractuous* cavities of the ear, and call by the term *anfractuosities* the sinuous depressions separating the convolutions of the brain.—T. S. Eliot, in Sweeney Erect (1920) cries *Paint me the bold anfractuous rocks Faced by the snarled and yelping seas.* It is a good, anfractuous word.

angard. Proud, boastful; boastfulness, arrogance. There may be a relation to Old Norse *agjarn,* insolence; there is no relation (though some confusion) with *angered.* Used in the 14th and 15th centuries, as in THE DESTRUCTION OF TROY (1400): *Angers me full evyll your angard desyre.*

angelica. See *angel-water.*

angelot. (1) A musical instrument, like a lute, used in the 17th century and in Browning's Sordello (1863). (2) a gold coin of France, minted by Louis IX; also by the English King Henry VI in Paris. It bore a representation of St. Michael subduing a dragon. From French *angelot,* diminutive of Latin *angelus,* angel; Greek *aggelos,* messenger (the angels were the messengers of God). (3) a small cheese, first made in Normandy, stamped with the coin, the *angelot.* Various recipes exist for the making of *angelots, angellet . . . and within a quarter of a year they will be ready to eat.*

angel-water. A perfume, fashionable in the 17th century. Also used as "a curious wash to beautify the skin." Short for *angelica-water.* The aromatic *angelica* (Medieval Latin *herba angelica*) was cultivated in England, after 1568, for cooking, for medicine—it was used as an antidote to poison and pestilence—and for a candy made from its root. Harvey used the term figuratively in a letter of 1592: *Converting the wormwood of just offence into the angelica of pure atonement.* Sedley in BELLAMIRA (1687) exclaimed: *I met the prettiest creature in new Spring Garden! her gloves right marshal, her petticoat of the new rich Indian stuffs . . . angel-water was the worst scent about her.*

anget. To recognize; to acknowledge. Appeared in several forms—*ongetan; anndgaeten*—from the 10th to the 14th century. It is the opposite of *forget,* which word is still quite necessary.

anhang. A 10th to 14th century form of *hang.* Chaucer uses it frequently, as in The Monk's Tale (1386): *Anhanged was Croesus, the proud Kyng.*

anhelation. Shortness of breath; panting; hence, (panting after) aspiration. Via Old French from Latin *ambi,* on both sides, doubtfully + *halare, halatus,* to breathe, whence *exhale.* Thus *anhelant,* breathing; *anheled,* breathed out with effort; *anhelose, anhelous,* panting, out of breath. To *anhele,* to puff; to pant for; eagerly desire. The figurative use developed as early as 1425, in Wyntoun's THE ORYGYNALE CRONYKIL OF SCOTLAND: *Constantynys sonnys three That anelyd to that ryawte* [royalty]; the reference is to the story of the three princes that desired, and divided, their father's kingdom, with the legend of the three rings, superbly retold in Schiller's NATHAN THE WISE.

anility. Dotage; a more scornful term than *senility. Senility* is from Latin *senilis,* senile, from *senex,* old man; *anility* is from Latin *anilis,* from *anus* (which if feminine meant old woman; if masculine, what she sat on). Hence, *anilar, anile, anicular,* like an old woman; over-fussy; imbecilic. BLACKWOOD'S MAGAZINE in 1841 scoffed at *the fopperies and anilities of fashion.* Another instance of its use is at *editrix.*

animalillio. A tiny creature, an animalcule. Howell (in FAMILIAR LETTERS; 1650) wrote: *As I was musing thus, I spyed a swarm of gnats waving up and down the ayr about me, which I knew to be part of the univers as well as I, and methought it was a strange opinion of our Aristotle to hold that the least of those small insected ephemerans should be more noble than the sun, because it had a sensitive soul in it, I fell to think that the same proportion which those animalillios bore with me in point of bignes, the same I held with those glorious spirits which are near the throne of the Almighty.*

anlace. A short two-edged knife or dagger, tapering to a point. Matthew Paris

(1259) Latinized it as *anelacius.* Also *anelas, analasse.* Used into the 15th century. Blount in his 1656 GLOSSOGRAPHIA (retranslating Matthew Paris) spelled it *anelate.* The word was revived by Scott and Byron (CHILDE HAROLD'S PILGRIMAGE, 1812): *The Spanish maid . . . the anlace hath espoused, Sung the loud song, and dared the deed of war.*

annes. Unity; concord, agreement; being by oneself, solitude. Also *annesse, anes.* Common until about 1300; revived in the 17th century in the form *oneness.*

anno. Latin, in the year of. Used in abbreviations, to indicate various dates. Quite current is *anno Domini,* in the year of our Lord—the Christian era, A.D. Less commonly encountered are: *anno hebraico,* in the Hebrew year, A.H. *anno hegirae,* in the year of the hegira (Arabic *hijrah,* separation, flight; the reference is to the forced journey of Mohammed from Mecca to Medina, 622 A.D.), A.H. *anno mundi,* in the year of the world (dated from 4004 B.C.), A.M. *anno orbis conditi,* in the year of creation, a.o.c. *anno urbis conditae,* in the year of the founding of the city (the Roman calendar, set at 753 B.C.), A.U.C. The last abbreviation may also be read as *ab urbe condita,* from the founding of the city; either way, the date is the same.

annothanize. See *indubitate.* The correct form, *anatomize,* is from Greek *ana,* apart + *tom-,* to cut. An *atom* is that which cannot be cut, i.e. the indivisible remnant —according to physics before the electron and the atom-bomb.

annoyous. Vexatious. Supplanted in the 16th century by *annoying.* Chaucer speaks, in THE PARSON'S TALE (1386) of *anoyouse veniale synnes.* Also *ennoyous* and *noyous.* The word is ultimately from *inodiosus,* Latin *in* with intensifying force + *odiosus* from *odium,* hatred, aversion.

annueler. A priest that celebrates anniversary masses for the dead. Chaucer in THE CHANOUNS YEMANNES TALE (1386) says *In Londoun was a prest, an annuellere.*

annuent. Nodding; adapted to nodding (as the muscles of the neck). Latin *annuare, annuatum,* to nod to. Thus *annuate,* to nod to; to direct by signs. Used in the 17th and 18th centuries.

anomphalous. Without a navel. From Greek *an-,* without + *omphalos,* navel. Medieval pictures show an anomphalous Adam and an equally smooth-bellied Eve, and many were the arguments as to whether they were thus correctly depicted, "not wanting nourishment in the womb that way."

anon. This word has shifted its sense. Originally Old English *on an,* into one; *on ane,* in one, it first meant in one company, all together; in accord, in unity. Then, in one course, straight ahead. *Anon to,* even to, as far as. *Anon so, anon as,* as soon as ever; *anon after, anon right,* immediately, at once; *soon anon,* quickly. Thus from the 10th into the 15th century. Man, however, is a tardy creature; *presently* used to mean in the present instant, at once; *anon* followed the same course so that by the 16th century *anon* meant, in a little while, in a while. Also *anon,* here, at this time (opposed to 'at that time,' mentioned or understood); Shakespeare in LOVE'S LABOUR'S LOST (1588) has: *Who now hangeth like a jewell in the eare of Celo the skie . . . and anon falleth like a crab on the face of terra. Ever and anon,* every now and then; in the same play *ever and anon they made a doubt.*

anonymuncle. An anonymous writer of no account. Combining *anonymous* (From Greek *an-*, without + *onyma,* name) and the diminutive ending from Latin *homunculus,* a little man, from *homo,* man. Charles Reade in his ESSAYS AND STUDIES (1869) sneers at the *anonymuncles that go scribbling about.* Today, with less modesty, they sign their columns, and might be called *scribuncles* (with, if you please, a pun on their material).

anophysial. Supernatural; metaphysical. A rare form from Greek *ano,* above + *physis,* nature.

anorexy. Lack of appetitie. From Greek *an-,* without + *oregein,* to reach for, desire. Richard Burton, in A MISSION TO GELELE, KING OF DAHOME (1864), rejoiced: *We bade farewell to anorexy.*

anothergates. Of a different sort (a different "gate," or way). Also *anothergaines, anotherguess, anotherguise, anotherkins.* Sidney in ARCADIA (1580): *If my father had not played the hasty fool . . . I might have had anothergaines husband.* Dryden in AMPHITRYON (1690): *The truth on't is, she's anotherghess morsel than old Bromia.* Butler in HUDIBRAS (1664): *When Hudibras about to enter Upon anothergates adventure . . .*

anred. Steadfast, constant; having a single aim or purpose. Old English *an,* one + *raed,* counsel, purpose. Used from the 9th into the 13th century. Also *anrednesse, anraednesse, onredness,* steadfastness; unanimity.

ansal. Two-edged; cutting both ways. Used both literally and figuratively, from the 16th century, but not often. Latin *ansa,* handle (handles come in pairs). In English *ansa, anse* (plural *anses, ansae*) is used for the handle-like projects of the ring around the planet Saturn. Johnson lists *ansated (ansate),* having handles, or something in the form of handles, but writers have seemed chary of its use.

anserine. Pertaining to a goose; by extension, stupid, foolish, silly. Also *anserous.* Latin *anser,* goose. Hood in his poem THE FORGE (1845) uses the word with reference to "goose-flesh": *No anserine skin would rise thereat, It's the cold that makes him shiver.* Sydney Smith in a letter of 1842 declared: *He is anserous and asinine.*

anspessade. A petty officer in the infantry (17th and 18th century); originally a cavalier whose horse was killed under him—he being then given minor rank on foot. The word was originally French *lancespessade,* after Italian *lancia spezzata,* broken lance; the *l* was misunderstood as the article *le,* the: *l'ancespessade.* Coleridge uses the term, *anspessate,* in his DEATH OF WALLENSTEIN (1800). Bailey's DICTIONARY (1751) gives lanspessade as well.

antecedaneous. Happening before; preliminary. From Latin *ante,* before + *cedere* to go. The ending *-aneous* is formed as in *contemporaneous, simultaneous, coetaneous Cp. absentaneous.*

antejentacular. See *jentacular.*

anteloquy. An actor's cue; a preface. From Latin *ante,* before + *loquium,* speech. Found only in the dictionaries, but even there sometimes (as in Cockeram's of 1623) misspelled *antiloquy.* See *antiloquist.*

antepast. Something taken before a meal, to whet the appetite. Hence, a foretaste; a forerunner. Latin *ante,* before + *pascere, pastum,* to feed; whence also *repast, pasture* [*pastry, pasty, patty, paste, pastel,* are from Greek *paste,* barley porridge; *pastos,* sprinkled; *passein,* to strew].

The word survives in Italian restaurants in the Italian form, *antepasto.* The English word was frequently applied to things other than food, as when THE LONDON QUARTERLY REVIEW (June, 1847) said: *It was, indeed, a part of the policy of the Romish church to encourage the Feast of Fools and other outbreaks of popular humor, in which popes and priests were ridiculed ad libitum; for the watchful guardians of the Spotless Hind were thus enabled to attend the antepasts of undeveloped heresies, which were not likely to be very dangerous so long as they could be represented as the outpourings of drunkenness or idiocy.*

antesupper. A display of viands before the eating of them. Osborn describes this 17th century practice in his KING JAMES (1658): *The Earl of Carlisle was one of the quorum that brought in the vanity of antesuppers, not heard of in our forefathers' time. The manner of which was to have the board covered at the first entrance of the ghests with dishes as high as a tall man could well reach, filled with the choicest and dearest viands sea or land could afford: and all this once seen, and having feasted the eyes of the invited, was in a manner thrown away, and fresh set on to the same height, having only this advantage of the other, that it was hot.*

anthomancy. See *aeromancy.* An extravagant passion for flowers was called *anthomania,* whence *anthomaniac.* THE LONDON TIMES of June 8, 1882 offered *a proof that anthomania is as real and potent as bibliomania.*

anthropinistic. Concerned with what relates to man. See *apandry.*

anthropomancy. See *aeromancy.* Also *anthroposcopy;* accent on the *pos.*

anthropophagi. Cannibals. From Greek *anthropos,* man + *phagein,* to eat. Shakespeare in OTHELLO (1604) speaks of *The Canibals that each other eat, the Antropophague.* The word is rarely used in the singular, as by Carlyle in SARTOR RESARTUS (1831): *That same hair-mantled, flint-hurling aboriginal anthropophagus.* In THE MERRY WIVES OF WINDSOR, Shakespeare speaks of an *anthropophaginian.*

anthropurgic. Wrought by man; acted upon by man. From Greek *anthropos,* man + *ergon,* work. Used only once, in 1838, but worth reviving.

antic. A grotesque or burlesque entertainment, or entertainer. Also *antique* (accent on the first syllable); survives in plural, *antics.* Hence, *to antic,* to make grotesque; to perform antics. Shakespeare in ANTONY AND CLEOPATRA (1606) says: *The wilde disguise hath almost antickt us all.* Browning (1871) uses *anticize,* to perform antics. Shakespeare has HAMLET (1601) *put an antic disposition on.* Death is often represented as a grinning skull; hence, in Shakespeare's RICHARD II: *Within the hollow crown That rounds the mortal temples of a king Keeps Death his court, and there the antic sits . . .*

antilapsarian. One that disbelieves in the doctrine of the Fall of man; also as an adjective, *antilapsarian heresies.* Latin *anti,* against + *lapsus, q.v.,* slip, fall.

antilibration. Counterpoising, weighing one thing against another. Latin *anti,* against + *librare, libratum,* to balance; *libra,* a balance. The word rhymes with *vibration.* De Quincey in WHIGGISM (1858) spoke of: *His artful antithesis, and solemn antilibration of cadences.*

antiloquist. One who contradicts; an opponent; one who speaks against something. Also *antiloquy,* contradiction. From Latin *anti-,* against + *loquor,* to speak. See *anteloquy.*

antimacassar. A covering, often hand-knitted by Victorian maidens, placed over the back of a sofa or chair, to protect this from the hair-oil of the Victorian gentleman. This popular hair-grease, *macassar oil,* was named from the district (native name *Manghasara*) of the island of Celebes, from which the manufacturers (Rowland & Son) averred that the ingredients were obtained. The antimacassar remains as an ornament; in 1875 G. R. Sims freed the Victorian housewife from the need of such protection by concocting a stainless hair-balm. Sims also concocted melodramas, such as THE LIGHTS OF LONDON (1881) and TWO LITTLE VAGABONDS (1896); along with Dickens in the novel, he was an apostle of the "gospel of rags." Some antimacassars are museum pieces.

antimnemonic. Something that weakens the memory. Also as an adjective, *antimnemonic unconcern.* The first *m* is unpronounced. Greek *anti,* against; *Mnemosynē,* Memory, daughter of Coelus and Terra (Heaven and Earth), was mother of the Muses. Coleridge (BIOGRAPHICA LITTERARIA; 1817) said: *The habit of perusing periodical works may be properly added to Averrhoes' catalogue of antimnemonics.* As an evil age passes many laws, so an ignorant age issues many periodicals.

antipelargy. A return of love or of a kindness; specifically, a child's caring for an aged parent. Greek *antipelargia,* mutual love; *pelargos,* a stork (supposedly a most affectionate bird—which is probably a reason why it was selected to bring the baby). The word, with the adjective *antipelargic,* mutually loving, occurs in 17th and 18th century dictionaries.

antipharmic. Overcoming poison. Greek *pharmacon,* poison; see *alexipharmac.*

antiphlebotomical. Relating to one that, as knowledge of medical treatment improved, was opposed to *phlebotomy* or blood-letting; opposed to bleeding. *Phlebotomy* is from Greek *phleb-,* vein + *temnein,* to cut.

antiphlogistian. One that, as scientific knowledge increased, opposed the *phlogiston* theory, the idea that there exists an element, fire, Also *antiphlogiston.* The word was also used as an adjective, equivalent to *antiphlogistic;* this term, however, was earlier, and developed two other senses: conteracting burns and inflammation; allaying excitement. Hood in MISS KILMANSEGG AND HER SILVER LEG (1840) said: *None more needs a Matthew to preach A cooling and antiphlogistic speech. Phlogiston* is from Greek *phlogistos,* burning; *phlegein,* to burn. *phlogistic,* inflammatory. *phlogisticate,* to render flammable, as in arson. Note that *Phlegethon,* the fiery river in Hades, (from the same root), gave us the 17th century adjectives *phlegethontal, phlegetheontic,* fiery, blazing. Byron in DON JUAN (1821) spoke of *Cogniac, sweet naiad of the phlegethontic rill!* A drink that made the throat cry for an antiphlogiston!

antipodize. To turn upside down. The *antipodes* (Greek *anti,* opposite + *pous, podis,* foot) were formerly pronounced with three syllables, thus developed a singular form, an *antipod, antipode;* Taylor, in MAD FASHIONS (1642) declared: *This shewes mens witts are monstrously disguis'd, Or that our country is antipodis'd.*

antre. (1) Old English (into the 13th century) for *adventure,* risk. (2) A cavern, a cave. Also (especially of body cavities), *antrum.* Via French from Greek *antron,* cave. Shakespeare in OTHELLO (1604) speaks of *antars vast, and desarts idle.* Keats in ENDYMION (1818): *Outshooting . . . like a meteor-star Through a vast antre;* Meredith in THE EGOIST (1879): *She . . . shunned his house as the antre of an ogre.*

antur. A short form of *adventure.* A book of the year 1400 was called the *Anturs of Arther. Cp. antre.*

anxiferous. Causing anxiety, as often a child's—or a nation's—behavior. The word has been repeated from 17th century dictionaries.

anythingarian. One that embraces any attitude that presents itself as timely or advantageous. Hence, *anythingarianism.* Thomas Brown (WORKS, 1704) spoke of *Bifarious anythingarians, that always make their interest the standard of their religion.* Swift, in his POLITE CONVERSATIONS (1738) picked up the term; when Lady Spark inquires as to a man's religion, Lord Spark answers: *He is an Anythingarian.* This is not a protestant faith.

anywhen. At any time. We still say *somewhere* and *anywhere,* but have lost the convenient and pleasant *somewhen, anywhither,* and *anywhen.* (*Anywhere* used to be written separately; before 1450, its forms were *owhere, oughwhere, aywhere.*) Carlisle in SARTOR RESARTUS (1831) wished you were able, *simply by wishing that you were anywhen, straightway to be then!* Similarly, *elsewhere* calls for as *elsewhen;* indeed Robert A. Heinlein, on its republication in 1953, changed the title of a story to ELSEWHEN. Often one would rather it were elsewhen than now.

apagoge. A proof of something by showing the absurdity of its not being; the type of argument called *reductio ad absurdum.* Pronounced in four syllables, accent on the *go.* Also *apogogy.* PHILOSOPHICAL TRANSACTIONS of 1671 said that *theorems may be demonstrated by the apagogick way.* Also *apogogic, apogogical.*

apair. To damage; to deteriorate. From Latin *em, en,* into + *peior-are,* to make worse. This word has had many forms in English: *ampayr, appere, appayr, empair,* etc. and—the form still current, *impair.* Chaucer in THE MILLER'S TALE (1386) laments that one should *apeyren any man, or him defame.*

apanage. Originally, provision made for the maintenance of younger sons of great families. Thus Richard Carew in THE SURVEY OF CORNWALL (1602) mentions that Belinus *had for his appanage Loegria, Wales, and Cornwall.* Later, it was applied to an appropriated possession; in the LONDON REVIEW of July 26, 1862, it was stated that *the diplomatic service . . . must always remain the apanage of the wealthy.* Then, figuratively, *apanage* was also applied to a quality or attribute that seems to go naturally with something else, as by Swinburne in his ESSAYS AND STUDIES of 1875: *This fretful and petulant appetite for applause, the proper apanage of small poets. Apanage* (accented on the first syllable) comes via French from Latin *ad,* to + *panare,* to supply, from *panis,* bread. It is sometimes spelled *appanage,* as by John Yeats in THE GROWTH OF COMMERCE (1872), referring to *the period when a 'New World' was the appanage of a European peninsula.*

apandry. Male impotence. Not in O.E.D. Greek *ap-,* away, off + *andros, anthropos,* man. O.E.D. does list *apanthropy,* love of solitude, desire to be away from men, and *apanthropinization,* withdrawal from concern with things relating to man. G. Allen in the quarterly MIND (1880) declared: *The primitive human conception of beauty . . . must have been purely anthropinistic . . . All its subsequent history must be that of an apanthropinisation . . . a gradual regression or concentric widening of aesthetic feeling around this fixed point,* man.

apanthropinization. See *apandry.*

aparage. See *apparage.*

apay. To please. Via French from Late Latin *adpacare; ad,* to + *pacare,* to appease, satisfy; *pax, pacem,* peace. Chaucer in TROYLUS AND CRISEYDE (1374) wrote (ah, fickle woman!): *She elleswhere hath now her herte apeyde.* Spenser used the word, in the sense of repay, requite, and it was revived by William Morris (1870) in the first sense; but it never quite died out in the past tense, as an adjective, *apayede, apaid, apaied, appayd,* satisfied, pleased; repaid, rewarded, as in Thomson's THE CASTLE OF INDOLENCE (1748): *Thy toils but ill apaid.*

apert. Open, manifest; clear to the understanding; straightforward, bold; outspoken, forward in manner. The last sense survives in the shortened form, *pert.* Via French from Latin *apertum,* open, *aperire,* to open. Confused, in some early uses, with Old French *espert* from Latin *expertus,* expert; *malapert,* from this form (Latin *malus,* bad + *appert, espert,* experienced) shifted its meaning by association with *apert,* and came to mean improperly frank, saucy, impudent. The ROMAUNT OF THE ROSE (1366) speaks of *Falsnesse that apert is.* Henry Hickman, in his ANIMADVERSIONS ON DOCTOR HEYLIN'S QUINQUARTICULAR HISTORY (1674) states: *There are in Zuinglius . . . most apert sentences from which it is gathered that God is the Author of sin.* Many words from this source have struggled to find place in the language: *apertement,* openly (14th century); *apertion,* opening, an opening (16th and 17th century) *apertive,* manifest (17th century); *apertly,* openly, plainly (13th to 18th century); *apertness,* frankness, plainness of speech (17th to 19th century)—one succeeded: *aperture.*

apheta. See *almuten.*

aphlogistic. Flameless. From Greek *a-,* without + *phlogiston,* flame. Applied in science to the *aphlogistic lamp,* invented by Sir Humphrey Davy, in which a glowing platinum wire consumes the fuel. Most modern illumination is aphlogistic, though a fireplace retains its charm. *Cp. antiphlogistic.*

apocrisiary. A person appointed (especially by the Pope) to give and receive answers. From Greek *apo-,* away, back + *crisis,* judgment. Used, from the 15th through the 18th century, of a papal nuncio.

apodiabolosis. The common word *apotheosis,* meaning to rank among the gods, to deify, is from Greek *apo-,* used as an intensifier, + *theoein,* to make a god of, *theos,* god. By analogy, in the 19th century was coined the word *apodiabolosis,* to devilify, to lower to the rank of devil. Accent on the *bol.* Thus in THE REALM of May 25, 1864, is the description: *With one base imbecile smugness, which is the very apodiabolosis of art.*

apogean. Proceeding from the earth. Also *apogeal; apogaeic, apogaic.* Accent on the *jee;* except the last, which has the accent on the *gay.* Greek *apo,* away; *gaia, ge,* the earth. Baroness Rosina Bulwer-Lytton in CHEVELEY; OR, THE MAN OF

HONOUR (1839) wrote: *When this enterprising and apogaeic old lady had gone up so high, she went still further, even to the moon.* We still speak of planets (or a person's fancies) being at their *apogee.*

apolaustic. Self-indulgent, seeking pleasure. Used in the Victorian age, when pleasure was seldom mentioned directly. Thus the SATURDAY REVIEW in 1880 spoke of *the lordly, apolaustic, and haughty undergraduate.* Sir William Hamilton, in his LECTURES ON METAPHYSICS (1836) suggested *apolaustics* for what Baumgarten was calling *Æsthetics;* but in the world of metaphysics the German term prevailed. In its basic meaning, however, the word is still widely applicable; we are an apolaustic world.

apollonicon. A powerful chamber organ, with keys and barrels, invented in 1817. H. Coleridge in his ESSAYS (1849) wrote: *Sing 'Songs of Reason' to the grinding of a steam apollonicon.*

apomecometry. This smooth-sounding word, scarcely used since the 16th century, should be renewed in our space-probing age. From Greek *apo-,* away + *mecos,* length + *metria,* measuring, it means the art or science of measuring distance. (The accent is on the *com;* but perhaps the six syllables are too many for our speedy days.)

apopemptic. Relating to farewell. From Greek *apopemptikos, apo-.* away + *pempein,* to send. Used in the 18th and 19th centuries. ENCYCLOPAEDIA BRITANNICA (1815) says *They dismissed them, following them to the altars with apopemptic hymns.*

apophoret. Though found only in 17th and 18th century dictionaries, *apophoret* (accent on the second syllable) is a smiling word for a present a hostess gives her guest (as at a wedding or a party, or for knowing when to take leave). It is from Greek *apo-,* away + *pherein,* to carry.

aposiopesis. A rhetorical device more often used than named, in which the speaker comes to a sudden stop, as if (or stating that) he is unable or unwilling to speak further. The accent is on the *pee.* Pope in THE ART OF SINKING IN POETRY (1727) calls it "an excellent figure for the ignorant." Goldsmith uses the term, in A CITIZEN OF THE WORLD (1762) to laugh at the tragedies of his day: *Observe the art of the poet . . . When the Queen can say no more, she falls in a fit. While thus her eyes are shut, while she is supported in the arms of Abigail (q.v.), what horrors do we not fancy! We feel it in every nerve; take my word for it, that fits are the true aposiopesis of modern tragedy.*

aposta. Bailey, in 1751, defines this as "a creature in America, so great a lover of men that it follows them, and delights to gaze on them." Obviously an 18th century word for woman.

apostasy. See *apotactical.*

apostil. This word of uncertain origin (perhaps from Latin *ad,* to + *postum, positum,* placed) means to write a note in the margin, or the note thus made. Motley, in THE RISE OF THE DUTCH REPUBLIC (1858) says that, in the opinion of Philip, the world *was to move upon protocols and apostilles.* A record of 1637 notes, of Charles I: *apostiled with his own hand.*

apostolicon. A cure for all kinds of wounds. Named because (like *apostle's ointment*) it is a mixture of twelve ingredients, thus enforced with the apostles' power of healing. In the Wyclif (1382) and the King James (1611) BIBLE, Jesus is called *the Apostle.* The twelve *apostles* were originally persons sent; Greek *apostolos,* messenger; *apo,* forth, away + *stellein,* to send.

apotactical. Renouncing; recreant. Greek *apo,* away, apart; *tasso,* to arrange; *apotassomai,* to bid adieu, renounce, abandon. *Apostasy* (Greek *stasis,* standing) means standing off, the renouncing of one's faith or allegiance; hence *apostate; apostatic, apostatical.* Bishop Hall in his tractate NO PEACE WITH ROME (1627) cried out upon *monsters of men . . . apotacticall and apostaticall miscreants.*

apotelesm. The casting of a horoscope (accent on the *pot*). Greek *apo,* off + *teleein,* to finish; *teleos,* complete; *telos* end, whence *teleology,* the doctrine of final causes. Literally *apotelesm* meant (17th century) the result, the sum and substance; one's horoscope settled one's outcome. Also *apotelesmatic, apotelesmatical* (accent on the *mat*), relating to the casting of horoscopes.

apozen. A decoction, an infusion. Also *apozume, apozeme;* Greek *apo,* off + *zeein,* to boil. Hence *apozemical.* Jonson in SEJANUS (1603) speaks of physic *more comforting Than all your opiates, juleps, apozems.*

appair. See *apair.*

appanage. See *apanage.*

apparage. An early form of *peerage,* noble rank. It is from Latin *ad,* to + *par,* equal, peer. Thus Stephen Hawes in THE EXAMPLE OF VIRTUE (1503) says: *She is comen of royall apparage,* and later speaks of *a gown of silver for great aparage.*

apparance. Preparation. From Latin *ad,* for + *parantem,* preparing, *parare,* to arrange. Richard Hooker, in his ECCLESIASTICAL POLITY (1594) complains of one who would *go about the building of an house to the God of heaven with no other apparance, than if his end were to rear up a kitchen.* Originally *apparatus* meant the work of preparing; then it came to mean the things involved in the preparation—e.g., 1767: *the gaudy apparatus of female vanity*—then the prerequisite instruments for an action (such as a scientific experiment).

apparitor. A servant or attendant, especially, of the Roman magistrates; hence, a minor court officer. Also a herald, an usher, an announcer; in this sense, also figuratively. More rarely, one that puts in an appearance; Carlyle in PAST AND PRESENT (1843) spoke of that Higher Court in which *every human soul is an apparitor.* The court officer might be used on questionable errands, as Landor implies in IMAGINARY CONVERSATIONS (1829): *The judges will hear reason, when the wand of the apparitor is tipped with gold.*

appease. See *pease.*

appere. A variant form of *appear.* Surrey's HOW NO AGE IS CONTENT WITH HIS OWN ESTATE (1537) uses this, in the poulter's measure (*cp. himpnes*): *Layd in my quiet bed, in study as I were, I saw within my troubled head a heape of thoughtes appere: And every thought did shew so lively in myne eyes That now I sighed, and then I smilde, as cause of thought dyd rise.*

applejohn. An apple supposed to be at its best when shriveled, keeping good for two years. Also *johnapple;* thus named because ripening on St. John's day. Sir John Falstaff (in Shakespeare's HENRY IV, PART

TWO; 1597) cannot endure an applejohn, because *the Prince once set a dish of applejohns before him, and told him there were five more Sir Johns and, putting off his hat, said, "I will now take my leave of these six dry, round, old, withered knights."*

applemose. A dessert made with the pulp of stewed apples, in the 14th and 15th centuries. Old English *mos,* pap, pottage. Also *applemoise, appulmoy, appulmoce,* and the like. A recipe of 1390 suggests: *Take apples and seethe hem in water. Drawe hem thurgh a stynnor. Take almande mlyke, and hony, and floer of rys, safron and powdor-fort, and salt; and seeth it stondyng.*

applesquire. The male servant of a procuress or prostitute. Frequent in the late 16th and early 17th century, as in the play WHAT YOU WILL: *Of pages, some be court pages, others ordinary gallants, and the third apple squires.* The term was possibly coined with thought of Eve's proffering, but it has been suggested that the costermongers, dealers in apples, were often intermediaries in intrigues.

apricate. To bask in the sun; to expose to the sun. Aubrey in 1697 wrote: *His lordship was wont to recreate himself in this place, to apricate and contemplate.* ('This place' was the top of the old gatehouse at Chelsea; once, while Sir Thomas More was apricating there with his dog, a wandering Tom o' Bedlam climbed up and wished to throw Sir Thomas over the battlements. "Let's throw the dog over first," said Sir Thomas. Over it went. "Now go down and fetch it up again." Tom o' Bedlam went down; Tom More locked the door, and continued his aprication.) Fire Island, New York, and Key West, Florida, are popular places to apricate. Note that the *apricot,* sometimes explained as from *in aprico coctus,* ripened in a sunny place, is via Latin *praecoctum,* early ripe, which sounded like the original Arabic name of the fruit, *al birquq.* The early European name was *Armenian apple. Aprique* is a rare word for sunny; Richard Tomlinson in his MEDICINAL DISPENSATORY (1657) avers that *the santal-tree fruticates best in aprike places.* See *beek.* Hence *aprication,* basking in the sun; *apricity,* the sun's warmth, as on an August afternoon, but also applied to the warmth of a sunny day in winter.

apricide. See *stillicide.*

aprike. See *apricate.* The accent is on the first syllable. With accent on the second syllable, *aprick* is a rare (13th century) verb meaning to spur on.

aqueity. Wateriness; the essence of water. *Cp. terreity.*

arace. Uproot; snatch away; tear. From Latin *ab,* away + *radicem,* root, whence also *radish.* One of the seven English nouns spelled *race* means (ginger) root. Under French influence, the word was sometimes spelled *arache.* Chaucer in TROYLUS AND CRISEYDE (1374) has *him soon out of your heart arace;* in THE CLERK'S TALE (1386): *The children from her arm they gonne arace.*

arachnean. See *orifex.*

arain. A spider. Also *erayne.* Via French from Latin *aranea;* Greek *arachne,* spider. For the story of Arachne, see *orifex.*

arbalest. A medieval weapon, a crossbow: a steel bow fitted to a wooden shaft, with a mechanism for drawing the bowstring taut and letting it slip. Arrows and bolts were the usual missiles; occasionally stones. The word had many forms—*arcubalist, arbalist, arblast, arbalust, alblast, alablaste, aroblast;* it is from Latin *arcus,* bow + *ballista* (*q.v.,* a larger but similar weapon). *Arbalester, arblaster, alblaster,* a soldier armed with an arbalest; also, the missile shot from the weapon. *Arbalestry,* the art or practice of crossbow shooting.

arbor. See *arbust.*

arbust. A shrub; a dwarf tree. Medieval Latin *arbuscula,* diminutive of *arbos, arbor,* tree. Also as a verb (17th century) *arbust,* to plant with trees. Also *arbustal, arbustive,* relating to shrubs or young trees. Other words for a dwarf tree or sapling are *arbuscle, arboret,* the latter favored by poets (Spenser, 1596; Southey, 1805; Milton in PARADISE LOST, 1667: *Among thick wov'n arborets and flours.*) From Latin *arbor,* tree, come many forms: *arboreal, arborean, arboral, arborical,* relating to trees. *arboricole,* dwelling in or among trees. *arborescent,* like a flourishing tree; with many branches; E. Burr in ECCE COELUM (1867) speaks of *God whose unity is arborescent with endless varieties of beauty and power. Arborous* (Milton, 1667; Coleridge, 1796), with many trees. There is quite a distinct word *arbor,* now used in the sense of a bower, shady retreat, covered walk. This was originally *herber,* Old French *herbier,* a place covered with grass, a garden of herbs; Latin *herba,* grass, herb. This became *erber;* it was pronounced *arbor* (as *clerk* is pronounced *clark*), then spelled as pronounced. In the 14th century this *arbor (arbour)* meant a garden of herbs, a grassy lawn; then, since fruit trees were planted on grass plots, an orchard; then (15th century) trees or vines trained on a framework or trellis—whence the current uses.

arcanum. A mystery; a deep secret. Hence, one of the great secrets of nature the alchemists sought to discover; therefore, a universal remedy, elixir of life. The word was often used in the plural, *arcana,* the dark mysteries. Latin *arcanus; arcere,* to shut up; *arca,* chest, *ark, arche* (13th and 14th centuries, *Noah's arche*). Also *arcanal,* of a secret nature, mysterious, dim; *arcane,* hidden from the common eye, secret. Boorde in THE BREVIARY OF HEALTHE (1547) wrote of *the eximiouse and archane science of physicke.* Scott in KENILWORTH (1821) noted *the pursuit of the grand arcanum.*

archlute. A long lute, with two sets of strings, one open, one stopped. Used for playing a thorough bass. Also *arcileuto, archilute.*

arctation. Constriction; the act of drawing close together. Used in medicine, but also figurative, as of the huddling together of children in fear. From Latin *arctare, artare; artus,* confined. There is an old English verb *art,* to cramp, restrict, press, used by Wyclif in his BIBLE (1382); Chaucer uses it in the sense of to press, to urge, in TROYLUS AND CRISEYDE (1374): *What for to speke, and what to holden inne, And what to arten.*

arcticize. To make frigid; to accustom to arctic conditions. *Cp. cynarctomachy.*

areach. See *arecche.*

aread. To decree; to declare by supernatural counsel, to prophesy; to declare; to guess; to advise. Old English *a,* out + *redan,* read. Also spelled *arede, areed.* Used from the time of King Alfred, about 875, to about 1650, by Gower, Tindale, Chaucer in TROYLUS AND CRISEYDE (1374): *What it is, I leye I kanne arede.* Later used, as a revival, by Spenser, by Milton in his tract on DIVORCE (1643): *Let me areed him, not to be the foreman of any ill-judg'd opinion.* The word is also used as a noun, advice, as by Lodge in EUPHUES' GOLDEN LEGACIE (1590): *Follow mine arreede.* In Spenser's THE FAËRIE QUEENE (1596) the Faun has bribed one of Diana's nymphs to tell him where the goddess bathes; when he beholds her, he laughs aloud in joy: *A foolish faune indeed, That couldst not hold thy selfe so hidden blest, But wouldest needs thine owne conceit areed. Babblers unworthy been of so divine a meed.*

arecche. To explain, state the meaning of; to speak. Also *areche, areccan.* Past tense forms included *arehte, araht, arought.* An emphatic form of *recche, reche,* to tell, say; to go (by mistake for *reach; arreche* was similarly confused with *areach*), to get at, to obtain; to deliver; to strike. Used (both *recche* and *arecche*) into the 15th century; Gower in CONFESSIO AMANTIS (1393) says: *Christ wroughte first and after taught, So that the deed his word arought.*

arefy. To dry up, parch. From Latin *arere,* to dry *(aridus, arid)* + *facere,* to make. Bacon in SYLVA SYLVARUM (1626) says that *the heat which is in lime and ashes . . . doth neither liquefy nor arefy.* A synonym for *arefied* is *arefacted,* withered.

arenate. To cover or mix with sand. From Latin *arena, harena,* sand, especially the sand-covered battle-'ring' of an amphitheatre. The verb exists only in dictionaries, but *arenation* is an 18th century medical term for a sand-bath. Many a person, on a sunny summer day at the seashore, indulges in an *arenation.* Hence also *arenous, arenose,* sandy, full of sand, like one's shoes when one comes home from the seashore.

areopagy. A conclave; a secret tribunal. Also *areopagus,* a high tribunal. Accent on the *op.* From *Areopagus,* Greek *Areios pagos,* the hill of *Ares* (Mars), where the highest judicial court of Athens held its hearings; hence, a high tribunal. An areopagite, a member of the tribunal. Also *areopagitic, areopagitical.* Sir Thomas Browne in CHRISTIAN MORALS (1682) said that conscience *sits in the areopagy and dark tribunal of our hearts.*

aret. To reckon; hence, to reckon to someone's account, to credit or blame. From Old French *areter; a,* to + *reter,* Latin *reputare,* to reckon, from *re-,* back + *puto,* to think. This word was very frequent in the 14th and 15th centuries; Chaucer used it many times, as when he asks the reader, if he find an error in his work, to *aret it to Adam Scrivener.* Spenser (whom others have followed) misunderstood *aret* as meaning to commit a charge to someone, to entrust; hence in THE FAËRIE QUEENE (1596): *The charge, which God doth unto me arrett . . .* When the English learned Latin, they associated this word with Latin *rectum,* meaning right; hence during the 15th and 16th centuries we find the word often spelled *arect, arrect.* Which is incorrect.

aretaics. The science of virtue. Four syllables; Greek *arete,* virtue. Grote in MORAL IDEAS (1865) said that in moral philosophy there are *two sciences . . . the science of virtue, aretaics . . . the science of happiness, eudaemonics.* In 17th century dictionaries we find *aretaloger* (Blount, 1656): *one that braggs or boasts of vertue in himself; a lyer.*

arfname. An heir. Old Norse *arfr,* inheritance; Old English *numa,* taker; *niman,* to take; see *nim.* Used from the 10th to the 13th century.

argal. Therefore. A perversion of Latin *ergo; cp. ergotize.* By extension, as a noun, a clumsy piece of reasoning. Shakespeare in HAMLET (1602) has the gravedigger reason: *He drownes not himselfe, Argal, he . . . shortens not his owne life.* THE TIMES of 23 August 1861 called *Mr. Buckle's argument as absurd an argal as ever was invented by philosopher or gravedigger.*

argh. Cowardly, timid; inert, sluggish, loath, reluctant; base, good-for-nothing. From the 9th to the 15th century, later in northern dialects. Also, as a verb, *argh,* to be disheartened, frightened; to frighten. *Me arghes,* I am afraid. Other forms included *arg, ergh, arwe, arewe, arwhe, arowe, arch, ergh, erf, arrow.* Also *arghship, arghth, arghness, arghhood,* cowardice, timidity. William Stewart in THE BUIK OF THE CRONICLIS OF SCOTLAND (1535) wrote: *King Duncane so arch ane man wes he.*

argosy. A large merchant ship of the middle ages. Also a *Ragusee,* a ship from *Ragusa* in Italy. *Ragusa* was also called in 16th century England, *Aragouse, Arragosa.* Other forms for *argosy* included *arguze, argosea, ragusye, argozee.* Shakespeare uses the word in THE TAMING OF THE SHREW (1596) and THE MERCHANT OF VENICE: *Argosies with portly saile Like signiors and rich burgers on the flood Do over-peere the pettie traffiquers That curtsie to them, do them reverence, As they flye by them with their woven wings.* There may later have been some thought, in connection with an argosy, of the *Argo* (Greek *argos,* swift) the ship in which Jason sailed in quest of the golden fleece, with his *argonauts* (Greek *nautes,* sailor). From a different story, but related in origin, comes *Argus,* a watchful guardian. Hence *Argus-eyed,* on the qui vive. This is from Greek *Argos-Panoptes* (literally, the swift all-eyes), who had 100 eyes sprinkled over his body. The jealous Hera set him to watch Io, whom Zeus was courting; he was killed by Hermes (Mercury), thence called *the Argus-queller.* When Argus died, Hera set his orbs in the peacock's tail, wherefore Spenser in THE FAËRIE QUEENE (1596) says: *Fayre pecocks . . . full of Argus eyes Their tayles dispredden wide.*

Argus-eyed. See *argosy.*

argute. Sharp; clear. From Latin *argutus,* from *arguere,* to, make clear, to assert—whence English *argue. Argute* tastes are sharp; *argute* sounds are shrill —Landor wrote to Barry Cornwall in 1864 of *a rich but too argute guitar; argute* persons are sharp, subtle, shrewd, especially in details. Thus the QUARTERLY REVIEW of 1818 speaks of *argute emendations of texts.* Browning, in ARISTOPHANES' APOLOGY (1875): *Thou, the argute and tricksy.* There is also an adverb, as in Sterne's TRISTRAM SHANDY (1762): *"You are wrong," said my father argutely.*

Ariachne. See *orifex.*

arietation. The act of butting, from Latin *arietatum, arietare,* to butt, from *aries,* ram. Used in the Middle Ages of the battering-ram. Bacon observed in his ESSAYS (1625) that *ordnance doe exceed all arietations;* Fuller in THE HISTORY OF THE HOLY WAR (1639) says that *Before ordinance was found out, ships were both gunnes and bullets themselves, and furiously ranne one against another. They began with this arietation.* The word was also used figuratively, as in THE MONTHLY REVIEW in 1797: *props of our old constitution against the arietations of democracy.* Now it seems democracy's turn to be arietated.

ariolation. Soothsaying. From Latin

ariolatum, hariolatum, from *hariolus,* soothsayer. Sir Thomas Browne in PSEUDODOXIA EPIDEMICA (1646) speaks of persons *deluding their apprehensions with ariolation, sooth-saying, and such oblique idolatries.* John Gaule in THE MAGASTROMANCER (1652), in addition to *ariolation,* uses *ariolist* and *ariolater* for soothsayer, also the verb: *to vaticinate and ariolate his Persian victory.* There are other forms, e.g., Cassandra was a foredoomed *ariole.* For methods of ariolation, see *aeromancy.*

arista. See *muticous.*

aristarch. A severe critic. Used from the 17th century; from *Aristarchos* (?220-150 B.C.), librarian at Alexandria, who rejected much of Homer as spurious. Plural *aristarchs, aristarchi.* Harington (1612) used *aristarchy* to mean severe critics as a body. Note that the first meaning of *aristocracy* (Greek *aristos,* best) was government by the best citizens; *aristarchy,* in that sense, is listed by O.E.D. as a spurious word. Samuel Johnson has by many been deemed an aristarch. Make your own choice among today's.

aristology. The art of dining. Greek *ariston,* luncheon + *logia,* talk. Used in the 19th century; also *aristological.* An 1864 cookbook was listed as *by an Australian aristologist. The Romans,* said M. Collins in PEN SKETCHES (1879) *defied all the rules of aristology by their abominable excesses;* for a contrary thought, see *vomitorium.*

armiger. This word comes directly from a Latin form meaning a bearer of arms; hence, a squire. Originally it meant a soldier who carried a knight's shield and spear. Later it was applied to a person entitled to bear heraldic arms (that is, a coat of arms). Shakespeare in THE MERRY WIVES OF WINDSOR (1598) speaks of *A Gentleman born . . . who writes himself Armigero.* In his AUTOBIOGRAPHY (1840) Thomes De Quincey uses the word in the second sense, and defines it. Blackmore in his rousing romance LORNA DOONE (1869) says of a wealthy man: *He . . . could buy up half the county armigers.*

armil. The word *armilla* was taken directly from the Latin in the description (1485) of the coronation of King Henry VII, for the "stole woven with gold and set with stones" that the Cardinal placed upon the King at the coronation. More frequently, however, perhaps from the association of its first three letters, *armilla* meant the royal bracelet. In the sense of bracelet the word is still used in archaeology. The Latin *armus* meant shoulder. The word *armil,* or *armilla* was also applied to an astronomical instrument, consisting of one or two circular loops so arranged that shadows on them indicated the recurrence of the equinoxes and solstices. The word *armillated,* wearing bracelets, aptly describes one whose arms are thus burdened.

arming. A wretched creature. Old English *earm,* poor. In the play THE LONDON PRODIGAL (1605), formerly attributed to Shakespeare, occurs the exlamation: *O here God, so young an armine!* The word was more frequent in the 11th, 12th, and 13th centuries.

armomancy. See *aeromancy.*

armozeen. See *ormuzine.*

arndern. See *aadorn.* Drayton's THE OWLE (1604) spoke of *the sad arndern shutting in the light.*

arnement. Ink, or its components. Via Old French *arrement* from Latin *atramentum,* ink; *atrum,* black. From the 13th through the 16th century. THE SEVEN SAGES (1320) neatly says: *He let him make a garnement As black as any arnement.* Thomas Lupton in A THOUSAND NOTABLE THINGS OF SUNDRIE SORTS (1586) offers a recipe: *Take arnement, hony, and the white of eggs.* (Some books are to be digested.)

aroint. This is a word much discussed by commentators, apparently coined by Shakespeare, to mean Begone! He uses it in MACBETH (1605): *Aroynt thee, Witch, the rump-fed ronyon cries,* and also in KING LEAR. The nearest to an earlier use seems to be an old Cheshire exclamation: *Rynt you, witch.* The word has been used by writers after Shakespeare; in Sir Walter Scott's works it appears seven times; both Robert Browning and Elizabeth Barrett Browning used it. In Cheshire, the milkmaids may say to a cow: *Roint thee!,* whereupon it moves off —"the cow being in this instance," Nares remarks in his 1882 GLOSSARY, "more learned than the commentators on Shakespeare."

Ronyon is an alternate spelling for *runnion,* which Samuel Johnson defines as a mangy creature, from French *rogne,* the itch. Shakespeare uses it not only in MACBETH but also in THE MERRY WIVES OF WINDSOR: *Out of my door, you Witch, you Rag, you Baggage, you Polecat, you Runnion.* No one seems to have followed Shakespeare in using *runnion* as a scornful term for a woman; in the only other recorded use (1655), the word refers to the male organ.

aromatizate. To spice, to render fragrant. Used in the 16th and 17th centuries. The more familiar *aromatize* (from the 15th century) was also used figuratively, as when Sir Thomas Browne (1646) spoke of Jews *aromatized by their conversion.* In the 17th century, a dealer in spices might be called an *aromatary.* Barroughs in THE METHOD OF PHYSICK (1624) wrote: *Let it be boiled upon the coales without any smoake long time together, wringing the reubarbe strongly, being bound in a peece of linnen cloth, clarifie it, and aromatizate it.*

arrant. Originally a variant of *errant,* wandering, present participle of Latin *errare,* to stray. The original form is still used in *knight errant.* In such expressions as *thief errant, arrant thief,* the term meant a roving robber or highwayman; hence, a professed, manifest thief; hence, anything manifest, downright; thorough (thoroughly bad). The word is quite common from the 14th century to about 1850, and is still used, as by Chaucer, Langland, Shakespeare, Fuller, Richardson, Fielding—TOM JONES (1749): *The arrantest villain that ever walked upon two legs*—Washington Irving, a half-dozen times, occasionally without opprobrious implications, as in THE SKETCH BOOK (1820): *a tight brisk little man, with the air of an arrant old bachelor.* More often there is an implication of evil—*arrant coward*—which sometimes becomes part of the meaning of the word, as in a letter (1708) of Pope: *You are not so arrant a critic . . . as to damn them without a hearing.* That would be a sign of an arrant ass!

arras. A tapestry fabric, usually woven with colored figures and scenes; a hanging made of this material, often far enough from the wall to conceal a person, as Hamlet stabs Polonius through the arras. The word occurs in several spellings—*ares, arays, aresse, arrace*—but it is from *Arras,* a French town where the fabric was made. Common since 1400, the word is most frequent in literature: Bacon,

Cowper, Byron, Scott; Carlyle in SARTOR RESARTUS (1831) speaks of *our dim arras-picture of these University years.*

arrect. See *aret.* There is also a verb *arrect,* to set upright; to set right, direct. See *arrectary.* As an adjective, *arrect* means set upright, pricked up (as a dog's ears); hence, on the alert. Bailey's DICTIONARY (1751), without any origin or instance, gives *arrectate,* suspected or accused of a crime.

arrectary. An upright post, especially the upright post of the cross. From Latin *arrect-,* past participle of *arrigere; ad,* to + *rigere, regere,* to straighten.

arrectate. See *arrect.*

arrestographer. A writer, or a collector and publisher, of arrets. An *arret* (also *arrest*) was a judgment, decision, decree; especially, of the French supreme court. The form *arrest,* used from the 15th through the 17th century, was supplanted by the French form *arret.* Scott in IVANHOE (1820) uses it figuratively, of an expert *in all matters concerning the arrets of love.*

arrha. An advance on sums to be paid; earnest-money; a pledge. Latin *arrha, arrato;* Greek *arrabon.* Used from the 15th into the 18th century. Also *arrhal,* relating to, or given as, a pledge.

arrhenotoky. Production of males only. See *thelyphthoric (thelytoky).* Also *arrenotoky.* Greek *arren,* male + *-tokos,* begetting. Hence *arrenotokous* (accent on the *not*).

arride. To smile at; to please. From Latin *arridere, ad,* at + *ridere,* to laugh, whence also *risible.* Mainly in the 17th and 18th century. Jonson in EVERY MAN OUT OF HIS HUMOUR (1599) has: *'Fore Heavens, his humour arrides me exceedingly.* Lamb in ESSAYS OF ELIA (1823): *That conceit arrided us most . . . and still tickles our midriff to remember.* The adjective *arrident* (accent on the long *i*) occurs, but rarely, meaning smiling, pleasant; Thomas Adams wrote, in 1616, of *a pleasing murderer, that with arrident applauses tickles a man to death.*

ars. Art; one of the seven arts. This is a direct borrowing of Latin *ars, artem*—which also included what we call science. A Master of Arts, or a Bachelor, was learned in the seven arts, which, until the advent of finer distinctions, were: arithmetic, geometry, music, astronomy, grammar, rhetoric, and logic. THE LEGEND OF POPE GREGORY (1300) said: *Gregorii couthe not well his pars, And wele rad and songe in lawe, And understode wel his ars.* Ars longa, vita brevis.

arson. A saddle, as the tyro has reason to feel. The word is thus used in KYNG ALYSAUNDER, 13th century. More strictly, a saddle-bow; Via Old French from Late Latin *arcionem;* Latin *arcus,* bow. One of the two curved pieces of wood or metal, knobs, at the front and the back of the saddle, to give the rider greater security. Thus we read in KING ARTHUR (1557): *The arson of his sadel brake, and so he flewe over his hors tayle.* The current *arson* is from Late Latin *arsionem;* Latin *ardere* (whence *ardent*), *arsum,* to burn.

art. To press; to urge. See *arctation.*

artolater. A worshipper of bread. Used in the 17th century against the Catholics, as by Lewis Owen in SPECULUM JESUITICUM (1629): *Dare you (artolaters) adore a piece of bread, for the living God?* Also *artolatry,* bread worship, from Greek *artos,* bread + *latreia,* worship. Used figuratively of one that gives preeminence to his "daily bread," to the material aspect of living.

artotyrite. An eater of bread and cheese. Greek *artos,* bread + *tyros,* cheese. In ecclesiastic history, a follower of Montanus (of the 2d century), who celebrated the Eucharist with bread and cheese. His most distinguished convert was Tertullian; the sect was finally suppressed under Justinian, by 565. With wine instead of religion, artotyrites flourish today.

artry. A 15th century contraction of artillery.

aruspicy. A variant of *haruspicy;* prophecy by inspecting sacrificed animals. See *aeromancy.*

arval. (1) A funeral feast, a wake. Also *arvel, arvill.* Old Norse *arfr,* inheritance + *öl,* ale, banquet. A feast (to celebrate the inheritance?) follows the funeral in many lands. Sometimes the late lamented would provide the banquet; in his will of 1459 John Alanson left an ox for his friends and relatives, *for my arvell.* There are many references to the *arvil-supper,* and to *arval-bread,* in 1875 *(averill-bread)* described as "funeral loaves, spiced with cinnamon, nutmeg, sugar, and raisins." (2) Related to ploughed land, from Latin *arvolis,* from *arvum,* arable land. The *Arval Brethren* were twelve priests of pagan Rome, whose task it was, by appropriate prayer and sacrifice, to ensure the fertility of the soil.

aschewele. To frighten away. Rarely used; from Old English *a-* + *schewel,* a scarecrow. Sidney uses *shewel* in his ARCADIA (1590). THE OWL AND THE NIGHTINGALE (1250) has a figure hanging: *There I aschwele pie and crow.* The *shewel* (also *sewel, sewell*) was used especially to frighten away deer.

ascititious. See *adscititious.*

asele. See *acele.*

asiden. Sideways, aslant. Also *asyden;* an early variant of *aside. Cp. acydenandys.* An old saying (in Ray's PROVERBS; 1691) spoke of things *all asiding as hogs fighting.*

asinego. A little ass; a fool. From Spanish *asnico,* diminutive of *asno,* ass. In Shakespeare's TROILUS AND CRESSIDA (1606), Thersites cries to Ajax: *Thou hast no more brain than I have in mine elbows; an asinego may tutor thee, thou scurvy-valiant ass!* The word is also spelled *asinico, assinego.*

askefise. A coward; especially, one that stayed home by the fire while his fellows went forth to combat. Swedish *aske,* ashes + *fisa,* to blow, to pass wind. Also *askebathe.* Used from the 13th to the 16th century. There was also a form *axwaddle,* defined by Nares: *One, who by constantly sitting near the fire, becomes dirty with ashes; an idle and lazy person.*

aslope. Slantwise. In origin this is probably from Old English *aslopen,* slipped away; *cp. adown.* It was used both literally and figuratively, the latter, for instance, in A WARNING TO FAIRE WOMEN (1599): *My hope is aslope, and my joy is laid to sleepe.* Also *aslopen,* fallen asleep; Middleton in BLURT MASTER CONSTABLE (1604) said *Good night, we are all aslopen.*

asmatographer. A writer of songs. This pompous word—which might be revived in humor or scorn—is from Greek *asma, asmat-,* song + *graphos,* writing. It is found only in 17th and 18th century dictionaries.

aspector. Beholder. Also *aspection,* the

action of looking at, of watching; this was the first meaning also of *aspect;* Bacon in SYLVA (1626) spoke of the tradition *that the basilisk killeth by aspect.* As a verb, *to aspect* (accent on the *pect*), to look for, expect; to look upon; to look upon with favor. The verb was also used in astrology, of one planet looking upon another. Hence, *aspectable,* visible, within sight; fair to look upon. Also *aspectabund,* expressive of countenance; *aspectant,* facing (each other); *aspected,* looked at; *aspectful,* of favorable aspect, benignant. J. Davies in EXTASIE (1618) spoke of *Lyons, dragons, panthers, and the like That in th' aspectors harts doe terror strike.*

asper. This word, directly from Latin *asper,* rough, harsh, wild—whence also *asperity*—was frequent in the 16th and 17th centuries; it was used by Caxton and Bacon. Chaucer earlier used it in both prose and poetry, as in BOETHIUS (1374): *Thou . . . makest fortune wrothe and aspere by thine inpacience.* The KALENDER OF SHEPHERDES (1503) declared that *Naturally a man is . . . aviricious as a dog, and aspre as the hart.* There was also a small silver Turkish coin called an *asper* (from Greek *aspros,* white; probably the same word as the Latin); in 1589 five aspers were "but two pence English." Scott uses this word in IVANHOE (1819): *I relieve not with one asper those who beg for alms upon the highway.*

asperge. See *aspersionating.*

aspersion. See *conspersion; aspersionating.* In warm weather, a cold aspersion may be quite welcome.

aspersionating. Casting slurs upon, unjustly defaming. There is no verb *aspersionate;* the noun *aspersion* has the (less common) verb *asperse.* The original meaning of *asperse* was to besprinkle, from Latin *ad,* at + *spergere, spersum,* to sprinkle. There is also an English verb *asperge,* which kept the meaning besprinkle, in connection with religious ritual. Since that which is sprinkled may become spotted, muddy, soiled, *to asperse* came to mean to bespatter with false, injurious charges; an *aspersion,* a false and damaging charge or insinuation. Shakespeare in THE TEMPEST (1610) still uses the term in its early sense of shower, spray: *No sweet aspersion shall the heavens let fall.* Fielding in TOM JONES (1749) shows the other use: *I defy all the world to cast a just aspersion on my character.* William Barriffe, in MILITARY DISCIPLINE (1635) makes the only use of the participle above, speaking of *private and frosty nips from aspersionating tongues.* Other words are retained for the ritual: *aspersorium,* the vessel to hold the holy water for sprinkling; *asperge, asperges, aspergill, aspergillum,* names for the brush with which the holy water is sprinkled. The Mass begins with the Latin words *Asperges me, Domine:* Sprinkle me O Lord . . .

aspheterism. Disbelief in private property; communism. Greek *a,* not + *spheteros,* one's own; *spheterismos,* appropriation. Accent on the *sfet.* Also *aspheterist.* Hence also *aspheterize,* to be a communist, to practice communism. This is the name used by the English Romantics (Coleridge; Southey) in their consideration of communal living. As Coleridge put it in 1794, *our aspheterising in Wales.*

asphodel. A common flower; the earlier form of the word, *affodil,* gave us *daffodil.* Poets turned it into an immortal flower, like *amaranth (q.v.),* growing in the Elysian fields. Milton in COMUS (1634) thinks it pleasant *to embathe In nectared lavers* *strewed with asphodel;* Tennyson tells us, in THE LOTUS-EATERS (1842): *Others in Elysian valleys dwell, Resting weary limbs at last on beds of asphodel.*

aspic. A form of *asp,* the small poisonous serpent found in Egypt and Libya; from Greek *aspis.* Also spelled *aspycke, aspike,* etc. Found chiefly in poetry, as Shakespeare's Antony and Cleopatra (1606): *This is an aspickes trail.* Used also by Jeremy Taylor, Addison, Lamb, Tennyson; in a figurative sense by George Daniel in TRINARCHODIA: HENRY V (1649): *Stung with the aspicke of invading fear.* The adjective, snaky, is not *aspic,* but *aspine.*

aspre. See *asper.*

assart. Forest land converted into arable land; a clearing in a forest; also, the action of grubbing up trees and bushes to make land arable. Also *assartment.* Via Old French from Latin *ex,* out + *sartare,* frequentative of *sarrire, saritum, sartum,* to hoe, weed. From the 13th century, *to assart,* to clear forest land; the noun appeared in the 16th century. It was illegal *to assart* without permission of the king or overlord, and usually paying *assart rents.*

assation. Roasting. From Latin *assare, assat-,* to roast. Thomas Love Peacock in HEADLONG HALL (1815) speaks of the *malignant adhibition of fire and all its diabolical processes of elixion and assation.* (See *adhibit.*) There is also a rare *assate,* to roast, and—only in the dictionaries—*assature,* a roast. For a discrimination, see *semiustulate.* The word might well be employed figuratively, as when a wife gives her husband (not at the table!) a rare assation.

assinego. See *asinego.*

assoil. To absolve, pardon, forgive: one said, when mentioning a dead person, *Whom God assoil!* Hence, to set free (from obligations); to acquit, to clear. Also, to clear up, solve (*soil, soyle;* 16th century); to refute; to clear one self of, to atone for, to discharge, get rid of; Spenser thus in THE FAËRIE QUEENE (1596): *Till that you come where ye your vowes assoyle.* Also *asoylen, asoyli, asoylle, assoilzie;* in Scotch law the term for to acquit is still to *assoilzie.* The forms are via Old French from Latin *ab,* from + *solvere,* to loosen, *dissolve.* A later form was *absoil;* and around 1500, directly from the Latin, was fashioned the form *absolve,* which supplanted *assoil.* Hence *assoilment,* absolution. Scott in THE ANTIQUARY (1816) has: *"God assoilzie her!" ejaculated old Elspeth. "His mercy is infinite." Oxford,* said De Quincey in his AUTOBIOGRAPHICAL SKETCHES in 1840, *might avail to assoil me.*

assoine. A variant of *essoin, q.v.* Both noun and verb. Also *asoyne, asunien, assoygne; assonzie* (Scotch verb form). Used from the 13th century.

assubtile. To *subtilize;* to refine. Also *assubtiliate.* Latin *ad,* to + *subtilis,* subtle, woven fine; *sub,* under + *tela,* web. Puttenham in THE ARTE OF ENGLISH POESIE (1589) speaks of *much abstinence* as *assubtiling and refining their spirits.* In his list of *many more like usurped Latine and French words,* Puttenham includes *methodicall, placation, compendious, assubtiling, prolixe, figurative, inveigle.* Of all his list, *assubtiling* alone has not survived.

assuefaction. The process of growing accustomed, or of making (someone) accustomed, to a thing. Thus also *assuete,* accustomed, practiced. Latin *as, ad,* to + *suescere, suetum,* to accustom, to grow used to; Old Latin *suere,* to make one's own; *suus,* one's own (whence also *suicide*). Bacon in SYLVA (1626) said that *assuetude of things hurtful, doth make them lose their force to hurt* (Pope expressed the idea otherwise, in his quatrain *Vice is a monster of so frightful mien, As to be hated, needs but to be seen; But seen too oft, familiar with her face, We first endure, then pity, then embrace*). The term *assuetude* has fallen into innocuous desuetude.

assyth. To satisfy; to compensate. Also *asyth, assithe, asith; cp. syth.* As a noun, *assyth,* satisfaction; also *assythment; assything,* giving satisfaction for an offence. Mainly in Scotland, 14th to 17th century. A York Mystery of 1450 said: *To hym will I make asith agayne.*

astart. To start up; to start (into existence), to happen, to happen to; to start off, to escape. The word existed in many forms in the 14th, 15th and 16th centuries; in the third sense above, it is probably a variation of the earlier *atstert.* Chaucer in THE FRANKLIN'S TALE (1386) says that no man may *from his death asterte.* Spenser uses the word several times, as in THE FAËRIE QUEENE (1596): *Out of her bed she did astart;* in THE SHEPHERD'S CALENDAR (1579): *No danger there the shephard can astert.*

astatic. With no tendency or ability to remain in one position. Greek *a,* not + *statos,* stable; *sta-,* stand. An astatic needle is one so set as to be unaffected by the earth's magnetism; an astatic youngster is unaffected by other things.

astert. To escape. An old variant of *astart, q.v.*

asterve. To die; especially, of hunger; to kill, destroy, starve out. Used from the 10th century, gradually replaced by *sterve, q.v.,* the early form of *starve.* (*Sterve* was pronounced *starve* as *clerk, clark.*)

asthenia. Weakness, debility. Greek *a,* not + *sthenos,* strength. Also *astheny.* Used in the 19th century; still a medical term. Hence, *asthenic, asthenical,* weak.

astrologaster. A foolish lying astrologer; a 'phony' fortune-teller. (There were, of course, astrologers that believed in the truth of the stars' telling.) The Latin ending *aster* originally meant somewhat like; hence, not genuine. In English it is used to mean a pretender, as in *grammaticaster, poetaster, politicaster*—the last especially pointing to disaster.

astromancy. See *aeromancy.*

ate. See *atel.*

atel. Hateful; hideous, foul. Also *atelich,* into the 13th century, as in Mapes THE BODY AND THE SOUL (1275): *The bodi ther hit lay on bere, An atelich thing.* Old Norse *atall,* fierce, dire; but *Ate* was the Greek goddess of discord: when not invited to a feast of the gods, she tossed in a golden apple with the message 'For the fairest'; the contest to win the apple led to the Trojan War. Hence *Ates* (two syllables), incitements to mischief; Shakespeare's LOVE'S LABOUR'S LOST (1594): *More Ates, more Ates! Stir them on!*

athanasy. Immortality. Also *athanasia;* Greek *athanasia,* from *a-,* without + *thanatos,* death. Bryant's poem THANATOPSIS is (Greek *opsis,* sight) "a view of death." Lowell in MY STUDY WINDOWS (1871) queries: *Is not a scholiastic athanasy better than none?* He seems to have achieved it.

atheticize. To set aside, invalidate. Greek *athetos,* invalid; *a,* not + *thetikos,* positive. Also *athetise,* to condemn as spurious; *athetesis.* Beverley in THE PRAISE OF THE GLORY OF GRACE (1701) asked: *Might he not even atheticize and disannul sin, and bring it even to nothing?*

athlothete. The judge, or awarder of prizes, at games. From Greek *athlos,* contest, *athlon,* prize + *thetes,* one who places.

atomy. (1) An anatomical preparation, a skeleton; hence, an emaciated person, a 'walking skeleton.' Shakespeare in HENRY IV, PART TWO (1597) has: *You starved blood-hound! . . . Thou atomy, thou!* This is a shortening of *anatomy,* the word being understood as *an atomy;* also by misunderstanding (*a*) the forms *natomy* and *nathomy* developed. *Cp. anatomy.* Gay in THE BEGGAR'S OPERA (1728), Smollett (1755) and Cooper (1823) used the word. (2) At atom, a mote. A use as though it were singular, of *atomi,* plural of *atomus,* a 16th century learned form of *atom*—via Latin from Greek *a,* not + *tomos,* cut. Shakespeare in AS YOU LIKE IT tells us: *It is as easie to count atomies as to resolve the propositions of a lover.* Hence, anything tiny; a mite, a pigmy. Shakespeare, in ROMEO AND JULIET: *Drawne with a teeme of little atomies Over mens noses;* Kingsley in THE WATER BABIES (1863): *I suppose you have come here to laugh at me, you spiteful little atomy.*

atonement. Reconciliation; harmony; the state of being *at one* with others. There was an earlier word, *onement,* with the same sense. Also *attonement, attonment.* The word was in use in the 16th century; the first occurrence of the surviving sense, expiation, is in the King James BIBLE (1611). More in RICHARD III (1513) spoke of men *having more regarde to their olde variaunce then their newe attonement.*

atrabiliarious. See *atramentaceous.* Also *atrabilar, atrabilarian* (also, as a noun, a hypochondriac), *atrabilarious, atrabilaric, atrabilary, atrabiliary, atrabilious, atrabilous.* Used mainly in the 17th and 18th centuries.

atramentaceous. Full of ink, like a poor writer's fingers; inky. Also *atramental, atramentarious, atramentary, atramentous, atramentitious,* all meaning inky; black as ink; of or pertaining to ink; hence, written or printed. *Atrament,* ink; blacking. Latin *atramentum; atrare,* to blacken, *ater,* black. Hence also *atrabiliarious, atrabilious,* affected by black bile—one of the four medieval humours—better known from the Greek, *melancholy.* See *humour.*

atretus. In Bailey's DICTIONARY (1751): "one whose fundament, or privy parts, are not perforated." From Greek *atretos, a-,* not + *tresis,* perforation. The noun *atresia* is used in pathology.

atter. *Atter* was a common word for poison, from 1000 to 1650; almost as early, it was used figuratively to mean bitterness; later (again in a physical sense) it was used of pus or other exudation from abscess or wound. From an olden belief that spiders are poisonous, *attercop* (*cop,* cup, round head) came to mean spider; the word was also applied to a venomous person. Also *ettercap; ethercap.* Bailey's DICTIONARY (1751), quoting Cumberland, gives "*attercob,* spider's web"; both spelling and meaning are in error. Our language is a tangled web. Other old forms include *atterlich,* bitter, venomous; *atterling,* a malignant person; *atterlothe* (Old English *lath, hostile*), an antidote for poison.

attercop. See *atter.*

aucupate. To lie in wait for; to hunt for; to win by craft. Literally, to go bird-catching; Latin *auceps, aviceps; avis,* bird + *capere, cepi, captum,* to catch. Hence *aucupation; aucupable,* fit for hunting, desirable. In the Water-Poet Taylor's WORKS (1630) we read: *Some till their throats ake cry alowd and hollo, To aucupate great favors from Apollo.*

audaculous. Timidly daring, slightly bold. Latin *audaculus,* diminutive of *audax, audacem,* bold, whence *audacious.* Sir Christopher Heydon in A DEFENCE OF JUDICIALL ASTROLOGIE (1603) wrote: *The ignorance hereof hath carried him too farre in this audaculous dispute.*

auf. See *ouph.*

aufyn. See *alfin.*

Augean. See *orgyan.*

augrym. See *algorism.*

aulary. Relating to a hall. Also *aularian.* As a noun, *aularian,* a member of a hall (as distinct from a college) at an English university. Greek *aule,* court, hall; *cp. aulic.* Used from the 17th century.

aulete. A flute-player. Hence *auletic.* Greek *auletes; auleein,* to play the flute; *aulos,* flute.

aulic. Courtly; relating to a court. Watson, in 1602, contrasted *aulicall, martial, and rural.* Greek *aule,* hall, court; *cp. aulary.* T. Adams in his COMMENTARIES (1633; 2 PETER) said: *God affects not aulicisms and courtly terms. Aulicism,* a courtly phrase. De Quincey (WORKS, 1853) spoke of investing the *homeliness of Æsop with aulic graces and satiric brilliancy.*

aumbry. See *ambry.*

aunt. In addition to its still current sense, *aunt* was commonly used in the 17th century as a light woman; a procuress or prostitute. One of Autolycus' songs in Shakespeare's THE WINTER'S TALE (1610) has a stanza: *The lark, that tirra-lyra chants, With heigh! With heigh! the thrush and the jay, Are summer songs for me and my aunts While we lie tumbling in the hay.* In this sense (and others) sometimes *naunt,* by improper shifting of *mine aunt* to *my naunt.* Shakespeare also uses *aunt* to mean an old gossip; in A MIDSUMMER NIGHT'S DREAM he has *the wisest aunt telling the saddest tale.*

aunters. At a venture, in any case. A 14th and 15th century form from *of aventure, by adventure.* Later used for *peradventure,* perhaps. *Cp. enaunter.* Also *auntre, aventurs, awnturs, anters.* Chaucer uses *auntre* as a verb, to venture, i.e. in THE REEVE'S TALE (1386): *I wol arise and auntre it, by my fay.* Hence *auntrous,* adventurous.

aurum potabile. A potion of minute particles of gold in an oil, to be drunk as a cordial. Directly from the Latin: drinkable gold. Quarles in JUDGMENT AND MERCY (1644) puns upon the potion: *Poverty . . . is a sickness very catching. The best cordial is aurum potabile.*

auspicy. See *aeromancy.*

austromancy. See *aeromancy.*

autangelist. This word, apparently the creation of N. Bailey (I found it in his 1751 DICTIONARY), might have more frequent use. It means one who is his own messenger. In Greek *auto-* means self; *aggelos,* messenger. Double *g* in Greek was given a nasal sound; an *angel* was a messenger of the Lord.

autem. See *pedlers French.* Also *altam, altham.*

autophoros. A person "caught with the goods," from Greek *auto-*, self + *phoreo, phero,* to bear. Found only in the dictionaries, but (with accent on the second syllable) not a bad word for "a thief with the thing he stole upon him."

avage. A payment made by tenants (especially of the manor of Writtel, Essex) for the privilege of feeding pigs in the manor woods. Also, *avisage.*

avarous. Avaricious. Originally *averous.* The word was changed by association with French *avare,* miser; Latin *avarus,* greedy. It is, however, from *aver* (also *havour; hawere, avyoure* and more; common from the 14th to the 17th century); Latin *habere,* to have. English *aver* meant wealth, property; in the plural, possessions; farm-stock. In DIVES AND PAUPER (1496) we read: *Unryghtfull occupyenge of ony . . . aver in this worlde, is called theeft.* Chaucer in THE PERSONES TALE (1386) says: *The avarous man hath more hope in his catel than in Jhesu Crist.*

avaunt. This word has had several meanings; among them, it came to be its own antonym. Via Old French *avanter* from Latin *vanitare,* to boast (frequentative of *vanare*) from *vanus,* empty, vain, it meant to speak proudly of, to boast, to praise, to *vaunt.* Chaucer (1386) used it so. As a verb, it was also an early form of *advance,* French *avant;* Latin *ab,* from + *ante,* before. It meant (as in Spenser, THE FAËRIE QUEENE; 1596: *To whom avaunting in great bravery*) to come forward. Then it was widely used as a command: *Avaunt!* Move on!—hence Begone! Thus the verb came to mean both to come and to go: its own opposite.

So many words have meant their own opposite that it has been suggested that in early times a polarity (a wide scale of meaning) was designated by one word, as *temper* and *humor* may still be good or bad; but in *humorous* and *He has quite a temper* (or *temperature*) become specific. Thus, in ancient Egyptian, *keu* meant strong and weak; in Hebrew, *sechel,* wise and foolish; *kieless,* to mock, to pray; *boruch,* blessed, cursed; in Latin, *sacer,* sacred, accursed; *altus,* high, deep; *clamare,* to shout, *clam,* secretly. In English, *with,* together, for, but in compounds as *withhold, withstand,* apart, against. So *cleave,* to hold tight together, to cut clean apart. A *fast* horse runs rapidly, a *fast* color runs not at all. To *let,* to allow, permit, also to hinder, as *a let ball* in tennis. *Seeded* raisins have the seeds removed; *seeded* bread has the seeds put in; similarly *dusted. Cp. dup; stickler (stightle); to-; trip, couth.* There are also pairs of words that look like antonyms, yet are almost identical in meaning: *sever, dissever; ravel, unravel; flammable, inflammable.* More of both sorts can easily be gathered.

avenage. From Latin *avena,* oats; the English word is accented on the first syllable. It is a term of feudal times, meaning a payment in oats, instead of service, to a landlord or feudal chief. The officer of the stable in charge of the provender was the *avener*—accent on the second syllable. Might well be used for any payment in goods instead of labor.

avenant. Convenient, agreeable, handsome. Via French *avenir* from Latin *ad,* to + *venire,* come; to be becoming. Used as a noun in the expression *at your avenant,* at your convenience.

avener. See *avenage.*

avent. To refresh with fresh air; hence, to open the *aventayle* for this purpose; by extension, to come out into the open air, to escape from confinement. Old French *esventer;* Latin *ex,* out + *ventum,* wind. Used especially in the 14th and 15th centuries. An *aventayle (aventail, avantaill, adventayle, aventaille)* was the mouthpiece of a helmet, usually kept raised to admit fresh air. Chaucer tells, in TROYLUS AND CRISEYDE (1374), *He drough a kynge by th' avantaille.* After the 15th century, Scott brought the word back in THE LAY OF THE LAST MINSTREL (1805): *And lifted his barred aventayle.*

aver. See *avarous.* Accent on the long ā; not to be confused with the verb *aver* (Latin *ad,* to + *verus,* true), to declare to be true.

avernal. Infernal, hellish. Also *avernian. Avern* (Latin *Avernus;* Greek *a,* without + *ornis,* bird) was a lake in Campania, which supposedly gave off a poisonous effluvium that killed all birds flying over it. By extension, the infernal regions, as in the famous words of the Æneid: *Facilis descensus Averno,* Easy is the road to hell. Both forms in English may be nouns, meaning a devil. In THE WYLL OF THE DEVILL (1550) at *the courte avernall,* Pamachios, we read, *doth cause all his avernals, forked types and annointed gentlemen to come to the readynge of the devylls testament and last wyll.*

averruncate. To avert, ward off. From Latin *a,* off + *verruncare,* to turn, often used in prayer: *bene verruncare,* to turn out well. The 17th century misinterpreted the word as from *ab,* off + *eruncare,* to weed off; whence it was used to mean to weed, to prune, to cut off what hurts. Thus De Quincey in THE CONFESSIONS OF AN OPIUM EATER (1821) speaks of *His decree of utter averruncation to the simple decoration overhead.* A long pole topped by shears worked from below by wire, for pruning high branches, is still called an *averruncator.* In its basic sense Butler in HUDIBRAS (1663) has: *Sure some mischief will come of it Unless by providential wit Or force we averruncate it.*

averty. See *verty.*

avetrol. A bastard. (Three syllables, accent on the last.) Roundabout, Old French *awotron,* from Latin *adulterum,* whence also *adultery.* Used in the 13th century romance of KYNG ALYSAUNDER: *Whar artow, horesone! whar? . . . Thou avetrol, thou foule wreche!* and into the 15th century.

aveugle. To blind; to hoodwink. Via French *aveugle* from Latin *ab,* away + *oculus,* eye. Sharington is quoted (1547) in Froude's HISTORY OF ENGLAND as being *so seduced and aveugled by the lord admiral.* The still current *inveigle* is from the same source, although it is suggested that Medieval Latin *aboculus* is a shortening of *albus oculus,* blind (literally, white eye).

avidulous. Although this word, meaning somewhat greedy, occurs only in dictionaries, the frequency of the quality produced a variety of words. *Avid* is from Latin *avidus,* from *avere,* to crave. John Bale, in THE IMAGE OF BOTH CHURCHES (1550) states: *Nothing is more avidiously to be desired. Avidulous* contains the diminifying root *-ul-. Avidous* is a stronger word, the *-ous,* from Latin *-osus,* meaning full of: *courageous,* full of courage; *pious,* full of piety.

avisage. See *avage.*

avision. A dream, a *vision;* a warning in a dream. Also *a visyon, avysioun,* and more; in the 16th century, often *advision.* Chaucer in THE NONNE PREESTES TALE

(1386) states that *A litil* or [before] he *was mordred . . . His mordre in his avysioun he say* [saw].

aviso. Information; a notification, dispatch; a formal notice. From Spanish *aviso,* but in the 16th century often spelled *adviso,* as though more directly from Latin *ad,* to + *videre, visum,* to see, whence English *advise, advice.*

avital. Ancestral, of long standing. Latin *avitus,* pertaining to the *avus,* grandfather. Pronounced *a-vý-tal* or *av́-i-tal.* Also *avitall, avitic, avitous* (accents on the *vit*). The 17th century spoke of *avital customs.*

avowtry. See *advowtrie.*

avulse. To pluck off, tear away. Latin *a,* from + *vellere, vulsum,* to pluck, pull, whence also *convulsion, revulsion.* Hence *avulsion,* the action of pulling away, plucking off; forcible separation; also, a portion torn off. Lamb in a letter of 1822 rejected the literal sense, saying that the eyes came away *kindly, with no Œdipean avulsion.*

awhene. To vex, trouble. Earlier *ahwene;* Old High German *hwennen,* to shake. Most of the English words beginning *wh* (e.g., *when, whither, while*) were originally forms in *hw* and are still to be pronounced with the breath before the *w. Awhene* was used from the 10th to the 14th century.

awk. Originally, with or from the left hand: hence, the wrong way, backhanded, perverse, clumsy. *To ring awk,* the wrong way: used of bells warning of evil, as a fire. *To sing awk* (of a bird), to call as an omen of evil. Hence, *awky, awkly; awkness,* clumsiness, perversity, wrongness. The same development occurs in words from Latin; *dexter, right,* gives us *dexterity,* while *sinister,* left, remains *sinister* in English. *Awk* was also used as a noun, untowardness; Bulwer in CHIRONOMIA (1644) wrote: *To fling words at his auditors out of the auke of utterance.* The word survives in the form *awkward,* which originally meant upside down, turned the wrong way.

axe. To ask. Forgotten in standard speech, this form occurs in the earliest printed books. In Caxton's ENEYDOS (THE AENEID; 1490), for example, we read that *a mercer came in to a hows and axed for mete, and specyally he axyd after eggys.* Incidentally, the *good wyf understode hym not,* until someone explained that by *eggys* he meant *eyren.*

axinomancy. See *aeromancy.*

axwaddle. See *askefise.*

ayenbite. See *agenbite.*

ayenst. An early form of *against;* also *ayen.* Sometimes used to mean in anticipation of, as when Cavendish in THE LYFFE AND DEATHE OF CARDYNALL WOOLSEY (1557) told of the coming of the King: *He came by water to the watergate without any noyse, where ayenst his commyng was layed charged many chambers. At whos landyng they ware all shot off, whiche made suche a romble in the ayer that it was lyke thonder.*

ayren. An early plural of *egg: eggs.*

ayword. See *nayword.*

B

babes-in-the-cradle. See *Hymen's torch.*

babion. An early variant of baboon. From the French; also *babian, babioun.* Used in the 17th century as a contemptuous term for a person. Massinger in THE PARLIAMENT OF LOVE (1624) says *Farewell, babions!* Also *bavian,* in which form the word appeared in Dutch. The *bavian* was a frequent comic figure in the old morris dance, where his long tail and tumbling antics added much to the jollity.

baccare. See *backare.*

bacchanal. See *bacchation.*

bacchation. Revelry; drunkenness. From the *Bacchantes,* revelers at the festival of *Bacchus,* Roman god of wine (and father of Hymenaeus, god of marriage). There is also a verb, to *bacchanalize* (accent on the first syllable), as well as the adjective *bacchant.* Thus Thomas Moore in his translation (1800) of the ODES of Anacreon: *Many a roselipped bacchant maid Is culling clusters in their shade;* and Byron in DON JUAN (1821): *Over his shoulder, with a bacchant air, Presented the o'erflowing cup.* Many a new baccalaureate has celebrated with a bacchation. The word *bacchanal,* still used of the revel (*bacchanalia*) was earlier used of the reveling person; by extension, one whose emotions are out of control. Thus Nashe in NASHES LENTEN STUFFE, OR THE PRAYSE OF THE RED HERRING (1599) tells jestingly the story of Hero and Leander, which Musaeus (500 A.D.) and Marlowe (1598) had more seriously told. Nashe ends, when the tide carries the corpse of Leander away: *At that Hero became a franticke bacchanal outright, and made no more bones but sprang after him, and so resigned up her priesthood, and left worke for Musaeus and Kit Marlowe.*

baccivorous. Berry-eating; like me in old-fashioned strawberry shortcake time; living mainly on berries. Latin *bacca,* berry. The accent is on the *siv.* Also *bacciferous,* berry-bearing; *bacciform,* shaped like a berry.

bace. A blow, a drubbing. In the 16th century. So O. E. D. *Bace* was also a variant of *base,* as the name of an old game, later called *prisoners' bars, prisoners' base.* By act of Parliament during the reign of Edward III, playing bace was prohibited in the avenues of Westminster palace while Parliament was in session. Spenser in THE FAËRIE QUEENE (1596) says: *So ran they all as they had been at bace, They being chased that did the others chase.*

bacharach. See *backrag.*

backare. Stand back! The origin is unknown; "Back there!"? At times spelt *bacare, baccare* and pronounced in three syllables, like a yokel pretending to Latin. Shakespeare, in THE TAMING OF THE SHREW (1596): *Bacare, you are mervaylous forward.* The word appeared in a proverbial saying, *Backare, quoth Mortimer to his sow.*

backberend. Carrying on the back. A 10th to 15th century term for a thief caught carrying off stolen property, especially venison in the forests. Sir Walter Scott revived the word, in THE FAIR MAID OF PERTH (1828). The term is sometimes modernized, to *backbearing,* whence the verb, to *backbear,* used in 16th and 17th century English forest laws, of carrying illegally killed deer.

backfriend. A pretended, a false, friend; an enemy masked as a friend. From the 15th century. *I have had backfriends,* said Southey (LIFE; 1827), *as well as enemies.* By a few in the 16th century, and Scott in QUENTIN DURWARD (1823) *backfriend* was used in the opposite sense, of a backer, a friend standing firmly at one's back.

backrag. A wine from *Bacharach,* a town on the Rhine; the flavor was much appreciated in the 17th century. Hence also *bacharach, backrak, bachrag, bachrach.* Fletcher and Massinger's THE BEGGAR'S BUSH (1620) has: *My fireworks and flapdragons and good backrack.*

bacon. (1) A rustic, a clown. Perhaps a shortening of *chaw-bacon.* In early England, the meat most eaten in the country was swine's flesh. Shakespeare in HENRY IV, PART ONE (1596) has Falstaff cry, when waylaying the travelers: *On, bacons, on! What, ye knaves! Young men must live. bacon-brains,* a 'fathead', a fool. *bacon-picker,* a glutton. *baconer,* a pig that will make good bacon. *baconize;* to make into bacon; also figurative, as when Burritt in A WALK FROM LONDON TO LAND'S END (1865) said that *magnipotent chimneys . . . puff their black breathings into the . . . sky above, baconising its countenance.* (2) A variant form of *baked,* past tense of *to bake.* Thus in Wyatt's poem of THE MEANE AND SURE ESTATE (1536) the country mouse envies her sister, the town mouse: *She fedeth on boyled, bacon meet, and roost . . . And when she list, the licor of the grape Doeth glad her hert till that her belly swell.*

baculine. The line of the flagellant. Relating to the rod, or to punishment by flogging. Thackeray in THE VIRGINIANS (1858) states that *the baculine method was a common mode of argument. Bacul* was used in the 15th century for a religious staff or crosier. From Latin *baculus,* a rod, the symbol of power, also used in English. Hence *baculiferous,* bearing a cane, like the dandy of yore. The common *bacillus* was named from its shape: Latin *bacillus,* little rod; diminutive of *baculus. Baculometry,* says Bailey in his DICTIONARY (1751), is *the art of measuring accessible or inaccessible distances or lines, by one or more staves.* The baculine schoolmaster is a fading phenomenon.

bad. See *badling.*

badeen. Frivolous, jesting. Via French *badine,* silly, from Late Latin *badare,* to gape. Its only literary use is in F. Spence's translation (1685) of THE SECRET HISTORY OF THE HOUSE OF MEDICIS: *a dialog completely bouffon, waggish, and badeen, between the head and the cap.* The noun from the same source remains in use, as in Disraeli's ENDYMION (1880), which warns: *Men destined to the highest places should beware of badinage.* We have used other forms: the verb *to badiner*—a character in Vanbrugh's THE RELAPSE (1697) wishes that *Loveless were here to badiner a little; badinerie*—Shenstone, in his WORKS AND LETTERS (1712) laments that *the fund of sensible discourse is limited; that of jest and badinerie is infinite; badi-*

neur—Pope wrote to Swift, on December 19, 1734: *Rebuke him for it . . . as a badineur, if you think that more effectual.* Many a badeen badger (*q.v.*) has built a reputation on a caustic tongue, as in the play THE MAN WHO CAME TO DINNER; the more insulting he is, the more his sycophants—and the audience—laugh.

badger. Two wholly different words, from origins unknown, ended in this form. (1) From the 16th through the 18th century, a *badger* was a peddler of victuals, buying especially corn and butter and cheese, later other provisions as well, from the farmers to sell at the market towns. In the 16th and 17th century there were many laws regulating (and trying to tax) their trade. There is also a verb, *to badge,* to hawk for sale. (2) The common fighting animal, between a weasel and a bear. This use is of course still common; but from it rose two by-products now less familiar. (a) *badger-drawing, badger-baiting.* The badger was a fierce fighter. It became a game in England to put a badger into a hole (usually a barrel) and set dogs to draw it out—the better 'sports' set one dog at a time against the doomed but valiant creature. Hence, *to badger* came to mean to constantly pester and persecute one who cannot escape. THE SATURDAY REVIEW of February 8, 1862, speaks of *The coarse expedients by which the Old Bailey advocate badgers and confuses a nervous witness.* Thomas Fuller, in THE HOLY AND THE PROFANE STATE (1642) anticipates this sense when he observes: *Erasmus was a badger in his jeers; where he did bite he would make his teeth meet.* The verb, however, refers to the actions of dogs and their masters. (b) *The badger-game.* In the 1920's there came to public attention a practice that goes at least as far back as Elizabethan days, consisting of a woman's luring a man to her chamber, whereupon her accomplice breaks in, plays the role of an outraged husband, then spares the man's life for as large a sum as can be extorted. Herbert Asbury in THE GEM OF THE PRAIRIE (1941) states *that John Hill and his wife Mary . . . are said to have been the first persons in Chicago to work the badger game.* (The spirit of the pioneer!) The woman partner was called the *badger-worker;* the man, the *badger*—though sometimes, loosely, the decoy was also called the *badger.* The whole game arose from living loosely. If the peddler *badger* is derived from Latin *bladium, blade* (of wheat) the two senses of the word approach one another in this game that may be played on a sower of wild oats.

badling. An effeminate man. The word was used from the 10th through the 17th century; it dropped out of use because the word *bad* had come to mean evil, and *badling* was consequently misunderstood. *Bad,* Old English *badde* (two syllables) originally meant homosexual; the change to its present meaning came in the 13th century.

badminton. See *batler.*

baetyl. Directly from Greek *baitylos,* this rare word means a meteoric stone held sacred. Such a stone, either because it was seen falling from another world, or because its structure is manifestly different from local terrene rocks, became the object of awe and adoration.

baffle. To disgrace; especially, of a recreant knight, to disgrace publicly; the punishment usually included hanging by the heels. A common Romance term; Provençal *bafar,* to mock, from *baf,* an exclamation of disdain (English bah!) Spenser in THE FAËRIE QUEENE (1596 tells:

And after all for greater infamie He by the heels him hung upon a tree, And bafful'd so, that all which passed by The picture of his punishment might see. Also to cheat, hoodwink, and then (17th century) the current sense, bewilder, confound, foil. Shakespeare in HENRY IV, PART ONE (1597) cries: *An I do not, call me villain, and baffle me!*

bagge. To leer; to look at sidewise; to glance aside. (Bailey in 1751 gives the meaning to swell, and *bagged* was used from the 15th through the 17th century to mean pregnant.) The origin of *bagge,* to leer, is not known, but the word was used in that sense by Wyclif (1380) and by Chaucer in THE BOKE OF THE DUCHESSE (1369): *The traiteresse false and full of guile . . . That baggeth foule and looketh faire.* The practice continues.

bagnio. Originally, a bath-house for hot and cold baths, sweating, and cupping; the 17th century equivalent of the Turkish bath. Italian *bagno;* Latin *balneum,* bath; *bagnio* was pronounced *ban-yo.* Also *banio, bagno, bannia, banniard, bagnard.* In the 17th century also, the word was used of an oriental prison or slave-pen. From the beginning, however, the bagnios were places of assignation and licentiousness; as early as 1624 *bagnio* was used to mean brothel. The same fate overcame the *hummum* (*hammam, hammaum*) or Turkish bath proper; Arabic *hammam,* hot bath, *hummum,* coal. *The Hummums* opened in Covent Garden in 1631; when the baths were suppressed for immorality, the place became a hotel. Hoadley in THE SUSPICIOUS HUSBAND (1747) bids: *Carry her to a bagnio, and there you may lodge with her.*

bagpudding. (1) A pudding boiled in a bag; in early use, with two ends. POOR ROBIN said in 1709: *True love is not like to a bag-pudding; a bag-pudding hath two ends, but true love hath never an end.* It was made with flour, with suet and plums, and was popular from Jack Horner's days at least to the Christmastides of my childhood. (2) A clown, a merry-andrew—perhaps from the inflated bladder that was his characteristic equipment. *Cp. jackpudding.*

baignoire. A box at the theatre at the level of the orchestra seats (English 'stalls'). *Baignoire* is a French word meaning a place or a vessel to bathe in, from *baigner,* to bathe. Browning, in RED COTTON NIGHT-CAP COUNTRY (1873), queries: *Should one display One's robe a trifle o'er the baignoire edge. Bain* was also used from the 13th through the 17th century, as a noun, bath, or as a verb, to bathe. It comes via the French from Latin *balneum,* bath. Twyne in his 1573 translation of THE AENEID says: *The launce . . . in virgins blood doth bayne.* Surrey (1557) uses the word metaphorically: *Salt tears do bayne my breast.*

There is another *bain,* of different origin (Old Norse *beinn,* straight, direct) that into the 19th century was used to mean ready, willing, supple, handy. Douglas in his 1513 translation of THE AENEID says: *To seek your old mother make you bane.* This in turn must not be confused with the word *bane,* a common Teuton word, which first meant murderer, then, as in Chaucer and in Henry More's PLATONICAL SONG OF THE SOUL (1647): *Brimstone thick and clouds of fiery bain,* meant anything deadly, and now is used to mean poison or (poetically) any great harm—but chiefly survives in the names of plants, as *dogbane, henbane, wolf's bane* and the like.

bain. See *baignoire.* Barnaby Googe tells, in his EGLOGS (1563): *Princely nymphs accompanied Diana in her baynes.* See also *balneum.*

bairman. Pauper. A variant spelling of *bare man;* not in the *O. E. D.* (1933) but often in the early law courts. Defined by Bailey (1751) as *a poor insolvent debtor, left bare and naked, who was obliged to swear in court that he was not worth more than five shillings and five pence.*

baisement. A kissing of the hands. Also *baisemain;* French *baiser,* to kiss + *main,* hand. In the plural, *baisemains,* respects. Spenser in THE FAËRIE QUEENE (1596) uses the Italian form *basciomani;* and in the 15th century (Caxton) *baisier,* a kiss. Farquhar in THE BEAUX' STRATAGEM (1707) has: *Do my baisemains to the gentleman, and tell him I will . . . wait on him immediately.*

bajardour. See *bajulate.*

bajulate. To carry (a burden). From Latin *bajulus,* porter; but see *badger.* Fuller, in his HISTORY OF THE WORTHIES OF ENGLAND (1662) speaks of *bajulating* provisions to London. Bailey in his DICTIONARY (1751) lists *bajardour,* a carrier of burdens.

bakemeat. A pastry, a pie. Also *baken meat, baked meat.* Used by Chaucer (1386), by Shakespeare in HAMLET (1602), and in THE WHITE DEVIL (1700): *As if a man Should know what fowl is coffin'd in a bak'd meat Afore it is cut up.* It might be four and twenty blackbirds.

baker's dozen. Thirteen. In the 16th century, when there were special pillories for cheating bakers (Heywood in his PROVERBS, 1562, includes: *I feare we parte not yeet, Quoth the baker to the pylorie*), a huckster was entitled by law to receive thirteen batches and pay for twelve, the extra batch (baking) providing his profit on resale. Nares (GLOSSARY; 1882) confuses the term: *It was originally called a devil's dozen, and was the number of witches supposed to sit down at table together in their great meetings or sabbaths. Hence the superstition relating to the number thirteen at table. The baker, who was a very unpopular character in former times, seems to have been substituted on this account for the devil.* Nares has found a mare's nest with this explanation. The unlucky thirteen is of course traceable to the Last Supper of Christ and the twelve apostles, but it goes farther back. In Norse mythology, Loki once intruded and made thirteen at a feast in Valhalla; Balder was slain. The baker's dozen was entirely commercial, there being a time within my memory when the local baker gave an extra roll or bun with every dozen, much as the neighborhood Chinese laundryman gave children come for the family's wash their first taste of lichee nuts. *Cp. himpnes.*

balaam. This word draws its meanings from the story of Balaam in the BIBLE: NUMBERS, 22-24. Balak, the King of Moab, summons Balaam to curse the children of Israel, new-come from Egypt. Balaam approaches on his ass; three times, when the ass holds back, Balaam beats it, until the ass finds words, and reproaches Balaam. Then the Lord opened the eyes of Balaam, and he saw the angel of the Lord standing in the way. And instead of the curse Balak desired, the Lord gave Balaam blessings to pour forth upon the children of Israel. Hence (1) directly, as in Milton's OBSERVATIONS ON THE ARTICLES OF PEACE (1648): *God has so dispos'd the mouth of these Balaams, that comming to curse, they have stumbled into a kind of blessing.* (2)

Balaamite, one that follows religion for the sake of gain; hence *balaamitical.* At each of the three places to which Balak brought him, Balaam demanded seven altars, seven bullocks and seven rams. (3) *balaam.* An article, or news items, of freak events, saved to fill odd spaces in a newspaper or magazine. From the phenomenon of the talking ass. Hence *balaam-box, balaam-basket,* a receptacle for such material.

balas. A delicate rose colored ruby. Via the French from Marco Polo's Latin *balascus,* from the Arabic *balakhsh,* from *Badakhshan,* a district near Samarcand, whence come the choice ones. Holinshed's CHRONICALES (1577): *a great bauderike* (see *baldric*) *about his necke of great balasses.* The word, revived by Scott—THE FORTUNES OF NIGEL (1822): *a carcanet (q.v.) of large balas rubies*—is now used by jewelers in the combination *balas ruby.*

balatron. A babbler; jester; buffoon; booby. Also *balatroon.* Latin *balatro,* with the same meaning; *blaterare, blateratum,* to babble; whence also *to blate, blaterate,* to babble, talk vainly; *blateration; blateroon*—all in the 17th century. Aphra Behn in SIR PETER FANCY (1678) wrote: *The affront this balatroon has offered me.* THE ILLUSTRATED LONDON NEWS of 10 November, 1883 mentioned *an interleaved copy of the Slang Dictionary* for *students of the balatronic dialect.*

balbutiate. To stammer, stutter. Latin *balbutire;* hence also *balbutient,* stammering, stuttering. The noun *balbuties* (four syllables) is still used in medicine.

baldachin. See *baudekin.*

baldrib. A thin person. Originally, a cut of pork nearer the rump than the sparerib. Middleton, in THE MAYOR OF QUINBOROUGH (1621) exclaims: *Thou art such a spiny baldrib.*

baldric. A belt, usually richly ornamented, worn over one shoulder and under the opposite arm, to support a sword, a bugle, or the like. The origin of the word is unknown, though it comes from Medieval Latin *baldringus,* perhaps related to Latin *balteus,* Old High German *balz,* English *belt.* A very frequent word in references to swords, it is also used figuratively, as in Frederic W. Farrar's LIFE AND WORK OF ST. PAUL (1879): *Let spiritual truth be their baldric.* The word is found in many spellings, as *baudrick, bawdrik.* It has been used, loosely, to mean a necklace, and metaphorically of the gem-studded belt in the sky, the zodiac—as in Spenser's THE FAËRIE QUEENE (1596): *Those twelve signes which nightly we do see The heavens bright-shining baudricke to enchace.* Spenser liked the image; his PROTHALAMION speaks of the twins of Jove *Which deck the baldric of the heavens bright.*

balductum. Curdled milk, buttermilk. Also, hot milk curdled with ale or wine. Used in the 15th century; also *balducta, balducktum, balduckstome.* By extension, in the 16th century, trashy writing, a farrago of words; a paltry, affected writer. Harington in 1596 speaks of a *balductum play.* POLIMANTEIA (1595) stated: *Because every balductum makes divine poetry to be but base rime, I leave thee (sacred eloquence) to be defended by the Muses ornaments, and such (despised) to live tormented with endless povertie.*

bale. This form belongs to three words, one obsolete, one poetic, and one practical and current. (1) *bale,* a great conflagration; hence, specifically, a funeral pyre. Old English *bael,* a blazing fire, cognate with Sanskrit *bhalas,* lustre. Used through the 16th century, and briefly revived by Scott in THE LAY OF THE LAST MINSTREL (1805): *On Penchryst glows a ba' of fire, And three are kindling on Priesthaughswire.* Spenser in THE FAËRIE QUEENE (1596: *He strove to cloak his inward bale, and hide the smoke that did his fire display*) uses it to mean fire of wrath, and thus fuses it with the second use. (2) *bale,* active evil; great torment. This is common Teuton, Old English *bealu,* Old Norse *böl.* The word was often paired, as its opposite, with *bote,* relief, *q.v.* It was marked obsolete in 17th century dictionaries, but was revived, as a vague but powerful word for destructive forces of evil, by 19th century poets. Thus Southey in THE DOCTOR (1834) says: *Death . . . calls up a soul from bale* and Bryant in Homer's ODYSSEY (1870) says: *Tidings of bale she brought.* (3) *bale,* a large bundle or package, as a *bale* of hay. This word is from Old High German *balla, palla,* or Greek *palla,* meaning a ball, then a round bundle. This sense, too, has an obsolete meaning (15th through 17th century) of a set of dice for a game—in those days, usually three. Scott tried to revive this meaning also in THE FORTUNES OF NIGEL (1822): *The Captain, taking a bale of dice from the sleeve of his coat . . .* This kind of bale has often brought the other. *Cp. hext.*

baleu. Ruby. A variant form of *balas, q.v.* Urquhart, in his translation of Rabelais, speaks of *a perfect baleu.*

balk. A ridge, as between two furrows or fields. From the 9th century. Also, a piece of ground carelessly unploughed; hence, *a balk,* a disappointment; *to make a balk,* to waste, to miss an opportunity. Also *baulk, balc, bawk;* in Old English it meant a division, either a ridge or a bar; hence also, a beam of wood (from the 13th century). This is the same word as *baulk* in billiards. Breton in THE PASSIONATE SHEPHERD (1604) inquired: *Who can live in heart so glad As the merrie countrie lad? Who upon a faire greene balke May at pleasure sit and walke . . . Or to see the subtill foxe, How the villaine plies the box . . .* N. McClure, in a note in 16TH CENTURY ENGLISH POETRY (1954) explains *plies the box* as 'plays a trick'; it seems rather to mean 'strikes the blow' that knocks out the victim, as when Green in his SHORT HISTORY OF THE ENGLISH PEOPLE (1874) tells us that Queen Elizabeth I *met the insolence of Essex with a box on the ear.*

balker. A man on a high point ashore, who signals to fishing-boats the direction taken by the schools of herring or other fish. From the 17th through the 19th century; 20th century devices make him unnecessary.

ballard. (1) A bald-headed person. Used by Wyclif (1382) in the BIBLE: KINGS 2 and Caxton (1485). (2) A musical instrument, described in Purchas' PILGRIMES (1625): *Their ballards are a foot above ground, hollow under, with some seventeen keyes on the top, on which the player strikes . . . with two strikes a foot long, with balls fastned on the end.* Evidently an early sort of xylophone.

ballista. An ancient weapon, shaped like a large bow stretched with thongs, for hurling stones. Also *balista.* The usual plural was the Latin form, *ballistae;* the word is from Greek *ballein,* to throw. The word was sometimes used for *arbalest, q.v.*

ballock. Once (politely) used in various compounds. Also *bealluc, ballok, balluk, balok,* and the like. Thus *ballock-cod,* the scrotum; *cp. cod. ballock-hafted,* with a handle shaped like a ball. *ballock-knife,* a knife worn hanging from the girdle. *ballock-broth* seems unrelated, being thus described in THE FORME OF CURY (1390): *Take eelys, and hilde hem, and kerve hem to pecys, and do hem to seeth in water and wyne, so that it be a litel over-stepid. Do thereto sage an oothir erbis, with few oynons yminced. Whan the eelis buth soden ynough, do hem in a vessel; take a pyke, and kerve it to gobettes, and seeth hym in the same broth; do thereto powdor gynger, galyngale, canel, and peper; salt it, and cast the eelys thereto, and messe it forth.* Hence also *ballop, ballup,* the front or flap of smallclothes.

balneum. A bath; bathing. This word is taken directly from the Latin; several other forms were also used, mainly from the 15th through the 18th century: *balne; bawne; balneo.* The usual implication was of a warm bath; *balneary* was used for a medicinal spring. *Balneal* and *balneatory* are adjectives; compounds include *balneography,* a treatise on baths; *balneology,* study of (medicinal) baths; *balneotherapy,* treatment by baths. Hence *balneation,* bathing. The *balneum Mariae* or *bain-Marie* is a chemical or culinary dishwarmer: a pan of hot (not boiling) water into which saucepans, etc. were put to keep them warm (supposedly so called from the mildness of the bath). *Cp. baignoire.*

bam. To hoax, deceive, impose upon, *bamboozle,* of which it is either the origin or a shortening. Both words arose in the early 18th century. Also a noun, a *bam,* a story or device intended as a hoax. Swift in his POLITE CONVERSATION (1738) observed: *Her ladyship was plaguily bamb'd.*

banausic. Mechanical (with implied scorn). From Greek *banausos,* mechanical, working with fire; *baunos,* forge. George Grote, in FRAGMENTS ON ETHICAL SUBJECTS (1871) joined a controversy: *that the teaching music as a manual art was banausic and degrading.*

bancalia. Equipment, such as covers and cushions, for benches and chairs. *Bank, banc,* is a common Teutonic word for bench—whence *mountebank* and *bankrupt. Cp. bankrout. Bancalia,* however, seems to occur only in the 17th and 18th century dictionaries—Bailey (1751) if not Barnum.

banderol. This word, in a dozen spellings, came through the French from the Italian *banderuola,* a diminutive of *bandiera,* banner. It meant the long narrow flag a ship flies from the mast-head, a streamer on a lance, or the like. Shortly after Spenser's use in THE FAËRIE QUEENE (1596) the word was forgotten, until revived by Sir Walter Scott in MARMION (1808): *Scroll, pennon, pensil, bandrol there O'er the pavilions flew.* After Scott, Washington Irving and others used the word. *Pensil* (spelled as though related to *pensile,* hanging, *pendent,* from Latin *pendere, pens-,* to hang, as in *suspense*) is a variant of *pencel,* a streamer. *Pencel* is a shortening of *penoncel,* a French diminutive of *penon,* English *pennon. Pencel* was frequently used from the 13th to the end of the 16th century, then it lapsed until revived by Scott, first in THE LAY OF THE LAST MINSTREL (1805): *Pensils and pennons wide were flung.* Chaucer and Malory also used the word *pencel* to mean a lady's token borne by her knight, e.g., Chaucer, TROYLUS AND CRYSEYDE (1374): *She made him wear a pencel of her sleeve.*

bandog. A dog tied up, as a guard or because it is fierce; hence, generally, a fierce dog; a mastiff, a bloodhound. Also *bonde-dogge, bandogge,* and more. Etheredge in LOVE IN A TUB (1669) wrote: *As fierce as a bandog that has newly broke his chain. To speak bandog and bedlam,* to talk furiously and madly. The word was also used figuratively, as in Ussher's *A Body of Divinitie* (1645): *Letting loose Satan, his bandog, to . . . molest the godly.* Scott, who revived the word in the 19th century, used it sixteen times.

bandon. Jurisdiction; authority; control. The plural, *bandons,* orders, commands. *In (at) one's bandon,* under one's control, at one's pleasure. Late Latin *bandum,* edict, a form of *bannum,* whence the marriage *banns.* An edict might often work to interdict; hence to ban came to mean to forbid; hence *banish, bandit.* Latin *bannum,* authority, was also used for the symbol of authority (*under one's bannum* might mean either); hence, *banner.*

bandore. Two words have been corrupted into this form. (1) The Greek musical instrument, *pandoura, q.v.* The name was given to a 16th, 17th, and 18th century wire-stringed instrument, used as a bass to the cittern, *q.v.* Shadwell, in BURY-FAIR (1689) hails *the best music in England . . . shawm and bandore.* The word easily became figurative, as in Heywood's THE FAYRE MAYDE OF THE EXCHANGE (1607): *What's her hair? Faith two bandora wires.* It has been further corrupted, into the forms *mandoline* and *banjo.* (2) From French *bandeau,* and with the same meaning, came *bandore,* a widow's head-dress. Thomas D'Urfey, in PILLS TO PURGE MELANCHOLY (1719), pictures *the buxom widow, with bandore and peak.* The musical *bandore* had three, four, or six wire strings.

bandrol. See *banderol.*

bane. See *baignoire.*

bankrout. An early form of *bankrupt,* perhaps with the idea of putting to rout. After Tarquin's violation, in Shakespeare's THE RAPE OF LUCRECE (1594), the poet declares: *Feeble Desire all recreant, poor, and meek, Like to a bankrout beggar wails his case.* The word *bankrupt* is via French *banqueroute* from Italian *banca rotta,* broken bench—the end being later refashioned after Latin *ruptus,* broken. The original money-changers (later bankers) worked in the open, on a bench. *Cp. scaldabanco; bancalia.*

banner. See *bandon.*

banneret. An old title, lower than baron, superior to bachelor and knight: a knight entitled to bring a company of vassals into the field under his own *banner.* From Old French *baneret,* bannered; *cp. bandon.* Later the title was awarded on the battlefield, for valiant deeds in the king's presence. Sometimes, when this occurred, the knight's pennon was cut to the shape of a banner (square)—whence the suggestion in Sir William Segar's HONOR, MILITARY AND CIVIL (1602): *I suppose the Scots do call a knight of this creation a Bannerent, for having his banner rent.* The official English heralds have not allowed the title since 1612, the year after the rank of *baronet* was created.

bannerol. See *banderol.*

bantling. A brat; a young child. Drayton in his ECLOGUES (1593) pictures *lovely Venus . . . Smiling to see her wanton bantlings game.* More often the word is a term of scorn; originally it meant bastard, probably a corruption of German *bänkling,* begotten on a bench. Thus, in Father KNICKERBOCKER'S HISTORY OF NEW

YORK (1809) Washington Irving mentions *a tender virgin, accidentally and unaccountably enriched with a bantling.* The word is also used figuratively, as when Byron wrote, in a letter of 1808: *The interest you have taken in me and my poetical bantlings . . .* These, who has not had?

baragouin. Unintelligible speech; jargon; double-talk. Breton *bara, bread + gwenn,* white—because of the astonishment of Breton soldiers at seeing white bread. The word *baragouin* was French, taken directly into English in the 17th century. Overbury in his CHARACTERS (1613; THE LAWYER) declared: *He thinks no language worth knowing but his barragouin.* From the Welsh *bara pyglyd,* pitchy bread, came a 17th century term for dark bread, *barapicklet, barrapyclid,* which did not grow into figurative use, like *baragouin.*

barathrum. A pit; especially, a deep pit at Athens, whereinto were hurled criminals condemned to die. In early English use, the pit of hell. By extension (a pit that cannot be filled) an insatiable extortioner or glutton. Massinger in A NEW WAY TO PAY OLD DEBTS (1633) exclaims: *You barathrum of the shambles!*

barato. A small amount of a gambler's winnings, given to the bystanders, for luck. From the Spanish. Mabbe in his translation (1622) of Aleman's GUZMAN DE ALFARACHE said *And, though I were no gamester, yet I might receive barato as a stander by.* A pleasant practice, recently foregone.

barber. Used figuratively for one that cuts things short, a curtailer. Jonson in THE SILENT WOMAN (1609) speaks of an *excellent barber of prayers.* Also in combinations: *barber-monger,* a frequenter of the barber, a fop. Shakespeare in KING LEAR (1605) has: *You whoreson cullyenly barber-monger, draw! barber's music,* discordant music—in scornful reference to the music made by waiting customers in a barber-shop, where a cittern was commonly left, in the 16th and 17th centuries, for such entertainment. Thus Pepys in his DIARY (5 June, 1660) records: *My Lord called for the lieutenant's cittern, and with two candlesticks with money in them for symbols, we made barber's music.* Dekker in THE HONEST WHORE (1604) has a woman called *a barber's citterne, for every serving man to play upon;* thus, a strumpet. *Cp. cithern.* Also, *barber's chair,* one in which all comers sit. Shakespeare in ALL'S WELL THAT ENDS WELL (1601) has: *Like a barber's chair that fits all buttocks;* hence also, a strumpet. Motteux in his translation (1708) of Rabelais spoke of *bonarobaes, barbers chairs, hedge-whores.*

barbery. A barber's shop; the art of the barber, shaving. French *barberie,* from Latin *barba,* beard. About 1690 laws were passed in England, seeking to separate the barber from the doctor: *Neither shall any chirurgeon there use barbery.* See *barbigerous.* A *barbet* is a small beard; the word is also applied to "bearded" creatures, as (1) a sort of poodle; (2) a hairy worm that feeds on the aphis; (3) a bird with tufts of bristles at the base of the bill.

barbican. An outer fortification to a castle or city wall; especially, a double tower over a gate or bridge. It was often made high enough to serve as a watchtower. Also *barbycon, berbikan, barbakane, barbygan,* and the like. Hence *barbicanage,* a tax paid for the building and maintenance of a barbican. In the 16th and 17th centuries, *barbican* was also used for a loophole in a wall, through which one might fire missiles. Spenser in THE

FAËRIE QUEENE (1596) has: *Within the barbican a porter sate.* After the 17th century, Scott renewed the word in KENILWORTH (1821), and figuratively in THE FAIR MAID OF PERTH (1828): *Dawn seemed to abstain longer than usual from occupying her eastern barbican.* In all, Scott used *barbican* 31 times.

barbigerous. Bearded. The word indicates pomposity—or a most imposing beard. From Latin *barba,* beard + *ger-,* bearing. See *abarcy.*

barbiton. A musical instrument, many stringed, a sort of large lyre. Also *barbitos.* For a use of the word, see *sambuca.*

barbula. A small beard; directly from the Latin, *barbula* being the diminutive of *barba,* beard. Randle Holme, in THE ACADEMY OF ARMORY (1688) sets it in its place: *The barbula or pick-a-divant, or the little tuft of hair just under the middle of the lower lip. Pick-a-divant* is French *pic à devant,* point in front. The last Republican alderman of New York City insisted (in the lingo of his native Montana) that my *barbula* is a *sonofabitch;* politer persons today prefer to call it an *imperial.*

barcelona. A kerchief of twilled silk, commonly worn about the neck in the early 19th century. Usually of bright color. From the Catalan city of *Barcelona,* whence also as goodly a couple as recent vicissitudes have brought to our shores.

bardash. See *burdash.*

bar'd cater-tra. False dice, so constructed that the four and the three very seldom come on top. Also *bard cater-tray, bar'd cater trea, barr'd quatre trois.* Dekker in THE HONEST WHORE (1604) says: *I have suffered your tongue, like a bar'd cater tra, to run all this while and have not stopt it.* Such dice (in a pair) make it very hard to cast a five or a nine; they were used in the game of dice called *novum (novem),* in which a toss of nine won. *Cp. fullam, langret.*

bardlet. A petty poet, a tyro at the versifying art. Also *bardling.* Both are 19th century coinages; Bailey in THE AGE (1858) cried: *So woe to you young bardlings scant of brains!*

bardocucullus. A crude woollen cloak, with a hood, worn by peasants (in France) and monks. Hence *bardocucullated,* wearing a cowled cloak. Motteux in his translation (1694) of Rabelais scorns *these monkhawks whom you see bardocucullated with a bag.*

bardolf. One of the dishes made when the English joyed to cook: *Bardolf. Take almond mylk, and draw hit up thik with vernage* [a strong, sweet white wine] *and let hit boyle, and braune of capons braied, and put therto; and cast therto sugre, cloves, maces, pynes, and ginger, mynced; and take chekyns parboyled, and chopped, and pul of the skyn, and boyle al ensemble, and in the settynge doune from the fire put therto a lytel vynegur alaied with pouder of ginger, and a lytel water of everose* [rose water], *and make the potage hanginge* [clinging, i.e., thick] *and serve hit forthe.* And if you do, invite me.

barleybreak. A game originally played by three couples, something like prisoners' base. Sidney described the game in ARCADIA (1580): *Then couples three be straight allotted there, They of both ends the middle two do flie; The two that in mid place. Hell callèd, were Must strive with waiting foot and watching eye To catch of them, and them to Hell to beare That they, as well as they, Hell may supply. There you may see that, as the middle* *two Do coupled towards either couple make, They, false and fearful, do their hands undo.* The game went on; when a couple was caught, it replaced the chasers; the last couple in Hell (supposedly staying there) ended the game. It was named because first played in a field, and the chased couple, if in danger, could *break*—separate—amid the *barley*. Also *barlebreyke, barlibreak, barleybrake.* Mackyn in his DIARY (1557) noted that *Master parsun . . . entryd into helle, and ther ded at the barlebrayke with alle wyffe of the sam parryche.* The game, played in Scotland into the 19th century, naturally developed many variations. Herrick, among others, played on the name of the central station, of the couple that was "it" and showed the forfeit on being caught—in an epigram of 1648: *We two are last in hell: what may we feare To be tormented or kept pris'ners here? Alas, if kissing be of plagues the worst, We'll wish in hell we had been last and first.*

barleyhood. A spell of bad temper induced by drink. *Barley* is used to mean malt liquor, which is made therefrom. Skelton said in THE TUNNYNG OF ELYNOUR RUMMYNG (1529) *And as she was drynkynge, she fyll in a wynkynge With a barlyhood.* Also, *to wear a barleycap,* to be tipsy; *a barleycap,* a tippler. Thus, and still, *John Barleycorn.*

barm. Bosom, lap. Used 9th through 15th centuries, from a Teutonic form related (*berm*) to *beran,* to bear. Also in combination, as in Chaucer's THE MILLER'S TALE (1386): *A barmcloth eek as white as morning milk.* There is also a *barm* that means the froth on poured beer or fermenting malt liquors; yeast—sometimes used figuratively, as when Landor, in IMAGINARY CONVERSATIONS (1828) declares: *Milton's dough . . . is never the lighter for the barm he kneeds up with it.*

Barmecide. See *stillicide.*

barnard. A lurking sharper; the decoy of the 16th century sharpers' gang. Also *bernard;* probably a variant of *berner,* originally the feeder of the hounds; *bran + ard,* a derogatory suffix as in *coward.* The *berner,* during a hunt, waited with extra hounds along the way the animal was expected to take. Dekker in THE BELMAN OF LONDON (1608) describes the work of the *barnard,* also Greene in A DISCOVERY OF COZENAGE (1591), which lists the usual team: *the taker up, the verser, the barnard, and the rutter . . . Comes in the barnard stumbling into your company, like some aged farmer of the countrey . . . and is so carelesse of his money, that out he throweth some fortie angels on the boords end.*

barrat. Fraud; distress; quarreling. A common Romanic word, accent on the first syllable, of doubtful origin, the first meaning of which was commerce, trade. Also *baret* (THE OWL AND THE NIGHTINGALE, 13th century), *barette.* One can see what the middle ages thought of business! A *barrator* was a cheater; in the 15th and 16th centuries, especially an ecclesiastic who buys or sells preferment, or a dishonest judge. From the 16th to the 18th century, the word was used mainly of rowdies, brawlers; hence *barratress,* a female brawler, virago; amazon. In law, it meant one who incites to discord or to law-suits; and *barratry* means such incitement. *Barratry* is also used, in law, of fraud at sea, especially of the captain against the owners—such as sinking or running away with the ship or its cargo.

barth. A warm, sheltered pasture for calves, lambs, and the like. Possibly from

Old English *beorgan,* to protect. From this source come also the verb *bergh,* to shelter, protect, save; *bergh* as a noun, protection; *berghless,* unprotected; *bergher,* a protector, saviour. All these are words of the 10th through the 13th century. *Bergher* was in those years used of the Lord.

bartholomew-pig. Prominently displayed roasted pigs were among the chief attractions at Bartholomew Fair, held annually on *St. Bartholomew's* Day (24 August) from 1133 to 1855 at West Smithfield, London. As Jonson pictures in his BARTHOLOMEW FAIR (1614) pregnant women were most fond of the flesh—or pretended a yearning to get to the fair. Davenant mentions the *Bartlemew pig That gaping lies on every stall Till female with great belly call.* Perhaps because on St. Bartholomew's Day (1572) Protestants were massacred in France and (1662) the English Uniformity Act (Bartholomew Act) was passed, the Protestants resented the day. They certainly resented the revelry of the Fair; there is little excess of satire in Jonson's Puritan's cry: *For the very calling it a Bartholomew pig, and to eat it so, is a spice of idolatry.* Shakespeare in HENRY IV, PART TWO (1597) applies the term to Falstaff: *Thou whorson little tydie Bartholmew bore-pigge.* Also *Bartholomew-baby,* a gawdy doll; a puppet. POOR ROBIN (1740) speaks of telling *farmers what manner of wife they should chuse, not one trickt up with ribband and knots, like a Bartholomew-baby; for such a one will prove a holiday wife, all play and no work.* Also *Bartholomew ware,* cheap and showy goods; used figuratively, as in a 1645 letter of Howell: *Freighted with mere Bartholomew ware, with trite and trivial phrases. Bartholomew-gentleman,* a man not to be trusted; a pickpocket (as often at the Fair).

bartizan. A battlemented parapet; a turret overhanging the top of a tower. Scott in THE EVE OF ST. JOHN (1801) has *He mounted the narrow stair, To the barbizan seat.* Scott uses the word also in MARMION and WAVERLEY, and in THE HEART OF MIDLOTHIAN (1818) he speaks of *a half-circular turret, battlemented or, to use the appropriate phrase, bartizan'd on the top.* The "appropriate phrase," however, rose from an error; the word was created by Scott. The early term used by Wyclif in 1395 and into the 17th century, was *bretticing, bratticing,* a temporary wooden parapet. *Bratticing* or *brattice-work* is still used, of supports of wood in a mine. But later historians accepted Scott's word as genuine.

bartolist. A skilled attorney. From a noted Italian lawyer, Bartolo, of the 14th century. Samuel Daniel, in a letter of 1602, wrote of *these great Italian Bartolists Called in of purpose to explain the law.* Portia, in THE MERCHANT OF VENICE, volunteered for the task.

barton. Originally, this was a threshing floor, Old English *bere-tun,* barley enclosure. Then it was used of a farm yard; especially, of the farm a lord kept for his own use. It was also applied to a chicken coop or larger pen, but the lord kept claim (1783) to *the eggs of the bartons of his demesne.* A book on HUSBANDRY by George Winter (1787) declares that *stale urine and barton draining are greatly preferable to dung.* In contrast, we are told of *a fine grove of Scotch and silver fir on the barton of Bridestow.* And Southey in THE POET'S PILGRIMAGE TO WATERLOO (1816) speaks of *Spacious bartons clean, well-wall'd around, Where all the wealth of rural life was found.*

barytone. A deep-sounding musical instrument. Applied to a bass viol invented by Joachim Fielke in 1687; in the 19th century, to a bass *saxhorn* (invented by the Belgian C. J. Sax, died 1865; his son is to be blamed for the *saxophone*). Greek *barys,* deep + *tonos,* pitch. Also *baritone,* in which spelling it is still applied to a singer between tenor and bass; *barritone, bariton, baryton.* In Greek grammar, *barytone* was used of a word not having the acute accent on the last syllable. Hence *barytonize,* to make a deep sound, as in Urquhart's translation (1653) of Rabelais, in which we are told Gargantua *would loll and rock himself in the cradle . . . monocordising with his fingers and barytonising with his tail.* (The O.E.D. defines this word-play as though Gargantua were a dog. *Cp. Mono-.*)

bas. A kiss. A variant of *bass, q.v.* Also *cp. basiate.*

base. Short for *prisoner's base,* the game. *Cp. barleybreak.* Spenser uses it in THE FAËRIE QUEENE (1596); Shakespeare in CYMBELINE (1611) speaks of *lads more like to run the country base, then to commit such slaughter.* Hence, *to bid base,* to challenge someone to chase one (as in the game); by extension, to challenge. Used by Shakespeare (VENUS AND ADONIS) and by Milton in ANIMADVERSIONS (1641): *I shall not intend this hot season to bid you the base through the wide and dusty champaine of the Councels.*

baselard. A dagger, usually worn at the belt. Used from the 14th through the 18th century, as in THE NEW LONDON MAGAZINE of 1788: *The Mayor, drawing his baselard, grievously wounded Wat (Tyler) in the neck.*

basery. See *basiate.*

bashaw. An early form of the Turkish title *pasha,* associated with haughty tyranny; whence *bashawism,* imperiousness. From Turkist *bash,* head. In the 16th century the word was also spelled *bassa, bassi, basha,* and the like. Fielding has, in JONATHAN WILD (1743): *He addressed me with all the insolence of a basha to a Circassian slave.* A *bashaw of three tails* was of high rank, with three horse-tails hung on his standard.

basiate. To kiss—in the 17th century. Latin *basium,* kiss; whence also *basial; basiation;* see *bass; deosculate.* Note also *basifugal (q.v.),* turning away from a kiss; but also, tending away from the *base:* Latin and Greek *basis,* a stepping, a pedestal; something to step or stand on; Greek *ba-,* to walk, go. The adjective *base* (Latin *bassus,* low) developed in the 17th century the noun *basery,* dishonorable dealing; Thomas Brian in THE PISSE PROPHET (1637) wrote: *They will hardly acknowledge their errours, and relinquish this basery.*—Meredith in THE EGOIST (1879) spoke of *love that . . . seems to the scoffing world to go slinking into basiation's obscurity.* A *basifuge* is one who or that which drives away kisses, as a two day's growth of beard, or bad taste.

basifugal. Fleeing its base; tending to fly from its base. Accent on the *sif.* It might be said that psychoanalysis attempts to basify the basifugal. But see *basiate.*

basil. See *basilicon.*

basilicon. An ointment of 'sovereign' virtue, from Greek *basilicos,* royal. The herb *basil,* used in royal bath or unguent, drew its name from this source; but the *basilisk (q.v.)* was drawn into the notion. A *basilica,* originally a royal palace, then a hall of justice granted by Roman emperors for religious use, is now a church, especially an early church, e.g., one of the seven principal churches of Constantine. There is an adjective *basilic,* royal; *the basilic vein* is the large vein from elbow to armpit.

basilisk. A fabulous serpent, whose very glance was mortal. It was marked by a crown-like spot on its head, hence the name. *basilisk* (little king; see *basilicon.*) It was hatched by a serpent from a cock's egg, hence also called *basilicock* (as in Chaucer's THE PARSON'S TALE, 1386) and *cockatrice* (in Wyclif's BIBLE, 1382, and King James', 1611; in Spenser's SONNETS of 1595 and Shakespeare's ROMEO AND JULIET of 1592: *the death-darting eye of cockatrice*) and *cokadrill.* The word, especially in adjective forms, is also used figuratively. Shakespeare in TIMON OF ATHENS (1600) cries: *With my basiliscan eyes May I kill all I see.* J. Wilson in BLACKWOOD'S MAGAZINE of 1828 speaks of the *fascinating and basiliskian glare of gorgeous and rhetorical embellishment.* Kingsley in WESTWARD HO (1855) uses a third form, speaking of *Our fair Oriana, and the slaughter which her basiliscine eyes have caused. Basilisk* was also used, beginning in the 16th century, as the name of a large cannon. *Culverin,* another cannon, comes via French *couleuvre* from Latin *coluber,* snake. There is also a shorter cannon called *battard* (from French bâtard, bastard), contracted from *culverin battard* or *battard-falcon.*

basin. See *basnet.*

basnet. A small, light helmet; smaller than a *basin.* Medieval Latin *basinetum,* diminutive of *bacin,* English *basin.* Also *basinet, bacinet, basynet, bassenet,* and more. When worn in battle without an *aventayle (q.v.),* the *basnet* was often covered by the great *helm,* which rested on the shoulders. *Such a stroke,* Lord Berners admires in his translation (1523) of Froissart, *that their basenettes were cloven.* DIVES ET PAUPER (1496) spoke figuratively of *the basynet of helthe, that is hope of the lyfe that is to come.* Scott, using *basnet* six times, brought it back into the vocabulary in the 19th century.

bass. A kiss. Common on all Roman tongues; Latin *basium,* kiss; *cp. basiate.* Also used as a verb, thus one of J. Heywood's PROVERBS (1562): *He must needs basse her.* Still known uses of *bass* include: (1) a fish of the perch species, earlier *barse;* (2) the inner bark of the lime or linden tree, earlier *bast;* (3) the deepest male voice; Greek *basis, base.* This deep-toned *bass* is pronounced *base,* but Pope rhymed it with *ass.* The word *buss,* which in one sense meant a two- or three-masted ship, a fly-boat; is also a corrupt form of *bass,* kiss, especially common since the 16th century, as a hearty word for a smacking kiss. Shakespeare also used the verb figuratively, as in TROILUS AND CRESSIDA (1606): *Yond towers, whose wanton tops do busse the clouds . . .* Tennyson refrains, in THE PRINCESS (1847): *Nor burnt the grange, nor buss'd the milking-maid.* Meredith, in VITTORIA (1866), urges: *Up with your red lips, and buss me a Napoleon salute.* Children in their teens, word-conscious and coy, used to play a game with this variation—e.g., *blunderbus,* to kiss the wrong party; *omnibus,* to kiss all the girls in the room. When Shakespeare in CYMBELINE (1609) says that Imogen must *Forget that rarest treasure of your cheek, exposing it . . . to the greedy touch Of common-kissing titan,* he meant the sun, which 'kisses' all alike, the good and the bad, the fair and the foul, the young and the old, the ascetic and the erotic. Quite an omnibuster!

bast. In addition to its scientific use, as the inner bark of certain trees (lime, linden), which is sold for matting; *bast* has meant (1) the fish, the *bass.* (2) *bastardy.* (3) *a bastard.* This sense is from Old French *bast,* a pack-saddle—which muleteers used for a bed; originally there was a phrase *fils de bast,* son of a pack-saddle. (4) to boast. Note that *bastard* was applied to many things of mixed genesis: a kind of cannon (16th century); a kind of cloth (15th and 16th centuries); a kind of galley used as a war-ship; a sweet wine—Shakespeare in HENRY IV, PART ONE (1596) says: *Anon, anon sir, Score a pint of bastard in the Halfe Moone.*

bastard. See *bast.*

bastinado. See *baston.*

baston. To thrash with a stick. The stick itself was also a *baston,* other forms for this were *batten, batoon,* and the current *baton. To bastinade, bastonate* (17th century), to beat. Also *to baste;* occasionally referred to as a *dry basting* (Shakespeare, THE COMEDY OF ERRORS, 1590: *Lest it make you chollericke, and purchase me another drie basting*) in contradistinction to the 'wet' *basting* given roasting flesh or fowl. Hence also a *bastinado, bastinade, bastonade,* as every schoolboy used to know. Shakespeare, in KING JOHN (1595) uses this figuratively: *He gives the bastinado with his tongue: our ears are cudgell'd.* In cards, since the 17th century, the ace of clubs (club, to beat with) was called *basto.* In Spanish, the whole suit of clubs is *basto;* the ace, *el basto.* And in the 14th century (translating *staff, stave*) a *baston* was a stanza of poetry.

bat. (1) A pack-saddle; used in combinations, as *bat-horse,* one that carries the baggage of military officers. *Cp. bast.* (2) To flutter, as the wings of a hawk, or the phrase *to bat an eye;* a variant of *bate, q.v.* The stick and the bird are both Old English; the former, perhaps associated through French *battre* with Latin *batuere,* to beat; the latter, replacing older forms such as *bakke, blaka,* in Scandinavian countries, where bats might be in any belfry.

bate. (1) To fight, to contend with blows or arguments. In the latter mood, replaced by *debate.* Also, to beat the wings (as a falcon or hawk) and flutter away from the perch. Hence, to be restless or impatient. Shakespeare in ROMEO AND JULIET (1592) bids night *Hood my unmann'd blood, bayting in my cheekes.* (2) To beat or flutter down; to end. In R. Brunne's CHRONICLE (1330) we read: *Bated was the strife.* Also, to cast down; hence, to humble, depress; to be dejected; to lower, reduce, lessen. In these senses, a shortening of *abate. At bate,* at odds, contending. The word is frequent in Shakespeare, in various senses. Hence *bated breath,* subdued breathing. *bateless,* that cannot be blunted; Shakespeare in THE RAPE OF LUCRECE (1593) has: *Haply that name of chaste unhappily set This bateless edge on his keen appetite. bateful,* quarrelsome. *batement,* lessening, *abatement. bate-breeding,* quarrel making, inciting to strife; Shakespeare in VENUS AND ADONIS speaks of *This sour informer, this bate-breeding spy.*

bathykolpian. Deep-bosomed. Also *bathykolpic;* Greek *bathos,* deep + *kolpos,* breast. Both forms have been used spelled with *uk, yc, uc.* The word *bathos,* descent from the sublime to the ridiculous, springs from Pope's satire BATHOS, THE ART OF SINKING IN RHETORIC (1728), a travesty of Longinus' essay ON THE SUBLIME. Hence *bathetic,* fashioned after *pathetic;* also *bathotic. While a plain and direct road is paved to their hypsos, or sublime,* said Pope, *no track has been yet chalked out to arrive at our bathos, or profund.* Other words formed with *bathy-,* deep, include: *bathyal,* of the deeper regions of the sea; *bathybic,* dwelling in the deeps, also *bathypelagic. bathylimnetic,* living at the bottom of a marsh or lake, like the ondines.

batler. A flat-sided stick with a handle, for beating clothes. Shakespeare in AS YOU LIKE IT (1600) has: *I remember the kissing of her batler.* Later editions say *batlet,* as though a diminutive of *bat.* The *battledore* was originally a *batler* or *beetle,* sometimes cylindrical for mangling, but usually flat. Hence, other instruments of that shape: a paddle, a wood for putting loaves into an oven; especially, a small bat for hitting the shuttlecock in the game also called *battledore.* Other forms of this word, common from the 15th century, were *batylledore, batyndore, batteldoor,* and the like. The word was also used figuratively, as by Lowell in 1879: *So they two played at wordy battledore.* The game, once vigorously enjoyed, has been replaced by tennis, ping-pong (table tennis) and, especially *badminton. Badminton,* from the country seat of the Duke of Beaufort, was also in the 19th century the name of a drink, a 'grateful compound' of claret, sugar, and soda-water. The *shuttlecock* (also *shittlecock, shoottlecock,* and more) was a piece of *cork* tufted with feathers, used as far back as the 15th century, and is used frequently (literally and figuratively) by poets and playwrights of the 16th and 17th centuries who, as Sears said later (1858) in ATHANASIA, *were only playing at shuttlecock with words.*

batlet. See *batler.*

batling. See *battle.*

Batrachomyomachia. See *cynarctomachy.*

battalia (pie). See *beatilles.*

battard. See *basilisk.*

battle. In addition to the too well known activity named by this word, to *battle* meant to furnish with battlements, and also—quite apàrt—to nourish, supply with rich pasture or food; also, to make soil fertile; hence, to grow fat, to thrive. In this sense the word was also spelled *batle, battel,* and is related to *batten.* The adjective *battle* meant nourishing; fertile, fruitful. Douglas in his AENEIS (1513) spoke of *battill gras, fresche erbis and grene suardis.* Hence also *batling pastures* (*battling, batteling*), nourishing, fertilizing; growing fat; Fuller in A PISGAH-SIGHT OF PALESTINE (1650) exclaimed: *A jolly dame, no doubt, as appears by the well-battling of the plump boy.*

battledore. See *batler.* Also: a *battledore* (short for *battledore-book*) was a horn book, a single sheet, with the alphabet thereon, covered with horn and fastened to a flat piece of wood with a handle. The shape of the wood gave it the name. Hence *battledore boy,* one learning his *a b c's.* Thus the old saying *He doesn't know a bee from a battledore* (sometimes *He doesn't know A B . . .*)

battologist. One that endlessly and uselessly repeats the same thing. Greek *battalogos; Battos + logos,* speaking. The form *battos* may be echoic of the sound of stuttering, but is supposedly derived from a Lacedaemonian named *Battus,* who in 630 B.C. founded the city of Cyrene, and is mentioned in Herodotus as the stuttering king. Hence *battological; battology;*

battologize. Southey in the QUARTERLY REVIEW of 1818 cried: *Away then with . . . the battology of statistics.*

baude. Joyous; forward; gay. Old French *baud,* gay; Old Low German *bald,* bold, lively. The adjective was used in THE ROMANCE OF THE ROSE (1400); the noun *baudery (q.v.),* jollity, was more frequent. There is also a verb *bawdefy,* to bedeck, to make gay. Somehow, in the transfer from French to English, *bawd*—perhaps compounded with *bawd,* earlier *bad,* a cat, a pussy, a rabbit, used in slang senses—came to be applied to a pander. Shakespeare in ROMEO AND JULIET (1592) cries *A baud, a baud!* meaning a hare; but in AS YOU LIKE IT (1600) he has Touchstone tell Audrey *We must be married, or we must live in baudrey.* The earliest form of *bawd* in the sense of pander (male or female) is *bawdstrot;* this became *bawstrop* and, especially in the plays of Middleton, *bronstrops,* as in A FAIR QUARREL (1617): *I say thy sister is a bronstrops.* Much better to be baude.

baudekin. An embroidered cloth, the warp of gold thread, the woof of silk; later, any rich brocade or heavy silk. The word, from *Baldacco,* the Italian name for *Bagdad,* has many spellings: *baldachin* (which was also applied to a canopy made of such cloth), *baldaquin, baudkin, bawdikyn, bodkin,* and more. Bulwer-Lytton in THE LAST OF THE BARONS (1843) says: *The baudekin stripes (blue and gold) of her tunic attested her royalty.*

baudery. (1) A variant of *bawdry.* (2) Gaiety, mirth. Chaucer in THE KNIGHT'S TALE (1386) speaks of *Beautee and youthe, bauderie, richesse*—a happy train! See *baude.*

baudrick. See *baldric.*

bauson. A badger, *q.v.* Also *bawson; bawsym, baucyne, boreson.* Hence *bauson-faced,* with a white mark on its face, like the badger. *bausond,* spotted; with white spots on a black or bay ground. From the qualities of the animal, applied in scorn to (1) a stupidly persistent man, (2) a clumsy fat man. Chatterton (1765) used *bawsyn* several times, to mean large. In LINGUA (1607) we read: *Peace, you fat bawson, peace!*

bavardage. Gay, jolly talk; teasing exchange; chatter. The word has softened: French *bavarder,* to prate, chatter; *bavard,* talkative; *bave,* saliva. Used in the 19th century; now both the word and the art are neglected.

bavian. See *babion.*

bavin. Brushwood; especially, a bundle of light wood (as for bakers' ovens) tied with one withe or band; a fagot is tied with two. The word was used figuratively, of slight things, as in Chapman's EASTWARD HOE (1605): *If he outlast not a hundred such crackling bavins as thou art;* and Shakespeare's HENRY IV, PART ONE (1596): *Shallow jesters, and rash bavin wits, Soon kindled and soon burnt.*

bawcock. Fine fellow. A jocular term of endearment, from French *beau coq,* fine cock, used in the same way. Shakespeare uses the word in TWELFTH NIGHT, and twice in HENRY V (1599) e.g.: *The King's a bawcock, and a heart of gold.*

bawdreaminy. Bawdy misbehavior. Used by Dampit, in Middleton's A TRICK TO CATCH THE OLD ONE (1608). Like Urquhart in his translation (1653) of Rabelais, Middleton liked to invent resounding words. Dampit, an unscrupulous usurer and a drunkard, when his serving maid —well, wench—Audrey tries to get him from his cups to his bed, favors her with fine examples: *Thou quean of bawdreaminy! . . . Out, you gernative quean! the mullipood of villainy, the spinner of concupiscency! . . . Out, you babliaminy, you unfeathered cremitoried quean, you cullisance of scabiosity!*

bawdrik. See *baldric.*

bawdstrot. See *baude.* Probably from *baude* (q.v.), lively + *strutt,* strut: one with an inviting walk. Also *baudetrot, baldestrot, baldystrot, bawstrop, bronstrops.* In Langland's PIERS PLOWMAN (1362) one manuscript has *bawdstrot;* another, *bawd.*

bawdy. See *baude.*

bawn. A fortified enclosure. From Irish *babhun,* of unknown origin. Spenser, in A VIEW OF THE PRESENT STATE OF IRELAND (1596) speaks of the *square bawns which you see so strongly trenched and thrown up.* The word is still used in Ireland, but now referring to the yard where the cows are milked, the cattlefold.

bawson. A frequent variant of *bauson, q.v.,* as applied to a person.

baxter. Baker. Originally feminine; from 10th through 15th century used of both sexes; thereafter masculine. In the 16th century, a new feminine form was fashioned: *backstress.* Sir Walter Scott used the word in THE HEART OF MIDLOTHIAN (1818): *One in appearance a baxter, i.e. a baker's lad, handed her out of her chair.* After about 1400, however, *baxter* was rarely used save in Scotland.

bayard. One that is self-confident through ignorance; one firmly equipped with blind assurance. Originally, *bayard,* a *bay* horse. Then, the name of the magic (bay-colored) steed King Charlemagne gave to Rinaldo. From some now forgotten story with a 'leap before you look,' *Bayard* became a type or symbol of blind recklessness. Also, *bayard's bun,* a kind of cake for horses. *To ride the bayard of ten toes,* to walk; similarly, *to go on shanks' mare.* Hence, *bayardly,* in blind self-confidence; *bayardism,* ignorant presumption. According to some versions of the story, *Bayard* was given not to Rinaldo alone but to him and his three brothers, sons of Agmon. The horse changed size according to how many of the brothers mounted him. He may still be heard neighing, we are told, in the Ardennes on Midsummer Day. There was also a man, *Bayard,* Pierre du Terrail, Chevalier de Bayard (1475-1524) distinguished under three kings, and called 'le chevalier sans peur et sans reproche.'

be-. As a prefix, *be-* is used to add force, or to make an active verb, in many Old English words. Chaucer is fond of the form. Among these may be listed: *bebay,* to bay about, hem in, surround; *beblast,* to blast completely, wither; *bebleed,* to make bloody; *beblind; beblister; beblot* (Chaucer, TROYLUS AND CRISEYDE, 1374: *Biblotte it with thy tears*); *bebroyde,* embroider; *beclip,* embrace; *beclose,* imprison; *beclout,* to dress up (as in a loincloth; usually a term of scorn) ; *becudgel; becurl; bedaff,* to make a fool of; *bedog, bedaggle,* to trail in the mire, *befoul; bedaggle,* to deceive; *bedight,* to equip, bedeck (Poe, EL DORADO, 1849: *Gaily bedight, a gallant knight*) ; *bedilt,* hidden; *bedoubt, bedoute,* to dread; *bedove, bedoven,* plunged, immersed; *bedwynge,* to restrain; *befong* (Old English *fon,* to grasp), to seize; *begab,* to fool with words, impose upon; *beghost,* to make a ghost of; *begin* (pronounced *bejin: gin,* a trap, 13th and 14th centuries), to ensnare;

bego, to go about, to encompass, to overrun, to beset—survives in the participle *begone,* as in *woe-begone; begod,* to deify; *begrede,* to weep for; *behest,* to promise (*land of behest* was a common term for land of promise; then the noun took on the sense of bidding, command: *at his behest*); *behight,* to promise, to hold out hope, to warrant; used (archaically, and improperly) by Spenser to mean to deliver, to command, to name, as in THE SHEPHERD'S CALENDAR: DECEMBER (1579) *Love they him called . . . But better might they have behote him Hate; behounce,* to adorn, deck out; *bejape,* to trick; *bekend,* known; *bekiss,* to cover with kisses; *belace,* to adorn with lace, to stripe, to beat until one's back is striped; *belack,* to find fault with; *belate,* to detain, delay—survives in *belated; belaud,* to load with praise; *belay,* to set things around, as ornamentation, to set armed men around, to besiege, to forestall, to waylay—survives in the nautical sense, to set a rope around a cleat, etc. so as to fasten it securely, hence, in sailor's slang, *belay there!* stop! (Tie youself up!); *belirt,* to deceive, to cheat; *belive,* to remain, also (confused with *beleave*) to go; *belouke,* to shut, to shut in or out, to encompass; *bemark,* to make the sign of the cross; *bemete,* to measure, measure out (Shakespeare, THE TAMING OF THE SHREW, 1596: *I shall so bemete thee with thy yard*); *beneaped,* left ashore by the *neap* tide, hence beyond reach of ordinary high water; *benight,* to darken, literally or figuratively, as of those *whom error doth benight; beray,* to dirty, befoul, cover with abuse; *berede,* to advise, to plan, to deliberate; *beseem,* to appear, to suit in appearance, befit, be fitting; *beshrew,* to make or wish evil, to invoke evil upon—later, mainly an exclamation (Shakespeare, MUCH ADO ABOUT NOTHING, 1599: *Marry beshrew my hand, if it should give your age such cause of fear;* Sir Walter Scott, THE FAIR MAID OF PERTH, 1828: *Beshrew me if thou passest this door with dry lips!*); *bespall, bespaul, bespawl,* to spatter with saliva, as some persons when they talk, also figuratively, as in Jonson's THE POETASTER (1602): *Bespawls The conscious time with humours, foam, and brawls; bespreng,* to sprinkle (Wordsworth, AT VALLOMBROSA, 1837: *The flower-besprent meadows*); *besprink,* besprinkle; *bespurt, bespurtle,* to sully, to smear with abuse; *bestead,* to assist, relieve, be of service to (Arthur H. Clough, in MACMILLAN'S MAGAZINE of August, 1862: *Thou vain Philosophy! Little hast thou bestead, Save to perplex the head; beswink,* to work hard for; *beteem,* to think proper, to grant, to allow (Shakespeare, A MIDSUMMER NIGHT'S DREAM, 1590: *Rain, which I could well Beteeme them, from the tempest of mine eyes; betine* (from *tine,* a late form of *tind,* tinder), to set on fire; *bewhapped,* utterly amazed, confounded; *bewray,* to speak evil of, to expose (especially to reveal bad things, or what one wanted to keep hidden) as in Shakespeare's CORIOLANUS (1607): *Our raiment And state of bodies would bewray what life We have led since thy exile.* And there are many more that buzzed in the Middle Ages.

beadle. A herald; a town-crier; a mace-bearer before authority; one that delivers or carries out the orders of officials. Used from the 10th century; also *bydel, beadel, bedell;* still *bedel* at Oxford and Cambridge Universities. The word was used figuratively, especially with allusion to the beadle as bringing punishment; thus in Shakespeare's KING JOHN (1595): *Her injurie the beadle to her sinne.* The dignity of a beadle was *beadlehood;* his jurisdiction, *beadlery*; his office, *beadleship*; his qualities as a class—i.e., stupid officiousness—as in Dickens' Oliver Twist (1838) *beadleism,* or *beadledom.* Cousin to Tweedledum. Guilpin in SKIALETHEIA ("Shadow of Truth"; 1598) prefers the satire to the amorous ode; even the strictest Plato, he avers, *Will of the two affoord the satyre grace, Before the whyning love-song shall have place: And by so much his night-cap's overawde As a beadle's better statesman than a bawde.*

beatilles. Literally 'little blessed things,' from a diminutive of Latin *beatus,* blessed. Also *beatilia, beatilla.* Originally applied to pieces of needlework by nuns, pin-cushions, samplers with pious mottos, and other knick-knacks. Hence, trinkets, trifles, odds and ends—finally, odds and ends baked in a pie: cocks' combs, sweetbreads, giblets in merry mixture. A good cook can make such a dish tasty indeed; Disraeli in VENETIA (1837) speaks of *that masterpiece of the culinary art, a grand battalia pie.*

beaver. See *bever.*

bebled. The past of *bebleed,* to cover or stain with blood, used almost always in the past tense. Used through the 15th century (Caxton, CHARLES THE GREAT, 1485: *The place was alle bybled*) and revived in the 19th by Kingsley. *Cp. be-.*

bedight. See *dight; be-.*

bedstraw (1) The straw, covered by a sheet, that formerly constituted the bedding of a second-best bed and lesser sleep-spots. (2) The straw within a mattress; hence, a mattress. Chaucer knew the danger; he cries in THE MERCHANT'S TALE (1386): *O perilous fyr that in the bedstraw bredeth!*

bedswerver. A person unfaithful to the marriage bed. Shakespeare in THE WINTER'S TALE (1611) has Leontes say of Hermione: *She's a bed-swerver, even as bad as those That vulgars give bold'st titles.*

beek. To bask in the sun, or before a fire. The word is probably a mild form of *bake.* Hence *beeking,* exposure to genial warmth. Cockeram (1623) defines aprication (*q.v.*) as *a beaking in the Sunne.*

beesom. See *besom.*

beetle. See *bottle.*

begarred. See *rochet.* Scotch *begary* (accent on the *gare*) was also a noun, used in the 16th century to mean variegated facings on a dress.

behoveful. Useful; expedient; fit; necessary; due. Also *behooveful; byhooful, behoful,* and more. Very common from 1380 to the 18th century. Shakespeare in ROMEO AND JULIET (1595) has: *We have culled such necessaries As are behooveful for our state tomorrow.*

bel-. Also *bell-;* but see *bell-.* This prefix, via French *bel,* beautiful, from Latin *bellus,* has entered into many English words. Some of those that have slipped out of common use are: *bellaria,* delightful foods, desserts; *bellaview,* a fair prospect; *bellibone,* a fair maiden (Spenser, in THE SHEPHERD'S CALENDAR, 1579, uses both this form and its reverse, *bonibel*); *bellify,* to beautify, also *bellish,* short for *embellish; bellitude.* The word *belle* was once good English, meaning pretty, and was employed in various phrases, as in Chaucer's THE WIFE OF BATH'S TALE (1386): *He that wolde han my bele chose* [my pretty thing] . . . Congreve in the Epilogue to THE WAY OF THE WORLD (1698) speaks of *Whole belles assemblées of coquettes and beaux;* Lady Montague in a letter of 1716 refers to the *belles passions.* But spare me a bellicose belle! Note that the *bellarmine,* a drinking-mug of capacious belly and narrow neck, took its name (and shape) as a Netherlands Protestant satire on Cardinal *Bellarmine* (1542-1621; beatified 1924). D'Urfey in PILLS TO PURGE MELANCHOLY (1719) listed *jugs, mugs, and pitchers, and bellarmines of state.*

belaccoil. Friendly greeting. Also *belaccoyle. Cp. bel-.* Spenser, in THE FAËRIE QUEENE (1596) *her salewed with seemly belaccoil, Joyous to see her safe after long toil.*

belamour. A loved one, a sweetheart; a lover, a mistress. *Cp. bel-.* Spenser, in THE FAËRIE QUEENE (1596), said: *But as he nearer drew, he easily Might scerne that it was not his sweetheart sweet, Ne yet his belamour, the partner of his sheet.*

belamy. Good friend. Often used (13th to 18th century) as a form of address. French *bel,* fair + *ami,* friend. Also *bele amys, bellamy. Cp. bel-.* Thus in a Towneley Mystery (1460) we read: *Welcom be thou, belamy!*

belgard. A kind look, a loving look. Italian *bel guardo.* Spenser uses the word in THE FAËRIE QUEENE and in his HYMNE IN HONOUR OF BEAUTIE (1596): *Sometimes within her eyelids they unfold Ten thousand sweet belgards, which to their sight Doe seem like twinckling starres in frostie night.*

belive. Speedily, eagerly; at once. *As blive,* as quickly as possible. Middle English *bi life, be live,* with life (liveliness). The ballad of ROBIN HOOD AND GUY OF GISBORNE has: *Fast Robin he hied to Little John, He thought to loose him blive.* Surrey (THE AENEID, 1547): *To bring the horse to Pallas' temple blive;* Spenser (THE FAËRIE QUEENE, 1596): *And down to Pluto's house are come bilive.* Later—by the same process of human procrastination as altered *presently* (which first meant at the present moment, immediately) *belive* (in the 17th century) came to mean by-and-by.

bell-. This prefix, from Latin *bellum,* war, has given us a number of English words. *Bellacity,* a spirit of warlikeness, is only in the 18th century dictionaries; likewise *bellatrice,* a female warrior, a virago. *Belliferous,* bringing war, is rare; and the common *belligerent* developed a dictionary form *belligerate,* to wage war. *Belligerous,* full of warlike spirit, is also rare; *bellicose* is more common in the same sense; *bellatory* has dropped out of use; *bellipotent,* mighty in war, is now used only to create a pompous effect. *Bellonian,* warlike, is from *Bellona,* the Roman goddess of war; an imposing and strong-willed woman might be called a *Bellona.*

bellarmine. See *bel-.*

belle. See *bel-.*

belomancy. See *aeromancy.*

belswagger. A swaggering bully or gallant; a pimp. The *bel* may be from the French, but the form *bellyswagger* also appeared. Used from the 16th into the 18th century. Dryden in THE KIND KEEPER (1678) cried: *Fifty guineas! Dost thou think I'll sell myself? . . . thou impudent belswagger.*

belvedere. See *gazebo.*

beme. A trumpet. Used from the 8th to the 15th century. Figuratively, parade, trumpeting; ARTHUR in 1400 spoke of a *Pater Noster wythout any beeme.* Hence, as a verb, to trumpet; to trumpet (loudly proclaim) a thing; to summon with trumpet-call.

beneme. See *benim.*

beneurte. Happiness. *Beneurous,* happy, is a 15th century borrowing. French *bienheureux.* Used by Caxton, in the GOLDEN LEGEND and other 15th century works, as the translation (1480) of Ovid's METAMORPHOSES: *Benewrte and honour laste her not longe.*

benevolence. Used since the 15th century for a gift of money, a contribution to help the poor. Used by various kings—first, Edward IV, in 1473—of a forced contribution imposed upon their subjects. There were, of course, many protests. Lord Digby in 1644: *so preposterous a name as of a benevolence, for that which is a malevolence indeed.* Pepys in his DIARY, 31 August, 1661: *The benevolence proves . . . an occasion of so much discontent everywhere, that it had better it had never been set up.* And in 1775 Chatham pointed out in Parliament: *The spirit which now resists your taxation in America is the same which formerly opposed loans, benevolences, and shipmoney in England.*

benim. To take away; to rob; to deprive. Also *beneme;* after 1500 usually *benum, benumb.* (*Benum,* to deprive, added a *b* by analogy with *dumb, limb,* etc. The meaning was gradually limited to depriving (a part of the body) of its capacity for feeling. *Numb* is a shortening from *benumb. Benim* was a common word from the 10th to the 16th century; Chaucer uses it several times—twice in THE PARSON'S TALE (1386): *the likeness of the devil, and bynymeth man from God . . . bynymeth from man his witte.* May ours be spared!

benison. Blessing. A shortening of the Latin *benediction,* which is now the usual English word. Shakespeare, in KING LEAR (1605), refers to *the bountie and the benizon of heaven.* Scott in THE FAIR MAID OF PERTH (1828): *I have slept sound under such a benison.* Back in 1755 Samuel Johnson in his DICTIONARY said of *benison:* "not now used, unless luricrously," but the word still survives in historical fiction and in poetry. *Cp. malison.*

benjamin. A short coat worn by men in the late 18th and early 19th century. Brewer derives it from the name of a tailor, but it is more probably a Biblical transference, Benjamin being the youngest brother of Joseph. An 18th century ladies' riding cloak was called a *joseph,* from the "coat of many colors" in the Bible. Thus Goldsmith in THE VICAR OF WAKEFIELD (1766) pictures Olivia *dressed in a green joseph, richly laced with gold, and a whip in her hand.* Peacock in NIGHTMARE ABBEY gives us the younger brother: *His heart is seen to beat through his upper benjamin.*

bennet. (1) An old stalk of grass, left in late winter and early spring; eaten then by cattle, or the seeds by birds. An early form of *bent* (*grass*). (2) An herb (often identified as the avens) which the middle ages believed drove the devil away; hence called (*herb*) *bennet,* Old French *beneite;* Latin *benedicta,* blessed. The ORIUS SANITATIS (1486) quotes Platearius: 'Where the root is in the house the devil can do nothing, and flies from it; wherefore it is blessed above all other herbs.' Urquhart in his translation (1653) of Rabelais, ascribes to it another quality: *Fervency of lust is abated by certain drugs, plants, herbs, and roots . . . mandrake, bennet, keckbuglosse.* [There is a different opinion regarding mandrake; *cp. mandragora.*]

benthal. Relating to (ocean) depths of over 1000 fathoms. From Greek *benthos,* deep of the sea; related to *bathos,* whence *bathysphere.* May also be used figuratively, as when one reveals his benthal ignorance.

benumb. See *benim.*

bergamask. A rustic dance. Italian *bergamasco,* of *Bergamo,* a province of Venice; the dance supposedly mocked its country ways. From the same town came the *bergamot,* a citrus tree and its fruit; also, the fragrant oil prepared from the fruit rind. There is also a *bergamot,* an excellent variety of pear (Turkish *beg-armudi,* prince pear). Shakespeare in A MIDSUMMER NIGHT'S DREAM (1590) says *Will it please you . . . to have a bergomask dance . . . Come, your burgomask.* Thackeray in PENDENNIS (1850) says: *A delightful odour of musk and bergamot was shaken through the house.* Among the CRYS OF LONDON (BAGFORD BALLADS; 1680) resounded: *Do you want any damsons or bergume pare?*

bergh. See *barth.*

berlaken. See *byrlakin.*

berne. Before 1400, a warrior; later, a poetic word for a man. Sometimes used interchangeably with *baron.* The corresponding feminine word was *burd,* lady; in poetical use, usually young lady, maiden. Frequent in ballads. The term *burd-alone* was used, of either sex, to mean all alone. The ballads have Sir Roland *riding burd-alane,* whereas King Henrie *lay burd-alane.*

berner. See *barnard.*

bersatrix. A rocker of cradles; a babysitter. From French *berceau,* cradle + *trix,* a feminine ending. Found in Bailey's DICTIONARY of 1751, but applicable 200 years later.

berwe. A shady place, a grove. Also *berowe.* Used from the 9th to the 15th century; surviving in place-names as *bere, beere, bear, ber.*

beshrew. See *shrew; be-.*

besmotered. See *smotherlich.*

besom. A bundle of rods used for punishment; a similar bundle used for sweeping, a broom; hence, anything used to cleanse or purify. A common Teutonic word, with variant spellings: *besme, besum, beesom, bissome,* etc. There are references to a *bessume* (1493) of peacock's feathers; to a *beasome* (1697) of laurel; to (1756) a birchen *beesom.* Lyly in EUPHUES (1580) says: *There is no more difference between them, than between a broome and a beesome.* Carlyle in THE FRENCH REVOLUTION (1837) says: *With steel-besom, Rascality is brushed back;* Tyndall in MOUNTAINEERING (1862): *Grandly the cloud-besom swept the mountains.* From its shape, a comet has been called (1566) *the fyrie boosome,* (1639) *a firie bissome.* Which is sweeping enough! However, a *besom-head* is a stupid or foolish person. And *beesome* (though not so listed in O.E.D., which gives that form in the quotation from Shakespeare here under *conspectuity*) is one form—as also *bisene, bysome, bisme, beasom, bysone*—of *bisson,* blind; part blind; blinding, as in Shakespeare's HAMLET (1602) with 'the mobled queen' *threatening the flame With bisson rheume.*

besonio. See *bezonian.*

bestad. An old form of the past participle of *beset.* Also *bestadds.* Used by Spenser in the AUGUST ECLOGUE, THE SHEPHERD'S CALENDAR (1579) and in THE FAËRIE QUEENE: *But both attonce on both sides him bestad.* This is a variant of *bested, q.v.*

bested. Placed, situated; settled; arranged; set with, ornamented. Also, placed in a certain situation, *hard bested;* troubled, *beset by* (earlier, *bested with*) fears, dangers, difficulties. Accent on the second syllable; not to be confused with *bested,* accent on the first syllable, past participle of *best,* to overcome, to worst. *Bested,* also *bestead, béstad, bestadde,* is the old past participle of *beset.* Gower in CONFESSIO AMANTIS (1393): *Whan they ben glad I shall be glad, And sorry whan they ben bestad.* Shakespeare in HENRY VI, PART TWO (1593) says: *I never saw a fellow worse bestead.* There was also a verb (from the 16th century) *to bestead,* to help, to be of service to; to take the place of, from *be + stead,* to prop, support, whence also *steady. At nights,* Woodhead thought in ST. TERESA (1669) of *our mantles of thick cloth which many times besteaded us.* We still say *stood us in good stead.*

bestented. Distended. In Herrick's HESPERIDES (1648), the poem OBERON'S FEAST gives the one literary use of this form (an emphatic form of *stent, stend,* which survives in *extend* and *distend*): *The sag And well bestented bees sweet bag.*

bestiate. To make beastly. Latin *bestia,* beast. Used in the 17th century especially of liquor, as by Owen Feltham in RESOLVES (1628): *Drunkenness . . . bestiates even the bravest spirits.* The verb was sometimes Anglicized to *beastiate. Bestiary* means (1) a fighter of wild beasts in the Roman amphitheatre; (2) a moralizing treatise, using animals to point lessons, as written in the Middle Ages. A *bestiarian,* however, is a friend of the animals, especially, in the 19th century, an antivivisectionist.

bet. Old form of *better,* comparative of *good.* For several hundred years both forms were used, but by 1600 *better* had supplanted *bet.* Gower in CONFESSIO AMANTIS (1393) says: *One jousteth well, another bet.* In the frequent expression *Go bet* (Chaucer, THE PARDONER'S TALE, 1386: *Go bet, quod he, and axe redily what cors is this*), *bet* means quickly.

betony. A plant, with spiked purple flowers, helpful to keep evil spirits from the house, but still more efficacious as a healer. Hence frequently used in foods. *Betony* is from the Late Latin *betonia, betonica;* Pliny (HISTORIA NATURALIS; 70 A.D.) called it *vettonica,* ascribing its discovery to a Spanish tribe, the *Vettones.* Barbour in ST. BAPTISTA (1375) said: *Quhare mene makis drink of spycery, Of betone thare is gret copy. Cp. copy; coltsfoot.*

bevel. Slanty, sloping; hence (figuratively), away from a straight line or course of behavior. Shakespeare in SONNET 121, says: *I may be straight though they themselves be bevel.*

bever. A drink; time for drinking; a sip and a bite between meals, especially in the afternoon. In the first sense (from Latin *bibere,* to drink) the word survives in *beverage.* Marlowe in DOCTOR FAUSTUS (1590) speaks of *thirty meals a day and ten bevers.* The word *bever* was also used as a verb, to take a snack; but there was another verb of the same form *bever,* from Old English *beofian,* to tremble, meaning to tremble, to quake, and still used in north dialects. [*Bever* was also a variant from—*bavour, baviere, beavoir*— of *beaver,* originally (in French) a child's bib; Old French *bave,* saliva; but used in English for the lower part of a visor, the movable face-guard of a helmet. Sometimes *beaver* was used for the visor. An early movable beaver is pictured on the effigy of Thomas, Duke of Clarence, who was killed in 1421. Shakespeare in HAMLET (1602) has Hamlet inquire about the ghost: *Then saw you not his face?* and Horatio answer: *Oh yes, my lord, he wore his beaver up.* Hence *beaver-sight,* eye-hole of a helmet. The word *beaver* is sometimes used to imply concealed (down) or exposed, revealed (up) as in Hamilton's query in POPULAR EDUCATION (1845): *Why should the author suppress this anecdote now that his beaver is up?*—The animal *beaver* is related to the Old Aryan form *bhebhou,* brown. A *visor*—*vizor, vysere, vesoure, vysour,* etc.—was originally the upper part of the face guard; more frequently, the whole front part, so that in use the term was interchangeable with *beaver.* This word is from French *vis,* face, as in *vis-à-vis,* face to face; but occasionally, as though connected with *videre, visum,* to see (*vision*), *visor* has been used to mean a hole—the *visures*—to see through in a *beaver.* Also *visiere, vizard;* these mainly in other senses: a countenance; a mask to conceal the face; hence, a false outward show. Spenser in THE FAËRIE QUEENE (1590) speaks of *the crafty cunning traine By which deceipt doth maske in visour faire.*]

bevue. An error of inadvertence. French *bes,* bad + *vue,* view. Also *bevew.* Used in the 18th and early 19th centuries. Scott in his MEMOIRS (Lockhart, 1839) said: *He will content himself with avoiding such bevues in future.* Ah, sweet content!

bezoar. An antidote, a counterpoison. Through French, Spanish, and Arabic from Persian *pad-zahr,* counterpoison, *zahr,* poison. The word had many spellings in English, as *besert, bezahar, beazer, bazar, bezoard.* It was applied particularly to a 'stone' (the *bezoar-stone*), believed to be an antidote, found in the digestive organs of ruminant animals, especially the wild goat of Persia, the bezoar-goat. Edward Topsell, in THE HISTORIE OF SERPENTS (1608) advises: *The juice of apples being drunk, and endive, are the proper bezoar against the venom of a phalangie.* The Earl of Monmouth, in his translation (1637) of Malvezzi's ROMULUS AND TARQUIN, uses the word figuratively: *Valor is a kind of besar, which comforts the hearts of subjects, that they may the better endure a tyrant's venom.* In the 17th and 18th century, the adjective, *bezoardic, bezoartic,* was sometimes used as a noun instead of *bezoar.* And in 1693 Sir Thomas Blount in his NATURAL HISTORY remarked that *everything good against poysons is commonly term'd bezoardical.* (*Bezoar* is pronounced in two syllables, with the accent on the first.)

bezonian. A raw recruit. Later, a beggar, a rascal. Shakespeare in HENRY VI, PART TWO remarks that *Great men oft dye by vile bezonians.* And Massinger, in THE MAID OF HONOUR (1632), speaks of the slut who would, *for half a mouldy biscuit, sell herself to a poor bisognion.* The word was originally *besonio.* It is from the Italian *bisogno,* need, want, applied in derision to the raw soldiers who came to Italy from Spain, in the 15th and 16th centuries, without proper equipment or means. Robert Johnson, in his translation (1601) of Botero's THE WORLD, AN HISTORICALL DESCRIPTION, speaks of *a base besonio, fitter for the spade than the sword.* Both forms, after a lapse of two centuries, were revived in historical novels: Scott in THE MONASTERY (1820): *Base and pilfering besognios and marauders;* Bulwer-Lytton in THE LAST OF THE BARONS (1843): *Out on ye, cullions and bezonians!*

bib. To drink; to tipple. The word may be imitative in origin, or from Latin *bibere,* to drink—probably imitative in origin. Also *beb.* Chaucer says, in THE REEVE'S TALE (1386): *This Miller has so wisely bebbed ale That as an horse he snorteth in his sleep.* The word was naturally very common, and developed many forms: *bibitory,* relating to drink; *bibacious,* fond of drink: a writer in BLACKWOOD'S MAGAZINE (1834) calls the middle class *bibacious more than health requires*; *bibacity, bibbery, bibation, bibition*; a *bibber, bibbler,* or a *biberon*; *bibbing,* also as a compound: FRASER'S MAGAZINE (1833) speaks of a *port-bibbing, goutbemartyred believer in the Tory faith.* To *bibble* is to keep on drinking—though *bibble-babble* takes its sense from the second part, and means long empty talk. *Bibesy* means a too great desire to drink; too many even today are afflicted with bibesy. The verb *bib,* to drink, survives in the form *imbibe.* Two current nouns were formed from it: *bib,* a fish that distends a membrane in its head as though filling it with liquid; and *bib,* the cloth tucked under a child's chin when it drinks. This *bib* was also applied to a neck cloth for adults, sometimes for protection, sometimes as adornment. Hence, one's best bib and tucker means one's best attire. See *tucker.* There is also a rare form *biberage* (influenced perhaps by *beverage*; see *bever*) meaning a drink given in payment. See *bibulate.*

biblio-. See *bibliopole.*

bibliomancy. See *aeromancy.*

bibliopole. A bookseller. During the 18th and 19th centuries many formal or pedantic terms, from Greek *biblion,* book, developed in the literary field. Often they were used for humorous effect. Among these are: *biblioclasm,* destruction of books; *biblioclast,* destroyer of books; *bibliognost,* an expert on books; *bibliogony,* production of books; *biblioklept,* a book thief; *bibliopegy,* the art of book-binding, hence *bibliopegist*; *bibliophagist,* a devourer of books, an ardent reader; *bibliopyrate,* a burner of books; *bibliopoly, bibliopolery,* bookselling; *bibliotaph,* one who 'buries' books by keeping them locked away. The still current *bibliophile* was contrasted with the *bibliophobe* but had its excess in the *bibliomane.* At which I (looking at my book-shelves) pause.

bibulate. To tipple; a humorous diminutive from Latin *bibere,* to drink, whence also *imbibe*; see *bib.* Used in the 18th and 19th centuries. BLACKWOOD'S MAGAZINE (1828) tells of persons who *bibulate gin and water with the housekeeper.* ST. JAMES'S GAZETTE of April 12, 1882, speaks of *the extraordinary capacity for bibulation displayed by the regular soldier.* The word *bibulous* was more frequently used; it meant both fond of drinking and (technically) able to absorb moisture; Cowper in his translation (1790) of the ODYSSEY speaks of *bibulous sponges.*

bicipital. Having two heads. In current anatomical use, as of a muscle (the *biceps*) , but applicable also to a committee with co-chairmen or a party with two leaders, or Siamese twins.

bidale. A party (ale-drinking) to which all the neighbors were bid, when, as Blount explained in 1656, "an honest man decayed in his estate is set up again by the liberal benevolence and contribution of friends at a feast." *Bidales* were forbidden in Wales by a law (1534) of King Henry VIII, and later in England by the Puritans. The practice, nevertheless—if not the word—survives.

bifarious. Ambiguous, capable of being interpreted in two ways; taking a dual stand, so as to be accepted according to the liking of each listener. The even more plural *multifarious* has survived. E. Ward in HUDIBRAS REDIVIVUS (1707) spoke of *Some strange, mysterious verity In old bifarious prophesy.* Sir Roger de Coverley frequently observed: "There is much to be said on both sides."

bigama. A woman living in bigamy. Also *bigame,* applied to a bigamous man or woman. A 15th and 16th century term, apparently no longer needed.

Big-endian. See *cynarctomachy.*

bigenerous. Hybrid; with characteristics of two genera. Nature has been generous. Guillim in his book on HERALDRY (1610) wrote of *a bigenerous beast of unkindly procreation.*

biggen. To recover weight and strength after illness; especially, one's strength after pregnancy; to grow big; to make big. Shakespeare uses the word as a noun, in the sense of a cloth wound round the head at night, as a comforting night head-dress, in HENRY IV, PART TWO (1598) as Prince Henry looks upon his father asleep with his crown on his pillow: *Sleep with it now! Yet not so sound and half so deeply sweet As he whose brow with homely biggen bound Snores out the watch of night.* (Quite a phenomenon, a snoring brow!)

bigote. The moustache. In Mabbe's translation (1623) of Aleman's GUZMAN DE ALFARACHE we read: *It seeming perhaps unto them that . . . the bearing their bigotes high, turn'd up with hot yrons . . . should be their salvation and bring them to heaven.* The word is Spanish, apparently unconnected with *bigot.*

bilbo. (1) A sword, of fine temper and elastic blade. Used by Shakespeare (THE MERRY WIVES OF WINDSOR, 1598) and other Tudor writers; revived by Sir Walter Scott, in WOODSTOCK (1826): *My tough old knight and you were at drawn bilbo.* Also transferred to the man who wears a sword, as by Shakespeare (again in THE MERRY WIVES): *I combat challenge of this latin bilboe.* (2) A long iron bar, with shackles for the ankles of prisoners, and a lock to fasten one end to the floor or ground. Shakespeare uses this sense in HAMLET. Both words are supposed to come from the city *Bilbao* (which the English called *Bilboa*) in Spain, a center of sword-making. The bars were supposedly shipped on the Spanish Armada (1588), to fetter the English prisoners; but the word, and the instrument, appear at least as early as 1557. From *bilbo,* sword, came the expression *bilbo-lord,* a swaggerer, a bully.

biliment. See *billyment.*

bill. See *glaive.*

billingsgate. Scurrilous and violent abuse. By the 16th century *Billing's Gate,* London, brought inevitably to mind the foul-mouthed workers (women as well as men) in the fish-market there, and by the mid-17th century the name of the gate was being used for the language there spoken. The Third Earl of Shaftesbury, in CHARACTERISTICKS (1710) speaks of *philosophers and divines who can be contented to . . . write in learned billingsgate.* The word is quiescent, but the practice still is loud. Bailey (1751) defines a *billingsgate* as "a scolding impudent slut." THE PRESENT STATE OF RUSSIA (1671) stated: *If you would please a Russian with musick, get a consort of billingsgate nightingales, which, joyn'd with a flight of screech owls, a nest of jackdaws, a pack of hungry wolves, seven hogs in a windy day, and as many cats with their corrivals . . .*

billyment. A variant form of *biliment,* itself short for *habiliment,* garment. Via French *habiller,* to clothe, make fit, from Latin *habilis,* fit, *able,* suitable, from the root *hab,* to have. Usually in the plural, *billyments,* garments, clothing.

bilynne. See *blin.*

bimana. Two-handed animals; men. From Latin *bi-,* two + *manus,* hand. One of the *bimanous* (or *bimanal*) tribe is a *bimane.* This is a late 18th and 19th century pedantic way (used first by Buffon and Cuvier, in their natural histories) of referring to the highest order of mammalia, of which man is the only known species.

birdsnie. My sweet one; a term of endearment. Used in 17th century plays. The *nie* (also *birdsnye*) means *eye;* old *myn eye* became *my nye.* R. Davenport in THE CITY NIGHT-CAP (1661) cried *Oh, my sweet birds-nie! What a wench have I of thee!*

birthdom. Inheritance, birthright. So in the O.E.D. In his notes to Shakespeare's MACBETH (1605), however, G. B. Harrison defines the word as meaning native land. Macduff is speaking, fled to England from Scotland and Macbeth's savagery: *Let us rather Hold fast the mortal sword, and like good men Bestride our downfall'n birthdome.*

biscot. Three words have taken this form. (1) A fine exacted in the 16th and 17th centuries, from landowners who failed to repair ditches, marsh banks, etc. The first syllable may be Old English *by,* borough, which survives in *by-law* and such names as *Derby.* The second is Old English *scot,* contribution, payment, which survives in the expression *scot free.* The *sc* was also pronounced like *sh,* whence *to pay one's shot* and (slang) *the whole shoot,* sometimes expanded, in mistake of its origin, to *the whole shooting-match.* Also, *to pay scot and lot* (*shot and lot*), to pay thoroughly, to settle with; Shakespeare puns on this in HENRY IV, PART ONE (1597): *Or that hot termagant Scot had paid me scot and lot too.* (2) To caress. From French *biscoter,* this is used in Urquhart's translation (1653) of Rabelais: *Wheresoever they should biscot and thrum their wenches.* (3) Biscuit. Also, a small one, *biscotin.* From the 16th to the 18th century the preferred spelling was *bisket;* then in imitation of modern French the spelling was changed to *biscuit* but the sound was kept the same. The Latin form would be *biscoctum panem,* twice-cooked bread.

bismer. Shame; mockery, scorn. Old High German *bismer,* ridicule, from *bi,* by + *smier,* smile. Also *bismere, bysmer, bismor, busmar, busmeyr,* and the like. *Bismer* is also a verb, to mock; and from 1300 to 1550 was applied to a person worthy of scorn. From the time of King Alfred (about 890) to the mid-16th century, the word was used, e.g. Chaucer, THE REEVE'S TALE (1386) *As ful of hokir and of bissemare.* (*Hokir,* contempt, abuse.)

bismotered. See *smotherlich.*

bissextile. Leap year, the year containing the *bissext.* Also *bisext, bisex, bysext.* Latin *bis,* twice + *sextus,* sixth. The calendar as improved under Julius Caesar created 'leap year,' by adding a day in February. This was inserted after February 24, the *sixth* day before the calends of March—which day was counted twice, making it *bissextile* (in English, both adjective and noun). Tomlinson (1854) pointed out a refinement of the Julian calendar: *Thus 1600 was bissextile, 1700 and 1800 were not so.* Mrs. Somerville had observed, a score of years earlier, that *if in addition to this, a bissextile be suppressed every 4000 years, the length of the year will be nearly equal to that given by observation.* That is one act of suppression we must remember and be ready to perform.

bisson. See *besom.* Perhaps from *biseonde; bi,* by, near at hand + *seonde,* seeing.

black acre. A name used in court, to distinguish one plot of ground from another: *black acre; white acre; green acre*—somewhat like "party of the first part" etc. The colors were perhaps originally chosen from various crops. After a time, *to black-acre* meant to litigate over land; in Wycherley's THE PLAIN DEALER (1677) the litigious widow is *Mrs. Blackacre;* her son *Jerry Blackacre* is so well trained by her in court procedure that he wins all of her land.

bladarius. A dealer in grain. Found only in the dictionaries (Bailey, 1751). *Blaed* was Old English, from a common Teuton form, for *blade* (of grass, as opposed to leaf)—though influenced by Latin *bladum,* Old French *bled,* corn, wheat. By the 11th century *blade* was transferred from plants to the broad flat part of an oar, a spade and the like; and by the 14th, to the *blade* of a knife and a sword.

blake. Pale. As a verb, to make or to become pale. This is from a common Teuton word *blikan,* shine, but in Old English it lost the sense of white from shining light, and came to mean white from lack of color—pale. Hence it was often confused, in form then in meaning, with that other word for absence of color, *black.* Figuratively (as listed by Bailey, 1751) *blake* also meant skin-white, i.e., naked. In various parts of England, the word took different hues, as ash-colored, pale yellow ("as blake as butter"), whence also *blakes* came to mean cow dung dried for fuel.

blas. (1) A *blast,* breath. A common Teuton term; Old Norse *blasa,* to blow. Used 10th through 14th centuries. (2) The supposed twofold motion of the stars, producing changes in terrestrial weather. The term *blas* was invented for this by Van Helmont (about 1640); he also invented the longer-lived word *gas.*

blate. (1) Pale; bashful; backward. Used from Old English through the 17th century, surviving in dialect. Scott tried to revive the word in QUENTIN DURWARD (1823): *You are not blate—you will never lose fair lady for faint heart.* (2) To babble, to prate. Pepys in his DIARY (1666) entered: *He blates to me what has passed between other people and him.* Loud talk and empty chatter being what they are, other words developed: *blaterate,* to babble; *blateration; blateroon,* a foolish talker. Also *blather; blether; bletherskate; blatherskite,* a noisy talker of nonsense. This word became common in the United States from the lines *Jog on your gait, ye bletherskate* in MAGGIE LAUDER (1650), which was a favorite song in the American Revolution. Burns, in TAM O' SHANTER (1790) speaks of *A bletherin, blusterin, drunken blellum.* Even Coleridge (1834) was annoyed by *blethering,* though he did not go so far (American-wise) as to call the offender a blethering idiot!

blaze. A variant form of *blazon,* to publish forth. Spenser begins his song to Queen Elizabeth, in the April Eclogue of THE SHEPHERD'S CALENDAR (1579): *Ye dayntye nymphes, that in this blessed brooke Do bathe your brest, Forsake your watry bowres, and hether looke, At my* *request: And eke you virgins that on Parnasse dwell, Whence floweth Helicon the learned well, Helpe me to blaze Her worthy praise, Which in her sexe doth all excell.*

bleb. A bubble of air, as in water or glass. Also *blebb.* An imitative word, making a bubble with the lips, like *bubble, blob, blubber, blobber,* etc. Also used as a verb, as in Clare's THE VILLAGE MINSTREL (1821): *While big drops . . . bleb the withering hay with pearly gems.*

blee. Color, hue; complexion. Also *blio, bleo, blo, ble, bleye.* (Note that this word is not related to Anglo Saxon *blae,* blue.) Used only poetically in Middle English; obsolete before Shakespeare, but frequent in early ballads and metrical romances, whence it was revived by 19th century poets, as Elizabeth Barrett Browning (1850): *The captain, young Lord Leigh, With his eyes so grey of blee.*

bleo. See *blee.*

blete. Naked, bare. Also *bleat.* From the 10th to the 14th century.

blethe. Timid, lacking in spirit. Also *bleath.* From the 10th to the 14th century.

blether. See *blate.*

bletonism. Divining; indicating "by sensation" the location of subterraneous springs. Derived from a *Mr. Bleton* who, according to the MONTHLY MAGAZINE of 1821 "for some years past has excited universal attention by his possessing the above faculty." A *bletonist, bletonite,* a practitioner with the divining-rod—whose most effective instrument was (naturally) of witch-hazel.

blin. From the prefix *be,* off and the common Teutonic *linnam,* to cease; used in English in the senses to stop, to stay, and to stay silent. Used by Chaucer and Spenser, who in THE FAËRIE QUEENE says *Nathemore . . . Did th' other two their cruel vengeance blin.* It also appeared as *bilynne,* etc. It was a frequent word from about 950 to about 1600, and would make a better exclamation than, say, "Cut it out!" Blin!

blissom. In heat. As a verb, to couple; used 16th through 18th century of a ram and a ewe. Hence, to be lustful, *to go ablissoming.*

blithemeat. A party or feast at the birth of a child. From *blithe,* merry. A term of the 17th and 18th centuries, *blithemeat* lingers in Scotland. In China, the feast is held at the next new moon. In the United States, the happy father hands out cigars.

blive. See *belive.*

blo. See *blue (blueman).*

bloman. A black man, Negro. See *blue (blueman).* Wright's DICTIONARY OF OBSOLETE ENGLISH (1849) lists *bloman: a trumpeter.* There are no instances of this use.

blomanger. An early English dish. It can be made with capon, or other fowl. Let us note, from Warner's ANTIQUITATES CULINARIAE (1791) the recipe for a *blomanger of fish: Tak a pound of rys, les hem wel and wasch, and seth tyl they breste; and let hem kele; and do thereto mylk of to pound of almandys; nym the perche, or the lopuster, and boyle yt, and kest sugur and salt also thereto, and serve yt forth.*

blonk. A steed, a war-horse. Also *blanka, blank, blonke;* Old High German *blanch,* white. Used from Beowulf to the 16th century; a poetic term.

blore. A violent blowing or blast. A favorite word of Chapman's; in his translation (1598) of THE ILIAD: *The west wind and the north . . . join in a sudden blore.* Sometimes used to mean the air: Chapman's THE ODYSSEY (1614): *Vanish'd again into the open blore.* Johnson's DICTIONARY (1775) calls it "an expressive word, but not used"; it has, however, lingered in poetry. There is also a verb *blore,* surviving in dialects, meaning to cry, to bellow. Both are probably imitative of sounds.

blowen. A wench; a prostitute. Also *blowing.* The O.E.D. gives all its examples in the 19th century; but Shadwell in THE SQUIRE OF ALSATIA (1688) has Cheatly remark to the booby country fellow he is trying to gull: *What ogling there will be between thee and the blowings! Old staring at thy equipage! And every buttock shall fall down before thee!*

blowess. A variant of *blowze, q.v.* Bishop Hall in his first SATIRE (1597) wrote: *Nor ladies wanton love, nor wandring knight, Legend I out in rymes all richly dight . . . Nor list I sonnet of my mistresse face, To paint some blowesse with a borrowed grace . . . Nor can I crouch, and writhe my fauning tayle To some great patron, for my best availe. Such hunger-starven trencher-poetry, Or let it never live, or timely die.*

blowze. A beggar's wench, a trull. Burton in THE ANATOMY OF MELANCHOLY (1621) says: *I had rather marry a fair one, and put it to the hazard, than be troubled with a blowze.* Bailey (1751) defines a *blowze* as "a fat, red-fac'd, bloted wench, or one whose head is dressed like a slattern." Shakespeare declares, in TITUS ANDRONICUS (1588): *Sweet blowse, you are a beautious blossome sure.* Hence also *blowzed, blowzing, blowzy.* Occasionally the word has a pleasant savour, as when Tennyson in THE PRINCESS (1847) speaks of *Huge women blowzed with health and wind and rain And labour.*

blue. This color word was very popular in compounds and phrases. Thus *blue apron,* a tradesman; hence, *blue-apron statesman,* a tradesman who interferes in politics. *blue beans,* bullets (of lead); *blue-beat,* to beat black and blue. *blue blanket,* the sky. *blue blood,* (one of) aristocratic heritage, from the Spanish idea that the veins of aristocratic families show through the skin a 'truer blue' than those of commoners. *blue bonnet,* also *blue cap,* a Scotsman. *To burn blue,* of a candle, to burn without red or yellow light: an omen of death, or sign of the presence of ghosts or the Devil. Shakespeare in RICHARD III (1594) says: *The lights burne blew! blue bottle,* a beadle; also a policeman. Shakespeare in HENRY IV, PART TWO says to a beadle: *I will have you as soundly swindg'd for this, you blue-bottle rogue.* Also *blue coat,* as in the American boy's taunt: *Brass button, blue coat, Couldn't catch a nanny-goat!* But *blue coat* likewise (Shakespeare, Dekker), being then the garb of lower servants and charity folk, was used to mean a beggar, an almsman. *blue-dahlia,* a rarity or most unlikely thing. *blue devil,* an evil demon; in the plural, *blue devils,* despondency, also *the blues.* Byron in DON JUAN (1823) declares: *Though six days smoothly run, The seventh will bring blue devils or a dun.* Also, the horrid sights in delirium tremens. *blue fire,* a stage light for eerie effects; hence (19th century) sensational, as *blue-fire melodrama. blue funk,* a spell of fright, nervous dread. *blue gown*; in Scotland, a licensed beggar; in England (17th century) a harlot; especially one in prison (where a blue gown marked her shame).

blueman, also *bloman, blamon,* a Negro. From the 13th to the 17th century, *blo* was used for blue, bluish black, lead colored. *blue hen,* in the expression *Your mother must have been a blue hen,* a reproof given to a braggart, from the saying, *No cock is game unless its mother was a blue hen. To shout blue murder,* to cry out more from fear than because of actual danger. *blue ruin,* a bad quality of gin; gin. *blue story,* an obscene or pornographic story. [In French, *conte bleu* is an old wives' tale; a lascivious or obscene story is *conte gras.*] Other *blue* compounds, like *bluebeard, blue stocking, blue ribbon,* remain well known. *Cp. red.*

blushet. A shy maiden; a modest girl (literally, little *blusher*). Jonson in THE STAPLE OF NEWS (1625) *Though mistress Band would speak, or little blushet Wax be ne'er so easy.* Jonson, who likes the word (and why not?) seems to be the only one that has used it.

bly. Likeness; aspect; character. Survives in dialects: *I see a bly of your father about you.*

boanerges. THE GOSPEL ACCORDING TO ST. MARK tells us that "Simon he surnamed Peter"; James and John, *he surnamed them Boanerges, which is, The sons of thunder.* As they became preachers, the word *boanerges* (four syllables; used as a singular noun) was applied to a loud or fiery preacher. It was also used figuratively; R. S. Hawker, in CORNISH BALLADS (1869) has: *Loud laughed the listening surges . . . You might call them Boanerges From the thunder of their wave.* Hence also *boanergism, boanergy,* for loud oratory or vehement denunciation.

boanthropy. "Man into ox": a madness in which a man imagines himself an ox, as was prophesied and fulfilled of Nebuchadnezzar in the BOOK OF DANIEL in the BIBLE. Also figuratively, as when a man becomes obstinate, stolid, stupid, or develops other unpleasant ways we can foist upon the patient ox.

bob. Among the forgotten meanings of *bob* are: a bunch of flowers; an ornamental pendant; an ear-drop; Goldsmith in SHE STOOPS TO CONQUER (1773): *My cousin Con's necklaces, bobs and all.* In the 17th century, *bobbed hair, a bob,* meant hair drawn into a bunch in the back, or with a bunched or tassel-like curl; also, a man's wig so made. Thus, *bob-wig, bob-peruke.* The refrain of a song: *to bear the bob,* join in the chorus; Lestrange in his FABLES (1692): *To bed, to bed, will be the bob of the song.* A trick, befoolment; *to give the bob,* to fool, mock, impose upon. A blow with the fist; a sharp rap; hence, a rap with the tongue, a rebuke—this sense combined with the one before, to develop the meaning, a taunt, scoff, bitter jibe; thus Shakespeare in AS YOU LIKE IT (1600): *He that a foole doth very wisely hit, Doth very foolishly, although he smart, Seeme senselesse of the bob.* Hence also the verb, as in Shakespeare's OTHELLO: *Gold, and Jewels, that I bob'd from him. To bob off,* to get rid of fraudulently. Also *blind-bob,* an early name for the game of *blind-man's buff.*

bobadil. A blustering braggart, a swaggering pretender to prowess. From the character *Bobadil,* in Jonson's EVERY MAN IN HIS HUMOUR (1598). Hence also *bobadilian, bobadilish; bobadilism.* Carlyle in THE FRENCH REVOLUTION (1837) speaks of *that bobadilian method of contest.*

bobance. Pride; pomp; boasting. Also *boban, bobant.* In the plural, *bobances,* "pomps and vanities." Chaucer in THE

WIFE OF BATH'S PROLOGUE (1386) has: *Certeinly I sey for no bobance Yet was I nevere withouten purveiance Of mariage.*

bodement. An omen; a presentiment; an announcement; from the 16th century. From the 14th century *bode* was used in the same sense; Chaucer in THE PARLEMENT OF FOULES (1374) mentions *The owl eke, that of death the bode bringeth.* Old English *bod,* related to *bid;* the earliest meaning of *bode* (10th century) was command; then message, tidings. But note also *bide, abode;* in the 14th, 15th, and 16th centuries, *bode* was used to mean a tarrying, waiting, delay. *But bode,* without delay. The first sense of the verb *to bode* was to announce, to teach; then, to proclaim; to command; to announce beforehand; to foretell, to portend. In Shakespeare's MACBETH (1605) when Macbeth is told that he is safe until Birnam forest come to Dunsinane, he exclaims: *Sweet boadments, good!*

bodkin. Originally, a short pointed dagger. So in Chaucer, and in Hamlet's soliloquy: *He himself might his quietus make with a bare bodkin.* Then used of similarly shaped instruments, for piercing holes in cloth, for fastening up or frizzling ladies' hair, etc. A *bodkinbeard* is one dagger-shaped. A *bodkin* is also a person squeezed between two others without proper room; hence, *to ride bodkin, to sit bodkin;* Thackeray in VANITY FAIR (1848) protests: *He's too big to travel bodkin between you and me.* The verb *bodkin* thence meant to squeeze in. The exclamation *Ods bodkins!,* however, is a corruption of *God's bodikin,* little body.

boeotian. A stupid fellow, blockhead, Gothamite. See *Gotham. Boeotia* was a region of ancient Greece proverbial for the stupidity of the natives. Hence *boeotize,* to behave like a fool; *boeotic. Boeotian* is also used as an adjective, stupid; it is pronounced *Bee-ocean.* Lockhart in VALERIUS (1821) spoke of an opportunity *which I should have been a boeotian indeed had I neglected.* Byron, in ENGLISH BARDS AND SCOTCH REVIEWERS (1809): *To be misled By Jeffrey's heart, or Lambe's boeotian head.*

boggard. A jakes, privy. Also *boghouse, bogshop.* From *bog* (never in literary use), 'to exonerate the bowels,' says the O.E.D.; to defile with excrement. "Martinus Scriblerus" in 1714 said: *He cast them all into a bog-house near St. James'.*

boist. A box, especially for ointment; a cupping-glass. Hence, *to boist,* to cup. Via Old French *boiste,* box (modern *boite*) from Greek *pyxis,* box. Also, later (like the French word), used in slang to mean a rude hut, a "joint."

boistous. Rough, rude; coarse; vigorous; roughly violent. From the 13th century; a common word, appearing in many forms, such as *boysteous, buystous, busteous, bustwys, boisteous, boystuous,* which by the 16th century were mainly gathered into *boisterous.* Hence also *boistousness, boistness,* and (a rare 17th century form) *boisture.* Surrey in a song of 1538 said: *I call to minde the navie great That the Grekes brought to Troye town: And how the boysteous windes did beate Their ships, and rent their sayles adown, Till Agammemnons daughters blood Appeasde the goddes that them withstood.* Euripides tells the story of the daughter's sacrifice in IPHIGENIA AT AULIS.

bombace. Raw cotton; cotton wadding; hence stuffing, padding. Also *bombage, bombase, bumbasie, bombasie, bombasine, bombazeen, bombazine.* The verb *bombase,* to stuff with cotton-wool, to pad—

Gascoigne in A VOYAGE TO HOLLAND (1572); *They march bumbast with buttered beer* — (originally accented on the second syllable; so in Byron; later, on the first) developed in the late 16th century the still current sense of the noun *bombast,* inflated language. It has been (erroneously) suggested that this later use of the word sprang from the name and manner of Paracelsus (1493-1541), whose full name was *Philippus Aureolus Theophrastus Bombastus von Hohenheim.* Which is bombastic enough!

bombard. The earliest type of cannon. Also *bumbard, boumbard.* It was introduced in the late 14th century, but did not prove effective. It was usually loaded with a stone, weighing sometimes 200 pounds. Also, from the shape, a leather jug for liquor; hence, a heavy drinker (17th century). Also, from the sound, a deep-toned wooden musical instrument, like a bassoon; *bombardo.* A *bombardman* was a pot-boy, bartender; a *bombardphrase* was a loud-sounding utterance, inflated language. Shakespeare mentions the drinking jug in THE TEMPEST and in HENRY IV, PART ONE (1596): *that huge bombard of sacke.* Thomas Heywood in PHILOCOTHONISTA, OR THE DRUNKARD OPENED, DISSECTED AND ANATOMIZED (1635) spoke of *the great black jacks and bombards at the Court, which, when the Frenchmen first saw, they reported . . . that the Englishmen used to drink out of their bootes.* (Champagne from milady's slipper?) Jonson in his translation (1640) of Horace's THE ART OF POETRY said: *They . . . must throw by Their bombard phrase, and foot and half-foot words.* Also *cp. sesquipedalian.*

bombast. See *bombace.*

bombazine. See *bombace.*

bombilate. To hum, to buzz. Derived by error from Latin *bombitatio, bombilation.* Also *bombinate, bombination,* as in Rabelais' riddle of the bombinating chimaera. (Rabelais, ridiculing the over-refined subtleties of the Schoolmen, posed "the most subtle question, whether a chimaera bombinating in a vacuum could eat up second intentions.")

bombycinous. Silken; pale yellow. Greek *bombyx,* silk-worm.

bomination. Short for *abomination*; used as an adjective, execrable, abominable. Nashe in HAY [Have Ye] ANY WORK FOR COOPER (1589), the title playing on the name of Thomas Cooper, Bishop of Winchester, whom he was attacking in the Martin Marprelate controversy, protests that he was misunderstood: *Non would be so groshead as to gather, because my reverence telleth Dean John that he shall have twenty fists about his eares more then his owne (whereby I meant in deede that manye would write against him by reason of his bomination learning, which otherwise never ment to take pen hand) that I threatned him with blowes and to deale by Stafford law.* [*Stafford law* is a play on English place names; law of the *staff,* i.e., the use of force; as they might say *I am going to Bedfordshire,* meaning to bed.]

bombylious. Buzzing, humming. Greek *bombylios,* a buzzing insect. *Cp. bombilate.*

bonaroba. A showy wanton. From Italian *buona,* good + *roba,* gown, stuff. Shakespeare has, in HENRY IV, PART TWO (1597): *We knew where the bonarobas were, and had the best of them all at commandment.* Scott revived the word, in THE FORTUNES OF NIGEL (1822): *Your lordship is for a frolic into Alsatia? . . . There are bonarobas to be found there.* [*Alsatia* was the cant name of the section of London under the White Friars; hence, a sanctuary for debtors and law-breakers; thence, a haunt of prostitutes and criminals.]

bongrace. A protection. From the French: *bonne,* good + *grace,* grace. Specifically, a shade hanging from a woman's bonnet to protect her face from the sun and, later, a broad-brimmed hat for the same purpose. A commentator of 1617 speaks of *bonegraces, now altogether out of use with us.* The word was also used figuratively, as by Thomas Heywood in TROIA BRITANICA (1609): *A grove through which the lake doth run, Making his boughs a bongrace from the sun.* Sir Walter Scott revived the word in GUY MANNERING (1815). On the sea, a frame of old rope etc. hung over a ship to protect it "from damage of great flakes of ice" (Bailey, 1751) and other encounterings was also called a *bongrace.*

bonibel. See *bel-.*

bonism. See *malism.* This 'best of all possible' worlds.

bookholder. A prompter in a theatre. Used in the 16th and 17th centuries. Nothing like the current *bookkeeper* or *bookmaker.*

boot. See *bote.*

boots-and-shoes. See *pattens-and-clogs.*

booze. See *bouse.*

bopeeper. A mask. Behind it, one plays *bo-peep. Bo-peep* is often used figuratively: *to play bo-peep* with one's creditors, with one's fancies, with the Almighty.

bora. See *borasco.*

borable. That may be bored (physically or mentally). Also *boreable.* Listed by Johnson (1755), who ought to have known. Hence, sophisticate.

borachio. A large leather bottle for wine, especially as used in Spain. From Spanish *borracha,* wine bag; *borracho,* drunkard. Also used in English for a man who is a 'wine bag'; in Shakespeare's MUCH ADO ABOUT NOTHING (1599) there is a character named *Borachio.* Greene's MAMILLIA, A LOOKING GLASSE FOR THE LADIES OF ENGLAND (1594) uses the word figuratively: *a borachio of kisses.* Bailey's DICTIONARY (1751) reminds us that borachios are the bottles we are warned against in the SCRIPTURES, MARK: "And no man putteth new wine into old bottles: else the new wine doth burst the bottles."

boraginaceous. See *bugloss. Borage* was used in cookery; see *eowte.*

borametz. "A strange plant in Scythia, like a lamb, which consumes the grass round about it." So says Bailey's DICTIONARY (1751). When all the grass is gone, the plant dies. There are many barren stretches in Scythia.

borasco. A violent squall. Via French from Catalan *borrasca,* Italian *burasca,* the intensive of *bora,* a severe north wind in the Upper Adriatic, from Latin *Boreas,* god of the winds. Both *bora* and *borasco* (also *borasque, burrasca*) were taken into English in the 17th century and used into the 19th.

borborygmite. A filthy fellow, especially in talk. *Borborygm,* from Greek *borborygmos,* rumbling in the bowels, is still a medical term. A *borborite* (Greek *borboros,* filth) was a nickname of some early heretics; used in the 16th and 17th centuries meaning one who holds filthy or immoral doctrines (applied, e.g., to the Mennonites). *Borborology* is filthy talk;

Shun obscene borborology and filthy speeches, said John Trapp in a COMMENTARY ON THE EPISTLES (1649).

bordar. A peasant (villein) of the lowest rank in the feudal system. He held a cottage, for which he did menial work (see *bordlode*) at his lord's pleasure. THE DOMESDAY BOOK (1087) used the Latin plural form *bordarii.* Land such a person was permitted to till was called *bordland;* he held it in *bordage.* The word *bordage* also meant the services he owed, which might include, besides drawing wood, drawing water, threshing, grinding corn and the like.

bordel. A house of prostitution; also, the act there perpetrated. Toone's GLOSSARY of 1834 suggests *bordel* may be from French *bord,* edge + *d'eau,* of the water, as the river shore was the most convenient place for such a house, witness "the stews at the bankside," and Dekker in THE GULL'S HORNBOOK (1609) suggests that the gallant take a house along the Thames, to ship his cockatrice away betimes in the morning. But *bordel* in Saxon and Old French meant a cottage, "which growing out of repute by being made common alehouses and harbours for lewd women," Toone admits, gave their name to the brothel. *Brothel* originally meant a good-for-nothing, a wretch, then a prostitute; a *brothel's house* was shortened to *brothel*; confused with *bordel,* it lost its meaning of wretch, and came to be used instead of *bordel. Brothel* is a variant of earlier *brethel,* wretch; the verb, *brethe,* to go to ruin. They are from Old English *brerthan,* to go to ruin, *brothen,* ruined. Sometimes the Italian form *bordello* was used (Jonson, 1598; Milton, 1642). Also *bordeler,* a keeper or frequenter of a *bordel; bordelry.* Chaucer, in THE PERSONES TALE (1386) speaks of *harlottis, that haunten bordels*; Carlyle, in LATTER-DAY PAMPHLETS (1850) said that *this universe . . . was a cookery-shop and bordel.*

bordlode. A service required of the *bordar (q.v.)* by the feudal lord: carrying timber out of the lord's wood to the lord's house.

borrel. See *burel.*

boscage. Woodland; sylvan scenery; especially, a picture of wooded land; a decorative design representing leaves or foliage. Also *boskage.* Late Latin *boscum,* wood. Sylvan paintings were *de rigueur* in the 17th century. Sir Henry Wotton, in THE ELEMENTS OF ARCHITECTURE called for *chearful paintings in feasting and banquetting rooms . . . landskips and boscage and such wild works in open terraces*; and a poem, THE CONFINEMENT, of 1679 states that *Boscage within each chamber must be shown, Or the mean pile no architect will own.* Rousseau in French, and North (in LIVES, 1734) in English used the word *boscaresque.* Hence *bosky,* wooded, as when Shakespeare in THE TEMPEST (1610) speaks of *My bosky acres, and my unshrubd downe.* In the 18th and early 19th century, *bosky* was also a common term for tipsy ('overshadowed'), as when BLACKWOOD'S EDINBURGH MAGAZINE in 1824 remarked that a gentleman *may be tipsy, bosky, cut, or anything but drunk.* Many a man's grown bosky in the boscage.

boswellize. To note a person's actions minutely; to write in the style of *Boswell's* LIFE OF JOHNSON (1791). Macaulay, in an essay of 1825, first spoke of *Boswellism.* Hence also *Boswellian.*

botargo. A relish of the roe of the mullet or tunny fish. Via Italian from Arabic *butarkhah*; Coptic *outarakhon,* from

Coptic *ou* (the article) + Greek *parixion,* pickle. Captain John Smith, in the new world (1616), called it *puttargo.* Hood, in MISS KILMANSEGG AND HER SILVER LEG (1840) speaks of *that huge repast With its loads and cargoes Of drink and botargoes At the birth of the babe in Rabelais.* In 1598 the recipe is given simply: "fish spawn salted." By 1751 it had grown more complicated; Bailey's DICTIONARY gives it: "a sausage made of eggs and of the blood of a sea mullet." In 1813 it is described as *Boutaraga, the roes of fish, salted and pressed into rolls like sausages.* It might be worth trying.

bote. Remedy; advantage; health. The verb *boten, botne,* to heal, lasted through the 14th century; but *bote* was replaced much earlier by *boot,* which survives in the phrase *to boot,* to the good, into the bargain. Often used in contrast to *bale, q.v.* Thus Chaucer in THE CANON'S YEOMAN'S PROLOGUE AND TALE (1386) prays: *God send every true man boote of his bale.* The word was extended to mean amends, compensation for injury, as in Stephen's LAW OF ENGLAND (1845): *If the great toe be struck off, let twenty shillings be paid him as bot.* From the phrase *to make boot of* (make advantage, profit) the word was confused with *booty,* plunder; thus Shakespeare in HENRY V (1599) speaks of bees that, like soldiers, *Make boote upon the Summers velvet buddes: Which pillage they . . . bring home. To boot* may sometimes be used as an intensifier, meaning futhermore, in addition; there is always the fellow, as the punster remarked, who is a scoundrel and a good one *to boot.* And we hope that one that deserves reward will not go *bootless. Cp. hext.*

bottle. (1) A dwelling, building. Used up to the 13th century. This sense survives in place names, such as *Harbottle.* (2) a bundle, especially of hay or straw. The remark about a *needle in a haystack* was originally *to look for a needle in a bottle of hay.* Chaucer in THE MAUNCIPLE'S PROLOGUE (1386) says: *Although it be not worth a botel hey.* Several combinations of *bottle,* container, have lapsed from use: *bottle-boot,* a leather case for a bottle; especially, one to hold the bottle firm while corking. *bottle-coaster,* a tray or stand for passing around a decanter; also *bottle-slide, bottle-slider. bottle-track,* the path in the ocean of a bottle thrown overboard; from such was made a *bottle-chart,* a chart of surface currents. *bottle-jack,* a jack for roasting meat, shaped like a bottle. *bottle-screw,* a corkscrew. *To pass the bottle of smoke,* used by Dickens to mean to join in a falsehood, to carry on a deceit. Also a *three-bottle man,* etc., one that drinks three (etc.) bottles of wine at a sitting; Leigh Hunt in THE EXAMINER (11 May, 1812) spoke of *six-bottle ministers and plenitudinous aldermen.* A *bottle-head,* a fool, is an alteration of *beetle-head.* A beetle is a sort of hand pile-driver, with a heavy weight for a 'head' and a handle sometimes three men used together. Hence, *dumb as a beetle; beetle-brain; beetle-head, blockhead, bottlehead. bottle-holder,* a backer; a second; in 18th century prizefights, the pugilists' attendants had a bottle ready, as they still do; Carlyle in FREDERICK THE GREAT (1858) referred to someone as *His Majesty's bottle-holder in that battle with the finance nightmares and imbroglios.*

bounce-Jane. A delicious dish, in 15th century cookery. *Take gode cowe mylk, and put hit in a pot, and sethe hit, and take sage, parsel, ysope, and savory, and other gode herbes, and sethe hom and hew hom smalle, and do hom in the pot;*

then take hennes, or capons, or chekyns; when thai byn half rosted, take hom of the spit, and smyte hom on peces, and do thereto, and put therto pynes and raysynges of corance, and let hit boyle, and serve hit forthe. Minced fowl boiled in milk with currants and herbs would be a delicious dish in the 20th century.

bouch. An allowance of food granted by a king or noble to his household or attendants on an expedition. Also *bouge, bowge, bouche,* and especially in the phrase *to have bouche in court.* French *bouche,* mouth; *avoir bouche en cour.* Hence, *to have bouch of court,* to eat and drink at the lord's expense.

bouchée. A small baked confection; a patty. French *bouchée,* mouthful; *bouche,* mouth.

boucon. Veal-steak rolled in bacon and gammon. From French *boucon,* a mouthful—which it seems succulently to be. See *gammon.*

bouffage. A satisfying meal. Old French *bouffage,* a meat that puffs the cheeks.

bouge. (1) A bag, a wallet; a skin-bottle; also *bowge, q.v.; bulge, bulch.* Latin *bulga,* a leather bag; the womb. Also, a bulge, a swelling; hence, *bowgework,* raised work. (2) Court rations; provisions. A variant of *bouche,* mouthful. *To have a budge-a-court, to be given free food and drink.*

bouillans. "Little pies of the breast of roasted capons minced with udders, etc." So in the 1751 DICTIONARY of Bailey, who seems to have been an 18th century gourmet.

bouksome. Corpulent. *Bouk* was an old word for belly; then for the trunk, then the body, of a man. After the 14th century *bouk* was used only in Scotland; *bouksome* was influenced by *buxom* and by *bulk.*—The result of too many a bouffage.

boun. To prepare, make ready; to dress; to betake oneself. Also *bown, bune, bowen, bowyn.* Used from the 13th to the 17th century; revived by Scott, in MARMION (1808): *Each ordering that his band Should bowne them with the rising day.*

bourd. Mockery. So in the early 14th century. Soon, however, the sense softened, to jesting, merriment, fun; a merry tale; a game, play. Also as a verb, to make game, to say things in jest; to play. R. Brunne in HANDLYNG SYNNE (1303) tells *how a bonde man bourdede wyth a knyght.* Also *burde, borde, boward, bowrde, bourde.* Hence *bourder,* a jester; a buffoon; a mocker. *Bourdful,* sportive. There was another verb, *to bourde, to burdis,* to joust; *bourdis,* tilting, fencing with lances; Old French *behourt,* lance. Caxton in GEOFFROI DE LA TOUR L'ANDRI (1483) said: *He is but a bourdour and a deceyver of ladyes.*

bourdon. (1) A pilgrim's staff; a club or cudgel; a spear-shaft. Apparently from Latin *burdonem,* mule; shifted from the pilgrim's mount to his staff. A *bourdonasse* (16th century), a light lance, with a hollow shaft; a similar javelin. Used from the 13th century; Urquhart in THE JEWEL (1652) pictured a man *with a palmer's coat upon him, a bourdon in his hand, and some few cockle shels stuck to his hat.* (2) A low undersong, while the leading voice sang the melody. Used from the 14th century; Late Latin *burdo,* drone, perhaps an echoic word. Chaucer used this rather common word, in the Prologue to THE CANTERBURY TALES (1386): *This somonour bar to hym a stiff burdoun, Was never trompe of half so greet a soun.* This sense grew into the form *burden;* indeed, *bourdon* is (3) an early variant of *burden, q.v.,* in all its meanings.

bouse. Liquor; a drinking-bout. Also a verb; Herrick says, in the HESPERIDES (1648): *But before the day comes Still I be bousing.* In nautical parlance of the 19th century, *to bowse up the jib* was to get drunk. *Bouse,* related to early Dutch *busen,* was usually pronounced *būz,* whence the still current *booze.* Sometime *booze* was used to imply drinking for good fellowship, as when Colman says, in his EPILOGUE FOR THE SCHOOL FOR SCANDAL (1777): *While good Sir Peter boozes with the Squire.* But, warns BLACKWOOD'S EDINBURGH MAGAZINE (1824): *Never boozify a second time with the man whom you have seen misbehave himself in his cups.* Some would cut off the last fifteen words.

bousy. See *semibousy.*

boutade. A sudden outburst; a sally. Also *boutado.* From French *bouter,* to thrust, to put, of Teutonic origin. Used in the 17th century; Swift in A TALE OF A TUB (1702) said: *His first boutade was to kick both their wives . . . out of doors.*

boutefeu. A firebrand, incendiary; an inciter to dissention and strife. French *bouter,* to put + *feu,* fire. Also *beautifew, boutfeu, boutefeau, botefeu, bowtifeu,* and more. A common 17th century word. North in THE EXAMINER in 1734 complained of *factious boutefews, bawlers for property and against popery;* Richardson in a letter to Mrs. Barbauld, in 1754, spoke of a *boutefeu editor.*

bouteselle. A call to arms: *boot and saddle,* the trumpet signal to put saddle on and mount horse. French *bouter,* to put + *selle,* saddle. *The sprightly chanticlere,* said Cleveland (POEMS, 1658), *Sounds boutesel to Cupid's knight.*

boutgate. A going about; by extension, circumlocution; equivocation, quibble. *About* + *gate* (*gait*), going. R. Bruce in a sermon of 1591 said: *The boutgates and deceites of the heart of man are infinite.*

bouts-rimés. A popular game of the late 17th and the 18th century, in which a set of rhymes is given a person, who must then compose the verses. Games of the sort are still played. French *bouts,* ends + *rimés,* rhymed. *Past, last; roam, home; deal, seal; old, manifold*—for an instance.

bove. An early form of *above.* Also *beufan, bufan, buven, buve, boven.* A compound of three forms: *by* beside + *uf,* up + *ana,* a suffix indicating motion from. The *a* in *above* also meant down from, as in the old *adown, q.v.,* which has permanently lost the *a.* Used through the 15th century, after which (in Spenser, Shakespeare—THE TEMPEST, 1610; *'Bove the contentious waves*—and later poets) it is thought of as a contraction of *above.*

bovicide. See *stillicide.* The term *bovicide* has been applied, humorously, to a butcher—whom it literally fits.

bovoli. See *fagioli.*

bower-maiden. A lady in waiting; a chambermaid. Also *bowermaid, bowerwoman.* From *bower,* a cottage, an abode—later used by poets as a vague term for an idealized dwelling, as in Goldsmith's THE DESERTED VILLAGE (1770): *Dear lovely bowers of innocence and ease!* Also *burmaiden, bourmaiden.* Wyclif (1380): *This gospel tellith not how Marie took a bourwoman, but went mekeli in hast to salute her cosyn.* Also in Scott; Tennyson in his play BECKET (1884) says: *My best bowermaiden died of late.*

bowge. A variant of *bouge, q.v.* In sense (1) also *bowger,* a purser, treasurer. In sense (2), used in the title of a satiric poem by Skelton, *The Bowge of Court* (1498).

bowssen. To immerse (suddenly, in a holy well, especially as a cure for madness). Also *boossen, bousen, bowsen.* It was apparently a treatment especially favored in Cornwall; the Cornish-Breton *beuzi* meant to drown. Carew in his THE SURVEY OF CORNWALL (1602) referred to the practice: *There were many bowssening places, for curing of mad men . . . if there appeared small amendment he was bowssened again and againe.* (The final *e* is presumably to emphasize his gain.)

bowyer. One that makes, or deals in bows. Also, a bowman. *Cp. fletcher.* Formed as was *lawyer,* save that archery is now seldom practiced.

box. See *balk.*

boy. Be with you. Also *boye.* Used in 16th and 17th century plays; superseded by *bye,* by, especially in *good-by,* God be with you.

boysteous. See *boistous.*

brabble. See *prabble.* It has been suggested that the word is a corruption of Medieval Latin *parabolare,* to harangue, Greek *para,* beside + *ballein,* to throw (whence also *parabola* and *parable*); but it is more probably echoic, like *babble,* but stronger, meaning a noisy quarrel, a petty discordant brawl. Shakespeare, in TWELFTH NIGHT (1601) has: *Heere in the streets . . . In private brabble did we apprehend him.*

bracery. Corruption. Short for *embracery, q.v.* A law of Henry VIII (Act 32, 1540) was entitled: *The bill of bracery and buying of titles.*

brache. A hound that hunts by scent; later, any kind of bitch hound (always feminine). A common medieval form, later usually *brach* (also *bracke, brasche, bratche*). The word was sometimes (as in Jonson's THE ALCHEMIST, 1610) used as a term of abuse, like *bitch* and her offspring today. For a list of dogs in Shakespeare, see *lyam.*

bradypeptic. Slow to digest. Meredith in THE EGOIST (1879) says: *For facts, we are bradypeptics to a man, sir.* Greek *bradys,* slow + *pepsis,* cooking, digestion. Hence also *bradypepsy, bradiopepsy, bradypepsia.* A *bradypod, bradypus,* a slowfoot.

bradypus. See *bradypeptic.* Greek *pous, podis,* foot. In zoology, used of the family of quadrupeds that includes the sloth.

brag. As a noun. In the current sense of boastful language, one might remember the words of Johnson's mother—which he recorded in THE RAMBLER (1752; No. 197)—when he envied a neighbor's finery: *Brag was a good dog, but Holdfast was a better.* Among less remembered uses of brag are: (1) a loud noise, as the blare of a trumpet. (2) Pomp, display; pompous behavior. Udall in RALPH ROYSTER DOYSTER (1553) said: *Ye must have a portely bragge, after your estate . . . Up man with your head and chin.* (3) When the YORK MYSTERY (1440) said: *Here are bragges that will not faile,* it meant by *brag* a large nail. (4) An 18th and early 19th century card game, later called *poker.* It was named from the *brag* or challenge of one player to the others, to match the value of his cards. As an adjective, from the 14th century, *brag* meant boastful, also spirited, mettlesome, lively. Spenser in THE SHEPHERD'S CALENDAR (1579;

FEBRUARY) used it as an adverb: *Seest how brag yond bullock beares . . . his pricked eares?* Also see *bragly.*

bragance. See *bragly.*

bragget. A drink of honey and ale fermented together. Chaucer in THE MILLER'S TALE (1386) says: *Her mouth was sweet as bragot.* Also *braket, brogat,* and the like. Bailey, in 1751, omits the ale, saying "of honey and spice"; the *O.E.D.* in 1933 says that "latterly the honey has been replaced by sugar and spice." Hardwick in TRADITIONS OF LANCASHIRE (1872) states that *Mid Lent Sunday is likewise called Braggat or Braggot Sunday, from the custom of drinking mulled or spiced ale on that day.*

bragly. Briskly; with pleasant show. Formed from the verb *to brag,* to sound loudly; to boast; to show off; whence also *bragance* (15th century), *braggade* (18th century), boasting, supplanted by *bragging.* Spenser in THE SHEPHERD'S CALENDAR (1579; MARCH) has: *Seest not thilke same hawthorne studde, How bragly it begins to budde?*

brahminicide. See *stillicide.* Also *brahmanicide.*

brand. See *brandle.*

brandewine. An early form of what is now called *brandy.* Also *brandwine; Dutch brandewijn,* burnt [distilled] wine.

brandish. See *brandle.*

brandle. To shake (both transitive and intransitive). From French *branler,* with the same meaning. Hence also in English, though rare, *branle,* to agitate, to toss about. Pepys in his DIARY for 1662 says: *They danced the brantle.* The dance, and the music for it, also appear as *branle;* and a 1581 translation of Tacitus says that the first legion was put *in branle* (agitation, confusion). The verb is also used of onanism. A more vigorous form of the same word is *brangle,* to shake vehemently, to brandish; to make uncertain; in THE MERRY DEVIL OF EDMONTON (1608), a man's title to a piece of property is, he is reminded, *brangled with thy debts.* Another French form of the same root word is *brandir, brandiss—,* from which comes English *brandish.* The words are related to the common Teuton *brand,* a sword, which in turn comes from Teuton *bran, brinnan,* to burn. The gleaming or waving of the sword, the flickering or brightness of the flames. Note also the rare *branskate* (*brand* + German *schatz,* treasure, tribute), a ransom paid so that a place will not be burned.

brandreth. A three-legged fire-grate; a gridiron. By extension, various other frameworks, as for a hay-rick; a rail around the opening of a well. Also *branrith, branlet, brandelette,* etc. Old Norse *brand,* burning + *reith,* carriage.

brandy-cowe. The washings of brandy casks, used in making inferior drinks.

brandy-pawnee. Brandy and water. Hindustani *pani,* water. Used by Thackeray in VANITY FAIR (1848).

brangle. See *brandle.*

branks. A bit and bridle for a scold: an iron framework to enclose the head, with a metal gag for the mouth. 16th and 17th centuries, especially in Scotland. The Newcastle Municipal Accounts of 1595 list: *Paid for carrying a woman through the town for scolding, with branks, 4 d.* Perhaps by humorous extension from this, *branks* was used in the 18th and 19th centuries for that mouth-closing disease, the mumps. T. N. Brushfield in OBSOLETE PUNISHMENTS (1858) gave various names: *a brank, the branks, a pair of branks, the scold's bridle, gossip's bridle and . . . 'a brydle for a curste queane.'*

branle. See *brandle.*

branskate. See *brandle.*

brant. Steep, sheer, straight. In 1544 Ascham, in TOXOPHILUS, wrote that *Hawarde . . . slew King Jamie even brant against Flodden Hill.* The word was also applied to a straight, unwrinkled forehead. The Scotch form is *brent*; Burns in his song JOHN ANDERSON MY JO (1789) says *Your bonny brow was brent.*

brantle. See *brandle.*

bratticing. See *bartizan.*

bravery. Swaggering; behaving like a bravo or reckless swaggerer. *For (in, upon) a bravery,* in defiance; in display of reckless daring, as a brag. Also, an adornment; finery; ostentatious show, pretense; flamboyance. Sometimes used to mean a person, or gallants as a class; Jonson in THE SILENT WOMAN (1609) says: *Hee is one of the braveries, though he be none o' the wits.* Lodge in AN ALARUM AGAINST USURERS (1584) declared: *Thy modest attire is become immodest braverie; thy shamefast seemelynes is shamelesse impudencie; thy desire of lerning to loitering love.*

bray. To beat small; crush to powder. In Coverdale's BIBLE: PROVERBS (1535) we read: *Though thou shuldest bray a foole with a pestell in a morter like otemeel, yet wil not his foolishnesse go from him.*

braythe. To rush up, to start up. Also *breythe, breathe, breat.* Old English *braegdan,* whence also *braid.* The earliest meaning of *braid* was to pull quickly, to make a jerky movement, move to and fro—hence also *broid, broider, embroider; brawde, browde, browder.* In EARLY ENGLISH ALLITERATIVE POETRY (14th century) we read that wine *warmed his hert and breythed uppe in to his brayn.* How often since!

breadberry. See *aleberry.*

brede. This word has many forms—*breed, bread, breid,* etc.—and three distinct meanings. It appears about the year 1000 in the sense of roast meat: *Swines brade is well sweet*—which sense lingers in the word sweet*bread.* About the same time it was used to mean width, or a measure of width; a will of 1554 leaves *one pair of fine sheets of two bredes and a half*; by 1600 this sense was taken over by the form *breadth.* In the 17th century *brede,* as a variant of *braid,* was used of tresses or threads or colors intertwined. This use lingered with the poets, as in Keats' ODE ON A GRECIAN URN: *with brede Of marble men and maidens overwrought.* Lowell pictures the three fates (the Parcae: Clotho, who held the distaff; Lachesis, who spun the events of our life; and the eldest sister, Atropos, who cut the thread) : *the ancient Three . . . Still crooning, as they weave their endless brede.* The form meaning to burn, or heat, is related to the words *breath* and *brood.* In all senses the word was also used as a verb; in THE PARLIAMENT OF DEVILS (1509) one of the fiends exclaims: *I will . . . in hell his soule brede.*

breech. A garment covering the loins and thighs; originally a *breech*-cloth, a loin-cloth; later reaching to the knees; after the 15th century and still current, in the plural and pronounced *britches,* coming below the knees and used as a dialect, humorous, or scornful word for *trousers.* The Geneva BIBLE translation of 1560 is called *the breeches Bible* because of Genesis 3: *They sewed figge tree leaves together, and made themselves breeches. To wear the breech* (later, *breeches*), to be boss of the household, usually said of the wife; Shakespeare in HENRY VI, PART THREE (1593) has: *You might still have worne the petticoat, And ne'er have stolne the breech from Lancaster.*

breme. Also *breem, brim,* etc. Originally, in Old English, this word meant famous, glorious. The sense was extended to anything great in its kind: brilliant color; loud sound; violent, raging storm. Hence it was often used by the poets of a fierce winter, or a fierce beast. Thus in 1400 we read of *beastes breme*; in 1526 of *the breme light of grace.* Lydgate in 1430 and Spenser in 1579 speak of *breme winter*; other poets follow them, as Thomson (1748) in THE CASTLE OF INDOLENCE: *Glad summer or the winter breme. Bremely* is also used in this manner—a song of 1500 says *That brymly beast*—but is usually the adverb, meaning brightly, loudly, or fiercely; Stanyhurst in his AENEIS (1583) says *At the windoors . . . moonshyne brimly did enter.*

The original English name for sulphur was *bernstone,* the burnstone. This was shifted to *brenstone*; then association with *brim,* fierce, may have changed it to *brimstone.* Similarly, in the 1250 poem of GENESIS and EXODUS, we read of the "stinken smoke" of the *brinfire.*

bren. An old form of *burn,* used by Chaucer. Also *brenne.*

brendice. A cup in which a person's health is drunk. From the Italian *brindisi,* but perhaps a corruption of the German Ich *bringe dir's* zu. A nonce-word: Dryden begins his AMBOYNA, 1673: *I go to fill a brendice to my noble Captain's health.* The verb *brince,* or *brinch,* meaning to drink or to give to drink, was fairly common in the 16th and 17th centuries; a Psalter of 1556 says: *The good at brink the clear doth drink, God brinche them gently so.*

brent. See *brant.*

breviate. To shorten; to abridge, to abstract. Used in the 16th and 17th centuries; Latin *brevis,* short—cp. motto on the New England gravestone of Henry Longbottom, age 13: *Ars longa, vita brevis.* The current form, of course, is *abbreviate.* Skelton, in MAGNYFYCENCE (1526) says: *By myschefe to breviate and shorten his dayes. Breviate* was also used as an adjective, meaning shortened, and as a noun, meaning a brief statement, a note, or a lawyer's brief. *How often,* says a poem of 1594 (ZEPHERIA) *hath my pen (my hearts solicitor!) Instructed thee in breviat of my case!* Hence also *breviately; breviation; breviator; breviature.* A *breviger* was, first, one who carries briefs; by extension, a begging friar.

breviloquence. Brevity in speech. Latin *brevis,* short; whence *brief* + *loquens, loquentem,* speaking. Hence *breviloquent,* as were the Spartans, hence *laconic*—from *Laconia,* the country of which Sparta (or Lacedaemon) was the capital. Lacedaemon was a son of Jupiter and Taygeta (daughter of Atlas); he married Sparta the daughter of Eurotas. [The Spartans never set out on an expedition or opened a battle save at the full moon, which shows they were lunatic as well as laconic. In the 15th and 16th centuries *lunatic,* in addition to meaning—from the 13th century—moonstruck, crazy, was used to mean influenced by the moon . . .

borne, said Greene in MAMILLIA (1583) *under the influence of Luna, and therefore as firme . . . as melting waxe.*] The proverbial brevity of Spartan speech is illustrated in their reply to Philip of Macedon's threat: *If I enter Laconia, I will level Lacedaemon to the ground.* The Spartans responded: *If.* Pope in a letter to Swift (17 August, 1736) said: *I grow laconic beyond laconicism;* breviloquence changed this to *laconism,* though Jeremy Collier (1697) noted that no *laconism* can match the language of the face. *Cp. chilonian.*

breythe. See *braythe.*

bricole. Indirectly, on the rebound. Originally the word was applied to a sort of catapult for hurling stones, and may be derived from a name, as *gun, Big Bertha,* etc. In the 16th century, when tennis was popular, the term was applied to a stroke (or to the rebound) when a ball was driven to hit the side wall, then bounce in the opponent's court. In the 19th century, the term was applied to a cushion-shot in billiards. In the 17th century, *bricole* was used figuratively; as late as 1798 Walpole speaks of a play's introducing *two courtiers to acquaint one another, and by bricole the audience,* with events offstage. The walls of the tennis courts were of brick, hence by error *bricole* sometimes became *brickwall,* as some today say *net ball* for *let* (hindered) *ball.* Thus Sidney in ARCADIA (1580) speaks of *music . . . which tho' Anaxias might conceive was for his honour, yet indeed he was but the brickwall to convey it to the ears of the beloved Philoclea.* Schoolboys copying their assignments must be careful lest, as F. Greville said in 1628, they *brickwall errors from one to another.*

bridal. See *givale.*

bridelope. This is the oldest English word for a wedding, meaning the run (*lope*) of the man bearing his choice to her new home, a ritual probably symbolizing the earlier actual carrying off of the woman. (We still use the term *elope.*) Many combinations of *bride* have been forgotten, e.g.: *bridebush,* a bush hung out at the local tavern in honor of the wedding; *bridecake; bridecup,* a cup of spicy drink offered the *bride-couple* before the *bridebed; brideknot, bridelace,* a wedding favor, or the band on the sprigs of rosemary worn at weddings; *bridestake,* a pole set up to dance around at the wedding, similar to the Maypole; *bridelock,* a word for wedlock until about 1250; *bridewain,* a wagon bearing the "hope chest" (topped by the spinning wheel adorned with blue ribbons) to the bride's new home. *Brideale* is a deliberate spelling, used by Cranmer in the Preface to his BIBLE of 1540, and for 300 years after, to remind readers that a *bridal* is really an ale-drinking, a party, for the *bride. Bridewell,* meaning a prison, is from *St. Bride's well* in London; near this holy well King Henry VIII had a house, which Edward VI donated as a hospital, later a house of correction. The word *bride* originally meant not a woman on the brink of marriage, but a daughter-in-law; the French word for daughter-in-law is *bru.* It is related to the root *bru,* meaning to *brew broth,* to cook—which in the primitive family was a task of the daughter-in-law.

brides-laces. See *Hymen's torch.*

brimstone. See *breme.*

brince. See *brendice.* Also *brinch.*

brinfire. See *breme.*

britzka. A fashionable carriage of the 19th century (from Polish *bryczka*), open, with room for reclining. Often mentioned in the current fiction, as Disraeli's CONINGSBY (1844) and Thackeray's VANITY FAIR (1848).

briviatic. Pertaining to a beggar. From Old Spanish *brivion,* a wandering beggar. In 1623, references to *the briviatick art.*

broadside. A sheet of paper printed on one side; usually large. Broadsides were the forerunners of newspapers; they might contain a decree, but more often a ballad or other verse based on a current happening. In the 18th century, also *broadsheet. Many of the fabliaux and comic poems,* said Wright (ESSAYS; 1861) *were issued as broadside ballads.*

broch. A prehistoric structure in Scotland (many remain on the Orkney and Shetland Islands): a round tower with inner and outer stone walls, between which the humans lived, while the central space was used to keep their cattle secure. Also *brough.* Old Norse *borg,* castle; Old English *burh,* surviving in *burgh* and *borough.*

brock. This common Celtic word developed many senses. (1) a badger. So used by Ben Jonson (1637) and Burns (1786). Hence *brock-faced,* with a face streaked like a badger's. (2) A dirty or stinking fellow. So in Shakespeare's TWELFTH NIGHT (1601): *Marry, hang thee, brocke.* (3) An inferior horse; so used by Chaucer (1386). (4) The larva of the frog-hopper, that froths upon leaves, leaving what is called "cuckoo-spit." (5) A three-year-old deer, a *brocket.* (6) As a verb, to *brock* is to talk complainingly, or in broken speech—again in Chaucer. *Brockish* means beastly, dirty.

brodekin. A boot reaching halfway up the calves; a buskin. French *brodequin,* Italian *borzacchino,* buskin. Used from the 15th through the 17th century; Urquhart in his translation of Rabelais (1653) has *brodkin blowes* for kicks. Revived in 19th century historical novels, as Thackeray's PENDENNIS (1850): *From their bonnets to their brodequins.*

broil. As a noun; tumult, turmoil, a disorderly quarrel. *To set in broil,* to create a disturbance; *broiler,* one that takes part in or instigates quarrels; *broilery,* dissension, disorder. Shakespeare has in HENRY VI, PART ONE (1591): *Prosper this realme, keepe it from civill broyles;* in SONNET 55: *And broils root out the work of masonry.* The senses overlap with *broil,* a state of great heat (from *to broil,* current today), as in Badington's A VERY FRUITFULL EXPOSITION OF THE COMMANDMENTS (1583): *What broyles of scorching lust soever the minde abideth.*

broke. See *gerning.*

bronstrops. A procuress, *bawd;* see *baude; bawdstrot.* Used in the 17th century, especially by Middleton; Webster alludes to Middleton when he remarks, in A CURE FOR A CUCKOLD (1661): *A tweak or bronstrops: I learned that name in a play.*

brontomancy. See *aeromancy.*

broom. A shrub, with large yellow or white flowers. Old English *brom;* Middle High German *brame,* whence also *bramble.* The petals of the broom were used to dye hard boiled eggs green, at Eastertide; they were thus doubly symbolic of fertility, so that the eating of them portended large families. Now folks use other colors. Wordsworth in TO JOANNA (1800) says: *'Twas that delightful season when the* *broom, Full-flowered . . . Along the copses runs in veins of gold.*

browet. Soup of the juice of boiled meat, thickened with other savory substances. Enjoyed in the 14th and 15th centuries. Also *brewet, bruet*; Medieval Latin *brodium;* Old High German *brod;* akin to and supplanted by *broth.* A COOKERY of 1440 gives a recipe for white almond soup, *blaunche bruet of almayn;* a Towneley MYSTERY (1460) : *broght me bruet of deer.*

brumal. Wintry; relating to the time of short days. Latin *brumalis,* relating to winter; *bruma,* short for *brevima,* shortest (day) . Hence *brume,* fog, mist. *Hail, with its glassy globes,* said J. Barlow in THE COLUMBIAD (1808), *and brume congealed.* Lowell in MY STUDY WINDOWS (1871) wrote: *What cheerfulness there was in brumal verse was that of Horace's.*

brummagem. A counterfeit coin (especially, counterfeit groats coined at Birmingham in the 17th century) ; a sham, showy imitation. Also *brummagemize, brummagemism, brummagemish.* The word is a corruption of *Birmingham,* a manufacturing town. A half-way stage of the formation is quoted at *shab.* A. K. H. Boyd, in RECREATIONS OF A COUNTRY PARSON (1861) watched *the vulgar dandy, strutting along, with his brummagem jewelry.*

brusole. "Stakes of veal well seasoned, laid in a stewpan between slices of bacon, and baked between two fires." The DICTIONARY (1751) of Bailey the epicure again gives a revivable recipe.

brustle. (1) To make a crackling or rustling noise; to move swiftly with such a noise; to *rustle,* to *bustle.* (2) An early form of *bristle,* as hair, or the mane of a beast, or the feathers of a bird; hence (as the peacock), to show off, to *bluster.* Fletcher in THE SPANISH CURATE (1622): *See where the sea comes, how it foams and brussels.*

brut. A chronicle. From the many medieval chronicles of *Brutus, Brut,* and his descendants in Britain, by Wace, Layamon, etc. There is also a 16th and 17th century verb *to brut,* to browse, as in Evelyn's ACETARIA, OR A DISCOURSE OF SALLETS (1699) : *marking what the goats so greedily brutted upon . . .*

brygge. An early variant of *bridge.* Not so listed in O.E.D. Apparently used in the sense of wharf or pier, by Cavendish in THE LYFFE AND DEATHE OF CARDYNAL WOOLSEY (1557) : *It semed to them that there shold be some noble men and strangers arryved at his brygge* [at the Thames' bank] *as ambassitors frome some forrayn prynce.* (Cavendish is telling of the coming of Henry VIII, masked, with companions dressed as shepherds, to a party at the Cardinal's.)

brynnyng. A variant form of *burning.* Skelton (WORKES; 1529; *cp. shyderyd*) declared: *Oure days be datyd To be chek matyd With draüttys* [moves] *of deth Stopping oure breth, Oure eyen synkyng, Oure bodys stynkyng, Oure gummys grynnyng, Our soulys brynnyng.*

bubble-bow An 18th century fashionable case for a lady's tweezers and the like. Used by Pope; explained by Arbuthnot in JOHN BULL (1712) as from *to bubble a beau,* to dazzle or fool a gallant. Also spelled *bubble-boy*; explained (in THE MONTHLY MAGAZINE of 1807) as *probably a misspelling for bauble-buoy, a support for baubles.* They now dangle from jingly bracelets or lie concealed in a purse.

buccellation. Division into tiny pieces. A 17th and 18th century dictionary word, from Late Latin *buccella,* morsel, from *bucca,* cheek.

buccinate. To blow a trumpet. Latin *buccina,* a crooked trumpet; whence also *buccinal* (pronounced *buck'sinall),* shaped like or sounding like a trumpet. But note that Latin *bucca* means cheek. The *buccinator* muscle is the muscle that forms the wall of the cheek, so called, says the O.E.D. (1933), "because it is the chief muscle employed in the act of blowing." It is at least as likely, however, that the reverse process is correct: that the trumpet was called *buccina* from the characteristic puffing of the *bucca,* cheek, to blow it, to buccinate. Sterne in TRISTRAM SHANDY (1760) says: *Directing the bussinatory muscles along his cheeks . . . to do their duty, he whistled Lillabullero.* A *bucculent* fellow is one agape, "blub-cheeked," as beholding a succulent morsel.

bucentaur. A large ship; a gaily decorated barge. Especially, the ship (*Bucentoro*) in which the Doge of Venice, on Ascension Day, went to wed the Adriatic by dropping a ring in it. From Greek *bous,* ox + *centauros,* the figure-head of the Doge's galley. Byron in CHILDE HAROLD (1818) states: *The Bucentaur lies rotting unrestored.* A 1658 account of Queen Christina of "Swedland" says that Her Majesty sailed *towards Bruxells in a bucentoro most richly adorned, and guilded within and without.*

bucksome. An old variant of *buxom.* Also *buhsum, bocsum, bowsome,* and more. The word first meant easily bowed, pliant; submissive; flexible—hence, good-natured, lively, gay—whence its current meaning.

bude-light. A light obtained by directing a stream of oxy-hydrogen gas over crushed egg shells. Invented (and named in 1835) by Sir Goldsworthy Gurney of Bude, Cornwall. Also *bude-burner,* of three concentric perforated rings.

bugloss. One of various boraginaceous plants; especially the prickly ox-tongue. Greek *bous,* ox + *glossa,* tongue; from the shape and roughness of the leaves. Used in cookery and medicine; Jonson in VOLPONE (1605) lists *a little muske, dri'd mints, buglosse, and barley-meale.* The boraginaceous plants belong to the genus *borage* (*burrage, burridge;* Latin *burra,* a shaggy garment), used in making claret cup and as a cordial. Steele in THE TATLER (1709; No. 31) speaks of *burridge in the glass when a man is drinking.*

bum. The buttocks. A very common word from the 14th to the 17th century; replaced by *bottom.* Used of a person, in contempt; sometimes *bum,* short for *bum-bailiff, q.v.;* used in combinations; see *bumrowl.* Harvey in his attack on Nashe in PIERCES SUPEREROGATION, OR A NEW PRAYSE OF THE OLD ASSE (1593; for Nashe's fling, see *gallimaufry*) cried upon *vaine Nash, railing Nash, craking Nash, bibbing Nash, baggage Nash, swaddish Nash, rogish Nash, Nash the bellweather of the scribling flock, the swish-swash of the presse, the bumm of impudency, the shambles of beastliness, the poulkat* [skunk] *of Pouls-churchyard, the shrick-owle of London, the toade-stoole of the realme, the scorning-stocke of the world.* Nashe had earlier (1591) as *Adam Fouleweather, Student in Asse-tronomy,* parodied a poor astrological prediction of Gabriel Harvey's brother Richard, and returned to the attack the next year in PIERCE PENILESSE HIS SUPPLICATION TO THE DIVELL, in which Nashe boasts: *Have I not an indifferent prittye vayne in spurgalling an asse? Spurgall* means to *gall,* injure, with the spur. It was also used figuratively, as when the Water Poet (WORKS; 1630) said: *Like to a post Ile runne through thicke and thin To scourge iniquity and spurgall sinne.* Many that run on that errand find themselves fallen on their bum.

bumbailiff. A bailiff; one that makes arrests. The term is one of contempt (*bum,* buttocks; *cp. bumrowl*), implying that the bailiff is close upon the debtor's back. The similar French word is *pousse-cul.* Shakespeare in TWELFTH NIGHT (1601) says: *Scout mee for him at the corner of the orchard like a bum-baylie.* The word was used by Washington Irving and Thackeray (1859). A similar word of scorn was *bumtrap; The noble bumtrap,* observes Fielding in TOM JONES (1749) *into the hands of the jailer resolves to deliver his miserable prey.* Tucker in THE LIGHT OF NATURE PURSUED (1768) spoke of *the two necessary ministers of justice, a bumbailiff and Jack Ketch.*

bumboat. A scavenger's boat for removing filth from ships on the Thames. Apparently from *bum,* buttocks + *boat;* a *bumbay* on a farm was a pool formed by draining dung, etc. *Bumboats* were made requisite for London harbor, by a law of 1685. They often carried robbers to the ships. As they also carried provisions to sell on the ships, the word *bumboat* (after the earlier practice ended) came to mean a boat carrying things to sell to ships anchored offshore. This 19th century use, frequent in the nautical novels of Frederick Marryat, is kept alive in Gilbert's H.M.S. PINAFORE (1878): Little Buttercup is a *bumboat woman.*

bumrowl. A bustle, or other protuberant part of the feminine skirts; especially, stuffed cushions or padding worn about the hips. *Cp. dress-improver.* Also *bum-roll; bum-barrel.* From *bum,* the buttocks. *Bum* was frequently combined, especially by 17th century playwrights. Thus *bum-blade, bum-dagger,* a wide one, for striking with the flat. *bumfodder* (Latin *anitergium; anus,* bum + *tergere,* to wipe), worthless literature; French *torchecul,* used in Urquhart's translation (1653) of Rabelais. A *bumbrusher* (18th century) a flagellant or flogger; a schoolmaster; hence (Peter Pindar, ODE, 1786) *bumproof to all the flogging of the* schools. In Jonson's THE POETASTER (1601) the lady Chloe, married to a plain citizen, complains: *Nor you nor your house were so much as spoken of, before I disbased myself, from my hood and my farthingal, to these bumrowls and your whale-bone bodice.* The next year, Warner in ALBION'S ENGLAND pictured another woman: *Supporters, pooters, fardingales above the loynes to waire, That be she near so bombe-thin yet she cross-like seems foure-squaire.*

burd. See *berne.*

burdash. A foppish adornment to a man's costume, in the reigns of Queen Anne and George I: a fringed sash, or a kind of cravat. Steele in THE GUARDIAN (1713) says: *I have prepared a treatise against the cravat and berdash.* Sometimes spelled *bardash,* and influenced by that word (meaning catamite, effeminate, from Arabic *bardaj,* slave). Butler in HUDIBRAS (1678) speaks of *Raptures of Platonick lashing And chast contemplative bardashing.* There is double play in Mrs. Centlivre's words of 1721 of an effeminate man *with your false calves, burdash, and favorites.* The last word meant curls dangling at the temples; but which meaning of *burdash* had she in mind?

burden. The bass, or accompaniment, of a song; see *bourdon.* By extension and more commonly, the refrain or chorus of a song or stanza. Figuratively, the main idea or tenor, or chief sentiment. *Cp. dildo*; for an instance of its use, see *whist.*

burel. A coarse woolen cloth; a garment made thereof; hence, plain clothing. Used from the 13th into the 17th century. The original color was probably reddish-brown, from Latin *burrus,* red. Other forms were *borel, borrel, burrell.* The French form *bureau,* from the fact that this coarse cloth (baize) was used for the top of a writingdesk, came to be used for the desk, and gave us the current *bureau.* The form *borrel, borel* (because the clergy never used such coarse cloth) came in the 14th century to be applied as an adjective, meaning belonging to the laity. Hence, by the 16th century, *borrel* (also *borowe, borou*), unlearned, rude, rough. Gascoigne in A HUNDRETH SUNDRIE FLOWERS (1572) said: *My borrell braine is all too blunt To give a gesse.* Spenser in THE SHEPHERD'S CALENDAR (1579) uses *borrell* to mean a plain fellow.

burn. Besides the current sense of *a burn,* the result of contact with excessive heat, *burn* as a noun was (1) a short form of *burden*; since the 14th century. (2) a spring, fountain; a brook. It was also used of water from a well—since the 9th century—and, poetically, of the sea. Hence also *burngate,* a water course; *burnside, burnhead, burnmouth*; now preserved in place names. *Burn,* as a brook, is still current in dialects. Note that the idea is related to burning, as a *torrent* is from Latin *torrere,* to scorch, whence also *the torrid zone.*

burridge. See *bugloss.*

burthen. A variant of burden (16th-18th century). See *dildo.*

buskin. A half-boot, reaching to the calf, sometimes to the knee. Especially, the high, thick-soled *cothurnus* worn by the tragic actors of ancient Greece, as opposed to the comic sock (*soccus*) or low shoe. Hence, *buskin* is used to signify tragic style or matter, as in the phrase *to put on the buskin.* In Spenser; Dryden (TROILUS AND CRESSIDA, 1679, Preface): *I doubt to smell a little too strongly of the buskin.* A *buskinade* is a kick with a *buskin*; see *brodekin.* Many writers use *buskined,* meaning shod with *buskins*; thus Shakespeare in A MIDSUMMER NIGHT'S DREAM (1590): *The bouncing Amazon Your buskin'd mistresse* and Pope in WINDSOR FOREST (1704): *Her buskin'd virgins*—without suggestion of tragedy. Marlowe in HERO AND LEANDER (finished by Chapman; 1598) pictures artificial birds singing on Hero's legs: *Buskins of shels all silvered used she, and brancht with blushing corall to the knee, Where sparrowes pearcht, of hollow pearle and gold, Such as the world would woonder to behold: Those with sweet water oft her handmaid fils, Which as shee went would cherupe through the bils.*

buss. See *bass.* Shakespeare in KING LEAR (1605) declares: *You have heard of the news . . . I mean the whisper'd ones, for they are yet but ear-bussing arguments.*

buxom. See *bucksome.*

by-and-by. Immediately. Thus *presently* originally meant at the *present* moment, at once. The dilatory tendency of human nature drew both terms to their current protraction. Merygreeke says of the title figure in Udall's RALPH ROISTER DOISTER (1553): *If any woman smyle, or cast on* *hym an eye, Up is he to the harde eares in love by-and-by.*

by-blow. A side stroke. Hence other meanings grew: (1) a calamity as a side effect of the main action, as in the statement that inequality is a by-blow of man's fall; (2) a blow that misses its aim, as in Bunyan's PILGRIM'S PROGRESS (1684): *Now also with their by-blows they did split the very stones in pieces;* (3) an illegitimate child—an unintended side-effect; thus Motteux in his translation (1708) of Rabelais remarks that *Kind Venus cured her beloved by-blow Aeneas;* and Browning in THE RING AND THE BOOK (1868) refers to *A drab's brat, a beggar's bye-blow.*

bycorne. See *chichevache.*

byental. An 18th century term for "the yard or privy member of a horse."

bynempt. Named; called. Old past participle of *bename.* Used in THE SHEPHERD'S CALENDAR (1579; JUNE) by Spenser.

byrespect. Attention paid to something other than the apparent purpose; a side aim; an ulterior motive. Used 16th to 18th century; Burkitt ON THE NEW TESTAMENT (1703) exclaimed: *How natural it is for men to seek Christ for sinister ends and byrespects!*

byrlakin. A contraction of *By Our Ladykin,* by our darling lady— referring to the Virgin Mary, and used as a mild oath. Also the simpler *byrlady—berlady, burlady, birlady, byleddy; bylakin, belakin, berlakin,* and more. Shakespeare swears *Berlady thirtie yeares* in ROMEO AND JULIET (1592) and *Berlaken, a parlous feare* in A MIDSUMMER NIGHT'S DREAM.

C

cabbage. See *caboche.*

cablish. Brushwood. Its disposition was covered by law. Originally the word meant trees or branches blown down by the wind.

caboche. To cut off the head (of a deer) close behind the horns. Via French from Italian *capocchia,* big head, from *capo,* head. It is sometimes spelled *cabage,* through confusion with the early verb *to cabbage,* to grow or come to a head (like the horns of a deer). As the head of the vegetable is removed when it has "cabbaged," so was the head of the deer.

cacafuego. A braggart; a spitfire (etymologically, the second letter of *spitfire* should be *h*: Latin *cacare,* Spanish *cagar,* to void excrement + Spanish *fuego,* fire). The word came into English as a term of contempt because it was the name of the Spanish galleon Drake captured in 1577. Bailey explains it, in 1731, as the name of a Spanish fly that by night darts fire from its tail. Fletcher in THE FAIR MAID OF THE INN (1625) cries: *She will be ravished before our faces by rascals and cacafugos, wife, cacafugoes!*

cachespell. Tennis. The 16th and 17th century term, from Flemish *caestespeel,* from French *chasse,* chase + *speel,* play. Also the Dutch *kaats,* place where the ball hits the ground. There were many spellings—*cachepule, kaichspell, cachespale,* etc.—in the 16th century, before the French name for the game, *tennis,* took its place.

cachexy. A depraved condition: of a person—body or mind—or of a state, as MACMILLAN'S MAGAZINE of November 1883 said that Ireland *lies fretful and wrathful under a grim social cachexy of distressful centuries.* From Greek *kakos,* bad + *exia, exis,* habit, state, *exein,* to have, to be in a condition. Hence also *cachectic, cachectical, cacexicate, cachexicate.*

Other English words come from Greek *kakos,* bad. *Cack,* to void excrement (see *cacafuego*); Cranmer in 1549 tells of a man who *cacked out the Devil.* The *fish cackerel* was a small Mediterranean fish, eaten only by the poor, so-called in scorn; others, as Johnson records in 1755, say that eating it is laxative. *cacodaemon,* an evil spirit, a nightmare; *cacodemoniac,* one possessed; *cacodemonic,* bringing misfortune. *cacochyme, cacochymic,* full of evil humors. *cacodorous. cacodox,* holding evil opinions: *cacodoxy. cacoethes* (4 syllables), an evil habit, an 'itch' to do, as the *insanabile cacoethes scribendi* (incurable itch to write) Addison (1713) quotes from Juvenal, saying it *is as epidemical as the small pox. cacolike* was a 16th and 17th century scornful perversion of *Catholic. cacology,* ill report; bad speaking. *cacomagician,* sorcerer. There are others, in medicine and prosody (*cacophonous, cacorhythmic,* etc). Jeremy Bentham, countering More's *Utopia,* supposes a *Cacotopia* or worst possible government. The O.E.D. (1933) probably errs in calling Bentham mistaken. Erasmus, when he wrote IN PRAISE OF FOLLY, was living with More, and the Latin title is a pun on More's name (as though IN PRAISE OF MORE: ENCOMIUM MORIAE). More punned in his title UTOPIA: the beautiful (*eu-*) place that is no (*ou-*) place. The world must be ever vigilant, to avoid *Cacotopia. cacozelia* (perverse imitation, like "copying the cough of genius" or the manners and tactics of a Hitler) is quite pervasive, easily caught. It is sometimes spelled *cacozeal,* which is, more properly, misdirected zeal; whence *cacozealot; cacozealous. cacozelia* (the term) was used especially in the 16th and 17th centuries, as by Spenser and Puttenham; Bulwer (1644) warns lest *imitation degenerate into cacozeale,* developing *a left-handed Cicero.*

cachinnate. To laugh loud and long, immoderately. From the 15th century, through Browning (THE RING AND THE BOOK, 1868); the practice extends farther. Scott, in GUY MANNERING (1815) mentions *the hideous grimaces which attended this unusual cachinnation.* Also *cachinnator; cachinnatory.* Sometimes in the theatre one can sympathize with Hawthorne, who in MOSSES FROM AN OLD MANSE (1846) *threatened instant death on the slightest cachinnatory indulgence.*

caco-. A combining form meaning bad or evil, from Greek *kakos,* bad. See *cachexy.*

cacodemon. See *cachexy; eudemon.*

cacography. (1) Bad handwriting. The opposite of *calligraphy.* (2) Bad spelling. The opposite of *orthography.* Also a bad system of spelling, such as—says O.E.D., abandoning historical perspective—"that of current English". Also *cacographic; cacographer.* Used from the 16th century. *Cp. cachexy.*

cacuminous. Pointed; of a tree, pyramidal in shape. Latin *cacuminem,* point, peak, top. Hence *cacuminate,* to sharpen, especially at the top, as with a stake; to shape like a pyramid; also *cacumination.* M. Collins in PEN SKETCHES (1879) wrote of *Luminous books* (*not voluminous*) *To read under beech-trees cacuminous.*

cad. See *cadcatcher.*

cadcatcher. A cheap article for sale, especially prepared to ensnare the undiscriminating. A 19th century term from *cad.* Before its current meaning of a vulgar person, *cad* grew through several senses. In the 17th century, it meant a goblin, a familiar spirit, as when Bishop King wrote in his POEMS (1657): *Rebellion wants no cad nor elfe But is a perfect witchcraft of itself.* In the 18th century, it was used for an unbooked passenger in a coach, whose fare was pocketed by the driver; in the 19th, for an assistant or helper; a cheap laborer; an omnibus conductor (Hood; Dickens, PICKWICK PAPERS; Thackeray, THE BOOK OF SNOBS); then as a school term (Eton, Oxford; in Scotland, *caddie*) for a fellow that did odd jobs, as around the sporting fields, then contemptuously, for a townsman (as opposed to a gownsman). Hence, the current use.

caddis. A yarn; a worsted tape, used for garters and the like; hence, short for *caddis ribbon* or *caddis garter.* Shakespeare uses it in THE WINTER'S TALE (1610): *He hath ribbons of all the colors i' the rainbow, points more than all the lawyers in Bohemia can learnedly handle, though they come to him by the gross—inkles, caddises, cambrics, lawns;* and in HENRY IV, PART ONE.

cade. (1) a barrel, from Latin *cadus,* a large earthenware vessel. From the 14th through the 18th century, especially a barrel of herrings holding six great hundreds (6 score in a great hundred); later the cade held 500. (2) A pet; a lamb or a foal raised by hand; hence, a spoiled or petted child. See *cosset.* (3) A kind of juniper bush, yielding *cade oil,* used by veterinarians. *To cade* may mean, from (1), to put into a keg or, from (2), to pamper.

cadent. Falling. Latin *cadentem,* falling; *cadere,* to fall. Shakespeare in KING LEAR (1605): *With cadent tears fret channels in her cheeks.*

Cadmean. Related to the Phoenician Cadmus, brother of Europa, founder of Thebes, who brought the alphabet to Greece. He killed a dragon and sowed its teeth, whereupon armed men sprang from the ground; he threw a stone amongst them and they at once attacked one another; all perished save five, who helped Cadmus build his city. From his legend come two uses of *Cadmean, Cadmian*: (1) Tennyson in a poem of 1868 speaks of *Dragon warriors from Cadmean teeth*; (2) *a Cadmean victory,* a victory involving the winner's ruin—like that of World War II and thereafter.

caducous. Fleeting, transitory; liable to fall; infirm, feeble. Also (15th through 17th century) *caduce, caduke.* Latin *caducus; cadere,* to fall. In biology, *caducous* is used of parts that fall off naturally when they have served their purpose. Caxton in the translation (1484) of THE CURIAL MADE BY MAYSTRE ALAIN CHARRETIER wrote: *Our lyf . . . ne hath glory mondayne ne pompe caduque wythoute adversyte.* And Biggs in THE NEW DISPENSATION (1651) noted *that caduce, specious and seductive chameleon, reason.*

caffa. A cloth, of rich silk, popular in the 16th century. Also *capha.* The Wardrobe Accounts of King Henry VIII (for 18 May, 1531) list *white caffa for the Kinges grace.* Cavendish in THE LYFFE AND DEATHE OF CARDYNALL WOOLSEY (1557) spoke of Woolsey's *habytt, which was other of fynne skarlett or elles of crymmosyn satten, taffeta, dammaske, or caffa, the best that he could gett for money.*

cagastric. Sent by an evil star; used by Paracelsus of certain diseases, fevers, or the plague. Also, under the baneful influence of a star. Thus *cagastrical;* from (?) *cacos-,* evil + *aster,* star; *cp. cachexy.*

caitiff. A captive; later, a poor wretch; a despicable wretch, a villain. In many spellings, including *caytive, chaytif,* via French from Latin *captivus,* captive. A very common word from the 13th through the 17th century. Also *caitifhede,* wretchedness; wickedness; *caitifly; caitifty,* captivity; wretchedness; villainy. Wyclif and Chaucer use the verb *caitive, caytifue,* to imprison. *Caitisned,* chained, listed in Bailey's DICTIONARY (1751) and elsewhere as used by Chaucer, is a 1560 misprint for *caytifued,* in Chaucer's TESTAMENT OF LOVE (1400).

calamist. A piper. From Latin *calamus,* reed, which is used in English as the name of various reeds and rushes, especially the sweet flag. In Whitman's LEAVES OF GRASS, the section of 45 poems first published in 1860 is called CALAMUS. Possibly from the curling leaves of rushes came Latin *calamistrum,* curling-iron, whence 17th century English (Burton, ANATOMY OF MELANCHOLY, 1621) *calamistrate* (accent on the *mis*), to curl or frizzle the hair. Also in the 17th century: *calamize,* to pipe or sing.

calash. A light carriage with low wheels and a removable top. Hence also, the folding hood of a carriage, a perambulator, etc. In the 18th and 19th centuries, a woman's hood, supported by whalebone or cane hoops, projecting beyond the face, as in Mrs. Gaskell's CRANFORD (1867); *Three or four ladies in calashes met at Miss Barker's door.* From French *caleche,* from the Slavonic, *kolasa,* wheel-carriage, *kolo,* wheel. A small two-wheeled carriage in Canada, usually without a cover, is still called a *caleche.*

calcate. To trample or stamp upon. From Latin *calcare,* from *calx,* heel. BLACKWOOD'S EDINBURGH MAGAZINE of 1822 remarks that *even a few supernumerary calcations would have been overlooked.* A *calcatory* was a 15th century term for a winepress, where the grapes are stamped upon. Combinations formed with *calcar,* such as *calcarine, calcariferous,* spur-like, bearing spurs, are from Latin *calcar,* spur, from *calx, calcis,* heel. *Calceate* is a 17th and 18th century term for shod, from Latin *calceus,* shoe. The *Fathers Calceate* were the moderate Carmelites, "of the rule relaxed," who did not go barefoot. Hence also *calced* and *discalced,* shod and unshod. *Calceolate* means shaped like a slipper, used in botany today, the genus *calceolaria. Calcimine,* however, *calcium* and its many compounds and related words, are from the Latin *calx, calcis,* meaning lime. The change of heat-rays from non-luminous to luminous, which Tyndall (1872) called *calorescence,* was earlier called *calcescence,* because it happened in the lime-light. I suppose *calcescence* is the main process in the creation of a Hollywood star.

calcey. Causeway. Also *calcetum.* Listed as old by Bailey, 1751.

calcium. See *calcate.*

caldese. See *chaldese.*

calendar. In addition to its still current senses (in use since the 14th century) *calendar* was used to mean a guide, a model—Chaucer (LEGEND OF GOOD WOMEN; 1385); Shakespeare (HAMLET; 1602): *He is the card or calendar of gentry.* Also, a list, as of canonized saints (17th century) or of prisoners awaiting trial (16th century); a record; Shakespeare (ALL'S WELL THAT ENDS WELL): *The kalender of my past endevours.* Also, a record in the sense of a sign; Lodge (EUPHUES GOLDEN LEGEND; 1590): *Nor are the dimples in the face the calendars of truth.*

calenture. A tropical disease afflicting sailors, who in delirium fancy the ocean to be a green field and wish to leap into it and play. It is also used figuratively, of a burning passion or zeal, as in a poem (1631) of Donne: *Knowledge kindles calentures in some. Pure chastity,* Bishop Thomas Ken piously observed in 1711, *excels in gust The calentures of baneful lust.* Congreve in LOVE FOR LOVE (1695) uses the word to mean the victims of the disease, as Ben exclaims: *I believe all the calentures of the sea are come ashore.*

calepin. A dictionary, especially a polyglot. Figuratively, a note-book; to bring one *to one's calepin,* to the limits of one's information, one's wit's end. From Ambrosio *Calepino,* of *Calepio,* Italy, an Augustine friar who in 1502 published a Latin DICTIONARY that was the standard for the century; an edition in eight languages was issued in 1609. *Taxations, monopolies, tolls,* protested Drummond of Hawthornden in 1649, *such impositions as would trouble many calepines to give names unto.*

calewise. Warmly. Latin *calere,* to be warm. In 18th century dictionaries.

calibogus. A mixture of rum and spruce beer, imbibed by misguided Americans in the 18th and 19th centuries; as L. de Boileau described it in his RECOLLECTIONS OF LABRADOR LIFE (1861), "more of the former and less of the latter."

calicrat. An ant. A 16th century term, apparently from *Callicrates,* a Greek artist, mentioned by Pliny, who specialized in sculptures—minute ivory carvings—of ants and other tiny creatures.

caligate. Wearing military boots. From Latin *caliga,* half-boot, worn by the Roman soldiers. A *caligate knight,* in the 16th century, was one that fought on foot.

caliginous. Obscure; dark. Latin *caliginem,* obscurity, mistiness. *Caliginosity,* dimness of sight. Used mainly in the 16th and 17th century, but Mrs. Piozzi is not the only one who commented (1794) on *the caliginous atmosphere of London*; and Bulwer-Lytton in THE CAXTONS (1849) has: *Her lone little room, full of caliginous corners and nooks.*

calino. A rascal. French *calin,* 'a beggarly rogue or lazie vagabond that counterfeits disease.' Nashe in LENTEN STUFFE (1599) spoke of *our English harmonious calinos.* The word may be corrupted from an Irish song, *calino custure me,* popular about 1600. Shakespeare in HENRY V (1599) makes Pistol, when his prisoner speaks French, respond in meaningless English: *Qualtitie calmie custure me.*

callet. A lewd woman, a strumpet. Also *calat, kallat, calot,* etc. Shakespeare in OTHELLO (1604): *A beggar in his drink Could not have laid such terms upon his callet*; Burns' THE JOLLY BEGGARS (1785): *I'm as happy with my wallet, my bottle and my callet.* As a verb *callet* means to scold, to rail, and sometimes the noun is used as a general term of abuse, meaning no more than 'a scold'—thus used in GAMMER GURTON'S NEEDLE (1575), by Skelton, by Stanyhurst, by Shakespeare (THE WINTER'S TALE, 1611): *A callat of boundless tongue, who late hath beat her husband, and now baits me.*

calliblephary. A coloring for the eye-lids. Greek *kallos,* beauty + *blepharon,* eye-lid. Accent on the *bleph.* Robert Lovell, in A COMPLEAT HISTORY OF ANIMALS AND MINERALS (1661) recommends: *the marrow of the right fore legge with soot . . . serveth for a calliblephary.* Modern maids have other modes.

callidity. Cunning, craftiness. From Latin *callidus,* skilful, crafty (in good or bad sense). Used in 16th, 17th and 18th centuries, but FRASER'S MAGAZINE in 1833 spoke of persons that *suspect their own intimate friends of callidity.* The formality of the term seems somewhat to lessen the offence.

callipygean. "Largely composed behind," as Sir Thomas Browne put it in 1646. From Greek *kalos, kallos,* beauty + *pyge,* buttocks. Also *callipygian, callipygous; cp. aischrology.* The word *kalos* was also used of moral values; the Greeks set in opposition *to kalon kai to aischron*; the Romans, *honestum et turpe*; the English, *virtue and vice.* And also *callipygy,* beauty behind. Lyly in EUPHUES (1580) tells, of the ancient artists: *Zeuxis having before him fiftie faire virgins of Sparta whereby to draw one amiable Venus, said, that fiftie more fayrer than those coulde not minister sufficient beautie to shewe the godesse of beautie, therefore being in dispaire either by art to shadow hir, or by imagination to comprehend hir, he drew in a table a faire temple, the gates open, and Venus going in, so as nothing coulde be per-*

ceived but her backe, wherein he used such cunning that Appelles himselfe, seeing this worke, wished that Venus would turn hir face, saying that if it were in all partes agreeable to the backe, he would become apprentice to Zeuxis, and slave to Venus. It may not be impious to note that another god himself said (BIBLE: EXODUS 33): *And it shall come to pass, while my glory passeth by, that I will put thee in a clift of the rock, and will cover thee with my hand as I pass by: And I will take away mine hand, and thou shalt see my back parts: but my face shall not be seen.* This takes us on philosophical roundings. —As might be expected of the Victorian era, THE ATHENAEUM of 17 October, 1885, speaks of *the callipygian luxuriance he so deplores.*

caltrop. A snare. Originally a trap to catch the feet of men or horses in war, and of hunted beasts; probably from Latin *calx,* heel + Old High German *trapo* (Latin *trappa*), trap. Spelled in many ways: *coltetraeppe, calteroope, calthrap, galtrop,* etc. In the 16th and 17th centuries, an iron ball with four prongs so arranged that one always pointed up, flung on the ground to hinder charging cavalry. Also used figuratively as by Dekker in THE WHORE OF BABYLON (1607): *If ever I come back I'll be a calthrop to prick my countries feet that tread on me.*

cam. See *kam.*

camarine. A fetid marsh or swamp. From *Camarina,* a town in Sicily beside a pestilential marsh. Thomas Newton in 1576 speaks of a man who can *wade into the very gulph and camarine of man's apparant wilfulnesse.* Paul Rycant, in his translation (1681) of Gracian's THE CRITICK, speaks of *camarines of customs, which use to envenome and infect the soule.*

cambium. (1) Exchange; a place of exchange. Late Latin *cambium,* exchange. A *cambist* was a dealer in bills of exchange; by extension, a manual of measures, weights, etc. Hence also *cambistry.* (2) One of the "alimentary humours" supposed to nourish the body; in 1708 Kersey's DICTIONARY lists three, the other two "being called gluten and ros." (3) The cellular tissue in which the annual growth of wood and bark takes place. By extension from (2) and still used in botany.

cambrel. A bent piece of wood or iron, on which butchers hung meat. J. Jackson in 1641 pictured a man crucified head downward, *like a sheep upon the cambrel.* Also *cambren,* perhaps the original form, Welsh *cam,* crooked (surviving in arms *akimbo*) + *pren,* wood.

camis. A light loose silk or linen dress; a shirt. Via Spanish *camisa* from Late Latin *camisia,* tunic, shirt. The French form is the familiar *chemise*; the English has many: *camus; camise* (from Arabic *gamiç,* which occurs in the KORAN but is probably borrowed from Latin); *camisole,* a negligee jacket; also, a straitjacket. Spenser in THE FAERIE QUEENE (1596) tells of a woman who *was yclad, for heat of scorching aire, All in a silken camus lily white.*

camisado. A night attack. The word, frequent in the 16th and 17th centuries, is literally (Spanish) "shirted"; see *camis.* The attackers wore a white shirt over their armor so as to be recognized by one another in the dark.

camlet. Originally a beautiful and costly eastern fabric, made—especially in the 16th and 17th centuries—of the hair of the angora goat. Also (and in French) *camelot,* from Arabic *kemel,* angora—

sometimes confused with *camel,* though the cloth was never made of camel's hair. There was also a "watered" camlet, with a wavy surface, and as a verb *to camlet* came to mean to mark with wavy lines; Edmund Bolton in his translation (1618) of THE ROMAN HISTORIES OF LUCIUS JULIUS FLORUS speaks of *cassocks chambleted with figures of palms.* The word was also used of a garment made of the material. Later camlet was made of mohair, then spun of wool and silk, then wool and linen or cotton. By 1815 tents were made of it, *of a kind of black blanket, or rather of coarse camlet.* Then it dropped out of use.

campestrial. Also *campestral.* See *champestrial.*

campion. An earlier (later, a Scotch) form of *champion.* The Late Latin was *campionem,* a fighter on the *campus,* a field for pugilistic contests—as the campus may still be. See *champestrial.*

canary. (1) A lively dance, or the music thereto. Also *to canary,* to dance. Shakespeare in ALL'S WELL THAT ENDS WELL (1601) has *a medicine That's able to breath life into a stone, Quicken a rock, and make you dance canari;* in LOVE'S LABOUR'S LOST, *jig off a tune, at the tongue's end, canary to it with your feet.* Other writers of the time usually employed the plural; Nashe (1592); Dekker in THE SEVEN DEADLY SINS OF LONDON (1606): *They would make all the hogges-heads that use to come to the house, to dance the cannaries till they reeld againe.* (2) A light sweet wine. Both of these come from the *Canary Islands,* which also gave their name to the yellow songster—but took it (Latin *canaria insula,* island of the dogs; *canis,* dog) from the dogs that used to roam there. Also (3) a quandary; an anticipatory malapropism by Mistress Quickly in THE MERRY WIVES OF WINDSOR: *You have brought her into such a canaries; the best courtier of them all could never have brought her to such a canarie.*

candicant. Waxing white, like the morning; whitish. *To candicate* is to turn (something) white; to grow white. Rare words both, ultimately from Latin *candidus,* white—whence also *candidate,* because aspirants to office in Rome wore a white toga. Dictionaries of the 18th century include *canitude,* hoariness, whiteness—probably in error from this source.

candlewaster. One that 'wastes candles' by study late at night. Applied in scorn to fruitless elucubration. Jonson in CYNTHIA'S REVELS (1599) speaks of *a whoreson bookworm, a candle-waster.* Shakespeare in MUCH ADO ABOUT NOTHING (1599) bids *Patch griefe with proverbs, make misfortune drunke With candlewasters.*

canephor. One that bears a basket on her head. Also *canephora, canephorus;* Greek *caneon,* basket + *phoros,* carrying. Applied in ancient Greece to a maiden bearing the sacred items for the feasts of Demeter, Bacchus, and Athena. FRASER'S MAGAZINE of 1849 said: *To be chosen canephor was as if 'Beautiful' were stamped on the lintel of a woman's door.*

canescent. See *canous.*

canicular. Relating to a dog. Latin *canicula,* diminutive of *canis,* dog. In Latin the diminutive was used to name the dog-star; thus usually also in English. The *canicular days,* the dog-days, around the rising of the dog-star (Sirius or Procyon), about 11 August. *Caniculars* has also been used to mean doggerel verses. Harvey in his FOURE LETTERS (1592) declared: *If Mother Hubbard . . . happen to tel one canicular tale, father Elderton and his sonne Greene will counterfeit an hundred* *dogged fables, libles, calumnies, slaunders, lies for the whetstone, what not, and most currishly snarle and bite where they should most kindly fawne and licke.*

canion. Used in the plural, of rolls of cloth "laid like sausages" round the bottom of breeches-legs. A style for men in the 16th and 17th centuries. Pepys in his DIARY of 24 May, 1660, says: *Made myself as fine as I could, with the linning stockings on and wide canons.* (The word was also spelled *cannons* and *cannions.*) Portraits of Henry III of France and his Court show costumes with cannions.

canitude. See *candicant.*

cankedort. A critical situation; "a woful case" (Bailey, 1751). Chaucer in TROYLUS AND CRISEYDE (1374) inquires: *Was Troylus nought in a kankedort?* Also (Medwall, 1500): *That were a shrewd crankdort.* The etymology is unknown.

canorus. Melodious; singing; resonant. Latin *canorem,* song; *canere,* to sing. De Quincey in his CONFESSIONS OF AN ENGLISH OPIUM-EATER (1822) breaks into *a long, loud, and canorous peal of laughter.* Lowell remarks in AMONG MY BOOKS (1870): *He chooses his language for its rich canorousness rather than for intensity of meaning.*

canous. Hoary; grey. Used in the 16th century; also *canois, canus;* Latin *canus,* hoary. Thus *canescent,* growing gray; rather hoary; dull white. Also *canescence;* R. Burton in EL MEDINAH (1855) wrote: *All colour melts away with the canescence from above. The sky is of a dead milk-white.*

cantankerous. See *conteck.*

cantharides. The dried beetle or Spanish fly; formerly used as an aphrodisiac. (Four syllables; plural of Greek *kantharis,* blister-fly.) Also *cantharids, cantarides.* Used figuratively, as by Jonson in THE POETASTER (1601): *I, you whoreson cantharides! was it I?* Burke in THE FRENCH REVOLUTION (1790): *cantharides to our love of liberty.* Guilpin in SKIALETHEIA ("SHADOW OF TRUTH"; 1598) said of satires and epigrams: *They are philosophicke true cantharides To vanities dead flesh. An epigrame Is popish displing* [discipline], *rebell flesh to tame: A plain dealing lad, that is not afraid To speak the truth, but calls a jade a jade. And Mounsieur Guulard* [Biggullet] *was not much to blame When he for meat mistook an epigrame, For though it be no cates, sharpe sauce it is To lickerous vanitie, youths sweet amisse.* We no longer use *amiss (q.v.)* as a noun; and, for the most part, we no longer use cantharides as an aphrodisiac.

cantle. A nook or corner; especially, a projecting corner of land. Hence, a corner sliced off; by extension, a slice of bread, a section of anything (especially, a segment of a circle or sphere), a separate part or portion. Also the bump at the back of a horse's saddle, the bar at the back of a camel's. Figuratively (Scotch), the crown of the head, as in *I'll crack his cantle for him.* Chaucer in THE KNIGHT'S TALE (1386): *For Nature has not taken his beginning Of no partie ne cantel of a thing.* Shakespeare uses the word in HENRY IV PART ONE (but see *scantle*); also in ANTONY AND CLEOPATRA (1606): *The greater cantle of the world is lost With very ignorance*—a remark not of an age but for our time.

capel. See *caple.* In alchemy *capel, cappell* was also the name for a large crucible or furnace.

capelclawer. A groom, a horse-scrubber. Hence, a scurvy fellow. So used in POLITICAL SONGS of the time of Henry III and Edward I, collected by Thomas Wright, 1839. *Cp. caple.*

capha. See *caffa.*

capilotade. A meat dish; in the 17th and 18th centuries, usually *capirotade*: of stewed veal, capon, chicken, or partridge minced, spiced, and laid upon several beds of cheese. Rabelais uses the form *cabirotade*; perhaps the word is from *capirote,* hood: a covered dish. Another old recipe worth re-trying. The word was applied figuratively to "a cooked-up story": Vanbrugh in THE CONFEDERACY (1705) has: *What a capilotade of a story's here!*

capistrate. To muzzle. A rare word of the 17th and 18th centuries, from Latin *capistrum,* halter, Latin *caput,* head.

caple. A horse. Also *caball* (not to be confused with *cabal, cabbala,* from the Hebrew), *capel, capul, capil, capylle* and the like (Drayton uses *cauple*) roundabout from Latin *caballus,* horse, which by French routes gives us *chevalier* and *cavalier.* Chaucer in THE FRERES TALE (1386) says: *Bothe hey and cart and elk his caples three.* Drayton (1603) pictures the course of the sun: *Phoebus took his lab'ring teame . . . To wash his cauples in the ocean streame.* Scott in IVANHOE (1819) revived the word, borrowing *my neighbour Buthan's good capul.*

capnomancy. See *aeromancy.*

capocchia. Simpleton, blockhead. Italian *capocchio,* from *capo,* head. The word in English is a suggestion by Theobald (1726; SHAKESPEARE RESTORED, which criticized Pope's edition of Shakespeare, after which Theobald was made the chief butt in Pope's DUNCIAD). Theobald suggests *capocchia* as the correct reading, in TROILUS AND CRESSIDA (1606): *Alas poore wretch: a poor chipochia.*

capot. To win all the tricks in the game (of piquet). The player who fails to make a single trick is *capot.* The game was introduced into England from France in the 17th century. *Capot* is also a variant spelling of *capote* (augmentative form of French *cape,* cape), a long mantle for women or cloak for men. *Capote* (Latin *caput,* head) is also used for a close-fitting hat, which fits the head almost like a skull-cap; Scott in KENILWORTH (1821) has this in the form *capotaine.* There is also a 16th and 17th century head-dress called *capuchon* (from the French augmentative of *capuche,* hood; Latin *caput,* head); this was sometimes simple as a cowl, but often twisted and piled upon the head as an adornment.

capotaine. See *copataine.*

capripede. A satyr. *Capriped,* goat-footed; Latin *caper, capri, caprem,* goat (whence the island and the *taxi*: short for *taxicabriolet*) + *pedem,* foot. Among words formed from *caprem* are *caprice* (still current), in the form *capriccio* used by Shakespeare (ALL'S WELL THAT ENDS WELL; 1601: *Will this caprichio hold in thee, art sure?*) and revived by Scott (REDGAUNTLET; 1824). *capricorn, capricornify,* to equip with horns; to cuckold: in 1665 *A wily wench there was . . . Who used to capricorn her husband's head. caprid, caprine,* relating to a goat. *caprizate,* to leap like a goat; used in medicine of an irregular pulse. The *caprifig* is the goat-fig, the wild fig; *caprification*; to *caprify,* to ripen artificially; specifically, to ripen figs by means of the puncture of insects, or of a small feather. Noted by Pliny in ancient times, extensive on the island of Malta, *caprification* is now considered both unnecessary and injurious.

capuchon. See *capot.*

capul. See *caple.*

caput mortuum. (1) A death's head (this is the literal translation of the Latin words), a skull. (2) In alchemy (and chemistry) the residuum after distillation or sublimation of a substance, the useless remains, 'good for nothing' (said Willis in 1681) 'but to be flung away, all vertue being extracted.' Hence (3) worthless residue. *Cp. terra damnata.* Bishop Thomas Ken, in his epic poem EDMUND (1700), speaking of a person that turns to religion late in life, observed: *His youthful heat and strength for sin engage; God has the caput mortuum of his age.*

carbonado. A steak (says Bailey, 1751) broiled on the coals. A piece of fish, flesh, or fowl (says the O.E.D.) scored across and grilled or broiled upon the coals. The idea of "flesh scored across" appealed to many writers—including Shakespeare: CORIOLANUS (1607): *He scotcht him and notcht him like a carbinado*; THE WINTER'S TALE (1611): *How she long'd to eate adders heads, and toads carbonado'd.* Hence *to carbonado* came to mean to slash, to hack—as again in Shakespeare, ALL'S WELL THAT ENDS WELL (1601): *Your carbinado'd face.* Washington Irving in THE ALHAMBRA (1832) speaks of a man *so cut up and carbonadoed that he is a kind of walking monument of the troubles of Spain.*

carcan. (1) An iron collar used for punishment, in the 13th through 16th centuries. (2) An ornamental collar or neckline, later called a *carcanet.* In the PROGRESS of Queen Elizabeth I, of 1572, we read that she received *one riche carkanet or collar of golde, having in it two emeralds.* Stanyhurst's AENEIS (1583) speaks of a *garganet heavy. Carcanet* was sometimes used for a circlet for the head; it might be, as in Herrick's HESPERIDES (1648), *a carkanet of maidenflowers,* or even (1876) *a carcanet of smiles.*

cark. A load, a burden; hence, trouble, troubled state of mind. Also *carke, kark.* Via old French *carkier* and Late Latin *carcare* from Latin *carricare,* to load, whence also *carriage*; the same Latin by another route gave Old French *cargier, chargier,* English *charge,* which also first meant a load. Used from the 14th century, frequent in the alliterative phrase *cark and care.* Spenser makes other pattern in THE FAËRIE QUEENE (1590): *Downe did lay his heavie head, devoid of careful carke. Cark* was also used as a verb, to load; to burden with trouble; to be worried, to toil anxiously. Thus Berkeley in ALCIPHRON (1732) wrote: *Old Bubalion in the city is carking, starving, and cheating, that his son may drink, game, and keep mistresses.*

carkanet. See *carcan.* Shakespeare said, in THE COMEDY OF ERRORS (1592): *Say that I lingered with you at your shop, To see the making of her carkanet*; Massinger, in THE CITY MADAM (1632): *Curled haires, hung full of sparkling carcanets, Are not the true adornments of a wife*—though many wives prefer them.

carkes. See *sloth.*

carline. Several words shaped into this form (always with a short *i*). (1) An olden coin of Naples and Sicily, worth less than a dime. Also *carlin*; from a ruler *Carlo,* perhaps Carlo I, 1266. (2) A woman; especially a scornful term for an old woman; Arbuthnot in JOHN BULL (1712) has Peg exclaim *There's no living with that old carline his mother!* Hence, a witch; in Burns' TAM O'SHANTER (1790): *The carlin caught her by the rump.* From Middle English *kerling,* feminine of *karl.* (3) A kind of plant, the *carline thistle,* also *caroline,* supposedly named after King *Carolus* Magnus, Charlemagne. (4) The yellow ball in *carline billiards,* played with two white, one red, one blue, and the *carline ball,* which holed in a center pocket scores six (Hoyle, 1820). (5) One of the pieces of timber supporting the deck-planks of a ship. Also *carling.* (6) Parched peas. Probably so-called because eaten on *Carling Sunday,* the fifth Sunday in Lent. This is, more properly, *Care Sunday,* with *care* in its early meaning, sorrow.

carlot. A fellow, peasant. A variant of *carl, churl. Churl* has come down from earliest English times; *carl* at that period was used in combinations, as *housecarl.* Both are common Norse and Teuton, from the same root, and survive in the names *Carl* and *Charles.* Both *carl* and *churl* went through the same shift of meanings. *Churl* first meant a male, then a husband (correlative to wife); *to churl* (10th and 11th centuries), to take a husband. Then it meant a plain man, a member of the lowest (third) rank of freemen. At this point *carl* also came into separate use, mainly as a countryman. Then—after the Norman Conquest—the Saxon *ceorlas* (*churls, carls*) came to be serfs. By extension, a boor, a rude ill-bred fellow. Hence *carlish, churlish,* the latter of which survives. Wyclif uses *churlhood;* Chaucer, *churldom.* Shakespeare, in AS YOU LIKE IT (1600) says: *He hath bought the cottage and the bounds That the old carlot once was master of.*

carminate. To card wool; to expel wind. From Latin *carminare,* from *carmen,* a card for wool. This original sense, though in 17th century dictionaries, was apparently never used in English. But in Renaissance medicine, certain substances were supposed to dilute the gross humours in the stomach and bowels that give rise to wind, and to comb them out like the knots in wool. Such medicines were therefore called *carminative;* their purpose was to expel flatulence. Note however that *carmination* is a rare word for incantation, charm, from Latin *carmen,* song.

carnation. Flesh-color. Latin *carnem,* flesh. Especially, in the plural, the flesh tints in a painting, the parts of a body drawn naked. Goldsmith in A CITIZEN OF THE WORLD (1760) exclaims: *What attitudes, carnations, and draperies!* The *carnation* is also a variety of cherry. The flower *carnation* was originally *coronation,* as in Spenser's SHEPHERD'S CALENDAR (1579): *Bring coronations and sops-in-wine, Worn of paramours.*

carnifex. See *excarnation.* Also *cp. carnation.*

carrack. A large ship, such as was used by the Portuguese in East Indian trade, also equipped for fighting. Chaucer, in THE SOMPNER'S TALE (1386) says: *Broader than of a carryk is the sail.* (Also in various manuscripts, *carrik, carike, caryke.*) Shakespeare has still another spelling, in THE COMEDY OF ERRORS (1590): *Spain, who sent whole armadoes of carrects.*

carranto. See *coranto.*

carriwitchet. A pun, a hoaxing question, a quibble. Ben Jonson has, in BARTHOLOMEW FAIR (1614): *All the fowle i' the Fayre, I mean, all the dirt in Smithfield (that's one of Master Littlewit's carwitchets now).* The word occurs (*corwhichet, carry-which-it,* etc.) in Dryden, Butler, Arbuthnot, and was revived by Scott in THE FORTUNES OF NIGEL (1822): *mortally wounded with a quibble or a carwitchet at the Mermaid.* A SLANG DICTIONARY of 1874 defines *carriwitchet: a hoaxing, puz-*

zling question . . . as, How far is it from the first of July to London Bridge?

carrucage. A tax levied on each carrucate of ground. From medieval Latin *carrucagium,* from *carruca,* plough. (All these words are also spelled with one *r.*) Also, *caruage.* A *carrucate* was as much land as could be tilled with one plough in one year. A plough had a team of eight oxen. The size of a *carrucate* varied with the nature of the soil. The terms *caruck* and *carue* (in error, *carve*; see *caruage*) were occasionally used in old law; they are shortened forms of *carrucate.*

caruage. See *carrucage. Caruage* was used in the 17th century to mean ploughing. It was sometimes spelled *carvage*; in early English *v* was printed as *u,* and some errors were made when *v* was first employed.

carus. Profound sleep or insensibility. From Greek *karos,* torpor. Phillips (1678) defines it as "a disease in the head which is caused by an overfull stomach and want of concoction"; Bailey (1751) describes it as "a sleep wherein the person affected being pulled, pinched, and called, scarce shows any sign of either hearing or feeling." The four degrees of insensibility are *sopor, coma, lethargy, and carus. Sopor* is also used in English, of a deep sleep, especially of a mentally or morally benumbed condition. It is direct from Latin *sopor,* deep sleep. Hence also *soporate,* to put to sleep, to stupefy; *soporation*; *soporiferous*; *soporose, soporous,* and the still current *soporific.*

cashier. See *cass. Cashier,* to dismiss, is a verb; the noun for one who dismisses is *cashierer.*

cashmarie. A fish-peddler; especially, one who brings fish from the seacoast to sell inland. A 16th and 17th century word: Old Northern French *cacher,* to hurry, to drive fast + *marée,* tide.

cass. To annul; to dismiss. From Latin *quasare,* to dash to pieces, which took on the meanings of Latin *cassare,* to bring to naught, from *cassus,* empty, void. After 1700 *cass* was gradually supplanted by *quash* and *cashier.* Rarely *cass,* to dismiss, was spelled *cash.* [The original meaning of *cash,* money, was money-box, French *casse* from Latin *capsa,* case, coffer. Only in English did it come, by transfer from the container to the thing contained—noticed also in the expression "He's fond of the bottle"—to mean money.] From *cass* also came *cassate,* to annul; *cassation,* cancellation.

cassan. See *pedlers French.*

cassolette. See *caxon.*

cassoon. See *caxon.*

castellan. The governor of a castle. Also *chastelain; chatelain* (feminine *chatelaine,* mistress of a castle; by extension, an ornament worn hanging at a lady's waist, as it were the keys of the castle—usually a series of loops or short chains attached to the girdle, with scissors, thimble-case and other such objects. Later applied to a bunch of such articles on a watch-chain or bracelet. CASSELL'S FAMILY MAGAZINE of October 1883 reported that *chatelaine bags are much worn again*). Other forms are *castellin, castelane, castelyn, castelain*; ultimately from Latin *castellum,* castle. Hence also *castellanship, castellany,* the lordship of a castle; the district under its control. Also *castellated,* built like a castle (e.g., with battlements); enclosed as in a castle, as were the 18th century cisterns and fountains of London; shaped like a castle, as Washington Irving in CHRONICLES OF WOLFERT'S ROOST (1840) described *stately dames, with castellated locks and towering plumes.*

casting. This word was used as a compound, in several terms. A *casting-box,* a box for shaking dice, then throwing them. *Castingcounters,* counters used in calculating, in *casting* an account. *Casting-bottle, casting-glass,* a container from which perfume was sprinkled: an Elizabethan dainty device, mentioned by Jonson in CYNTHIA'S REVELS (*bottle*; 1600) and EVERY MAN OUT OF HIS HUMOUR: *Faith, ay: his civet and his casting-glass Have helpt him to a place among the rest.*

castorides. See *lycisk.*

castrametation. The act, art, or science of laying out a camp; the pattern or outline of a camp set down. Latin *castra,* camp + *metari,* to measure. *Cp. chester.* Also *castral,* pertaining to a camp. The Romans, when they occupied Britain (55 B.C. to the 6th century), laid out many camps, as can be seen from such place names as *Lancaster, Westchester, Leicester.* In *Worcestershire* the early British, the Roman, and the Saxon combine to give us the name of a sauce.

cata-. A Greek combining form (also *cat-, cath-*) meaning down, reflected back, used up, etc. In many current words. Also in some less known: *caballative,* tending to throw down; Peacock in HEADLONG HALL (1815) mentions *a machine containing a peculiar cataballative quality; catabaptist,* a 16th and 17th century term for one opposed to the sacrament of baptism; *catachthonian* (Greek *chthon,* earth), underground: Pluto was *a catachthonian Zeus; catadupe* (Greek *doupos,* thud, sound of a heavy fall), a cataract; originally, of the River Nile, used figuratively by Lodge in WITS MISERIE AND WORLDS MADNESS (1596): *In the catadupe of my knowledge I nourish the crocodile of thy conceit.* The *Catadupes* are (17th century) the dwellers by the cataracts of the Nile. A *catafalque* is a platform to hold a coffin, in church or movable, used in elaborate funeral ceremonies. *Cataglottism* is a scornful dictionary word for "a lascivious kiss," a tongue-kiss. *Catallactic* means in exchange; Ruskin in UNTO THIS LAST (1862) warns: *You may grow for your neighbor . . . grapes, or grapeshot; he will also catallactically grow grapes or grapeshot for you, and you will each reap what you have sown*; in 1831 Whately suggested the name *catallactics* for "the science of exchange." *Catamidiate* is a rare (17th century) term for to defame, to hold up to open shame. A *catamite* is not formed from *cata-,* but is a corruption of *Ganymedes,* the name of the cup-bearer of Zeus. *Cataphor,* a coma (in 17th century medicine; see *carus*). *Cataphysical,* contrary to nature; DeQuincey in his AUTOBIOGRAPHIC SKETCHES (1839) says he has seen portraits of Scott with a *cataphysical pile of forehead. Catoptric,* relating to a mirror, or to reflection. It is good to pause for reflection. Then continue: *cataskeuastic* (17th century), constructive. *catasophistry,* quibbling, deception. *catasta,* a platform on which slaves were exhibited for sale; a torture-bed; the stocks (pedantic); Kingsley in HYPATIA (1853): *Standing an hour on the catasta to be handled from head to foot in the minimum of clothing. catastaltic,* restraining, cutting short. *catasterism,* a constellation; a collection of legends of the stars; Greek *katasterismoi* was the title of such a collection attributed to Eratosthenes (3d century B.C.). *catathleba,* a fabulous monster of 14th century England; *catawampus,* a fierce and fabulous monster of 19th century United States; *catawampous,* fierce, destructive.

Bulwer-Lytton in MY NOVEL (1853) did not like *to be catawampously chawed up by a mercenary selfish cormorant of a capitalist.*

catafalque. See *cata-*. Old French *chafault, chafauld,* whence also English *scaffold.* The origin of the word is unknown; the first part may not be the Greek *cata-*. Also *catafalco, catafalc, catafalk.* The forms were used since the 17th century; by Evelyn in his DIARY (1641), Landor (1831), Browning; by Francis Thompson figuratively in A CORYMBUS FOR AUTUMN (1888): *Heaven's death-lights kindle, yellow spark by spark, Beneath the dreadful catafalque of the dark.*

cataglottism. See *cata-*. The humour of lovers.

cataplasm. A poultice, plaster—in the 17th century made with herbs and flour, or (1612) of bread crumbs, milk, and a little saffron. In the 19th century (1866), *the well known mustard plaster or cataplasm.* Shakespeare knew it too; in HAMLET (1602), Laertes puts a poison on his sword *So mortal that but dip a knife in it, Where it draws blood no cataplasm so rare, Collected from all simples that have virtue Under the moon, can save the thing from death That is but scratched withal.*

catastrophe. When *Falstaff,* in HENRY IV, PART TWO (1597), cries euphemistically to Mistress Quickly: *Away, you scullion! you rampallion! you fustilarian! I'll tickle your catastrophe,* the meaning of the last word centers in the second syllable: I'll give you a drubbing, and you'll deem it a disaster.

catchpenny. Designed to lure purchasers; also, an item or article of little value, concocted merely to sell. Thus Wesley (WORKS; 1785) said: *The late pretty tale of her being the Emperor's daughter is doubtless a mere catchpenny.* Other terms of the same significance are: (first, in the theatre) *claptrap,* a device to ensnare applause; *potboiler,* something whose sole function is to earn money to 'keep the pot aboiling.' Hence, a shoddy work.

cate. Usually in the plural. See *acate.*

catekumeling. A young *catechumen,* a convert being instructed before baptism. Thus *catechesis* (accent on the *kee*), oral instruction to a beginner; *catechism,* an elementary treatise, especially in the form of question and answer. Greek *kata,* thoroughly + *echein,* to sound, ring; *eche,* sound; English *echo.* In Shakespeare's HENRY IV, PART ONE (1596), Falstaff asks (and answers) a series of questions about honour, concluding: *Honour is a meere scutcheon, and so ends my catechisme.* Langland in THE VISION OF PIERS PLOWMAN (1377) has: *To baptise barnes that ben catekumelynges.*

catel. An old form of *cattle.*

cateran. A troop or band of fighting men, especially Scotch Highlanders. Irish *ceithern* (the *th* became silent, hence English *kern,* a peasant, a rustic, an Irish foot-soldier). Hence also, one of the band, a fighting man, a marauder. Used from the 14th century, renewed by Scott, who used it some 30 times. Lowell in MY STUDY WINDOWS (1870) speaks scornfully of a man with *the statecraft of an Ithacan cateran.*

catercap. The 'mortar board,' the four-cornered hat once worn by presbyters and now by academics. Also, the wearer thereof. *Cater,* four. Hence, *catercapt.* In THE PROTESTACYON OF MARTIN MARPRELAT (1589), in the face of imminent arrest, the author declares that, *notwithstanding* *the surprizing of the printer, he maketh it known unto the world that he feareth neither proud priest, Antichristian pope, tiranous prelate, nor godlesse catercap: but defieth all the race of them by these presents.*

cater-cousin. A close friend. In Tudor times, *cousin* was used by close friends, without blood relationship; in AS YOU LIKE IT Shakespeare has Rosalind and Celia say, *Sweet my coz.* Jonson suggests that *cater-cousin* meant *quarter-cousin,* "from the ridiculousness of calling cousin or relation to so remote a degree," but there is no ridicule intended, in the use of the word. It may be from *cater,* to care for, to feed, *cater-cousins* being those that have eaten together, as *companions* means those that have broken bread together. Shakespeare used the expression in THE MERCHANT OF VENICE (1596): *His maister and he (saving your worships reverence) are scarce catercosins;* and writers since have followed him.

caterpillar. See *complice.*

catha. See *queth.*

catharan. One that admits his superior purity; a puritan. Also *catharian, cathare, catharist, catharite.* Applied to various religious sects. While O.E. (Matthew Sutcliffe) in A BRIEFE REPLIE TO A CERTAINE . . . LIBEL (1600) said: *The catharistes do boast much of their merits,* Donne in a sermon of 1616 turned the other way and declared: *The catharists thought no creature of God pure.* The word is from Greek *katharizein,* to make clean, to purify, purge; *katharos,* clean, whence also *cathartic.* Hence also *catharize,* to purify (usually, by a ceremony); *catharm,* a purging, purgation.

catholicon. A universal remedy. Greek *catholicon,* universal, whence also *catholicity* and the *Catholic* faith. The word *catholicon,* in the sense of a universal or comprehensive treatise, was applied by Johannes de Balbis de Janua in 1286 to his noted Latin grammar and dictionary, whereafter the name catholicon has been applied to other dictionaries. The word has been used, figuratively, to mean faith, inspiration, wit—and as by Baker in a translation (1638) of Balzac's LETTERS: *A good wife is a catholicon, or universal remedy for all the evils that happen in life.* More literally Sir Thomas Browne in RELIGIO MEDICI (1642) declared: *Death is the cure of all diseases. There is no catholicon . . . I know but this.*

cat-o'-nine-tails. A whip with a short handle and nine lashes; in early use the lashes were knotted for the inflicting of greater pain. Until 1881 the use of the cat-o'-nine-tails was allowed in the British army and navy; Gilbert uses the shortened form, *the cat,* in a pun in H.M.S. PINAFORE (1878), when Deadeye Dick reassures the startled sailors by telling them *"It was the cat"* they heard.

catoptric. Relating to a mirror, or to reflection. Also, the science of reflection—for an instance of this use, see *alchemusy;* in this sense, now used in the plural, *catoptrics.* Also tricks of reflection; an apparatus or device for producing such effects. *With Dutch patience,* said Evelyn in his DIARY (1644), *he shew'd us his perpetual motions, catoptrics, magnetical experiments;* and Burton declared in THE ANATOMY OF MELANCHOLY (1621): *'Tis ordinarie to see strange uncouth figures by catoptricks.* Such tricks of vision still amuse at fairgrounds and play places.

catoptromancy. See *aeromancy.*

catso. A rogue; a fraudulent beggar. Also *catzo.* Also used as an exclamation From

Italian *cazzo,* the male generative organ. Ben Jonson in EVERY MAN OUT OF HIS HUMOUR (1602) speaks of *nimble-spirited catsos.* Both Urquhart (1653) and Motteux (1708) use the word in their versions of Rabelais, as might be expected (Motteux): *Catso! Let us drink!* The noun naming the activity of a catso, *catzery,* is used in Marlowe's THE JEW OF MALTA: *Who when he speaks, grunts like a hog, and looks Like one that is employed in catzerie.*

caudle. A warm, soothing drink. From Latin *calidum,* warm. Bailey (1751) says it is made of ale or wine with sugar and spices; earlier writers (Woodall, 1612) add the yolk of an egg; the O.E.D. (1933) says these are mixed with a thin gruel. All agree the drink was served mainly to women in childbed (and to their visitors). Pepys (1660) used to drink *a caudle* when he went to bed. Fuller in THE HOLY AND THE PROFANE STATE (1642) speaks of a ship that cast out *much sugar, and packs of spices, making a caudle of the sea round about.* From the idea of its comforting, *a caudle of hemp-seed* was used, ironically, to mean hanging (rope being made from hemp); thus Shakespeare in HENRY VI, PART TWO (1593): *Ye shall have a hempen caudle then.*

cautel. A crafty device or trick; trickery; a precaution. *Cautela,* in Roman law, was an exception made as a precaution, from *caut-,* the past stem of *cavere,* to take heed (*cp. caveat*); this also gives us English *caution,* but the two forms developed different meanings. *Cautelous* means wary, heedful (*cautious*), but more commonly deceitful, wily, as in Shakespeare's CORIOLANUS (1607): *Your son . . . caught With cautelous baits and practice.*

caveary. An early variant of *caviar.* Shakespeare used *caviarie*; Swift, *caveer.* Also *gaveare, kavia, cavery, cavialy, chaviale.* Enjoyed in England since the 16th century, always as a luxury. Thus Hamlet (in Shakespeare's play; 1601) said: *For the play, I remember, pleased not the million; 'twas caviarie to the general.* And E. Blount in his OBSERVATIONS (1620) remarked: *A pasty of venison makes him sweat, and then swear that the only delicacies be mushrooms, caveare, or snails.*

caveat. A warning. Latin *caveat,* let him beware; *cavere, cautum,* to beware, whence also *caution; cavus,* wary. *Cp. cautel.* The root *cav,* watch, ware, via *cavira, cura,* also gave us *cure, secure* and endless *curiosity.* It survives in the (Latin) warning *Caveat emptor,* let the buyer beware, which is a principle of common law. It was often used in titles, as in Harman's A CAVEAT OR WARENING FOR COMMON CURSETORS, VULGARELY CALLED VAGABONDES (1567). Budgell in THE SPECTATOR (1712; No. 365) said: *I design this paper as a caveat to the fair sex.* Perhaps it is the other sex that needs it.

cavel. See *javel.*

cavenard. A villain. Probably a corruption of, or error for, *caynard, q.v.* It occurs in HAVELOCK THE DANE (1300): *Hede cavenard! Wat dos thu here at this pathe?*

caxon. (1) An 18th century style of wig. James Cawthorn, in some verses of 1756, has: *Though that trim artist, barber Jackson, Spent a whole hour about your caxon.* The word is probably drawn from someone's name. (2) A chest of ore ready to be refined. From Old Spanish *caxon,* augmentative of *caxa,* case, chest. The French form gives us English *caisson*; the Italian, *cassoon* (18th century; in the 17th, *casson*). A *cassolette* was a small box or vessel, usually with a perforated cover, in which perfumes were burned or savorous essences allowed to spread their perfume. A larger box (in which, for instance, a broken leg in plaster might be set to rest) was—in the 16th and 17th centuries—a *cassole.*

caynard. A sluggard; a scoundrel. French *cagnard,* Italian *cagna,* bitch, feminine of *cane,* dog. Thus the word is tantamount to the current slang *bitch,* though its use seems to have been milder, as in the Prologue to Chaucer's THE WIFE OF BATH'S TALE (1386): *See, olde caynard, is this thine array?*

caytive. See *caitiff.*

ceaze. A variant form of *seize.* Rowlands in his satire LOOKE TO IT: FOR ILE STABBE YE (1604; *cp. Vulcan's brow*) attacked the glutton, that *hast a nose to smell out any feast, a brazen face to ceaze on every messe, That undertakest nothing with good will Unlesse it be thy puddinghouse to fill. Ile stabbe thee.*

cecils. A mixture of minced meat, onions, anchovies, crumbs of bread, chopped parsley, and seasoning; make them into balls, with an egg; sprinkle them with fine crumbs, and fry them of a yellow brown. An early 19th century savory sort of meatball.

cecity. Blindness. From Latin *caecus,* blind. A *cecograph,* developed in the 19th century, was a writing-instrument for the blind. A tendency to blindness, or partial blindness, is *cecutiency;* Sir Thomas Browne (1646) said that in moles there is *no cecity, yet more than a cecutiency.* Degrees of blindness are not exact; from *stone blind,* blind as a stone, completely blind, Shakespeare developed *gravel blind* and *sandblind. Sandblind,* however, is really *samblind, sam* (related to *semi-*), half + *blind. Cecity* may also be used figuratively, as by Disraeli in THE AMENITIES OF LITERATURE (1841): *the cecity of superstition.*

ceduous. Suitable for felling, as a straight tree or a battered prizefighter. Latin *caeduus; caedere,* to fell. Used in the 17th century. *Cp. caducous.*

ceint. See *seynt.*

celation. Concealment. From Latin *celare,* to conceal. In 19th century English law, especially concealment of pregnancy or birth.

celature. Embossing; an embossed figure. From Latin *caelare,* to emboss, engrave. Jeremy Taylor in THE GREAT EXEMPLAR OF SANCTITY (1649) says: *They admitted even in the utensils of the Church some celatures and engravings.*

celebrious. Crowded (of an assembly hall); hence, festive. From Latin *celebrem,* honored by an assembly. Hence, renowned, famous—in this sense also *celebrous.* From this source we have the well-known *celebration* and forms akin. A rare (humorous) form for 'most noted' (from the Latin superlative) is *celeberrimous.*

celestinette. An 18th century musical instrument. Walpole described it in a letter to Sir W. Hamilton, 19 June, 1774: *I heard a new instrument yesterday . . . It is a copulation of a harpsichord and a violin; one hand strikes the keys and the other draws the bow . . . The instrument is so small it stands on a table, and is called a celestinette.*

celeusma. A battle-cry or watchword; specifically, the call that gives the time to rowers. From Greek *keleuein,* to order. Often the rowers in large vessels propelled by oars would sing hymns and psalms by way of celeusma.

celostomy. Hollowness of sound; speaking with the mouth hollow. Accent on the second syllable. From Greek *koilos,* hollow + *stoma,* mouth. Used in the 16th and 17th centuries, when actors needed Hamlet's advice.

celsitude. High rank, eminence; dignity; exalted character; height. Also used as a title of respect: *His Celsitude* (Late Latin and in English, 17th century). From Latin *celsus,* lofty; seen also in *excel, excelsior.* In the sense of height the word may still be used humorously, as by Scott in REDGAUNTLET (1824): *Peter Peebles, in his usual plenitude of wig and celsitude of hat.* The form, *celsity,* with the same meaning, appears in 17th century dictionaries.

cenacle. See *cenation.*

cenation. Dining. From Latin *cenare,* to dine. Latin *cena* was the mid-day or afternoon meal, eaten in the *cenacle. Cenacle,* dining room, is used especially of the upper chamber where Christ and his disciples ate the Last Supper. *Cenation* and *cenatory* (as in *cenatory garments*) are 17th century words, used e.g. by Sir Thomas Browne (1676). *Cp. coenaculous.*

ceneromancy. See *aeromancy.*

cenobite. See *eremite.*

centure. See *seynt.*

cephalotomy. See *kephalotomy.*

cepivorous. Feeding on onions. Latin *cepa,* onion; hence also *cepous,* like an onion.

cerastes. A horned serpent. Greek *keras,* horn. Actually a poisonous viper of Africa and Asia, with a projecting scale over each eye; loosely used to suggest a horrid snake. Thus Cary in his translation (1814) of Dante's INFERNO: *Adders and cerastes crept Instead of hair, and their fierce temples bound.* For its use by Milton, see *ellops.*

ceratine. Sophistical and intricate (of an argument). Greek *keratinos,* horny, *keras,* horn. Given in 17th and 18th century dictionaries, taking its meaning from "the fallacy of the horns" (the horns of a dilemma), in Diogenes Laertius (3d century A.D.): *"If you have not cast a thing away, you have it: but you have not cast horns; therefore you have horns."* The ceratine perplexity is more commonly created by such questions as "Do you still beat your wife?"

ceration. Covering with wax; softening a substance that will not liquefy. A term in alchemy. Via French *ceration* from Latin *cerare,* to smear with wax, from *cera,* wax. Johnson in THE ALCHEMIST (1610): *Name the vexations and the martyrizations of metals in the work . . . Putrefaction, solution, ablution . . . calcination, ceration and fixation.* Also, from Greek *keros,* wax, comes *ceruse,* white lead, especially as a cosmetic; also a verb *ceruse,* to paint the face. Used in plays of Massinger and Jonson (SEJANUS, 1603): very common in the 17th and 18th centuries; Macaulay in his life of Samuel Johnson (1849) remarked that the old bumbleton's *eyesight was too weak to distinguish ceruse from natural bloom.*

ceraunite. Thunderstone. Greek *keraunos,* thunderbolt. A piece of meteoric iron, or an arrow-head of prehistoric times (formerly thought to be a thunderbolt). A *ceraunoscope* was a machine used in the Greek theatre to imitate thunder.

Cerberean. Related to Cerberus, the three-headed watchdog at the entrance to the infernal regions, in Greek and Roman mythology. According to Hesiod, Cerberus had fifty heads. Hence used of the fierceness of the beast, or the keenness of his guard, or the noise of his barking. Milton in PARADISE LOST (1669) has: *A cry of Hell Hounds never ceasing bark'd With wide Cerberean mouths*; Coleridge in BIOGRAPHIA LITTERARIA (1817) speaks of the *Cerberean whelps of feud and slander.* Orpheus quieted Cerberus with his lyre; Hercules fought him; but Aeneas stopped each mouth with a cake. Hence *a sop to Cerberus* is a gift to appease a fierce or angry person in authority (guardian, head-waiter, etc.).

cerebrosity. Wilfulness; a state of brainstorm. Used by Sidney (1586) and other euphuistic extravaganzists—as Anthony Wood, in his LIFE (1647): *To admit . . . a meer frog of Helicon to croak the cataracts of his plumbeous cerebrosity before your sagacious ingenuities.* The *plumbeous cerebrosities* comes right out of Sidney. A *cerebrose* person is 'mad-brained.'

ceromancy. See *aeromancy.*

cerule. An early form of *cerulean.* Also *ceruleal, ceruleous.* In early use (Spenser and others) as in Latin *caeruleus,* the word meant the dark blue of the sky or the dark green of the sea, and was occasionally applied to leaves and fields. After the 17th century it was tinted only of the sky. Byron, in DON JUAN (1821), uses the word humorously, to mean a blue-stocking: *O ye who make the fortunes of all books! Benign ceruleans of the second sex!*

ceruse. See *ceration.*

cervelat. (1) A short thick sausage, "eaten cold in slices," says Bailey (1751). He does not give the recipe, but on his recommendation you may serve a lot. (2) From the shape, a short reed musical instrument. Also *cervalet.*

cervicide. See *stillicide.* Latin *cervus,* stag. If it was the King's deer, the offence —as Robin Hood knew—was regarded gravely.

cessant. See *couth. Cessant* was used in the 17th and 18th centuries, meaning intermittently, at intervals; a scientific observer of 1746 recorded: *I personally knew a Gentleman . . . who cessantly winked with one eye.*

cestus. (1) A belt; especially a marriage girdle, unloosed by the bridegroom on the wedding night. From Greek *kestos,* stitched. In particular, the love-belt of Aphrodite, which made her irresistible. Yet Addison in THE SPECTATOR (1712) seems to prefer *Venus without any ornament but her own beauties, not so much as her own cestus.* Also used figuratively; there is a pathetic tone, today, in Carlyle's words (in FREDERICK THE GREAT, 1865): *The brightest jewel in the cestus of Polish liberty is this right of confederating.* (2) An ancient boxer's glove: a band made of thongs of bull-hide, with strips of iron and lead. Latin *caestus,* perhaps from *caedere,* to strike, more probably the same word as (1), *cestus,* girdle, band. In our degenerate times the *cestus* has dwindled to the brass knuckles, and it is no longer the boxer that wears them.

chad. I had. Old English *Ich,* I + *had.* Many verbs, especially the auxiliaries, through the 17th century in dialects, were combined with *ch.* Thus *cham,* I am; *chave,* I have; *chard,* I heard; *chill,* I will; *chold, chud,* I would; etc. Many in Sir Thomas More (1510-1540); RALPH ROYSTER DOYSTER (1553); GAMMER GURTON'S NEEDLE (1575), and later plays including

Shakespeare's KING LEAR (1605): *Chill not let go zir . . . and 'chud a bin zwaggerd out of my life.*

chaetophorous. Bristle-bearing; hence (pedantically humorous), in need of a shave. Pronounced *kye;* accent on the *toff.* Greek *chaite,* hair + *phoros,* bearing.

chafe. To warm, to heat. Hence, to inflame the feelings, to excite. Used in both senses since the 14th century. The current sense, to rub (so as to warm) developed in the mid 15th century. Also *chauffe, chaufe, chaff,* and more; via Old French from Latin *calefacere; calere,* to be warm (whence the *calories*) + *facere,* to make. (In many English words—*gauge; Ralph; safe—au* became long *a.*) A *chafer* (*chaver, chaufer*) from the 14th century, was a *chafing-dish,* a portable stove or warming-pan; the 18th and 19th centuries revived the forms *chauffer, chauffet.* Spenser in THE FAËRIE QUEENE (MUTABILITY; 1596) pictures Spring wearing a garland on his head, *from which as he had chauffed been The sweat did drop.*

chaffron. See *chamfrain.*

chaldese. To trick; to play a mean turn. Perhaps from *Chaldees,* the idea being that astrologers are cheats. Butler in HUDIBRAS (1664): *He stole your cloak and picked your pocket, Chews'd and caldes'd you like a blockhead.* For *chews'd,* see *chouse.*

chalon. A blanket or other bed-cover. Perhaps from *Chalons-sur-Marne,* a town in France where the material was made. Chaucer in THE REEVE'S TALE (1386) pictures *a bed With schetys and with chalouns fair i-spred.* The manufacturer of *chalons* was a *chaloner,* quite busy in the 14th and 15th centuries.

chamade. A beat of drums or peal of trumpet, calling to a parley. Portuguese *chamada, chamar,* from Latin *clamare,* to call—whence also the current *clamor* and *exclamatory* impulse of our time.

chamber (a verb). (1) To confine, enclose. Shakespeare in KING RICHARD II (1593): *The best blood chamber'd in his bosom.* (2) To restrain. (3) To provide with a *chamber,* as *the chambered nautilus.* (4) To lodge in a *chamber,* or as though in one. Heywood in THE GOLDEN AGE (1611): *You shall no more . . . chamber underneath the spreading oaks.* (5) To indulge in lewdness, to seek a *chamber* for wanton ends. Scott in WOODSTOCK (1826): *What—chambering and wantoning in our very presence!*

chamberdekin. A poor (impoverished) scholar from Ireland, who attended Oxford, especially in the 15th century, but did not belong to any college. Often he acted as a servant for noblemen at the university; hence *chamber-deacon.* Bailey, in 1751, defines *chamber-dekins* as *Irish beggars, in the habit of poor scholars of Oxford, who often committed robberies etc. and were banished the kingdom by Henry V.* The modern counterpart sells magazines from door to door "to pay his way through college."

chamberer. (1) A lady's maid; a *chambermaid.* (2) A concubine. In earlier use, these two forms usually had the feminine final *e;* thus *chamberere, chambriere, chambryere.* (3) A *chamberlain;* a valet. (4) A frequenter of ladies' chambers; a gallant; a wanton. Shakespeare in OTHELLO (1604) says: *I . . . have not those soft parts of conversation That chamberers have.*

chamfrain. The frontlet of an armed horse, for a knight in feudal times. Also *chamfron, chaufrayne;* (15th and 16th centuries) *cheveronne, chieffront; chafron,* *chaffron, shaffron, shaferne; shamfron, shawfron,* and more. Scott revived the word in IVANHOE (1820; *chamfron*). The frontlet was often ornamented with engraved designs; ST. JAMES'S GAZETTE of 20 June, 1884 mentioned *a chamfrein chased with a combat of two horsemen.*

champerty. (1) Division of lordship; partnership in power. From French *champart,* originally a division of the field, or a part of the produce going to the overlord, Latin *campi pars,* part of the field. Chaucer in THE KNIGHT'S TALE (1386) is emphatic: *Wisdom ne richesse, Beautee ne sleighte, strength, hardynesse, Ne may with Venus holde champartie.* Lydgate, misinterpreting this passage, used the word as though it meant rivalry; a few others, especially in the 16th century, followed him. (2) a combination or partnership for an evil purpose; especially, in law, a conspiracy to help a litigant in return for a share of the disputed property. Something of this sort, however, is common practice in accident suits.

champery. Contending in the lists. Old French *champier,* to fight in a field; whence also *champion* etc.

champestrial. A variant of *campestrial, campestral,* pertaining to the fields. Also *champestre.* The *ch* forms are from the French; *fête champêtre,* a rural festival or party. Many English words, from *camp* to *champignon,* come ultimately from Latin *campus,* field.

chancemedley. Inadvertency; largely accidental. Used in law, from the 15th century, especially in the phrase *manslaughter by chance-medley,* homicide by misadventure. The word is sometimes used to mean pure chance, but more precisely means a mixture of intention and chance. Thus Brimley in an essay of 1855 inquires: *Why does . . . Hamlet after murdering Polonius die by chancemedley?*

chandler. See *chandry.*

chandry. A short form (especially used in the 17th century) of *chandlery,* a place where *candles* are kept; candles and other provisions sold by a retail dealer. By the 19th century, *chandler,* as a retail dealer, was somewhat contemptuous; Dickens in SKETCHES BY BOZ (1836) says: *The neighbors stigmatized him as a chandler.* Falstaff says to Bardolph, in Shakespeare's HENRY IV, PART ONE (1596): *Thou hast saved me a thousand marks in links and torches, walking with thee in the night betwixt tavern and tavern; but the sack that thou hast drunk me would have bought me lights as good cheap at the dearest chandler's in Europe. Chandler* also meant the officer who supervised the candles in a household; also, a support for candles, a *chandelier.*

changeling. (1) A fickle person; a waverer; a turncoat. (2) A person or thing secretly substituted for another. Especially, of a child—particularly, of an ugly or stupid child—supposedly left in infancy, by the fairies, in exchange for the real (and of course beautiful and bright) child stolen. Hence, a half-wit (as in Pepys' DIARY, 28 December, 1667). Shakespeare in A MIDSUMMER NIGHT'S DREAM (1590) has the King of the Fairies say: *I do but beg a little changeling boy, to be my henchman.* [Note that Oberon refers to the child taken; the word usually refers to the child left amongst us humans.]

chantepleure. Title of a 13th century French poem, to those that sing (*chanter*) in this world but will weep (*pleurer*) in the next. By extension, a mixture or alternation of joy and sorrow. Chaucer in

ANELIDA AND ARCITE (1374) has: *I fare as doth the song of Chantepleure, for now I pleyne and now I play.*

chaogenous. Born out of chaos. Like the cosmos, and the *chaogenous* hero-gods of Hesiod.

chaomancy. See *aeromancy.*

chapbook. A pamphlet containing tales, ballads, or other examples of the popular literature of the 15th to 18th centuries. The name was not contemporary, but created (in the 19th century) by collectors, from *chapman* (*q.v.*) + book.

chape. A metal plating, used as a cover or ornament. Especially, the extra covering on the point of a scabbard; by extension, the tip of a fox's tail, which resembles this—also by extension, the sheath or scabbard itself. Also *chaip, schape, cheap.* Hence as a verb, *to chape,* to furnish with a chape; Chaucer in the Prologue to THE CANTERBURY TALES (1386) pictures five well-to-do merchants (*An haberdassher and a carpenter, A webbe, a dyere, and a tapicer*), each fit to be an alderman: *hir* [their] *knyves were chaped noght with bras But al with silver wroght ful clene and weel.* There was also a *chape* (14th to 16th century) short for *achape* (Old French *achaper, eschaper*), escape. In Shakespeare's ALL'S WELL THAT ENDS WELL (1601) a French lord speaks of the prisoner *Monsieur Parolles, the gallant militarist* [military expert]—*that was his own phrase—that had the whole theoricke of warre in the knot of his scarfe, and the practise in the chape of his dagger.*

chapman. A dealer. From Old English *ceap,* barter + *man.* Later (16th century on) an itinerant dealer, a peddler; more rarely, a broker, or a customer. Hence also *chapmanable,* marketable; *chapmanry*; *chapmanship,* in which "the children of the east" excelled. *Chap-money* (*chapmanry* is also used in this sense), a small sum returned to the purchaser when payment is made, an old way of allowing a discount. Thomas Freeman in RUBBE, AND A GREAT CAST (1614; *cp. sute*) puns in his praise of George Chapman, who *commeth near'st the ancient commicke vaine, Thou hast beguilde us all of that sweet grace: and were Thalia to be sold and bought, no chapman but thyselfe were to be sought.* From George to John, still dealing in good plays.

char. See *chare.* In addition to its current senses, *char* was an early form of both *chair* and *car*; it meant a cart; by extension, a cart-load. Also, a *chariot,* as in Hobbes' Homer (1677): *For all his flaming horses and his charre.*

charactery. Writing; expressing thought by symbols. Shakespeare in THE MERRY WIVES OF WINDSOR (1598) says that *Fairies use flowers for their characterie.*

charbon. *A charbon* (French *charbon,* charcoal, pustule) is used in English for the disease anthrax (19th century). In Shakespeare's ALL'S WELL THAT ENDS WELL (1603), however, the Clown refers to *young Charbon the puritan and old Poysam the papist*; the names are labels and probably from the French *chair bon,* good flesh, and *poisson,* fish, alluding to the diet of the two faiths on 'fast' days.

chare. (1) The return of a time, day, or season; hence, time, occasion. Also *char, cherre, cyrr, chewre, chore.* Hence, a turning back; *againchar, gainchar,* repentance. *On char,* on the turn, in the act of shutting; this survives in the form *ajar*: "When is a door not a door?" By extension, a turn or stroke of work; this sense survives in English *charwoman* and American *chore(s).* Also *charfolk, chairfolk* (17th century), temporary servants. Hence (from the sense of turning) a name for a narrow lane or wynd, in parts of England, since the 13th century. *chare* is also a verb, indicating the actions named above. (2) An old form of *chary,* careful. (3) In names of dishes from France, flesh, meat (French *chair,* Latin *carnem,* flesh). Also the flesh (pulp) of certain fruit, as in: *chardecoynes, chardeqweyns, chardequynce* (15th and 16th centuries), a quince preserve; *chare de wardon,* a preserve of Warden pears; a COOKERY BOOK of 1425 states: *Charwardon. Take pere Wardonys, seethe hem in wyne . . .* Good for any pere!

charet. An earlier form of *chariot,* until the mid-17th century. Used widely in the King James BIBLE (1611). In France a *charette* was two-wheeled; a *chariot,* four-wheeled. Hence *chareter,* early for *charioteer.* Spenser in THE FAËRIE QUEENE (1596) has *She bad her charett to be brought.*

charientism. A species of irony, couching a disagreeable sense in pleasant terms. Later called *euphemism,* like saying "He stretches the truth" instead of "He lies."

chark. See *jar.*

charlet. A sort of omelet. The recipe is in THE FORME OF CURY (1390): *Take pork, and seeth it wel. Hewe it smale. Cast it in a panne. Breke ayrenn* [eggs], *and do therto, and swyng it wel togyder. Put therto cowe mylke and safroun, and boile it togyder. Salt it, and messe it forth.*

charneco. A kind of wine, drunk in the 16th and 17th centuries. Also *charnico, charnaco.* Shakespeare in HENRY VI, PART TWO (1593) proffers it: *Here's a cuppe of charneco,* but we have lost its savour. It may be named from a village near Lisbon. The term degenerated, so that in 1775 Ash defined it: *charneco (a cant word), any kind of strong liquor which is like to bring drunken fellows to the stocks.*

chasmophile. A lover of crannies and crevices; a haunter of holes. Hence *chasmophilous.* In botany, *a chasmophyte* is such a plant as Tennyson apostrophized: *Flower in the crannied wall, I pluck you out of the crannies, I hold you here, root and all, in my hand, Little flower—but if I could understand What you are, root and all, and all in all, I should know what God and man is.*

chassis. An early form (also *shashes, shasses*) of *sash,* a window-frame; especially one fitted with paper or linen (before the widespread use of glass). Thus Urquhart in his translation (1693) of Rabelais speaks of *chassis or paper-windows.*

chatelaine. See *castellan.*

chaterestre. A female chatterer. Feminine of *chaterere,* which was the early form of *chatterer.* THE OWL AND THE NIGHTINGALE (13th century) exclaims: *Site nu stille, chaterestre!* A less pleasant word than *chatmate, q.v.*

chatmate. A companion in conversation. Nashe in LENTEN STUFFE (1599), speaking of the fair Hero, mentions *the toothlesse trotte her nurse, who was her onely chatmate and chambermaide.*

chaud-mellé. A sudden flare of fighting, out of the heat of roused passion; hence, a killing without premeditation. French; literally, hot broil; *melee.* Also *chaud-mella* (15th and 16th centuries); by some 17th century writers altered to chance-medley, *q.v.*; thus Blackstone in his COMMENTARIES (1769): *Chance-medley, or (as* *some rather chuse to write it) chaud-medley.*

chauffe. See *chafe.*

chaundrye. A variant of *chandlery,* the place where candles were kept. In Tudor times, this was an important room; Cardinal Wolsey had three servants in his chaundrye. As Cavendish tells, in THE LYFFE AND DEATHE OF CARDYNALL WOOLSEY (1557), in addition to a score of men in his hall kytchen: *In his privy kytchen he had a master cooke who went dayly in dammaske, satten, or velvett with a chayne of gold abought his nekke; and ii gromes, with vi laborers and children to serve in that place. In the larder there a yoman and a grome; in the schaldyng house a yoman and ii gromes. In the scollery there ii persons. In the buttery ii yomen and ii gromes, with ii other pages. In the pantrie ii yomen; ii gromes and ii pages, and in the ewrie lykewyse; in the seller iii yomen, ii gromes and ii pages, besides a gentilman for the monthe. In the chaundrye iii persons. In the wafery ii.* For food and drink alone, 67 servants. The *ewrie* (*ewery, ewry, yewrie*) was the room where table linen, towels, and water ewers (pitchers with a wide spout, to bring water for washing the hands) were kept. The *wafery* was the kitchen for biscuits (flat cakes). It is little wonder that one of the charges in the arrest of Cardinal Wolsey for high treason (1530) was that he sought to be grander than the king.

chawdron. A sauce, made with chopped entrails and spices; hence, entrails, especially as used for food. Also *chawdon, chalderne, chaldron, chawdre,* akin to *chowder*; ultimately (by long popular mouthing) from Latin *calidus,* hot. It is interesting to note that, in the early chowder (from Breton fishermen to Newfoundland to New England) there was often a goodly dash of cider or champagne. *Soups,* said THE LITERARY WORLD (Boston, U.S.A.; 15 November 1884), *are divisible into four groups: viz. clear, thick, purées or bisques, and chowders.*

cheap. As a noun: Bargaining; buying and selling. So used from the 8th century. Hence, a market. This sense is preserved in names, such as *Cheapside, Eastcheap.* Hence also, price, value. *Good cheap,* a bargain; Chaucer in the Prologue to THE WIFE OF BATH'S TALE (1386) says *To great cheap is holden at litel price. Dear cheap,* high prices, scarcity. *Niggard cheap,* close economy, niggardliness. *(At) good cheap,* on advantageous terms; this phrase, shortened, gave us the still known adjective *cheap,* which is not often appropriate today. Other forms included: *cheapable* (16th century), valuable. To *cheapen,* to bargain for; a *cheapener, cheaper,* a bidder. *cheaping,* marketing, buying and selling; *cheapild,* a marketwoman. Sir George Wheler, in A JOURNEY INTO GREECE (1682) wrote: *Here is very good bread and wine, and good cheap I believe.*

cheer. Face; countenance; aspect, mien; hence, disposition, mood (as shown in the face). Also *chere, chire, cheyr, cheare, chaire,* and the like. *To make a cheer,* to put on a (pleased, angry, etc.) expression. *What cheer? (with you? make you?),* How are you? Used from the 13th century to the 17th, lingering in poetry. Sackville, in A MIRROR FOR MAGISTRATES (1563): *With ruful chere, and vapored eyes upcast.* Shakespeare, in A MIDSUMMER NIGHT'S DREAM (1590): *All fancy sicke she is, and pale of cheere.* Blake, in SONGS OF INNOCENCE (1783): *So I piped, with merry cheer.*

cheese. Used in several combinations now lapsed: *cheeseparing,* a thing of little value; the concern of a niggard. Shakespeare in HENRY IV, PART TWO (1597) says: *I doe remember him at Clements Inne, like a man made after supper, of a cheese-paring. cheese and cheese,* two ladies kissing, or riding on one horse. *To make cheeses* (of school-girls), to spin around and suddenly sink, so that petticoats and skirt spread all around, inflated—vaguely resembling a cheese; hence, a deep curtsey. Used by Thackeray in THE VIRGINIANS, and throughout the 19th century. Other combinations whet the appetite.

chemise. See *camis.*

cherisaunce. Comfort, support. French *cherir,* to cherish; *chère,* cheer. So Toone's GLOSSARY (1834). Chaucer's ROMAUNT OF THE ROSE (1370) has: *For I ne know no cherisaunce That fell into my remembrance.* It is likely that Bailey's *cherisaunie* (*q.v.*) is a misprint for *cherisaunce.* But *cherisaunce* itself is a misprint, listed as a 'spurious word' in O.E.D. See *chevisance.*

cherisaunie. A pleasant word in dictionaries, which Bailey (1751) lists as 'old,' and defines as 'comfort.' With glass and book on a wintry night, before a fireside I seek my cherisaunie. But see *cherisaunce.*

cherry-pit. A hole into which children try to throw cherry-stones; the game of throwing them. Shakespeare in TWELFTH NIGHT (1601) says *'Tis not for gravity to play at cherry-pit with Satan*; Randolph in THE JEALOUS LOVERS (1632) has: *Your cheeks were sunk So low and hollow they might serve the boys For cherripits.*

chertee. Fondness, affection; dearness (in price). Latin *caritatem,* from *carus,* dear. An early form of *charity,* which first meant love. Spelled *chiertee, cherte, chierte* by Chaucer. Sometimes used in the sense of cheerfulness, as though related to *cheer. Chertes,* says Bailey (1751, attributing the use to Chaucer), are merry people. [In geology there is a kind of quartz called *chert,* whence also *cherty,* like hornstone, *chert.*] A frequent 14th and 15th century expression was *to have* (or hold) *someone in chertee.*

chese. A variant form of choose. Wisely in THE PARLEMENT OF THE THREE AGES (1350; in the old 4-beat alliterative verse): *And chese me to the chesse that chefe is of gamnes: And this es life for to lede while I shalle lyfe here.*

chessner. A player at chess. Middleton uses the term in his play, A GAME AT CHESS (1624; for which he was censured because it satirized court policy in regard to the Spanish marriage): *Yonder's my game, which, like a politic chessner, I must not seeme to see.* My good friend Motty is an ardent chessner, keeping me on the qui vive.

chester. A city or walled town; originally, the site of a Roman camp. Latin *castra,* camp. The Latin word survives in English in place names, taking three forms, as in *Lancaster, Worcester, Westchester.* Used from the 9th to the 13th century, thereafter historically. *Cp. castametation.*

chete. See *pedlers French.*

chevachance. Chivalry; the spirit of the true gentleman. Used in the 16th century. See *chevisance.*

chevachee. See *chyvachie.* Old French *chebauchie. cavalcata,* riding; Medieval Latin *caballicare, caballicatum,* to ride; *caballus,* horse.

chevaline. Pertaining to the horse; especially, of its flesh as food. The LONDON

TIMES of 5 October, 1864, speaks of *cold horse pie, and other chevaline delicacies,* not appreciated in the western hemisphere.

chevance. Fortune; acquired wealth. Hence, achievement in other fields. *To make chevance* is to raise money, borrow. Also *chievance, chevaunce*; from Old French *chever,* to finish, to accomplish, *chef* (*chev-*), head. Hence also *achieve.* But see *chevisance.*

cheverel. Kid leather. Old French *chevrelle,* diminutive of *chèvre,* she-goat; Latin *capra,* whence *caper, capricious, cabriolet*; *cp. capripede.* Also *cheveril.* Kid leather was noted for its pliancy and capability of stretching, whence various figurative uses. Thus Shakespeare, in ROMEO AND JULIET (1592): *Here's a wit of cheverell, that stretches from an inch to an ell broad*; in TWELFTH NIGHT (1601): *A sentence is but a chev'rill glove to a good witte, how quickly the wrong side may be turn'd outward*; in HENRY VIII (1613): *the capacity of your soft chiverell conscience. Cheverel conscience* was a frequent phrase —still too widely applicable.

chevese. Mistress, concubine. A common Teuton term. *Chevese-born* was euphemistic for bastard.

chevetaine. Early form of chieftain, until the mid-17th century.

cheville. Originally a peg, a plug; then, a meaningless or unnecessary word used to complete a verse or round off a sentence.

chevisance. Bringing to a head; comfort; help; hence an expedient, a device; shiftiness; ability to shift; provision, supply; booty. *To make a chevisaunce* was to arrange a loan; hence (in a bad sense), a shift to get money; *to make chevisaunce of* was to convert to one's profit (with bad implications). From Old French *chevir, chevissant,* to finish, succeed with, etc.; see *chevance.* The word *chevisance* was widely used (14th and 15th centuries) in these many senses. Spenser, in the Gloss to the SHEPHERD'S CALENDAR (1579) misunderstood the word, confusing it with *chevance* and *chivalry,* as in THE FAËRIE QUEENE (1590): *Shameful thing It were t' abandon noble chevisaunce For show of peril, without venturing.* This error was repeated, as late as 1849 by Bulwer-Lytton in KING ARTHUR: *Frank were those times of trustful chevisaunce,* and 1880 by Shorthouse in JOHN INGLESANT: *When the northern gods . . . rode on their chevisance, they went down into the deep valleys singing magic songs.* More prosaically, a *chevisancer* was (a rare word for) a money-lender, usurer. Also *chevisance,* a flower, possibly the wallflower (not the lorn maiden); *cp. pawnce.*

chevise. The verb form of *chevisance, q.v.,* meaning to accomplish; to provide for, help; to raise money, etc.

chibol. See *ramolade.*

chichevache. There was an Old French bogy, to scare children into good behavior, an imaginary monster called *chinceface,* thin-face, ugly-face. This was changed, in English, to *chichevache,* ugly cow, and used of a monster that fed only on patient wives, hence was always starving. Chaucer, in THE CLERK'S TALE (1386) ironically warns women to avoid humility, *lest chichevache you swallow in her entrail.* Lydgate in 1430 wrote a poem *Chichevache and Bycorne. Cp. palmer.* This *bycorne,* as the poem tells, is a fabulous monster that fed on patient husbands, hence was always fat. The name *bicorn,* which means two-horned, may be an allusion to the traditional horns of the cuckold. In the 15th century, the term *bicorne* was applied to a two-pronged pitchfork.

chickweed. A small plant, earlier called *chickenweed.* It was formerly used for feeding caged birds (linnets; goldfinches). The Elizabethans enjoyed it in salads. THE SHEPHERDS KALENDER (1503) advised: *Take chickweed, clythers, ale, and oatmeal, and make pottage there with.*

chideress. A female scold or brawler. Also *chidester.* Manuscripts of Chaucer's THE MERCHANT'S TALE (1386) spell this *chidestere, chidystere, chydester*: *A chidester and waster of thy good.*

childwit. "A power to take a fine of a bondwoman who has been gotten with child without her owner's consent": Bailey, 1751. Paid to the woman's lord, by English law, 10th to 16th century. Also *childwite*; Old English *wite,* penalty, satisfaction.

chiliad. (Pronounce the *ch* as *k.*) A collection or group of 1,000 things; the millennium. From Greek *chiliados,* from *chilioi,* thousand. In the 17th and 18th centuries, tables of logarithms were called *chiliads.* A *chiliast* is one that believes Christ will reign on earth, in person, for a thousand years.

chilindre. A cylindrical, portable sundial, carried before there were watches. Greek *kylindros,* cylinder; in Medieval Latin *chilindrus* and in Italian *cilindro* meant this kind of dial. Chaucer in THE SHIPMANNES TALE (1386) says: *And let us dine as soon as that ye may for by my chilyndre it is pryme of day.* Also *chylendre, chilandre, chilyndre, chylawndur.* They could not agree on the spelling, but it gave them the time.

chilonian. Succinct. In 17th and 18th century dictionaries; also *chilonic.* From *Chilon,* one of the seven wise men of ancient Greece, whose utterances were brief and to the point. Not so abrupt as *laconic, q.v.*

chimer. See *cymar.*

chiminage. A toll paid for passage through a forest. Usually collected in behalf of the lord who had had the way cleared, sometimes also by the local Robin Hood. *Chimin* was a 17th century legal term for road; Law Latin *chiminus,* French *chemin*; *camino real* is Spanish for royal way, highway—and the title of an American play (1953) by Tennessee Williams. Latin *caminus,* however, means furnace; English *chimney.*

chinch. Niggardly. Originally *chiche,* a Middle English word meaning parsimonious; thin; see *chichevache.* Hence also *chincherd,* niggard; *chinchery, chincery* (in Chaucer *chyncherie*), miserliness. (In the United States, *chinch* is still a name for the bed-bug.)

chine. The spine, or part of the back along the vertebral column. French *échine*; Latin *spina. To bow the chine* (often *back and chine*), to pay homage. By extension, of meat: the cut left of a hog when the sides are cut for bacon; a saddle of mutton; ribs or sirloin of beef. By transference (19th century) a crest or ridge of land. Kingsley, in TWO YEARS AGO (1857): *Crawling on hands and knees along the sharp chines of the rocks.* Cooper in THE PIONEERS (1823) served *a prodigious chine of roasted bear's meat.*

chipochia. See *capocchia.*

chirocracy. Government with a strong hand; by physical force. Greek *cheir,* hand + *kratia,* rule; accent on the *rock.* Hence also: *chirocosmetics,* the art of adorning the hands. *chiroponal* (Greek *ponos,* toil), relating to or involving manual labor. *chironomy,* the art of gesticulation. *chiromachy,* a fist-fight; a hand-to-hand battle. *chirosopher,* one learned as to the hand. *chirosophist,* one that practices sleight of hand; one that reads palms, a *chiromancer,* a *chiroscopist. chiroscopy,* palmistry. *chirotony* (accent on the *rot*), voting by show of hands; also *chirotonia;* to *chirotonize,* to vote by show of hands.

chiromancy. See *aeromancy.*

chirurgeon. An early form of *surgeon.* Also *chirurge* (in the 16th century). Ultimately from Greek *cheiro,* hand + *ergos,* working. Hence also *chirurgeonly, chirurgery, chirurgical, chirurgy. Cp. chyurgerie.*

chis. Fastidious, dainty in eating; choice, exquisite. From the 7th through the 15th century. Also *chise, chys, chyse.*

chisan. An inviting early dish; also *chysanne.* One recipe runs: *Take hole roches and enchys, or plays* [or other fish] *but choppe hom on peces, and frie hom in oyle; and take crustes of bredde, and draw hom with wyn and vynegur, and bray fygges, and draw hom therewith; and mynce onyons, and frie hom, and do therto, and blaunched almondes fried, and raisinges of corances* [raisin'd, i.e., dried, currants], *and powder of clowes and of ginger and of canelle, and let hit boile, and then do thi fissh in a faire vesselle, and poure thi sewe above, and serve it forthe colde.*

chitarrone. A 17th century musical instrument, used for basso continuo. Like the *cithern* or *cittern, gittern, zither,* it was developed from the Greek *cithara, q.v.,* which was triangular, with from seven to eleven strings. There is one in the New York Metropolitan Museum of Art collection.

chlamys. A short mantle worn by men in ancient Greece. Used historically and poetically (also, in botany, for the floral envelope).

chopin. A liquid measure. From the French *chopine,* half a *chope.* It seems to have varied; the French measure was about an English pint. In Scotland, about a half-pint, which was almost a quart by English wine measure. Also *choppin, choppyne, schopin*—but see *chopine.* The word was used from the 13th into the 19th century; Smollett in HUMPHREY CLINKER (1771) mentions a *call for a chopine of two-penny.* Hence, as a verb, to tipple; Urquhart in his translation (1653) of Rabelais speaks of *chopining and plying the pot.*

chopine. A shoe raised above ground by a cork sole. Apparently from Spanish *chapa,* plate of metal, then a thin cork sole. English writers in the late 16th and 17th century associated the word with Italy, especially Venice, spelling it *cioppino,* but it is not in the Italian dictionaries. The soles, apparently, were made thicker and thicker; we hear in 1577 of *choppines a foot hygh from the ground.* Jonson in CYNTHIA'S REVELS (1599) says: *I do wish myself one of my mistresses choppini.* In Shakespeare's HAMLET (1602) we hear: *Your Ladyship is nearer heaven than when I saw you last, by the altitude of a choppine.* Also *chopin, chapiney, chipeener, cheopine,* etc. They were little worn in England, except onstage, but the 19th century historical novelists (Scott, THE FORTUNES OF NIGEL, 1822; Reade, THE CLOISTER AND THE HEARTH, 1861) wrote as though the chopine were a normal part of a 17th century English costume.

chouse. A cheat, a trick; a swindler; also, a gull, a cheat's victim. Johnson (1755) defines chouse as "a man fit to be cheated." Originally *choush, chiaus,* a Turkish messenger. There is a 1609 story of an agent from Turkey who "chiaused" the Turkish merchants of £4,000. Jonson plays on the two senses in THE ALCHEMIST (1610): *D. What do you think of me, that I am a chiause? F. What's that? D. The Turk was here—As one would say, Do you think I am a Turk? . . . This is the gentleman, and he is no chiause.* Also *chowse, chews* (see *chaldese*). Also as a verb, to dupe, to defraud; a Law Report of 1886 queries: *Is it to be said that they are to be choused of their remedy?*

chout. The sum of one-fourth of the revenue of a province in India, exacted by neighboring Mahrattas in payment for immunity from plunder. Also, payment to the judge of one-fourth the value of property in litigation. Abolished by the 19th century.

chowder. See *chawdron.*

chowse. See *chouse.*

chrematist. A student of the science of wealth; a political economist. *Chrematistics* was suggested by Gladstone (1858) as a better name than 'political economy.' Greek *chrematizein* meant to consult (or to respond as) an oracle; thence (from the main purpose of consulting one), to make money; *chrema, chremat-,* thing required; money. From the first meaning came the (rare) English word *chrematistical,* oracular.

chreotechnics. The applied or useful arts (commerce, manufacture, agriculture). Greek *chreia,* use + *techne,* an art.

chrestomathy. A collection of choice passages, especially as used to learn a language. Greek *chrestos,* useful + *matheia,* learning, as also in *mathematics. Chrestomathics* is a rare word for the field of useful learning. *Chrestomathy* (accent on the *tom*) has been largely replaced by *anthology* (Greek *anthos,* flower + *legein,* gather).

chrisom. (1) Oil and balm, for sacramental use; hence, any unguent. In these senses, it was a popular pronunciation and spelling of *chrism* (as folk say *prisum* for *prism,* etc.); Greek *chrisma,* anointing, whence also to *christen* and the *Christ.* In Romanic, *chrisma* became *cresma,* French *crême,* English *cream.* (2) A head cloth, to keep the *chrism* from being rubbed off before the anointed new-born is baptized. If the child died within a month of baptism, the *chrism* was used as the shroud; if it lived, the cloth or its value in money was given to the church at the mother's purification ceremony. (Because of the high rate of infant mortality in China, the celebration of a son's birth is held after a month, at the first full moon.) (3) Also *chrysom,* a child dying before baptism. *chrisom child, christom child,* an infant still in its *chrisom;* hence, an innocent babe. The Hostess in Shakespeare's HENRY V (1599) says, in her picture of Falstaff's dying: *A' made a finer end and went away an it had been any christom child.* (4) Hence, in general, an infant, an innocent; later, especially in dialects, a fool.

chroma. Bailey (1751) gives three meanings for this word (from Greek *chroma,* color); it is not in the O.E.D. proper, but appears in the Supplement, as meaning "purity or intensity as a colour quality." Bailey: (1) "color, gracefulness"; (2) "in music, the graceful way of singing, with quavers and trilloes"; (3) "in rhetoric, a color [figure], set-off, or fair pretence."

chromatocracy. A ruling class of a particular color; government by a group of a particular color.

chronogram. Writing, certain letters of which form a date. THE ATHENAEUM (No. 2868) related: "Thus, in 1666, when a day of national humiliation was appointed in the expectation of an engagement between the English and Dutch navies, a pamphlet issued in reference to the fast day, instead of bearing the imprint of the year after the usual fashion, had this seasonable sentence at the bottom of the title-page: LorD haVe MerCIe Vpon Vs. It will be seen that the total sum of the figures represented by the numeral letters (printed in capitals) gives the requisite date 1666." Hence *chronogrammatic, chronogrammic, chronogrammatical; chronogrammatist.* A single line of verse that contains a chronogram is a *chronostichon* (accent on the *nos*).

chryselephantine. Of gold and ivory. Greek *chrysos,* gold + *elephantinos,* of ivory; *elephas, elephant-,* elephant, ivory. The word was especially applied, in the 19th century, to ancient Greek statues (often of wood) overlaid with ivory and gold, including the Olympian Zeus and the Athene Parthenos of Phidias.

chrysom. See *chrisom.*

chrysostomic. Golden-mouthed. THE MONTHLY REVIEW of 1816 says: *By the majestic of his chrysostomic eloquence.* From Greek *chrysos,* gold + *stomat-,* mouth. Also *chrysostomatical.* Applied to various ancient orators, it became the surname of (Saint) John Chrysostom (345?-407), priest at Antioch, bishop of Constantinople, banished (404) to Armenia despite (or because of) his popularity with the people. Even the golden-mouthed must control his tongue.

chuff. See *cuffin.*

chyurgerie. An early form of *surgery*—usually fatal. Also *chiurgery*; likewise *chirurgeon, q.v.* The English word for a measure of work (*energy*) is *erg.*

chyvachie. A horseback expedition; a raid; a campaign. Also *chevachee, q.v.; chivachee, chyvauche,* and more. Chaucer in the Prologue to THE CANTERBURY TALES (1386) says: *He hadde ben somtyme in chyvachie In Flaundres, in Artoys, and Picardie.*

cibaries. Victuals, provisions. Plural; Latin *cibaria,* things used for food; *cibus,* food. See *pote.*

cicisbeo. A cavalier *servente*; a recognized gallant of a married woman. In Italy, 15th through 18th century. Pronounced *chi-chis-baý-o.* Mentioned by Sheridan in THE SCHOOL FOR SCANDAL (1777), but the pious Wesley exclaimed (1782): *English ladies are not attended by their cicisbys yet; nor would any English husband suffer it.* The practice was a growth from the troubadour days of medieval southern France.

ciclatoun. Scarlet cloth; later, cloth of gold. A precious stuff through the Middle Ages. The word was obsolete by 1400; Spenser guesses at what Chaucer meant by it. Chaucer (SIR THOPAS, 1386): *His robe was of Syklatoun That coste many a Jane, Ciclatoun,* also *sikelatoun, syclatowne, shecklaton,* etc., is from Arabic *siqilatun,* from Persian *saqirlat, sakarlat,* whence also English *scarlet.*

cicurate. To tame; to render mild or harmless. Latin *cicur,* tame. Sir Thomas Browne in PSEUDODOXIA EPIDEMICA (1646) tells of poisons *so refracted, cicurated, and subdued, as not to make good their . . . destructive malignities.* Cotton Mather, in

THE ECCLESIASTICAL HISTORY OF NEW ENGLAND (1702): *Nor did he only try to cicurate the Indians.* The verb was sometimes shortened to *cicure.* Hence *circuration,* domestication.

cid. A valiant man, a great captain (Bailey, 1751). A title (Arabic, *es Sayd,* my lord) given to Ruy Diaz, Count of Bivar, champion of Christianity against the Moors in Spain, 11th century. Title also (LE CID, 1637) of the greatest play by Corneille, which Cardinal Richelieu disliked and the newly formed French Academy condemned.

cillibub. See *sillabub.*

cinct. Girt, girdled; surrounded. Latin *cingere, cinctum,* to gird. Hence *cincture,* a belt; an encompassing; an embrace; the environment. The *cincture of sword* was the ceremony of girding on a sword when made a duke or an earl. To *cincture,* to girdle, encircle—as the head of the Indian when Gray in THE PROGRESS OF POESY (1757) speaks of *their feather-cinctur'd chief.* Shakespeare uses *cincture* to mean belt in KING JOHN (1595): *Now happy he whose cloak and cincture can Hold out this tempest.*

cinereous. Ash-colored. Also *cinereal, cineritious.* Latin *cinerem,* ashes. Thus *cinerescent,* inclining to ash-color, grayish; *cinerulent,* full of ashes; of the texture of ashes. *Cinereous crows,* Morse recorded in his AMERICAN GEOGRAPHY (1796) *brave the severest winter.* Another instance of the use appears at *vinaceous.*

circum-. Around. Used in many English words, some familiar, some forgotten. Thus *circumaggerate,* to heap around; *circumcursation,* running around, rambling in discourse; *circumambages,* ways of getting around (someone): women are the *circumambagious* sex; *circumdolate,* to cut around, to deceive; *circumfulgent,* shining all around. *circumcellion,* a 4th century fanatic who roamed from monastery to monastery, especially in Africa where—Burton reports in THE ANATOMY OF MELANCHOLY (1621)—they preached and practiced suicide; later, a vagabond, a tavern hunter—a type far from extinct. *Circumdate,* to surround; *circumforane -al, -an, -ous,* vagrant, wandering from market to market, fair to fair, like the medieval jugglers and the strolling players: Addison in THE SPECTATOR (1711) says *I mean those circumforaneous wits, whom every nation calls by the name of that dish of meat which it likes best . . . in Italy, maccaronies; and in Great Britain, Jack Puddings. Circumgyral,* in circling wreaths or whirls, as *circumgyral smoke. circumplication,* a wrapping or folding around; *circumspicious,* seeing all around; *circumspicuous,* easily seen all around; *circumterraneous, circumterrestrial* (like the stratosphere and the moon); *circumvoisin,* neighboring on all sides.

circumbendibus. See *recumbentibus.*

circumbilivagination. See *circumquaque.*

circumcellion. A vagabond monk; originally, one of the 4th century Donatist fanatics in Africa, who roved from house to house. Latin *circum,* about + *cella,* cell. Cotton Mather in MAGNALIA CHRISTI AMERICANA (1702) remarked: *There was the phrensie of the old circumcellions in those Quakers.* Hence, in general, a vagabond, a haunter of public houses. *Cp. circum-.*

circumquaque. Circumlocution; a coined word, like *circumbendibus, circumbilivagination, circumbilivigation. To circumbilivaginate,* to speak in a roundabout way; to talk in circles. *Cp. circum-.* These are mainly 17th century pedantically humorous terms. Goldsmith, in SHE STOOPS TO CONQUER (1773) says *With a circumbendibus, I fairly lodged them in the horse-pond.* (This is the most lasting of these coinages.) Urquhart in his translation (1693) of Rabelais says: *That is spoke gallantly, without circumbilivaginating about and about.* J. Heywood in THE SPIDER AND THE FLIE (1556) wrote: *What (quoth the flie) meaneth this circumquaquie?* and in his PROVERBS (1562) said: *Ye set circumquaques to make me believe . . . that the moone is made of greene cheese.* [Note that *green,* in the expression *green cheese,* means unripe—hence not golden like a ripe cheese, but pale yellow. In the same way, blackberries are red when they are green.]

cit. Short for *citizen.* Also *citt.* Feminine (used by Dryden, 1685), *citess;* Johnson (1751) used *cit* as a feminine. *Cit* was used in the 17th and 18th centuries, usually with some measure of scorn, for a townsman as opposed to a squire, or a tradesman as opposed to a gentleman. Pope in a SATIRE of 1735 asks *Why turnpikes rose, and now no cit or clown Can gratis see the country or the town.* The Prologue to Hannah Cowley's THE RUNAWAY (1776) pictured the Londoner, still seeking the countryside, scorned by the actor: *Let cits point out green paddocks to their spouses; To me, no prospect like your crowded houses.*

cithara. An ancient Greek and Roman musical instrument. It has had many medieval and modern variants; see *citole; cithern.*

cithern. A guitar-like instrument, strung with wire. Popular in the 16th and 17th centuries. Latin *cithara.* Also *gittern, cittern;* see *bandore.* Bacon in SYLVA (1626) states that an Irish harp *maketh a more resounding sound than a bandora, orpharion, or cittern, which have likewise wire strings.* The head of the *cittern* was often grotesquely carved; hence *cittern-head* was used as a term of scorn, as in Shakespeare's LOVE'S LABOUR'S LOST (1588): *Holofernes: I will not be put out of countenance. Berowne: Because thou hast no face. Holofernes: What is this? Boyet: A citterne head.* Sometimes called *cither;* a Tyrolese form of the instrument is called *zither.* The cithern had eight strings divided into four pairs (courses). It was commonly kept in barber shops for the use of the waiting customers. Also see *orpharion.*

citole. A stringed instrument, perhaps at first like the ancient cithara—which was triangular, with from seven to eleven strings—but probably later with fewer strings, and sometimes box-shaped. The strings were strummed with the fingers (the cithern, bandore, and other wire-stringed instruments were struck with a plectrum. See *cithern.*) The citole was very popular in the 13th, 14th, and 15th centuries; Chaucer in THE KNIGHT'S TALE (1386) says: *A citole in her right hand hadde she.*

cittern. See *cithern;* also for *cittern-head.*

civet. (1) a carnivorous animal, in appearance between a fox and a weasel. Hence, the musky, oily secretion in the anal pouch of this animal; especially the African *civet-cat;* used in making perfumes. Thus Shakespeare, in AS YOU LIKE IT (1600): *Civet is of a baser birth than tar, the very uncleanly flux of a cat.* Hence, a perfume. The term *civet-cat* was applied (in ridicule) to a person highly perfumed. (2) An old word for chive. (3) a way of preparing chicken or hare:

first frying it brown in lard, then stewing it in broth. Served with bread toasted, soaked for an hour in wine, then strained and spiced. This *civet* sounds a succulent dish.

clack-dish. A beggar's cup: a wooden dish with a cover the beggar would clack down as an appeal. Also *clapdish*. Shakespeare knew the device; MEASURE FOR MEASURE (1603): *and his use was, to put a ducat in her clack-dish.* "The last of her race," sitting on a door-step, is pictured in 1861; now the beggar rattles coins in a tin cup.

clam. See *clem.*

clancular. Secret; clandestine, underhand. In the 17th and 18th centuries; the commoner form in the 16th century was *clanculary*. From Latin *clanculum,* diminutive of *clam,* secretly.

clapperclaw. To strike and scratch. From two uses of the hand. Figuratively, to revile. The Epistle to the First Quarto of Shakespeare's TROILUS AND CRESSIDA (1609) recommends it as *a new play, never stal'd with the stage, never clapperclawd with the palms of the vulgar.*

clapperdudgeon. A beggar; a rapscallion. The word is probably from the beggar's rapping on his *clapdish* (see *clack-dish*) with the handle of his *dudgeon, q.v.* The 16th century play GEORGE A GREEN said: *It is but the part of a clappedugeon To strike a man on the street.*

claptrap. See *catchpenny.*

clarry. See *piment.*

claudicate. To limp, to be lame. Latin *claudus,* lame. Also figuratively, as *claudicant arguments.* Rare after 17th century.

clavicymbal. See *clavis.*

clavicytherium. Also, *clavichord.* See *clavis.*

clavis. A key; especially, to a cipher. A 17th and 18th century term, directly from Latin *clavis,* key. Hence also *clavicular,* pertaining to a key (also to the *clavicle,* "little key," the collar-bone). The *clavicymbal,* a 15th to 17th century name for the early harpsichord; *clavicytherium,* a sort of harpsichord, an upright spinet, of the same period. A *claviger,* a key-keeper; one that carries a key—but also (Latin *clava,* club) one that carries a club; also *clavigerous. Clavis,* key, from the sense, key to a cipher came also to mean a glossary (key to a language).

claymore. See *morglay.*

cleam. See *clem.*

cleap. See *clepe.*

cleave. See *avaunt. Cleave,* to hew asunder, to split, had early English forms *clofen, clufan,* akin to Greek *gluf-,* to carve. In the 14th century it became fused with *cleave,* earlier *clive,* to stick, a common Teuton term related to *climb* and *clay.* Wyclif in 1382 said that the husband should *cleave to* (not *cleave*) his wife.

cleeves. An old form of *cliffs,* plural of *cliff.*

clem. To pinch as with hunger, to starve. From a Teuton form *clamm*; the early English noun *clam* meant the act of squeezing together, then anything that holds tight (such as a *clamp* and the shellfish *clam,* whence the current slang *to clam up,* to refuse to talk, shut the lips tight). But the verb *clam,* to clutch, hold tight, lost that meaning in favor of the sense to smear, from Old English *clasman,* to anoint, daub, smear, whence current *clammy.* There was also (12th to 19th century, now dialectic) a verb *cleam, cleme,* to smear. Thus the original sense of pinching, squeezing, was lost in all the verbs, though surviving in the noun forms. Jonson in THE POETASTER (1601) exclaims: *I cannot eat stones and turfs . . . What, will he clem me and my followers? Ask him an he will clem me.*

clench (noun). A play on words. Used in the 17th and 18th centuries. Dryden in his ESSAY ON DRAMATIC POESY (1668) says of Shakespeare: *He is many times flat, insipid; his comic wit degenerating into clenches, his serious swelling into bombast.* Pope says scornfully, in THE DUNCIAD (1728): *One poor word a hundred clenches makes.*

Clench has a major meaning, that which *clenches* or grasps; it is a variant of *clinch,* as in a prize fight. It is a causal form of *cling;* to *clinch* is to make *cling.* In a pun or other play on words, two unconnected ideas are made to stick together. Usually the auditor (if he has paid to listen) is also stuck. A *clincher,* in the sense of something that settles an argument, comes from the verb *to clinch,* to bend the point of a nail back into what it's been driven through, as in the old story of the two boasters (*cp. palmer*). Said the first: "I drove a nail through the moon last Thursday night." "I can vouch for that," said the second, " 'cause I went around to the back and clinched it."

cleombrotan. Characterized by the abandonment of one's present goods for the sake of an unknown, perhaps imaginary, but it is hoped better future. From *Cleombrotus,* a young man of Ambracia in Epirus, who after reading in Plato's PHAEDO the discourse on the immortality of the soul, leapt into the sea to go at once to that better after-life. Aesop tells a cleombrotan story of a dog with a bone in its mouth that sees its image in the water.

cleopatrical. Extravagantly luxurious. After the ways of Cleopatra, Queen of Egypt, wife of Ptolemy Dionysius, mother of a child of Julius Caesar, mistress of Marc Antony. *Cleopatra's nose* came to mean the essential element—from the remark by Blaise Pascal (died 1662): *If the nose of Cleopatra had been shorter, the whole face of the earth would have been changed.* Bishop Hall in his SATIRES (1597) exclaimed: *Oh, cleopatrical! what wanteth there For curious cost, and wondrous choice of cheere?*

clepe. To call; to call on, appeal to; to summon; to call to witness; to speak to; to name. A very common word with a range of meanings, used in many forms from the 8th through the 18th century: *clipian, clep, cleap, clip.* Especially frequent in the 16th century was the form *yclept,* named; as in Shakespeare's LOVE'S LABOUR'S LOST (1588): *Judas I am, ycliped Machabeus;* this has survived as an archaism, as in Byron's DON JUAN (1823): *Microcosm on stilts, yclept the Great World.* The forms occur throughout early literature, frequent in Chaucer, in Spenser—VISIONS, 1591: *I saw the fish (if fish I may it cleepe) . . . the huge leviathan*—and in Shakespeare—HAMLET, 1604: *other nations . . . clepe us drunkards.* Hence *cleper,* one who calls; *cleping,* a name; a vocation; Wyclif in 1382 urged that *ye walk worthily in the cleping in which ye ben clepid.*

clepsydra. An instrument anciently used (Bailey, 1751, says by the Egyptians) to measure time by the running of water out of one vessel into another; a water-clock. Similarly, the instrument using the fall of grains of sand to tell time was a *clepsammia. Clepsydra* is from Greek *kleps,* from *kleptein,* to steal (whence also *kleptomaniac*) + *hydor,* water.

clerk. Originally in English (10th century), an ordained officer of the church. Hence, a person of book learning; one able to read and write; a scholar; a pupil. Greek *kleros* meant piece of land, estate, heritage; *klerikos,* relating to an inheritance; by the 2d century this came to be applied to those that carried on the Christian inheritance; i.e., *the clergy, the clerics.* Caxton in his Prologue to ENEYDOS (THE AENEID; 1490) spoke of *that noble poete and grete clerke Vyrgyle*; elsewhere he mentioned *Plato the sage . . . and his clerke named Aristotle.*

cleromancy. See *aeromancy.*

clicket. The latch of a gate or door; any lid, valve, or other catch that shuts with a click. Also, a latch-key, as in Chaucer's THE MERCHANT'S TALE (1386). Also, rattling bones as an accompaniment to music (usually plural); a device for making a clicking sound, carried by beggars in France, as the *clack-dish, q.v.,* in England. Hence, a chattering tongue, a woman (1611) *whose clicket is ever wagging.*

clinch. See *clench.*

cline. To bow, to incline. Used in the 15th century, perhaps shortened from *accline, incline,* and in the 16th century, perhaps from the Greek *klinein,* to cause to slope, *recline*; Greek *kline,* a bed, *klinikos,* pertaining to a bed, whence English *clinic.* Carew, in his translations from Tasso (1594) has: *shamefast and downe clyned eyes.*

clinic. See *cline.* In early use (17th to mid 19th century), *a clinic* was a person confined to bed; especially, one who deferred baptism to the death-bed, "a wash for all our sins" said a commentator of 1666, "when we cannot possibly commit any more." Hence *clinic baptism.* A *clinic convert,* one converted when sick or dying: "When the devil was ill, the devil a monk would be; When the devil was well, the devil a monk was he!"

clinquant. Glittering, as with gold; tinselled; showy. Also *clinkant, clincant, clinquent.* Shakespeare speaks of *The French, all clinquant* in HENRY VIII (1613); Fletcher and Rowley in THE MAIDE IN THE MILL (1623) mentioned *a clinquant petticoat of some rich stuff, To catch the eye.* The word was also used as a noun, and figuratively (false glitter), as in FRASER'S MAGAZINE for 1839: *the worst portion of the silly bits of clinquant strung together, and called gems of beauty.*

clip. (1) To embrace. Shakespeare in CORIOLANUS (1607) has: *Let me clip ye In armes as sound, as when I woo'd in heart.* (2) To cut short (still used); slang from this was the meaning to cheat, to cozen. Many a wanton has clipt a man (sense 1) to clip him (sense 2). Shakespeare in LOVE'S LABOUR'S LOST (1588) puns: *Judas I am, ycliped* [*ycleped,* called] *Machabeus.—Judas Machabeus clipt, is plaine Judas.*

clipse. Old form of *eclipse.* Also *clips, clypse, clippis,* and the like. Phaer, in his translation (1558) of the AENEID, tells us that *Coribantes beat their brasse the moone from clips to cure.* Hence *clipsi, clipsy,* dark, obscure; in the ROMAUNT OF THE ROSE (1400) we read that love is *now bright, now clipsi of manere.*

cloacinean. See *ajax.*

clipsome. Fit to be embraced. A lightsome word for a winsome lass.

clodpate. A blockhead. Also *clodpoll, clodpole.* A 17th century favorite—Shakespeare, in TWELFTH NIGHT (1601): *This letter being so excellently ignorant . . . he will find it comes from a cloddepole*—and surviving (as in Thackeray, 1840, and Browning, 1878) well into the 19th.

close-stool. A covered chamber-pot set in a stool. Used from the 15th century. *Cp. ajax.* Shakespeare in ALL'S WELL THAT ENDS WELL (1601) presents *a paper from Fortune's close-stool to give to a nobleman.* Milton in THE READIE AND EASIE WAY TO ESTABLISH A FREE COMMONWEALTH (1659) girded at *chamberlains, ushers, grooms, even of the close-stool.*

cloud-kissing. A most pleasant adjective for what we more crudely call a *skyscraper.* Shakespeare in THE RAPE OF LUCRECE (1594) speaks of *cloud-kissing Ilion.* Other such combinations include *cloud-gloom, cloud-glory, cloud-serpent; cloud-cleaver; cloud-coifed, -compacted, -courtiered, -girt.* Also various terms for those whose thoughts are 'in the clouds': *cloud-castle, cloud-world, cloud cuckooland* (Aristophanes, THE BIRDS). The *cloud-assembler, cloud-compeller* was Zeus, but these terms were used in the 19th century, with pedantically humorous application to a heavy smoker. Also *cloud-headed,* confused.

cloud-monger. One that foretells by observation of the clouds. Used by Scott in DEMONOLOGY (1830); *cp. aeromancy.*

clough. A steep-sided ravine or valley, usually with a swift stream coursing through. Sometimes applied to the steep sides, as though it were a form of the word *cliff.* Pronounced *cluff* or *clau;* common from the 14th to the 17th century; later in dialects, as a rocky glen.

clow. A mill-dam; more often, a sluice or floodgate that controls the flow of water, as into a mill-wheel or a tidal river. Also *clowys, clew, clough.* Originally *clowes, clowis,* mistaken (like *pease,* whence *pea*) in the 15th and 16th centuries for a plural. It is ultimately from Latin *clausa,* a closed way.

clumperton. A silly fellow, a clown. From *clump, clumper,* to tread heavily, clumsily.

clumse. Benumbed with cold; hence stupid, stolid, awkward; later, in dialects, surly, 'an awkward customer.' Also *clomps, clumps.* Bailey (1751) defines *clumps* as 'a numpskull.' The word has been replaced by the later form *clumsy.*

clyster. "A fluid medicine of different qualities," says Bailey (1751), "to be injected into the bowels by the fundament." From Greek *klyster,* from *klyzein,* to wash, drench. Sometimes for nutrition, usually as an enema—the common word for enema, 14th through 17th century. Also *clister,* or beginning with *g.* Also used figuratively, as by Greene in GREENES MOURNING GARMENT (1590): *My purse began with so many purging glisters to waxe not only laxative, but quite emptie.* In the interlude of THE FOUR P'S (see *palmer*) the 'pothecary's lie is a story of a man with an eight days' constipation; when a clyster is administered the result is so violent that a stone wall miles away is knocked down and the stones tumble into a stream so that one can walk over dry-shod.

co. In Tudor cant, short for *cove.* See *pedlers French.*

coacervate. To heap up, to accumulate. Also *coacerve.* From Latin *co-,* together + *acervare,* to heap. Used 14th through 19th century; items may be *coacerved but not commixed.*

coal. In various phrases: *black coal* (*charcoal,* as opposed to *white coal,* wood; used to make a black mark), a mark or sign of censure. In PASQUILS RETURN (1589) we read: *He gives the English a dash over the face with a blacke coale, and saith: Traistre Angloi* [Perfidious Albion]. *Precious coals!* was a 16th and 17th century exclamation, for emphasis or surprise. *To blow the coals,* to rouse the flames of passion. *To blow hot coals,* to rage fiercely. *To blow cold coals,* to strive in vain; *a cold coal to blow at,* a hopeless task. *To carry coals,* to perform menial tasks; hence, to submit to insults or degradation. Shakespeare uses this phrase in the opening of ROMEO AND JULIET (1592) and plays on it to indicate cowardice in HENRY V: *Nym and Bardolph are sworn brothers in filching, and in Calais they stole a fire-shovel: I knew, by that piece of service, the men would carry coals.* This phrase has been obscured by the now obsolescent expression *to carry coals to Newcastle,* to do something absurdly superfluous. Also *coal-blower,* a scornful term for an alchemist, a quack scientist; also, a *blow-coal. coal-kindler,* one that stirs up strife.

coax. See *cokes.*

cob. Used in many senses, some (as *corncob*) surviving. The general notion is of something stout, or roundish, like a head (*cop,* Latin *caput,* head). Among the less familiar meanings are: (1) a leading man in a group; (2) a wealthy man, especially a miserly one; (3) a big, lumpish man; (4) a male *swan* (q.v., also *cobswan*; the female is a *pen*). In plural (5) testicles; (6) "small balls or pellets with which fowls are usually crammed"—an 18th century trick to fill them out for market. (7) A small lump of anything, as bread, or coal; (8) the head of a red herring: Jonson in EVERY MAN IN HIS HUMOR (1598) has: *The first red herring that was broil'd in Adam and Eves kitchin do I fetch my pedigree from . . . his cob was my great-great-mighty-great grandfather.—Cob-knights* were those "dubbed in clusters." A *cobloaf* is a bun made with a round head—used figuratively as a term of abuse in Shakespeare's TROILUS AND CRESSIDA (1606), where Thersites is provoking Ajax, who calls him *cobloaf!* and whoreson cur!, then strikes him. Also see *spincop.*

cock. This word has had many meanings, figuratively or by extension from the domestic fowl. Applied to men, it meant a night watchman; especially, one that arouses slumberers. Chaucer in the Prologue to THE CANTERBURY TALES (1386) says: *Amorwe whan that day gan for to sprynge Up roos oure hoost and was oure aller cok.* The spout for letting liquor out of a cask had a stopper like a *cock's comb;* hence (15th to 18th century) it was called *a cock;* Shakespeare in TIMON OF ATHENS (1607) says: *I have retyr'd me to a wasteful cocke, and set mine eyes at flow.* It is probably from this sense that the meaning penis developed. From the 13th century *gock* and then *cock* were used, as a euphemistic perversion of *God,* in mild oaths. Chaucer speaks of *cokkes bones;* for another reference, see *gis.*

cockatrice. See *basilisk.* Occasionally *cockatrice* is used in error for *crocodile.* In the 16th, 17th, and 18th centuries, it was applied to men as a term of scorn—Bacon (1622): *this little cockatrice of a king*—and, especially by the dramatists, to women in the sense of strumpet, whore. Thus Dekker, in THE GULL'S HORN-BOOK (1609), advises a gallant to secure a lodging by the waterside, for its convenience to avoid shoulder-clapping (summons for debt) and *to ship away your cockatrice* *betimes in the morning.* The glance of the (serpent) cockatrice was fatal—it could, by looking in a mirror, kill itself—to everybody save one that had eaten rue. For another instance of the word, see *coney.*

cocket. A document from the customs-house—or the seal on it, that validates it—certifying that duty has been paid. From 13th to mid 19th century. Also, the customs-house; the duty to be paid. Supposedly from Latin *quo quietus est,* by which he is quit: the words with which the receipt ended. There was also (16th and 17th centuries) an adjective *cocket,* from *cock,* rooster, equivalent to the current *cocky.*

cockquean. Variant of *cuckquean, q.v.*

cockshoot. See *cockshut.*

cockshut. Twilight. Perhaps from the time when poultry are shut up for the night. It was often spelled *cockshoot,* however, and may be a shortening of *cockshoot time.* A *cockshoot* was a glade or clearing in a wood, through which the woodcock and other birds might dart or 'shoot,' to be caught by nets at the edge of the clearing. This was used figuratively by Ogilby in his version (1651) of Aesop: *When loud winds make cockshoots thro' the wood, Bending down mighty oaks, I firm have stood.* Florio (1598) defines *cockshut* as the time 'when a man cannot discern a dog from a wolfe.' Shakespeare in RICHARD III (1594) tells that *Thomas, the Earl of Surrey, and himself, Much about cockshut time, from troop to troop, Went through the army, cheering up the souldiers.*

cod. See *codpiece.*

codding. See *codpiece.*

codling. A variety of apple, somewhat tapering; especially, a variety that could be cooked while still unripe. Hence, a raw youth, as when in THE ALCHEMIST (1610) Jonson hails the arrival of *a fine young quodling.* Also *codlin, querdlyng, codlyng, quadling,* and more. Shakespeare in TWELFTH NIGHT (1601) similifies: *As a squash is before tis a pescod, or a codling when tis almost an apple. Hot codlings* were roasted apples, sold in the London streets from the 17th century. A folk song of 1825 ran: *A little old woman, her living she got, By selling hot codlings, hot, hot, hot.* By 23 February, 1881, THE DAILY TELEGRAPH lamented: *Hot codlings may now be sought for in vain.* The word *codling* may have come from *coddle,* one meaning of which was to cook (we still have *coddled eggs,* cooked gently; but *coddled pease* were roasted; and *hot codlings* may also have meant roasted peas). *Codling* also may mean a small *cod* (fish); also, the scrotum; *cp. codpiece.* Sylvester, in his translation (1605) of Du Bartas, wrote of *The wise beaver who, pursu'd by foes, Tears off his codlings, and among them throwes.*

codpiece. A bagged appendage in the front of the tight-fitting hose or breeches worn by men (15th to 17th century), often ornamented. Herrick in HESPERIDES (1648): *If the servants search, they may descry, In his wide codpeece, dinner being done, Two napkins cramm'd up, and a silver spoone. Codpiece-point,* the lace with which the codpiece was fastened. The word was often used for the organs it covered but did not conceal, as in Shakespeare's MEASURE FOR MEASURE (1603): *Why, what a ruthless thing is this in him, for the rebellion of a codpiece to take away the life of a man!* In LOVE'S LABOR'S LOST, Cupid is called *king of codpieces.*

God, Old English *codd,* was a common word for a bag; by extension, the *codfish,* bag fish; a purse; the belly; and—most commonly 14th through 17th century—the scrotum; by extension, the *cods,* the testicles. *Cp. ballock.* In TITUS ANDRONICUS *That codding spirit they had from their mother* plays on two senses: jesting, and lecherous.

coemption. Cornering the market; buying up the available supplies. Literally (Latin *co-, com,* together + *emere, emptum,* to buy: *caveat emptor,* let the buyer beware; *cp. caveat*) the word means joint purchasing; Chaucer in his translation (1374) of Bothius thus understood the word: *coempcioun that is to seyn comune achat or bying to-gidere.* And in ancient Rome, one type of marriage ceremony consisted of the husband's buying the wife and the wife's buying the husband; this too was called *coemption.* Bacon in his ESSAYS (1625, ON RICHES) said that *monopolies, and coemption of wares for resale, where they are not restrained, are great means to enrich.*

coenaculous. Fond of suppers, as one that enjoys a midnight snack. Should preferably be *cenaculous*: Latin *cenaculum,* supper-room, dining room; *cp. cenation.* Leigh Hunt in BACCHUS IN TUSCANY (1825) spoke of *people grossly coenaculous.*

coenobite. See *eremite.*

cogitabund. Deep in thought. Accent on the first syllable; it slips to the fourth in the alternate form *cogitabundous.* Used in the 17th and 18th centuries; later, to give a ponderously humorous effect. Also *cogitabundation, cogitabundity, cogibundity,* deep meditation. Carey in his POEMS (1734) pressed the humor: *His cogitative faculties immersed In cogibundity of cogitation.* Cog within cog!

cohonestation. Honoring with one's company. A word out of the formal 17th and 18th centuries. "I deeply appreciate your cohonestation":—any author, to his readers.

coif. A close-fitting cap, covering top, back, and sides of the head, tied under the chin, worn outdoors by both sexes. Later, a sort of night-cap, but worn in the day by women, indoors or under the bonnet. Hence, also, a close-fitting skull-cap (iron, steel, later leather) worn under the helmet. Also, the white cap worn by lawyers as a sign of their profession, especially, by a serjeant-at-law; hence, the position of serjeant-at-law; in these uses from the 14th century. In Scotland, from the 17th century, the headgear of a married woman; as Scott explains, in a note to THE LADY OF THE LAKE (1810): *The snood was exchanged for the curch, toy, or coif, when a Scottish lass passed, by marriage, into the matron state.* Thus *The lassie has lost her silken snood* was used to mean she was no longer a virgin, yet not a wife.

coign. A corner. Also *coigne.* Older spelling of *coin, quoin* via French from Latin *cuneus,* wedge, corner. [The verb meant to strike hard or press in with a wedge, hence our money, the value, etc., impressed upon the *coin.*] Shakespeare in MACBETH (1605) says: *No jutty frieze, buttrice, nor coigne of vantage, but this bird Hath made his pendant bed.* Scott in THE HART OF MIDLOTHIAN (1818) repeated: *As if the traders had occupied with nests . . . every buttress and coign of vantage, as the marlett did in Macbeth's castle.* Scott used *coign of vantage* again in MARMION and in QUENTIN DURWARD; thereafter, George Eliot, Browning, and others took up the phrase.

coint. This is an old form of *quaint,* which (in many spellings) came from the Latin *cognitum,* known, from *cognoscere,* to find out, as in *recognize.* The English *coint, cwointe, quhaynte, quaint,* etc., at first meant wise, then skilful. It was then applied to things skilfully made, so as to look beautiful; then to persons of beautiful dress or refined speech. Gradually it was applied to those too particularly dressed, foppish, and to those that adorned their speech with affectations and conceits, especially as with an old-fashioned elegance. By this gradual course, *coint* in 1225 became *quaint* in its present sense by 1795, in Southey's JOAN OF ARC: *many a merry ballad and quaint tale.* In the sense of skilled in speech, Shakespeare in HENRY VI, PART TWO (1590) says *Show how queint an Orator you are,* and Dryden in his ÆNEID (1697) says *Talk on ye quaint Haranguers of the Crowd.*

coistrel. In origin a variant of *custrel, q.v.,* and ranging through the same senses: a groom; a lad; a rascal. Also *coystrel, coisterel,* etc. More emphatic in sound, this form was the more common, especially in chronicles and plays, 16th through the 18th century, as in Shakespeare's TWELFTH NIGHT (1601): *He's a coward and a coystrill that will not drink to my niece.* For another instance, see *tib.*

cokes. A fool, a simpleton. A frequent term in the 16th and 17th centuries. Also *coaks, coax, coxe.* The origin is unknown, though the creature is still familiar. The word survives in the verb *to coax,* which originally meant *to make a cokes of,* to fool. Jonson in THE DEVIL IS AN ASS (1616) wrote: *Why, we will make a cokes of thee, wise master; we will, my mistress, an absolute fine cokes.* Samuel Johnson in 1755 called *coax* "a low word"; it has become gentler if not more genteel.

colbertine. A kind of lace, "resembling network," open, with a square ground, worn in the 17th and 18th centuries—"of the fabric of Monsieur *Colbert,* Superintendent of the French King's manufactures," says a FOP'S DICTIONARY of 1690. Also *colverteen.*

colcannon. Potato and cabbage pounded together in a mortar and stewed with butter. An 18th and early 19th century Irish dish. From *cole,* cabbage (as also in *coleslaw*) + *cannon,* from the ball with which the pounding was done.

cole. See *coleprophet.* Also, of course, the *cole* (*kail, kale*) family of vegetables, as in the Scottish *kailyard,* vegetable garden.

coleprophet. A pretender to knowledge of the future; a false diviner. Also *colprophet, collprophet,* these forms in the 16th century; in the 17th century, also *coldprophet.* From *cole,* a conjuring trick; a deceiver, sharper; used from the 14th century. In the 17th and 18th centuries, *coal, cole* were used to mean money; *to post the cole,* to pay down the money. General Burgoyne in his play THE LORD OF THE MANOR (1781) wrote: *Come, my soul, post the cole; I must beg or borrow.*

coleron. Doves. An old plural of *culver,* dove. Also *culfre, culefre, colvyr,* and many more, the word being very common from the 9th to the 14th century. Hence *culver-hole, culver-house,* a dove-cote. Scott in THE LAY OF THE LAST MINSTREL (1805)—*Falcon and culver, on each tower, Stood prompt their deadly hail to shower* —uses *culver* for *culverin,* for which see *basilisk.*

colibus. "The humming-bird, which makes a noise like a whirlwind, though it be no bigger than a fly: it feeds on dew, has an admirable beauty of feathers, a scent as sweet as that of musk or ambergrease." So Bailey (1751), following Kersey (1715). The O.E.D. (1933) gives the name as *colibri,* from the French after the Carib original; but Browning in SORDELLO (1840) uses *colibri* as a plural. Kingsley, in WESTWARD HO! (1855): *that's a colibri; you've heard of colibris? Frank looked at the living gem which hung, loud humming, over some fantastic bloom.*

colin. Quail—as my friend of that ilk never does. From the Mexican word *colin,* for the American quail, a pretty bird unfortunately also tasty; known likewise as the bob-white.

coll. A hug around the neck. Short for *accole, accoll,* with the same meaning, from French *a,* to + *col,* neck, Latin *collum.* The word had other meanings: (1) a dupe, a simpleton. This sense also appears as *cull* and *gull.* (2) ale. This is an 18th century use, especially at Oxford. (3) a bundle (of wood), a cock of hay. There is also a verb *coll,* to poll, shear; Ascham uses it (*coul*) for paring an arrow-feather. This is probably from the Scandinavian; Icelandic *kollr,* shaven crown, polled beast.

collabefaction. A wasting away, decaying. A 17th and 18th century dictionary word, from Latin *collabefacere,* to cause to collapse.

collachrymate. To weep together. Also as an adjective, mingled with tears, accompanied by weeping. Rare; 16th and 17th centuries.

collactaneous. Suckled together, nursed with the same milk. A 17th century dictionary word: *col,* together + *lact-,* milk.

collation. See *decollation.*

colliby. See *collybist.*

collice. See *cullis.*

colligate. To bind together, to connect (literally, or logically). From Latin *col-, com-,* together + *ligare,* to bind, as in *ligature.* From the 16th to the 19th century; still used in formal writing; Andrew Lang in MYTH, RITUAL, AND RELIGION (1887) says that *The explanation . . . colligates it with a familiar set of phenomena.* Hence *colligance,* attachment together, connection; *colligation;* H. More in AN ILLUSTRATION OF THE BOOK OF DANIEL (1685) speaks of *the admirable union or colligation of the Soul of the Messias with the eternal Logos.*

collimate. To close an eye so as to aim at a target; to adjust a telescope to the proper line of sight. Used in Latin by Kepler in 1604, hence into modern languages—by error for *collineate,* from Latin *col-, com-,* together + *lineare,* to make a straight line, *linea,* line. There are also, in English, the technical terms *collinear, collineate,* etc.

colliquate. To melt or fuse together. Used in medieval alchemy and Renaissance medicine, but also figuratively, as in Holland's translation (1603) of Plutarch's PHILOSOPHIE: *Who being severed apart in body, conjoin and colliquate, as it were perforce, their souls together.* Hence also *colliquative; colliquefaction; colliquescence,* readiness to become fluid. *Colliquament* is the melted substance; in the 17th century, the thin fluid that is the earliest sign of an embryo in the egg, *the white colliquament out of which the young one is formed.*

collistrigiated. Pilloried. Also *collistrigium, collistridium,* pillory. These two are direct from Medieval Latin, from *collum,* neck + *strig-, strigere,* to bind (as also in English *stringent*). *Collistrigiated* is a rare

17th century word, remaining in 18th century dictionaries.

collop. Fried egg on bacon; later called *collops and eggs, collops* being used to mean the bacon; by transference *collop* was used for any piece of fried meat. Bailey (1751) defines it as "a cut or slice of flesh meat." Hence, a piece of flesh on something, as a fold of flesh, that shows good condition; also, a cut from something; by extension, an offspring, as in Shakespeare's THE WINTER'S TALE (1611): *To say this boy were like me . . . my dearest, my collop.* The word was occasionally used in threats (as to children): "I'll cut you into collops!" The day before Shrove Tuesday is still known as *Collop Monday,* it being traditional then to eat fried bacon and eggs.

colluctation. Wrestling; conflict. Also *colluctance, colluctancy.* Rare 17th century words—though Lamb in his discussion of Marlowe (about 1818) said that Faustus' last scene *is indeed an agony and a fearful colluctation.* Latin *col-,* together + *luctari,* to wrestle.

collugency. Mutual sorrow. Latin *col-,* together + *lugere,* to mourn. In Urquhart's translation (1693) of Rabelais: *This ruthful and deplorable collugency.*

collybist. Money-changer; usurer; miser. Also *collibist.* Greek *kollybistes,* money-changer; *kollibos,* small coin. From 14th through 17th century; Bishop Hall in his SATIRES (1598) has: *Unless some base hedge-creeping collybist Scatters his refuse scraps on whom he list.* From the same source (possibly influenced by Latin *collibere,* to please; *col-,* together + *libet,* it pleases), *colliby* was a 14th and 15th century word meaning a small present.

collyridian. One of a sect called heretical, of the 4th and 5th centuries, who offered cakes to the Virgin Mary as Queen of Heaven. From Greek *kollyra,* roll of coarse bread. From the use of a moist pellet of such bread as a poultice, Greek *kollyrion,* poultice, then eye-salve, came with the same meaning into Latin and English as *collyrium.* Also (13th to 17th century) *collyrie, colorye, colirie,* etc.; (16th century) *collyre.* In the 17th century *collyrium* grew more general, to mean any application (including cosmetics) for the eyes; in the 18th century (again from the moist pellet) the word was also used for a suppository. In its application to the eyes, the word was also used figuratively; thus Emerson in REPRESENTATIVE MEN (1847) says: *Great men are thus a collyrium to clear our eyes from egotism.*

collyrium. See *collyridian.*

coimar. (1) a kind of pear, from a town in Alsace. (2) a kind of fan, popular in the reign of Queen Anne. Pope, in his MARTINUS SCRIBLERUS PERI BATHOUS, OR THE ART OF SINKING IN POETRY (1727), wrote that *the bride . . . with an air divine her colmar ply'd.* See *cosins.*

colon. See *commation.*

coloquintida. An early form of *colocynth,* the bitter-apple, a kind of gourd, from the fruit of which a purgative drug was made. Also *coloquint, coloquintid, coloquinto, coloquinty.* Shakespeare in OTHELLO (1604) speaks of a food *as bitter as coloquintida. Cp. acerb.*

colour. Used from the 13th century, *color* from the 15th. Also *colure, coulur, collor, colowre, cooler, collour, culler,* and more. Among its senses, we may note: (1) outward appearance, false show; a pretext or cloak over the facts; hence, alleged reason, excuse. Used from the 14th century; Hampole's PSALTER (1340): *That under colour of goed counsaile bryngis til syn.* Shakespeare in THE TWO GENTLEMEN OF VERONA (1591) says: *Under the colour of commending him, I have access my own love to prefer* [advance]. (2) Nature, kind. Shakespeare in AS YOU LIKE IT says of the wrestling: Le Beau *You have lost much good sport.* Celia: *Sport! of what colour?* (3) An allegory, a parable, a figure of speech. Hawes in THE PASSE TYME OF PLEASURE (1509) remarked: *For under a colour a truthe may aryse, As was the guyse in olde antyquyte.*

colpon. See *culpon.*

colter. See *coulter.*

coltsfoot. A plant, growing low on the ground; its yellow flowers appear before its leaves. It is named from the shape of the leaves; though some suggest the reference is to the colt that bore Jesus into Jerusalem (BIBLE; MATTHEW 21). The root fibres were dried in the sun, then dipped in saltpeter and used as tinder to light lamps. More significantly, the Greeks smoked the plant as a cure for coughs; the Romans used it for the same purpose, calling it *tussilago* (still its scientific name) from *tussis,* cough; the Old English infused the flowers and drank the liquor as a cure. The plant was also called *filius ante patrem* (the son before the father) because the flowers appeared before the leaves. Steele in THE TATLER (No. 266; 1710) says: *Upon the table lay a pipe filled with bettony and coltsfoot.*

colubrine. Snake-like; wily, crafty. Latin *colubra,* snake (feminine). *Coluber* is a current zoological term for a genus of snakes—now, but not formerly, limited to harmless snakes. In zoology, *colubrine* is still the adjective for snake-like. In earlier (16th through 18th century) use, it was applied to persons, as in Skelton's poems (1528) *His county pallantyne Have coustome colubryne With code viperyne, And sectes serpentyne. Colubrine* was also used, in the early 17th century, as a variant name for an early cannon, a culverin.

columbuck. An aromatic wood. Used, said Dunton's LADIES DICTIONARY (1694) *in their chambers to keep out unwholesom aires.*

comb. See *compt.*

comeling. A newcomer; anyone not a native to a place; by extension, a novice. Common in 13th, 14th and 15th centuries, used into the 19th, carrying some measure of scorn, as Harrison in THE DESCRIPTION OF ENGLAND (1587) speaks of *the comeling Saxons.*

comessation. Eating together; especially, riotous feasting. Latin *comedere,* to devour, *com-,* altogether + *edere,* to eat, whence also English *comestible. Comessation* may also be related to Greek *komos,* revel, hence it is often linked with *ebrietas,* drunkenness; see *ebriety.* The NEW TESTAMENT of 1582 speaks of *fornication . . . envies, murders, ebrieties, commessations* (which the King James version, 1611, renders as revellings). *Comestion,* eating, was also used in the 17th century of devouring by fire.

comicar. A writer of comedies. Used (once) by Skelton, 1523: *Master Terence, the famous comicar.*

comitate. To accompany. Latin *comitari, comitatus; comes, comitem,* companion. Used in the 17th century, as in Vicars' translation (1632) of the AENEID: *Achates kinde Aeneas comitated.*

comma. See *commation.*

commacerate. To harass, torment. Latin *com-,* altogether + *macerare,* to soften, weaken, enervate, hence torment. A rare

16th century word, as in Nashe's HAVE WITH YOU TO SAFFRON-WALDEN (1596): *one true point whereof well set downe wil more excruciate and commacerate him . . .*

commation. A short lyrical passage in a drama. From Greek *kommation,* diminutive of *komma,* comma—which in relation to Greek writing means 'a group of words less than a colon'; hence, a short part of a sentence, or any short passage or period, as in Shakespeare's TIMON OF ATHENS (1607): *No level'd malice Infects one comma in the course I hold.* A *colon* (Greek *kolon, member,* limb) is a rhythmical division of a sentence, a clause or group of clauses written as a line, and taken as a standard of measure. *Commation* is a word current critics have overlooked. *Commatic,* however, means like a *commos,* consisting of short measures. A *commos* is a lament sung in alternate parts by a character and the chorus in a Greek tragedy; it is from Greek *kommos,* beating (one's head and chest in lamentation), from *koptein,* to strike.

commensal. A messmate, a boarder. From Latin *com-,* together + *mensalis,* pertaining to the table, *mensa,* table. The eucharist, commented Bishop Hall (1624) makes us *commensals of the Lord Jesus.* The word *commensal* is still used in biology, of a plant or animal that lives attached to or as tenant of another, sharing its food. The host may also be called a *commensal.* The *commensal* is to be distinguished from the parasite, which eats the body of its host.

commentitious. Feigned, fictitious; lying. Also *commentitial.* A 17th century term, as in Bentley's DISSERTATION ON THE EPISTLES OF PHALARIS (1699): *as false and commentitious as our Sibylline Oracles.* From Latin *com-,* altogether; *comminisci, comment-,* to invent, from the inceptive form of *mentiri,* to lie. There is also the rare (nonce-word) *commentiter,* liar (which sounds rather close to *commentator,* as Daniel Featley put it, in THE DIPPERS DIPT, 1645: *No expositors, but impostors; no commentators, but commenters, nay rather commentiters.* And that was before the nights of radio!)

commetics. "Things which give beauties not before in being, as paints to the face; differing from *cosmetics,* which are only to preserve beauties already in possession." Thus Bailey's DICTIONARY, 1751: not in the O.E.D. A usable word, save that every woman wishes to be thought "in possession."

comminate. To threaten with (Divine) vengeance. Latin *com-* (with intensive force) + *minari,* to threaten. One of Donne's SERMONS (1625) exclaims: *How many without any former preparatory cross or comminatory or commonitory cross . . . fall under some one stone.* From Latin *com* + *monere, monit-,* to warn, *commonitory* means reminding, warning. There was a verb *commonish* (accent on the second syllable), to warn; these forms have been supplanted by *admonish, admonitory, admonition,* etc. Also *commonefaction,* warning, reminder; used in the 17th century. Note that *monitory* means warning; *monetary* means relating to *money*—which is probably from *Juno moneta,* the warning Juno, in whose temple grounds the Roman mint was established. Thus while the love of money is the root of all evil, *money* in itself bears a warning.

comminute. To pulverize; to break into small portions, as a large estate into building lots. Hence, *comminuible* (accent on the *min*), that may be broken into small particles; Sir Thomas Browne in PSEUDODOXIA EPIDEMICA (1646) said that *a diamond steeped in goats bloud, rather encreaseth in hardness . . . the best we have are comminuible without it.* THE SATURDAY REVIEW in 1860 spoke of *the comminuted political condition which is just now so noxious to his country.*

commode. As an adjective: convenient, suitable. Used in the 17th century. Via French from Latin *com,* together + *modus,* measure. Applied to women in the 18th century, meaning accommodating, usually with bad implications. Steele in THE CONSCIOUS LOVERS (1722) speaks of *one of those commode ladies who lend out beauty for hire.* Hence, as a noun: (1) a procuress. This sense was also used figuratively, as when Cibber in the Epilogue to his version of JULIUS CAESAR (1721) spoke of making *the tragic muse commode to love.* (2) A small piece of furniture for holding a chamber pot. (3) A tall headdress for women, worn especially in the late 17th and early 18th centuries, built on a wire framework, often with silk or lace streamers hanging over the shoulders. The *commode,* however (as Addison pointed out in his essay on LADIES' HEADDRESS IN THE SPECTATOR, 1711, No. 98), never *aspired to so great an extravagance as in the 14th century, when it was built up in a couple of cones or spires, which stood so exceedingly high on each side of the head, that a woman who was but a pigmy without her headdress appeared like a colossus upon putting it on.* This headdress was also called a *fontange* (from French *Fontanges,* the estate of a mistress of King Louis XIV). The olden fontanges, Addison continued, *were pointed like steeples, and had long pieces of crape fastened to the tops of them, which were curiously fringed, and hung down their backs like streamers.*

commonefaction. See *comminate.* Accent on the *mon.*

commonitory. See *comminate.*

common-kissing. See *bass.*

commorant. Resident. Latin *com-,* together, altogether, + *morari,* to tarry, *mora,* delay. Especially a member of the Cambridge Senate resident in the town (no longer in a college)—until 1856, when the requirement of residence was abolished. Also *commorance, commorancy,* abiding, residence (all accented on the first syllable). *Commoration,* dwelling, sojourning; a *commoratory* is (17th century) a dwelling-place. Note however that *commorient* (Latin *mori,* to die) means dying together; *commorse* (Latin *morsus,* bite, as also in *morsel* and *remorse;* see *agenbite*) means compassion, pity.

commorient. See *commorant.* Buck in THE HISTORY OF . . . RICHARD III (1623) wrote of *the same compatient and commorient fates and times. Compatient* means either suffering together, or sympathetic; *compatience* (14th through 16th century), compassion.

commorth. A collection to help someone. Welsh *cym-,* together + *porth,* support, help. A commorth (*comorth*) might be made at a wedding, or at the first Mass of a new priest, or to redeem a murderer or felon. Apparently the practice was abused, for laws were passed against taking a *commorth,* under Henry IV (1402) and again under Henry VIII (1534).

commos. See *commation.*

companage. The things eaten (not drunk) along with bread, as butter, cheese, meat. Via Old French from Latin *companagium, com-*, with + *panis,* bread —whence also *companion,* originally, one who shares bread, bread-fellow. In use 14th through 17th century. Chaucer, in THE SHIPMAN'S TALE (1386) uses *companable,* sociable, friendly; this also appeared as *compinable, cumpynable, compenable, compynabil,* and the like; these have been supplanted by *companionable.*

compatient. See *commorient.*

compellate. To address (by name), to call, call upon, as one may *compellate a saint.* Hence *compellation,* a calling upon; a name or form of greeting, an *appellation* (the current term in this sense); a reproach, reproof, calling to account. Bastwick in THE LETANY (1637) wrote: *The worst things are varnished over with finest names and compellations.* Note that *compellative* means related to address, to a word used as a title; *compellatory* means compulsory; *compellant, compellent* mean compelling, constraining; Richard Congreve in ESSAYS (1873) spoke of *the compellent contagion of great examples.*

compenable. See *companage.*

comperendinate. To put off from day to day. From legal Latin *comperendinare,* to postpone to the third day after; *com* + *perendie,* day after tomorrow. A 17th and 18th century dictionary word. Also *comperendination* (where the *end* is in the *middle*).

compinable. See *companage.*

complice. An assistant to another in a matter; especially, a confederate in crime. From *com-,* together + *plic-,* folded. By 1600 the second sense was dominant; it is the only meaning given by Johnson (1755). *Complice* has been supplanted by *accomplice.* In the 15th and 16th centuries, the word was used frequently in connection with politics: a rebel or a traitor *and his complices.* Shakespeare in RICHARD II (1595) lists *Bushy, Bagot, and their complices, The caterpillars of the commonwealth.* A *caterpillar* was one that preyed upon society, a rapacious devourer. From the 15th to the end of the 17th century, it was usually doubled in force as a play on words: a *caterpillar,* as one that devours the green leaves and young shoots of a healthy state; and a *piller,* as one that *pillages.* A *piller,* robber, plunderer, was common English from the 14th century. *To piller,* to pillage; also *pillery,* pillage.

complosion. Clapping; striking together. From Latin *complodere, complosus, com-,* together + *plaudere,* to clap. A 17th and 18th century word, covering sounds from the snapping of the thumb and middle finger to *the complosion of the air* that causes thunder. The more violent *explosion* has survived (as we may not future explosions).

comportance. One's bearing, carriage (implying approval); agreement, compliance. Latin *comportare,* to carry together. Spenser in THE FAËRIE QUEENE (1590): *Goodly comportaunce each to other beare, and entertain themselves with courtsies meet.*

compossibility. Possibility of two things at the same time, or together. Also, *compossible,* able to be at the same time. The idea plagued 17th century thinkers; Samuel Jackson, in COMMENTARIES UPON THE APOSTLES CREED (1630) argued *the mutual compossibility of actual particular cogitations with virtual continuance of some main purpose;* Ralph Cudworth, in a TREATISE CONCERNING ETERNAL AND IMMUTABLE MORALITY (1688) cried out that *the compossibility of contradictions destroys all knowledge.*

compotation. A drinking bout; Latin *com-*, together + *potare,* to drink. Usually mild; we hear in 1862 of *a stately compotation with the Abbot,* which probably was little more than a symposium (which is Greek for drinking together). *Compotation* may, however, be a humorous euphemism for a gay party; *compotate* was a 17th century verb meaning to carouse.

compt. Well combed (Latin *comere, comptus,* to comb, to adorn); hence, spruce, polished. Also applied to style: elegant. Hence also *comptly*; *comptness.* Replaced by the verb forms from *kemb,* to dress the hair, a common Old Teuton word now current as *comb*: *kempt,* spruce; more frequently (alas!) *unkempt.* Both *kemb* and *comb* were used, humorously, to mean thrash; thus in Skelton's works (1566): *His wife would divers times in the week kimbe his head with a three-footed stool.* See *kemb.*

comrogue. A fellow-rascal. Used since the 17th century, often satirically or humorously for *comrade.* Jonson in THE MASQUE OF AUGURS (1621) uses it seriously: *You and the rest of your comrogues shall sit disguised in the stocks.*

comse. A short form of *commence,* used in the 13th and 14th centuries. Hence *comsing,* commencing; *comsement,* commencement. Langland in PIERS PLOWMAN (1377) says *Dyinge . . . unknitteth al kare and comsynge is of reste.*

comus. A revel; a drinking-bout. Greek *komos,* whence *comedy* (*komos* + *aoidos,* singer; *aeidein,* to sing); *kome,* village, may be the source of *komos,* merrymaking. In English, after Milton's COMUS (1634), used mainly as a name for the god of revelry.

conable. Suitable; agreeable; convenient. A 14th and 15th century contraction of *covenable,* itself an early form of *convenable.* From Latin *convenire,* to agree, *com-,* together + *venire,* to come. These forms, along with an intermediate *conveniable,* gave way by the mid 18th century to *convenient.*

conceptious. Ready to conceive; prolific. Shakespeare in TIMON OF ATHENS (1607) bids: *Ensear thy fertile and conceptious womb, Let it not more bring out ungrateful man!*

concinnate. To put together neatly; to arrange well; also *to concinne. Concinnate terms* are terms of studied elegance. *Concinnity* is skilful putting together; congruity; beauty of style. In music, a *concinnous discord* is a discord to be resolved to a concord. From the 16th century; Bishop Reynolds in 1640 speaks of *that knitting quality of love to which he elsewhere properly ascribeth the building, concinnation, and perfecting of the Saints.*

concion. An assembly; an oration before an assembly, a public harangue. Latin *concionem, contionem,* shortened from *conventionem,* convention, *com-,* together, *venire, ventum,* to come. These forms retained the literal (physical) sense; for the figurative sense, to come together, to agree, see *conable. Concion* was used in the 16th and 17th centuries, along with other forms: *concional, concionary,* relating to an assembly or a speech; *concionate,* to harangue, to preach; *concionator,* orator; *concionatrix.*

conchomancy. See *aeromancy.*

concitate. To provoke, stir up, prick forward. Also *concite.* A *concitatrix* was a woman who roused one to an action. These are 15th and 16th century words (Latin *com-*, together + *citare,* to move); supplanted by *incite* and *excite;* a *concitatrix* (any woman) can do both.

conclave. A private room or place; especially, the room where the cardinals meet for the naming of a pope. Latin *con,* together + *clavis,* key. Also used figuratively, as in Bacon's THE NEW ATLANTIS (1626): *the secret conclave of such a vast sea.* Hence, the assembly of cardinals for the election of a pope; loosely, the body of cardinals, as in Shakespeare's HENRY VIII (1613): *I thanke the holy conclave for their loves.* From these, the current sense of a private assembly. Hence, *conclavical. conclavist,* one in a *conclave* (or an attendant on a cardinal in conclave; each cardinal is allowed two).

conculcate. To trample upon. From Latin *com* (with intensive force) + *calcare, calcatum,* to tread, *calx,* heel; see *calcate.* Used in the 16th and 17th centuries, mainly by religious writers, as Bishop Hooper in CHRIST AND HIS OFFICE (1547): *the conculcation of His precious blood.*

concupiscible. (1) Ardently to be desired, worthy of rousing lust. Sterne in TRISTRAM SHANDY (1762) states: *Never did thy eyes behold . . . anything in this world more concupiscible.* (2) Eagerly desirous. Shakespeare reports, in MEASURE FOR MEASURE (1603): *He would not, but by gift of my chaste body To his concupiscible intemperate lust Release my brother. Concupiscence, concupiscency, concupitive* and *concupiscible* all take the accent on the *cue.* The forms are from Latin *con,* with intensive force + *cupere,* to long for. *Cupid* was the god of desire. Our 'irrational nature' was divided by Platonic philosophers into two faculties or appetites, the *irascible* and the *concupiscible.*

concupy. A variant of *concuby,* short for *concubine. Concubine,* a mistress, is from Latin *con,* together + *cubare,* to lie. In the form *concupy,* there is implication of the word *concupiscence,* as when Thersites remarks in Shakespeare's TROILUS AND CRESSIDA (1603), referring overtly to Troilus' sword: *Heele tickle it for his concupie.*

conditaneous. Appropriate for pickling or preserving. A 16th and 17th century word. Over a century earlier was *condite,* as a noun, a preserve; an adjective, pickled; a verb, to preserve, to pickle. Also *conditure,* pickling, seasoning. From Latin *condire, conditus,* to preserve, earlier *condere,* to put away, preserve, *com-*, together + *dare,* to give, to put. In the 17th century *condite* was (rarely) used in the sense of *recondite,* abstruse. From the meaning 'to preserve, pickle' came the still current *condiment,* spice; also used figuratively from 1430—*Make it savory with the condiment of thy wisdom,* until today.

condog. To agree. Accent on the second syllable; used since the 16th century. Perhaps originally a facetious substitution of the more formal *dog* for *cur* in the verb *concur;* Lyly's GALLATHEA (1592) makes that juxtaposition. In Heywood's THE ROYALL KING (1637) the clown says to the bawd: *Speake, shall you and I condogge together?*

conductitious. Hired; employed for wages or reward; open to hire. From the 16th century; also *conduction,* hiring—used especially of a venal person. J. Smith in OLD AGE (1666) spoke of the *rubs and petulant endeavours of all conductitious detractors;* Sydney Smith in his WORKS

(1818), of *the conductitious penmen of government.*

condul. An old variant of *candle.* Its plural form was *condlen.*

coney. A rabbit. Latin *cuniculus,* rabbit, burrow. Long the usual term (whence *Coney Island,* New York), *rabbit* being the word for the young *coney.* In many spellings: *cony, cunin, conynge; cunning* (to the 16th century), *cunnie, cunny* (16th to 18th century), rhyming with honey. The earliest use of the word, however (*cunig, cunin,* about 1200) was as a rabbit-skin. By the 15th century, it was a term of endearment for a woman, then a nickname for her intimate parts. The most common special use, from the 16th through the 18th century, was *cony,* an easy mark, a gull—the victim of the *cony-catcher,* made popular by Greene's books on *conny-catching* (1591). Shakespeare in THE MERRY WIVES OF WINDSOR (1598) says *There is no remedy: I must conicatch, I must shift;* two years earlier, in THE TAMING OF THE SHREW, he cries: *Take heed signior Baptista, lest you be coni-cacht in this businesse.* Thus *conyhood,* the state of a dupe. Also, *to cony,* to act the rabbit, to be fearful, seek to hide. The many words for a rabbit warren—*conyhole, conygreene, conygree, conyearth, conygarth, conyger, cunnery,* and more—were also used with sexual implication.—Massinger and Dekker in THE VIRGIN MARTIR (1622) punningly and cunningly exclaim: *A pox on your Christian cockatrices! They cry, like poulterer's wives, 'No money, no coney'.*

confabulate. To chat; Latin *com* + *fabula,* a tale, whence *fable.* Used 15th to 18th century; poets (Cowper, 1785; as recently as Browning, 1873) speak of the *confabulation* of birds. *Confabulation* is still used, humorously, of a conference, shortened at times to *confab.* In the 15th century, the verb was sometimes shortened to *confable.*

confarreation. (Five syllables.) A wedding. Especially, the solemn marriage of the ancient Romans, usually before the Pontifex Maximus and ten witnesses, and solemnized with a spelt-cake. Latin *confarreationem,* from *com-,* with + *farreum,* a spelt-cake; *far, farris,* grain, spelt. *Confarreate, confarreated,* married in that wise. Used in English in the 16th and 17th centuries; later, historically. See *diffarreation.*

conference. See *decollation.*

confricate. To rub together. Latin *com* + *fricare,* to rub. Hence also *confrication* (14th through 18th century) and (from 17th century) *confriction. Confricatrice, confrictrice* (in Bailey, 1753), a Lesbian, tribade (Greek *tribad-,* from *tribein,* to rub).

congee. See *congy.*

congeon. A dwarf; hence, a half-wit; hence a term of derision (especially applied to a child). Also *conjon.* Probably from Late Latin *cambionem,* a changeling, *cambire,* to change. A changeling (child of an incubus or demon substituted for a human child) grew up to be a dwarf, or deformed (that is, so distorted a child manifestly was not naturally born to such fine parents!). Mainly used in the 12th through the 15th century.

conger. A large salt-water eel, caught for food along the coasts of Britain. It attains a length of ten feet, and may be behind some of the sea-snake stories. *Conger-douce, conger-doust* (*doust, dust*), eel dried and powdered for soup. Also *kunger, cunger, congre, coonger, congar.*

Both *conger* and *conger-head* were used as terms of abuse for a man; Shakespeare uses *conger* in HENRY IV, PART TWO (1597); Dekker in THE HONEST WHORE, PART TWO (1630) says: *She nibbled but wud not swallow the hooke, because the cunger-head her husband was by.*

congree. To join in agreement. French *gré,* liking. In the 16th century, *gree* was a common shortening of *agree. Agree, ad,* to give accord *to*; *congree, com,* to give accord together. Shakespeare in HENRY V (1623 edition) speaks of government *congreeing in a full and natural close.* The 1600 quarto edition, however, has *congrueth with a mutual consent,* and Shakespeare's form may be *congrue*; Latin *congruus,* agreeing, suitable, *congruere,* to meet together, whence also *incongruous.*

congy. A dismissal; formal leave to depart; a farewell gift to a beggar; a bow, a courtesy on departing (later applied to any bow). Used in English, 15th to 17th century; later, felt to be a French word, *congé.* Also *congee, conge, coungy*; roundabout from Latin *commeatus,* leave to pass; *com,* together + *meare, meatum,* to pass. Also as a verb; to give leave, to license; to permit to depart; to dismiss; to take ceremonious leave. Shakespeare in ALL'S WELL THAT ENDS WELL (1601) says: *I have congied with the Duke, done my adieu with his neerest.* Armin in A NEST OF NINNIES (1608) said: *Sir William, with a low congy, saluted him; the good lady, as is the courtly custom, was kist of this nobleman.* Lamb in ESSAYS OF ELIA (IMPERFECT SYMPATHIES; 1833) said: *I do not like to see the Church and Synagogue kissing and congeeing in awkward postures of an affected civility.*

conjugial. Conjugal. From Latin *conjugium,* connection, marriage, *conjugem,* spouse; from *com-,* together + *iugo* (also *iungo*), to bind. *Conjugial* was introduced in 1794, in the title of Swedenborg's DELIGHTS OF WISDOM CONCERNING CONJUGIAL LOVE, to distinguish his special concept of marriage, "an union of souls, a conjunction of minds." *Cp. scortatory.*

connictation. Winking. Latin *com-,* together + *nictare,* to wink. A 17th and 18th century dictionary word, still good for humorous use. *Nictate* and *nictitate,* and their noun forms in *-ion,* are mainly medical terms.

connudate. To strip naked. Latin *com-,* together + *nudus,* bare. A 17th and 18th century dictionary word, *connudation* is just the term for the practice of 20th century nudist colonies.

connyng. See *ammove.*

conquassate. To shake violently. Latin *com* (with intensive force) + *quassare,* frequentative of *quatere,* shake. Also *conquassant,* shaking violently (used of a woman in travail); *conquassation.*

conrey. See *corrody.*

consarcination. Patching together; hence, a heterogeneous gathering; F. Saunders, in the Preface to A SALAD FOR THE SOLITARY (1853) calls the book *a consarcination of many good things for the literary palate.* Also *consarcinate,* to patch together; used mainly in the 17th century. The HISTRIOMASTIX (1610) aptly remarks that stage plays are *consarcinated of sundry merry, ludicrous officious artificial lies.*

consciuncle. A conscience most minutely particular. A derisive nonce-word coined by Bishop Hacket in 1670, still fit for Burns' *unco guid.*

consentaneous. Agreeing; agreeable (to); unanimous; also, happening at the same time—in this sense supplanted by *simultaneous.* From Latin *consentaneus,* agreeing; *consentire*: *com-*, together + *sentire,* to feel. Richardson in CLARISSA HARLOWE (1748) speaks of the *consentaneousness* [accord] *of corporal and animal faculties.*

conskite. To befoul with ordure, as when one's bowels are loosed with fear. Thus Urquhart in his translation (1653) of Rabelais said: *He had conskited himself with meer anguish and perplexity.*

consobrine. A sister's son, as Cockeram lists it (1623); a cousin. Latin *com,* together + *soror,* sister. Hence *consobrinal* (accent on the *bry*), related as a cousin. J. Hannay in SINGLETON FONTENOY, R.N. (1850) spoke of *two avuncular baronets, a consobrinal lord.*

consoude. An herb of healing virtues. One, for the Romans; the medieval herbalists found three, which they labeled *consoude major, media, minor*: respectively, the comfrey, the bugle, and the daisy. The word *consoude* (also *consowde, consolde*) is via Old French from Latin *consolidare,* whence also *consolidate; com* (with intensive force) + *solidare,* to make firm, to heal. By the 16th century, popular confusion with *sound,* whole, had changed the spelling to *consound.* In both spellings, the word was also used as a verb, as when Gerarde in his HERBAL of 1597 advises: *Fit consounding plaisters upon the greeved place.*

consound. See *consoude.*

conspectuity. Power of sight. An irregular form from Latin *conspectus,* sight (*conspectus* was used in the 19th century, to mean a comprehensive survey; a summary but general view). The word was coined by Shakespeare in CORIOLANUS (1607): *What harme can your beesome conspectuities gleane out of this charracter?* For *beesome* (*bisson,* purblind) see *besom.*

conspersion. Sprinkling. Latin *com-,* altogether + *spargere,* to sprinkle. Lancelot Andrewes (1607) and Jeremy Taylor (1649) in sermons use the word—Andrewes: *of that conspersion whereof Christ is our firstfruits*—to mean the dough for the sacramental wafer. To *consperge* is to besprinkle, to strew all over. For a time, this word was a rival of *aspersion,* which meant a sprinkling, a shower; then *conspersion* faded and *aspersion* drew to its special, figurative use.

conspissation. Thickening; condensation. Latin *com* (with intensive force) + *spissare,* to thicken; *spissus,* thick, dense. Also to *conspissate;* used 15th through 17th century.

conspue. See *conspute.*

conspurcation. Defilement, pollution. From Latin *com* (with intensive force) + *spurcare,* to befoul; *spurcus,* unclean. Also *conspurcate,* verb—and adjective; W. Sclater in a Biblical exegesis (1619) declared: *Never saw the Sun a people more conspurcate with lust.*

conspute. To spit upon; to despise. Latin *com* (with intensive force) + *spuere, sputum,* to spit. Hence also *conspue,* and the still current *sputum.* Used from the 16th century; still found, as when THE SATURDAY REVIEW of 27 September, 1890 vented the statement: *The only thing criticism has to do with the Shakespeare-Bacon craze is to conspue it!* Now the adherents of Oxford claim the day.

constult. To play the fool with; to become as big a fool as those around. Latin *com,* together + *stultus,* foolish; whence also to *stultify.* The Water Poet in THE

WORLD'S EIGHTH WONDER (1630) said: *Some English gentlemen with him consulted And he is nat'rally with them constulted.*

constupration. Ravishing; deflowering. Latin *com* (with intensive force) + *stuprare,* to ravish; *stuprum,* violation. *Constupration,* and the verb *constuprate,* were favorite words in the 17th century; John Bale (1550): *The good ghostly father that constuprated two hundred nuns in his time*; Burton in THE ANATOMY OF MELANCHOLY (1621): *Their wives and loveliest daughters constuprated by every base cullion;* Algernon Sidney of Sydney, in DISCOURSES CONCERNING GOVERNMENT (1683): *Romulus and Remus, the sons of a nun, constuprated, as is probable, by a lusty soldier.* The world has little changed.

consuetude. Custom; habit; the unwritten law of established custom. Also, more formally (19th century) *consuetitude.* Latin *consuetudo,* short for *consuetitudo*; *consuescere, consuetum,* to accustom, to grow accustomed; *com,* together, altogether + *suescere, suetum,* to make one's own; *suus,* one's own—whence the more lingering *desuetude,* occasionally innocuous. Hence *consuete* (14th to 17th century), accustomed; *consuetudinal,* pertaining to custom; *consuetudinary,* according to custom. A *consuetudinary* is a book of customs; also, a book of the ritual and ceremonial usages of a religious body. By way of Old French contraction to *coustume,* this Latin word also grew into English *custom.* Emerson in his ESSAYS (1844; PRUDENCE) speaks of *the sweetness of those affections and consuetudes that grow near us.*

contabescence. A wasting away, decay. From Latin *com* (with intensive force) + *tabescere,* to pine, to melt; inceptive of *tabere,* to waste away; *tabes,* a wasting, decay. Used in 17th and 18th centuries; still used in botany to mean atrophy of anthers, so that no pollen is formed.

contabulation. Joining of boards to form a platform or floor. Latin *com-,* together + *tabula,* table, plank. Hence also the verb, to *contabulate.* Used in the 17th and 18th centuries.

conteck. Strife; quarrelling; also, to contend, to quarrel, to dispute. From the Old French, perhaps *con-,* against + *teche,* to touch. Common in English (like the action it describes) since the 13th century. A *contecker* is a quarrelsome person; also *contakkour, contacker*; hence *contackerous,* which in the 20th century is dialectic or slang as *cantankerous.* Chaucer in THE KNIGHT'S TALE (1386) has *contek with bloody knife and scharp manace.*

contemn. To despise. Used from the 15th century; surviving in the noun, *contempt.* Latin *con* (with intensive force) + *temnere,* to despise; Greek *temnein,* to judge. In the 16th century the form *to contempne* was used. Hence *contemner,* a scorner; *contemnible,* despicable. The sense of this verb fused with, or was lost in, that of *to condemn.*

contentation. Contentment. Also, satisfaction of a claim, or one's conscience. Common from the 15th to the 17th century. Occasionally misused for *contention,* strife, from *to contend. Contention* is from Latin *contendere, contentum*; *con,* against + *tendere,* to stretch, strain; whence also *tendency, distend, tentative, tempt* (*temptare,* to handle, test, intensive of *tendere*), *tendon, tent. Content, contentation* are from *contineo, contentum*; *com,* together + *tenere,* to hold, whence also *tenacious, tenant, continent.* King James I tried to act (so he said in 1603) *for the contentation of our subjects.*

contesseration. Close bond of friendship. Latin *com-*, together + *tessera* (*hospitalis*) a square tablet: broken in half, between two friends, so that the generations after them might know the friendship. In the 17th century, John Donne (in a Sermon of 1620) and others use *contesseration* to apply to baptism into the brotherhood of the church, or to the Eucharist.

contignation. Joining together (of beams); the manner or state of being joined. Latin *com-*, together + *tignum,* building material, piece of timber. Used by Donne (1630), Evelyn (1641), Burke (1796), and other 17th and 18th century writers. Also figuratively (Burke): *Linked by a contignation into the edifice of France.* The verb is *contignate,* to join together with, or as with, beams.

continge. To come together; to happen. Latin *com-*, together + *tangere,* to touch. The verb seems to be in dictionaries only; much more widely used was the noun *contingence,* touching, contact; a happening, a thing that happens by chance—which by the mid-19th century was supplanted by the still current *contingency.*

contingerate. To approach the borders of. Latin *com,* together + *tangentem,* touching; *tangere, tactum,* to touch; whence also *tangent, tactile, intangible, contact, tactless.* A word coined by the Water Poet (1630) satirizing learned coinages, inkpot terms. *Yet I with nonsense could contingerate, With catophiscoes terragrophicate, And make my selfe admir'd immediately By such as understand no more then I.*

contortuplicated. Twisted and entangled. Latin *contortus,* twisted together + *plicatus,* folded. Still used in botany; in the 17th century also figurative (1648): *the snarl'd and contortuplicated affairs of the State.*

contrist. To make sad. French *contrister;* Latin *com* (with intensive force) + *tristare,* to sadden; *tristis,* sad. *Contristate* was used in the 17th century (by Bacon and others) with the same meaning. Bacon also noted, in THE ADVANCEMENT OF LEARNING (1605), that Solomon observed *that in spacious knowledge there is much contristation.* The shorter verb, *contrist,* was used into the 19th century, by Urquhart in his translation (1653) of Rabelais; by Sterne in TRISTRAM SHANDY (1761); in the 1625 translation of Boccaccio's DECAMERON: *that your contristed spirits should be chearfully revived.* Many works have that purpose today.

contriturate. To pulverize. Latin *com* (with intensive force) + *tero, tritus,* to rub, to grind—whence also English *detritus,* debris. In Scott's THE FORTUNES OF NIGEL (1822), King James calls himself *the very malleus maleficorum, the contunding and contriturating hammer of all witches, sorcerers, magicians. To contund* is to pound, bruise, pound to pieces (as in a mortar): Latin *com* + *tundere, tusus,* to beat. The past participle form of this gave us the English verb *contuse,* to bruise (especially as with a blunt instrument that does not break the skin); this has survived in the noun form, *contusion.*

contund. See *contriturate.*

contusion. See *contriturate.*

convail, convale. This simple form meaning to recover strength or health, was replaced by *convalesce* in the 19th century. *Convale* is from Latin *con,* altogether + *valere,* to be strong. From *valere* came *valescere,* to grow strong, whence *convalesce.*

convenable. See *conable.*

convertite. A convert. Especially common in the 16th and 17th centuries, renewed by Scott and others in the 19th. Shakespeare in KING JOHN (1595) has: *But since you are a gentle convertite, My tongue shall hush againe this storme of warre.* BLACKWOOD'S EDINBURGH MAGAZINE of 1839 recognized the newly-won's fervor: *With all the zeal of a new convertite.* Especially, a repentant magdalen; so Browning in THE RING AND THE BOOK (1868); John Weever in ANCIENT FUNERALL MONUMENTS (1631) said: *This church was built by a female convertite, to expiate and make satisfaction for her former sinnes; and . . . was called Hore-Church at the first.* Also *to convertise, convertyse, convertize,* to convert. A *convertist* is a professed convert, or a professional convert or converter (used in scorn). A *convertite* may be used of one honestly won over to a faith (Marlowe, THE JEW OF MALTA; 1592) or to an opinion or course of action, as in KING JOHN. It may also be used in scorn, as when Lamb confesses his IMPERFECT SYMPATHIES (ESSAYS OF ELIA; 1833; *cp. congee*): *I do not understand these half convertites. Jews christianizing —Christians judaizing—puzzles me. I like fish or flesh.*

conviciatory. Railing, abusive. *To conviciate* is to revile; Latin *com* (with intensive force) + *vitiare,* to spoil, corrupt, make faulty; *vitium,* a fault. Also *convitiatory;* and there is a rare (16th-17th century) noun, *convicy,* reviling, abuse. Thomas James, in A TREATISE OF THE CORRUPTION OF SCRIPTURE BY . . . THE CHURCH OF ROME (1611) wisely warned against *convitiatorie arguments, which do but ingender strife.* J. C. Hobhouse, in A JOURNEY THROUGH ALBANIA . . . (1813), encountered *the Greeks, whose convitiatory language is most violent and abusive.*

cony. See *coney.*

conyger. A rabbit warren. Also *conygarth, conygrate, conygree, conygreen; conynger, cunnerie, conery*—and a dozen other forms of this very common word, from the 10th into the 19th century. It was also called *conyhold, conyhole,* and—though not until the 17th century—*conywarren.* See *coney.*

conynge. A variant of *coney, q.v.*

cop. See *spincop.*

coparcenary. Joint share in an inheritance; joint ownership. *Com-,* together + Old French *parçonerie,* partnership; Latin *partitionem,* dividing, whence also English *partition.* Also *coparcenery.* Thence also *coparcener,* a co-heir or copartner. From the 16th century; replaced in the late 19th century, in the second sense, by *copartnership* and *copartner.*

copataine. A high-crowned hat, shaped like a sugar-loaf. Shakespeare, in THE TAMING OF THE SHREW (1596): *Oh fine villain, a silken doublet, a velvet hose, a scarlet cloak, and a copataine hat.* Scott in KENILWORTH (1821) speaks of a *capotaine* hat. Perhaps he thought the word related to *cap;* but its most frequent forms are *copintank, copentank, coptank,* and the like. There are also forms including *coptanct, copple-tanked,* which mean wearing such a hat. References to this style of hat are frequent through the 16th century, and the hat may be seen in the art of the period, but (although *cop* was slang for head) the origin of the word is unknown. Stranger styles have been seen since.

cope (as a noun). Originally a long cloak worn outdoors as an outer garment; a common English word until the 18th century; in this sense, supplanted by *cape,* another form of the same word. By extension: (1) a tablecloth. (2) In the phrases (a) *cope of Night,* pall of night —Gower, Addison, Southey; (b) *cope of lead,* coffin (15th to 17th century); (c) *cope of heaven,* Chaucer, Spenser, to Swinburne—in this sense sometimes just *the cope*: Shakespeare, PERICLES (1608): *The cheapest country under the cope*; hence used to mean height, expanse, firmament, as by Coleridge and Tennyson. (3) A canopy; Milton in PARADISE LOST (1667): *Bad angels seen Hovering on wing under the cope of Hell*; Longfellow in EVANGELINE (1847): *the cope of a cedar. Cp. copeman.*

From another source—Old French *cop* (Modern *coup*), blow—comes *cope,* encounter, shock of combat; by extension, *to gain cope of,* to gain advantage over. Still another *cope* (related to *cheap*) was a 16th century word meaning bargain; a large sum was called *God's cope.* May God's cope be wi' ye!

copeman. A dealer, merchant. In late 18th century, a receiver of stolen goods. Also *copesman, copemaster, copesmaster. Cp. copesmate.* (Also, a person wearing a *cope;* 19th century.) *Cope,* to deal satisfactorily with—in OTHELLO (*is again to cope with your wife*), to have intercourse —is from French *couper,* to strike, earlier *colper*; Latin *colaphus,* blow of the fist. Jonson in VOLPONE (1605) says: *He would have sold his part of Paradise For ready money, had he met a copeman.*

copener. Paramour. From *copen,* Middle English *copnien,* to long for. Used from the 9th through the 14th century. Also *copynere.* In THE SEVEN SAGES (1320), *The pie saide, 'Bi God Almight! The copiner was here tonight.'*

copesmate. A person with whom one *copes*; an adversary. Hence, a love partner, paramour. Hence, a partner or colleague; a partner in marriage, spouse; by extension, a confederate (cheat) at cards or other gaming; more vaguely, often with contempt, a fellow. Also *copemate; cp. copeman.* Lisle in his translation (1625) of Du Bartas: *Fooles, idiots, jesters, anticks, and such copesmates as of naughtworth are suddenly start up.* Jonson, in EVERY MAN IN HIS HUMOUR (1598): *O, this is the female copesmate of my son.* Shakespeare in THE RAPE OF LUCRECE (1593): *Mis-shapen Time, copesmate of ugly Night . . . eater of youth, false slave to false delight, Base watch of woes, sin's packhorse, virtue's snare.*

copintank. See *copataine.*

copist. A 17th and 18th century variant of *copyist.*

coppice. A grove of small trees, grown for periodical cutting. Via Old French *copiez* from Late Latin (Salic Law) *colpus,* blow, stroke; Greek *kolaphos,* blow. Treated as a plural, *coppice* (*copys*) developed the forms *copy, coppy;* more often it was shortened to *cops,* surviving as *copse.* Milton, in LYCIDAS (1637) speaks of *the willows and the hazel copses green*; Goldsmith in THE DESERTED VILLAGE (1770) has: *Near yonder copse where once the garden smiled.* Shakespeare in LOVE'S LABOUR'S LOST (1588) has: *Upon the edge of yonder coppice.* Shakespeare does not have Macbeth's sentry cry, on seeing Birnam Wood move toward Dunsinane: *Cheese it, the copse!*

coprolite. A stony round fossil, originally (or thought to be) animal dung. Greek *kopros,* dung + *lithos,* stone, whence also *lithography,* etc. *Kopros* has given us several English words, including *coprophi-*

lous, fond of, or feeding on, dung, by extension, fond of "obscene" literature; *coprophory,* purgation. *Coprolite* is accented on the first syllable; all the others, on the second. Swinburne in an essay on Ben Jonson (1889), hopefully chauvinist, exclaimed: *All English readers, I trust, will agree with me that coprology should be left to Frenchmen.*

copse. See *coppice.*

copy. Abundance; fullness; resources; power. Latin *copia,* multitude; whence also *cornucopia,* horn of plenty. Used from the 14th century. (In Medieval Latin, from such phrases as *facere copiam describendi,* to give the power of setting down, came the meaning of *copy,* a transcript.) For an instance of its use, see *betony.*

coquet. Amorously familiar; flirtatious. French *coquet,* diminutive of *coq,* cock; after the strut of the rooster. As a noun *coquet* was used of either sex—Gay in THE BEGGAR'S OPERA (1728) says: *The coquets of both sexes are self-lovers, and that is a love no other whatever can dispossess*—until the mid-18th century, when *coquette* was adopted for the woman, and the male *coquet* became obsolete. The verb *coquet, coquette* and the noun *coquetry* are still prevalent.

coraggio. The Italian word for courage, used in English as an exclamation. Shakespeare in ALL'S WELL THAT ENDS WELL (1601), and in THE TEMPEST (1610): *Coragio, Bully-Monster, Coragio!* Also Macaulay, in his DIARY of 1850: *But coraggio! and think of* A.D. *2850. Where will your Emersons be then?*

corance. See *crants.*

coranto. (1) A lively dance. From Italian *coranta,* "a kind of French dance"; also *courante,* directly from the French. It was danced at a lively triple time; hence *coranto* was used in general for lively; Middleton in MORE DISSEMBLERS BESIDES WOMEN (1627) has *Away I rid, Sir; put my horse to a coranto pace.* Shakespeare knew the dance; HENRY V (1599) has: *They bid us to the English Dancing Schools, And teach lavoltas high, and swift carrantos. Cp. galliard; pavan; lavolta.* (2) a news-letter, or early newspaper. Modified, like the above, by the Italian, but from French *courante,* current. Used in the 17th century, as in Burton's ANATOMY OF MELANCHOLY (1621): *New books every day, pamphlets, currantoes, stories.* Also *currant, curranto.* The currantos came to be noted for their feigned stories, so that *coranto* was synonymous with *liar.* Thus the Water Poet (WORKS; 1630) slily wrote: *It was reported lately in a currant that a troope of French horse did take a fleete of Turkish gallies, in the Adriaticke sea, neere the gulph of Venice. The newes was welcome to me, though I was in some doubt of the truth of it; but after, I heard that the horses were shod with very thicke corke; and I am sure I have heard of many impossibilities as true as that.* That's one for the horse marines (*q.v.*)!

corat. A dish, recipe given in THE FORME OF CURY (1390): *Take the noumbles* [entrails] *of calf, swyne, or of shepe; parboile hem, and skerne hem to dyce; cast hem in gode broth, and do thereto herbes. Grynde chyballs* [*chibol*: rock onion—between onion and leek] *smalle y-hewe. Seeth it tendre, and lye it with yolkes of eyrenn* [eggs]. *Do thereto verjous, safronn, powdor-douce, and salt, and serve it forth.*

corbel. A raven. Via Old French *corbel* from Latin *corvellum,* diminutive of *corvus,* raven. The *corbel's fee* was part of a deer left by the hunters for the ravens (for good luck and propitiation). From its shape, in profile like a raven's beak, *corbel* was used by architects in Medieval France and England to mean a projection, jutting out from the face of a wall, to act as a support. It was usually a plain, unadorned architectural feature (although Spenser in THE FAËRIE QUEENE, 1596, speaks of *a bridge . . . with curious corbes and pendants graven faire*) until Scott seized on the term in THE LAY OF THE LAST MINSTREL (1805) and gave it decorations: *The corbels were carved grotesque and grim.* Since then, historical novelists (and some historians) have elaborated the decorations.

Latin *corvus,* raven, apparently had another diminutive, *corvetto,* from which a variant of *corbel* came into English—*corbet,* with the same architectural significance. Chaucer used this in THE HOUS OF FAME (1384): *How they hate in masoneryes As corbetz and ymageryes.* This passage was misunderstood, and 17th and 18th century dictionaries define *corbet* and *corbel,* erroneously, as "a niche in a wall, for a statue, etc." So even Britton's DICTIONARY OF THE ARCHITECTURE OF THE MIDDLE AGES, in 1838.

corcousness. Corpulency. Listed by Bailey (1751) as an old word. The adjectives *corcy, corsy, corsive,* big-bodied, were used from the 15th into the 17th century. From French *corsé,* having body; *cors,* body, Latin *corpus. Corsive* was more frequently used as a variant of *corrosive,* as Jonson speaks of *corsive waters* in THE ALCHEMIST (1610). Topsell, in THE HISTORIE OF SERPENTS (1608), tells that Podagra went *to the house of a certain fat, rich, and well-monied man; and quietly laid herself down at the feet of this corsie sire. Podagra* (gout) is from Greek *pous, pod-,* foot + *agra,* a catching: a trap for the foot. This is the story of the origin of gout. Life insurance statistics have further woes for the corsy.

cordovan. See *cordwain.*

cordwain. Leather, originally of goat skins, later of split horsehides. Much used for shoes by the upper classes in the Middle Ages. Named from *Cordova,* Spain, whence the leather came. Used from the 12th through the 16th century; revived by Scott in REDGAUNTLET (1824), but since 1590 largely replaced by the form *cordovan,* reborrowed directly from the Spanish and still used.

coriander. A plant from the Levant, naturalized in parts of England, the fruit whereof is used for flavoring. Also (*coriander-seed*; from the shape), 18th and early 19th century slang for money. Ozell in his translation (1737) of Rabelais, wrote: *Which they told us was neither for the sake of her piety, parts, or person, but for the fourth comprehensive p, portion; the spankers, spur-royals, rose-nobles, and other coriander seed with which she was quilted all over.* Coriander was also used in the fumigation, part of the incantation ceremony to summon spirits, who appeared within the wreathing and writhing smoke.

Corinthian. (1) Elegant in style. Emerson in his essay on BEHAVIOUR (1860) says: *Nothing can be more excellent in kind than the Corinthian grace of Gertrude's manners.* Arnold, on the other hand, speaking of literary style, contrasts it with *the warm glow, blithe movement, and soft pliancy of life,* as in the Attic style, and with *the over-heavy richness and encumbered gait of the Asiatic*; the Corinthian style *has glitter without warmth, rapidity without ease, effectiveness with-*

out charm. (2) In various uses, from the reputation for profligacy and dissipation of the inhabitants of *Corinth.* When Shakespeare in TIMON OF ATHENS (1607) says: *Would we could see you at Corinth,* he means a house of ill fame. When in HENRY IV, PART ONE he has: *I am . . . a corinthian, a lad of mettle, a good boy,* the implication is of profligate idling, gay licentiousness. In 19th century England the word was used for a man about town, a 'swell'; also, especially in the United States, an amateur yachtsman, a wealthy sportsman. Among phrases: *to act the Corinthian,* to commit fornication; also *to corinthianize,* to be licentious; to be a (costly) prostitute. *It falls not to every man to get to Corinth* (not every one can afford it), said Plutarch: the courtesans there, notably Lais, as Demosthenes commented, spurned many suitors and set enormous prices on their favors. Lais might ask 10,000 Attic drachmae (some $3,000) for a night's companionship.—*Corinthian brass* was an alloy (perhaps of gold, silver and copper) highly valued for ornaments; but also, figuratively, it was used to mean effrontery, shamelessness. Hence *corinthian,* brazen. St. Paul, in his first EPISTLE TO THE CORINTHIANS (the BIBLE) said: *It is reported commonly that there is fornication among you;* but from other aspects of the Biblical account Andrew Lang refers to the 'old saying' that Pater in MARIUS THE EPICUREAN (1885) worded as follows: *There is but one road that leads to Corinth.* The meaning here is that the way of evil is broad, with many tracks (the early Protestants might instance: All roads lead to Rome); but there is only one road, straight and narrow, to righteousness. The *Corinthian* (vs. the *Doric* and the *Ionic*) is the lightest and most ornate of the three orders of Grecian architecture, its column being identifiable by the bell-shaped capital adorned with rows of acanthus leaves. Ruskin in THE STONES OF VENICE (1851) says that *the two orders, Doric and Corinthian, are the roots of all European architecture.*

cormarye. Another olden dish, from THE FORME OF CURY (1390): *Take coliander, caraway, smale grounden; powder of pepper and garlec y-grounde in rede wyne. Medle alle these together, and salt it.* [A goodly start!] *Take loynes of pork, rawe, and fle of the skyn, and pryk it welle with a knyf, and lay it in the sawse. Roost thereof what thou wilt, and keep that that fallith therefrom in the rosting, and seeth it in a possynet* [*posnet*: small pot, skillet] *with faire broth, and serve it forth with the roost anoon.*

cornage. A feudal rent, calculated by the horned beasts (French *corn, corne,* horn): one in every ten was set apart for the overlord. *Cornage* is interesting because of the misunderstandings of later historians and lexicographers. Littleton (1574) said that it was land granted because the tenant engaged himself to blow a horn as warning of a (Scotch or other) enemy raid; this error is repeated in Blackstone's COMMENTARIES (1767). Also, misread as *coruage, coraage,* it was explained in the 17th century as an unusual imposition, a levy of corn.

cornardy. Folly. A 14th century word, from Old French *cornard,* a cuckold, a horned person; *corn,* horn. See *cornute.*

cornemuse. A hornpipe; an early form of the bagpipe. Not every loyal Scot approved of it; BLACKWOOD'S EDINBURGH MAGAZINE of August 1882 said: *Long before the cornamouse (father of the bagpipe) sent its execrable Sclavic notes up the Highland straths.* Chaucer in THE

HOUS OF FAME (1384) mentioned the instrument; Mrs. Palliser (in BRITTANY; 1869) said that it is the national instrument of Western and Southern France. It may have wailed with the builders of the pyramids.

cornute. Horned; in various figurative senses. (1) a retort used in distilling; 17th and 18th centuries. (2) a forked pennon; 17th century. (3) a cuckold—common 14th through 18th century; in this sense, the Italian form *cornuto* was often used, as in Shakespeare's THE MERRY WIVES OF WINDSOR (1598): *the peaking cornuto her husband.* Hence also *cornardy,* state of being deceived or horned; folly. (4) a dilemma; the "horned argument," see *ceratine.*—Hence also the verb, popular among playwrights into the 18th century, *to cornute,* to give horns, to cuckold. Thomas Jordan, in a poem of 1675, pillories jealousy: *He that thinks every man is his wife's suitor Defiles his bed, and proves his own cornutor.*

corody. See *corrody.*

corposant. A glowing ball of electrical discharge sometimes seen on a church steeple or a ship's mast; I have seen one atop the Empire State Building. From Portuguese *corpo santo*; Latin *corpus sanctum,* holy body, body of a saint. Since *St. Elmo* is the patron saint of sailors, this phenomenon is also called *St. Elmo's fire* or *St. Elmo's light.* See *furole.*

corpse-candle. (1) A thick candle used at wakes. (2) a flickering light seen in a churchyard, believed by many to be an omen of death. Used in 17th, 18th and 19th centuries; Tennyson in HAROLD (1876) speaks of *Corpse-candles gliding over nameless graves.*

corrade. To scrape together; hence, to collect. Latin *com-,* together + *radere, rasus,* whence also *razor.* The *cor-* is also taken as though it were an intensive; in this use *corrade* means to scrape away, to wear away by scraping. A 17th century word, also used (from the past participle) in the form *corrase*; the noun, scraping together, was *corrasion.*

corrige. To correct; to punish. Latin *com-,* altogether + *regere,* to make straight. *Corrigenda* are things that must be corrected, as *agenda* are things to be done. *Corrige* was used in the 14th and 15th centuries (by Chaucer in BOETHIUS, 1374); *corrigendum* was taken directly from the Latin in the 19th century.

corrivate. To flow together. Small streams by *corrivation* grow into rivers. From Latin *com-,* together + *rivalis,* of the bank; *rivus,* stream. A *rival,* was, originally, a fellow from the opposite bank of the stream; a *corrival* is one of two or more rivals of equal status. Burton, in THE ANATOMY OF MELANCHOLY (1621) misused *corrivate* and *corrivation,* reversing the process, as though a large stream were dividing, as for irrigation.

corrody. An allowance for maintenance; a pension. Also *corody*; *corradie, corradye,* and the like; Romanic form *conredo,* making ready; whence English *conrey,* equipment, company equipped to fight, used in the 14th century. Accent on the *core.* Originally (in feudal time) the right of free quarters, supplied by the vassal to the lord on his circuit; or an abbot to the king; later, in the form of an annual payment. The last sense became dominant, hence the word lapsed with the Reformation.

corsned. The easiest of the three major medieval tests for guilt. Ordeal of bread: a piece of bread (about an ounce) consecrated by the priest, to be swallowed by persons accused of a crime "wishing it might be their poison, or last morsel, if they were guilty." So said Bailey in 1751, by which time the word was purely historical. *Corsned* was a Saxon test. Old English *corsnaed, cor,* choice, trial + *snaed,* bit, piece, *snidan,* to cut. In the ordeal of fire, if the red-hot iron does not burn you, you are innocent. In the ordeal of water, if when bound and thrown in you do not sink, you are guilty. Most ordeals—and *corsned* with them—were abolished in the early 13th century; ordeal of water was used as a test for witches until comparatively recent times.

corsy. See *corcousness.*

corybant. Originally, a priest of the Phrygian worship of Cybele, who performed with noisy, turbulent dancing; hence, a reveler. Hence *corybantiasm, corybantic* frenzy. The plural is usually *corybantes;* Chaucer (in BOETHIUS, 1374) has *coribandes;* Drummond of Hawthornden in his poems of 1649 has *corybants.* The O.E.D. defines *corybantiate,* to act like a *corybant;* but Bailey in his DICTIONARY (1751) has "*corybantiate,* to sleep with one's eyes open, or be troubled with visions that one cannot sleep." In this sense, *corybantiating* is well known today. For another instance, see *clipse.*

corymb. A cluster of ivy-berries or grapes. Before the 19th century used only in botany. Also *corymbus,* the Latin form. De Quincey in THE ENGLISH MAIL-COACH (1849) speaks of *gorgeous corymbi from vintages.* Hence *corymbiate, corymbiated,* set with clusters of ivy-berries. The word has also been used in the sense of wreath or garland, as by Francis Thompson, who entitled one of his colorful poems (1888) *A Corymbus For Autumn.*

coryphée. The chief dancer in a ballet; by extension, a ballet dancer. In Greek drama the *koryphaios* was the leader of the chorus, *koryphe,* head, top. Hence also, the leader of a party, sect, group, etc.

cos. A short form of *coss, q.v.*

cosaque. A fancy paper (originally French, brought to England in the 19th century) for wrapping bon-bons; especially, the kind that explodes when pulled open. Named humorously from the unexpected, irregular firing of the Cossacks.

coscinomancy. See *aeromancy.*

cose. To make oneself *cosy.* Harriet Parr ('Holme Lee'—why should she pick this *homely* pseudonym?) in ANNIE WARLEIGH'S FORTUNES (1863) spoke of Rachel's *cosing with a delightful new novel in her sofa corner.*

cosher. To feast; to live free of charge with kinsmen. A 17th century use, from Irish *coisir,* entertainment. By the 19th century, *cosher* had come to mean (1) to pamper; (2) to chat with familiarly. *Coshery,* entertainment for himself and his followers exacted by an Irish chief—as John Dymmok put it in A TREATISE OF IRELAND (1600)—"after Easter, Christmastide, Whitsuntide, Michaelmas and all other times at his pleasure." Hence a *cosherer,* one who lives on others. In the 16th and 17th century, laws vainly sought to suppress the practice.

cosins. An 18th century style of stays, named from the maker. Pope in THE ART OF POLITICKS (1729) inquired: *Think we that modern words eternal are? Toupet, and tompion, cosins and colmar Hereafter will be called by some plain man A wig, a watch, a pair of stays, a fan.*

coss. "Rule of coss," the term for *algebra,* until the 16th century. From Italian *cosa,* thing, translating Arabic *shai,* thing, the word for the unknown quantity (x) of an equation. *Coss* is also (1) an Old English (mainly Scottish) word for barter, trade —both noun and verb; (2) a measure of length in India, varying from a little over one mile to a little over two. From Sanskrit *kroça,* originally a call, calling distance. There were stentors in those days. (3) An old form of *kiss,* which has continued; more often *cosse, q.v.*

cosse. A variant form of *kiss.* In SIR GAWAYNE AND THE GRENE KNIGHT (1360), the Green Knight's lady, tempting Sir Gawain, gently reproaches him with the suggestion that a true knight *couth nat lightly have lenged so long with a lady Bot he had craved a cosse by his courtaysye, Bi sum touch of summe trifle at sum tales ende.*

cosset. A lamb (or other quadruped) brought up by hand, a cade lamb. See *cade.* Also *cossart.* Hence, a pet, a spoiled child. Not used before the 16th century. To *cosset,* to fondle, to pamper, was used 17th through the 19th century. A *cossety* child (or cat) is one that expects and likes to be petted and pampered.

costable. Expensive. A 15th and 16th century word, supplanted by *costly.* Also (14th through 17th century) *costage,* expense, expenditure, cost; (in the 13th and 14th century) *costning. Costal,* however, means related to the ribs; Latin *costalis,* from *costa,* rib.

costard. A large apple. Originally probably a ribbed one, from Old French *coste,* rib. Applied in derision to the head, as in Shakespeare's KING LEAR (1605), where Edgar in disguise says to Oswald: *Ise try whether your costard or my ballow be the harder.*

costay. This is an old form, from the French *costoyer,* of the verb to *coast.* The spelling *coast* did not become usual until about 1600. The Latin *costa* meant rib or side. Lydgate in THE COMPLAINT OF THE BLACK KNIGHT (1430) says *And by a river forth I gan costay. Costeaunt* is a 14th century word (used by Gower) for bordering, alongside.

costermonger. Originally an apple-seller —*costard,* apple; *monger,* dealer. Thence, a pushcart salesman; also used figuratively —Miss Mitford (1812) *From all the selected fruits of all the poetical costermongers . . . could ye choose nothing more promising than this green sour apple?*— and as a term of abuse—Shakespeare, HENRY IV, PART TWO (1597): *Virtue is of so little regard in these costermonger times.* (the *monger* is pronounced *mun' ja.*) Hence also *costermongering, costermongery, costermongerdom.* Also, tout court, *coster.* Various other combinations have been used, such as *costerditty,* street song; *costerwife,* a woman with a stall for selling apples and the like. *Cp. applesquire.*

costile. See *custile.*

costning. See *costable.*

costnung. Temptation. Old English *costnian, costian,* to tempt. Used 10th into 13th century.

costrel. A bottle for holding wine or less inviting liquid; especially one with an ear by which it could be hung at the waist. Later, a small keg. Very popular, 14th through 16th century. Chaucer in THE LEGEND OF GOOD WOMEN (1385) shrewdly says (three manuscripts spell it *costret;* three, *costrel*): *And therewithal* *a costrel taketh he And said 'Hereof a draught, or two, or three.'* Perhaps in confusion with *costard, q.v., costrel* was also used (in the 17th century) to mean the head.

cothurnus. See *buskin.* Sometimes *cothurnus* is shortened to *cothurn.* Also, meaning shod with the *cothurnus,* hence tragic: *cothurnal, cothurnate, cothurnic, cothurnian.*

cotidian. Also *cotidial.* See *cotydyan.*

cotquean. A housewife. From *cot,* house +*quean,* woman; not to be confused with *cuckquean, q.v. Cotquean* later became a term of abuse, meaning a vulgar, scolding woman; finally (16th to 19th century) a man that fusses over and meddles in affairs that should be the housewife's. In this sense, *to play the cotquean,* to be a (male) busybody in household affairs. When Capulet (in Shakespeare's ROMEO AND JULIET, 1592) says: *Look to the bakt meats, good Angelica, Spare not for cost,* the Nurse replies: *Go you cot-queane, to, Get you to bed.* Ben Jonson piles it on, in THE POETASTER (1601) : *We tell thee thou angerest us, cotquean; and we will thunder thee in pieces for thy cotqueanity.*

cottabus. A diversion of ancient Athenian youth, which consisted in the young man's drinking some wine, invoking his mistress' name, and throwing the rest of the wine into a metal basin. If it struck fairly, with a clear sound, and none spilled over, it was a sign the girl would favor him. Greek *kottabos; kottabeion,* the metal basin for the game. *Cottabus* was a popular game, and developed more complicated forms; e.g., a number of little cups might be set floating in the basin, and he whose tossed wine sank the most cups would win a prize. Sometimes the mistresses floated in the wine.

cotydyan. An old form of *quotidian,* daily. Also *cotidian, cotidial.* Caxton in POLYCRONICON (1482) truly declared: *Historye is a perpetuel conservatryce of thoos thynges that have be doone before this presente tyme, and also a cotydyan wytness of bienfayttes, of malefaytes, grete actes, and tryumphal vyctoryes of all maner peple.*

coulant. Flowing. A pleasant 17th century word; French *coulant,* present participle of *couler,* to flow, whence also *coulee.* Lithgow in THE TOTALL DISCOURSE OF THE . . . PAINEFULL PEREGRINATIONS OF LONG NINETEEN YEARES TRAVAYLES (1632) states: *Epiphanio calls it Chrysoroas, that is . . . coulant in gold.* A sunny stream, pardy!

coulter. The front blade in a plough, making the vertical cut in the soil, which is then cut horizontally by the share. Old English *culter,* Latin *culter,* knife. Also *colter.* The King James BIBLE: SAMSON (1611) : *To sharpen every man his share and his coulter;* so also in Chaucer (1386). The word is in Burns' well-known TO A MOUSE; whence Hardy's figurative use in THE MAYOR OF CASTERBRIDGE (1889) : *That field-mouse fear of the coulter of destiny.* For Shakespeare's use, in HENRY V (1599), see *fumitory.*

count palatine. A noble that within his territory had the powers that elsewhere belonged to the sovereign alone. Originally, in the later Roman Empire, a count (*comes*) of the palace (*palatium,* palace), with supreme judicial authority; in the German Empire and in England it came to have the meaning above. Also *Earl palatine.* Shakespeare in THE MERCHANT OF VENICE (1596) speaks of one with *a better bad habite of frowning then the count palatine.* His fief was a *county,* but this word was sometimes used for the man; a few lines earlier in the same play, Shakespeare said: *Than is there the countie palentine.* The terms were also used figuratively, of one with complete authority in any field; Nashe in THE UNFORTUNATE TRAVELLER (1594) has Jacke Wilton say: *There did I (soft, let me drinke before I go anie further) raigne sole king of the cans and blacke jackes* [leather bottles for liquor], *prince of the pigmeis, countie palatine of cleane straw and provant* [army issue of arms and supplies], *and, to conclude, lord high regent of rashers of the coles and red herring cobs.*

countermate. Opponent, rival. Used in the 16th century.

countour. (1) An accountant; the officer that assisted in collecting and auditing county dues, in the 13th and 14th centuries. (2) especially in the phrase *the common countor,* a legal pleader, a serjeant-at-law. *Countour* is an early form of *counter,* one that *counts.* A poem on Edward II in 1325 mentioned *contours in benche that standeth at the barre.* In the first sense, Chaucer in the Prologue of THE CANTERBURY TALES (1386) says of the *ffrankeleyn*: *A shirreve* [sheriff] *hadde he been and countour.*

county palatine. See *count palatine.*

coup-gorge. A cut-throat (literally, from the French). As a military term (15th-17th centuries), a spot in which one must surrender or be cut to pieces.

couplement. (1) Joining two things together. Spenser in PROTHALAMION (1596) speaks of *love's couplement*; Shakespeare in SONNET XXI more figuratively says: *Making a coopelment of proud compare With sun and moon, with earth and seas rich gems.* (2) The things joined: a couple. Again Spenser (THE FAËRIE QUEENE, 1596), and Shakespeare in LOVE'S LABOUR'S LOST (1588): *I wish you the peace of mind, most royall cupplement.*

courante. See *coranto.* Swift but sliding steps (as opposed to leaping). Sometimes *corant, currant*; in the 18th century *courante* replaced *coranto*; *courante* is the only word used for the music, the tune of the dance.

court-cupboard. A movable sideboard, used to display plate and other silver service. Shakespeare, in ROMEO AND JULIET (1592): *Remove the court-cubbord, looke to the plate.* Scott revived the word in KENILWORTH (1821).

courtepy. A short coat or tabard of coarse material, worn in the 14th and 15th centuries. Dutch *korte,* short + *pie, pij,* a coarse woolen coat, a *peacoat.* Used by Langland (1362) and Chaucer (see *overeye* for quotation); revived by Bulwer-Lytton in THE LAST OF THE BARONS (1843): *Going out in that old courtpie and wimple—you a knight's grandchild.*

court-hand. The style of handwriting used in the English law-courts, from the 16th century until abolished by statute under George II. Commonly referred to; by Shakespeare in HENRY VI, PART TWO (1593).

court holy water. Fair words without sincere intention; flattery. Also *court-water. Court-holy-bread* was used in the same way. Shakespeare, in KING LEAR (1605): *O nunkle, court holy-water in a dry house is better than this rainwater out o' doore.*

courtship-and-marriage. See *Hymen's torch.*

cousin. As early as the still current sense (1300) was the use of *cousin* to mean any relative more distant than brother or sister. Legally, the next of kin, thus in Shakespeare's KING JOHN (1596) it refers to a grandchild. A king (15th to 18th century) might call another monarch, or a high noble, *cousin.* Also, a close friend; thus Celia in Shakespeare's AS YOU LIKE IT: *I pray thee, Rosalind, sweet my coz, be merry. Coz* (*q.v.*) was a frequent abbreviation of *cousin*; also *cosin, kosin, cozyn, cossen, cosyng,* and many more—at times it was linked with *cozen, q.v.*; *to make a cousin of,* to deceive, impose upon, cheat; *to prove a cousin to,* to prove a deceiver. Medieval Latin *cosinus,* perhaps from *consanguineus*; *com,* together + *sanguineus,* of blood; *sanguis,* blood. *Cp. aunt.* While sometimes traced to Latin *consobrinus,* cousin of the mother's side, *cousin* was the term used, from medieval times, in translation of a royal writ: *dilecto consanguineo nostro: to our well-beloved cousin.* In the 18th century, *cousin* was used for a strumpet; Motteux in his translation (1708) of Rabelais listed *cousins, cullies, stallions, and bellibumpers.* A *Cousin Betty* was successively a strumpet, a beggar, a madwoman (usually begging); similarly *Cousin Tom,* a bedlamite beggar. Also *cousin brutes,* fellow men; *to be cousin to,* to be akin, related; Chaucer in the Prologue to THE CANTERBURY TALES (1386) says: *The wordes moote be cosyn to the dede.*

cousoner. See *cozen.* Awdelay in THE FRATERNITYE OF VACABONDES (1565) devoted a chapter to *The Company of Cousoners and Shifters.* The author of THE DEFENSE OF CONNY-CATCHING (1592) spoke of *such secret villanies as are practised by cosoning companions.*

couth. (1) A variant of *could, couldeth*; for an instance, see *cosse.* (2) Known, familiar; kind, agreeable, pleasant. *Couth* is the past participle of the Old English verb *cunnan,* can (*ken*), which originally meant to know; it still means know how to, in such expressions as "I can play the violin," "I can speak Urdu." *Couth* is one of a number of English words of which the simple form has lapsed from use, while a compound remains: we may still call an unmannerly person *uncouth. Uncouth* (from the 9th century) meant unknown, strange; marvelous; solitary, desolate. Shakespeare's AS YOU LIKE IT (1600) says: *If this uncouth forrest yeeld any thing savage, I will either be food for it, or bring it for foode to thee.* Milton in L'ALLEGRO (1632) bids: *Hence, loathed Melancholy! . . . Find out some uncouth cell, Where brooding darkness spreads his jealous wings And the night raven sings.* Applied to persons, *uncouth* meant unfamiliar, strange; ignorant; hence (since the 18th century) uncultured, rude. Other compounds of which the simple form is forgotten are *ineffable, inscrutable, insuperable, innocent, incessant.* We retain both *complete* and *incomplete,* etc. We still use *fatigue* and *indefatigable,* but we have forgotten the two families *fatigable, fatigate, fatigation* and *defatigable, defatigate, defatigation.* We still say *avail* and *prevail,* but the veil has been drawn over *vail, q.v.* We use *connect, regard,* as well as their compounds; but, while one may at times be *disgruntled, gruntle* has had little use since the 17th century. We have *turbulence, disturbed, perturbed,* but *turb* (save as a noun, in the sense of swarm, crowd, troop) scarce even came upon the tongue. We still may speak of a man as *ruthless,* but *ruth* (*q.v.*) stands amid alien corn and *ruthful* long has lapsed. Other simple forms listed in this dictionary are: *complice, effable* (see *nefandous*), *dure, gressile, minish, pervious, peccable, rupt* (see *ruptile*), *mersion, sightly, sist, spatiate, suscitate, vastation* (see *vastity*), *ustulation* (*ustion*), *verberate, vestigate, sperate, suade, tire, lumination* (see *relume*), *spectable, tendance, trusion.* Also see *pease, semble, ligate, paration, sperse. Flammable* is coming back into currency, partly because *inflammable* is longer and is more likely to be misunderstood on the back of gasoline trucks. *Cp. avaunt.*

There are also words that have survived only in a set phrase. One seldom hears of a person *off* tenterhooks, or at the *beginning* of his tether, or, conceivably, *wrong* as a trivet! We always *take* umbrage, though trees may fairly be said to give it; we speak of *umbrageous boughs*; for an instance, see *patulous.* We are often *in* a quandary; one humorist even claims to have spent ten years there, but rarely has anyone announced that he is, or has come, *out of* a quandary. Nor, indeed, *out of* clover. Who has been in *low* dudgeon, or *low* jinks, or in *coarse* fettle? This could go lengthily on, if one didn't grow gruntled.

cove. (1) To hatch, to sit upon. Also *couve, couvey, covie*; roundabout from Latin *cubare,* to lie. Used in the 16th and 17th centuries. (2) A small room, a bedchamber, an inner chamber. Common Teutonic; Old Norse *kofi,* hut, cell. From this comes the still current sense of a sheltered place among the hills and woods, or along the shore. (3) A fellow, a chap. Possibly related to Scotch *cofe,* pedlar; it also appears as *co, coff, cofe, coffin.* It is Tudor thieves' and beggars' cant; see *pedlers French.*

covenable. See *conable.*

covent. The earlier form of *convent,* from Anglo-French *covent, couvent*; Latin *convenire, conventum,* to come together, whence also *convene.* The form survives in place-names, notably *Covent Garden,* London.

covershame. A cloth over nakedness; a cover over infamy. Also, the shrub savin (Juniperus Sabina) used to produce abortion. Gayton in THE ART OF LONGEVITY (1659) said: *Thou cover-shame, old fig-tree.* Dryden in THE SPANISH FRIAR (1681) asked: *Does he put on holy garments for a covershame of lewdness?*

coverslut. A garment to hide slovenliness; hence, an apron. A decoration, as in architecture, covering deformity or ugliness. Also used figuratively, as by Burke (1795): *rags and coversluts of infamy.*

covin. A confederacy; a conspiracy. From Old French *couvin, couvaine, convine,* from Latin *convenium, com-,* together + *venire,* to come. Also *covyne, kouveyne, covene, coven, convyne,* and the like. By extension, fraudulent action; secret device. A *coviner,* a *covinous* person, is one guilty of fraud. Frequent in the 14th century (Douglas; Gower uses several forms) and into the 17th; Scott revived the word in THE FAIR MAID OF PERTH (1828): *Such burghers as have covine* [secret agreement] *and alliance with the Highland clans.* Among nations in our time, covins are not unknown.

cowl. (1) A monk's hood; a monk's garment, hooded but sleeveless, covering the head and shoulders. Hence, a monk. Also used figuratively, as in Kingsley's THE WATER-BABIES (1863): *By the smoky town in its murky cowl.* Ultimately from Latin *cucullus,* hood of a cloak, from the root *cal, scal,* to hide, whence also *occult, squalor, calix, hole, hall, hell.* (2) A tub or large vessel for water and other liquids; especially a large one with two ears, to be carried on the shoulders of two men, on a *cowl-staff*. The *cowl-staff* was in every household, and made a handy weapon. Shakespeare uses it in THE MERRY WIVES OF WINDSOR (1598) when Falstaff is carried out and dumped into the water: *Go, take up these cloathes heere, quickly: Wher's the cowle-staffe?* Also *coule, coll, colt, cole, coal* + staff. This *cowl* is possibly from Latin *cupella,* a small cask, diminutive of *cupa,* cask, vat, from the root *cub,* bend, lie, whence also *incumbent, succubus, hump, hoop, heap. To ride on a cowl-staff,* to carry one, or to be carried, on a pole mockingly through the streets, a medieval popular punishment, as for a man who lets his wife wear the breeches. In ARDEN OF FAVERSHAM (1592) it was no less than the constable they took *and carried him about the fields on a colt-staffe.* May you deserve no such ride!

coxcombic. Relating to or resembling a coxcomb; foolishly conceited; vainly ostentatious. Also *coxcombical*; *coxcomical*; Scott in THE MONASTERY (1820) refers to *that singularly coxcomical work, called Euphues and His England.* Hence, *coxcombalities,* actions or things coxcombical.

coystril. Also *coystrill.* A form of *coistrel, q.v.*

coz. Short for cousin, *q.v.* A form of familiar address, to relatives or good friends, 16th to the 19th century. Shakespeare has "sweet my Coz"; "gentle Coz", in several plays.

cozen. To cheat. A most popular word,, 16th-18th centuries. Also *cosen, cooson, cousin, cozon,* and the like. Two origins are suggested: (1) From *cousin,* as persons sought to be entertained by claiming kinship—especially rife in Ireland; see *cosher.* (2) From Italian *cozzone,* horse-trainer, crafty knave. Shakespeare uses *cozen* in several plays, e.g., MERRY WIVES OF WINDSOR (1598) : *By gar I am cozoned;* ALL'S WELL THAT ENDS WELL: *Sawcie trusting of the cosin'd thoughts Defiles the pitchy night;* and in THE RAPE OF LUCRECE: *Her rosy cheek lies under, cozening the pillow of a lawful kiss.* Hence *cozenage* (also in various spellings), an act of cheating, a piece of trickery; *cozener, cousoner,* etc.; *cozenry.* The "gull-groper" in Dekker's LANTHORNE AND CANDLE-LIGHT (1608) tells the gull that *the dice are made of womens bones, and will cozen any man.*

crab. The wild apple, now known as the *crab-apple.* Used since the 15th century; also *crabbe*; *scrab.* Its sour taste made it as distasteful as the cultivated apple is delicious; thus Shakespeare in KING LEAR (1605) says: *She's as like this, as a crabbe's like an apple.* Browning (1878) figuratively called his poems *crabs: weak fruit of idle hours.* Crabs, however, were used for making verjuice, and were tasty roasted or preserved. In SONGES AND SONNETTES (1557) a poem in praise of "the pore estate" declares: *Such as with oten cakes in poore estate abides, Of care have they no cure* [worry], *the crab with mirth they rost.*

crachoun. See *craddon.*

crack-halter. A rogue; a gallows-bird. One who will some day crack (strain) the halter by which he is being hanged. A term of abuse (sometimes friendly), especially in the 16th and early 17th century playwrights. Also a *crackrope,* similarly either abusive or playful. Motteux in his translation (1708) of Rabelais mentions *about a score of fusty crackropes and gallowclappers.* Shirley in LOVE IN A MAZE (1631) cried: *You do not know the mystery: this lady is a boy, a very* *crackrope boy.* Dekker in NORTHWARD HOE (1607; the one direction these plays didn't *hoe* you was South) says of a talebearer: *Fetherstone's boy, like an honest crack-halter, layd open all to one of my prentices.*

cracknel. A light, crisp cracker, usually curved or hollow. Also *crackenelle, crackenal,* and the like. As Lord Berners put it, in his translation (1523) of Froissart: *Whan the plate is hote, they cast of the thyn paste thereon, and so make a little cake in maner of a crackenell, or bysket.* In English *biscuit;* in the U.S., *cracknel* has been replaced by *cracker* or *cookie.*

craddon. A coward. Also *crawdown; crathon, craton,* with the same meaning, may be other forms of the same word. Used 14th to 17th century. There is also a form *crachoun,* which conveys more scorn, suggesting French *crachat,* spit. There is also a form *craddant, crassant.* Hence *craddenly, craddantly, crassantly,* cowardly. So many forms seem to indicate that the species was widespread.

crambe. Originally c a b b a g e (Greek *krambe*); used by Jovenal (*crambe repetita*) to mean a distasteful repetition. Hence applied in English (16th through 18th century) for a wearying repetition of words or ideas. *Crambe,* as noun or verb, was sometimes used for *crambo, q.v.*

crambo. A name for two games. (1) A player starts with a word or line of verse; each other in succession must give one that rhymes with the first. If any repeats a rhyme, all cry 'Crambo!' and he pays a forfeit. This game was popular in the 17th and 18th centuries; I used to play a variation of it as a child, not quite so long ago. (2) *Dumb crambo*: one group must guess a word set by the other group. The guessers are told what the word rhymes with; then they act in dumb show one word after another until they hit the right one. A variant of this game, with questioning aloud, called "the game" or charades, is still played. Other senses in which *crambo* has been used are (3) rhyming (used contemptuously); (4) a fashion of drinking (early 17th century); (5) a variant of *crambe, q.v.*

crame. Originally (Old High German *chram, cram*) an awning; in English, a booth where goods are sold at a fair. Hence, a pedlar's stock of wares. Used 15th through 18th century; longer (as *krame, kraim*) in Scotland. Hence *cramer, creamer, crammer, craimer, kramer,* one who sells goods at a booth; a peddler.

cramp. See *crome.*

crankdort. See *cankedort.*

cranreuch. Hoarfrost. Used as an adjective in Burns' TO A MOUSE (1785): *The winter's sleety dribble, An' cranreuch cauld!*

crants. A garland, a chaplet. Old High German *kranz.* Also *corance.* Shakespeare, in HAMLET (1602), of the drowned Ophelia: *Yet here she is allowed her virgin crants* (Some versions have the word *rites*). Later, *crants* were garlands of white paper hung in the church for a young girl's funeral; the practice continued (in Yorkshire) into the 19th century.

crappit-head. The head of a haddock stuffed with the roe, oatmeal, suet, and spices. Apparently from Dutch *krappen,* to cram: a stuffed head. A Scotch 19th century notion of a delicacy, though Edward Ramsay in his REMINISCENCES (1861) sets down: *Eat crappit heads for supper last night and was the waur o't.*

crassantly. See *craddon.*

crassitude. Thickness. Latin *crassus*, thick; whence English *crass*, corresponding to the slang sense of 'thick.' At first this was simply a measuring term, used from the 15th century (*not five feet in length, and much less in crassitude*); then, by transference (17th century), gross ignorance, stupidity, extreme dullness of intellect. *Cp. inspissate.* Mortimer Collins in MARQUIS AND MERCHANT (1871) said that *Amy, not being afflicted with crassitude, soon did her work admirably.*

crastin. The day after; especially, after a feast-day or holiday. Used in the 16th and 17th century; via Old French from Latin *crastinum*, adjective form of *cras*, tomorrow. Hence the rare verb *crastinate*, to put off till tomorrow, which never found favor in English. Things seem more lingeringly, less malingeringly, delayed when we just *procrastinate*.

crayton. Also *critone*. A simple dish of the 14th century: *Tak checonys, and scald hem, and seth hem, and grynd gyngen, other pepyr, and comyn; and temper it up with god mylk; and do the checonys theryn; and boyle hem, and serve yt forth.*

crebrity. Frequency. Latin *creber*, frequent. Also *crebrous*, frequent. Used in the 17th and 18th centuries.

crathon. See *craddon*.

craton. See *craddon*.

credenda. Things to be believed. Plural of *credendum*, gerundive of *credere*, to believe. Used in the 17th and 18th centuries of religious matters, items of faith, and usually opposed to *agenda*, things to be done, "works." In the 19th century, the word was sometimes given a political application, as by Louis C. Miall in THE NONCONFORMIST of 1841: *Is the power of selecting the credenda of the nation to be vested in the civil magistrate?* That power is being widely manipulated today.

cremasters. Suspenders. Greek *kremaster*, from *krema-*, to hang. Accent on the second syllable. Still used in anatomy and entomology, but a superfine word for a super-fashionable haberdashery.

cremosin. An early form (Spenser) of *crimson*. Also *cremoysin, cremsin, cremysn.*

crepine. See *crespine*. Also spelled *crispyne, krippin, creppin,* and the like.

crepundian. A toy, a rattle. Hence, an empty talker, one who rattles on. Latin *crepundia*, a rattle, from *crepare, crepitum*. to rattle, tinkle; whence *crepitare*, to crackle, etc. (see *creve*) and English *crepitation*, crackling; *crepitate*, to crackle, (17th and 18th centuries) to break wind. Although idle talk continues, *crepundian* was used mainly in the 16th and 17th centuries. Nashe (Greene's MENAPHON, 1589) speaks of *our quadrant crepundios, that spit 'ergo' in the mouth of every one they meet.*

crepuscular. Pertaining to twilight. Also *crepusculine, crepusculous*; the first two favored by poets. I can still remember a lad of sixteen, who wrote, as a classroom blackboard exercise, a sonnet *To Certain Crepuscular Murmurers*—before he subdued his poet's heart to his biophysicist mind. Also *crepuscule, crepusculum*, twilight. Latin *crepusculum* is a diminutive, related to *creperum*, darkness, *creper*, dark. The Romans opposed *crepusculum*, the dusk of evening, to *diluculum* (*lux, lucis* light), the dusk of dawn. In the 17th century, however, the forms *dilucid*, clear, manifest (Latin *dis-*, apart; *lucere*, to shine, be clear); *dilucidate, dilucidation, dilucidity* were used—later supplanted by *lucid* and *elucidate*, etc.

crespine. A variant of *crêpe* (Old French *crespe*) with some special senses: (1) a net or caul, of gold thread, silk lace, etc., for the hair; worn by ladies of the 14th and 15th centuries. (2) a fringe of lace, for a hood; or for a bed, dais, and the like; 17th and 18th centuries. (3) "a sort of farce wrapt up in a veal caul"; also *crepine*; French *crépine,* the caul around the viscera. Listed by gastronome Bailey; still flavorous.

cresset. An iron basket in which a fire was lighted, to be hung on a pole or suspended from a roof, as a beacon; also used in the early theatre. Used from the 13th through the 16th century; till applied to a fire-basket on a wharf. Hence *cresset-light.* Used figuratively, as by Scott in WOODSTOCK (1826), of the moon's *dim dull cresset;* by Bryant in CONSTELLATIONS (1877): *The resplendent cressets which the Twins uplifted.*

creticism. Lying. The 17th and 18th century dictionaries also give the form *cretism.* Also *cretize,* to play the Cretan, to lie, cheat. From *Crete,* and the reputation its enemies gave it. *Creticism* should wherever possible be distinguished from criticism.

creve. To split, burst. THE MIROUR OF SALVACIOUN (1450) has: *The roches . . . creved both uppe and doune.* Via French *crever,* to burst, from Latin *crepare, crepitum,* to rattle, to make resound, to crack; whence also (see *crepundian*) *crepitation, decrepit, crevice, crevasse.*

crevecoeur. A style of woman's hair, worn in the 17th century: *the curl'd lock at the nape of the neck, and generally there are two of them.* Literally, heartbreaker.

crewels. The king's evil. French *écrouelles,* scrofula. Also *cruels.* Up to the 17th century; revived by Scott in THE HEART OF MIDLOTHIAN (1818): *a beloved child sick to the death of the crewels.* Scrofula was called "the king's evil" because, from the reign of Edward the Confessor (1042) until that of Queen Anne, it was believed the disease could be cured by the royal touch. The last person to be thus touched in England was Samuel Johnson, at the age of two and a half, in 1712, by Queen Anne. On Easter Sunday of 1686, King Louis XIV of France touched 1600 sufferers, saying "The King touches you, may God cure you." Apparently, God worked on Samuel Johnson.

crine. See *cryne.*

cristallomancy. See *aeromancy.*

crithomancy. See *aeromancy.*

critickin. A petty critic; a critic. Southey (1843) cried: *Critickin, I defy you!* Also *criticling, criticule, criticaster.* Hence *criticasterism, criticastry.* Mainly 18th and 19th century terms, used by authors suffering from *criticophobia,* which FRASER'S MAGAZINE of 1836 says *has possessed the mind of every great author.* Swinburne in UNDER THE MICROSCOPE (1872) belabors *the rancorous and reptile crew of poeticules who decompose into criticasters. Cp. medicaster.*

critone. See *crayton.*

cro. Compensation for the killing of a man, according to his rank. Also *croy.* In 1609, by statute, *cro of an Erle of Scotland is seven tymes twenty kye* [cows].

crocheteur. A porter. Used in the 16th and 17th centuries. French *crochet,* hook (for lifting bundles; *cp. crotchet*); but the English crocheteur (*crochetor*) was distinguished by his whip. Beaumont and Fletcher, in THE HONEST MAN'S FORTUNE (1613) exclaim: *Rescued? 'Slight I would*

Have hired a crocheteur for two cardecues, To have done so much with his whip.

croisee. Old form of *crusade.* Also *croiserie.*

crolle. A variant of *crull, q.v.*

crome. A hook; especially, a long stick with a hook at the end, to pull down boughs of a tree, etc. Also *cromb, cromp.* In the 14th and 15th centuries, *crome* was sometimes used to mean the claw of a wild beast. From an Old English form *cromb, cramb,* crooked, hooked. So, in the 16th and 17th centuries, *cramp,* an iron bar with the end bent as a hook; a *cramp* word is one hard to decipher. The senses of *cramp,* hook, crook, and *cramp,* the hooking or contracting of a muscle, grew confounded.

cronyke. An early variant of *chronicle.* Caxton in POLYCRONICON (1482) stated that *the detestable actes of such cruel personnes ben oftymes plantyd and regystred in cronykes, unto theyr perpetuel obprobrye and dyvulgacion of theyr infamie, as thactes of Nero and suche other.*

crosbiter. See *crossbite.*

croshabell. A prostitute. One of Peele's JESTS (1598) is headed: *How George gulled a punk otherwise called a croshabell—a word but lately used,* he explains, *and fitting with their trade, being of a lovely and courteous condition.*

crossbite. To cheat; originally, to outwit a cheater, to 'bite the biter.' Also, to censure stingingly. Also *crosbite*; hence *cros(s)biter.* A frequent word in 16th and 17th century plays and pamphlets; thus Greene in his *A Groat's Worth of Wit, Bought with a Million of Repentance* (1592) speaks of *the legerdemaines of nips, foysts, conicatchers, crosbyters.* In the particular cheat sometimes called the badger game (see *badger*) Dekker (1608) said: *The whore is then called the traffick. The man that is brought in, is the simpler. The ruffian that takes him napping is the crosbiter.*

crotchet. Originally, a small hook (French *crochet,* diminutive of *croche,* hook; women still *crochet* with a small hook; *cp. crocheteur*). By transference, many other meanings, among them: (1) an ornamental hook, a brooch; Steele in THE TATLER (1710) tells of *a crochet of 122 Diamonds, set . . . in silver.* (2) a hook-shaped symbol for a note in music; (3) a whimsical fancy; a perverse and peculiar notion. Shakespeare plays on both these senses in MUCH ADO ABOUT NOTHING (1599): *Why these are very crotchets that he speaks, Note notes forsooth, and nothing.* From (3) came (4) a fanciful device or construction. Less literarily and more literally (5) a bracket, in typography [*crotchets*]. A dealer in odd conceits and deliberately perverse opinions is a *crotchet-monger.*

crowd. The common Teutonic noun and verb, to press; a large press of persons, though used from the 10th century, and by Shakespeare (as in HENRY V; 1599), was not common in English until the 17th century. In the 14th century, two other words took this form. (1) *crowd,* an underground vault, a crypt. Via French from Late Latin *crupta,* Latin *crypta.* A will of 1501 asked that the maker *be buried in the crowde of Saint John Baptist in Bristow.* (2) A Celtic musical instrument, at first with three strings; later, with six, four played with a bow and two with the fingers, an early form of the fiddle. From Welsh *crwth,* paunch, bulging box; *croth,* belly, womb. By extension, a fiddle. A fiddler was also *a crowd,* or *a* *crowder.* Butler in HUDIBRAS (1664) spoke of men *That kept their consciences in cases, As fidlers do their crowds and bases.* From its big-bellied flowers, the figwort was called *crowdy-kit.*

croy. See *cro.* Bailey in his DICTIONARY (1751) defines *croy*: "(Scotch Law) a satisfaction that a judge, who does not administer justice as he ought, is to pay to the nearest of kin to the man that is killed." Bailey (not to be confused with Old Bailey) has his law confused.

croysade. Old form of *crusade.* Also *croysada, croysado, croyserie.*

crudy. A variant of *curdy*: like *curds* (the coagulated part of soured milk; the liquid part is the *whey,* as Miss Muffet knew). Also *cruddy;* in the 14th, 15th, and 16th centuries, *crodde, crudde, crude* were as common as *curde, courd, curd.* Shakespeare has *curdied* in CORIOLANUS (1607); *crudy* in HENRY IV, PART TWO: *A good cherris sack hath a twofold operation in it. It ascends me into the brain, dries me there all the foolish and dull and crudy vapors which environ it . . .* Some editors, however, explain *crudy* here as a form of *crude.* From the Latin *crudus,* raw, came Latin *crudelis,* rough, fierce, whence English *cruel.* Thus *crude* and *cruel* are of the same origin. We may note 15th century *crudelity,* an early form of *cruelty*—listed by Caxton (CATO; 1483) as the third sin. Also *crudefaction,* the making of something crude, rough, unripe.

cruels. See *crewels.*

cruent. Bloody; also, cruel. Latin *cruentus,* from *cruor,* gore. Also *cruentate, cruentous;* both rare. The (supposed) bleeding from the wounds of a body when the murderer comes by was called *cruentation.*

crull. A variant of *curled, curly.* In Chaucer's Prologue to THE CANTERBURY TALES (1386), he speaks of *A Young Squier . . . with locks as crulle as they were laid in presse.* From their shapes were named what Irving in THE LEGEND OF SLEEPY HOLLOW (1818) calls *the doughty doughnut . . . the crisp and crumbling cruller.*

crumenically. As the purse is concerned (Latin *crumena,* money-bag). Used for humor, as when Coleridge wrote, in a letter of 1825, *I am interested, morally and crumenically.* Spenser, in THE SHEPHERD'S CALENDAR (1579) uses *crumenal,* purse. Bailey (1751) lists *crumenial,* of a purse.

crush-room. A hall or lobby of a theatre or opera house, where the audience might —"promenade," says the O.E.D., but the word itself has other implications—during intermissions. An early 19th century term.

crustade. "A kind of dainty pye," deservedly popular from the 14th to the 17th century. From French *croustade,* Latin *crusta,* a hard surface, a crust (as of ice, etc.), *crustum,* pastry. By way of *crustarde, custade,* the form (and about 1600 the recipe) changed to the current (sometimes currant) *custard.* The earlier *crustade* was a dish of minced flesh, eggs, herbs, and spices, with a little broth or milk, baked in a crust (at times with fruit instead of meat).

cryne. (1) Head of hair. Latin *crinis,* hair. Thomas Chatterton has a roundelay (1778) "My love is dead, Gone to his death-bed All under the willow tree," with the line: *Black his cryne as the winter night.* The etymological spelling was used by Sylvester in his translation (1614) of Du Bartas: *Priests, whose sacred crine felt never razor;* also in prosaic reference in the BRISTOL JOURNAL of October 1768: *hose of goatskin, crinepart outwards.* (2) To shrink, shrivel. This verb is probably from Gallic *crion,* to wither. Used from the 15th into the 18th century, it was revived by Scott (THE HEART OF MIDLOTHIAN, 1818) and used in a letter of Jennie Carlyle (1849) : *He had grown old like a golden pippin, merely crined, with the bloom upon him.*

cryptarch. A secret ruler, as would be the head of the modern 'gang' in violent fiction. Greek *kryptos,* hidden + *archos,* ruler. Thus *cryptarchy,* secret government or control. Other English forms from *kryptos* include: *kryptocephalous* (accent on the *seph*), with the head concealed; *cryptocerous,* with concealed horns, like a cuckold; *cryptorchis, cryptorchid,* a man whose testicles are not in his scrotum; *cryptology,* secret or code speech; *cryptonym,* a secret name or password; *cryptodynamic,* possessing or relating to hidden force; and a number of words specially combined, such as *crypto-insolence,* veiled insolence. In times of religious persecution, many of the persecuted faith outwardly conform to the persecuting faith while retaining an inward conviction; thus THE CONTEMPORARY REVIEW of April 1888 noted *the large number of Christians who professed Islam but remained crypto-Christians.*

cryptomancy. See *aeromancy.*

crystallomancy. Also *cristallomancy.* See *aeromancy.*

cuckingstool. A chair in which an offender (a scold or disorderly woman; a fraudulent tradesman) was fastened, and either exposed to the public jeers or ducked in a pond (often a filthy place) or stream. The original chair, for greater shame, was in the shape of a close-stool; hence the name *cucking-stool; cuck,* to void excrement. Hence also *cuck-stool.* Used from the 13th century. As this idea waned, other associations developed the forms *cuckquean-stool, coqueen-stool; ducking-stool* (from the 16th century). *To cuck,* in the 17th century, to punish by putting in the *cucking-stool.* The penalty is listed in Blackstone's COMMENTARIES (1769).

cuckold. A man that has a faithless wife. The word was always used in derision. It is derived from the bird, the *cuckoo,* which lays its eggs in another bird's nest. The word was very common from the 13th to the 18th century, and took many forms, including *cukeweld, cowckwold, cockhole, cookcold, cuckot, cuckhold.* Hence the verb, *to cuckold* (*cuckoldize*), used by Shakespeare in OTHELLO (1604) and THE MERRY WIVES OF WINDSOR, in which latter he also says *Hang him, poor cuckoldly knave.* Also *cuckoldom, cuckoldry, cuckoldage* (as often *old age* has been). In Jonson, Chapman, and Marston's EASTWARD HOE (1604) Touchstone says: *If you be a cuckold, it's an argument you have a beautiful woman to wife; then you shall be much made of; you shall have store of friends, never want money; you shall be eased of much o' your wedlock pain; others will take it for you . . . If you be a cuckold and know it not, you are an innocent; if you know it and endure it, a true martyr.* This closing point had been earlier developed by Florio, in SECOND FRUTES (1591), where in Chapter Nine Caesar demonstrates that a cuckold must go to heaven: *If he knowe it hee must needs be a patient, and therefore a martir. If he knowe it not, hee is an innocent, and you knowe that martires and innocents shall be saved, which if you grant,* *it followeth that all cuckolds shall obtaine Paradise.* To which Tiberio shrewdly rejoins: *Mee thinks, then, that women are not greatlie to bee blamed if they seeke their husbands eternall salvation, but are rather to be commended, as causes of a worthie effect.* Caesar shrugs his shoulders, but adds: *Woman was sometimes called woe-man.* He speaks no more favorably, however, of the husband, *that ruffian-like fellowe that studies nothing but bellie-cheere and foolosophie, and that with such diligence putts nothing in practise but the madmatikes.*

cuckquean. A female cuckold; also as a verb. Formed from *cuckold,* husband of an unfaithful wife, and *quean,* from Anglo-Saxon *cwene,* woman; Greek *gyne,* whence *gynecology. Quean* and *queen* are related; *queen* comes directly from Anglo-Saxon *cwen,* lord's wife. *Cuckquean* was common in the 16th and 17th centuries, as in Brome's THE MAD COUPLE (1652): *You can do him no wrong . . . to cuckold him, for assure yourself he cuckqueans you. Cuckquean,* also *cockquean, cucquean,* is not to be confused with *cotquean, q.v.*

cucupha. A cap with spices quilted into it, worn in the 17th century for head ailments. Accented on the first syllable; also *cucufa.* A spice-cap. The idea of fragrance as well as color in headgear is not unattractive.

cucurbit. A retort, originally shaped like a gourd, used in alchemical processes; usually as the lower part of an *alembic, q.v.* Later (16th century), a cupping-glass. A small cupping-glass was a *cucurbitule, cucurbittel.* Other forms are *concurbite, cocurbite.* French *courde,* whence English *gourd,* is from the same source, Late Latin *curbita;* Latin *cucurbita,* a gourd, later a cupping-glass. Chaucer in THE CANON YEOMAN'S PROLOGUE (1386) speaks of *cucurbites and alambikes eek.*

cudden. A born fool. A term favored by 17th century playwrights. Wycherley, in 1698, says *The fools we may divide into three classes, viz. the cudden, the cully, and the fop. The cudden a fool of God Almighty's making.* The *cully* is one who is cheated or imposed upon. *Cullies* make, said Carlyle in his MISCELLANIES (1833): *the easy cushion on which knaves and knavesses repose.* A fop (see *fob*) also first meant a fool, or to fool, cheat; as in Shakespeare, OTHELLO (1604): *I . . . begin to find myself fopt in it;* KING LEAR (1605): *Wise men are grown foppish.* In the 17th and 18th centuries, *fop* developed the special senses: (1) a conceited person, a pretender to wit or wisdom; (2) one foolishly concerned with his appearance, a dandy. In these senses, it developed other forms: *fopdoodle, fopling, foppet, foppotee*—all meaning simpleton in regard to manners or dress, and all contemptuous. To *fopple* (18th century) was to behave like a ridiculous dandy. Dryden knew there's no fool like an old fool, in his FABLES (1700) he pictures *the slavering cudden, propped upon his staff.* And there is the old saying: *Give a cudden a mink wrap, it is still but a cudden's coat.*

cuerpo. Used in the Spanish phrase *in cuerpo* (literally, in the body; Latin *corpus*), without the outer garment, in undress; by extension (often humorously), naked. Frequently used, however, to mean stripped to the waist. Used by 17th and 18th century playwrights and novelists; e.g., Fletcher in LOVE'S CURE (1625): *Boy, my cloake and rapier; it fits not a gentleman of my ranck to walk the streets in querpo;* Jonson in THE NEW INN (a failure of 1629): *Your Spanish host is never seen in cuerpo, Without his paramentos, cloke, and sword.*

cuffin. A man, a fellow, a cove. Also *cuffen, cuffing.* Mainly 16th and 17th century thieves' cant; used by the playwrights. Note that *cuff* and *chuff* were used always in a bad sense: a miserly old fellow; *chuff* also was applied to a boor, a rude countryman. *A queer cuffin,* a churlish fellow; hence, a justice of the peace. Scott revived the phrase *queer cuffin* in THE HEART OF MIDLOTHIAN (1818).

cuish. A thigh-piece. Plural, usually *cuisses,* armor for the front of the thighs. Also *quyssewes, cuissues* (14th century); *quysseaux, cusseis, cushes, cuishes,* and the like; also *cuishard, cuisset, cuissot;* (15th century) *cussan.* Via Old French *cuisseaux;* Italian *cosciale;* Latin *coxale; coxa,* hip. Shakespeare in HENRY IV, PART ONE (1596) says: *I saw young Harry with his bever on, his cushes on his thighs.* Used by Pope, Dryden; Scott in THE LORD OF THE ISLES (1814): *Helm, cuish, and breastplate stream'd with gore.*

cuisses. See *cuish.*

cullion. Testicle. Usually in the plural. From Latin *culleus,* a sack (in which a parricide was sewed up and drowned), a testicle; Greek *koleos, kouleos,* sheath. Chaucer, in THE PARDONER'S TALE (1386): *I would I had thy coillons in myn hand.* (For *pardoner,* see *palmer.*) Other manuscripts read *coylons, colyounnys, culyons.* By extension, *cullion,* rascal; as in Shakespeare's HENRY VI, PART TWO (1593): *Away, base cullions!* Hence *cullionly* (in KING LEAR; revived by Scott), rascally, base; *cullionry,* rascally conduct. *Cp. cullyenly.*

cullis. A strong broth (as "beef-tea") made of flesh or fowl boiled and strained; especially, as used for the sick. So made 15th through 17th century. Spelled in many ways: *colys, culys, collesse, collice, coolisse* and several more; ultimately from Latin *colare,* to strain, whence also English *colander.* In the 18th century, a cullis grew into a savoury soup: 'Use for a cullis, a leg of veal and a ham . . . take onions . . . thicken with cullis, oil, and wine.' The word was also used figuratively, from its use to nourish—as in Lyly's EUPHUES (1580): *Expecting thy letter, either as a cullis to preserve or as a sword to destroy*—and occasionally in irony (to mean a beating); Fletcher's THE NICE VALOUR (1625): *He has beat me e'en to a cullis* shows the development toward D'Urfey's PILLS TO PURGE MELANCHOLY (1719): *a cullise for the back too.* Hence the verb *cullis,* to beat to a jelly.

cullisance. A badge or a sign, a mark of rank. Also *cullisen, cullizan.* A corrupt form of *cognizance.* See *bawdreaminy.* Jonson in EVERY MAN OUT OF HIS HUMOUR (1599) has: *I'll keep men . . . and I'll give coats . . . but I lack a cullisen.*

cully. See *cudden.*

cullyenly. A variant form of *cullionly.* For an instance of its use, see *barber; cp. cullion.*

culpon. A piece cut off; hence, a slice, strip, shred. In the 18th century this became *coupon.* Also *to culpon,* to cut, to slice; (16th and 17th centuries) to border or ornament with strips or slices of a different-colored material. Old French *colper; couper,* to cut; from Latin *colaphus,* Greek *kolaphos,* a blow. Chaucer, in THE KNIGHT'S TALE (1386): *He hath anon commanded to hack and hew The okes old, and laie them all on a rew, In culpons well araied for to brenne.* A 15th century cookbook recommended: *Take eeles culponde and clene wasshen . . .*

culter. See *coulter.*

culver. A pigeon. From 8th century; in Spenser (SONNET *89*), on to Tennyson and Browning. Hence, a term of endearment (mainly in the 13th through 15th centuries). Perhaps from the timidity of the dove, Bailey's (1751) DICTIONARY lists *culvenage,* faintheartedness. *Cp. coleron.*

culverin. See *basilisk.*

culys. See *cullis.*

cumber. See *cumberworld.*

cumberworld. A useless person or thing, that needlessly encumbers the world. In Chaucer's TROYLUS AND CRISEYDE (1374). The verb *cumber,* used from the 14th into the 19th century, has been largely replaced by *encumber.* Note that the original sense was to overwhelm, destroy; then harass (body or mind); then hamper, burden. The present *disencumber* was preceded by the verb *uncumber,* to free from a burden, used from the 15th century. There was a saintly woman named Wylgeforte, most beautiful, who prayed for a beard, that she might be uncumbered of suitors and lead a holy life. *Women changed her name to St. Uncumber,* said Sir Thomas More in a DYALOGE of 1529, *because they reken that for a pek of otys she wyll not fayle to uncumber theym of theyr husbondys.* Michael Woode explained (1554) that *if a wife were weary of a husband, she offered oats at Poules to St. Uncumber,* and More elaborated: *For a peck of oats she would provide a horse for an evil housebonde to ride to the deville upon.* In the United States, although the desire is unchanged, the saint has been Renovated.

cunctation. Delaying; delaying action. From 16th into the 19th century. Herrick, in HESPERIDES (1648), cried: *Break off delay, since we but read of one That ever prosper'd by cunctation.* The "one" is *Fabius Cunctator,* the Roman Quintus Fabius Maximus Verrucosus, surnamed *Cunctator,* Delayer; in the Second Punic War (218-201 B.C.) the Fabian tactics of harassing the enemy while avoiding direct combat broke Carthaginian Hannibal's military strength. Hence the *Fabian Society* in England (founded 1884) which believed in the advance of Socialism by gradual degrees, of which the best known member was Bernard Shaw. Hence also the adjective forms *cunctatious, cunctative, cunctatory,* prone to delay.

cupshotten. Drunken, "in his cups." *Cupshotten and swilling fool!* cried Urquhart in his translation (1693) of Rabelais. More, in a DYALOGE of 1529, remarked: *If a maide be suffred to ronne on the brydle, or be cup shotten, or wax too prowde . . . Cup-shotten* was in use since the 13th century; in the 16th, the shorter form *cupshot* (*cup-shot, cupshott*) also appeared, as in Herrick's HESPERIDES (1648): *A young enchantress close by him did stand Tapping his plump thighs with a myrtle wand; She smiled: he kissed: and kissing, culled her too; And, being cupshot, more he could not do.*

curch. See *coif. Curch* is by error from *curches*; Old French *couvrechés,* plural of *couvrechef,* cover head, whence *coverchief, kerchief.* A square piece of linen, used instead of a cap. Used, mainly in Scotland, from the 15th century.

curdcake. As described in THE QUEEN'S ROYAL COOKERY of 1713: *Take a pint of curds, four eggs: take out two of the whites, put in some sugar, a little nutmeg and a little flour, stir them well together, and drop them in, and fry them with a little butter.*

curiosity. This word, from Latin *curiosus,* full of pains; *cura,* trouble, care, pains, had had many meanings. The O.E.D. lists 18 major senses of the form *curious, q.v.,* only two of which are still current. Among those of *curiosity* are: carefulness; scrupulousness; accuracy; skill arrived at by these qualities; Shadwell in THE VIRTUOSO (1676) says, of swimming: *You will arrive at that curiosity in this watery science, that not a frog breathing will exceed you.* By extension, excessive attention, undue fastidiousness; an undue subtlety. A pursuit to which one gives great attention; a hobby. Also, of things: careful or elaborate workmanship; elegance. Ingeniousness in art or experiment. A vanity, an object or matter on which much concern is lavished. This sense survives in the familiar *curiosity-shop.* Ascham in THE SCHOLEMASTER (1568) said that *Caesars Commentaries are to be read with all curiositie;* Barclay, in THE MIRROR OF GOOD MANNERS (1510): *Though I forbid thee proude curiositie Yet I do not counsell nor move thee to rudenes;* Wyclif (WORKS; 1380) spoke of men that *traveilen not in holy writt but veyn pleies and curioustees.*

curious. Early meanings of *curious* (Latin *curiosus,* full of *cura,* care) include: (1) careful, taking pains, as in Chaucer's THE SHIPMAN'S TALE (1386): *For to keep our good be curious.* (2) anxious, concerned, as in Shakespeare's CYMBELINE (1611): *And I am something curious . . . To have them in safe stowage.* (3) fastidious, particular, cautious, as in Shakespeare's THE TAMING OF THE SHREW (1596): *For curious I cannot be with you, Signior Baptista.* (4) careful in observation, particular about details, as in Shakespeare's ROMEO AND JULIET (1592): *What curious eye doth quote deformities?* Scott revived senses (3) and (4) together, in KENILWORTH (1821) saying that men, in arranging their hair, *were very nice and curious.* One must not be too curious, though one be not feline.

curkle. To call as does a quail. An echoic word. Urquhart in his translation (1693) of Rabelais mentions *curring of pigeons . . . curkling of quails.*

currant. See *coranto.*

curry favor. See *favel.*

curse. See *precurrer.*

cursitor. See *cursorary.*

cursorary. A Shakespearean variant of *cursory;* used in HENRY V (1599): *We have but with a cursorary eye Ore-viewed them.* Latin *currere, cursum,* to run, whence *discursive, course, discourse, excursion, corsair;* not related to *curse.* Note *cursorial,* relating to or adapted for running. Also *cursitor* (*cursetor, cursitour*); Latin *cursor,* runner. (1) One of 24 clerks of the Court of Chancery, who made out all writs *de cursu,* i.e. of the usual run or routine; each had his own shire or shires. The post was abolished in 1835. By extension, a secretary. (2) A runner, messenger. Fuller in THE WOUNDED CONSCIENCE (1646) uses this figuratively: *The spirits, those cursitors betwixt soul and body.* (3) A wanderer, vagabond, tramp. Harman in 1567 wrote a book titled *A Caveat or Warening, for commen cursitors vulgarely called vagabones.*

curtal. A horse, later any animal, that has lost its tail, or had its tail cut short. Romanic *corto,* French *court,* short. Also used as a term of contempt for a rogue or a drab; Cotgrave's DICTIONARY (1611) lists *a hedge-whore, lazie queane, lowsie trull, filthie curtall.* Toone's GLOSSARY (1834) states: *A dog whose tail had been cut off by the effect of the forest laws, to hinder him from hunting, was called a* *curtail dog; and by abbreviation, a worthless dog is at this day called a cur.* Shakespeare in THE COMEDY OF ERRORS (1590) has: *She had transform'd me to a curtull dog, and made me turne i' th' wheel. Cur,* however (first in the phrase *cur-dog*), is probably related to Norse *kurra,* to growl, grumble. The verb *curtail* was originally *curtal,* to make a *curtal* of, to dock the tail; its ending changed by association with *tail* or (17th century) with French *tailler,* to cut. Note that *cutlass* (Old French *coutelas,* a large knife; *coutel, couteau,* knife), being a short sword, was given many forms: *curtelace, curtalax;* Spenser mistook this and in THE FAËRIE QUEENE (1596) pictures Priamond using *spear and curtaxe both,* while *With curtaxe used Diamond to smite,* as though *curtaxe* were a short-handled *ax. Curtal* was also a man wearing a short coat; *the curtall Friar* was Friar Tuck in the Robin Hood ballads, whence Scott rather vaguely revived the phrase (IVANHOE, 1820): *Now, sirs, who hath seen our chaplain? Where is our curtal friar?* In the 18th century, *curtal* was also used for a cutpurse, or petty thief that cut pieces from fabrics displayed out of shop windows. —H. Cogan, in his translation (1653) of Pinto's TRAVELS pictured *six pages apparelled in his livery mounted on white curtals.*

curtsey man. See *pedlers French.*

curule. In the phrase *curule chair,* a seat shaped like a camp-stool with curved legs, but of costly wood inlaid with ivory, occupied by the highest magistrates of ancient Rome. Hence, *curule,* pertaining to high civic office, eminent. The word was used in English in the 17th century; it was revived by Scott in THE HEART OF MIDLOTHIAN (1818); Butler shifted its application in HUDIBRAS (1663): *We that are merely mounted higher Than constables in curule wit.*

curvify. To grow curved; to make curve or bend; to curl. Jordan in DEATH DISSECTED (1649) speaks of *Irons to curvifie your flaxen locks, And spangled roses that outshine the skie.*

cury. Cookery. A bookful of delicious dishes is bound within THE FORME OF CURY (1390). The word is roundabout from Latin *coquus, cocus,* cook; *coquere, coctum,* to cook, to ripen, whence also *concoction; precocious, biscuit* (French *bis,* twice + *cuire, cuit,* to cook; whence also *cuisine.*) The Latin *coquere* was used figuratively to mean to think out, to plan, as in modern slang: *What's cooking?* Trevisa in the HIGDEN ROLLS (1387) declared *They conne ete and be mury Withoute grete kewery.*

cussan. See *cuish.*

custard. See *crustade.* The recipe now used dates from about 1600.

custile. A long, two-edged dagger. A 15th century weapon, from Old French *coustille.* Also *costile.* See *custrel.*

custos. Custodian; keeper; guardian. From 15th through 17th century regarded as an English word, plural *custoses;* revived in the 19th century (e.g., in Thackeray's THE NEWCOMES, 1855) as though direct from the Latin, plural *custodes.* Also *custosship* (accent on the first syllable), the office of custos.

custrel. An attendant on a knight. Used 15th through 17th century; Old French *coustillier,* soldier armed with a *coustille;* see *custile.* Later degenerated to mean knave, rascal; in this sense possibly influenced by *custron, q.v.* In this sense, also, more frequently in the form *coistrel, q.v.*

custron. A kitchen-knave. Hence, a base fellow, a rascal. From Old French *coistron,*

Late Latin *cocistronem,* cook's helper, *coquere, coctus,* to cook. See *custrel; coistrel.*

cutchery. See *kedgeree.*

cutty. See *sark. Cutty* is a Scotch or Northern Dialect word.

cutwaist. An insect. Latin *in* + *sectum,* cut; *cutwast, cutwaist,* is an English rendering. Thus also the Greek, *entomology; en,* in + *tomos,* cut. Topsall introduced the English form in THE HISTORIE OF SERPENTS (1608); it did not survive the pressure of foreign terms in science.

cyclamen. A plant, with beautiful early-blooming flowers. Also called sow-bread, the fleshy root bulbs being a favorite food of swine. The name is from Greek *kyklaminos,* circular; *kyklos,* circle—the shape of the root. The cyclamen was highly esteemed for a love-philtre; but Gerard (HERBALL; 1597) was so afraid of its abortive effects that he set a criss-cross fence of sticks about the plant in his garden, lest women stepping over it be cursed with a miscarriage.

cygnet. See *swan.*

cymar. A loose light garment for women; also, a chemise. Also *simarre.* A favorite word in exotic poetry and fiction since the 17th century, usually as the only garment left on, as in Scott's THE TALISMAN (1825): *Disrobed of all clothing saving a cymar of white silk.* A *chimer,* from the same source, old French *chamarre,* was a loose upper robe; especially, a bishop's, to which his lawn sleeves were attached. It was of scarlet silk until Queen Elizabeth's time, when Bishop Hooper changed it to more sober black satin. Mrs. Browning brought this form back into use, in a poem (1850): *This purple chimar which we wear.*

cynarctomachy. Fighting of dogs and bears; bear-baiting. Greek *kynos,* dog + *arctos,* bear + *machia,* fighting. Butler in HUDIBRAS (1663) declared *That some occult design doth ly In bloudy cynarctomachy.* [The *arctic* region is the region not of the polar bear but of the Great Bear constellation.] The *Batrachomyomachia,* the *battle* of the *frogs* and the *mice,* is a mock epic written in ancient Greece in Homeric style; it is sometimes used as a symbol of a war over trivial things, like the *Big-endian* and *Little-endian* war (over which end of the shell of a soft-boiled egg to open, to eat it from the shell) in GULLIVER'S TRAVELS (1726; LILLIPUT): *The books of the Big-endians have long been forbidden.* Carlyle (in FRASER'S MAGAZINE; 1832) said: *Its dome is but a foolish Big-endian or Little-endian chip of an egg-shell compared with that star-fretted dome.*

cynocephali. See *acephalist.*

cyprian. Licentious, lewd; also, a licentious person; a prostitute. Literally, of *Cyprus,* an island in the eastern Mediterranean, anciently known for the worship of Aphrodite. Used from the 16th century. THE SATURDAY REVIEW in 1859 spoke of *the cyprian patrol which occupies our streets in force every night;* but forty years earlier J. H. Vaux in his MEMOIRS told of *a very interesting young cyprian whom I . . . attended to her apartments.*

cyule. A boat. From Late Latin *cyula,* which is from Old English *ciol,* whence *keel,* boat. Holland in his translation (1610) of Camden's BRITAIN wrote: *Embarqu'd in forty cyules or pinnaces, and sailing about the Picts' coasts . . . in every ciule thirtie wives.*

czaricide. See *stillicide.*

D

dacity. Energy; activity; capability. Shortened from *audacity;* Latin *audax, audacem,* spirited. Sampson in THE VOW BREAKER (1636) declared: *I have plaid a major in my time with as good dacity as ere a hobby-horse on 'em all.*

dacryopoeos. Things, according to Bailey (1751) "which excite tears from their acrimony, as onions, horseradish, and the like." A number of English medical terms have been formed from Greek *dacry,* tear. Hence, *dacryopoetic,* producting or causing tears, like a 'tear-jerker' screen-play.

dactyliomancy, dactylomancy. See *aeromancy.*

daddock. Rotted wood. Blount (1674), and Bailey after him, call it "the heart or body of a tree thoroughly rotten," and suggest the word is a corruption of *dead oak.* Its etymology is unknown.

daedal. Skilful, inventive. From *Daedalus,* the legendary inventor and architect, who built the Labyrinth for the Minotaur in Crete. When King Minos imprisoned Daedalus and his son Icarus (they first devised the Labyrinth, then showed Ariadne how Theseus could escape from it), Daedalus fashioned wings on which they flew away. Despite his father's warning, the presumptuous Icarus flew too near the sun; his wings melted off, and he fell into what was thereafter known as the Icarian Sea. Daedalus landed safely in Sicily.

The word *daedal* was also applied to the earth, as inventive of many forms; variously adorned, as in Spenser's THE FAËRIE QUEENE (1596): *Then doth the daedale earth throw forth to thee Out of her fruitful lap abundant flowers.* Hence also *daedalian,* skilful, ingenious. Both these forms are also occasionally used in the sense of labyrinthine, mazy—as *daedalian arguments;* or as in Keats' ENDYMION: *By truth's own tongue, I have no daedal heart!* Hence *daedalize,* to make intricate.

daff. (1) A person deficient in sense or in courage; one who is *daft.* So Chaucer, in THE REEVE'S TALE (1396). Hence *to daff,* to play the fool; to make sport of. (2) to remove, to take off. A variant of *doff,* to do off. Thus Shakespeare in THE LOVER'S COMPLAINT (1597) has *There my white stole of chastity I daff'd.* Hence, to thrust aside, as Shakespeare in HENRY IV, PART ONE (1596) speaks of Prince Hal *that daft the world aside*; or to put off, as in OTHELLO (1604): *Every day thou dafts me with some device, Iago. Daffing the world aside* was a frequent phrase, after Shakespeare. Johnson, misunderstanding Shakespeare's usage, erroneously taking the past form for the present, put in his DICTIONARY (1755) a non-existent verb, to *daft.*

daffadowndilly. A poetic—and to some extent still a popular—form of *daffodil,* which itself is a variant of *affodill,* which is a corruption of *asphodel,* which is directly from Greek *asphodelos. Strew me the ground with daffadowndillies,* cried Spenser in THE SHEPHERD'S CALENDAR (1579); the inevitable rhyme appears in Henry Constable's poem DAIPHENIA (1592): *Diaphenia like the daffadowndilly, White as the sun, fair as the lily, Heigh ho, how I do love thee!* Fair flower of spring.

dag. A pendant; anything short and pointed, as the straight horn of a young stag. Diminutive of *dagger,* from French *dague,* dagger. Hence (1) the points of a cloak or dress slashed at the bottom as an ornament (Chaucer and the 15th century). (2) The top of a shoelace (15th to 18th century). (3) A lock of wool about the hinder parts of a sheep, dirty and draggling. (4) A hand-gun or heavy pistol (of the 16th to the 18th century). The O.E.D. sees no connection between this use of *dag* and *dagger,* but the publisher of this volume has in his collection a weapon that is at once a dagger and a gun. In the 16th and 17th century *dag and dagger* was a frequent phrase; Johnson (1751) hence mistakenly defined *dag* as *dagger.* For an instance of its use, see *slop.* Note, however, French *dague,* dagger; and *to dag* meant to stab (14th century) before it meant to shoot.

There is also a word *dag* of Norse origin, used from the 17th century (and in dialects) to mean dew, or a gentle rain or mist.

dahet. A curse upon! An imprecation, possibly from Old (Merovingian) French *Deu hat,* God's hate. Also *dathet, dathait, dait.* In early uses, with the verb *have,* as in THE OWL AND THE NIGHTINGALE (1250): *Dahet habbe that ilke best* [every beast] *That fouleth his owne nest.* Used to the 15th century.

dainty. As a noun. Estimation, honor; delight, joy. By extension, fastidiousness. Old French *dainté,* pleasure, titbit; Latin *dignitatem,* worthiness; *dignus,* worthy, whence also *dignity, indignation.* (Eliezer Edwards, in WORDS, FACTS, AND PHRASES, 1881, says that the first meaning of *dainty* was a venison pasty, from French *daine,* a deer. A pleasant thought, but oh dear!) In the sense of fastidiousness, Shakespeare has, in HENRY IV, PART TWO (1597): *The King is wearie Of daintie, and such picking grievances.* As joy, Dunbar in TWA MARYIT WEMEN (1508): *Adew, dolour, adew! my daynte now begynis.* Also, *to make dainty,* to hold back, scruple, refuse. Shakespeare has, in ROMEO AND JULIET: *ah ha, my mistresses! which of you all Will now deny to dance? She that makes dainty, she, I'll swear, hath corns.*

daisy. The *Bellis perennis,* "a familiar and favorite flower," says the O.E.D. Old English *daeyes eage,* day's eye; its white petals fold in at night, hiding its central sun until the dawning. In olden times, it was an emblem of fidelity; knights and ladies wore them at tourneys, and Ophelia gathered them, to be strewn on her grave. There is indeed beauty, as Spenser sees it in THE SHEPHERD'S CALENDAR (1579) in *the grassye ground with daintye daysies dight.*

daltonism. Color-blindness; especially, inability to discriminate red and green. From John Dalton, English chemist (1766-1844), who developed the atomic theory —and was afflicted with color-blindness. The word was first used (1827) by Prof. Pierre Prevost of Geneva; it was objected to by the British, in that it associates a great name with a physical defect (as though the crippling from infantile paralysis were called *Rooseveltism*); the word is therefore seldom used in English, though *daltonisme* is the current French term. A *daltonian* is a person afflicted with color-blindness.

damoclean. Relating to *Damocles.* Also (19th century), *damoclesian*; the sword of *Damocles.* Damocles was not the king, but a flatterer in the train of Dionysius the Elder, tyrant of Syracuse, an unscrupulous plunderer—to keep Jupiter warm, he replaced the golden mantle on the god's statue with a woolen one—impious, savage, suspicious, credulous. He was, however, a shrewd commander; he invented the catapult, and held his throne for 38 years, dying in 368 B.C. When Damocles expressed envy of Dionysius' happy state, the king made Damocles ruler for a day. All went merrily—until Damocles noticed, over the throne on which he sat, a sword suspended by a horse hair. Dionysius' symbolism was so obvious and so apt that *the sword of Damocles* has been often used to refer to the thread by which all fortune hangs.

dandeprat. See *dandiprat.*

dandiprat. A small coin (3 halfpence) of the 16th century. A contemptible or insignificant fellow; a dwarf. Applied in friendly intimacy to a little child. Also *dandeprat, dantiprat.*

dapatical. Sumptuous; costly. Late Latin *dapaticus,* from *dapem,* feast. A 17th and 18th century dictionary word; *cp. dapifer.*

daphnomancy. See *aeromancy.* Greek *Daphne,* a nymph loved by Apollo, fleeing whom she was, at her own entreaty, changed into a bay-tree (laurel). Hence winners of "the bays"; hence champions in the games Apollo sponsored were crowned with laurel.

dapifer. One who serves at table; a steward; a waiter. Latin *dapem,* feast (see *dapatical*) + *ferre,* to bear. A 17th and 18th century word.

dapinate. To provide or serve dainty meats, as among *les amis d'Escoffier.* Latin *dapem,* food; *cp. dapifer.*

dapocaginous. Mean-spirited; of little worth. A 17th century term (accented on the *cadge*) from Italian *dapoco,* of little (value).

dariole. A crustade, *q.v.* From the 14th century; but by 1650 the recipe had changed and a *dariole* was a cream tart. In that sense Scott revived the word in QUENTIN DURWARD (1823): *Ordering confections, darioles, and any other light dainties he could think of.*

darkhede. See *darkmans.*

darkmans. Night. Originally 16th century thieves' cant; also *crackmans,* a hedge; *lightmans,* daytime, etc. See *lib*; *pedlers French.* Used by 16th and 17th century playwrights (Dekker, THE ROARING GIRL, 1611, e.g.), revived by Scott in GUY MANNERING (1815): *Men were men then, and fought other in the open field, and there was nae milling in the darkmans.* The regular early English word for darkness was *darkhede* (10th to 14th century).

darnel. A grass; especially (*lolium temulentum*), one that grows as a weed in corn, supposed to make dim the eyesight. Joan of Arc (La Pucelle) in Shakespeare's HENRY VI, PART ONE (1597) mocks the English for having corn *full of darnel.* Hence, figuratively, weeds, tares, evil things that grow amidst us; H. Barrow in John Greenwood's COLLECTION OF CERTAINE SCLAUNDEROUS ARTICLES GYVEN OUT BY THE BISSHOPS (1590) spoke of Satan *sowing his darnel of errors and tares of discord amongst them.*

darraign. An early variant of *deraign, q.v.* Also *darrain, darrein, darrayne, darrein, darreyne.*

darrein. Final. An old legal term, from the 13th century. Via Old French *darrain, derrein*; Late Latin *deretranus; de retro,* behind. Especially in the phrase *darrein resort,* last resort. But also see *darraign.*

dathet. See *dahet.*

daub. See *dealbate.* The earliest meaning in English was to plaster; hence, to lay on crudely.

daw. See *dawkin.*

dawgos. See *dawkin.*

dawkin. A fool; a slattern. Diminutive of *daw,* the bird (jackdaw); applied contemptuously, in the same senses. A jingle of 1565 says: *Then Martiall and Maukin, a dolt with a dawkin, might marry together.* Bailey (1751) gives the variant form *dawgos.*

daysman. An umpire, a mediator. *Day,* as a verb, meant (1) to dawn; in this sense, also *daw.* (2) to appoint or set a day; hence, to appoint a time for decision, for arbitration. Thus also *dayment, daying* (15th to 17th century), arbitration. Lupton in 1580 uttered a sound lament: *to spende all . . . that money and put it to dayment at last.* Hervey in his MEDITATIONS (1747) wrote that *Death, like some able daysman, has laid his hand on the contending parties.* The public suffers today from reluctance to call upon daysmen.

dealbate. (Three syllables.) To whiten. From Latin *de* + *albare,* to whiten; *albus,* white. The Old French form of this, *dauber,* gave English *daub.* T. Whitaker, in THE TREE OF HUMANE LIFE (1638), ventured the suggestion that *Milke is blood dealbated or thrice concocted. Dealbation,* the action of bleaching, whitening; but *dealable,* that which may be dealt, or dealt with.

deambulate. To walk, to walk about. A common 16th century word, used into the 19th century; now supplanted by *perambulate* and its forms. Skelton in a poem of 1529 has: *They make deambulations With great ostentations.* A *deambulatory* (also *deambulatour*) was a place to walk in for exercise; especially, a cloister.

deartuate. To dismember. Latin *de,* from + *artus,* joint, member; whence also *articulate.* A 17th century word. Hence, *deartuation.*

dearworth. Honorable, noble; costly, precious; highly esteemed, beloved. Also *dearworthy.* A common word from the 9th into the 15th century. Also *derworth, deorwurthe, direwerthe, dereworth, derwarde,* and the like. Hence *dearworthily,* honorably; *dearworthiness.* As late as Tottel's MISCELLANY (1577) we read of *a dearworth dame.*

debacchate. To rage like a bacchanal; to revile like a drunkard. Prynne, in HISTRIO-MASTIX (1633) speaks of folk that *defile their holiday with . . . most wicked debacchations and sacrilegious execrations.*

debellate. To vanquish, to put down by war. Latin *debellare,* to subdue, *de-* down + *bellare,* to fight; *bellum,* war. Also *debel, debell.* Hence *debellation,* vanquishing; *debellator*; *debellative,* tending to overcome. Note however that *debellish* (also used in the 17th and 18th centuries) meant to dis-embellish, to rob of beauty. How soon are the winners of beauty contests debellished belles! It is the inner beauty that lengthily holds the eye.

debellish. See *debellate.*

debile. Weak, feeble. Latin *de,* from (the opposite of) + *habilis,* able; *habere,* to have, to be able. Hence also 17th century *debilitude,* replaced by *debility*; *debilitated*; to *debilite* (15th and 16th centuries) to weaken, to *debilitate.* Shakespeare uses *debile* in ALL'S WELL THAT ENDS WELL and in CORIOLANUS (1607): *For that I have not washed my nose that bled, or foyl'd some debile wretch . . . You shout me forth In acclamations hyperbolical, As if I loved my little should be dieted In praises sauced with lies.*

deblateration. Blabbling overmuch, prating. See *quisquilious.* Latin *deblaterare, deblateratum,* to blab out; *blaterare,* to prate, from the root *bal-, bar-,* to bleat, stammer. Stevenson in THE BRITISH WEEKLY of 27 April, 1893, wrote from the South Seas: *Those who deblaterate against missions have only one thing to do, to come and see them on the spot.*

deboshed. An early form of debauched. Shakespeare, in KING LEAR (1605) speaks of *Men so disorder'd, so debosh'd, and bold.* Revived by Scott, in WOODSTOCK (1826): *Swashbucklers, deboshed revelers, bloody brawlers.* Used by Lowell and others, with a less specific and milder sense than *debauched.*

decachinnate. To scorn. Late Latin *de,* down + *cachinnare, cachinnatum,* to laugh, whence also *cachinnation.* In 17th century dictionaries.

decadist. Amid the various forms of decay, decadence, decadescence (the initial stages), it is interesting to note the appearance of the *decadist,* a poet (such as Livy) that writes in *decades,* that is, sections subdivided into ten parts. The 'perfect number' of the Pythagoreans, 10, was called the *decad* (Latin *decem,* ten). We usually think of a *decade* as a period of ten years, but the French Republican calendar of 1793 substituted for the seven-day week a *decade* of ten days—the last day of which, *Décadi,* replaced Sunday as a day of rest—and *decadary* means relating to such a ten-day period; *decadic,* related to counting by tens, as in the metric system.

decant. To sing (or say) over and over. Also *decantate.* Coryat in his CRUDITIES (1611) mentions *the very Elysian Fields, so much decantated and celebrated by the verses of poets.* From Latin *de,* off + *cantare,* to sing. The still current use of *decant,* to pour out (as into a *decanter,* from which wine is decanted into the glasses) is from the Latin of the alchemists, *decanthare*; *de,* off + *canthus,* the 'lip' of a jar, by transfer from Greek *canthos,* corner of the eye. The word was especially applied to pouring off the clear liquid, leaving the sediment or lees. Holmes used this sense figuratively in THE POET AT THE BREAKFAST-TABLE (1872) considering it unfortunate *if you are not decanted off from yourself every few days or weeks.*

decarnation. Stripping of the flesh; deliverance from carnality. Latin *de,* off + *carnem,* flesh. Thus Walter Montague in DEVOUT ESSAYS (1648) said: *God's incarnation enableth man for his decarnation, as I may say, and devesture of carnality.* Hence *decarnate,* unfleshed, not in the flesh; THE READER of 16 December, 1865, remarked: *Logic Comte never liked, but it became to him at last a sort of devil decarnate.*

decaudate. To untail, remove the tail. Latin *de,* off + *cauda,* tail. NOTES AND QUERIES in 1864 observed that *The P was originally an R which has had the misfortune to be decaudated.*

decollation. A beheading. Latin *de,* from + *collum,* neck. Burke in his ESSAY ON THE SUBLIME AND THE BEAUTIFUL (1756) remarks that *a fine piece of a decollated head of St. John the Baptist was shewn to a Turkish emperor.* The word was also used figuratively, as when Sir Thomas Browne (1646) said: *He by a decollation of all hope annihilated his mercy.* The verb *decollate,* in the 17th century, was used in the short form *decoll.* Although the French invented the guillotine expressly for *decollation,* the French form *decolletée* means merely cut low around the neck, or wearing a dress low-cut.

Note also that *decollation* and *collation* are not opposites. Indeed, they are not related. *Collation* is from Latin *collatum,* past participle of *conferre,* to bring together—as in a *conference.* About 410 John Cassian wrote COLLATIONES PATRUM. . . , which in 540 St. Benedict ordered to be read in his monasteries before the last service of the day (Compline); the word *collation* was applied to the reading, and then to the light repast that followed it; hence, any light repast. A *collatitious* work is one produced by conference, by working together—as the organs of the digestive tract, stomach, intestines, bowels, are called the *collatitious* organs. They were often subjected to exenteration (*q.v.*) after their owner's decollation.

decorrugative. Tending to remove wrinkles, as (many women hope) ointments or (more probably) peace of mind.

decorticate. To remove the bark, rind, or husk; hence, to strip off what conceals, to expose; to flay (figuratively). Latin *de,* from; *cortex, corticem,* bark. Hence *decortication.* Waterhouse in ARMS AND ARMOUR (1660) wrote: *Arms ought to have analogie and proportion to the bearer, and in a great measure to decorticate his nature, station, and course of life.* THE LONDON REVIEW of 16 August, 1862, said: *It is impossible to decorticate people, as the writer now and then does, without inflicting pain.*

decrepitation. The roasting (of a salt or mineral) until it no longer crackles with the heat. Latin *de,* away + *crepitare,* to crackle, frequentative of *crepare,* to crack. Also *decreptitate,* the verb. From this literal sense have come the applications to mankind in *decrepitude* (16th and 17th century, *decrepity,* 17th century, *decrepitness;* 18th century, *decrepidity*); *decrepit,* limp, with all the 'crackling' vitality burned away.

decussated. Intersected, formed by crossing lines, like an X. There is a rare verb, to *decuss,* to divide crosswise; to cross out, from Latin *decussis* (X), probably from *decem,* ten and *as,* a Roman coin. The English word is known mainly from Johnson's ponderously humorous definition (1755) of *network: anything reticulated or decussated, at equal distances, with interstices between the intersections.* Johnson's definition may well be decussed.

dedalian. Another form of *daedal, q.v.*

deem. See *deemster.*

deemster. A judge. *Deem* originally meant opinion, judgment, as in Shakespeare's TROILUS AND CRESSIDA (1606) where Cressida cries: *I true? how now? what wicked deeme is this?* The verb *deem* also first meant to pronounce judgment; it is closely related to *doom.* A less frequent form of *deemster,* though phonetically more regular, is *dempster,* which also meant judge, but in Scotland until the 19th century was used for the officer of the court who (after the judge's decision) pronounced sentence, or *doom,* upon the prisoner. In current use, *deemster* refers specifically to one of the two Manx judges, one presiding over the northern, one over the southern, division of the Isle of Man.

deer. A beast. The original sense of this common Teuton word was an animal, a quadruped, as distinct from birds and fishes. This meaning survived into the 16th century, although the restricted meaning was also in use by 1100. The word is probably from the root *dhus,* to breathe; as *animal* is from *anima,* breath. Shakespeare used *deer* in the general sense in KING LEAR (1605), when he said, of Tom the cat (echoing the early 14th century poem SIR BEVES): *But mice, and rats, and such small deare Have been Tom's food for seven long yeare.*

defatigation. See *couth.*

defeature. (1) Undoing, defeat (16th and 17th centuries). (2) Frustration. Old French *desfaiture; desfaire,* to undo; Latin *de,* from + *factura,* making, doing; *facere, factum,* to make, do; whence *factotum, manufacture, factitious;* that's a *fact.* (3) Disfigurement, defacement. In this sense, mainly copied from Shakespeare, who thus used the word in VENUS AND ADONIS and in THE COMEDY OF ERRORS (1590): *Care-full houres with times deformed hand Have written strange defeatures on my face.*

defecate. To clear of dregs and impurities; to purify; to refine; to purge. Latin *defaecare, defaecatum; de,* from + *faeces,* dregs, excrement. Laneham in a letter of 1575, said: *I am of woont jolly and dry a mornings; I drink me up a good bol of ale, when in a sweet pot it iz defecated by al nights standing the drink iz the better, take that of me, and a morsel in a morning with a sound draught iz very holsome and good for the eysight.* It is also used figuratively, as by Burton in THE ANATOMY OF MELANCHOLY (1621) declaring that Luther *began upon a sudden to defecate, and as another sun to drive away those foggy mists of superstition.*

defenestration. The act of throwing out of a window. Latin *de,* from + *fenestra,* an opening for light. The word has a place in history, because *the defenestration of Prague*—21 May, 1618; the hurling of Imperial commissioners out the window by insurgent Bohemians—was immediate cause of the Thirty Years' War. It plays a part also in theatrical lore. A group in an upper room of an 18th century tavern were arguing the value of silence onstage. Garrick took no part in the discussion, but began to walk to and fro, cradling in his arms an imaginary infant. After a minute or two, he walked toward the window, then the others leapt to their feet in an impulse to rush: Garrick had defenestrated the child.

defensum. An enclosure; fenced ground. Indeed, *fence* is a shortened form of *defence; fencible,* capable of making defence, hence liable for military service; also, capable of being defended, strong. Spenser in THE FAËRIE QUEENE (1590) declares: *No fort so fensible . . . but that continuall battery will rive. Defensum* is in Bailey (1751); not in O.E.D. (1933). It helps us, however, to grind teeth at the perhaps unintended paronomasia in Robert Frost's MENDING WALL (1914): Before I built a wall I'd ask to know What I was walling in or walling out, And to whom I was like to give offence. (There is, of course, no offence intended.)

deferve. To boil down. Latin *de* + *fervere,* to boil, whence also *fervent. Deferve* was used in the 15th century. Later (from the 18th century) but more common was *defervescence,* cooling down; Latin *de* + *fervescere,* to begin to boil; English *defervesce,* to begin to cool; also *defervescent.* These terms were used both of liquids and of human emotions; the contrary progression—*effervescence*—has survived. Less remembered are *effervescible;* and *effervency,* the condition of being overheated, of issuing forth in a heated state, as occasionally the water in an automobile.

deflorate. An early form of *deflower.* Used in the 15th century of a woman; in the 19th, of a plant. Hence *defloration.* Note that *deflorator* has also been used (17th century) of one that culls the choicest parts of a book or author.

defunctive. Pertaining to dying. *Defunct* has been preserved, as a euphemistic reference to the dead, but the adjective has lapsed. Shakespeare uses both: *defunct* in HENRY V and CYMBELINE; in THE PHOENIX AND THE TURTLE (1601): *Let the priest in surplice white That defunctive music can, Be the death-divining swan.*

deipnosophist. A master of the art of dining, like my fellow-member of les amis d'Escoffier, Moritz. Accent on the *nos;* Greek *deipnos,* dinner + *sophistes,* a wise man, a master. There are also a few words coined for special use: *deipnodiplomat,* one that forwards affairs of state at dinners; *deipnophobia,* dread of dinner-parties. *Deipnosophistai* was the title of a widely read work, about 230 A.D., by the Greek Athenaeus, picturing the wide-ranging discussions of a group of men dining together. Hence also *deipnosophistic; deipnosophism.* BLACKWOOD'S EDINBURGH MAGAZINE in 1836 exclaimed: *Let me . . . luxuriate in the . . . paradisiacal department of deipnosophism.*

deitate. Made into a god, deified, as the Pharaohs and the Caesars. Used in the 16th century. Latin *deitas,* from *deus, dei,* god. Three syllables, accent on the *dee.*

deivirile. See *theandric.*

delator. An informer. The verb *delate* is from a Latin frequentative form of the verb that gives us English *defer;* Latin *delatare* from *deferre, delatum,* to carry down or away. Both verbs in English meant the same as in Latin; *delate* took on the meanings deliver, report, accuse. Hence *delatory,* pertaining to accusing or informing (of criminal activity). Gibbon in THE DECLINE AND FALL OF THE ROMAN EMPIRE (1776) refers to *a formidable army of sycophants and delators. Delator* and *delatory* are also early forms of *dilator,* a delaying, and *dilatory,* tending to cause delay; slow, tardy—as in Shakespeare's OTHELLO (1604): *Wit depends on dilatory time* and Addison's SPECTATOR reference (1711, No. 89) to *women of dilatory tempers, who are for spinning out the time of courtship.* These two forms are from *diferre, dilatum,* to carry or hold back or apart; hence, to delay. There is still another word *dilator* (accented on the second syllable; the other is accented on the first), early *dilater,* from the verb to *dilate,* to stretch, to spread wide; this is from Latin *dilatare,* from *dis-,* apart + *latus,* wide. The verb *dilate,* to delay, has not been used since the 17th century. Men who *delate* (inform) we still have with us. To confound confusion, there are also the forms *deletory* and *deletorious,* relating to the act of *deleting* or rubbing out; Jeremy Taylor in his A DISSUASIVE FROM POPERY, addressed (1647) to the people of Ireland, says that confession *was most certainly intended as a deletory of sin,* and gout, we are told, is *a perfect deletory of folly.* The form *de-*

letorious, blotting out (from Latin *delere, deletum,* to efface) was confused (even in the Latin) with *deleterious,* harmful, from Greek *deleterios,* noxious; *deleter,* destroyer. Thus the word *deletery* was used in the 16th and 17th century to mean a noxious drug, a poison, but also in the 17th century to mean an antidote, that wipes out poison. In the latter sense it was often used figuratively: *deleteries of the sin;* Episcopacy, said Jeremy Taylor (1642) *is the best deletery in the world for schism.* One can perhaps, now, sympathize with Byron's lament in DON JUAN (1821): *'Tis pity wine should be so deleterious, For tea and coffee leave us much more serious.*

deleniate. To soothe. From Latin *delenire; de,* down; *lenis,* soft, mild, soothing. Sometimes spelled *delineate,* in orthographical confusion with *delineate,* to draw, to trace in outline, from Latin *de + linea,* line. The 17th and 18th century dictionaries also give the form *delenifical* (accented on the third syllable), soothing, pacifying. A 'modern' mother does not tender the delenifical nipple.

deleterious. See *delator.*

deletory. See *delator.*

delf. That which is delved (dug): a hole, a pit, a quarry, a mine, a grave. Used from the 13th through the 18th century. The plural is *delfs, delphs,* or *delves.* Spenser in THE FAËRIE QUEENE (1590) speaks of *Mammon in a delve;* Shelley in the HYMN TO MERCURY (1820) also uses this form. The verb *to delve* is from a common Teutonic form. The glazed earthenware originally made at *Delft* in Holland may be called *delft* or *delf,* as Swift in his poems (to Stella) of 1723: *A supper worthy of herself, Five nothings in five plates of delf.* The original name of the town in Holland was *Delf,* from the *delf,* the ditch or canal, that runs through it.

Delian. (1) Relating to *Delos,* an island of Greece, birthplace of the divine Apollo and Artemis. Hence, from their realms, *the Delian twins,* the sun and moon (17th century). (2) Relating to the oracle at Delos. From the oracle's statement that a plague in Athens would end when Apollo's altar, which was of cubical shape, was doubled, *the Delian problem,* the doubling of the cube, the finding the square root of two. (3) Nashe in LENTEN STUFFE (1599) speaks of Hero as Leander's *mistress or Delia.*

delibate. To taste, sip; take a little of; cull; pluck. Fuller in a sermon of 1655 spoke of a soul *unacquainted with virgin, delibated, and clarified joy.* Latin *de,* from + *libare, libatum,* to take as a sample, to taste, sip; pour—whence also *libation.* Also *delibation,* a taste; a slight knowledge; a portion culled or extracted. Mede in his Biblical commentary on ACTS (WORKS; 1638) said: *Nor can it be understood without some delibation of Jewish Antiquity.*

deliber. An old and simpler form of *deliberate.* Also *delibere, delybre* (15th and 16th centuries), *deliver.* Latin *deliberare; de,* from + *librare, libratum,* to poise, balance; *libra,* balance, pair of scales. *Deliber* was also used in the sense of to decide, to resolve, as when Caxton in POLYCRONICON (1482) said: *I have delybered too wryte twoo bookes notable.*

deligible. Worthy of being chosen. From Latin *deligere,* to choose; *de-,* down + *legere,* to propose, to name; *lex, legis,* a motion, a proposal of a bill—later, by extension, a bill that has passed, a law—whence *legal, legislate,* and further complications. If only all that were eligible were deligible!

delignate. To remove the wood. Latin *de,* from; *lignum,* wood. Fuller, in THE CHURCH-HISTORY OF BRITAIN (1655) gives the only recorded instance of its use: *Dilapidating (or rather delignating) his bishoprick.*

delineate. See *deleniate.*

deliquium. A failure of the vital powers, a swoon; a failure of light; a melting away. Two Latin words fused in this form, and are tangled in other English words. Latin *delinquere; de,* down + *linquere, liqui, lictum,* to leave, forsake; and *deliquescere, deliqui,* to begin to melt, to pine away, *de* + *liqui,* to be fluid; *liquare, liquatum,* to make fluid, to liquefy. *Delinquere* came to mean to lapse, hence to commit a fault, whence English *delinquency* and *delinquents; delict,* an offence, and the legal (Latin) phrase *in flagrante delictu,* in the very act of committing the crime; also (as in Scott's IVANHOE, 1820), *in the flagrant delict.* Other English words from these forms include *deliquesce, deliquiate, deliquate,* to dissolve, melt; *delique,* a failure (*deliquium*); *deliquity,* guilt. Sydney Smith in a letter to Singleton in 1837 uses *deliquescent* humorously, as dissolving in perspiration: *Striding over the stiles to church, with a second-rate wife—dusty and deliquescent—and four parochial children, full of catechism and bread and butter.* Burton in THE ANATOMY OF MELANCHOLY (1621) speaks *of a man who carries bisket, aquavitae, or some strong waters about him, for fear of deliquiums.* Carlyle in THE FRENCH REVOLUTION (1837) said: *The assembly melts, under such pressure, into deliquium; or, as it is officially called, adjourns.* Whitlock in ZOOTOMIA (1654) declared: *Death is a preparing deliquium, or melting us down into a menstruum, fit for the chymistry of the resurrection to work on.*

delirous. A 17th century form of *delirious.* Also *deliry,* delirium.

delitability. Delightfulness. Also *delite, delitable,* delightful. Old French *delitier,* to delight; Latin (*de,* from + *legere, lectum,* gather, bring together) *deligere, delectum,* to choose, select; hence *delectum,* chosen, therefore *delectable* and (via French) *delightful.* All three English forms are from the same Latin word.

delitescent. Concealed, latent. Latin *de,* away + *latescere,* inceptive of *latere,* to lie hid, whence *latent.* Used from the 17th century; also *delitescence, delitescency.* The Preface to an 1805 reprint of Brathwait's DRUNKEN BARNABY speaks of *republishing this facetious little book after a delitescency of near a hundred years.* Sir William Hamilton in his LECTURES ON METHAPHYSICS (1837) declared: *The immense proportion of our intellectual possessions consists of our delitescent cognitions.* Praise be!

deme. (1) A judge, a ruler. An old Teutonic form, related to *dom,* doom. Used from the 8th to the mid-13th century. (2) A township of ancient Attica. Greek *demos,* township; hence, the people—whence the trials and virtues of *democracy.* The *academe* or *academy,* the athletic field and grove near Athens where Plato taught, took its name from the Athenian legendary hero *Academus* (*Akademion; aka,* gently; *demion,* of the people.) Shakespeare in LOVE'S LABOUR'S LOST (1588) says: *Our court shall be a little achademe.* Lowell in a poem of 1870 speaks of *That best academe, a mother's knee. Academe* is reserved for Plato's school, or grove of learning, leaving *academy* for the modern institution.

demean. Behavior; treatment (of others). Spenser in THE FAËRIE QUEENE (1596) has: *All the vile demeane and usage bad, With which he had those two so ill bestad. Cp. bestad.* The early form of *demeanor.* Also a verb, to behave; manage; employ; deal with. The sense of *demean,* to lower, developed about the 18th century, probably by analogy with *debase*; the earlier and natural English form for this sense is *bemean,* which was superseded by *demean.*

demesne. Possession; then, an estate possessed. By extension, land subject to a lord, *domain*—which is another form of the same word. Spelled in many ways, *demean, demeigne,* etc., via French from Latin *dominicus,* of the lord, *dominus,* lord, *demesne* is pronounced *demean.* The word has been in common use since the 13th century, but for the past 150 years has been mainly limited to historical or poetic uses, as in Keats' sonnet-reference (1816) to the wide expanse *That deep-brow'd Homer ruled as his demesne.* Shakespeare used the word smilingly in ROMEO AND JULIET (1595) : *I conjure thee by Rosaline's bright eye . . . By her fine foot, straight leg, and quivering thigh And the demesnes that there adjacent lie.*

demiceint. A belt of gold or silver in front, silk or other material behind; a girdle with ornamental work only in front. Latin *demi,* half; Old French *ceint,* Latin *cinctum,* girdle; *cingere, cinctum,* to bind; *cp. ceint.* Also *dymysen, dymison, demicent.* Many 15th and 16th century records refer to such items as *a dymysen with a red crosse harnossid with silver wrought with golde; my dymyson gyrdylle and my coralle beydes.* The word faded, but the fashion survives.

demonifuge. See *demonocracy.*

demonocracy. Government by demons. Greek *daimon,* a ministering spirit; *kratos,* rule. The *daemon* of Sophocles was by him called a *daimonion,* a divine principle. The Jews added the sense of evil to the idea demon; this was followed (of Socrates and in general use) by the Christion Fathers, whence the current sense. There is also the form *demonarchy,* rule by a demon (Greek *arche,* rule), which seems a better word to employ than *demonocracy,* lest one elide a syllable. One may, if necessary, have recourse to a *demonifuge, diabolifuge,* a charm against evil spirits.

demonomancy. See *aeromancy.*

dempster. See *deemster.*

den. See *dene.*

dene. A bare sandy tract by the sea. Bailey's DICTIONARY (1751) calls *dene* 'a small valley,' and *dena* 'a hollow place between two hills' but (spelled *den, dene,* or *deane*) the word seems in most uses closer to the still current *dune.* It was used in the 13th and 14th centuries in the phrase *den and strand*: *den,* the privilege of fishermen to spread and mend or dry their nets on the denes at Great Yarmouth; *strande,* their privilege to deliver their herrings freely at the Great Yarmouth port. *Dene* is also used (1) as a separate form *by dene,* of the adverb *bedene,* together; (2) to mean ten (Latin *deni*) ; (3) as a variant spelling of *den, din,* or *dean.*

dentiscalp. A toothpick. Latin *dens, dentem,* tooth (whence the *dentist* and more) + *scalpere,* to scratch; *scalprum,* a knife, a chisel; *scalpellum,* a little knife, whence the surgeon's *scalpel.* The *scalp* we used to associate with the Indians is a form of *scallop*, a shell-shaped vessel; hence, top of the head. *Dentiscalps*, comments W. King in 1708, *vulgarly called toothpicks.*

deoculate. To deprive of eyes, or of sight. Lamb uses this word—its only recorded use—in a letter of 1816 to Wordsworth: *Dorothy, I hear, has mounted spectacles; so you have deoculated two of your dearest relations in life.*

deodand. (Latin *deo dandum*, that which is to be given to God). A gift to expiate the divine wrath; in old English law, a chattel that, having caused the death of a person, was forfeit to the Crown, to be applied to pious uses. Sometimes the money value was given instead, as when a jury of 1838 laid *a deodand of £1500 upon the boiler or steam engine of the Victoria.* The deodand, granted since the 13th century, was abolished in 1846.

deonerate. Unload, relieve of a burden. Latin *de-*, down + *onerare*, to load; *onus, oneris*, a burden; whence also *onerous*. Used mainly in the 17th century, of both literal and figurative burdens.

deosculate. To kiss eagerly. Latin *de-*, (in the sense of 'down to the bottom,' completely) + *osculare, osculat-*, to kiss, whence *osculation*; *os*, mouth. The verb (defined by Cockeram, 1623, as 'to kiss sweetly') is confined to the dictionaries; the practice is less restrained. The noun *deosculation*, though also rare, was used in the 17th and 18th centuries. See *bass*.

depaint. See *depeint*.

depascent. Eating greedily; consuming. Latin *de*, down + *pascere, pastum*, to feed, whence *pasture, pastor*. Hence *depasture*, to consume by grazing, eat out of pasturage, used (1596) by Spenser and (1858) by Carlyle. Stubbes in his ANATOMY OF ABUSE (1583) wrote of *The wicked lives of their pastors (or rather depastors).* In the 19th century, *depascent* was used as a medical term, meaning eating away; from the 17th, *depastion*, consumption—*a wasting depastion and decay of nature.*

depeach. To send away quickly; to get rid of. So O.E.D. Bailey, however, in 1751 defined *depeach* as to acquit, thus linking it by contrast with *impeach*. Both (with opposed prefixes: *de-*, down, off; *im*, in, on) are via French from Latin *pedica*, snare; *ped-*, foot. From the same source, with the prefix *ex-* comes English *expedite*. *Depeach* was used in the 15th, 16th and 17th centuries.

depeculate. To embezzle; used of public officials preying upon public funds. Hence, *depeculation*.

depeditate. To deprive of feet, or the use thereof. Hence, *depeditation*, the cutting off of a foot or feet. Johnson is reported, in the TOUR TO THE HEBRIDES (1773), to have punned on *the depeditation of Foote.* (Samuel Foote, player and playwright, 1720-1777, who had a leg amputated in 1766; he was called the English Aristophanes. Johnson was not on punning terms with Richard Head—who in any event was not decapitated.)

depeint. A variant of *depaint*, to set forth or represent, to portray. Also *depeinct, depinct, depict*—the last of which has survived. A verb, *to depeint*, but more frequent (13th to 16th century) as the past participle; LAUNCELOT (1500): *with wordis fair depaynt.* Spenser in THE SHEPHERD'S CALENDAR (1579; APRIL) has: *The redde rose medled with the white yfere, In either cheeke depeincten lively chere.*

dequace. To crush. Also *dequass*. Better known in the simple form *quash*. From Latin *de-*, down + *quassare*, frequentative of *quatere, quass-,* to shake; hence, to break. The compound form is rare; it appears in THE TESTAMENT OF LOVE (1400): *Thus with sleight shalt thou surmount and dequace the evil in their hearts.*

deraigne. To vindicate; especially, to vindicate or maintain a claim by single combat; hence, to settle by single combat; *to deraign battle,* to wage single combat to decide a claim, to engage in battle; more generally, to line up for battle (so Spenser; so Shakespeare in HENRY VI, PART THREE, 1953: *Darraigne your battell, for they are at hand*) ; hence, to line up, to array, to order, to arrange. Also *dereyne, dereine, darraign, derene,* and more; Old French *deraisnier,* to render a reason, defend; Latin *de,* from + *rationem,* reckoning. But also *deraigne,* to put into disorder, disarrange (16th to 18th century) ; Old French *desregner,* to put out of rank; replaced by *derange.* The second *deraigne* also was used of those discharged from religious orders; hence *deraignment* (16th and 17th centuries), discharge from a religious order.

dern. Dark, sombre, solitary; hence, secret; hence sly, deceitful, evil. Chaucer in THE MILLER'S TALE (1386) has: *Ye must been ful deerne as in this case.* The word appears from BEOWULF (10th century) to Scott who in WAVERLEY (1814) speaks of the *dern path. Dern* is also used as a noun, in the senses: a secret; secrecy; a place of concealment; darkness. The word was common in Old Teutonic; there is also a verb *dern,* to hide, to keep secret. Other early forms are *derned, darned,* hidden; *dernful,* dreary; *dernly,* secretly; *dernhede* (1300) and *dernship* (*darnscipe,* in the ANCREN RIWLE, 1225), secrecy.

derring-do. Desperate courage. So Sir Walter Scott, in a note to Ivanhoe (1818), on the passage: *Singular . . . if there be two who can do a deed of such derring-do.* Also *dorryng do, derring doe;* Spenser in THE FAËRIE QUEENE (1596) speaks of *dreadful derring doers.* The form was originally *daring to do,* in Chaucer's TROYLUS AND CRISEYDE (1374) : *Troylus was nevere unto no wight . . . in no degre secounde In dorynge to do that longeth* [that which belongeth, is proper] *to a knyght.* Other manuscripts had *duryng do* and *dorryng don.* Lydgate in his TROY-BOOK (1420) said that Troilus was the equal of any in *dorryng do, this noble worthy wyght.* The 16th century editions printed this *derrynge do.* Then Spenser in THE SHEPHERD'S CALENDAR (1579; OCTOBER) spoke of those *who in derring doe were dreade,* explained *derring doe* in the gloss as 'manhood and chevalrie'—and the new word was launched. Spenser used it again in the DECEMBER eclogue and twice in THE FAËRIE QUEENE, then Scott, Bulwer-Lytton, Burton in his translation (1885) of THE ARABIAN NIGHTS and other historical novelists gave currency to the goodly knight of derring-do.

desipience. Folly; idle trifling. THE SPECTATOR of 17 September, 1887, spoke of *the maturity of sweet desipience.* Also *desipiency.* Latin *de,* from + *sapere,* to taste, to have taste, to be wise. Hence *sapid; insipid,* tasteless, *sapience,* wisdom. Thus *desipient;* used since the 17th century; Stevenson in THE TIMES (2 June, 1894) : *in his character of disinterested spectator, gracefully desipient.*

dess. A table; early variant of *dais.* Spenser in THE FAËRIE QUEENE (1596) pictures Shamefastnesse, who *ne ever once did look up from her desse.* Hence the verb *desse,* to pile in layers, used by farmers (17th-19th centuries) of stacking straw or hay. Hence *dessably,* well arranged.

desuete. Out of use, like *desuete* itself, though revived by Max Beerbohm, from 18th century dictionaries and *innocuous desuetude.*

deuterogamy. Second marriage. Greek *deutero-,* second + *gamos,* marriage. Goldsmith, in THE VICAR OF WAKEFIELD (1766) uses both *deuterogamy* and *deuterogamist.* THE ECHO of 7 September, 1869, expressed the English law: *We do not allow deuterogamy until the primal spouse is disposed of by death or divorce.*

devirginate. To deflower. Also an adjective, ravished. Hence *devirgination; devirginator.* Also *divirginate.* Used from the 15th century. Chapman in MUSAEUS (1600) said: *Fair Hero, left devirginate, Weighs, and with fury wails her state.* R. Ellis in his COMMENTARY ON CATULLUS (1889) speaks of *Night the devirginator.* Stubbes in THE ANATOMIE OF ABUSES (1583) rails at the theatre: *Whereas you say there are good examples to be learned in them, truely so there are, if you will learn falshood, if you will learn cosonage, if you will learn to deceive, if you will learne to playe the hypocrit, to cog, to lie and falsify, if you will learne to jest, laugh, and fleare, to grinne, to nodde and mowe; if you will learne to play the Vice, to sweare, teare, and blaspheme both heaven and earth, if you will learne to become a baud, uncleane, and to divirginate maides, to defloure honest wives; if you will learne to murther, flay, kill, picke, steale, rob, and rove; if you will learne to rebell against princes, to commit treason, to consume treasures, to practise idlenesse, to sing and talk of bawdie love and venerie; if you will learne to deride, scoffe, mocke, and floute, to flatter and smooth, if you will learne to play the whoremaister, the glutton, drunkard, or incestuous person; if you will learne to become proud, hautie, and arrogant, and finally, if you will learne to contemne God and all his lawes, to care neither for heaven nor hell, and to commit all kind of sinne and mischiefe, you need to goe to no other schoole, for all these good examples you may see painted before your eyes in enterludes and plaies.* This is such a detailed indictment as in our day Dr. Fredric Wertham (with illustrations to boot) levels against crime "comic" books for children.

dewitt. To lynch. As *lynch law* comes from a practitioner (or place of practice), so *to dewitt* comes from a victim. Two victims: the brothers John and Cornelius *De Witt,* Dutch opponents of William III, Stadtholder of the United Provinces, were murdered by a mob in 1672. Their name was used, in connection with mob violence, into the 19th century, as by Macaulay in his HISTORY OF ENGLAND (1855).

dewtry. A potion prepared from the thorn-apple, employed to produce stupefaction. Also *deutery, doutry, dutra, deutroa, dutry*; varied from *datura*; Sanskrit *dhattura,* the name of the plant (Datura Stramonium). Its powers were thought similar to those of the nightshade. Butler in HUDIBRAS (1678) wrote: *Make lechers and their punks, with dewtry, commit phantastical advowtry.* Fryer (1698) pictures the Indian practice of widow-burning (suttee): *They give her dutry; when half mad she throws herself into the fire, and they ready with great logs keep her in his funeral pile.* On the other hand, said Ken in HYMNOTHEO (1700): *Indian dames, their consorts to abuse, Dewtry by stealth into their cups infuse.*

dey. A dairy-woman; a maid servant. Used from early times, Old English *daege,* maid; *dag,* dough. From the 14th to the 18th century, a man in charge of a dairy —milking, tending cows—might also be called a *dey* (*deie, dai, daie*). A *deyhouse* was a dairy.

deyite. An old form of *deity.*

deyntie. An old form of *dainty, q.v.*

deywife. A dairy woman, dairymaid. *Cheese,* said Trevisa in his translation (1398) of Bartholomeus' DE PROPRIETATIBUS RERUM, *slydeth out bytwene the fyngres of the deyewife.* Also *deywoman.* Scott (1828, THE FAIR MAID OF PERTH) renewed the use of this form, after Shakespeare's LOVE'S LABOUR'S LOST (1588): *For this damsell I must keepe her at the parke, shee is alowd for the day-woman.*

dia. Used now as a pharmaceutical compound, to mean consisting (mainly) of; as a noun, a compound. Also *dya*; *cp. diamerdes.* In the 14th, 15th, and 16th centuries, *dia* was used as a separate word, e.g., *goats' milk dia.* Lydgate in a poem of 1430 said: *Drugge nor dya was none in Bury towne.*

diablogue. See *endiablee.*

diabolifuge. See *demonocracy*; *endiablee.*

diamerdes. Consisting of dung. Also *diamerdis. Cp. dia.* For an illustration of its use, see *sinapize.* Greek *dia* was used often (as a separate word; combined as a prefix in Latin) for medicaments, condiments, etc., meaning made up of, consisting of. Some of these have been used in English, among them *diabotanum,* a plaster of herbs; *diacaryon,* a preparation of walnuts; *diacopraegia,* of goat's dung; *diacrommyon,* of onions; *diacydonium,* of quinces—marmalade; *diapapaver,* of poppies; *diatrionpipereon,* of three kinds of peppers; *diazingiber, diazinziber,* of ginger.

Diana. The goddess of the moon, patroness of virginity and of hunting. Latin *Diana,* corresponding to Greek *Artemis*; French *Diane,* whence also English *Diane, Dian.* Used in various ways. As an adjective, unsullied: *snow of Dian purity.* With reference to Diana of the Ephesians (BIBLE; ACTS 19); by making silver shrines for her Demetrius made "no small gain": a source of wealth; (1681) our *woolen manufactures which is our Diana.* In alchemy (from the color of the moon), silver: *Sol,* gold; *Mercury,* quicksilver; *Venus,* copper; *Mars,* iron; *Jupiter,* tin; *Saturn,* lead. *Dian's bud,* the wormwort (*q.v.*) was used as an antaphrodisiac, or a cure for love-blindness, to keep maids virgin. A good blossom for a girl to wear on her first date.

diascord. A medicine made of dried leaves of the plant *Teucrium Scordium,* with other herbs. Used from the 16th century. Also *diascordium*; see *alkermes.* Greek *dia,* made up of + *scordian,* the plant water-germander. Scott in THE ABBOT wrote: *With their sirups, and their julaps, and diascordium, and mithridate, and My Lady What-sha-call'um's powder.* Sovereign remedies, all.

diasper. An early form of *jasper.* Also *diasprie. Not of marble,* said R.D. in HYPNEROTOMACHIA (1592), *but of rare and hard diasper of the East.*

dicacity. Jesting speech, banter, raillery. From Latin *dicacem,* sarcastic; *dicere,* to speak. The form *dicacious,* defined by Wright (1869) as talkative, is defined in the O.E.D. as pert of speech, saucy. Rarely *dicacity* was used to mean talkativeness, or mere babbling, as *the dicacity of a parrot.* Heywood in PLEASANT DIALOGUES (1637) says *His quick dicacitie Would evermore be taunting my voracity.* It would be pleasant if those given to dicacity had equal capacity for sagacity—and veracity.

dicephalous. Two-headed. Greek *di,* two + *kephale,* head. Also *dicephalism; dicephalus,* a two-headed creature, like truth or Mr. Lookingbothways, cousin to old Mr. Turncoat.

dicker. As a noun. Ten; especially as a unit of exchange: a parcel of ten hides or skins. Roundabout (Old English *dicor*) from Latin *decuria,* a company or parcel of ten; *decem,* ten. In trade with the American Indians, *dicker* became a verb, to deal in skins; hence, to bargain, haggle, barter, trade. By extension, *a dicker,* a lot, a large but vague number or amount, as in Sidney's ARCADIA (1580) *Behold, said Pas, a whole dicker of wit.*

dictitate. To declare. From Latin *dictitare,* the emphatic form of *dictare, dictatum,* to pronounce, to say often—itself the frequentative form of *dicere, dictum,* to say. From these forms come *dictate* and *dictum, predict* and more beyond fear of *contradiction.* In STAFFORD'S HEAVENLY DOGGE (1615) we are told: *No doubt the old man did dictitate things, the knowledge whereof would have beatified all happy wits.*

didymate. Paired, as twins. Greek *didymos,* twin; see *didymist.* Also *didymated; didymous.* The forms survive in scientific use. Also *didynamy,* twinship.

didymist. A sceptic. Also *didymite. Cp. didimate.* Greek *didymoi,* twins; by extension, testicles, in which sense Bailey gives the word in his 1751 DICTIONARY. The meaning sceptic comes from "doubting Thomas," the apostle that wavered in his faith: Thomas' surname was *Didymos,* twin. BLACKWOOD'S EDINBURGH MAGAZINE (1822) has: *His Lordship is a Dydimite in politics and religion . . . he must put forth his finger to touch, ere he be convinced.*

diffarreation. Divorce. The opposite of *confarreation, q.v.* On this occasion "the breaking of bread" also broke the union.

diffugient. Dispersing. Latin *dif, dis,* apart + *fugere,* to flee. The form *diffugous* (accent on the *dif*) is defined in 18th century dictionaries as flying off in different directions—like the man that was tied to four horses. Thackeray in THE ROUNDABOUT PAPERS (1860) says: *Tomorrow the diffugient snows will give place to spring.* A pleasant prospect!

digastric. Double-bellied. Greek *di-,* two + *gastr-,* belly, whence also *gastronome,* one skilled in what goes into the belly. *Gastronomy* was first used as the title of a poem by Berchoux (French, *Gastronomie,* 1801) ; the ending was formed after *astronomy.* While *digastric* is used in anatomy, of certain muscles (as that of the lower jaw) that have twin swellings, in another sense a gastronome must be careful lest he become digastric.

dighel. Secret, obscure. Old High German *tougal, dougal,* secret. Used until the 14th century. Also *dighelness,* secrecy; *dighelliche, dighenliche,* secretly. Layamon, in 1205, wrote: *Fourth riht faren we him to, digelliche and stille.*

dight. This was a most common word, from early times. Its original sense was to dictate, compose a speech, letter, etc.—related to German *Dichter,* poet, and Latin *dictare, dictatum,* to *dictate*; *dicere, dictum,* to speak. Many other senses developed. (1) To appoint, ordain. Thus by Chaucer in TROYLUS AND CRISEYDE (1374);

revived by Scott in MARMION (1808): *The golden legend bore aright, 'who checks at me, to death is dight.'* (2) To keep in order, to deal with, to use—then, to abuse. By extension, to deal with sexually. Chaucer uses this sense several times, as in THE WIFE OF BATH'S PROLOGUE (1386): *Al my walkynge out by nyghte Was for tespy wenches that he dighte.* (3) To dispose, put, remove. To put into a specific state; e.g., *to dight to death.* So used by Gower (1393); North in his translation (1580) of Plutarch, from which Shakespeare drew his classical plots; Scott in HAROLD THE DAUNTLESS (1817). (4) To compose; construct, make; perform. Spenser in THE FAËRIE QUEENE (1596): *Curst the hand which did that vengeance on him dight.* (5) To equip, set in order; array, arrange; prepare, make ready. Morris in his version (1887) of THE ODYSSEY has: *This Queen of the many wooers dights the wedding for us then.* (6) To array, dress, adorn. *To dight naked,* to strip. Palsgrave in 1530 set down the saying: *A foule woman rychly dyght semeth fayre by candell lyght.* Spenser in THE SHEPHERD'S CALENDAR: JANUARY has: *Thy summer prowde with daffadillies dight.* For another instance of *dight,* adorned, see *blowess.* Spenser also gave the word an erroneous meaning, to lift, in THE FAËRIE QUEENE: *With which his hideous club aloft he dights.* (7) To direct; to direct oneself, to go. Chaucer says in THE MONK'S PROLOGUE: *And out at dore anon I moot me dighte.* (8) To repair, put to rights; to cleanse from rust, to polish; Chaucer in THE ROMAUNT OF THE ROSE speaks of arrows *shaven wel and dight.* Among the forms in which the word appeared are *dihtan, dyghte, dyte, dyth.* Meanings (5) and (6) are still used occasionally, by poets. Poe in EL DORADO (1849) has his gallant knight *gaily bedight.*

digladiation. Crossing of swords, hand-to-hand fighting; more often, wrangling, verbal disputation. Latin *di, dis,* asunder + *gladiari; gladius,* sword, whence also the flower *gladiola; gladiator.* Also *digladiator;* to *digladiate,* to contend, dispute. Used since the 16th century. Hales in GOLDEN REMAINS (1656) spoke of *mutual pasquils and satyrs against each others lives, wherein digladiating like Eschines and Demosthenes, they reciprocally lay open each others filthiness to the view and scorn of the world.*

dilaceration. A tearing to pieces. *Dilacerate* (sometimes *delacerate*) is an emphatic form of *lacerate,* from Latin *dis-,* asunder and *lacerare,* to tear; *lacer,* mangled, torn. The riddles of the Sphinx, observed B. Montague in 1805, *have two conditions annexed . . . dilaceration of those who do not solve them, and empire to those that do.* See *exenteration; dilaniation.*

dilaniation. A ripping or cutting to pieces. Latin *di-,* apart + *laniare, laniatum,* to tear; *lanius,* butcher. Frequent, especially figuratively, in 16th and 17th century sermons. We read of *the dilaniation of Bacchus,* and Overbury in a letter to Cromwell (1535) exclaimed *There be many perverse men, which do dilaniate the flock of Christ.* See *dilaceration.*

dilate. (1) To delay. (2) To spread wide. See *delator.*

dildo. (1) A nonsense word used in refrains, as *Sing trang dildo lee.* Shakespeare in THE WINTER'S TALE (1611) plays the innocent in the servant's words of Autolycus: *He has the prettiest love-songs for maids; so without bawdry, which is strange; with such delicate burthens of 'dildos' and 'fadings', 'jump her and thump her'; and where some stretch-mouth'd rascal would, as it were, mean* *mischief, and break a foul jape into the matter, he makes the maid to answer, 'Whoop, do me no harm, good man'; puts him off, slights him, with 'Whoop, do me no harm, good man.'* A *burthen, burden* was a refrain, 'carried along.' A *fading* was a 16th and 17th century lively dance; but Partridge in SHAKESPEARE'S BAWDRY suggests that in the passage quoted *fadings* implies the die-away languor at the end of love-making. *With a dildo* was the refrain of a popular risqué song; hence (2) A name for the phallus. Therefore applied contemptuously to a man. Hence, also, to objects of phallic shape, as a sausage-like curl on an 18th century wig; R. Holme in THE ACADEMY OF ARMOURY (1688) said: *A campaign wig hath knots or bobs, or a dildo on each side, with a curled forehead.* Jonson in THE ALCHEMIST (1610) comments on a practice still familiar in public toilets today: *Madame, with a dildo, writ o' the wall.*

dilligrout. A mess of pottage, offered to the King of England on his Coronation Day, by the lord of the manor of Addington in Surrey. It was by this service that the manor was held, the first lord (named Tezelin, in the Domesday Book) having been the King's cook. The word is a corruption of the Latin phrase *del girunt,* possibly "by which it should be held." The last service of the *dilligrout* was at the Coronation Banquet of George IV, 1820.

dilling. A child born when the parents are old. So Bailey, in 1751. The O.E.D. suggests that it may be a corruption of *darling* (little dear), applied to the youngest child. In country dialects (*dilling pig*), the word is applied to the weakling of a litter.

dilucid. See *crepuscular.*

dimble. A deep, shady dell, a dingle, *q.v.* Frequent in 16th and 17th century verse. Jonson in THE SAD SHEPHERD (1637) says: *Within a gloomy dimble she doth dwell, Downe in a pitt, ore-grown with brakes and briars.* For another instance, see *slade.*

dime. See *disme.*

dimication. Contention, fighting. Latin *dimicare, dimicatus,* to contend. Mainly in the 17th century; used later for humorous or deliberately ponderous effect.

dimidiate. To divide into halves; to reduce to half. Latin *di, dis,* asunder + *medium,* middle; hence also *dimidiation. Dimidiated,* halved, but also *dimidiate* as an adjective; Lamb in his POPULAR FALLACIES (ESSAYS OF ELIA; 1825) says that the author of TOM BROWN'S SCHOOL DAYS *allows his hero a sort of dimidiate pre-eminence:—Bully Dawson kicked by half the town, and half the town kicked by Bully Dawson.*

dingle. A deep dell. Used since the 13th century, but appearing in literature only from the 17th. Milton applied the word—in COMUS, 1634: *I know each lane, and every alley green, Dingle, or bushy dell of this wild wood*—to a hollow in a forest; use since then has continued the association. For a further instance, see *slade*; *cp. dimble.*

dipsas. A serpent whose bite was fabled to cause a raging thirst. From Wyclif (1382) through Milton (PARADISE LOST, 1667: see *ellops*) and Shelley, who in PROMETHEUS UNBOUND (1821) says: *It thirsted As one bit by a dipsas.* The plural is *dipsades.* From Greek *dipsa,* thirst, whence *dipsomaniacs.* Sylvester in his translation (1618) of Du Bartas says: *Gold bewitches me, and frets accurst My greedy throat with more than dipsian thirst.*

dipsian. See *dipsas.*

diral. Terrible; dire (of which it is a rare alternate form); pertaining to the Furies. Latin *Dirae,* the Furies, the *dire* ones. The Romans also borrowed the Greek euphemistic appellation of the Furies: *Eumenides,* daughters of kindness. There is also an infrequent (16th-18th century) noun *dirity,* dreadfulness, as in a sermon of Hooker (1586): *So unappeasable is the rigour and dirity of his corrective justice.*

direption. Pillaging; snatching away; dragging apart (as when a man is tied by the legs to two stallions whipped off in different directions *Cp. diffugient*). From Latin *di-,* asunder + *rapere, reptum*—whence also *rape.* Fairly common (as was the sacking of captured towns) 15th-18th century.

dirity. See *diral.*

disannul. An emphatic form of *annul.* It was used by Shakespeare (THE COMEDY OF ERRORS, 1590: *Our laws . . . Which Princes, would they, may not disanull*), but since the 17th century has been largely supplanted by the simple form *annul.* The opposite course was taken in the case of *shevel, sheveled,* which have been supplanted by *dishevel, disheveled,* with the same meanings. Other instances where the prefix (instead of forming antonyms, as *connect, disconnect,* etc.) intensifies the meaning are *embowel, disembowel; sever, dissever; simulation, dissimulation.* Also *loose, unloose; flammable, inflammable; ravel, unravel.*

discalceate. Barefoot. Also *discalced.* Latin *dis-,* away, off + *calceare,* to shoe; *calceus,* a shoe; *calx, calcis,* heel. *Discalceate* was first used of friars or nuns whose order was barefoot, then in more general application; *discalceation*—more common in the Eastern lands—is the action of taking off the shoes in reverence. In the West men more usually take off their hats.

discandy. To dissolve from a candied or solid state. Also *discander.* Shakespeare uses *discander in* ANTONY AND CLEOPATRA (1606), but also: *The hearts . . . to whom I gave their wishes, do discandie, melt their sweets On blossoming Caesar.*

discerp. To dismember; pull to pieces; to pluck or tear off; sever. Used from the 15th century. Latin *dis,* apart + *carpere,* pick, pluck; with other prefix, English *excerpt* (picked from). Hence *discerpible, discerptible; the soul,* said the CONTEMPORARY REVIEW in 1867, *is discerptible, and perishes with the body.* East Apthorp, however, in his LETTERS ON THE PREVALENCE OF CHRISTIANITY (1778) presented an alternate view: *His principle was, that the human soul, discerped from the soul of the universe, after death was re-fused into the parent-substance. discerptibility,* divisibility, was defined by Johnson (1775) as 'liableness to be destroyed by disunion of parts.' Also *discerption,* the action of pulling to pieces, of tearing off; a portion thus severed. *discerptive,* tending to pull to pieces, promoting division ("in the ranks," or in a party).

discinct. Ungirt; loosely clad. Hence *discincture,* ungirding; Latin *dis,* away + *cingere, cinctum,* to gird; see *cinct.* When a knight was disgraced, he suffered *discincture,* 'the depriving of the belt.' The word was also used figuratively; Trapp in his COMMENTARIES (1647: LUKE) declared: *A loose, discinct, and diffluent mind is unfit to serve God.* Landor in his WORKS (1846) tells: *In the country I walk and wander about discinct.*

discomfish. See *scomfit.*

discount. Literally, to count off, whence the current financial sense. It was also used to mean to leave out of account, to disregard; to subtract, deduct, detract from. Thus Butler in HUDIBRAS (1664): *For the more languages a man can speak, His talent has but sprung the greater leak; And for the industry he has spent upon't Must full as much some other way discount . . . Yet he that is but able to express No sense at all in several languages Will pass for learneder than he that's known To speak the strongest reason in his own.*

disembogue. To come out of land-waters into the sea; to flow out, to flow into; hence, to pour forth, to empty out. The *disembogue, disembogure,* the mouth (of a river or strait). Via the Spanish: *dis* + *en,* in + *boca,* mouth. Maynarde in his account of DRAKE'S VOYAGE (1595) stated that Sir Thomas Baskerville *talked with such as hee hearde intended to quit companie before they were disembogued.* De Quincey in a letter of 1823, on education, said: *The presses of Europe are still disemboguing into the ocean of literature.* Pope in THE ODYSSEY (1725) mentions *the deep roar of disemboguing Nile* (a sound I should like to hear!); three years later in THE DUNCIAD he moves in more familiar waters: . . . *by Bridewell all descend* (*As morning-pray'r and flagellation end*) *To where Fleet-Ditch with disemboguing streams, Rolls the large tribute of dead dogs to Thames, The King of dykes! Than whom no sluice of mud With deeper sable blots the silver flood.* From this let us turn to AN ADDRESS TO THE HOPEFUL YOUNG GENTRY OF ENGLAND, which in 1669 declared that wit does not need *to call a deity down upon the stage, to make its way open and disembogued.*

disgregate. To separate, scatter, go apart, disintegrate. The opposite of *congregate.* From Latin *dis-,* apart + *gregare,* to collect; *gregem,* flock. In a sermon of 1631, Donne said: *The beams of their eyes were scattered and disgregated . . . so that they could not confidently discern him.* This is based on the then current theory of vision, which held that visual rays might be scattered (rendered divergent), thus confusing or obscuring the sight. Bishop Andrews in a sermon of 1626 said that without concord *a gregation it may be, but no congregation. The con is gone; a disgregation rather.*

disguise. An alteration of a fashion or style; a new, ostentatious or distinctive fashion. Latin *dis, de,* apart + Romanic *guisa* from Old High German *wisa,* manner, mode, appearance—whence English *wise* (the noun, surviving in phrases and as a suffix: *in this wise; lengthwise, crosswise*). Also as a verb; the first sense (from the 14th century) was to alter the style or appearance, to make different, to transform. The intent of concealment also developed in the 14th century; it became dominant by the 17th. Whetstone in AN HEPTAMERON OF CIVILL DISCOURSES (1582) said: *In this cittie there was an old custome . . . that what man so ever committed adulterie should lose his head, and the woman offender should ever after be infamously noted by the wearing of some disguised apparrell.*

disheveled. See *disannul.*

dishonest. Used as a verb from the 14th into the 17th century, meaning: to dishonor, bring disgrace upon; to defame, calumniate; to violate, defile; to deform, render ugly or repellent. Whetstone in AN HEPTAMERON OF CIVILL DISCOURSES (1582) pictured Andrugio, to save his life, beseeching his sister Cassandra to give herself to Lord Promos: *Thou shalt be deflowred, but not dishonested.*

dislimn. To efface the outlines of, erase, blot out; to become effaced, to vanish. Shakespeare in ANTONY AND CLEOPATRA (1606) says: *Sometimes we see a clowd that's dragonish, A vapour sometime like a beare or lyon, A towered citadel, a pendent rock . . . That which is now a horse, even with a thoght The racke dislimes and makes it indistinct As water is in water.*

disme. Tenth. An early form of the common *dime;* Old French *disme,* Latin *decima,* a tenth part, *decem,* ten. Also, *to dime, disme* (15th to 17th century) to take a tenth of; to divide into tenths. From the 14th to the 17th century, especially the tithe or the share for the church or the government. Also a 'tithe' of war, every tenth man slain, as in Shakespeare's ANTONY AND CLEOPATRA (1606): *Let Helen go. Since the first sward was drawn about this question, Every tithe soul, mongst many thousand dismes, Hath been as dear as Helen.*

disour. Via Old French from Latin *dicere,* to tell. A story-teller, a reciter of gestes; a jester. See *dizzard.*

disperson. To insult; treat like a dog. Latin, *dis,* away from + *persona* (originally, mask), person; dignity. ALEXANDER (1400) said: *For spyte he spittis in his face, Dispises him despetously, dispersons him foule.*

displant. Shakespeare first took this word out of its literal sense, in ROMEO AND JULIET (1592); hence it developed the sense of removing persons from their settlements (*plantations;* Spenser speaks in 1596 of countries *planted with English . . . shortly displanted and lost*). Hence also, to root up; to supplant; Shakespeare in OTHELLO speaks of *the displanting of Cassio.* THE LONDON QUARTERLY REVIEW of June 1847 quoted Shakespeare: *'Hang up philosophy! Unless philosophy can make a Juliet, Displant a town, reverse a prince's doom, It helps not, it prevails not; talk no more!' But Dante, in the same Verona, found not merely an adequate but an apt substitute for his lost love in the religious stoicism of the day.*

dissemble. See *semble.* AN ASYLUM FOR FUGITIVE PIECES, in 1785, printed anonymously the now noted lines: *Perhaps it was right to dissemble your love, But why did you kick me downstairs?*

distain. To stain; to discolor, dirty; hence, to defile, dishonor. Via Old French from Latin *dis,* away + *tingere, tinctum,* whence *tinge, tint, tincture.* In the first sense, Spenser in THE FAËRIE QUEENE (1590) says: *I found her golden girdle cast astray Distaynd with durt and blood.* In the second, Shakespeare has, in THE RAPE OF LUCRECE (1594): *The silver-shining queen he would distain; her twinkling handmaids too;* and in RICHARD III: *You having lands, and blest with beauteous wives, They would restraine the one, distaine the other.*

distrain. To press, squeeze; confine, restrain; constrain, compel; to seize, confiscate; to tear off, tear asunder. Chaucer speaks in THE PARLEMENT OF FOULES (1381) of *The gentyl faucoun that with his feet distraynyth The kyngis hand.* Spenser says in THE FAËRIE QUEENE (1590): *That same net so cunningly was wound That neither guile nor force might it distraine.* Shakespeare in RICHARD II (1583) cries: *My fathers goods are all distraynd, and sold.* The word was very common from the 13th to the 17th century, being used in law: *distrain,* to hold as a forfeit to ensure the fulfilment of an obligation; later (18th century) to sell chattels to satisfy a debt, especially arrears of rent; *to distrain upon* a person, to enforce such a sale.

divirginate. See *devirginate.*

dizzard. A fool. Perhaps originally a variant of *disour, q.v.,* but soon linked with *dizzy.* A frequent 16th and 17th century term of contempt, used into the 19th century, as in D'Israeli's CURIOSITIES OF LITERATURE. More than one man that prides himself on being a wizard is by his friends esteemed a very dizzard.

doak. See *dolk.*

docible. See *indocible.*

doddard. A tree (especially, an oak) that has lost its top branches (by decay). The Old English verb *to dod* meant to blunt the top of a thing; hence, to clip a person's hair or an animal's horns—*dodded,* clipped, polled, hornless—and by extension, to behead. The *doddings* are the cuttings (e.g., the wool cut near the tails of sheep). A *doddle* is a pollard; also, an infirm person. To *doddle* is to shake the head, or walk feebly about, as in Urquhart's translation (1653) of Rabelais: *dodling his head;* or to toddle or waddle, as when THE SPECTATOR of 6 December, 1884, speaks of *a pretty girl . . . with a quantity of little pigs doddling about in front of her. Doddy-pate* and *doddypoll* are 15th through 18th century terms for blockhead, fool; they are related to the verb *dote,* to be foolish, which is related to *dod*—a 'dodded poll' being a sign of a simpleton, it seems. And *dotard* is another form of *doddard.*

doit. A trifling sum; a very little. Originally (perhaps via Norwegian *dveit,* a piece cut off, *dvita,* to cut) a Dutch coin worth half an English farthing. Shakespeare in THE TEMPEST (1610) says: *They will not give a doit to relieve a lame beggar;* Mrs. Carlyle in a letter of 1849 exclaimed: *As if anybody out of the family of Friends cared a doit about W. Penn!*

doke. See *dolk.*

dole. This common form came into the language from three sources; it has had many meanings. (1) Old English *dal, dael,* whence also *deal.* The state of being divided; division. Hence, a portion (16th to 18th century, a portion of a common field); one's portion or lot in life: *Happy man be his dole.* From this meaning came the current uses of *dole,* a gift made in charity, food *doled out.* (2) Late Latin *dolium,* grief, whence French *deuil;* Latin *dolere,* to grieve, to suffer; *dolor,* grief, pain, anguish; also in English, *dolor.* Hence *dolorific, doloriferous,* causing pain, suffering grief. Grief, mental distress; mourning; lamentation. To *make dole,* to lament; *dolent,* mournful; clothes, weeds *of dole,* mourning garments. Also pain; also, that which rouses sorrow, a piteous thing. A *dole tree* (19th century, e.g., Stevenson, *dule tree*), a gallows, a hanging-tree. From this *dole* also came *indolency, indolence,* which first meant freedom from pain, insensibility or indifference to pain; thus, also, an *indolent ulcer,* one causing no pain. From this came the current meaning of *indolent,* lazy; Addison in verses of 1719 wrote: *While lull'd by sound, and undisturb'd by wit, Calm and serene you indolently sit.* An *indolent* man, however, may find himself in need of a *dole.* (3) Greek *dolos,* deceit. Guile, deceit; deliberate mischief; in Scotch law, *dole* means the malicious or evil intent that makes a misdeed a crime. Thus Chambers in his CYCLOPAEDIA

(1753) stated: *Under dole are comprehended the vices and errors of the will, which are immediately productive of the criminal act.* Hence also *dolose,* intentionally deceitful; maliciously intended; *dolosity,* hidden malice; deceitfulness. Lord Cranford in THE MANCHESTER GUARDIAN (31 July, 1861) wrote: *Without accusing his . . . learned friend of being dolose, he did accuse him of having misled their lordships.*—The word *dole* took many forms, among them *dool, dule, deol, del, doylle, dol, doale, doel, dowle, duyl, duill, dulle.* In hunting, said Turberville in his VENERIE (1576), *the houndes must be rewarded with the bowels, the bloud and the feete . . . it is not called a reward but a dole.* Milton used the word figuratively in his APOLOGY FOR SMECTYMNUS (1642): *Who made you the busy almoner to deal about this dole of laughter and reprehension?* A *dole-window* was a window from which doles were distributed, as to a breadline.

dolk. A dimple, a dint or tiny hollow. Also *doke, doak.* THE SPECTATOR of 20 January, 1866, mentions a *little doke in the end of the nose.*

dolose. See *dole.*

dolphin. An early variant of *dauphin;* used by Shakespeare. The French *dauphin* was derived from *delphinus* (the name of the fish), the proper name of the lords of the Viennois, whose province was thence called *Dauphiné.* The last lord of *Dauphiné,* Humbert III, on ceding the province to Philip of Valois, in 1349, stipulated that the title *dauphin* should thereafter be borne by the heir to the throne of Naples.

domable. Tamable. From Late Latin *domabilis,* tamable, from *domare,* to tame. The frequentative form of *domare* was *domitare,* whence English *domitable,* a rare form, surviving in the negative, *indomitable,* untamable. Bailey's DICTIONARY (1751) also gives *domation* and *domature,* both meaning taming—which the O.E.D. (1933) ignores.

dondaine. A medieval engine for hurling stones. Lydgate (1430) spells it *dondine,* but rhymes it with *attayne.*

donet. A grammar; hence, a primer in any field. Also *donat.* From Aelius *Donatus,* a 4th century scholar whose elementary Latin grammar (ARS GRAMMATICA) became the standard.

doniferous. Bearing a gift, as Santa Claus come Christmastide. The word, found in 17th and 18th century dictionaries, may be traced to Virgil's lines in Book II of the AENEID: "Men of Troy, trust not the horse! Whatever it is, I fear the Greeks even bearing gifts"—*Timeo Danaos et dona ferentes.*

donjon. Early form of *dungeon.* The old spelling is usually retained for the meaning 'the great tower or innermost keep of a castle.' The word is from Late Latin *domnionem,* castle, from *domnus, dominus,* lord, whence also *dominion.* A 1678 translation of Gaya's THE ART OF WAR explains *donjon* as *a place of retreat in a town or place, to capitulate in with greater security in case of extremity*—a definition of realism, but hardly of romance. Scott was fond (as in MARMION, 1808) of *the battled towers, the donjon keep.*

dool. See *dole.*

doom. See *deemster.*

dop. An old form of *dip,* as noun and verb. Hence, a bow, a quick curtsey. Jonson in CYNTHIA'S REVELS (1599) remarks: *The Venetian dop, this.*

dor. As a noun: (1) An insect that flies with a humming sound. Also *dorr, dore, doar.* Probably echoic in origin. Also *dor-bee, dor-fly; dumble-dor,* the dung-beetle. Also, a drone bee; hence, an idler, a lazy drone, a *dor-head.* (2) An old form for *dare.* (3) An old form for *deer.* (4) Mockery, making game (of); *to give one the dor, to put the dor upon.* Milton in THE APOLOGY FOR SMECTYMNUS (1642) wrote that he *brings home the dorre upon himself.* (5) A simpleton, a fool. Jonson in CYNTHIA'S REVELS (1599) uses *give him the dor,* also: *This night's sport, Which our court-dors so heartily intend.* As a verb: (a) *dor, dorr, durr,* to make dim or dull (color); to deaden. Holland in his Pliny (1601) says of colors: *The lightnesse or sadnesse of the one doth quicken and raise, or els dorr and take downe the colour of the other.* (b) *dor, dorre,* to make game of, mock, confound. 'Smectymnus' in his ANSWER (1641) said: *This is but a blind, wherewith the Bishop would dorre his reader. To dor the dotterel,* to hoax a simpleton. The form *dotterel* is related to *dote; cp. doddard.* Also *dottrel, dotrill,* and more. It meant a silly person; especially, one whose intellect is decayed. It was also applied to a kind of plover, because the bird (like a fool) allows itself to be easily taken; and to a doddered tree. *Thy words,* said Bauldwin in his TREATISE OF MORALL PHILOSOPHIE (1547), *savour of old idle dottrels tales.*—This should suggest some new answers to the old riddle: When is a door not a door?

dorbel. A dull-witted pedant; a foolish pretender to learning. From Nicholas *Dorbellus* (Nicholas de Orbellis, died 1455), a professor of Scholastic Philosophy at Poitiers, a follower of Duns Scotus (whose name gave us *dunce*). Hence also *dorbelish, dorbellical,* stupid, clumsy. Nashe in PIERCE PENNILESS (1592) spoke of *sheepish discourse . . . uglye, dorbellicall and lumpish.* When the dorbel rings, the dunce enters. *Dunce* has remained.

dorrye. See *hastlet.*

dorse. See *dossal.*

dorter. A sleeping-room; sleeping quarters; especially in a monastery. *Cp. dossal.* Also *dortour, dortore, dortoire*; Old French *dortour, dortoir*; Latin *dormitorium,* dormitory; *dormitare,* to be sleepy, fall asleep; *dormire, dormitum,* to sleep. A common word from the 13th to the 17th century; Nashe in PIERCE PENNILESS (1592) said: *It will make them jolly long winded to trot up and downe the dorter staires.* Bishop Andrewes in a sermon of 1626 spoke of a cemetery as *a great dortor;* Heywood in PROVERBS (1562) said: *The mouth is assynde to be the tounges dorter.* Silence is golden.

dossal. (1) An ornamental cloth for the back of a seat, especially a throne, or for the back of an altar. Bulwer-Lytton in HAROLD (1848) pictures a hawk *perched on the dossal of the Earl's chair. Cp. antimacassar.* (2) A pannier, a basket carried on the back, or two such hanging over the back of a beast of burden, as Chaucer mentions (1384: *dosser*) in THE HOUS OF FAME. Also *dossel, dosel, dosser, dorse, dorsel.* Old French *dossel,* from *dos* (Latin *dorsum*), back. From the general sense "back" various other forms have come. A *dorter* (*dortour*) *q.v.,* is a sleeping-room, dormitory. *To dorse* was 18th and 19th century boxing slang for to knock down (flat on the back); Wilson in NOCTES AMBROSIANAE (1826) wisely remarked that *the straight hitting . . . soon dorsers your roundabout hand-over-head* hitters. *Dorty* (perhaps, however, another word) meant sulky, then saucy, haughty; *dort, dortiness,* *dortiship,* all meant ill-humor, the sulks. A *dosser* is one who sleeps at a cheap lodging-house; a *happy dosser* (19th century) was one who slept wherever he could find a place. To *doze,* which of course does not require one to lie on the back, is apparently from the Scandinavian. The word does not appear in literary English before the 17th century, but the practice dates at least as far back as schools and churches. One cannot always keep one's eyes fixed on the dossal!

dotant. One that dotes, a simpleton. A variant of *dotard;* see *doddard.* Shakespeare has, in CORIOLANUS (1607): *Such a decay'd dotant as you seem to be.*

dotard. See *doddard.* Also *dotehead,* blockhead; *doter.*

dotterel. See *dor.*

douce-ame. A sweetly savory dish, recipe in THE FORME OF CURY (1390): *Take gode cowe mylk, and do it in a pot. Take parsel, sawge, ysope, savray, and oother gode herbes, hewe hem, and do hem in the mylke, and seeth hem. Take capons half yrosted, and smyte hem on pecys, and do thereto pynes and hony clarified. Salt it, and color it with safron, and serve it forth.*

doucet. A sweet thing; applied to various fruits (apple, grape), then to dishes. Also *dowcet, dulcet.* A 15th century recipe called for pork, honey, pepper, and flowr, baked "in a cofyn." In the plural, a special delicacy, the testicles of a deer; Sir Walter Scott in WOODSTOCK (1826) speaks of *broiling the . . . dowsets of the deer upon the glowing embers with their own royal hands.* There was also a sweet-sounding sort of flute (as in Chaucer's THE HOUS OF FAME, 1384) called the *doucet.* From French *doucet,* diminutive of *douce,* Latin *dulcis,* sweet. In a poem of 1640 we read: *Heer's dousets and flappjacks, and I ken not what.*

dought. See *douth.*

doundrins. Afternoon drinkings. Bailey (1751) lists these as in Derbyshire, but today they are ubiquitous.

dout. To put out, extinguish. From *do + out.* Also *dout, douter,* an extinguisher. Used from the 16th into the 18th century. *Cp. dup.* Rastell in A HUNDRED MERRY TALES (1526) said *Dout the candell and dout the fyre.* Shakespeare in HAMLET (1603) notes that *the dram of base Doth all the noble substance often dout To his own scandal.*

douth. Virtue, power; good deed; manhood. Early English, from a common Teutonic form. Early *dugan,* to be good. Later appears as *dought* (18th century), perhaps a back-formation from *doughty,* also related to *dugan. Doughty* is now archaic or humorous.

dowlas. A coarse linen. Also *dowlace, doulas;* (in Scotland, late 15th century) *douglas.* The word is from the town of *Doulas* in Brittany. A similar linen cloth, apparently finer, was called *lockram* or *lockeram,* from the nearby town of *Locronan,* 'cell of St. Roman.' *Lockram* was used for the cloth, and for articles made from it, from the 15th into the 18th century; Scott revived the word (*lockeram*) in THE ABBOT (1820). Shakespeare in HENRY IV, PART ONE (1596) says: *doulas, filthy doulas . . . they have made boulters of them. Dowlas* was a very common cloth (linen, made of flax) in the 16th and 17th centuries; then the word began to be used of a strong calico substitute for the linen. The shift in meaning is shown in a trial recorded in PROCEEDINGS AT THE SESSIONS OF THE PEACE, April 1733; Goody

Baker and Goody Trumper are arguing over the theft of a linen cap, of 'an ordinary coarse cloth.' Tr. *Coarse, but what sort I say?* B. *Why, it was of flax.* Tr. *Flax; very well! Now my brother's cap was made of dowlas, and this cap here is dowlas, I'll take my oath on't; and pray Goody Baker, do you call dowlas flax?*

down. See *adown.*

doxy. (1) Mistress; wench. From the 14th century (first as slang: the mistress of a beggar or a vagabond), prostitute; then wench; later, sweetheart. Shakespeare has a refrain in THE WINTER'S TALE (1611): *With hey, the doxy over the dale.* (2) Opinion, especially in regard to religion. Since the 18th century. Warburton, followed by John Quincy Adams (1778) and countless others, remarked: *Orthodoxy is my doxy; heterodoxy is the other man's.* Greek *doxa,* opinion.

draconian. (1) Severe, harsh; characteristic of *Draco,* archon of Athens in 621 B.C., said to have established a severe code of laws. *I never much admired,* said Gifford (in Smiles' J. MURRAY) in 1819, *the vaunt of draconianism, 'And all this I dare do, because I dare.'* Also *draconism,* severity. (2) Relating to a *dragon;* Greek *drakon,* dragon. THE DAILY TELEGRAPH (10 November, 1880) recorded that, *in the course of one of these draconian performances . . . the mummer's tail came off.* Other forms with the same meanings are *draconic, draconical; dracontic*—used of the dragon only; also *dracontine.* A precious stone supposedly found in the dragon's brain was the (four syllabled) *draconites* (*dracontites, dracondite*). In astronomy, *dracontic,* relating to the moon's nodes: the ascending node of the moon's orbit is known as *the dragon's head;* the descending, *the dragon's tail.* In palmistry, the *dragon's tail* is the discriminal line between the hand and the arm.

draff. Dregs, refuse; swill for swine; especially, the refuse or grains of malt after brewing. Hence *draffish,* worthless. The word appears in various proverbs: Heywood (1546), *Draffe is your errand, but drinke ye woulde;* Shakespeare (THE MERRY WIVES OF WINDSOR, 1598), *Still swine eats all the draffe;* Ferguson (1598), *As the sow fills the draff sours.* Also in combinations: *Thanks is but a draff-cheap phrase.* A *draffsack,* a big paunch; a lazy glutton; Chaucer in THE REEVE'S TALE (1386): *I lye as a draf-sak in my bed.* The word was also used figuratively, as in Chaucer's THE LEGEND OF GOOD WOMEN (1385): *To wryte the draff of stories, and forgo the corn.*

dragon's tail. See *draconian.*

dragon-water. A medicinal drink, frequently prescribed in the 17th century. The Water Poet (WORKS; 1630) spoke of *dragon-water in most high request.*

dratchell. See *drazel.*

draught. From the general sense of drawing (dragging) or pulling, other meanings arose. These include: (1) drawing of breath. (2) a team of horses. (3) a take, quantity of fish in one *draught* of the net; specifically (19th century), 20 lbs. of eels. (4) the distance a bow can shoot. (5) a move at chess or other game; *the draught of a pawne,* Beale noted in CHESS (1656) *is only one house at a time. Cp. drautt.* (6) a current, flow. Also, the bed of a stream; a ravine. (7) The entrails of an animal when drawn out; the *pluck, q.v.* (8) A cesspool, sewer. Shakespeare in TROILUS AND CRESSIDA (1606) exclaims: *Sweet draught: sweet quoth-a?*

sweet sinke, sweet sure. Hence, a privy (also *draught-house*); Shakespeare in TIMON OF ATHENS cries: *Hang them, or stab them, drowne them in a draught.* Hence also, a voiding of the bowels.

drautt. A variant form of *draught, q.v.* For an instance of its use, *see brynnyng.*

draw-glove. A game (*draw-gloves; drawing gloves*) known only from literary references; played 15th to 18th century. It seems to have been a race to see who, when a certain word was unexpectedly spoken, could first draw off his (or her) gloves. Herrick in HESPERIDES (1648) refers to it twice, in addition to his little poem *Draw-Gloves: At draw-gloves we'll play And prethee let's lay A wager, and let it be this: Who first to the sum Of twenty shall come, Shall have for his winning a kiss.*

drazel. A slut. So in 17th century use; the 18th and 19th centuries used the forms *dratchell* and *drotchell,* as George Eliot in ADAM BEDE (1859): *She's not a common flaunting dratchell, I can see that.* These are all variants of *drossel, q.v.*

dreary. See *dririmancy.*

dreche. A variant of *dretch, q.v.*

drede. An old form of *dread.*

dredge. A comfit, a sweetmeat; especially, one containing a grain of spice. In the form *dragée* (19th century) one that has medicine in the center. The candy *dredge* (*drage, dragie, dregge*; at first, two syllables) came roundabout from the Greek *tragemata,* spices. Hence, *dredge-box, drageoir, dragenall,* a box to hold sweets; Lord Berners in his translation (1525) of Froissart lists *two dredge-boxes of golde.* [The verb *to dredge,* to bring up from the water, occurs first in the 16th century; it is probably a variant of *drag.*]

dree. To do, perform, commit; to endure, suffer (especially, *to dree one's weird,* to endure one's fate; the three fates are *the weird sisters*); to endure, to last. Also a noun. And an adjective, heavy; long-suffering; long-lasting. Very common, 10th through 16th century; thereafter archaic, though revived by Sir Walter Scott (as in a letter of 1810: *I was dreeing penance for some undiscovered sin at a family party*) and others. Robert Bridges uses the noun in a poem of 1890: *The half-moon . . . shrinketh her face of dree* [trouble]. Lydgate in a poem of 1430 says: *The first year of wedlock is called pleye, the second dreye, and the third year deye.* Lucky those that reach *day* so soon! [But beware! *deye* is an old form for *die.*]

drepee. A dish, described in THE FORME OF CURY (1390): *Take blanched almandes, grynde hem, and temper hem up with gode broth; take oynouns a grete quantité, perboyle hem, and frye hem, and do thereto. Take smalle bryddes* [birds], *perboyle hem, and do thereto pellydore, and a lytel grece.*

dress-improver. A mid-Victorian term for the bustle; so named because it amply covered the posterior (though probably the ladies figured that while it dimmed the outline it accentuated the appeal). Lustier times called this article the *bumrowl, q.v.*

dretch. To trouble in sleep; to torment. As a noun, *dretch, dretching,* trouble. From the 9th century. Also, from the 13th century, *to dretch,* to delay, linger; protract. Also *dreche, dracche, drecche*; not known in other languages. Malory in MORTE D'ARTHUR (1485): *We alle . . . were soo dretched that somme of us lepte oute of oure beddes naked.* Chaucer uses the word in both senses.

dreynt. Drenched. An early form of the past tense and past participle of *drench.*

drightin. A lord; hence, the Lord, God. Also *drighton, drighten*; sometimes shortened to *dright. Dright* was also an Old English word—to the 13th century—meaning army; Gothic *go-draughts,* soldier. Hence *drightman,* warrior. *drightfare,* march, procession, throng. *drightin* was used from BEOWULF to the 15th century. Hence *drightness, drihtnesse,* majesty, godhead. *drightful, drightlike,* noble. In SIR GAWAYNE AND THE GRENE KNIGHT (1360) we are assured: *Ful wel con Drightin shape His servauntes for to save.*

dririmancy. See *aeromancy.* Reade in THE CLOISTER AND THE HEARTH (1861) has: *I studied at Montpelier . . . There learned I dririmancy, scatomancy, pathology . . .* The reference here is to diagnosis rather than divination. The form *driry* is a variant of *dreary,* which first (Old Saxon *dror*; Old Norse *dreyri,* gore) meant gory, bloody; then horrid, dire, cruel—then sad, melancholy, and finally the current dismal, gloomy. BEOWULF shows the first meaning, as does Spenser in THE FAËRIE QUEENE (1590): *With their drery wounds.*

dromond. 'A great vessel of the class of long ships'; one of the largest of medieval vessels, used in commerce and war. Also *dromon, dromoun, dromund, dromonde.* Greek *dromon,* large vessel; *dromos,* running, course, as also in *dromedary,* 'ship of the desert,' a fleet breed of camel. The word was not used after 1500 except historically, as by Scott in THE FAIR MAID OF PERTH (1828): *I have got the sternpost of a dromond brought up the river from Dundee.*

drore. A 15th century dish: *Take vele or motun, and smyte it on gobettes, and put it in a pot with watur, and let it sethe; and take onyons, and mynce hom, and do thereto, and parsel, sauge, ysope, savery, and hewe hom smale, and do hit in the pot, and coloure hit with saffron, and do thereto powder of pepur, and of clowes, and of maces, and alaye it wyth yolkes of rawe eggus and verjus; but let it not sethe after, and serve hit forthe.*

drosomely. Honey-dew; manna. Greek *drosos,* dew; *meli,* honey. Four syllables, accent on the second. A pleasant word, in Bailey (1751), although the O.E.D. ignores it.

drossel. A slut. Also *drosell, drossell*; *cp. drazel.* Used from the 16th century. Warner in Albion's England (1602) said: *Now dwels each drossell in her glasse.* Origin unknown; probably not related to *dross,* though the O.E.D. defines this as scum, recrement, or extraneous material thrown off . . .

drotchell. See *drazel.*

druery. See *drury.*

drumble. An inert or sluggish fellow, a 'drone.' Also in the names of insects, *drumble-, drummel-, dumble-*: a *drumble-bee,* a *humble-bee, bumble-bee*; *drumble-dore,* a clumsy insect; hence, a heavy, sluggish, stupid person. Hence, *to drumble,* to drone, mumble; to move sluggishly. In this sense, used by Shakespeare (MERRY WIVES OF WINDSOR; 1598); revived by Scott (THE FORTUNES OF NIGEL; 1822): *Why, how she drumbles—I warrant she stops to take a sip on the road.* There are two other verbs, *to drumble*: (1) to sound like a drum (*the drumbling tabor*; 17th century). (2) to trouble, disturb; to make *drumly* or turbid. *Drumly,* cloudy (of the sky), turbid (of water) was used from the 16th into the 18th century. And from Dutch *drommeler,* a boat, a heavy-set man, English in the 16th and 17th centuries used *drumbler, drumler,* for a small but fast boat, especially used as a privateer or by pirates.

drumly. See *drumble.*

drury. It is amusing to think that the two great (licenced) theatres of England for two centuries, drew their names from the same mood. *Covent Garden* was *convent* garden; *Drury Lane* was modesty (sobriety) lane. So at least Bailey (1751), defining *drury* as modesty. The O.E.D., however, will have none of this. It lists *drury* as one of many different spellings of *druery,* which means love, especially illicit love; a love token or gift; a sweetheart. *Druery* (ultimately from Old French *dru, drut,* lover, akin to German *traut,* beloved, whence also Old English *drut,* darling) was common from the 13th through the 15th century; Chaucer in SIR THOPAS (1386) says: *Of ladies love and druerie Anon I wol you tele.* In SIR GAWAYNE AND THE GRENE KNIGHT (1360) the Green Knight's lady tempted Sir Gawain: *The lady loutes adoun And comlyly kisses his face; Much speche thay ther expoun Of druries greme and grace.*

drut. See *drury.*

dryad. A wood nymph, a spirit that inhabits trees. Greek *dryas,* plural *dryades; drys, dryos,* tree. Hence also *dryadic.* By transference, a sylvan maiden, a denizen of the woods. *Young Health,* said Warton in BATHING (1790), *a dryad-maid in vesture green.* In bathing, one is more likely to meet a *neread, q.v.*

duan. A poem; a canto of a long poem. A Gaelic word, first used in English by Macpherson in OSSIAN (1765). Burns and Byron followed him.

dub (noun). A pool of water, especially, a muddy pool, as of rain water on a dirt road; also, a deep pool in a shallow stream. Used from the 16th century; still in Scotland. Burns uses it in TAM O'SHANTER (1790): Stevenson in KIDNAPPED (1886) has: *'Here's a dub for ye to jump.'*

duckingstool. A chair on the end of a plank, for plunging scolds, dishonest tradesmen, and other offenders, into water and public obloquy. One on wheels, so that the offender might be more widely exhibited, was called a *ducking-tumbrel.* See *cuckingstool.*

dudgeon. (1) A kind of wood used for handles, as of knives; probably boxwood. Hence, a hilt made of this wood; Shakespeare has in Macbeth 1605 *I see . . . on thy blade and dudgeon, gouts of blood.* Hence, from *dudgeon-dagger,* shortened to *dudgeon,* a dagger. (2) Perhaps the same word, from "looking daggers" (?), came to mean resentment, anger. Scott in THE ANTIQUARY (1816) says *They often parted in deep dudgeon*—but usually the preceding adjective is *high*—no one has ever been seen *in low dudgeon.* See *couth; clapperdudgeon.*

duke. (1) As a verb, to behave like a duke (with an implication of ostentation); Shakespeare in MEASURE FOR MEASURE (1603) says: *Lord Angelo Dukes it well in his absence.* (2) The castle in chess. A 17th century term, explained by Middleton in A GAME AT CHESS (1624): E. *There's the full number of the game; Kings, and their pawns, queen, bishops, knights, and dukes.* J. *Dukes? they're called rooks by some.* E. *Corruptively. Le roch, the word, custodiè de la roch, The keeper of the forts.* (3) In phrases. *To dine with Duke Humphrey,* to go dinnerless. Supposed to have arisen in the 17th century, from Sir Humphrey's Walk in old St. Paul's, London, where persons would loiter in hopes of an invitation to dinner; if they received none, they *dined with Duke Humphrey.* Also 17th century, *the Duke of Exeter's daughter,* a rack-like instrument of torture, used in the Tower of London, supposedly invented by the Duke. Similarly, *Scavenger's daughter,* invented by Sir W. Skevington, Lieutenant of the Tower. The *gunner's daughter,* cannon to which a seaman was lashed, to be flogged. There was also *Madame Guillotine.*

dulcarnon. A dilemma; a person perplexed. The phrase *at dulcarnon,* at one's wit's end. Chaucer in TROYLUS AND CRISEYDE (1374), "Crisseide" remarks: *I am, til gȯd me bettre minde sende, At dulcarnon, right at my wittes ende.*

dulcet. See *doucet. Dulcet* survives as an adjective, meaning sweet, agreeable to sight, sound, or taste. Earlier forms include *dulce* (noun and adjective); *dulcean; dulceous; dulcid,* sweet; *dulcifluous,* sweetly flowing; *dulciloquent,* with honeyed words; and of course the *dulcimer,* on which the damsel played in Coleridge's KUBLA KHAN. The *dulcimer* occurs earlier, in Pepys' DIARY (23 May, 1662) and Milton's PARADISE LOST (1667), and is the earliest prototype of the piano.

dulcify. To sweeten (in taste or disposition); to mollify, to appease. *Cp. dulcet; edulcorate.* Hence also *dulcity, dulcitude,* sweetness. And *dulcoamare,* bitter-sweet. *Dulcify* was also used, in the 19th century, to mean to speak sweetly or in bland tones. In alchemy, it was used of washing soluble acids out of a substance; Subtle asks, in Jonson's THE ALCHEMIST (1610): *Can you sublime, and dulcefie?* Lamb's famous essay on roast pig in ELIA (1822) rejoices in *intenerating and dulcifying a substance . . . so mild and dulcet as the flesh of young pigs.*

dulcimer. See *dulcet.*

dule. See *dole.*

dulia. Servitude; used in the Roman Catholic religion of the minor type of veneration, of saints and angels, as contrasted with *latria, q.v.* Greek *douleia,* servitude; *doulos,* slave. Hence, though rarely, *dulically* and *dulian.*

dun. In phrases. A. *Dun is in the mire:* (1) "Everything is at a standstill." (2) A Christmas game. A log is brought into the room, and the cry is raised that *Dun* (the cart-horse; *dun* was from the 14th century a common name for a horse—from the color) *is stuck in the mire.* Two persons pretend to be trying vainly to pull Dun out; more join them—in the play, there are "sundry arch contrivances to let the ends of it fall on one another's toes" and other sources of merriment. Finally, Dun is drawn out of the mire, and put on the fire. B. *Dun is the mouse*: "The task is done." This is a jesting way of saying something is settled, or completed, by a nonsense pun on the color of a mouse. Shakespeare alludes to both these phrases, in the verbal play of ROMEO AND JULIET (1592). Romeo, before the masked ball at the Capulets', is aweary: *The game was nere so faire, and I am done.* Mercutio: *Tut, dun's the mouse, the constable's owne word. If thou art dun, weele draw thee from the mire Of this sirreverence love wherein thou stick'st Up to the ears.*

dungeonable. Shrewd, "deep." In the 17th and 18th centuries. From the figurative use of the noun, as applied to a person of profound learning. Boswell in his JOURNAL OF A TOUR TO THE HEBRIDES

(1773) tells us: *Lady Lochbury said 'He was a dungeon of wit.'*

dup. To open (as a gate or door). So the O.E.D.; Edward's WORDS, FACTS, AND PHRASES (1912) as plausibly says, to fasten. The word *dup* is a contraction of *do up.* Shakespeare has, in HAMLET (1602): *Then up he rose, and don'd his clothes, and dupt the chamber door.* The slang *dub* meant either to open or to fasten; it is a corrupt form of *dup,* which may also have had either meaning. Formed in the same way were *don, do on; doff, do off; dout, q.v.*

durance. Continuation, duration. The noun of the verb *dure, q.v.* Also *durancy;* superseded by *endurance.* Hence, a stout, durable cloth (16th to 18th century), used figuratively by Cornwallyes in his ESSAYS (1601): *I refuse to wear buffe for the lasting, and shall I be content to apparrell my braine in durance?* The word is dimly remembered, from historical romances, in the sense of imprisonment, especially *in durance vile.* In this sense it is akin to *duress* (also from Latin *durus,* hard), which first meant hardness, roughness, violence; then firmness; then forcible restraint, imprisonment. Shakespeare in HENRY IV, PART TWO (1597) says that Doll *is in base durance, and contagious* [pestilential] *prison.*

dure. (1) An early form of *endure,* used from the 13th through the 17th century. The form *during,* now used as a preposition, was originally a participle of *dure.* French *durer,* to last; Latin *durare,* to harden, be hardened, last; *durus,* hard. Hence also, as an adjective (2) hard. Related to *dour.* Even in the 19th century, Bulwer-Lytton (in HAROLD; 1848) wrote: *In reply to so dure a request.* Marlowe and Nashe in DIDO (1594) had: *I may not dure this female drudgery.*

durgen. An undersized creature; a dwarf. Also *durgan.* Fielding in THE TRAGEDY OF TRAGEDIES; OR TOM THUMB (1730) has a character cry: *And can my princess such a durgen wed!*

dustyfoot. See *piepowder.*

duty. That which is due. That which one ought—from Late Latin *debutus,* from *debere, debitus,* whence also *debt,* that which one owes. Due respect, as in Chaucer's THE KNIGHT'S TALE (1386), *That good Arcite . . . Departed is with duetee and honour Out of this foule prison of this life.* A slave has obligations (Latin *ob + ligare,* to bind); a free man has duties. As Henry Fielding said in 1730: *When I'm not thanked at all, I'm thanked enough; I've done my duty, and I've done no more.* Thomas Jefferson, whom many profess to admire, said in 1789: *My great wish is to go on in a strict but silent performance of my duty; to avoid attracting notice, and to keep my name out of newspapers.* The satiric use of the word was first emphasized by W. S. Gilbert, who in RUDDYGORE (1887) playfully remarks that duty must be done and *Painful though that duty be, To shirk the task were fiddle-de-dee.* After him, more condescendingly, Oscar Wilde remarked: *Duty is what one expects from others* and Bernard Shaw: *When a stupid man is doing something he is ashamed of, he always declares that it it his duty.* In the wake of these cynical remarks (while customs duty is always hated) moral duty has been increasingly disregarded. The word, if used today, often arouses a surprised distaste. *O tempora!*

dwale. (1) Delusion; deceit; a deceiver, a transgressor; a heretic. Used in these senses from the 10th through the 13th century. (2) A soporific drink; a stupefying dose (as of the juice or an infusion of belladonna). Chaucer in THE REEVE'S TALE (1386) says: *Hem needed no dwale.* Thus, 14th-18th century. The verb *dwale* had as alternate forms *dwole, dwell.* It first meant to confuse, to lead into error; to stun, stupefy. Thence, to remain for a time, in a condition or a place. Hence the meaning in which the form *dwell* has survived. Chaucer also used *dwale* to mean the *deadly nightshade,* the plant from which belladonna and atropine are extracted, the most sinister of all the witches' brew.

dwell. See *dwale.*

dwole. See *dwale.*

dya. See *dia.*

dyslogistic. Expressing dispraise. The opposite of *eulogistic.* THE SPECTATOR of 2 July, 1887, speaks of *the dyslogistic names by which it pleases each side to denominate its opponents.*

dyspathy. Aversion. The opposite of *sympathy.* Hence, *dyspathetic.* Also *dispathy.* Lowell in a letter of 1886 remarks: *What you say of Carlyle is . . . not dyspathetic.*

E

eagre. A tidal wave; especially, the high crest of the tide's rushing up a narrowing estuary—as in the Humber, Trent, and Severn rivers. Also *eager, higra, hyger, eger, egre*; *agar, q.v.*; *aegir, eygre,* and more. Sir Francis Palgrave (1851) wrote it *eau-guerre,* as though 'warring waters.' Drayton in POLYOLBION (1612) wrote: *with whose tumultuous waves Shut up in narrower bounds, the higre wildly raves.* Dryden in a THRENODY of 1685 wrote that *His manly heart . . . like an eagre rode in triumph oer the tide.*

ean. To bring forth lambs, to *yean.* Also *eanian, enen, enye, eyne.* Thus *eaned,* born (used of a lamb); *eanling,* a young lamb. Shakespeare in THE MERCHANT OF VENICE (1596) tells of *all the eanelings which were streakt and pied. Dire as a smiting haile,* said Daniel in an ECLOGUE (1648), *to new-ean'd lambs.*

ear. See *unear'd.* Also *earer,* a plowman, in Wyclif's BIBLE (1382; ISAIAH).

ear-bussing. See *buss.*

earik. See *eric.*

earling. See *airling.*

easement. (1) Relief from pain or annoyance. Chaucer has, in THE REEVE'S TALE (1386): *Some esement has lawe yshapen us.* Hence, *stool of easement,* toilet; *dogs of easement,* a second string to relieve tired dogs on a hunt. (2) Refreshment, comfortable board and lodging. So revived by Scott in THE MONASTERY (1820). (3) Advantage, comfort, enjoyment. Also revived by Scott, in THE HEART OF MIDLOTHIAN (1818). (4) The right to use something not one's own, as a roadway through a neighbor's ground, or water from his spring—as a legal term, this is still current.

eath. Easy, smooth; gentle, ready, susceptible; comfortable, at ease. Also *eith, eth, eeth,* and the like. Hence *ethi modes,* gentle of mood, from which came *edmod,* gentle, humble, meek; also *edmede, athmod, admod, edmodi.* Into the 13th century, *edmede* was also used as a noun, meaning gentleness, humility; so *edmodness. Eathly,* easy; hence, trifling, of short duration; of low station, mean nature, little worth. *Eaths,* easily; also, *uneaths,* with difficulty. THE ROMAUNT OF THE ROSE (1400) well observes: *A foole is eith to bigyle* [beguile]. An old Scotch proverb, with less general truth, declares: *God's bairns are eath to lear* [learn=teach].

ebberman. One that fishes below bridge, commonly at *ebbing* water. From *ebb* + *er,* one who + *man.* Also *hebberman.* Used in the 18th century, along the lower Thames.

ebriety. Drunkenness. Habitual drunkenness is *ebriosity. Ebrious,* tipsy; copiously drunk, *ebriose.* Latin *ebrius,* drunk. Note that *inebriety* and *inebrious* are not negatives; the *in-* is intensifying. *Cp.*

couth. See *comessation.* Ebriety from wine is for the pleasure of the journey; from whisky, for the relaxing after the trip. From beer? That must have a reason, too.

ebuccinate. To trumpet forth. Hence *ebuccinator;* as Becon declared in NEWS OUT OF HEAVEN (1541): *The ebuccinator, shewer, and declarer of these news, I have made Gabriel.* See *abuccinate.*

ebulum. Elderberry wine. From the name of the (dwarf) elderberry tree. An English recipe of 1713 suggests making a white ebulum with pale malt and white elderberries. Apparently a countryside favorite in the 18th century; red ebulum is still common, home-made, in the United States.

eccaleobion. An aid to the coming of life. Greek *ekkaleo bion,* I evoke life. Pronounced in six syllables, accent on the *by.* Thus, applied in 1839 to an egg-hatching apparatus invented by O.W. Bucknell. Also used figuratively, as in HARPER'S MAGAZINE (1880): *Willis's* HOME JOURNAL *was at one time a very eccaleobion for young writers.*

ecce. Behold. Latin, used in phrases, especially *Ecce Homo* (THE BIBLE: JOHN 19); hence, a representation of Christ with the crown of thorns. *Ecce signum,* behold the sign; Shakespeare in HENRY IV, PART ONE (1596) has Falstaff (after his rout at the misfired robbery at Gadshill, when he 'lards the lean earth as he walks along') telling of his fierce battle and his miraculous escape, declare: *I am eight times thrust through the doublet, four through the hose; my buckler cut through and through; my sword hacked like a handsaw—ecce signum!* Hence also *ecceity,* the quality of being present (used mainly in the 16th century).

eccle. See *ettle.*

ecdysiast. See *abarcy.*

eche. *Eche* and *eke* are very common English words, Old English *ecan,* Old Teutonic form *aukjan,* related to Latin *augere, auxum* (whence English *auxiliary*) and to Greek *auxanein,* to increase. As a verb, *eche* (*ich, eke, ayke, eak, etc.*) meant to increase, to add, to prolong, to supplement (*eke out*), as Shakespeare in the Prologue to HENRY V (1599) asks the audience to *still be kind And eech out our performance with your mind.* As a noun, *eche* (*eke*) meant something added, especially, an extra piece on a bell rope. *To eken* meant to the bargain, in addition, as did also *on eke* and *eke* (as an adverb): in addition, moreover, also; as Sterne said in TRISTRAM SHANDY (1759): *Supposing the wax good, and eke the thimble.* As an adjective *eche* also meant everlasting; *in eche,* forever. *An eke-name* was an added name (like *Plato,* Broad-shouldered; *Oedipus,* Swell-foot); folk-etymology transferred the *n,* making it *a neke-name,* whence *nickname. Cp. napron.* The act of enlarging or adding was *eking,* as when Spenser laments in THE SHEPHERD'S CALENDAR (1579): *But such eeking hath made my heart sore*—but *eking* is also used as that which serves to *eke* out, as by D'Israeli in QUARRELS OF AUTHORS (1814): *Suppressed invectives and eking rhymes could but ill appease so fierce a mastiff.* Enough of this eking! By way of reverse English, note that *an eker,* water-sprite, is a 14th century mistake for *a niker,* a water-sprite, mermaid, a common Teutonic form related to Sanskrit *nij-,* to wash. Other forms, for water-elf, mermaid, are *nix, nixie.* Kingsley in HYPATIA (1853) elucidates: *'What is a nicor, Agilmund?' 'A sea-devil who eats sailors.'*

eckle. See *ettle.*

edipol. A mild oath; an inkhorn asseveration. Originally itself an oath: Latin *edepol, ex,* out + *deus,* god + *Pollux*; By Pollux! Dekker in THE GENTLE CRAFT (1600) draws it from obscurity for humorous use: *Away with your pishery pashery, your pols and your edipols!*

editrix. The feminine form of *editor,* usually applied in scorn, as by THE LONDON QUARTERLY REVIEW (September, 1847), discussing the novels of George Sand, *semivir obscoenus,* and claiming that these works—if translated, and *an attempt is now being made by an English editrix*—will help bring on that *new religion which is to recognize virtue and vice as developments of human nature equally respectable—that moral code of which adultery and incest are to be the cardinal virtues, and marriage the unpardonable sin—when that glorious consummation is reached, we shall have something to substitute for the anile dogmas and outworn precepts of the Gospel.*

edmede. Also *edmod.* See *eath.*

edulcorate. To sweeten; to soften. Latin *e,* out + *dulcor,* sweetness, whence also *dulcify q.v.,* to make sweet, as coffee or one's disposition. In THE CHARACTER OF ITALY (1660) we read: *We will allay the bitterness of this potion with the edulcorating ingredients of their virtues.* Hence *edulcorator,* one who or that which sweetens. *Swines dung,* farmers were told by Worlige in 1669, *is supposed to be a great edulcorator of fruit.*

effable. That can be (or lawfully may be) put into words. Used in the 17th century; later (as by Longfellow in THE DIVINE TRAGEDY, 1871) only in contrast with *ineffable.*

effervency. See *deferve.*

eft. (1) A second time, again; after. A common word from the 9th to the 16th century. Used also in combinations: *eft-castle,* the after-part of a ship, opposite of *forecastle; eftsith, eftsithes,* once more, from time to time; *eftsoon, eftersoon, eftsoons,* a second time, afterwards, or (in modern archaic use, as in Coleridge's THE ANCIENT MARINER, 1798) immediately. Shakespeare, in PERICLES (1608): *Eftsoons I'll tell thee why.* (2) Perhaps as a corruption of *deft;* used in this manner only by Dogberry in Shakespeare's MUCH ADO ABOUT NOTHING (1599): *Yea, marry, that's the eftest way.* Dogberry is an ancestor of Mrs. Malaprop. (3) An ewt, or a newt. CELIA'S ARBOUR (1878) by Besant and Rice says: *We used to hunt as boys for . . . the little evvet, the alligator of Great Britain.* But Lyly earlier (EUPHUES, 1580) warned: *All things that breed in the mud are not efts.*

eftsoons. See *eft.* In Spenser's PROTHALAMION (1596) *Eftsoons the nymphs, which now had flowers their fill, ran all in haste . . .*

egelidate. To thaw; to render liquid. Latin *e,* out + *gelidus,* frozen. Davies, in THE HOLY ROODE (1609): *Then should my teares egelidate his gore.*

egest. To expel; especially from the body, by perspiration, bowel-evacuation, etc. Hence *egestion,* which follows *digestion.* Latin *e,* out + *gerere, gestum,* to carry. The waste materials are the *egesta.* T. Adams in his EXPOSITION (1633) of the SECOND EPISTLE OF PETER queries: *What* [is the] *rich apparel, which man takes up in pride, but that the worm hath egested in scorn?* Note, however, that *egestuose, egestuous* means needy, extremely poor; *egestuosity* (Latin *egestas*), poverty. THE BRITISH APOLLO of 1709 (No. 64) spoke of *clothing the egestuosity of your matter with pompous epithets.*

egestuosity. See *egest.*

eggment. Instigation, inciting, *egging on.* The verb *to egg,* to incite, urge on, was used from the 13th century; another form from the same Teuton root is *edge; to edge on* was used in the 16th and 17th centuries in the same sense. In his CHRONICLES (1577), Holinshed stated: *He accused the moonks of manie things, and did therewith so edge the king against them.* Also *egger, egger on,* an instigator. Chaucer in THE MAN OF LAWES TALE (1386) declared: *Sothe is that through wommannes eggement Mankind was lorn and damned aye to die.*

egredouce. (1) A piquant sauce. Literally, sharp-sweet. (2) A dish; the recipe is in THE FORME OF CURY (1390): *Take conynges* [rabbits] *or kydde, and smyte hem on pecys rawe, and frye hem in white grece. Take raysons or coraunce, and fry hem, take oynouns, parboile hem, and hewe hem smalle, and fry hem. Take rede wyne, sugar, with powdor of pepor, of gynger, of canel; salt, and cast thereto; and let it seeth with a good quantité of white grece, and serve it forth.*

egritude. Sickness. Also *aegritude;* Latin *aeger; aegrotus,* sick; *cp. egrote.* R. Baron in THE CYPRIAN ACADEMY (1647) wrote: *Now, now we symbolize in egritude And simpathize in Cupid's malady.* An *aegrotant* was a sick person. Also *aeger,* a note certifying that a student is sick, used in the 19th century at English universities; *aegrotat* (literally, he is sick), a certificate that a student is too ill to go to class or examination.

egrote. To feign sickness. From Latin *aegrotus,* sick. Accented on the second syllable, this word, found in 18th century dictionaries, might well find place in current speech.

eirack. A hen of the first year. Also *earack, erock.*

eirenicon. A proposal intended to make peace; an attempt to clear away differences. Greek *eirene,* peace, whence the name *Irene.* Hence also *eirenic, irenic,* pertaining, or tending, to peace. An *eirenarch* was an ancient officer corresponding to justice of the peace. *We wait with interest,* said THE PALL MALL GAZETTE of 19 June, 1886, *to see Mr. Chamberlain's response to the new eirenicon.* In the suspicious atmosphere of today, an eirenicon is called a 'peace offensive.'

eirmonger. An egg-dealer. Middle English *eiren,* eggs. Used in the 13th and 14th centuries.

eisel. Vinegar. Via French from Late Latin *acetillum,* diminutive of *acetum,* vinegar. Also *eisell, aisille, ascill, eysell, aysell,* and more. Used in HAMLET; see *woot.*

eke. See *eche; cp. eyas.*

elaboratory. A 17th and 18th century form of *laboratory. Every great person,* said Evelyn in ST. FRANCE (1652), *pretends to his elaboratory and library.*

elamp. To shine forth. Giles Fletcher in CHRIST'S VICTORY (1610) tells us *The cheerful sun, elamping wide, Glads all the world with his uprising ray.*

elaqueate. To disentangle. From Latin *elaqueare, e,* out + *laqueus,* snare, noose. Found in dictionaries from the 17th century.

elatrate. To call out, to speak violently. From Latin *e,* out + *latrare,* to bark;

hence to rant, roar, bluster. A 17th century dictionary word.

elder-gun. A pop-gun; a toy gun made of the hollow shoot of an *elder,* the young branches of which are pithy. Shakespeare in HENRY V (1599): *That's a perilous shot out of an elder gunne.* Note also, in his THE MERRY WIVES OF WINDSOR, *heart of elder,* faint heart, in humorous contrasting allusion to *heart of oak,* stout heart.

eldritch. Weird, ghostly; frightful, hideous. Also *elphrish,* probably derived from *elf.* And *eldritch, elraige, eldrich,* and the like. James I in his ESSAY ON POESIE (1585) spoke of *the King of Fary . . . with many elrage incubus rydant. Elf* is a common Teuton form, used by extension of a child or other diminutive creature. Shakespeare in KING LEAR uses it as a verb—*Ile . . . elfe all my haires in knots*—to twist, to tangle, as might a mischievous elf; hence, *elf-locks* (ROMEO AND JULIET), tangled hair. Also *elf-skin* (HENRY IV, PART ONE), a small thin fellow.

elenge. See *alange.*

eleutherian. Pertaining to freedom; as a noun, a deliverer. Greek *eleutheros,* free. *Eleutherian Jove,* Jove (Zeus) as the protector of freedom. Hence *eleutherism,* a zeal for freedom; W. Taylor in 1802 spoke of *a Miltonic swell of diction and eleutherism of sentiment.* When excessive, this is called *eleutheromania.* Carlyle in THE FRENCH REVOLUTION (1837) says: *Eleutheromaniac philosophedom grows ever more clamorous . . . nothing but insubordination, eleutheromania, confused, unlimited opposition in their heads.* "If there's a government," as the Irish rebel roared, "I'm agin it!"

elf. See *eldritch.*

ellingness. See *alange.*

ellops. A serpent. In ancient times Greek *ellops, elops* was applied to either a fish or a serpent. Milton in PARADISE LOST (1667) includes it in a catalogue of horrid snakes: *Dreadful was the din Of hissing through the hall, thick swarming now With complicated monsters, head and tail, Scorpion and asp and amphisbaena dire, Cerastes horned, hydrus, and ellops drear And dipsas . . .*

elsewhen. See *anywhen.*

elucidate. See *crepuscular.*

elucubration. Studying or composing by candle-light or burning the midnight oil; the product of such activity, a literary work (with emphasis on the work; *cp. ergasy*). Also *elucubrate,* to compose in the late hours; *elucubrationary; elucubrator.* Latin *ex,* out + *lucubrare,* to work at night; *lucubrum,* signal fire; *lux, lucem,* light: *Fiat lux!* Note that *lucubrate* and *lucubration* were also used in English; the *ex* did not change the meaning. Painter in THE PALACE OF PLEASURE (1566) spoke of *Histories, chronicles, and monumentes, by the first authors and elucubrators.*

emacity. An itch to be buying. Latin *emere,* to buy; *Caveat emptor,* Let the buyer be ware! Everyman's wife, in America, is noted for her emacity. Also *emptional,* that may be purchased—but of a person, *emptitious,* venal, open to a price. A market place was an *emptory;* as in Ray's FLORA (1665): *The flower-market, the common emptory of trash and refuse.*

emball. To wrap up; to make a bundle of. Thus Hakluyt in his VOYAGES (1599): *The marchandize . . . they emball it well with oxe hides.* More literally, to put inside a ball or sphere; but in this sense used figuratively, as by Browning in ARISTOPHANES' APOLOGY (1875): *As lark emballed by its own crystal song.* Shakespeare uses *emballing* in HENRY VIII (1613), the O.E.D. states "Probably used in indelicate sense; explained by commentators as 'investing with the ball as the emblem of royalty.'" Commentator G.B. Harrison explains the meaning as 'assault.' The context makes it clear that, while a Victorian might call it indelicate, Shakespeare is punning on the scepter and sex. An old lady of the court is speaking to Anne Bullen, who says she does not wish to be a queen. The lady says: *If your back cannot vouchsafe this burden, 'tis too weak Ever to get a boy.* Anne: *How you do talk! I swear again I would not be a queen For all the world.* Lady: *In faith, for little England You'd venture an emballing. I myself Would for Carnarvonshire.*

embarquement. The act of placing under *embargo* (Italian *imbargo*; Latin *in* + *barra,* bar). Also *imbargement, embargement.* Shakespeare in CORIOLANUS (1607) uses the word in the sense of hindrances, prohibitions: *Nor sleep nor sanctuary . . . The prayers of priests nor times of sacrifice, Embarquements all of fury, shall lift up Their rotten privilege and custom 'gainst My hate to Marcius.*

emblaze. To set forth by coat-of-arms, banner, or other heraldic devices. Thus Shakespeare in HENRY VI, PART TWO (1590): *Thou shalt weare it as a herald's coat, To emblaze the honor that thy master got.* Also *emblazon,* to portray conspicuously; to celebrate, make illustrious. Hence, *emblazonry,* heraldic devices, symbolic ornament; gorgeous colorful display; colorful (sometimes verbal) embellishment; *emblazure.* Milton preferred the form *imblazonry;* for quotation, see *horrent.*

embracer. *Bashful* at first, said Sir. W. Jones in a song of 1794, *she smiles at length on her embracer.* This meaning is quite common; it comes via French *embrasser* (*bras,* arm) from Latin *in,* in + *bracchium,* arm. The forgotten word *embracer* is from French *embraser,* to set on fire, hence to entice, of Teutonic origin; and from the 15th through the 18th century an *embracer* was one who sought corruptly to influence a jury. Henry VII passed laws in 1487 against *embracery;* 400 years later THE TIMES (31 March 1887) mentioned a case in which *the plaintiff . . . was charged . . . with the offence of embracery.* THE TIMES was referring to an attempt to influence a verdict. *Cp. bracery.*

embrew. See *imbrue.*

eme. An uncle; originally, a mother's brother; more loosely, an elderly friend. From BEOWULF to the mid-18th century; Drayton in POLYOLBION (1612) mentions *Henry Hotspur and his eame the Earl of Rochester.* Scott revived the word in THE HEART OF MIDLOTHIAN (1818). *Eme* is also a variant form of *ant, emmet.*

emeute. A riot or uprising of the people. Directly from the French; from *émouvoir,* to agitate, rouse. Gilbert in THE PIRATES OF PENZANCE (1880) pictures the policemen *threatened with emeutes.*

emication. A shining forth, as the glory of the Lord. Also, the sparkling out of carbonaceous and certain other liquors. From Latin *e,* out + *micare,* to vibrate; to gleam, flash, shine. The verb *emicate* is also used in the sense of to spring forth, to appear, as when Motteux in his translation (1708) of Rabelais heavily speaks of *the studious cupidity, that so demonstratively emicates at your external organs.*

emmew. See *enew. Emmew* is also a variant of *immew,* to put into a *mew;* see *mews.*

emollient. Something that softens or soothes. Latin *e,* with intensive force + *mollire,* to soften; *mollis,* soft. Also an *emollitive*; *emollition,* the act of softening; *emolliment,* softening, assuaging, soothing. The forms are not to be confused with *emolument,* benefit, reward, salary; Latin *emolimentum,* profit; probably from *emoliri,* to bring out by effort; *e,* out + *moliri,* to strive, to toil. Gilbert in the apostrophe in THE PIRATES OF PENZANCE (1880) addresses Poetry as *Divine emollient!*

emphyteusis. A hereditary lease; perpetual right in property belonging to another. Medieval (from Roman) law; the word is from Greek *emphyteusis,* implanting. The tenant on such land was called *emphyteuta, emphyteuciary, emphyteuticary.* For quotation, see *stillicide.* What a man is likely to do when a place is his 'for keeps' may be judged from Blount's definition (1656) of an *emphyteuticary: he that maketh a thing better than it was when he received it.* May your life so render you!

empiricutic. A one-time variation of *empiric, empirical,* based on trial only; by extension, quack. Also, in the Folios, *emperickqutique*; *emperickti*c; hence some editors print *empirictic.* Shakespeare, in CORIOLANUS (1607), *The most soveraigne prescription in Galen is but empiricutic; and to this preservative, of no better report then a horse-drench.*

emptitious. See *emacity.*

emulous. Desirous of imitating; jealous, envious; (of things) closely resembling. Also, filled with the spirit of rivalry; greedy for praise or power. Shakespeare in TROILUS AND CRESSIDA (1606) says: *He is not emulous, as Achilles is.* Also *emulatory;* of the nature of fond imitation; *emulable,* worthy of being used as a model, Shakespeare in HAMLET: *Pricked on by a most emulate pride.* Hence *emulator,* a rival; a zealous imitator; used in the Douay BIBLE (1609)) of God—*God is an emulator:* one that brooks no rival. Feminine forms were *emulatress, emulatrix.* An early meaning of the verb was to vie with, rival; Shakespeare in THE MERRY WIVES OF WINDSOR has: *I see how thine eye would emulate the diamond.*

en-. This prefix is most common, with several uses. (1) To place in or on, as *enambush*; *encouch*; Shakespeare in RICHARD II (1593: *Within my mouth you have engaol'd my tongue*); *enlabyrinth; enstage; enzone,* to engirdle. (2) To put on or cover with, as *endiadem*; Drummond of Hawthornden in a poem of 1630 pictures the *enchariotéd* sun making gold the world: *Phoebus in his chair Ensaffroning the sea and air. enspell,* to cast a spell upon; *enstomach,* to give courage to; *enwood,* to cover with trees. (3) To make, or bring to a condition or state: *encalm,* becalm; *endrudge,* to enslave (oneself); *enfamous;* Shakespeare has in LOVE'S LABOUR'S LOST (1588) *enfreedoming thy person; engarboil,* to throw into confusion or commotion; *enwoman.* (4) As an in-intensive, for emphasis (sometimes with the added idea of *in*): *endazzle; endiaper,* to variegate, dapple; *enwed; enwisen,* to make wise.

enacture. Behavior; act; performance. Shakespeare in HAMLET (1604) has *The violence of either grief or joy Their own enactures with themselves destroy, Where joy most revels, grief doth most lament; Grief joys, joy grieves, on slender accident.*

enascent. Just coming into being. E. Darwin in his poem THE BOTANIC GARDEN (1791) spoke of *enascent leaves;* also, *The new annals of enascent time.*

enatation. Escape by swimming; swimming out. Also *enatant,* coming to the surface. Rare words, of the 17th and 18th centuries.

enaunter. Lest by chance. A variant of *on aunter,* French *en aventure.* Similar to *if peradventure. Cp. aunters.* Spenser in THE SHEPHERD'S CALENDAR (1597; FEBRUARY) says: *Anger nould* [would not] *let him speake to the tree, Enaunter his rage mought cooled be.*

encheason. See *anchesoun.*

enchiridion. A handbook, a concise guide. Greek *en,* in + *cheir,* hand + *-idion,* a diminutive suffix. Coverdale in his translation (1541) of THE OLD FAITH, states that Moses made *an enchiridion and sum of all the acts of his time.* Bailey in his 1751 DICTIONARY defines *enchiridion* as 'a small portable pocket book,' and the term indeed fits the pocket-size books of today.

endiablee. To put the devil into, to possess with Satan. Via French *diable,* devil, from Greek *diabolos,* devil (the chief slanderer); *diabole,* slander; *dia, across* + *ballo,* to throw: to throw across, to accuse, to slander. Also *endiablement,* possession by the devil. North in THE EXAMINER of 1734 spoke of *such an one as might best endiablee the rabble, and set them abawling against Popery.* More directly from the Greek come the too currently *diabolic* things, and such less familiar forms as *diablotin,* a little devil, imp of Satan; *diabolarch, diabolarchy* (accents on the *ab*), chief of the devils, rule of the devil. *diabolify, diabolize.* A *diabolifuge* is something to drive away the devil. A dialogue of (or talk about) devils is a *diabologue.* The doctrine of the devil, or devil lore, is *diabology,* more formally *diabolology.* In several of these forms, the *o* after *b* may be omitted; thus *diablifuge, diablogue.* These words were used in the 17th, 18th, or 19th century, when *diablodoxy,* if not *diabolocracy,* was more prevalent. As that *diabolish* (accent on the *ab*) authority Baudelaire remarked: "The cleverest ruse of the devil is to persuade us he doesn't exist."

endore. See *hastlet.*

enemious. Hostile. Also *enmious; enemiable,* with the feelings of an enemy. Thus *enemicitious, inimicitious, inimicitial, inimicous,* mainly 17th century forms replaced by *inimical.* Sterne in TRISTRAM SHANDY (1761) spoke of driving the gall *from the gall-bladder . . . of his Majesty's subjects, with all the inimicitious passions which belong to them.* More in THE HISTORIE OF KYNG RYCHARDE THE THIRDE (1513) spoke of an action as *no warning, but an enemious scorne.*

energumen. One wrought upon or possessed by a devil; hence, a fanatical devotee. Latin *energumenus;* Greek *energoumenos,* past participle of *energeein,* to work upon; *en,* in + *ergon,* work. Accent on the *gyu.* Used in the 17th and early 18th centuries; renewed by Scott and others in the 19th. Morley in MACMILLAN'S MAGAZINE of February 1885, spoke of *the seeming peril to which priceless moral elements of human character were exposed by the energumens of progress.* Also *energumenist,* one possessed by devils; Gaule in SELECT CASES OF CONSCIENCE, CONCERNING WITCHES AND WITCHCRAFT (1646) sought to discriminate: *The* *meerly passive be simply deemoniacks, but not energumenists.*

enew. To plunge into the water. Also, to drive into the water, as a bird of prey would another bird. French *en,* in + *eau,* water; Provençal *aigua;* Latin *aqua,* as in *aquatics.* Used from the 15th into the 17th century; in Shakespeare (MEASURE FOR MEASURE; 1603) it has been misprinted *emmew* and *enmew,* explained by some commentators as 'keep in the coop'—the bird fears to come out. Shakespeare says: *This outward-sainted deputie Whose settled visage and deliberate word Nips youth i' the head, and follies doth enmew As falcon doth the fowle, is yet a devil.* The BOOK OF ST. ALBANS (1486) made the sense clear: *Yowre hawke hath ennewed the fowle in to the ryver.*

enfeoff. To put a person in possession of a fief, land and other property held under a feudal lord. Also, to give over as a fief; hence, to surrender, to give up (something). Also *enfeffe, enfief, infeoff,* and the like. Used figuratively in both senses; in the second, when Henry IV (in Shakespeare's play; 1596) warns his son, Prince Hal, against the dangers of too great familiarity with the people, by instancing his own predecessor: *The skipping King, he ambled up and down . . . Mingled his royalty with capering fools . . . Grew a companion to the common streets, Enfeoff'd himself to popularitie.*

engastrimyth. A ventriloquist. From Greek *engastrimythos; en,* in + *gastri,* of the belly + *mythos,* speech. Also, in 17th century dictionaries, *engastromich.* Sylvester in his translation (1598) of Du Bartas has: *Al incenst, the pale engastromith . . . speakes in his wombe.* Urquhart, in his translation (1693) of Rabelais, speaks of the *engastrimythian prophetess.* The word was used occasionally in the 19th century, but by then had been largely supplanted by *ventriloquist,* from Latin *ventri,* of the belly + *loquor,* to speak—whence also *eloquent* and a flood of words.

engraff. To graft in; an early form of *engraft.* Used since the 15th century. Also *ingraff.* Used by Swinburne (ATALANTA IN CALYDON; 1864) meaning to beget. Shakespeare used it in the passive voice, meaning to be closely attached: HENRY IV, PART TWO (1597): *You have beene so lewde, and so much ingraffed to Falstaff.*

ennead. "The first square of an odd number"—17th century. Three syllables. Greek *enneas, enneados,* nine. Hence, a set of nine persons or things; Porphyry, who studied under Plotinus in Rome (262 A.D.) divided the works of his teacher into six enneads. Also *enneatic,* occurring once in nine days, months, throws of dice, etc. The *enneatical year,* every ninth year of life. Nine was, in many periods (especially as three contained in itself), deemed the perfect number.

ennoyous. See *annoyous.*

enow. A variant of *enough.* Also *ynoghe, anowe, ynowe,* etc. *Enow* was the Middle English plural of *enough;* thus one might have sugar or coal *enough;* but men, ships, slips *enow.* Today the two are interchangeable, save that *enow* is archaic or poetic, as in *Ah, wilderness were paradise enow.*

ensconce. To furnish with *sconces,* to fortify; to shelter; to hide; to get into a place for security or concealment. From *en,* into + *sconce,* small fortification, earthwork; Old French *esconse,* shelter, hiding-place. Shakespeare in THE COMEDY OF ERRORS (1590) says: *I must get a sconce for my head and insconce it too;*

in THE MERRY WIVES OF WINDSOR: *I will ensconce mee behinde the arras.* Butler in HUDIBRAS (1678) described *A fort of error to ensconce Absurdity and ignorance.*

ensear. To dry up. The *en* is intensive + *sear, sere,* dry. Shakespeare in TIMON OF ATHENS (1607) has: *Ensear thy fertile and conceptious wombe.*

enseygned. See *admonish.*

ensiferous. Bearing a sword. From Latin *ensis,* sword + *ferre,* to carry. In dictionaries from the 17th century. More frequent in use is *ensiform,* sword-shaped, which is used scientifically of leaves, cartilage (appended to the breast-bone), and antennae.

ensorcell. To enchant. Used by Wyatt in 1541; revived by Meredith in the amusing THE SHAVING OF SHAGPAT (1855): *a sorceress ensorcelled,* and used by both Payne (1883) and Burton (1886) in their translations of THE ARABIAN NIGHTS, that prime collection of ensorcellings.

entach. To spot; to stain, defile; to imbue with (good or evil quality). Used by Chaucer. Also *entech, entatch*; Old French *en,* in + *tache,* spot, trait of character; Latin *tangere, tactum,* to touch (related to *attach*) whence also *tangent, contact, intact, tactless; integrity, entire* (Latin *integer,* not touched, whole). Skelton (WORKS; 1489) declared: *Of elephantis tethe were the palace gatis, Enlosenged with many goodly platis Of golde, entachid with many a precyous stone.*

enucleation. Clarification, explanation, getting out the 'kernel' of the matter. Latin *enucleare, enucleatum*; *e,* out + *nucleus,* kernel—whence the *nucleus* of an atom or an idea. The converse of giving some one 'the story, in a nutshell.' Also *enucleate,* to make clear, explain. Butler in HUDIBRAS (1678) exclaimed: *Oh! that I could enucleate And solve the problem of my fate.*

eoan. Pertaining to the dawn; eastern. Greek *eos,* dawn. Shelley in LIBERTY (1822) says: *The morning-star Beckons the sun from the eoan wave.*

eotand. A variant of *eten, q.v.*

eowte. A dish; the recipe is given in THE FORME OF CURY (1390): Eowtes of flessh. *Take borage, cool, langdebef* [beef tongue] *persel, betes, orage, avance, violet, sawray, and fennel, and when they buth soden, presse hem wel smale, cast hem in gode broth, and seeth hem, and serve hem forth.*

epact. (1) The number of days from the new moon at the beginning of the calendar year. (2) The extra, intercalated day in Leap Year; the extra days in any calendar, as the ancient Egyptian, which had twelve months of thirty days and five epacts. From Greek *epaktos; epagein,* to intercalate, from *epi,* on + *agein,* to bring. There were special gods to be worshiped and rites to be performed on these *epagomenic* days.

Ephesian. A boon companion, a roysterer. Shakespeare in THE MERRY WIVES OF WINDSOR (1598) has: *It is thine host, thine Ephesian, calls.* Brewer in THE DICTIONARY OF PHRASE AND FABLE suggests that this contains a pun on *pheeze,* to flatter: *a-pheeze-ian*; *cp. feeze (5). Ephesian letters* are magic characters; many of the people of Ephesus, at the admonition of Paul, burnt their books of magic—so many books that (BIBLE; ACTS, 19) "they counted the price of them, and found it fifty thousand pieces of silver." And there was a great riot at the theatre and the temple of Diana, on whose fair statue Ephesian letters were wrought.

ephestian. Domestic, not foreign. Greek *ephestios,* of the family; *epi,* upon + *hestia,* the hearth. A rare word, used in the 17th century.

ephialtes. Nightmare; a demon that leaps upon people and causes nightmare. A 17th century term, probably from Greek *epi,* upon + *allesthai,* to leap. A demon in female form, supposedly having carnal intercourse with men in their sleep, was a *succubus;* from Latin *sub,* under + *cub-,* root of *cumbere,* to lie. In the feminine forms *succube* (two syllables) and *succuba,* the word also meant a strumpet; Jonson in THE ALCHEMIST (1610) has: *I walked naked between my succubae.* The forms were quite common from the 14th century. C.K. Sharpe in the Preface to Law's MEMORIALS (1818) tells us that Benedict of Berne *for forty years . . . had kept up an amatory commerce with a succubus called Hermeline.* This, despite the fact that in 1797 the ENCYCLOPEDIA BRITANNICA had assured its readers: *The truth is, the succubus is only a species of the nightmare.* Barham in THE INGOLDSBY LEGENDS (1838) cries: *Oh! happy the slip from his succubine grip That saved the Lord Abbott.* The demon that sought carnal intercourse with women in their sleep was the *incubus;* Latin *in,* upon + *cumbere,* to lie. There were civil and ecclesiastical laws concerning *incubi,* in the Middle Ages. The incubus also consorted with witches, who had a pet term for it, *incuby.* In the 17th century, *incubus* began also to be used of any great burden, hanging on one like a nightmare. A miser, brooding over his wealth, was called (17th century) an *incubo.* From the same Latin source come the brooding terms relating to *incubation.* One possessed by an ephialtes was sometimes said to have gone witch-riding.

epicaricacy. Rejoicing at, or taking joy in, the misfortunes of others. From Greek *epi,* upon + *chara,* joy + *kakon,* evil. Bailey's DICTIONARY (1751) spells it *epicharikaky;* the accent falls on the *ick.* The O.E.D. (1933) ignores the word, but alas! the feeling is not so easily set aside.

epicene. Partaking of the characteristics of both sexes; adapted to, used by, both sexes; by extension, effeminate. Also as a noun, one that has characteristics of both sexes. Greek *epi,* upon + *koinos,* common—used in Latin and Greek grammar of nouns that (without change of gender) may denote either sex. Fuller in his WORTHIES OF ENGLAND (1661) spoke of *those epicoene and hermaphrodite convents, wherein monks and nuns lived together.* Jonson wrote a play (1609), *Epicoene; or, The Silent Woman*—the 'woman' turns out to be a man. Referring to the fact that male actors performed the female parts, FRASER'S MAGAZINE in 1850 said: *Even Shakespeare sometimes slides into the temptation which this epicenism presents to unlicensed wit.* Shakespeare took advantage of all conditions of the theatre of his day; of this *'epicenism',* in the frequency with which his women (played by males) disguise themselves as men; Rosalind plays on the condition in the Epilogue to AS YOU LIKE IT.

epicrisis. Critical appreciation of literature. The O.E.D. (Supplement) gives only the specific meaning: an appendix to each book of the OLD TESTAMENT, giving for that book the number of letters, verses, and chapters, and the middle sentence. Hence also *epicritic,* a learned critic of literature. As an adjective, *epicritic* was suggested by H. Head (in BRAIN, 1905) to designate recently developed, finer sensations of touch—opposed to the earlier *protopathic.* Many, however, have questioned such a distinction.

epideictic. Adapted for display; used to show off; especially, among the ancients, of orations to display one's ability. Also *epideiktic, epideictical*; Greek *epideiktikos; epi,* upon; *deiknunai,* to show. Farrar in THE LIFE OF CHRIST (1874) said: *He would not work any epideictic miracle at their bidding.*

epiky. Reasonableness, equity—as opposed to rigid law, to the strict letter. Greek *epi,* according to + *eikos,* likely, reasonable. Also *epicay, epicheia.* Latimer in a Sermon of 1549 declared: *For avoydyng disturbance in the communewealth, such an epiky and moderacion may be used.*

epithalamic. Related to a wedding, or to a nuptial song. Also *epithalamial.* From *epithalamium, epithalamy, epithalmie,* a song or poem in praise of the bride and groom, with a prayer for their well-being. Greek *epithalamion; epi,* upon + *thalamos,* bridal chamber. Hence *epithalamize,* to compose a nuptial song; the composer is an *epithalamiast.* Spenser in 1595 wrote an *epithalamion.* Stockton in his noted story THE LADY OR THE TIGER (1884—and still no one knows which!) pictured dancing maidens *treading an epithalamic measure.*

equiparate. To reduce to a level; to level, raze. Latin *aequiparare, aequiparatum,* to put on an equality; compare; *aequus, equal* + *par,* like. Hence *equiparable, equiparant, equiparate* (adjective), equivalent, of equal importance. *Equiparance,* equivalence; *equiparation,* the act of placing on an equal footing; the act of comparing; a comparison. All save *equiparable* and *equiparation* accent on *quip*; all were used mainly in the 18th century, as in Vicars' translation (1632) of THE AENEID: *King Latines throne this day I'le ruinate And houses tops to th' ground aequiparate.*

erayne. See *arain.*

erbolat. A dish of herbs and eggs; recipe in THE FORME OF CURY (1390): *Take parsel, myntes, saverey, and sauge, tansey, vervayn, clarry, rewe, ditayn, fenel, southrenwode; hewe hem, and grinde hem smale; medle hem up with ayren. Do butter in a trape, and do the fars thereto, and bake, and messe it forth.*

erbowle. A dessert or compote; recipe in THE FORME OF CURY (1390): *Take bolas* [*bullace*: a wild plum] *and scald hem with wyne, and drawe hem with a styomor. Do hem in a pot. Clarify hony, and do thereto, with powdor fort, and floer of rys. Salt it, and florish with white aneys, and serve it forth.*

erding. An abode, a dwelling. Also *earding.* Thus *erding-stow,* dwelling-place. Used from the 10th to the 14th century. From *erd* (earth), land where one dwells, one's country. *erd-folk,* people of the land. Used from BEOWULF to the 14th century. Old English *eard,* land; Old Saxon *ard,* dwelling; Old High German *art,* ploughing; Old Norse *orth,* harvest. Also a verb, *erde,* to live, to inhabit; to exist in a place or condition. *Erde* is also an old form of *earth.*

erede. Lacking counsel. Also *eirede.*

erege. A heretic. Spanish *herege*; Old French *erege*; Latin *haereticus*; Greek *hairesis,* a sect. Also *erite* (12th century; *erege* is a 14th century form).

eremite. An early form of *hermit,* lingering in poetry and for archaic effect. Greek *eremites*; *eremia,* a desert; *eremos,* uninhabited. The *eremite* (from the 3d century) was a Christian solitary, distinguished from the *coenobite, cenobite* (Greek *koinos,* common + *bios,* life), who was withdrawn from the world but lived in a religious community. The two types are included in the *anchoret* (*anchorite, ancorite, anachorete*); Greek *ana,* back + *choreein,* to withdraw), one that has withdrawn from the world. In a SONNET (1616) Drummond of Hawthornden has: *Framed for mishap, th' anachorit of love.* Milton in PARADISE LOST (1671) used *eremite* with suggestion of its literal sense: *Thou spirit who ledst this glorious eremite Into the desert;* Bulwer-Lytton in EUGENE ARAM (1832) speaks of *the twilight eremites of books and closets.* Also *eremitage, eremiteship, eremitism; eremital, eremitary, eremitic, eremitical, eremitish;* and *eremic* (accent on the *ree*), pertaining to the desert.

erendrake. A messenger; ambassador. Used from the 9th to the 13th century. Also *aerendwreca, erndraca, aerndrache, herindrak,* and more. Old English *aerende,* errand + *wrecan,* to tell.

erept. To snatch away, to carry off. Hence *ereption.* Latin *eripere, ereptum; e,* out + *rapere,* to snatch. Bishop Joseph Hall in A PLAINE AND FAMILIAR EXPLICATION (BY WAY OF PARAPHRASE) OF ALL THE HARD TEXTS OF THE WHOLE DIVINE SCRIPTURE (1633) noted *The suddaine and inexpected ereption of Isaac from his imminent and intended death.* THE ATHENAEUM of 1865 (No. 1951) went to pagan mythology to observe: *Pluto erepts Proserpine.*

erer. Former; before. Also *aerra, earre, erur, earar,* and the like. Used from the 9th into the 15th century; as an adverb, *erer* was replaced by *ere.*

erf. Cattle. Hence, *erfe-blood,* blood of animals; *erf-kin,* the race of animals, cattle. As *cattle* originally meant capital, goods, so *erf* originally mean inheritance; Old Norse *arfi*: it is related to Greek *orphanos,* English *orphan;* Latin *orbus,* bereft. Thus words tell us of early ways. *Erf* was used until the 14th century. [There is a 19th century form *erf,* from the Dutch—also originally meaning inheritance—used in South Africa for a garden plot, usually of about half an acre.]

ergasy. A literary production, an elucubration. Greek *ergasia; ergon,* work. R. Humphrey in his translation (1637) of St. Ambrose spoke of *ending the whole ergasie or tractate with it.*

ergotize. To quibble; to wrangle. Also *ergot, ergoteer.* From Latin *ergo,* therefore, used in English to introduce the conclusion of a syllogism. The combinations, from this frequent use in argument, came to be applied to those that liked to dispute, or disputed sophistically. Thus *ergoteer, ergoteerer, ergoteur,* a wrangler, a disputatious fellow; *ergotism,* arguing, quibbling; *ergotic,* sophistical, jumping to conclusions; *ergotist,* a quibbler, a pedantic reasoner. Urquhart in his translation (1653) of Rabelais said: *After they had well ergoted pro and con, they concluded* . . . THE NINETEENTH CENTURY (September, 1881) stated that *Mr. Gladstone and this famous ergoteur are the only people living who have boundless faith in reasoning.* More today render it at least lip-service.

eric. A pecuniary payment, as compensation for murder or other violent crime, accepted in Ireland into the 17th century. Also *eriach, earike, erycke, earik;* Irish *eiric.* Spenser noted it, in THE STATE OF IRELAND (1596): *In the case of murder . . . the malefactor shall give unto them* [the friends] *or to the child, or wife of* *him that is slain a recompence, which they call an eriach.* R. Bagwell commented on it, in IRELAND UNDER THE TUDORS (1885): *This blood-fine, called an eric, was an utter abomination to the English of the sixteenth century.*

eringo. See *eryngo.*

erite. See *erege.*

errant. See *arrant.*

errhine. A medicine (not snuff) that causes sneezing. Greek *errhinon; en,* in + *rhin,* nostril, whence also *rhinosceros. Cp. sternutation.* Also, a plug of lint put into the nose, steeped in such a medicine.

erst. Formerly. Also *erest; arst, earst, earest,* and more. The superlative of *ere,* before: the most before, i.e., the first, earliest, soonest. *not erst,* not before. *on erst,* in the first place. *then at erst,* then at the earliest. Spenser uses *at erst,* to mean at once, right now. A very common word, beginning to grow old in Shakespeare's time (it occurs in his early plays, HENRY VI, PART TWO, 1590; AS YOU LIKE IT), but lingering in poetry.

erubescent. Blushing. From Latin *e,* out + *rubescere,* to grow red; *rubere,* to be red; *ruber,* red. In 18th century dictionaries. Thackeray in PENDENNIS (1849) says: *The Major erubescent confounded the impudence of the young folks.*

eryngo. The root of the sea holly, candied, eaten as a sweetmeat, supposed to have aphrodisiac properties. Also the Latin form *eryngium;* and *eringo, ringo.* In Shakespeare's THE MERRY WIVES OF WINDSOR (1598) Falstaff exclaims: *Let the sky rain potatoes, let it thunder to the tune of 'Green Sleeves,' hail kissing-comfits, and snow eryngoes; let there come a tempest of provocation, I will shelter me here*—then he embraces Mistress Ford. *Colchester,* said Evelyn in his MEMOIRS (1656), *is also famous for oysters and eringo root.*

esbatement. Amusement, diversion. Apparently applied originally to boxing and wrestling; *esbatement* comes via Old French from Latin *ex,* out + *battere,* to beat. Used in the 15th and 16th centuries.

esbrandill. To shake. Old French *esbrandeler* (modern *ebranler*) from a Teutonic stem *brant,* to quiver (like fire), to burn. Hence the *brand* in the burning. Queen Elizabeth, in a letter of 1588, declared emphatically: *Never shall dread of any mans behavior cause me doo aught that may esbrandill the seat that so well is settled.*

escal. Fit to eat; pertaining to food. From Latin *esca,* food; whence also *esculent,* good to eat, as *the esculent snail. Escal* is found only in 17th and 18th century dictionaries; *esculency* is slightly more common.

esclavage. A necklace of several rows of gold links, named from its resemblance to the chains of a slave. French *esclavage,* slavery. By extension, any similar adornment, as triple rows of beads or jewels. Colman and Garrick in THE CLANDESTINE MARRIAGE (1766) inquire: *How d'ye like the style of this esclavage?* A time nearer to our own affected the *slave anklet,* which for a while transferred the application from the physical resemblance to the idea, and was worn as a sign that one's affections were in bondage.

esculent. See *escal.*

esemplastic. Unifying; molding into a unity. Also *esemplasy* (accent on the *em*), the unifying power of the imagination.

Greek *es,* into + *en, eis,* one + *plastikos; plassein,* to mold. The words were first used by Coleridge (BIOGRAPHIA LITTERARIA; 1817), probably a transmutation into Greek forms of Schelling's German term *ineinsbildung,* forming into one. The words are almost always used in conscious echo of Coleridge.

eslargish. To extend the range or scope of; to set (oneself) at large, free. A 15th century word; replaced by *enlarge.* Caxton in his translation (1483) of GEOFFROI DE LA TOUR L'ANDRI wrote that *God moveth him self to pyte and eslargyssheth his misericorde.*

esmay. An earlier form of *dismay.* From Old French *esmaier,* to trouble; *ex,* out + a Teutonic root; *magan,* to be able. Gower said, in CONFESSIO AMANTIS (1393): *I am . . . so distempred and esmaied.*

esne. An Old English slave. Pronounced *eznie.* From a Tetuonic root, *asnjo-,* harvester; *asano-,* harvest. Revived by Scott in IVANHOE (1820): *Esne art thou no longer.*

esoteric. See *acroamatic.*

espadon. A long two-handed sword. Spanish *espadon,* augmentative form of *espada,* sword. Used 15th, 16th, and 17th centuries. BLACKWOOD'S EDINBURGH MAGAZINE (May, 1881) recorded *the horseman's huge espadon of six feet long.*

espringal. A medieval catapult, for hurling heavy missiles. Also *springald; espringold.* Some lighter ones shot winged arrows of brass. *Springal, sprynhold, springold,* etc., also were very commonly uesd from 1450 to 1650, to mean an upstanding youth. Thus Beaumont and Fletcher in THE KNIGHT OF THE BURNING PESTLE (1613) exclaim: *Sure the devil, God bless us, is in this springald.* Scott in OLD MORTALITY (1816) and IVANHOE (1819: *This same springal, who conceals his name . . . hath already gained one prize*) revived the word; Byron and others followed.

essexed. Well rounded in the calf of the leg. Originally, *Essex calf,* a calf grown in Essex county; then used contemptuously of a native of the country. By punning practice, *Essex-growth,* development of the calf of the leg; *You would wish,* we read in the play LADY ALIMONY (1659), *that his puny baker-legs had more Essex growth in them. A good legge,* said the Water Poet (WORKS; 1630) *is a great grace if it be discreetly essex'd in the calfe, and not too much spindled in the small.* Then this was a man's; now, rather a woman's, concern.

essoin. To offer excuse for non-appearance in court; to accept an excuse, to let off. Also, as a noun, an excuse; the offering of an excuse. *Day of essoin, essoin-day,* first day of court term, when excuses may be submitted. An *essoin* might be for illness, king's service, holy pilgrimage, and the like. The word was common from the 14th century, also *essoyne, assoine, essonyie*; via Old French *essoignier*; Medieval Latin *ex,* out + *sonia, sunnis,* lawful excuse; Gothic *sunja,* truth. Hence *essoiner,* one that presents the excuse for the absentee; *essoinee,* one excused; *essoinment.* Spenser in THE FAËRIE QUEENE (1590) has: *From everie worke he challenged essoyne, For contemplation sake.* In THE UNIVERSAL REVIEW (November, 1889) we read: *In the high court of night Be thou essoiner for us unto death.* Death grants no long essoining.

estive. See *aestivate.*

estovers. Necessaries allowed by law. Old French *estovoir, est à avoir,* it is to have, it is needed. Specifically (13th to 18th century): wood a tenant may take from his landlord's estate for essential repairs; alimony; maintenance for an imprisoned felon. *Cp. hereyeld.*

estre. Condition, way of life; state of things. Also *eastre, ester, hester, esture, aistre*; Old French *estre,* to be. Hence, a place, a region where one is; an estate. In the plural, dwellings; quarters; inner rooms; paths in a garden, and the like. Used from the 13th to the 16th century (Lydgate; Gower; Chaucer).

eten. A giant. Also *ettin, eont, eotand, eotend, eatand, yhoten, etayne, eitin,* and the like. Hence *etenish,* gigantic. From the 13th century, when giants were common—although it's in 1549, in the COMPLAYNT OF SCOTLANDE, that we glimpse *the taiyl of the reyde eythyn witht the three heydis*—into the 17th century. Beaumont and Fletcher remark in THE KNIGHT OF THE BURNING PESTLE (1611): *They say the King of Portugal cannot sit at his meate but . . . the ettins will come and snatch it from him.* The opposite of an eten was a *droich,* a dwarf. Also *droigh*; perhaps altered from *duerch, duergh,* variant forms of *dwarf.* Used especially in Scotland, 16th and 17th centuries. Also *droichy,* dwarfish. The BANNATYNE MANUSCRIPT (1568) contains *Ane little Interlud, of the droichis part of the play.* This begins: *Hiry, hary, hubbilschow.* In it the dwarf (representing Plenty) complains that *for eild* [age] he has dwindled from the size of his ancestors, the giants Hercules, Fin Ma Cowl, Gog Magog—each such a one as *wold apoun his tais* [toes] *up stand And tak the starnis* [stars] *down with his hand And sett thame in a gold garland Aboif his wyvis hair.* Similarly, the dwarf that teased Gulliver in Brobdingnag was only thirty feet tall.

eth. Also (Spenser, THE SHEPHERD'S CALENDAR, 1579) *ethe.* See *eath.*

ethnagogue. A leader of a nation—with some of the same implication of charlatanry or self-seeking as in *demagogue,* literally, a leader of the people. Greek *ethnos,* nation (whence *ethnic*) + *agogos,* leader. Also *ethnarch* (Greek *archos,* ruler), ruler of a people, also used in ancient times for the governor of a province (as in the Roman Empire, where a province held a people).

ethology. (1) The portrayal of character by mimicry. Only in 17th and 18th century dictionaries. (2) The science of ethics. (3) Used by J. S. Mill (1843) and since, as the science of character-formation. From Greek *ethos,* character + *logos,* a talker. A mimic, thus, is an *ethologist.*

ethopoetic. Representing character or manners. Greek *ethos,* character +*poietikos*; *poieein,* to make, represent. Hence *ethopoeia,* delineation of character; moral portraiture. Urquhart in THE JEWEL (1652) spoke of a man pranking, with *a flourish of mimick and ethopoetick gestures.*

etiolation. The action or process of becoming, or the state of being, pale or colorless. The verb is *etiolate* or *etiolize;* from Norman *étieuler,* ultimately from Latin *stipula,* straw. Used in the 18th and 19th century; by scientists to refer to plants; but Charlotte Brontë in JANE EYRE (1848) has: *I . . . left a bullet in one of his poor etiolated arms,* and THE NORTH BRITISH REVIEW of 1844 said that *Newton smoked himself into a state of absolute etiolation.*

etna. A spirit-lamp; especially, one shaped like an inverted cone on a saucer, used in the 19th century for heating a small amount of liquid. Also *aetna.*

Named from the volcano, *Mt. Etna.* THE ENGLISH MECHANIC of 18 March, 1870, announced *an etna with which I can produce a pint of boiling water in eight minutes.*

ettercap. See *atter.*

ettle. To intend, to purpose; to ordain, destine; to aim, direct; direct one's course; to arrange, set in order, prepare. Also to guess, conjecture. A common word from the 12th century; after the 14th mainly in northern dialects. Among its forms were *atlien, attle, ahtil, atthill, eitle, attile, ettelle.* Hampole in THE PRICKE OF CONSCIENCE (1340) mentioned a daughter *the whilk he luved specialy and eghtild to mak hir qwene of worshepe.* Hence *ettle, ettling, ettlement,* intention; endeavor—*ettle* was also used (18th century) to mean opportunity; *ettling* (13th century) to mean conjecture; *withouten eni etlunge,* without any guessing, unquestionably. *Ettler,* a schemer; an aspirant. Scott in THE MONASTERY (1820), reviving the word, said: *They that ettle at the top of a ladder will at least get up some rounds.*

euchologion. A prayer-book. Greek *euche,* prayer + *log; legein,* to say. Also *euchologue, euchology.* Used in the 17th and 18th centuries; the first form, mainly in reference to the Greek Church. Lingard in his study (1844) of THE ANGLO-SAXON CHURCH refers to *the liturgical and euchological forms of her worship.* Hence also *euctical,* relating to prayer; supplicatory.

euciliast. See *abarcy.*

euclionism. Miserliness; stinginess. From *Euclio,* the miser, in Plautus' AULULARIA, THE POT OF GOLD. Nashe, in LENTEN STUFFE (1599), declared: *Those grey beard huddleduddles . . . were strooke with such stinging remorse of their miserable euclionisme and snudgery.*

eucrasy. A sound mixture of qualities; health, well-being. Greek *eukrasia,* good temperature; *eukratos,* well-tempered; *eu,* good + *kra-, kerannunai,* to mix. Hence *eucratic,* happily blended—of a drink or a person's characteristics. Used in the 17th and 18th centuries.

euctical. See *euchologion.*

eudemonic. Conducive to happiness; *eudemonics,* devices or appliances that increase comfort or happiness. Also *eudaemonic;* Greek *eudaimonikos; eudaimonia,* happiness; *eu,* good + *daimon,* guardian, spirit. Hence *eudemon, eudaemon,* a good angel—which strictly should be called an *agathodemon;* Greek *agathos,* good. M. Conway in DEMONOLOGY (1879) observed: *The Japanese are careful to distinguish this serpent from a dragon, with them an agathodemon.* Also *agathodemonic.* The notion 'composed of good and evil' is caught in the term *agathokakological* (Greek *kakos,* bad); Southey in THE DOCTOR (1843) says that *indeed upon the agathokakological globe there are opposite qualities always to be found.* In the same work he says: *The simple appendage of a tail will cacodemonize the eudaemon.* Hence *eudemony* (accent on the *dem*), *happiness,* prosperity; Martineau in TYPES OF ETHICAL THEORY (1885) observes that *the best defence of the invariable eudaemony of virtue proceeds from Shaftesbury.* May you bury the shafts of misfortune in spreading eudemony!

Eumenides. See *diral.*

eumorphous. Well-shaped.

eunomy. Good government; good laws well-administered.

euonymous. Well named; appropriately named. To call the plant spindletree (prickwood) *euonymus,* as the ancients did, was probably a euphemism, for Pliny notes that its flowering was a presage of pestilence. *Cp. diral* (*Eumenides*). THE SATURDAY REVIEW in 1864 grew facetious over *The Peace Society and its euonymous president, Mr. Pease.* An American columnist used to print euonyms, under the label *aptronymics.*

euripe. A variant of *euripus,* a channel of violent and uncertain currents. Originally a proper name, of the channel between Negropont and the mainland. Used, often figuratively, in the 17th, 18th, and 19th centuries; thus Drummond of Hawthornden asked, in 1649: *What euripe . . . doth change as often as man?* And THE PALL MALL GAZETTE of 16 February, 1884, remarked: *Although all nations are nowadays more or less unquiet, Paris seems to lie in a very euripus of change.* Plus ça change . . .

evagation. Wandering of one's thoughts: listed in the 15th century as a 'branch' of accidia, one of the seven deadly sins. See *accidie.* In the 17th century, *evagation* was used of a more literal wandering, as of clouds or (they feared) of planets. It was also then applied to a digression (in speech or writing) and to a (pleasant) departure from propriety, as when Walton (1638) remarked: *You married men are deprived of these evagations.*

eventration. The act of cutting open the abdomen. Via French from Latin *ex,* out + *ventrem,* belly. Also used more generally; in FALSE BEASTS (1875) Frances Cobbe refers to the camel and *the animal's provision of water, which his master could always reach . . . by the simple process of eventration.* To *eventrate,* to draw (as when one was hanged, drawn, and quartered); *cp. exenteration.* Also *eventricness, eventriqueness,* great corpulence; used figuratively by Waterhouse in A SHORT NARRATIVE OF THE LATE DREADFUL FIRE IN LONDON (1667), when he said that if London must *be borne with till its humors be sweetened, and its eventriqueness be reduced . . . then to no purpose is this waste of rage.*

everose. Rose water. Also *everrose.* Used in cosmetics and cookery; for an instance of the latter, see *bardolf.*

evisceration. See *exenteration.*

evitable. See *couth*; *evite.* A. Walker, in BEAUTY IN WOMEN (1836) pronounces the obiter dictum: *The scarcely evitable consequence of great fortune . . . will ever be the ruin of the rich.*

evitate. See *evite.*

Evite. A woman wearing little clothing. Humorously derived from Eve. Our bathing beaches had antecedents; Addison in THE GUARDIAN (1713) remarked (No. 134) on *there being so many in all public places, who show so great an inclination to be Evites*; and again (No. 142) said *that the Evites daily increase, and that fig-leaves are shortly coming into fashion.*

evite. To avoid. From Latin *e,* out + *vitare,* to shun. Common in 16th and 17th centuries; thereafter used mainly in Scotland. A less common form was *evitate* (used by Florio in his translation, 1603, of the ESSAYS of Montaigne; by Shakespeare in THE MERRY WIVES OF WINDSOR, 1598: *She doth evitate and shun A thousand irreligious cursed hours*) with the noun *evitation* and the adjective *evitable* (surviving in the negative, *inevitable*).

eviternal. The early form of *eternal*; Latin *aeviternus,* from *aevum,* age, was shortened to *aeternus.* Johnson in 1755 defined *eviternal* as "of duration not infinitely but indefinitely long"; but the use of the word does not justify his limitation. He was seeking a distinction where there was no difference. The basic form of the word is *aeviternal, q.v.*

evoe. The exclamation of the orgiac Bacchanalian celebrants. From Greek *evoi.* Shelley in PROMETHEUS UNBOUND (1819) says: *Like maenads who cry loud Evoe! Evoe!* Carlyle wrote in his MISCELLANIES (1830): *The earth is giddy with their clangour, their evohes.*

ewry. See *chaundrye.*

exallotriote. Fetched from a foreign land. Coined by Bulwer-Lytton (THE CAXTONS; 1849): *O planeticose and exallotriote spirit*—as from Greek *ex,* out + *allotrios,* foreign; *allos,* other.

exaration. Tracing characters upon wax or stone; hence, writing. Also, a written work. From Latin *ex,* out + *arare,* to plough, applied figuratively to digging (characters) into wax. W. H. Morley said (1840) in his discussion of THE ARABIAN NIGHTS: *The story in the Persian MS . . . is written in three different hands. The first part . . . has been apparently added since the exaration of the other two.*

exaugurate. (1) To render unhallow, cancel the *inauguration.* (2) To augur ill fortune.

excarnation. (1) The separation of the soul from the body; opposite of *incarnation* (Latin *carnis,* flesh). (2) Stripping off the fleshy parts; growing lean. The verb is *excarnate*; *excarnous,* without flesh. *Excarnificate* is to butcher, to torture, to cut to pieces (Latin *carnifex,* executioner; *carnifex* was used as an English word in the 16th and 17th centuries, and revived by Scott in THE FORTUNES OF NIGEL, 1823. J. Martineau, 1882, mentions *the chief carnifex undertaking the high-born folks.*) Evelyn in SYLVA (1664) advises sowing black cherry stones *in beds immediately after they are excarnated.* See *carnation.*

excecation. Putting out the eyes; blinding—literally and figuratively. Hall in his CHRONICLES of 1540 said that *the people of Scotland . . . is utterly excecated.* A frequent word in 17th century sermons, as (1588) of Pharoah's *obduration and excecation in wilful wickedness.* Latin *caecus,* without light; blind. Appius Claudius (Roman consul, 307 B.C., builder of the Appian Way) was given the agnomen *Caecus,* blind; whence (diminutive) Cecil, feminine *Cecile, Cecilia*—as in St. Cecila (died 230) patron saint of music, celebrated in Dryden's *Ode for St. Cecilia's Day.*

excerebrate. (1) To clear out of the mind. From Latin *ex,* out + *cerebrum,* brain. S. Ward, in THE LIFE OF FAITH (1621) asks whether faith *hath not soveraigne virtue in it to excerebrate all cares, expectorate all fears and griefs?* (2) To beat out the brains of. Thus in 17th and 18th century dictionaries. Hence, *excerebrated,* brainless, witless.

excrement. That which grows out, as hair, nails, feathers. By extension, an excessive outgrowth, as when Warner in ALBION'S ENGLAND (1606) says that *wit so is wisedomes excrement.* Shakespeare uses the word in THE COMEDY OF ERRORS: *Why is Time such a niggard of hair, being as it is so plentiful an excrement?* and in LOVE'S LABOUR'S LOST (1588): *It will please his grace to dallie with my excrement, with my mustachio.* The word is from Latin *excrementum*; *ex,* out + *crescere,* to grow; it has been replaced by *excrescence.* The *excrement* that survives is from Latin *ex* + *cernere, cretum,* to sift, whence also *secrete, secret, secretary, secretion; concern, discern,* and the frequent *indiscretion.*

excubant. Keeping watch. From Latin *ex,* out + *cubare,* to lie down; *cumbere,* to lie; *cp. succubus.* An *excubitor* is a sentinel; G. White observed, in 1775, that the swallow *is the excubitor to the house-martins . . . announcing the approach of birds of prey.*

exculcate. To trample out, to eradicate. From Latin *ex,* out + *calcare,* to stamp; *calc-,* heel. The opposite of *inculcate;* what many 'modern' parents do with good manners in their offspring.

excuss. (1) To shake off, get rid of (as dust, or undesired qualities). (2) To shake out the contents; hence, to investigate; to probe the truth from someone. (3) In 18th century law, to shake out one's property, i.e., to take a man's goods for debt. From Latin *excutere, excussus; ex,* out + *quatere,* to shake. (In Latin the verb also meant to search by shaking one's robe.) The word was often in religious mouths, especially in the 17th century, as when Bishop Hall (1620) spoke of *the just excussion of that servile yoke.*

exenteration. The act of removing the entrails, disemboweling. *Exenterate* is from Latin *ex,* out + a Late Latin verb from Greek *enteron,* intestine. When a man was condemned to be hanged, drawn, and quartered, the drawing was *exenteration. Cp. eventration.* The word was also used figuratively, as in Lamb's praise (1808) of Ford's play THE BROKEN HEART: *I do not know where to find, in any play, a catastrophe so grand, so solemn, so surprising, as in this . . . The fortitude of the Spartan boy who let a beast gnaw out his bowels till he died, without expressing a groan, is a faint bodily image of this dilaceration of the spirit, and exenteration of the inmost mind, which Calantha, with a holy violence against her nature, keeps closely covered till the last duties of a wife and queen are fulfilled.* A slightly more familiar word is *evisceration* (Latin *e-,* out + *viscera,* the internal organs). This was used both literally and figuratively, as to *eviscerate* one's brains; in the 17th century it was frequently applied in an image of the spider, which *'eviscerates* itself' to weave its web. Coleridge in TABLE-TALK, 27 October, 1831, wonders *if a certain latitude in examining witnesses is . . . a necessary mean towards the evisceration of truth.* Back in 1636, W. Ambrose was suggesting that writers might thrive if they *exenterate old stories;* his advice has been well taken.

exhibition. Maintenance, support; especially, an allowance of money for one's support; a gift; a prize-sum or scholarship at a university. Used from the 15th century. The verb *to exhibit* had the same range of meaning; to grant; provide, furnish; defray (expenses). Latin *ex,* out + *habere,* to have, to hold. Shakespeare in OTHELLO (1604), speaking of being false to one's husband, has Desdemona ask: *Wouldst thou do such a deed for all the world?* and her servant Emilia reply: *Marry, I would not do such a thing for a joint ring, nor for measures of lawn, nor for gowns, petticoats, nor caps, nor any petty exhibition; but for the whole world —why, who would not make her husband a cuckold to make him a monarch? I should venture Purgatory for't.* In TWO GENTLEMEN OF VERONA he declares: *What maintenance he from his friends receives, Like exhibition thou shalt have from me.* King Lear complained that his daughters put him on a set allowance: he was *con-*

fin'd to exhibition. The current sense of the word developed in the 17th century.

exilient. Exulting; bounding; alert, active. From Latin *exilire; ex,* out + *salire,* to leap (like the *saltimbancos* who leapt on a bench to sell their wares; *saltimbanco* has been used since the 17th century for a quack). Hence *exilience,* rapture, exultation; *exiliency* has this meaning, but also any outburst; Heylin in CYPRIANUS ANGLICUS (1662) speaks of *some exiliency of human frailty.*

exility. Thinness, meagreness; poverty. Also fineness of texture; hence, subtlety. The adjective *exile* was used from the 15th into the 19th century to mean meagre, shrunken, thin, as when Bacon in SYLVA (1626) speaks of a voice *made extreme sharp and exile, like the voice of puppets.* An *exile theory* is fine-spun, subtle. The words are from Latin *exilis,* thin, scanty; *ex,* out + *agilis* from the root *ag-,* weigh. (To *exile,* to banish, is from *ex* + *salire,* to leap; *cp. exilient.*)

eximious. Choice, excellent, distinguished. From Latin *eximere, exemptus; ex,* out + *emere,* to take (whence also *exempt,* which first meant taken out, removed, then removed out of obligation or influence, etc.) In the 16th and 17th centuries, *eximious* was frequently used; since then, it has been mainly humorous or satiric, as in Carlyle's FREDERICK THE GREAT (1865): *Oh ye wigs, and eximious wig-blocks, called right-honourable!* (A wig-block was a block of wood shaped like a head, on which a wig rested when not in use; its like may be seen in many shops —and, in the Carlylean sense, parlors— of today.)

exinanite. To void, deprive of force; to reduce to emptiness, to humble. Accent on the *in.* Latin *ex,* out + *inanis,* empty, whence *inane.* The BIBLE (PHILIPPIANS, 2; 1582) said that Jesus, being in the form of God, *exinanited himself;* the King James Version (1611) says "made himselfe of no reputation." Also, in the 17th century, *exinanitiate,* and the noun *exinanition.* Donne in an Essay of 1631 spoke of the Lord's *replenishing the world after that great exinanition by the generall deluge;* he also used the word referring to emptying oneself of pride— thus meaning abasement, humiliation— in a Sermon of 1627: *This exinanition of ourselves is acceptable in the sight of God.*

exion. Action. A blunder of Mistress Quickly, in a legal matter, in Shakespeare's HENRY IV, PART TWO (1597): *I pray ye, since my exion is enter'd . . . let him be brought in to his answer.*

exitial. Destructive, ruinous, fatal. That is, resulting in one's *exit;* from Latin *exire, exitus; ex,* out + *ire,* to go. Other forms, used 16th-18th centuries, are *exitiable, exitiose, exitious.* Other forms for *exit* were *exitus, exition, exiture* (the last also used in medicine, of a running sore or abscess). Mushrooms, said Evelyn in his ACETARIA, OR A DISCOURSE OF SALLETS (1699) are *malignant, exitial, mortal, and deleterious.*

exoculation. The action of putting out the eyes; blinding—often as part of a torturing or (an early) judicial sentence. *Cp. abacinate.* Southey in RODERICK, THE LAST OF THE GOTHS (1814) has a note: *The history of Europe during the dark ages abounds with examples of exoculation.* There are instances of it in the Elizabethan drama, including the exoculation of old Gloucester in Shakespeare's KING LEAR.

exoneration. See *oner.*

exornation. Adornment. Used mainly by 16th and 17th century rhetoricians, as T.

Wilson in THE ARTE OF RHETORIQUE (1553): *Exornacion is a gorgiousse beautifiynge of the tongue with borowed wordes.* From Latin *ex* (with intensive effect) + *ornare,* to embellish. *Exorn, exourn, exornate* were verbs, largely supplanted after the 17th century by *adorn.*

exosculation. A 'smack,' a hearty kiss. Latin *ex* (with intensive force) + *osculari,* to kiss; *osculum,* a little mouth, *os,* mouth. *Cp. bass; osculation.* Used in the 16th and 17th centuries. The verb *exosculate,* to kiss heartily, is hopefully in the dictionaries, but found no literary use.

exoteric. See *acroamatic.*

expeccation. Removal of sin or of guilt. From Latin *ex,* away + *peccare,* to sin. Used (only) by Donne in a Sermon of 1631: *It is . . . this expeccation . . . this taking away of sins formerly committed, that restores me.*

expergefacient. Rousing; that which causes one to awake. The noun was used in THE MECHANIC'S MAGAZINE of 1823, of an early alarm clock: *The newly invented hydraulic expergefactor rings a bell at the time when a person wishes to rise.* From Latin *expergefacere; expergere,* to arouse + *facere,* to make. *Ex* is used as an intensive; so is *per* in *pergere,* to make haste, continue; *regere,* to lead straight, to guide. The action of awakening someone, or the state of being aroused, is *expergefaction.* Used since the 17th century; Howell in THE PARLEY OF BEASTS (1660) says that he, *after such a long noctivagation . . . returned to my perfect expergefaction.* R. North, in his LIVES (1734) coined a new form: *I should perceive a plain expergiscence though I had no sense of drowsiness.*

experiment. Experience; practical knowledge. Also, practical proof; a specimen. Both *experience* and *experiment* are from Latin *experiri, expertum,* to try. *Experience* first (14th century) meant putting to the test; *to make experience of,* to make trial of. Once one is experienced, however, the trial (*experiment*) is over; one has become *expert.* Thus Bacon, in the most compact of all English essays (1598), says that *expert men can execute, and perhaps judge of particulars, one by one; but the general counsels, and the plots and marshalling of affairs, come best from those that are learned.* Caxton in POLYCRONICON (1482) recommends history *to yong men . . . and to old men, to whome long lyf hath mynystred experymentes of dyverse thynges.*

expetible. Desirable. Latin *ex,* out + *petere,* to seek. Used in 16th, 17th, and 18th centuries.

expiscation. Investigation; "fishing out." From Latin *ex,* out + *piscari,* to fish; *piscis,* fish. Chapman uses the verb *expiscate* in his translation (1611) of THE ILIAD; his own poem (1605) on Jonson's SEJANUS speaks of *the Castalian head: In expiscation of whose mysteries Our nets must still be clog'd with heavy lead.* An investigator is, hence, an *expiscator,* though this form is rare. But indeed those that can expiscate the truth walk not on every highway.

exprobration. Speaking reproachfully; a scolding. Also, *to exprobrate, exprobate,* to reproach; to make clear (to one's shame). Latin *ex,* out of + *probrum,* shameful action. The second form of the verb came by association with *to reprobate. Reprobation, reprove* are from Latin *reprobare, reprobatum,* to reject; *re,* back + *probare,* to esteem, approve; *probus,* good, honest, whence *probity. Reproach* (French *proche,* near) is via French from

Late Latin *repropiare,* to bring near again; *re,* again + *prope,* near; applied figuratively to bringing a fault back to one's attention. Norton in his preface to Grafton's CHRONICLE AT LARGE (1569) says he will refrain from listing Grafton's good deeds, *because the rehearsall in particularitie cannot but have some affinitie with exprobration.*

exsibilate. To reject scornfully; to hiss off the stage. From Latin *ex,* out + *sibilare,* to hiss. Thus Bishop Barlow declared, in 1601: *Cardinal Allen hath long since exibilated this rash illation.* American audiences are quite restrained, and sit suffering before plays that deserve swift exsibilation.

extispice. See *aeromancy.* Urquhart in his translation (1693) of Rabelais, uses the form *extispicine;* Bailey (1751) has *extispice;* the most frequent form is *extispicy.* One that inspected the entrails of the sacrificial victims was an *extispex,* from Latin *exta* (used also in English), entrails + *specere, spex-,* to look at.

extraneize. To make extraneous, i.e., to remove. Four syllables, accent on the *strain.* Urquhart, in his translation (1653) of Rabelais: *To extraneize the blasting mists and whirlwinds upon our vines;* H. Clarke, in SCHOOL CANDIDATES (1788): *To extraneize the blasting mists and whirlwind of immorality upon the minds of youth.* Omit one *e,* and *extranize* has present values. Thus also *extranate* (Latin *natus,* born), originating from outside, as opposed to *innate.* Originating from outside was the first meaning of *extraneous,* which is current in the sense of outside, irrelevant; earlier forms are *extraneal, extranean, extranear. I desist* (said T. Gainsford in 1618; few since have followed him!) *from all extraneal and superfluous discourses.*

extravagate. To wander, figuratively: away from; into; at will; beyond proper bounds. Latin *extra,* beyond, outside + *vagari,* to wander, whence *vagrant.* Also the current *extravagance,* a spending beyond proper bounds. Also *extravage,* to go beyond the sphere of duty; to talk off the subject, to ramble; used in the 17th and 18th centuries. Wordsworth in THE PRELUDE (1805) speaks of *schemes In which his youth did first extravagate.*

extravasate. To force out of its proper container; to escape. Accent on the *trav.* Used from the 17th century (Latin *extra,* out + *vas,* vessel), mainly in chemistry and physiology; but De Foe in his HISTORY OF THE DEVIL (1726) said: *If he be not in the inside . . . I have so mean an opinion of his extravasated powers . . .*

extund. To drive out or away. Not used in English in the literal sense, to hammer out, from Latin *ex,* out + *tundere,* to hammer.

exturb. To hustle off, get rid of. Latin *ex,* out + *turbare,* to agitate; *turba,* tumult; whence also *disturb.* Whence also *exturbation,* removal, hustling away (of someone).

exul. An early form of *exile,* used, e.g., in Spenser's COLIN CLOUTS COME HOME AGAIN (1595). An *exulant* is one living in exile. *Cp. exility.*

exungulation. Paring the nails. Latin *ex,* out +*ungula,* diminutive of *unguis,* claw. *Exungulated* (of animals), with the hoofs pulled or cut off. To *exungulate* is also (in preparing food, perfume, or medicinal prescriptions) to cut off the white part of rose petals.

exustion. Burning up. S. Parker, speaking (1720) of the burning of Sodom and Gomorrah, said: *The frightful effects* *which this exustion left are still remaining.* Some think the wrathful divine exustion has begun again. The verb *exust,* to burn up, was used into the 19th century; the form *exust* was also used as an adjective, burnt or dried up. From Latin *ex,* out + *urere, ustum,* to burn; whence also *combustion.* Also *exustible,* capable of being consumed by fire.

exuviae. Cast skins, shells and other coverings of animals; figuratively, cast-off articles of apparel. Thackeray in CATHERINE (1840) looks at the old-clothes man and wonders at *the load of exuvial coats and breeches under which he staggers.* FRASER'S MAGAZINE in 1855: *Crabs of mature age and full size cease to exuviate.* Huxley in 1880: *The young crayfish exuviate two or three times in the course of the first year.* Ah, youth, youth!

eyas. A young hawk, taken for training; a nestling. This is an altered form of *nyas* (*a nyas* became *an yas,* from oral misunderstanding, as *a nadder* became *an adder; nickname* shows the converse error; *cp. eke*); French *niais* (which is used to mean childish, foolish); Latin *nidus, nest.* The spelling *eyas* as influenced by Middle English *ey,* egg, and also by *eyry* (*aery, airie*; a hawk's nest). The word was used figuratively, usually in scorn, of young men. Thus Rosencrantz in Shakespeare's HAMLET (1602): *An ayrie of children, little yases, that crye out on the top of question*—in allusion to the boy actors of the Blackfriars, for a time serious rivals of Shakespeare's company. Thus *eyas-thoughts,* unfledged, inexperienced thoughts; *eyas wings,* untried wings. Of a lively youngster Shakespeare inquires (MERRY WIVES OF WINDSOR): *How now, my eyas-musket, what newes with you?* [A *musket* was the male of a sparrowhawk; the word is a diminutive of Romanic *mosca,* Latin *musca,* fly; Latin *muscus,* musk. The gun took its name from the bird, as did the *falcon,* etc.]

eymery. An old form of *ember*; ashes. Also *eymbre, eymbery.*

eyot. A small island. Also *ait.* Hence *eyoty,* like an island.

eyren. An old plural of egg: eggs. Also *eyrone, eyroun*; *ayren.*

F

fabaceous. Like a bean. Latin *faba,* bean. Used in the 18th century. Figuratively, lanky, 'skinny.'

fabian. See *cunctation.* Propertius used the phrase *licens Fabius* of the Fabian priests of Pan, who had the privilege of licentious conduct at the Lupercalia; hence late 16th century references (Florio; Nashe) to a *flaunting fabian,* a roisterer.

fabulose. Fond of fables and myths, like Moritz Jagendorf. A 17th century term modern folklorists could use.

facete. See *inficete.*

facient. One that does, acts, performs. Latin *facientem,* present participle of *facere,* to do, to make. Bishop Hacket in his MEMORIAL TO ARCHBISHOP WILLIAMS OF YORK (1670) inquired: *Is sin in the fact, or in the mind of the facient?* The word fills a gap in current speech.

facinerious. A variant of *facinorous, q.v.* The variation occurred in Latin; *facinorem* or *facinerem.*

facinorous. Extremely wicked, infamous; grossly criminal. The word, naturally, is accented on the *sin.* From Latin *facinorosus,* full of bad deeds; *facinus,* a (bad) deed; *facere,* to do. Also *facinerose* (in the dictionaries), *facinerious, facinorious,* as in Shakespeare's ALL'S WELL THAT ENDS WELL (1601): *He's of a most facinerious spirit.*

fackins. See *fegs.*

fact. A deed, a thing done. Latin *facere, factum,* to do. Hence, used of a noble deed or exploit (earlier *fait;* this sense survives in *feat*); also as an evil deed, a crime. The last was the most common meaning in the 16th and 17th centuries; it survives in the phrases *accessory after* (*before*) *the fact. In the very fact,* in the very act. The current sense, of a thing that is so, developed in the 17th century. *Fact* was also, more rarely, used to mean guilt, as when Massinger in THE EMPEROR OF THE EAST (1632) said: *Great Julius would not rest satisfied that his wife was free from fact, but, only for suspicion of a crime, sued a divorce.*

facund. Eloquent; also a noun, eloquence; *facundity.* Latin *facundus.* Hence *facundious,* fluent, glib. *facundate,* to make eloquent (a 17th century term; not to be confused with *fecundate;* Latin *fecundus,* fruitful). The words are from a form of Latin *for, fari, fatum,* to speak; whence also the *forum* and one's *fate:* that which has been spoken. Lord Berners (Sir John Bourchier) in his early 16th century translations used simple terms, apologizing for not using *fresshe ornate polysshed Englysshe* on the ground that he was unequipped with *the facondyous arte of rethoryke.* Warner in ALBION'S ENGLAND (1606) knew how often eloquence displays but *facundious fooles.*

faddity. An oddity that is the moment's fad. A late 19th century word.

fadge. A very common verb, from the late 16th century. (1) To fit, be suitable, to fit in with; to get along well with. (2) To agree; to fit together; to piece together (*fadge up*). (3) To fit in with; hence, to get along, thrive. *It won't fadge,* it won't succeed. *Fadging,* well matched, well suited, fitting. There is also a noun *fadge,* with the basic sense of something flat: a flat bundle (of pieces of leather, etc.); a large flat loaf; a dumpy person. Hence *fadgy,* unwieldy; corpulent. Fuller in THE HISTORY OF THE WORTHIES OF ENGLAND (1661): *The study of the law did not fadge well with him*; Milton, in the Preface (1643) to his treatise on DIVORCE: *They shall . . . be made, spight of antipathy, to fadge together*; Wycherley in THE COUNTRY WIFE (1675): *Well, sir, how fadges the new design?*

fading. See *dildo.* The word is possibly from Irish *feadan,* pipe, whistle; but in Cornish *fade* meant to dance from town to country, a sort of *morris, q.v.*

faex. See *fegs.*

fage. To coax, to flatter. Common in the 14th and 15th centuries. Also *faging,* flattery; *fager,* flatterer. A *fage,* a deceit; in Bailey (1751) defined as 'a merry tale.'

fagioli. Beans; kidney beans. From the Italian. Jonson in CYNTHIA'S REVELS (1600) says: *He doth learn to make strange sauces, to eat anchovies, macaroni, bovoli, fagioli, caviare. Bovoli* are periwinkles, snails.

fagot. Still occasionally in use, meaning a bundle of sticks, tied together for firewood, *fagot* had various other meanings. Its origin is unknown, though its meaning is similar to Latin *fascis,* which in the plural, *fasces,* was applied to the bundle of rods with an axe in the middle, carried before the highest magistrate as a symbol of his authority, the revival of which in modern Italy gave name to the *Fascist Party.* In England *faggot* is the preferred spelling; other forms were *faggat, faget, fag(g)ald.* Forgotten meanings include: An embroidered figure of a bundle of firewood, which recanted heretics had to wear on their sleeve, as a sign of what they had deserved. Similarly, *to fry a faggot,* to be burnt alive; *fire and faggot,* the stake, burning alive; *to bear a faggot, to carry a faggot,* to have renounced heresy. *Fagot* was also used of bundles of other things, in general. Also (from the shape) a rolled cake of chopped liver and lights, mixed with gravy and stuffed into a sausage-skin (19th century). From the 16th into the 19th century, a term of abuse for a woman; Lodge in CATHAROS (1591) tells us: *A filbert is better than a faggot, except it be an Athenian she handfull.* (*Filbert,* a term rather of endearment, after the color and comparatively low height of the hazel tree.) In the 17th century, *fagot* came to be used of a man quickly hired to answer "Here!" in a shortage of soldiers at mustertime; hence, one used to fill a deficiency; also, a dummy. From this came the 19th century use *faggot, faggot-vote,* one manufactured to help carry an election, as by temporarily transferring to persons not otherwise qualified enough property to entitle them to vote. Thus in the DAILY NEWS of 16 April, 1879, a candidate averred that he *had not the slightest doubt he would win, unless he were to be swamped by faggots.* Bishop Montagu, in one of his DIATRIBES (1621) cried out: *You deserved to fry a fagot!*

fain. Glad, well-pleased. Also *fagen, fein, fayen, feene, vein, vayn, fyene, feign* and more. *Full fain, glad and fain.* In the phrase *fain to,* glad to; then, content to, as the lesser of two evils; hence, necessitated, obliged, as when D'Israeli in THE AMENITIES OF LITERATURE (1841) remarks that *Ascham, indeed, was fain to apologise for having written in English.* Also apt, wont; favorable, well-disposed; Spenser, in THE FAËRIE QUEENE (1596): *Whose steadie hand was fain his steed to guyde;* Rossetti, in DANTE AND HIS CIRCLE (1850): *I . . . saw Love coming towards me, fair and fain. I would (had) fain,* I would gladly . . . *Fain* was also a verb, to be glad (of, on); to make glad, hence to welcome; to rejoice in. There was an old proverb (echoed by Scott): *Fair promys maketh fools fain.*

faintise. Deceit, pretence. Also feebleness, cowardice. From *faint, feint.* Also *feintise, feyntise, fayntes, fantise, fayntise.* In the first sense, THE DESTRUCTION OF TROY (1400) has: *Ere he fain any faintes;* in the second, Harding's CHRONICLE (1470) states: *They fought without feyntise.*

fairing. A present on the occasion of a fair; hence, any complimentary gift; especially, *fairings,* sweets or cakes sold at a fair. Also, *to go afairing,* to go for a good time to the fair. *A day after the fair* (16th century), too late. *To give (get) one's fairing,* to give (get) one's just deserts. Deloney in JACK OF NEWBERIE (1597) has the widow watching her servant John (Jack), whom she hoped to marry, *till at last it was her lucke upon a Bartholomew day (having a fayre in the towne) to spie her man John give a pair of gloves to a proper maide for a fayring, which the maiden with a bashfull modesty kindly accepted, and requited it with a kisse, which kindled in her an inward jealousie.* Shakespeare, in LOVE'S LABOUR'S LOST (1588): *We shall be rich ere we depart, If fairings come thus plentifully in.*

fait. See *fact; cp. faytour.*

falbala. A trimming for petticoats and other garments; a flounce. Also *falbeloe, fallbullow; furbelow.* (Origin unknown; not from a *fur* trimming, *fur below.*) In the plural, *furbelows,* it came to be used (in the 18th century) of overdecorative, showy trimming or ornaments; hence figuratively, *rhetorical furbelows.* NEW CRAZY TALES (1783) lists things to be found in London's second-hand shops, on Monmouth Street: *The rags of peasants, and the spoils of beaus, Mix'd with hoop-petticoats and falbeloes . . . Here on one hook I oftentimes have seen The warrior's scarlet and the footman's green; And near a broken gamester's old roqu'laure The tatter'd pawn of some ill-fated whore; Hats, bonnets, scarves, sad arguments of woe, Beavroys and riding-hoods make up the show.*

fambles. See *pedlers French.*

famular. A domestic servant. So Bailey (1751). Hence *famulary,* relating to servants; *famulate,* to serve; *famulative,* suitable for service; serving. The Latin *famulus,* servant (plural, *famuli*) is used in English of the helper of a scholar or a magician; thus Carlyle in THE FRENCH REVOLUTION (1837) states that *the magician's famulus got hold of the forbidden book, and summoned a goblin;* Thackeray in HENRY ESMOND (1852) notes that *faithful little famuli see all and say nothing.* Such, a century later, are hard to find.

fanger. (1) A guardian. One who takes (hold) care of another. The first meaning of *to fang* was to lay hold of. (2) One who captures. (3) That with which one captures (e.g., a claw, a tooth; but often figurative). Dekker in IF IT BE NOT GOOD, THE DEVIL IS IN IT (1612) said: *All the craft in that great head of yours cannot get it out of my fangers.*

fangle. A fashion, especially in the phrase *new fangle,* always contemptuous. By extension, a silly piece of foppery or fuss; a fantastic contrivance. Lyly in EUPHUES (1579) speaks of *A pedlers packe of new fangles.* Originally *newfangle* was applied to a person, meaning eager for novelty. Hence the verbs: *to new fangle,* to dress in new fashion; *to fangle,* to fashion, to trick out. Also *fanglement,* the act of fashioning; a contrivance (usually in scorn). Shakespeare in CYMBELINE (1611) says: *Be not, as is our fangled world, a garment Nobler than that it covers.*

fantastic. A person full of absurdities, fancies, whimsies. Shakespeare in ROMEO AND JULIET (1597) speaks of *limping antique affecting fantasticoes.*

fap. Drunk, 'tight.' Shakespeare in THE MERRY WIVES OF WINDSOR (1598) has Bardolph exclaim: *I say the gentleman had drunk himself out of his five sentences*—Evans corrects him: *It is his five senses. Fie, what the ignorance is!* Bardolph goes blithely on: *And being fap, sir, was, as they say, casheered.*

farandman. A *faring-man;* a traveler. From *farand,* an old participle of *fare* + man. In many cases, the stranger (vagabond or pedlar) had little help from the law, but in Scotland (15th-18th century) the *Law of Farandman* provided that a pedlar could bring a townsman to trial for theft or felony 'within the third flowing and ebbing of the sea.'

farce. See *fastuous.*

fard. (1) Motion, impetus; hence, a violent onset. Related to *fare;* used 16th-18th century. (2) Paint for the face, especially a white paint. F. Barrett in UNDER STRANGE MASK (1889) spoke of *the enamels and fards employed to conceal the mark of Time's finger;* Sir G. Mackenzie in THE RELIGIOUS STOIC (1663) used the word figuratively: *the fard of eloquence.* Also, *to fard,* to paint the face; hence, to embellish, to gloss over, as in Scott's OLD MORTALITY (1816): *Nor will my conscience permit me to fard or daub over the causes of divine wrath.* In the 15th century, painting the face—or the effect thereof—was called *fardry.* Fardry today (as Hamlet protested to Ophelia) is common practice.

fardel. (1) A bundle; a collection (as *a fardel of myths*); a burden. Also, something to wrap things in. Via Old French and Spanish (*fardo*), possibly from Arabic *fardah.* Hence also *fardellage,* a package (15th-16th centuries); *fardlet,* a little bundle (15th-17th centuries). There are two other words spelled *fardel.* (2) A fourth part of anything. From *fourth* + *deal.* Hence, plural, quarters, pieces, fragments. (3) Profit. A form of *fore-deal.*—Carew, in his translation (1594) of Huarte's EXAMINATION OF MEN'S WITS, says: *I have always held it an errour, to hear many lessons of divers matters, and to carry them all home fardled up together.* One fardel at a time! But there is always Shakespeare: (1602) Hamlet, in his greatest soliloquy, asks *Who would fardels bear?* and in THE WINTER'S TALE (1611) we find: *There lies such secrets in this farthel and box, which none must know but the King.*

farrago. A confused agglomeration, a hodgepodge. Latin *farrago,* mixed fodder for cattle; *farrem,* grain, corn. By the 16th century, the form *farrage* was used for fodder. Canning in his POETICAL WORKS (1827) said: *No longer we want This* *farrago of cowardice, cunning, and cant.* Hence *farraginary* (16th century) and, more frequently since 1600, *farraginous.* Southey in THE DOCTOR (1843) spoke of *farraginous notes;* Reade in ALL THE YEAR ROUND for 3 October, 1863, declared that *Bailey was one of the farraginous fools of the unscientific science.*

farthingale. A framework of hoops, usually of whalebone, worn under ladies' dresses to spread them wide; the petticoat under a hoop-skirt. Via Old French *vertugalle* from Spanish *verdugato,* a farthingale, from *verdugo,* rod. Bailey's DICTIONARY (1751), however, suggests the word is a corruption of French *"vertu gard,* i.e., the Guard of Virtue, because young women, by hiding their great bellies, preserve the reputation of their chastity." The farthingale was worn from the mid-15th well into the 19th century. Dekker in WESTWARD HOE (1607) tells that women must *learn how to wear a Scotch farthingale.* Evidently the women learned; J. G. Strutt in SYLVA BRITANNICA (1830) informs us that *the maids of honour had just stripped off their farthingales.* Others preferred to die in them; Rhoda Broughton in NANCY (1873) recalls *the faithful, ruffed and farthingaled wife on the fifteenth century tomb.*

farthingdeal. See *thirdendeal.*

fastigiate. To make pointed at the top; to taper to a point; to form into or with gables. Rarely, *fastigate.* Latin *fastigare,* to sharpen. Hence *fastigium,* a gable point; the upper ridge of a roof; a peak or summit. Also, as an adjective, *fastigiate,* tapered up to a point. *fastigious,* gabled; figuratively, pompous, pretentious; G. H. in his translation (1670) of G. Leti's HISTORY OF THE CARDINALS wrote: *They thought the title too eminent and too fastigious for them.*

fastrede. Firm in purpose; steadfast. Old English *faest,* fast + *raed,* counsel, purpose. From the 8th into the 14th century, as in THE OWL AND THE NIGHTINGALE (1250): *He is nu ripe and fastrede.*

fastuous. Haughty; pretentious, ostentatious. From Latin *fastuosus,* full of pride, *fastus (farstus),* arrogance, haughty contempt. This is probably (meaning "puffed up" with pride) akin to Latin *farcire, fartus,* to stuff, whence English *farce,* which first meant stuffing. [Then the word *farce* was applied to the extra words "stuffed in" between *kyrie* and *eleison* in church singing; later to interpolated 'gags' and buffoonery.] Collier in 1707 attacked *a pompous display of a fastuous learning;* many in the 17th century objected to fastuosity.

fate. See *fatuate.*

fathom. The embracing arms (in the plural; in the singular, bosom). Hence, one to be embraced, the 'wife of thy bosom'; Dekker in SATIROMASTIX (1602) speaks of *thy bride . . . She that is now thy fadom.* Also, *to make a fathom,* to stretch the arms to their full extent. From this come the meanings of measurement, whether it be physical (Shakespeare, THE WINTER'S TALE, 1611): *the profound seas hides In unknowne fadomes* or the stretch of one's comprehension (Shakespeare, OTHELLO): *Another of his fadome, they have none. Fathom* was so used from the 8th century, the meaning of *fathoms deep* coming toward the end of the 15th. In the same range of meanings, from the 13th century, *fathom* has been used as a verb, to encircle with extended arms—*trees,* wrote Scott in his JOURNAL for 1828, *so thick that a man could not fathom them;* to embrace, also *to fathom together*—*lascivious Delilahs,* said Thomas Adams

(WORKS; 1629), *fadomed him in the arms of lust;* to measure (17th century); to get to the bottom of, see through, thoroughly understand (17th century, and still current).

faticane. A prophet; especially one in verse. Latin *fatum, fati,* fate + *canere,* to sing. A rare 17th century word, used by John Gaule in THE MAGASTROMANCER (1651): *What fatuous thing is fate, then, that is so obvious . . . as for the faticanes to foretell?* More frequent were the compounds with Latin *dicere,* to speak: *fatidic,* concerning prophecy; *fatidical,* gifted with prophetic power; *fatidicate,* to prophesy; *fatidicency,* divination (accents on the *tid*). There is also the rare compound with Latin *ferre,* to bring: *fatiferous,* bringing on one's fate, deadly, mortal. NOTES AND QUERIES for 1864 mentions *those fatidical women, who . . . ruled the destinies of the nation.*

fatidical. See *faticane.*

fatiferous. See *faticane.*

fatigate. See *couth.*

fatuate. To act foolishly, to be silly. A verb in the 17th and 18th centuries. Other forms were *fatuant,* behaving foolishly; *fatuate* (as an adjective, in Jonson's THE POETASTER, 1601), *fatuated,* silly; these have been replaced by *fatuous;* the form survives in *infatuated.* The forms are ultimately from Latin *fatuus,* speaking by inspiration, hence insane, simple, silly; *fari, fatum,* to speak, *fatum,* spoken, hence the utterance of an oracle, hence destiny —whence English *fate.* If you look silly, it may be the fat you ate—but that need not be your fate!

faunic. Wild; of the woodland; rude; relating to a *faun.* Also *faunal. Fauna* was a countryside goddess, sister of *Faunus.* Linnaeus used her name for his book *Fauna Suecica* (1746) sequel to his *Flora Suecica* (1745); hence the current meaning, the animal life of a region. *Faunus* was the Greek *Pan* (Greek-Roman *p* became Teutonic *f,* as *pod,* English *podiatry, foot*). Hence *a faun,* a demigod of the countryside; for one of his bits of mischief, *see areed;* feminine, *fauness.* But *a faunist* is a student of the *fauna* of a region. *faunship,* state of being a faun; used by Hawthorne in THE MARBLE FAUN (1860).

faunt. A child. Also *fauntekin, fauntelet,* a little child, an infant. Hence *fauntelte,* childishness. Shortened from Old French *enfaunt;* French *enfant;* English *infant;* Latin *in,* not + *fantem,* speaking; *fari, fatum,* to speak; *cp. fatuate.* The English forms were used in the 14th century, but may have faint echo in Little Lord *Fauntleroy* (literally, the King-child).

faust. Happy; lucky. *Faustus* (as in Marlowe's play, 1588) is Latin for favored, from *favere, faustus,* to favor. E. Johnson in THE RISE OF CHRISTENDOM (1890) pictures *the Emperor . . . ascending the Capitol amidst faust acclamations in the Hebrew, Greek and Latin tongues. Faustity, faustitude,* good luck. Hence also *fauterer, fautor,* a favorer, abettor, partisan; *fautive* (of, to), favorable.

favel. The color, fallow, of a horse; hence, a fallow horse. Also *favell.* Then the *favel* (horse) was taken as a symbol of deceit and cunning; R. Edwards in the PARADISE OF DAINTY DEVICES (1576) exclaims *Oh favell false!* Hence, *favel,* flattery; *to curry favel,* to use insincere flattery to win favor. Hence, a *curry-favel,* a flatterer to win favor—corrupted by folk etymology (as early as 1500) to *curry favor.* Wyatt (OF THE COURTIERS LIFE;

1536) speaks of cloaking a vice with the nearest virtue, *As dronkenes, good fellowshippe to call . . . And say that favell hath a goodly grace In eloquence; and crueltie to name Zele of justice.*

favonian. Favorable, propitious, gentle. Latin *Favonius,* the west wind. From 1650. Keats (1821): *Softly tell her not to fear Such calm favonian burial.*

fax. The hair of the human head. Also *feax, facts, faix, vaex, vax.* From BEOWULF to 1600; survives in names, as *Halifax, Fairfax.* A *faxed star* is a comet, its tail being likened to hair. Rolland in THE COURT OF VENUS (1560) has: *With countinance and facts virginall.*

fay. See *fegs. Fay,* as short for *faith,* was common from 1300 to 1600; used by Chaucer and Spenser. *Fay,* as short for *fairy,* was common from 1350 to 1750, used by Gower, 1393; Collins, 1746, and is still used for archaic flavor.

fayned. A variant form of *feigned.* Pronounced in two syllables. One of Wyatt's best sonnets (1540) begins: *Unstable dreme according to the place Be steadfast ons, or else at leist be true: By tasted sweetenes make me not to rue The sudden losse of thy false fayned grace.*

fayring. See *fairing.*

faytour. An impostor; especially, a vagrant who pretends to be ill or to tell fortunes. Also *faitor, fayter*; Old French *faitor,* doer; Latin *factor,* from *facere, factum,* to do. (A thing done is a *fact, q.v.*) There was also a 14th and 15th century verb *fait,* to act or speak falsely, to beg on false pretence; to lead astray. Spenser (the gloss explains the word as 'vagabonds') in THE SHEPHERD'S CALENDAR (1579; MAY) says: *Those faytours little regarden their charge.* Scott uses the word often, as in THE FAIR MAID OF PERTH (1828): *Yonder stands the faitour, rejoicing at the mischief he has done.*

feague. (1) To whip. A 17th century word; the 16th century has the term *bumfeage,* to spank. Etheredge in SHE WOULD IE SHE COULD (1668) says: *Let us even go into an arbour, and then feague Mr. Rakehell.* (2) To finish off, 'do for'; Wycherley in LOVE IN A WOOD (1672) plans a *sly intrigue That must at length the jilting widow fegue. To feague a horse* was (1785, Grose's DICTIONARY) "to put ginger up a horse's fundament, to make him lively and carry his tail well." (3) *To feague away,* to set in brisk motion (as violins); to stir in one's thoughts. *To feague it away,* to work at full power, as Villiers in THE REHEARSAL (1672): *When a knotty point comes, I lay my head close to it . . . and then I fegue it away i' faith. Feague* (also *feak, q.v.*) as a noun, was used of a slattern, a sluttish woman.

feak. A dangling curl of hair. Marston, in THE METAMORPHOSIS OF PIGMALIONS IMAGE (1598) speaks of a man that *Can dally with his mistress dangling feake, And wish that he were it. Feak* is also a variant form of *feague, q.v.* Also, in falconry, *feak,* to wipe the beak after feeding. Also (16th into 19th century) to twitch, to pull (as one's vest); to fidget, busy oneself with trifles.

fease. See *feeze.*

feat. As an adjective, common from the 14th to the 18th century. Fit; apt; dexterous; becoming; neat (sometimes exaggeratedly; hence, affected, over-fastidious). Via Old French *fait* from Latin *factum,* made; *facere,* to make. Shakespeare in THE TEMPEST (1610) says: *Looke how well my garments sit upon me, Much feater than before.* Hence *feateous, featous, q.v.* Also *featish* (rare, 19th century), elegant; in good condition or health. *featless,* clumsy, inept, foolish (16th century). An anonymous epigram (SONGES AND SONETTES; 1557) *Of a new maried student* runs: *A student at his boke so plast That welth he might have wonne, From boke to wife did flete in hast, From wealth to wo to runne. Now, who hath plaied a feater cast Since jugling first begonne? In knitting of himself so fast Him selfe he hath undonne.*

featеous. See *featous.* The nymphs in Spenser's PROTHALAMION (1596) *with fine fingers cropt full featеously The tender stalks on high.*

featous. Well formed; artistically fashioned; elegant. In the Prologue to THE CANTERBURY TALES (1386) Chaucer says *Full fetise was her cloak. Featous* is via Old French *fetis* from Late Latin *facticius,* made, well made. It was understood in the 15th, 16th, and 17th centuries, however, as from *feat* (Old French *fait,* Latin *factum,* made, well made) plus an adjective ending, hence various adjective forms developed: *featly, featеous, featish, featuous. Cp. feat. Featly,* fitly, nimbly, deftly, precisely—Shakespeare in THE WINTER'S TALE (1611) has *She dances featly*—has not wholly lapsed from use.

feces. Preferably *faeces.* Also *faecal, faecical.* Hence *fecula,* less often *faecula,* sediment; plural *feculae.* See *fegs.*

fecula. See *feces.*

fedifragous. Faithless; treaty-breaking. From Latin *foedus,* compact, whence also federation, + *frag-, frangere, fractum,* to break, whence also *fragile, fraction, fracture,* and the like. *Fedifragous* (accent on the *if*) is a 17th century word, as also the rarer noun, *fedifraction,* breach of faith or covenant. Vicars' translation (1632) of Virgil said: *And let great Jove heare thus, whose thunders great Do truces tie, fright the fedifragous.* We could use Jove today.

fedity. Foulness, loathsomeness, material or spiritual. Also *feditee, foedity;* Latin *foeditatem,* from *foedus,* foul. Fotherby in ATHEOMASTIX (1619) states: *All these delicacies . . . when they come into the belly, they are wrapped up together in one and the same foedity.* The word was common in 16th and 17th century sermons.

fee-simple. Land held by the owner and his heirs forever, without restriction as to the heirs. *In fee-simple,* in absolute possession. *Fee* (Old Teutonic *fehu;* Old Aryan *peku;* Latin *pecunia,* money) meant property, wealth, hence cattle (*wild fee,* deer); then (by 900 A.D.) money. *Fee-simple* meant pure, absolute property, as opposed to *fee-tail,* property *entailed,* restricted to a specific class of heirs (Old French *taillier,* to cut, to fit, to limit; whence *tailor*). Shakespeare in HENRY VI, PART TWO (1593) says: *Heere's the Lord of the soile come to seize me for a stray, for entering his fee-simple without leave.* The word was extended to apply to anything held permanently or absolutely, also used figuratively, as by Burton (1621); Cowper (1781); also Shakespeare, in ALL'S WELL THAT ENDS WELL: *He will sell the fee-simple of his salvation,* also in THE MERRY WIVES OF WINDSOR: *If the devil have him not in fee-simple.*

feeze. As a noun: a rush, a swift impetus; a violent impact. Thus Chaucer (THE KNIGHT'S TALE, 1386). *In a feeze,* in a state of alarm or perturbation. Also *pheese; fese, fesyn, veeze, fease, feaze.* Lowell in THE ATLANTIC MONTHLY (December, 1855) said: *I am in a feeze half the time.* From the literal meaning come two phrases: *to* *fetch (take) one's feeze,* to take a short run before leaping; *to take one's full feeze,* to start at top speed. As a verb: (1) to drive, drive away, put to flight. (2) to impel, urge on. (3) in threats, to 'fix,' to beat, to finish off; Shakespeare in the Induction to THE TAMING OF THE SHREW (1596) says *I'l pheeze you infaith.* (4) to twist, to turn as a screw. (5) to insinuate into good graces, to flatter, be obsequious.

fegary. An early variant of *vagary.* Also *figary, fleegary.* Richardson in CLARISSA HARLOWE (1748) says: *The world must stand still for their figaries.* The word was also used to mean gewgaws, trifling fineries of dress, as in Tennant's drama CARDINAL BEATON (1823) : *As braw a hizzie, with her fardingales and her fleegaries, as ony.*

fegs. A corruption of *fay,* faith, used in exclamations and as a mild form of swearing. Also *i' fegs, q.v.* Sometimes in forms with *-kin,* a diminutive (as in *odds bodkins,* a corrupt euphemism for *God's bodykin*). Many variants have been used, especially by the playwrights: Jonson (1598, EVERY MAN IN HIS HUMOUR) : *By my fackins!* (1610, THE ALCHEMIST) : *How! Swear by your fac?* Heywood (1600, EDWARD I, PART ONE) : *No, by my feckins!* Middleton: *By my facks, sir!* Vanbrugh: *No, by good feggings.* Also *faiks, faix, fecks, fags.* These forms led to confusion with *faex, fex, dregs,* excrement (Latin *faex, faecem*; the plural of which, *faeces,* is the form that has survived in English), *faeces, feces,* which may also have been in the minds of the playwrights.

felicide. See *stillicide.* Latin *feles, felis,* cat. Note that Latin *felix, felicem* means happy, which gives us many English forms, including *felicitate* (as a verb, to make happy; to congratulate), used as an adjective in Shakespeare's KING LEAR (1605) : *I am alone felicitate In your deere Highnesse love.*

felicitate. See *felicide.*

fell. (1) The skin or hide of an animal; the human skin (as in the phrase *flesh and fell*) ; sometimes, the flesh just beneath the skin. Also, a fleece; thick, matted hair *(a fell of hair)*. Shakespeare in AS YOU LIKE IT (1600) has: *We are still handling our ewes and their fels you know are greasie.* A common Teuton word, related to *film*; also to Greek *pella,* English *pelt,* skin. (2) A high hill; a stony stretch of high land; a field atop a hill. From the Scandinavian; used from the 14th to the 18th century. In the 16th and 17th centuries used of marshy land, as in Drayton's POLYOLBION (1612). (3) Rarely, from Latin *fell, fel,* gall, *fell* was used in the sense of bitterness, rancor, as in Spenser's THE FAËRIE QUEENE (1590) : *Untroubled of vile fear or bitter fell. Cp. firth.*

femetary. An early variant of *fumitory, q.v.* Also *femetorie.*

femicide. See *stillicide.*

fenage. Hay crop. Via French from Latin *faenum,* hay. Used in the 17th century.

fencible. See *defensum.*

fend. See *forfend.*

fenerate. To lend money at interest. Latin *faenerare, faeneratum*; *faenus,* interest. Hence, *feneration,* lending money at interest; usury. Also *feneratitious,* given to usury; *feneratorial,* pertaining to usury; *fenerator,* a money-lender, usurer. Barckley in his DISCOURSE OF THE FELICITIE OF MAN (1598) declared that true love *hath respect only to his friends necessitie, without merchandize or feneration.*

feng. An early (12th and 13th century) form of *fang.* See *fanger.*

fennel. A plant, with fragrant yellow flowers. From it a sauce was made, eaten especially with salmon or eel; in earlier times, as a cure for overweight. Henry VIII used it; Falstaff refers to it as one reason for Prince Henry's liking Poins: he *eats conger with fennel.* The word *fennel* is from Latin *foenum,* hay: hay-scented. Fennel was also a symbol of flattery; mad Ophelia gave a sprig of it to Claudius who had flattered his way to the throne. The seed was taken for the hiccough; it was used, boiled in wine, for snakebite, as effectively as most other remedies of the time. In ancient Greece, *fennel* was also used to take off weight; the Greeks called it *marathon,* that which makes thin; and Browning in PHEIDIPPIDES (1880) sets the battle of Marathon on the *fennel-field.* Fennel was also thought good for the eyesight; we are told that serpents rubbed it on, to clear their vision. The corpulent might try it as a sauce; if the fennel doesn't reduce their weight, the fish diet may.

fenow. A variant of *finew, q.v.* For an instance of its use, see *panary.*

feracious. Prolific, bearing abundantly. From Latin *ferax, feracis; ferre,* to bear. From the 17th century; Carlyle in PAST AND PRESENT (1843) wonders at the *world so feracious, teeming with endless results.* (This is not a misprint for *ferocious.*) Hence, *feracity,* fruitfulness; also (of persons), profit.

feral. (1) Deadly, fatal; pertaining to the dead; funereal, gloomy. Latin *feralis,* pertaining to funeral rites. A *feral sign* in astrology portended doom. The EIKON BASILIKON (1648) spoke of *such a degree of splendour, as those ferall birds shall be grieved to behold.* (2) Wild, uncultivated —applied often to domesticated plants or animals that have reverted to a wild state. Hence brutal, savage; BLACKWOOD'S EDINBURGH MAGAZINE in 1838 spoke of a potent charm which *converts the feral into the human being.*

ferblet. Effeminate. Old English *forblete,* to make soft; *blete,* soft. Used in the 13th and 14th centuries.

ferd. (1) A military expedition. The word is used in this sense in Old English only; it is related to *fare,* journey. By extension, an army; a host; a great number; a troop, a band. Hence *ferdfare,* payment for exemption from military service (10th to 14th century); *ferdwit,* payment (in lieu of punishment) for murder committed in the army. (The Irish extended this privilege to civilians; *cp. eric.*) (2) Fear, terror. A noun use, in the 14th and 15th centuries, of *ferd, feared.* Hence also *ferdlac, ferdlayk,* terror; *ferdful,* fearful, dreadful; afraid, wary. Chaucer pictures a state of panic in THE HOUS OF FAME (1384): *He for ferde lost hys wyt.*

fere. As a noun. A companion (one that *fares* with another) as a *meatfere, playfere, suckingfere.* Hence, to *choose, have, take, unto (one's) fere.* Hence, a spouse, a mate; an equal. Thus *without fere,* without equal; *in fere, yfere,* together; *al in fere,* all together, altogether. By extension, companionship; a company, a party; also, ability, health. As an adjective, healthy (able to *fare*), strong; often in the phrase *whole and fere.* As a verb. (1) To *fare,* to journey, proceed, go on; behave; take place, happen. (2) To be proper, to be fit. (3) To be a companion to, accompany; to join, unite; to join together, provide with a consort. *Fere* was also a variant form of *far, fear, feer* (fierce), *ferry,* and *fire.* Other forms of the word were *vere, fer, feare, phere, phear.* Venus, Chapman reminds us in his translation (1611) of the ILIAD, which kept Keats awake—Venus was *the nuptial fere Of famous Vulcan.* Coleridge took up the word for THE ANCIENT MARINER (1798): *Are these two all . . . That woman and her fleshless pheere?* Southwell (POEMS, 1595) using the form to mean companion, punned: *Feares now are my pheares.*

ferial. This word has had odd shifts of sense. Latin *feria,* holiday, was originally applied, in ecclesiastical English, to weekdays (as opposed to the Sabbath) that called for certain observances, as Ash Wednesday. Hence, a weekday; then, a weekday on which no holy day or holiday falls. Thus *ferial,* pertaining to a weekday, as opposed to a festival. But there also continued in use the sense of a weekday to be especially observed; hence *ferial,* pertaining to a holiday; from the 15th through the 17th century, a *ferial day, ferial time* meant that the law courts were closed; Mrs. Byrne in UNDERCURRENTS OVERLOOKED (1860) said that Admiral Mackan *ordered that all works in the navy should be suspended on ferial days.* Hence *feriate, feriot,* vacation, holiday; also *ferie*; in his THRE LAWES (1538) Bale spoke of *Sondayes and other feryes.* And the rare verb *ferie, fery,* to keep holiday; *To abuse the sabbothe,* cried Hooper in A DECLARATION OF THE TEN HOLY COMMAUNDEMENTES (1548), *is as mouche as to fery unto god, and work to the devill.* Also *feriation,* cessation of work, holiday taking. Sir Thomas Browne in PSEUDODOXIA EPIDEMICA (1646) exclaimed scornfully: *As though there were any feriation in nature!*

ferk. See *firk.*

ferly. Here is one word, four parts of speech. As an adjective (from the 9th century), sudden, unexpected; frightful, terrible; strange, wonderful; wonderfully great. The same, as an adverb. As a noun, a marvel, a wonder; wonder, astonishment. *What ferly,* what wonder! As a verb, to wonder; to amaze. The noun and the verb do not occur before the 13th century. *Ferly* is from Old English *faer,* whence *fear* + *lic,* like, *-ly.* Also *ferlich, ferrely, farley, fearely, ferley. Cp. forferly.* Chaucer in THE REEVE'S TALE (1386) asks: *Who heard ever swilke a ferlie thing?* SIR GAWAYNE AND THE GRENE KNIGHT (1360) said that *Mo ferlies on this folde han fallen here oft Then in any other that I wot.* Longland's VISION OF PIERS PLOWMAN (1377) opens invitingly: *In a somer seson whan soft was the sonne I shope me in shroudes as I a shepe were, In habite as a heremite unholy of workes, Went wyde in this world wondres to here. Ac on a May mornynge on Malverne hulles Me byfel a ferly . . .*

fescue. A twig, a small piece of straw—sometimes used in allusion to the Biblical mote in one's neighbor's eys. Hence, a small stick or pointer used to help children learn. Common 14th through 17th century. Also as a verb, *fescue,* to guide in reading, with a stick (which may be a pointer or used to rap one over the knuckles); Milton in ANIMADVERSIONS . . . SMECTYMNUS (1641) speaks of a child *fescu'd to a formal injunction of his rote-lesson.*

festinate. Hasty. From Latin *festinare,* to hurry; *festinus,* in haste, quick. Shakespeare in KING LEAR (1605) has *Advise the Duke where you are going, to a most festinate preparation. Festinate* is also a verb, to hasten—mainly of the 17th century, but used by Shelley in a letter of 1812. Shakespeare also uses the adverb, in LOVE'S LABOUR'S LOST (1588): *Bring* *him festinatly hither.* To Suetonius we owe the caution *Festina lente,* make haste slowly, also rendered The more haste, the less speed. Noun forms are *festinance, festinancy, festination,* haste—as when one proceeds with festination towards one's destination.

fet. An early form, replaced by *fetch.* Also in phrases: *to fet again,* to bring to, restore to consciousness. *To fet in,* to take in a supply of. *To fet off,* to pick off (as a marksman does), to kill. *In fine fet,* short for *fettle, q.v.* Used from Beowulf; in the 15th and 16th centuries, mainly in the past forms. Chaucer, in THE SOMPNER'S TALE (1386): *Forth he goth . . . and fat his felaw.* Udall, in RALPH ROYSTER DOYSTER (1553): *Shall I go fet our goose?*

fettle. As a verb. To gird up, make ready, put in order; to get ready, to busy oneself; to fuss. Old English *fetel,* root *fat,* to hold. As a noun, a basket-handle; a girdle, a bandage. From the idea of being readied, *fettle* came by the 18th century to mean condition, state, trim, especially in the phrases *in good fettle, in high fettle* and—surviving because of the alliteration—*in fine fettle.* No one, however, seems to be *in foul fettle,* although Holmes in THE PROFESSOR AT THE BREAKFAST-TABLE (1859) remarks that the young man John is *in frustrate fettle.* I hope that yours is fine!

feuage. See *focage.*

feud. Also *feudum.* See *allodium.*

feu de joie. A bonfire; especially, one for a celebration or merrymaking. Direct from the French; literally, fire of joy. Used from the 16th century. Also (19th century), a military salute, consisting of guns fired in quick succession down one rank and up the next, so as to make a long continuous sound.

feuillantine. A small tart, filled with sweetmeats; an 18th century delicacy. The *Feuillantines* were French nuns, in the convent of whose order the pastry was probably first concocted.

feuillemort. See *filemot.*

feverfew. A plant, also called *feverfoylie; fettertoe; featherfew, featherfoy, featherfoil* (the leaves are a little like feathers). It was supposed to allay fever; the name is Late Latin *febrifuga;* Latin *febris,* fever + *fugare,* to drive away, whence also *fugitive.* Feverfew was the main ingredient in Henry VIII's *Medyicine for the pestilence;* but in the year of America's first blow for independence Adam Smith calculated that half of England's working class never reached maturity, cut down in the main by fevers, in spite of feverfew.

fever-lurden. The disease commonly called laziness. The name is coined in imitation of other disease-names; see *lurdan.* Also *feverlurgan, feverlurgy, fever lordeyn.* Jamieson (1808) explains *feverlargie: two stomachs to eat, and none to work.*

fex. See *fegs.*

feyntise. See *faintise.*

fico. See *fig.* The Italian form is *fico;* Latin *ficus,* fig.

fidge. See *fig.*

fidimplicitary. Putting full trust in another. Church Latin *fides implicita,* implicit faith. Urquhart in THE JEWEL (1652) speaks of *fidimplicitary gown-men . . . satisfied with their predecessors' contrivancês.* For another instance of its use, see *quisquilious.*

fidious. Short for *perfidious.* Thus used in Shirley's ARCADIA (1640): *Oh! fidious rascal! I thought there was some roguery.*

fig. In addition to the delicious fruit (in the north, usually dried and often pressed), *fig, figge, fygge, fico,* has had several other meanings. (1) A poisoned fig to get rid of a person; also *Spanish fig, Italian fig;* thus Gascoigne in HERBES (1577) warned lest thou *suppe sometimes with a magnifico, And have a fico foysted in thy dish. To fig away,* to get rid of with a poisoned fig, as in early Renaissance Italy: Pope Sixtus Quintus (died 1590). (2) Anything small, mean, or contemptible; also *a fig's end, a dried fig. Never a fig,* not the tiniest bit. Shakespeare in OTHELLO (1604) says: *Virtue? A figge; 'tis in ourselves that we are thus, or thus.* And in THE MERRY WIVES OF WINDSOR: *A fico for the phrase.* This moves toward (3) a contemptuous gesture: putting the thumb between the next two fingers, or into the mouth. Hence, *to give the fig,* to make this gesture; to hold in contempt. (There is an obscene allusion in Italian *fica.*) *To fig,* to insult with this gesture. For the insulting uses, *fig, figo, fico* were the preferred forms. There were other uses of *fig,* not derived from the fruit. (4) *To fig* (16th to 18th century), to move briskly, to jog about. This is a variant of *fike, fidge,* and the surviving *fidget.* Middleton in A CHAST MAYD IN CHEAPE-SIDE (1620) wrote: *Their short figging little shittlecock* [shuttlecock] *feet;* Urquhart in his translation (1693) of Rabelais: *their . . . figging itch, wrigling mordicancy.* (5) *To fig* (19th century) *to feague,* to make lively or spirited, *to fig up.* Also *to fig out,* to dress smartly. *In full fig* (possibly here *fig* is an abbreviation of *figure*), all dressed up; De Quincey (1839): *All belted and plumed, and in full military fig.* (6) *To fig* (16th to 18th century), to pick pockets. *Figboy,* a pickpocket. *Figging law,* the art of pickpocketry. *Figger,* a boy lifted to a window to filch the display.

figary. See *fegary.*

figee. A dish of sour milk and fish, eaten in the 14th century. Also *fygey;* Old French *figé,* a dish of curds; *figer,* to curdle. The name was soon confused with that of the fruit *fig,* and in the 15th century *figee* (now also *ffygey, fygee, figge*) was described as *figs* boiled in wine, or other forms of cooked figs.

figo. See *fig.*

figure-flinger. A figure-caster, an astrologer. *Figure-casting,* said Archbishop Abbot in his EXPOSITION UPON THE PROPHET JONAH (1600), *to judge of nativities . . . is a lying vanity. Figure-flinger* is a term of contempt for one who indulges in such practices; it was used from the 16th into the 18th century. Hearne in his REMINISCENCES (1723) stated: *Being much addicted to astrology, he gave over his trade and set up the trade of figure-flinging and publishing of almanacs.* Both terms were also applied (*figure-casting* by Swinburne in his STUDIES OF SHAKESPEARE, 1880) to persons that took a literal view of the world, 'casting,' calculating, with numerical figures only.

fike. (1) To move restlessly, to fidget. See *fig.* A very common word from the 13th century, still used in the 19th. The Scandinavian forms meant to move briskly, eagerly; and *fike* with this implication is probably the source of our most frequently unprinted four-letter word. (2) To flatter, to fawn; to deceive. Also *fyke.* Old English *gefic,* deceit, probably related to *faken,* deceit, whence (perhaps) *fake.* Hence also *fikeling,* flattery, in the CHRONICLE of Robert of Gloucester (13th century); *fikenung,* deceit (12th century).

filbert. See *fagot.*

fildor. Gold thread. Directly from French *fil,* thread + *d'or,* of gold. Also *fildore, fyldor.* Used into the 14th century, as in GAWAIN AND THE GREEN KNIGHT: *Folden in wyth fildore about the fayre grene.*

file. As a verb. In addition to the usual senses, to march in line; to rub smooth with a file (by extension, to polish, to perfect; Shakespeare in SONNET 85, 1600: *Precious phrase by all the Muses fil'd*), *file*—in this sense related to *foul*—was from the 14th to the 17th century (later, as *'file*) used as an early form of *defile.* Shakespeare in MACBETH has: *For Banquo's issue have I fil'd my mind.* As a noun. (1) A girl; especially, a concubine, a whore. Used in the 14th century. Old French *file*; Latin *filia,* daughter. (2) A worthless person of either sex. 14th and 15th centuries; related to *foul.* (3) *File, foyl, foyl-cloy, file-cloy,* a pickpocket (17th and 18th century). In the Motteux translation (1708) of Rabelais: *Pickpockets, divers, buttocking-foiles*: the last word is explained in Bailey's DICTIONARY (1721): *Bulk and file is, when one jostles you while another picks your pocket.* (4) The word *file,* meaning a line or rank, originally meant a thread; French *fil,* Latin *filum,* thread; *filare,* to spin, draw out threads. Hence, the thread of life; Sidney's OURANIA (N. Baxter, 1606): *The fatall sisters would not cut her file.* Also, the thread or tenor of a story; a catalogue, list. *To accept the files,* to open one's ranks for a charging enemy to enter, so as then to close upon him. *The common file,* the 'common herd'; Shakespeare in CORIOLANUS: *The common file—a plague! Tribunes for them!—The mouse ne'er shunn'd the cat as they did budge From rascals worse then they.* Tourneur in THE REVENGER'S TRAGEDY (1607) spoke *A word that I abhorre to file my lips with.*

filemot. The color of a dead leaf. The word is a 17th century corruption of French *feuille morte,* dead leaf. Also in the forms *feuillemort, fillemort, foliomort, philemort, philamot.* Browning in SORDELLO (1840) says: *Let Vidal change . . . His murrey-coloured robe for philamot, And crop his hair.*

filius ante patrem. See *coltsfoot.*

filoplume. See *filoselle.*

filoselle. A kind of floss silk, used in the 17th century; a cloth made of silk and wool. Also *filosella, philizella, philosella*; influenced by Latin *filum,* thread; but more directly via Italian from Late Latin *follicellus,* cocoon; *follis,* bag, whence also English *follicle.* The long thin feather of some birds, with an almost invisible stem, is called a *filoplume,* literally, thread-feather.

fimashing. See *fumishing.*

fimble. (1)"Hemp early ripe"; so Bailey, 1751. A corruption of French *femelle,* female; in popular terminology, the female hemp. Actually, what is called the *fimble* is the male plant of hemp, which yields a shorter and weaker fibre than the *carl hemp* or female plant. Popularly, the weaker fibres were called female, *fimble;* the stronger, *carl,* male. (2) A ring for fastening a gate. (3) (As a verb) to touch lightly and frequently with the tips of the fingers, as a woman may fimble a jewel at her breast; to move over or through without harming, as a scythe may fimble (i.e., not cut) the grass.

fimetic. See *fumishing.*

findal. That which is found, treasure-trove. By transference (what the mind lights upon), an invention. From 10th to 17th century. Used in the plural, *findals,* of goods from wrecked ships. The law does not quite concur in the olden claim Finders keepers.

fine. A a verb. Among lapsed uses are: To pay for the privilege of not holding, or running for, an office. Pepys in his DIARY for 1 December, 1663, noted that Mr. Crow *hath fined for alderman.* From the noun, which is from Latin *finem,* end (settlement). To make pure, to refine; to grow clear; to make beautiful, *to fine up.* From the adjective, which is from Latin *finire, finitum,* finish (whence also *infinite*), in the sense of *putting a finish* or polish on a thing. Mulcaster in THE ELEMENTARIE (First Part; 1582) spoke of *use and custom having the help of so long time and continuance wherein to fine our tung.*

finew. Mouldiness; mould. Also as a verb, to grow mouldy, to make mouldy. *Finewy, finewed,* mouldy. The last form existed (16th-18th century) in many variations: *fenowed, finnowed, vynued, vinewed, vinnowed, vinnied, whinid*; Shakespeare in TROILUS AND CRESSIDA (1606) has: *Speake then you whinid'st leaven, speake!*

finitor. Horizon. A translation of Greek *horizon*; Latin *finitor* from *finire,* to bound, *finis,* boundary, end. Used in 16th and 17th century astronomy.

firk. This was a very common word from the 10th into the 19th century. Also *ferk*; in some senses related to *fare*; a variant of *fike, q.v.* Among the meanings were: (1) To bring, to help on the way, to urge along; (2) to drive, to drive away; (3) to rouse (*firk up*); (4) to speed along, to move quickly or suddenly; to draw (a sword) hastily (*firk out*); (5) to beat, whip; (6) to raise (money), to cheat, to rob. Used in many 17th century plays: Jonson, THE ALCHEMIST (1610): *He . . . puffs his coals Till he firke nature up, in her own center*; Fletcher, RULE A WIFE AND HAVE A WIFE (1624): *These five years she has firkt a pretty living*; Shakespeare, Henry V (1599): Boy: *He says his name is Monsieur Fer.* Pistol: *Monsieur Fer. I'll fer him, and firke him, and ferret him.* The word was often used with sexual implications. In the 17th century, *firk* was also used as a noun, meaning a sudden blow (with a whip or a sword); a prank, caprice; a trick, subterfuge.

firman. Passport, license, permit. Originally an order issued by the Sultan of Turkey or other near-Eastern potentate; Persian *ferman,* Sanskrit *pramana,* command. Used literally in 17th and 18th centuries, more widely in the 19th, as in Barham's INGOLDSBY LEGENDS (1840): *a German . . . Paid his court to her father, conceiving his firman Would soon make her bend.*

firmance. See *firmitude.*

firmitude. Steadfastness of purpose; the state of being *firm.* Also *firmity*—though at least once (in Audelay's POEMS; 1426) *firmity* was used as a short form of *infirmity*: *To succour ham, in here fyremeté.* Other forgotten forms from *firm* include: *firmation,* the action of making firm, but also ratification, *confirmation.* To *firmify,* to make firm; to become firm; it would be a surprise to behold 'Casper Milquetoast' firmify. Also *firmance,* the holding firm; confinement; especially *to keep (put) in firmance,* but *to make firmance to* was to pledge loyalty to; thus Bellenden in his translation (1536) of Boece's HISTORY AND CHRONICLES OF SCOTLAND: *Als soone as Gillus was maid kyng . . . to stabil the realme to him with sickir* [surer] *firmance, he tuk the aithis* [oaths] *of his pepil.* Robert Copland in his translation (1542) of the FOURTH BOKE OF THE TERAPEUTYKE

[Therapeutic] OR METHODE CURATYFE OF CLAUDE GALYEN remarked: *They do use these names, dyspathies, metasyncrises, imbecyllitees, fyrmytudes, and sondry other such names.* Here *dyspathy, q.v.,* the opposite of *sympathy,* is used to mean antagonism (lack of susceptibility) to a disease; *metasyncrisis* is a medical term, explained later by Copland as "mutacyon of the state of pores and smal conduites." Further discussion must be dismissed with firmitude.

firth. A variant of *frith, q.v. Firth,* in the sense of grove, was the preferred form in the frequent phrases, in alliterative verse, *firth and fell, firth and field, firth and fold.*

fisking. Bustling, frisking, scampering. From the verb, *to fisk.* Usually scornful, as when the DICTIONARY OF THE CANTING CREW (1700) defines gadding-gossips: *waygoing women, fidging and fisking everywhere.* Even more so, in Harvey's PIERCES SUPEREROGATION (1593), against Nashe: *He hath little witt, less learning, lest judgement, no discretion, vanity enough, stomacke at will, superabundance of selfeconceit, outward liking of fewe, inward affection to none . . . no reverence to his patrons, no respect to his superiors, no regard to any but in contemptuous or censorious sort, hatred or disdaine to the rest, continuall quarrels with one or other (not such an other mutterer or murmurer, even against his familiarest acquaintance), an evergrudging and repining mind, a ravenous throte, a gluttonous mawe, a dronken head, a blasphemous tongue, a fisking will, a shittle nature, a revolting and rennegate disposition, a broking and huckstering penne, store of rascall phrases, some little of a brabling scholar, more of a raving scould, most of a roisterly servingman, nothing of a gentleman, lesse then nothing of a fine or cleanly artist.* [*Shittle* means fickle, flighty, unstable; also *shittle-brained, shittle-witted.* It is another form of *shuttle,* as in *shuttlecock; cp. batler.*] The Rules of Civility (1675) in THE ANTIQUARY stated: *Fisking and pratling are but ill ways to please.*

fitchet-pie. A pie made with apples, onions, and bacon. A North of England favorite.

fitchew. A polecat. Also *fitch, fitchet, fitcher, fitchole, fitchock.* The first and last forms were applied to persons, in contempt ("the skunk!"); Shakespeare in OTHELLO (1604), when Bianca, the prostitute, enters, Cassio exclaims: *'Tis such another fitchew! Marry, a perfumed one.* (In the mating season, the polecat is exceedingly demonstrative—and odorous.)

fitment. A making fit, preparation; that which is fit; one's duty. Used only in Shakespeare before the 19th century; then (often in the plural, *fitments, fittings*), in the sense of furniture, furnishings. In Shakespeare's CYMBELINE (1611): *'Twas a fitment for The purpose I then followed;* in PERICLES the Bawd complains of the consistently virtuous Marina: *We must either get her ravished or get rid of her. When she should do for clients her fitment and do me the kindness of our profession, she has me her quirks, her reasons, her master reasons, her prayers, her knees; that she would make a puritan of the devil, if he should cheapen* [bargain for] *a kiss of her.*

fizgig. An emphatic form of *gig,* which to Chaucer meant a frivolous person; to Shakespeare, a whipping-top. Hence *fizgig* (also *fisgig, fisguigge, fizzgig*), a gadabout woman; a top or whirligig; especially, one that makes a whizzing sound as it spins. Also, a hissing kind of firework, sometimes called a *serpent.* Also—possibly another word, from Spanish *fisga,* harpoon, *gar,* spear—*fizgig,* a harpoon; this was corrupted into *fishgig.* From the sound of the word, *fizgig* was later (19th century) used in the sense of a gim-crack, a piece of tawdry finery, a silly notion, an absurdity, as Southey in THE QUARTERLY REVIEW of 1822 spoke of *the banderoles, the humgigs, and fizzgigs of superstition.* A *gig* (also *giglot, gixy, q.v.*) meant also a giddy, frivolous girl; THE PLOWMAN'S TALE (1395) said: *Some spend their good upon their gigges, And finden them of greet aray.* Also (from the 16th century) a fancy, joke, whim; (from the 18th) fun, glee; *in high gig, on the (high) gig,* having lots of fun. Rogers in NAAMAN (1642) spoke of *any idle tale, or gigge of a geering, gibing wit.*

flabel. A fan. The Latin *flabellum,* fan, is used as an English word for a fan carried in religious ceremonies or courtly procedure; *The bishop's pastoral staff,* William Maskell notes, in IVORIES ANCIENT AND MEDIAEVAL (1875), *has not dropped out of use like . . . the flabellum. Flabellum* is the diminutive of *flabrum,* a gust of wind; *flare, flatum,* to blow, whence an *inflated* tire or ego. *Flabel* is also used as a verb—*flabbell'd by the north winds,* says Urquhart in his translation (1653) of Rabelais. Hence *flabellation,* fanning. The botanists and zoologists ring the changes, with *flabelliform, flabellifoliate,* and the like. In music, wind-instruments were in the 18th century referred to as *flabile.*

flacket. A bottle or vessel. The 1539 BIBLE (SAMSON) says: *Isai toke an asse laden with breed, and a flacket of wyne.* Also (possibly from the shape) a puff or bunch of hair, such as might hang on each side from beneath a lady's cap (16th and 17th centuries).

flag-fallen. Unemployed. Used first (16th and 17th centuries) of actors; the playhouse flag was lowered where there was no performance. Rowley in the appropriately entitled THE SEARCH FOR MONEY (1609) included *foure or five flag-falne plaiers, poore harmlesse merrie knaves, that were neither lords nor ladies, but honestly wore their owne clothes.*

flagitate. To importune, to demand earnestly. From the 17th century. Hence, *flagitation,* an earnest or passionate request. (Occasionally *flagitation* has been used in error for *flagellation.*) Latin *flagitare,* to demand earnestly; *flagitium,* eagerness; hence, a passionate deed, a burning shame, an outrage. This shift in meaning was carried over into English. *flagitious,* extremely wicked, villainous; *flagition, flagitiousness,* villainy, burning shame. Riches, said J. Keeper in 1598, are *the infamous offspring of covetousness, and guilty even of the same flagition.*

flagon. A large bottle for holding wine or inferior liquors; especially a metal one (carried by pilgrims before scofflaws) with a screw top. Urquhart in his translation (1653) of Rabelais points out that *the bottle is stopped . . . with a stoppel, but the flaggon with a vice.* Also, a large bottle for use at table, usually with a handle, a spout, and a lid. Scott, in THE FAIR MAID OF PERTH (1828), says: *He set the flagon on the table, and sat down.* A right good start!

flam. Possibly a shortened form of *flim-flam* or *flamfew.* (1) *Flim-flam.* A reduplication expressing contempt, common from the 16th century: idle talk; a cheap trick or petty attempt to deceive; nonsense. Probably from the Scandinavian; Old Norse *flim,* a lampoon; *flimska,* mockery. Hence *flambuginous,* sham, nonsensical, as in the SPORTING MAGAZINE of 1813: *The flambuginous sea-monster, known by the name of the Non-Descript.* (2) *Flamfew.* A trifle, a gew-gaw; a gaudily dressed woman. Also *flamefew, flamfoo.* This word is a corruption of French *fanfelue;* Medieval Latin *famfaluca,* a bubble, a lie. (3) Hence *flam* (from the 17th century): a fanciful notion, a whim; a sham story, a deception, a cheap trick; humbug, flattery. Common, in these senses, in the dramatists, as in Fletcher's THE HUMOUROUS LIEUTENANT (1625): *Presently, with some new flam or other . . . she takes her chamber.* There are three other words with the form *flam.* (a) *Flam* (from the sound), a signal on a drum: a quick beat, each stick just once, in rapid succession. (b) A watery, rushy place, where the *flambe* (blue flag, iris) grows. (c) A torch; short for *flambeau. Flam* is also a verb, to mock, to deceive; as when Ford in THE WITCH OF EDMONTON (1658) complains: *—And then flam me off with an old witch.*

flamfew. See *flam.*

flampoint. A pie with pointed pieces of pastry as ornaments. Also *flaumpeyn, flampett, flampoynte.* A recipe for *pork flampoint* is given in THE FORME OF CURY (1390): *Take gode enturlarded porke, and sethe hit, and hewe hit, and grinde it smalle; and do therto gode fat chese grated, and sugur, and gode pouder; then take and make coffyns of thre ynche depe, and do al this therin; and make a thynne foyle of paste, and cut oute thereof smale pointes, and frie hom in grese, and stike hom in the farse, and bake hit, and serve hit forthe.*

flatlings. Flat on the ground; (of a blow) with the flat side; (of motion) horizontally, on level ground. Also *flatling;* (16th and 17th centuries) *flatlong.* THE MIROUR OF SALVACIOUN (1450) said: *The knyghtes upon the grounde laide then the crosse flatling.* Scott revived the word in IVANHOE (1820): His *sword turned in his hand, so that the blade struck me flatlings;* so also Morris in THE EARTHLY PARADISE (1868).

flaun. See *flawn.* Stubbes in THE ANATOMIE OF ABUSES (1583) listed *some custardes, some cracknels, some cakes, some flaunes, some tartes . . .*

flaw. (1) A detached piece. Old Norse *flaga,* related to *flag* as in *flagstone,* and to *flake.* Thus: a snowflake; a spark. A fragment; especially, the point of a horseshoe nail broken off by the smith after it has gone through the hoof. Hence, *not worth a flaw.* Thus also, a broken piece; a break, a faulty place—whence the still current meaning, a fault. Shakespeare uses it figuratively in ANTHONY AND CLEOPATRA (1606): *Observe how Anthony becomes his flaw.* 2) A sudden gust or burst of wind; a short spell of bad weather (rain or snow and wild wind). Hence, a sudden onset, a burst of passion; a sudden tumult. Thus Shakespeare in MACBETH: *O, these flawes and starts . . . would well become A woman's story.* From its stirring in the wind was named the *flaw-flower,* a delicate plant also called the anemone (Greek *anemos,* the wind). Most piteously we read, in Shakespeare's KING LEAR: *This heart shall break into a hundred thousand flawes.*

flawn. A sort of custard or cheese-cake, made flat. Old High German *flado,* flat cake; West German form *flapon;* English *flapjack.* Perhaps related to Greek *plathanon,* cake-mold; *platys,* broad—whence the *platypus* and the philosopher *Plato.* Common, 14th to 18th century, as in the saying *flat as a flawn.* Also *flaun.* Scott revived the word, wisely remarking in THE ABBOTT (1820) : *He that is hanged in May will eat no flaunes in Midsummer.* Dekker, in SATIROMASTIX (1602), applies the word to a flat hat: *Cast off that blue coat, away with that flawne!*

flayflint. One so mean that he would flay a flint if he could, to profit by it. An earlier form of *skinflint* (which dates from 1700). *Flay* was often spelled *flea,* as *tea* and *tay* were interchanged, all with the long *a* sound; Shadwell in THE MISER (1672) cried: *A pox on this damn'd flea-flint!*

fleam. (1) A river. Especially applied, 14th-16th century, to the Jordan: *the flem Jordan.* Also, an artificial channel, such as a mill-stream; in this sense the word survives in dialects. Also as a verb, *fleam,* to flow; thus R. Buchanan wrote in 1863: *As the vapours fleam'd away, behold! I saw . . . a nymph.* (2) In medical use, a blood-letting instrument, a lancet. Via French and Latin from Greek *phlebotomon; phleb-,* vein + *temnein,* to cut.

fleawort. A plant the seeds of which were used to inspire prophecy. Its name comes from its supposed virtue in destroying fleas; the ancients, more literal-minded, named it Latin *pulicaria* (*pulicem,* flea), Greek *pyllion,* because the seeds resembled fleas. In the 16th and 17th centuries, it was used for ulcers, and (Lloyd, THE TREASURIE OF HEALTH; 1550) *a bath made of the decoction of flewort taketh away all goutes.* In Henry VIII's herb garden, fleawort and fennel (*q.v.*) were favorite plants.

flebile. Mournful (especially of literary or oratorical style). Used in the 17th and 18th centuries. The verb *fleble* (14th century) meant to grow weak. The two forms are from Latin *flebilis,* deplorable, to be wept over; *flere,* to weep, to lament. By way of Old French *fleible, fieble,* this gave us the still common English word *feeble,* pitiable, weak.

fleegary. See *fegary.*

fleer. A mocking look or speech; "a deceitful grin of civility" (Johnson). As a verb, to laugh in a coarse or impudent manner, to sneer; to smile fawningly. Common from the 17th century; Shakespeare in OTHELLO (1604) has: *Mark the fleeres, the gybes and notable scornes That dwell in every region of his face.* Carlyle in his REMINISCENCES (1866) gives us the one use of the word in a pleasant sense, an *innocent fleer of merriment.*

flemaflare. See *fleme.*

fleme. Exile, flight; a fugitive, an outlaw; to put to flight, chase, outlaw, banish. Common from the 9th to the 16th century; the early noun form from the verb *to flee*; replaced by *flight,* from *to fly.* Hence several Old English words, including (1) *flemaflare,* the right to forfeit an outlaw's property (in Bailey's DICTIONARY, 1751); (2) *flemensfirth,* the entertaining of a banished person; hence, a penalty exacted by the king for such entertainment. Old English *flymena fyrmth,* entertainment of fugitives. Old charters give this in many forms, as *flemenfremith, flemeneferd, flemenefenda.*

flemensfirth. See *fleme.*

fleshment. Excitement from a first success. From the verb *to flesh,* which in the 16th and 17th centuries meant to give a hawk (falcon, hound) some of the flesh of the first game killed, to excite it to further hunting. Hence, to initiate or harden to warfare; to harden (as in a course of evil); to incite; to inflame—by extension, to gratify (rage or lust); Shakespeare has, in ALL'S WELL THAT ENDS WELL (1601): *This night he fleshes his will in the spoyle of her honour.* Swift wrote, in A TALE OF A TUB (1704): *Fleshed at these smaller sports, like young wolves, they grew up in time to be nimble.* In Shakespeare's KING LEAR Oswald complains that Kent beat him *And in the fleshment of this dread exploit Drew on me here again.*

flet. The floor or ground beneath one's feet. A common Teutonic form; *flato,* flat. Hence, a place, a hall, the inner part of a house; a storey of a house, a suite of rooms on one floor, an apartment—in this sense Scotch until the mid-19th century; now *a flat.* Especially in the phrase *fire and flet* (sometimes *fleet*), fire and houseroom, often used in wills, as one of 1533: *to fynd the said wife . . . mete and drink, fyer and flet.*

fletcher. A maker of arrows; a dealer in bows and arrows. By extension (rarely), an archer. From French *flèche,* arrow. A common word until the 19th century; it survives as a name.

fleuron. A puff of pastry, for garnishing. So Bailey's DICTIONARY (1751). Also, from the shape (French *fleur,* flower), a flower-shaped ornament in architecture, printing, numismatics.

flexanimous. Persuasive, affecting; having power to bend the mind. From Latin *flectere, flexus,* to bend (whence *genuflect, reflect, flexible*) + *animus,* mind. Used in the 17th century, mainly in religious contexts, as when T. Adams (1633) speaks of *that flexanimous Preacher whose pulpit is in heaven.*

flibbertigibbet. A gossipy or frivolous woman; a devil. The first form (in a 1549 sermon of Latimer; in the first sense) was *flibbergib;* then *flebergebet, fliberdegibek,* and many more. Harsnet, in his DECLARATION OF EGREGIOUS POPISH IMPOSTURES (1603) said that *Frateretto, Fliberdigibbet, Hoberdidance, Tocobatto were four devils of the round, or Morrice;* hence Shakespeare took *the foule Flibbertigibbet* of KING LEAR (1605). Scott in KENILWORTH (1821) called the boy Dickie Sludge flibbertigibbet; hence, a mischievous, impish-looking urchin; a restless and grotesque person. Also *flibbertygibberty,* flighty, frivolous.

fligge. See *fraight.*

flim-flam. See *flam.*

flimmer. To burn unsteadily, as though near to dying out. An echoic word, suggesting quiet, or slight continuing or lessening action; thus *simmer, shimmer, glimmer, dimmer.* Per contra, rapid and violent movement is suggested by such words as *bash, dash, gash, hash, clash, lash, flash, plash, splash, slash, mash, smash, gnash, crash, thrash.* And as horror tends to constrict the throat, so *ghost, ghoul, ghastly, aghast.* The sound may be an echo to the sense.

flirt-gill. A light or loose woman. Also *flirt-gillian; gill-flirt. Gill* (Remember Jack and *Jill*) is a pet form of *Juliana.* Not in print before Shakespeare, who in ROMEO AND JULIET (1592) cries: *Scurvy knave, I am none of his flurt-gils;* Beaumont and Fletcher, in THE KNIGHT OF THE BURNING PESTLE (1613): *You heard him take me up like a flirt gill, and sing bawdy songs upon me.*

flite. Also *flitte, flight, flyt, flyte, fleyte.* See *flyting.*

floccify. To consider worthless. From the Latin *floccus,* a lock (of hair) + *facere,* to make, especially in the negative; *nec* *tamen flocci facio,* I do not care a straw. *Floccify* is a 17th and 18th century dictionary word; *floccipend,* to regard as of no account (*pendere,* to weigh, esteem) was somewhat more frequently used, as by W. Thomson, who observed in 1882 that the Bacon-Shakespeare field was one *prone to floccipend odd locks of thought from woolly-headed thinkers. Floccinaucical* means inconsequential; *floccinaucity,* a matter of little consequence. These forms are shortened from *floccinaucinihilipilification,* the habit of estimating things as worthless. This is a humorous combination of words linked in a rule of the widely used Eton Latin Grammar; Southey (1816) and Scott (1829) borrowed it from Shenstone, who in a letter of 1741 said: *I loved him for nothing so much as his flocci-nauci-nihili-pili-fication of money.*

floccinaucinihilipilification. See *floccify.*

florentine. A pie; especially, a meat pie with crust on top only. Various *florentine* recipes have survived. One is for *apple florentine*: baking apples, sugar, and lemon, under a crust. One of 1700 calls for *minced meats, currans, spice, eggs, etc., baked.* THE QUEEN'S ROYAL COOKERY of 1713 gives more detailed directions: *Take a leg of mutton or veal, shave it into thin slices, and mingle it with some sweet herbs, as sweet marjoram, thyme, savory, parsley, and rosemary, being minced very small, a clove of garlick, some beaten nutmeg, pepper, a minced onion, some grated manchet, and three or four yolks of raw eggs, mix all together, with a little salt, some thin slices of interlarded bacon, and some oister-liquor, lay the meat round the dish on a sheet of paste, bake it, and being baked, stick bay leaves round the dish.*

florilegium. An anthology. From Latin *flos, floris,* flower + *legere,* to choose, gather. A translation into Latin of the Greek *anthologion*; the Greeks had a word for it that survived.

fluctuous. Full of, or resembling, waves. Latin *fluctus,* wave. Used literally and figuratively, since the 16th century. Leigh Hunt in his AUTOBIOGRAPHY (1850) suggests a classification: *waves, wavelets, billows, fluctuosities, etc.*

flummery. A food: *from this small oatmeal, by oft steeping it in water and cleansing it, and then boiling it to a thicke and stiffe jelly, is made that excellent dish of meat which is so esteemed in the West parts of this Kingdome, which they call wash-brew, and in Chesheire and Lankasheire they call it flamerie or flumerie.* So Markham in THE ENGLISH HUSWIFE (1615). The word is from Welsh *llymru,* the *fl* being the English attempt to capture the sound of Welsh double *l.* Goldsmith in A CITIZEN OF THE WORLD (1760) speaks of supping on *wild ducks and flummery.* A common London street cry in the 18th century was *Flummery! Buy my flummery!*

flurch. A multitude, a great many; spoken of things, not of persons, as a flurch of strawberries. So Bailey, 1751, listing it as "North Country." It is not in the O.E.D. (1933), though anyone that will ignore a flurch of strawberries will turn from Izaak Walton and hunt red herrings in the wood.

flyting. Wrangling, contention; scolding; a reproach; abusive speech. Also *fliting; flyte, flite*; these two also were used as a verb, to wrangle; strive; scold. Used from the 10th century. Since the 15th century, also, a scolding-match; especially, in Scotch poetry, an invective in which each of two persons alternately abuses the other in tirades of vituperative verse. Hence *fliting-free,* unrestrained in rebuke or abusive speech. Also *fliter, flyter,* one that disputes; a scold. The words were rarely used, except in dialect, after the 16th century, until revived in the historical novels of Scott (OLD MORTALITY, 1816; THE ANTIQUARY). THE PARLEMENT OF THE THREE AGES (1350) remarked: *Fole is that with foles delys* [deals with fools]. *Flyte we no lengare! Cp. rouncival.*

fnast. To pant, snort. Also a noun, breath. Used from the 10th to the 14th century. Also *fnest;* related to Greek *pneuma,* air, breath. Also *fnese,* to sneeze; to snort; Chaucer, in THE MANCIPLE'S PROLOGUE (1386): *He speketh in his nose and fneseth faste.* Wyclif in his translation of the BIBLE (JEREMIAH; 1382) wrote: *Fro Dan is herd the fnesting of his hors.*

fob. To cheat. Used since the late 16th century; German *foppen,* to deceive. Hence also *fop; cp. cudden.* Also, to bring in, or palm off, by trickery. *To fob off,* to put off by a trick or with a cheap substitute. Shakespeare, in HENRY IV, PART TWO (1597): *I have been fub'd off and fub'd-off, from this day to that day;* CORIOLANUS (1607): *You must not think To fobbe off our disgrace with a tale.* A very common word, to the late 19th century; THE TIMES of 25 July, 1895, remarked that *if a . . . novel cannot be fobbed off upon the . . . people of London . . . it is rusticated.* Hence *fobbery,* a sham, deceit. From *fob,* a small pocket (German *fuppen,* to pocket stealthily) comes the verb *to fob,* to pocket, with implication of thievery or deceit; Lover in HANDY ANDY (1842) notes that *The gentlemen in black silk stockings . . . have been fobbing fees for three weeks.* A watch *fob* is a ribbon, with metal or other such ornament, by which the watch can be lifted (usually, by the wearer) from the small pocket (*fob*) in the front of the trousers.

focage. Hearth-money, a tax (12-pence) upon every hearth-fire, exacted at times in medieval England. Latin *focus,* hearth. Also *feuage, fuage,* from French *feu,* fire. While there is no call for a revival of this, the modern fireplace might restore to use the word *focary,* one who tends the hearth-fire.

focillate. See *refocillate.*

foedity. See *fedity.*

foin. (1) The beech-marten, or the fur of this animal. Via French *fouine* from Latin *fagum,* beech-tree; the animal feeds on beech-mast. Also *foyn.* A *foins-bachelor* was one that (16th and 17th century) wore a gown trimmed with *foins* in the London civic processions. (2) A thrust or push with a pointed weapon. *To cast a foin at,* to make a thrust at. This sense came via Old French *fouine, fouisne,* from Latin *fuscina,* a fish-spear. It was more common as a verb, to thrust, from the 14th to the 17th century; revived by Scott, as in WOODSTOCK (1826): *The fellow foins well.* Shakespeare uses *foin* twice in HENRY IV, PART TWO (1597) with sexual significance, as when Doll Tearsheet asks Falstaff: *When wilt thou leave fighting o' days and foining o' nights?*

foison. Abundance; plentiful harvest; nourishment; hence, vigor, vitality; in the plural, resources. Also *foyson, fusioun, fuzzen, fizon, fizzen,* and the like. Old French *fuison,* Latin *fusionem; fundere, fusum,* to pour. Hence *foisonable,* productive; *foisonous,* full of energy, fruitful; *foisonless,* weak, lacking nourishing properties. Shakespeare in THE TEMPEST (1610) hails *Earths increase, foison plenty, Barns* *and garners never empty.* Thomas Walkington, in THE OPTICK GLASS OF HUMORS (1607) used the word figuratively: *The foison of our best phantasies.* Lamb, in his FAREWELL TO TOBACCO (1810) cried: *Africa, that brags her foison, breeds no such prodigious poison.* Perhaps that fateful rhyme explains why the word *foison* passed from favor; tobacco grows more tardily obsolete.

foliomancy. See *aeromancy.*

follify. To jest, to play the fool. Also (Keats in ENDYMION; 1818) *to folly,* to act foolishly. Thus *follery* was an old form for *foolery; folliness,* foolishness. Via Old French *fol, fool* (also *folt, q.v.*) from Latin *follis,* bellows, puffed cheeks, possibly from the idea of being blown about by every wind or whimsy. Gilbert in THE YEOMEN OF THE GUARD (1888) wrote: *Here's a man of jollity, Jibe, joke, jollify! Give us of your quality; Come, fool, follify!*

folt. A fool. Also *folet, foult.* Hence *folthead, foltry,* folly. *Cp. follify.* In the 14th and 15th centuries; also as a verb, *to folt,* to act like a fool; *folted, foltish,* foolish. Drant in his translation (1566) of Horace's SATIRES wrote of *the foolishe frantycke foultes.*

foltron. An herb mixture, steeped; and the liquid strained therefrom, drunk in the 18th century. Wesley (WORKS; 1748) advised: *Try foltron, a mixture of herbs to be had at many grocers, far healthier, as well as cheaper, than tea.* Most awesome of such mixtures are blended by the Chinese.

fon. As a noun, a fool. Spenser in COLIN CLOUT'S COME HOME AGAIN (1595) has: *Ah! Cuddy (then quoth Colin) thous a fon.* From the 13th century. As an adjective, silly. Also *fonly, fonnish.* As a verb, to lose savour, become insipid. In this sense, the word is found only in the past participle, *fond.* By extension, to be foolish or infatuated, to be silly. From this springs the current *fond.* Also, to make a fool of; then more mildly, to *fondle,* to toy with. From this sense came the verb, *to fun,* to cheat, to hoax, to make fun of, which lapsed in the 15th century, but left the current noun, as in *Life may still be fun.*

fond. Also *fondnes,* foolishness. Wilson in THE ARTE OF RHETORIQUE (1553) declared that *the occasion of laughter, and the meane that maketh us merie . . . is the fondnes, the filthines, the deformitee, and all suche evill behavior, as we see to bee in other.* The hunched back; the slipped-on banana peel. See *fon.*

fonnell. A 14th century dish; recipe in THE FORME OF CURY (1390): *Take almandes unblanched, grynde hem and drawe hem up with a gode broth. Take a lombe, or a kidde, and half rost hym, or the thridde part. Smyte hym in gobbettes, and cast hym to the mylke. Take smale briddes yfested and ystyned, and do thereto sugar, powder of canell, and salt; take yolkes of ayren harde ysode, and cleeve atwo, and ypanced with floer of canell, and florish the seme above. Take alkenet fryed and yfondred, and droppe above with a feather, and messe it forth.*

fontange. A tall head-dress; a knot of ribbon on a lady's head-dress. Worn in the 17th and 18th centuries. Named from a mistress of Louis XIV of France. Addison in THE SPECTATOR (1711; No. 98) observed: *These old-fashioned fontanges rose an ell above the head; they were pointed like steeples, and had long loose pieces of crape, which were fringed, and hung* *down their backs.* Tate's THE CUCKOLDS HAVEN (1685) spoke of *fontanges of seven stories. Cp. commode.*

foolometer. A standard for measuring folly. (Accent on the *om.*) The term was coined by Sydney Smith in a letter of 1837; the device to be used as a test of public opinion. THE LONDON QUARTERLY REVIEW (June, 1847) remarked, of the court jester: *The foolometer of a European king in the middle ages was employed to mark the temperature of the public mind in an age of hypocrisy and terrorism . . . Anxiety to hear the truth, coupled with a wish to represent it as a folly, is the real causation of court jesters.* Our age has its various systems of opinion polls.

fop. See *cudden.* Hood in MISS KILMANSEGG AND HER SILVER LEG (1845) announced: *There's Bardus, a six-foot column of fop, A lighthouse without any light on top.*

forcible feeble. A weak person who makes great show of strength (physical or moral). Shakespeare first used the expression as a play on a name, in HENRY IV, PART TWO (1597); Shallow calls: *Francis Feeble!* but Falstaff rejects him as a recruit: *Let that suffice, most forcible Feeble.* The term came into wider use in the 19th century, as in Disraeli's CONINGSBY (1844): *Italics, that last resort of the forcible feebles.*

foredeal. An advantage. See *afterdeal.*

forfare. To pass away, decay, perish; to destroy. The past participle, *forfare, forfard,* meant worn out (as with labor, travel, age); Gower in CONFESSIO AMANTIS (1393) wrote: *As it were a man forfare Unto the woode I gan to fare. Thong Castle,* said the CHRONICLE of Fabyan (1494) *is now forfaryn.*

forfend. To forbid, prohibit; to avert, prevent. Shakespeare cried, of Joan of Arc, in HENRY VI, PART ONE (1591: *Now heaven forfend, the holy maid with child?* In KING LEAR, Regan asks the double-dealing Edmund, who has been making advances to her sister: *But have you never found my brother's way To the forfended place? Adam and Eve syneden,* said Wyclif in a sermon of 1380, *by etyng of the forfendid appul. Forfend* is from *for,* with the sense of prohibition or opposition (to *forsay* is to renounce) + *fend,* to defend, to strive. Hence, *to fend (off, back),* to ward off; *to fend for,* to provide for, look after. The phrase *to fend and prove* meant to quarrel, wrangle; Vanbrugh said, in THE FALSE FRIEND (1702): *Instead of fending and proving with his mistress, he should come to . . . parrying and thrusting with you. The prestis,* said Wyclif in his BIBLE translation (1382; 2 KINGS), *ben forfendid to eny more takyn monee of the peeple.*

forferly. To astonish greatly. From *ferly, q.v.* Used in the 13th and 14th centuries, only in the past participle; CURSOR MUNDI (1300) has: *Ful forfarled then war thai.*

forfex. A pair of scissors. The Late Latin word, used humorously in English, as in Pope's THE RAPE OF THE LOCK (1714), *The peer now spreads the glittering forfex wide, To inclose the lock.* Note also *forficate,* shaped like a pair of scissors, and *forficulate*: (1) shaped like a small pair of scissors; (2) as a verb, to feel a creeping sensation, as though a *forficula* (earwig) were crawling over one's skin; Bulwer-Lytton said in THE CAXTONS (1849): *There is not a part of me that has not . . . crept, crawled, and forficulated ever since.*

forficulate. See *forfex.*

forfret. Gnaw, corrode, devour. Hence *forfretten,* wasted away, destroyed, as in the translation (1440) of Palladius ON HUSBANDRIE, when he declares there is no help can save *the long endurid, old, forfreton vine.*

forgetive. Inventive, creative. Coined by Shakespeare, in HENRY IV, PART TWO (1597), of the brain: *A good sherris-sack . . . makes it apprehensive, quick, forgetive, full of nimble, fierie, and delectable shapes.* Not related to *forget*; probably from *forge* (via Old French from Latin *fabricare,* to make; whence *fabrications*), meaning good at forging. Writers after Shakespeare have used the word, as Cary in his translation (1814) of Dante's PURGATORY: *O quick and forgetive power!*

forhele. To hide. Old English *helan,* to hide. Past participle, *forholen.* Used by King Alfred, and into the 15th century, as in THE BABEES BOOKE (1430): *Schewe* [show] *it to thy freendis, and forhile thou it not.*

formication. A feeling as though ants were crawling over one's skin. Latin *formica,* ant. Hence *formicate,* to crawl like ants; by extension, to swarm with living beings; Lowell, in his JOURNAL (1854) of his trip to Italy, speaks of *an open space, which formicated with peasantry.* In 'modern' city households of the 1940's, a *formicary* (ant-hill enclosed in glass) was almost as common as an aquarium of tropical fish. Zeus, noted for his amorous transformations, turned into a swarm of ants to woo the nymph Klytoris, a formidable formicatory approach.

forsary. A galley-slave. Via Old French *forsaire* from Latin *forcia, fortia,* from *fortis,* strong (by force). King Henry VIII freed some *forsares* in 1546; but Strype in his ECCLESIASTICAL MEMORIALS (1721) of Henry's reign refers to *a proclamation . . . that . . . every such author . . . be committed into the galleys, there to row in chains, as a slave or forsary.* Also *forsar,* and *forsado,* from the Spanish galleys, which doubtless for some years held many English forsaries.

forsay. See *forfend.*

forsooth. In truth. Old English *for + sooth,* truth. See *sooth.* Very common, 9th through 16th century; also in phrases *forsooth and forsooth; forsooth and God; forsooth to say.* From the 17th century, used almost always as a mark of irony or derision, as in Pepy's DIARY for 25 March, 1667: *By and by comes Mr. Lowther and his wife and mine, and into a box forsooth, neither of them being dressed.* Also humorously or disdainfully: *a forsooth,* an affected speaker (Jonson, 1604: *a forsooth of the city*); *to forsooth,* to treat with (mock) ceremony, also in Pepy's DIARY, 1661. Bailey, in 1751, indicates a current style of address: "*forsooth,* a title of respect and submission used by a servant to a mistress, etc." "Please close the window." "Forsooth."

forspend. To spend completely, to exhaust; hence, to wear out. Since Anglo-Saxon times rarely used except in the past participle. Thus Sackville in THE INDUCTION (1563) to THE MIRROR FOR MAGISTRATE: *Her body small so withered and forspent.* Lamb in his essay on VALENTINE'S DAY (1821) speaks of *the weary and all forspent postman.* Lanier, in A BALLAD OF TREES AND THE MASTER (1884) fondles the word: *Into the woods my Master went, Clean forspent, forspent. Into the woods my Master came, Forspent with love and shame.*

forswat. Covered with sweat. Very common, 14th-16th century; even the King, said Barbour in his BRUCE (1375), was *wery forswat.* Sidney in his ARCADIA (1580) speaks of *a couple of forswat melters.*

forthink. (1) From Old English *for,* away, off + *thyncan,* to seem. To displease, cause regret to; to be sorry for. Thus Chaucer in TROYLUS AND CRISEYDE (1374) : *a thing that might thee forthenke.* (2) From Old English *for* + *thencan,* to think. To despise; to be reluctant; to regret; to change one's mind. One of Heywood's PROVERBS (1562) is *Better foresee than forthink.*

forthy. For this reason, therefore. Also *forthi, forthe.* Thus Henryson in his MORALL FABILLIS OF ESOPE (1480) said: *The morning mild, my mirth was more forthy.* Also *notforthy, nought for thy,* nevertheless; Barbour in his BRUCE (1375): *Undir the mantill nochtforthi He suld be armyt prevaly* [privily, secretly]. Also *what forthy,* what of that? And *forthy the, forthy that,* because; Maundeville relates, in 1400: *Thare also great King Nabugodonosor putte the three childer in the fyre, forthi that they held the right beleve.*

forwander. To weary oneself with wandering; to wander far and wide. Spenser pictures, in THE FAËRIE QUEENE (1590) *a weary wight forwandring by the way.*

forwean. To pamper, spoil by over-indulgence. Hence, *forweaned,* insolent. The word is from the 14th century, the act is perennial.

fother. A load, a cart-load; hence, a lot, a great quantity. Chaucer in THE KNIGHT'S TALE (1386) speaks of something *That coste largely of gold a fother. To fall as a fother* was used of a crushing blow. In the 18th and 19th centuries, there was a verb *to fother,* meaning to cover a sail with oakum, etc., to stuff a leak; also, to stop a leak in this way. A NAVAL CHRONICLE of 1800 said: *By foddering, and those excellent pumps, we kept her above water.*

fouch. The fork of the legs; especially, the hind quarters of a deer. *To fouch,* to cut (a deer) into quarters. Also *furch.* Old French *fourche,* fork. Other English forms were *forche, fourche, fowche.* Urquhart in his translation (1693) of Rabelais has: *My heart like the furch of a hart in rut dothe beat within my breast.*

fouldre. A thunderbolt. Also, *foudre.* Old French *fouldre*; Latin *fulgur,* lightning flash. Hence to *foulder,* to flash or thunder forth; *fouldering, fouldring.* Chaucer in THE HOUS OF FAME (1384) speaks of *That thing that men call foudre That smoot sometime a tower to powdre.*

foumart. The polecat, skunk. Old English *ful,* foul + *mearth,* martin. Also *folmarde, fulmerde, foulmart,* and the like. Applied to a man as a term of contempt; Jonson in A TALE OF A TUB (1633) : *Was ever such a fulmart for an huisher To a great worshipful lady, as myself!*

fourteener. A line of fourteen syllables; later often printed in two lines of four and three iambic feet respectively; two such broken lines constituted the standard ballad form. See *himpnes.*

foutre. "A word of contempt, equivalent to 'A fig for you!'" So Toone, in 1834. Used in the phrases *A foutre for; I care not a foutre.* Old French *foutre,* Latin *futuere,* to have intercourse. Also *foutra, fouter, fowtre, foutree, foutir.* Used in English since the 16th century; sometimes contemptuously applied to a person. Shakespeare, in HENRY IV, PART TWO (1597) cries *A footra for the world, and worldlings base.* Marryat has. in PETER SIMPLE

(1833): *O'Brien declared that he was a liar and a cowardly foutre.*

foxship. The character of a fox; astuteness, cunning. Sometimes used mockingly as a title. Shakespeare in CORIOLANUS (1607) queries: *Had'st thou foxship To banish him that struck more blows for home Than thou hast spoken words?*

foy. (1) Faith, allegiance; also used as an exclamation. From French *foi,* faith. (2) A parting drink, entertainment, or gift. French *voie,* way, "on your way." Also, a party before a wedding and the like; a tip. Richardson says, in PAMELA (1741): *Under the notion of my foy, I slid a couple of guineas into the good woman's hand.* (3) (As a verb) to bring provision to ships; to assist ships in distress; hence also *foy-boat* and *foyer,* one who goes to assist those in distress. Not to be confused with *foyer* in a theatre, where those in distress go.

foyn. See *foin.*

fracid. Rotten ripe, hoary and putrefied. So Bailey, 1751. From Latin *fracidus*; *frax, fracis,* lees of oil. It was once thought that (as in a letter of 1655) insects were *Natures recreation, which she out of the fracid ferment of putrifying bodies doth form.*

fraight. A variant form of *freight,* burden. Used in the 16th century; also *fraught.* Originally (15th century) *freight* meant the hire of a vessel to carry goods; also, passage-money. *To take freight,* to take passage, as in De Foe's ROBINSON CRUSOE (1719). Southwell in LOSSE IN DELAYES (1593) advised: *Crush the serpent in the head, Break ill egges ere they be hatched. Kill bad chickens in the tread; Fligge* [fledged], *they hardly can be catched. In the rising stifle ill, Least it grow against thy will . . . Single sands have little waight, Many make a drowning fraight. Tender twigs are bent with ease, Aged trees doe breake with bending; Young desires make little prease* [pressure], *Growth doth make them past amending.*

fraise. See *froise.*

frampold. Cross, disagreeable; (of a horse) mettlesome, fiery. Also *frampard, frampull, frampled, frompered* (Bunyan, 1688). Shakespeare, in THE MERRY WIVES OF WINDSOR (1598) remarks: *She leads a very frampold life with him.*

franion. A person of free or loose behavior; usually applied to a man; but Spenser (THE FAËRIE QUEENE, 1596) speaks of a woman as a *fair franion.* Lamb, in a poem of 1810, speaks of *Fine merry franions, Wanton companions.* Also spelled *fronion, frannion, frannian.* The old play KING EDWARD IV PART ONE said: *He's a frank franion, a merry companion, and loves a wench well.*

frannian. See *franion.*

frape. A mob, the rabble. Also *frapaille,* camp-followers, rabble. Used mainly in the 14th and 15th centuries. In the 16th and 17th centuries *to fraple,* to wrangle, bluster; *frapler,* blusterer, bully. The verb *frap* (French *frapper*), to strike, to whip, was common from the 14th to the 18th century, and thereafter in dialects. A *friar frapart,* originally a flagellant friar, in the 15th and 16th centuries, especially among non-Catholics, meant a libertine monk. The whipped confection, a *frappé,* was borrowed more recently from the French. Other forms from the same source are (17th century) *frappish,* peevish, and (19th century) *frappant,* striking, impressive. In Jonson's CYNTHIA'S REVELS (1599) is the accusation: *Thou art . . . a frapler, and base.*

fream. To rage, to roar. We are told (through the 16th and 17th centuries) that, especially at rutting time, *an hart bellows, a buck groyns . . . a boar freams.* Hence *frement,* roaring; *fremescence,* a rising sound; Carlyle in THE FRENCH REVOLUTION (1837) says: *Fremescent clangour comes from the armed Nationals . . . Confused tremor and fremescence, waxing into thunderpeals, of fury stirred on by fear.*

fremd. See *frenne.*

fremescence. See *fream.*

frendent. Gnashing the teeth. Latin *frendentem,* present participle of *frendere,* to gnash the teeth. From the root *fri,* to rub, earlier *ghri,* related to *grind, grist.* Lane in the CONTINUATION OF CHAUCER'S SQUIRE'S TALE (1616) wrote of *His frendent horse of manie colors pied.*

frenne. Strange. More commonly, a stranger, a foreigner, an enemy. Used in the 16th century. Also *fren;* altered from *frend,* correctly *fremd,* a common Teuton term meaning foreigner, enemy; also as an adjective, foreign, wild, hostile, strange, unusual. It is related to *from.* Child's collection of BALLADS has one that sings: *I wish I had died on some frem isle, And never had come home!* Spenser uses *frenne,* foe, in THE SHEPHERD'S CALENDAR (1579; APRIL): *So now his friend is chaunged for a frenne*—with a gloss explaining that the form of the word was influenced by *forenne,* foreign.

fret. As a verb. (1) To devour. A common Teutonic compound: *for + etan,* to eat; German *fressen.* Hence, to consume, to destroy. Used from BEOWULF to the 15th century; Chaucer in THE LEGEND OF GOOD WOMEN (1385) has: *into a prysoun . . . cast is he Tyl he should fretyne be.* The word grew milder, and is still used in the senses of to gnaw; to irritate, annoy; to worry. (2) To adorn with interlaced embroidery, as of silver or gold; to decorate elaborately. To form a pattern on; to variegate. Shakespeare in JULIUS CAESAR (1599) states that *Yon grey lines That fret the clouds, are messengers of day.* This sense seems to overlap the first, and a third, (3) to rub, chafe—via Old French from Late Latin *frectatum; frictare, frictatum,* to rub, frequentative of *fricere, frictum,* to rub, whence much *friction.* Sidney in the ARCADIA (1580) has the lover, seeing his mistress in the orchard, avow that *the apples, me thought, fell downe from the trees to do homage to the apples of her breast;* and he pictures a steed *milk white but that upon his shoulder and withers he was fretned with red staines as when a few strawberies are scattered into a dish of creame.* Delicious sense of imagery in those Arcadians! There were also (16th and 17th centuries) two verbs of the same forms, *fretish, fretize,* (A) to chill, benumb; from a lengthened form of Old French *freider* (French *froidir; froid,* cold) and (B) a variant of *fret,* to adorn, used especially in architecture, of the capitals of columns. Urquhart's translation (1693) of Rabelais speaks of *frettized and embowed seelings.* In the 13th century, from the first verb, *fretewil* was used, to mean voracious. And in the 17th century, a *fretchard* was an easily irritated, peevish person; *the angry fretchard,* said William Fenner (WORKS; 1640) *praies for patience and meeknesse and yet sets downe without it.* (There was also a verb *to fratch,* used in the 15th century to mean to squeak, to make a strident noise, and in the 18th, to scold, to quarrel.

Hence *fratcheous, fratchy, frachety,* quarrelsome; *fratcher,* a scold.)

fricandeau. The word is French, the recipe is Scotch: thin slices of veal, rolled with bacon and stuffed. Also *fricandel, fricadelle, fricando.* An 18th century delicacy, apparently spoiled by the English, for Bulwer-Lytton in DEVEREAUX (1829) observed: *I think her very like a fricandeau—white, soft, and insipid.*

frigerate. To cool. Latin *frigerare, frigeratum,* to cool; *frigidus* (adjective), cold; *frigus, frigoris* (noun), cold. *Frigerate, frigeration, frigeratory* are in 17th century dictionaries; only the noun seems to have been used, and all three were overlooked in the 20th century wave of *refrigeration.* Other forms forgotten include *frigidal, frigidious,* very cold; *frigiferous, frigorific,* producing cold (Shelley, 1810: *A frigorific torpidity of despair chilled every sense*); *frigitate, frigorify,* to cool, to freeze; *frigidize* was also used figuratively, as when Lady Gower tried *to frown her down and frigidize her.* Through the 17th and 18th centuries (still debated in the 19th) *frigoric* was supposed to be an imponderable substance that made things cold; Rumford (Tyndall said in his study of HEAT, 1863) *maintained with great tenacity the existence of 'frigorific rays.'* And—a rare 19th century use—a *frigot* is a person of frigid temperament.

frim. Vigorous; abundant in sap, juicy; plump, full-fleshed. From BEOWULF into the 19th century. Thus Drayton in POLYOLBION (1613): *My frim and lusty flank Her bravery then displays.*

friskin. One that likes to *frisk,* a gay, lively person. Nashe in HAVE WITH YOU TO SAFFRON-WALDEN (1596) said: *His wench or friskin was footing it aloft on the greene.* Also, a brisk lively action, encounter, or frolic; a *frisking. It was the custome of some lascivious queans,* said Burton in THE ANATOMY OF MELANCHOLY (1621), *to dance friskin in that fashion.*

frith. (1) Peace; freedom from molestation; hence, a game-preserve. From a common Old Teutonic root *fri-,* to love; related to *friend.* (2) (In this and the following sense, interchangeable with *firth, q.v.*) A stretch of wooded land; land covered with underbrush only, or a space between woods; hence brushwood, and (by extension) a hedge, especially one of brushwood; hence also, a fish-weir of brushwood. The origin of this word is unknown; it may be related to *fir.* (3) An arm of the sea. Used first in Scotland, reaching England by 1600; related to Scandinavian *fjorthr, fjord.* These are all very common, the first two meanings from the 9th century. *Frith,* peace, was used only historically after the 14th century; the other two are still to be found, as in Tennyson's IN MEMORIAM (1850): *The friths that branch and spread Their sleeping silver thro' the hills.* In the Middle Ages, the *frith-stool* was a (stone) seat near the altar in a church, which gave supposedly inviolable protection to one seeking sanctuary.

frith-stool. See *frith.*

fritiniency. Twittering; the noise of insects. Sir Thomas Browne in PSEUDODOXIA EPIDEMICA (1646) says of the cicado that its *note or fritiniancy is far more shrill then that of the locust.* Linklater in POET'S PUB (1929) records a conversation: *'The most significant noise of earth is the singing of birds,' said the professor with determination. 'Fritinancy,' declared the young man beside the fire.*

froise. A pancake with bacon in it. From the 14th century. Ultimately from Latin *frigere, frictum,* to fry. Also *fraise, froys,* etc. Gower in CONFESSIO AMANTIS (1390) tells of a man who *brustleth as a monkes froise When it is throwe into the panne.* Served, we are told, with a sweet sauce—the best is maple syrup. Good, too, even though (MONTHLY MAGAZINE, 1819) *the general . . . threw the froize out of the window.*

fronion. See *franion.*

frore. Frozen; bitterly cold. Also *froren, frorne; frory.* The old past participle of *freeze.* Used since the 13th century; Spenser in THE SHEPHERD'S CALENDAR (1579; FEBRUARY) uses *frorne*; Milton in PARADISE LOST (1667): *The parching air Burns frore, and cold performs th' effect of fire.*

frowze. A lady's wig, probably with frizzed hair. Also *frowes, fruz, frouze.* Worn in the 16th and 17th centuries. When Lady Jane Grey was on the scaffold, as Foxe told in ACTES AND MONUMENTS (1563), *she untyed her gowne, and the hangman pressed upon her to helpe her off with it, but she desiring him to let her alone, turned towardes her two gentlewomen, who helped her of therwith, and also with her frowes, past, and neckerchefe, geving her a fayre handkerchefe to knit about her eyes.* [*past* (*paste, payst*) was an ornamental headdress, probably with a *pasteboard* foundation; Greene in his VISION (1592) spoke of the bride *very finelie dizond in a little cappe, and a fair paste.*]

fructuous. See *infructuous.* Also *fructuate,* to bear fruit, literally or figuratively, as plans or ideas fructuate; *fructuation, fructuosity. Fructure,* the use or enjoyment of the fruits (of a tree or an activity).

frumenty. Hulled wheat boiled in milk, seasoned with sugar, cinnamon and other condiments. Also, a variety of wheat; especially, wheat mashed for brewing. Other forms of this word, common since the 14th century, include *furmety, fromenty, formety, frummetry, frumentary.* Latin *frumentum,* corn; from the root *frugi-,* fruit, produce. Beaumont and Fletcher, in BONDUCA (1614) have: *He'll find you out a food that needs no teeth nor stomack; a strange formity will feed ye up as fat as hens i' the forehead.* Massinger in THE BONDMAN (1623) pictures a man *licking his lips Like a spaniel o'er a furmenty pot.*—A person in a dilemma (19th century) was said to be in a *frumenty sweat.*

frush. To strike; to dash down; to crush. Also, to rush violently, to rub violently; to break, to be crushed. Also used technically: (1) to rub straight the feathers of an arrow; (2) to dress a chub; (3) to carve a chicken. Via Old French *fruissier* from a popular Latin form *frustiare,* to shiver into pieces; Latin *frustum,* fragment. Hence also *frushy,* brittle, liable to break. Also *frust,* a fragment, as in Sterne's TRISTRAM SHANDY (1765): *Such a story affords more pabulum to the brain than all the frusts, and crusts, and rusts of antiquity, which travellers can cook up for it.* Hence also *frustulum,* a small fragment; *frustulent, frustulose,* consisting of, or full of, small pieces.

frust. See *frush.*

frustraneous. Vain, useless, ineffectual. Latin *frustrari,* to disappoint; *frustra,* in vain. The 15th and 16th century verb, *fruster,* has been superseded by *frustrate.* Hence also *frustrable,* that can be rendered ineffectual; *frustrative, frustratory,* tending to balk. *Frustratory* was used in the 15th and into the 18th century; *frustrative,* in the 18th and 19th. Milton in his EIKONOKLASTES (1649) scorned *a most insufficient and frustraneous means.*

fucatory. See *infucation.*

fucus. A cosmetic, a coloring for the face. Latin *fucus* (Greek *fucos*), rock-lichen, used in English of a genus of seaweed. The lichen was a source of red dye, used as a cosmetic. Hence also figuratively, a false coloring, pretense, as when Young cries, in NIGHT THOUGHTS (1742): *Of fortune's fucus strip them, yet alive.* Hence *fucation,* painting the face, dissembling; *cp. infucation.* Adjectives are *fucal, fucate, fucatious, fucose, fucous,* painted, fair-seeming, falsified, deceitful. All especially in the 17th century, which gives us also the statement: *Frequent are fuco'd cheeks.* H. Hutton in FOLLIES ANATOMIE (1619) wrote: *Joves constant Daphne, timorous, perplext, His fucall arguments doth still confute.*

fulgor. See *fulgurate.*

fulgurate. To flash like lightning. Latin *fulgere,* to lighten. Many English words have come from this source: *fulgor, fulgour,* a dazzling brightness, splendor; *fulgur,* lightning (noun); *the fulgural science* means divination by lightning, and the priest that interprets the lightning was called the *fulgurator. Cp. fulminate. Fulgure* and *fulgurity* were other 17th century words for lightning. *Fulgurations* were lightning flashes, but in "chymistry" (Bailey, 1751) *fulguration* is *an operation by which all metals, except gold and silver, are reduced into vapours.* Carlyle in his essay on Diderot (1833) said that Diderot could talk *with a fulgorous impetuosity almost beyond human.*

fullam. A kind of false die, for cheating at dice. Also *fulham; cp. langret; bar'd cater tra.* Probably originally a *fullan,* a full one: loaded at the corner; though the O.E.D. also offers the conjecture that it may be from Fulham, "once a noted haunt of gamesters," an idea Nares (1822) had brushed aside: "nor is it very likely that gambling should have flourished in so quiet a village." A *high fulham* ensured a cast of 4, 5, or 6; a *low fulham* of 1, 2, or 3. Shakespeare in THE MERRY WIVES OF WINDSOR (1598) cries: *Let vultures gripe thy guts: for gourd, and fulham holds: And high and low beguiles the rich and poor.* Butler in HUDIBRAS (1664) builds a figure with the word: *One cut out to pass your tricks on With fulhams of poetick fiction.*

fulmart. See *foumart.*

fulminate. To thunder and lighten; to explode; to burst forth into violent or condemnatory speech; to denounce vehemently. The Latin *fulmen,* a thunderbolt, especially one that starts a conflagration, is also used as an English word. Other English forms are *fulminancy; fulminatory; fulmineous, fulminous. Cp. fulgurate.* Poets are less likely to use the verb *fulminate* than the form *fulmine,* which Spenser used literally, and Milton (followed by Tennyson and echoed by Lowell) used of speaking fiercely: *fulmined over Greece.*

fumacious. Fond of smoking.

fumade. A smoked herring (pilchard). Recommended by Fuller (1661) with oil and lemon. Also *fumatho, fumado, fair maid.* Spanish *fumado,* smoked.

fumage. "Smoke farthings"; hearth-money; a tax paid in Anglo-Saxon times, for every chimney in the house.

fumatory. A place set apart for smoking. In these days of *lubritoria* for automobiles, and the like, it is surprising that our motion-picture palaces do not have *fumatories* for the *fumacious, q.v.*

fumets. See *fumishing.*

fumidity. The state of being vaporous or fuming. Latin *fumidus,* English *fumid;* Latin *fumus,* fume. Over many factory cities (I write on the hottest recorded August 31) it isn't the heat, it's the fumidity.

fumishing. The excrement of wild animals (as the deer); also *fumet* (usually plural). From French *fumer,* Latin *fimare,* to dung; *fimus,* dung. Hence also spelled *fimashing.* Also (15th through 17th century) *fime,* dung. *Fimicolous,* inhabiting dung, is a scientific term applied to half a hundred fungi. Also *fimetarious, fimetic.* Ruskin, in THE NINETEENTH CENTURY for 1880, speaks of the *necessary obscurities of fimetic Providence* . . . A deer that's famishing will yield little fumishing. *Fumet* (Latin *fumus,* smoke, *fume*) was also used of the smell of game when high, of game flavor, as in Swift's STELLA AT WOOD PARK (1723): *A haunch of venison made her sweat, Unless it had the right fumette.*

fumitory. A plant (*Fumaria*) often mentioned by medieval and Renaissance writers; as *fumyterre water,* it was recommended for leprosy, choler, the itch, scurf, and tetters. Also *femetary; fumeterre, fumitery, femiter, fumiter,* and more; Latin *fumus terrae,* smoke of the earth, from the way the green-gray herb covered the earth. Chaucer lists the herb in THE NUN'S PRIEST'S TALE (1386): *Of lauriol, centaure, and fumeterre;* Shakespeare in HENRY V (1599): *Her fallow leas The darnel, hemlock, and ranke femetary Doth root upon while that the coulter rusts That should deracinate such savagery.*

fun. See *fon.*

funambulant. A rope-walker. Also *funambulator, funambule, funambulist* (current), *funambulo.* A *funambulus* (plural *funambuli*) was a rope-dancer, as indeed they all were, in the measure of their ability. Hence also *funambulic, funambulous, funambulatory.* Latin *funem,* rope + *ambulare, ambulatum,* to walk, whence *amble, preamble, ambulance* (originally a 'traveling hospital'). To *funambule, funambulate,* to walk on a stretched rope, tight or slack. The same words may be applied even though the 'rope' is wire. Sir Thomas Browne in CHRISTIAN MORALS (1682) used the word figuratively: *Tread softly and circumspectly in this funambulatory track and narrow path of goodness.*

furacity. Thievishness. Also *furacious,* thievish. Latin *furari,* to steal; *furax, furacem,* thievish. The word was used in the 17th and 18th centuries, then became pedantic, then became rare. The attitude it denominates has not grown less common.

furbelow. See *falbala.*

furca. A gallows. Latin *furca,* a two-pronged fork (whence English *furcate,* forked); hence, a fork-shaped prop, a triangular brace; hence, from that support, a gallows. Bailey (1751) speaks of a 13th century law, *furca and fossa* (Latin *fossa,* ditch) whereby male felons were hanged; female, drowned. *A furca for you!* was a fighting curse; though see *fig.*

furch. See *fouch.*

furfuration. The shedding of the skin in small particles like bran (Latin *furfur,* bran); the falling of dandruff when the hair is combed.

furibund. Raging with fury. Also *furybound, furebund.* Jonson in THE POETASTER (1601) includes *furibund* in a list of inkhorn words; Carlyle in THE FRENCH REVOLUTION (1837) speaks of *a waste energy as of Hercules not yet furibund.*

furmenty. See *frumenty.* Spelled *furmenty* by Mrs. Gaskell and others in the 19th century.

furnage. Baking; the price paid for permission to bake. Also *fornage*; via French from Latin *furnus,* oven, whence also *furnace.* In feudal days, tenants paid *furnage* to use the lord's oven, or not to use it (for permission to have an oven of their own).

furole. (Bailey, 1751): "of *feu,* fire, and *rouler,* to roll, French. A little blaze of fire appearing by night on the tops of soldiers' lances; or at sea on sailyards, which whirls and leaps in a moment from place to place: it is sometimes the forerunner of a storm. If there be two, it is called *Castor* and *Pollux,* and is supposed to portend safety, but if but one, it is called *Helena,* and is thought to forebode shipwreck." (Helen, sister of the luckier twins Castor and Pollux, who were worshiped as gods, was tangled in the Trojan War that brought disaster on both vanquished and victor.) Other names for *furole* are *corposant, q.v.,* and *St. Elmo's fire.*

fuscous. Dusky, swarthy, of sombre hue. Latin *fuscus,* dusky. Used since the 17th century. De Quincey in a letter of 31 July, 1855, wrote: *Some confused remembrance I had that we were or ought to be in a relation of hostility, though why, I could ground upon none but fuscous and cloudy reasons.* Ivor Brown in I GIVE YOU MY WORD adduces an amusing instance from a play, THE DEVIL AND THE LADY, that Tennyson wrote at the age of fourteen. A character, finding the Devil disguised as a woman, exclaims: *What jejune, undigested joke is this, To quilt thy fuscous haunches with the flounced Frilled, finical delicacy of female dress? Hast thou dared to girdle thy brown sides And prop thy monstrous vertebrae with stays?* In technical terms *fusco* is a combining form meaning dull, dusky: *fusco-ferruginous,* dull rust-colored; *fusco-piceous,* dull reddish-black; *fusco-testaceous,* dull reddish-brown.

fust. A wine-cask (15th century); by extension, a smell "as of a mouldy barrel" (Johnson, 1755); *cp. fustilugs.* Hence, *to fust,* to become mouldy, stale-smelling. *He that made us,* says Shakespeare in HAMLET (1604), *gave us not That capabilitie and god-like reason To fust in us unusd.*

fustigate. To cudgel. Latin *fustigare, fustigatum,* to beat to death; *fustis,* a knobbed stick. Used from the 17th to the mid-19th century; now only for humorous effect. The Earl of Bristol exclaimed, in 1667: *Heaven send him a light hand, to whom my fustigation shall belong!* Hence also *fustigator,* whipper.

fustilarian. A term of contempt. Perhaps compounded from *fustilugs* (*q.v.*), with the ending *-arian* implying old (as in *centenarian,* etc.). For an instance of its use in Shakespeare, see *catastrophe.*

fustilugs. A fat, frowzy woman (*fusty,* mouldy + *lugs,* implying heavy). Burton in THE ANATOMY OF MELANCHOLY (1621) states that *every lover admires his mistress, though she be . . . a vast virago, or . . . a fat fustylugs. Fusty* (from *fust,* a wine cask, *q.v.*) was used to mean stale (wine too long in the cask); then mouldy bread; then anything no longer fresh; seedy, dull.

Shakespeare in TROILUS AND CRESSIDA (1606) says *At this fusty stuff The large Achilles . . . laughs out a lowd applause.* Hence *fusty-rusty,* out-of-date, old-fashioned; ill-humored.

fusty. See *fustilugs.*

fyke. See *fike.*

fylfot. A cross cramponee, a swastika. This symbol, sometimes turning clockwise, sometimes counter-clockwise, is found in many lands at many times. The Greeks formed it by a combination of the letter *gamma* (Γ) four times at right angles, and called it a *gammadion.* The American Indians had a cross representing the four directions; on the end of each limb stood the god of the wind, north, east, south, west. The figure was often used in series as a decoration; hence *fylfot,* to *fill the foot* of a stained glass or painted window. But it also, from prehistoric times, was taken as a mystical or magic symbol; hence *swastika,* from Sanskrit *svastika,* well; *su,* good + *as,* to be. Recent use has belied the ancient meaning. A *fylfot* (pronounced fill′-fot) was also called *the cross of Thor.*

G

gabelle. A tax. Used in the 15th and 16th centuries as *gabel, gable*; related to *gavel, q.v.* The word was then forgotten; revived as a foreign word (French *gabelle),* referring to Italy and France; especially, the tax on salt in France before the French Revolution. Dickens, in A TALE OF TWO CITIES (1859) calls the farmer-general (tax collector) *M. Gabelle.*

gaberdine. A loose upper garment of coarse material, as worn by pilgrims, hence, by beggars; after Shakespeare in THE MERCHANT OF VENICE (1596), applied to Jews. In THE TEMPEST Shakespeare has Trinculo, come upon Caliban in the storm, for protection *creep under his gaberdine,* whence the word is sometimes used to mean protection, as when Lord Bentinck in the CROKER PAPERS for 8 September, 1847, said: *They have crawled into the House of Commons under the gabardine of the Whigs.*

gad. See *garabee*; *cp. gadling.*

gadbee. See *garabee.*

gadfly. See *garabee.*

gadling. Originally, a companion, from the Old English *gaed,* fellowship + *ling* (diminutive personal suffix, as in *darling, duckling*). Then it was applied to a companion on a trip; hence, to a traveler, and finally to a vagabond. From the sense of wanderer, by back-formation came the verb *to gad,* whence also a *gadabroad* and the more frequent *gadabout. Gadling* appears from BEOWULF (10th century) through the 17th century, as in a poem by Wyatt in Tottel's MISCELLANY (1542): *The wandring gadling, in the summertide, That finds the Adder with his reckless foot.*

gaffer. An old man, a "grandfather." Sometimes used as a title or form of address, to a man below the rank of Master, as when Scott in THE FAIR MAID OF PERTH (1828) says: *You have marred my ramble, Gaffer Glover. Gaffer* was probably a contraction of *godfather,* with the vowel changing to *a* because of association with *grandfather.* So, for the female, with *gammer, q.v.* Occasionally used humorously, as when Randolph in HEY FOR HONESTY (1651) says: *This same gaffer Phoebus is a good mountebank and an excellent musician.*

gain. An adjective. Used first (10th century) of roads: straight, direct; *the gainest way,* the shortest way. Old Norse *gegn,* straight, favorable, helpful. Hence, ready, well-disposed, kindly; available, convenient, useful. Also *geyn, gane, gayne.* The early form *gegn* (Modern German *gegen*) meant both directly towards and (as a consequence) opposite to, contrary to, *against.* Hence as a prefix, *gain-* meant against, or in return (as a counter-stroke); it survives in *gainsay*; it was used in *gainsaw,* a contradiction; *gainspeaker,* an opponent; *gainbuy,* to redeem, also *gain-*

buying. Also *gaincall,* to revoke, withdraw. *gainchare,* a way of returning, means of escape. *gainshire,* the barb of a fishing-hook; a barb on the tang of a knife, to prevent its coming free of the handle (the term is still used in cutlery). *gainstand,* opposition. *gainstrive,* to oppose. *gainturn,* a turning back, evasion. From the adjective *gain* was formed a second adjective, *gainly,* (*ganely*), proper, becoming; helpful, gracious; graceful, shapely—the opposite of the still current *ungainly.* The original sense of *gain* is preserved in the Midland proverb: *Roundabout is sometimes gainest:* The longest way round is the sweetest way home.

gain-. See *gain.*

gainchar. See *chare; cp. gain.*

gainsay. See *againsay; gain.*

gaipand. A variant form of *gaping.* The ending *-and* was frequent for *-ing* in early Northern and Scottish words. In a lyric of Dunbar (1508) we are reminded that *Deth followis lyfe with gaipand mowth.*

gair. See *gore.*

galage. An early form (in Chaucer; in Spenser's THE SHEPHERD'S CALENDAR, 1579) of *galosh.* Also *golosh, galoge, galache, galoshoes,* etc. The *galage* was a wooden shoe or sandal with leather thongs; later (17th century), an overshoe. Spenser's gloss explains *galage* as 'a start-uppe or clownish shoe,' clownish meaning peasant's.

galantine. See *galentine.* Chaucer in TO ROSEMOUNDE (1400) *Nas never pyk walwed in galauntyne As I in love am walwed and ywounde.* The spelling *galantine* grew from folk association with (French) *galant* (*cp. gallant*), agreeable, pleasing.

galanty show. A shadow show; shadows of miniature figures are thrown on a wall or screen. Also *gallantee, gallanty;* accent usually on the *ant.* Performed in the early 19th century, by 1860 Mayhew declared (in LONDON LABOUR AND THE LONDON POOR): *The galantee show don't answer, because magic lanterns are so cheap in the shops.* It has, however, survived in children's play; I saw a lively production of a galantee show in a children's camp last summer.

galder. See *sigalder.*

gale. (1) A plant, the bog-myrtle, also called *sweet gale,* from the twigs of which *gale-beer* is made. Crabbe in THE BIRTH OF FLATTERY (1807) says: *Gale from the bog shall yield Arabian balm.* (2) The current sense of a very strong wind was long softened, in poetry and figurative discourse, to a gentle breeze. Addison, in THE SPECTATOR (No. 56, 1711): *He felt a gale of perfumes breathing upon him;* Massinger, in THE DUKE OF MILAN (1623): *One gale of your sweet breath will easily Disperse these clouds;* Marvell in a letter of 1669 hopes for *some unexpected gaile of opportunity.* (3) A periodical payment of rent, or the rent thus paid. *Hanging-gale,* rent in arrears. Used from the 17th into the 19th century; perhaps a contraction of *gavel, q.v.* (4) Singing, a song; merriment. This sense is related to Old English *galen,* to sing; Italian (and thence English) *gala*—but this sense died in the 14th century; KYNG ALYSAUNDER in the 13th century said: *The nyghtyngale In woode, makith mery gale.*

galentine. A sauce. Also *galyntyne; cp. galantine.* A recipe is given in THE FORME OF CURY (1390): *Take crustes of bred, and grynde hem smalle. Do thereto powdor of galyngale, of canel, gyngyves, and salt it. Tempre it with vynegar, and* *draw it up thrugh a straynor, and messe it forth.* Hence, a dish of sopped bread and spices. Later used of other dishes, as veal, chicken, or other white meat, boned, tied, boiled, and served cold in its jelly.

galingale. A mildly aromatic root of East India, used in medicines and in cookery. Bailey in 1736 listed as tasty condiments *cardamums, cloves, cubebs, galangal, ginger, mace, and nutmegs.* The word is via French and Arabic from Chinese *Ko-liang-kiang,* mild ginger from Ko (in Canton province). Also applied to the English sedge. Especially, a dish seasoned with *galingale,* as in Beaumont and Fletcher's THE BLOODY BROTHER (1616): *Put in some of this* [poison], *the matter's ended; dredge you a dish of plovers, there's the art on't; or in a galingale, a little does it.* Tennyson pictured the land of the Lotus-Eaters (1833): *Border'd with palm and many a winding vale, And meadow, set with slender galingale.*

galiot. See *galliot.*

gallant (verb; accented on the second syllable). To play the gallant; to flirt with; to escort. *To gallant a fan* was to break a fan (intentionally, but as though by accident), so as to win permission to present a better one. Thus Addison in THE SPECTATOR, No. 102 (1711): *I teach young gentlemen the whole art of gallanting a fan. N.B. I have several little plain fans made for this use, to avoid expense. Gallant* is related to *gala;* Old French *galer,* to make merry. Other forms are *gallantise,* courtliness, *gallantry; gallantize,* to play the gallant, to court (Urquhart in his translation, 1693, of Rabelais has *to gallantrize it*); *to be gallantified* was used humorously (17th century) meaning to be whipped.

galleon. See *galliot.*

galley. See *galliot.*

galliard. As an adjective: valiant, sturdy; full of high spirits, lively, gay; spruce, gay in looks. Also *gaillard, galyeard, gagliard,* and more. Chaucer in THE COOK'S TALE (1386) says: *Gaillard he was as goldfinch in the shawe.* As a noun: (1) A man of spirit; a gay fellow, a man of fashion. (2) A lively dance, in triple time. Shakespeare asks, in TWELFTH NIGHT (1601): *Why dost thou not goe to church in a galliard, and come home in a carranto? Cp. coranto; pavan.* Hence *galliardise,* gaiety, revelry; a merry prank.

galliass. See *galliot.*

galligaskin. A kind of tight-buttocked wide hose or breeches worn in the 16th and 17th centuries; later, it became a term of ridicule for breeches wide at the knee. French *garguesque,* from Italian *grechesco,* Greek style (*alla grechesca*). Usually plural; also *gaskins; gallybreeches; gallyslops; gallygaskins, garragascoyne, galigascon, and more.* Also, from its appearance, the flower the cowslip. Used figuratively in THE POETICAL REGISTER of 1794: *While in rhyme's galligaskins I enclose The broad posteriors of thy brawny prose.* Sterne says, in TRISTRAM SHANDY (1761): *His whole thoughts . . . were taken up with a transaction which was going forwards . . . within the precincts of his own galligaskins.*

gallimaufry. A dish, hashed out of odds and ends; hence, a confused or ridiculous mixture; a foolish medley. Also, a haphazardly mixed assemblage, or collection of persons; Shakespeare in THE MERRY WIVES OF WINDSOR (1598) says: *He wooes both high and low . . . he loves the gallymawfry.* Occasionally applied in scorn to a person, a Jack-of-all-accomplishments, a fellow of many parts. Thus *gallimaufrical,* mixed up; miscellaneous. As a verb, *to gallimaufry,* to confuse, to make mincemeat of; also, a *gallimaufrier,* one who messes or mixes things up. Nashe, attacking Gabriel Harvey in STRANGE NEWES (1593; for Harvey's thrust, see *bum*), concluded: *From this time forth for ever, ever, ever, evermore maist thou be canonized as the nunparreille of impious epistles, the short shredder out of sunday sentences without lime, as Quintillian tearmed Seneca all lime and no sande; all matter and no circumstance; the factor for the fairies and night urchins, in supplanting and setting aside the true children of the English, and suborning inkehorne changelings in their steade, the gallimafrier of all stiles in one standish, as imitating everie one, and having no seperate forme of thy owne; and to conclude, the onely feather-driver of phrases, and putter of a good word to it when thou hast once got it, that is betwixt this and the Alpes. So bee it worlde without ende. Chroniclers heare my praiers.* This one has heard.

galliot. A small swift boat, propelled by sails and oars; especially, one used in Mediterranean waters. Hence, a sailor or rower on a galley (slave or free); by extension (15th century), a pirate. Also *galiote, galyete, galyote, galleot.* Via French, and Italian *galeotta,* diminutive of Latin *galea,* galley. The *galley* was a low, one-deck sea-going vessel, propelled by sails and oars; the rowers were usually slaves or condemned criminals. The *galliass—galleass, galliace, galeaze—*was larger than a *galley* and used mainly in war. The *gallivat—galleywat, gallevat—*was larger than a *galliot*; it was used in the Eastern seas, and had a triangular sail. The *galleon* was a ship of war, higher but shorter than the *galley*; after the 15th century, however, *galleon* was used mainly for the large merchantmen with which the Spanish carried on trade with their possessions in America. Also *galion, galeoon, galloon.* For a while, because of the British privateers' raids on Spanish shipping, *galleon* was used to mean a fine catch, a prize, as in Farquhar's THE BEAUX STRATAGEM (1706): *This prize will be a galleon . . . I warrant you we shall bring off three or four thousand pound.*

galp. (1) To yelp. Caxton's translation (1481) of THE HISTORYE OF REYNART THE FOXE stated: *He mawede and galped so lowde that martynet sprang up.* Old Saxon *galpon,* to boast; Dutch *galpen,* to bark, yelp; *yelp* is another form of this word. By association with *gape,* however, *galp* more frequently (14th to 17th century) meant to yawn, to gape; to vomit forth; also to gape after in desire, as in the AENEIS of Stanyhurst (1583), which pictures *Charybdis with broad jaws greedelye galping.* Chaucer in THE SQUIRE'S TALE (1386) has: *With a galpyng mouth them alle he keste.*

gambade. One of the forms of *gambol*; also *gambad, gambado, gambawd, gambauld, gambal, gamboil, gambole.* Via French from Italian *gambata,* leap; *gamba,* leg—English slang speaks of a girl's *gams*; French *jambe.* The word meant first the leap or curvet of a horse; then, a leap in dancing or play; then, a frolic. *Gambado* (frequent in the 19th century, after Scott's use in THE MONASTERY, 1820) had the same meanings, but from the 17th century was also used of leather leggings or, especially, of a boot attached to a saddle, to protect the rider's leg from wet and cold. *Gambol* is used as both noun and verb; *gambade* was revived by Scott as a noun only—as a leap: QUENTIN DURWARD, 1823, *Each fresh gam-*

bade of his unmanageable horse placed him in a new and more precarious attitude—of a prank: JOURNAL, 1825, *To Southey I wrote . . . touching on . . . his innocence as to those gambades that may have given offence.*

gammadion. See *fylfot.*

gammer. An old woman, a "grandmother." A lusty old English comedy is *Gammer Gurton's Needle* (1575) by J. Still. Hence, *to gammer,* to idle, to go gossiping about. See *gaffer.*

gammon. A ham; the bottom of a flitch of bacon, with the hind leg; a smoked ham. From pressing one's ham against the victim, *to give gammon,* in 18th century thieves' slang, was used to mean to press against a man while a confederate picks his pocket. By extension, to distract the victim's attention in any way; hence *gammon,* idle talk, chatter; nonsense, humbug. In this sense, the word is often used as an exclamation, as in Thackeray's THE ROSE AND THE RING (1855): *"Gammon!" exclaimed his Lordship.* Also in the sense of nonsense, phrases were used such as *gammon and patter* (also meaning the stock phrases in any field) and—from what was often served with smoked ham, *gammon and spinach. Gammon* is from Old Norman French *gambon,* ham, *gambe,* leg; modern French *jambon; cp. gambade. What a world of gammon and spinnach it is!* says Miss Moucher in DAVID COPPERFIELD. *Heigh ho!* says Anthony Rowley.

ganch. To execute by impaling on stakes or hooks. The victim was raised by a pulley, then let fall. Women in the Near East were drowned; men were *ganched.* Also *gaunch. Cp. furca.* The word was also applied to a boar's gashing with its tusks. A ganched man might hang for several days before he died. Spanish *gancho,* Italian *gancio,* hook. The noun *ganch* named the apparatus used for such execution.

gangrel. A vagabond. (Middle High German *gängeln,* to walk about + the ending with depreciative connotations, as in *mongrel, wastrel,* etc.) Used from the 16th century; by Burns (1785, THE JOLLY BEGGARS), Scott (1815, GUY MANNERING), Morris (1870, THE EARTHLY PARADISE). Also, by association with *gangling,* a lanky, awkward person.

gantry. A large four-legged wooden stand, for barrels and wine-casks. Also *gauntry.* THE TEA-TABLE MISCELLANY (1724) edited by A. Ramsey, says: *I . . . paid him upon a gantree As hostler wives should do;* Scott in OLD MORTALITY (1816) shows the negation of this practice: *The housekeeper . . . is neither so young nor so handsome as to tempt a man to follow her to the gauntrees.*

gar. To do, to make; to cause, to make (someone) do (something) as *What garres thee greete?* (*q.v.*) in Spenser's THE SHEPHERD'S CALENDAR (1579; APRIL). A common word from the 13th century; later mainly Scotch and dialectal. Burns in TAM O' SHANTER (1790) has: *He screw'd the pipes and gart them skirl;* Scott in THE ANTIQUARY (1816): *Ye like to gar folk look like fools.*

garabee. A 17th century variant of *gadbee,* which was a stronger term for *gadfly,* horse fly, that bites horses and cattle and makes them *gad about. To have a gadfly* (*in one's cap*) is not the same as having a bee in one's bonnet, or a flea in one's ear; it means to be fond of *gadding about.* Thus Lyly in SAPPHO (1591): *My mistresse, I thinke, hath got a* *gadfly; never at home, and yet none can tell where abroade. Gadfly* is also used figuratively (1) of a person that *gads about;* (2) of one that worries or torments another, as when Irving says in THE SALMAGUNDI PAPERS (1808): *It is our misfortune to be frequently pestered . . . by certain critical gad-flies.* Browning in ARTEMIS PROLOGIZES (1842) speaks of *A noisome lust that, as the gadbee stings, Possessed his stepdame.*

garboil. Confusion, tumult; a brawl, a hurlyburly. Also a verb, to agitate, disturb. The word is via Italian *garbuglio;* Latin *bullire,* to boil. A common word for a common condition in the 16th and 17th centuries. Also *garboyle, garbroyl,* and the like. Stanyhurst began his translation (1582) of Virgil's AENEID (Arms and the man I sing): *Now manhod and garbroyls I chaunt;* Hood mocks this in his sixth SATIRE (1597): *Manhood and garboiles shall be chaunt with chaunged feete . . . If Jove speake English in a thundring cloud, Thwick thwack, and rif raf, rores he out aloud. Fie on the forged mint that did create New coyne of words never articulate.* Stanyhurst had said: *Of ruffe raffe roaring, mens herts with terror agrysing. With peale meale ramping, with thwick thwack sturdilye thundring.*

gardyloo. A warning cry (especially in Edinburgh, 18th and 19th centuries) before throwing slops out of the window. From French *gare de l'eau*—by error; the correct French would be *gare l'eau,* watch out for the water. Also *garde loo, jordeloo. To make the gardyloo* is to throw out the slops. Sterne used the word in A SENTIMENTAL JOURNEY (1768); Smollett, in HUMPHREY CLINKER (1771); Scott both literally (*She had made the gardyloo out of the wrong window*) in THE HEART OF MIDLOTHIAN (1818) and figuratively: *The overwhelming cataract of her questions, which burst forth with the sublimity of a grand gardyloo.* City boys on roof tops fill bags with various liquids and drop them streetward without the caveat of a gardyloo.

gare. See *gere; gore.*

garganet. See *carcan.*

gargat. The throat. Also *gargaz, garget.* Hence *gargarise, gargarism,* a gargle; to *gargarize, gargrise,* to gargle. An echoic word, from the Greek. Hence also the name of Rabelais' large-gulleted voracious giant, *Gargantua,* used in various forms: *gargantuan,* enormous (in size and especially in appetite); a *gargantuism,* an outlandish idea.—Chaucer in THE NUN'S PRIEST'S TALE (1386) tells that *The fox stert up at oones, And by the gargat hente Chaunteclere.*

garlic. A lively jig; danced in the 17th century. This sense and the surviving sense are combined in the word-play of R. Tailor's THE HOG HATH LOST HIS PEARLE (1614): Player: *That shows your more learning, sir. But, I pray you, is that small matter done I entrusted you for?* Haddit: *A small matter! You'll find it worth Meg of Westminster, although it be but a bare jig.* Player: *O lord! Sir, I wish it had but half the taste of garlick.* Haddit: *Garlick stinks to this; if it prove that you have not more . . . than e'er garlick had, say I am a boaster of my own works; disgrace me on the open stage, and bob me off with ne'er a penny. Garlic* (the vegetable) is Old English *gar,* spear + *leac,* leek; *cp. gere.*

garnison. See *warison.*

gasconade. Extravagant boasting; a boastful tale. Also *gasconado, gasconnade. Gasconade* was also used as a verb, to boast, to tell tall tales with oneself as hero. A *Gascon,* from *Gascony* in southwestern France, was proverbially a boaster —specimens of the species are exhibited in Rostand's CYRANO DE BERGERAC (1898; Cyrano lived 1619-1655). Smollett in a song of 1771 wrote: *A peacock in pride, in grimace a baboon, In courage a hind, in conceit a Gascoon.* Hence *gasconader,* a braggart, boaster.

gast. To terrify; also, to ruin. *For gast,* for fear. Also *ghast, gaast.* The form *gast* was also a noun, fright, and an adjective, terrified. In this sense also *agast,* surviving as *aghast; gastly, gastful; gastness.* As a noun, *gast* was also an early form of *ghost.* The translation (1422) of SECRETA SECRETORUM said: *Thou shalte have many rynnynge engyns to make horribill sownes to gasten thyn enemys.* Shakespeare in KING LEAR (1605) has: *Or whether gasted by the noyse I made, Full sodainely he fled.* In the second sense of the verb, we read in Wright's specimens of early LYRICAL POETRY: *Whet helpeth the, my suete lemmon, my lyf thus forte gaste?* [What good does it do you, my sweet mistress, my life thus for to ruin?]

gastromancy. See *aeromancy.*

gastronome. See *digastric.*

gaum. (1) (Verb) (a) to handle; especially, to fondle or mishandle a female. R. Fletcher, translating (1656) the EPIGRAMS of Martial, said: *Each lad took his lass by the fist and . . . squeezed her and gaumed her.* Also *goam.* (b) To smear with a sticky substance. Also *gome.* Hence *gaumy,* daubed, smeary; sticky. (c) To stare vacantly, to gawk, to look like a fool. All these were common, shading into dialect use, 17th into the 19th century. (2) (Noun) (a) heed, attention, notice; understanding. More commonly *gome* (13th to 16th century); but the other spelling lasted into the 19th century in compounds: *gaumless,* stupid, lacking sense; *gaumlike,* with an intelligent air; *She were a poor, friendless wench,* says Mrs. Gaskell in SYLVIA'S LOVERS (1863), *but honest and gaumlike.* (b) *Gome,* also *guma, gom,* etc., a man. This was a common Teuton word, its root *ghomon* being related to Latin *homo, hominis,* man. It survived in poetic use into the 16th century, and was the original ending of *bridegome,* wedding man, later corruped into *bridegroom.*

gaunch. See *ganch.*

gauntry. See *gantry.*

gavel. The word *gavel,* meaning first a mason's hammer for leveling, then a presiding officer's mallet, was first used in the United States in the 19th century; its origin is unknown. Two earlier words had the same form. (1) From Early English (Anglo-Saxon) until the 16th century, *gavel* meant first tribute, then rent. *To set to gavel* was to rent out. This word was Old English *gafol,* related to *giefan,* to give. An especial kind of rent (in Kent, in Wales; from the 16th century, more widely) gave tenure *in gavelkind;* namely, on the tenant's death the land did not go to the eldest son, but was divided equally among his sons. [Edwards, in WORDS, FACTS, AND PHRASES (1912) stated that *gavelkind* is composed of Saxon *gif ael kynd,* give to all children. *Kynd* gives us *kin,* and *kindred;* also, via the German, *kindergarten.* Edwards was probably wrong.] In Ireland, on an occupant's death, the land went back to the tribe (sept) and was redivided among the tribesmen; hence, *gavel,* a partition of land amongst the sept. In these various uses, *gavel* was also a verb. A legal action against a tenant for non-payment of *gavel* was called *gavelet,* probably from *gafol* + *laetan,* to let (hinder). (2) From the 15th into the 19th century, *gavel* was a pile of corn cut and lying, waiting to be bound into a sheaf. Also *javelle. To lie on the gavel* was to lie unbound. The O.E.D. (1931) says the early Old French meaning was heap; but note also English *gavelock, gavelot, javelot* (French *javelot*), a spear for casting, a *javelin.* The word *gavelkind* has been used figuratively by many writers, since Donne's Sermon of 1627: *For God shall impart to us all a mysterious gavelkind, a mysterious equality of fulness of glory to us all*: Carew (1639) and Fuller (1661), of God; Hallam (1838) and Lowell (1869) of books: *All that is worth having in them,* said the last, *is the common property of the soul—an estate in gavelkind for all the sons of Adam.*

gavelkind. See *gavel.*

gavelock. See *gavel.*

gaylede. Another delightful dish of 15th century England. TWO COOKERY-BOOKES (1430) tells how: *Take almaunde mylke and flowre of rys, and do therto sugre or hony, and powder gyngere; then take figys, and kerve them ato, or roysonys* [raisins] *yhole, or harde wastel* [*q.v.*] *ydicyd and coloure it with saunderys* [sandalwood] *and sette it and dresse hem yn. Sawnderys, sanders, saundres,* and enough more to prove its popularity: sandalwood was a frequent ingredient of dishes, listed from the early 14th century. We find mention in THE PILGRIMAGE OF PERFECTION (1526) of *a precyous tree: whereof the stock is saundres, the barke synamon, and the fruit nutmygges or maces.* A true chef's dream!

gazebo. A turret or lantern on a housetop; hence, a raised room overlooking or in a garden; a belvedere. Pronounced ga-zeé-bo, the word may be a humorously formed imaginary Latin future "I shall see," from *gaze,* but its earliest uses have Oriental allusions (1752: *the elevation of a Chinese tower or gazebo*) and it may be a corruption of an eastern word. The term *belvedere,* with the same meaning as *gazebo,* is from Italian *belvedere,* a beautiful sight; *bel, bello,* beautiful + *vedere,* to see. Webster in THE DEVIL'S LAW CASE (1623) wrote: *They build their palaces and belvederes With musical water-works;* Harvey in a DIALOGUE (1755) in Southey's COMMONPLACE BOOK observed: *Over this recess, so pleasingly horrid . . . arose an open and airy belvidere.* I miss the view from the gazebo friends of mine used to enjoy in Hillcrest Park.

geason. Barren, unproductive; by transference (scantily produced) rare, scarce, uncommon; hence rare, unusual, extraordinary. A common word (*gesne, gayson, gesen,* etc.), 10th into the 17th century. *Cp. peason.* Also used as a noun (16th century): a rarity. Udall in his paraphrase of Erasmus (1548) spoke of *precious stones that are gayson to be found.* That charming song of 1584, *Fain would I have a pretie thing To give unto my ladie,* has a stanza: *Some goe here and some go there, wheare gazes be not geason, And I goe gaping everywhere But still come out of season.* A legended shield was described, in a verse to Bossewell's ARMORIE (1572): *The siege of Thebes, the fall of Troy, in beaten massie golde, dan Vulcan hath set out at large, full geazon to beholde.*

geck. A simpleton, a dupe; an expression or gesture of derision or contempt. *To get a geck,* to be tricked; *to give one the geck,* to mock or to trick one; *to geck at,* to mock or scoff at. The verb *geck* means to mock; to trick, to cheat, but also to toss the head as in scorn; *to geck up the head.* Shakespeare uses the noun (*gecke*) in CYMBELINE, also in TWELFTH NIGHT (1601), when Malvolio protests: *Why have you suffer'd me to be imprison'd . . . And made the most notorious gecke and gull That ere invention played on?*

gelasin. A dimple in the cheek that comes with smiling. Greek *gelasinos; gelan,* to laugh. Sampson Lennard in his translation (1612) of Charron's WISDOME, spoke of *the cheeks somewhat rising, and in the middle the pleasant gelasin.* Also *gelastic,* risible, causing or related to laughter. Both, naturally, are pronounced with a soft *g.* T. Brown had a prescription: *My friendly pill,* he said (WORKS; 1704) *causes all complexions to laugh or smile . . . which it effects by dilating and expanding the gelastic muscles, first of all discover'd by myself.*

gelastic. See *gelasin.*

gelatia. "A whyte precyous stone," said John de Trevisa, in his translation (1398) of Bartholomeus' DE PROPRIETATIBUS RERUM, "shapen as an heyll [hail] stone: and it is so calde that it never hetith wyth fyre." Also *gelacia.* Probably from a fusion of Latin *gelare,* to freeze and *chalazias,* Greek *chalassa,* hail. The gelatia was admired into the 17th century; no samples of it seem to be in rings or necklaces today.

geloscopy. See *aeromancy.*

gemel. Twin; in the plural, *gemels,* twins. Used from the 14th to the 18th century, in various forms: *gemell, gemmal, gemoll, gemmell;* also *gemew, gimbal, gimmal, gimmer.* Via French from Latin *gemellus,* diminutive of *geminus,* twin—the plural of which was also used in English; see *gemini. Gemew* (Old French *gemeau;* French *jumeau*) also had other forms: *gemow; gewmew, gymmew, jemowe,* and more; likewise *gimball, gimbole, gimble, gimbald; gimmall, gimal, gymell, gemoll, gymmal, gimmel*—all with the same variations of meaning. These included: a pair of anything, such as a double door; a two-part harmony; a hinge or other two-part joint or device for fastening, as a hook and eye; especially (late 15th and the 16th century) a finger-ring that could be divided and worn as two rings; also *gemel-ring, gemowe-ring, gimmal-ring.* Greene in 'MENAPHON (1589) declared: *Twas a good world . . . when a ring of rush would tie as much love together as a gimmon of gold*—each lover wore one circlet. Shakespeare uses the word of a two-part driving mechanism in clockwork, when the French Reignier describes the fighting English in HENRY VI, PART ONE (1591): *I think by some odd gimmors or device Their arms are set like clocks, still to strike on, Else ne'er could they hold out so as they do. Gimmors,* in this use, is close to the mid-20th century *gimmick.*

gemelliparous. Bearing twins. Accent on the *lip.* Latin *gemellus,* twin + *parere,* to bring forth. *Cp. gemel.*

gemew. See *gemel.*

gemini. In addition to the constellation Castor and Pollux (Latin *gemini,* twins; *cp. gemel*) this form—also *gemyni, gemony, jeminy, geminies, jimminy,* and more—has meant a couple or pair; especially, a pair of eyes. Shakespeare in THE MERRY WIVES OF WINDSOR (1598) says: *Else you had look'd through the grate, like a geminy of baboones;* Quarles in EMBLEMES (1635): *He that daily spies Twin babies in his mistress' geminis. To* *play the gemini,* to behave like Castor and Pollux, who could never both be in the same place; i.e., to never be where the one looking for you is. Also *By Gemini!, Oh jiminy!,* a mild exclamation of surprise or displeasure—this is perhaps a euphemism for *Jesu domine,* Jesus our Lord.

genethliacs. See *aeromancy.*

geniculation. The act of kneeling; *geniculate,* to kneel, to bend at, or like, the knee. Latin *geniculum,* diminutive of *genu,* knee. Used in the 17th century; *genuflection, genuflexion,* introduced a century earlier, proved a hardier term, but implies a bending in worship.

gent. Noble; having the qualities expected of those of high birth, *gentle,* courteous, (of ladies) graceful. From Latin *genitum,* past participle of *gignere,* to beget. From meaning *born,* the Latin *gentum* came to mean born of Roman blood; then well-born; hence, noble in conduct. Villiers, in THE REHEARSAL (1672) speaks of a man *so modest, so gent.* Spenser, who uses the word 14 times in THE FAËRIE QUEENE (1590) there says, for example, *He loved, as was his lot, a lady gent.* The form *gent* was supplanted by *gentle,* from French *gentil,* and by *genteel,* re-adopted from *gentil* in the late 16th century.

gentylnes. A variant form of *gentleness,* which in the 16th century was used to mean kindness, generosity. Among the HUNDRED MERRY TALES (1526) is the story of the man who married a dumb wife, went to great pains to have her cured, then found her so unendingly talkative that he had himself made deaf. Rabelais refers to this story; Anatole France made a play of it. There is also the story of a woman who was told that the disease afflicting her pigs could be charmed away with the use of a cuckold's hat. She tries to borrow one from her neighbors, but is (rather naturally) rebuffed; thereupon she determines to arrange to have one of her own, from her husband. The story has a moral: *It is more wysdome for a man to trust more to his owne store than to his neyghbours gentylnes.*

geomancy. Also *gemensye.* See *aeromancy.* In China, *geomancy* flourished under the Liang Dynasty (502-566 A.D.), along with the introduction of kites and firecrackers.

gere. (1) A sudden fit of passion, a whim; a wild, changeful mood. By 1600 *gere* was replaced by *gare,* with the same meaning; *gare* lasted a century. *Gare-brained,* heedless, with swift-changing moods. Chaucer used *gere* several times, as in THE KNIGHT'S TALE (1386): *Into a study he fell suddenly, as doon these lovers in their queynte geres.* Also *gery, gerful,* capricious, in the same tale: *Right as the Friday, soothly for to telle, now it shyneth, now it rayneth faste, Right so can gery Venus overcaste The hertes of her folk; right as her day Is gerful, right so changeth she array.* (Friday is the day of Venus; Freya—for whom Friday is named—is the Scandinavian goddess of love.) Love indeed is gery! (2) *gere, gaer,* more commonly *gare,* earlier *gar,* a spear, a javelin; used from BEOWULF into the 13th century—in the 14th century misused for a sword. Surviving in the *garfish* and the pungent *garlick,* the spear leek.

gerfalcon. A large falcon, such as was used to hunt herons. *Cp. tercel.* Various suggestions have been made as to the source of the first syllable; in 1188 Giraldus Cambrensis suggested that it was from *gyrare,* to gyrate, from the circling of the bird in air. Greek *hieros,* sacred, has also been suggested; most likely source is Old High German *gir,* vulture; *giri,* greedy. The word has been used in English since the 14th century, with many mentions of a *milk white gerfauk.* Norton in his translation (1891) of Dante's INFERNO spoke of *Caesar in armor, with his gerfalcon eyes.*

german. Full; closely akin. Said of children of brothers and sisters, as *sister-german,* first cousin; loosely used of other kinship, as in Shakespeare's TIMON OF ATHENS (1607): *Wert thou a leopard, thou wert germane to the lion.* Also *germain, germeyn, germayne, germane, jarman, jermaine,* and the like. Latin *germanus,* in the same sense; *germen, germinem,* sprig, sprout, bud; also used in English to mean germ; by Shakespeare first, in MACBETH, and in KING LEAR: *And thou all-shaking thunder, Strike flat the thicke rotundity o' th' world, Crack natures moulds, all germaines spill at once That makes ingratefull man.* Shakespeare uses *german* in HAMLET—*The phrase would be more germaine to the matter, If we could carry cannon by our sides*—in the sense of closely connected, pertinent, relevant; this sense has continued, usually with the spelling *germane.*

gerning. A variant form of *girning*: grinning; grumbling. In Marston's THE SCOURGE OF VILLAINIE (SATIRE TEN; 1599) we read: *But roome for Tuscus, that jest-monging youth, Who nere did ope his apish gerning mouth But to retaile and broke anothers wit. Broke* is to trade in it; it survives in the noun *broker.* Note that *girn* means to grin; but also, to show the teeth (as in anger), to snarl; to complain constantly. Hence *gernative,* relating to or addicted to complaining; Middleton in A TRICK TO CATCH THE OLD ONE (1608) cried: *Out, you gernative queane! Girn* also meant to ensnare, to catch in a *girn,* a noose or trap; it was so used in the 14th century (replaced in England by *gin;* but *girn* survived in Scotland into the 19th century). *Gin* was short for Old French *engin,* engine, used in English since the 12th century. At first *gin* (*q.v.*) meant skill, artifice; then, an artifice, an instance or a product of cleverness; a trick, a device, an instrument. Then it was specifically applied to various instruments: a snare, a trap, for game; a device for torture, as the rack; a crane, for lifting weights; a weapon, for casting stones; a bolt or bar to fasten a door. Hence, *to know the gin,* to know how to open something, or how to get in. Spenser in THE FAËRIE QUEENE (1590) says *Typhoeus joynts were stretched on a gin.* Typhoeus may well have been gerning.

gerocomy. The science of the treatment of the aged. A word already existing when *gerontology* (not in the 1931 O.E.D. nor the 1953 WEBSTER) was coined for the same purpose. Greek *geras,* old + *komia,* tending. It would be flattery to suggest that the new word was devised because the old had an unfortunate adjective—*gerocomical*: *It is my earnest desire,* said J. Smith in his 1666 treatise on OLD AGE, *that physicians would study the gerocomical part of physick more than they do.* The form *gerocomian* would serve just as well. Bailey in 1751 gives the form *gerontocomy* (accent on the *toc*) for the noun; he also lists *gerontocomium,* an old-folks' home. Note also *gerontarchy, gerontocracy,* government by the old. Plants (and sometimes persons) native to "the old world" (the eastern hemisphere) have been called *gerontogenous* (accent on the third syllable, *todj*). May your years be gerocomical!

gerontology. See *gerocomy.*

gery. See *gere.*

gest. This word, very common from the 14th century into the 19th, occurred in Middle English mainly in the plural, meaning deeds, *gests, gestes,* from Latin *gesta,* exploits, *gerere, gestum,* to perform. Spenser in MOTHER HUBBERD'S TALE (1591) speaks of the *fond ape . . . into whose brest Never crept thought of honor, nor brave gest.* Hence, a story or romance; *the English gest, the French gest,* metrical chronicles of England, of France; hence, *in gest,* in verse, like the metrical romances. Later, *gest* came to mean an idle tale; then a satirical remark; in this sense, it was supplanted in the 16th century by the form *jest.* By another path, from the same Latin *gerere, gestum,* to act, to perform, *gest* was used to mean one's carriage, the movement of one's limbs, as when Garth in his translation (1717) of Ovid's METAMORPHOSES says: *The bold buffoon . . . Their motion mimics, but with gests obscene.* In this sense, the word has been supplanted (gradually, 16th and 17th centuries) by *gesture.* There is another *gest* (earlier *gist,* from Old French *gist, gît,* lie; see *gist*) which meant a stopping place, a lodging; then especially the stops or stages of a journey, of a royal progress; then the time allotted for a stop on the journey. In the last sense we see the word in Shakespeare's THE WINTER'S TALE (1611): *I'll give him my commission To let him there a month behind the gest Prefix'd for's parting. Gest* is also a verb. In the expression *gested and done* it means performed; its usual sense is to sing or tell tales (like a professional *gester*). Thus there is the protest in THE PARSON'S TALE (1386) of Chaucer: *I kan not geeste, Rum, Ram, Ruf by letter.* The effects of drinking are quite evident on a four-handled cup in the Museum at Salisbury (England) that bears the date 1692 and the inscription: *Here is the gest of the barly korne, Glad ham I the cild is born.*

gesture. See *gest.*

gib. (1) A cat, especially a male cat. *Gib* is a pet name of *Gilbert. To play fy gib,* to look or speak threateningly (as though scolding—*Fie!*—a cat). *To play the gib* (of a woman), to be quarrelsome; hence *gib* was used as a term of reproach for an old woman; Drayton in HEROIC EPISTLES (1598) piles it on: *Beldam, gib, witch, nightmare, trot.* Also *your gibship,* in scorn of a woman. A *gib-cat, gibbed-cat,* a gelded male cat. (2) The form *gib* also (Latin *gibba*) meant hump—used from the 15th century; hence *gibbous,* protruberant; *gibbose; gibbousness, gibbosity.* (3) Also (16th century) *gib,* a hook; *gibby* or *gibby-stick, gib-stick, gibbey,* a stick with a hooked or curved handle; also a candy in that shape, like a peppermint cane.—*'Sblood,* says Falstaff in Shakespeare's HENRY IV, PART ONE (1597), I am as *melancholy as a gib-cat.* In HAMLET, the Prince, bitterly taunting his mother, alludes to the King in several ways: *For who that's but a Queen, fair, sober, wise, Would from a paddock, from a bat, a gib, Such dear concernings hide?*

gibbet. A hanging-post, gallows. In later use the two were distinguished, the *gallows* consisting of two uprights and a crosspiece; the *gibbet,* of an upright post with projecting arm. Hence, *gibbetation,* hanging. To *gibbet,* to kill by hanging; to hang so as to hold up to public contempt; to hold in infamous notoriety. Thus Goldsmith in A CITIZEN OF THE WORLD (1762) tells of a man that *unknowingly gibbeted himself into infamy,* *when he might have otherwise quietly retired into oblivion. Wickedness,* says Burke in THE FRENCH REVOLUTION (1790) *walks abroad; it continues its ravages, whilst you are gibbeting the carcass, or demolishing the tomb.*

gibbose. See *gib.*

gig. See *fizgig.*

gigant. The early form of *giant,* 10th into the 17th century. Via Latin *gigantem,* from Greek *gigas, giganto-.* This form of the Greek word survives in *gigantic,* which was preceded in English by *gigantean* and *gigantal;* thus Urquhart in his translation (1653) of Rabelais says: *This gigantal victory being ended, Pantagruel withdrew himself to the place of the flaggons.*

gigantomachy. The war of the giants against the gods. Also *gigantomachia;* Greek *gigas, giganto-,* giant + *mache,* battle. *Gigantomachize,* to rebel as did the giants; thus Jonson in EVERY MAN OUT OF HIS HUMOUR (1599): the *goggle-eyed Grumbledories would ha' gigantomachiz'd.*

gigget. See *gigot.*

giglot. A wanton woman; rarely, also, a dissolute man. Shakespeare in HENRY IV, PART ONE says: *Young Talbot was not born To be the pillage of a giglot wench.* The influence of the word *giggle* developed the forms *giglet, gigglet,* and softened the meaning (18th and 19th centuries) to a laughing, romping girl. *Cp. fizgig.* Thus Shakespeare cries, in MEASURE FOR MEASURE (1603): *Away with those giglets,* whereas in Chambers' JOURNAL OF POPULAR LITERATURE for 1885 we find the query: *Why should female clerks in the postal service consist of pert giglets hardly out of their teens?* Hence *giggly* means prone to giggle, but *gigly* (15th through 17th century) meant lascivious.

gigman. A narrow-minded, conventional member of the middle class. *This was not a nobleman,* said Carlyle (MISCELLANY, 1830), *or gentleman, or gigman, but simply a man!* Carlyle, who coined the word, explained it by quoting from a trial (of Thurtell): "What do you mean by 'respectable'?" "He always kept a gig." [This *gig* is not 'a romping girl,' but 'a light two-wheeled one-horse carriage.'] Hence, *the gigmania of the times; gigmanism,* the typical middle-class attitude; *gigmanity,* the group that manifests this attitude. Mrs. Grundy was a *gigwoman.*

gigot. A leg or haunch (of mutton or veal); a slice; a minced meat or sausage. Also, a leg-of-mutton sleeve. From the French; also *gigget, jigotte, jigget.* M. Scott in THE CRUISE OF THE MIDGE (1834) said that *a good practical sermon should be like a jigot o' mutton, short in the shank and pithy and nutritious.* A 1676 recipe for *roast gigget of mutton: Take your gigget with cloves and rosemary, lard it, roast it, baste it with butter, and save the gravy, and put thereto some claret wine, with a handful of capers; season it with ginger and sugar, when it is boiled well, dish up your gigget, and pour on your sauce.*

gigour. A musician. Among the many meanings of *gig, gige,* was a noise; also, apparently, a high-pitched musical instrument. The word *gigour* occurs in the 13th century GESTE OF KING HORN: *Hi sede hi weren harpurs, And sume were gigours.*

gilder. A snare, especially for small animals and birds. Also *gildire, gylder, giller, gildard, gildert.* Hampole, in the PSALTER of 1340, said: *Godis luv and Godis word . . . sall kepe him fra the gildire of the devele.* A 19th century *gildert,* for catching birds on snow, was a slip noose of horsehair tied to a line. Bread tempted the birds through the loops, which entangled their legs as they rose to fly off. *Gilder* was also a verb, to ensnare, as in CURSOR MUNDI (1300): *Now is man gildred in ivels all; His awn sin has made him thrall.*

gilenyer. A cheat, a swindler. Old French *Ghillain, Gilain,* a pseudo-name for a swindler, related to *guile, wile, wily.* Also *gileynour, golinger.* Used in the 18th century, mainly in Scotland. Also *gilenyie,* a device, a trick. There is a Scotch proverb (mid-18th century): *The greedy man and the gielainger are well met.* Robert of Gloucester's CHRONICLE (13th century) has *gileyspeke* (*guilty* or *guily talk?*), meaning a cunning trick.

gileyspeke. See *gilenyer.* Too much of our current use of words is gileyspeke.

gill. See *jill.*

gilliflower. A flower scented like a clove, especially the pink. Old French *girofle, gilofre,* clove; via Latin from Greek *karyophyllon; karyon,* nut + *phyllon,* leaf, the clove-tree. It was a most popular flower, judging by the multiplicity of forms of the name, which include *gilver, gillifloure, gillyflower, gelofer, gyllofyr, gilliver, jilliver, gerafloure, Julyflower, gillowflower.* References to it abound in the poetry of the 15th, 16th, and 17th centuries. Greene in MENAPHON (1589) said: *He that grafteth jillyflowers upon the nettle, marreth the smell.* The word was also applied to a woman: (1797) '*gilliver,* a light-heel'd dame'; (1855) '*A jilliver,* a wanton woman in the last stage of her good looks. A July flower, or the last rose in summer.' There were several sorts of *gillofer* distinguished by Lyte in his translation (1578) of Dodoens' NIEWE HERBALL, among them the *feathered gillofers,* the *turkie gillofers, Aphrican gillofers,* and also the *sops-in-wine, q.v.*

gimble. See *gemel.*

gimmor. See *gemel.* Other early editions of HENRY VI have *gimmals, gimmers, gimmalls.*

gin. Skill, ingenuity; cunning; artifice. *Quaint of gin,* clever in planning; deftly contrived. An instance of ingenuity, a clever device or stratagem; especially, a spring or other trap for catching game. A device for torture; a fetter. *To know the gin,* to know how to do something, usually (16th and 17th centuries) with dishonest purpose. *Gin* is shortened from French *engin,* engine. *Cp. gerning*; for an instance of its use, see *woodcock.*

gipon. See *smotherlich.*

gipser. A pouch or purse, usually hung from the girdle. Also *gypcyere, gypsire, gipciere* and the like. Chaucer, in the Prologue to THE CANTERBURY TALES (1386): *A gipser al of silk Heeng at his girdel.* Planché's HISTORY OF BRITISH COSTUME (1834) lists *A gypsire of purple velvet garnished with gold.*

girandola. A revolving wheel from which rockets are fired for holiday, or jets of water spurt; a series of jets in an ornamental fountain. Via Italian, from Greek *gyros,* circle, whence *gyrate.* Also *gyrondola.* Used from the 17th century. By way of French came the alternate form *girandole* (*girondel, gironell*) which later developed two other meanings: (1) (From the 18th century) a branched candlestick, especially as a bracket on a wall; (2) (19th century) an earring or pendant; especially, one with a large stone surrounded by smaller ones. THE MORNING STAR (29 June, 1868) reported a fireworks show: *The whole wound up with a girandole of two thousand rockets.*

gird. See *gride.*

girdlestead. The place for the girdle, i.e., the waist. Used from the 14th century; Chaucer in THE ROMAUNT OF THE ROSE (1366) has: *Hise shuldris of a large brede, And smalish in the girdilstede.* Swinburne extends it to the lap, in TRISTRAM OF LYONESSE (1882): *There fell a flower into her girdlestead Which laughing she shook out.*

girlery. A gathering of girls, girls collectively. A *girleen* (Irish), a young girl. Note that from the 13th to the 15th century, *girl* was used for a child of either sex; then *knave girl* was used to mean boy; by 1550 *girl* had become restricted to the feminine kind. The origin of the word is unknown, but there is a Scotch verb, *to girl,* to thrill, to whirl, to be giddy. *Girlie* is a term of endearment for a little *girl,* but a *girling* is a young fish (salmon). Meredith says of a character in ONE OF OUR CONQUERORS (1891): *The silly girly sugary crudity has given way to womanly suavity.* Yet it's pleasant to watch the ways of growing girlery.

girn. See *gerning.*

girondel. See *girandola.*

gis. Jesus. A euphemism; also *jysse, jis, gisse, gys.* Used in mild exclamations, as in mad Ophelia's song in Shakespeare's HAMLET (1602): *By gis and by Saint Charity, Alack, and fie for shame! Young men will do't, if they come to't; By cock, they are to blame.* Note that *By cock* here is another euphemism, replacing *By God*—with one of the bard's bawdy puns.

gisarme. A weapon, a spear, says Bailey (1751) with two points or pikes; the O.E.D. (1931) says it has a long straight blade sharpened on both sides. The word had many spellings, from the 13th into the 16th century, e.g., *guisarme, gyssarn, giserne, gysyryne* (all with a hard *g,* not *j*); Kingsley in THE WATER BABIES (1863), by whose time it was an antique, speaks of *a whole cutler's shop of lances, halberts, gisarines.*

gist. See *gest. Gist* had several meanings; it comes from Old French *gist, gît,* from *gésir,* to lie; Latin *jacere, iacere,* to lie. (The current sense, as in *the gist of the matter,* is from *gésir en,* to lie in, to depend upon.) The sense of a place to stop (for rest and refreshing) was applied to the halting-places of migratory birds. By extension *gist* was used to mean refreshment. Another sense (short for *agist, q.v.*) meant pasturing, or the right to pasture cattle; *to gist* was to take in or put out cattle to pasture (at a price). And that is the gist of it.

gittern. A musical instrument, like the guitar, strung with wire. Also *ghittern, getron, gyterne, guthorne, guiterne; guiterre,* whence *guitar.* Also *cithern, q.v.* Used from the 14th to the 17th century; revived (the word) by Scott in OLD MORTALITY (1816). Hence, *to gittern; a gitterner.*

givale. An annual feast, free, given in certain parishes (especially in Kent, up to the 17th century) with money bequeathed for the purpose. Also *give-ale, gifeale, yevall, yeovale, gevall.* A will recorded in the 16th century makes fair provision: *Alsoe I will that specially my feoffees and executors see that the yeovale of St. James be kept for ever.* Note that the wedding feast, the *bridal,* is *bride + ale.*

givel. To heap. Related to *gavel, q.v.* HAVELOK THE DANE (1300) had: *He cast a panier on his bac, With fish giveled as a stac.*

gixy. A wench; a lively lass. Coined after *gig, q.v.,* as *trick, tricksy; Nan, Nancy,* etc. Urquhart in his translation (1693) of Rabelais noted that Hans Carvel *entred into a very profound suspition that his new-married gixy* was unfaithful to him. In a dream the devil came to Hans and gave him a ring: as long as he wore this, he would know when his wife was unfaithful. "Hans woke, and his hand was pressed In passion's nest. And then Hans ruefully knew His dream was true."

glaik. Originally a flash of light, that dazzled; hence, a deception (usually in the plural); *to give one the glaiks,* to swindle; *to get the glaiks,* to be cheated. The verb, *to glaik,* meant to dazzle; to gaze wantonly or idly; to deceive, trick; to pervert. *Glaikery,* wanton or giddy conduct. In Scotland (from Henryson, 1450, through Burns, as in TO THE UNCO GUID, 1786) *glaikit* meant foolish, flighty, giddy. Although probably of different origin, *gleek* was used (both as noun and verb) in almost the same senses as *glaik*: a jibe; *to give one the gleek,* to mock, make sport of, play a trick upon. (*Gleek* was also a game at cards—3 persons dealt 12 cards each, with 8 held as a 'stock'—from the 16th into the 19th century. Shakespeare, in A MIDSUMMER NIGHT'S DREAM (1590) has Bottom say: *Nay, I can gleeke* [jibe] *upon occasion.* Rarely, *gleek* is used to mean a coquettish glance, as in Jonson's CYNTHIA'S REVELS (1599): *Coy glances, glickes, cringes, and all such simpering humours.*

glair. The white (of an egg); hence, any similar substance. Hence, *glaireous, glairy,* viscid, slimy. Chaucer in THE CANON YEOMAN'S TALE (1386) lists *unslakked lime, chalk, and the gleyre of an ey* [egg].

glaive. A sword. Perhaps from Latin *gladius,* sword; but the earliest (French and English) meaning was lance; then, bill; then, sword. Also *gleyve, gleave, gleve, glayve, glave.* Also, a swordsman. (A bill was a blade fastened to a long handle.) Also, a lance set up as the finish-post in a race, taken as a prize by the winner; hence, a prize. Coverdale in CERTAIN MOST GODLY LETTERS . . . quotes Bradford (1555): *Cast your eies on the gleve ye runne at, or els ye wil loose the game.* Naturally Scott revived the word, in IVANHOE (1820). Lowell in a poem of 1869 speaks *Of the glaived tyrant and long-memoried priest.*

glamoury. See *gramarye.*

glaucous. Of a pale green passing into greyish blue. Greek *glaukos,* sea-color. Shelley in PROMETHEUS UNBOUND (1820) has Panthea say *Ere-while I slept Under the glaucous caverns of old Ocean.* Also *glaucy,* mainly in poetry, as in Barnes' madrigal in PARTHENOPHIL (1593): *Sleep Phoebus still, in glaucy Thetis' lap.* The color of olive-tree foliage, and keen eyes.

glaver. Used in the 14th century as a noun, meaning chatter; then and into the 18th century as a verb, meaning to talk deceitfully, to flatter. Also *glavir*; *cp. glother. To glaver on* was to lavish blandishments on. Hence *glavery,* flattery. Jonson in THE POETASTER (1601) says: *Give him warning, admonition, to forsake his saucy glavering grace.*

glaze. To stare. So first used by Shakespeare, in JULIUS CAESAR (1601): *Against the Capitoll I met a lyon Who glaz'd upon me, and went surly by.* Jesperson in his searching study of LANGUAGE (1922) suggests that *glaze* is here a blending of *gaze* and *glare*. Lewis Carroll's "portmanteau words" in ALICE are well known; Jesperson lists such telescoping as a regular process in the development of language. It is obvious in slang, *brunch* for *breakfast* + *lunch*. It has occurred in many other words, such as *flush, flash* + *blush*; *good-bye, good-night* + *godbye* (God be by ye); *knoll, knell* + *toll*; *slender, slight* (*slim*) + *tender*; *slide, slip* + *glide*; *twirl, twist* + *whirl*. The other *glaze* is a variant of Middle English *glasen, glas,* modern *glass*. Shakespeare's word was used again in the 19th century (as by Peter Pindar) and is preserved in dialect. Despite all which, the context makes it possible that Shakespeare meant the word in the original sense: the lyon *glazed,* i.e., looked glassily, upon him.

glebe. The soil; cultivated land; especially, land assigned to a clergyman as part of his benefice. A very common word, 14th to 18th century; thereafter mainly used poetically. Sometimes used to mean a clod, or a small lump (this was the Latin sense: *gleba, glaeba,* clod); also figuratively (1583): *Judas Iscariot, for a gleib of geir, betrayed his Master. Glebose, glebulent, glebous,* abounding in clods; clod-like. *Gleby* soil, however, is rich, fertile soil.

glede. The bird the kite. From Old Teutonic *glid,* to glide. Also *gled, glead, gleed*. Note that *gleed,* however (also spelled *glede*), is a different word (related to *glow*) meaning a live coal, an ember; sometimes a fire; hence also, a beam of light. This word was often used figuratively, as by Chaucer in the Prologue to THE REEVE'S TALE (1386): *Four gleedes han we which I shall devise: Avaunting, liyng, anger, covetise* (boasting, lying. . . , coveting). Hence also *gledy,* glowing hot, as in the Prologue to Chaucer's THE LEGEND OF GOOD WOMEN (1385): *Constreyned me with so gledy desire.*

glee. As a noun. This word has been common, in many senses, from the 8th century. It took its current sense of delight, lively joy, as early as 1250, but even in this sense the word died out during the 16th and 17th centuries. Johnson in his DICTIONARY (1755) notes: "It is not now used, except in ludicrous writing, or with some mixture of irony and contempt." In the 18th century, the sense of lively joy was revived, and it has continued. The earliest uses of the word, in Old and Middle English, were mainly poetic. The now obsolete uses of *glee* include: (1) Entertainment, sport; making sport of one, mockery. *To have glee,* to make sport; *to make one's glee on* (*of*), to make sport of. (2) Musical entertainment, playing; music; a musical instrument; especially, a musical composition for three or more voices, (strictly, without accompaniment). (3) Mirth, rejoicing (originally, a stronger feeling than in present use). *There glads him no glee,* nothing gives him pleasure. *To make a person good glee,* to welcome him heartily. Hence *glee,* a state of exaltation or prosperity; a person who brings one joy (1610): *Thou art my glee.* Hence also, bright color, beauty; a frequent 16th century phrase was *gold and glee*; Spenser's THE FAËRIE QUEENE (1590) has: *Not for gold nor glee will I abide by you. Glee-beam,* a harp (poetical); *glee-craft,* minstrelsy; *gleeman,* a professional entertainer, a minstrel; *glee-dream,* the pleasure of minstrelsy. Scott in THE LADY OF THE LAKE (1810) has: *Thou hast now glee-maiden and harp.* As a verb. There is a verb *glee,* to make merry, to gladden; but the proper form of the verb is *glew,* which was very common, 9th into 14th century, meaning to make merry; to play music; to entertain. From a different source, *to glee,* also to *gledge, to gleg,* to squint, to look at with one eye (as when taking aim); to have a cast in one eye. Which is no cause for glee.

gleed. See *glede.*

gleek. See *glaik.* In Gower's words to Pistol, in Shakespeare's HENRY V (1599)—*I have seen you gleeking and galling at the gentleman*—there is a forward-looking pun, because the gentleman, Fluellen, will soon force Pistol to taste of the leek he was leering at. *Gleek* was also used, in the card game of *gleek,* to mean a set of three court cards of the same rank held in one hand; by extension, any trio, set of three. *Cp. mournival.* Thus THE BRITISH APOLLO (1710) irreverently alluded to the three fairest Greek goddesses, come to Mount Ida and the Trojan prince, contesting the golden apple, prize of beauty: *Like Paris with his gleek of wagtails on Ida.*

glew. See *glee.*

glomerate. To roll or gather into a ball or rounded mass. Latin *glomus,* a ball, whence also English *glome,* a ball (as of yarn), used figuratively in Browne's RELIGIO MEDICI (1643): *There is therefore a secret glome or bottom of our days. Glomeration* is a heaping together; a cluster of things; the word has been supplanted by *agglomeration* and (more widely used) *conglomeration.* De Quincey in CASUISTRY (1840) spoke scornfully of *the glomeration of moonbeams upon moonbeams.*

glomery. The (Latin) grammar school, associated with the early English universities (12th to 15th century). The head of the school was the *Master of Glomery* (Latin *Magister Glomeriae*); a pupil was a *glomerel.* The words are (like *glamour*) corruptions of *grammar;* see *gramarye.*

gloosing. See *prick.*

glossolalia. See *glother.* My friend Harry Starr knows a woman who is (he assures me) a *glossolalipop.*

gloterie. An early (13th century) variant of *gluttony.*

glother. To flatter; to cajole. *Cp. glaver,* with the same meaning. *Gloze* also meant flattery and to flatter; Greek *glossa,* tongue; also *gloss.* Both *gloss* and *gloze* (following the Greek senses: tongue; foreign tongue; explanation) came also to mean to make a marginal note, explanation; also (still current) *to gloss over. Glother* was used until the 16th century; when *gloss* came into use, supplanting *glother* and to some extent *gloze,* which was first used in the 14th. What today is called 'double-talk'—the use of incomprehensible polysyllables, or meaningless combinations of apparently meaningful sound—was in the 19th century called *glossolalia,* 'the gift of tongues.'

gloze. See *glother.*

gluteal. Relating to the buttocks. Also *glutaeal, glutean.* Greek *gloutos,* rump. The buttock is composed of three powerful *glutei muscles*: the *gluteus* (*glutaeus*) *maximus, medius, and minimus.*

glyptic. Relating to engraving, especially on precious stones. Greek *glyphein,* to carve, engrave, whence *hieroglyphics,* sacred carvings. A *glyptician* (19th century) was a lapidary; *The famous Kohinoor,* said THE TIMES OF 20 July, 1883, *was recut by a great Dutch glyptician after it came into the possession of the*

Queen. Sir S. Ferguson in his study (1887) of THE OGHAM INSCRIPTIONS said one must be *prepared to recognize familiar forms, though in glyptical masquerade.*

gnathonical. Sycophantic. The parasite in the play THE EUNUCH, by Terence, is named *Gnatho* (Greek *gnathos,* jaw). Terence's play was imitated by Udall in RALPH ROISTER DOISTER (1554); in the 16th and into the 18th century *gnathoes and parasites* was a fairly frequent phrase. Urquhart in THE DISCOVERY OF A MOST EXQUISITE JEWEL (1652) *thinks no better of adulatory assentations than of a gnatonick sycophantizing, or parasitical cogging.* Hence also *gnathonism,* sycophancy, used by Coleridge (1838): *gnathonize,* to flatter, to play the lickspittle. *Cp. thrasonical. gnathic,* of course, means relating to the jaw; the *gnathopods* are the jaw-footed crustacea, like the lobster and the crab. The earlier forms apply to humans, as the coy words in Greene's HISTORY OF ORLANDO FURIOSO (1590); *Knowing him to be a thrasonicall madcap, they have sent me a gnathonicall companion, to give him lettice fit for his lips.*

gnavity. Activity, quickness. Latin *gnavus, navus,* diligent, active. A 17th and 18th century dictionary word.

gnede. Niggardly, miserly; scarce, scanty, small. Thus *gnede of* (gifts), sparing with. *To make the gates gnede,* to go straight to one's destination. Used from BEOWULF into the 15th century. *Ask me thy will,* we read in CURSOR MUNDI (1300), *for am I noght of givetes* [gifts] *gnede.*

gnide. To rub between the hands; to bruise, crush; to rub out. Also, to crumble away (as though rubbed). Also *gnodde, gnudden.* Used from the 9th to the 14th century. Also *tognide*; see *to-.* In ARTHUR AND MERLIN (1330) we read: *Herbes he sought and fond And gnidded them.*

gnoff. A churl, boor. (East Frisian *gnuffig,* coarse, ill-mannered). Also *knuff.* Chaucer's THE MILLER'S TALE (1386) begins; *Whylom ther was dwellinge at Oxenford a rich gnof.* A story of 1575 speaks of *The country gnooffes Hob, Dick, and Hick, with clubs, and clouted shoon.*

gnome. (1) A member of one of the four groups of spirits that (supposedly) inhabited the four elements: sylphs (air), gnomes (earth), nymphs (water) and salamanders (fire). A gnome moves through earth unobstructed, as a fish through water, a bird through air. Paracelsus, who first used the word, may have invented it, or may have shaped it from *genomus,* for Greek *geo,* earth + *nomos,* order, law. A female *gnome* is a *gnomide.* (2) A short pithy statement of a general idea, a proverb, maxim. Greek *gnome,* thought. Hence *gnomic, gnomical. gnomology,* a collection of maxims, the sententious element in discourse. There was also (3) *gnomon,* an indicator; Greek *gnomon,* indicator, *gno-* (English *recognize*), *gignoskein,* to perceive, judge, *know.* Especially: the post or plate on a sundial; the nose; the teeth of a horse (indicating its age), etc. Hence *gnomonic,* pertaining to the sundial, or the measurement of time thereby. *Gnomon* was also used for a carpenter's square; hence, in the 17th century, a rule, a canon of belief or action, a *gnome.* Symonds in his essays on THE GREEK POETS (1873) observed that *many of the sublimer flights of meditation in Sophocles are expansions of earlier gnomes.*

gnomon. See *gnome.*

gobbet. A piece of anything cut or broken; especially, a piece of raw flesh, frequent in the phrase *to cut* (*chop, hack*) *into gobbets.* Hence, a lump or mass; a mouthful. Old French *gobe,* a mouthful, *gober,* to swallow. Whence also English *gob,* the mouth; *to give gob,* to scold, abuse; *gift of the gob,* fluency of speech —later, *gift of the gab.* Langland said, in PIERS PLOWMAN (1393): *So hope Ich to have of Him that is al-myghty A gobet of Hus grace.*

gobbet-royal. A sweetmeat of the 14th century; literally, a mouthful for a king. A Durham account book of 1362 listed *cofyns of anys comfyt and gobetes reale.* A *coffin* of anise confection was a case made of pastry, such as a pie-crust.

goderheal. Prosperity, good fortune. Also as an exclamation, Good luck! *To goderheal,* with good fortune, successfully. Also *goderhele, goderhayl, godder-haile,* and the like. Used into the 15th century.

godfright. Pious, devoted; God-fearing. Also *godfyrht, godfurht, godfruct, godfriht.* From the 10th into the 13th century. Hence, *godfrightihead,* piety, devotion.

godivoe. A chopped meat or fish pie, made in the 17th and 18th centuries. French *godiveau,* probably from *veau, veal.* A pie, said Phillips in 1706 "filled with a delicious farce made of veal and several other kinds of meat; or else of carps, pikes, and other fish, for days of abstinence." Chopped eel was also used for the godivoe. Not only the word but the recipe is too greatly neglected.

goety. Black magic; witchcraft by use of evil supernatural spirits. Greek *goes, goet-,* sorcerer; *goaein,* to wail, cry (as in summoning the evil powers). Hence *goetic, goetical*; the *e* is a separate syllable. *Cp. theurgy.* A *goetian* (sometimes also *a goetic*) was a sorcerer. The words were occasionally spelled *geoty, geotic,* by confusion with *geo-,* earth. They are rarely still employed, as by C. S. Lewis in his ENGLISH LITERATURE IN THE 16TH CENTURY (1954), reminding us that many believers (like King James in his DEMONOLOGY, 1597) felt that even good magic (*magia,* high magic, white magic) was *all a snare and would lead you into the goetic sort in the end.* Lewis pointed out that the audiences of Marlowe, Chapman, and Shakespeare believed in such a magician: *'He to his studie goes'; books are opened, terrible words pronounced, souls imperilled.* Of Prospero and Dr. Faustus, Lewis continues: *Nor could anyone at that date hear the soft and timely 'I'll drown my book' without remembering the earlier magician who had screamed too late 'I'll burn my books'. All the difference between fire and water is there.* Many thinkers of the Renaissance, Lewis added, allowed *the use of evil spirits when enslaved by magia and not given dominion over us by goetia.* Thus Bacon thought the aim of the magicians *noble*; like him, they sought knowledge for the sake of power, *'as a spouse for fruit', not a 'curtesan for pleasure'.* Also, Lewis pointed out that white magic presumed power in man, whereas the widespread (and still spread) belief in astrology reduced man to a puppet: *the little creatures who dreamed of controlling the winds and raising the dead were in reality only the stars' tennis-balls.* Thus A MIDSUMMER NIGHT'S DREAM is Shakespeare's play of faerie; THE TEMPEST, his play of magia; MACBETH, his play of goety.

goliard. A wandering scholar or ribald clerk, often the author of satirical Latin verse; an educated jester, of France, Germany, and England, especially in the 12th and 13th centuries. The *goliards* claimed to be followers of a Bishop *Golias*—but *goliart* was the Old French word for glutton (French *gueule, gullet*) from Latin *gula,* the *gullet;* hence, appetite, gluttony. Langland in PIERS PLOWMAN (1377) speaks of a *goliardeys, a glutton of words.* Chaucer in the Prologue to THE CANTERBURY TALES (1386) says of the Miller with the thumb of gold: *He was a jangler and a golierdis.*

golilla. A stiff starched collar, worn in Spain in the 17th century. Also *golille, golilia, golila, golillio.* Spanish *golilla,* diminutive of *gola* (Latin *gula,* whence *gullet*), throat. A *gullable* (now *gullible*) person is one who will swallow anything, i.e., believe any tale. *Cp. gull.* Wycherley in THE GENTLEMAN DANCING-MASTER (1673) said: *I had rather put on the English pillory than this Spanish golilia.*

gome. See *gaum.* Also *gomenlich,* manly. *gome-graith,* armor. We read in THE PARLEMENT OF THE THREE AGES (1350; in the old 4-beat alliterative verse): *I was als everrous* [eager] *in armes as outher of youre-selven, And as styffe in a stourre on my stede bake, And as gaye in my gere as any gome ells And a lelly byluffede with ladyes and maydens.*

goose. (1) A foolish person. See *widgeon.* (2) A hiss, as in the theatre—not the more vulgar sound meant today by the expression *give him the bird.* Also, sibilation in general; Tennyson in his MEMOIRS (1897) says that to write good blank verse requires a *fine ear for vowel-sounds, and the kicking of the geese out of the boat.* When an audience disliked a performance, the actors used to say (18th and early 19th centuries): *The goose is in the house.* (3) In special combinations: *All his geese are swans,* He always exaggerates; thus, *to turn every (a) goose into a swan. Sound (all right) on the goose* (in U.S. politics), on the right side. *The old woman is picking her geese,* It is snowing. Also see *Winchester goose. To shoe the goose,* to spend one's time in unnecessary labor. *Goose without gravy* (in the British navy): a flogging that does not draw blood. *To say bo to a goose (boe, boh, booh),* to speak; usually this expression is used in the negative; Blackmore put it coyly in CRADOCK NOWELL (1866): *Bob could never say 'Bo' to a gosling of the feminine gender.* (4) A game, also called *fox and geese,* played from the 16th to the 19th century; on a squared board with counters (17, in 1801); every fourth and fifth square pictured a goose, and doubled the move of a player landing thereon. Goldsmith in THE DESERTED VILLAGE (1770) refers to *the royal game of goose;* Byron in DON JUAN (1823) made play with this idea: *For good society is but a game, The royal game of goose, as I may say.* (5) A tailor's smoothing-iron; the handle had the shape of a goose's neck. Shakespeare plays on this meeting when the porter in MACBETH (1606), opening the gate of hell, extends the invitation: *Come in, taylor; here you may rost your goose.*

gore. (1) Dung; filth; slime. From the 8th century. By extension (from the 16th century) clotted blood, blood shed in battle; this sense lingers. In the 16th and 17th centuries *gore-blood* was used to mean clotted blood. *What!* cried Wesley (WORKS; 1774) *To whip them for every petty offence, till they are all in gore blood?* Hence also *to gore,* to besmear with blood, to lie soaking in blood; *They left them goaring in their blood,* said Stanyhurst in his DESCRIPTION OF IRELAND (1577), *and gasping up their flitting ghosts.* Gilbert and Sullivan entitled a comic operetta (1887) *Ruddygore,* then more mildly *Ruddigore.* The word is from Old High German *gor;* Old Norse *gor,* the cud in animals, slimy matter. (2) From Old English *gar,* spear (also *gare,* and via French *geron, giron* English *gyron*) the shape of the spear-head came in the word *gore, gair,* to mean (9th century) an angular promontory, then (from the 13th century) a triangular strip of land, a wedge-shaped strip between two larger fields. By extension, a triangular piece of cloth, as the front section of a skirt, the lap of a gown; loosely, a skirt. *Under gore,* under one's clothes. Also, the opening in the breast of a waist or gown; Skelton in PHILIP SPAROWE (1529) wrote: *My byrde so fayre That was wont to . . . go in at my spayre And crepe in at my gore Of my gowne before.* It may be from this *gore,* spear, that there developed the still current verb, *to gore,* to pierce.

gossip. See *sib.*

gossoon. A young man; a serving-man, lackey. Maria Edgeworth in IRISH BULLS (1802) remarks that *even the cottiers and gossoons speak in trope and figure. Gossoon* is a transformation of *garsoon,* from French *garçon,* boy.

gotch. An earthenware jug, big-bellied. Hence *gotchy,* bloated, swollen. Also *gotch-gutted,* corpulent; *gotch-bellied.* Used in the 16th and 17th centuries.

Gotham. A village the inhabitants of which are proverbial for their folly. *A wise man of Gotham* is a fool. Used since the 16th century; applied by Washington Irving (SALMAGUNDI, 1807) to New York City. Hence *Gotham parish,* a place where fools live; *Gotham College,* training ground of a fool; *Gotham quarrel*: while the two fools belabor one another, a bystander makes off with the stakes. A *Gothamist* is a simpleton; a *Gothamite* is a New Yorker.

gothele. 'To make a noise, as water does when a hot iron is placed in it.' So Herbert Coleridge in his DICTIONARY OF THE OLDEST WORDS (1863). Accented on the first syllable of its two; but three syllables in *godelen, godeley.* The O.E.D. calls it echoic, and defines it as 'to make a low rumbling noise, as bubbles rising through water, or as is heard in the bowels.' *Cp. borborygmite.* Hence, to slander. Used into the 15th century.

gowpen. See *yepsen.* Used from the 14th century, especially in Scotland. Hence *gowpenful,* a double handful; Carlyle in a letter of 1852 wrote that *An old Russian countess yesternight sat playing gowpansful of gold pieces every stake.*

gracile. Slender, lean. Latin *gracilem,* slender. Also *gracill, gracilent* (18th century), *gracilious* (17th century). *gracilescent,* growing slender; narrowing. *gracility,* slenderness, leanness. Not to be confused (as it sometimes is) with *graceful,* from Latin *gratia,* thanks, attractiveness; *gratus,* pleasing, whence also *grateful.* Among poets and fictioneers of the 19th century, the sound of the word affected its sense; it was used as meaning gracefully slender; e.g., in HARPER'S MAGAZINE (April, 1888): *Girls . . . beautiful with the beauty of ruddy bronze,—gracile as the palmettoes that sway above them.*

graffito. A drawing, or writing, scratched on a wall; scribbling on a wall. Italian *graffito; graffio,* a scratch; Greek *grapho* meant first to *grave* (*engrave*), scratch; that is, to write in stone; hence to write and all the English consequences: *graphic; photograph* (Greek *photos,* light), drawing with light; on to the recently renewed study of *graphology,* retrieved from palmistry and *graphomancy*; *cp. aeromancy*. Although used mainly of such scrawlings left on ancient walls (Pompeii; Rome) the word has been elsewhere applied, as in Dowden's LIFE OF SHELLEY (1886): *She sang pleasantly; and could scribble such graffiti as may be found in school-girls' copy-books.* Surely the word has use, of walls today.

graim. See *grame*.

graith. To make ready, to prepare; hence to equip, to array. In HOBIE NOBLE (in Child's BALLADS, 1775) we hear that *Hobie has graithd his body weel.* Chaucer uses *graith* in THE REEVE'S TALE (1386). The word is from Old Teutonic; the Old English form was *geraede*, the prefix *ge* + *raidh*, whence English *ready*. *To graith in the grave* was to bury. *Graithing* meant preparation, hence also furniture, attire; SYLVESTRA (1881) by Annie Ellis says *The lass was . . . willing, but sadly in want of graithing. Graithness* (not used since the 15th century) meant readiness.

graking A 13th century variant of *graying*, early dawn. Also *griking*. Used in the romance of KYNG ALYSAUNDER.

gramarye. In the 14th and 15th centuries *gramarye* meant *grammar* (being an early form of that word, ultimately from Greek *gramma*, letter); then learning in general. In the 15th century learning fell under suspicion, and was associated with magic; hence *gramarye* came to mean occult learning, necromancy. Scott in THE LAY OF THE LAST MINSTREL (1805) brought this use back into currency. Another form was *glamoury*, which also meant magic; as a spell: *to cast the glamour over one*; Scott (in the same poem) used this form also; but it has come into current use as the white magic of enchanting beauty and charming enticement.

grame. Anger; grief. Also, in the plural, troubles (in the 12th century, devils). Also *graim, greme. Grame* also was an adjective, sorrowful; and a verb, as in the phrase *It grames me.* The word is related to *grim*. Wyatt in his poem THE LOVER'S APPEAL (1557) inquires *And wilt thou leave me thus? Say nay! Say nay! for shame! To save thee from the blame Of all my grief and grame.*

gramercy. Thank you. Also as an exclamation of gratefulness, or surprise: Mercy on us! Old French *grant merci*, great thanks. *No gramercy*, no special merit; also *What gramercy. . . ?*, what reason. . . ? In Greene's A NOTABLE DISCOVERY OF COOSENAGE (1591) the coney said to the verser (*cp. pedlers French*): *"Now gramercy, sir, for this tricke," saith the connie. "Ile domineere with this amongst my neighbors."* Gramercy Park, New York is from Dutch *Krummersee*, crooked (arm of the) sea, which there bent into Manhattan Island.

grange. Originally a *granary*, a repository for grain; Toone (1834) said it was the place where monasteries deposited their rents (paid in grain.) Medieval Latin *granagium*; Latin *granum*, grain. Toone's notions must be taken with a grange of salt. Later, *grange* was used of a farm with its various outbuilding; then, a country house. *There, at the moated grange*, says Shakespeare in MEASURE FOR MEASURE (1604), *resides the dejected Mariana.* The word was often applied figuratively, as in Spenser's THE FAERIE QUEENE (1596): *Ne have the watry foules a certain grange Wherein to rest.*

grangerize. To illustrate a book by adding prints and other clippings. A frequent

18th and 19th century practice, especially in contemporary histories. From James *Granger,* whose BIOGRAPHICAL HISTORY OF ENGLAND (1769) left blank pages for the purpose. Hence *grangerism; grangerizing, grangerization;* a *grangerizer, grangerite.* THE NEW YORK TRIBUNE of 13 January, 1889, announced: *The portraits of actors will be paged separately, with blank backs, for the benefit of grangerizers.*

grangousier. One that will swallow anything—physically or mentally. Also *grandgosier;* used from the 16th century, the name of the father of *Gargantua* in Rabelais: French *grand,* great + *gosier,* throat. Meredith in THE ADVENTURES OF HARRY RICHMOND (1871) speaks of *our grangousier public.*

grassator. A rioter, bully, footpad. Latin *grassator,* from *grassari, grassatus,* to riot, to lie in wait, to attack. Hence *grassation,* assault; Donne (1610) speaks of *violent grassations.* The verb *grassate,* to rage, and the adjective *grassant,* raging, were used mainly of disease, though North spoke in 1734 *of thieves, malefactors, and cheats, everywhere grassant.*

graval. A form of *gravel;* see *gravel-blind.* Ascham in THE SCHOLEMASTER (1570) warned that *any labor may be sone gravaled, if a man trust alwaies to his own singuler witte, and will not be glad sometyme to heare, take advise, and learne of an other.*

gravel-blind. See *sandblind.* Revived by Scott in THE HEART OF MIDLOTHIAN (1818; first use after Shakespeare's), and used since then (Prescott; Hood) to mean nearly *stone-blind: sand, gravel, stone.* E. Gilliat in THE FOREST OUTLAWS (1887) uses words often true today: *There be a power of signs to tell us what's coming, if we were not gravel-blind.* Other combinations of *gravel* have been used. *Gravelly* means abounding in, or resembling *gravel; gravely* (two syllables), seriously, with dignity. *Gravel-stone* has been used figuratively, as in JACOB'S WELL (1440): *Thise gravelstonys, that is, coveytous thoutys* [thoughts]; Dryden in his rendering (1697) of the GEORGICS of Virgil reminds us that *Bees bear gravel-stones, whose poising weight Steers thro' the whistling wind their steddy flight. To gravel,* to run aground (of a ship); hence, to be stuck in the mud; to smother or choke with gravel; to confuse, perplex, puzzle; Shakespeare in AS YOU LIKE IT (1600) has Rosalind, disguised as a boy, giving Orlando advice on how to make love; Orlando says *I would kiss before I spoke.* Rosalind: *Nay, you were better speake first, and when you were gravel'd for lacke of matter, you might take occasion to kiss. Very good orators, when they are out, they will spit, and for lovers lacking—God warn us!—matter, the cleanliest shift is to kisse.*

graveolent. Foul-smelling, fetid. Latin *gravis,* heavy + *olere,* to smell. Hence also *graveolence.* The accent is on the second syllable, *e.* Used 17th into the 19th century; applied to rancid butter, bad eggs, hell; also figuratively as in Bulwer-Lytton's ENGLAND AND THE ENGLISH (1833): *He strives to buoy himself from the graveolent abyss of his infamy.*

greave. (1) Brushwood; a thicket. Plural, twigs; branches. Old English *graefa,* related to *grove.* (2) The sandy shore of a stream; French *grève;* related to *gravel.* (3) In plural only, *greaves,* the skin over animal fat, cooked for crackling. If the fat is melted for tallow, the *greaves* forms a sediment which, removed, was pressed into cakes for dogs, fish-bait, etc. German *Griebe.* (4) Armor for the leg below the knee (usually in the plural); hence, the skin. Chaucer and Spenser were among those that used the first sense, which was common from the 10th century through the 16th: Spenser in THE FAËRIE QUEENE (1590): *It is best . . . that ye do leave Your treasure . . . Either fast closed in some hollow greave, Or buried in the ground from jeopardy.* The most frequent use was as the armor: Milton (1671, SAMSON AGONISTES), Pope, Byron; Tennyson in THE LADY OF SHALOTT (1832): *The sun came dazzling thro' the leaves and flamed upon the brazen greaves Of bold Sir Lancelot.*

gree. Several words joined in this common form, very frequent in the 14th, 15th and 16th centuries, but lingering into the 19th. (1) *gree,* a step (Old French *gré* from Latin *gradum,* step), a degree, literally or as a stage in a process, a degree in rank, etc. *Cp. congree*; *grise.* In law (e.g., of matrimony) *greis defendant* was a forbidden degree (of relationship). Hence also, the highest degree, pre-eminence, victory; the prize for a victory: *to bear (get, take, win) the gree.* All senses of *degree,* which supplanted *gree*; thus Chaucer says in THE MERCHANT'S TALE (1386), quoting Seneca: *There is no thing in gree superlative, As saith Senek, above an humble wyf.* (2) From Old French *gré* (modern French *de bon gré,* with good will) from Latin *gratus,* pleasing, came English *gree,* good will. *To take (accept, receive) in gree,* to take in good part. Chaucer uses this sense also; likewise Spenser in THE FAËRIE QUEENE (1590): *Which she accepts with thanks and goodly gree. To do (make) gree,* to give satisfaction (for an injury); *unto gree,* as an indemnity; *by his gree,* of his own accord; *of the gree,* voluntarily; *out of gree,* against one's will; amiss. (3) In the 16th century, *gree* was used to mean weeping. mourning: Chatterton revived this in a poem of 1768, as a verb: *Round his holy corse to gre.* As a verb, *gree* was an early form (15th into the 18th century) of *agree,* in all its meanings; thus Shakespeare in SONNET 114 (1600) has: *Mine eye well knows what with his gust is greeing.* The form *gre* was also used, in every sense. God grant you (as they said in the 15th century) gree and grith!

green (in various combinations). *green-bag,* a lawyer; originally, the green cloth bag in which barristers carried their papers. Wycherley in THE PLAIN DEALER (1677): *You green bag carrier, you murderer of unfortunate causes, the clerks ink is scarce off your fingers.* Thus *What's in the green bag?* What's the charge against me? *green baize, green table,* a gaming table. *green box,* an upper box at a theatre. *green cheese*; see *cheese*; the O.E.D. suggests the variegated surface of the moon may have suggested a round cheese with streaks of green from sage. *greencoat,* a scholar in certain charity schools; Westminster had *black-coat, blue-coat,* and *greencoat schools. green goose,* a simpleton. *To give a girl a green gown,* to roll a girl (in amorous sport) on the grass; hence, *to wear a green gown,* to have lost one's virginity. Green was, indeed, associated not only with country simplicity (*greenhorn*) and country freshness, and vigor or unripeness, callowness, but with amorous activity, as in the ballad of *greensleeves* (*Lady Greensleeves*) and in such references as in Jonson's BARTHOLOMEW'S FAIR (1614), when two loose women are being readied: *Ursula, take them in, open thy wardrobe, and fit them to their calling. Green gowns, crimson petticoats; green women, my lord mayor's green women! guests o' the game,* *true bred. greenhead,* an immature or untrained intellect; *greenheaded,* inexperienced. *greenkin,* a person (a little one) clad in green. *greenman,* a savage; especially, a man dressed in greenery, to play a wild man of the woods in a masque or outdoor show. *greenroom,* a theatre lounge for the performers; *to talk green-room,* to gossip of the theatre. Jerome K. Jerome in ON THE STAGE in 1885 remarked: *Where a green-room was originally provided, it has been taken by the star or the manager, as his or her private room. green rushes,* fresh rushes spread on the floor of a house for an honored guest that is a stranger; hence, an exclamation of surprise at seeing one long absent; N. Breton in WONDERS WORTH HEARING (1602): *Greene rushes, M. Francisco! It is a wonder to see you heere in this country. greenwax,* a seal on documents delivered to sheriffs by the Exchequer; hence, a fine, an amercement (as ordered by such a document); GOD SPEED THE PLOUGH (1500) laments: *Then commeth the grenewex which greveth us sore. green way* (*green gate*) the pleasant road, the broad road, the primrose path; Milton in a Sonnet of 1674 wrote: *Lady, that in the prime of earliest youth Wisely hast shunned the broad way and the green* (*broad,* as opposed to *strait and narrow*). *greeny,* verdant; vigorous; Queen Elizabeth (rendering Boethius; 1593) spoke of *happy griny youth*; she was then sixty, far beyond the age of *green-sickness* (an anemia that affects girls at puberty), though still in some ways *green.*

greet. Two words coalesced in this form. (1) To *greet,* to salute, to hail, to welcome, still current, had now forgotten uses. Its earliest senses, lost during the Old English period, were to approach, to take in hand; hence (surviving into the 15th century), to attack. KYNG ALYSAUNDER (13th century) had: *With his launce he him grette.* Also, to offer congratulations (unto); so used by Spenser, several times in THE FAËRIE QUEENE (1596). (2) To *greet,* to weep, lament; beseech with tears; cry out in supplication or anger. This word (also as a noun, lamentation) was common from the 8th century, continuing in Scots through the 19th, as when Stevenson wrote, in CATRIONA (1893): *I sat down and grat like a bairn.* There were many variants: Present tense, *gret, grate, griet, greit*; past, *grett, gretid, grete, grat*; past participle, *graten, igroten, greten, gret, grutten.* Hence *greeter,* one that salutes or one that cries. *Greetingful,* sorrowful, tearful; *greetingless,* unsaluted, unwelcome; *greety,* inclined to shed tears. In THE SHEPHERD'S CALENDAR (1579; AUGUST), Spenser has: *Well decked in a frocke of gray.—Hey, ho, grey is greete,* with the gloss: 'weeping and complaint.' A very rare use—only in Greene's JAMES IV (1591) and Shakespeare's PERICLES (1608): *It greets me as an enterprise of kindness*—is *greet,* to gratify.

Gregorian. (1) Relating to Pope Gregory I (in the Holy See 590-600), as *Gregorian water,* holy water; *Gregorian chant.* (2) The *Gregorian calendar* was established by Pope Gregory XIII, in 1582; hence *Gregorian style,* new style; *Gregorian epoch.* (3) A wig worn in the 16th and 17th centuries, supposedly intraduced by one *Gregory,* a barber on the Strand. Braithwait in THE HONEST GHOST (1658) speaks of one *who pulling a little downe his gregorian, which was displac't a little by hastie taking off his bever, sharpening his peake and erecting his distended mouchatos, proceeded in this answere.* (4) A member of an 18th century society (often mentioned along with the Freemasons); referred to by Pope, Smollett, Crabbe. (5) The *gregorian-tree,* the gallows; in the 17th century: *a gregory,* a hangman—from *Gregory* Brandon, common hangman of London under James I, succeeded by his son, "*Young Gregory,*" who died in 1649. Also (6) *gregory* (*gregory-powder*), compound powder of rhubarb; named after the Scotch Doctor James *Gregory* (1758-1822). Being ill-tasting, it was often mixed with honey or other pleasant comestibles, hence used figuratively, as in THE PALL MALL GAZETTE (28 August, 1886): *However beautifully the gregory-powder of morality is apparelled in the currant jelly of story . . .*

greking. Daybreak; dawn. Akin to *grey.* Used 14th, 15th and early 16th centuries, *the greyking of the misty morn* of English letters. Also *graking, q.v.*

greme. See *grame. Gremeful,* sorrowful; *greming,* angry.

gremial. Also *gremious.* Relating to the lap or bosom; hence, protecting, intimate. (Latin *gremium,* lap, bosom, therefore shelter.) Hence also, dwelling within the "bosom" of an alma mater; *gremials* (16th into the 19th century) were resident, active members of a university or society. A 1669 harangue against prostitutes called for *a repentance that will snatch you out of their gremial graves.*

gressible. Able to walk. Latin *gradi, gressum,* to walk, whence human *progress.* The play TIMON (1600) speaks of *a two legd living creature, gressible, unfeathered*: the standard definition of a man. Hence also *gressile, gressive; gressorial,* adapted for walking. The simple forms from the Latin hardly survive in English (*cp. couth*), but we still use many compounds: *grade, gradation, retrograde, gradual, graduation, degree; congress, disgression,* and all the avenues of *aggression.* P. T. Barnum, whenever the crowd at his circus sideshow grew large, had a sign put up reading: *This way to the Egress*; many spectators, expecting to behold a feminine marvel or monster (such as an ogress), went through the door and found themselves outside . . . Terrestrial creatures may be classified as walking, flying, or crawling: *gressile, volatile, or reptile.*

gressop. A 13th century form for *grasshopper.* Used in the 77TH PSALM.

gressorial. See *gressible.*

grey. As a noun, in various applications from the color: a badger, the fur of a badger. An old man (in Chaucer, 1386). *A greyhound*; also *a grew, a grewhound; to grew,* to hunt with greyhounds, was used in Scotland into the 19th century; from *grew,* Greek, as though the dog were Grecian. *A pair of greys,* two grey horses; by extension from this, in 19th century slang, *a grey,* a coin with two heads or two tails, for cheating gamblers.

gride. A variant form of *gird*—not the *gird,* to encircle, that gives us *girdle,* but an early (12th century) verb meaning to strike, to pierce, to thrust; surviving in the figurative sense, *to gird at,* to make thrusts at, to mock. The form *gride,* used by Lydgate, Spenser, then later writers, meant to pierce with a weapon, to wound, then to cut or scrape, with a rasping sound. Spenser used it first in THE SHEPHERD'S CALENDAR (1579; FEBRUARY): *The kene cold blowes through my beaten hyde, All as I were through the body gryde*—to which the gloss gives 'perced'—and several times in THE FAËRIE QUEENE. Note that *gryde, gryed* was also the past tense form of *grye,* to shudder, an infrequent verb that occurs in the 14th century GAWAIN AND THE GREEN KNIGHT: *So agreved for greme he gryed within.*

gridelin. A color: white and red; pale purple or red. Literally (French *gris-de-lin*) flaxgrey. Used from the 17th century. Killigrew in THE PARSON'S WEDDING (1663) averred: *And his love, Lord help us, fades like my gredaline petticoat.*

grimalkin. An old she-cat; a term of contempt for a bossy old woman; a witch. See *merkin.* Swift (1745) speaks of *grimalkin eyes*; Lord Chesterfield, in THE WORLD, No. 185 (1756) declared: *I am not henpecked; I am not grimalkined; I have no Mrs. Freeman with her Italian airs; but I have a wife more troublesome than all three.*

gripple. Gripping, tenacious; griping, niggardly. Also *gripel, gripul, griple*; *grippal* (Scott, 1814, WAVERLEY). Used from the 10th century; by Spenser in THE FAËRIE QUEENE (1590): *He gnasht his teeth to see Those heaps of gold with griple covetise.* Middleton in ANYTHING FOR A QUIET LIFE (1626) exclaimed *that a man of your estate should be so gripple-minded and repining at his wife's bounty!* Thence *grippleness,* niggardliness, greed; also, greedy desire; *grippy* (19th century), *gripulous* (17th century), avaricious, grasping; a 1633 Exposition of PETER (THE BIBLE) stated that *liberality is in medio* [*cp. mesothesis*] *between gripulousness and profuseness.*

grise. (1) A variant of *grece,* from *gree,* step. See *gree.* The plural (French *greis*) English *grise, grize, greece, grece, grees* was taken as a collective singular, flight of steps, stairway, and developed new plural forms, such as *greces, greeses.* (2) *gris, grys, grice, grise, greyce,* the color grey; also, a kind of grey fur (14th to 16th century). *Grisamber* was an early form of *ambergris.* In the 14th and 15th centuries, *grise* (3) was used as an adjective, a variant of *grisly* (from the 12th century), terrible, fearful. Also (4) the verb *to grise,* to shudder at with terror or abhorrence; to tremble in great fear; *to agrise. It grises me* (13th and 14th centuries), it makes me shudder with fear; I am afraid. Shakespeare uses *grise,* step, in OTHELLO; in TIMON OF ATHENS (1605): *Who dares, In purity of manhood stand upright And say "This man's a flatterer"? If one be, so are they all, for every grise of fortune Is smoothed by that below*; and in TWELFTH NIGHT when Viola says: *I pity you.* Olivia: *That's a degree to love.* Viola: *No, not a grize, for 'tis a vulgar proof That very oft we pity enemies.*

grith. Guaranteed security (under the laws of King Cnut, 1000); safe conduct. Old Norse *grith,* home; in the plural, truce, pardon, sanctuary. *To take grith,* to take sanctuary. *Church-grith,* sanctuary within the precincts of the church; *hand-grith,* protection under the King's hand. By extension, *grith* came to mean peace, in which sense it was often associated with *frith, q.v.* Hence also, quarter in battle, *to give grith*; *without* (*en*) *grith,* without mercy. Also, in Scotland, the closing of criminal courts at Christmas and other times when the King's peace was granted to criminals. *Grithman,* one who has taken sanctuary; the place of sanctuary might be a *grith-stool, grith-place, grith-town. Grith* and its compounds were common from the 10th to the 15th century.

grobian. A slovenly person, a boor. Also, *grobianism.* From an imaginary medieval *Grobianus,* taken by writers in 15th and 16th century Germany as the supreme boor. *This tree of gulls,* says Dekker in his Preface to THE GULL'S HORN-BOOK (1609), *hath a relish of grobianism.* Burton in *The Anatomy of Melancholy* (1621) makes a remark that should give hope to despairing mothers of adolescents: *Let them be never so clownish, . . grobians and sluts, if once they be in love, they will be most neat and spruce.*

grog. A drink, originally of rum and water. Hence, *seven-water grog,* a very weak mixture. Admiral Vernon, of the British Navy, was called *Old Grog* because of his *grogram* cloak [from French *gros grain,* coarse grain (cloth)]; in August 1740, the Admiral ordered half rum, half water, to be served to the sailors instead of their regular allowance of neat spirits. The nickname *grog* was transferred from the Admiral to the drink. The word *groggy,* tipsy (sometimes, punch-drunk), survives. Hence various combinations: *grog-blossom,* the red nose of the drunkard; *grog-fight,* a drinking party (last New Year's Eve I saw three men lying in Times Square, and traffic diverted, after such a 'party'); *grog-shop* or *groggery; groggified,* tipsy.

grot. (1) A small particle, fragment. Related to *grit, grout, groats,* grain. Chaucer in THE FRIAR'S PROLOGUE (1386) has: *I shall him quiten every grot.* (2) Weeping, lamentation; *to grote* was to bewail. Both of these senses are found from the 9th to the 15th century. (3) Beginning in the 16th century, *grot* was also used, especially in poetry, as a form of *grotto;* Johnson in THE RAMBLER, No. 108 (1753) mentioned *a natural grot shaded with myrtles.*

groundling. One that frequented the pit or 'ground' of a theatre—in Elizabethan days, he stood on the bare ground before the stage. Hence, a rude person of uncultivated taste. Shakespeare used the word in a famous passage of HAMLET (1602)—*O it offends mee to the soule, to see a robustious perywigpated fellow teare a passion to tatters, to verie ragges, to split the ears of the groundlings*—and most instances since are reverberations of that use. Lamb, however, in REFLECTIONS IN THE PILLORY (1825) spoke of the stocks as *that domicile for groundling rogues and base earth-kissing varlets.*

growtnoll. A blockhead; a 'great noddle.' Also *groutnoll, grouthead, growthed,* and more. Used from the 16th century; Urquhart's translation (1653) of Rabelais revels in the forms: *Noddie meacocks, blockish grutnols, doddi-pol-jolt-heads.*

grue. (1) A grain, a tiny bit. Old French *gru,* grain, meal, related to *gruel.* Mainly in the negative: *no grue, not a grue,* not a bit. (2) A crane (the bird); hence, *to grue,* to call like a crane. Latin *gruem,* crane; French *grue.* (3) Shivering, shuddering. *Grueful,* horror-struck. As a verb, *to grue,* to shiver, shudder; to feel horror or terror; to shrink from something; later, to thrill, as when H. Coleridge in a poem of 1849 wrote: *His every member grueing with delight.* Since the 13th century the main use was as the verb, to be troubled in heart, to feel terror, to shudder—whence *gruesome* has survived.

gruntle. The snout of a pig; by transference, disrespectfully, a person's face. Also, a little grunt. Other forms were *gruntill; grunkle* (Scotch). Hence, *to gruntle,* to make a sound like a swine; to grumble, complain. *Disgruntled* is, obviously, with one's nose out of joint. *Cp. couth.*

gryde. See *gride.*

guarish. See *warish.* Used often by Caxton (1480); also by Spenser in THE FAËRIE QUEENE (1590): *All his wounds, and all his bruses guarisht.*

guary. The Cornish name (15th and 16th centuries) of the miracle play. Also *garye.* Carew in his CORNWALL (1602) called it *a kinde of enterlude, compiled in Cornish out of some scripture history, with that grossenes which accompanied the Romanes Old Comedy.*

guerdon. A reward or requital. Roundabout via Old French from Old English *witherlean; wither* (German *wieder*), again + *lean,* payment. Used from Chaucer to Tennyson, as both noun and verb; Shakespeare in MUCH ADO ABOUT NOTHING (1599) says: *Death in guerdon of her wrong Gives her fame which never dies.* Hence also *guerdoner; guerdonable; guerdonize; guerdonless;* also *guerdoun.*

guidon. A pennant, forked or pointed at one end, borne at the head of a company of soldiers; the officer that carries this standard; the company that fights under it, a troop. French; related to *guide.* In the 17th century the forms *guydhome, guidhome, guidhim, guidone* show the notion that the word was from *guide-homme,* guide for men. Shakespeare has the Constable of France say, in HENRY V (1599): *I stay but for my guidon. Take the field!*

guimbard. The name of what is commonly known as a jew's-harp. Pronounced with a hard *g;* accent on the *gim.*

gulch. To swallow greedily (from the sound). Hence *gulch,* a glutton; *gulch-cup,* a tosspot; *gulchin,* a little glutton (in 17th and 18th century dictionaries). In addition to this sense, and its current meaning of a narrow ravine, especially one where gold may be found, a *gulch* is a heavy fall, as in wrestling; *to come down gulch.* As a glutton or drunkard, Jonson uses the word in THE POETASTER (1601): *You'll see us then, you will, gulch, you will?* In the sense of plunging heavily Clare (1821) speaks of *fly-bit cattle gulshing in the brook.*

gull. This word has had many meanings. (1) The throat, gullet (Latin *gula,* gullet). Hence *to gull,* to eat voraciously; to cram—to fool, cheat, trick, *make a gull of.* The common bird the *gull,* though the word is of different origin, has become associated with these senses, as in *greedy gulls; gull-catcher,* a cheater. (2) *Gull,* also *gule, gool,* yellow. From this, probably, a fish not fully grown; a bird not yet fledged, as in Shakespeare's HENRY IV, PART ONE (1596): *As that ungentle gull the cuckoo's bird Useth the sparrow.* From these senses (3) *gull* came to mean a simpleton, an easy mark; so Shakespeare (1594), Milton (1645), Dickens (1838), Stevenson (1885). Dekker in 1609 wrote a satiric guide for gallants in London, called *The Gull's Horn-Book.* Hence also *gullage,* cajolery into deception. By extension, a *gull* meant a deception, a false report, as in Shakespeare's MUCH ADO ABOUT NOTHING (1599): *I should think this a gull, but that the white-bearded fellow speaks it.* (4) By enlargement from *gullet, gull* was also used in the sense of *gully,* a channel made by a swollen stream; *to gull,* to wear down or sweep away, make ruts in.—Poe in 1849 commented on *the pertinacity of the effort to gull,* but Washington Irving twenty-five years earlier remarked: *Nothing is so easy as to gull the public.* The public is indeed *gullable*—the later forms *gullible* and *gullibility* are still widely around.

gybe. See *pedlers French.*

gypon. See *smotherlich.*

gyromancy. See *aeromancy.* Walking in a circle (divided into zones) until falling from dizziness, the prophecy dependent upon the zone in which one fell. It's simpler to play roulette.

gyve. A fetter, a shackle for the leg. Usually in the plural: *gives, guives, guyves*; the word was probably once pronounced with the *g* hard, as in *give;* now the *g* is soft, as in *gem.* A common word (and instrument) since the 13th century. The word was often used figuratively. Shakespeare in THE LOVER'S COMPLAINT (1597) speaks of *Playing patient sports in unconstrained gives;* Disraeli, in CONINGSBY (1844), of *the gyves and trammels of office. Gyve* was also used as a verb, to fetter; as by Shakespeare in OTHELLO: *I will give thee in thine own courtship.* CIRCUMCISION (15th century) declared: *My wittis be so dull with rudenes, And in the cheynes of ignoraunce gyved.*

H

hab nab. Hit or miss; at a venture; at random; anyhow. Probably from Old English *habbe,* to have; *nabbe,* not to have. Also *hab or nab*; later, *hob a nob, hob or nob, hob and nob*; Shakespeare in TWELFTH NIGHT (1601) says *hob, nob is his word; give't or take't.* Used from the 16th century; in the 18th century it was used when glasses were lifted to drink: *Hob or nob,* come what may. Hence, *to drink hob or nob,* to drink together in companionship—whence the current use of *hobnob* today.

habergeon. Also *haberjoun*; *cp. acton.* See *smotherlich.*

hadiwist. Vain regret; the heedlessness that results in this. Also *had-I-wist,* literally, if I had known. Used from the 13th to the 17th century. Gower in CONFESSIO AMANTIS (1390) wrote: *Upon his fortune and his grace Cometh hadiwist full ofte a place.* The BABEES BOOK (1460) warned: *Kepe thee well from hadde-y-wyste.* There was a common 16th century proverb: *A wise man saith not, had I wist.*

haecceity. Thisness; the quality of being this and nothing else. Pronounced *hike-see-ity. Haec* is Latin for *this.* See *thisness.*

haffet. Also *halfet, halfhed, haffat.* See *swith.*

haggaday. A door latch; especially, on a cottage door, a latch on the inside with nothing projecting on the outside; there is a thin slit in the door, into which a nail or a slip of metal is inserted to raise the latch. Also *havegooday.* Probably from, or altered to relate to, *"Ha' good day,"* used in leave-taking.

haha. Apart from the sound of laughter, but perhaps arising as an exclamation of surprise, *haha* has been used since the 17th century (also *aha, ah ah, ha! ha!, hahah, haw-haw*) for a sunken fence, a trench, ditch, or other boundary to a garden that does not obstruct the view and is not visible until one is nigh into it. R. S. Surtees in SPONGE'S SPANISH TOUR (1852) tells of a hound that *ran a black cart-colt, and made him leap the haw-haw.* The word was also used figuratively; Mason in his EPISTLE TO SIR W. CHAMBERS (1773) wrote: *Leap each ha-ha of truth and common sense.* It became an 18th century fashion, as De Foe noted in his TOUR OF GREAT BRITAIN (1769) to be *throwing down the walls of the garden, and making, instead of them, hawhaw walls.*

half. In various combinations. *half-bull,* a pontifical letter of a new pope before his coronation—the *bulla* being stamped with only one side of the seal, the side representing the apostles. *half-cap,* a slight and almost discourteous salute; Shakespeare in TIMON OF ATHENS (1607): *With certaine halfe-caps, and cold moving nods, They froze me into silence. half-dike,* a sunken fence, a haha. *half-labor,* a way of paying rent: half the crops or other product of the tenant's toil, that went to the landlord. *halfheaded,* stupid. *halflang, halfling,* a stripling, one not fully grown. *halfman,* a eunuch. *halfkirtle,* a short-skirted, loose bodied gown, commonly worn by courtesans; hence, a courtesan; Shakespeare in HENRY IV, PART TWO: *You filthy famish'd correctioner! if you be not swinged, I'll forswear half-kirtles. halfner,* one that shares 50-50 (16th century). *half-seas-over,* midway toward a goal; Dryden in 1700: *I am half-seas over to death*; the sense of half-drunk came in the 18th century. *half-tongue,* of a jury half of whom were foreigners, as used to be allowed in England, in criminal prosecution of a foreigner. *half-word,* an insinuation; so used by Chaucer.

halfendeal. See *thirdendeal.*

halidom. Holiness; a holy place, a chapel; a holy relic—by which one might take an oath; hence, since the 16th century, *By my halidom,* often used as a mere exclamation, e.g., in Shakespeare's TWO GENTLEMEN OF VERONA (1591): *By my hallidome, I was fast asleep.* In the 16th and 17th centuries, the word was often spelled *halidam, holidam, holydame,* as though referring to 'Our Lady.' It is from Old English *halig* (German *heilig*), holy + *dom,* state.

halieutics. The art or craft of fishing, or a treatise thereon. *Halieutic,* relating to fishing. Greek *halieutikos*; *halieutes,* fisher; *halieuein,* to fish; *hals,* the sea. Sir Thomas Browne in his treatise on VULGAR ERRORS (1646) mentions *four books of cynegeticks or venation, five of halieuticks or piscation. Cynegetics,* hunting, the chase, is also a 17th century word, from Greek *kyn-,* dog + *hegetes,* leader. President Eisenhower is an expert in halieutics as compared with President Washington, who fished two hours in the Hudson without so much as a nibble—which may be why many presidents after Washington have taken up halieutics.

haliography. Writing about the sea. Although the word was used mainly in the 17th and 18th centuries, the practice lures many; in the early 1950's there was a flood of *haliographic* volumes. The word is from Greek *hals, hali-,* the sea + *graphia,* writing; but note that *hals* also means salt (the sea is salt) as in *halogen,* salt-forming, and *haligraphy* is a treatise or writing on the nature of salts.

halitus. Vapor. Latin *halitus,* breath; *halare,* to breathe, whence *inhale, exhale* and all our living. Hence *halituous,* of the nature of vapor, accompanied by vapor, as the *halituous heat* of these late summer days. Hence, also, the too current *halitosis,* literally, full of breath.

halomancy. See *aeromancy*

haltersack. Gallows-bird; 'a bundle fit for the rope.' Used in the late 16th and the 17th century, especially by the dramatists. Beaumont and Fletcher, in THE KNIGHT OF THE BURNING PESTLE (1609) said: *If he were my son, I would hang him up by the heels, and flea him, and salt him, whoreson haltersack!* and in FOUR PLAYS IN ONE declared: *Thy beginning was knapsack and thy ending will be haltersack* [born bastard, to die hanged].

haluwen. See *imene.* A variant of *hallow,* which, as a noun, meant a saint.

hamesucken. Assaulting a person in his own home; a serious crime in Old England. The word is still used in Scotland. Also *hamesoken, homsokne*; *hamfare.*

hamiform. Hookshaped. Latin *hamus,* hook; the *a* is long.

hand. This common Teutonic word developed numerous offshoots. Less remembered ones include: *hand-adventure,* single combat; *hand-bolt,* a handcuff. *hand-canter, hand-gallop,* easy paces, with the horse well under control. *handfast,* a firm grip; Shakespeare in THE WINTER'S TALE (1611) says: *If that shepheard be not in handfast, let him flye*; also, manacled; also, wedded by joining hands; Malory in the MORTE D'ARTHUR (1485): *Anon he made them handfast and married them*; thus, *to handfast,* to contract in marriage. *hand-friend,* a friend at hand in need. *handgrith* (10th century) protection given by the king's hand. *hand-habend,* with the (stolen) goods, an Old English law term. *hand-loose,* free from restraint. *handlings* (10th to 14th century), hand to hand. *hand-maker,* one that profits fraudulently. *handsal,* to hand over; a 13th century verb. *hand-sale,* a bargain bound by a *handshake*; *hand-sale weight,* weight (for a sale) judged by poising the article in the hand. *handsmooth,* level as though smoothed by the hand; hence, downright, without qualification. *handsome* originally meant easy to handle, to deal with or use; hence *handsome is as handsome does. handtame,* mild, gentle; *handtamed,* subdued. *handwhile,* a short span of time; Hawkins in his translation (1646), YOUTH'S BEHAVIOR; OR, DECENCY IN CONVERSATION AMONGST MEN, advised: *Contradict not at every handwhile, that which others say.*

hand of glory. A charm. Originally, a *mandrake* root shaped like a hand. The term is a translation of French *main de gloire,* which is a popular corruption of *mandegore, mandragore,* mandrake. Scott in THE ANTIQUARY (1816), tells of what the charm later consisted: *De hand of glory . . . is hand cut off from a dead man, as has been hanged for murther, and dried very nice in de shmoke of juniper wood.* Such a charm was buried with precious metals, to make them double overnight.

handsaw. The obvious meaning, a saw used with one hand, occurs in Shakespeare's HENRY VI, PART ONE (1596): *My buckler cut through and through, my sword hackt like a handsaw.* There is less immediate point to the noted remark in Hamlet: *I am but mad north north-west: when the wind is southerly, I know a hawk from a handsaw.* It is plausibly suggested that *handsaw* here is changed from dialectal *harnsa,* for *hernsew.* This is itself a variant of *hernshew, hernshaw, heronsaw, heronshew, heronshaw,* and more, from Old French *heronceau,* a little *heron.* Thus the expression would mean: I know the bird of prey from the bird it preys on, I know my nose from my eyebrow. Early lexicographers (Cotgrave, 1611, followed by Johnson, 1755) took the ending *shaw* (*q.v.*) to mean wood, and explained *hernshaw, heronshaw,* as a wood where herons breed. A menu of 1440 called for *pygge rosted . . . and hernesewes. The young heronshowes* (1620) *are by some accounted a very dainty dish.*

handsel. A token of good luck; specifically, a gift as a token of good wishes for the New Year or a new occupation, a marriage, the first sale of the day, and the like. Probably in origin 'a giving of the hands,' a handshake, or a gift in the hand. Also *hancel, hansel.* By extension, the first sum received (on a new day, or as a first instalment); hence, the first trial or experience or specimen of a thing —usually with hope or sense of good luck. *Bring him a six-penny bottle of ale,* Jonson has in BARTHOLOMEW'S FAIR (1614); *they say a fool's handsell is lucky.*

handy-dandy. A game played since the 14th century, in which an object is shaken in the two hands held together; the hands are suddenly closed, and one must guess which holds the object. Usually the question was asked in a verse e.g., *Handy-pandy, Sugar-candy, which hand will you have?* Hence, used of two things when it doesn't matter which is chosen; also, a shifting, as from hand to hand; an object held in the closed hand, a covertly proffered bribe. *To play handy-dandy,* to juggle or toy with as though of no value; Carlyle, in FREDERICK THE GREAT (1862): *You cannot play handydandy with a king's crown.* Also *handidandy*; *handy-bandy*; *handy-spandy*. Shakespeare in KING LEAR (1605) says, *Change places, and handy-dandy, which is the justice, which is the theefe?*

hans. A frequent nickname of *Johannes*; Jack. In the phrase *hans en kelder* (Dutch, Jack in the cellar), an unborn child. Used by Dryden in THE WILD GALLANT (1663); Lovelace in a poem (1649) says: *Next beg I to present my duty To pregnant sister in prime beauty, Who well I deem (ere few months elder) Will take out hans from pretty kelder.* Cleveland, the next year, used *kelder* figuratively: *The sun wears midnight; day is beetle-brow'd, And lightning is in kelder of a cloud.*

hanse. A company, or merchants' guild; especially one engaged in foreign trade. Also, the initiation fee of such a guild; the privileges the guild possessed. Specifically (from the 13th century), a political and commercial league of Germanic towns, *the Hanseatic League.* It had a house in London; it had many privileges and monopolies.

hansel. See *handsel.*

hap. (1) Chance, fortune; hence, good fortune (whence the present meanings of *happily* and *happiness*; *haply* still means by chance). Chaucer, in THE LEGEND OF GOOD WOMEN (1385) says: *Hap helpeth hardy man alday.* Milton, in PARADISE LOST (1667), said the serpent *wish'd his hap might find Eve separate. Hap* was also a verb; Shakespeare says, in THE TAMING OF THE SHREW (1596): *Hap what hap may, I'll roundly go about her.* (2) To cover; Hogg, in THE QUEEN'S WAKE (1813) pictures *Her bosom happed wi' flowerets gay.* Especially, to cover to keep warm; Nashe in A WONDERFULL, STRANGE, AND MIRACULOUS ASTROLOGICALL PROGNOSTICATION (1591) says that he *shall hop a harlot in his clothes all the year after.* This was perhaps slantwise reference to the word *hap-harlot,* used in the 16th and 17th century to mean a coarse or ragged coverlet. (3) To seize (Dutch *happen,* to snatch). In 16th and 17th century legal writings. (4) To turn to the right. A Scotch term, used as a call to a horse; opposite of *wynd,* to turn to the left. Hence the 18th and 19th century expression *neither to hap nor to wynd,* meaning without turning, on a straight course.

hap-harlot. See *hap.*

happy family. See *Hymen's torch.*

haqueton. See *acton.*

hards. See *suckeny.* Thus *harden,* a coarse fabric made from hards. Also *herden, hurden.* Hence Brome in THE CITY WIT (1652): *You hurden smocked sweaty sluttery!* Hards were in use at least from the 8th century.

hare-finder. A man that spies the hare in form. *The first point,* said a 1616 country guide, *for the killing of the hare,* *consisteth in finding out her forme.* The *form* was the lair in which the hare—*a wery hare in a fourme,* said Chaucer (1386)—lurks crouching. Benedick in Shakespeare's MUCH ADO ABOUT NOTHING (1599) wonders whether Claudio is jesting: *Doe you play the flowting jacke, to tell us Cupid is a good hare-finder and Vulcan a rare carpenter? Come, in what key shall a man take you?* [Cupid, of course, was blind; Vulcan was a blacksmith.]

harengiform. Shaped like a herring; good for dragging across a trail.

hariolation. See *aeromancy.* Verb forms, meaning to soothsay, to divine, were (16th century) *hariolize;* (17th and 18th centuries) *hariolate*—also used to mean to practice ventriloquism; and (once, in the 19th century) *hariole.*

hariot. See *heriot.*

harlot. A vagabond, rogue, rascal, knave. Medieval Latin *arlotus,* glutton. Also, a male servant. Sometimes, loosely, equivalent to the now current fellow, good fellow. A common word since the 12th century; not applied to a woman until the 15th, but common in such application in 16th century Biblical references. The word was also used to mean the pointed boots worn in the 14th century. Chaucer uses the word often, as of the Somonour in the Prologue to THE CANTERBURY TALES (1386): *He was a gentle harlot and a kynde, A bettre fellawe sholde men noght fynde.*

harpocratic. Observing, or relating to, silence. The Romans placed a figure of *Harpocrates,* god of silence, with finger held on mouth, at the entrance to their temples, as a sign that the mysteries of religion were not to be revealed to the people. The god was derived (by error) from the Egyptian dawn-god *Harchrot* (*Horus,* the sun) represented as a child with finger to lips. Dawn, the day's birth, was shown as a child without speech, an *infant* (Latin *in,* not + *fans,* speaking; *fari,* to speak). A spell of *harpocracy* might spare us much hypocrisy.

harrish. An old variant of *harsh.*

harsnet. See *haslet.*

haruspicy. See *aeromancy; cp. aruspicy.*

haskard. A man of low degree; a base or vulgar fellow. Also *haskerd.* Hence *haskardy,* such persons collectively; also, baseness. Caxton in his LIVES OF THE FATHERS (1491) wrote: *As . . . he came out of the hous of a comyn woman, he met with a lewd haskarde, whyche for to doo the sayd synne of lechery went to the hous.*

haslet. A piece of meat for roasting; especially, the entrails or fry of a hog or other animal. Also *hastelet; harslet; hasselet, harcelet, harsnet,* and more. Old French *hastelette,* roasted meat; diminutive of *haste,* a spit; Latin *hasta,* spear. *Cp. hastlet.* Used from the 14th century. Frere in his translation (1872) of Aristophanes' THE FROGS says: *Keep quiet—and watch for a chance of a piece of the haslets.*

hastary. A spearman. Latin *hastarius,* from *hasta,* spear. Hence *hastal,* spear-shaped (in natural histories of the 17th century; the scientific term today is *hastate.*)

hasteler. The roasting-cook; the turnspit. Latin *hasta,* spear; *hastelaria* (Late Latin), place where broaches were kept. Also *hastler; cp. haslet; hastlet.*

hastelet. See *haslet.* And *cp. hastlet.*

hastlet. A preparation of fruit. The word is a form of *haslet, q.v.,* and so listed in the O.E.D. THE FORME OF CURY (1390) gives the recipe: *Take fyges iquarterid; raysons hool, dates and almandes hool: and ryne hem on a spyt* [from which the delicacy takes its name], *and roost hem; and endore hem as pome dorryes, and serve hem forth. Endore* has no relation to the witch but *(en,* in + *d'or,* of gold; as also *pome dorryes,* golden apples) means to gild. As a term in cookery, it means to make shiny, as pie-crust with the yolk of egg.

hatchment. An escutcheon; especially, a square or diamond-shaped background on which are the armorial bearings of a dead person, often placed on his former home. The word is a shortened variant form of *achievement,* which also once had this special sense. Shakespeare in HAMLET (1602) has *No trophee, sword, or hatchment o're his bones.* It was also used figuratively, as in John Fletcher's VALENTINIAN (1614): *My naked sword Stands but a hatchment by me, only held To shew I was a soldier.*

hauberk. See *smotherlich.*

haulte. An early variant of *haughty. Cp. haut.* Elyot in THE BOKE NAMED THE GOVERNOUR (1531) said: *Yet is not majestie alwaye in haulte or fierce countenaunce, nor in speche outragious or arrogant, but in honourable and sobre demeanure . . .*

hausture. The action of sucking in. Latin *haurire, haustum,* to draw up, drink in; whence also, *exhausted.* Hence also (16th and 17th centuries) *to haust,* to draw in, drink up. *A haust,* a draught. W. Watson, in QUODLIBETS (1600): *To drinke up the Thames at a haust. haustellate (haustellous, haustellated),* adapted for sucking, is used in entomology; it is from the diminutive *haustellum* of Latin *haustrum,* a machine for drawing water. T. Adams in A SERMON ON LUKE (1650) spoke of men *with an avarous hausture to lick up the mud of corruption.*

haut. An early form of *haught, haughty. Cp. haulte.* The *gh* was added in the late 16th century, under the influence of Saxon words with *gh.* The *h* was added in Old French, under the influence of German *hoch,* high. The word is from Latin *altum,* high. In English *haut* was a noun (ORDER OF CRYSTEN MEN, 1502: *the soverayne hautes of heven*), a verb (ARTHUR, 1400: *He daunted the proude and hawted the poure*), and an adjective, as in Skelton's COLYN CLOUTE (WORKES; 1529): *Thus eche of other blother* [gabble] *The tone against the tother; Alas, they make me shoder. For in hoder moder The church is put in faulte, The prelates ben so haut.*

hautain. An early form of *haughty;* see *haut.* Also *hautein, hawteyne, hauten,* and the like. *Hautainesse, hautainety, hautynete,* haughtiness, arrogance. *Hautain* was also (15th century) used to mean courageous; also loud. Chaucer in THE PARDONER'S TALE (1386) says: *In churches whan I preche, I peyne me to han an hauteyn speche.* Also literally high, high-flying; Chaucer in THE LEGEND OF GOOD WOMEN says: *Ne gentil hawtein faucoun heroner.*

havel. See *javel.*

havelon. Double-dealing; guile; doubling on one's tracks, as a fox. Used in the 14th and 15th centuries; also *havyloune, havilon.* Langland in PIERS PLOWMAN (1377) denounced those *that useth these haveloунes to blende* [confuse] *mennes wittes.*

haveour. See *haviour.*

haviour. The fact of having, possession; property; deportment, *behaviour.* Originally *aver,* then (15th century) *avoir,* directly from the French. Association with English *have* added the *h,* and the forms *haviour, havour, haveour* (which Spenser used five times) developed by 1500. Then the word was associated with *behave,* and by 1600 *haviour* had come to mean one's bearing, deportment. Then the sense of possessing grew obsolete; then (by the 18th century) *haviour* was replaced by *behaviour.* Caxton in THE GAME AND PLAY OF THE CHESSE (1474) says: *He took all his havior and he put it on a ship.*

hay. See *heydeguyes.*

haybote. Wood or brush for repairing fences. Also *heybote*; from *hay,* a hedge; see *heydeguyes.* Also, the right to take such wood from the landlord's estate or from the common. In legal writing, especially after the 16th century, the allowance of wood is called *hedge-bote.* Such wood was included among a tenant's *estovers, q.v.*

hayward. An officer of a manor, township, or parish, in charge of fences and enclosures, to keep cattle from breaking through (from the common) into enclosed fields. *Hay* + *ward,* guardian. Also *heiward, haiward, haward.* The post seems to have lasted into the 19th century. Wyclif (1380) wrote: *The emperor . . . makede hise bishopis haywardis of the world.* Note, however, that the *hay* hereintended is not the grass for fodder but the hedge; see *heydeguyes.*

heal. See *hele.*

heald. See *hield.*

heart of elder. See *elder-gun.*

heartbreaker. See *lock.*

heavenric. The kingdom of heaven; heaven as the abode of the blessed. Anglo-Saxon *heofona rice,* kingdom of the heavens. (German *Reich,* kingdom.) Also *heavenrich, heovenryke.* Used into the 15th century. In THE LAND OF COCKAYNE (13th century) *heavenriche* is used for the sky.

hebdomad. The number seven; a group of seven. Greek *hebdomas, hebdomad-,* seven. Hence: a week; also, the seven superhuman beings of some gnostic systems. Thus *hebdomadal,* consisting of, relating to, or lasting seven days; by extension, changing every week, fickle. *hebdomary, ebdomary, hebdomadary, hebdomatical, hebdomadic,* weekly; pertaining to the days of the week. [The first three of these forms, in the Roman Catholic Church, are applied to a member of a chapter, in a monastery or convent, who takes weekly turn in performing the sacred offices.] *The secondary cit,* says G. Colman in BROAD GRINS (1802), *From London jogs hebdomadally down And rusticates in London out of town.* Southey in THE DOCTOR (1837) referred to *the hebdomad, which profound philosophers have pronounced to be . . . a motherless as well as a virgin mother.*

hebe. "The first hair appearing about the genital parts; also the parts themselves; but more especially the time of youth, at which it first appears." So Bailey, 1751. From *Hebe* (two syllables), Greek goddess of youth and spring. Since she is pictured as the cup-bearer on Olympus, *hebe* came also to mean a barmaid, a waitress. Likewise, an attractive young woman (whether waitress or no). *Her violet eyes,* Tennyson admired (1842), *and all her hebe bloom.* Beauty being by no means allied with sluggishness, there is no relation between Greek *Hebe* and Latin *hebes,* blunt, dull; *cp. hebetation;* note that *hebetic* may be used to mean relating to puberty.

hebenon. A substance with a poisonous juice, mentioned by Gower (*hebenus*), Marlowe (in THE JEW OF MALTA, 1592), and Shakespeare, as in HAMLET (1602), where the late King's ghost explains: *Upon my secure bower thy Uncle stole With juice of cursed hebenon in a vial.* The Quartos spell it *hebona;* also *hebon.* Various conjectures—German *eibenbaum,* the yew; *ebon, ebony; henbane*—have failed to fix the substance.

hebetation. The act of making, or the fact of being, dull or blunt. Latin *hebes, hebetis,* dull; *hebere,* to be dull, sluggish. *Cp. hebe.* Hence English *hebetate,* to make or to be dull or blunt; used in the 16th and into the 19th century. In the 16th century *hebete* was also used as a verb, to make dull; *hebescate,* to grow dull or blunt. Also *hebetant,* making dull. Both *hebetate* and *hebete* were also used as adjectives meaning dull, sluggish; Fitzgerald (translator of the RUBAIYAT of Omar Khayyam) wrote in a letter of 1840: *I am becoming more hebete every hour.* The 19th century chose more elaborate forms; *hebetize,* to make dull; *hebetude,* used in the 17th century for dullness, sluggishness, lethargy, became in the 19th *hebetudinosity;* Leigh Hunt, in THE INDICATOR (No. 37, 1820) used the adjective: *dull, uninformed, hebetudinous.*

hebetude. See *hebetation.*

heder. A male sheep; especially one from about eight months to the first shearing. From *he* + *deer,* which originally was the general term for animal; Anglo-Saxon *deor,* wild animal; German *Tier,* The female was called the *sheder.* Spenser has, in THE SHEPHERD'S CALENDAR (1579; SEPTEMBER): *He would have devoured both hidder and shidder,* explaining in the gloss 'he and she, male and female.'

hederigerant. Ivy-bearing. The ivy (Latin *hedera*) was sacred to Bacchus, and often worn in garlands or wreaths. Several English words are from the Latin root. *hederaceous, hederal, hederiferous, hederiform* (accent on the first syllable) are mainly b o t a n i c a l terms; *hederated* (crowned with ivy) and *hederigerant* are poetic. Thus M. Collins in THOUGHTS IN MY GARDEN (1876) says: *Nymphs hederigerant, Wine that's refrigerant, These are the joy of poets and gods.*

hedge-bote. See *haybote.*

hedgepriest. An illiterate priest. A contemptuous term of the 16th and 17th centuries; Green in his SHORT HISTORY OF ENGLAND (1874) harked back to *the whole body of the clergy, from Pope to hedgepriest.* But *cp. patrico.*

hedysma. A sweetening for medicine. The plural is *hedysmata;* the word is from Greek *hedys,* sweet. It is in Bailey's DICTIONARY (1751). Although ignored by the O.E.D. (1933), it would have tempted the rhyming talent of W. S. Gilbert, who knew that one must always gild the philosophic pill.

heerdis. See *suckeny.*

heete. See *hight.*

hegira. See *anno.*

hele. To hide, keep secret; to cover, cover in; to keep silent. The Aryan root is *kel,* as in Latin *celare,* to hide; *conceal; occult.* Also *heal; helian, hel; hell.* Hence the abode of the dead, *hell,* the coverer up. Caxton in his translation (1483) of

THE GOLDEN LEGEND: *But the preest alwey heled his synne.* BOLD BURNET'S DAUGHTER, a 17th century ballad, has the lines: *Although I would heal it never so well, Our God above does see.* Hence also *hele,* concealment; *heler, healer, heeler,* a person or thing that hides or covers up; figuratively in the 14th century: *The eyelids are the helers of the eyes;* proverbially, of a receiver of ill-gotten goods: *The heler's as bad as the stealer.*

hell. See *barleybreak; hele.*

hellebore. A plant (e.g., the Christmas rose) ; also, the drug extracted therefrom. From ancient days its medicinal and poisonous properties were known; in medieval and Elizabethan times it was highly esteemed as a cure for madness. So popular was it that the O.E.D. lists 15 derivative terms, such as *helleborate,* prepared with hellebore; *helleboric,* relating to it; *helleborose, helleborous,* full of, or related to, it. *I am represented,* protested Sir W. Hamilton as late as 1856, *as one who would be helleborised as a madman for harbouring the absurdity.* The name itself took many forms, among them *elebre, elevre, helleborus, helleboraster, hellebory.* Bishop Hall in THE INVISIBLE WORLD (1652) said: *These errors are more fit for hellebore than for theological conviction;* and in 1830 Scott (DEMONOLOGY) spoke of *wretches fitter for a course of hellebore than for the stake.* Today the preference is for insulin.

helo. Bashful; shamefaced. Also *helaw, halo, hala.* Used in the 17th century, lingering in dialect. Shadwell in THE SQUIRE OF ALSATIA (1688) has a character urge: *Kiss her, I say,* to get the response: *I am so hala, I am ashamed.* [*Alsatia,* in addition to being no-man's land, debatable ground, between France and Germany, was in 17th and 18th century slang the precinct of the White Friars in London, sanctuary for debtors and criminals; hence *Alsatia,* a sanctuary or hideout for criminals; *an Alsatian,* a criminal in sanctuary or hiding.] A helo fellow blushes when he says Hello.

helobious. Palustrine, dwelling in marshes. Greek *helos,* marsh + *bios,* living. From the 18th century *helodes* has been an adjective meaning swampy; also, as a noun, a medical term for swamp fever. The bullfrog is helobious, Its habitat, the marsh. To feel it wakens phobias; Its love notes, rudely harsh. We often wonder how frog, You fascinate the cowfrog.

hemerology. A day-book, a calendar. Greek *hemera,* day + *logos,* word, account. Used in the 17th century. Also *hemerologe, hemerologium.* Hence *ephemeral.*

hempseed. The seed of the hemp plant, used for prophecy. Besides employing it for fumigation (smoke whirls, within which the powers of darkness appeared) and for magic brews, folk used it in other ways to reveal the future—as pictured in Gay's THE SHEPHERD'S WEEK (1714): *This hempseed with my virgin hand I sow, Who shall my true-love be, the crop shall mow.* From the fact that the fibres of *hemp* are used to make rope, many expressions developed. Thus *young hemp,* a graceless boy, an 18th century juvenile delinquent. In the 16th century, *hempstring, stretchhemp,* a gallows-bird; *hempseed,* a fellow fit for hanging. Southey in 1843 used *hempstretch* of a person hanged. *Cp. honeysuckle.* Thus *hemp-sick,* arrested for a capital crime; then one dies of a *hempen fever.* Shakespeare in HENRY IV, PART TWO (1597) has: *Do, do, thou rogue; do, thou hempseed.*

henbane. A plant, with dull yellow flowers streaked with purple. Its narcotic and poisonous properties are acknowledged in the O.E.D.; the poison is *hyoscyamine.* Mixed with like sinister herbs and the blood of bats, henbane was long used to make a murky incense for summoning the powers of darkness. It was also called *hennebone* and, more pleasantly, *henbell.* The Water Poet in his PRAISE OF HEMPSEED (*q.v.*; 1630) limits its power: *No cockle, darnel, henbane, tare or nettle Neere where it is can prosper, spring, or settle.*

hend. At hand; handy; skilful with the hands; clever; gentle, courteous, comely. A very common word from the 10th century, by the 14th *hend* was applied conventionally, as a term of courtesy, to persons of quality. The same form was used as an adverb, also as a verb, meaning to hold in the hand, to grasp, as in Spenser's THE FAËRIE QUEENE (1596): *As if that it she would in pieces rend, Or reave out of the hand that did it hend.* The word is related, in origin as well as meaning, to *hand.* It developed other forms: *henden,* near; *hendly, hendily,* courteously, gently; *hendness, hendiness, hendship,* courtesy, gentleness; *hendy,* with the various meanings of *hend,* from *handy* to polite. Note that *hend, hende* are also old forms for the plural of *hand.* For a more active form of the verb *hend,* see *hent.*

hene. To stone. Old English *han,* stone, whence also *hone.* Used from the 10th to the 14th century; THE LEGEND OF THE ROOD (1300) tells of a man they *ladde without the toun, and henede him with stones. Cp. tohene* (*to-*).

hent. To lay hold of, to catch, to grasp. In this basic sense the word is used both by Spenser (THE SHEPHERD'S CALENDAR, 1579: *His harmful hatchet he hent in hand*) and by Shakespeare (THE WINTER'S TALE, 1611: *Jog on, jog on, the footpath way, And merrily hent the stile-a*). The word was very common from the 10th to the 17th century, and developed further meanings: to lay hold of and take away; to seize; to strike; to meet with, to experience; to arrive at; to pluck up (heart, courage); to perceive. *To hent in* (*upon*) *hand,* to undertake; *to hent one's way,* to go. Also as nouns, *hent, henting,* the act of seizing; grasp, apprehension. A *henter* (Chaucer), one who grasps. Chaucer also uses the verb of a man who took for good purpose; in the Prologue to THE CANTERBURY TALES (1386), we read: *All that he mighte of his friendes hente, On bookes and his lernynge he it spente.* For another quotation, see *gargat.*

heptachord. See *scolion.*

here. An armed host; hence, a multitude. A common Teuton word, with root *har,* war, whence also to *harry*; *harbor* (originally, army shelter); *harbinger* (also originally, army shelter, then an official going ahead of the king to arrange lodgings). Also *haere, her, heere.* In the more general sense, we read in the 14th century KYNG ALYSAUNDER that *tygres, olyfaunz* [elephants] *and beres Comen flynge with grete heres.* Many compounds were formed from *here,* used in Old and Middle English; among them: *hereburne,* a coat of mail; *heredring* a warrior; *herefeng,* booty; *heregang,* an invasion, also *herefare* (used by 17th century antiquaries); *heregeld,* army tax, especially, the tribute paid to the Danish host, also *hereyeld*; *herekempe,* a warrior; *heremarke,* a standard; *heretoga,* an army leader (German *Herzog,* duke); *hereweeds,* armor. Oddly enough, *here* was also an adjective (BEOWULF to the 15th century) meaning mild, gentle, pleasant.

heredipety. Legacy-hunting. Latin *heredium,* legacy + *petere,* to seek. Hence the adjective, *heredipetous.* Accent on the *dip.* In Milman's HISTORY OF LATIN CHRISTIANITY (1855) we read: *Heredipety or legacy hunting is inveighed against, in the clergy specially.* Today it may mark the man that marries a millionaire's daughter. A lexicographer's sons-in-law are seldom heredipetous. There is but coincidental similarity to *serendipity, q.v.*

hereword. Word of praise; renown, glory. From Old English *herian,* to praise + *word.* Used until the 14th century. Likewise *hereworth,* worthy of praise, admirable. Hence the verb *hery,* to praise, in common use (Chaucer, Spenser) from 735 into the 17th century.

hereyeld. In Scotland, equivalent to *heriot, q.v.* 'The *yield* to the *here.*' Also *herield, herezeld, hyrald, herrezeld*; actually, a variant of *heregeld*; see *here.*

hereyesterday. The day before yesterday. Probably a corruption of *ereyesterday.* Used in the 17th century.

hericide. See *stillicide.*

herigaut. An upper garment, worn by both men and women in the 13th and 14th centuries. Also *herigald, herygoud.*

herile. Pertaining to a master. Latin *herus,* properly *erus,* master of the house, lord. *Herility,* mastery, mastership.

heriot. In Old English, *heriot* meant military equipment, from *here,* army + *geatwe,* trappings. In feudal times it came to mean, first, military equipment (horse, arms, etc.) restored to a lord on the death of his vassal; then, the yielding to the lord of the best living beast of the dead vassal; later, a fixed sum of money usually was given instead of the beast. In Scotland the similar payment was the *hereyeld, q.v.* Also *hariot, haryotte, heriet,* and the like. Hence *heriotage*; *heriotable,* subject to *heriot.* The word was later applied to similar payments in other places; for example, in Guinea (18th century) the eldest son was sole heir, but was obliged to present a slave *by way of heriot* to the king.

hern. (1) A corner, nook, hiding-place. Old English *hyrne,* corner, angle; Old Teutonic form *hurnjon,* whence *horn.* Hence *hirnstone,* cornerstone. Also *hirn, hyrne, heorne, heryn,* and more. (2) An old or poetic form of *heron*; also *herne.* (3) An old or dialect form of *hers* (correct in the 14th century); Wyclif in his BIBLE (1388; KINGS, BOOK TWO) wrote: *Restore thou to hir alle thingis that ben hern. Hern,* a corner, lasted from the 9th to the 19th century; Chaucer in the Prologue to THE CANON YEOMAN'S TALE (1386) speaks of *lurkynge in hernes and in lanes blynde.*

hernshaw. See *handsaw.*

hership. Harrying, plundering; a raid. Hence ruin, distress—the result of harrying; also, booty, plunder, especially cattle driven off. Old English *here, q.v.,* army; *herja,* to harry; Old Norse *herskapr,* harrying (*sk* was pronounced *sh,* as in *ski*). Used from the 14th through the 17th century; too common, especially along the Scotch border. It was revived by Scott in WAVERLEY (1814): *the committing of divers thefts, reifs, and herships upon the honest men of the Low Country.* In a note in THE HEART OF MIDLOTHIAN four years later, Scott states that *her'ship may be said to be now obsolete; because, fortunately, the* *practice of 'plundering by armed force,' which is its meaning, does not require to be commonly spoken of.* On a larger scale, under other names, the practice continues.

hery. See *hereword.*

hesperian. Relating to the west (the ancient Greeks meant Italy; the Romans meant Spain); to the place where the sun sets, the land of the evening star. Greek *Hesperia,* the land of the west; *Hesperus,* the evening star. The *Hesperides* were the nymphs (3, 4, or 7, according to the tale), daughters of *Hesperus.* With a never-sleeping dragon, they guarded the tree of the golden apples in the Isles of the Blest, beyond the Pillars of Hercules at the western edge of the world. Ruskin in MODERN PAINTERS (1860) names four Hesperides: *Aeglé,* Brightness; *Erytheia,* Blushing; *Hestia,* Spirit of the hearth; *Arethusa,* Ministering. From the guardians, *Hesperides* came to be used for the garden, the Isles of the Blest, the Fortunate Islands; hence, a golden land of promise, of beauty and happiness, in the unreached west. Go west, young man! Shakespeare in PERICLES (1608) used the word as singular, referring to Antiochus' daughter—*See where she comes, appareled like the spring!—Before thee stands this fair Hesperides, With golden fruit, but dangerous to be touch'd.* Hence *hesperian, hesperidian, hesperidean,* relating to the fortunate islands, idyllic, wonderful. References to the story were very common in the 16th and 17th centuries; Milton uses it several times, e.g., in COMUS (1634) warningly: *Beauty like the fair hesperian tree Laden with blooming gold, had need the guard Of dragon-watch.*

hest. Bidding, command. A common word, 10th into 17th century. Shakespeare, in THE TEMPEST (1610), has: *O my father, I have broke your hest to say so.* Revived by Scott (THE HEART OF MIDLOTHIAN, 1818: *Christian or heathen, you shall swear to do my hest*), the word was used by Carlyle and others. *Hest* comes from Old Teutonic *haitan,* to call upon by name, whence also *hight, q.v.* It developed the transposed meaning of vow, promise (close to modern *behest*); also, by a misunderstanding of the first sense, *hest* was used to mean will, purpose, determination, as in Dunbar's POEMS (1520): *He handled her as he had hest* and in Carlyle's CROMWELL (1845): *Swallowing in silence as his hest was.* Hence as a verb, *to hest,* to command; to promise.

hext. A variant form of *highest.* Also *hexist.* Found in the medieval proverb: *When bale is hext, boot is next;* a little later: *When bale is highest, boot is nighest.* Sackville differs, in lament at the fall of Troy in A MIRROR FOR MAGISTRATES (1563): *O Troy, Troy, there is no boot but bale.*

heydeguyes. A 16th and 17th century country dance, a variation of the *hay.* Perhaps the *hay* of *Guy* or *Guise;* there was also a 15th century French dance known as the *German hay, haye d'allemaigne.* Also *haydeguy, heyday guise, hydegy, hydaygies,* and a number of other forms that attest its popularity. Spenser in THE SHEPHERD'S CALENDAR (1579) goes *With heydeguyes, and trimly trodden traces.* In addition to the still current meaning of mown grass, hey (*hay*) meant (1) a net for catching rabbits and other small game; (2) a hedge; especially one erected, not grown, sometimes called *dead hey* as opposed to the *quick hey,* a hedge of living bushes or trees; (3) a serpentine country dance. Hogarth in THE ANALYSIS OF BEAUTY (1753) said: *One of the most* *pleasing movements in country dancing is what they call 'the hay': the figure of it, altogether, is a cypher of S's, or a number of serpentine lines interlacing or intervolving each other. Hay* was also an exclamation (in fencing) on hitting an opponent; in Latin the cry was *habet,* he has it, when a gladiator was struck. Hence *hay,* a home-thrust; Shakespeare in ROMEO AND JULIET (1592) cries: *Ah the immortall passado, the punto reverso, the hay.*

hickock. An early variant of *hiccough, hiccup.* Also *hicket, hitchcock,* and more. Donne in POLYDORON (1631) said: *Laughter is the hickock of a foolish spleen, but he notes himselfe judicious, or stupid, that changeth not his countenance upon his owne talke.*

hidder. See *heder.*

hidduous. A variant form of *hideous;* 16th century, Northern and Scotch. Lyndsay in THE MONARCHE (1553) told that before the Flood *The watter was so strang and fyne They wold nocht laubour to mak wyne,* and recorded that when God struck the workers on the tower of Babel with confusion of tongues, the *schaddow of that hidduous strenth* was already six miles long. [Query: How long is the shadow of a foot-high bush at break of day?] Note the apparent sound of the word *strength,* a pronunciation still on many lips. The rich nasal clangor is lost.

hide. A measure of land, used in Saxon England and into the 12th century: the amount deemed adequate for a free family and its dependents; roughly, as much as could be tilled with one plough in a year (by some measures, 120 acres of arable land). Hence, *hidegeld, hidegild, hidage,* a tax paid on a hide of land. But see *hidegild.*

hidegild. A fine paid in lieu of a flogging. From Old English *hide,* skin + *geld, gyld,* money. Also *hidegeld, hydegild.* See *hide* for another use of the word.

hidels. A hiding-place. *In hidels,* in secret. Common from 10th to 15th century. In the 14th century the forms *hidel* and *in hidel* came into use, *hidels* being erroneously taken as a plural. The phrase *but hidel* meant without hiding, openly. Also *hudles, hydels, hydeles,* and the like; the same without *s.* Also *hidel-like,* secretly; *hideling,* a person given to secrecy or concealment.

hield. To bend; to slope; to bow to, to submit; to sink, decline, fall; to bend one's course; to turn aside; also, to bend toward, to incline to, to favor. Used literally or figuratively, from the 9th to the 16th century. Also used transitively: to bend something; to pour out (by tilting the container); this too was used figuratively, as *to hield his wrath.* The word *hield* was likewise used as a noun, meaning a slope, an incline; *on held,* in a bent-over posture. Hence, figuratively, an inclination; also, a decline, as in Nashe's LENTEN STUFFE (1599): *His purse is on the heild.* Among other spellings of this common word were *heald, heeld, helde, hulde, heel* (in nautical use, as when a ship inclines, *heels over*). As the twig is hielt . . .

hierapicra. A bitter purgative. Greek *hiera,* sacred + *pikra,* bitter. Also *hickery-pickery, higry-pigry,* and the like. *Hierapicra* has the accent on the first syllable, pronounced *high.* It was used from the 14th into the 18th century; used figuratively also, as in a sermon (1639) by Bishop Ward: *There is too much of this bitter zeal, of this hierapicra in all our books of controversies.*

hierde. An old form for *herdsman.* Also *hierdess,* shepherdess.

hieromancy. See *aeromancy.*

Highgate. In the phrase *sworn at Highgate,* put through a ludicrous ritual. Highgate was a spot on a hill, on the north road to London, where about 1600 a gate was erected, for the collection of a toll for the Bishop of London. Taverns naturally were opened nearby; at these, it became the custom to require an oath of all that stopped there before entering London. The traveler was sworn on a pair of horns fastened to a stick—that is, on pain of cuckoldry—never to kiss the maid when he could kiss the mistress; never to eat brown bread when he could get white; never to drink small beer when he could get strong. [*Cp. small beer.*] Then he was fit to be trusted in the big city.

hight. Called, named. Thus Sidney (1580) : *Even he, the King of glory hight.* This form has survived, poetic or archaic, as in Irving's SALMAGUNDI PAPERS (1808): *A little pest, hight Tommy Moore.* From Old English *haitan* (*cp. hest*), this was one of the commonest verbs from the 8th to the 15th century; forms still survive in dialects. It meant to command, bid; call, summon; call (by name), name. It was also used in the phrase *I hicht,* I assure you. It had many forms. In the present tense, *hat, hot, hiht, hight, hete*; Chaucer in THE MAN OF LAW'S TALE (1386) : *To grete God I heete.* In the past tense, *heht, heycht, hight, hahte, heet, heitte*; *hote* (by error; Spenser in THE SHEPHERD'S CALENDAR, 1579) : *A shepheard trewe, yet not so true as he that earst I hote.* Spenser also uses the word (archaic by his time) in senses not elsewhere found: THE SHEPHERD'S CALENDAR, *Say it out, Diggon, whatever it hight*; THE FAËRIE QUEENE, *Charge of them was to a damsel hight . . . But the sad steel seiz'd not, where it was hight.* As a noun, *hight* had the same meanings as *hest*: a command; a promise, a vow. But also *hight* (from *hie*) meant exertion, haste; and (from Old Teutonic *hycgan,* to hope) meant hope, glad expectation, joy. These two forms (haste; joy) were less common, lasting from the 10th scarcely beyond the mid-13th century. *Hight* was also an early variant spelling of *height.* With these nouns were verbal meanings: *hight,* to hope, to rejoice, to exult; by transference, to adorn, beautify, set off. Hence *highter,* an embellisher. Also *hightle* (14th and 15th centuries), to adorn; *hightly* (11th to 13 century), hopeful, joyous; delightful. We had a hightly journey.

higra. See *eagre*; *agar.*

higry-pigry. See *hierapicra.*

hilasmic. Propitiatory. Greek *hilasmos,* propitiation. Used in the 19th century.

hilding. Something or someone worthless; applied to a beast (as a horse), a man or (less commonly) a woman. Perhaps *hilding* is from *hield* (*q.v.*), to bend down, to turn waywardly. Shakespeare uses the word in ALL'S WELL THAT ENDS WELL (1601), in CYMBELINE: *A base slave, a hilding for a livery, a squire's cloth*; in ROMEO AND JULIET: *Out on her, hilding*; and as an adjective in HENRY IV, PART TWO (1597) : *Some hielding fellow, that had stolne The horse he rode on.*

himpnes. A variant of *hymns.* Gascoigne in CERTAIN NOTES OF INSTRUCTION (1575) wrote that the most frequent verse form of his day, the *poulter's measure . . . although it be nowadays used in all theames, yet in my judgement it would serve best for psalmes and himpnes. Poulter's meas-*

ure was a rhymed couplet, an Alexandrine (12 syllables) followed by a fourteener. Its name was drawn from the practice of the *poulter* (poultryman) of giving two extra eggs with the second dozen. *Cp. baker's dozen.* For an example of *poulter's measure, see appere.* The fourteener rhymed couplet, broken into lines of four and three feet (thus with the rhyme in the second and fourth lines) became the common "short meter" of the metrical psalms and the popular ballads, renewed (1798) in Coleridge's RIME OF THE ANCIENT MARINER. Sternhold's metrical version of 19 of the Bible PSALMS (1547; all the PSALMS, 1562) popularized the form, but by his monotonous iambics with many monosyllables—*And with my voyce upon the lorde I do both cal and crye, And he out of his holy hyl Doth heare me by and by*—contributed to the later quest of more varied diction.

hind. In addition to its still current uses (noun: the female of the deer; adjective, posterior, as *the hind quarters*), *hind,* earlier *hine,* meant a servant, especially a farm servant; hence, a rustic, a boor. Shakespeare uses all senses of the noun. In AS YOU LIKE IT (1600) Touchstone proves he can ring the rhymes on Rosalind—*For a taste: If a hart do lack a hind, Let him seek out Rosalind*; servant in the same play and MERRY WIVES OF WINDSOR; rustic in LOVE'S LABOUR'S LOST and HENRY IV, PART ONE. The use as rustic also occurs in Milton (1645) and Jonson, who in EVERY MAN OUT OF HIS HUMOUR (1599) protests: *Why should such a prick-ear'd hine as this, Be rich?*

hindermate. A spouse who is a *hindrance.* In his COMMONPLACE BOOK (1843) Southey noted: *There are hindermates as well as helpmates in marriage.* [*Helpmate* was coined in the 18th century, modeled on *helpmeet,* a spouse. *Helpmeet,* however, is the result of a misreading, a running together, of two words in THE BIBLE, GENESIS: *an help meet* (suitable) *for him,* meaning Eve.] Thus *hindersome,* obstructive, harmful (from the 16th century); *hinderyeap,* cunning, deceitful (11th and 12th centuries); *hinderful,* impious, evil (13th to 16th century). A *hinderling,* a mean or degenerate person; also (11th century) *on hinderling, hindforth,* backwards; (19th century) *hinderlings,* buttocks, as in Scott's ROB ROY (1818).

hippocampus. A seahorse, with two fore feet and a dolphin's tail, such as drew the chariots of the sea-gods. In a letter of 1606, Drummond of Hawthornden speaks of a 'stately' Cheapside pageant representing *Neptune on a hippocampus, with his Tritons and Nereids.* Greek *hippos,* horse + *kampos,* sea-monster. Also *hippocamp.* Hood, in MISS KILMANSEGG AND HER SILVER LEG (1840) finds the creature jovial: *hearty as hippocampus.*

hippocaust. The burning of a horse in sacrifice. The word is used in 19th century discussions of (east) Indian practice.

hippocras. A cordial, of spiced wine. This was a very popular drink, 14th to 17th century. The word is a corruption of *Hippocrates,* name of "the father of medicine," Greek physician of the 5th-4th century B.C., whose ethical code is the basis of the *Hippocratic oath* taken by doctors today. Chaucer uses *hippocras* of the doctor himself, saying in THE DETHE OF BLAUNCHE (1369) that no physician can heal, *Noght ypocras, ne Galyen.* The wine for this drink was strained through a cloth called *hippocras bag* or *hippocras sleeve.* Chaucer in THE MERCHANT'S TALE (1386) says: *He drynketh ypocras clarree and* *vernage Of spices hote tencreesen his corage*; Heywood in EDWARD IV, PART ONE (1600): *We'le take the tankards from the conduit-cocks To fill with ipocras and drinke carouse.* There seems no reason why the drink should not be popular: *Take of cinamon 2 oz., of ginger ½ oz., of grains ¼ oz. Punne* [pound] *them grosse, and put them into a pottle* [2 quarts] *of good claret or white wine, with half a pound of sugar; let all steep together, a night at the least, close covered in some bottle of glasse, pewter, or stone; and when you would occupy it, cast a thinne linen cloath or a piece of a boulter over the mouth of the bottle, and let so much run through as you will drink at that time, keeping the rest close, for so it will keep both the spirit, odor, and virtue of the wine and spices.* Next rainy day would be a good time to occupy it.

hippocrene. The fountain of inspiration; the draught that poets drink. Hippocrene (Greek, fountain of the horse; it flowed from a rock on Mt. Helicon where the hoof of Pegasus struck) was the name of a fountain sacred to the Muses. *O for a beaker,* cried Keats in the ODE TO A NIGHTINGALE (1820), *Full of the true, the blushful hippocrene.*

hippocrepian. Relating to, or shaped like, a horseshoe. Greek *hippos,* horse + *krepis,* shoe. Also *hippocrepiform,* still used in zoology. On many a field, in the balmy season, men can be seen tossing horseshoes for the hippocrepian championship.

hippodame. A horse-tamer or trainer. Also *hippodamist* (19th century). Spenser, however (THE FAËRIE QUEENE, 1590: *Infernall hags, centaurs, feendes, hippodames*), confused the word with *hippocamp* (see *hippocampus*), or perhaps with *hippotame,* an early form of *hippopotamus.*

hippodrome. See *peridrome.*

hippuric. Relating to the urine of horses. Greek *hippos,* horse + *ouron,* urine. For an illustration of its use, see *hircine.*

hircicide. See *stillicide.*

hircine. Goat-like. Latin *hircus,* goat. Also *hircic,* relating to a goat. The forms *hircine, hircinous, hircose* are used especially in connection with the goat-smell, rank; by extension, lewd, lustful. Hence *hircosity,* rankness; lustfulness. *They stinken as a goat,* says Chaucer in THE YEOMAN'S TALE (1386); *Wanton as youthful goats,* says Shakespeare in HENRY IV, PART ONE (1597). Kane in THE GRINNELL EXPEDITION (1854) described the bear as *most capricious meat . . . One day he is quite beefy and bearable; another hircine, hippuric, and damnable.*

hircocervus. A creature out of medieval natural history, supposedly half goat, half stag. Latin *hircus,* goat + *cervus,* stag. K. W. in CONFUSED CHARACTERS OF CONCEITED COXCOMBS (1661; THE INFORMER) wrote: *He's a clubfooted . . . large-luggd eagle-ey'd hircocervus, a meere chimera, one of the devils best boys.*

hiren. A siren to hire: a seductive woman; a prostitute. A transfer from the seductive woman in Peele's lost play, *The Turkish Mahamet and Hyrin the Fair Greek* (1594); *Hyrin* being a corruption of the name *Irene,* Greek *Eirene.* In Shakespeare's HENRY IV, PART TWO (1597): *Down, down, dogs! Down, faitors! Have we not hiren here?,* the word may be a direct use of the proper name, parodying Peele, for Pistol's next words parody the "pampered jades of Asia" in Marlowe's

TAMBURLAINE (1587). T. Adam in THE SPIRITUAL NAVIGATOR (1615) said: *There be sirens in the sea of this world. Sirens? Hirens, as they are now called . . . What a number of these sirens, hirens, cockatrices . . . in plaine English harlots, swimme amongst us!*

hispid. Rough, bristly. Latin *hispis, hispidem,* with rough hairs. Used from the 17th century; also *hispidity.* Hence *hispidulate, hispidulous,* somewhat hispid. Used still in zoology and botany, the word has been used figuratively, as (1848) in *the harsh and hispid law.*

hobnob. See *hab nab.*

hoddypeak. See *peagoose.*

hodermoder. Confusion. See *hody-moke.*

hodgepoker. A mischievous hobgoblin. *Hodge* was often used as a typical name for the English rustic; *poker,* one that annoys, hence the devil. Also *hodgepocher.* Florio (1598) lists, as the meaning of *fistolo: a hobgoblin, a hag, a sprite, a robingoodfellow, a hodgepocher. Cp. hodgepot.*

hodgepot. A stew of various meats and vegetables. Also *hotchpot, hotch-potch, hodgepodge.* The earliest form was *hotchpot, hotch,* to shake, mix + *pot.* It was changed to *hodge* probably because of the wide use of the name *Hodge* to mean a farmer or countryfellow in general. *Hodge* is a nickname for *Roger.* Hence, *hodge-razor,* a razor to sell to a greenhorn; hence Carlyle used the term to mean something made only to sell, a sham—in his MISCELLANEOUS ESSAYS (1843; DR. FRANCIA): *Hodge-razors, in all conceivable kinds, were openly marketed, 'which were never meant to shave, but only to be sold!'* The other meanings of *hodge-podge* are still used. *Cp. olio.*

hodgepudding. A pudding made with many ingredients. Shakespeare uses the word figuratively, of the big-bellied Falstaff, in THE MERRY WIVES OF WINDSOR (1598): Ford: *What, a hodgepudding? a bag of flax?* Mistress Page: *A puft man?*

hodge-razor. See *hodgepot.*

hody-moke. Secrecy, concealment; hence intrigue; hence muddle, confusion, trouble. Also, one who keeps things secret; hence, a hoarder, a miser. This is one of a group of terms with the same meaning, from the 15th century: *hudder-mudder, huckermoker, hokermoker*; the form that has survived is *hugger-mugger,* sometimes shortened to *hugger-mug. In hugger-mugger,* secretly. Speaking of Polonius, in Shakespeare's HAMLET (1602), the King says *We have done but greenly In hugger-mugger to inter him. Hugger-mugger* and *hugger* are also verbs, meaning to keep secret, to act or meet in a clandestine manner, to act in a muddled way. (*Hugger* also, in the 18th and 19th centuries, especially in Scotland, meant a stocking without a foot.) Mary Charlton in THE WIFE AND THE MISTRESS (1803) spoke of someone who had *saved a mort of money . . . and behold, it was all hugger-muggered away.*

hogmanay. The last day of the year; also, a gift given on that day. Especially in Scotland and northern England, since the 17th century. The children go from house to house, singing carols and crying *Hogmanay!—hagman heigh; hanganay; hogmynae*—in hope of a present. A similar custom had developed earlier in France, to the cry of *Aguillanneuf!* Note, however, that *hogmoney* was the name given to the early 17th century coinage of the Somers (now Bermudas) Isles: copper pieces, silvered, with a hog on the obverse.

Perhaps children there got hogmoney for hogmanay.

hogoo. A high or piquant flavor; a relish; a highly flavored dish. Also, a 'high' or putrescent flavor, an offensive taste or smell, a stench. Also *hogo, hough goe, how go, huggo,* and the like; corruptions of French *haut gout,* high taste. Walton in THE COMPLEAT ANGLER (1653) favors garlic: *To give the sawce a hogoe, let the dish (into which you let the pike fall) be rubbed with it. Hogoo* is also used figuratively, as by Crowne, in his play SIR COURTLY NICE (1685) : *Lock up the women till they're musty; better they should have a hogo, than their reputations.*

hoker. Also *hokir.* See *bismer.*

holethnos. A primitive race, that has preserved its racial integrity. Greek *holos,* whole, entire + *ethnos,* nation, race. Hence also *holethnic.* Other compounds formed from *holos* include, in addition to the still current *holocaust* (*kaustos,* burnt) : *holocryptic,* thoroughly secret, e.g., of a code or cipher that can be read only by those with the key. *holograph* (adjective or noun), written entirely in one's own hand; also *holography. holophrasis* (accent on the *off*), the expression of a whole phrase or complex idea by one word; also *holophrastic,* as in polysynthetic languages.

holidam. An early form of *halidom, q.v.* Some editions of Shakespeare use this form.

hollowpampered. Feeble. Used by grandiloquous Pistol, in HENRY IV, PART TWO (1598) : *Shall pack horses, and hollowpampered jades of Asia, Which cannot go but thirty miles a day, Compare with Caesars, and with Cannibals, and Trojan Greeks?* Shakespeare is playing on Pistol's pretentious ignorance: *Cannibals* should be *Hannibals;* Greeks were not Trojans. The passage is a parody of well-known lines in Marlowe's TAMBURLAINE, PART II, where the conqueror Tamburlaine's chariot is drawn by captive kings: *Holla, ye pampered jades of Asia. What! Can ye draw but twenty miles a day?*

holo-. See *holethnos.*

holor. A fornicator, a debauchee. Also *hulour, hullw, holour, holer, holyer* (not to be confused with *holier*), *houlloure,* and more. A common term, 13th through the 15th century. The word is from Middle High German *huorer,* whorer; but this form came into English via Old French, and the first *r* became *l* as Latin *peregrinus* became French *pelegrin,* English *pilgrim; cp. peregrine.* Hence *holorie, holoury,* fornication. Chaucer in the WIFE OF BATH'S PROLOGUE (1386) has: *Thou seyst that every holour wol her have.*

holp. An old past tense of *help*: helped. Used by Shakespeare in MACBETH (1606) : *He rides well, And his great love, sharp as his spur, hath holp him To his home before us.*

holt. A copse, a grove. Used from the 8th century (BEOWULF), often in the phrase *holtis hie,* which may have led to the 16th and 17th century use of *holt* to mean a wooded hill. Scott differentiates, in THE WILD HUNTSMAN (1796) : *The timorous prey Scours moss and moor, and holt and hill.* Hence *holtfelster, holtfeller,* a woodcutter.

homager. One that owes *homage* to a king or overlord; hence, an humble servant. Used figuratively, as by Shakespeare in ANTONY AND CLEOPATRA (1606): *Thou blushest Anthony, and that blood of thine Is Caesar's homager.*

homuncle. A diminutive man. Latin *homunculus,* diminutive of *homo,* man. From the 17th century; also *humuncio, homuncule; homuncular,* tiny. Max Beerbohm, with pedantic inaccuracy, used the form *homoncule* to designate a jockey.

honeysuckle. In Shakespeare's day, *honeysuckle* was a name of the red clover; hence *honeystalks* (TITUS ANDRONICUS; 1592) stalks of clover. Note that in HENRY IV, PART TWO, the Hostess uses *honeysuckle* for *homicidal* and *honeyseed* for *homocide.* Falstaff has said: *Throw the quean in the channel;* she retorts: *Throw me in the channel! I'll throw thee in the channel. Wilt thou? Thou bastardly rogue! Murder! Murder! Ah, thou honeysuckle villain! Wilt thou kill God's officers and the King's! Ah, thou honeyseed rogue! Thou art a honeyseed, a man-queller, a woman-queller . . . Thou hempseed!*

hoplite. A heavy-armed foot-soldier of ancient Greece. Greek *hoplon,* piece of armor, heavy shield; weapon. FRASER'S MAGAZINE (1851) said that *the heavy-armed hoplitic angler, as he may be called, returns generally from his expedition laden only with disappointment.* Hey for the piece of string and the bent pin!

hoplochrism. Weapon salve (says Bailey, 1751): the anointing of arms. Greek *hopla,* arms + *chrism,* anointing. Most of the *hoplo-* compounds are zoological, as *hoplognathous,* with armed jaws; more literary (and forgotten) are *hoplarchy,* rule of arms, by armed force; *hoplomachy* (accent on the second syllable; *ch* like *k*), a battle of heavily armored forces; hence, *hoplomachist,* one who fights heavily armed or in heavy armor.

hore. The earlier form (10th to 16th century) of *whore.* Also see *horowe.* Indo-European *qar-*; Latin *carus,* dear; Old Irish *cara,* friend; Lettish *kars,* lascivious. The spelling *wh* became current in the 16th century. The pronunciation *hoor* was common from the 17th century into the 19th, persisting in dialects; it seems a milder sound than the scornful *hoar.* The BIBLE (LUKE) of 1382 speaks of *this thi son, which devouride his substaunce with hooris.* Sometimes used as a general epithet of scorn or anger, as in GAMMER GURTON'S NEEDLE (1575): *Gyb, our cat, in the milk-pan she spied . . . 'Ah, hore! out, thefe!' she cryed aloud.*

horecop. See *horowe.*

hornbook. A sheet of paper covered with a thin strip of horn, mounted on wood with a projecting handle. On the paper were the alphabet, the ten digits, and often the Lord's Prayer. Hence, an elementary presentation of a subject, an *absey-book, q.v.* A later, simpler form, as a piece of varnished cardboard, from its shape was called a battledore. Dekker uses the word satirically in his title (1609): *The Gull's Horn-Book;* Shakespeare plays on the cuckold's horn in LOVE'S LABOUR'S LOST (1588): *Yes, yes, he teaches boyes the horne-book: What is Ab spelled backward with the horn on his head?*

horologe. A device for telling the time. Also *horometer; horologium; horology; orloge, orlegge, orlyge, horlege, horrelage,* and many more; common from the 14th to the 17th century. Also applied to chanticleer, the cock, *horloge of the dawn.* Shakespeare in OTHELLO (1604) says: *He'll watch the horologe a double set*—stay awake twice around the clock. The word is via Old French (without the *h*) and Latin from Greek *hora,* time + *logos,* telling. Hence also *horologer, horologist,* clockmaker; announcer of the hours.

horography, horologiography, the art of making dials; a record of the hours; a description of timepieces. J. Smith in SELECTED DISCOURSES (1652) said: *This world indeed is a great horologe to itself, and is continually numbering out its own age.* A *horoscope* is, of course, a viewing of the hour (of one's birth).

horowe. Filthy, foul; slanderous. Thus Chaucer in THE COMPLAINT OF MARS (1374): *Somtyme envyous folke with tongues horowe departen them alas.* The more usual spellings were *hory, horry, hoory,* as the word is from Old English *hore* (*hor, hoore*), meaning filth, defilement. But *hore, q.v.,* is also an old spelling of several words: *oar, hoar, hour, whore.* Note also that *horecop, horcop* (meaning bastard; from *whore + cop*) was a common 15th and 16th century term of abuse.

horrent. Bristling. Thus Milton in PARADISE LOST (1667): *Inclos'd with bright imblazonrie, and horrent arms*; figuratively, Carlyle in his MISCELLANY (VOLTAIRE, 1829): *A life . . . horrent with asperities and chasms.* Also, shuddering, horrified.—A number of English words have come from Latin *horrere,* to bristle, to stand on end; to tremble; to shudder at; to dread—most commonly, *abhor.* Also *horre,* to hate (15th and 16th centuries; supplanted by *abhor*); *horrend, horrendous,* terrible, frightening: E. Hooker in editing (1683) John Pordage's THEOLOGICA MYSTICA exclaims upon *damnings most dreadful . . . execrations horrendous, blasphemies stupendous.* Also *horrescent,* shuddering; *horriferous,* inducing *horror*; *horrific,* causing horror: Urquhart in his Rabelais (1693) has: *Now you have heard a beginning of the horrifick history.* Also *horring,* abhorrence; *horrious,* causing horror; both used in the 16th century. And more that are horrible and horrid, including *horrisonant, q.v.,* and *horripilation,* 'gooseflesh'; the standing of the hair on end through fear.

horripilation. See *horrent.*

horrisonant. Making a horrid sound. Also *horrizonant*; *horrisonous*; accents on the second syllable. *Cp. horrent.* Latin *horrere,* to make the hair stand on end. Nashe in STRANGE NEWES (1593) scorns to teach Gabriel Harvey (*cp. bum; gallimaufry*) *the true use of words, as also how more inclinable verse is than prose, to dance after the horrizonant pipe of inveterate antiquitie.*

horsebread. A "bread" of beans, bran, and other fodder, used as a delicacy or a supplementary food for horses. Like horsemeat now, horsebread was sometimes palmed off on humans; an English Guild regulation of 1467 required that *non baker that shalle bake eny horsbrede, kepe any hostre* [inn]. Jonson in EVERY MAN OUT OF HIS HUMOUR (1599) cried: *You threadbare, horsebread-eating rascals!*

horse-marine. See *marinorama.*

hortensian. See *hortus.*

hortulan. See *hortus.*

hortus. Latin, a garden. Hence (in the 17th and 18th centuries), a woman's privy parts. *Hortus siccus,* an arranged collection of dried plants; also used figuratively, as by Gray in a letter (1763) to Wharton, speaking of Cambridge, *where no events grow, though we preserve those of former days by way of hortus siccus in our libraries.* In the 16th and 17th centuries, the word *orchard* was sometimes (pedantically) altered to *hortyard.* Other English words from *hortus* are *hortal,* cultivated (of flowers, as opposed to wild;

also figuratively); *horticolous,* growing in the garden; *ortolan* (via the Italian), *hortulan, hortensial, hortensian,* relating or belonging to a garden. This makes considerable horticulture! Perhaps because God Almighty first planted a garden—still the purest of human pleasures.

hortyard. A 16th and 17th century spelling of *orchard,* as though from Latin *hortus.* See *hortus. Orchard* was Old English *ortyeard,* later *orceard;* by 1200 *orchard.* North (1580) in his Plutarch spoke of *pety larceny, as robbing mens horteyardes and gardens of fruite.*

hostelity. Hospitaly. From *hostel,* an inn; *hostel,* except for hikers, has been largely replaced by *hotel. Hostelity* is not to be mistaken (as sometimes it might) for *hostility.*

hotchpotch. See *hodgepot.*

hothouse. Originally (15th century) a bath house with hot baths. The CHURCHE OF YVELL MEN (1511) spoke of *bordelles, tavernes, sellers, and hote houses dissolute, there as is commytted so many horryble synnes.* As this quotation shows, the word soon came to mean a brothel, as in Shakespeare's MEASURE FOR MEASURE (1603) *wherein Mistress Overdone professes a hothouse, which I think is a very ill house too.* The glass hothouse, for strawberries, flowers, and the like, came into use in the 18th century.

housel. As a noun: a sacrifice; the consecrated aspects of the Communion; the Mass or Eucharist. Old English *husl;* Gothic *hunsl,* sacrifice; the pre-Teutonic form was *kwnt;* Sanskrit *cwanta,* tranquil. The word was borrowed from Old English for the Christian use. Earlier as a noun, it became more frequent as a verb, *to housel,* to administer, or to receive, the Communion; hence, to purify by ceremonial expiation or lustration. [*Lustration,* a cleansing; Latin *lustrare, lustratum,* to purify, from *luere, lustrum,* to wash, whence also English *lustrum;* see *lustre.*] In the ballad of SIR ALDINGAR, (1650) in Child's collection, *'A priest, a priest,' says Aldingar, 'Me for to houzle and shrive!'* In Topsell's THE HISTORIE OF FOURE-FOOTED BEASTS (1607) we read: *The Athenians, when they houseled their army . . . did it with hogs, sheep, or buls . . . and at last slew and offered them to Mars.* Hence *unhouseled,* not sanctified by the Eucharist, as Shakespeare says in HAMLET (1602): *Cut off even in the blossomes of my sinne, Unhouzzled, disappointed, unnaneld.*

houseleek. A succulent plant, with pink flowers, and leaves forming a rosette close to the root. It grows on walls and roofs of houses. It guarded the house against the thunder-god, but was effective only on his day, thunder-day, Thursday (Thor, Norse god of thunder), hence it has been widely supplanted by the lightning-rod. The houseleek was also pressed for its juice, which was drunk in the 17th century.

hubristic. Insolent. Greek *hubris* (*hybris*), that overweening pride which leads to a fall; often, in ancient drama, a character's tragic flaw. Also *hybristic.* Used in the 19th century.

hugger-mugger. See *hody-moke.* HAMLET grew out of it.

huisher. An early form of *usher.* Also *husher, huissier, hushier.* Old French *huisier; huis,* door; popular Latin *ustium,* Latin *ostium,* door; *os,* mouth. For an instance of the use of *huisher,* see *foumart.*

hullur. See *holor.*

humour. Originally, fluid, moisture. Latin *humorem, umorem,* moisture, whence also *humid.* In medieval physiology, the word *humours* was applied to the four chief fluids of the body, which supposedly determined a person's complexion and temperament. These *cardinal humours* were the *blood,* the *phlegm,* the *choler,* and the *black choler* or *melancholy,* also called the black humor, and, from the Latin, *atrabile;* Shakespeare has, in LOVE'S LABOUR'S LOST (1588) : *Besieged with sable coloured melancholie I did commend the blacke oppressing humour to the most wholesome physicke of thy health-giving ayre.* From the sense of *humour* as disposition (*good humor, bad humor*) , the word scaled to its other senses. A man in whom *blood* was the dominant humour was of *sanguine* complexion: ruddy, courageous, confident, amorous, though with the loom of apoplectic seizures in older age. The *choleric* was originally active, ever busy. The *phlegmatic* and the *melancholic* need no further word. Jonson's two plays *Every Man In His Humour* and *Every Man Out of His Humour* use the word in its physiological sense. Shakespeare, who uses the word often, was more fluid in his application, as in HENRY V (1599) : *I have an humor to knocke you indifferently well . . . and that's the humor of it.*

hurr. A variant of *hore, q.v.* For an instance of its use, see *preostend.*

hurricano. An early variant of *hurricane.* Shakespeare, followed by Drayton, used the word for a waterspout, as in KING LEAR (1605) : *Rage, blow, you cataracts, and hyrricanos spout.*

husting. In Saxon times (*hus-thing*: house-assembly) a special council called by the king. In King Cnut's reign (1016-35) the *hustings-weight* set the standard for precious metals. The word *husting* (usually plural) was later used of the highest court of London; also, of the temporary platform from which nominations for Parliament were made; hence, the parliamentary election proceedings. Commenting on Macaulay's words against the "Jewish disabilities" in Parliament, THE LONDON QUARTERLY REVIEW (September, 1847) said: *The principle, then, which is to receive its final triumph and complete development in a Judaizing parliament, is that the end of government has nothing to do with religion or morality; that 'an essentially Christian government' is a phrase meaning just as much as 'essentially Protestant cookery' or 'essentially Christian horsemanship'; that government exists solely for purposes of police—and that therefore—(to quote the words of Lord J. Russell himself the other day on the London hustings)—'a man's religious opinions ought not to affect his civil privileges'. But the misfortune is that the proposition involved in this great principle is both philosophically untenable and historically false.*

huswife. A variant of *housewife*—as in *hussy,* and, like *hussy,* used for the less respectable senses of the term: a light, pert or gadabout woman; an undependable wife. Shakespeare applied the term *huswife* to Nature and to Fortune.

hydra. A fierce monster (or person), multiplex, destructive, and almost impossible to destroy. Originally the many-headed snake of the marshes of Lerna, near Argos, in Greek mythology; its heads grew again as fast they were cut off; Hercules in his second 'labour' destroyed the monster. Greek *hydra,* with the same meaning; in English, also *ydre, hyder, idra, hidra, hydre.* Chaucer (1374) spoke of doubts as many and as recurrent as *hydra heads;* Spenser (1590), of *spring-headed hydres;* Milton (1667), of *Gorgons and hydras and chimeras dire.* Shakespeare in OTHELLO (1604) declares: *Had I as many mouthes as hydra, such an answer would stop them all.* The word was often used figuratively, as in Daniel's SONNETS TO DELIA (1592): *And yet the hydra of my cares renews Still newborn sorrows of her fresh disdain;* and Hannah More in COELEBS IN SEARCH OF A WIFE (1808) declared that selfishness *is the hydra we are perpetually combating.*

hydromancy. See *aeromancy.*

hydromel. A drink, supposedly a favorite of the ancient Greeks, of honey and water mixed. Greek *hydros,* water + *meli,* honey. It was used in 15th and 16th century England as a medicine. When fermented, it was called *mead*—though Howell in a letter of 1645 identifies the two drinks: *In Russia, Moscovy, and Tartary, they use mead . . . this is that which the ancients called hydromel.* Probably the Greeks enjoyed it fermented, too.

hydroptic. With an insatiable thirst. The medical term (thirsty as a man with *hydropsy* or *dropsy*) is *hydropic; hydroptic* is favored by the poets. Thus Donne in A NOCTURNAL UPON ST. LUCY'S DAY (1649) says *The general balm th' hydroptic earth hath drunk,* and Browning in A GRAMMARIAN'S FUNERAL (1855) has *Soul-hydroptic with a sacred thirst.*

hydrus. A horrid watersnake. Greek *hydros,* watersnake; *hydratis,* wetness. Used by Milton in PARADISE LOST (1667); see *ellops*—but probably another form of *hydra, q.v.*

hyger. See *agar.*

hymen's torch. The flower the yellow crocus. Named after Greek *Hymen,* god of marriage. Cullers of flower lore may trace an entire amatory train in the folk names of flowers: (1) *lad's love;* (2) *none-so-pretty;* (3) *kiss-me-over-the-garden-gate;* (4) *true-lovers' knot;* (5) *courtship-and-marriage;* (6) *brides-laces;* (7) *babes-in-the-cradle;* (8) *happy family*: (1) southernwood, (2) saxifrage, (3) wild pansy, (4) herb paris, (5) meadow sweet, (6) dodder, (7) lords and ladies, (8) wall pepper. You can also follow a course to *maid's ruin* (southernwood) or *mournful widow* (field scabious), faithful wearer of *hymen's band.*

hyne. An old form of *hence,* away from here, departed. Thus *gone hyne,* is no more. Also *heir* and *hyne,* in this world and the next. *Hyneforth, hyneforward, hyneward*; henceforth, hence. Rolland in THE COURT OF VENUS (1560) said *God ordanit luve to be baith heir and hine.*

hyomancy. See *aeromancy.*

hyomandibular. Pertaining to the *hyoid* (tongue) bone and the lower jaw; hence used in pedantic humor of a tireless talker, as a person of *persistent hyomandibular performance.* Hyomandibular exercise is a favorite feminine sport.

hyper-. A combining form from the Greek, as a prefix meaning over, beyond, above, in excess, extreme. Thus *hyperanarchy. hyperaphic,* extremely sensitive to touch. *hyperaspist* (Greek *aspis,* shield), a defender, champion. *hyperborean* (*boreas,* north wind), relating to, or an inhabitant of, the extreme north of a country or of the planet; also, stronger than the North wind: Thackeray in THE VIRGINIANS (1859) said: *He blew a hyperborean whistle, as if to blow his wrath away*; accent on the *bore,* as if to bore your ear-drum. *hyperbyssal,* of extreme profundity, as a sea-hole or (in ponderous humor) a mind. *hypercarnal. hyperdeify,* to exalt above God. *hyperdisyllable,* word of more than two syllables; polysyllable. *hyperhypocrisy. hyperideation,* extreme mental activity or restlessness. *hyperlatinistic*; so Coleridge (1819) called Sir Thomas Browne. *hypermagical.* Southey (1826) spoke of *hypermiraculous miracles. hypermodest. hypernephelist,* one that goes above the clouds; also, a dealer in day-dreams and extravagant fancies. *hypernomian,* beyond the scope or the reach of the law. *hyperochality,* eminence of rank or position. *hyperpathetic* (too deep for tears). *hyperplagiarism. hyperprophetical. hyperthetical,* superlative. *hyperterrestrial,* beyond the earth; *hyperuranian,* beyond the heavens; *hypercosmic,* beyond the ordered universe. Spacemen disembark.

hypo-. The Greek prefix *hypo,* down, under, too little, less, has not, like its antonym *hyper, q.v.,* become a readily combined English form. It remains, however, in some current words, a *hypochondriac, hypocrisy.* Less remembered words include *hypocorism* (Greek *koros,* child), a pet-name; *hypocoristic*; applied also to euphemistic terms, as when Farrar in his CHAPTERS ON LANGUAGE (1865) asked his readers to *Imagine the power and danger of this hypocoristic process in times when it was fashionable to fling a delicate covering over the naked hideousness of vice. hypocrify,* to play the hypocrite; also *hypocrise. hypogastrian,* pertaining to the belly, especially if it hangs low. *hypogeal, hypogean, hypogeus* (long or short *i* sound; accent on the *gee*), underground; growing underground; also *hypogene*; *in the great hypogenic laboratory of nature,* said the LIBRARY OF UNIVERSAL KNOWLEDGE in 1880, *rocks have been softened and fused. hypogeum, hypogaeum,* an underground chamber. *hypothecate,* to give as a pledge, to pawn, mortgage; *cp. impignorate. hypothec* was the legal term for an item (piece of land, goods, etc.) given as security; hence *hypothecal, hypothecary, hypothecarious,* relating to a security; *a pawnbroker's side door,* we read in 1856, admits the *hypothecative philosopher.* Which is, alas, far from hypothetical!

hyssop. An aromatic herb, often used in medicinal decoctions, such as *hyssop-wine.* Its twigs were used, in Jewish rites, for sprinkling; hence, *a hyssop,* a sprinkler for holy-water, an aspergillum. In the BIBLE (I KINGS; 4) we hear that Solomon *spake of trees, from the cedar tree even unto the hyssop that springeth out of the wall*; whereafter the hyssop has been taken (as by Cowley, 1663; Browning, 1878) as the type of a lowly plant. St. John states that the sponge with vinegar offered to Jesus on the Cross was *put upon hyssop.* Several allusions in the BIBLE imply what is made explicit in the Fifty-First PSALM: *Purge me with hyssop, and I shall be clean.* Therefore Paracelsus called chemistry (alchemy) the *hyssopic art,* the art of purifying metals.

I

iatric. Relating to medicine; medical; medicinal. Greek *iatros,* healer, *iasthai,* to heal. Also *iatrical.* (The first *i* is long). Hence *iatrology,* the science of medicine. THE ENGLISHMAN'S MAGAZINE of February 1865 mentioned, of Aesculapius, *The iatric powers with which he is credited.* Burton in THE ANATOMY OF MELANCHOLY (1621) spoke of *iatromathematical professors,* meaning persons that applied astrology in their medical practice; but in 17th century Italy a school of *iatromathematicians* arose, whose system of physiology and medicine was based on mechanics and mathematics.

Icarian. (1) Over-ambitious or presumptuous; leaping high to one's own ruin. From Icarus, son of Daedalus (*cp. daedal*), who in escaping from Crete, despite his father's warning flew so high that the sun melted the wax that held his wings, and he fell into the Aegean (Icarian) Sea. Thus Disraeli has, in CONINGSBY (1844): *Your Icarian flight melts into a very grovelling existence.* (2) Relating to an ideal republic, as described in *Voyage en Icarie* (1840) by Etienne Cabet, who later founded (and named *Icaria*) several communistic settlements in the United States. Nordhoff, in his history of COMMUNISTIC SOCIETIES IN THE U.S. (1875) used the word of persons: *The Icarians reject Christianity* (which had its communism before them).

icasm. A figurative expression. Greek *eikasma,* simile; *eikazein,* to make like, to depict; *eikon,* likeness, whence English *iconoclast,* image-smasher. Hence *icastic,* figurative. Henry More in the MYSTERY OF INIQUITY (1664) stated: *The difficulty of understanding prophecies is in a manner no greater, when once a man has taken notice of the settled meaning of the peculiar icasms therein.* A rare, but a good, word, icasm.

icche. To move, to stir. In Ormin's ORMULUM (1200) we read: *He . . . icchedd himm a litell up.* Also *icchen.* The word was used into the 14th century, whereafter it appeared as *hitch* or *itch.*

icelet. An icicle. Also, prettily, an *ice-candle.*

ichthyomancy. See *aeromancy.*

iconoclast. See *mythistory*; *icasm.*

iconomancy. See *aeromancy.*

icteritious. Jaundiced. Greek *ikteros,* jaundice; also, a yellowish-green bird the sight of which supposedly cured persons afflicted with the disease. In the 17th century, the word was used figuratively, as when Bishop William Barlow wrote, in his ANSWER TO A NAMELESS CATHOLIC'S CENSURE (1609): *His gall overflowes, and he must void it by his pen in his icteritious pamphlet.*

icunde. Nature; kind; inheritance; native land. Used until the mid-13th century. Old English *gecynd*; *cynd,* nature, *kind.* Hence, as an adjective, *icunde,* natural, native; *icundelich,* naturally, as in THE OWL AND THE NIGHTINGALE (1250): . . . *faleth icundeliche.*

icusse. To kiss ('mutually,' adds the O.E.D.). The past participle was *icust,* which must not be confused. The word is an early form of *kiss* (Old English *gecyssan*; *cyssan*).

idio-. For words beginning with this form (from Greek *idios,* one's own, personal, private, peculiar) see *idiopathy.*

idiopathy. An individual or personal state of feeling. Greek *idios,* one's own, personal, private + *pathos,* feeling. The accent falls on the *op.* Among the many forms compounded from *idios,* mention might be made—will be made—of *idiorepulsive,* self-repelling; *idiocrasy,* a 17th century short form of *idiosyncrasy*; *idioglottic,* using words of one's own invention, like James Joyce; *idiolatry,* self-worship (a nonce-word but a widespread status); *idiorrhythmic,* living in one's own way (especially, of monasteries that allowed freedom to the individual; opposed to *coenobitic*); *idioticon, q.v.* a dictionary of words of one dialect or region.

idioticon. A dialect dictionary. Greek *idiotikos*; *idiotes,* a private person; *idios,* private, peculiar, one's own. Related to *idiom,* French *idiotisme*; the *idiotish, idiotic* branch of the word came by a different social pathway.

idoneous. Apt, suitable. Latin *idoneus.* Also *idoneal.* Hence *idoneity, idoneousness,* suitability, aptitude.

i'fegs. In faith. By my faith. See *fegs.* A favorite oath of 17th and 18th century playwrights. Also (Jonson, 1610) *i' fac*; (Fletcher, 1625) *i' fex*; (Wycherley, 1673) *y' facks*; (Steele, 1709) *i'fackins.* Fielding (1742) and others omit the apostrophe: *ifags; ifacks*; Congreve uses it as a statement, in THE OLD BACHELOR (1687): *Nay, dear Cocky, don't cry; I was but in jest, I was not ifeck.* Also (Wycherley, 1672) *i'fads.* Those playwrights swore a lot, i' fegs!

igly. See *ugsome.*

ignaro. An ignoramus. (Italian *ignaro,* ignorant.) Used in the 17th century as a common noun, probably from Spenser's use of it as a name, in THE FAËRIE QUEENE (1590): *His name Ignaro did his nature right aread.*

ignavy. Sluggishness, sloth. (Accent on the first syllable.) From Latin *ignavus,* idle, sluggish; *in,* not + *gnavus,* busy, industrious. Carlyle, in a pamphlet of 1850, exclaimed: *Nations, sunk in blind ignavia, demand a universal-suffrage Parliament to heal their wretchedness.* It seems to take more than a century for the cure.

ignivomous. Vomiting fire. (From Latin *ignis,* fire + *vomere,* to vomit.) The accent falls on the *ni* (short *i*). Obviously of volcanoes, but frequent, figuratively, in 17th century sermons and pamphlets, as in Harsnet's A DECLARATION OF EGREGIOUS POPISH IMPOSTURES (1603): *What a monstrous coil would six or seven ignivomous priests keep in hell!*

ignoscency. Forgiveness; forgiving spirit. Accent on the *no.* Latin *in,* not + *gnoscere, notum,* to take notice of; root *gno,* to know, as also in *ignore, ignorant*; *recognize.* To *ignore* first meant to be ignorant of; the meaning 'to pay no attention to' was first applied in the 19th century. Trapp in his COMMENTARY (1647; I CORIN-

THIANS) speaks of *innocency and ignoscency*. Note, however, that *ignote* means a person unknown, or (as an adjective) unknown; *ignotion,* an ignorant and erroneous notion; *ignotism,* a mistake due to ignorance.

illaqueate. To ensnare, entangle, as in a noose; Latin *in* + *laqueare,* to snare; *laqueus,* noose, net; remembered in the goodly *Dr. Laqueur.* See *laqueat.* Hence also *illaqueate,* ensnared; *illaqueation; illaqueable.* Coleridge (in his LITERARY REMAINS, collected 1834), says: *Let not . . . his scholastic retiary versatility of logic illaqueate your good sense.*

illation. The act of inferring, drawing a conclusion from premisses. From Latin *inferre, illatum,* to *infer; in,* in + *ferre,* to carry. *Cp. exsibilate.* NOTES AND QUERIES (1886) said: *It is permissible to smile at such an illation.*

illect. To entice, allure, charm. *It were therefore better,* said Elyot in THE GOVERNOUR (1531), *that no music be taught to a noble man, than . . . he should . . . by that be illected to wantonness.* From Latin *illicere; in* + the root *lacere,* to entice, related to *laqueus,* a snare, a noose. See *illaqueate; allect.* The form *illect* developed more complicated forms: *illective,* attractive; *illectation,* enticement; but also *illecebration,* allurement, and *illecebrous* (accent on the *le,* short *e*), alluring, also used by Elyot: *The illecebrous dilectations of Venus.* Note that, with the prefix *de,* down, the common words *delightful, delicious, delectable,* are from the same source. Thus we are all ensnared.

imblazonry. See *emblaze.*

imbrue. To stain, defile. Hence, to stain (one's hand, sword) with blood (slaughter). Also, to soak or steep in any moisture. The word is via French from Latin *in,* in + *bibere,* to drink. There is burlesque in Shakespeare's having Pistol cry, in HENRY IV, PART TWO (1597): *What? shall wee have incision? Shall wee embrew?* There is sound advice in the BABEES BOOK of 1430: *With mouth embrowide the cuppe thou not take.* There is more poetic use in Spenser's THE FAËRIE QUEENE (1590): *Some bathed kisses, and did soft embrew The sugured licour through his melting lips;* likewise, in Keats' ode TO AUTUMN (1819): *And little rills of crimson wine imbrued His plump white arms and shoulders, enough white For Venus' pearly bite.*

imene. Shared or owned in common. Old English *gemaene;* Latin *communis.* Hence *imennesse,* communion, fellowship. *I bileve,* said the COTTON HOMILIES of 1175, *on holi chirche, imennesse of haluwen.* [*haluwen,* hallowed folk, saints.]

immane. Monstrous; huge, enormous; inhumanly cruel or savage. Latin *in,* not + *manus,* hand: not to be contained in or measured by the hand. Chapman in his translation (1615) of THE ODYSSEY, speaks of *a man in shape immane.* Hence *immanity,* monstrousness, monstrosity. *Immanity,* however, came to be regarded (16th and 17th centuries) as the opposite of *humanity,* more monstrously cruel than *inhumanity,* as in John Foxe's THE BOOK OF MARTYRS (1587): *Not to be accounted inhumanity but rather immanity and beastly cruelty;* Bentley, in his DISSERTATION UPON THE EPISTLES OF PHALARIS (1699): *Phalaris the Tyrant came to that degree of cruelty and immanity, that he devour'd sucking children.* Shakespeare uses *immanity* in HENRY VI, PART ONE. Evelyn in SYLVA (1679) inquires: *What immane difference then is there between* *the twenty-fourth of February and the commencement of March?*

immarcessible. See *marcescible.*

immew. See *emmew.*

immorigerous. See *morigerous.* (Accent on the *ridge.*)

imp. I. As a noun. A shoot of a plant, a sapling; hence, a young person, a scion. Thence, a shoot or slip used for grafting. As applied to persons, a child, at first of a noble family (14th to 18th century) but by the 16th century used in such phrases as *an imp of serpents, imp of Satan.* Hence *an imp,* a little or minor devil; especially, an attendant or paramour of a witch. From this came the softening to the sense, a mischief-maker; now, mischievous child. From the sense of a grafted slip, also: a piece added to anything, as an extra line to a bell-rope so that more than one can pull. (2) As a verb. To plant or transplant shoots; to graft. To engraft, as into a family by marriage; Bishop Joseph Hall in his CONTEMPLATIONS (1615) said: *Nothing is more dangerous than to be imped in a wicked family; this relation too often draws in a share both of sinne and punishment.* In falconry, *to imp,* to engraft feathers on a bird, to improve its flight; hence, to increase one's powers, to enable higher flights; Nashe punned in THE RETURN OF . . . PASQUILL (1589): *such an eccho as multiplies every word . . . and ympes so many feathers into every tale, that it flyes with all speede into every corner of the realme.* Thus Spenser in his HYMN TO HEAVENLY BEAUTY (1596) is *Gathering plumes of perfect speculation, To impe the wings of thy high flying mynd.* Also, to add on, to lengthen, enlarge; Lyly in MIDAS (1592) draws the dreadful image of *a woman's tongue ympt with a barbar's*—no ear would have rest! Also (rarely) *to imp,* to clip; the O.E.D. suggests that this developed through a misunderstanding of the use in falconry, but it is probably by transfer in the process: before a thing is grafted on, it must be cut off. Bishop H. King (POEMS; 1657) said: *God shall imp their pride, and let them see They are but fools in a sublime degree.* Finally, *to imp,* to mock, to poke fun at, as would an imp. Gray used the noun light-heartedly, in verses of 1750: *Thereabouts there lurk'd A wicked imp they call a poet.* Peter Pindar remarked (1792) that often Fortune *with an eagle's pinion imps an owl.* What is at first imposing may betray itself as less important. But in matters of high import, watch out for the imp.

impair. See *apair.*

impavid. Fearless. From Latin *in,* not +*pavidus,* fearful. Thackeray in PENDENNIS (1849) remarked that *Calverley and Coldstream would have looked on impavidly.* These forms appeared only in the 19th century; in the 17th, *impavidity* was used, in the sense of foolhardiness: *impavidity, or lack of just fear.*

impawn. See *impone.*

imperseverant. A form in Shakespeare's CYMBELINE (1611) for *imperceiverant,* not *perceiving,* imperceptive, undiscerning. The positive form *perceiverant* was used (once?) in the 16th century. Shakespeare says: *The lines of my body are as well drawne as his . . . yet this imperseverant thing loves him in my despight.*

impeticos. Put into petticoats; invest in a woman (?). The Clown's word in Shakespeare's TWELFTH NIGHT (1601) when he turns away with nonsense Sir Andrew's tipsy question: *I sent thee sixpence for thy lemon* [leman: sweetheart]. *Hadst it?* —*I did impeticos thy gratillity* [gratuity], *for Malvolio's nose is no whipstock. My lady has a white hand, and the myrmidons are no bottle-ale houses.* Sir Andrew: *Excellent! Why, this is the best fooling when all is done. Now, a song.* Sir Toby: *Come on, there is sixpence for you—let's have a song.* Sir Andrew: *There's a testril of me too.* The Clown sings *O mistress mine.* A *testril* was a variant of *tester* (*testourn, testorn,* and more), originally *teston* (Old French *teston,* French *tête,* head) applied first to the shilling (20 pence) of Henry VII, the first English coin to have a true portrait; then to other coins. Many of these sank in value; by Shakespeare's day, *tester, testril,* meant sixpence.

impetre. Chaucer in his translation (1374) of BOETHIUS, uses this form, for the verb *impetrate,* to obtain by request or entreaty; to bring about; also, to entreat, to beseech. The words are from Latin *impetrare,* to procure, *im* (with intensive force) + *petrare,* to bring to pass, perhaps influenced by *petere,* to beseech, entreat. Even in Roman times the word had religious applications, Latin *patratus* was the priest who ratified (performed the rites at) an agreement; in English *impetration* was used especially of the pre-obtaining of church benefices (in Catholic times) which were within the grant of the King. Hence also *impetrative, impetratory,* related to obtaining by request, as in Taylor's HOLY DYING (1651): *Alms . . . are preparatory to, and impetratory of the grace of repentance.* (The accent goes way back to the *imp.*) *Impetrant,* that obtains; *impetrable,* that may be obtained; capable of obtaining or effecting, successful, as Nashe uses it in his LENTEN STUFFE (1599): *How impetrable he was in mollifying the adamantinest tyranny of mankind!*

impignorate. To pawn, to pledge. Latin *in* + *pignor-,* from *pignus,* a security, a pledge, a pawn. *Cp. hypo-* (*hypothecate*). Used in English from the 16th century; also *impignoration,* as in Hakluyt's VOYAGES (1598): *all arrestments, reprisals, and impignorations of whatsoever goods and marchandises in England and Prussia . . . are from henceforth quiet, free, and released.* From the 17th century the simple forms were also used: *pignorate,* to give or to take as a pledge; *pignoration*; *pignorative,* pawning; *pignoratitious,* relating to pawning or things pawned.

impigrity. Diligence, quickness, alertness. From Latin *in,* not + *piger, pigris,* sluggish, slow. In 17th and 18th century dictionaries. Also *impigrous* (accent on the *imp*), diligent, quick, ready.

impinguate. To fatten. Latin *in,* in + *pinguis,* fat. Thus Gideon Harvey, in MORBUS ANGLICUS (1666) states that Rhenish wines *do accidentally impinguate.* Many a person today keeps close watch on calories for fear of impinguation.

impleach. To interweave, entwine. After Shakespeare's use (1597; quoted under *skainsmate*) the word was renewed by Tennyson (TIMBUCTOO, 1829: *The fragrance of its complicated glooms and cool impleached twilights*) and by Swinburne (TWO DREAMS, 1865: *Where the green shadow thickliest impleached Soft fruit and writhen spray and blossom*).

implete. Replenished; filled. Latin *in,* in + *plere, pletum,* to fill; whence also *complement, complete*; *implement*; *plethora* is from the Greek form *plethein,* to fill. *Implete* is listed by Puttenham in THE ARTE OF ENGLISH POESIE (1589) as a word "not so well to be allowed by us"; it was used through the 17th century, then dropped. (19th century America used *implete* as a verb, to fill.) Other words on Puttenham's list—*audacious, egregious, compatible*—have, in spite of his disapproval, lingered.

impoak. Also, *impoke.* See *insachel; poke.*

impone. To place or set upon, to impose; to impose upon; to 'lay' upon, to wager. Latin *im, in,* on + *ponere, positus,* to place; whence *imposition.* Shakespeare is the only writer that has used the word in the sense of to wager (HAMLET, 1623 edition; the Quartos have *impound, impawn'd*): *The King sir has wag'd with him six Barbary horses, against the which he impon'd as I take it sixe French rapiers and poniards*—and as the effeminate Osric is speaking, the spelling may be intended to indicate an affected pronunciation of *impawn,* to pledge; to put in hazard.

imposterous. Relating to an *impostor* or *imposture.* Latin *im, in,* on + *ponere,* to set, place; *cp. impone.* A number of forms were used in the 16th and 17th centuries: *impostorious, impostorous, impostrate* (*the impostrate quagmires of this abortive age*), *impostrous, imposturious.* For the noun *imposture* (which was also a 17th century verb: *The devil's a witch, and has impostur'd them*), there were also the forms *impostry, impostery, impostory, impostury, impostorism, imposturage.* Apparently the *impostor* (*imposter, impostour*) and the *impostress* (*impostrix*) flourished in those years.

imposthume. An inner swelling; a purulent cyst; an abscess. Also *impostume, emposteme, imposthim,* and more. Roundabout from Greek *apostema.* Used from the 14th century, often figuratively. In the 17th century the verb *impostumate,* to cause an impostume in, was used, also in figures, as in a 1592 letter of Nashe: *To corrupt the air and impostumate mens ears with their pan-pudding prose.* Shakespeare in HAMLET (1601) says: *This is the imposthume of much wealth and peace, That inward breaks, and shows no cause without Why the man dies.*

impotionate. Poisoned. Medieval Latin *impotionare, impotionatum,* to poison; *im,* in + *potionem,* draught, especially a poisoned draught. Also a verb, to poison. Used in the 16th century. Also used figuratively; Stubbes in THE ANATOMIE OF ABUSES (1583) is speaking of *pride* when he says: *I am sure there is not any people under the face of heaven, how savage and brutish soever . . . that hath drunke so deep of this impotionate cup as England hath.*

impresa. An emblem with a motto; also, the motto. Used figuratively by Greene in MENAPHON (1589) *There was banding of such lookes, as every one imported* [signified] *as much as an impreso.* Also *impressa, impreza.* Drummond of Hawthornden (1649) distinguished between an *emblem* and an *impresa* in that the words of the former merely explain the design, whereas the words of the latter complement the figure.

inablutible. See *abluted.*

inamissible. That cannot, or is not liable to, be lost. *As this is irremediable and irrecoverable,* said Jeremy Taylor in 1649, *so is the other inamissible.* Divines (17th into the 19th century) used to say that *virtue is inamissible in heaven* (do not confuse this with *inadmissible*), and Catholics speak of the continual appearance of saints in the world as *the inamissibility of justice* (or *of righteousness*).

inaniloquent. Talking foolishly, babbling. *Inane* (Latin *inanis* + *loquent,* talking). In 17th and 18th century dictionaries. Also *inaniloquence,* an instance of which is an *inanilocution.* Page the wise men of Gotham.

incardinate. See *incarnate.*

incarnadine. Originally this was an adjective (16th century), meaning flesh-colored. There was a slightly earlier verb, *to incarn,* to cover with flesh, make flesh grow, embody in flesh—as in THE MIRROR FOR MAGISTRATES (1563): *The duke of Glocestre that incarned devyll. Cp. incarnate.* Since Shakespeare's use in MACBETH (1605), however, *incarnadine* has meant colored blood-red or, as a verb, to redden. After the murder of the King, Macbeth exclaims: *Will all great Neptune's ocean wash this blood Clean from my hand? No, this my hand will rather The multitudinous seas incarnadine, Making the green, one red.* Lady Macbeth responds: *A little water clears us of this deed,* not knowing that she will later lament: *What, will these hands ne'er be clean? . . . Here's the smell of the blood still. All the perfumes of Arabia will not sweeten this little hand.*

incarnate. This not wholly unremembered word was used by Shakespeare (HENRY V, 1599; TITUS ANDRONICUS) only in reference to the devil in human shape. He also used, in the same sense, the forms *incardinate, incarnal, incarnation.*

incatenate. To enchain; to link together. From Latin *in,* in + *catenare, catenatum,* to bind with chains; *catena,* chain. Goldsmith's CITIZEN OF THE WORLD (1762) speaks of persons *triflingly sedulous in the incatenation of fleas, or the sculpture of a cherry-stone.*

incense. See *insense.*

inclip. To enclose; embrace. Used first by Shakespeare, in ANTHONY AND CLEOPATRA (1608): *What ere the ocean pales, or skie inclippes, Is thine, if thou wilt ha't.*

inconvenytys. An old variant of *inconveniences.* Caxton in POLYCRONICON (1482) praised history, because through it a man *can be reformed by other and straunge mennes hurtes and scathes, and by the same to knowe what is requysyte and prouffytable for his lyf, and eschewe suche errours and inconvenytys by whiche other men have been hurte and lost theyr felycyte.*

incony. Delicate, pretty, choice. The word was popular, especially among playwrights (Marlowe, Middleton, Jonson) around 1600. Shakespeare used it twice in LOVE'S LABOUR'S LOST (1588): *My sweet ounce of man's flesh, my inconie Jew . . . most sweet jests, most inconie vulgar wit.* There are several guesses as to its origin; it may be a corruption of French *inconnu,* unknown, hence rare, hence choice.

incrassate. To thicken, to condense; to dull, stupefy. Latin *crassus,* thick, *crass.* Also as an adjective, as in a sermon of Hammond's (1659): *Their understandings were so gross within them, being fatned and incrassate with magical phantasms.* Also *incrassant,* thickening; *incrassative,* able to thicken; *incrassation, incrassion.* Used from the 17th century; current as scientific terms.

incremation. A 19th century form (Huxley; Thackeray in PENDENNIS, 1849) of *cremation.* From Latin *in,* in + *cremare,* to consume by fire. Note that in the earlier (17th century) adjective the *in* means not; *incremable,* that cannot be burnt; thus

Sir Thomas Browne in PSEUDODOXIA EPIDEMICA (VULGAR ERRORS, 1646) says: *They conceive that from the skin of the salamander, these incremable pieces are composed.*

increpate. To scold, rebuke. Latin *in,* against + *crepare,* to make a noise, creak. Hence *increpative, increpatory,* chiding, rebuking; *increpation,* reproof, rebuke. Used in the 16th and 17th centuries, especially in sermons.

incroyable. A dandy, a fop; first used in 1795 of the French. Via French, literally, unbelievable—as one was, to behold—from Latin *in,* not + *credere,* to believe. Supposed to have been borrowed from or influenced by a favorite phrase of the time: *C'est vraiment incroyable,* It's really incredible! Carlyle in SARTOR RESARTUS (1831) asks mockingly: *Wert thou not, at one period of life, a buck, or blood, or macaroni, or incroyable, or dandy, or by whatever name . . . such phenomenon is distinguished?*

incubus. See *ephialtes.*

indagate. To search into, investigate. From Latin *indagare,* to investigate, hunt for, explore. Hence *indagator, indagation*; *indagacious,* inclined or eager to investigate; *indagative,* characterized by seeking; *indagatory,* relating to or of the nature of investigation. The word was occasionally (in the 17th century) spelled as though confused with *indicate;* thus in 1653 we find mention of *the soul, the indigatrix of all things.*

indefeasible. That cannot be defeated, done away with, removed, forfeited, wiped out. Used since the 16th century; the word is via Italian *indefessibile* from the Latin. The noun *defeasance,* annulment, is via French *desfaire,* to undo, from Latin *de,* from, down + *facere, factum,* to make, to do. Symonds in THE GREEK POETS (1873) said: *Beauty is the true province of the Greeks, their indefeasible domain.* Addressing the season in A CORYMBUS TO AUTUMN (1888), Francis Thompson says: *Thou hold'st of God, by title sure, Thine indefeasible investiture.*

indentured. Bound by an *indenture,* as an apprentice or servant, especially, for service in the colonies. A man would *indenture* himself for a number of years' service in the New World, in exchange for which his master paid the expenses of the voyage and his keep. The word is from *indent,* from Latin *in,* into + *dentem,* tooth. An *indenture* was originally a deed or contract written in duplicate on one piece of parchment, which was then cut between the copies in a wavy or indented line; putting the two pieces together would identify the documents. Sometimes a signature or other matter was written between the copies and the cut made through it. Hence, an agreement; especially, that of an apprentice with a master or of a man binding himself to serve in a colony. *To take up one's indentures,* to receive the other copy at the expiration of the apprenticeship or service. Also *indenture English,* extravagant legal phraseology; Ascham in THE SCHOLEMASTER (1568) wrote: *As if a wise man would take Halles Cronicle, where much good matter is quite marde with indenture Englishe, and first change strange and inkhorne tearmes into proper and commonlie used wordes.* W. Taylor in THE MONTHLY MAGAZINE of 1808 noted that *indentured bond-slaves are shipped from Liverpool and Glasgow, for Canada, and independent North America, in considerable numbers*; THE DAILY NEWS on 7 January, 1878, voiced *misgivings as to the* *expediency of extending the indentureship system, which in other colonies has notoriously provoked grave scandals.*

indigate. See *indagate.*

indigenate. Of native origin; an early form of *indigenous;* also, *indigenary, indigenal, indigenital.* An *indigene, indigena,* a native. Latin *indu,* an early form of *in* + *gen-, gignere, genitum* (whence *genital*), to bear, to be born. *Indigenity,* the state of being native. Note that *indigent,* lacking, deficient; poor—*indigency, indigence*—are from Latin *indu* + *egere,* to want. And that *indigerable,* that cannot be *digested,* is from *dis,* apart + *gerere, gestus; digerere,* to set in order, to digest. *Indigest,* undigested, crude, shapeless, confused, was in use from the 14th century; Shakespeare used it as a noun, a shapeless mass, in KING JOHN (1595): *You are born To set a forme upon that indigest, Which he hath left so shapeless and so rude.*

indigest. See *indigenate.*

indigete. A hero regarded as the patron deity of his city or country. A common practice among the ancient Egyptians, Greeks, and Romans; of their rulers, it became routine. The COMPLAYNT OF SCOTLANDE (1549) mentioned *Amasis the sycond, quhilk was the last kyng and indegete of the Egiptiens,* explaining: *Indigetes war goddis of Egipt quhilkis hed beene verteouse princes quhen thai lyvit.*

indigitament. A local or special name of a god, as Pluvius (of the rain) for Jupiter. The Latin *indigitamenta* (associated with *digitus,* finger; *cp. indigitation*) were books listing the names of the gods and indicating their rituals. *The indigitaments of old deities,* said W. Burton in A COMMENTARY ON ANTONINUS HIS ITINERARY (1658), *were often inscribed to rivers; as Belisama, a name of Minerva, to the river Rible.*

indigitation. The act of pointing out; indication; demonstration; a declaration. Also, calculating or conversing by means of the fingers; also, interlocking the fingers of two hands, as children used to sit in school or sweethearts walk. Also to *indigit, indigitate,* to proclaim, to call by name, to point out, to point to; to interlock fingers. Latin *indigitare, indigitatum,* associated with *digitus,* finger (whence also the ten *digits*) but probably different in origin and originally meaning to invoke a god; hence, to call upon, to proclaim, to declare. *Cp. indigitament.* The sense, to point out, to point to, is of course sprung from the association with *digitus.* Sir Thomas Browne in PSEUDODOXIA EPIDEMICA (1646) declared that *Juvenall and Perseus were no prophets, although their lines did seeme to indigitate our times.*

indign. Unworthy. Used from the 15th century; Latin *in,* not + *dignus,* worthy; whence also *dignity. Indignation* first meant the act of treating a person as unworthy of attention or regard; earlier, *indignancy, indignance;* Spenser in THE FAËRIE QUEENE (1590): *With great indignaunce he that sight forsooke. To indign* (from the 15th century), to be indignant at, to resent; to treat with indignity. Shakespeare in OTHELLO (1604) has: *All indign and base adversities make head against my estimation.*

indocible. Incapable of being taught. From Latin *in,* not + *docere, doctus,* to teach—whence also *doctor, doctrine,* and more. Note that *docere* also gives English both *docible,* apt to be taught (16th through 18th century), and the still current *docile,* easily taught; hence, submissive to training. Hence also *indocile,* untractable; *indocility,* unruliness. But also (17th into the 19th century) *indocibility,* incapability of being taught; Jeremy Taylor in 1647 speaks of *pevishness and indocibleness of disposition.* As early as 1666 we find comment on the English *indocible humor.* Some pupils likewise seem indocible.

indoles. Innate character. Latin *indu,* within + root *ol, or,* to grow. This root appears in many words, including *abolish, adolescent, adult, origin, order, abortive, proletariat.* In English, *indoles* (three syllables, accent on the *in*) has been used from the 17th century. THE QUARTERLY REVIEW of July 1882 said: *Every language has its own indoles.*

indomitable. See *domable.*

indubitate. As an adjective: certain. Latin *in,* not + *dubitare, dubitatum,* to doubt; *dubius,* moving two ways, *duo,* two; whence also *dubious, doubt, duplicity* (twice folded). Used from the 15th century (Caxton) into the 17th; by Shakespeare in LOVE'S LABOUR'S LOST (1594): *The magnanimous and most illustrate King Cophetua set eye upon the pernicious and indubitate beggar Zenelophon; and he it was that might rightly say, Veni, vidi, vici; which to annothanize* [*anatomize,* analyze] *in the vulgar . . .* —the affected letter by Don Adriano de Armando which Boyet is reading, in Shakespeare's play, tells how King Cophetua married the beggar-maid (whose name in the legend is Penelophon). As a verb, *indubitate,* to render doubtful; to call in question; Sir Thomas Browne in PSEUDODOXIA EPIDEMICA (1646) wrote of the devil: *He would make men believe there is no such creature as himself . . . and contriveth accordingly many ways to conceale or indubitate his existency.* Over 200 years later Baudelaire phrased this: "The cleverest ruse of the devil is to persuade us he doesn't exist."

inebriety. See *ebriety.*

inescate. To entice, to allure. From Latin *in,* in + *esca,* bait, food. Prynne, in HISTRIOMASTIX (1633) cries out upon *all the inescating lust-inflaming solicitations . . . that either human pravity or Satan's policie can invent.* Hence also *inescation. Inescatory* was used, more literally, in the 19th century: *inescatory traps, and others with snares.* From Latin *esca* also came *inesculent,* not edible; Peacock in CROTCHET CASTLE (1831) says: *I care not a rush* (*or any other aquatic and inesculent vegetable*) *who or what sucks up either the water or the infection.* See *escal.*

infatuated. See *fatuate.*

infaust. Unlucky, ill-omened. See *faust.* A fairly common word, 17th into 19th (Bulwer-Lytton; Lowell) century. Motteux, in his translation (1708) of Rabelais, exclaimed *O most infaust who optates there to live!*

infibulation. Fitting with a buckle or clasp; especially, the fastening of the sexual organs, the application of a chastity lock. From Latin *in,* in + *fibula,* a fastening, shortened from *figibula* from *figere, fixus,* to fasten, to *fix. Infibulation* (the word) was English, 17th into the 19th century; the sexual practice was applied to young male singers by the Romans, to girls among many primitive peoples, to women by the medieval Crusaders. The verb is listed in 17th and 18th century dictionaries, but DeQuincey in his essay on Sir W. Hamilton (1847) says *'Infibulate' cannot be a plagiarism, because I* *never saw the word before; and, in fact, I have this moment invented it.* John Bulwer, in ANTHROPOMETAMORPHOSIS (1650), describes masculine infibulation as "buttoning up the prepuce with a brass or silver button."

inficete. Not witty. *Facete* is an older form of *facetious.* Peacock in CROTCHET CASTLE (1831) uses three forms: Mr. E: *Sir, you are very facetious at my expense.* Dr. F: *Sir, you have been very unfacetious, very inficete, at mine.* The forms are from Latin *facetus,* polite, urbane; hence, merry, witty, jocose.

inficious. Given to denying—*inficious adversaries*; a rare word, used in the 17th century. *Inficiate,* to deny (Latin *infitiae,* denial; *in,* not + *fateri,* to confess). *inficial,* relating to or characterized by denial, also *inficiation, inficiative, inficiatory* are found only in 17th and 18th century dictionaries.

infound. See *infund.*

infrication. The action of rubbing in. Also *infriction.*

infructuous. Barren, unfruitful; fruitless. The affirmative form was more common, used from the 14th into the 19th century; T. Adams in THE DEVIL'S BANQUET (1614) wrote: *It was as populous as fructuous; and at once blessed with pregnancie both of fruits for the people and of people for the fruits.* Hence *infructuosity.*

infrunite. Senseless, silly. A 17th and 18th century word.

infucation. The painting of the face. *To infucate,* to color the face, found first appearance in 17th century dictionaries. The practice, among savage men and civilized women, antedates that by centuries. Latin *in,* on + *fucare,* to paint, rouge; *fucus,* cosmetic paint. In the 16th century, *fucate* was used as a verb; also, an adjective, painted, artificially colored; hence, disguised, counterfeit. Also *fucation,* painting, counterfeiting. *fucatious,* fair-seeming, deceitful. Yet few women have true *fucatory* skill. The O.E.D. lists *infucation* as never used; but Marion Mainwaring in MURDER IN PASTICHE (1954) rediscovered the word, saying of the great Nappleby of Scotland Yard: *This time the frills, the infucation, the periphery of childishness, were of his own providing.*

infude. See *infund.*

infula. A religious head ornament of ancient Rome. A twisted woolen fillet, usually red and white, worn by priests and suppliants, also put upon sacrificial victims. Also *infule.*

infund. To pour in; to infuse, steep. Latin *in + fundere, fudi, fusum.* A primer of 1559 said: *By infunding thy precious oil of comfort into my wounds.* Also *infude, infound,* the latter usually in figurative use, as when More in RICHARD III (1513) wrote of *the great grace that God giveth and secretly infowndeth in right generacion after the lawes of matrimony.* To some extent these forms have been supplanted by the current *infuse.* Hence, an *infundible,* a funnel; *infundibular,* funnel-shaped.

infuneral. To bury, entomb. Giles Fletcher wrote in CHRISTS VICTORIE (1610): *Disconsolat (as though her flesh did but infunerall Her buried ghost) she in an arbour sat . . . weeping her cursed state.*

infurcation. A forked expansion, e.g., a spreading of the legs.

infuscation. The act of darkening; the state of being dark. *Infuscate* was an adjective, darkened; or a verb, to render dark. In the translation (1650) of Caussin's ANGEL OF PEACE, we read that *the eternall City . . . was infuscated with the sooty vapours of a brutish warre.*

ingraff. See *engraff.*

ingravescent. Growing more severe; growing worse. Latin *in* (with intensive force) + *gravescere,* to become heavy; *gravis; gravidus,* heavy. Hence *ingravescence.* Also *ingravidate,* to load, weigh; render gravid; impregnate; Fuller in THE HOLY AND THE PROFANE STATE (1642) speaks of persons *ingravidated with lustfull thoughts.* Hence *ingravidation,* the act of rendering gravid; pregnancy.

inhearse. Used by Shakespeare (SONNET 86; 1598) to mean entomb: *Was it the proud full sail of his great verse, Bound for the prize of all too precious you, That did my ripe thoughts in my brain inhearse, Making their tomb the womb wherein they grew?*

inimicitious. See *enemious.*

inkhorn. A small portable container, originally made of horn, for writing-ink. Used from the 14th century. Also *inkehorne; ynkehorne. Ink-horn mate, inkhorn varlet,* a scribbler. The word was widely used, in the late 16th and early 17th centuries, in such phrases as *inkhorn term, inkhorn word, inkhorn language,* to mean a pedantic or bookish word (usually of Latin or Greek derivation). Hence, *inkhornism; inkhornist.* Puttenham in his discourse on ENGLISH POESIE (1589) lists *irrevocable, irradiation, depopulation and such like . . . long time despised for inkehorne terms.* For another instance, see *lightskirts.* Many persons even today too often inkhornize.

inkle. (1) A kind of linen tape; a piece of this. *Unwrought inkle,* the yarn from which this tape is made. Autolycus, we are told in Shakespeare's THE WINTER'S TALE (1611), *hath ribbons of all the colours i' the rainbow, points . . , inkles, caddysses* [see *caddis*], *cambrickes, lawnes.* In combinations: *inkle-beggar,* one that pretends to sell tape, as today pencils; *inkle-eloquence,* cheap, tawdry flow of words—THE WESTMINSTER MAGAZINE of 1774 remarked: *I have seen a powdered coxcomb of this gawzy make . . . flatter himself with the power of his inkle-eloquence. Thick* (*great*) *as inkle-weavers,* intimate—"the inkle-looms being so narrow and close together." *Cp. nonesopretty.* (2) As a verb, *inkle,* to hint, to let something be known. Hence, to guess at, surmise, get an *inkling* of; Blackmore has, in LORNA DOONE (1869): *She inkled what it was.* In the 16th century, *inkleth* meant a hint or surmise; this has survived in the form *inkling. Inkless,* of course, means without ink; *inknot,* to tie in, to ensnare (the *k* is silent, as in *knot*)—Long's translation (1879) of the AENEID speaks of a smitten snake: *The rest, Retarded by the wound, delays it there Inknotting knots and twisting round itself.*—My fountain pen, a moment ago, was inkless.

inknot. See *inkle.*

inly. Inwardly; in the heart or spirit; in a way that goes to the heart or essence, hence, intimately, fully. Used from the 9th century; also *innlice, inliche*; (15th century) *endly.* Used by King Alfred; Chaucer; Emerson (POEMS; 1847): *Friends year by year more inly known*; Spenser explains it as 'entirely' in a gloss to THE SHEPHERD'S CALENDAR (1579; May): *Their fondnesse inly I pitie.*

innate. See *extraneize.*

inquiline. A lodger; a sojourner. Accent on the *in*; Latin *in* + *colere,* to dwell. In zoology, still used of a creature that lodges in another's nest.

inquinate. To pollute; to corrupt. Also *inquination.* Used from the 15th century, popular in the 17th. Sir Thomas Browne used the word more than once; in 1646: *An old opinion it was of that nation, that the ibis feeding upon serpents, that venomous food so inquinated their . . . eggs within their bodies, that they sometimes came forth in serpentine shapes*— and in 1682: *The soul may be foully inquinated at a very low rate, and a man may be cheaply vitious, to the perdition of himself.*

insachel. To pack, put into a *satchel.* Urquhart, in his translation (1693) of Rabelais, spoke of papers *impoaked, insacheled, and put up in bags. Impoaked* means put into a *poke* or pocket. See *poke.* French *ensacher,* to put into a *sack.*

insacyatly. See *sloth.*

insapory. Ill-tasting. A rare word, neatly applied to *coho or coffee* by Sir Thomas Herbert in his RELATION OF SOME YEARS TRAVAILE . . . INTO AFRIQUE AND THE GREATER ASIA (1638): *However ingrate or insapory it seems at first, it becomes grate and delicious enough by custom.* Once, it would seem, coffee was caviar to the general.

insculpt. To carve, engrave, sculpture on something. Used in the 15th, 16th, and 17th centuries. Also *to insculp; to insculpture* (18th century). *Insculpture,* a figure, design, or inscription carved upon something, was used in the 17th century, first by Shakespeare in TIMON OF ATHENS (1607): *On his gravestone this insculpture which With wax I brought away.*

insense. As a noun (16th and 17th centuries), the inner sense, essential significance. As a verb, to inform. Used from the 14th century; from the 17th, mainly in dialects. Also *insence, incense, incence.* Shakespeare in HENRY VIII (1613) says: *I thinke I have incenst the Lords o' the Councell, that he is . . . A most archheretic, a pestilence That doth infect the land.* [G. B. Harrison's edition, 1948, 1952, has a footnote explaining *incensed*: 'made angry, with the accusation that.' Shakespeare's spelling led Harrison to the other word *incense* (meaning both to perfume and to anger, by divergent paths) from Latin *incendere,* to set on fire.]

inspissate. Thickened. Also a verb, to thicken; Latin *in* + *spissare, spissatum,* to thicken; *spissus,* thick. *Cp. crassitude.* Hence *inspissant,* something that thickens; *inspissation,* the action (or an act) of thickening; BLACKWOOD'S EDINBURGH MAGAZINE of 1839 said: *He could imbibe sixteen tumblers of whisky punch, without any other external indication than a slight inspissation of speech.* Noted is Johnson's remark, quoted by Boswell, 16 October, 1769: *In the description of night in Macbeth, the beetle and the bat detract from the general idea of darkness—inspissated gloom.*

intempestive. Untimely, unseasonable; inopportune. Latin *in,* not + *tempestivus,* seasonable; *tempus,* time. [Note that our *tempest* (Latin *tempestas*) first meant season, then weather, then bad weather. A number of English words indicating a scale have tipped: *humor* (*q.v.*) once meant one's disposition; *temper* usually today implies a bad (uncontrolled) *temper.*] Hence *intempestivity,* untimeliness. Also *intempestuous,* altered from *intempestivous,* which took no root in English. Venner in THE BATHS OF BATHE (1621) shows that the distrust of tobacco is nothing our day has newly found, as he went *reproving the too too licentious, liberall, and intempestive taking of it.*

intenebrate. See *intenerate.*

intenerate. To make tender, soften, mollify. Johnson prayed, according to Boswell (23 April, 1753): *I hope they intenerate my heart.* (Daniel used the same expression in a Sonnet of 1595, as the well-read Johnson probably knew.) D. Gray in his WORKS (1861) wrote: *The teeming South Breathes life and warm intenerating balm.* The verb *intenebrate,* of course, means to darken, to obscure. Latin *tener,* tender; *tenebrae,* the shades, darkness. Hence, *inteneration,* softening; *intenebration,* darkening, obscuring.

intrinsicate. As an adjective, entangled. A variant of *intricate;* perhaps developed from *intrince, intrinse* (though *intrinsicate* is recorded earlier). Shakespeare uses both forms. In KING LEAR (1605): *Such smiling rogues as these, Like rats, oft bite the holy cords a twaine, Which are t' intrince t'unloose.* In ANTONY AND CLEOPATRA (1606; the serpent of the Nile talking to the asp): *Come thou mortal wretch, With thy sharpe teeth this knot intrinsicate Of life at once untye: poore venomous foole, Be angry, and dispatch.* As a verb, to probe, to enter intimately. [Both forms are by confusion with Italian forms. The adjective joins *intricato,* intimate, with the form of *intrinsicato,* familiar. The verb is a development from *intrinsicare,* to become familiar with, to understand, a reflexive form of *intricarsi,* to become familiar or friendly with some one else.] H. Cross in VERTUES COMMONWEALTH (1603) wondered *to heare how some such clouting beetles rowle in their loblogicke, and intrinsicate into the major of the matter, with such hidebound reasons.*

intussusception. Absorbing within oneself; the taking in of immaterial things, such as ideas. Latin *intus,* within + *suscipere, susceptum,* to take up; *sub,* under + *capere, captum,* to take, whence also *captive.* Max Muller in his study of THE SCIENCE OF LANGUAGE (1861) took the *view of the gradual formation of language by agglutination, as opposed to intussusception.* THE MONTH for June 1898 observed that *like language, dogma is modified by desuetude, by intussusception, by neology.*

inveigle. See *aveugle.*

invultuation. The making of an effigy or likeness; especially, of a waxen image of a person for witchcraft to work through. Also *invultation.* Medieval Latin *invultuare, invultare,* to make a likeness; *in,* in + *vultus,* countenance, likeness. Used in the 19th century (not by those that employed the waxen figure).

inwit. Conscience; inner awareness. See *agenbite.*

irenic. See *eirenicon.*

irremeable. Without possibility of return. Latin *ir, in,* not + *re,* back + *meare,* to go, pass. This word, used from the 16th century, was sometimes taken as meaning *irremediable,* without possibility of cure. Dryden's AENEID (1697) said: *The chief without delay Pass'd on, and took th' irremeable* way. Pope in the ILIAD (1720) said: *My three brave brothers, in one mournful day, All trod the dark irremeable way.* Johnson (widely read but here with different application) wrote in a letter to Mrs. Thrale (3 October, 1767): *I perhaps shall not be easily persuaded . . . to venture myself on the irremeable* *road.* Today we think less undeviatingly of matrimony.

irrorate. To bedew, to sprinkle. From Latin *in* + *rorare,* to bedew; *ros, rorem,* dew. A recipe of Lovell (1661) pleasantly suggests: *They are to be fried and irrorated with the juice of oranges.* Rawley in his edition (1638) of Bacon's HISTORY NATURAL AND EXPERIMENTAL OF LIFE AND DEATH says that *to the irroration of the body, much use of sweet things is profitable.* This, many women have known.

irrumpent. Bursting in. Latin *irrumpere; in,* in + *rumpere, ruptus,* to break—whence also *rupture; irruption; interrupt.* Although *irrumpent* is a useful word, it occurs only in 17th and 18th century dictionaries.

iswonk. Past tense form, used by Chaucer, of *swink, q.v.* In earlier times 10th to 13th century) *iswink, iswinch* were also used, meaning to toil. *Cp. y-.*

iwis. See *wit.*

izle. Hoarfrost. Also *izebelle,* an old variant of *icicle.*

J

jack. A pet form of John, used in many senses and combinations. Especially, *Jack,* a name for a representative of the common people. *Every man Jack,* every single one. Hence, a low-bred or ill-mannered fellow; Shakespeare uses it several times in this sense (MERCHANT OF VENICE, 1597, *bragging Jacks;* RICHARD III; ROMEO AND JULIET: ANTONY AND CLEOPATRA). *To play the jack,* to play mean tricks; THE TEMPEST: *Your fairy . . . has done little better than plaid the Jacke with us.* Also, the figure of a man that strikes the bell on a clock; *Jack o' the clock* (RICHARD II). In musical instruments (virginal, spinet, harpsichord), an upright piece of wood on the back of the key-lever: press the key, the jack rises and an attached quill plucks the string. Shakespeare uses it as though it were the key: *How oft,* he says in SONNET 128, *Do I envie those jackes that nimble leape To kisse the tender inward of thy hand.* A measure of drink, half a pint (1787, Yorkshire); a quarter of a pint (1877, Lincolnshire), apparently as thirsts shrank. In this sense, half the northern *Gill* (associated in many references to *Jack and Jill,* in various senses). Shakespeare in THE TAMING OF THE SHREW (1593) puns on *jacks and jills,* boys and girls, and measures for drinks (jugs) in Grumio's ordering the household preparations: *Be the jacks fair within, the jills fair without, the carpets laid, and everything in order?* In the old game of bowls (somewhat like the Scotch curling), a *jack* was a smaller bowl for the players to hit; Shakespeare says in CYMBELINE: *Was there ever man had such lucke? When I kist the jacke upon an upcast, to be hit away?* This was also called the *jack-bowl.* Other uses, in combination, include: *Jack among the maids,* a gallant, a ladies' man. *Jack at a pinch,* one always ready, a handy person. *Jack in office,* a pompous, self-important petty office-holder. *Jack in the low cellar,* an unborn babe. *Jacks o' both sides,* "claw-backs and pickthanks," fellows that smile on both of two rivals or rival parties. *Jack-o'-the-green,* a figure of the May-pole gaiety, decked with ribands and flowers, carrying a garlanded staff. *Jack's alive,* a 19th century game: a burning piece of paper or match is passed around; whoever is offered it must accept it; the one in whose hand it burns up or goes out must pay a forfeit. Until then, each one receiving it cries "Jack's alive!" There was also a *jack,* short for *jacket,* used from the 14th century for a sleeveless, padded leather jacket worn by soldiers and in fencing. It is probably from this that the waxed leather jug was called a *jack. To the buttery-hatch,* said MUCEDORUS (1598), *to Thomas the butler for a jack of beer. jack-a-dandy,* a conceited, affected fellow, a fop; *jack-a-dandyism.*

jack-a-lantern. Originally, a night watchman. Also a will-o'-the-wisp, friar's lantern; hence, something misleading or elusive. Also *jackalentern, jack-o'-lantern, jack-a-lanthorn.* Sheridan in THE RIVALS (1775) has: *I have followed Cupid's jack-a-lantern, and find myself in a quagmire.* Rarely used as a verb: Meredith in ONE OF OUR CONQUERORS (1891) pictured: *His puckish fancy jack-o'-lanterning over it.*

jack-a-Lent. A figure shaped like a man, set up to be thrown at, originally during Lent; later, at amusement parks. Also *jack-a-lent; jack-o'-Lent.* Hence, a butt; also, a puppet; a contemptible person. Shakespeare in THE MERRY WIVES OF WINDSOR (1598) has: *See now how wit may be made a jacke-a-Lent when 'tis upon ill imployment . . . You little jack-a-Lent, have you bin true to us?*

Jack Ketch. The hangman. Jack Ketch (*Catch, Kitch*) was the common executioner from about 1663 to 1686; he seemed so bloodthirsty when the Duke of Monmouth and other political offenders were executed that his name was given to the hangman in the Punch and Judy show, newly introduced (Punchinello) from Italy; thereafter, it became the common term for an executioner, especially in the late 17th and early 18th centuries.

jackman. See *pedlers French.*

jackpudding. A buffoon; especially, a clown serving a mountebank. Also as an adjective, *jackpudding nonsense.* Used since the 17th century. Also *jackpuddinghood. Cp. bagpudding.* Fielding in THE COVENT GARDEN JOURNAL (1752) protested that *writers are not . . . to be considered as mere jackpuddings, whose business it is only to excite laughter.*

jactation. A restless tossing of the body. From Latin *jactare,* frequentative of *iacere,* to throw. Even in Roman times the verb developed the sense of tossing words about; that is, of boasting; hence in English *jactation,* boasting, ostentatious display. *Jactator* (17th and 18th centuries), a boaster. Hence also *jactance* (from the 15th century), *jactancy* (from the 17th) boastfulness, vainglory. The Latin developed still another form, *jactitare,* to throw out publicly, often with implication of a false statement to harm someone; hence also in English *jactitation,* a boastful public declaration: especially *jactitation of marriage,* false declaration that one is married to a person, for the advantages that may ensue. There were laws covering this in England for four centuries; the DAILY NEWS recorded a case in 1892.

jakes. A privy. See *ajax.* In Shakespeare's KING LEAR (1605) we find both forms: *I will tread this unbolted villain into mortar, and daub the wall of a jakes with him . . . . None of these rogues and cowards but Ajax is their fool.* The word is short for *Jacques' house* (*Jack's house*; *Jack* being a common term for man. Today we make similar reference to *the John*). A *jakes-farmer,* cleaner of the *jakes.*

jar. This was originally an echoic word, meaning to make a harsh sound. Similar are *charre, gorre, churr, chirr, chirk, chark. Jar* was also used of a clock's ticking; Shakespeare in RICHARD II (1593) has: *My thoughts are minutes and with sighs they jarre Their watches on unto mine eyes.* By extension, *to jar,* to wrangle, to dispute; Marlowe in HERO AND LEANDER (finished by Chapman; 1598) says that *Hero's lookes yeelded, but her words made warre; Women are won when they begin to jarre. Thus having swallow'd Cupid's golden* *hooke, The more she striv'd the deeper was she strooke.*

jarke. See *pedlers French.*

jaunce. Listed in the Sussex dialect GLOSSARY of 1875 as meaning a weary journey. That was the original meaning of *jaunt* (which now means a light and easy pleasure trip). However, the verb *jaunce* (16th century) meant to make a horse prance up and down, to cavort; and *jaunce* in the second Quarto of Shakespeare's ROMEO AND JULIET (1592) may be an error for *jaunte;* the first Folio has *jaunt: Lord how my bones ake; fie what a jaunce have I had!* Carlyle in REMINISCENCES (1866) said of a honeymooner, *He was on his marriage jaunt.*

javaris. A swine in America, which has its navel upon its back. So Bailey's DICTIONARY (1751); our folklorists might make something of this back-bellied critter, which the O.E.D. ignores. The nearest the DICTIONARY OF AMERICANISMS (1951) can come is to list the *javalina (havalena),* a piglike animal of the Southwest. Page Moritz Jagendorf; he'll have (or find, or invent) a tale of the javaris.

javel. A rascal. Also *jawvell, jevel, javill.* Likewise *havel, cavel,* a worthless fellow; possibly from *cavel,* a stick of wood. Used since the 14th century. Spenser in MOTHER HUBBERDS TALE (1591) noted that *Expired had the terme, that these two javels Should render up a reckning of their travels.* Roper reported (THE LIFE OF SYR THOMAS MORE; 1557) that when More was preparing himself for his execution (the executioner by custom receiving the clothes the victim wore), *as one that had bine invited to some solempne feaste, chaunged himself into his best apparell, which Master Lieutenant espienge, advised him to put it off, sayenge that he that should have it was but a javill. "What, Master Lieutenant," quoth he, "shall I accompte him a javill that shall doe me this day so singuler a benefit?—Javel* was also, in the 15th and 16th centuries, a northern word for jail; *javeler,* jailer. A wordbook of 1483 reads: *a javelle, gaola, ubi a presone.*

javelot. See *gavel.*

jejune. It is not this word, but its meaning, that is frequently forgotten. It has no connection with *juvenile,* being from Latin *jejunum,* fasting, abstinent; hence, barren, feeble; spiritless, dry; insignificant, trifling. It developed these meanings in Latin, and carried them all into English. Thus J. Beale in the PHILOSOPHICAL TRANSACTIONS of 1670 wrote of *poor and jejune people, who are accustomed to drinks almost as weak as water.* The most frequent application of the word is to speech or writing that seems dull, insipid, flat. Hence *jejunery* (rare); *jejuneness, jejunity.* The 'seconde subtyll gutte' (1398) of the intestine is called the *jejunum* because it is usually found empty in autopsies.

jemmy. (1) A dandy, a fop. Also, in the phrase *Jemmy Jessamy (Jessamine),* an effeminate or great fop. In the 18th century, a scale of eight degrees of sophisticate was listed: *a greenhorn, jemmy, jessamy, bright, flash, puzz, pizz, and a smart.* (2) a riding-boot. (3) a light cane. A London street cry of the 18th century was: *Come buy my pret-pret-pretty leetle jem-em-emmy sticks!* (4) a great-coat. (5) a burglar's crowbar. See *jessamy. Jemmy* is a pet-form of the name *James.* In all these meanings, the form *jimmy* was sometimes used; for the 5th, *jimmy* has survived.

jentacular. Relating to breakfast. Latin *ientare,* to breakfast. Amherest, in his TERRAE FILIUS: OR THE SECRET HISTORY OF THE UNIVERSITY OF OXFORD (1721) declared: *Nothing more . . . can be expected from these jentacular confabulations.* Alexander Knox in a letter to Jebb (1811) wrote: *I therefore wish to close at this ante-jentacular hour.* Hence *jentation,* breakfasting, breakfast. Jeremy Bentham (died 1832) used to speak of his exercises in his garden as his *antejentacular and postprandial circumgyrations.* The O.E.D. gives only 19th century references for *prandial* (Latin *prandium,* luncheon), dinner and *postprandial,* the latter mainly jocular: *postprandial potations, postprandial oratory.* In Latin *prandium* (*prae,* before + *dies,* day) originally was breakfast; then, a late breakfast, usually of bread with fish or cold meats, eaten near noon; in England noon was at first the dinner hour. HARPER'S MAGAZINE for July 1883 spoke of *expenses legal, medical, funereal and prandial.*

jess. A short strap, fastened one to each leg of a hunting hawk; on its free end was a ring to which the leash was attached. Also *ges* (plural *gesses*), *chess, gest.* Also used figuratively as in Shakespeare's OTHELLO (III iii; 1604) and Braithwait's THE ENGLISH GENTLEMAN (1630): *Intangled with the light chesses of vanity.*

jessamy. A form of *jessamine, jasmine.* Hence, a yellow color; a perfume of jasmine. By extension (one that perfumes himself, or wears a sprig of jessamine), a dandy, fop. See *jemmy.* Another list than given there names the eight degrees of sporting sophisticate (1753): *greenhorn, jemmy, jessamy, smart, honest fellow, joyous spirit, buck, and blood.*

jesse. A genealogical tree of Jesus, from *the root of Jesse* (ISAIAH, xi). Often used on church wall or window, or formalized in a candlestick.

jest. See *gest.*

jetto. The spurt of water, or an opening therefor, in a fountain. French *jet d'eau; jeter,* to throw + *d'eau,* of water. Evelyn recorded in his DIARY for 22 October, 1644: *The garden has . . . fountaines, especially one of five jettos.*

jetton. A counter; an early form of the chips for calculating the score in cardgames. It was a piece of metal, ivory, etc., with an inscription or design; hence, a token, a medal. From French *jeter,* to cast; to cast up, calculate. The jetton became a collectors' item; Snelling in 1769 wrote a book entitled *View of the Origin, Nature, and Use of Jettons or Counters, especially Those Known by the Name of Black Money and Abbey Pieces.*

jill. As *Jill,* a common name for a girl: *every Jack shall have his Jill*—whether or not she come tumbling after. It is a variant of *Gill,* short for *Gillian, Juliana,* a very common Middle English name. By deterioration, *jill* (also *gill; jillet, jelot, gillot;* and *gilliver* from *gilliflower, q.v.*) came to mean a giddy or flighty girl, a *jilt;* then, a loose woman. The original sense of *jilt* was a non-virgin; a strumpet; a kept woman; the current sense in *to jilt,* to raise hopes in love then cast off, may be of another origin. The Water Poet (WORKS; 1630) tells: *But the mad rascall, when hee's five parts drunke, Cals her his drab, his queane, his jill, or punke, And in his fury 'gins to royle and rore, Then with full mouth, he truely calls her whore.*

jockteleg. A large clasp knife. This word was used mainly in Scotland and northern England, from the 17th into the 19th century. It took various forms: *jactaleg, jackylegs, jockylegs,* and the like. There is an unverified suggestion that such knives were imported, and first made by *Jacques de Liege,* whence by corruption *jockteleg.* It is more likely that the large knife was worn at the side of the leg, *jack* being a word commonly applied to many tools. For quotation, see *keelivine.*

jocund. Cheerful, merry, gay. A common word, especially favored by poets, since Chaucer's TO ROSEMOUNDE (1380): *Therewith ye ben so mery and so jocunde.* The *o* came into the word by association with Latin *jocus,* joke, jest; the word is from Latin *jucundus,* pleasant, from *juvare,* to help, to please. Hence also the rare English forms *jucund, jucundity* (16th, 17th, 18th centuries). *Jocund* was used by Shakespeare (ROMEO AND JULIET, 1592: *Jocond day Stands tiptoe on the misty mountains' tops*), by Milton (L'ALLEGRO, 1632: *And the jocond rebecks sound*), by Scott and more. Also *jocundary*; and the nouns *jocundity, jocundness, jocundry.* With Milton let us call the Muses to *favour our close jocondrie*—or if we must, say with Byron *We'll wear our fetters jocundly.*

joint-stool. A stool with the parts joined (fitted) together, as made by a skilled hand. In 16th to 18th century expressions, (possibly with reference to the new-style privy or close stool) used to ridicule or insult: *I cry you mercy, I took you for a joint-stool*; used by Lyly (1594), Shakespeare, allusively in THE TAMING OF THE SHREW (1596) and in full in KING LEAR, and more.

jonathan. (1) An instrument for lighting pipes (19th century). (2) A stand for holding toast and the like, with legs, but also hooks, so that it may be hung on a grate. (3) *Brother Jonathan,* the United States collectively, as *John Bull* for England; or a representative citizen. Said to be Washington's appellation (recalling the BIBLE: SECOND BOOK OF SAMUEL, i) for Jonathan Trumbull, Governor of Connecticut. Lowell in THE BIGLOW PAPERS (1848) contrasted the English and the American: *To move John you must make your fulcrum of solid beef and pudding; an abstract idea will do for Jonathan.* Now *Brother Jonathan* has given way to *Uncle Sam.*

jordan. A pot or bottle used by alchemists and medieval doctors. Often used to hold urine for analysis; hence, a chamber-pot. So used by Chaucer (1386) and Shakespeare (HENRY IV, PART ONE; 1596; II i). By extension, as a term of abuse, a dolt, a foolish fellow.

jorum. A large drinking-bowl, a punch-bowl; the contents thereof; especially, a bowl of punch. From the 18th century (Fielding; Goldsmith in SHE STOOPS TO CONQUER, 1773: *Then come put the jorum about, And let us be merry and clever.*) Also used to mean a large quantity, as when ST. JAMES'S MAGAZINE of December 1872 speaks of someone's being *treated to a jorum of gossip.*

joseph. See *benjamin.*

jouissance. (1) Possession (of something good), enjoyment (of); pleasure, delight. French *jouissance*; *jouir,* to enjoy; Latin *gaudere,* to rejoice. All our *joy* and *rejoicing* come from the same source. The English word was also spelled *jouisance,* *joysaunce, jouysaunce,* and the like. Spenser in THE SHEPHERD'S CALENDAR (1579) is glad *To see those folkes make such jouysaunce.* The 17th century misread the old *u*—*u* being often used for *v*—and spelled the word *jovisaunce* (as in *jovial,* which, however came from *Jove,* Jupiter, and meant the disposition of one born under the influence of the planet Jupiter) in editions of Spenser and elsewhere, as in GOD'S PLEA (1657) by Reeve: *We cannot abdicate wonted jovisances.*

jovial. See *jouissance.*

jucund. See *jocund.*

jugulate. To slit the throat of, to slay. Latin *jugulum,* collar-bone, throat, neck. Also *jugulator,* cut-throat. Ivor Brown in A WORD IN YOUR EAR (1945) suggests that Thackeray was thinking of Elizabethan songs—"Cuckoo, jug-jug, pu-we, to-witta-woo"—when he spoke of the *jugulation* of a pseudosongstress. (She probably deserved the word in its basic sense!)

jumbal. A sweet cake, made since the 17th century. Also *jumble.* Often baked in the form of rolls or rings; Holmes in ELSIE VENNER (1860) speaks of *hearts and rounds, and jumbles, which playful youth slip over the forefinger before spoiling their annular outline* with a bite. A recipe from THE CLOSET OF RARETIES (1706): *Take a pound of fine wheat flower, and as much white sugar, mix them into a paste with the beaten whites of eggs; put to the paste a pound of blanched almonds well beaten, and half a pound of sweet butter; add half a pint of cream, and so mould it all well together with a little rosewater. Shape them into forms, and bake them in a gentle oven.*

jump. See *souse.*

Jupiter. The supreme god of the Romans. From *Zeus* (the highest Greek god) or *Jove* + *pater,* father. Hence, the largest of the planets. Also *cp. Diana.* Also in names of plants: *Jupiter's beard, Jupiter's eye,* the *houseleek, q.v. Jupiter's nut,* the walnut, upon which the gods lived in the Golden Age; *Jupiter's staff,* the mullein.

justaucorps. A tight-fitting garment; especially, a woman's outer garment of the 17th century. Also *justacor, justycoat; chesticore,* and more. From the French *juste,* right + *au corps,* to the body. Pepys in his DIARY for 26 April, 1667, has the entry: *With her velvet cap . . . and a black just-au-corps.* THE WESTMINSTER GAZETTE of 28 July, 1896, observed that in the Pyrenees *the women look gorgeous in red justaucorps.*

K

kam. Awry, crooked. From the Celtic; Welsh *cam,* crooked; hence (also in English) *cam,* perverse, obstinate. Shakespeare, Motteux (in his translation, 1708, of Rabelais) used the *k* form, which Johnson gives in his DICTIONARY (1755). *Clean kam,* also *kim kam,* quite crooked, perverse, contrary to the purpose; Shakespeare has, in CORIOLANUS (1607): *This is clean kamme.* The 17th century might say: *Everything went kim kam,* or *all this chim-cham stuff.* Hence also the verb *kimbo,* to set awry; crooked—like an arm *akimbo.* Richardson in CLARISSA (1748) thinks it ill *for a wife to come up with kemboed arm.* May you not have to cry, as Aubrey in 1692: *This year all my businesses and affairs ran kim-kam.*

kankedort. See *cankedort.*

kaput. (Current slang, from German, for defeated, wholly out of it). See *capot.*

kedgeree. An Indian dish much favored by the English in the 18th and 19th centuries: rice boiled with split pulse, onions, eggs, butter, and condiments. The English variety usually added cold fish, but served it hot. In the 17th century it was simpler: *kitsery,* pounded beans and rice boiled together. Also *cutchery, ketchery, quicharee.* Often served as part of the English breakfast.

keech. A lump of fat, the fat of a slaughtered animal rolled into a lump. In Shakespeare: HENRY IV, PART TWO: *Did not goodwife Keech the butchers wife come in then?* In HENRY VIII (referring to Cardinal Wolsey, son of a butcher) : *I wonder That such a keech can with his very bulke Take up the rayes o' th' beneficiall sun And keepe it from the earth.* Some commentators on HENRY IV, PART ONE explain *tallow catch* as *tallow keech.*

keel. As a verb, to cool. From the 9th century; Old English *coelan*; a common Teutonic form, *koljan,* whence also *cool.* Hence, to cool a hot liquid by stirring; by extension, to cool the passions, make less violent or ardent, to mitigate, lessen; to cool down, to lessen, grow less; HOW A MERCHANDE DYD HYS WYFE BETRAY (1460) said: *The marchandys care began to kele.* Shakespeare's song in LOVE'S LABOUR'S LOST (1588) runs *While greasie Joane doth keele the pot.* The HALI MEIDENHAD (1230) urges the man *to kele thi lust,* and a PENITENTIAL PSALM of 1508 sought to *kele the hete of unlawful desyre.* Thus in Merlin (1450), *The kynge yet was not keled of the love of the stiwardes wif.*

keelivine. A wooden pencil. Also *keelie vine*; *keelivine pen,* a pencil. *Keel* was a reddish iron-ore used (15th to 19th century) for marking sheep. *Vine* referred to the wood (cedar) into which the *keel* (and later, lead) was put. The word was used in the 18th and 19th centuries; it also took the form *killow,* which in the 17th century (Johnson, 1755, also gives *cullow; collow* meant soot) was used to mean graphite. FRASER'S MAGAZINE of October 1833 has: *In a hole he had jocktolegs, keelavine-pens . . . or whatever else he could purloin.*

keep. As a noun. Care, attention; *to nim (take, give) keep,* to take notice; hence, care in watching. Hence, a place for keeping something, a cupboard, a meat-safe (to keep flies from flesh in summer: 17th century), a reservoir for fish; a clasp, button, or lock. Especially (translating Italian *tenazza,* hold), the innermost, strongest, central tower of a castle, which served as the last defence; a stronghold. Thus Burke in a letter of 1796: *Like the proud keep of Windsor rising in majesty of proportion, and girt with the double belt of its kindred and coeval towers.* Scott gave the word fresh life for historical stories.

kemb. An early form of *comb,* which replaced it (also *kemm*) by the 17th century. See *compt.* The form *kemb* developed several meanings: to beat; to lacerate with a rake or comb; figuratively, to smooth, make elegant, as in Chaucer, THE SQUIRE'S TALE (1386): *So peynted he and kembde at point devis As wel hise wordes as his countenaunce.* Whence also *kempt,* combed, surviving in *unkempt. kempster,* a comber (of wool), originally female, the male being *kember. Cp. kemp.*

kemp. (1) A champion, a strong and brave warrior or athlete. From the 8th century. (2) A cask or small barrel (14th and 15th centuries). (3) A coarse hair, as of the eyebrows. Chaucer in THE KNIGHT'S TALE (1386) says: *Lik a grifphon looked he aboute, With kempe heeris on hise browes stoute.* Later, a hair of this kind amid wool. (4) A contest, especially of reapers to see who can finish first. Hence, to *kemp,* to fight, to contend with. Also *kemper, kemperyman,* a contender.

kempkin. See *kilderkin.*

kempt. See *compt; kemb.*

kenodoxy. Vainglory; the empty desire of praise or repute. Greek *kenos,* empty + *doxa,* glory, opinion; *dokein,* to seem. A word that has fit application today, though found only in 17th and 18th century dictionaries.

kephalotomy. The act of beheading. Greek *kephale,* head + *tomos; temnein,* to cut, as in *atom,* uncuttable, indivisible portion, *appendectomy,* and many more. The more usual form in English is *cephalo-*; but either form of this word is in deliberate quest of pedantic humor, as when THE SATURDAY REVIEW of 15 February, 1890, referred to *the violent kephalotomic method for the abatement of party spirit proposed by Swift.*

kepi. An early 19th century French military cap, with a flat top sloping toward the front, and a horizontal peak. Now used historically. In OF WHALES AND MEN, R. B. Robertson (1954) remembers: *A century ago, in the days of corsets and kepis and before steel and plastics pushed our flesh and the flesh of our women in ways God never intended it to go, whalebone was the most valuable part of the baleen whale.*

keraunoscopy. See *aeromancy.* Accent on the *nos* (short *o*). Greek *keraunos,* thunder and lightning; the thunderbolt. (Thunder alone was *bronte,* as with Charlotte.) Hence Greek *keraunoscopia,* the observation of thunder and lightning; divination therefrom.

kern. See *cateran.*

keyn. See *ky*; *cp. soke.*

kibe. A chapped chilblain, especially on the heel. Hence, *to tread upon one's kibe,* to annoy. Shakespeare in HAMLET (1602) says: *The toe of the pesant comes so neere the heeles of our courtier, hee galls his kibe.* And the CONTEMPORARY REVIEW of June 1883 said of suicide: *How closely this spectre follows on the kibes of pleasure and extravagance.*

kichine. An old form of *kitchen.*

kickshaw. (1) A fancy dish; not a substantial English recipe, but one of those 'somethings' the frivolous French concoct. From French *quelque chose,* something; hence *kick-choses, kickshaws*; this was later treated as a plural, whence 17th century *kickshaw.* Shakespeare in HENRY IV, PART TWO (1597) calls for *a joint of mutton, and any pretty little tiny kickshawes.* (2) By extension, anything elegant but trifling or unsubstantial; in Shakespeare's TWELFTH NIGHT (1601) we hear Sir Andrew Aguecheek: *I delight in masks and revels sometimes altogether,* and Sir Toby Belch: *Art thou good at these kickshawses, knight?* Milton, in his essay on EDUCATION (1644) applies the word to persons: *The Monsieurs of Paris to take our hopeful youth . . . and send them over back again transformed into mimicks, apes, and kickshoes.* As early as 1658 we find protest against *the kickshaw language, which these chameleon times love to feede on*—a pattern of speech and writing never since wholly set aside.

kicksie-wicksie. A whim or erratic fancy. Also *kickie-wickie*; *kicksey-winsey, kicksy wincy, kickshiwinches*; probably humorous variants of *kickshaw, q.v.* Shakespeare uses the first two forms (according to the edition) in ALL'S WELL THAT ENDS WELL (1601), as a jocular term for a wife: *He weares his honor in a boxe unseene That hugs his kicky-wicky heare at home, Spending his manly marrow in her arms, Which should sustain the bound and high curvet Of Mars's fiery steed.*

kilderkin. A cask, half a barrel in size. Also *kempkin, kinkin,* via Dutch, perhaps from Latin *quintale,* fifth. By a statute of 1531, the beer *kilderkin* contained 18 gallons; that for ale, 16. There was also a *kilderkin* of butter, 112 pounds. The word was used figuratively, as by Peele in EDWARD I (1593): *Pluck out thy spigot, and draw us a fresh pot from the kinderkin of thy knowledge.* And the cask grew smaller; thus Dryden says in MACFLECKNOE (1682): *A tun of man in thy large bulk is writ, But sure thou'rt but a kilderkin of wit.*

killcow. A swashbuckler, braggadocio; person (that thinks he is) of importance. From *kill* + *cow,* the cow being the most unwarlike of creatures. Richard Harvey in PLAINE PERCEVALL THE PEACE-MAKER OF ENGLAND (1590) exclaimed: *What neede all this stir? this banding of kilcowes to fight with a shadow?* Nashe in return (*cp. bum; gallimaufry*) calls Gabriel Harvey *the kilcow champion.*

killcrop. An insatiable brat, presumed to be a changeling substituted for the genuine child. *Near unto Halberstad,* we read in Henry Bell's translation (1652) of Luther's COLLOQUIA MENSALIA, *was a man that also had a killcrop, who sucked the mother and five other women dry, and besides devoured very much.*

kimbo. See *kam.*

kinchin. See *pedlers French.* This word was from the German: *kindchen,* a little child. In English it appeared also as *kinchyn, kynchin,* and sometimes *kitchin, kitchen.*

kinkin. See *kilderkin.*

kipsey. A small wicker-basket. Perhaps a diminutive of *kipe,* basket; *kipe* has been common since the year 1000, though now only in dialects. Also *kibsey, kybzey.* Gervase Markham, in COUNTRY CONTENTMENTS (1615) advises: *With a gathering hook, gather those which be full ripe, and put them into your cherry-pot, or kybzey, hanging by your side or upon any bough you please.*

kirat. An earlier form of *carat,* "the weight of 3 grains." Arabian *qirat*; Greek *keration,* little horn; fruit of carob tree (locust bean); hence, a small measure. Turner in A NEW HERBALL (1568) says that *if one kirat of it be given in wine, it maketh a man wonderfully dronken.*

kiss. Used in various phrases, among which might be mentioned: *to kiss the book,* to swear by kissing the Bible. *to kiss the cup,* to drink. *to kiss the post,* to arrive too late and be shut out. *to kiss the rod,* to accept punishment submissively. *to kiss the stocks,* to be placed in the stocks; similarly, *to kiss the clink.* A *kiss-cow* is one that 'kisses the cow for the milk,' stoops to indignities for a consideration; also used as an adjective, as in THE NEW MONTHLY MAGAZINE in 1840: *We have no such kiss-cow tastes.* A *kiss-me-quick* was (19th century) a small bonnet set far back on the head; also, a curl of hair in front of the ear. As names of various flowers. The heartsease has been called *kiss-me, kiss-me-at-the-garden-gate.* Love-in-a-mist is also *kiss-me-twice-before-I rise.* Southernwood is called *kiss-me-quick-and-go,* perhaps because it is also called *boy's love—maiden's ruin.* Also try *kissing.*

kissing. *kissing-comfit.* A small sweet confection for perfuming the breath. For a quotation from Shakespeare, see *eryngo.* This of course invited a kiss, and was sometimes called a *kissing cause,* as in SWETNAM ARRAIGNED (1620): *Their very breath is sophisticated with amber-pellets, and kissing causes.* A *kissing gate,* one that opened in a U-shaped enclosure, so that but one person could go through at a time; a kiss was the accepted fare. THE WESTMINSTER GAZETTE of 7 November, 1896, noted *the disappearance of the last of the kissing-gates on Parliament Hill. kissing-strings,* strings of a bonnet tied under the chin, the ends hanging. Scott in THE HEART OF MIDLOTHIAN (1818) remarks that *the old-fashioned terms of manteaus, saques, kissing-strings, and so forth, would convey but little information even to the milliners of the present day.* Also try *kiss.*

kiss-me-over-the-garden-gate. See *Hymen's torch.*

kist. A northern form of *chest,* used from the 13th century. Applied especially to (1) Noah's ark, (2) the basket into which the infant Moses was put, (3) a coffin. Also (in Scotland, from the 17th century) a verb, to put into a chest or coffin. *I wad fain see thee kisted,* I wish that you were dead.

kith. See *kithe.*

kithe. To make known: by words, to announce, tell; by acts, to show, prove, indicate; to make manifest, to exhibit, discover; to appear; to show oneself; to acknowledge, admit, recognize. *Kithe* (also *kythe, kyth, kith, kuthe*; and in the past forms *kydde, kithed, kudde, ikid, icud,* *kyde,* etc.) was very common from the 9th to the 16th century. Chaucer used it, as in the LEGEND OF GOOD WOMEN (1385): *I shall anon it kythe . . . She kytheth what she is.* Scott sought to revive the word in THE FORTUNES OF NIGEL (1822) in the sense of prove: *It would have kythed Cellini mad, had he never done ony thing else.* The noun form, *kith,* went through more changes of meaning: knowledge, acquaintance; especially, knowledge of proper behavior; (as early as the 9th century) the country one knows, one's native land; then, persons known and familiar. *Kith and kin* originally meant country and kinsfolk; later, friends and relatives; by the mid-18th century it had become merely a loose phrase for kinsfolk. Sometimes it was corrupted to *kiff and kin,* as in Middleton's A CHASTE MAID IN CHEAPSIDE (1620): *A mayd that's neither kiffe nor kin to me.* In his BUIK OF THE CRONICLIES OF SCOTLAND (1535) Stewart spoke of *the grit wonder and miraclis that tha kid.* No kidding!

kittle. To tickle; hence, to excite, rouse (usually pleasantly); to puzzle with a riddle (tickle one's curiosity); also, to 'tickle' the fiddle and the like. This was a common word from the 10th century, and is still used in Scotland. Also *kickle.* Hence, as an adjective, *kittle,* ticklish, hard to handle, risky (a 'ticklish' situation), delicate. TRUTH for 11 September, 1890, said: *Cleopatra is a kittle character for a London theatre, unless played by some French actress who has no character to lose.*

knar. A rugged rock; a knot in wood, especially a knob on a tree-trunk. By extension, a thick-set fellow. Chaucer in the Prologue to THE CANTERBURY TALES (1386) has: *He was short scholdred, brood, a thikke knarre.*

knotgrass. A plant, of interbranched and knotted creeping stems, with tiny pink and crimson flowers. It was used—particularly the variety called *male knotgrass*—to stunt growth, especially of the boys that played female roles in the Tudor theatre. Shakespeare in A MIDSUMMER NIGHT'S DREAM (1590) cries: *You dwarfe! you minimus, of hindring knotgrasse made.* Beaumont and Fletcher in THE COXCOMB (1612) declare: *We want a boy extremely for this function, Kept under for a year with milk and knotgrass; In my time I have seen a boy do wonders.* Which is better treatment than accorded boys whose voices were to be kept soprano.

kony. Fine, fit for a king. German *König,* king. In 18th century dictionaries. *Kony* is also a variant of *coney, q.v.*

kramer. See *crame.*

ky. A variant plural of *cow: kine.* For an instance of its use, see *sigalder.* The form *keyn* is used some ten lines later in the poem.

kyriolexy. The habit of using literal expressions. In 19th century dictionaries; Greek *kyrios,* authoritative, proper + *lexia,* speaking; *lexis,* speech, word, as also in *lexicographer,* a harmless drudge.

L

lac. See *lake.*

lace. To catch in a net or snare; to variegate, streak with color (originally, from gold and silver lace); hence, to lash, whip (leaving streaks of the lash); to cut lines along the breast of a bird, for cooking—*laced fowl. Lace* is via Old French from Late Latin *laciare,* Latin *laqueare,* to ensnare. *Cp. laqueat.* To *lace coffee,* from about 1675 to 1725, was to add sugar; Addison, in his satiric notes for A CITIZEN'S DIARY (SPECTATOR; 1711) wrote: *Mr. Nisby of opinion that laced coffee is bad for the head.* In most instances, a *laced* beverage is one to which a dash of brandy has been added. *Laced mutton* (sometimes just *mutton*), a strumpet, prostitute—perhaps from wearing a bodice; or, with the waist drawn tight. In Shakespeare's THE TWO GENTLEMEN OF VERONA (1591), Speed says of Julia: *Aye, sir. I, a lost mutton, gave your letter to her, a laced mutton, and she, a laced mutton, gave me, a lost mutton, nothing for my labour. Lost mutton,* of course, suggests the more serious *lost sheep,* which would also include the laced mutton.

lachrymae. Latin for tears; used by Beaumont and Fletcher; see *sippet. Lacrima (lachryma, lachrymae) Christi,* a strong, sweet red Italian wine; sometimes just *lacrima (lacrimae)*: literally, the tears of Christ. Also *lachrymable,* tear-worthy; *lachrymabund,* with tears ready to fall; *lachrymation,* weeping. *lachrymental,* mournful. (All these, instead of *chry,* may be spelled *cri* or—naturally—*cry*). Caxton has a rare use of the verb, in his translation (1490) of THE BOOK OF ENEYDOS: *Thenne she began somewhat for to lachryme and sighe upon the bed.* Fielding in THE AUTHOR'S FARCE (1731) boasted: *Tokay I have drank, and lacrimae I have drank.* Archaeologists have guessed that the tiny phials found in ancient Roman tombs were intended to hold tears, and call them *lachrymatories* (accent on the *lack,* which refers to evidence). Carlyle in his MEMOIRS OF LORD TENNYSON (1842) declared: *There is in me what would fill whole lachrymatories, as I read.* The word was humorously applied to a lady's handkerchief, as in THE NEW MONTHLY MAGAZINE in 1825: *Women will be stationed in the pit with white cambric lachrymatories, to exchange for those that have become saturated with the tender tears of sympathy.* And that was before women went to enjoy a good cry at the movies. *Sunt lacrimae rerum.*

lack. See *lack-Latin.*

lackland. A person that owns no land; hence, a common person. Cardinal Vaughan in THE WESTMINSTER GAZETTE of 29 August, 1899, declared that the transference *of the great commons of England to the rich created a lackland and beggared poor.* King John of England, the Plantagenet, who ruled 1199-1216, was called *John Lackland, a common appellation of younger sons,* said the PENNY CYCLOPAEDIA of 1839, *whose age prevented them from holding fiefs.*

lack-Latin. One that knows little or no Latin. Especially (16th century) *Sir John Lack-Latin,* a representative name for an ignorant priest. It was with a sigh for a vanishing generation that Brander Matthews (1914) remarked: "A gentleman needs not know Latin, but he should at least have forgotten it."—Shakespeare used *lack* to form several compounds: *lack-beard* (MUCH ADO ABOUT NOTHING); *lack-brain* (HENRY IV, PART ONE); *lack-linen,* shirtless (HENRY IV, PART TWO); *lack-love* (A MIDSUMMER NIGHT'S DREAM); *lack-lustre* (AS YOU LIKE IT; 1600), the melancholy Jacques is describing Touchstone: *And then he drew a diall from his poake: And looking on it with lacke-lustre eye, Says very wisely, "It is ten o'clock."* Several (Byron, Dickens) have used *lack-lustre* after Shakespeare. Once, in CYMBELINE, Shakespeare uses *lack* as an abbreviation for *good lack* or *alack,* an interjection of sorrow, alas!

laconic. See *breviloquence; chilonian.*

laconicum. The sweating-room of a bath. Named from the *Laconians* (Spartans), who first used such a room.

lacrima. See *lachrymae.*

lacunate. To make holes; dig ditches. Latin *lacuna,* hole, pit; *lacus,* lake. In English *lacuna, lacune,* is used of a gap, a blank space; a missing portion, as in a manuscript or an argument. The plural is *lacunae.* Several adjective forms have been used: *lacunal, lacunar, lacunary,* relating to lacunae; *lacunose, lacunous,* characterized by, full of, lacunae. Also *lacunulose,* with tiny gaps or hollows. And *lacunosity.* The terms are still used in science—botany, medicine, astronomy—less often in general reference. W. Taylor in MEMOIRS (Robberd; 1814) said: *He could trust to his extempore eloquence for supplying the lacunes of his text. Lacuna* is the Latin diminutive of *lacus,* a larger hollow—which naturally becomes filled with water and is a *lake.* Hence *lacustrial, lacustrian, lacustrine,* pertaining to a lake; *lacuscular,* of a small lake, a pond, pool. A *lacustrian* was a lake-dweller; the *lacustrine period* is the prehistoric age when (in Europe) dwellings in lakes (on high poles) were common, as the *lacustrine habitations* of Switzerland (accent on the *cuss*).

lacustrine. See *lacunate.*

lac virginis. (1) A cosmetic; used in the 15th, 16th and 17th centuries. Literally (Latin), milk of the Virgin. Nashe in PIERCE PENNILESSE HIS SUPPLICATION TO THE DIVELL (1592) said: *She should have noynted your face over night with lac virginis.* (2) A wine; perhaps a translation of German *Liebfraumilch.* BLACKWOOD'S EDINBURGH MAGAZINE said, in a poem of 1820: *The parsons should grow misty On good lac virginis or lachryma Christi.*

lad's love. See *Hymen's torch.*

lag. There are several words of this form; first, as verbs. (1) *to lag,* to be bedraggled; to be or to make wet or muddy; Bunyan in THE HOLY WAR (1682) warns, of new garments: *Let them not lag with dust and dirt.* (2) To drag after one; to fall behind, the still current sense. (3) To carry off; to send to penal servitude, transport; to catch; De Quincey observed (1847) that *Aladdin himself only escaped* *being lagged for a rogue and a conjurer by a flying jump after his palace.* (4)—Technically: to cover with *lags* (staves, strips of felt, etc., to cover a barrel, a boiler, and the like). There were nouns corresponding to these various verbs, and compounds. Shakespeare in HENRY IV, PART ONE (1596) has: *I could be well content To entertaine the lagge-end of my life With quiet hours.* From *lag,* the hindmost person; *lags,* what's left when liquor is emptied from a vessel, dregs, came the use of *lag,* the lowest class, the meanest sort of persons, as by Shakespeare in TIMON OF ATHENS: *The Senators of Athens, together with the common lag of people.*

laic. (1) A variant of *lake, q.v.,* meaning play. (2) A variant of *lay,* pertaining to the *laity,* not of the church. Also used as a noun, meaning a *layman,* one not of the clergy. Lamb in IMPERFECT SYMPATHIES (ESSAYS OF ELIA; 1833) points out that oath-taking creates a sort of double standard of truth: *A great deal of incorrectness and inadvertency, short of falsehood, creeps into ordinary conversation; and a kind of secondary or laic truth is tolerated, where clergy truth—oath truth—by the nature of the circumstance, is not required.*

lake. (1) An offering, sacrifice; a gift. To receive something *to lake,* as a gift. Related to Old English *lician,* to please, to like; used from BEOWULF into the 13th century. (2) play, sport, fun; a contest. In the plural, games, goings on. Old High German *leich,* song; Gothic *laiks,* dance; Teutonic *laikan,* to play. *Cp. laic.* (3) a fine linen, used for shirts. First used in Chaucer's RIME OF SIR THOPAS (1386): Old Saxon *lakan,* mantle. (4) a reddish pigment, or the color produced thereby. This is a variant (17th century) of the earlier *lac* (Hindustani *lakh*; Sanskrit *laksha*). *Lac* is a dark red resinous crust on trees, produced by the prick of an insect. The incrusted twigs are called *sticklac;* the resin broken off the twigs is called *seedlac;* melted and formed into thin plates, it is *shellac.* (5) a small stream, or a channel for water; specifically (Wright; 1869): "an open part of the river, or the waters in a fen, when a hard frost sets in, in a drowned year; to which the wild fowl resort for food." Old English *leccan,* to moisten; related to *letch, lick, leak.* This sense combined with Latin *lacus,* basin, tub, pond, to produce the still current sense. (6) a pit, a den (as of lions); a grave; an underground dungeon; a winevat. These are extensions of the sense of Latin *lacus;* they all developed in the 14th century. Thornley in his translation (1657) of the charming DAPHNIS AND CHLOE said that Daphnis *out of the lake, tunn'd the wine into the butts.* The PRYMER of 1400 uses the word (in the sense of pit or dungeon) figuratively: *He ladde me out of the laake of wretchednesse.* Also the verb, *to lake,* to color red; to make an offering or sacrifice to; to play, sport. This sense was extended: to sport with, to make sport of, mock; to leap, move quickly, to fight; to play amorously; to take holiday from work; to be out of a job. *Let the lasses,* said T. Cutwode in CALTHA POETARUM: OR THE BUMBLEBEE (1599): *give over leaking in the greene.*

lambitive. A medicine to be taken by licking, often given (in the 17th and 18th centuries) on the end of a licorice stick. Latin *lambere, lambitus,* to lick, whence *lambent* flames. Also *lambative, lambetive*; Steele in THE TATLER (1710, No. 266) has: *Upon the mantle tree . . . stood a pot of lambetive electuary.*

lampad. Almost always in the plural: *lampads,* in the BIBLE: REVELATIONS, the "seven lamps of fire burning before the throne, which are the seven spirits of God." Greek *lampas, lampad-*, lamp, has given English a number of forms: *lampadary* (1) an officer of the Eastern church, in charge of the lighting, (2) a cluster of lamps, a candelabrum. A *lampadephore* was a torch-bearer, especially, (a *lampadist*) a competitor in a torch-race, in a *lampadedromy, lampadrome, lampadephoria.* A *lampadias* (Bailey's DICTIONARY, 1751) is a shooting-star resembling the flame of a torch; I saw one in August 1953. For *lampadomancy* see *aeromancy.* The adjective *lampyrine* means shining; it has been applied in zoology to the genus of glowworms.

lampadomancy. See *aeromancy; cp. lampad.*

lamprophone. An instrument (megaphone, or electrical device) for increasing the intensity of sound. Greek *lampros,* bright, shining; *cp. lampad.* Also (19th century, for the deaf), *lamprophoner.* A clear, sonorous quality or state of the voice is called *lamprophony.*

lancinate. To pierce, thrust through. Latin *lancinare, lancinatus,* to tear to pieces, was changed in meaning (in Cooper's THESAURUS, 1565) by association with *lance.* In the Near East, lancinated chunks of meat are cooked before an open fire. Donne, in a Sermon of 1630, declared that *Every sin is an incision of the soul, a lancination.* An acute, piercing pain is *a lancinating pain.*

land-carrack. A woman—with disrespectful implications; Iago is speaking of his envied master (Shakespeare, OTHELLO; 1604). Woman is a 'vessel': *Honour unto the wife, as unto the weaker vessel,* says the BIBLE (I PETER): hence, various vessels have been used as figurative terms for woman. In Elizabethan days, a *land-frigate* was a woman, usually a strumpet; Iago makes the same implication when he speaks of Othello's secret marriage: *Faith, he tonight hath boarded a land-carrack.* See *carrack.*

land-damn. To make a hell on earth for. Shakespeare thus uses it (unless the text be corrupt) in THE WINTER'S TALE (1611): *You are abus'd, and by some putter on, That will be damn'd for't; would I knew the villaine, I would land-damne him.*

langle. To fasten with a thong; especially, to tie together the legs of an animal to prevent its straying. Also, as a noun, a thong for such binding; a hobble. Probably from Latin *lingula,* thong, diminutive of *lingua,* tongue; but no intermediate French word has been found. Trapp in his commentary (1647) on the BIBLE: ROMANS wrote of *this carcase of sin to which I am tied and langold.*

langrage. A kind of shot for cannon, 17th into the 19th century, of bolts, bars, and other irregular pieces of iron, used especially against the rigging and sails of enemy vessels. Also *langridge, langrel, langrill.* Nelson in 1796 declared: *It is well known that English ships of war are furnished with no such ammunition as langrage.*

langret. A false die, used by sharpers of the 16th and 17th centuries. Gilbert Walker's A MANIFEST DETECTION OF THE MOST VYLE AND DETESTABLE USE OF DICE-PLAY (1550; echoed by Dekker's THE BELMAN OF LONDON, 1608) explained it as *a well favored die that seemeth good and square: yet is the forhead longer on the cater and tray than any other way, and therefore holdeth the name of a langret.* The extra length keeps the four or the three on the bottom; hence such a die is also called a *bar'd cater-tra, q.v. Cp. fullam.*

langridge. See *langrage.*

lanspessade. See *anspessade.*

lant. Urine; especially, stale urine, gathered for various industrial uses. The word is Old English, used from the 10th century. Hence *to lant, to lantify,* to moisten or mix with urine. *Cp. lotium.* A. Wilson's THE INCONSTANT LADY mentioned *a goodly peece of puff paste, A little lantified, to hold the gilding.* Among the cosmetic and gustatory uses of *lant* was the practice of putting it into ale; there are several 17th century references to this, as in THE TINKER OF TURVEY (1630): *I have drunke double-lanted ale, and single-lanted, but never gulped down such Hypocrenian liquor in all my life.*

lanterloo. A card game, later called *loo.* The knave of clubs, called *pam,* was the highest card. *Cp. pam; loo.* The name is from a meaningless refrain to a French song, *lanturelu;* akin to the earlier *laturelure, toora loora* as the Irish might sing. *Lanterloo* was very popular in the 17th century, and was mentioned frequently by the dramatists. Etheredge in SHE WOULD IF SHE COULD (1668) has *playing at lanterloo with my old Lady Loveyouth and her daughter;* Crowne in SIR COURTLY NICE (1685) refers to a man as *the very pam at lantereloo, the knave that picks up all.*

laodicean. Lukewarm; indifferent in politics, religion, etc. Christ's message to the church of the Laodiceans was "Because thou art lukewarm, and neither cold nor hot, I will spue thee out of my mouth." In ROBERT ELSMERE (1888), by Mrs. Humphry Ward, we read: *You will loathe all this laodicean cant of tolerance.* (The word is pronounced lay-odd-i-seé-an.) Hence also *laodiceanism,* lukewarmness, indifference. Not only in ours but in many times the middle-of-the-way man was scorned as (FORTNIGHTLY REVIEW, December 1877) a *laodicean liberal.*

lap. See *lapidable.*

lapicide. See *stillicide.*

lapidable. Worthy of being stoned. In 17th and 18th century dictionaries. Phillips (1706), however, perhaps with a lassie on his lap, defined *lapidable* as marriageable, fit for a husband. Originally *lap* meant a fold in a garment; especially a fold of the toga over the breast, serving as a pocket or pouch; the use of this, in such phrases as *the lap and bosom of the Church,* led to the current sense. Latin *lapis,* stone, has given us many English forms, e.g., *lapidify,* to turn to stone; *cp. lapidity. lapidescence,* turning to stone, as was the lot of those that looked Medusa in the eye; petrifaction (Latin *peter,* rock, on which the Catholic church stands).

lapidity. The essence of stoniness. Latin *lapis, lapidem,* stone. Note that *a lapicide* is a stonecutter; also *a lapidary, a lapicidary.* To pelt with stones, to stone to death, is *to lapidate;* hence *lapidation;* a *lapidator* is a man presumably without sin. *lapidose, lapidous,* abounding in stone; stony (also figuratively, of one's disposition). The diminutive of *lapis* was (Latin) *lapillus;* whence English *lapilliform,* pebble-shaped; *lapilli,* pebbles, especially tiny stones belched from a volcano; a mass or heap of such pebbles is *lapillo. Lapis* itself is used in the name of various stones: *lapis calaminaris, lapis causticus, lapis divinus, lapis infernalis, lapis lazuli,* and more. Permit the thought to lapse. Rather, turn to the 19th century, which, seeking essences, spoke of the *lapidity* of stone, the *aureity* of gold. Earlier (16th and 17th centuries) *aureation* referred to the gilding of one's speech; gilded speech, the use of *aureate* terms, especially polysyllabic coinages from Latin. Also *aureal* (Latin, *aureus*) golden. Thus Lydgate in the Prologue to his CHRONICLES OF TROY (1430) said: *And of my pen the traces to correcte Which barrayne is of aureat lycoure.* Further examples might be greeted, if not with lapidation, at least with lapidity.

lapsus. A slip, an error. Familiar in the Latin expression *lapsus linguae,* a slip of the tongue; not so well remembered, though with frequent occasion, in *lapsus calami,* a slip of the pen (*calamus,* reed). Chaucer blamed any *lapsus calami* in his writings on *Adam Scrivener* (John Doe, his scribe); Rabelais proclaimed that any passage in his works found heretical was merely *lapsus calami.*

laputan. Chimerical, visionary, absurd. Also *Laputian.* Aristophanes in his play THE CLOUDS kept Socrates suspended above earth in a basket, to show that the philosopher is always up in the air. Swift in GULLIVER'S TRAVELS (1726) set *Laputa,* an island in the air, for his philosophers. They went about lost in chimerical schemes; 'flappers' with inflated bladders had to tap the thinkers with inflated egos, to bring them back to awareness of their surroundings. Yet Herschel in his FAMILIAR LECTURES ON SCIENTIFIC SUBJECTS (1866) suggested that *After all, Swift's idea of extracting sunbeams out of cucumbers, which he attributes to his Laputan philosophers, may not be so very absurd.* Poe (1849) used *laputically,* to mean in the manner of the Laputans.

laqueat. Ensnared. Latin *laqueare, laqueatus,* to ensnare; *laqueus,* noose. Hence *laqueary, laquearian,* related to a noose, or armed with a noose (as a gladiator; so used by Byron in CHILD HAROLD, 1818). A *laquear,* in architecture, is a ceiling laced with network. Also see *illaqueate.* Rolland in THE COURT OF VENUS (1560) pictured one *laqueat with lust of luif.*

lar. A household god. In Roman references, plural *lares,* the guardian gods of the house. They were usually linked with the *penates* (three syllables; *penus,* the inner shrine in the temple of Vesta; hence, a sanctuary), the gods of the hearth and home. In English, both were used figuratively for one's home. Occasionally (16th and 17th centuries) *lar* was used in more familiar fashion, as a domestic sprite; Florio in MAZZARUOLO (1598) spoke of *a lar in the chimney.* The part of a Roman house where the *lares* were kept was the *lararium.* Walpole in a letter of 1775 said: *I am returned to my own lares and penates—to my dogs and cats.* Thomas Pitt was, said THE ATHENAEUM of 20 July, 1889, *through his sons and daughters, the great lar of not fewer than five families in the English peerage.*

larbar. A withered or worn-out person. Used 15th to 17th century. Also as an adjective; THE BOOK OF ST. ALBANS (1486): *He is meegre, larbre, and leene.*

lardon. A piece of bacon or pork, inserted into meat in the process of *larding.* Also *lardoon, lardun, lardet*—"to put into rostemeate," said Florio in 1598; "drawn through with a large larding-pin," said Eliza Acton (MODERN COOKERY) in 1845. Urquhart tells, in his translation (1653) of Rabelais: *The lardons or little slices of bacon, wherewith I was stuck, kept off the blow.*

laron. A robber. Also *laroun, la-roone, larrone.* Old French *laron*; Latin *latro-*

nem; cp. latrociny. The English form *ladrone* (*ladren, laydron, latherin, latheron*; accented on the first syllable) was a (mainly Scotch) term of reproach: scoundrel, blackguard. Shakespeare in THE MERRY WIVES OF WINDSOR (1598) cries *O Diable, Diable: vat is in my clossett? Villanie, La-roone: Rugby, my rapier!*

last in hell. Also, *last couple in hell.* See *barleybreak.*

latifundian. Owning, or one who owns, a large estate. Latin *latus,* broad + *fundus,* estate. Hence also *latifunds, latifundia,* large estates. Used from the 17th century, as by Roger North in EXAMEN (1734): *Although the interest of a very latifundian faction was concerned.*

latimer. An interpreter. Old French *latimmier,* transformed from *latinier,* one that knows *Latin.* Milton was Cromwell's *latimer.* Also *latymer, latynier, latynere.* Layamon's BRUT (1205) declared: *He was the bezste latimer that aer com her.*

lation. Movement from one place to another; motion. From Latin *latus,* past participle of *ferre,* to carry. Frequent in 17th century scientific writings, reaching into poetry as in Herrick's HESPERIDES (1648): *Make me the straight and oblique lines, the motions, lations, and the signes.*

latitate. To lie hid, to lurk. From Latin *latitare, latitatus,* to lurk, frequentative of *latere,* to hide, whence English *latent.* The verb *latitate* seems to have occurred only to the 17th and 18th century dictionary makers, but *latitation,* lying concealed, and *latitancy,* especially in the sense of hiding away for the winter, hibernation, have been used. The *latitancy* of the ovum and the spermatozoon is their lying in wait for one another (so it was thought, into the 19th century) after insemination.

latrant. Barking, snarling. Latin *latrare,* to bark. Hence also *latration. We have no three-headed dog,* said the NEW MONTHLY MAGAZINE in 1824, *chained at the gate of Tartarus to startle the visitants by his trilinguar latrations.* The word may be used physically—as by M. Green in SPLEEN, 1737: *Whose latrant stomachs oft molest The deep-laid plans their dreams suggest*—or figuratively, as of *a latrant critic,* who rather snarls in ink than passes judgment.

latria. The deepest worship, due to God alone. Via Latin church terms from Greek *latreia,* service; *latreyein,* to serve with prayer. The adjective forms are *latreutic, latreutical.* A lesser form of worship is *dulia, q.v.*

latrociny. Highway-robbery, brigandage; a company (or a government) of thieves. Latin *latro, latronem,* a mercenary soldier; hence, a freebooter, highwayman, brigand. *Cp. laron.* In the 17th century *latron,* thief, was used in English; Meredith revived it in THE EGOIST (1879). Other forms are *latrocination, latronage,* thievery.

latten. A mixed metal, yellow; brass or something like it, often hammered into thin sheets or drawn into wire. Also *laten, laton, latin, latun; lattinne, latton,* and the like. Chaucer in the Prologue to THE CANTERBURY TALES (1386) says *He hadde a croys of laton ful of stones.* Shakespeare in THE MERRY WIVES OF WINDSOR has Pistol call Slender a *latten bilbo* (see *bilbo*) because he is tall, thin, and blond (brass-color). Later in the scene, there is a pun on *latten* and the *Latin* language; such puns were perpetrated fairly often in the 17th century, as by Sir N. L'Estrange in 1655, fathering the phrase on Shakespeare, who was supposed to be godfather to one of Jonson's children, and after the christening said: *I' faith, Ben, Ile e'en give him a douzen good Lattin spoones, and thou shalt translate them.* The truth of this tale, said Nares in 1882, "has latterly been questioned."

lavender. A washerwoman; early and rarely also a washerman. Old French *lavandier, lavandiere*; Latin *lavanda,* things to be washed; *lavare,* to wash, *cp. laver.* The plant probably derived its name from being used (at least as early as the 16th century) for perfuming baths or for laying in newly washed linen; it may, however, be from *lividual,* diminutive of *lividus,* livid, bluish, shifted in form by association with the use. A *lavendry* (14th to 16th century) was a laundry. *To lay in lavender,* to store away carefully for future use; hence (15th and 16th centuries) to pawn; to put where one can do no harm, as in prison. References to such pawning are frequent; Chapman in EASTWARD HOE (1605) says: *Good faith, rather then thou shouldest pawne a rag more Ile lay my ladyship in lavender, if I knew where.* Greene in THE UPSTART COURTIER (1592) pictured a persistent evil: *The poore gentleman paies so deere for the lavender it is laid up in, that if it lie long at a broker's house, he seems to buy his apparell twice.*

laver. A basin or water-jug for washing the hands; later, a larger basin or cistern; applied especially to the basin for the ablutions of priests. Latin *lavare,* to wash, whence the still used *lave* and *lavatory.* Also, the basin of a fountain; Evelyn in his DIARY for 18 January, 1645, wrote of *many stately fountaines . . . casting water into antiq lavors.* Pepys has it in his DIARY too (14 June, 1664). By extension, from the religious use, a spiritual cleansing or cleansing agency; baptism was (16th and 17th centuries) often called *the laver of new birth.*

laverock. An Old English name for the *lark.* Also *laverk, leverock* (Izaak Walton, 1653), *lavroc, lavercok,* and more. Chaucer in THE ROMAUNT OF THE ROSE (1366) says *Ther mighte men see many flokkes Of turtles and laverokkes;* Coleridge in THE ANCIENT MARINER (1798) has: *Sometimes adropping from the sky I heard the lavrock sing.* For the blithesome bird that heralds the dawn, *laverock* is a pretty name.

lavolta. A lively dance for two persons, with many "high and active bounds." For quotation, see *coranto.* W. Tennant in THE THANE OF FIFE (1822) says: *Like spark from fire lavolting through the dance.*

law. See *low.* The meaning hill persists in Scotland. Wilson in NOCTES AMBROSIANAE (1825) wrote: *Ilk forest shaw and lofty law Frae grief and gloom arouse ye.* In addition to this and to the still current senses, law (*lagh, lauch*) in the 15th and 16th centuries was used to mean legal fee, share of expense.

lawnd. An old form of *lawn.* Also *laund.* In both senses, fine linen, and a grassy glade. Shakespeare in HENRY VI, PART THREE (1593) says: *Under this thick grown brake we'll shroud ourselves, For through this laund anon the deere will come.*

lay. As a noun. (1) A lake, pool; 10th to the 15th century. (2) law; religious law; faith. *Cp. laic.* (3) A short poem, to be sung; a tune. (4) A bill, a reckoning. (5) A wager, bet. *Even lay,* an even chance; also *fair lay, good lay,* or the reverse. Shakespeare uses the word in this sense several times: the verb is still current. (6) Short for *allay,* alloy; *lay* *metal,* a kind of pewter. (7) A prostitute. Influenced by the verb, also the erotic sense of the noun, *a good lay;* but in origin a false singular from *layes,* a loose woman, taken as a plural, from *Lais* the Greek courtesan. Hence *layesian,* a prostitute. Herbert in his TRAVELS (1638) said: *Till by inquiry I saw it came from greedy novelty, I thought them layesians; but it seem'd I erred.* A *laystall* was a dump, or a dunghill, as in Spenser's THE FAËRIE QUEENE (I v; 1590); used figuratively by the Water Poet (WORKS; 1630): *These are the right patternes of an industrious bawd, for shee picks her living out of the laystall or dunghill of our vices.*

laystall. See *lay.*

lea. A stretch of open ground; meadow, fallow, grassland. Common—*leah, lee, laye, ley*—from the 9th century. There are two other words with the form *lea*: a scythe (since the 15th century) and (since the 14th) a measure of yarn, seventh part of a hank (19th century: worsted, 80 yards; cotton and silk, 120 yards). The *lea* for land may also be an adjective, meaning unploughed, fallow, also in the expression *to lie ley,* to lie in grass; and it is common in English place-names, as *Shipley,* sheep meadow.—*So might I, lying on some pleasant lea . . .*

leach. In addition to the current senses (to wet, to pour a liquid through, etc.) *leach* as a noun had several uses. (1) A perforated vessel for pouring water over a substance; especially to make lye from wood ashes. This is the same word, in origin, as *letch,* a ditch, a pool. (2) A variant of *leech* (*q.v.*), a physician. (3) A variant of *leash;* especially, the leather thong attached to the *jess* (*q.v.*) of a hawk. (4) A slice or strip of meat. Especially, a dish of sliced meat, eggs, fruits and spices in jelly or gelatine. *Dry leash,* a sort of gingerbread with dates, etc.; *white leach,* with almonds in gelatine. In the 15th century, a *leche-frye* was made with calves' feet. Also a verb; *cp. leche.*

leal. A variant form of *loyal* and *legal*—both of which (the first via French) are from Latin *legalis; lex, legem,* law. Also *lel, leyll, lele, leale,* and more. Hence *lealty,* loyalty.

leam. (1) A light; a gleam or flash. Common since BEOWULF, also as a verb, to shine, gleam, light up. Also *leem, leme, lym, lyme,* and the like. *Hail, my Lord, leamer of light,* says one of the York Mystery plays (1440). (2) The husk (not the shell) of a nut; *a brown leamer,* a nut with a brown husk, i.e., a ripe nut. *To leam* is to remove the husks of nuts. The first sense is the more common, as in Dunbar's THE THISTLE AND THE ROSE (1503): *All the houss illumynit of hir lemys.*

leaping-house. A brothel. A coinage of Shakespeare, in HENRY IV, PART ONE (1596): *What a divell hast thou to do with the time of the day? unlesse hours were cups of sacke, and minutes capons, and clocks the tongues of bawdes, and dialls the signes of leaping-houses, and the blessed sun himselfe a faire hot wench in flame-colored taffeta.* Shakespeare also, in CYMBELINE, uses *leaping-time* to mean youth.

lease. (1) A *lease,* as few realtors will admit, is a lie—or was a lie, from the 9th century to the 15th. [*Lease,* in the current sense of a contract conveying land or buildings, etc., was first used in the 15th century; it is related to French *laisser,* to let, leave. In this sense, a *lease-parole,* in the 16th and 17th centuries, was a verbal agreement.] The early *lease*

—also used as an adjective, false, lying—is related to *lose* and *loose,* and survives as a suffix meaning without, *-less,* as in *senseless. Cp. leesing. Withouten lease,* truthfully, was a common phrase in Middle English poetry; Chaucer in THE LEGEND OF GOOD WOMEN (1385) puts it: *Thus seyt the book withoutyn ony les.* Also *leasing, lesing,* falsehood, lying; a lie. Spenser in COLIN CLOUT'S COME HOME AGAIN (1595) says: *No leasing new, nor grandams fable stale.* Shakespeare used the word in TWELFTH NIGHT; Scott revived it in THE TALISMAN (1825) : *Satan is strong within you . . . and prompts thee to leasing.* Hence also *to lease,* to tell lies; *a leaser,* a liar; also a *leasing-monger,* dealer in lies. (2) *To lease,* to gather; especially, to glean; used in 11th and in 14th century tellings of the Biblical story of Ruth and Boaz. Hence *leasing,* gleaning. Edwards (WORDS, FACTS, AND PHRASES, 1912) relates this word to *lea, q.v.,* a field; but there was Old English *lesan,* to gather. It's better to hold your lease.

leash. A set of three. This use, common from the 14th into the 18th century, and used occasionally later—Tennyson in GARETH AND LYNETTE (1859) uses it as a vague plural: *Then were I wealthier than a leash of kings*—rose from the original and still current use of the word, as a strap for holding in dogs. In hunting, commonly three hounds were strapped together, hence *a leash* of hounds meant three. This was extended, first to deer, hares, foxes, and the like, then to things in general. Shakespeare in HENRY IV, PART ONE (1596) says: *Sirra, I am sworn brother to a leash of drawers . . . Tom, Dicke, and Francis.* Jonson, in THE SILENT WOMAN (1609) : *kept my chamber a leash of days for the anguish of it.* The TRAVELS of Baron Munchhausen (1792) boast: *I have acquired precisely nine hundred and ninety-nine leash of languages.* Quite a lease (*q.v.*) of words!

leasing. See *lease.*

leatcher. A variant form of *lecher.* Thomas Freeman in RUBBE, AND A GREAT CAST (1614; *cp. sute*) addressed Shakespeare, the many-sided: *Vertues or vices theame to thee all one is: Who loves chaste life, there's Lucrece for a teacher: Who list read lust there's Venus and Adonis, True modell of a most lascivious leatcher.*

lecanomancy. See *aeromancy.*

leche. An early form of *leach, q.v.* Also an early variant of *leech, lich, like.* As a verb, *to leche,* to slice, was frequent in cookery directions, and in names of dishes, as *lechefryes, lechelardis.* In the plural, *leches,* slices, cakes. See the recipe at *monamy.*

lechne. To administer medicine; hence, to heal, cure. An old Teutonic term, whence also *leech*; *cp. leechcraft.* Also *lecnian, lacnian, lechnien.* Used into the 15th century; Langland in PIERS PLOWMAN (1393) says: *Lame men he lechede.*

lectistern. A feast (among the ancient Romans) at which the statues of the gods were lifted from their pedestals and laid upon couches, with fine food set before them. Latin *lecti,* couch + *sternere,* to spread. Used by Addison (1702) in the Latin form, *lectisternium.*

lectual. Pertaining to bed; confined or proper to be confined in bed. Lectual activity is not necessarily unrelated to intellectual.

leden. Latin (to the 13th century only; then), the language of a people. Also *leed; boc-leden,* book language. The word was an early north European mispronunciation of Latin *Latinum,* confused with Celtic *leden, leoden,* language. Other forms were *lede, lyden, ledone, lidene, ledyn, lidden, leaden,* and the like. Spenser in THE FAËRIE QUEENE (1596) has: *He was expert in prophecies, And could the ledden of the gods unfold.* From the 14th into the 17th century, poets used *leden* also of the 'language' of birds, as Drayton in POLYOLBION (1612): *The ledden of the birds most perfectly shee knew.*

leechcraft. The art of healing. *At leechcraft,* under medical care. From *leech,* to heal; used from the 12th century into the 17th, as by Fletcher in THE LOYALL SUBJECT (1618): *Have ye any crack maidenhead, to new leach or mend?*; revived by Scott in IVANHOE (1820): *Let those leech his wounds for whose sake he encountered them.* Also *leche, liche, leach*; from the 9th to the 14th century, *lechne q.v.,* to give medicine, to heal. Also, 19th century, *to leech,* to bleed by applying *leeches.* The blood-sucking worm was probably named because it served as a *leech,* a physician.

leese. (1) The earlier form of *lose,* in all its senses. A common Old English word, continuing through the 16th century. (2) To loose, to relax, to unfasten; hence, to set free, release. This also was used into the 17th century, as by Middleton in YOUR FIVE GALLANTS (1608): *Keep thou thine own heart . . . I leese you again now.* From the past forms *lorn, loren,* came the noun *lorel,* meaning a 'lost' soul, a worthless fellow, a blackguard, used by Chaucer (1374) and rather frequent (Spenser, THE SHEPHERD'S CALENDAR, 1579: *Thou speakes lyke a lewde lortell*), often in contrast to *lord.* A *cock lorel, cocklorel,* was a jolly but thorough rogue; Gascoigne in 1577 spoke of *a piece of cocklorels musicke . . . such as I might be ashamed to publish in this company.* This form came from the name of the captain of the boat containing a varied assortment of rogues, of all trades, in the satiric poem *Cocke Lorelles Bote* (printed, 1515, by Wynkyn de Worde). From another past tense form of *leese, losen* (lost), came a form *losel,* also meaning a lost one, a scoundrel; later, with weakened force, a ragamuffin, a ne'er-do-well. This form, from the 14th century, lasted longer, being used by Carlyle (1832), and Browning in A BLOT IN THE 'SCUTCHEON (1843): *Wretched women . . . tied By wild illicit ties to losels vile.* Both these nouns developed further forms: *lorelship, loselism, loselry,* rascality, lewdness; *lorelly, loseling, loselly, loselled,* rascally, lewd; lazy. Note that *leeser,* from the two verbal meanings, developed several senses, two contradictory; (1) a loser; hence (2) a destroyer; (3) a deliverer: Wyclif (in the second sense) speaks in 1380 of *lesars of mennys soulis*; a PSALTER of 1300 (in the third sense) speaks of God as *my helper and leser mine.*

leesing. This is an old word that meant its own opposite. It was very common, as a verb, *to leese, q.v.,* from the 9th century. The root was Gothic *leus, laus, los,* akin to Greek *lyein,* Latin (*so*) *luere, solvere,* to loosen, whence also *solve, dissolve, dissolute,* etc. From the Gothic root came *lose, loss, loose,* and the ending *-less. Cp. lease.* In the train of the sense *lose* came the meaning to be lost, to come to ruin; hence, *leesing,* destruction, perdition. In the train of the sense *loosen* came the meaning to unfasten, open, release; hence, *leesing,* deliverance, redemption. The verb had many forms, including *leosen, lyese, lesse, leze*; in the past, *ylore, losen, lorin, lorne, lorn.* Spenser uses *lore* and *lorn* to mean to forsake, forsaken; THE FAËRIE QUEENE (1590): *After he had faire Una lorne, Through light misdeeming of her loialtie.* Langland in PIERS PLOWMAN (1362) said: *Of his leosinge I lauhwe* [laugh] *Ac for his wynnynge I wepe.* Rolland in THE COURT OF VENUS (1560) cried: *Peradventure thay wold yow leis of cair*; earlier the PSALTER (Hampole's, 1340) said: *We are lesyd of syn.* Wherewith we may leese these thoughts of *leesing.*

leesome. (1) Lovable; pleasant. Middle English *leofsum; lief* + some. Used since the 12th century. Burns in his song IN SIMMER WHEN THE HAY WAS MAWN (1792) sighs for *The tender heart o' leesome love, The gowd and siller canna buy.* The form *leesome lane,* however, is a variant of *leelane,* all by one's lone. (2) Lawful; permissible; right. This sense is from Middle English *lefsum, leave* (permission) + some. In the same sense *leeful (leveful, laifull, lyefull,* etc.) was used from the 13th century to Burns (FOR A' THAT AN' A' THAT, 1814). The form *leesome (lesume, leisom, leifsome,* etc.), lawful, was used from the 14th century into the 18th; Douglas in his AENEIS (1513) said: *So that it lesum be Dido ramane In spousage bound. Blind brutal boy,* said Montgomery in 1600, in a sonnet on Cupid, *that with thy bow abuses Leill* [loyal] *leesome love by lechery and lust.*

leet. (1) A court which lords of some manors were privileged to hold, once or twice a year; the jurisdiction of such a court; hence, a district in general. (2) A list of persons eligible for certain offices; hence, *to be in leet, on the leets,* etc. *Short leet,* a select list of candidates. (3) In phrases *two-leet, two-way-leet, three leet,* etc., a crossway. THE READER of 21 October, 1865, speaking of a vacant professorship, said: *The patrons are the Faculty of Advocates and the Curators, the former having the right of presenting to the latter a leet of two, from which the appointment must be made.* For a further instance of its use, see *waive.*

lege. An old form of *league, ledge, liege.* These are listed in O.E.D. Shakespeare, however, uses *lege* for *allege* in THE TAMING OF THE SHREW (1593), when Grumio protests: *Nay, 'tis no matter, sir, what he leges in Latin.*

lege de moy. A lively 16th century dance. Skelton in THE TUNNYNG OF ELYNOUR RUMMYNG (1529) said: *She made it as koy as a lege de moy.*

legem pone. Cash down; ready payment. These are the first two (Latin) words of the fifth section of PSALM 119, which opens the Matins service on the 25th of the month; March 25 was quarter day, when payments were due. Hence, in the 16th and 17th centuries, *legem pone* was used to mean payment, as when Motteux in his translation (1694) of Rabelais said: *They were all at our service, for the legem pone.* Harvey in his NEW LETTER (1592) said bluntly: *Without legem pone, wordes are winde.*

legion. A devil. This roundabout use of the word is drawn from the devil challenged by Jesus in the BIBLE (MARK, 5): *And he asked him, What is thy name? And he answered, saying, My name is legion: for we are many.* Thus, in general, *their name is legion* (often with capital *L*) means they are innumerable. But Shakespeare in TWELFTH NIGHT (1601) says: *If all the divels of hell be drawne in little,* *and Legion himselfe possest him.* The word *legion* is via French from Latin *legionem; legere, lectum,* to choose (whence *select, elect*), to levy. It was used first of the levied forces of Rome, the *legion* of at first 3,000 men, later 6,000 footmen. Hence, any large body; any great number. *The poor curate's wife,* said Charles T. C. James in THE ROMANTIC RIGMAROLE OF A TIME OUT OF TOWN (1891), *with the legion family clothed from the odds and ends of her rich sister's cast-offs.*

leguleian. A petty befogged lawyer, a pettifogger; also as an adjective, pertaining to petty or verbal questions of the law. Accent on the third syllable, *lee;* Latin *leguleius,* a little dealer in law; *lex, legem,* law. Also *leguleious*: Henry More in AN EXPLANATION OF THE GRAND MYSTERY OF GODLINESS (1660) decried *the leguleious cavils of some pragmatical pettifoggers.*

leighton. A garden. From Old English *leac,* leek + *tun,* enclosure. Used from the 10th into the 18th century. Also *lahtoun, lectun, leyton.* Up to the 14th century, a gardener was called a *leightonward.*

lele. See *leal.*

leman. A person beloved by one of the opposite sex. From Middle English *leofman, lief (q.v.)* + *man.* Sometimes referred to husband or wife, but as early as 1275 it had taken on the implication of illicit lover or mistress. Hence *lemanry,* illicit love. A translation (1671) of Erasmus' COLLOQUIES spells the word oddly (though perhaps fitly): *It may be his wife ith' meantime had got herself another lemon and therefore she acknowledged not her husband.* The word was often applied metaphorically, as in a poem of Hartley Coleridge (1833): *Hope Love's leman is, Despair his wife.*

leme. A variant form of *leam, q.v.*

lere. To teach; to guide; to learn. Also *learen,* later *learn; laren, ler, leryn, leir, lear.* A common Teutonic word; whence also *lore.* Note that (although this sense is now vulgar) as early as 1200 *learn* meant to teach; Shakespeare uses it in THE TEMPEST (1610): *The red-plague rid you For learning me your language.* Hence *lered,* learned; Chaucer says in THE DOCTOR'S TALE (1386): *For be he lewed man or ellis lered.* [The earliest meaning of *lewd* was lay, not in holy orders; hence, unlearned, artless, vulgar; belonging to the lower orders.] The expression *lered and lewed* was common from the 12th to the 16th century; *This lewde and learned,* said Ascham in THE SCHOLEMASTER (1568), *by common experience know to be most true.*

lesing. See *lease.*

let. See *avaunt.* "Without *let* or hinder." Hamlet cries, when Horatio would stop him from following the Ghost: *By heaven, I'll make a ghost of him that lets me!* Hence, *let-game* (Chaucer in TROYLUS AND CRISEYDE; 1374), one that interferes with a game: a "kibitzer," a spoilsport.

letabund. Joyful. Latin *laetabundus; laetari,* to be joyful. Used (rarely) in the 16th century.

letating. Making glad. Latin *laetare,* to rejoice, make glad; *laetus,* cheerful. Motteux in his translation (1694) of Rabelais said that pleasant notes *wake your soul with their letating sound.* A rare but pleasant word.

letch. (1) A stream flowing through boggy land; a muddy ditch; a bog. A variant form of *leach, q.v.* Also *lache, latch.* Used from the 12th century. (2) A craving; inordinate desire. Perhaps a variant of *latch*; used from the 18th century. Grose (1796) defines it as 'a whim of the amorous kind, out of the common way.' Something like a *yen,* of more recent slang; but it has other applications, as when De Quincey (BENTLEY, 1830) stated: *Some people have a letch for unmasking impostors, or for avenging the wrongs of others.* Recent slang has used *letch* as a short form of *lecher.*

letelorye. A dish. Also *lethelory.* The O.E.D. gives *lete* as a separate word, 'meaning obscure'. THE FORME OF CURY (1390) gives a simple but inviting recipe for *letelorye*: *Take ayren, and wryng hem thurgh a stynnor, and do thereto cowe mylke, with butter, and safron, and salt, and seeth it wel. Leshe it* [*lash*: beat]. *And loke that it be stonding, and serve it forth.* Have some scrambled eggs!

lethied. Forgetful; pertaining to or causing forgetfulness or oblivion. Also *lethean, lethaean,* which are still used; *lethy, leathy.* Marston in THE INSATIATE COUNTESS (1613) spoke of a devil that *drown'd thy soule in leathy faculties.* Shakespeare in ANTONY AND CLEOPATRA (1606) speaks of a *lethied dulnesse*; some editors reshape this to *lethe'd*; from the river *Lethe,* one of the rivers that flowed in Tartarus, of which the dead drank; it gave them forgetfulness of all they had seen, heard, or done. Latin *letum, lethum,* meant death; in the 17th century *lethean* was occasionally used as meaning deadly; *lethed,* dead. Also, from the 17th century, *lethiferous, letiferous,* and (19th century) *lethiferal,* causing death, deadly, fatal. Lowell uses this figuratively in THE BIGLOW PAPERS (1848): *I have noted two hundred ond three several interpretations, each lethiferal to all the rest. Leth,* hatred, related to *loath,* was used from the 9th to the 15th century. The *lethal* dose is still used in detective stories.

leuco-. This is a combining form, from Greek *leukos,* white, used mainly in chemistry and medicine; also in a few words of other import. *leucanthous,* white-flowered. *leucocholy,* coined after *melancholy, melan,* black; Gray in a letter of 27 May, 1742, wrote: *Mine . . . is a white melancholy, or rather leucocholy, for the most part; which, though it seldom laughs or dances, nor ever amounts to what one calls joy or pleasure, yet is a good easy sort of state.*

levant. As a noun, the East, the countries of the East. Pronounced with the first syllable accented by Milton (PARADISE LOST, 1667: *Forth rush the levant and the ponent winds*); usually, with the accent on the second. Via French from Latin *levare,* to lift (whence *levitation*), to raise, to rise—here, of the rising sun. Hence, an easterly Mediterranean wind, a *levanter.* Also, a kind of leather, mainly from Morocco. Hence, *to levant,* to make (other leather) look like levant morocco. Also (from the verb), a bet made with the intention of absconding if it is lost —used in the phrases *to come the levant, to run (throw) a levant,* among 18th century playwrights (Vanbrugh; Cibber) and novelists (Fielding). As a verb, to run away; especially of a bookmaker or bettor, to abscond. From Latin *levare,* but probably via Spanish *levantar la casa,* to break up housekeeping; *levantar el campo,* to break camp. Also *levant me!,* a mild imprecation, usually followed by *but,* or a negative (18th century): *Levant me, if I don't turn the tables on him tonight!* Thackery in BRIGHTON (1847) observed that *Guttlebury House was shut up by the lamented levanting of the noble earl.*

levedi. A variant form of lady, which is from Old English *hlaf,* loaf + *dig,* to knead. SIR ORFEO (1320; *cp. urn; rud*) pictured *a quen of priis That was ycleped Dame Herodis, The fairest levedi, for the nones, That might gon on bodi and bones, Ful of love and of godenisse.*

level-coil. A noisy game formerly played at Christmas: each player in turn must leave his seat, which another takes. Played in the 16th and 17th centuries; later called *Going to Jerusalem* (the route was crowded; Mary had to seek shelter in a stall). From French *(faire) lever le cul,* to make (someone) lift his buttock. Later, in the interest of decent speech, the game was called *level-sice, levell-suse*; French *assise,* seat; as Sylvester in his translation (1608) of Du Bartas wrote: *Ambitious hearts do play at level sice.* The word came to be used generally: *to keep level-coil,* to engage in noisy sport or noisy activity or riot. Also, as an adverb, alternately, each in turn. Nashe, in THE UNFORTUNATE TRAVELER (1594): *The next daie they had solempne disputations, where Luther and Carolostadius scolded levell-coyle.* Ben Jonson, in A TALE OF A TUB (1633): *Young Justice Bramble has kept level-coyl Here in our quarters, stole away our daughter.*

leven. (1) A short form of *eleven.* (2) An old form of *leaven,* as in *leavened bread.* (3) A variant of *levin, q.v.* As a verb, to flash brightly. Hence *levening,* lightning.

lever. Preferable. This is the comparative form; also *liever*; the simple survives in the expression *I'd as lief . . .* Thus *liefer was (were) to me,* I had rather. As a noun, *lever* was used in the 14th century as short for *believer* (in God); and, in the 18th century, *lever* was a variant form of *levée,* a (king's, queen's, or noble's) rising or morning reception. Wyatt in his sonnet FAREWELL LOVE (1535) says to the blind god: *Thy sherpe repulce that pricketh ay so sore Hath taught me to sett in tryfels no store, And scape fourth, syne libertie is lever.*

leverock. See *laverock.*

levesel (two syllables). A bower of leaves, a canopy. From Old English *leaf + sele* (French *salle*), hall, room. Also *lefsale, leefsel,* etc. Chaucer, in THE REEVE'S TALE (1386) has the clerk's horse standing *behind the mill, under a lefsel.*

levet. A trumpet call for awakening. Italian *levata,* Latin *levare, levatus,* to raise. The word was used in the 17th and 18th centuries, then supplanted by the French word *reveille.*

levigate. To smooth, polish; to reduce to a paste or smooth powder. From Latin *levigare, levigatus,* to smooth; *levis,* smooth. Hence also *levigation; levigable*: (1) able to be smoothed: Evelyn in POMONA (1664): *Useful is the pear-tree . . . for its excellent colour'd timber, hard and levigable;* (2) able to be powdered; Browning in CHRISTMAS EVE: *Dust and ashes levigable.*

levin. Lightning. Used from the 13th century, as noun and as verb, especially by poets: Gower, Chaucer, Dunbar, Spenser, Scott, Poe, Longfellow, Swinburne. Other forms were *leven, leyven, levyn, leaven.* Hence *levining.* Also combined, as in *levin-brand* (earlier *brond*), *levin-fire, levin-darting.* Spenser in THE FAËRIE QUEENE (1596) speaks of *when the flashing levin haps to light Upon two stubborne oakes.* For a use of *levin-brond,* see *quooke.*

levisomnous. Light-sleeping; watchful. Latin *levis,* light + *somnus,* sleep. In 17th and 18th century dictionaries. I am a levisomnous soul.

lew. Warm, sunny; sheltered from the wind (related to *lee*); tepid, *lew-warm,* later *lukewarm.* As a verb, to make or to be warm; to shelter. In the Wyclif BIBLE (1382; REVELATIONS) we read: *For thou art lew, and nether coold, nether hoot.*

lewdster. A low lewd fellow. See *penster.*

lexicon. A word-book; a list of words or names. Hence, the range of items, or of knowledge, in a field; Swift in THE USE OF IRISH MANUFACTURES (1724) scorned *all silks, velvets, callicoes, and the whole lexicon of female fopperies.* Greek *lexikon (biblion),* (book) of words; *lexis,* word, diction; *leg-,* to speak (Latin *legere,* to read). The word *lexicon,* referring to a dictionary, was long limited to those of Greek, Hebrew, Syriac, or Arabic. It is best known today in the phrase usually misquoted from Bulwer-Lytton's RICHELIEU (1839): *In the lexicon of youth, which fate reserves For a bright manhood, there is no such word as—Fail.* [From the same play comes the always half-quoted observation: *Beneath the rule of men entirely great, The pen is mightier than the sword.*]

lexiphanes. A user of polysyllabic or bombastic phraseology. Greek LEXIPHANES, phrasemonger, was the title of a DIALOGUE of Lucian (2d century A.D.): *lexis,* word + *phan-, phainein,* to show. Hence *lexiphanic; lexiphanicism; lexiphanaticism,* excessive and long-continuing bombast. D'Israeli in THE AMENITIES OF LITERATURE (1841) spoke of *the encumbering lexiphanicisms of the ponderous numerosity of Johnson.*

leye. Flame, blaze, fire. *On leye, a leye,* on fire. Old English *lieg,* related to *light.* Also *ley, lai, lyė, leyhe, lyghe,* and the like. Common from BEOWULF.

liatico. A red Tuscany wine; from *Aleatico.* Also *leaticke, leathick.* Drunk in the 17th century.

lib. This was a common form, with various meanings. (1) From the 8th century; a charm. (2) As a verb. From the 14th century, to castrate; also, figuratively, to cut off, as when Fulke wrote in TWO TREATISES AGAINST THE PAPISTS (1577): *In the latter end, where he libbeth off the conclusion of Origens wordes . . .* In the 17th century, to suckle, to suck persistently. From the 15th century (also *lyp*), to sleep; defined in a CANT DICTIONARY of 1700 as *lib, to tumble or lye together.* Middleton and Dekker wrote in THE ROARING GIRL (1611): *Oh I wud lib all the darkemans.* [*Lightmans,* the day; *darkmans,* the night; thieves' cant of the 16th to 18th century.] Hence *libbege,* 16th to 18th century cant for a bed.

libanomancy. See *aeromancy.* Greek *libanos,* incense. [Latin *libare, libatum,* to taste, to pour out, gave English *libation,* whence *libant* (long *i*), tasting, touching lightly.] Also *libaniferous, libanophorous,* (accents on the third syllable), *libanotophorous,* producing or bearing incense.

libbard. An early variant of *leopard,* used by Shakespeare in LOVE'S LABOUR'S LOST (1594). Boyet is interrupting the show presented by "the pedant, the braggart, the hedge priest, the fool, and the boy." The fool, Costard, says *"I Pompey am—"* Boyet: *You lie, you are not he.* Costard: *"I Pompey am—"* Boyet: *With libbard's head on knee.* Some editors suggest that this refers to Pompey's coat of arms; Sherwood in 1632 said old-fashioned garments had such a head on elbows or knees.

liberticide. See *stillicide.*

libido. The post-Freudian spread of this word may deserve the reminder of its earlier use. In the BIBLE (I JOHN) appear the warnings against the lust of the flesh (*voluptas*), lust of the eyes (*curiositas*), and pride of life (*vana gloria*). Marlowe in his day was accused of these enormities; Beard's THEATRE OF GODS JUDGMENTS (1597), for example, described him as "suffering his lust to have the full raines". St. Augustine (died 430 A.D.) in his CONFESSIONS stressed this triple danger. In his commentary on the saint, AUGUSTINUS (1641), Cornelius Jansenius listed the urges as *libido sentiendi, libido sciendi, libido excellendi*: lust to experience, to know, to surpass. Pascal (died 1662) in his PENSÉES stressed not pride but the will (the flesh, the mind, the will) and therefore made the third urge *libido dominandi,* lust to dominate. These desires mark the main figures of Marlowe's plays.

lich. Form, shape; hence, body; also, the trunk or torso; especially, the dead body, corpse. This was the common word from early times. Also *liche, lych, litch, like, lyke, leech, leach.* ALISAUNDER OF MACEDOINE (1370) has: *Liliwhite was hur liche.* Hence, *lichamly,* pertaining to the body, bodily; in the flesh; carnal. Many compounds were formed from *lich* (*lych, lyk*): *lichbell,* a handbell rung before a corpse. *lichfowl, lich-owl,* the screech owl; its cry was held an omen of death. *lich-lay,* a tax to provide a churchyard. *lich-gate,* a covered gateway to the churchyard, where the corpse is set down until the minister arrives; *lich-stone,* a stone at the lich-gate, on which the coffin rests. *lich-way,* a path on which a corpse has been borne to burial (we are all born to burial); in some regions, such a procession was taken as establishing a right of way. *lich-wake, lychwake, lyke-wake,* the night watch over a dead body; Chaucer in THE KNIGHT'S TALE (1386) has: *Ne how that lych wake was yholde Al thilke night . . . kepe I nat to seye.* Also *licham* (*lich,* body + Old English *hama,* shape, covering), the fleshly garment of the soul, the living body; especially, the body as the seat of desire and appetite. Audelay in a poem of 1426 wrote: *To sle* [slay] *the lust of her lycam and her lykyng.*

licious. Short for *delicious;* possibly, also, the origin of *luscious.* Also *licius.* Used from the 15th to the 17th century.

licitate. To bid for, set a price on. Latin *licitari; liceri, licitum,* to make a bid. Also *licitation,* bidding; putting up the price; offering for sale at auction. *licitator,* a bidder at an auction. *Ecclesiastical persons,* said a pamphlet of 1601, *are not to study how to murder princes, nor to licitate kingdoms.* That would indeed be illicit! The form *licit,* lawful, is from Latin *licere, licitum,* to be permitted.

lick-. Several compounds of the common word *lick* (verb since the 10th century, noun only from the 17th) have been used in derogatory senses. Among these are *lick-box,* one that likes sweets; *lick-dish, lick-fingers, lick-ladle, lick-platter, lick-pot, lick-sauce, lick-spigot, lick-trencher,* all used for either a glutton or a parasite. A *lick-boots, lick-foot, lick-spit, lick-spittle, lick-twat,* a sycophant, a parasite. *Lick-penny* is a spendthrift, or a money-consuming diversion, that 'licks up' the pennies. Also, *the lickpot,* the first finger. *Lickster* (feminine), one that licks. Among old proverbs with the verb *lick* are: *Wele wotith the cat whos berde she likkith* and *He is an evyll cooke that can not lycke his owne fyngers.*

lickerish. Pleasant to the palate, hence sweet, delightful; skilful in preparing dainties; fond of delicious fare, having a keen relish for pleasant things, especially food and love. Hence, lustful, wanton. Also *liquorish* (*q.v.*), *liccorish, licorish*; in another form, *lickerous, liquorous, lykerowse, likerose,* and many more—all of them variants of *lecherous.* From Old High German *leccon* (French *lécher*), to lick, as when one licks the lips. Shakespeare in TIMON OF ATHENS (1607) has *licourish draughts and morsels unctious. The holy man,* said Southey in THE QUARTERLY REVIEW of 1828, *had a licorish tooth. Go to, Nell,* warned Heywood in EDWARD IV, PART ONE (1600), *ye may be caught, I tell ye; these be liquorish lads.* Chaucer pictures a lady (in THE MILLER'S TALE, 1386): *And sikerly she hadde a likerous eye*; Hoccleve called adultery (1420) *this likerous dampnable errour.* Bacon, said Wilson in THE HISTORY OF GREAT BRITAIN (JAMES I; 1652), *was one of those that smoothed his way to a full ripeness by liquorish and pleasing passages.* Note the warning, however, in THE BOOK OF THE KNIGHT OF LA TOUR (1450): *No woman shulde ete no lycorous morcelles in the absens . . . of her husbond.*

licour. An old form of *liquor.* Chaucer wrote in 1386: *Here biginneth the Boke of the Tales of Caunterbury. Whan that Aprille with his shoures sote The droghte of Marche hath perced to the rote, And bathed every veyne in swich licour, Of which vertue engendred is the flour . . . Than longen folk to goon on pilgrimages.*

lief. Beloved, precious, agreeable; desirous, glad, willing. From Old English times *lief* and *liefly* (in many forms, such as *leof, lef, leef, lefe, leave, liff, lyve*) have both been used as adjective and as adverb. *Liefis me, leeze me,* dear is to me, I'd like to; *liefer were,* I'd rather. *Cp. lever. I'd as lief* is sometimes still used. Spenser in THE FAËRIE QUEENE (1590) uses it in the first sense: *my liefest lord she thus beguiled.* The word was often paired with its opposite, *loath,* as by Peele in THE ARRAIGNMENT OF PARIS (1584): *Well, Juno, whether we be lief or loth, Venus hath got the apple from us both.* Sometimes *lief* was used (10th to 15th century) as a substitute for *Sire!,* when addressing a superior; sometimes it was used to mean beloved, as by Spenser in COLIN CLOUT'S COME HOME AGAIN (1595): *Colin my liefe, my life.* Other forms were *leefkyn,* darling (16th century); *leeftail,* desirable, much in demand, selling quickly (17th into 19th century); *liefhebber* (17th and 18th century), lover, amateur.

liflode. Sustenance in living. Also *lifelod.* Early forms of *livelihood.*

lift. The sky; the heavens (in this sense, sometimes plural); the air, the atmosphere. Related to *loft, aloft*; German *Luft,* air. Also in combinations: *liftlike,* like the heavens; *lift-fowl,* high-flying birds. Used from BEOWULF to the 15th century; later in Scotland, as in RURAL LOVE (1759): *The dearest lass beneath the lift,* and in Burns' WILLIE BREWED A PECK O' MAUT (1780): *It's the moon, I ken her horn, That's blinkin' in the lift saw hie. To lift* meant, originally, to move up into the air; hence a modern *airlift* doubles the idea.

ligate. Bound. From Latin *ligare, ligatum,* to bind. Found as an adjective in 17th century dictionaries; more frequent —from the 16th century—as a verb, to tie;

to tie up, especially in surgery. A prescription of 1599 advised: *Open a blacke henne on her backe, applye and also ligate her on his head.* Hence *ligation,* a binding; also used figuratively, as by Sir Thomas Browne in RELIGIO MEDICI (1643): *The slumber of the body seems to be but the waking of the soul. It is the ligation of sense, but the liberty of reason.* And, also in the 17th century, *ligatory* was used where we now say *obligatory.*

ligby. A bedfellow; a mistress. From *lig,* a variant of *lie + by,* beside; used in the 17th century. Lacy in SAUNY THE SCOT (1667; a prose rewriting of Shakespeare's THE TAMING OF THE SHREW) said: *He means to make one of your lasses his wench—that is, his love and his ligby.*

lightmans. Daytime. See *lib; pedlers French.*

lightskirts. A woman of easy virtue (whose skirts are not hard to lift). Bishop Hall in his eighth SATIRE (1597) complains that Solomon *is become a newfound sonetist, Singing his love, the holy spouse of Christ, Like as she were some lightskirts of the rest, In mightiest inkhornismes he can thither wrest.*

limbec. A favorite poetic form (both as noun and as verb) of *alembic, q.v.* Also *limbeck, lembyck, lymbique,* and the like. Used from the 16th into the 19th century; thus Hood in MISS KILMANSEGG AND HER SILVER LEG (1840) speaks of *the limbeck of pride and vanity.* As a verb, to distill or extract the essence, *limbeck* was often used figuratively to mean to rack one's brains (to extract ideas or sense). Donne in A NOCTURNAL UPON ST. LUCY'S DAY (about 1613) says: *I, by love's limbec, am the grave Of all that's nothing.* That's quite a distillation, even for Cupid! Shakespeare puts the word on the lips of Lady Macbeth, urging her husband to the murder of the King: *His two chamberlains Will I with wine and wassail so convince That memory, the warder of the brain Shall be a fume, and the receipt of reason A limbeck only* [a still in which the thoughts will whirl].

limbmeal. See *limmel.*

lime. As a noun. (1) A viscous sticky substance prepared from holly bark, used to catch small birds. Used from the 7th century. Latin *limus,* mud; the West Aryan root, *li,* appears in Latin *linere,* to smear. Often used figuratively, as by Shakespeare in TWO GENTLEMEN OF VERONA (1591): *You must lay lime to tangle her desires By walefull sonnets.* (2) Limit, end; used in the 15th century. Also the current senses, the fruit and the cement. As a verb. (1) To smear with birdlime; to ensnare. Also figuratively, as when Shelley in his DEFENSE OF POETRY (1822) declares that *Lucretius had limed the wings of his swift spirit in the dregs of the sensible world.* (2) To foul, defile. (3) To copulate (with), to be coupled (to); THE ROXBURGHE BALLADS (1682) declare: *But France is for thy lust too kind a clime, In Africk with some wolf or tyger lime.* (4) To dress with lime; put lime into. Shakespeare plays on this use when he says, in THE MERRY WIVES OF WINDSOR (1598): *Let me see thee froth, and lyme.* Hence, *limed,* smeared, sticky; said of hands ready for pilfering; also, *lime-fingered. Lime-fingers,* a thief; thievish inclinations. Purchas' PILGRIMAGE (1613): *They are light-footed and lime-fingred. Cp. limerod.* Shakespeare cried, in HAMLET (1602): *Oh limed soul, that strugling to be free, Art more ingag'd.*

limerod. Another name for *lime-twig,* a *twig* smeared with *lime, q.v.,* for catching birds. Chaucer in THE MONK'S TALE (1386) pictures *The feeld of snow, thegle* [the eagle] *of black therinne Caught with the lymerod.* The *lime-twig* is used figuratively by Dekker (1607), Milton (1634), Smollett (1771, HUMPHREY CLINKER: *There are so many lime-twigs laid in his way that I'll bet a cool hundred he swings before Christmas*), Byron (1821) and, as a verb, by Landor in IMAGINARY CONVERSATIONS (1829): *He allowed his mind to be lime-twigged and ruffled and discomposed by words. His fingers are lime-twigs* was said (17th century) of a thievish person.

limitour. A friar licensed to beg within specified limits. Also *limiter, friar limiter, lymitour.* Chaucer, in THE WIFE OF BATH'S TALE (1386) praises *The grete charitee and prayeres Of lymytours and othere hooly freres.* Also Spenser (1591) and J. Heywood in THE SPIDER AND THE FOX (1556): *There never was fryer limiter that duckt so low, where beggyng won him twenty cheeses.*

limitrophe. On the border; also, a border land. Latin *limes, limitis,* a cross-path, a boundary + Greek *trophos,* supporting; originally used of lands that supplied frontier troops. It was in 1826 that an Englishman wrote: *Russia has already absorbed, within its empire, that great limitrophe nation which might have been a barrier against further progress.*

limmel. Limb from limb, piecemeal. Also *limbmeal, limmeal, limb-mull.* Shakespeare cries, in CYMBELINE (1611): *O that I had her here, to tear her limb-meale.* Butler (REMAINS, 1680) speaks of a man who *tears cards limbmeal without regard of age, sex, or quality, and breaks the bones of dice.*

lin. To leave off, cease. Common from BEOWULF into the 18th century. Milton protests, in his treatise on DIVORCE (1643): *We should never lin hammering out of our own hearts, as it were out of a flint, the . . . sparkles of new misery to ourselves.* Also *linn* (*q.v.*), *linnan, leen*; in the past tense, *lann, lind, lynned.* Related to Old Norse *linr,* soft, yielding. Swift used the word in 1710, in an old proverb: *When the year with M.D. 'gins, Without M.D. it never lins*—and then he explained it.

lingam. A representation of the phallus, worshipped among the Hindus as an aspect of the god Siva. Also *linga, lingum, lingham.* Macaulay (1843) spoke of the cult, *linganism.* The corresponding female organ is the *yoni* (directly from the Sanskrit; akin to Latin *geni,* whence the *genitals*). Hence also *yonic,* as in *yonic symbolism.* ASIATICK RESEARCHES (1799) said: *The navel of Vishnu, by which they mean the os incae, is worshipped as one and the same with the sacred yoni.* [The *os incae,* or interparietal bone, found sometimes in man and regularly in some other mammals, is a sort of 'third eye' or 'navel of the skull.'] R. Tomas (AN AMERICAN IN JAPAN; 1857) observed *several stones, of four feet in height . . . which appeared to be lingams.*

lingot. A 15th to 19th century variation of *ingot,* a mould for casting metal, or the metal in the shape thus cast.

linguished. Skilled in languages. Used in the 17th century, as when the Water Poet in his ELEGY ON PRINCE HENRY (1630) says of his Muse: *Mean time she 'mongst the linguish'd poets throngs, Although she want the helpe of forraigne tongs.*

linguosity. Talkativeness. Latin *linguositatem; linguosus,* talkative; *lingua,* tongue,

+ *-osus,* full of. A 17th and 18th century dictionary word for a perennial quality.

linn. (1) The linden tree; also, the wood of that tree. Used since the 15th century, now mainly in dialects. (2) A cascade; a rapids; a pool into which a cataract flows; a deep, narrow ravine. Also *lynne, lin.* Common since the 10th century, though since the 17th century mainly Scotch. Used by Scott in MARMION (1808) and THE HEART OF MIDLOTHIAN (1818): *If you come here again, I'll pitch you down the linn like a football.* The form survives in English names, as *Brooklyn.*

lipogram. A work written without any word that contains a specific letter or letters. Greek *lip-* from *leipein,* to leave, to be lacking + *gramma,* letter. Pindar wrote an ode without the letter *sigma;* Lope de Vega wrote five novels, each omitting a different one of the five vowels. Tryphiodorus wrote an ODYSSEY the 24 books of which each in order omitted a letter of the Greek alphabet. Addison in THE SPECTATOR (1711, No. 62) lists as "false wit" *anagrams, chronograms, lipograms, and acrosticks.* Hence *lipogrammatic, lipogrammatism, lipogrammatist.* Note that *lipography,* however, is used for the *unintentional* omission of a letter.

lippen. To trust to, in, or with; to rely on. *To lippen for,* to expect confidently; *to lippen in* (*upon*), to expect from. The word was used from the 11th century; until the mid-16th, it appeared also as *licken* (*to*), to trust in, and *litten,* to rely on. Since the 17th century it has survived mainly in Scottish and dialects. Thus Stevenson in CATRIONA (1893) says: *I would lippen to Eli's word.*

liquorish. See *lickerish.* Although some of the forms coincide, there is no relation between this word and *liquorice, licorice, lickerish,* etc., the sweet candy (once a medicine) made from the plant root. The candy is via French and Latin from Greek *glykyrriza; glykys,* sweet (whence also *glucose,* etc.) + *rhiza,* root. There is also *liquorish,* fond of liquor, touched with liquor, as *a liquorish eye*—not that of Chaucer's lady.

liss. Release; mitigation, abatement; cessation, end; hence, comfort; tranquillity, peace; joy, delight. Thus Chaucer in THE HOUS OF FAME (1384) wrote: *Ther sawe I Joves Venus kysse And graunted was of the tempest lysse.* Also *lisse, lithe.* The first meaning of *lithe* was soft, gentle; comfortable, warm. The form *lisse* had other meanings as well: A kind of silk gauze (19th century); Stowe in UNCLE TOM'S CABIN (1852) mentions a *snowy lisse crape cap.* Also (a variant of *lease*), several items in the technique of weaving: the cylinders of the loom; or rings of small cord fastened to the threads of the front cloth. As a verb, *to lisse* (*les, lis, lys, lysse*), to mitigate, lessen pain; to comfort; to abate, cease; to be relieved of. Chaucer in TROYLUS AND CRISEYDE (1374) says: *Lat us lyssen wo with other speche.*

lissom. A 19th century variation of lithesome. Also *lissome.* Mary Mitford in OUR VILLAGE (1824) wrote: *They are . . . so much more athletic, and yet so much lissomer—to use a Hampshire phrase, which deserves at least to be good English.* Tennyson, Jefferies, and others made it so. Saintsbury in his CORRECTED IMPRESSIONS (1895) speaks of a *marvellous lissomeness . . . of thought.*

list. (1) Short for *listen.* (2) To be pleasing to. An impersonal verb form, common Teutonic; also *leste, lyste, lust,* and more. *Me list,* I like, I desire. Bishop Hall, in the Prologue to his SATIRES (VIR-

GIDEMIARUM; 1597) said: *I first adventure: follow me who list, And be the second English satyrist.* The word lingered in poetry; Lowell in THE VISION OF SIR LAUNFAL (1848) tells that the musing organist *First lets his fingers wander as they list And builds a bridge from dreamland for his lay.*

litation. A sacrifice; the act of sacrificing. Latin *litationem*; *litare,* to offer a (successful) sacrifice. Thomas Stanley in THE HISTORY OF PHILOSOPHY (1661) declared that *the terrestrial gods . . . delight in banquets, and mournings, and funeral litations.*

lite. (1) A short form of *delite,* which was an early form of *delight,* both noun and verb. Used in the 13th and 14th centuries. (2) An early variant of *light.* (3) An early variant of *little* (9th to 15th century). *a lite, alite,* a little, a few. *A* (or *by*) *lite and lite,* little by little; Chaucer has, in THE SOMPNER'S TALE (1386): *Ever it wasteth lyte and lyte awey.* Also, as a verb, *lite* (*litte, lytyn, lyte, light*), to expect, wait, delay; to trust to, rely (on). So used, 13th to 16th centuries, later in dialects. The English suffix *-lite* is a variant through the French of Greek *lithos,* stone (as in *lithography*), as in *chrysolite, coprolite.*—Chaucer in THE ROMAUNT OF THE ROSE (1366) uses *lite* in the sense of small: *Upon this dore I gan to smite, That was so fetys and so lyte*; and in THE HOUS OF FAME: *Me thougt she was so lyte That the lengthe of a cubit Was lengere than she.*

lith. (1) A limb. *Lith from lith,* limb from limb. Used from the 8th century. Also, a joint. *Out of lith,* out of joint. Frequent in the phrase *lith and limb.* In carving, neat work cuts right at the lith (joint); hence figurative uses, such as Rutherford's in a letter of 1637: *To hold off an erroneous conclusion in the least wing or lith of sweet sweet truth.* (2) A slope. Early times (BEOWULF) to the 14th century; later in dialect; preserved in place names. The same root is in the verb to *lean* and in *ladder.* (3) A body of men; by extension, help. (13th to 15th century.) Also, in alliterative references to *land and lith,* people, vassals. In the ANTURS OF ARTHUR (1400) we read: *Here I gif Sir Galerone . . . Al the londes and lithes . . .* (4) An early variant of *light.* (5) An early verbal form, *he lith* for *he lieth.* As a prefix or a suffix, *lith* (Greek *lithos,* stone) is used mainly on biological and pathological terms; also *monolith,* though in mineralogy the usual ending is *-lite, q.v.* Thus *litholatry,* stone-worship.

lithe. See *liss.*

lither. Bad, wicked; ill-tempered; worthless; (of the body) withered, impotent; foul, pestilential; (from the 15th century) lazy, spiritless, sluggish. (Pronounced with a short *i.*) *Lither lurden,* lazy lout; *the lither lurden,* the 'disease' of laziness. For an instance of this use, see *abbey-lubber.* As a noun, evil; evil men. Also, a sling. [This form is related to a very early *lethro,* leather.] Hence, as a verb, *to lither* (1) to shoot from a sling, to let fly. (2) To act wickedly, to do harm. A *litherback,* a slothful person; *litherhead,* wickedness. These were all used from the 6th century, and developed many forms, including *lethre, luther, luthur, lytheir, liethur, liddyr, ledyr.* In the 16th century the adjective *lither* developed the sense (from the meaning, weak) of pliant and (of sky or air) yielding; thus Shakespeare in HENRY VI, PART ONE (1591) cries *Thou antique Death . . . Two Talbots winged through the lither skie In thy despight shall scape mortalitie.*

lithomancy. See *aeromancy.*

litster. A man who makes his living by dyeing. Used by Chaucer, and into the 18th century.

Little-endian. See *cynarctomachy.*

livelihood. Before it meant a means of living (which has been current since the 13th century), *livelihood* (from the 10th to the 15th century) meant the course of life, a lifetime; the manner of one's life; hence, conduct. Also, from the 16th century, it was used as a variant of *liveliness,* as when Shakespeare in ALL'S WELL THAT ENDS WELL (1601) observes: *The tirrany of her sorrowes takes all livelihood from her cheeke.*

livering. (1) A liver pudding made into a sausage. Chapman in his translation (1624) of Homer's BATRACHOMYOMACHIA (BATTLE OF THE FROGS AND THE MICE) spoke of *lyvrings* (*whiteskinnd as ladies*). (2) Short for *delivering*; delivery; provision of entertainment. In the romance of KYNG ALYSAUNDER (13th century) we read: *Ther was fair hostell, and lyvereyng.*

lob. In addition to its current uses in mining, cricket, tennis, and thieves' slang (a till; *lob-crawler,* robber of tills), *lob* had various other senses. *Cp. lobscouse.* (1) *lob,* also *lop,* a spider (9th to 14th century). Chaucer (1391) speaks of *a webbe of a loppe.* (2) A lump, a heavy, unwieldy piece; also a nugget (of gold), a large amount (of money). By extension, a pendulous lump or object, the wattles of a cock, ornament on spurs, scabbard, and the like. Also, a lumpy person, a bumpkin, lout. Hence, as an adjective, clownish, clumsy, stupid; the 17th century spoke of *loblogic.* By transference from the bumpkin, the word moved mildly into the fairy world. Beaumont and Fletcher record, in THE KNIGHT OF THE BURNING PESTLE (1613): *There's a pretty tale of a witch . . . that had a giant to her sonne, that was cal'd Lob-lie-by-the-fire.* Taking that name as title of her book, Mrs. J. H. Ewing (1873) explained: *Lob-lie-by-the-fire—the lubber-fiend, as Milton calls him—is a rough kind of brownie or house elf.* The sort of modern Puck that arranges the magic in Barrie's DEAR BRUTUS (1918) is *Mr. Lob.*

loblolly. See *lobscouse.*

lobscouse. A sailor's dish: meat and vegetables stewed. Also *scouse; lob's course, lap's course, lobskous.* Hence, *lobscouser,* a sailor, a tar. A thick gruel served to sick sailors was called *loblolly,* which thence became a general term for a ship-doctor's medicines. The form *lob* (*q.v.*) was a dialectal term, meaning to bubble (as porridge in boiling), also, to eat or drink noisily; *lolly* was dialectal for broth or porridge. Hence also *loblolly,* a bumpkin, a boor. Thus *loblolly boy,* a helper to a ship's surgeon; *loblolly lamb,* a bumpkin, a rustic. Also *loplolly, laplolly*; Mrs. Piozzi related (1786) that Samuel Johnson *asked an officer what some place was called and received for answer that it was where the loplolly man kept his loplolly.* Smyth's SAILOR'S WORD BOOK in 1867 called *'lap's course' one of the oldest and most savoury of the regular forecastle dishes*; perhaps he was being respectful to age, for E. Ward in THE WOODEN WORLD DISSECTED (1706) said: *He has sent the fellow . . . to the Devil, that first invented lobscouse.*

lobsterize. To move backwards. *Cp. palinal.* Sylvester in his translation (1605) of Du Bartas wrote: *Thou makest rivers the most deafly deep To lobstarize* (*back to their source to creep*). Nares (1882), commenting that this motion is of a crab rather than of a lobster, adds, of the word: *The author did well to explain himself in a parenthesis; but he would have done better had he left it out.* Yet many a man might ponder the term when he reflects that a word once spoken goes not back into the mouth.

lock. Short for *lovelock,* so called because it secured a loved one: a long strand of hair, hanging at the left ear, often plaited and tied with a riband. Fashionable among men in the 16th and 17th centuries; King Charles I wore one until 1646. William Prynne wrote a treatise *The Unlovelyness of Lovelocks,* objecting also in his HISTRIOMASTIX (1632; for this aspersion on the king, he was imprisoned in London Tower, was fined £5,000, and had his ears sliced): *More especially in long, unshorne, womanish, frizled, love-provoking haire, and lovelockes, growne now too much in fashion with comly pages, youthes, and lewd, effeminate, ruffianly persons.* Dogberry, in his usual confusion (Shakespeare, MUCH ADO ABOUT NOTHING; 1599) mixes his terms: *And also the watch heard them talk of one deformed: they say he wears a key in his ear, and a lock hanging by it.* Locks were also artificial. They were worn by women as well; Pepys in his DIARY for 29 October, 1666, records: *My wife (who is mighty fine and with a new pair of locks).* From the supposed effect of the *lovelock,* it was sometimes called a *heartbreaker*; Butler in HUDIBRAS (1664) said: *Like Samson's heart-breakers it grew In time, to make a nation rue.*

lockram. See *dowlas.*

locofoco. (1) A self-lighting match, a lucifer; also, a self-lighting cigar. Bartlett's GLOSSARY of 1859 explained: *In 1834, John Marck opened a store in Park Row, New York, and drew public attention to two novelties. One was champagne wine drawn like soda-water from a fountain; the other was a self-lighting cigar, with a match composition on the end. These he called locofoco cigars.* The coined word may have been borrowed from the *loco* of the then new *locomotive,* imagining the syllable to mean self-moving + *foco* as an echoic addition, possibly with thought of Italian *fuoco,* fire. (2) A Democrat (1845-1900); especially (1835-1845) a member of the 'Equal Rights' section of the Democratic Party. The *locofoco cigar* was patented 16 April, 1834. The match was earlier. In 1835, at a Democratic Party meeting in Tammany Hall, New York, the gaslights were suddenly turned out by the conservatives, to black out the more radical 'Equal Rights' faction—which, warned of the trick, pulled out *locofocos* and candles, by the light of which the meeting proceeded. The antimonopolists who used the matches were dubbed *Locofocos.*—In England, the match made of a splinter of wood with inflammable substance ignitable by friction, was called after the legendary creatures that first brought fire to mankind. [Note that, in both Greek pagan and Christian story, the bearer of fire to men is treated as evil, as giving man hybris, pride, the aspiration to equal the god: Prometheus is perpetually gnawed by a vulture; Lucifer (Latin *lucem,* light + *fer,* bearer) was the rebel archangel (BIBLE, ISAIAH 14): *Lucifer* was the name of *Satan* before his fall.] The speech of the plaintiff's counsel, in Jones vs. Watts, was published in JOHN BULL for 28 November, 1831: *Mr. Jones had, some time ago, invented a match to produce an instantaneous light . . . and he had given his ingenious invention the name of pro-*

methean . . . Subsequently the plaintiff invented another description of match, which he designated with the frightful name of lucifer. For the lucifers he had not . . . secured his right as the patentee . . . The defendant made an exact imitation of the lucifer match. The adjective *luciferous* may have meant (17th to 19th century) bringing or emitting light; or—*luciferous; lucifrian, luciferan, luciferian*—devilish, satanic, often with thought of the sin of pride. Thus Marston in PYGMALION (1598) : *From haughty Spayne, what brought thou els beside, But lofty lookes, and their lucifrian pride?* The word *Promethean,* on the other hand (save when it bore allusion to the punishment), meant resembling Prometheus in art or skill. The name *Prometheus* means forethought; Prometheus is supposed to have made man out of clay, and to have taught man many arts. In revenge, Zeus sent Pandora to Prometheus, who foresaw the trouble she would bring, but his brother Epimetheus (afterthought) accepted her, and her box, when opened, released all the troubles and distempers that have afflicted mankind. Hope alone remained, at the bottom of the box. Pandora, the first woman, was fashioned out of clay by Hephaestus (Vulcan), the fire-god, as Prometheus was the fire-Titan; and it was Hephaestus that chained Prometheus to the rock, for the vulture eternally to gnaw his vitals. Shakespeare in LOVE'S LABOUR'S LOST (1588) says: *Women's eyes . . . are the ground, the bookes, the academs, From whence doth spring the true Promethean fire.* Milton in THE REASON OF CHURCH GOVERNMENT (1641) wrote: *With a kind of Promethean skill to shape and fashion this outward man into the similitude of a body.* Darwin in his JOURNAL OF RESEARCHES . . . DURING THE VOYAGE OF THE BEAGLE (1845) recorded: *I carried with me some promethean matches, which I ignited by biting.* The *lucifer* was a friction match, such as is still used; the *promethean* was described by Tidy in THE STORY OF THE TINDER BOX (1889): *In the year 1828, prometheans were invented. They consisted of a small quantity of chlorate of potash and sugar, rolled up tightly in a piece of paper. Inside the paper-roll is placed a small sealed glass-bubble containing sulphuric acid. On breaking the bulb, the mixture fired, igniting the paper-roll.* The simplest lighting device is still the locofoco.

lodemale. A trunk. From BEOWULF to the 15th century, *lode* meant a journey, a way; then a watercourse; then a channel; hence, leading, guidance, and a leading or vein of metal ore in a mine, the current sense. Originally *lode* and *load* were the same word; the two forms took different senses. The 14th century COER DE LION said: *Geve hym . . . loode males . . . ful off ryche preciouse stones.*

lofword. Praise. As early as BEOWULF, and into the 16th century, *lof* (*loob, loff, loif, love*; related to *love*) was used meaning praise, then price, value (13th century); A. Scott in his POEMS (1560) wrote: *For loif and not for lufe* [love]. A *lofsong* was a song of praise; but *lofsom, lofsum* are early variants of *lovesome.* By the 14th century there was confusion with *love* indeed, and *lofword,* meaning praise, was spelled *luffeword, luveword, loveword.*

loggat. A stick, a stake; especially in the game of *loggats* (also *logget, logat, locket*): Sticks are tossed at a stake; the nearest (or the one that knocks it down) wins. This was a country game, played since the 16th century at sheep-shearing feasts and the like; somewhat like pitching horseshoes.

Shakespeare in HAMLET (1602) reflects: *Did these bones cost no more the breeding but to play at loggets with 'em? mine ake to thinke on't.*

logodaedalus. One who is cunning in, or clever with, words. Greek *logos,* word + *daidalos,* cunning; see *daedal.* Also *logodaedale, logodaedalist.* Hence *logodaedaly,* skill in adorning with words. CORYAT'S CRUDITIES (1611) has: *He is a great and bold carpenter of words, or (to express him in one like his own) a logodaedale.* In his COMMENTARY ON THE SONG OF SOLOMON (1650) Trapp, on the other hand, scorns *those logodaedali, learned asses, that prophanely disdain the stately plainness of God's blessed book.* As might be expected, *logos* has given English many words. Among those 'forgotten' there may be resuscitated: *logocracy,* government by words, as in Washington Irving's SALMAGUNDI PAPERS (1808): *Their government is a pure unadulterated logocracy; logodiarrhe, logodiarrhœa,* an uncontrolled flow of words; *logofascinated* (used by Urquhart), fascinated by words; *logolatry,* worship of words, undue regard for words, or for the literal truth. A *logogriph* (Greek *griphos,* fishing basket, riddle) is a riddle in verse, giving synonyms of a word to be guessed or of its anagrams. Jonson ponders (1637): *Had I . . . weav'd fifty tomes of logogriphes, or curious palindromes.* Walpole in a letter of 1765 wrote: *All I can send your ladyship is a very pretty logogriphe, made by . . . Madame du Deffand.* Several forms have been used in English based on *logomachy,* a battle of words: a *logomach, logomachist,* one who fights over words, or verbal subtleties; *to logomachize.* In his POLITICAL ECONOMY (1848) Mill had to defend his field against *the reproach of logomachy.* This, indeed, is the essence of much philosophical disputation.

logomancy. See *aeromancy.*

logophobia. See *aeromancy.*

long. Short for *belong.* Rowlands, in HUMORS ORDINARIE (1607) cried: *Bid me go sleepe; I scorne it with my heeles, I know my selfe as good a man as thee: Let goe mine arme I say, lead him that reeles, I am a right good fellow, doest thou see? I know what longes to drinking, and I can Abuse myself as well as any man.*

longanimity. Forbearance, long-suffering. Common, especially in religious use (*the longanimity of God*) from the 15th to the 18th century. In a TRACT of 1724, Warburton exclaims: *Constancy is a word too weak to express so extraordinary a behavior, 'twas patience, 'twas longanimity.* Even more of a lay application appeared in THE SPECTATOR of 11 January, 1890: *His longanimity under the foolishness of the young woman is really marvellous.* Lowell misused the word, as though it meant long-drawn, in THE BIGLOW PAPERS (1861) and in CAMBRIDGE THIRTY YEARS AGO (1854): *He is expected to ask a blessing and return thanks at the dinner, a function which he performs with centenarian longanimity.* It is the listener that needs longanimity.

long-purple. One of the flowers Ophelia culled. See *stone.*

loo. (1) A mask, usually velvet, worn by 17th century ladies "to protect the complexion." Often a half-mask, or with the lower part of lace. Also *loup* (pronounced *loo*); the word is from French *loup,* wolf (Latin *lupus*), used in the same sense. (2) A game at cards, popular in the 17th and into the 19th century. The game was an early form of whist (*3-card loo;* also *5-card loo*); a player who does not take a trick is *looed;* he must put a specified sum into the 'kitty.' The word *loo* also meant the fact of thus losing, *being loo,* and also the forfeit, the amount paid in. In *3-card loo,* the cards are counted as in whist; in *5-card loo,* the highest card is the Jack of Clubs, called *Pam;* thus Pope in THE RAPE OF THE LOCK hails *Ev'n mighty Pam, that Kings and Queens o'erthrew And mow'd down armies in the fights of lu.* An earlier form of the game (from which this name was shortened) was called *lanterloo, q.v.*

lora. See *metheglin.*

lorain. See *loricate.*

lordane. See *lurdan.*

lordswike. A traitor. Old English *hlaford,* lord + *swica,* deceiver. Used into the 14th century, as in the 1325 CHRONICLES OF ENGLAND (reprinted in Ritson's METRICAL ROMANCES): *For he was loverdsuyke, Heo ladden him to Warewyke . . . Ther his heved wes of smyte* [Because he was a traitor, they led him to Warwick . . . there his head was smitten off].

lorel. See *leese.*

lorespell. A lesson, a sermon. A *loresman* was a teacher. Used from the 10th through the 14th century. Hence also *loring,* teaching; Spenser in THE FAËRIE QUEENE (1596) says: *They . . . Her wisdom did admire, and hearkned to her loring.* We now treasure folklore.

lorette. A prostitute. Borrowed from French; used in the 19th century, when many such frequented the environs of the Church of *Notre Dame de Lorette,* in Paris. Thus the PALL MALL GAZETTE of 9 September, 1865, spoke of *the brilliant ball given by the aristocracy of the Parisian lorettes—for even lorettism has its aristocracy.* Note that a *lorettine* is a nun of an order of *Our Lady of Loretto.*

loricate. To put a protective coating on; e.g., military armor, or clay on a chemical retort (18th century) "before it is set over a naked fire." Latin *loricare, loricatus,* to clothe in mail; *lorica,* a leather cuirass or corselet of thongs; *lorum* (*vlorum*), a leather strap or strip. Hence also in English, *loric* (Browning, 1855), a cuirass, more often *lorica; lorum, lore,* a thong, a rein. By way of Late Latin and old French, *lorain* came into English meaning the straps of a horse's harness, often jewelled or studded with metal. Hence (French *lorenier, loremier*) from the 12th to the 19th century, English *lorimer,* maker of mountings for horses' bridles, of bits and other small iron ware; a worker of wrought iron. Hence *lorication* (by error, occasionally, *lorification*), covering with a protective coat.

lorimer. See *loricate.*

loring. See *lorespell.*

loripede. A hobbler; figuratively, a person of weak will or scant endurance. From Latin *lorum,* strap + *pedem,* foot. *Cp. loricate.* Used in a sermon by Jeremy Taylor, 17th century.

lorn. See *leese. Lorn* in the sense of forsaken, lonely, bereft, first appeared in the 16th century, perhaps as a result of the incorrect use of *leese,* as by Spenser in THE FAËRIE QUEENE (1590): *After that he had faire Una lorne* [deserted], *Through light misdeeming of her loyaltie.*

losel. See *leese.*

losenger. A flatterer; a deceiver; a lying rascal. Also *loseniour, losengeour, loosinger,* and many more; the word and its other forms were common from the 14th through the 16th century. Thus *losengery, losengry, losangerie,* flattery, deceit; *losengeous* (this 17th century form was rare), flattering, lying; *to losenge,* to flatter, to praise fulsomely. Provençal *lauzenga;* Old French *loenge* (French *louange,* praise); ultimately from Latin *laudem,* praise, whence also things *laudatory.* There is no relation between this word and *lozenge,* which originally referred to the 'diamond' shape, in heraldry. Chaucer in THE LEGEND OF GOOD WOMEN (1385) said: *In youre court is manye a losenger;* of what society is this not true today?

lossom. An old variant of *lovesome,* worthy of love, lovely. Also *lossum, lossome, lufsum, lussom,* and more. In the 18th century, *lovesome* was also used to mean amorous, loving. Hence *lovesomehead* (14th century), *lovesomeness* (from the 10th century). Also, from the 10th to the 13th century, the pleasant *lovewende,* beloved, loving, lovely.

lostell. See *a lostell.*

lostling. A little person or thing lost. Raymond in his STATISTICS OF MINES . . . WEST OF THE ROCKY MOUNTAINS (1870) spoke of *the great 'lost river' which bursts out of the vertical side of the cañon of the Snake—a torrent from the solid rock; a foundling rather than a lostling.* A river that is a lostling drops in Xanadu, as described in Coleridge's KUBLA KHAN

loteby. A lover; a paramour. From *lote,* to lie concealed. Chaucer, in THE SECOND NUN'S TALE (1386) speaks of a man found *Among the saintes buriels lotynge.* Both words were used from the 13th into the 15th century; Audelay, in a poem of 1426, says: *He would here sell that he had bought . . . And takys to him a loteby.*

lotium. Stale urine, used by barbers (15th to 18th century) as a hair wash, etc. Latin *lavare, lautum, lotum,* to wash, whence also the current form, *lotion. Cp. lant.* In Jonson's THE SILENT WOMAN (1609), heaping execrations upon a barber, Morose says: *Let him be glad to eat his sponge for bread;* Truewit adds: *And drink lotium to it.*

lotophagous. Lotus-eating; hence, day-dreaming, idly drifting. Also *lotophagist,* lotus-eater, day-dreamer; *the lotophagi* (Greek *lotos,* lotus + *phagein* to eat. On the coast of Africa near the Syrtes [large shifting sandbanks, one near Leptis, one near Carthage, dangers to navigation; hence *syrtis,* a dangerous region of the sea, a quicksand. See *syr.*] dwelled the *lotophagi,* who cultivated the *lotos*—not the Egyptian flower, the water lily, but a tree of hard black wood of which statues were carved, perhaps the nettle tree or the date-plum—and invited visitors to eat of its fruit. Those that ate forgot their home, and lived in a dreamy idleness. Pidgeon, in AN ENGINEER'S HOLIDAY (1882) recorded: *Thus lotophagously sailing, we landed one morning on a beautifully wooded point.*

lough. See *low.*

louk. (1) An old form of lock. (2) To pull up or out; to weed (corn). Also *louker,* one that weeds. These were early words, common through the 15th century, developing various forms, including *luken, lowke, luke, look, luk, loc.* As a noun, used by Chaucer to mean a boon companion, in THE COOK'S TALE 1386): *Ther is no theef with-oute a lowke, That helpeth hym to wasten and to swoke Of that he brybe can or borowe may.*

lout. As a verb: (1) To bend, stoop; make obeisance; to bow, submit. Used from the 9th into the 19th century. In MERLIN (1450), we read: *The archebisshop lowted to the sword, and sawgh letters of golde in the steel*; In Conan Doyle's THE WHITE COMPANY (1891): *I uncovered and louted as I passed.* Also *luten, lowte.* (2) To lurk, lie hid; sneak. Used 9th to 16th century; Gower in CONFESSIO AMANTIS (1390) said that love *luteth in a mannes herte.* (3) To mock, treat with contempt; also, *to lout someone out of something.* Udall in RALPH ROYSTER DOYSTER (1553): *He is louted and laughed to skorne, For the veriest dolt that ever was borne;* Shakespeare in HENRY VI, PART ONE (1591): *I am lowted by a traitor villaine, And cannot helpe the noble chevalier.* Hence *louter,* a worshipper; *louting,* bowing, cringing; Keats in a letter to J. Taylor (23 August, 1819): *Is this worth louting or playing the hypocrite for?*

love-drury. Love-making; courtship. Also, a love-token. Havelock (1300) said: *Til that she were tuelf winter old, And of speche were bold; And that she couthe of courteysye Gon, and speken of luve-drurye.* This is a longer form of *drury, q.v.*

lovee. One that is loved; an 18th century term. Richardson in SIR CHARLES GRANDISON (1754) said: *The lover and lovee make generally the happiest couple*; he should have added, when each is both.

love-in-idleness. The wild pansy. Its amatory powers were celebrated in its various names: *heartsease; come-and-kiss-me; call-me-to-you*; and—most appealingly—*herb-constancy.* Drop but its juice upon the errant eye—as Oberon with Titania (A MIDSUMMER NIGHT'S DREAM; 1594): *Yet marked I where the bolt of Cupid fell: It fell upon a little western flower—Before milk-white, now purple with love's wound, And maidens call it love-in-idleness.*

lovelock. See *lock.*

lovertine. Fond of making love. A 17th century coinage, after *libertine.* Dekker in THE PATIENT GRISSILL (1603): *These gentlemen lovertine, and my selfe a hater of love.* (The early *libertine* sought political, not amatory, freedom.)

lovewende. See *lossom.*

low. (1) A flame. See *alow.* (2) A hill, especially one round or conical. Old English *hlaw*; Teutonic root *klei,* to slope; related to English *lean*; Latin *clivus,* hill, English *declivity*; Greek *klinein,* to make lean; *kline,* bed; English *clinic.* In this sense, also *law.* By extension, a burial mound. (3) A variant form of *lough,* Scotch *loch,* a lake; river; water. (4) Short form of *allow*; as a noun, permission. Also in dialect from the verb, as *I low, I allow,* I admit.

lown. As an adjective. Calm (of person or weather; gentle, quiet, mild. Sheltered, cozy, snug. As a noun. Calm, tranquility; shelter. Also a verb, to calm, to lull; to shelter. Used in the north and Scotland from the 14th century. Note that *lown* was also an early variant of *loon,* a stupid fellow, a boor; also, a rogue (*a false loon*); an idler. *To play the loon,* to act like a rascal. *Lord and loon,* of high birth and low. Of a woman, a strumpet, a concubine. The origin of the word is unknown; there is no connection with slang *loon, loony,* from *lunatic,* moonstruck; Latin *luna,* the moon. Iago's song in Shakespeare's OTHELLO (1604] rhymes the word with *crown*: *With that he call'd the tailor lown.*

lowte. A variant of *lout, q.v.*, especially in the sense of to bend; to make obeisance. Spenser used *lowted* in THE SHEPHERD'S CALENDAR (1579; JULY) with the gloss 'did honour and reverence'; also in THE FAËRIE QUEENE: *He faire the knight saluted, louting low,* and again: *Thrise lowted lowly to the noble maid.* After him, Drayton used *lowting lowe* in POLY-OLBION (1612); Scott, *louted low* in ROKEBY (1813).

loxotic. Oblique; awry, distorted in direction or position. Also *loxic*; Greek *loxos,* oblique. Still used in science (botany, medicine, mathematics; *loxodromic chart,* Mercator's projection; *loxodromics,* the art of oblique sailing).

lozen. A thin pastry-cake. Enjoyed in the 14th and 15th centuries, with cheese and wine. From Old French *loseingne,* a variant of *losange* whence English *lozenge.* Hence *lozen* was later (17th century) used for a lozenge-shaped pane of glass, etc. Fountainhall's JOURNAL of 1665 noted: *One of his servantes brook a lossen.*

lu. A variant of *loo, q.v.*

lucent. See *luculent.*

lucid. See *crepuscular.*

lucifer. See *locofoco.*

lucigenous. See *luculent.*

lucripetous. Eager for gain. Latin *lucrum,* gain (whence the current *lucre*) + *petere,* to seek. Used in the 17th century. Also *lucrify,* to put to gainful use; *lucrific, lucriferous,* bringing gain; *lucrous,* gainful, covetous (J. G. Cooper, in THE TOMB OF SHAKESPEARE, 1755: *Free from the muck-worm miser's lucrous rage*).

luctiferous. Mournful; gloomy. Latin *luctus,* sorrow + *fer,* bearing. Also *luctific, luctual, luctuous.* Hence *luctisonous, luctisonant,* mournful sounding. To *luctuate* was (18th century) to render mournful or gloomy, as with bad news or black drapes. Susan E. Ferrier in THE INHERITANCE (1824) mentioned *an equipage and attendants of—of—of the most luctiferous description.*

lucubrate. See *elucubration.*

luculent. Full of light, shining; brilliant; *lucid.* Thus Thomson in THE SEASONS: WINTER (1746): *Luculent along the purer rivers flow.* Jonson in EVERY MAN OUT OF HIS HUMOUR (1599) speaks of a *most debonaire, most luculent ladie.* Also *lucid; lucent,* shining, luminous, but also translucent, clear, as in Keats' EVE OF ST. AGNES (1820): *lucent syrops, tinct with cinnamon.* Latin *lux, lucem,* light. *Cp. crepuscular. Lucific,* producing light; *lucifugous* (accent on the *sif*), shunning the light; *lucigenous,* begotten or born in the daytime.

lud. (1) A euphemistic form of *Lord,* used especially in mild oaths of the 18th century, and by clerks and lawyers in court. (2) In the plural (and Scotland), the buttocks. Also, *luddock,* buttock. (3) A variant form of *loud.*

lumination. See *relume.*

lunatic. See *breviloquent; lown.*

lune. (1) A leash for a hawk. Also *lewne;* a variant form of *loyn.* This is via Old French *loigne* from Latin *longus,* long; in English, *loyn,* a length (of cord); hence, a leash. (2) Anything shaped like a crescent or half-moon. French *lune;* Latin *luna,* the moon. From the idea that the moon brings on *lunacy* came (3) *lunes* (plural), fits of frenzy, mad streaks, tantrums; spells of whimsy. Shakespeare uses *lunes* in THE MERRY WIVES OF

WINDSOR and THE WINTER'S TALE (1611): *These dangerous, unsafe lunes i' th' king —beshrew them!* Symonds in THE RENAISSANCE IN ITALY (1883) states that *Their tales for the most part are the lunes of wanton love.*

lungis. A long, lank, ludicrous lout; also, a laggard, a slowpoke. Also *lungeis, longis, lundgis;* Latin *Longinus,* the Roman centurion that pierced Jesus with a spear, but linked with Latin *longus,* long. Minsheu in THE GUIDE INTO TONGUES (1617) defines *lungis: a slimme slowback, a dreaming gangrill, a tall and dull slangam, that hath no making to his height, nor wit to his making.* Beaumont and Fletcher in THE KNIGHT OF THE BURNING PESTLE (1611) cry: *How dost thou, Ralph? Art thou not shrewdly hurt? The foul great lungies laid unmercifully on thee.*

lunt. A slow match; a torch. *To set lunt to,* to light. Also smoke, especially from a pipe; hot vapor. Dutch *lont,* match; *lonstock,* matchstick, gave us English *linstock* (*limstock, linestoke, lyntstock*), a three-foot staff, pointed to stick in the ground or a ship's deck, with a forked head to hold a lighted match; used from the 16th century, for firearms, rather than tobacco. *To lunt,* to kindle; to smoke (a pipe); (of smoke) to rise up, to curl. Hence *lunting,* smoking, glowing; (of the eyes) flashing. There was also a Danish *lunte,* lazy, used of a horse, spiritless, tame. A HISTORY OF JAMES VI (1588) mentioned a man that *had a loose lunt, quhilk negligently fell out of his hand amang the great quantity of poulder.*

lupanar. A brothel. Also, adjectives, *lupanal, lupanarian.* From Latin *lupa,* she-wolf, which was used figuratively (by Cicero, Livy, Juvenal) of a cheap prostitute (as equipped with wolf's teeth). *Cp. lupine.* R. Buchanan in THE PALL MALL GAZETTE (20 September, 1886) wrote, in not very good English: *It is a very phenomenal city whose existence can only be determined by its lupanars and its sewers.*

lupicide. See *stillicide.*

lupine. Relating to a wolf; wolf-like; savage, fierce. Also *lupous; lupus* is still used of the constellation the wolf, and in the 16th century was used of the animal: *the lupus in a lamb skyn lappit.* Latin *lupinus,* adjective of *lupus,* wolf. Not to be confused with *vulpine* (Latin *vulpes,* fox), fox-like; crafty, tricky. Jonson calls one of his plays (1606; via the Italian) *Volpone; or The Fox.* Certain humans were supposed transformed, or capable of transforming themselves, into volves; *cp. were:* Emma Phipson in ANIMAL LORE IN SHAKESPEARE'S TIME (1883) spoke of *ravages imagined to be committed by them in their lupine state.*

lurdan. A loafer, a vagabond. Used from the 13th to the 18th century as a term of scorn or abuse; revived (in THE ABBOT, 1820) by Scott. John Rastell, in THE PASTYME OF PEOPLE (1529) suggested that the word came from Lord Dane, because the conquering Danes kept the husbandmen as serfs and made these dependents call them Lord Dane, until the word became a term of abuse. This idea affected the spelling: *lordane, lordan, Lord-Dane.* Bailey, in his 1751 DICTIONARY, varied the story: because the Danes "injoined the better sort of people to maintain a *Dane* in their houses as a spy and a curb upon them." The word *lurdan* actually came into the language (Bailey admits this is "full as likely") from French *lourdin,* sluggish fellow; *lourd,* heavy. The word is also used as an adjective, worthless, lazy, ill-bred; Tennyson in PELLEAS AND ETTARRE (1870) speaks of *lurdane knights.*

luscous. One-eyed. Latin *luscus;* hence *luscition,* dimness of sight. A 17th century term.

luskin. A sluggard, a lazy or idle fellow. Also *lusk.* There was also a verb, *to lusk,* to lie hid; to skulk; to lie idly or lazily; used from the 14th into the 17th century. Hence *lusking,* skulking; idling; *luskish, lusk,* sluggish, lazy. It does seem a bit like old-time slander for Sir Thomas More to have said, in THE CONFUTACYON OF TYNDALES ANSWERE (1532): *Frere Luther and Cate Calate hys nonne lye luskynge togyther in lechery. Well may they bee cowards,* said Holland in his version (1600) of Livy, *and play the idle luskes.*

lusorious. Relating to or used for sport or as a pastime. Of speech or writing: in a playful style. Also *lusory;* Latin *lusorius,* belonging to a player; *lusor,* player; *ludere, lusus,* to play; whence also *ludicrous, delusive, allude,* and all the *illusions* that play upon us. In the 17th century, *lusory* was also used for *delusory, illusory,* deceptive. Shaftesbury in CHARACTERISTICKS (1711) said that *God, as a kind tutor, was pleased to . . . bear with his anger, and in a lusory manner cxpose his childish frowardness.* Disraeli in CURIOSITIES OF LITERATURE (1823) observed: *There is a refined species of comic poetry, lusory yet elegant.*

lust. See *list.*

lustration. See *housel.*

lustre. Also *lustir, luster.* (1) A period of five years. Occasionally used for four years, as in college references. Also *lustral* and (directly from Latin) *lustrum;* probably from *luere, lavere,* to wash. The *lustrum* was originally the purificatory sacrifice made for the people by the censors, after the census. The first year of the lustrum, during which the census was taken, was the *lustran* (Latin *lustrum annum*). *Lustral* is also an adjective, relating to the lustrum or to purification by sacrifice. Thus *lustrant. lustrical day,* Christening day. *lustrific,* purifying; *lustrative, lustratory. lustrable,* that which may be purged. Latin *lustrare, lustratum,* to make bright, to purify by propitiatory sacrifice; hence English *to lustrate, to lustre; lustration. Lustratory* is humorously applied to washing, as in *lustratory applications of the brush.* (2) A den; a cave (17th century), From Latin *lustrum* (from *luere*) a bog; a wilderness, a haunt of beasts; hence (in Latin) a house of ill fame; debauchery. (3) Latin *lustrare,* to make bright, is associated with *lux, lucem,* light (*luc-strare*); hence, in addition to the still current sense of shining by reflected light, sheen (*lustrious, lustrant, lustry, lustreful; lustrement; lustrification; lustrify. lustring, lutestring, q.v.; lustrée,* a glossy silk fabric), other meanings developed: *lustre,* a lustrous wool. a thin dress material, of cotton warp and woollen weft, highly lustrous. a glass ball set among lights to increase the brightness. a prism of glass hanging from a vase or a chandelier; often pendants of these tinkled with wafted air. a chandelier. Lady Mary Wortley Montagu (a bluestocking and perhaps the first English woman writer of note) in a letter to her sister (8 September, 1716) described the magnificence of the apartments in Vienna: *All this is made gay by pictures and vast jars of Japan china, and large lustres of rock crystal.* And at table *the variety and richness of their wines is what appears the most surprising; the constant way is to lay a list of their many names upon the plates of the guests along with their napkins, and I have counted several times* *to the number of eighteen different sorts, all exquisite in their kinds.*

lustring. Also *lustrine.* See *lutestring.*

luteous. Pertaining to mud; muddy. Latin *lutum,* mud. There was also a yellow weed the Romans called *lutum,* whence in English scientific works since the mid-17th century, *luteous* might be used for a color, deep orange yellow. Hence (19th century) *lutescent,* inclining toward yellow, as tan shoes or a jaundiced complexion.

lutestring. A glossy silk fabric; a garment or ribbon made thereof. Elizabeth Browning, in AURORA LEIGH (1856): *As if you had . . . held your trailing lutestring up yourself.* Walpole in his MEMOIRS OF GEORGE III (1797) used the word figuratively, of *a very pretty lutestring administration which would do very well for summer wear.* Hence, *to speak in lutestring,* to use silken, polished phrases. The word is probably a corruption of *lustring,* with the same meaning, from *lustrine,* which is both English and French; named because of the *lustre* of the fabric. Also, of course, *lutestring* means a *string* for a *lute.*

luther. See *lither.* [This was not a mock by the Catholics.] Also *lutherhood, lutherness,* wickedness; used in Robert of Gloucester's CHRONICLE (13th century).

lutulent. See *maculate.* Hence *lutulence,* muddiness; mud. Also see *luteous.*

luxury. The early meaning of this word was lasciviousness, lechery, lust. Also (16th and 17th centuries) *luxurity.* Used from the 13th century, *luxury* developed its current sense in the 17th century. In Latin *luxuria* meant lust; *luxus* was the Latin word for abundance, for sumptuous enjoyment. Chaucer in THE MAN OF LAW'S TALE (1386) cries *O foule lust of luxurie!* Thersites in Shakespeare's TROILUS AND CRESSIDA (1602), considering Cressida and Diomedes, exclaims: *How the devil luxury, with his fat rump and potato-finger, tickles these together! Fry, lechery, fry!*

lyam. A leash for hounds; hence, a dog. Also *lyme, lyalme, lyemme, lym, leame, leon.* Ultimately from Latin *ligamen,* binding; *ligare,* to tie. Shakespeare, in KING LEAR (1605) lists: *mastiff, greyhound, mongrill, grim, Hound or spaniell, brache, or lym.* A *lyam-hound,* a bloodhound. The word was used throughout the 17th century, and revived by Scott (WAVERLEY, 1819); also, in THE LAY OF THE LAST MINSTREL (1805): *Stout Conrade, cold . . . Was by a woodman's lyme-dog found.* The term was applied to a person in Beaumont and Fletcher's PHILASTER (1611): *Oh, hee's a pernitious limhound, turne him upon the pursue of any lady.*

lychwake. See *lich.*

lycisk. A fabulous beast, hybrid of wolf and dog. Greek *lykos,* wolf. In Guillim's book on HERALDRY (1610) two hybrids are together: *castorides, dogges ingendred by a fox and a bever; lyciscus, of a wolfe and a mastiffe.*

lye. As a verb, in cookery: to thicken (sauces, soups, etc.). Used in the 14th and 15th centuries. Thus, TWO COOKERY-BOOKS (1430): *Take vele . . . and hakke it to gobettys . . . and lye it with flowre of rys.*

lye-pot. An ornamented vessel to hold *lye* (a cosmetic) for use as a hair-wash. In Nashe's LENTEN STUFFE (1599) we read that the fabulous queen *Semiramis ranne out with her lie-pot in her hand, and her black dangling tresses about her shoulders.*

lyfkie. A bodice. Also *leefekey.* Dutch *lijfken,* diminutive of *lijf,* body. In Lyly's EUPHUES (1579), we read: *Their spots, their lawnes, their leefekyes, their ruffes, their rings Shew them rather cardinalls curtisans then modest matrons.*

lymytour. See *limitour.*

lyncean. Keen of vision, like the lynx. Latin *lynceus,* Greek *lygkeios; lygx,* lynx. There may also be allusion to *Lynceus,* one of the Argonauts, noted for his sharp sight. He was reputed to have the power to see through stone walls. Hence also *lynceous.* Used from the 16th into the 19th century, as in the HYPNEROTOMACHIA (1592): *Yet with a lincious eye, I never left to examine . . . the extreme beauty of the excellent nymph.*

lynne. See *lin, linn.*

M

ma. Also *maa.* Early forms for *make, may, me, more, my.*

mab. See *mob.*

macarism. The sharing, or state of sharing, another's happiness; taking pleasure in others' joy; (in religious reference) beatitude. Greek *markarismos*; *makar,* happy. Hence also *macarize,* to deem happy or blessed. Whately makes it clear in his COMMONPLACE BOOK (1864) : *A man is admired for what he is, macarized for what he has, praised for what he does . . . The words 'felicitate' and 'congratulate' are used only in application to events, which are one branch only of 'macarism' . . . To admiration, contempt seems to be the direct contrary; censure, to commendation; pity, to macarism.*

macaroni. A dandy, an exquisite of the late 18th century, who affected the fashions and tastes of continental society. The word grew fashionable from the *Macaroni Club* (1760), which took its name from the Italian food, then little eaten in England, hence highly esteemed by these young blades. For a somewhat different use, see *circum-* (*circumforaneous*). Horace Walpole in a letter to the Earl of Hertford (1764) spoke of: *The Maccaroni Club* (*which is composed of all the travelled young men who wear long curls and spying glasses*). The OXFORD MAGAZINE of June 1770 elaborated: *There is indeed a kind of animal, neither male nor female, a thing of the neuter gender, lately started up amongst us. It is called a macaroni. It talks without meaning, it smiles without pleasantry, it eats without appetite, it rides without exercise, it wenches without passion.* Hence also, *macaronism, macaronyish.* See *macaronic.*

macaronic. Verse, usually burlesque, in which are mingled words of various languages; originally, Latin and the native tongue. Bailey (1751) defines *macaronics* as verses in which the native words of a language are made to end in a Latin termination. The word was first used in this sense by Teofilo Folengo ("Merlinus Cocaius") for his BOOK OF MACARONICS, published in 1517. In the second edition, Folengo says he took the name from *macaroni,* "a sort of powdered wheaten paste with cheese, coarse, rude, and rustic." Hence also, as an adjective, *macaronic,* jumbled, mixed as in a medley. From the desire of the dandy, the exquisite, the fashionable young gentleman of the 1750's and 1760's to enjoy what he considered the superior tastes of Europe, came the *macaroni* (*q.v.*). Those that remember the *zoot-suit* watch chains of the 1940's will smile at the follies of 1780; *It is the custom, you know, among the macaronies,* said Madame D'Arbley in her DIARY for 9 December, 1783, *to wear two watches.* As late as 1823, at the horse races, *macaroni stakes* were those ridden by gentlemen, not professional jockeys. Even earlier, however, the term had come to be used in mockery; THE MONTHLY MAGAZINE (III, 1797) spoke of *this fanciful aera, when macaroni philosophers hold flirtation with science*; and most dwellers to the west of the North Atlantic recall (though they may have forgotten the meaning of the word) the Revolutionary song *Yankee Doodle came to town, Riding on a pony; Stuck a feather in his hat and called it macaroni* . . . Yankee Doodle dandy.

macro-. See *macrobian.*

macrobian. Long-lived. A *macrobiote* (accent on the *by*) is one that lives long. Greek *makros,* long, large + *bios,* life. Also *macrobiotic. Macro-* and its converse *micro-,* short, small, are used in many scientific terms. Some of the more general but presently overlooked words formed from them are: *macrognathic,* with large or protruding jaws; *macrology,* speaking at great length. *macroscian,* one having a long shadow; hence used of persons when the sun (or a light) is low behind them; also as a noun, a person in the arctic regions. *macrosmatic* (Greek *osme,* smell), capable of smelling from afar. Also *microcosmetor* (accent on the *coz;* Greek *cosmein,* to set in order; *cosmos,* order, the ordered universe; hence *cosmetics* that put order upon the fair sex), the "essence" or principle of life—used by Dolaeus. *micrological,* minute or detailed in discussion; *micrology,* discussion of petty matters, hair-splitting. *micronymy,* the use of shortened words for naming things, as in science (TNT) or in politics (SPQR; UNESCO). *microphily,* a friendship between persons of different rank or standing, a 'small' man with a great. *micropsychy* (17th century), timidness, pusillanimity; also *micropseuchy. microtherm* (Greek *therme,* heat, whence *thermometer*), relating to cold regions, dwelling or growing on mountains or in the polar zones; as a noun, a person that enjoys the cold, a "polar bear."

macromancy. See *aeromancy.*

macropicide. See *stillicide.* Greek *makrapous,* kangaroo; *makros,* long + *pod pous,* foot.

mactation. The action of killing; especially, of ritual sacrifice. Latin *mactare, mactatum,* to slay; hence also *to mactate*; a *mactator,* a killer; one that officiates at a ritual killing. In the HISTORY OF EGYPT (1838) M. Russell referred to *the deity before whom the mactation is about to be performed.*

maculate. Spotted, stained; polluted. Often used in opposition to *immaculate,* as in Shakespeare's LOVE'S LABOUR'S LOST (1594), where Armado protests: *My love is most immaculate white and red,* and his page, Moth, retorts: *Most maculate thoughts, master, are masked under such colors.* Latin *macula,* spot, is used as a scientific term in English; also *macule. macular,* relating to *maculae,* spots. From the 15th century there were verb forms, *macule, maculate,* to spot, to pollute. Bradshaw in THE LIFE OF SAINT WERBURGE OF CHESTER (1513) wrote that *a sensuall prynce . . . purposed to maculate this vyrgyn gloryous.* In the 17th and 18th centuries, *maculature* was in the dictionaries, as blotting paper, or a waste sheet of printed paper. T. Adams wrote, in THE DEVIL'S BANQUET (1614), of the *lutulent, spumy, maculatorie waters of sinne*: *maculatory,* apt to defile; *lutulent* (Latin *lutum,* mud), muddy; see *luteous.* Thus *maculation,* defilement; Shakespeare in

TROILUS AND CRESSIDA (1606): *I will throw my glove to death himselfe, That there's no maculation in thy heart.*

maculomancy. See *aeromancy.*

madrean. A spice; used in the 14th and 15th centuries in making conserves. Apparently a sort of ginger.

Mae West. See *nun-buoy.* (Not she!)

magia. White magic; the employment of benevolent supernatural powers for good ends. The opposite of black magic, or *goety, q.v.*

magiric. Relating to cooking. (Soft *g* followed by long *i*; *jy.*) Also *magirological.* Greek *mageiros,* cook. Hence also *magirist, magirologist,* expert at cooking; *magirology,* the art of cookery. PUNCH (21 May, 1892) spoke of *immortal contributions to mageiristic lore.* Since Greek *mageia* is magic, we may admit the relationship; as THE SCHOOL OF GOOD LIVING (1814) observed, *from the very first appearance of magirology in Greece, it produced effects absolutely magical.* For current evidence, consult LES AMIS D'ESCOFFIER.

magnific. Eminent; glorious; munificent. Imposing, exalted; highly eulogistic. In later use, occasionally suggesting the pompous, grandiloquent. Latin *magnus,* great + *fic*; *facere,* to make. Also *magnifical.* Milton in PARADISE LOST (1667) speaks of *Thrones, Dominations, Princedoms, Vertues, Powers, If these magnific titles yet remain Not meerly titular.* Caxton (ENEYDOS; 1490): *This gentylman was . . . of name magnyfyque.*

maid's ruin. See *Hymen's torch.*

main. As a noun. Physical strength; force, power. Shakespeare in TROILUS AND CRESSIDA (1606): *with all our main of power*; frequent in the phrase used in the nursery rhyme of the man who had "scratched out both his eyes": *"With all his might and main,* he jumped into another bush And scratched them in again." Also, the chief part, main body (MERCHANT OF VENICE V. i. 97; HAMLET: *against the main of Poland*). *The main point,* chief concern (HAMLET II. ii. 56). *The mainland* (KING LEAR III. i. 6). The ocean (KING JOHN II. i. 26; RICHARD III. iv. 20; OTHELLO II. i. 3, 39). A broad expanse (SONNET 60: *Nativity once in the maine of light Crawles to maturity*). The object aimed at, goal; Webster in THE DUCHESS OF MALFI (1623): Bosola: *You say you would fain be taken for an eminent courtier?* Castruccio: *'Tis the very main of my ambition.* In the 19th century, *to turn on the main,* to begin to weep copiously; from the *main,* the chief pipe, drain, or other duct for water. Thus Dickens in THE PICKWICK PAPERS (1837): *Blessed if I don't think he's got a main in his head as is always turned on.* Also *main,* short form of *domain*; *mains* (from the 16th century), a farm attached to a mansion house. In dice (the game of hazard), *main, maine, mayne*: a number (from 5 to 9) called by the caster before he throws; if he 'throws in' or 'nicks' that number, he wins; if he 'throws out' aces, or deuce and ace ('crabs') he loses. If any other number, he keeps throwing until that number (his 'chance') comes again, when he wins, or his *main* comes, when he loses. This was a very common use of *main,* 15th to 19th century; it was extended to apply to a match at bowling, boxing, shooting, and to *a main at cocks,* cock-fight. *A Welsh main* (1770) starts with say, 16 pair of cocks; the 16 winners are matched, then the 8 winners, and so till one triumphs as in a tournament at tennis. Shakespeare uses *main* in the gaming sense, in HENRY VI, PART TWO and in HENRY IV, PART ONE: *Were it good To set the exact wealth of all our states All at one cast? To set so rich a main On the nice hazard of one doubtful hour?*

mainour. Stolen goods found on the thief when he is apprehended. From Old French *maneuvre,* hand work. Also *manor, manner* (especially *with the manner, in the manner,* in the act), *meinor.* Shakespeare puns, in HENRY IV, PART TWO (1597): *O villain, thou stolest a cup of sack eighteen years ago, and were taken with the manner.* The 1611 version of the BIBLE (NUMBERS) gives directions that include: *If a man lie with her carnally . . . and there be no witness against her, neither she be taken with the manner . . .* The word was used from the 13th into the 17th century; Scott revived it in THE FAIR MAID OF PERTH (1828).

makeless. (1) Without a husband. Shakespeare in SONNET 9 (1598) says *The world will waile thee, like a makelesse wife.* From the year 1000, *make* as a noun meant match, mate, equal; *the make,* the like. Chaucer in THE COMPLAYNT OF MARS (1374) says: *God gif every wyghte joy of his make!* Hence (2) *makeless,* matchless, without equal. So used from the 13th into the 17th century, later in dialects. THE MIRROR FOR MAGISTRATES (Buckingham; 1563) wrote of *a makeles prynce in ryches and in myght.*

makeweight. A small quantity added to make up a certain weight; especially, in the 15th, 16th, and 17th centuries, a small candle added to whatever is being sold, to make a pound. Hence, an insignificant person or thing, used to fill a gap or the like. Thus Paine in his COMMON SENSE (1776) said of America: *By her dependence on Britain she is made the make-weight in the scale of British politics.* Anna Seward in a letter of 1793 said: *It is no custom of Shakespeare's to give us merely makeweight epithets.* Hallam in his INTRODUCTION TO THE LITERATURE OF EUROPE (1839) derided *an incestuous passion brought forward as the makeweight of a plot, to eke out a fifth act.* In the 19th century, an extra slice of bread sometimes used to make up the legal weight of a loaf. It was a moment of deep pathos in LITTLE GERTY, THE LAMPLIGHTER'S DAUGHTER (1876), when the hungry child confesses she has eaten the makeweight.

makke. A dish, recipe given in THE FORME OF CURY (1390): *Take drawen benes, and seeth hem wel. Take hem up of the water, and cast hem in a mortar; grynde hem al to doust, til thei be white as eny mylk. Chawf* [heat] *a litell rede wyne, cast there among in the gryndyng, do thereto salt, leshe it in dishes. Thanne take oynons, and mynce hem smalle, and seeth hem in oile, til they be al bron; and florissh the disshes, and serve it forth.*

malapert. Saucy, impudent; a presumptuous person. Bailey (1751) suggests that the word is from Latin *male,* ill + *partus,* gotten, bred; or else from *male* + *apert,* ready. *Cp. apert.* The O.E.D. says its meaning shows that it was understood as though from *mal* + *apert,* bold, hence improperly bold—but that it is from Old French *malapert,* used by Eustache Deschamps as the opposite of *appert, espert* (English *expert*), clever; hence it should have been used to mean clumsy. However, Shakespeare in TWELFTH NIGHT (1601) says *I must have an ounce or two of this malapert blood from you,* and Scott in THE BETROTHED (1825) continues this meaning: *you are too malapert for a young maiden.*

male. In addition to the fecundating sex, *male* had other meanings. (1) An apple, apple-tree. Also *male-apple*; Latin *malum,* apple. THE SONG OF SONGS (1400 BIBLE) said: *As the male is plentivouse of apples . . . so is my derlyng among sones.* (2) The human essence; so used in 15th and 16th century phrases. *The male wryes, the male wrings,* something is wrong, the evil case is thus. A poem of Lydgate (1430) reads: *The male so wryes, That no kunnyng may prevayl . . . Ayens a wommans wytt.* Also, *to wring one on the males,* to harm one, trouble one.

malebolge. A pool of filth; in the 19th century used figuratively. Hence also *malebolgian,* very filthy. THE PALL MALL GAZETTE (16 October, 1883) spoke of *This malebolgic pool of London's misery.* Occasionally *malebolgia*; the middle *e* is pronounced; the word is Italian, the name Dante gave to the eighth circle in Hell, which contained ten concentric circular pits, of filth, burning pitch, etc. THE SCOTSMAN of 12 July, 1894, said: *The channels that feed this devouring malebolge are the newspapers and the telegraph offices.* We might add the radio, not to more than mention television.

malebouch. The voice of evil; evil-speaking personified. From LE ROMAN DE LA ROSE (1230), in which it is the name of an allegorical person. French *malebouche,* evil mouth; at one point in the poem he is called *Wikkid-Tonge.* Also *male boush.* Used by Gower (1390), Lydgate, Churchyard (1594) and more.

male journey. Used in the 15th century for a severe defeat in battle. Old French *male journee,* evil day.

malengin. Evil machination; fraud; guile. Old French *mal,* evil + *engin,* device. Spenser in THE FAËRIE QUEENE (1590) speaks of *such malengin and fine forgery.* Milton (1641) said that the Protector Cromwell's brother *through private malice and malengin was to lose his life.*

malheur. Misfortune. Direct from French *malheur,* earlier *maleur*; *mal,* evil + *eur,* fortune; *eur* is shortened from Latin *augurium,* fortune, *augury.* Also *maleheure, malure, mallure,* etc. Used from the 15th into the 18th century, as in CHAUCER'S DREAM (1500): *I wofull wight full of malure, Am worse than dead.*

malicho. See *miche.*

malism. The doctrine that life on earth is essentially or predominantly evil, and so the world. Latin *malum,* evil. Hence also *malist,* one that holds this doctrine; *malistic.* The word is a 19th century coinage, used often as stronger than pessimism, as in Tollemache's book (1896) on JOWETT: *Jowett's optimism verges on pessimism, or, let us say, his bonism verges on malism.* Latin *bonus,* good; and may you have a good bonus!

malison. A curse. The word is a shortening of the more common *malediction,* from Latin *malum,* evil + *dicere, dictum,* to speak. *Cp. benison.* The word was also a verb, as in A. King's translation (1588) of Canisius' CATECHISM: *To malesone any, by giving thame to the devil, in wisching thame sicknes, deathe or any evill.* Also *malisun, malysun, malescun, malysoun, malicoun, mallison,* and more. The CURSOR MUNDI (1300) said bluntly: *His malison on tham he laid*; Kingsley in HEREWARD THE WAKE (1865) did little more: *Farewell, and my malison abide with thee!*

malkin. See *merkin.*

mallecho. See *miche.*

malmeny. A very popular dish of the 14th and 15th centuries. The name developed many forms, including *mawmenny, momene, mawmene, mameny.* A number of recipes survive, some with wine, so that the name may be related to *malmsey, q.v.* Here is one from THE FORME OF CURY (1390) : *For to make mawmenny: Take the chese, and of fless of capons or of hennes, and hakke smale. Take mylke of almandes, with the broth of freish beef, other freish flessh, and put the flessh in the mylke, other in the broth, and set hem to the fyre, and alye hem up with floer of rys, or gaftbon, or amydon, as chargeant as the blank desire* [to taste], *and with yolkes of ayren an safron for to make it yellow. And when it is dresst in dishes with blank desire, styr above clowes de gilofre, and strew powdor of golyngale above, and serve it forth.*

malmsey. A strong sweet wine. Also *malvoisie;* both forms are corruptions of *Monemvasia,* the place in Greece where the Malmsey grapes were first pressed. *Malmsey* is now also made in Spain, Madeira, and the Canary isles. A pleasant drink since the 14th century. Also *mammesey, mamulsye, mawlmsey; malvasia, mavasie, malvesin, mauvesyn, mawissie,* and more.

malominous. Of evil omen. Used in the 17th century, as in a translation (1658) of Cyrano de Bergerac's SATYRICAL CHARACTERS: *I saw it encompasst by a million of male-ominous creatures.*

malshave. A caterpillar. Used from the 10th to the 14th century; also *malshrag;* surviving in some 19th century dialects: Isle of Wight, *mallishag;* Hampshire, *maleshag;* Gloucester, *moleshag.* Trevisa (Higden, POLYCHRONICON; 1387) wrote: *Thanne as the grete flye folweth the tras of the malschave, so after other wo com the pestilence of the Ismaelites.*

malvoisie. See *malmsey.*

malure. See *malheur.*

mammet. See *maumet.*

mammock. To break or tear into fragments or shreds. Also, a scrap or shred. Shakespeare has, in CORIOLANUS (1607): *Hee did so set his teeth, and teare it. Oh, I warrant how he mammockt it.* Milton in OF REFORMATION IN ENGLAND (1641) declared: *The obscene and surfeted priest scruples not to paw and mammock the sacramentall bread as familiarly as his tavern biscuit.*

man. See *agate.*

manavlins. Small or supplementary items, odds and ends; especially as added bits to eat. Used in the 19th century. From it, *to manarvel* (accent on the *ar*), to pilfer small stores; sailor slang. Also *malhavelins, manablins, manarolins, menavelings, manavalins. He'd a stool and table too,* said R. Boldrewood in ROBBERY UNDER ARMS (1889), *this Robinson Crusoe cove. No end of manavalins either.*

manbote. A fine paid to an overlord, in the feudal system, for the loss of a man. Used from the 10th to the 13th century; after that, historically. See *bote.*

mancation. Mutilation; maiming. An 18th century term; Latin *mancare, mancatus,* to maim; *mancus,* one-handed, maimed. The root is *man-, min-,* meaning less, whence also *membrane; member; mean.* Latin *manus,* hand, whence *manual, manuscript, manure, manufacture* (note *manuduce,* to direct, point the way;

manuducent, guiding; *manumise, manumiss, manumit,* to excuse or release from an obligation, to free; *manumissable,* capable of being freed; *manumotor,* a vehicle propelled by mechanism worked by hand; *manuporter,* one that carries by strength of hand; see *manuduction.*) *manus* is from the root *ma-, man-,* to measure, whence also *administer, month, moon.* The hand was often used as a base for measurement: *a handful;* the height of a horse.

manchet. The best kind of wheaten bread. Used from the 15th to the 18th century; also *manchette, mayngote, mengyd, manged,* and more. The origin is obscure; French *paindemaine* had the same meaning; hence the English word might be related to *main,* hand or *main,* chief. There was a 19th century *manchette,* a trimming on the bottom of the sleeve of a woman's dress, a cuff; diminutive of *manche,* used in both English and French for a sleeve, from Latin *manus,* hand. Also, a bread in Rouen, France, called *manchette* from its shape. *Manchet,* however, refers to the quality; also, to a loaf of that quality. *Of bread made of wheat we have sundry sortes,* said Harrison, in England (in Holinshed's CHRONICLES; 1577), *wherof the first and most excellent is the manchet, which we commonlye call white bread, in Latin primarius panis.*

manciple. An officer in charge of purchasing provisions, as at a monastery or college. Latin *mancipium* meant a bondslave, which sense also came to English *manciple;* Latin *manus,* hand + *capere* (*cipi, cepi*), *captum,* to take; whence a host of words: *concept, inception, captor, captive, emancipation,* etc. Chaucer, in the Prologue to THE CANTERBURY TALES (1386) praises his man: *A gentil maunciple was ther of a temple Of which achatours myghte take example For to be wise in byynge of vitaille.*

mandible. See *manducate.* R. Head in THE ENGLISH ROGUE (1680) spoke of gathering up *geese, hens, pigs, or any such mandible thing we met with.*

mandilion. A loose coat, later sleeveless. In the 16th century (*mandilyon, mandillian*) worn by servants and soldiers. Also *mandill,* a loose overcoat, sometimes worn by knights over their armor. The word is ultimately from Arabic *mandil,* a sash, a turban-cloth—which in turn may be from Latin *mantellum,* cloak; *mantelum,* towel, napkin, mistaken as a diminutive of the later *mantum*—from which also have come *mantilla, mantle,* and *mantua* (an alteration of French *manteau* by connection with the city of *Mantua*), *manteau, manto, mantlet, mantelet,* all meaning various types of cloak or gown. Also *manteel* and, possibly by error from this, *mantevil, mandevil,* with the same meaning as *mandilion.*

mandola. A large sort of mandolin. Also mandora, mandore. *Cp. bandore.*

mandom. The world of man. Created by Elizabeth Barrett Browning in A DRAMA OF EXILE (1844): *Without this rule of mandom, ye would perish—beast by beast Devouring.*

mandorla. Any almond-shaped object, or decorative space. Italian *mandorla,* almond. A 19th century term; C. C. Perkins in ITALIAN SCULPTURE (1883) mentioned *Christ seated within a mandorla.*

mandragora. A plant used (especially in poetry) as a narcotic. Also *mandragores, mandragon, mandrage, mondrake, mandrake.* Shakespeare has Cleopatra cry:

Give me to drink mandragora; more notably, in OTHELLO (1604), Iago says: *Not poppy, nor mandragora, Nor all the drowsy syrups of the world Shall ever medicine thee to that sweet sleep Which thou owedst yesterday.* Sometimes the word was used as a term of abuse, as in HENRY IV, PART TWO: *Thou horson mandrake.* The root of the mandragora was often forked, and vaguely resembled a man, hence legends grew around it. It was supposed to produce fecundity in women; it was by virtue of Rachel's desire for Leah's son's mandrakes (BIBLE, GENESIS 30) that Jacob's fifth son was born. One name of Venus was *Mandragoritis.* And Macchiavelli made an amusing play on this theme . . . A mandrake root shaped like a human hand was greatly valued as a charm; it was called *hand of glory,* translating French *main de gloire,* a hopeful transformation of *mandragoire, mandragora* . . . To pluck a mandrake root was fatal; the accepted method was to tie a dog to it and chase the dog—which then died instead of the master. As it was uprooted, the mandragora screamed: Shakespeare in ROMEO AND JULIET tells of *Shrieks like mandrakes' torn out of the earth.* Also *mandrake apple,* the fruit of the mandragora; *mandrake wine.* Burton in THE ANATOMY OF MELANCHOLY (1621) says: *A friend's counsel is a charm, like mandrake wine.* The effect depends upon the dose: a little is an aphrodisiac; more makes one unduly vain; still more makes one an idiot; another sip makes one a corpse.

manducate. To chew, to eat. Late Latin *manducare,* Latin *mandere,* to chew, whence English *mandible,* capable of being eaten, and the *mandible,* still current for the lower jaw of fishes, the upper jaw of insects, and either the lower or the upper part of the beak of birds. Hence also *manducable, manducatory,* fit for eating. *Manducation,* though used since the 17th century to mean the act of chewing, has been used especially of the partaking of the Eucharist, as by Lamb in ESSAYS OF ELIA (1821): *The received ritual having prescribed these forms to the solitary ceremony of manducation.* The *manger* from which horses and cattle eat (and which was bed for the new-born Jesus) is via French from Latin *manducare.* From the Jesus story, *manger* has also been used to mean a crib; and to stand symbolically for the Nativity: *the blissful mystery of the Manger and the Cross. Manger* also, from the 14th to the 17th century (as in Chapman's EASTWARD HO; 1605) meant a banquet. Hence also the rare (15th century, ROWLAND AND OLIVER) *gramaungere,* a great meal. *Manger blanc* was the 16th century term for what is now called *blanc mange.* Thus *mangery* (*mawngery, maynery, mangrie;* 14th and 15th centuries) a ceremonial feast; a festivity; luxurious gourmandizing. Not by the dog in the manger.

maness. A 16th and 17th century feminine of *man.* As in the Bible (1594): *The man said, This nowe is bone of my bones, and flesh of my flesh: she shall be called mannes, or mannish, because she was taken out of man.* It was such a school of etymology that says *woman* was formed because she brought *woe* to *man.* Yet some things feminine may still be called *mannish.*

manger. See *manducate.*

mangonel. A medieval engine of war, for casting stones. Greek *magganon* [whence also *mangle,* machine for pressing clothes after washing. The earliest mangle was a wooden chest filled with stones, which by straps round a roller was worked to exercise the pressure of the weight on the cloth spread over a table underneath.] Historical writers revived the word: Southey in JOAN OF ARC, 1795; Scott in IVANHOE (1819): *You may win the wall in spite both of bow and mangonel.*

mangonize. To dress up (inferior wares) for sale; also, to deal in slaves. Latin *mango, mangonem,* a furbisher; a monger, a slavedealer; from the root *mac-, mag-,* big; to *magnify*. The English *monger* and its compounds stem from *mango*. Hence *mangony, mangonism,* the art, craft, or practice of furbishing things for sale; also (17th and 18th centuries), the treatment of plants so as to produce changes and new varieties. A *mangonist,* one that dresses up wares for sale. Used by the 17th century dramatists (Marston; Jonson).

manicon. An herb, a variety of nightshade (*cp. dwale*), supposed to induce madness. The name is from Greek *mania,* madness; *mainesthai,* to be insane. Thus Butler in HUDIBRAS (1678): *Bewitch hermetick-men to run Stark staring mad with manicon.*

mankind. As an adjective. Human; male; (of a woman) virago-like, fierce. Also *mankeen,* infuriated, fierce, mad. Wright (1869) also defines *mankeen* as marriageable, eager for a man. Udall in RALPH ROYSTER DOYSTER (1553) cries: *Come away! By the matte, she is mankine. I durst adventure the losse of my right hande, If shee dyd not slee hir other husbande.* Shakespeare in THE WINTER'S TALE (1611) is equally roused: *Out! A mankind witch! Hence with her, out o' doors.*

man-midwife. In the 17th century used figuratively. Suckling in AGLAURA (1638) speaks of *that old doting man-midwife Time.* Jonson in THE STAPLE OF NEWS (1625) said: *There are a set of gamesters within, in travell* [travail] *of a thing call'd a play . . . and they have intreated me to be their man-midwife, the Prologue.*

man-milliner. Used figuratively, from the 18th century, to mean one engaged in or fond of trivial occupations or adornments. Hence, *man-millinery,* apparel (or activity) on which attention is lavished trivially or beyond its desert. Hazlitt in POLITICAL ESSAYS (1814) said: *The 'Morning Herald' sheds tears of joy over the fashionable virtues of the rising generation, and finds that we shall make better man-milliners, better lacqueys, better courtiers than ever.* Scott in a letter of 22 August, 1819, remarked that *there goes as much to the manmillinery of a young officer of hussars as to that of an heiress on her bridal day.*

manner. See *mainour.*

manqualm. Plague, pestilence. Herbert Coleridge in his DICTIONARY OF THE OLDEST WORDS (1863) lists it, in Robert of Gloucester's CHRONICLE (13th century), as meaning slaughter of men: *so great manqualm that monimon* [many men] *al unburied lay.*

manqueller. Murderer; executioner. Also *manquelle.* As a verb, *manquell,* to murder. Also *manquelling,* manslaughter, homicide. Shakespeare plays on the softened idea of *to quell,* to subdue, in HENRY IV, PART TWO (1597): *Thou art a honyseed, a manqueller, and a womanqueller.*

manred. (1) Homage. Hence, vassals, those whom a lord may call to arms; a supply of men to fight. (2) The leader of the men called to fight; also, the control or government of the armed forces. (3) Carnal intercourse. This sense occurs only in Layamon's BRUT (1205): *He wolde monradene habben with than maidene.* Also *manratten, manrade, manryd, manredyn,* and more. The Scotch (15th to 18th century) used the form *manrent; bond (band) of manrent,* a pledge to be friend to all the other's friends, and foe to all his foes. Thus the Earl of Somerville, in the family MEMOIRS (1679): *To be obleidged and bound in mandred . . . to be with one another in all actiones.*

manse. A shortened form of *amanse, q.v.* Also *mance, monse.* Used into the 15th century. Langland in PIERS PLOWMAN (1377), wrote: *And now worth this Mede ymaried all to a mansed schrewe.* Hence *mansing,* cursing; a curse. *Manse* is also a shortened form of *mansion,* as in Hawthorne's tales and sketches (1846), *Mosses From an Old Manse.*

mansuetude. Gentleness, meekness. Also *mansuete,* gentle, tame; *mansuefy,* to tame (in 17th century dictionaries); thus *mansuefaction,* taming. Latin *mansuescere,* to tame; *manus,* hand + *suescere,* to grow accustomed; see *consuetude.* Chaucer in TROYLUS AND CRISEYDE (1374) says: *she . . . stod forth mewet, mylde and mansuete;* in THE PARSON'S TALE: *The remedye agayns ire is a vertu that men clepen mansuetude, that is debonairetee.*

mantevil. See *mandilion.*

mantic. Relating to divination or prophecy. Used also, but rarely, as a noun, the art of divination. Greek *mantis,* prophet, diviner; the root is *man,* as in *mania*—here referring to 'the divine madness,' inspiration. Hence also *mantical. manticism,* the practice of divination. A type of locust is called the *mantis,* diviner, particularly *the praying mantis,* which in characteristic pose has its forelegs crossed so as to suggest hands folded in prayer. The many ways of seeking to plumb the future have given rise to a host of words ending—the adjective, with *mantic;* the noun, with *mancy.* For some of these, see *aeromancy.*

manticore. A 'kind of serpent,' described in various ways; the O.E.D.'s favorite picture gives it the body of a lion, the head of a man, the quills of a porcupine, and the tail (sting) of a scorpion. The word is from Aristotle's *mantichoras,* but the better manuscripts have *martichoras,* probably 'man-eater' in Old Persian, from *martiya,* man + the root *xar,* to eat. Other forms and descriptions include *mantichora* (with double rows of teeth in its mouth), *monecore, mantissera, marticora* (of a red color, a man's head 'lancing out sharp prickles from behind'). The creature flourished in writings from the 13th to the 17th century; but Kingsley's WATER BABIES (1863) mentions *unicorns, firedrakes, manticoras.* Two of the forms of the word became quite distinct: (1) *mantegar.* Arbuthnot in 1714 (MARTINUS SCRIBLERUS) spoke of *the glaring cat-a-mountain . . . and the man-mimicking manteger.* The word came to be used of a kind of baboon. (2) *mantiger.* This might be a changeling (lycanthrope) that can assume the form of a tiger; it was also used (17th to 19th century) of a man as fierce as a tiger; Tylor in PRIMITIVE CULTURE (1871): *The Lavas of Birma, supposed to be the broken-down remains of a cultured race, and dreaded as man tigers.* Skelton, cursing (1529) the killer of Philip Sparrow, his little friend's bird, prayed that *the manticors in the mountaynes Myghte fede them on thy braynes!*

mantlet. See *mandilion.*

manubiary. Relating to the spoils of war. Latin *manubiae; manus,* hand. Also *manubial.* A *manubiary column* was a column branched like a tree, on which trophies and the spoils of war were hung. Hence *manubrium,* a handle, haft; *manubrial; manubriated,* with a handle. Other words formed from Latin *manus,* in addition to *manure,* originally work by hand, and to the large, still current group around *manufacture,* to make by hand, include *manuduct, manuduce,* to lead by hand, to guide, *manuduction, manuductory; manumotor,* an engine or device worked by hand; *manuscribe,* to write by hand, surviving in *manuscript; manustupration,* a 19th century form based on an etymological idea of *masturbation; manutergium,* a hand-wiper, i.e., a towel.

manuduction. Guidance, direction; means of guidance; a guide. Also *manuduce, manuduct,* to guide; *manuducent, manuductive,* guiding, leading by the hand; *manuductor,* a guide, director, orchestra conductor; *manuductory.* Latin *manu,* by the hand + *ducere, ductum,* to lead. These forms were used mainly in the 17th century. H. L'Estrange in GOD'S SABBATH (1641) said that *Adam and the succeeding Patriarchs . . . were manuducted and guided by an unerring spirit.* Sir Edward Dering in A COLLECTION OF SPEECHES IN MATTERS OF RELIGION (1642) shook his head to think that *young students . . . wander for want of manuduction.* Today it is often for want of heeding it.

marantic. Relating to or characterized by wasting away. Greek *marantikos,* from *marainein,* to wither, *marasmos,* wasting away. Hence also *marasmus, marasme,* a wasting away; *marasmic, marasmous.* Milton has a sonorous Homeric catalogue in PARADISE LOST (1663): *Convulsions, epilepsies, fierce catarrhs, Intestine stone and ulcer, colic pangs, Demoniac phrenzy, moping melancholy And moon-struck madness, pining atrophy, Marasmus, and wide-wasting pestilence, Dropsies, and asthmas, and joint-racking rheums.* More than a marantic ranting!

marcescible. Liable to wither or fade. Bailey (1751) lists *marcessibility, marcessibleness; marcescent* (applied to a plant, withering but not falling off) was more common. Latin *marcescere,* to fade, the inceptive of *marcere,* to be faint, droop, wither. Use in the BOOK OF COMMON PRAYER made the negative *immarcescible* (usually erroneously changed to *immarcessible*) more common still; there are several 16th and 17th century references (1542, 1548) to *the immarcessible crowne of glory* (in 1543 *uncorruptible* was substituted; in 1662, *never-fading*). In 1640 we find it more strongly: *Palms of victory and immarcessible ghirlands of glory and triumph to all eternity.* Hence *immarcescibleness, immarcessibleness,* imperishableness.

marcid. Weak; exhausted; withered, decayed. Also *marcidious; marcidity.* Latin *marcidus,* withered; *marcere,* to wither; *cp. marcescible.* T. Taylor in his translation (1822) of Apuleius, wrote: *She dismissed her marcid eyes to sleep.*

marigold. A plant, with bright yellow flowers. Also *marrygold; marygolde.* It was used in medicine (with herbs and thyme, it might be made into an unguent that enables a mortal to see the fairies). Its flowers were made into a conserve, and used for flavoring soup or giving a brighter color to cheese. The flower opens when the sun shines, and turns to follow the sun; hence it was called in Latin *solesequium* (sun-follower) and through the countryside *husbandman's dyall.* Lyte in his translation (1578) of Dodoens' NIEWE HERBALL said: *The conserve that is made of the floures of marygoldes . . . cureth the trembling of the heart.* Sir Thomas Overbury in A WIFE NOW THE WIDDOW OF SIR T. OVERBURY (1613) said: *His wit, like the marigold, openeth with the sun.*

marinorama. A wide seascape; a panorama of the sea. Various words have been used in English, roundabout from Latin *mare,* sea. In science, *maricolous,* sea-dwelling; *marigenous,* produced by or in the sea—both with accent on the second syllable. *To marill* was a 17th century term for to pickle in brine—*marilled trout* —also *to marinade, marionate*; now, *to marinate.* A *marina* (19th century; Washington Irving used *marino*) is a boardwalk or other promenade along the seashore. *marinage* (16th century), *marinary* (17th), seamanship. *marinal* (17th century), relating to the sea; nautical; salty—from the 14th to the 17th century, *marinal,* a mariner; whence also *marinaller, maryneller,* a sailor. A *marine* was earlier (17th century) a *marine soldier*; as a noun the word was used (14th—17th centuries) to mean the country along the coast; also (16th and 17th centuries) a sailor; then it became restricted to its current use of a soldier stationed on a ship. *Tell that to the marines—the sailors won't believe it!* occurs in Scott's REDGAUNTLET (1824), but Byron the year before referred to it as "an old saying". *marined* is still used in heraldry for an animal the lower part of whose body is like a fish, as mermaids and certain monsters. [Drama critic John Chapman has one of the rare mounted specimens of a furred trout.] Note that a *marinist* is a disciple or imitator of the Italian Giovanni Battista *Marini* (1569-1625) whose elaborate literary style, labeled *marinism,* is comparable to Spanish *gongorism* and English *euphuism.* In the 18th century, *horse-marine* was used for a seahorse; in the 19th, it was used humorously (Scott, 1824, in ST. RONAN'S WELL; O. W. Holmes, 1860) for an imaginary company of mounted marines—hence, men out of their element, unfit for their work, fish out of water. William H. Lingard used the term in nonsense lyrics: *I'm Captain Jinks of the Horse Marines, I feed my horse on pork and beans, And often live beyond my means: I'm a Captain in the Army.* Brought from London to New York in 1868, this song was a sensational success; in 1901 Clyde Fitch wrote a play, *Captain Jinks of the Horse Marines,* which gave Ethel Barrymore her first star role. Note, however, that in the 1870's and 80's there actually were cavalrymen, *horse-marines,* used in British maritime or seacoast action. They are, of course, the regular troops of the Swiss Navy. Also, along canals in pre-motor days, the boy leading the horse that towed the barge was humorously called a *horse-marine.* Tell *that* to the marines!

marine. See *marinorama.*

marrow. A companion, partner, mate (husband or wife); one's equal, one's match in a contest; one of a pair, as glove, shoe, pistol; Colvil in THE WHIGS SUPPLICATION (1681) wrote: *Some had bows but wanted arrows; Some had pistols without marrows.* (This example is given in the O.E.D., but possibly *marrows* is here used in the still current sense of the pith and essence of a thing: i.e., ammunition, as the bows lacked arrows.) *Marrow,* mate, was used from the 15th century. *The toune,* said Dalrymple, translating (1596) Leslie's HISTORY OF SCOTLAND, *standes in sa pleisand a place, that it hes na marrow.*

Mars. The Roman god of war (Greek *Ares*). Earlier *Mavors*; hence (16th and 17th centuries) *mavortial, mavortian,* warlike; *a mavortian,* a warrior. Hence *Mars,* war; a great warrior. Also, the fourth planet from the sun, between the Earth and Jupiter. *Cp. Diana.* Red is the color of martial ceremony or deed. *The field (camp) of Mars,* the Campus Martius, Rome. *The hill of Mars,* the Areopagus, Athens.

martel. (1) A hammer. Also *martews, marteaulx, marteaux.* After the 15th century, the word was used especially of a large hammer used as a weapon in war. Thus *martel-de-fer,* iron hammer. The grandfather of Charlemagne was Charles *Martel* (the Hammer; 689?-741). (2) *martels,* a medieval French game (Rabelais calls it *martre*; Ronsard, *martes*), 'fivestones.' (3) An old form of *marten, martin,* the animal. (4) A short form of *Martilman, Martinmas* (mainly Scotch). Spenser in THE FAËRIE QUEENE (1596) uses *martel* as a verb: *Her dreadfull weapon . . . Which on his helmet martelled so hard . . .* Hence *martelaise, marteleise, martileys,* a fighting with hammers; a sound hammering.

martin. (1) A fool, a dupe. So used in the 16th and 17th centuries, perhaps from the bird (the bird *martin,* of the swallow family, and the animal, *martin, marten, marton,* survive); Fletcher in THE ISLAND PRINCESS (1621) remarked: *We are all meere martins.* (2) A monkey. From the name given the monkey in the story of REYNARD THE FOX. Also, *martin-drunk;* Nash in PIERCE PENNILESSE (1592) lists various kinds of drunkard, including *lion-drunk; the sixt is martin drunke, when a man is drunke and drinkes himselfe sober ere he stirre.* (3) From *St. Martin; Martinmas,* 11 November. *martin chain,* a chain of imitation gold. *martin dry,* a pear that ripens about Martinmas. *St. Martin's evil,* inebriety. *St. Martin's rings, -stuff, -ware,* imitation, counterfeit. *St. Martin's summer,* what in the United States is called Indian summer (as occurring about Martinmas); Shakespeare uses this figuratively in HENRY VI, PART ONE: *This night the siege assuredly Ile rayse: Expect St. Martins summer, halcyons dayes.*

martinet. (1) An early name for the bird, the *martin, q.v.,* being its diminutive form. (2) The demon whose function it was to summon (and to dismiss) assemblies of witches. Noted by Jonson in THE MASQUE OF QUEENS (1609). (3) A military engine, for hurling large stones. (4) A system of military drill, devised by General *Martinet,* of the army of the French King Louis XIV. Hence, the current sense, a strict disciplinarian, a stickler for form.

martingale. To bet 'double or nothing'; to continue doubling one's stake after losing, in the hope of eventual recovery, if one's funds can endure the strain. A 19th century gambling term.

maship. A shortened form of *mastership;* used in salutation and direct address. Also *mashippe.* THE DEFENCE OF CONNY-CATCHING (1592) inquires: *Is not this coosenage and connycatching, Maister R[obert] G[reene], and more daily practised in England, and more hurtful, then our poore shifting at cardes, and yet your mashippe can winke at the cause?* Public abuses, he presses the point, are more to be attacked than private peccadills. Times have little changed.

masquin. A masquerade; a costume for a masquerade. Also *masken, masquine.* The form is possibly a corruption of *masking.* R. Franck in NORTHERN MEMOIRS (1658) spoke of *the Church of Rome . . . where matins are metamorphosed into masquins, collects translated into collations.*

mastigophoric. Carrying a scourge or whip. Also *mastigophorous.* Used for pedantic humor, in the 19th century, as by Peacock in HEADLONG HALL (1816); Sydney Smith (WORKS; 1826) wondered *what this medium boy can do while his mastigophorous superior is frowning over him.* The first form is accented on the *for;* the second, on the *goff.* They are from Greek *mastix, mastig-,* scourge, + *phoros,* bearing. In the 17th century, *mastigophore* was used of an usher that walked with a whip, ahead of a procession or an important person, to clear a way through a crowd. As a combination, *-mastix* appears at the end of special words, such as *infantomastix,* scourge of children, and in titles, as Prynne's *Histriomastix* (1632; Latin *histrio,* actor, whence *histrionics*) and Dekker's *Satiromastix* (1602, attacking Jonson).

mataeology. Useless or unprofitable discourse. Greek *mataios,* vain + *logia,* discourse. Hence *mataeologue, mataeologian,* an empty talker. Also *mataeological,* vain, empty. *mataeotechny,* a profitless science. (All the forms may simplify the *ae* to *e.*) Urquhart in his translation (1653) of Rabelais spoke of *the doting mateologians of old time.*

math. A mowing; the crop that is mowed. Used from the 10th into the 17th century; Bishop Hall in HARD TEXTS (1633; AMOS) noted the reservation of *the first mowing thereof for the King's use (which is wont to be sooner then the common mathe).* The word survives in the compound *aftermath.*

mathemancy. See *aeromancy.*

matutine. In or relating to the early morning; early. Accent on the *mat.* Also (accent on the *tyoot*) *matutinary* and the still occasional *matutinal.* Latin *matutinus; Matuta,* goddess of dawn; from the root *ma,* to shape, produce, grow—whence also *maternal* and *maturity.* Thackeray in his PARIS SKETCH-BOOK (1839) pictured *the matutinal dews twinkling on the grass.* Dunbar in his POEMS (1500) looked at the morning star: *Up sprang the goldyn candill matutyne.*

maugre. (1) Ill will, displeasure. Often in the phrase *to can (con) maugre.* Used from the 14th into the 16th century. Malory in the MORTE D'ARTHUR (1485) has: *I have heard moche of your maugre ageynst me.* Also *bongre maugre,* willy-nilly. From the phrase *in (the) maugre of,* despite the ill-will of, came the separate use of *maugre* as an adverb meaning in spite of, notwithstanding. Spenser in THE FAËRIE QUEENE (1596) bids: *Tell what thou saw'st, maulgre whoso it heares.* This use was very common from the 12th century, lasting into the 19th. Spenser also (in the same poem) uses the word to mean A curse upon!: *Yett, maulgre them, farewell my sweetest sweet!* The phrase *maugre his (my) head (cheek, teeth, eyes, heart,* etc.) meant In spite of all he (I) could do; Chaucer in THE DETHE OF BLAUNCHE (1369) has: *Maugre myn heed, I muste have tolde her or be deed.* Motley in his HISTORY OF THE UNITED NETHERLANDS (1860) stated: *He may see your Highness enjoy your blessed estate, maugre the beards of all confederated leaguers.* (2) As a verb, to show ill-will to; to oppose, to defy. Thus Webster, in APPIUS AND VIRGINIA (1609): *Whose bases are of marble, deeply fixt To mauger all gusts* *and impending stormes.* Also in Shakespeare's KING LEAR (V iii 131).

maumet. A false god; an idol. This word, a corruption of *Mahomet* (due to the medieval notion that Mohammed was worshipped as a god), took many forms, among them *mawmet, maummet, mawmot, mawment, mamet, mommet.* It ranged through various shades of meaning: (1) anything one worships as a god; thus Chaucer in THE PARSON'S TALE (1386): *Every florin in his coffer is his mawmet.* (2) An image of Christ or the saints. So applied by Protestants, especially in the 16th and 17th centuries. (3) An image; a doll, puppet; a person of grotesque appearance; thus Shakespeare in HENRY IV, PART ONE (1596): *this is no world To play with mammets.* (4) A person who is the 'puppet' or tool of another; then, a general term of contempt, as in Shakespeare's ROMEO AND JULIET: *A wretched puling foole, A whining mammet . . .* Hence, *maumeter,* an idolater; *maumetrous,* idolatrous; *maumetry,* idolatry, heathenism, idolatrous beliefs; idols collectively.

maund. (1) A wicker or other woven basket, with handle. A common word from early times (7th century); also *mond, mand, mawnd, moane, maun, mawn, mound.* Shakespeare in A LOVER'S COMPLAINT (1597) says: *A thousand favors from a maund she drew Of amber, crystal, and of beaded jet.* (2) A basketful; a measure of capacity (varying with place and commodity): 8 bales of unbound books; a gallon of small fish, etc. Also in India and Western Asia, a *maund* (a different word, from Hindi *man*) was 100 pounds troy weight. (3) Begging; from the verb *to maund,* to beg. In the 18th century, various begging impostures were described: *footman's maund,* a sore (made with unslacked lime, soap, and iron rust) on the back of the hand, as though bitten or kicked by a horse; *tum-maund,* pretense and make-up of an imbecile; *soldier's maund,* pretense of a wound in the left arm; *mason's maund,* pretense of a broken arm as by a fall from a scaffold. Also *maunder* (verb), to beg; (noun), a beggar. *Maunder* also meant (1) to grumble, complain, mutter; Swift in his JOURNAL TO STELLA (28 April, 1711): *I hate to buy for her; I am sure she will maunder.* (2) To move in a dreamy, idle fashion, *maunder along*; to talk or walk in a dreamy fashion (as from dotage or imbecility); this sense may have been influenced by *meander.* Also *maunderer,* a grumbler; a beggar; similarly *maundering, maunding.* Carlyle in SARTOR RESARTUS (1831) objects to folks' *mumbling and maundering the merest commonplaces.*

mavortian. See *Mars.*

mawmenny. See *malmeny.*

mawmet. See *maumet.*

mazard. A bowl, a drinking cup; originally, one made of hard wood. Also, *mazzard; mazer.* Old High German *masar,* an excrescence of hardwood; a large knob or knot) on a tree; later, a maple tree, a drinking cup of such wood. Both forms were used, by extension (from the shape) to mean the head; by Shakespeare in OTHELLO (II iii) and in HAMLET (1602), of the skull: *Chapless, and knockt about the mazard with a sextons spade.* Jonson in one of his court masques (1620) said, *If I had not been a spirit, I had been mazarded.*

mazomancy. Greek *mazos,* breast, whence also the *amazon.* See *aeromancy.*

meacock. A weakling; a coward; an effeminate man. Perhaps from French *mi-*

coq, half-rooster. Also *maycocke, meicocke, mecock.* Shakespeare has, in THE TAMING OF THE SHREW (1594): *How tame, when men and women are alone, a meacock wretch can make the curstest shrew!*

mead. A fermented (alcoholic) mixture of honey and water. This is a very old Aryan word; Sanskrit *medu,* honey, sweet drink. Priscus in 448 A.D. remarked that the Huns used *medos* instead of wine. Chaucer in THE MILLER'S TALE (1386) says *He sent her piment meeth and spyced ale.* Addison in THE SPECTATOR (No. 383, 1712) remarked: *A masque . . . asked him if he would drink a bottle of mead with her.* Milton uses the word (*meathes*) of a drink from a berry. Also see *hydromel; metheglin, mulse. Mead,* of course, is also short for meadow.

mealy-mouthed. Soft-spoken; applied to excessive delicacy of speech, prudery, or to hypocrisy, sycophancy; to one that does not venture to speak his mind. Hence, *mealy-mouthedness.* The word is usually related to *meal,* flour; but E. Edwards (in WORDS, FACTS, AND PHRASES, 1881) points out that Shakespeare uses *honey-mouthed* and suggests that *mealy-mouthed* may have come from Latin *mel,* English *mell,* honey. Dekker in THE GENTLE CRAFT (1600) says *This wench with the mealy mouth, is my wife, I can tell you.* The word *mealy* alone sometimes has the same meaning, as in (1697; Leslie, SNAKE IN THE GRASS) *thy mealy modesty.* The term was also used, more generally, to mean over-scrupulous, as in Malkin's translation (1809) of GIL BLAS: *You are not mealy-mouthed about receiving a commoner into your pedigree.*

meandrian. Winding. This is a pleasant 16th century variation of *meandering,* from *Meander,* a river in Phrygia noted for its winding course. Hence also *meandriform,* of a winding or labyrinthine shape; *meandrous, meandry.*

mechal. Adulterous. Also *michall;* Greek *moichos,* adulterer. Used several times by Heywood, as in THE RAPE OF LUCRECE (1608): *That done, straight murder One of thy basest grooms, and lay you both Grasp'd arm in arm in thy adulterate bed, Men call in witness of your mechall sin.*

meconomancy. Greek *mekon,* poppy. See *aeromancy; cp. mecop.*

mecop. The poppy. Flemish *men,* German *mohn,* poppy + *kop,* head. Note, however, Greek *mekon,* poppy, whence several English terms. *meconium,* opium. *meconology, meconologia,* a treatise on opium. *meconophagism* (accent on the *off*), opium-eating; hence *meconophagist,* as De Quincey.

medicaster. An incompetent physician; a quack. The feminine is *medicastra.* F. Hering in his ANATOMY (1602) declared that *another medicastra, a ratling gossip . . . commended a drench.* Duffield in his version (1881) of Don Quixote said: *A queen may be leman to a medicaster.* The ending *aster* is used of an incompetent or a pretender, as also in *poetaster, criticaster* (*cp. critickin*); do not add *forecaster, schoolmaster,* or—*disaster!*

medlar. The tree, or the fruit of the medlar tree: like a small brown apple, with a large cup-shaped 'eye'; good only if eaten when decayed until it is soft and pulpy. By transference, the word is given a sexual significance, in several plays of Shakespeare. Lucio in MEASURE FOR MEASURE (1604) says: *They would else have married me to the rotten medlar.* In ROMEO AND JULIET we read: *Now will he sit under a medlar-tree And wish his mistress were that kind of fruit As maids* *call medlars when they laugh alone. Oh, Romeo, that she were, oh that she were An open et cetera, thou a poperin pear!* There is a pun here on *medlar* and *meddler,* one that would *meddle* with her. What 'maids call medlars' is hidden in the phrase *open et cetera,* which is a euphemism for *openarse,* the old name of the *medlar,* from the shape of the disk between its calyx-lobes. Chaucer uses *openers* in the Prologue to THE REEVE'S TALE (1386); Killigrew in THE PARSON'S WEDDING (1663) employs the figure: *as useless as openarses gathered green.* A *poperin* (*poprin*; not in O.E.D.) pear is one from Poperinghe, a town in West Flanders, but here used to refer to the male organs. Further pursuit of this would lay one open to what my father used to call a *waylay-for-meddlers,* such as once almost cost me a finger's end.

meer. A variant for (1) *mare*; female horse; (2) *more*; (3) *mayor*; (4) *mere, q.v.* Also *meere.*

meinie. A family, household. Hence: a body of retainers, attendants; a retinue, suite, train. By extension, a company of persons employed together, an army, ship's crew, congregation, etc. Also, the men of a chess set; thus in MERLIN (1450) we read: *The pownes, and all the other meyne were golde and yvory freshly entailled.* From the 14th century, by confusion with *the many, meinie* was also used to mean a large number, a multitude; hence (of persons), the common herd, the masses. This was a very common word from the 13th into the 17th century; it developed many forms, among them *maynee, meingne, maine, meine, meyny, meney, mainy, meny.* Via Old French *meyne, mesnie,* it is from Latin *mansionem,* house, household, whence also English *mansion.* Wyclif (WORKS, 1380) observed: *No weddid man oweth to leve his wife and children and meyne ungoverned*—advice that has not lost its value in 600 years. *God's meinie*: (1) the angels, (2) the poor, as the Lord's especial concern. As a multitude, Barrie used the word in MARGARET OGILVY (1896): *You get no common beef at clubs; there is a manzy of different things all sauced up to be unlike themselves.*

mell. (1) To speak, to say. Also *mele; maelenn, meile; melle, meddle, medle,* and more. Old English *maethel,* discourse. Used from the 9th to the 15th century. (2) To mix together, combine; hence, to associate, to have intercourse with; to mingle in combat; to concern oneself (with); to meddle. This was a common word from the 13th century, used by Gower (1390), Chaucer, Spenser (THE FAËRIE QUEENE, 1590: *With holy father sits not with such things to mell*). Dying out in the 17th century, *mell* was revived by Burns (1786) and Scott (IVANHOE, 1819; QUENTIN DURWARD, 1823: *Draw in within the courtyard—they are too many to mell with in the open field*), and was fairly frequent through the 19th century. (3) To beat severely. This verbal meaning is from the noun *mell* (1) a heavy hammer—used also in phrases: *dead as a mell,* quite dead; *to keep mell in shaft,* to keep things going: Mrs. Carlyle wrote, in a letter of 6 October, 1831: *Carlyle is reading today with a view to writing an article —to keep mall in shaft. Mell,* as a noun, also was used to mean: (2) honey—Greek *meli*; whence many compounds, such as *mellisonant,* sweet-sounding; (3) a tail (of a horse; a rare 18th century use); (4) the last sheaf of corn in a season's harvest. This was usually cause for gaiety or celebration; hence, *mell-day, mell-supper*; a *mell-doll* was an ear from the *mell-sheaf* dressed like a baby girl, carried on a pole by a woman, amid the romping reapers.

melliloquent. Speaking sweetly. Latin *mel,* honey. More common were *mellifluent, mellifluous,* sweet as honey (mainly of the voice or speech); but also literally sweetened with or as with honey. Shakespeare has, in TWELFTH NIGHT (1601) *A mellifluous voice, as I am true knight;* Francis Meres in PALLADIS TAMIA (1598) hailed *mellifluous and hony-tongued Shakespeare.*

menalty. See *mesnalty.*

mendaciloquence. Ease and fluency in the telling of lies. The gracious word *mendaciloquent* occurs only in 17th and 18 century dictionaries, but a HISTORY OF LONDON CLUBS in 1710 refers to *a witty and famous gentleman in the art of mendatiloquence.* Hence *mendacity. Cp. mendicity.*

mendicity. The condition of a beggar; the practice of begging. Latin *mendicus; mendicare,* to beg. [*Mendacity,* the quality of being *mendacious;* the practice of lying, is from Latin *mendacem,* prone to lying, false; *mendax* from the form *mentnax; mentiri,* to lie. *Cp. mendaciloquence.*] Other forms for begging are *mendicanting* (17th century); *mendication* (17th into the 19th century, mainly of begging religious orders); and the earlier (15th century) *mendience.* Through the 15th century a beggar, *mendicant,* was called a *mendivaunt.*

mene. Fellowship, friendly intercourse. Old English *gemaene.* Used in the 13th century. Also *mene* was a variant form of (1) *men,* (2) *mean,* (3) *meinie, q.v.*

meng. This is an early form of *mingle,* used from the 8th into the 17th century. It is from a common Old Teuton root, whence also Old English *ge-mang,* modern *among. Meng,* in its various tenses, had many forms, among them *myng, mengde, mengid, menkit, meynt, imengd, imenget, ymeint.* Gower, in CONFESSIO AMANTIS (1390) says: *Warm milk she put also thereto With honey meynd.* Sylvester in his translation (1608) of Du Bartas, has: *Their country-gods with the true God they ming.* Hence *menged,* mixed, confused; *menging,* a mixture; disturbance (of mind).

menialty. See *mesnalty.*

mensk. Humanity; courtesy; reverence; honor; an honor; an ornament. A common word from the 13th into the 16th century, from Old Norse *mennska,* humanity, related to English *man.* As a verb *mensk* meant to reverence; to dignify; to adorn. Hence *menskful,* honorable, stately, gracious; *menskless,* ungracious; *mensking* (14th century), honor, courtesy. The Scotch form of the word, still in use in the 19th century, was *mense;* Scott in ROB ROY (1818) says: *We hae mense and discretion, and are moderate of our mouths.*

mental. Relating to the chin. See *mentulate.* A *mentonierre* was a piece of armour, attached either to the helmet or to the breastplate, to protect the neck and chin. A prizefighter as well as a thinker may receive a mental shock.

mentiferous. Relating to thought-transference, telepathic. Suggested about 1880, as a label for the 'ether' through which 'thought-waves' were supposed to travel. A word for the ESP-men.

mentimutation. Change of mind. Latin *mens, mentis,* mind + *mutare, mutatum,* to change; frequentative of *movere, motum,* to move, whence *motion, motive.* Used in the 17th century; the author,

"B," of DISCOLLIMINIUM (1650) claimed: *I shall be allowed the full benefit of all the . . . illaqueations, extrications . . . mentimutations, rementimutations . . . that I can devise.*

mentulate. Largely equipped with the outward manifestation of masculine potency. Also *mentulated;* Latin *mentula,* penis, from the root *men,* to project. Latin *mentum,* chin; one meaning of the English word *mental* is, relating to the chin. The ending *ul* is a diminutive; *mentula,* a little projection. The relation of this to the mental processes has never, despite Freud, been fully analyzed.

mercer. A dealer in textile fabrics; a dealer in small wares. Latin *mercem,* merchandise. Common from the 12th century. Also *mercership* (rare), *mercery,* the business or wares or shop of a *mercer. The Mercery,* the Mercer's Company (in London since the 14th century). The process of preparing cotton goods for dyeing, *to mercerize,* is named from the discoverer of the process (1844), *John Mercer.* The original word survives also in *Mercer Street,* just west of Broadway in the business section of New York.

mercury. The Roman god (Greek *Hermes*) of traders and thieves, of eloquence and feats of skill; presider over roads; guide of the dead to their new abode; messenger of the gods, and mischiefmaker. Pictured as a young man with winged sandals and hat, holding the caduceus. Hence *mercury,* a signpost; also, a newspaper; a messenger, a bearer of news (Shakespeare, RICHARD III, II i; 1594); a go-between, especially, in amatory instances (Shakespeare, THE MERRY WIVES OF WINDSOR, II ii). Also a nimble live-by-his-wits; a dexterous thief (Jonson, EVERY MAN OUT OF HIS HUMOUR, I ii; 1599). The planet nearest the sun. *Cp. Diana.* And used as an emblem of liveliness, wittiness, or inconstancy; wit. Congreve in THE OLD BACHELOR (1693) said he *was as able as yourself and as nimble too, though I mayn't have so much mercury in my limbs* (probably with reference also to the element *mercury,* quicksilver, named after the volatile god). Walpole in GEORGE II (1797) said: *He had too much mercury and too little ill-nature to continue a periodical war.*

merd. See *merdaille.*

merdaille. The rabble. Used in the 14th century. The ending means a heap, a group; similarly *canaille,* the rabble, meant literally a pack of dogs (Latin *canis,* dog). Latin *merda,* excrements, dung (French *merde*) was used in English from the 15th to the 18th century in the forms *merd, merde, mard.* Hence *merdiferous,* carrying or farming dung; *merdivorous,* feeding on dung; *merdous, merdose,* full of or covered with dung or ordure. Burton in THE ANATOMY OF MELANCHOLY (1621) said that *to dispute of gentry without wealth, is . . . to discusse the originall of a mard.* Cleveland in THE RUSTICK RAMPANT (1658) wrote: *This merdaille, these stinkards, throng before the gates.*

mere. This form embraces several words. (1) The sea; in poetry, a lake; in dialect, a marsh or fen. Old Saxon *meri,* sea, pool; Latin *mare.* (2) A boundary; a landmark. Related to Latin *murus,* wall. Also used figuratively, as by Spenser in THE FAËRIE QUEENE (1590): *So huge a mind could not in lesser rest, ne in small meares contain his glory great.* (3) A short form of *merman* or *mermaid.* As an adjective: (a) from Old English *maere,* came *mere,* famous, illustrious, noble. (b) *mere,* from

Latin *merus,* undiluted, pure, has had a long development: (wine) not mixed with water; pure (as in the phrase *mere Irish,* common in the 17th and 18th centuries, and a term of distinction not disparagement); hence, absolute, entire, all that it is said and supposed to be (Shakespeare in OTHELLO, 1604, speaks of *the mere perdition of the Turkish fleet*). This sense lasted until 1800, but about 1600 the present sense also came into use: no more than it is said to be, barely that and of little importance.

merel. A counter or piece used in the (15th to 17th century) game of *merels.* It was a game something like draughts or a primitive checkers; also called *marl, merrills, morals, miracles,* and more frequently *morris, q.v.* Hyde in his HISTORIA NERDILUDII (1694), mentioned *three men's morals, nine men's morals, and nine penny miracle*—according to the number of pieces used in the game. The name was also applied to various out-of-doors games, such as "fox and geese" and "hop scotch"; also to a place where the game was played, as in Shakespeare; see quotation under *morris.*

merenda. A light meal, what James Mabbe, in his translation (1622) of Aleman's THE ROGUE called an "inter-mealary repast." A 17th and 18th century word.

meresauce. Brine for pickling. From *mere (1)*; also *mersaus, miresauce*; Latin *muria salsa,* salt pickle; *mare,* the sea, whence *marinated* and the ones you "tell it to." See *marinorama.* Occasionally used in butchery, as recorded of the man that (Fabyan, CHRONICLES; 1494): *slewe the sayde servauntes of his brother, and hacked theym in small pecys, and cast them after in meresawce. Marinated herring* is pickled in what the 14th, 15th, 16th, and 17th centuries called *meresauce.*

meresman. A surveyor; specifically, a man appointed to determine the boundaries of a parish. See *mere (2).*

merestone. A stone erected as a landmark or guide. From *mere (2).*

mereswine. A porpoise; sometimes, a dolphin. From *mere (1).* Used from the 8th century; Carlyle in a letter of 1822 says: *Waugh fixed his eye on an enormous mereswine.* Dr. Daniel Tuke, in his CHAPTERS IN THE HISTORY OF THE INSANE IN THE BRITISH ISLES (1882) says that in earlier times *a skin of mereswine* was made into a whip to drive the devil out of a person possessed.

meretriculate. To deceive as does a harlot. A rare word, in a play by Chapman (MAY DAY; 1611): *I have not been matriculated in the University, to be meretriculated by him.* Other forms were more frequent: Latin *meretrix,* harlot (from *merere, meritus,* to deserve, to be entitled to; to earn; to work for hire, whence also *merit* and *meritorious* service) was used in English in the 16th and 17th centuries; the first meaning of *meretricious* was, relating to or characteristic of a harlot. Hence also *meretric, meretricial, meretrician,* other forms of *meretricious*; *meretricate,* to play the whore, to behave lasciviously. Bacon in THE NEW ATLANTIS (1626) observed: *The delight in meretricious embracements (wher sinne is turned into art) maketh marriage a dull thing.* T. Brown carried the idea along; his DECLAMATION IN DEFENCE OF GAMING (1704) declared: *Take from human commerce meretrician amours, and you will find a horrid confusion of all things, and incestuous lusts disturb every family.*

merkin. This is a variant of *malkin,* a diminutive of *Maud. Malkin* became a general term of contempt, meaning a slattern; then it was applied to a mop or (in the navy) to a sponge on a stick, for cleaning cannon; also to a scarecrow or grotesque effigy. It was also used as a name for a witch (in Shakespeare's MACBETH, 1605, *Grimalkin,* gray *malkin*), hence, for a cat. In the form *merkin,* a pussy, it was used for the female "pudendum," and also (15th to 18th century) for a wig or counterfeit hair for a woman's privy parts. Just as the small-pox (so common that, in the 18th century, servants were sought that had already recovered from the disease, hence could not contract it and infect their masters) disfigured the face, so the great pox often left traces farther down, which a merkin might mercifully mask.

merocracy. Government by a part. Used in the 17th century. Greek *meros,* part. *mero-* is used as a combining form in many scientific words, as *meropia,* dullness of sight, partial vision; *merorganize* (19th century), to bring to a partially organized state.

meropic. Able to speak. Greek *merops,* speaking. A 19th century word; also *merop.* Badham in PROSE HALIEUTICS felt that mute creatures are *as capable of jealousy and resentment as loud-tongued meropic man!* Not to be confused with *meropia* (Greek *meros,* part + *ops,* eye); *cp. merocracy.* There was also a form *meropie* (16th century), *merops* (17th), bee-eater, the name of a bird, taken directly from the Greek.

meroure. Lamentation; sorrow. Latin *maeror; maerere,* to mourn. In the MIROUR OF SALVACIOUN (1450) we read: *In whas absence . . . evre sho contynuyd in weping and in meroure.*

mersion. Dipping; especially, the act of dipping in water for baptism. Latin *mergere, mersum,* to dip, to plunge—which from legal Latin, to sink one cause within another, gives us *merge, merger. Mersion,* used in the 17th century, was replaced by *immersion.*

merveilleux. An extravagantly bedecked fop of the "Directory" period in France (1795-99; ended by Napoleon's coup d'état of 18 Brumaire—9 November—1799). The fine lady of the time was a *merveilleuse.* (These are the French forms for *marvellous.*) About the same time there strutted the *inconcevable* (inconceivable) and minced the *incroyable* (unbelievable). The *merveilleux* tried to revive the costumes of classical Greece; the *merveilleuse,* commented the DAILY NEWS of 19 October, 1892, *walked half naked in the Champs Elysées.*

mervilous. An early form of *marvellous,* used by Shakespeare in HENRY V (1599).

meschant. Wicked; wretched; also, a wretch, a villain. Common from the 15th to the 18th century; also *mischaunt, mishant, mechant,* and more. Old French *mescheant; mescheoire,* to be unlucky; Latin *mis,* wrong + *cadere,* to fall. Pepys in his DIARY for 6 September, 1664, wrote: *Cromwell, notwithstanding the meschants of his time, which were the Cavaliers . . .* Also *meschantness, meschancie,* wickedness; *meschantery,* an evil deed.

meschyne. A bad woman. Caxton (ENEYDOS; 1490) wrote of *a meschyne . . . that joyeth her to recite . . . more lesying than trouth.* The word is a variant of *mesquine,* feminine of French *mesquin,* mean, sordid. *Mesquin* was used as an English adjective in the 18th and 19th centuries; Kingsley in AT LAST (1871) spoke of *the mesquin and scrofulous visages, which crowd our alleys.*

mesnalty. The estate of a *mesne lord;* the condition of being a *mesne lord.* Via

French from Latin *medianum,* mean, middle; the *s* is silent, long *e.* The *mesne lord* was one who, though below the king, was above other lords, who held their estates from and owed fealty to him. As the feudal system lapsed, the word *mesnalty* (*mesnality*), shifting to *menalty,* was applied to the middle class. It should not be confused with *menialty,* persons of *menial* rank, the condition of being a *menial,* which is from *meinie, q.v.,* household. Hall in his CHRONICLES (1548; Henry IV) noted: *The evil parliament for the nobilitie, the worse for for the menaltie, but worste of all for the commonaltee.*

mesothesis. Something put in the middle, serving as a balance, or to reconcile two opposed principles, etc. Accent on the *soth.* Also *mesothet.* Greek *mesos,* middle + *thesis,* putting, *theton,* placed. These —also *mesothetic, mesothetical*—are 19th century terms. Froude in THE NEMESIS OF FAITH (1849) spoke of *the final mesothesis for the reconciling of the two great rivals, Science and Revelation.* Kingsley in ALTON LOCKE (1850) was more sprightly: *A curious pair of 'poles' the two made; the mesothet whereof, by no means a 'punctum indifferens,' but a true connecting spiritual idea, stood on the table—in the whisky bottle. Mr. Carlyle,* said FRASER'S MAGAZINE in 1837, *avoids the synthetical, as well as the analytical, and looks down upon both from the mesothetical.*

mesquin. See *meschyne.*

messuage. (Pronounced in two syllables: mess-swaje.) A portion of land in the English countryside, usually that rented for a dwelling and its attendant buildings and grounds. Tennyson, in EDWIN MORRIS (1842) says *They wedded her to sixty thousand pounds, To lands in Kent and messuages in York.* Robert Arden, a widower with eight daughters, preparing to marry a widow with children of her own, on July 17, 1550, made a settlement of his Snitterfield property, including *a messuage in the tenure of one Richard Shakespeare.* Later Richard's son John married Robert's daughter Mary; to them was born a son named William Shakespeare, who has not been forgotten.

mestive. Sad, mournful. Latin *maerere, maes-,* to be sad; *maestitia,* melancholy, sorrow. Also *mestful* (the 16th century uses *this mestfull verse . . . most mestfull bird am I*). Hence *mestifical,* rendering sad.

mete. See *metecorn.*

metecorn. An allowance of food (originally, corn) to servants, to hospital inmates, and the like. The verb *mete,* common since the 9th century and still current (*to mete out*), means to measure, to supply. There was a noun *mete* (15th century into the 19th) meaning goal, boundary, frequent in the phrase *metes and bounds.* There were also two other verbs: *mete,* to paint, design (10th into the 13th century) and *mete,* to dream, especially in the phrase *me mette* (*sweven*), I dreamed (a dream). Chaucer has, in THE PARLIAMENT OF FOULES (1381): *The lovere met he hath his lady wonne.* Hence *meting,* a measuring; or a dreaming, a dream; *Joseph,* said Chaucer in THE DETHE OF BLAUNCHE (1369), *red so The kynges metynge.*

meteoromancy, meteoroscopy. See *aeromancy.*

metewand. A measuring rod. Also *metestick, metepole*; Shakespeare in THE TAMING OF THE SHREW (also the 1611 BIBLE) has *meteyard. Cp. metecorn.* Used from the 16th century; often figuratively, as by

Ascham, in THE SCHOLEMASTER (1568); Coleridge (1810), Lowell, in his essay on Lessing (1866): *He continually trips and falls flat over his metewand of classical propriety.*

methe. Measure, proportion; hence, moderation; modesty, gentleness, consideration, kindness. The word is from a common Teuton root *mae-,* to measure, whence also *mete, meter*; see *metecorn. Methe* was used in English from the 10th to the mid-15th century; a Coventry Mystery of 1450 has: *Amos spak with mylde methe.* Note that *methe* was also an old spelling of *mead, q.v.* The verb *methe* meant to moderate; hence, to have mercy on, to spare. Thus *metheful, methely,* moderate, gentle; *metheless,* immoderate. Less often *metheful, methful* (from Old English *methe,* weary) meant weary, worn. An early catechism (1357) said that *The seventh virtue and last is methe or methefulnesse* (temperance): *Give us to drink in meth!*

metheglin. A spiced or medicated variety of *mead, q.v. Methe* was an early form of the word *mead,* but *metheglin,* the Welsh term, is also related to Welsh *meddyg,* healing (Latin *medicus*) + *llyn,* liquor. Pepys in his DIARY for 25 July, 1666, said *I drinking no wine, had metheglin for the King's own drinking.* Said C. Butler in THE FEMININE MONARCHIC, OR A TREATISE CONCERNING BEES: *Methaeglen is the more generous or stronger hydromel, being unto mede as vinum to lora.* (*Vinum* is wine of the first pressing; *lora,* wine of the last pressing, or from the skins of the grapes.)

metic. A resident alien; especially, one in an ancient Greek city, where resident aliens were allowed certain privileges of citizens. From Greek *metoikos*; *meta,* beyond + *-oikos,* dwelling; *oikein,* to dwell. The accent falls on the first syllable. THE SPEAKER of 23 January, 1904, declared: *The British imperialists . . . have found that the rich metics are their masters.*

meticulosity. See *sollicitudinous.*

meting. See *metecorn.* The translation (1430) of THE PILGRIMAGE OF THE LYF OF THE MANHODE said: *I wolde weene al were lesinge* [see *lease*], *or elles that it were meetinge.*

metoscopy. See *aeromancy.*

mewlyter. A variant form of *muleteer,* one that tended mules. Of Cardinal Wolsey we read in Cavendish's LYFFE (1557): *In the stabyll he hade a mayster of his horsses; a clarke of the stable, a yoman of the same; a sadler, a farrier, a yoman of his charyot, a sompter man* [driver of pack horses], *a yoman of his stirrope; a mewlyter; xvi gromes of his stable, every of them kepyng iiii great geldyngs.*

mews. A group of stables around a yard or alley. Originally, the royal stables at Charing Cross, London; so called because on that site the royal hawks were formerly *mewed.* The word is either singular or plural. *To mew* is to moult, or change feathers; also used figuratively, as by Chaucer in TROYLUS AND CRISEYDE (1374) and Fletcher and Massinger's THE LITTLE FRENCH LAWYER (1620): *'Tis true, I was a lawyer, But I have mewd that coat, I hate a lawyer.* Milton used the verb as meaning to mature. The word is via Old French from Latin *mutare,* to change. A *mew* was a cage for hawks, especially while *mewing*; by extension, a coop for birds, as when fattening. Chaucer in the Prologue to THE CANTERBURY TALES (1386) has: *Ful many a fat partrich hadde he in muwe.* The phrase *in mew,* cooped up, was quite common. Hence *mew* was used of any place of confinement, as by Spenser in THE FAËRIE QUEENE (1590): *Captiv'd eternally in yron mewes.* Sometimes *the mews* was applied to the alley around which the stables were grouped; it survives as a street name, as in *Washington Mews,* New York City.

meyne. An old form of *meinie, q.v.* Also *meyn, meynee. Meyne* was also a variant of (1) *many,* (2) *mean,* (3) *mien.*

meynt. Mingled. Spenser's THE SHEPHERD'S CALENDAR (1579; NOVEMBER). The past participle of *meng, q.v.*

mication. A popping up of the fingers, as in the game of *mora.* Latin *micare,* to move quickly, to flash; to stretch out the fingers suddenly—the game is an ancient one. *Mora* is played in two ways: (1) one person snaps up a number of fingers, the other simultaneously calls a number (or cries 'Odd' or 'Even'), trying to guess correctly; (2) one person snaps up a number of fingers, the other instantaneously shows the number of fingers (or calls the number) that added to the first man's fingers makes ten. The loser pays a forfeit.

miche. (1) A loaf of bread. From Old French, possibly related to Latin *mica,* crumb. Hence *michekin,* a roll, a cake. Used from the 13th into the 17th century. (2) A forked stick; to support a lowered mast; as the shaft of a pump; as the sight, for aiming a cannon. Used in the 15th and 16th centuries. Much more common was the verb *miche* (from the 13th into the 19th century), to pilfer; to skulk, lurk hidden; to play traunt. Thus Lyly in EUPHUES (1590) asks *What made the gods so often to trewant from heaven, and mych here on earth, but beauty?* A *micher* was a petty thief; a sneak; (16th and 17th centuries) a pander, a go-between. Also *michery,* pilfering, cheating. Shakespeare in HAMLET (1602) has the cry: *Marry, this is miching malicho!* The last word, associated by a guess with Spanish *malhecho,* misdeed, is often printed *mallecho;* the phrase means some sort of furtive evil.

mickle. Great, big, large; much. A common Teuton root, *mikilo-*; Greek *megalo-,* whence several English words. Also *michel, muchel, mekel,* and more; in Scotland, often *muckle. Mickle-mouthed,* large-mouthed; *micklewame,* the stomach (of an ox, ready to cook). *Mickledom, mickleness, micklehead,* magnitude, greatness. The *micklemote* or *micklegemote* was the Anglo-Saxon great council, called by the king. There is an old (now Scotch) proverb: *Many a pickle* [little] *makes a mickle.*

micro-. See *macrobian.*

microbicide. See *stillicide.*

micromancy. See *aeromancy.*

midden. A dungheap. From the Scandinavian; Danish *mydding,* from *mygdynge; myg,* muck + *dynge,* heap. Used in proverbs, as *Any cock can crow on his own midden.* Note that *kitchen-midden* means a prehistoric refuse-heap, of shells and bones whereamong are often found stone implements and other relics of early man. This is also used figuratively, as in *a mental kitchen-midden.* Kingsley used the simple word figuratively when he spoke (1859) of *that everlasting midden which men call the world.* This may have been, however, a far echo of *middenerd* (also *middle-erd,* Norse *midgard*), used from the 8th to the 14th century to mean the earth, thought of as midway between heaven and hell. *Middenstead* meant the place where a dunghill is formed; figuratively, Swinburne in his STUDY OF BEN JONSON (1889) speaks of *a very midden-stead of falsehood and of filth.* By a different road, Old High German *mist,* dung, but influenced by *mix,* the form *mixen* also came to mean dungheap. This too came into proverbs: *Better wed over the mixen than over the moor,* Better wed a neighbor than a man from far away. Thomas Hardy in THE TRUMPET-MAJOR (1880) uses it figuratively: *We will let it be buried in eternal mixens of forgetfulness.*

midovernoon. Midafternoon, 3 P.M. Also used figuratively, of the passing years, as in a HYMN of 1430: *At undren to scole I was sett . . . At mydday I was dubbid knyght . . . At high noon I was crowned king . . . At midovernoon I droupid faste, Mi lust and liking went away.* [*Undern, undren,* originally the third hour of the day, 9 A.M. Then, a meal eaten at that hour. Gradually, as folk came to eat later, *undern* came to mean a later hour, until by the 16th century (when it dropped from the tongue, save in dialects) it had passed through noon—15th century—and meant the afternoon or early evening.]

midsummer men. A plant (sedum telephium), which maidens picked on Midsummer Eve (June 23, MIDSUMMER DAY being June 24) to test their lovers' faithfulness, according as the leaves bent to the right or to the left. Midsummer Day was a time of festival. The *midsummer moon* being thought especially conducive to lunacy, *midsummer madness* (Shakespeare, TWELFTH NIGHT, III iv; 1601) meant the height of madness; hence, *to have but a mile to midsummer* (used from the 15th century), to be somewhat mad. THE CONNOISSEUR (No. 56; 1755) related: *I likewise stuck up two midsummer men, one for myself, and one for him. Now if his had died away, we should never have come together. A Midsummer Night's Dream* is Shakespeare's play of faery fantasy.

milce. Mercy, forbearance. Old English *milts, milds,* whence also *mild.* Other forms were *mildce, milge, mulce, mylse, milche*; also *milth, milthness.* Used from the 6th to the 14th century, often in phrases with *grace* or *mercy.* Hence, as a verb, to have mercy on; be kind, compassionate or gracious to. *Milcer,* one that shows mercy; also *milceful, mildful, milful, milce-witter,* merciful, gracious. Robert of Gloucester's CHRONICLE (1297) had: *He . . . hopede for to finde of hir betere mulce and grace.*

minacious. Threatening, menacing. Latin *minacem; minari,* to threaten. (From the same Latin words, via the French, comes *menace.*) *Minacy* was a 16th century term meaning *menace. Minaciousness,* the state of being threatening; *minacity,* threatening, denunciation. These words were used mainly in the 16th and 17th centuries, but lingered into the 19th. The adjective has been replaced by *minatory,* which in the 16th and 17th centuries was occasionally used as a noun; Evelyn in his DIARY for 22 September, 1686, spoke of *the Emperor sending his minatories to the King of Denmark.*

mince. The original use of *mince,* to cut into little pieces, has survived, delightfully in winter *mince-meat* for pie. The word is via French from Latin *minutia; minutus,* minute. But other senses have come and gone. By extension, *mince* came to mean to diminish, to make little of; then, especially in the phrase *to mince the matter,* to make light of. In Shakespeare's OTHELLO (1604): *Iago, thy honesty and* *love doth mince this matter.* This sense survives in the negative phrase, *not to mince matters.* Hence, to speak so as not to shock, to limit oneself within the bounds of propriety and decorum, as *to mince an oath,* to substitute a euphemism for the crude oath. Hence, to speak with affected elegance; and by extension, to walk with affected delicacy, with short steps and over-preciseness. *The daughters of Zion are hautie,* says the KING JAMES BIBLE: ISAIAH (1611), *and walk with stretched forth necks, and wanton eyes, walking and mincing as they go, and making a tinkling with their feet.* Shakespeare uses the word in several senses; thus in KING LEAR (1605): *Behold yond simpring dame . . . that minces virtue.* Hence *minceative, minsitive,* affected, given to *mincing.*

minchen. A nun. Old English *mynecenu,* feminine of *munuc,* monk. Also *minching, monchyn, menchon, mention.* Used from the 10th to the 17th century, *minchen* survives in names, such as *Minchen Lane.* In the 18th and 19th century, some (archaistic) writers referred to a nunnery or conventual building as a *minchery.*

mineral. Among the less remembered uses of this word are: recondite; deeply buried; thus Donne in an essay of 1615: *Nothing was too minerall, nor centrick, for the search and reach of his wit.* Material; the third of the Martin Marprelate tracts (1589) was a broadside entitled: *Certaine Minerall and Metaphisicall Schoolpoints to be defended . . .* Also *mineral virtue,* the special power (according to the alchemists) that engendered metals.

mineramancy. See *aeromancy.*

ming. See *meng.*

minibus. A small conveyance, carrying few passengers. Latin *minimus,* the fewest; coined in the 19th century after *omnibus* **(Latin, for everybody).** The abbreviated *bus* covers all sizes.

minikin. A little woman—a term of endearment. Although often balanced with *manikin,* which is a diminutive form of *man, minikin, menyking, minnekin* is from *minne,* love (as in the medieval *Minnesinger*) + the diminutive *kin.* From its use for love songs, the gut for the treble string of the lute or viol was called the *minikin,* or *minikin string. To tickle the minikin* meant to play the lute or fiddle, but was often used by 17th century dramatists with a play on the first meaning. From the application to the treble string, *minikin* was also used of a high-pitched voice; Marston in ANTONIO AND MELLIDA (1602) asks: *What treble minikin squeaks there?* The word is also used as an adjective, meaning tiny, delicate, dainty, or (disparagingly) affected, mincing; of a voice, shrill. *Minikin name,* a pet name. Thackeray in the ENGLISH HUMOURISTS OF THE 18TH CENTURY (1851) says that pastorals *are to poetry what charming little Dresden figures are to sculpture; graceful, minikin, fantastic. Surely,* said Glapthorne in THE HOLLANDER (1640), *surely the minikin is enamoured on me!*

minimifidian. One inclined to put the least possible faith in something, such as tales of flying saucers. Sometimes contracted to *minifidian.* Both forms may also be used as adjectives. Also *minimifidianism,* coined by Coleridge in AIDS TO REFLECTION (1825). *Lady Bloomfield's supernatural stories,* reported THE SPECTATOR (2 December, 1882) *are not of a kind to challenge the scrutiny of a minimifidian in pneumatology. Pneumatology* (Greek *pneuma,* breath, air, spirit) was the science or theory of spirits. In the 17th century it was in the division of *Special Metaphysics,* which dealt with God, angels, demons, and the human soul—in its study of the last of these, it was the early term for psychology. Hence also *pneumatological, pneumatologist. Cp. pneumo-.* Jonson in his comments (1765) on Shakespeare's HAMLET observed: *According to the pneumatology of that time, every element was inhabited by its peculiar order of spirits.*

minimus. A tiny or insignificant creature. *Cp. minikin.* Latin *minimus,* least; *minim* was used as an English adjective, meaning extremely small. In calligraphy, a single down-stroke, especially the short stroke at the beginning of some letters (m, n, u, w, etc) ; Dekker and Webster in WESTWARD HOE (1607) wrote: *She took her letters very suddenly, and is now in her minoms. Minim* was also used to mean a contemptible person, or a tiny creature; Browning in a poem of 1873 said: *This insect on my parapet,—Look how the marvel of a minim crawls!* Shakespeare in A MIDSUMMER NIGHT'S DREAM (1590) cries *Get you gone you dwarfe, you minimus.*

minion. A beloved, darling, favorite; a favorite child, servant or animal; a royal favorite. Shakespeare, in HENRY IV, PART ONE (1596) : *A sonne . . . Who is sweet Fortune's minion, and her pride.* In each of these senses the tone deteriorated, so that minion came to mean a mistress; a spoiled pet; one raised beyond desert by favor. The word was also used figuratively, as when John Day in PEREGRINATIO SCHOLASTICA (1640) smiled upon *Violets, roses, and lillies, and like mineons and darlings of the spring.* The word may be related to Old High German *minnja, minna,* love (as in the *Minnesinger*) or to Celtic *min,* small. Among its orthographic forms are *minyon, mynion, mignyon, minnion. Minion* was also an adjective, dainty, elegant; and a verb, to treat as a minion, to caress. Also *minionize* (1) to play the wanton, (2) to raise to the position of a favorite, to *minionship. It is no wonder,* exclaimed Bryce in THE AMERICAN COMMONWEALTH (1888), *if he helps himself from the city treasury and allows his minions to do so.* [Note that *minion* is also the Hebrew word for a quorum for prayer: ten males over 13 years old. Thus you can guess what happened when Principal Edward Kelly, in an elementary school in a Jewish neighborhood, rang his bell and with pedantic humor said to the responding monitor, Abraham Cohen: "Boy, fetch me a minion!"]

minish. An early form of (1) diminish, (2) mince. From Late Latin *minutiare,* to lessen; *minutum,* minute.

miniver. A fur; especially used as lining and trimming for ceremonial costumes. It may have been the white Siberian squirrel; it had a smaller pattern than *vair, q.v.*—the word *miniver* being from French *menu,* Latin *minutus,* minute + *vair.* Also *meniver, menevayr, menevoir, minifer, menyvere,* and the like. *Pured miniver, miniver pure,* has been taken to mean pure white; it really is French *meniver puré, powdered miniver*; i.e., spotted with tiny strips of miniver. Nathaniel Ward in THE SIMPLE COBBLER OF AGGAWAM (1647) attacking the fancified fashions of the American gentlemen, said: *It seems in fashion for you to . . . dapple your speeches with new quodled words. Ermins in minifer is every man's coat.*

minsitive. See *mince.*

minuity. A trifle. Via Old French from Latin *minutus,* minute. Shelton in his translation (1612) of DON QUIXOTE averred: *I would not have my soule suffer in the other world for such a minuity as is thy wages.*

minulize. To warble softly. Tourneur in THE TRANSFORMED METAMORPHOSIS (1600) wrote: *The thrush, the lark, and nightsjoy nightingale There minulize their pleasing laies anew.*

miradical. Speaking marvelous things. Latin *mirus,* wonderful + *dicere,* to speak. In Bailey's DICTIONARY, 1751. Also listed in 17th century dictionaries in the form *miridical.*

mirador. A turret atop a house (especially in Spain; Spanish *mirar,* to look) commanding a view. Originally, a watchtower. Also *miradore.* Dryden in THE CONQUEST OF GRANADA (1670) wrote: *Your valiant son, who had before Gain'd fame, rode round to ev'ry mirador.*

mirandous. Wonderful. Latin *mirandus,* worthy of wonder, the gerundive form of *mirari,* to wonder at; whence also *miracle.* The feminine of the gerundive, *miranda,* is used as the name of the heroine in Shakespeare's THE TEMPEST (1611).

mird. To venture; to sport amorously. Mainly in Scotland, since the 16th century. A song of 1768 has the line: *He there wi' Meg was mirdin' seen.* As a noun, *mird* is a variant of *merd; cp. merdaille.* Cokaine in his translation (1669) of OVID spoke of *oyntments made of the spawn of snakes, spittle of Jews, and mird of infants.*

miridical. See *miradical.*

mirific. Working wonders; rousing astonishment, marvelous. Also *mirificent,* working wonders; accent on the *if.* And *mirifical; mirificence.* Used since the 15th century; BLACKWOOD'S EDINBURGH MAGAZINE (1853) pointed to *the mirific diminishment of the contents of the brandy-bottle.*

mis-. Prefixed to many words, mainly verbs, *mis-* adds to the meaning the idea of error, of doing wrongly, badly, perversely, mistakenly, as in Shakespeare, KING JOHN, 1595: *Thou has mispoke, misheard; Be well advis'd, tell oer thy tale again.* In words of ill or sinister import, *mis-* intensifies the meaning, as in Shakespeare, PERICLES (1608): *The passions of the mind, That have their first conception by misdread.* Among many others, we may note *misgraffed,* badly matched, in Shakespeare's A MIDSUMMER NIGHT'S DREAM (1590): *The course of true love never did run smooth, But either it was different in blood . . . Or else misgraffed, in respect of years.* Also *misken,* to be ignorant of; *miskissing,* improper kissing, or kissing the wrong party; *misliterate,* ignorant, unlearned; *misqueam, misqueme,* to displease, offend; *misseeming,* false appearance, as in Spenser's THE FAËRIE QUEENE (1590): *With her witchcraft and misseeming sweet; mistime, mistide,* to happen amiss, to come to grief, as in Chaucer's TALE OF MELIBEUS (1386): *He that hath over-hard a heart, atte last he shall mishappe and mistyde*; *mistrow,* to mistrust, disbelieve; *miswoman,* manhandle, also a noun, one unworthy to be called a woman.

miscreance. False belief; misbelief. Used from Gower (CONFESSIO AMANTIS, 1390) to Ruskin (FORS CLAVIGERA, 1876). Spenser, for the form *miscreaunce* in THE SHEPHERD'S CALENDAR (1579; MAY) supplies the gloss, 'despair, or misbeliefe.' The form *miscreant,* as a noun, heretic, unbeliever, still appears as an imprecation in historical novels—probably after Shakespeare, who in RICHARD II (1593) exclaims: *Thou art a traitor, and a miscreant!*

miscreate. Ill-shaped, abortive, misformed. Also *miscreated.* Spenser in THE FAËRIE QUEENE (1590) says: *For nothing might abash the villein bold Ne mortall steele emperce his miscreated mould.* Henley in THE SPECTATOR (No. 396, 1712) wrote of *that mongrel miscreated (to speak in Miltonic) kind of wit, vulgarly termed the pun.* Shakespeare (HENRY V; 1599), Browning (THE RING AND THE BOOK; 1868), and Swinburne (SONGS BEFORE SUNRISE; 1871) use *miscreate*; Swinburne: *Fancies and passions miscreate By man in things dispassionate.* But also *to miscreate,* to create amiss, used since the 17th century; Meredith in THE TRAGIC COMEDIANS (1880) has: *The thick-featured sodden satyr of her miscreating fancy.*

miso-. A combining form (also *mis-*) from Greek *misos,* hatred; *misein,* to hate. The opposite of *phil-, q.v.* Among the forgotten forms with this prefix (less numerous than those of love) are: *misobasilist,* a hater of kings. *misocapnist,* a hater of smoking. *misogrammatist,* a hater of learning; also *misomusist. misopede, misopaedist,* a child-hater. *misopogonist,* a hater of beards. *misosophist* (accent on the second syllable), a hater of wisdom; also *misosophy. misoxeny,* hatred of strangers. Also *misology,* hatred of reason, of learning; *misologist. misoneism* (accent on the *nee*), hatred of what is new, of novelty; *misoneist; misoneistic.*

misproud. Arrogant; proud without basis for pride. Robert Manning of Brunne in HANDLYNG SYNNE (1303) said: *Gyf thou for strenkthe be mysproute And hast bostful wordys and loude . . .* Shakespeare in HENRY VI, PART THREE (1593) has: *Impairing Henry, strength'ning misproud Yorke.* After the 17th century, Scott took up the word in THE LADY OF THE LAKE (1810): *Thy misproud ambitious clan.*

missel. An old form (8th to 16th century) of *mistletoe.* Note that the proper Christmas use of the *mistletoe* requires that, each time a girl is kissed under it, a berry be plucked from the mistletoe sprig, and when there are no more berries the kissing privilege is over.

mistake. To misjudge, misunderstand. This sense is current; *mistaken,* however, has taken a curious course. Some words (*cp. avaunt*) have two meanings that are antonyms; others have a forgotten meaning (see *prevent*) that is the opposite of the present one. Such a word is *mistaken.* Since to *mistake* meant to misunderstand, *I am mistaken* meant I am misunderstood. Thus Ascham in THE SCHOLEMASTER (1568) observed that *Erasmus is mistaken of many, to the great hurt of studie.* This sense survives in the phrase *mistaken identity.* By the mid-16th century, however, the error was transferred from object to subject, and *mistaken* began to mean not misunderstood but misunderstanding. Thus Shakespeare in TWELFTH NIGHT (1601) says: *And she (mistaken) seemes to dote on me. I am mistaken* now means I am in error, I made a mistake. A similar shift has occurred with the participle *surprised.* The verb *to surprise* may still mean to catch in the act, but *surprised* currently means not caught but astonished. It was in the early 19th century that the lexicographer—when his wife caught him kissing the maid-servant and exclaimed "Why, Husband, I am surprised!"—drew himself up and said: "No, Madame. You are astonished; I am surprised." That, of course, cleared up the situation.

mistihede. Obscurity; mystery; mystical significance. Chaucer in THE COMPLEYNT OF MARS (1374) asks: *What meneth this? what is this mistihede?*

mithe. To conceal; to dissemble; to lie concealed, escape notice. A common word, 8th through the 13th century. Thus CURSOR MUNDI (1300) rules: *Qhen yee fast, then shall yee show gladnes with your sembland blith, and so your fasting shall yee myth.*

mithridate. An antidote to poison; a universal medicine or preservative. Named after *Mithridates VI,* King of Pontus, who sought to make himself immune to poison by constantly taking antidotes. Also *mithridaticon, mithridatium, mithridatum; mithrydate, metridate, medridate,* and the like. A host of 16th and 17th century prescriptions call for *mithridate,* as in S. Kellwaye's DEFENSE AGAINST THE PLAGUE in 1593: *Take a great onyon, make a hole in the middle of him, then fill the place with mitridat or triacle, and some leaves of rue . . .* D'Urfey in THE COMMONWEALTH OF WOMEN (1686), scorns the notion: *Fools may talk of mythridate, cordials, elixers.* D'Urfey puts the accent on the myth. The word was often extended to refer to any preservative, as by Lyly in MIDAS (1592): *That which maketh me most both to sorrow and to wonder, is that music (a methridat for melancholy) should make him mad.* Lodge in PHILLIS (1593) cried: *Oh pleasing thoughts, apprentises of love, Forerunners of desire, sweet methridates The poison of my sorrowes to remove, With whom my hopes and feare full oft debates.* Hence, *mithridatic,* immune (like Mithridates); Helps in REALMAH (1868) said: *Poison has no more effect on my mithridatic constitution than ginger-beer.* Mithridates, defeated by Pompey, committed suicide in 63 B.C.

mitten. See *mittent.*

mittent. Sending. Latin *mittentem,* present participle of *mittere, missum,* to send, whence also *missive, missile, mission, intermittent. Mittent* was used in the 17th century; particularly, in the physiology of the four humours (see *humour*), of the body part (*part mittent*) that *sent vicious humours to the part recipient.* There is no connection with *mitten* (though the words fit to a *t*); note that in the 18th century, a *mitten* was a glove that covered the arm but not the fingers.

mixen. See *midden.* In the same sense we also find (16th to 19th century) *mixhill, maxhill, maxul.*

mo. An early form of more. Also *ma, moo, moe.* Gascoigne in his POSIES (1575) caught the old proverb *the mo the merrier.*

moanworthy. Worthy of lament, pitiful, as *her moanworthy story.* The word was used (once) in the 16th century.

mob. This word, used for a tumultuous crowd, is short for Latin *mobile,* easily moved, fickle. This was used in the phrase *mobile vulgus,* the fickle crowd, the excitable common people. In this sense, *mobile* (three syllables) has also become an English word; Lord Chief Justice Jeffries, in his Charge given at the City of Bristol, 21 September, 1685, exclaimed: *Up starts a poppet prince, who seduces the mobile into rebellion!* (*Cp. poppet.*) D. Defoe in THE TRUE-BORN ENGLISHMAN (1701) says *He grants a Jubilee, And hires huzzas from his own Mobilee.* From the 17th century there have been a verb and a noun *mob* (also *mab*). The verb meant to muffle up the head; hence, to go in disguise, hence to frequent low company; also, to dress untidily. Gay, in an ECLOGUE of 1720 speaks of a woman at the theatre: *in the gallery mob'd, she sits secure*; Defoe in 1727 speaks of those that *go amobbing*. As a noun, *mob* meant (1) a strumpet. R. Head has, in THE ENGLISH ROGUE (1665): *We kist and parted; I sighed, she did sob; she for her lusty lad, I for my mob.* (2) négligé attire, a *mob-dress*; Swift in the JOURNAL TO STELLA (1710) speaks of *ladies all in mobs undrest.* (3) a *mob-cap,* a cap worn indoors by women in the 18th and 19th centuries; Dickens in DAVID COPPERFIELD describes one "with side-pieces fastening under the chin." Moore in his MEMOIRS (1828) says of a woman, after the fashion for *mob-caps* had faded: *Her beauty was gone; her dress was even prematurely old and mob-cappish.* In the 18th century, a *mobbed-head* was a harlot; also, by way of a play upon the idea of a night-cap, a *mob* was fashionable slang (as in the plays) for a drink. Note, however, that *mobbie, mobee* is from the Carib *mabi,* meaning a West Indian fermented drink made of sweet potatoes, with ginger and snake-root; also applied to peach and apple brandy.

moble. This is a variant of *mob, q.v.* As an adjective *moble* was an early form of *mobile.* As a noun, *mobles,* movable goods, personal property. As a verb, to muffle; also *mobble.* Shakespeare in HAMLET (1603) inquires: *Who had seen the mobled queene?* [This is not to be interpreted as *mob-led,* led by the *mob.*] Ogilby in AESOP (1668) spoke of being *mobbled nine days in my considering-cap.* How many today will spend nine minutes thus?

mochell. A variant of *mickle, q.v.* Spenser used the form *mochell* in THE SHEPHERD'S CALENDAR (1579; FEBRUARY).

moff. See *moph.*

moidore. This word, which rolls on pirate tongues in many a rousing tale, names a gold Portuguese coin; Portuguese *moeda d'ouro,* money of gold. Also *moedore, moydor, moider.* Accepted in England in the early 18th century, at an evaluation of about 27 shillings, the coin gave its name to such a sum, as a general term. Thus Leslie Stephen, in HOURS IN A LIBRARY (1874) speaks of *tangible subjects which he can weigh and measure and reduce to moidores and pistoles.* Many a desperado has committed murders for moidores.

moiety. A half, a half-portion. Hence, jestingly, in the 18th and 19th centuries (Charles Lamb, 1829), one's better half. Also *mediety*; *moiety* is via Old French from Latin *medietatem,* middle point; *medium,* middle. By extension, one of two parts; one's share; a small portion or amount. Shakespeare uses the word in HENRY IV, PART ONE, HAMLET, KING LEAR, SONNET 46, and the dedication to THE RAPE OF LUCRECE (1593): *The love I dedicate to your Lordship is without end: wherof this pamphlet without beginning is but a superfluous moity.*

molestious. Troublesome, molesting. Also (all in the 16th century) *molestous, molestuous.*

moliminous. Laborious, marked by great effort. Latin *molimen,* effort; *moliri,* to strive, to exert oneself. In medicine, *molimen* (plural *molimina*) is used of the effort the human system makes to perform a natural function. *Molition,* an effort;

also, a device or contrivance by which something is done.

moll. This is a shortening of *Molly,* a pet-name for *Mary.* Since the 17th century, it has been used to mean a prostitute, or especially, the unmarried female companion of a vagrant or thief. This sense survives in the phrase *gangster's moll.* It probably was first applied from *Moll Cutpurse,* nickname of a notorious wench of the 17th century, made a character in several plays (e.g., Middleton and Dekker's THE ROARING GIRL, 1611). *Moll Thompson's mark* was a slang phrase of the 18th century; *Take away this bottle, it has Moll Thompson's mark on it: Moll Thompson's mark,* her initials, MT, empty. (Thus, the seven letters one speaks on pouring the last drops from a bottle: OICURMT.) In the same years, *Moll Blood* meant the gallows; Scott in THE HEART OF MIDLOTHIAN (1818) has: *Three words of your mouth would give the girl the chance to nick Moll Blood.*

mollescent. See *mulcible.*

molliate. To make soft, smooth, or easy. Latin *mollire,* to soften. Also *molliable, mollifiable,* that can be softened or soothed. *mollicine, mollicinous,* softening; in Latin used of *mollicinum emplastrum,* soothing plaster. *mollifaction, mollification;* nouns of action surviving in the verb, *to mollify. mollificative,* something that soothes or softens; also, as an adjective, that causes softening or soothing. These are mainly 17th and 18th century terms.

mollitious. See *mulcible.*

moly. A magic herb, given by Hermes to Odysseus (in Homer's ODYSSEY) to preserve him from the enchantments of Circe. Bailey, 1751, calls it "a sort of wild garlick"; it has been identified with other flowers. It was described as having a white flower and a black root, a fact played upon by later writers, as Lyly in EUPHUES (1580). Tennyson uses the word literally when he pictures his Lotos-Eaters *propped on beds of amaranth and moly.* (See *amarant.*) Lodge uses it figuratively in PHILLIS (1593): *He had love's moly growing on my pappes, To charm a hell of sorrow and mishappes.*

molybdomancy. See *aeromancy.*

mommet. See *maumet.*

monamy. A dish. From French *mon ami,* my friend. A 15th century recipe: *Take thick creme of cow mylke, and boyle hit over the fire, and then take hit up and set hit on the side; and thane take swete cowe cruddes and press out the qway* [curds . . . whey], *and bray hom in a morter, and cast hom into the same creme, and boyle al togedur; and put thereto sugre, and saffron, and May buttur; and take yolkes of ayren strayned, and beten, and in the settynge downe of the pot bete in the yolkes thereto, and stere hit wel, and make the potage stondynge* [standing by itself: let it harden]; *and dress fyve or seaven leches in a dissh, and plaunt with floures of violet, and serve hit forthe.*

monchelet. A dish. (The form *monche* is an early variant of *munch,* but this dish is more inviting.) A recipe is in THE FORME OF CURY (1390): *Take veel other moton, and smite it to gobettes. Seeth it in gode broth. Cast thereto herbes yhew, gode wyne, and a quantitie of oynouns mynced, powdor fort, and safroun; and alye it with ayren and verjous; but lat not seeth after.*

monestar. An old form for *monastery.* Also *monester.*

monetary. See *comminate.*

mongcorn. A mixture of two kinds of grain (usually wheat and rye) sown together. It made an excellent bread, the usual type in religious houses before their suppression in England; hence also *monkcorn.* The word is from *mong,* a mingling + *corn. Mong,* a mingling; hence also intercourse, then commerce, was common from the 12th to the 15th century, and survived in dialect into the 19th. It was also applied to mixtures of various kinds of meal, such as ground *mongcorn.* The verb *mong* (9th to 16th century) meant to traffic (with), to barter. From the same source comes the common word *among,* mixed with, often shortened to *mong.* In 19th century England, *a muncorn team* meant a team of horses and oxen mixed.

monger. A trafficker, a dealer. From *mong,* to traffic; see *mongcorn.* The *g* is hard, as in *Mongol.* From the 16th century (both alone and in compounds) *monger* has implied a petty or disreputable traffic. A character in Ford's THE LADIES TRIALL (1639) protests that he is *no monopolist of forged corantos, monger of gazettes.* [See *coranto* (2).] Hence also *monging, mongering, mongery.* Among terms of scorn compounded with this form are *fashion-monger, mass-monger, news-monger, pardon-monger, salvation-monger, scandal-monger, whoremonger, word-monger.*

monitory. See *comminate.*

mono-. A combining form from Greek *monos,* alone, only, one, used in many scientific and technical terms. Also *monodiabolism,* belief in a single devil, or spirit of evil; usually as opposed to the God of good. *monogoneutic* (Greek *goneuein,* to beget), having one brood a year. *monocephalous,* a monster of one head and two bodies, like a fairy-tale ogre. *monochord,* a musical instrument of one string over a sound-board; used in the 11th century to teach the intervals in plain song; there is an obscene implication in Urquhart's translation (1653) of Rabelais: *He would nod his head, monochordizing with his fingers; cp. barytone. monochromic,* having, or showing, only one color. *monocracy,* government by one person, autocracy; *monocrat; monocratic. monocule,* a one-eyed creature, as a cyclops (plural *cyclopes*); also *monoculist, monoculite,* one-eyed person; *monoculus,* one-eyed being. *monodynamism,* the doctrine that all natural activity is the manifestation of a single force, such as Shaw's 'life force' —note that De Quincey, however, (1823), used *monodynamic* to mean having only one talent: *monodynamic men. monoglot,* speaking only one language, written in one language; a person that knows but one language. *monogyny,* the practice of marrying only one wife (at a time); a woman might similarly practice *monandry. monology,* the monopolizing of the conversation. *monomachy,* single combat, accent on the *om;* also *monomachist. monohemerous,* lasting but a day, accent on the *he; monemerous. mononeirist,* a person that has never dreamed but once, or that cherishes a single dream; Walpole says that Locke was a *mononeirist. monongahela* (only spelling puts this here; it is an Indian name, of a river in Pennsylvania, where there were many 'moonshine' stills; hence), American rye whiskey; Dicey in SIX MONTHS IN THE FEDERAL STATES (1863) wrote: *Where the cigar-case was always ready, and the flask of monongahela was always full. monophagous,* eating one sort of food only; Ruth Draper has a sketch of four ladies at luncheon, on four monophagous diets; *monophagy,* the eating of one sort of food only, also, eating alone. *monopode,* a man (fabled by Pliny, mentioned by Lowell) having but one foot, yet under which umbrella-like he might shade himself from the sun, also called a *sciapod* (Greek *skia,* shadow), plural *sciapodes,* four syllables, accent on the *ap*; these sciapodous folk lived—so they say—in Lybia. *monopoler, monopolian, monopole,* early forms for *monopolist*; also *monopolite. monopolylogue,* an entertainment in which one performer represents various characters; great artists in the field, *monopolylogists* supreme (accent on the *lill*) are Ruth Draper and Cornelia Otis Skinner; Hood puns on the word in TO A LADY ON HER DEPARTURE FOR INDIA (1845) : *Go where with human notes the parrot dealeth In mono-polly-logue. monorchis,* a person with but one testicle; the adjective is *monorchid* (the flower is named from the shape of its tuber). *monota,* a one-handled jar; especially, an ancient Greek vase with one handle. *monotome,* bound or included in one volume, as a *monotome edition* of Shakespeare; *monotomous,* let us hope not monotonous. *monotroch,* a vehicle with one wheel; Scott (1828) applied the word humorously to a wheelbarrow (Greek *trochos,* wheel). *monoxylon,* a canoe or other craft hewn from one piece of timber (Greek *chylon,* wood); the adjective is *monoxylous,* as in reference (19th century) to *the monoxylous artificers of Britain's prehistoric times.*

monoepic. See *poly* (*polyepic*).

monongahela. See *mono-.*

montance. See *mountance.*

monthly. Madly; as influenced by the moon. An English development like *lunatic*; Latin *luna,* the moon. Also *moonling,* a fool. (Jonson, THE DEVIL IS AN ASS; 1616). Middleton and Dekker in THE ROARING GIRL (1611) declare: *The man talks monthly . . . I see hee'l be starke mad at our next meeting.*

monticulous. With little projections or hills. Latin *montem,* mountain. In 17th and 18th century dictionaries. In the 19th century *monticulose,* covered with little elevations; also *montiform,* shaped like a mountain.

montigenous. Born on the hills, born amid mountains. So in Bailey (1751). From Latin *montem,* mountain + *gignere, genitus,* to beget. (The root *gen* has given us many English words, from *genus* and *genital* to *generous* and *generalissimo.*)

montjoy. A commemorative cairn. From the French *mont,* hill + *joie,* joy. A heap of stones piled by travelers, often with a cross atop, to mark the spot where one of them, dying en route, lies buried. Urquhart, in his translation (1653) of Rabelais, gives it another application: *Finally they found a montjoy or heap of ordure and filth*—the more common memento of travelers.

mooch. This verb has moved through various meanings; it is related to *miche, q.v.,* and to *munch.* Also, with the same pronunciation, *mouch*; but other sounds came with other forms: *mowche, moache, modge,* and the like. There was also a frequent noun, *moocher, moucher.* The main meanings of the verb were: (1) to pretend to be poor, so as to beg, or to escape borrowers. (2) to play truant (from the 17th century); in the 19th century, to play truant in order to pick blackberries; hence, to go picking. (3) to loaf, loiter. Jerome K. Jerome in THREE MEN IN A BOAT (1889) said: *All the inhabitants . . . come out and mouch round the lock with their dogs, and flirt, and smoke.* (4) to pilfer. (5) to sponge, to permit others to pay for the party. This sense is current slang. (6) In this sense usually *mouch* (French *mouche,* mouth): to eat greedily, gobble up. In Dekker and Webster's SIR THOMAS WYAT (1607), the clown exclaims: *O poore shrimpe, how art thou falne away for want of mouching!*

moonling. A simpleton. In Jonson's THE DEVIL IS AN ASS (1616): *I have a husband . . . But such a moonling, as no wit of man Or roses can redeeme from being an asse.* In spite of this scorn, *moonling* is a soft word for a witless one. Note that a *moon-man* (Shakespeare, HENRY IV, PART ONE, 1597) is one that works by night; especially, a nightpad, robber.

moot. A meeting, encounter. Hence, an assembly, especially one that forms a legislative or judicial court. In Anglo-Saxon and early English days there were the *gemot, witenagemot, burg-mote, hall-mote, hundred-mote,* and more. Hence *moot,* an action at law, a plea; an argument, disputation. At Gray's Inn (and the English Inns of Court since the 16th century), the discussion of a hypothetical case, by students, for practice; a case for such discussion. Hence, as an adjective, *a moot case, a moot problem,* debatable, doubtful, not decided. This was a very common word from the 9th to the 17th century; related to *meet.* The verb *to moot* meant to converse, then to argue, especially, to argue a doubtful case, or an imaginary case for practice. A *mooter* was a speaker, especially one who argued in court or in a *moot hall* in the Inns of Court. Earlier, a *moot hall* was a place where the *moot* (council of court) meetings were held; also in the *moot-house* or on the *moot-hill, mote hill.* The *moot* cases and *mooters* were often satirized; thus Skelton in COLYN CLOUTE (1529): *Stand sure, and take good fotyng, And let be all your motyng, Your gasyng and your totyng;* and James Gilcrist in THE INTELLECTUAL PATRIMONY (1817): *Probably neither the one nor the other understands what he is writing about more than a big school-boy or mooting babbler.*

moph. A 19th century name for an instrument consisting of a pair of compasses, one leg of which is made like the leg of a pair of calipers. From this 'cross-breed' structure it was given the name of *hermaphrodite,* shortened to *mophrodite,* then to *moph* or *moff.*

mora. See *mication.* We still play the game, though we've forgotten the name.

morcellate. To break (something) into small portions. Via French *morcel, morceau,* whence English *morsel;* Latin *mordere, morsum,* to bite, to break into fragments; *cp. mordacity. Morcellement,* division into small portions; used especially of land. THE PALL MALL GAZETTE of 3 July, 1889 (prior to any Soviet action) noted: *In the South peasant proprietors own most of the land, and the morcellement is in many cases excessive.* From the 18th century, *morceau* was used in English to mean a short piece, a musical or literary composition. Williams ('Anthony Pasquin') in THE CHILDREN OF THESPIS (1788) wrote: *She purloined the stool on which Kemble had writ The choicest morceaus of his Jesuit wit.*

mordacity. Propensity to biting; a biting or stinging quality, physically or in speech; mordancy. *Mordant* is directly from the present participle of French *mordre,* to bite; Latin *mordere; mordacem,* biting; *cp. mordicancy.* Hence also *mordacious,* biting, prone to bite. Barrow in a Sermon of 1677 said: *He hath little of the Serpent (none of its rancorous venom, of its keen mordacity).*

mordell. The share of her late husband's property to which a widow was entitled (16th century), as representing her 'morning gift.' Possibly influenced by Latin *mors, mortis,* death, but contracted from *morgen,* morn, morrow + *dael,* deal. This is related to Medieval Latin *matrimonium ad morganaticam,* marriage with morning-gift. See *moryeve.* A *morganatic marriage* (as between a man of high rank and a woman of lower) is one in which she and her issue have no claim to succeed to the possessions or dignities of the father, being entitled only to the customary "morning gift" on the day after the wedding-night. In the morganatic marriage, the man takes the woman with his left hand. She was not a concubine, but a wife. Sometimes it was the woman who had the higher rank, in a morganatic marriage; sometimes (especially in Germany), although the woman was not raised to her husband's rank, the children were allowed rights of succession. In all such cases, if the man died first, his widow received the mordell.

mordicancy. The quality of being biting or pungent. Also *mordicant, mordicative, mordificative,* biting, pungent; Latin *mordicare, mordicatum,* from *mordere, morsum,* to bite, whence *morsel* (a goodly bite) and *mordacity, q.v.* In the 17th century, *mordicate,* to sting, strike with a biting pain. For a use of *mordicancy,* see *fig.*

morena. A brunette. The word is probably related to *More, Moor.* A dark cloth was called *morella,* a dark, bitter cherry, *morello,* in the 17th century. Pepys in his DIARY of 18 December, 1661, says that he went *To church, where . . . I spent most of my time looking on my new morena.*

morganatic. See *mordell.* In some recent instances, rather than face the problems of morganatic marriage, men have relinquished their own dignities and rights of succession.

morgenstern. A club the head of which is studded with spikes. The word has been used since the 17th century. The weapon was sometimes called a *morning star,* which is a literal translation of (German) *Morgenstern.* Conan Doyle, in MICAH CLARKE (1889) speaks of *pike or half-pike, morgenstiern, and halbert.*

morglay. A sword. Originally, the name of the sword of Sir Bevis, one of King Arthur's knights. From the Gaelic; Welsh *mawr,* great + *cleddyf,* sword. Reversing the order of these words gives us *claymore,* the two-edged broadsword of the ancient Scottish highlanders. This word has been common in historical accounts, poems, and novels (Johnson, Boswell, Burns, Campbell, Scott) since the mid-18th century. Stanyhurst in his translation (1582) of the AENEIS, said: *And bootless morglay to his sydes he belted unhable.*

moria. Folly. Greek *moria; moros,* foolish. Used in the 17th century; in the 19th it was used, in medicine, for a monomania the victim of which believed himself to be brilliant and distinguished. In 1510 Erasmus wrote his PRAISE OF FOLLY, with the punning Latin title, ENCOMIUM MORIAE, while a guest of Sir Thomas More. [More himself in 1516 used the punning title UTOPIA, the beautiful (*eu-*) place (*topos*) that is no (*ou-*) place.] Hence also *morology* (*q.v.*), foolish talk; *morologist,* one that talks foolishly; a student of foolish talk. A *morosoph, morosophist* (Greek *sophos,* wise) is a foolish pretender to wisdom; a foolish pedant (the word occurs in Urquhart's translation, 1693, of Rabelais); reverse the situation for the quite current *sophomore.* Hence also *morosophy, morosophistry.* R. Carew in translating (1607) Estienne's WORLD OF WONDERS said that the old preaching developed a sermon so as *to make one part allegorical, another anagogical, and a third tropological: whereas they should have made one part morological, another mythological, and a third pseudological.*

morient. Dying. Latin *morientem,* dying; *mori,* to die. Used in the 17th century. Somewhat more common is *moribund,* at the point of death or extinction. Also, a person about to die. Hence, *moribundity.* Carlyle in THE FRENCH REVOLUTION (1837) bade us take heed of *the wail of a moribund world;* it seems to some louder now. The greeting of the gladiators to the Roman Emperor, when they entered the arena: *Morituri te salutamus,* We who are about to die salute thee.

morigerous. Obedient, submissive. Latin *mos* (plural *mores*), custom + *gerere,* to carry; the phrase *morem gerere* meant to comply with a person's wishes. In the play TIMON (1600) we hear: *Timon, thou hast a wife morigerous; She is the only comfort of my age.* Also *morigerate,* obedient; *morigeration,* obedience, deference, obsequiousness. Hence the negative form (used in the 17th and 18th centuries) *immorigerous,* disobedient, obstinate, rebellious; uncivil, rude. *Immorigerousness,* rebellious obstinacy; Jeremy Taylor (1649) declared that *All degrees of delay are degrees of immorigerousnesse.*

morion. A helmet, worn without visor, in the 16th and 17th centuries. Also *murren, morioune, murrian, moriam, murreowne,* and the like; possibly from Spanish *morra,* crown of the head. For an instance of its use, see *stour.*

morology. Foolish discourse; humorously, the science that deals with fools. Hence also *morologist, morological;* Greek *moros,* foolish; *cp. moria. Moron* is the name of the fool in Moliere's LA PRINCESSE D'ELIDE (1664); *moron* was adopted as a classification, in 1910, by the American Association for the Study of the Feeble-Minded; the O.E.D. captures this in its Supplement, the main volume listing *moron,* a variety of salamander. J. Melville's DIARY (1596) warns against *corrupt communication, morologie, aeschrologie.*

moromancy. See *aeromancy.*

morris. (1) A morris dance, or a group of morris dancers. The word is from Moorish, but the dance (16th and 17th centuries) was a native form. Persons in costume—usually of the Robin Hood stories, Maid Marian, Friar Tuck, and more—engaged in grotesque and fantastic movements, sometimes dancing from town to town. Southey in WAT TYLER (1817) has: *Since we were boys together, and played at barley-brake, and danced the morris.* Latimer in a Sermon of 1552 said: *Such fellows are more meet to daunce the morrice daunce, than to be admitted to preache.* Hence also *morris-bell, morris-feast, morris-mate. Cp. fading.* (2) A variant form of *merels;* see *merel.* Shakespeare in A MIDSUMMER NIGHT'S DREAM (1590) avers: *The nine mens morris is filled up with mud.*

mort. There are a half dozen words with this form, all but the first of unknown origin. (1) Death; especially, the kill, of a hunted animal. Also, as in *to blow a mort,* the note on a horn at the death of the deer (Scott, Browning). This was a common word since the 13th century (Latin *mors, mortem,* death, *morior, mortuum,* to die); later it was occasionally used to mean a corpse. (2) A wax candle, or a set of wax candles. 14th through 16th century. (3) A 3-year-old salmon. Since the 16th century. (4) Lard, pig's grease. Since the 17th century, probably of Celtic origin. (5) A great deal, a large quantity. Used by Sheridan in THE RIVALS (1775) and Dickens in DAVID COPPERFIELD (1850); for a quotation, see *hody-moke.* (6) A girl or woman; especially, among 17th and 18th century playwrights, a loose woman. Also *mot, mott.* Motteux, in his translation (1708) of Rabelais, speaks of *Those whom Venus is said to rule, as . . . morts, doxies.* Rogueries of the 16th and 17th centuries list several varieties of *mort*: the *walking mort* was a vagabond wench; the *kinching mort* (German *Kindchen,* little child) was a teen-ager, already old in sin, or a babe carried by a beggar to win sympathy and alms; *cp. pedlers French.*

mortifer. A bringer of death. Latin *mortem,* death + *ferre,* to bear, bring. Hence *mortiferous, mortific,* death-dealing, death-producing. Used from the 16th into the 19th century (*mortifer* only once, in the 17th). *Whenever you sin,* counselled S. R. Maitland in THE DARK AGES (1844), *do not wait in mortiferous security until your wounds putrefy.*

mortress. A dish. Mentioned by Langland (1377), Chaucer (1386) and Bacon (1626), it has won admittance to the O.E.D., which is not overhospitable to good old English cooking. Also *mortrel, morterel; mortreux, mortrews, mortesse,* and more. It seems to have been popular. A recipe is given in THE FORME OF CURY (1390): Mortrews. *Take hennes and pork, and seeth hem togydre. Take the lyvre of hennes and of the pork, and hewe it smalle, and grinde it alle to doust. Take brede ygrated, and do thereto, and temper it with the self broth, and alye it with yolkes of ayren, and cast thereon powder fort; boile it, and do therein powder of gynger, sugar, safroun, and salt, and loke that it be standing* [hardened], *and floer it with powdor of gynger.* A cookery-book of 1430 lists *mortrewes of fysshe . . . caste therto sugre and salt, and serve it forth as other mortrewys.*

moryeve. Morning-gift (Scotch, *morwyngift;* 16th century). See *mordell. Moryeve* has purely a sentimental association with *eve,* being from Old English *moryen, morgen,* morrow + *yifu, gifu,* gift—the gift made to the wife on the morning after the marriage was consummated. As this gift was sometimes specified in advance, as part of the marriage arrangements, *moryeve* was sometimes used as meaning dowry. *Moryeve* was superseded, about 1400, by *morning-gift.* The practice lingers, as a sign of true love.

mothering. See *simnel.*

motion. A puppet show, or a puppet therefor. Hence, contemptuously, a person. Used by the pamphleteers and playwrights of the 16th and 17th centuries: Nashe, Jonson, Shakespeare (TWO GENTLEMEN OF VERONA; 1591: *Oh excellent motion!*); Swift in the ODE TO SIR WILLIAM TEMPLE (1689) used the figure: *As in a theatre the ignorant fry, Because the cords escape their eye, Wonder to see the motions fly.*—*Motion* as a verb used to mean, to propose, to recommend, to petition; to be tempted.

mouch. See *mooch.*

moul. An earlier form of *mould,* in both senses: to grow mouldy; to form into a shape. Also *muwlen, moule, mowl.* Chaucer uses it in the former sense, in the Prologue to THE MAN OF LAW'S TALE (1386): *Lat us nat moulen thus in idelnesse.* In a poem of 1789 D. Sillar urges spending your "siller" while it's fresh: *Your pickle cash Will ly an moul, like ither useless trash.*

mountance. Amount, value. Old French *montance; monter,* to rise. Chaucer has, in THE MANCIPLE'S TALE (1386): *Noght worth to thee in comparison The montance of a gnat.* Sometimes also (from the 14th into the 17th century) *mountenance, mowntenawnce, mountenesse.* Josselyn in AN ACCOUNT OF TWO VOYAGES TO NEW ENGLAND (1674) said: *They satisfy themselves with a small quantity of meal, . . . which taken to the mountenance of a bean would satisfy both thirst and hunger.* Quite a meal!

mournful widow. See *Hymen's torch.*

mournival. A set of four aces, kings, queens, or jacks, held in one hand (in the game of *gleek, q.v.*). Also *mornyfle, mournaval, mournifal, murnival, mournevall.* The term is from French *mornifle,* which originally meant a slap in the face. By extension from its use in the card game, *mournival* came to mean a set of four, a quartet, as *gleek* came to mean a set of three. In Jonson's A STAPLE OF NEWS (1625) are the cry and the answer: *Let a protest goe out against him.—A mournivall of protests; or a gleeke at least!*

mousehunt. A woman-chaser, a "wolf." So Lady Capulet calls her lord—*Aye, you have been a mousehunt in your time*—in ROMEO AND JULIET (1595). Shakespeare refers to a woman as a mouse in LOVE'S LABOUR'S LOST, TWELFTH NIGHT, and HAMLET.

moyle. See *rochet.*

muchwhat. Nearly, almost, "pretty much." Used from the 15th to the 17th century, especially frequent 1625-1705. Collier (MARCUS AURELIUS; 1701) observed that *the world in a dream, and the world out on't, will appear muchwhat the same thing.* Earlier, *muchwhat* was used as a noun, meaning many matters; in GAWAIN AND THE GREEN KNIGHT (14th century), we read: *Thus thay meled* [spoke; see *mell*] *of muchquat til mydmorn paste.*

muckender. A handkerchief; a bib. From the 15th century. Also *mokedore, mucketter, mocketer, muckinger.* Related to French *mouchoir,* handkerchief. A coventry mystery play of 1450 says: *Goo hom, lytyle babe, . . And put a mukador aforn thi brest.* The Earl of Dorset wrote, in a scornful poem TO HOWARD ON HIS PLAYS (1706): *For thy dull fancy a muckinder is fit To wipe the slabberings of thy snotty wit.*

mues. An old form of *mews, q.v.*

mugient. Lowing, bellowing. Latin *mugientem,* present participle of *mugire,* to bellow. A 17th century word; Sir Thomas Browne (1646) uses the noun, *mugiency.*

Mulciberian. Like Vulcan. *Mulciber* was a Roman epithet of Vulcan, the blacksmith, from *mulcere,* to stroke. Thackeray, in THE CURATES' WALK (1847) exclaims: *What powerful Mulciberian fellows they must be, those goldbeaters!*

mulcible. That may be soothed or appeased. Latin *mulcere,* to stroke, to soothe. Whence also *mulcify,* to soothe. Used in the 17th century. *mollify,* to render soft or tender, has been used since the 15th century. It is from Latin *mollis,* soft, whence also the less common *mollition,* softening; *mollity,* gentleness; *mollescent,* growing soft, mild; softening. *mollitude,* softness, effeminacy, hence wantonness. *mollitious,* effeminate, luxurious, sensuous; Browning in SORDELLO (1840) speaks of *mollitious alcoves gilt Superb as By-*

zant-domes the devils built. By such things, as R. Sanders said in 1653, our earthly *sorrows are somewhat mulcified.*

mulier. Legitimate (used of a child). Latin *mulier,* woman, was used in English in the CURSOR MUNDI (1375) to mean wife: *Isaac his son of mulier was.* In the 16th and 17th century, there was frequent opposition, in wills and other documents, of *bastard ainé* (eldest) and *mulier puisné* (youngest). Hence *mulierly,* legitimately, *muliery,* legitimate offspring, *mulierty,* legitimacy. In the original Latin sense of the word, we had English *muliebral,* pertaining to women; *muliebrious,* effeminate; *muliebriousness,* effeminacy; *muliebrity,* womanliness, womanhood. Hence *mulierous, mulierose* (four syllables, accent on the *mu*), fond of women; Reade in THE CLOISTER AND THE HEARTH (1860) asks: *Prithee tell me; how did you ever detect the noodle's mulierosity?*

mulligrubs. A state of depression or low spirits. *In his mulligrubs; sick of the mulligrubs,* sometimes used of the stomachache. The word seems to have been a grotesque invention, but some spellings try to shape it toward meaningful forms: *mouldygrubs, male-grubbles, mulligrumphs,* and the like. The word was used by Nashe (1599), Fletcher (1619), and Dryden (1678); Scott in his JOURNAL for 19 September, 1827, said: *Surely these mulligrubs belong to the mind more than the body.* Medical opinion tends, a century later, to strike a middle way.

mulse. A liquor of honey mixed with water or wine; boiled together, says Bailey (1751). Latin *mulcere, mulsum,* to sweeten. A 16th and 17th century word; see *mead.* In the same centuries a similar drink was called *melicrat, melicrate,* from Greek *meli,* honey + *kra-,* to mix. Such drinks were very popular in ancient times, and for several centuries in England, often being used to offset the bitterness of medicines.

mumblecrust. A toothless person; a beggar. Used as a name or nickname in plays, as Madge Mumblecrust in Udall's RALPH ROYSTER DOYSTER (1553).

mumble-news. A tale-bearer (in contempt). Shakespeare in LOVE'S LABOUR'S LOST (1588) has: *Some carry-tale . . . Some mumble-newes . . . Told our intents before.*

mumbudget. Silence! Mum! A command to keep still. Perhaps originally the name for a children's game that called for silence, as in the crossing signals of Shakespeare's THE MERRY WIVES OF WINDSOR (1598): *We have a nayword, how to know one another. I come to her in white, and cry Mum; she cries Budget, and by that we know one another.* Butler in HUDIBRAS (1663) shows the full use: *Have these bones rattled, and this head So often in thy quarrel bled? Nor did I ever winch or grudge it, For thy dear sake.* (*Quoth she:*) *Mumbudget.*

mumchance. (1) A kind of game at dice. (2) A masquerade. In the DIURNAL OF REMARKABLE OCCURRENTS THAT HAVE PASSED WITHIN THE COUNTRY OF SCOTLAND . . . 1575, we read: *At evin* [evening] *our soveranis maid the maskrie and mumschance, in the quhilk the Quenis grace, and all hir Maries and ladies were all cled in men's apperrell.* As the masquerade was often a mumming (silent pantomime) *to play mumchance* came to mean to preserve silence. Hence, as a verb, to masquerade; to be silent; as a noun (3) silence, a silent person; as an adjective, silent, doggedly silent. Flatman in HERACLITUS RIDENS (1681): *Conscience, that* *was so clamorous before, is mumchance, and says nothing to the matter.*

mumpsimus. An old fogey; an obstinate adherent to old and erroneous ways; also, an old notion or tradition pigheadedly retained after it has been proved untenable. The term became popular in the 16th century after the story in Pace's DE FRUCTU (1517) of an illiterate priest who always said *quod in ore mumpsimus* ('which we now take into our mouth') in the Mass, and when corrected said: "I will not change my old *mumpsimus* for your new *sumpsimus.*" The priest perhaps knew the Old English word *to mump,* to munch; to move the jaws as though chewing; also, to mumble, mutter; to grimace with the lips. The Water-Poet Taylor in URANIA (1615) spoke of a man with *Not a tooth left to mumpe on beanes and pease.* A *mump* was a 'mouth' (as made when sounding the word *mump*), a grimace. In THE LADY MOTHER (1635; Bullen's OLD PLAYS) we are told: *Gallants now court their mistress with mumps and mows as apes and monkes do.* Gascoigne in THE SUPPOSES (1575) exclaims: *If this olde mumpsimus . . . should win her, then may I say . . . farewel the sight of my Polynesta.* Old mumpsimus would put aside young sumpsimus indeed!

mundicide. See *stillicide.* Hence also *mundicidious,* as when Nathaniel Ward in THE SIMPLE COBLER OF AGGAWAM (1647) roundly declared: *A vacuum and an exorbitancy are mundicidious evils.* Ward had not heard of the H bomb.

mundify. To cleanse, purify; to make oneself spruce. Latin *mundus,* clean. Used from the 16th century; Richardson in CLARISSA HARLOWE (1748) has: *mundified . . . from my past iniquities.* Hence also *mundifier, mundificant, mundification, mundificative.* A COUNTRY GENTLEMAN'S VADE-MECUM of 1699 recommends a beau new-come to the city *to steer to the next barber's shop, to new rig and mundifie.*

mundungus. Offal, refuse; then particularly, a poor quality of tobacco, foul smelling. The word is a humorous twist from Spanish *mondongo,* tripe—also used in English for a dish of tripe. (*Tripe* has likewise been turned to disparaging uses.) The word was sometimes shortened to *mundung* (17th and 18th centuries), doubtless with a play on the second syllable. Shadwell in THE HUMORISTS (1670) pictures a reveler *with a glass of windy-bottle-ale in one hand, and a pipe of mundungus in the other.*

murenger. An officer (into the 17th century) in charge of keeping the city walls in repair. Also *murager, muringer, maringer, murenger.* Latin *murus,* wall; Medieval English *murager.* [There is a tendency to add an *n* before a *g*; Greek *gg* became *ng* in Latin (*aggelos, angelus; angel*); English *passage* and *message* similarly developed the agent-forms *passenger* and *messenger.*] We read in a MUNICIPAL CORPORATION REPORT of 1506: *The charter of Henry VII provides that the mayor and citizens of Chester may yearly choose . . . two citizens to be overseers of the walls . . . called muragers.*

muricide. See *stillicide.* The word *muriform* (found only in dictionaries) is given as meaning like a mulberry, from French *mûre,* mulberry, or like a mouse, from Latin *mus, murem,* mouse. The word *murine* has been used to mean like a mouse, as when Topsell in THE HISTORY OF FOUR-FOOTED BEASTS (1607) speaks of *the murin wantonnesse of Xenophon.*

murklins. In the dark. *Murk, mirk* (*myrce, merck, mark, myrk*), darkness.

Common from the 10th century; Shakespeare in ALL'S WELL THAT ENDS WELL (1601) says: *Ere twice in murke and occidental dampe Moist Hesperus hath quench'd her sleepy lampe.* Also a verb *murk, murken,* to grow dark; *murk,* to darken, obscure; blacken; also used figuratively, as in a Coventry Mystery play (1450): *With sum myst his wittys to murk. Murk* was also used as an adjective, as well as *murky, murkful, murkish, murksome, mirksome*; Spenser in THE FAËRIE QUEENE (1590): *Through mirksome aire her ready way she makes.*

murlimews. Foolish antics. A coined word, used in the 16th and 17th century, frequently in attacks on the Catholics, as when Hollyband (1593) spoke of the *crossings which the papistical priests do use in their holy water, to make a meadlew muse.* Lyly, if he wrote THE MAIDES METAMORPHOSIS (1600), said: *Good master wizard, leave these murlemewes, and tell Mopso plainly, whether Gemulo . . . shall win the love of the fair shepherdess, or not.*

murrey. (1) Mulberry color; a mulberry-colored cloth. Latin *morum,* mulberry; *cp. muricide.* Such a cloth, from its popularity, then its cheapness, became a term of contempt for a woman, as in Middleton's MICHAELMAS TERME (1602) *I'll take no notice of her—scurvy murrey kersey.* Jonson, in EVERY MAN OUT OF HIS HUMOUR (1599) says: *I had on a gold cable hatband . . . which I wore about a murrey French hat.* (2) A stew of veal, prepared with mulberries. A 15th century dish, before the English lost the art of cooking: *Take molberys, and wryng a gode hepe of them through a cloth; nym vele . . .*

muskin. Johnson, in THE CONNOISSEUR (No. 138; 1756): *Those who . . . call a man a cabbage . . . an odd fish, and an unaccountable muskin, should never come into company without an interpreter.* Johnson himself failed to provide one. In the 16th century, however, *muskin* was used to mean a pretty face; hence, one's darling, sweetheart. It was also (17th century) a variant form of *misken,* a titmouse. (A *titmouse,* in case you've forgotten, is a tiny bird—of several species, including the chickadee—hence itself has been used as a term of endearment. So, by the way, has *cabbage*—in French: *mon chou*—with which Johnson started.)

mutch. In the 15th, 16th, and 17th centuries, a night bonnet; later, a (linen) cap for an infant or an elderly lady. Queen Victoria, in MORE LEAVES (1884) says: *The old mother, Mrs. Brown, in her white mutch, . . and a few neighbours stood round the room. Cp. coif.* Hence, *mutchless,* bare-headed.

mutchkin. A liquid measure, about three-quarters of an imperial pint (15th century) or—what would you expect?—one-fourth of the old Scots pint. In THANES OF CAWDOR (1591) we find: *Item three muskingis aquavitye.* Scott in WAVERLEY (1814) has: *He whistled the 'Bob of Dumblain,' under the influence of half a mutchkin of brandy.*

muticous. Beardless; awnless, lacking an arista. Also *mutic.* [The *awn* is the beard on a head of barley, and other grain or grass. The *arista* is the same; it was earlier *acrista,* from the Latin root *ac,* sharp + *arista,* most, best. *The Arista* is the honorary society of the New York City high schools.] The number of muticous tutors in our leading colleges seems always small. They may be mutic, but they are not mute.

mutton. A loose woman; see *lace.* Shakespeare in MEASURE FOR MEASURE (1604) uses it in this and the literal sense, as Lucio abuses the Duke, accusing him in one phrase of lechery and impiety (eating meat of a Friday): *The Duke, I say to thee again, would eat mutton on Fridays. He's not past it yet, and I say to thee he would mouth with a beggar though she smelt brown bread and garlic.* The word was frequent in 16th and 17th century pamphlets and plays; also *muttonmonger*; and in the 17th century there were *muttontuggers* at Oxford. They are still to be found at universities.

mycterism. A gibe, a sneering comment. Greek *mykterismos*; *mykter,* nose. Used occasionally since the 16th century; listed by Saintsbury, in THE HISTORY OF CRITICISM (1900) among the figures of rhetoric: *sarcasm, asteism . . . mycterism, a kind of derision which is dissembled, but not altogether concealed.*

mylate. A dish. THE FORME OF CURY (1390) gives a recipe for *mylates of pork. Hewe pork al to pecys, and medle it with ayren and chese igrated. Do thereto powder fort, safron, and pyneres, with salt. Make a crust in a trape, bake it wel thereinne, and serve it forth.*

mynekin. Also *mynchen.* See *minchen.*

myomancy. See *aeromancy.* Chambers' CYCLOPEDIA of 1727 remarks: *Some authors hold myomancy to be one of the most ancient kinds of divination; and think it is on this account that Isaiah (lxvi, 17) reckons mice among the abominable things of the idolater.*

myrionymous. Having many names. From Greek *myrios,* countless + *onym-,* name. In earliest religion, there seems to have been a vague, undifferentiated power attributed to all things. Later, each stream, each tree, each thunderclap, each emotion and quality had its specific deity. Gradually various of these attributes and powers were clustered about a single god, so that his potency was judged by the number of his names. Early Egyptian writings speak of Isis the ten-thousand-named, of Isis *myrionyma*; and in the KORAN Allah's majesty and might find expression in his hundred names.

myrtite. Myrtle wine. The drink was used in ancient Greece; the word has been English since 1400. In the 17th century, *myrtite* was advised as an antidote to snake-bite.

myse. Louse. Used (15th century) in reference to the third plague of Egypt in the days of Moses. A York Mystery play (1440) cried: *Lorde, great myses bothe morn and none* [noon] *bytis us full bittirlye.* Hence *mysely,* lousy.

myssemetrynge. A variant form of *mismetering,* spoiling the meter. Hawes in THE PASSE TYME OF PLEASURE (EXCUSACYON OF THE AUCTORE; 1509) said: *Go, lytell boke, I pray god thee save Frome myssemetrynge by wronge impressyon.* (In the early days of printing, the script was read aloud to the typesetter.) The prayer may still stand authors in good stead.

myst. A priest of the mysteries; a magician; one initiated into mysteries. Originally *mystes* (Greek *mystes*; *myein,* to close the lips or eyes; one vowed to keep silence) . *Mystes* was mistaken for a plural; hence the form *myst.* Riveley in his Funeral Sermon (1677) for the Bishop of Norwich said *There are few kinds of literature but he was a mystes in them. Mystery* is of two sources: (1) as above, meaning in ancient Greece a secret religious ceremony. It was usually used in the plural. The most famous *mysteries* were those of Demeter at Eleusis, *the Eleusinian mysteries.* A teacher of candidates for initiation into the *mysteries* was a *mystagogue.* From this word come the religious uses, *the mysteries of the Passion* and the like; also, the meaning, something hidden or secret. (2) Via Medieval Latin *misterium* from Latin *ministerium,* service, occupation; used in this sense in English too, as in Chaucer's THE PARSON'S TALE (1386). Hence handicraft, craft; guild. The phrase *art and mystery,* of cookery, of the trade of woollen draper, etc., was part of the usual indenture of an apprentice. Hence also skill, craftsmanship, as in Shakespeare's ALL'S WELL THAT ENDS WELL (1601): *if you think your mysterie in stratagem can bring this instrument of honour again into his native quarter . . .* Our modern magicians, however, cannot match the olden breed; let them try as they may, they'll none of them be myst.

mythistory. Legend; history mixed with fables and tales. *Mytho-* is a combining form, from Greek *mythos,* myth. Some of the less remembered words in this group are: *mythoclast* (Greek *klastes,* breaker), a destroyer of myths—as *iconoclast* is a destroyer of images or idols (real or figurative); *mythoclastic. mythoplasm,* the creation of myths; also *mythopoeism,* hence *mythopoeic, mythopoetic.* A *mythopoeist* is a maker of myths; a *mythopoet* is a poetic maker of myths.

N

nad. An early form of had not. Also *nadde, nade.* Especially common 1300 to 1450.

naeve. A spot, blemish. Latin *naevus.* Dryden in his ELEGY ON LORD HASTINGS (1649) has: *So many spots, like naeves, our Venus soil; One jewell set off with so many a foil.* Also used figuratively, as by Aubrey (LIVES; 1697) : *He was a tall, handsome, and bold man; but his naeve was that he was damnable proud.* Hence *naevous, naevose,* maculate.

nag. In addition to the old horse—being driven into oblivion by the "tin Lizzie," but once used as a term of abuse for a person, as when Shakespeare in ANTHONY AND CLEOPATRA (1606) cries upon *Yon ribaudred nagge of Egypt—whom leprosy o'ertake!—nag* has the still current meaning, as a verb, to constantly scold, to keep up a dull gnawing pain. The original sense of this word was to gnaw, to strip off bark or covering; its past participle was *nakt,* whence probably *naked.* See *nake. The Water Poet* (WORKS; 1630) extended the equine *nag* to *naggon: My verses are made To ride every jade, But they are forbidden Of jades to be ridden, They shall not be snaffled Nor braved nor baffled; Wert thou George with thy naggon That fought'st with the draggon, Or were you great Pompey My verse should bethump ye, If you, like a javel, Against me dare cavil.*

naiant. Swimming. Also *nayaunt;* via Old French *noiant,* present participle of *noire* from Latin *natare, natatum,* to swim; *cp. natatile.* Used from the 16th century, especially in heraldry.

nait. See *nowt; yate.*

nake. To strip, to lay bare. First used in the 14th century, 500 years after the adjective *naked.* See *nag.* Also *naken,* to strip. One sense of *naker, q.v.,* is one that denudes. It occurs in Chaucer and Douglas; Tourneur in THE REVENGER'S TRAGEDY (1607) cries *Come, be ready; nake your swords!*

naker. A kettle-drum. From Persian *naqara. Naker* meant also (1) one that denudes; *cp. nake.* (2) *nacre.* The drum occurs only in the 14th and 15th centuries, as in Chaucer's THE KNIGHT'S TALE (1386): *pypes, trompes, nakers, and clariounes*—until revived by Scott in IVANHOE (1819): *A flourish of the Norman trumpets . . . mingled with the deep and hollow clang of the nakers.*

nanity. A state of abnormal deficiency. Greek *nanos,* stunted. Hence also *nanism,* the state of being dwarfed. The process of dwarfing trees is *nanization.* All were used in the 19th century. There is no relation with *inanity,* from Latin *inanis,* empty.

napron. The original form of *apron.* By folk usage, *a napron* became *an apron.*

Nape (15th century), *napery, napkin* (via Old French from Latin *mappa,* towel, napkin) preserve the *n.* The opposite transfer occurred (*cp. eche*) when *an eke-name* became *a nickname.* Also see *valanche.*

nar. An early form of *near, nearer.* Used from the 9th century. Also *narre. narrest,* nearest.

nard. An aromatic ointment, of ancient use; also, the plant that yielded it. See *spikenard.* Wyclif's BIBLE (John, xii; 1382) tells that *Marie took a pound of oynement spikenard, or trewe narde, precious.* Poets like the word, from Skelton (1526): *Your wordes be more sweter than ony precyous narde* to Browning (PARACELSUS, 1835): *Heap cassia, sandal-buds and stripes Of labdanum, and aloe-balls, Smeared with dull nard.*

nare. A nostril. Usually in the plural; from the 14th century, but mainly in 17th century verse, as in Jonson's EPIGRAMS (1616) and Butler's HUDIBRAS (1616): *There is a Machiavilian plot, Though every nare olfact it not.*

nas. (1) was not (*ne was*). Chaucer, in BOETHIUS (1374): *I nas not deceived, quod sche* (with a double negative). (2) has not (*ne has*). Spenser, in THE SHEPHERD'S CALENDAR (1579): *For pittied is mishappe that nas remedie.* (3) never was (*ne'er was*). Chaucer, in THE MAN OF LAW'S TALE (1386): *No where so busy a man there nas And yet he seemed busier than he was.*

nat. (1) An early form of *mat.* Used in the 14th, 15th, and 16th centuries, especially of *natts* "for the wyves to knele on when they come to be churched." (2) An early form of *not,* used by Chaucer, Langland, Lydgate, and (1575) in GAMMER GURTON'S NEEDLE: *Nay, but I saw such a wonder as I saw nat these vii yere.*

natatile. Able to swim. Latin *natare,* to swim. *Natability* is the capacity to float. Note that *natalitial, natalitious* mean related to one's birthday, one's *natal* day, from *nasci, natus,* to be born. And that *natal* also means related to the *nates* (Latin), the buttocks.

nath. A contraction of *hath not. nathe,* the nave of a wheel. *nathless, natheless,* nevertheless. (From the 9th into the 19th century.) *nathemore,* nevermore; never the more. *nather,* neither.

natheless. See *nath.*

natomy. See *atomy.*

navigator. A laborer working on a canal or other earthwork (18th century); soon shortened to *navvy.* When Bob, in THE TICKET-OF-LEAVE MAN (1863) wonders who will deliver his warning of the burglary plot, the drunken navigator nearby says that he will. "You?" "I, Hawkshaw, the detective." *See ticket-of-leave.*

nawighte. An old form of *naught.* Also *nawight, nawiht.* But also see *wight, thwite.*

nayless. Accepting no refusal. Sylvester in THE MAIDEN'S BLUSH (1618) said: *Like a naylesse wooer, Holding his cloak, shee puls him hard unto her.*

nayward. In the direction of "nay," tendency to reject. Shakespeare in THE WINTER'S TALE (1611): *Ile be sworne you would beleeve my saying, How ere you leane to th' nayward.*

nayword. (1) Refusal, saying nay. A late use, as in BLACKWOOD'S EDINBURGH MAGAZINE of April 1898: *There will be no hasty nayword from me.* (2) A watchword, a password. Used into the 19th century; apparently first by Shakespeare (twice) in THE MERRY WIVES OF WINDSOR (1598);

see *mumbudget.* Shakespeare also seems to use the word in the sense of a laughing-stock, a byword, as when Maria in TWELFTH NIGHT (1601) says of Malvolio: *If I do not gull him into a nayword, and make him a common recreation, do not think I have wit enough to lie straight in my bed.* Some editions print this as *an ayword;* wherefore THE GENTLEMAN'S MAGAZINE (1777) says that *nayword* meaning a byword *is probably a crasis* [combination] *of an ayeword.*

neaks. See *sneaks.*

neat. See *nowt.* Hence also *neatherd,* a cowherd.

nebulochaotic. Hazily confused. A 19th century word of apt description. Macdonald (MARY MARSTON; 1881) spoke of *the altogether nebulochaotic condition of her mind.* Note also *to nebulate,* to become cloudy or vague. *nebule,* a cloud, a mist, a mental cloud; Blackmore in CRIPPS THE CARRIER (1877) spoke of *nebules of logic, dialectic fogs, and thunderstorms of enthymem.* To *nebulize,* to become or render indefinite. By extension (Sidney in ARCADIA, 1578; also in Latin), a *nebulon,* an idler, a worthless fellow.

necial. Funeral, sepulchral. Latin *necialis; necem,* death.

neckverse. A verse (usually the first verse of the 51ST PSALM, in Latin) the reading of which saved one's neck. By virtue of the Biblical text "Touch not mine anointed, and do my prophets no harm" any person in holy orders brought before a secular court (later, any one that could read—being thus potentially a cleric) could plead privilege of clergy. The Bishop's commissary, always present, pronounced *Legit* (he reads). A branding on the hand might then be inflicted, instead of the common felon's hanging. The 51ST PSALM begins, in English: *Have mercy upon me, O God, according to thy loving-kindness: according unto the multitude of thy tender mercies blot out my transgressions.* Shipley in his GLOSSARY (1872) mentioned the *deputy of the bishop . . . appointed to give malefactors their neck-verses, and judge whether they read or not.* An old song, reprinted in THE BRITISH APOLLO (1710) satirically ran: *If a monk had been taken For stealing of bacon, For burglary, murder, or rape, If he could but rehearse (Well prompt) his neck-verse, He never could fail to escape.*

necromancy. See *aeromancy.*

nectarel. Like nectar; fragrant. In TO HIS MISTRESSES (HESPERIDES, 1648) Herrick says: *For your breaths too, let them smell Ambrosia-like, or nectarel.* Also *nectareous, nectarious, nectarous,* full of or like nectar; *nectarean, nectarian,* as Gay in his verses on WINE (1708) : *Choicest nectarian juice crown'd largest bowles.*

necyomancy. See *aeromancy.*

needfire. Fire produced by the vigorous friction of dry wood (as when the Boy Scouts imitate the Indians). In the 15th and 16th centuries (and later) such a fire was held to possess magical properties, especially for the healing of cattle. Thus an extract from the PRESBYTERY BOOK OF STRATHBOGIE (1644) informs us that *It was regraited by Mr. Robert Watsone that ther was neidfire raysed within his parochin . . . for the curing of cattell.* Also, *to take needfire,* to start to burn spontaneously; Stewart in his translation (1535) of THE BUIK OF THE CHRONICLIS OF SCOTLAND wrote: *That tyme his stalf, in presens of thame all, it tuik neidfire richt thair into his hand.* Scott, in THE LAY OF THE LAST MINSTREL (1805), used the word to mean bonfire or beacon—*The ready page with hurried hand Awaked the needfire's slumbering brand*—and to some extent that use has persisted.

nef. The *nave* of a church. French *nef;* Latin *navem,* ship. Also, an incense-holder shaped like a boat; also called (15th and 16th centuries) *navet, navette*; and (19th century) *navicula* (Latin, diminutive of *navem,* ship). Also, *nef,* a silver or gold vessel in which napkins, saltcellar, etc., for the lord's table were kept; *every officer of the household,* said Maria Edgeworth in HELEN (1834), *making reverential obeisance as they passed to the nef.*

nefandous. Abominable, unmentionable. Latin *ne,* not + *fandum,* what ought to be spoken, gerundive of *for, fari, fatum,* to speak. *Nefandous* was used from the 17th into the 19th century (Southey); in the 15th and 16th centuries a shorter form was used, *nefand.* The printer Caxton in 1490 cried out against a *grete, horribyle, nephande, and detestable cryme.* Note that *ineffable* (cp. *effable*) has developed the opposite connotation, of something good beyond the power of words to express, as *ineffable happiness. Unspeakable* usually has unpleasant connotations; *unutterable* may swing with the emotions, either way.

neghtsom. Propitious. A 13th century form of *nighsome, q.v.* Used in the translation of the PSALMS.

negus. A mixture of hot water, sugar, and wine, sometimes otherwise flavored. Named after Colonel Francis *Negus* (died 1732), Master of the Horse under George I. Walpole said in a letter of 4 August, 1753: *Montagu understood the dialect, and ordered a negus.* The wine was usually sherry or port.

nemn. To name, to call, to mention. Common from the 9th to the 15th century. Forms include *nemny, mempnen, nempe, nempt,* from a Gothic form *namn,* name. Spenser has, in THE FAËRIE QUEENE (1590): *Much disdeigning to be so misdempt, Or a war-monger to be basely nempt.* In Brittany, the English storyteller ends his tale (1320; *cp. levedi*), the harpers made *a lay of gode likeing, And nempned it after the king: that lay 'Orfeo' is yhote* [past tense of *hight: called*]. *God is the lay, swete is the note. Thus com Sir Orfeo out of his care. God graunt ous alle wele to fare.*

nemophilist. A lover of the woods (such as Wordsworth). From Greek *nemos,* glade + *philos,* loving. [Not to be confused with Latin *nemo,* nobody, used as a name, *Captain Nemo,* by Jules Verne, and in an early comic strip.] Hence also *nemophilous, nemophily.* Hence *nemoral,* related to or frequenting groves or woods; *nemorose, nemorous,* woody, "shadowed and dark with trees." Evelyn in SYLVA (1679) said that *Paradise itself was but a kind of nemorous temple, a sacred grove planted by God himself.*

nenuphar. An early name for the waterlily—still used. The word, though now applied to the white or yellow varieties, is roundabout from Sanskrit *nil,* blue + *utpala,* lotus. Elyot in THE CASTEL OF HELTH (1533) recommends *syrope of violettes, nemipher, or the wine of sweet pomegranates.*

nepenthe. A drink that brings forgetfulness of woe. Also *nepenthes.* Referred to in Homer's ODYSSEY (*nepenthes pharmakon*) and ever since, a favorite of poets, Spenser to Shelley. Chesterfield in THE WORLD (1754, No. 92) said: *Gallons of the nepenthe would be lost upon him. The* *more he drinks, the duller he grows.* Shelley associates the plant *nepenthe* (which yields the drug) with *moly* and *amaranth, q.v.* Lyly in EUPHUES (1580) inquires: *Where is . . . that herb nepenthes that procureth all delights?*—sweet bringer of delicious oblivion.

nephromancy. See *aeromancy.*

nepos. A grandson; a nephew. Also *nepote.* Directly from Latin *nepos, nepotem,* which in Latin came also (by natural descent) to mean a spendthrift. Hence English *nepotation,* riotousness. *Nepotious,* over fond of one's nephews. *Nepotism,* now applied generally to favoritism, was first applied to the Popes' granting high posts to their nephews "or other relatives," says the O.E.D., *nephew* being at times a euphemism for an unacknowledged son. (The Popes, of course, could not marry.) Symonds in his brilliant study of THE ITALIAN RENAISSANCE (1886) speaks of *the most brilliant display of nepotistical ambition in a Pope.*

nepotation. Riotous wasting. See *nepos.*

neread. A sea-nymph, a mermaid. Three syllables. The more usual form of the word, especially when reference is to Roman or Greek mythology, is *nereid,* from *nereides,* children of *Nereys,* an ancient sea-god. Cowper in RETIREMENT (1781) speaks of *Nereids or dryads, as the fashion leads, Now in the floods, now panting on the meads.*

Neroic. Related to Nero; C. Claudius *Nero,* Emperor of Rome, 54-68 A.D. Also *Neronian, Neronic. To Neronize* (from the 17th century) : to label as resembling Nero; to corrupt like Nero; to tyrannize over like Nero. Hence also *Neronist, Neronism.*

neroly. A perfume; also the essential oil it is made from, distilled from the flowers of the bitter orange. Developed in the 17th century—*I have neroli, tuberose, jessimine, and marshal,* said Shadwell in 1676—and named after an Italian princess.

Neronize. See *Neroic.*

nescient. Ignorant. Also *nescious.* Latin *nescire,* to be ignorant; *ne,* not + *scire,* to know. Hence *nescience.* Used since the 17th century. Carlyle in SARTOR RESARTUS (1831) speaks of *the miserable fraction of science which united mankind, in a wide universe of nescience, has acquired.*

nescock. A fondling; a bird (then a child) that has never been away from home. Originally *nest-cock,* also *nestcockle,* the last-hatched bird in a nest.

nesebeck. A medieval dish, apparently of duck prepared with flour and ground figs. Please notify me if you experiment successfully.

nesh. This common word (Gothic *hnasqus,* soft) has gone through many shifts of meaning, from a basic sense of soft in texture or consistency. Thence: tender, succulent—*the nesh tops of the young hazel.* Slack, negligent, lacking in energy or diligence; timid; tender, gentle, mild. Hence, easily yielding to temptation, inclined to wantonness—Wyclif in his version (1382) of the BIBLE. Tender, delicate, weak (George Eliot, THE MILL ON THE FLOSS, 1860). The phrase *in nesh and hard* means under any and all circumstances. Also from the 9th to the 16th century, *nesh* was used as a verb, to make soft. Ripley in 1471 counselled the women: *Nesh not your wombe by drinking ymmoderately.*

ness. A promontory, a cape (of land). Also *naes, nesse, naisse*; *nase*; related to *nose, nese.* From the 12th century to the 17th, later in Scotland, *nese* was used for *nose*; in the 15th and 16th centuries, it was also used for a headland. Also *nese-end,* tip of the nose; *neselong,* face downwards (i.e., the length of the nose); *to nese,* in the 17th century—Jonson, THE SAD SHEPHERD, 1637—to smell. BEOWULF has *naess*; Morris in THE EARTHLY PARADISE (1868) says: *We stood Somewhat off shore to fetch about a ness.*

netheless. See *nath.*

nether. See *anether.*

neuf. (1) A sword-knot. Via French *neu, nou,* from Latin *nodum,* knot. (2) A variant of *nieve, q.v.,* fist. Jonson in THE POETASTER cries: *Reach mee thy neufe!*

neuft. A variant of *newt*; *an ewt*; *eft.* Spenser in THE FAËRIE QUEENE (1590) uses *ewftes. What!* exclaims Jonson in BARTHOLOMEW FAIR (1614), *Thou'lt poyson mee with a neuft in a bottle of ale, will't thou?*

newel. A novelty, something new; news. A 15th century variant of *novel*; later, also *newell*; *newelry,* a novelty; *neweltry,* newness, novelty. [There is also a *newel,* roundabout from Latin *nucem,* nut, which means the central post of a winding stair, and other such items in carpentry and architecture.] Spenser in THE SHEPHERD'S CALENDAR (1579; MAY) tells: *He was so enamored with the newell That nought he deemed deare for the jewell.*

newfangle. See *fangle.*

Newgate. The name of a noted London prison, whose inmates have been recorded since 1773 in the *Newgate Calendar.* Shakespeare has, in HENRY IV, PART ONE (1596): Falstaff: *Must we all march?* Bardolph: *Yea, two and two, Newgate fashion* (chain-gang style). Several compounds were formed from the term, among them: *Newgate bird,* jailbird; *Newgate frill (-fringe),* a narrow strip of beard under the chin; *Newgate knocker,* a lock of hair curled back from the temple to the ear. Also *Newgated,* confined in *Newgate*; *Newgateer,* a prisoner there; *Newgatory* (Hood, 1845; Ruskin, 1877), related to *Newgate,* with a pun on *nugatory,* worthless.

nicker. See *eche.* In Kingsley's HYPATIA (1853) we find: *"What is a nicor, Agilmund?" "A sea-devil who eats sailors."* Various other meanings have been attached to this form: a cheater; an 18th century hoodlum, who used to break London windows by throwing coppers at them; also, usually in the plural, the game of marbles (preferably *knickers*); also, a person's snicker, a horse's neigh.

nickname. See *eche.* As a verb, *nickname* also is used to mean to misname (16th through 19th century; Coleridge in BIOGRAPHIA LITERARIA, 1817; Byron, in DON JUAN, 1824; Shakespeare in HAMLET, 1602: *You lisp, and nickname God's creatures*; Shelley in QUEEN MAB, 1813: *The fool whom courtiers nickname monarch*) or to mention by mistake or to assert wrongly, as when in Shakespeare's LOVE'S LABOUR'S LOST (1588) the King says: *The virtue of your eye must break my oath* and the Queen retorts: *You nickname virtue: vice you should have spoke.*

nictate. See *connictation.*

niddering. See *nithing.*

niderling. See *nithing.*

nidget. An old form (16th to 18th century) of *idiot.* Sometimes used, later, to mean a trifler. Toone (1834) quoting

Camden (1605) states that the word then meant coward, one who 'refused to come to the royal standard.' He quotes, however, for the sense idiot (*an idiot* becoming *a nidiot, nidget*), Middleton and Rowley's play THE CHANGELING (1621): *'Tis a gentle nigget; you may play with him as safely as with his bauble.* Hence *nidgery,* foppery, trifling foolishness; *nidgetty,* trifling.

nieve. A fist. Common since the 13th century; recently only in dialects. The word appeared in many forms, including *nief, neve, nive, niv, neyf, nave, naive, nef, neave. Cp. neuf.* Shakespeare in A MIDSUMMER NIGHT'S DREAM (1590): *Give me your neafe, Mounsieur Mustardseed;* HENRY IV, PART TWO: *Sweet knight, I kisse thy neaffe.* Hence *nieveful* (*nieffeful,* etc.), a handful.

nifle. A trifling thing; a foolish or fictitious story. The word, recorded first in Chaucer—THE SOMNOUR'S TALE (1386): *He served them with nyfles and with tryfles* —was, especially from 1550 to 1650, used together with *trifle.* Hence, a flimsy garment. Also *nifling,* trifling, of little worth.

nig. A mean or miserly person. Also *nigon.* Used from the 14th into the 16th century, this form was replaced by *niggard.* Langland, Chaucer (*negarde;* in THE ROMAUNT OF THE ROSE, 1366: *A full gret fool is he, ywys, That bothe rich and nygart is*), and Shakespeare passed the word on. Hence also *niggardess, niggardise, niggardness, niggardship, niggardy, niggardliness; niggardize.* Caxton in his LIVES OF THE FATHERS (1491) tells that *among the brethern there was one, which was merveyllously scarse and nygardouse* (*niggardous*).

niggard. See *nig.*

niggle. (1) Cramped handwriting. Charlotte M. Yonge in THE DAISY CHAIN (1856) said that *Ethel's best writing was an upright disjointed niggle . . . a still wilder combination of scramble, niggle, scratch, and crookedness.* (2) To work or to move about, in a trifling or ineffective way; to be overly critical; to cheat. (3) To copulate with. A *niggler* is therefore (a) a lascivious person; (b) one who works ineffectively (especially in the arts), producing trifling or over-detailed or minute work.

nighin. To draw *nigh.* Also *nighen, nehyen, neigh* (as in *neighbor,* near farmer) and the like. *Nighsome* (*q.v.*) handy; favorable, gracious. Hence *nighsomeness.*

nighsome. Favorable, gracious. Also *neghsom, neghtsom.* Latin *prope,* nigh; hence in the 13th and 14th centuries, *propitius,* nigher (therefore favorable), was translated *nighsome.*

nightertale. See *nyghtertale.*

nightingale. See *sigalder.*

nightshade. See dwale. The berries of different varieties of *nightshade* are narcotic or poisonous. The *deadly nightshade* is also called *belladonna* (beautiful lady); from it is extracted atropine. The juice of belladonna enlarges the pupil of the eye, enhancing its attractiveness but weakening its vision; love is blind. The word was often used figuratively, as when O. Winslow in THE INNER LIFE (1850) declared: *Satan has ever sought to engraft the deadly nightshade of error upon the life-giving Rose of Sharon.*

nigon. See *nig.* The 15th century tale of Sir Bevis says *Thus men shall teche other . . . Of mete and drynke no negyn to be.* Hence also *nigonry, nigonship.*

nigromancy. Early form of *necromancy.* See *aeromancy.*

nigs. See *sneaks.*

nim. To take. A very common Teuton form; the root *nem* is related to Greek *nemein,* to possess. Found in English into the 17th century, in the various senses of *take,* including to steal, and to take off, to steal away. Gay, for example, in THE BEGGAR'S OPERA, has: *I expect the gentleman about this snuff-box, that Filch nimm'd two nights ago in the Park.* Hence *nimmer,* a thief, especially a petty one; *nimming,* pilfering; taking bribes.

nimbification. The process of cloud formation. Latin *nimbus,* cloud. *Nimb,* however, has shifted its sense from cloud to halo; *nimbated,* provided with a halo.

nimfadoro. An effeminate fellow. Probably a humorous or contemptuous elongation of *nymph.* Jonson in EVERY MAN OUT OF HIS HUMOUR (1599) queries: *What brisk nimfadoro is that in the white virgin boot there?*

nimiety. Excess, superfluity, redundancy. From Latin *nimis,* too much, as in the famous phrase of Terence, *nequid nimis,* nothing too much. *Nimiety* is pronounced in four syllables, accent on the second syllable, with long *i.* Coleridge in his TABLE TALK for 2 June, 1834, said *There is a nimiety . . . in all Germans.* Hence *nimious,* excessive, used since the 15th century.

niminy-piminy. Mincing, affected; lacking in spirit or vigor. Found first in THE MONTHLY REVIEW (1801), *a smirking countenance and mimeny pimeny lisp.* A reduplicated imitation of mincing speech. Used by Leigh Hunt, Thackeray, Stevenson, and remembered from Gilbert's PATIENCE (1881): *A Japanese young man, A blue-and-white young man, Francesca di Rimini, miminy-piminy, je-ne-sais-quoi young man.* A bit more coarsely, the form *nimpy-pimpy* has been used. And Hazlitt remarked (1884) *There was no niminy-pimininess about Johnson . . . He always said what he thought.*

nine-worthiness. See *worthy.*

ninnybroth. Coffee. A 17th and 18th century term. *Ninny,* a simpleton, is probably a shortening of *an innocent.* From it, in the 19th century, came *ninnyish; ninnyism; ninnyship.* From the 16th century, a thorough simpleton was a *ninnyhammer;* Urquhart in his translation (1653) of Rabelais preferred *ninnywhoop.* Of a group of coffee drinkers HUDIBRAS REDIVIVUS (1705) remarked: *Their wounded consciences they heal With ninnybroth.*

nipcheese. A purser of a ship. In the 18th and 19th centuries. Also, a mean, niggardly person. Used as an adjective, as when Sala in LADY CHESTERFIELD (1860) referred to *this nipcheese, candle-end saving, pebble-peeling . . . principle.* A *pebble-peeler,* of course, is a skinflint. So is a nipcheese. So, in one sense, is a *nipper,* though this may also mean a boy helper; a quick lad; a pickpocket—one that *nips,* in various senses of the verb.

nipper. See *nipcheese. Nippers,* among other things, meant handcuffs and pince-nez eyeglasses. *To nipper,* to take into custody.

nipperkin. A small vessel for liquids, containing no more than half a pint; also, that amount of liquor. Used from the 17th century. Hardy in THE MAN HE KILLED (1914) says: *Had he and I but met By some old ancient inn, We should have set us down to wet Right many a nipperkin.*

nippitate. A fine ale, or other good liquor; hence, as an adjective, of prime quality. Also with Latin or Italian endings, *nippitato*; *nippitatum*; the most frequent, *nippitaty*. Nashe, in SUMMER'S LAST WILL (1600) complained that *never cap of nipitaty in London came near thy niggardly habitation!* Urquhart in his translation (1693) of Rabelais, sums up one *Weltanschauung* (another nearly forgotten word! The world has grown too small): *'Tis all one to me, so we have but good bub and nippitati enough.*

nis. (1) In Scandinavian folklore, a friendly goblin, which frequents barns and farmhouses. Identified with the Scotch *brownie* and the German *kobold.* (2) An early contraction of *is not,* also *none is; cp. nys.* Used from the 9th century; by Spenser; by Sidney in ARCADIA (1586): *Nothing can endure where order n'is.* (The introduction of the apostrophe marked the dying of the form.)

nithe. Envy, hatred. Also a verb, to envy, to hate. A common Teutonic form, used in English into the 14th century. Also *to nither,* to thrust down, abase, humble; oppress. (This is related to *nether,* lower, and is perhaps a different word; it was used until the mid-16th century, later in dialects.) Also *nytherian, nidder, nether.* Thus *nithful,* envious, malicious.

nithing. A base coward, a most despicable wretch. A common Teuton word. By misreading of the *th* (Saxon *thorn*), the form *niddering* developed, the O.E.D. says in 1596; Bailey in 1751 gives the forms *niderling* and *niding.* Scott, reviving the word in IVANHOE (1819) speaks of *threatening to stigmatize those who staid at home as nidering.*

nitor. Brilliance, splendor. Latin *nitor,* brightness; *nitere,* to shine. Hence *nitid,* shining: *all her nitid beauties.* Also *nitidity,* brightness, trimness.

nix. A water-elf. See *eche; nixie.* Also (from German *nichts,* nothing) nothing, nobody. *Nix!* as a signal meant somebody's coming. *Keeping nix,* keeping watch so nobody will surprise one. Ainsworth in ROOKWOOD (1834) coined a phrase which has been copied by Hood, Thackeray, and more: *Nix my dolly, pals, fake away.* The first three words mean chuck it, never mind.

nixie. A water-nymph. See *eche.* This form, a diminutive of *nix, q.v.,* was first used by Scott, in THE ANTIQUARY (1816) and in THE PIRATE (1821): *She who sits by haunted well Is subject to the nixie's spell.*

nocent. *Cp. couth. Nocent* was used from the 15th into the 18th century, rather rarely later. Also *nocence, nocency.* From Latin *nocentem,* harmful; *nocere,* to hurt, whence not only *innocent* but *innocuous.* There was no English form *nocuous,* but harmful was represented by *nocible* (15th century, Caxton), *nociferous* (18th century, Evelyn), and *nocive, nocivous* (16th and 17th centuries) T. Adams in THE FATAL BANQUET (1620) has: *I would iniquity was not bolder than honesty, or that innocence might speed no worse than nocence.* Milton in PARADISE LOST (1667) speaks of Adam before the fall: *Nor nocent yet, but on the grassy herb Fearless, unfeared, he slept.*

noctivagant. Wandering by night. The accent is on the *ti,* short *i.* Also, *noctivagous. Noctivagation* was prohibited and punishable by fine where there was a curfew, as in many towns into the 17th century. For a sample of its use, see *expergefacient.*

noie. Also *noy.* See *noyous.*

noise. As a noun, in special senses: (1) rumor; especially evil report, slander, scandal. Hence, reputation. A Towneley Mystery of 1460 said: *Thou has an yll noys of stelyng of shepe.* Occasionally, high repute, note, *making a noise in the world.* (2) An agreeable or melodious sound. Thus from Chaucer (1366) to Coleridge, THE ANCIENT MARINER (1798): *It ceased; yet still the sails made on A pleasant noise till noon, A noise like of a hidden brook.* (3) A company (of musicians). This was a frequent 16th and 17th century use; Jonson in THE SILENT WOMAN (1609): *The smell of the venison, going through the street, will invite one noyse of fidlers, or other.* In Deloney's JACKE OF NEWBERIE (1597): *They had not sitten long, but in comes a noise of musitians in tawny coates, who (putting off their caps) asked if they would have any musicke. The widow answered no, they were merry enough. "Tut," quoth the old man, "let us heare, good fellowes, what you can doe, and play mee The Beginning of the World." "Alas," quoth the Widow, "you had more need to hearken to the ending of the world." "Why, Widow," quoth hee, "I tell thee the beginning of the world was the begetting of children, and if you finde mee faulty in that occupation, turne mee out of thy bed for a bungler."* Although it is perhaps the most popular in actual use, *a noise of musicians* is one of the large series of "nouns of assemblage" originally humorous or ironic in intent, such as *a gaggle of gossips, a frown of critics, a prowl of proctors, a dampness of babies, a charm of fairies, a duty of husbands, a questionnaire of wives*—many of which are gathered (*s.v.* Sports Technicalities) in Eric Partridge's useful USAGE AND ABUSAGE. He omits *a glee* (or *a pest*) *of punsters* and *an obsolescence of lexicographers,* but includes *a galaxy of milkmaids, a gush of poets, a superiority of young people*—and (modestly enough) *a covey of partridges.* Wycherley in THE PLAIN DEALER (1674) protested: *I cou'd as soon suffer a whole noise of flatterers at a great man's levee.*

noli-me-tangeretarian. One that stands rigidly firm, as though saying: Touch me not! Try not to move me! Landor in his EXAMINATION OF SHAKESPEARE (1864) declared: *If a dean is not on his stilts, . . he stands on his own ground: he is a noli-me-tangeretarian.* There are, also, women of the sort. *Noli me tangere* (Latin: Touch me not; used in the BIBLE: JOHN, 20, when the resurrected Christ appears to Mary Magdalene) has had several uses: (1) an eroding ulceration of the face; hence, an abomination. Smollett in HUMPHREY CLINKER (1771) says: *She's a noli me tangere in my flesh, which I cannot bear to be touched.* (2) Someone or something not to be tampered with. Whitlock in ZOOTOMIA (1654) said: *Learning was no such noli me tangere, in the Apostles account.* (3) A picture of Christ appearing to Mary Magdalene. (4) A warning against meddling or interfering; this sense may still be used.

nolition. Unwillingness. Used in the 17th century as the converse of *volition.* Latin *nolle,* to be unwilling. Precisely, in A HUMBLE ENDEAVOUR . . . ABOUT THE FREE ACTIONS OF MEN (1690) Corbet pointed out that *between volition and nolition there is a middle thing, viz. non-volition.*

noll. The top of the head; the head, usually in good-humoured scorn; the noddle. Also *nowl, noul, knoll, nole.* See *totty. Noll* is really a double of *knoll,* top, summit—applied to the head. It was used from the 9th century; later often in the phrase *drunken noll;* hence, by transference, *a noll,* a drunken fellow, a stupid fellow. By the 16th century, it was usually associated with drunkenness, as in Spenser's THE FAËRIE QUEENE (1596): *Then came October full of merry glee; For yet his noule was totty of the must.* The word is also played upon in Garrick's impromptu epitaph for Oliver Goldsmith: *Here lies Nolly Goldsmith, for shortness called Noll, Who wrote like an angel, and talked like poor Poll.*

nolt. A variant form of *nowt, q.v.* Used from the 15th century; in the 19th, by Carlyle.

nonce. Occasion, purpose. The word occurs only in phrases: *for the (very) nonce,* for the particular (present) purpose, on purpose; hence, temporarily. In Middle English, and archaically later, often used as a metrical tag, of vague meaning, rhyming with *stones* and *bones (banes).* Thus, in a ballad of 1400: *The lyon hungered for the nanes, Ful fast he ete raw fless and banes.* Leigh Hunt, in a poem of 1832: *A cup of good Corsican Does it at once; Or a glass of old Spanish Is neat for the nonce.* The word *nonce* is a transfer (like *a newt* for *an ewt,* etc.) from Old English *for than anes,* for that once. Also *with the nones,* on condition (that); *in the nonce,* at that moment, at once; *at the very nonce,* at the very moment. Thus Browning, in CHILDE ROLAND TO THE DARK TOWER CAME (1855): *Fool, to be dozing at the very nonce, After a life spent training for the sight!* A *nonce-word,* a word created *for the nonce,* for that particular occasion.

noncome. A standstill. Perhaps a humorous shortening of *non compos mentis,* not master of one's mind; perhaps a substitute for *nonplus,* the state of being *nonplussed,* at a loss. Used by Shakespeare in MUCH ADO ABOUT NOTHING (1599): *We will spare for no witte I warrant you: heere's that shall drive some of them to a noncome.* The speaker is Constable Dogberry, whose command of words is distinctively dogberrial.

nonesopretty. An article of feminine adornment, worn in the 17th and 18th centuries. By some other name, it is doubtless still being displayed. There were listed, in 1700: *webb-cane and leather hooping, gartering of all sorts, nonesoprетties, pins and needles, inkle and spinnel.* Also a flower; see *Hymen's torch.*

nonesuch. A person or thing unparalleled. Thus Rowlands in MORE KNAVES YET? (1613): *The very nonesuch of true courtesie.* Richardson in PAMELA (1741) bids: *Come to bed, purity! you are a nonesuch, I suppose.* Occasionally the word is used of something unequalled in a bad sense, as in Hickeringill's THE HORRID SIN OF MAN-CATCHING (1681): *These are the great plagues, the nonesuch pests of all society.*

nook-shotten. Abounding in nooks, points of land. Thus Shakespeare in HENRY V (1599): *A slobbry and a durtie farme In that nooke-shotten ile of Albion.* The verb *to nook* means to hide in a corner; to set in a corner, conceal. Since in HENRY V the Constable of France is speaking, while enemy English are on his soil, the editor (G. B. Harrison) may have a point when he explains *nook-shotten*: "pushed in a corner; i.e., remote and barbarous."

nooscopy. Examination of the mind. Pronounced with the first *o* long, the second short but receiving the accent. Also *nooscopics, noology.* Greek *noos, mind; cp. nous.* Bentham in 1816 divided *nooscopics* (accent on the *scop*) into *plasioscopic* and *coenonesioscopic.* These two words should be forgotten.

noria. A device for raising water from a well; the device as well as the word came via Spain from the Arabs. It consisted of a revolving rope or chain of pots or buckets that were filled below and emptied when they came to the top. Townsend in his JOURNEY THROUGH SPAIN (1792) said: *Every farm has its noria.* Knight in his DICTIONARY OF MECHANICS (1875) said: *The true Spanish noria has earthen pitchers secured between two ropes which pass over a wheel above and are submerged below.* A cool and refreshing drink!

norice. An old form (used by Chaucer) of *nourice,* which is an old form of *nurse.* Hence also, in the 15th century, *norry,* to nurse; also as a noun, *norry,* a foster-child, a pupil.

nortelry. Education. An old form, from Middle English *nortour,* nurture. Chaucer in THE REEVE'S TALE (1386) has: *What for her kynreed and her nortelrye, That she had lerned in the nonnerye.*

nosegay. A bunch of flowers; what better to make the nose gay? Also, a representation of this. By extension, anything pleasant, especially to sight, taste, or smell. T. Hawkins (1626) spoke of *the nosegay of the elect*; Swift (1738), of *a choice flower in the nosegay of wit.* Goldsmith in THE GOOD-NATURED MAN (1768): *I have a drop in the house of as pretty raspberry as ever was tipt over tongue . . . the last couples we had here, they said it was a perfect nosegay.* God grant you many such!

nosism. A sense of superiority on the part of a group. Latin *nos,* we, is the plural of *ego,* I; thus *nosism* is to a group what *egotism* is to an individual. The word *nosism* is also employed to name the practice of using the "editorial" we, of employing a plural for an ordinary singular. BLACKWOOD'S EDINBURGH MAGAZINE (1819) said that the *nosism of the other luminaries of the Lake School is at times extravagant enough, and amusing enough withal.* Don't you know such folks!

nostoc. This is the form of the word as coined by Paracelsus; it appears also as *nostoch, nostock*; Bailey in 1751 gives *nostick.* It is a genus of unicellular algae, but more interestingly defined in Charlton's translation (1650) of Van Helmont's PARADOXES: *nostoch understandeth the nocturnall pollution of some plethoricall and wanton star, or rather excrement blown from the nostrills of some rheumatick planet . . . in consistence like a gelly, and so trembling if touched.* Also called, until the 19th century, *star slough, or star-shot gelly . . . a substance that falls from the stars.*

noteye. A 15th century dish of various ingredients, garnished with nuts: *Take smal notys and breke theme; take the kyrnellys and make hem whyte . . . plante therwith thin mete and serve forth.*

nothal. Not authentic, spurious. Greek *nothos,* spurious. Used in the 18th century.

notheless. See *natheless.*

nother. A variant form of: *nether; an other* (becoming *a nother*); *no other; neither* (earlier variant, *nouther*). Tindale in his Biblical EXPOSITIONS, JOHN (1531): *We . . . love you all alyke, nother love we one more and another lesse.*

Skelton in his poem WARE THE HAUKE (1539): *Nor yet dronken Bacchus; nother Olibrius, nor Dionisyus.*

nothous. Spurious. Nothous words are not infrequent, in various dictionaries; the supplementary volume of the O.E.D. gives a list of them. *Nothous* seems to be one of such spurious words; *cp. nothal.*

nothynge. A variant form of *nothing. Nothing* was often used as an adverb, meaning not at all. For an instance, *see sloth.* Often the phrase *nothing at all* was used; then *nothing* meant *not.* Thus, in the letter Ralph Roister Doister (in the play of that name, by Udall; 1553) has sent to the wealthy widow: *Sweete mistresse, whereas I love you nothing at all, Regarding your substance and richesse chiefe of all; For your personage, beautie, demeanour and wit I commende me unto you never a whit. Sorie to heare report of your good welfare*—wherein the misplaced punctuation naturally enrages the *deare coney, birde, sweteheart, and pigany* to whom the would-be love letter was addressed.

notionate. Whimsical, full of notions; headstrong, obstinate. So used in the 19th century. More rarely, in the 17th, *notionate* was a verb meaning to come at by thinking. A *notionist* (from the 17th century) was one that formed notions (Lamb, in a letter; 1825: *such a half-baked notionist as I am*), especially odd or crotchety ideas; one that held extravagant religious opinions was a *high notionist.* Sewel in his HISTORY OF THE QUAKERS (1720) exclaimed upon *a high notionist, and rich in words.*

noughteness. Worthlessness. Hence, wickedness—which has lost force in *naughtiness.* Similarly *noughtie,* worthless, hence wicked, has become *naughty.* Ascham in TOXOPHILUS (1545) spoke of men's selling *noughtie wares;* More in UTOPIA (in English, 1551), of *my endevour to pluck out of hys mynde the pernitious originall causes of vice and noughtenes.* The world still needs that pluck.

noule. A variant form of *noll, q.v.*

nous. This Greek word for intellect (*nous, noos,* mind) was used in English, 17th into the 19th century, for common sense, intelligence. Pope in THE DUNCIAD (1729): *Thine is the genuine head of many a house, And much divinity without a nous.* Also Byron in DON JUAN (1819). A story in THE GRAPHIC of 8 November, 1884, said: *I am glad that my people had the nous to show you into a room where there was a fire.* In early 19th century (university) slang, *the nous box* was the head.

nouthe. An early form (used by Chaucer) of *now.* Also *nowthe.*

novation. A simpler form for *innovation. Novation* was common in Scotland from 1560 to 1650; Chapman in BUSSY D'AMBOIS (1607) uses the word to mean a revolution. Hence also *novator, novatrix;* J. B. Rose in his translation (1866) of Ovid's METAMORPHOSES said *Nature the novatrix remoulds the frame.* Also *novaturient* (17th century), desirous of novelty or change.

novelant. Also *novelist, novelism.* See *novity.*

novercal. Relating to, or resembling, a stepmother. Latin *noverca,* stepmother (from the root *nu,* now). Also *novercant,* behaving like a stepmother; the Rolls of Parliament of 1472-3 wished *to kepe in remembrance . . .* their *noble actes, pryncipally in execution of justice, ayenst* *novercant oblivion, ennemy to memorye.* Also (16th century) *noverk,* a stepmother.

novity. An innovation; novelty, newness. Used since the 15th century; especially common in the second sense in the 17th century. Latin *novitatem; novus,* new. Via Late Latin *novellum,* new, *novel,* came a group of English words: *novelant,* a newsmonger; *novelist,* an innovator (very common in this sense in the 17th century), a newsmonger; *novelism, novelry,* newness, *novelty.* Steele in THE TATLER (1710) and Goldsmith in his HISTORY OF ENGLAND (1764) still used *novelist* in the sense of bearer of news. When Morgan, in ALGIERS (1728) first used the word to mean writer of a *novel* (story) he felt it necessary to explain: *Such opportunities of gallantizing their wives, as the French and other novelists, I mean novel-writers, would insinuate.*

novum. A game of dice in which the principal throws were nine and five. Shakespeare mentions it in LOVE'S LABOUR'S LOST (1588): *Abate throw at novum, and the whole world againe Cannot pricke out five such.*

nowt. Cattle, oxen. Sometimes singular, a bullock, an ox. A common Norse term; Old English *neat,* an animal of the ox-kind, used in English from the 8th into the 19th century. Also *nolt. Cp. tate.* When William Morris, in JASON (1867) said *The herdsmen drave Full oft to Cheiron woolly sheep, and neat,* he did not mean neat (i.e., clean) sheep. The word is related to Old Teutonic *naut-, neut-,* to possess. There is, from this, an English word *nait* (14th to 17th century), to possess, to use, to enjoy. *Cp. pestle; vendible.*

nowthe. Now. Used from 1200 to 1400. Also *nouthe.*

noyau. A brandy liqueur flavored with the kernels of fruits. Old French *noyal, nuial,* from Latin *nucem,* nut. Canning in THE ROVERS (1797) exclaimed: *This cherry-bounce, this loved noyau, My drink forever be.*

noyous. See *annoyous.* Also, as both verb and noun, *noy, noie,* trouble. An early form of *annoy, annoyance,* though traced via Old French *nuire, noire,* to Latin *nocere,* to harm; *cp. nocent.* Also *noyment, noyance, noyant, noying.*

nubia. A soft fleecy shawl, or wrap for the head and neck, popular in the late 19th century. Latin *nubes,* cloud. The CONFESSIONS OF A FRIVOLOUS GIRL, 1881, records: *Emerging therefrom, five minutes later, in my nubia and snowy wrap . . .*

nubility. Readiness for marriage. Latin *nubes,* cloud, veil; whence *nubere, nuptum,* to don the (marriage) veil, whence also English *nuptials. Nubile* means (a girl) of marriageable age; the other forms, however, have brought into English only the primary sense: *nubilation,* cloudiness; *nubilate,* to cloud over, to render obscure (also used figuratively); *nubiferous,* cloud-bringing, obscuring; *nubilose, nubilous,* cloudy, vague—as in Peacock's MELINCOURT (1817): *Pointing out innumerable images of singularly nubilous beauty.* Many airplanes find themselves *nubivagant* (accent on the second syllable), journeying among clouds.

nuddle. To push or rub with the nose; to press close to the ground in this manner (of animals); hence (of humans), to grovel.

nudification. The act of laying bare. A *nudifier,* however, is an early term for a *nudist,* applying mainly to one that indulges in self-disclosure.

nudiustertian. Of the day before yesterday. Latin *nudius tertius,* short for *nunc dies tertius* (*est*), it is now the third day. Used in the 17th century. *The nudiustertian fashions are already old.*

nugacity. Triviality, trifling. Latin *nugax, nugacem,* trivial; *nugari, nugatum,* to jest, play the fool, talk nonsense. The Latin word *nugae,* trifles, was used in the same sense in 19th century English. Hence also *nugal, nugacious,* trifling; more often *nugatory, nugatorious,* worthless; *nugament,* a trifle, a trifling opinion. Myles Davies in his ATHENAE BRITANNICAE (1716) scorns the *quisquilian nugaments.* (*Cp. quisquilious.*) *nugator* (17th century), a trifler, a worthless fellow; *nugate,* to act foolishly or to talk nonsense. *There may be some difficulty,* remarked Henry More in REMARKS ON TWO LATE INGENIOUS DISCOURSES (1676), *but there is no nugality at all.*

nullifidian. A sceptic. Latin *nullus,* no + *fides,* faith. *Cp. minimifidian.* Used since the 16th century; Scott in OLD MORTALITY (1816) says *In their eyes, a lukewarm Presbyterian was little better than a Prelatist, an anti-Covenanter, and a nullifidian.*

nulliverse. A world without unity, that turns upon no intellectual or spiritual center. Coined in the 19th century; Latin *nullus,* no, in place of *uni-,* one + *vertere, versum,* to turn. *The world,* said William James in MIND (1882) *is pure incoherence, a chaos, a nulliverse, to whose haphazard sway I will not truckle.*

numb. See *benim.*

nummamorous. Money-loving. Latin *nummus,* coin + amorous. Also *nummiculture; nummicultivated.* Charles Reade in THE EIGHTH COMMANDMENT (1860) said: *The dagger stroke that slew Marlowe in his twenty-ninth year, struck down a heaven born and nummicultivated genius.* Hence also *nummary, nummular, nummulary,* pertaining to money; *nummularian* (15th century), a money-changer. Also, in Motteux' translation (1694) of Rabelais—*Large heaps of numms to fill your largest coffers*—*numm,* a coin.

nummulary. See *nummamorous.*

nun-buoy. A buoy (especially one fastened to a ship's anchor) widely circular in the middle and tapering toward each end. Used in the 18th century. In the 16th and 17th centuries, a child's top, also a fisher's cork float, of this shape was called a *nun.* A *Mae West,* on the other hand (20th century), is a life-preserver or buoy tapering toward the center, named from the hour-glass shape affected (during the 1890's) by the type of character the actress Mae West represented, especially "Come up 'n' see me sometime" Diamond Lil.

nuncheon. A slight refreshment of liquor, originally taken in the afternoon; then it moved ahead and became equivalent to luncheon, its own hour being given over to afternoon tea. From Middle English *none,* noon + *shench,* draught, cup. See *shenk.* Also *nonsenches, nunchings, nuntions* (usually with a final *s* until the 17th century); *nuncion, noneshyne, nunching*—and *nunch.* Jane Austen in a letter of 1808 wrote: *Immediately after the noonshine which succeeded their arrival, a party set off for Buckwell.* Urquhart in his translation (1694) of Rabelais, says there is *no dinner like a lawyer's and no nunchion like a vintner's. A monk's nuncheon*: "as much as another man eats at a large meal." Defined by Johnson (1755) as "a piece of victuals eaten between meals", *nuncheon* has been used also by Scott (NIGEL; 1822), Browning (PIED PIPER OF HAMELIN; 1845). *Luncheon* was first used in 1580. *Lunch* (first used in 1591, translating Spanish *lonja de tocino,* piece of ham) meant a hunk, a piece; it may be a variant of *lump* (note *hump* and *hunch*). Johnson defined *luncheon*: "as much food as one's hand can hold". These two words replaced *nuncheon* for the snack between breakfast and dinner. There was for a long time no formal noon meal, though there was often an afternoon dinner, among the non-working classes, at three, and a supper about ten. The Almacks Club in 1829 declared the word *luncheon* unsuited to "polished society"; Macaulay in 1853 objected to *the detested necessity of breaking the labours of the day by luncheon.* Until World War I (says Arnold Palmer in MOVABLE FEASTS; 1952) many London business men had only a glass of wine and a biscuit between breakfast and dinner. A genuine old-fashioned nuncheon.

nuncle. A variant of *uncle.* Used since the 16th century; by Shakespeare in KING LEAR (1605). Also *nunky.*

nuncupate. To call out, to name; to vow. Hence, to make an oral statement (will); to dedicate (a work to someone). Latin *nuncupare, nuncupatum,* to call; *nomen,* name + *capere,* to take. Hence also *nuncupation,* the act of designating; Usk in THE TESTAMENT OF LOVE (1388) says that *images ben goddes by nuncupacion.* More frequently used in the adjective form, *nuncupative* (accent on the *nun* or the *cue*), oral; nominal, so-called. Jeremy Taylor in his DUCTOR DUBITANTIUM (1660) warns against leaving important items unwritten: *Nuncupative records are like diagrams in sand, and figures efformed in air.*

nyggyshe. A variant form of niggardly. More in UTOPIA (1551) said that *there nothynge is distrybuted after a nyggyshe sort, nother there is anye poore man or begger.*

nyghtertale. A variant form of *nightertale,* the night-time. Always in a phrase: *a, by, of, on, upon, with,* (*the*) *nightertale,* by night, during the night. Chaucer in the Prologue to THE CANTERBURY TALES (1386) has: *By nyghtertale He sleep namore than dooth a nightingale.*

nym. A variant of *nim,* to take. For an illustration of its use, see *murrey.*

nymphlin. A little nymph; a charming lass. Graves in EUPHROSYNE (1773): *Well-pleas'd she sees her infant train Of nymphlins sporting on the plain.*

nympholepsy. This word is forgotten less often than its meaning, as it is often used when *nymphomania* is intended. *Nympholepsy* is a state of rapture inspired in men by nymphs; hence, an urge toward something unattainable. De Quincey in his RECOLLECTION OF THE LAKES AND THE LAKE POETS (1839) said: *He languished with a sort of despairing nympholepsy after intellectual pleasures.* And Bulwer-Lytton in GODOLPHIN (1833) said that *the most common disease to genius is nympholepsy—the saddening for a spirit that the world knows not.* Hence *nympholept;* Bulwer-Lytton in RIENZI has: *The very nympholept of freedom, yet of power —of knowledge, yet of religion!* and Birrell in OBITER DICTA (1884): *The nympholepts of truth are profoundly interesting figures in . . . history.* Also *nympholeptic.* Thus a *nymphomaniac* is a woman obsessed with sex; a *nympholept* is a devoted and often ascetic man.

nys. A variant of *nis,* none is; is not. Used from the 10th into the 17th century; Spenser in THE SHEPHERD'S CALENDAR (MAY, 1579) says: *Thou findest faulte where nys to be found.*

nysot. A wanton girl. Originally a variant diminutive of *nice.* Skelton in the interlude MAGNYFYCENCE (1520) has: *Where I spy a nysot gay, That wyll syt ydyll all the day.*

nystagmus. A constant squinting; a drowsiness; an inability to fix one's attention. (Still used, more specifically, in medicine.) Also *nystagmic, nystallic,* drowsy. Greek *nystagmos,* drowsiness; *nystagma,* a nap; *nystaxo,* to nod, to be sleepy.

O

oaf. See *ouph.*

ob. (1) A wizard. Hebrew *obh,* a necromancer. (2) Short for *obolus,* a Roman coin; used in English of a halfpenny. Thus in Shakespeare's HENRY IV, PART ONE (1596) Pointz reads a list: *Item, sack, two gallons . . . 5 s. 8d.; Item, anchovies and sack after supper . . . 2 s. 6d.; Item, bread . . . ob.* and Prince Hal cries: *O monstrous! but one half-pennyworth of bread to this intolerable deal of sack!* (3) In the phrase *ob and sol,* abbreviated in old books of divinity: *objection and solution*; therefore, subtle disputation. Burton in THE ANATOMY OF MELANCHOLY (1621) speaks of *a thousand idle questions, nice distinctions, subtleties, obs and sols.* An *ob-and-soller* is a subtle disputant, as in Butler's HUDIBRAS (1678): *To pass for deep and learned scholars Although but paltry ob-and-sollers.* (4) *ob.* Abbreviation of *obiit,* died; used in lists to indicate the date of a person's death. (5) *ob-.* The Latin preposition, used in many words as a prefix; also in many English (17th and 18th century, some earlier) words, as an intensive, or with the meaning, in the opposite direction. Thus (Chaucer) *obombrid,* clouded over. Among words thus formed in English are *obacerate,* to stop one's mouth, 'shut one up'; *obambulate,* to walk about; *obcaecation,* blindness (mental or moral); *obdulcorate,* to sweeten thoroughly; *obnubilate,* to hide or cover as with a cloud, used also of mental obfuscation; *obreptitious,* containing a falsehood for the sake of obtaining something, *obreption,* seeking something by deceit, from *ob* + *repere,* to creep. The converse of this is *subreption,* seeking something by suppressing the truth. [*Obscene* is from *ob* + *scaena,* stage, scene: not to be put on the stage, indecent.] Also *obserate,* to lock up; *obstipate,* to block or stop up, to stuff, to produce constipation (mental, moral, or physical); *obstreperate,* to make a loud noise—Sterne in TRISTRAM SHANDY (1765) has: *Thump—thump—obstreperated the abbess . . . with the end of her goldheaded cane against the bottom of the calash.* Other forms of this word survive, e.g., *obstreperous. Obstupefaction* is an emphatic form of *stupefaction. Obtemper, obtemperate* (since the 15th century), to obey, comply. *Obumber,* to overshadow, obscure (Chaucer's *obombrid*); but *obumbilate* is probably a scribe's error for *obnubilate*; *obumbrate,* to overshadow; *obvelate,* to veil over, to conceal, also *obvele. Obvolve,* to wrap around, muffle up, disguise. (6) In the German phrase *als ob,* as if: the philosophic and aesthetic doctrine of Hans Vaihinger, formulated in 1878, the idea that things should be accepted 'as if' they were so.

obeliscolychny. A light-house; light-bearer. Greek *obeliskos,* a small spit (whence also *obelisk*) + *lychnion,* lamp-stand. Accent on the penult, *like.* Motteux in his translation (1694) of Rabelais says: *We were conducted . . . by those obelisco-*

lychnys, military guards of the port, with high-crown'd hats.

obganiate. To annoy with needless repetitions. Latin *obgannire, oggannire,* to yelp at; *gannio,* to bark, snarl. Hence *obganning* (16th century; plural, *obgannynges*), needless, seemingly endless, repetition.

obliterature. The act or fact of doing away with, or of so being done. Replaced by *obliteration.* G. Hickes in TWO TREATISES ON THE CHRISTIAN PRIESTHOOD (1711) spoke of *a perfect obliterature of all injuries.* Comic books may also achieve a perfect obliterature.

obnounce. To announce that the omens are unfavorable (as might a Roman magistrate, thus preventing or voiding some public action). *Obnunciation,* the announcing of bad news or ill omens; hence, the dissolving of the (Roman) assembly. *To obnunciate* is defined, in 17th century dictionaries, to tell ill news.

obsequious. (1) Submissive, compliant to another's will. This sense, in use from the 15th century, survives. (2) Dutiful in performing funeral services; appropriate to *obsequies.* Both words and meanings are via French from Latin *ob,* towards, facing + *sequi,* to follow. Shakespeare uses the word in both senses; (1) in THE MERRY WIVES OF WINDSOR (1598); (2) in TITUS ANDRONICUS (V iii 152) and in HAMLET: *The surviver bound In filiall obligation . . . To do obsequious sorrow.*

obstringe. To put under obligation. Latin *ob,* upon, over + *stringere, strictum* (whence also *strict, constrict,* etc.), to bind. Hence *obstrictive, obstriction.* Milton in SAMSON AGONISTES (1671) tells that God *hath full right to exempt Whomso it pleases Him by choice From national obstriction.* The translation (1660) of Amyraldus' TREATISE CONCERNING RELIGION shows the background of a current Soviet practice: *It was never lookt upon as unjust or strange, for those who are obstringed one to another by those bonds to partake in the punishment of their relatives.*

obsurd. To deafen; to dull the hearing or the wits. Used in the 17th century; but absurd argument still obsurds the legislators of the world.

Occamism. The doctrine of 'the invincible doctor,' *William of Occam,* of the first half of the 14th century. *Occam's razor,* the principle of parsimony, the advice that the simplest explanation that covers all the points, or the simplest means of attaining the desired end, is the best. Copernicus deduced by applying Occam's razor that the earth revolves about the sun; how much more complex the mathematics to explain how the sun and planets revolve about the earth!

occamy. An imitation silver; hence, a base metal. Also used figuratively, as when Sir Francis Palgrave in 1857 spoke of *the dawning spirit of conventional honour gilding the ockamy shield of chivalry.* The word is a corruption of *alchemy,* by which it was sought to convert base metals into silver and gold.

ochlochracy. Mob-rule; government by the mob, as for a time in revolutions. Greek *ochlos,* crowd; *cp. ocracy.*

ocivity. Sloth. Via French from Latin *ocium, otium,* ease; whence also *otiose; otious* (17th century), leisurely, idle, at ease. *Cp. otiation.* In English, *otium* is occasionally used; Thackeray in PENDENNIS (1849) says: *Mr. Morgan was enjoying his otium in a dignified manner, surveying the evening fog, and enjoying a cigar.*

Scott (THE MONASTERY; 1820) and others have used the Latin phrase *otium cum dignitate,* dignified ease. The term *otiosity* usually puts more emphasis on the idleness, the state of being unemployed. This form was earlier *ociositie;* Caxton in POLYCRONICON (1482) spoke of *alle thoos men whiche thurgh the infyrmyte of our mortal nature hath ledde the moost parte of theyr lyf in ocyosyte,* rebukingly; but Thackeray in VANITY FAIR referred with but mild satire *to a life of dignified otiosity such as became a person of his eminence.*

ocker. See *oker.*

ocracy. Usually a suffix, meaning government by (the particular group or class named in the rest of the word, as *tradeocracy, bureaucracy*), *ocracy* has (like *ism*) been used as a separate form; for instance, in THE SPEAKER of 14 July, 1894: *Erect the great pillar of human brotherhood on the ruins of all the ocracies.*

ocreate. Wearing boots. Also *ocreated. Ocrea* is used as an historical term, being Latin for the greave or legging of the Roman infantryman and countryman. *Ocreate* is still used in botany and ornithology, of formations like leggings or boots; the nightingale is an ocreate bird.

oculate. To set eyes on. Latin *oculus,* eye. In the play EVERY WOMAN IN HER HUMOUR (1609) we hear of *Diana bathing herself, being occulated by Acteon. Oculation* also meant the same as *inoculation,* to put in little eyes or buds (like the 'eyes' of a potato).

od. (1) A euphemistic shortening of *God,* used in mild imprecations, especially in the 17th and early 18th centuries. Congreve in LOVE FOR LOVE (1695) ejaculates: *Odd! I have warm blood about me yet.* Also used in many phrases, mainly as a possessive: *od's bodikins, od's wounds* (*odsoons*), *odzooks* (*hooks*) and many more fantastic. In some cases—as in Shakespeare's THE MERRY WIVES OF WINDSOR (1598): *od's me*—the *od's* may be short for *God save.* (2) *od,* a supposed force permeating all nature, especially manifest in magnets, heat, light, and mesmerism. Postulated by Baron Von Reichenbach (1788-1869) and widely discussed if not accepted in the 19th century, before electricity (as in atomic energy) moved the notion into more scientific channels. Hence *odic,* relating to the force called *od;* Reichenbach photographed *odic lights.* The form was used in compounds to indicate specific aspects of the universal force: *biod,* the pervasive force in animal life; *chemod; heliod* (of the sun), etc. Elizabeth Barrett Browning in AURORA LEIGH (1856) mentioned *That od-force of German Reichenbach Which still from female finger-tips burns blue.*

odam. A son-in-law. From the 10th to the 13th century. Don't swear!

odontomancy. See *aeromancy.*

oeillade. A glance; especially, an amorous glance, an ogle. Directly from the French; also *oeyliade, aliad, eliad, illiad,* and more. Shakespeare uses the word in KING LEAR and in THE MERRY WIVES OF WINDSOR (1598): *Pages wife . . . examined my parts with most judicious illiads.*

oenologist. A connoisseur in wines. The forms *oeno, oino,* from Greek *oinos,* wine (*oine,* vine) are used interchangeably in various English words, including: *oenogen* (*gas*), the fumes of wine (Peacock in MELINCOURT; 1817). *oinomania,* mad craving for wine, the mellowest form of *dipsomania. oinophilist,* a lover of wine.

oinopoetic, relating to wine making; inspired by wine. In ancient Greece, an *oenochoe* (inocko-ee) was a vessel used for dipping the wine from the big bowl and filling the cups. Hence *oenanthic,* relating to (specifically, in chemistry, having the characteristic odor of) wine. With varied courses, serve the apt oenanthic treasure.

oenomancy. See *aeromancy.*

oenomel. A drink, wine mixed with honey. Favored of the ancient Greeks; *oinos,* wine + *meli,* honey. Used figuratively, as by Elizabeth Barrett Browning (WINE OF CYPRESS; 1844): *Those memories . . . Make a better oenomel.*

oint. An early form of *anoint.* Via French *oint; oindre,* from Latin *unguere, unctum,* to anoint, whence *unguent, unction.*

oker. To increase by interest (of money); to lend at interest; to take interest. From the 12th to the 15th century, usually mentioned as an abomination or a crime. Also as a noun, usury. Old English *wokor,* increase, related to Latin *augere, auctum,* to grow, increase, whence also *augment* and *auction.* Also *ocker, okyre, ocur, ockar, okker,* and more. Hence *okerer,* usurer, one that takes interest for lending money. Lyndesay in 1552 links *fornicatoris and ockararis;* Skene in 1609 recorded: *All the gudes and geir perteining to ane ockerer, quhither he deceis testat or untestat, perteins to the King.*

old. Among the meanings at one time acquired by this common old word, from the notion of long practice and experience it came to mean experienced, skilled, as when Defoe said in COLONEL JACK (1722): *The Germans were too old for us there.* And from the notion of long continuance *old* came to mean abundant, plentiful, as in the quotation under *blowen,* and when Shakespeare has, in MACBETH (1606): *If a man were porter of hell-gate, he should have old turning the key.* This sense also appears in THE MERRY WIVES OF WINDSOR, MUCH ADO ABOUT NOTHING, THE MERCHANT OF VENICE, and—*News! old news!*—THE TAMING OF THE SHREW. In KING LEAR, in Edgar's song on the heath, *old* is used for *wold,* forest, wooded downs; open country.

olio. A dish, originally Spanish and Portuguese, made with pieces of meat and fowl, bacon, pumpkin, cabbage, turnips and what more you will, stewed or boiled and highly spiced. Spanish *olla,* Portuguese *olha* (both pronounced *olya*), Latin *olla,* pot. By extension, any dish of many ingredients; see *hodgepot.* Thence applied to any heterogeneous mixture; Disraeli in TANCRED (1847) spoke of *an olio of all ages and all countries.* Especially, a mixture or collection of various artistic or literary pieces; a musical medley. The Duchess of Newcastle in 1655 wrote a book entitled: *The Worlds Olio: Nature's Pictures drawn by Fancie's Pencil to the Life.* THE SATURDAY REVIEW of 7 June, 1884, explained a new form: *The second part of a minstrel show is the 'olio'—and this is only a variety entertainment, of banjo-playing, clogdancing, and the like.* Current burlesque revivals of melodramas of the 1890's usually add an olio that includes acrobats and singing waiters.

olive-branch. (1) A token of peace or good-will, a peace offering. This meaning is drawn from the BIBLE: GENESIS 8, when the dove returns to Noah on his ark, bearing an olive-branch, a sign that the Lord's wrath was slaked. (2) Usually in the plural: *olive-branches,* children. This is from the BIBLE, PSALM 128 (Coverdale's version, 1535: *Thy children like the olyve* *braunches rounde aboute thy table*). Jane Austen in PRIDE AND PREJUDICE (1796) reported: *The rest of his letter is only about . . . his expectation of a young olive-branch.*

omittance. A Shakespearean form, for *omission.* Used in AS YOU LIKE IT (1600): *Omittance is no quittance.*

omophagous. Eating raw flesh. Hence *omophagist.* Greek *omos,* raw + *phagia,* eating. The *omophagia* was a feast of Bacchus, whereat the frenzied celebrants tore apart live goats, and ate their steaming entrails. THE PALL MALL GAZETTE of 13 December, 1884, recorded a woman that *cut from the victim's palm a piece of flesh and ate it raw—a literal omophagist.* A favorite dish of today's omophagists is *Steak Tartare,* chopped beef eaten raw with raw onion.

omophore. One who bears things on the shoulders, as Aeneas his father Anchises, from Troy. Greek *omos,* shoulder + *phoros,* bearing. Tylor in PRIMITIVE CULTURES (1871) mentions *the gigantic omophore of the Manichaean cosmology.* Hercules became an omophore for a day, in Atlas' stead. Many mythologies have world-bearing creatures; elephants, turtles, and other sturdy omophores.

omoplatoscopy. See *aeromancy.*

omphalomancy. Foretelling how many children a woman will have, by the number of knots in the unbilical cord of her first-born. Greek *omphalos,* navel. Also, the gaining of mystical insight by steadily contemplating one's navel. See *aeromancy.*

omphalopsychite. A person that induces lengthy (and perhaps hypnotic) reverie by steadily contemplating his umbilicus. Also *omphalopsychic.* Used in the 19th century. Greek *omphalos,* navel + *psyche,* spirit, soul.

oneiric. Relating to dreams. Greek *oneiros,* a dream, has been used for a number of English words. Among these, we may note: *oneirocrisy, oneirocriticism, oneirocritics,* the art of interpreting dreams; hence, an *oneirocritic, onirocritic,* such as Joseph in the BIBLE; also *oneirocrite,* a judge or interpreter of dreams. *oneiropompist,* a sender of dreams; one that makes another dream (Greek *pompos,* sending). *oneiroscopy, oneiromancy,* see *aeromancy.* Another term (15th century) for divination by dreams was *sompnary.*

oner. To burden. Also *onerate.* Latin *onerare, oneratum,* to load, burden; *onus, oneris,* a burden. *Onus* is a current English word. Also *onerous;* earlier forms of the adjective were *onerable, onerarious, onerose.* Hence, *onerosity.* An *onerary* (18th century) was a ship of burden; *oneration* (17th century) was the action of loading; especially, of loading the stomach with food. Hobbes in LEVIATHAN (1651) spoke of *all onerations and exonerations of the body.* In the sense of *onus,* burden, fault, developed also the still current *exonerate,* to unload, to clear of fault. Joye in his EXPOSITION (BOOK OF DANIELL; 1545) exclaimed: *Behold with how few single pure and easye institucyons Christ ordened and not onered his churche.*

onfang. To receive, accept; to receive in the mind, conceive; to conceive (a child); to undertake. Used from the 9th to the 14th century. The EARLY ENGLISH PSALTER (13th century) sang: *In wickedness onfanged am I, And in sinnes me onfong mi mothre fortly.*

ongin. To begin. Very frequent until the 13th century; the form *agin* remained until the 14th; thereafter, replaced by *begin.*

ongle. A claw. French *ongle;* Latin *ungula,* hoof, claw, talon; diminutive of *unguis,* nail. Caxton in his printing (1484) of Aesop's FABLES said of the lion: within his *ongles he took the rat.* Used into the 17th century.

onion-eyed. Ready to weep: readily weeping; with the eyes full of tears (as though watery from peeling onions). Shakespeare in ANTONY AND CLEOPATRA (1606) says: *Looke they weepe, And I an asse, am onyon-ey'd.*

onomancy, onomatechny. See *aeromancy.*

onychomancy. See *aeromancy.*

oo. Ever, aye. So given by Herbert Coleridge in his DICTIONARY OF THE OLDEST WORDS (1863), with reference to Wright's SPECIMENS OF LYRIC POETRY (of the 13th century). The O.E.D. quotes it from Wyclif's BIBLE (REVELATIONS; 1382) as a word—pronounced long *o*—for Greek *omega,* the last letter of the alphabet: *I am alpha and oo, the bigynnyng and the endyng.* (The Greek alphabet has two forms of the letter *o*: *omicron,* little *o,* and *omega,* great *o*—like Great Claus and Little Claus in the fairy-tale.)

oologist. A collector of birds' eggs; a country boy. Hence *oologize,* as Lowell in MY STUDY WINDOWS (1870): *The red squirrel, I think . . . oologizes; I know he eats cherries.* Greek *oon* (long *o* followed by short *o*; two syllables), egg. Newton in the 1875 ENCYCLOPEDIA BRITANNICA observed: *The greatest scientific triumph of oologists lies in their having fully appreciated the intimate alliance of the Limicolae with the Gaviae.* The many words with the prefix *oo-* (two syllables) include *ooscopy,* divination from eggs; *cp. aeromancy.*

open etcetera. See *medlar.*

operose. Laborious; hard-working; involving much labor, elaborate (as of a style in painting or writing). Latin *opus, operis,* work; the plural is *opera,* whence the Metropolitan.

oph. See *ouph.*

ophicleide. See *serpent* (3). Hence also *ophicleidist,* a performer on that instrument; also, *ophicleidean,* relating to it.

ophiomancy. See *aeromancy.*

opie. An opiate; opium. Also *opye, opi.* From Latin *opium;* Greek *opion,* poppy-juice, diminutive of *opos,* vegetable juice. Chaucer uses the word more than once, e.g., in THE KNIGHT'S TALE (1386): *A clarree maad of a certeyn wyn Of nercotikes and opie of Thebes fyn.*

opificer. A maker; a workman. (Accent on the *pif.*) Also *opifex.* Latin *opus,* work, and the forms *fex, fic,* from *facere,* to make, do. Thus *opifice,* the making of a work; the thing made, as an *edifice* (which has survived). The words were used mainly in the 17th century, though as late as 1761 Sterne in TRISTRAM SHANDY said: *So many playwrights and opificers of chitchat have ever since been working upon . . . my uncle Toby's pattern.*

opime. Rich; plentiful; sumptuous; splendid. Also *opimous.* Henry More in MYSTERY OF INIQUITY (1664) spoke rebukingly of *those great and opime preferments and dignities which thy ambitious and worldly minde so longingly hankers after.*

opimian. A most celebrated ancient Roman wine, best in the vintage of A.U.C.

633, when Opimius was consul. Shirley in FRASER'S MAGAZINE for February 1863 said: *The cry for light will not be silenced, though we . . . pour the hundred-yeared opimian before the shrine of Apollo.*

opsigamy. Marriage late in life. Greek *opse,* late + *gamos,* marriage. J. McCulloch, in THE HIGHLAND AND WESTERN ISLES OF SCOTLAND (1824) said: *Nor is there any danger of Donald's being flogged for opsigamy by the Highland nymphs as the Spartans were of old.*

opsimathy. (Accent on the second syllable.) Study late in life; learning acquired late. Greek *opse,* late + *mathe,* learning, whence *mathematics.* Hence *opsimath,* 'a laggard in learning'; not a dunce, but one like Rabbi Akiba ben Joseph (flayed by the Romans in 132 A.D.), who started his studies when he was forty years old.

opsony. Anything eaten with bread to give it relish. In ancient Greece and Rome this usually was fish (as it might today be caviar, smoked salmon, or pickled herring.) Greek *opsonion*; *opson,* cooked meat, relish, dainty. Hence also *opsophagist,* eater of dainties.

opsophagist. See *opsony.* A frequenter of pastry-shops, confectioners, and true purveyors of "delicatessen."

optate. To choose, especially between two alternatives. Also to *opt. Optable,* to be chosen, desirable. For an illustration of the use of *optate,* see *infaust.*

orangebutter. Another lost delicacy. A recipe is in THE CLOSET OF RARITIES (1706): *Take new cream two gallons* [ours is a meager time!], *beat it up to a thickness, then add half a pint of orange-flower-water, and as much red wine, and so being become the thickness of butter, it retains both the colour and scent of an orange.—Orange-flower water* was used also for perfume; its making was described in THE ACCOMPLISH'D FEMALE INSTRUCTOR (1719): *Take two pounds of orange-flowers, as fresh as you can get them, infuse them in two quarts of white wine, and so distil them, and it will yield a curious perfuming spirit.*

ordinary. As a noun. (1) A church officer or a civil judge who has authority by right of his position; an officer in charge of a convent; a staff of officers in regular service; a church officer whose function was to give the neckverse, *q.v.,* or to prepare the condemned for death. From the 13th century. In the 17th century, a prompter in the theatre. *In ordinary* (of a ship) laid up for repairs. (2) A prescribed or customary procedure; a regular custom; a church manual. (3) A customary, regular fixed meal; hence, a fixed allowance of anything. By extension (16th century), a public meal regularly offered at a fixed price in a tavern, table d'hôte; hence, the persons frequenting such a meal. By further extension, a tavern where such meals are provided; a dining-room. Thence, a gambling game played at a tavern. A very common word. *Here,* said a book of 1502, *endeth the booke named the Ordynarye of Crysten Men . . . emprynted in Flete Strete by Wynken de Worde.* For another instance of the word's use, see *whetstone.*

orectic. Characterized by appetite or desire. Used in the 18th and 19th centuries mainly in philosophical and medical works. Greek *orektos,* longed for; *oregein,* to stretch out, grasp for, desire. Symonds in THE RENAISSANCE IN ITALY (1881) speaks of *that blending of the reason with the orectic soul which we call will.*

ored. Adorned or covered with ore or metal. Feltham in RESOLVES DIVINE, MORALL, AND POLITICAL (1623) cried out upon *obscene scurrilities that the stage presents us with . . . or'd and spangled in their gaudiest tyre. Oredelf* (*ore* + *delve,* dig) was the early term (to the 17th century) for the right a man might claim to the minerals dug in his ground.

orfever. A goldsmith (15th century; rare). More common in the 15th century, and revived in the 19th, was *orfevrerie,* the work of a goldsmith. Via French from popular Latin *aurifabrum,* a worker in gold. *Orfrays, orfray, orphis, offreis,* are variant forms of *orphrey,* which came ultimately from Latin *aurum,* gold + *Phrygius,* Phrygian. The original form had an *s,* but was taken for a plural, so that the forms without *s* came into use. *Orfray* meant gold embroidery; a richly embroidered stuff, especially an ornamental border on an ecclesiastical garment. Thynne in 1599 distinguishes between *orefryes* 'a weved clothe of golde' and 'goldsmythe woorke,' *orfevrerie.* Chaucer in THE ROMAUNT OF THE ROSE (1366) says *Of fyn orfrays hadde she eke A chapelet so seemly on.* A York Mystery of 1415 lists *orfevers, goldbeters, monemakers.*

orgeat. A syrup, or a cooling drink made therefrom. In the 15th century it was made from barley (French *orge,* from Latin *hordeum,* barley) and was apparently no tastier than the oatmeal water I was sometimes allowed to drink, from pails waiting to refresh the marchers in the Police Parades of my childhood. As late as 1843 Thackeray (MISCELLANEOUS ESSAYS) speaks of *pulling a queer face over a glass of orgeat* (*pronounced orjaw*). Later, the syrup was made from almonds, or from orange-flower water, and presumably made a more succulent drink. Hannah More (but that was in BAS BLEU, 1786) exclaimed: *Nor be the milk-white streams forgot Of thirst-assuaging, cool orgeat.* Probably to be preferred to the current "colas"!

orgulous. Proud; swelling, violent; splendid. Also *orgillous, orgueilous, orguillous, orgullows.* From *orgueil, orguil, orgul,* pride. *Orgueil* is direct from the French (12th century), presumably from an Old High German form *urguol,* renowned. *Orgueil* has not been used since the 16th century, save as a fresh borrowing from the French. The 15th century also used *orgulity,* pride. Shakespeare used the adjective in TROILUS AND CRESSIDA (1606): *From iles of Greece The princes orgillous, their high blood chaf'd Have to the port of Athens sent their shippes.* The word then dropped from the language, until revived by Southey (1808), Scott (1820), Bulwer-Lytton (in HAROLD, 1848: *This our orgulous Earl shall not have his triumph*) and subsequent journalists.

orgyan. Relating to or marked by revelry, excessive indulgence, or debauchery. From *orgy, orgie,* originally (Greek *orgia,* the plural, also used in English) secret rites, especially a nocturnal festival in honor of Bacchus, god of the vintage; hence, rites or secret observances in general; especially, those marked by licentiousness. The more usual adjectives are *orgiac, orgial, orgiastic, orgic.* The state of excitement at orgies, *orgiasm,* used by Milman (HISTORY OF CHRISTIANTY; 1840) of *the working of a divine influence upon the soul,* has been confused with the similar but more explosive state of *orgasm,* as *orgiastic* and *orgastic* may be confused or fused. One that celebrates orgies is an *orgiast.* Nor should *orgyan* be confused with *Augean,* which is applied (1) to a tremendous, a Herculean, task; (2) to a tremendous gathering of filth, figuratively, of corruption; *Augean stable.* The fifth labor of Hercules was to clean the stables of *Augeas* (*Augias*) king of Elis. In the Augean stables had been kept an immense number of oxen and goats; Hercules removed the filth from the never-cleaned stables by diverting into them the course of the river Alpheus (some legends say, the Peneus). Cleansing politics would be an Augean task, but one would have to start with human nature.

orifex. Old form for *orifice,* opening. Used by Marlowe (TAMBURLAINE, PART TWO; 1590) and Shakespeare. Latin *os, orem,* mouth + *-ficium* from *facere,* to make. Hence also *orifacture,* the act of making with the mouth (17th century, e.g., Marvell), as of soap-bubbles. Nashe in THE UNFORTUNATE TRAVELER (1594) wrote: *O orificiall rethorike, wipe thy everlasting mouth*—more properly *orifical,* making with the mouth; hence, bombastic. Troilus, when he discovers the loose behavior of Cressida (Shakespeare's TROILUS AND CRESSIDA; 1606) exclaims: *This is, and is not, Cressid! Within my soul there doth conduce a fight Of this strange nature, that a thing inseparate* [inseparable, indivisible] *Divides more wider than the sky and earth, And yet the spacious breadth of this division Admits no orifex for a point as subtle As Ariachne's broken woof to enter. Ariachne* fits the rhythm. Many critics call it a slip of Shakespeare's. It may, however, represent a telescoping of two Greek legends: (1) *Arachne,* daughter of a dyer of Colophon, was so skilful with the needle that she challenged Minerva. Arachne wove into her work the amours of Jupiter with Aegina, Alcmene, Antiope, Asteria, Callisto, Danae, Dione, Electra, Europa, Klytoris, Laodamia, Leda, Maia, Niobe, Pyrrha, Semele—not to mention his wives, Metis, Themis, Eurynome, Ceres, Mnemosyne, Latona, and Juno. But who can defeat a goddess? In despair, Arachne hanged herself; Minerva changed her into a spider, whence *arachnean,* like a spider's web, gossamer, and the hosts of the *arachnida.* (2) *Ariadne,* daughter of Minos II of Crete, was also involved with thread; she gave Theseus a ball of thread to unroll as he went into the Labyrinth, so that he could retrace his steps after killing the Minotaur. He carried her away, but at the island of Naxos abandoned her. *Arachne* telescoped with *Ariadne* gives *Ariachne.* Shakespeare is often wiser than his critics.

orison. A prayer. From Old French *oreisun, orison* (French *oraison*); Latin *orationem,* whence also *oration.* Common in English from the 12th to the 19th century. Shakespeare in HAMLET (1602) has the Prince say: *Soft you now, the fair Ophelia? Nymph, in thy orizons Be all my sins remembered.* Less pious is the Urquhart translation (1653) of Rabelais: *To the same place came his orison-mutterer.*

ormete. Boundless, immense; excessive. Old English *or,* without + *maete,* mean; *metan,* to measure. Used up to the 14th century.

ormod. Spiritless, despondent; despairing. Old English *or,* without + *mod,* mind, *mood.* Used into the 13th century.

ormuzine. A silken fabric popular in the 16th and 17th centuries. The name is from *Ormuz,* a port near the entrance to the Persian gulf, frequented especially by Portuguese traders. Also *ormasi, armosie, armozeen.* Hakluyt in his VOYAGES (1599) speaks of *armesine of Portugal.* The term *armozeen* was applied particularly to a plain stout silk, usually black, used for clerical gowns, mourning scarfs, and the like. The Scotch used the form *ormasi.*

orniscopy, ornithomancy. See *aeromancy.*

orped. Stout, strenuous, valiant; of animals, fierce, furious. Hence *orpedlich, orpedly,* bravely; *orpedness, orpedship,* bravery. Used through the 15th century. Gower in CONFESSIO AMANTIS (1390) seeks *some orped knyht to slay this lord.* Trevisa in the POLYCHRONICON HIGDEN (ROLLS), translated 1387, said: *The Emperour dede nothing orpedliche.*

orpharion. A large lute-like instrument, with from six to nine pairs of metal strings, played with a plectrum. Invented, the story goes, by John Rose of London about 1560, the orpharion was popular through the 17th century. *Cp. cithern.* Jonson in THE POETASTER (1601) cries: *Another Orpheus! an Arion riding on the back of a dolphin*; and the name *orpharion* is a combination of *Orpheus* and *Arion*—telescoping the two mythical musicians. Drayton in his ECLOGUES (1593) said: *Set the cornet with the flute, The orpharion to the lute.* Enjoy the music!

orphery. See *orfever.*

orrery. A mechanism representing the motions of the planets about the sun. Invented about 1700 by George Graham, made by the instrument-maker J. Rowley, it was named (by Dean Swift) after a purchaser, Charles Boyle, Earl of *Orrery.* Young in NIGHT THOUGHTS (1742) said of something belittling, it *dwarfs the whole, and makes an universe an orrery.* Lowell in his ITALIAN JOURNAL (1854) said: *When that is once done, events will move with the quiet of an orrery.* Sir John Herschel in his ASTRONOMY (1833) said, speaking of the magnitudes and distances of the planets: *As to getting correct notions on the subject by drawing circles on paper or, still worse, from those very childish toys called orreries, it is out of the question.*

ort. Usually in the plural, *orts,* scraps left over from a meal, or fodder left by cattle; refuse leavings; hence as a term of contempt, *to make orts of,* to treat shabbily. Shakespeare uses the word in THE RAPE OF LUCRECE (1593), in TROILUS AND CRESSIDA; and in TIMON OF ATHENS: *some slender ort of his remainder*; George Eliot, in SILAS MARNER (1861): *Their feasting caused a multiplication of orts, which were the heirloom of the poor.* Used figuratively in the 17th century, as when would-be wags followed the nimble-tongued for the orts of wit that fell from their mouths.

orth. Breath, breathing. A common Teutonic word, for breathing out. By extension, wrath. Used 10th to 13th century.

orthangle. A rectangle. Greek *orthos,* right, as in *orthodoxy* (*doxos,* opinion). Used in the 17th century.

ortolan. See *hortus.*

oryctomancy. Greek *oryktos,* dug up. See *aeromancy.*

oscitate. To yawn from drowsiness. Latin *oscitare, oscitatum,* to gape; *os,* mouth + *citare,* to move, actuate. Hence *oscitant,* yawning, drowsy; *oscitation, oscitance, oscitancy.* These, however, developed the further sense of inattention, hence negligence. All the forms have been in use since the 17th century. THE NATION (New York, 15 February, 1900) said: *That they all went astray owing to a coincidence of* *oscitancy is clearly beyond belief*—and readers rushed for a dictionary.

osculation. See *exosculation.* An *osculary* was something to be kissed; Latimer in his SERMON BEFORE THE CONVOCATION of 1537 spoke of *manuaries for handlers of reliques . . . oscularies for kyssers.* A representation of Christ or the Virgin Mary, to be kissed during Mass, was called an *osculatory*; this form survives as an adjective, as when Thackeray in PENDENNIS (1849) said: *The two ladies went through the osculatory ceremony.* Also *osculable,* capable of being kissed; worthy of kissing, lovely. *osculant,* kissing. *osculum,* a formal kiss; *osculum pacis* (Latin), the kiss of peace. *osculatrix,* a female that kisses; also, the developable surface generated by the tangents of a non-plane curve; *osculation* is used in mathematics for kissing—contact—of a higher order, touching at three or more points. The mathematicians have a point.

ossomancy. See *aeromancy.*

otherwhere. A good Shakespearean form, for which we have substituted *elsewhere, some where else.* Romeo says of himself: *This is not Romeo; he's some otherwhere.* I'll say more of this some otherwhile.

otiation. Taking one's ease. Latin *otiari, otiatum; otium,* leisure. Hence, *otiant,* at leisure, indolent, doing nothing—the usual state of most actors. *Cp. ocivity.* Puttenham in THE ARTE OF ENGLISH POESIE (1589) spoke of those that manage *to seeme idle when they be earnestly occupied . . . and do busily negotiat by coulor of otiation.* Negotiation through otiation is a good trick.

otium. See *ocivity*; *otiation.*

oubliette. A dark and usually secret dungeon, reached only by a trap-door in the ceiling, often with a farther pit below, into which a prisoner might be plunged. (14th century French *oubliette,* a little forgotten place; *oublier,* to forget.) Occasionally used as a verb, as by Tennyson in his play BECKET (1884): *Could you keep her Indungeon'd from one whisper of the wind, Dark even from a side glance of the moon, And oublietted in the centre.*

ought. Past of *owe,* in all its senses. Thus Greville, in THE LIFE OF SIR PHILIP SIDNEY (1652) spoke of his *understanding heart that knew what was due to itself, and what it ought to others . . . the respect inferiors ought to their superiors.* A collection of CONCEITS in 1639 mentioned *a gentleman who had ought him money a long time.* He ought to have paid.

oundy. Wavy. Also *ounded*; *owndy, ownde.* Latin *undare, undatum,* to curl, flow in waves; *unda,* wave. The water-sprite via French is *Ondine* (superbly acted by Audrey Hepburn in Giraudoux' play of that name); via German, *Undine.* Hence also English *undulate*; *inundation.* An *ounding* was an adorning with wavy lines; Chaucer in THE PARSON'S TALE (1386) speaks of *the cost of embrowdynge the degise endentynge barrynge owndynge palynge wyndynge or bendynge and semblable wast of clooth in vanitee.*

ouph. This word probably originated in a typographical error: *ouph* instead of *auph, oph, oaph,* variants of *oaf.* The word first occurs in the 1623 edition of Shakespeare, in THE MERRY WIVES OF WINDSOR: *We'll dress like urchins, ouphes, and fairies, green and white.* The form was copied by later writers; naturally by Chatterton: *Ouph and fairy, light your fires,* and by Swinburne in TRISTRAM OF LYONESSE (1882): *Or how shall I trust* *more than ouphe or elf Thy truth to meward, who beliest thyself?*

Oaf, which was earlier *auf,* meant at first the child of an elf; especially, one substituted for a human child borne away by the elves or fairies, a changeling; hence, a deformed or half-wit child; a fool, a booby. Steele in THE TATLER, No. 248 (1710) speaks of marriages *between the most accomplished women and the veriest oafs.* The plural was also used in the form *oaves.* The expression *oaf-rocked* ('rocked' in the cradle) meant fool-born; either a booby from birth, or spoiled by over-indulgence from the start. The earlier form, *auf,* is related to Old Norman *alfr,* fairy, whence English *elf;* but the *auf* and the *oaf* are always the fairy's child, the changeling. And any babe stupid or deformed is obviously a changeling!

ouranic. See *uranical.*

ouranomancy. See *aeromancy.*

ourn. See *urn.*

ousel. Originally a name of the blackbird or the thrush; applied to a person of dark hair or complexion. Also *ouzel, woosel.* "And how doth . . . your fairest daughter and mine, my god-daughter Ellen?" asks Shallow in Shakespeare's HENRY IV, PART TWO (1597) and Silence replies: *Alas, a black ouzel!*

outrance. The last degree or limit, beyond bounds, as in *to fight* (*to the*) (*at*) *outrance,* to the death. The word is the same as in French (*combattre à outrance,* 13th century), ultimately from Latin *ultra,* beyond. The word was pronounced like *out* until about 1400, then the present (French) sound *oo* began to take its place, and (as *outmost* became *utmost*) the spelling frequently became *uttrance,* even *utterance.* Holland in his version (1601) of Pliny has: *As if sword-fences were brought into the lists to fight at outterance.* The return to *outrance* may be a later direct reborrowing from the French. Sometimes the French phrase *à outrance* is used (*à l'outrance* is incorrect).

outray. (1) To go beyond the bounds (literally), or (figuratively) to be excessive; to put out of bounds, expel. (2) An old form of *outrage,* in its various uses. (3) From the 17th century, to flash out as a ray; to excel in radiance. Thus Benlowes in THEOPHILA (1652) has: *Thou outray'st all diamonds of the skies.* Chaucer uses the word in the first sense, in his BOETHIUS (1374): *They ne sholden not owtrayen or forlyven from the vertues of hyr noble kynrede.*

outrecuidance. Excessive self-esteem or self-confidence; arrogance; presumptuousness. Via 12th century French *outrecuider* from Latin *ultra,* beyond + *cogitare,* to think. Scott revived the word; in IVANHOE (1819) he has: *It is full time . . . that the outrecuidance of these peasants should be restrained.* See also *surquedry.*

outwring. To press or force out, as by wringing. Chaucer in THE LEGEND OF GOOD WOMEN (1385) speaks of *tears falsly outwronge.*

overblow. To blow excessively. To blow (a thing) over, upset by blowing. To blow across the top of something; to blow past. To blow over, pass away; first of a storm, then of the passions. To blow up excessively; to cause to swell (with pride, etc.). Shakespeare in THE TAMING OF THE SHREW (1596): *To smile at scapes and perils overblowne;* Nashe in PIERCE PENILESSE (1592): *after the broyle was somewhat overblowne;* Kingsley in THE ROMAN AND THE TEUTON (1864): *overblown with self-con-*

ceit. Many verbs may have *over* as a prefix or as a following adverb; originally, the meanings overlapped; now, usually *over* as a prefix means excessively, *over* as a following adverb means again or across—as in *overact, act over; overbid; overdo; overeat; overheat; overload.* In some cases the meaning is the same either way: *overhang, hang over;* but notice *a hangover.* In still other cases, there is a greater difference in meaning, as with *overcome, come over; overlook; overrule; override; overtake. Cp. overeye.* One must not overreach.

overcrow. To crow over, exult over; to triumph over, subdue. Spenser in THE FAËRIE QUEENE (1590) wrote: *Then gan the villein him to overcraw.* Shakespeare in HAMLET (1602) has: *The potent poison quite overcrowes my spirit.* Scott, reviving the word, gives credit for its earlier use to Spenser.

overeye. To observe. Used by Shakespeare in the Induction to THE TAMING OF THE SHREW (1593). *overcome,* to take by surprise, in Macbeth; to come about, happen, in Chaucer's TROYLUS AND CRISEYDE (1374). *overglance,* to cast the eye over, in Shakespeare's LOVE'S LABOUR'S LOST. *overest,* the uppermost; Chaucer in the Prologue to THE CANTERBURY TALES (1386): *Ful thredbare was his overest courtepy. overlive,* to outlive, in Shakespeare's HENRY IV, PART TWO. *overscutched,* over-beaten, switched a lot, the *overscutched huswife* of HENRY IV, PART TWO probably means a trollop: *A came ever in the rereward of the fashion, and sung those tunes to the overscutcht huswives, that he heard the car-men whistle.* There is also the suggestion, however, that *overscutched* means overworked, worn out in service; Scott uses it in this sense in THE BRIDAL OF TRIERMAIN (1813): *For harp's an overscutched phrase, Worn out by bards of modern days.*

overplant. To transplant. So used, 10th to 14th centuries; Wyclif in his BIBLE (LUKE; 1388) wrote: *Be thou drawun up bi the rote, and be overplauntid in to the see.* In the 19th century, *overplant,* to plant excessively: *overplanted gardens;* when the price was high (U.S. FISHERIES REPORT; 1887) *overplanting of oysters.*

overscutch. See *overeye.*

overture. (1) An opening, orifice, hole. From the 13th to the 18th century; both literal and figurative. (2) An open, exposed place. Spenser in THE SHEPHERD'S CALENDAR (1579) has: *The wastefull hylls unto his threate is a playne overture.* (3) The opening up of something; revelation, disclosure. Used by Shakespeare in THE WINTER'S TALE, and in KING LEAR (1605): *It was he That made the overture of thy treasons to us.* The still current sense of a beginning dates from the 16th century; in music, from the mid-17th. In the 16th and 17th centuries, some writers confused *overture* with *overturn, overthrow;* thus Nashe in CHRIST'S TEARS (1593): *Consider, howe his threats were after verified in Jerusalems overture.* In a troublesome passage in CORIOLANUS—*When steele grows soft as the parasites silke, Let him be made an overture for th' warres—overture* may mean overthrower: "When a soldier turns flatterer, he brings dishonor on war"; some editors improve matters little by changing the word to *coverture,* which would seem the opposite of an overture.

overweening. See *ween.* Richardson in PAMELA (1742) notes that *Half the misunderstandings among married people are owing to . . . mere words, and little cap-*

tious follies, to overweenings, or unguarded petulances. The word has survived mainly as an adjective, as in Shakespeare's TWO GENTLEMEN OF VERONA (1591): *Go base intruder, overweening slave.* John Aubrey (1697) said: *No reason satisfies him but he overweenes, and cutts some sower faces that would turn the milke in a fair ladie's breast.*

oxymel. A drink or syrup of vinegar and honey, used from Saxon times into the 19th century, as a medicine. Greek *oxys,* sour + *meli,* honey. Elyot gives one formula in THE CASTEL OF HELTHE (1533): *Oximell is, where to one part of vyneger is put double so moche of honye, foure tymes as moche of water.* That ought to clear the throat!

oyez. Hear! A call (usually three times) by the public crier or court officer, to command silence and attention. The word is from Old French *oiez, oyez,* imperative form of *oir,* to hear; Latin *audiatis.* Pronunciation shifted, and the word was sometimes thought to be *O ye(z),* O you people; or *O yes;* hence it is sometimes spelled *oyes.* Hence the humorist Barham can say, in his INGOLDSBY LEGENDS (1842): *But when the crier cried 'O Yes!' the people cried 'O No!'* Lyly in his CAMPASPE (1584, remembered for its song "Cupid and my Campaspe played At cards for kisses; Cupid paid.") has *O ys, O ys, O ys, all manner of men, women, and children.*

oyster-chevit. A dish. A recipe is in THE CLOSET OF RARITIES (1706): *Take three quarts of large oysters, wash them from grit, strain their own liquor through a linnen cloth, and parboil them in it. Then wash them in warm water, dry them in a linnen cloth, and mince them very small. Season them very lightly with salt, pepper, and beaten cloves, mace, cinnamon, and carraway seeds beaten, a little handful of raisins of the sun, and six or seven dates, strew'd with a few currans, a little sugar, and half a pint of white wine. Put these into small pans with crust, and well buttered; bake them gently and serve them up on a plate with sugar scraped on the lid.* THE ACCOMPLISH'D FEMALE INSTRUCTOR (1716), a rival publication (*cp. orange-butter*), gave an even more packed recipe, with *barberries preserved or pickled, mace in blades,* for making *oyster-pie.*

ozokerit. An aromatic fossil resin, waxlike. It was first found in Moldavia, and named (in German) *ozokerit,* from Greek *ozo,* I smell + *keros,* beeswax. Also *ozocerite, ozokerite.* BLACKWOOD'S EDINBURGH MAGAZINE of September 1884 announced: *The ozokerite or earth wax of Galicia is found in great abundance.* Edwards, in WORDS, FACTS, AND PHRASES (1912) said that ozokerit *when properly prepared makes candles of exquisite beauty.*

P

pabulous. Abounding in fodder or food. Also *pabular, pabulary,* relating to forage or food. *Pabulum,* directly from the Latin, is properly applied to food of plants and animals; its use for human food is pedantic or humorous. It is, however, applied figuratively, as when Sterne in TRISTRAM SHANDY (1765) declares: *Such a story affords more pabulum to the brain than all the frusts, and crusts, and rusts of antiquity.* The Latin root *pa-* is also the source of *pasture, pastor,* and *pater* (father, the feeder of the family).

pacate. To make peaceful. As a verb, this is rare; in the 17th century *pacate* was used as an adjective meaning pacified, tranquil: *a pacate, humble, self-denying mind.* Latin *pacare, pacatus,* to pacify; *pacem,* peace. Hence also *pacative,* calming, sedative; *pacation.* Coleridge remarked, in his essay ON THE CONSTITUTION OF THE CHURCH AND STATE (1830): *Reasonable men are easily satisfied; would they were as numerous as they are pacable!*

pacolet. A magic horse, which can convey one instantly whithersoever one may desire. Also used of a very swift steed. In the 16th and 17th centuries, usually the phrase *Pacolet's horse* was used; later *pacolet* alone—as now *a frankenstein* is often used for *Frankenstein's monster. Pacolet* was the name of a dwarf (in the romance of Valentine and Orson) who made a magic horse of wood that could transport him instantly to any desired place. Thus Sidney, discussing the drama's 'unity of place' in his APOLOGY FOR POETRIE (1580) said: *I may speake . . . of Peru, and in speech digresse from that, to the description of Calicut; but in action, I cannot represent it without Pacolets horse.* The pacolet is the western equivalent of the magic carpet.

pactitious. Done or settled by agreement. Latin *pactum,* agreement (English *pact*), *paciscere, pactum,* to come to an agreement, the inceptive form from *pacare,* to make peace. *Cp. pacate.* The word is found only in 17th and 18th century dictionaries.

pad. A toad. Generally pictured in the Middle Ages (as Shakespeare phrases it in AS YOU LIKE IT) as ugly and venomous; hence, *a pad in the straw,* a lurking or hidden danger. In the 17th century, *pad* came into use as slang for path, the road. Hence, *on the pad,* tramping; *to stand pad,* to beg by the way; *gentleman* (*knight, squire*) *of the pad,* highwayman. Also, *footpad.* By the end of the 17th century, *pad* was used alone, to mean highway robber. *Pad,* the toad, by the 14th century developed a diminutive *paddock,* which was applied to both the toad and the frog (Wyclif's BIBLE: EXODUS in 1382 uses *froggis;* in 1388 *paddokis*). Spenser in THE SHEPHERD'S CALENDAR (1579; DECEMBER) pictures *The grieslie todestoole . . . And loathed paddocks lording on the same.* The word was applied to an evil person (or a familiar spirit in the shape of a toad), as in Shakespeare's MACBETH (1605) *Padock calls anon: faire is foule, and foule is faire.* For another quotation, *cp. gib.* Hence *to pad,* to rob, as in Sedley's THE MULBERRY GARDEN (1668): *What, ladies, come apadding for hearts here, in your vizards? . . . What, rob us of our liberties without a word? not so much as Stand and deliver?* What chance has a man against a wizard in a vizard? [Both *wizard* (now male) and *witch* (now female) were earlier applied to either sex.]

paedonymic. See *podalic.* Also *paidonymic.* The practice of giving paedonymics is *paedonymy* (accent on the *don*); it is found among some primitive peoples.

pagany. The land, domain, or state of mind of the pagans; pagandom. Also *payeny, paeni, paygne, paynye,* and the like; via Old French *paienie; paien,* whence English *payen,* pagan; Latin *paganus,* of the country, rustic; *pagus,* a province, the countryside. *Cp. paynim.* Lord Berners in THE BOKE OF DUKE HUON OF BURDEUX (1533) said: *He slew Sorbryn, the moost valyant knyght in all pagany.* Thus also *paganalian,* relating to the rustic feasts and festivals (May Day, Thanksgiving, country fairs) which in Roman times were held in each *pagus* or rural district and called *paganalia;* English, *paganals.*

pagled. Made pregnant; big with child. *To paggle,* to bulge, swell out. Nashe in LENTEN STUFFE (1599) pictured the gods deciding Hero's fate after she had drowned herself for love of Leander: *For that she was pagled and timpanized* [made drum-like], *and sustained two losses under one, they footebald their heads together* [went into a huddle]—and turned her into a fish, the herring. Inscrutable are the ways of the gods.

palaceous. See *palacious.* Note that *paleaceous* means chaffy; covered with chafflike scales. Its uses extend from botany to architecture; Chambers' CYCLOPAEDIA (SUPPLEMENT; 1753) described the Roman *receptaculum* (waiting-room): *Its surface is sometimes naked, and sometimes paleaceous.*

palacious. A 17th century form, supplanted by *palatial.* Thus Dekker in BRITTANNIA'S HONOR (1628) spoke of *faire, spacious, and pallacious houses.* Note that *palaceous* is a scientific term meaning spade-like, spade-shaped; from Latin *pala,* shovel. *Palaceward,* toward the palace, is used by Chaucer in TROYLUS AND CRISEYDE (1374): *As was his wey to wende to paylaysward.*

paladin. A knight errant; a renowned champion. Originally one of the twelve peers of Charlemagne's court, of whom the *Count Palatine* was foremost. Via French *paladin,* Italian *paladino,* from Latin *palatinus,* belonging to the palace; whence also English *palatine.* An earlier form in English was *palasin,* applied especially to a lady of the court, from Old French *palaisin.* Daniel, turning in DELIA (1592) to contemporary love, cried *Let others sing of knights and palladins!*

paleaceous. See *palaceous.*

pale-maille. A mallet for striking a ball; also, the game played therewith. Italian *palla,* ball + *maglio,* mallet; Latin *balla* + *malleus,* hammer; whence *malleable.* Also *pallemaile* and other forms; those surviving are *pellmell* and *pall-mall.* The game, popular in 16th century Italy, France, and Scotland, and 17th century England (introduced there by James I), consisted of driving a wooden ball through an arch of iron in the ground (or, as the O.E.D. describes it, through a suspended ring) at the end of a long alley; the one doing this in the fewest strokes won. The game thus seems a simple form of what we call *croquet.* King Charles II played *pale-maille* on the *mall* in St. James's Park—where, Gilbert-and-Sullivaniacs will remember, the minx Iolanthe was heard to remark she'd "meet him after dark and give him one."

palestral. Pertaining to wrestling; athletic. Also *palaestral; palestric, palestrical.* The *palaestra,* Greek *palaistra* (*palaiein,* to wrestle), was an ancient gymnasium, a place for the teaching and exercise of wrestling and other athletics. Hence, since the 15th century, the practice of wrestling or athletics; also used figuratively, as when Thomas P. Thompson in EXERCISES, POLITICAL AND OTHERS (1840) feared the time *when the conduct of criminal justice is but a palaestra or course of exercise, to be turned on occasion against perhaps the most deserving members of the community.* A *palestrian* was a wrestler. Chaucer in TROYLUS AND CRISEYDE (1374) spoke of *the feste and pleyes palestral.*

palfrey. A riding-horse, but not a war-horse; especially, a small saddle-horse for ladies. Used since the 12th century, lingering in romantic and poetic use. Also *palefrai, paulfrey,* and more. The word is via French from Greek *para,* beside, extra + Latin *veredus,* light horse. In Portuguese, Spanish, and Italian, forms ending *-freno* developed, under the influence of Latin *frenum,* bridle; these came into English in *palfrenier,* a man in charge of horses; Thackeray in his PARIS SKETCH-BOOK (1840) commented: *He calls his palfrenier a groom.* Other forms of this word were *palfreynyer; palfreyour, palfreur, palfrer,* these three untouched of the bridle (*frenum*). D'Urfey, in his PILLS TO PURGE MELANCHOLY (1719) tells that *A palphry proud, prick'd up with pride, Went prancing on the way.* This was a word Scott could not miss: *A maiden on a palfrey white* comes early in his telling.

palimpsest. Writing material that can be used over again, the first writing wiped or rubbed off. Greek *palin,* again + *psestos,* scraped; *psao, psen,* to rub smooth. Hence, parchment or other material used for a second time; this sense survives, applied to old manuscripts. Also used figuratively, as by De Quincey in SUSPIRIA (1845): *What else than a natural and mighty palimpsest is the human brain?*

palinal. Moving backward; relating to or characterized by backward motion. Greek *palin,* backward, whence also *palindrome.* Thus *palinate,* to move backward, retrogress. The word is used in science, as of the lower jaw in mastication; but it may well have figurative use; *cp. lobsterize.*

palinure. A pilot. From *Palinurus,* the pilot of Aeneas, as told in Vergil's AENEID. Used in the 17th century, mainly figuratively, as by Fuller in JOSEPH'S COAT, DAVID'S SIN (1640): *The winding shelves do us detain Till God, the palinure, returns again.*

Palladian. (1) Relating to Pallas Athene, the goddess of wisdom, whom the Romans called Minerva. The name *Pallas* may come from (a) *Pallas,* a giant, son of Tartarus and Gaea, whom Athene killed —flaying him and using his skin for armor; (b) Greek *pallo,* brandisher: as goddess of war she was pictured brandishing a spear; (c) Greek *pallas,* virgin. The adjective *Palladian* was used in English to mean inspiring wisdom; Milton in the AREOPAGUS (1644): *all his considerate diligence, all his midnight watchings, and* *expence of Palladian oyl . . .* (2) Relating to the style of the Italian architect Andrea Palladio (1518-1580), who indiscriminately mixed the classical orders. Micklethwaite in MODERN PARISH CHURCHES (1874) said *Europe has never seen a worse style than the Palladian;* Ruskin in THE STONES OF VENICE (1851): *We shall get rid of Chinese pagodas, and Indian temples, and Renaissance Palladianisms, and Alhambra stucco and filigree, in one great rubbish heap.* It seems the Palladian style is good to have forgotten; but not the Palladian lamp—which, however, must be not rubbed but lighted. Note that *palladic* and *palladious* refer to the chemical element *palladium;* and *cp. ancile.*

palladium. See *ancile.*

palliament. A robe; especially, the white gown worn by a Roman candidate for the consulship. Latin *pallium,* cloak; *palla,* a long robe. Thus Shakespeare (1588): *Titus Andronicus, the people of Rome . . . Send thee by me . . . This palliament of white and spotlesse hue, And name thee in election for the Empire.* To *palliate* was originally to cover, as with a cloak; then to disguise, conceal; then to conceal the enormity of an offence, to excuse, to tone down.

palliard. A vagabond, who slept on the straw in barns. From French *paille,* straw. Hence, a dissolute rascal; a lecher, a debauchee. Raleigh in his HISTORY OF THE WORLD (1614) spoke of Sardanapalus: *A most luxurious and effeminate palliard he was* and of Jupiter: *He gave himself over wholly to palliardize and adultery.* Thus *palliardize, pallardry,* lechery, fornication. *To palliardize,* to fornicate; to be a procurer of. T. Milles in 1619 records that Charlemagne's *eldest daughter was found palliardizing (paillardising) with . . . Eginhard, his secretary.* A straw shows which way the wind blows.

palliate. See *palliament.*

pall-mall. See *pale-maille.* The mallet, the game, the alley along which the game was played—then a London street developed from such an alley, a center of London club activity.

palm. The palm tree is a transferred use of Latin *palma,* palm of the hand, because of the shape of the leaves. As a highly prized tree, *palm* was applied to a distinguished person; Shakespeare in TIMON OF ATHENS (1607) says: *You shall see him a palme in Athens againe.* Also, a form of tennis, somewhat like the present handball, popular in the 15th and 16th centuries; also *palm-play.* A regulation of the English Gilds (1467) read: *Item, that no man play at tenys or pame withyn the geld halle.* Surrey in prison in Windsor (1537) recalled his happy youth there: *The palme play, where, dispoyled* [stripped] *for the game, With dazed eies oft we by gleames of love Have mist the ball, and got sight of our dame . . .*

palmary. (1) Relating to the palm of the hand. This sense is current in anatomy, etc. (2) Bearing the palm; holding or deserving first place or highest prize; excellent; of prime importance; main, chief. As a noun, *palmary,* a token of victory. John Quick, in A SERIOUS INQUIRY . . . WHETHER A MAN MAY LAWFULLY MARRY HIS DECEASED WIFE'S SISTER (1703) declared that *the palmary argument for these marriages . . . is this, their great expediency.*

palmaster. One that reads character or fortune in the palm of the hand. More vaguely, a fortune-teller. Also *palmastrer; cp. medicaster.* Hoby in his translation

(1561) of Castiglione's THE COURTYER, declared that, *as there can be no circle without a centre, no more can beawty be without goodnesse . . . And therefore is the outwarde beawtie a true signe of the inwarde goodnes, and . . . it is seene that palmastrers by the visage knowe manye tymes the condicions, and otherwhile the thoughtes of menne.*

palmer. (1) A palm tree. Medieval Latin *palmarius*; Latin *palma.* (2) A ferule, or a flat stick for striking the palm of the hand in punishment. The word was used from the 14th through the 17th century; the punishment persisted in the schools of my childhood. (3) One who palms objects (cards and the like) in sleight of hand, or in cheating. (4) One who had made the pilgrimage to the Holy Land, as a sign of which he carried a palm branch or leaf—hence, often, a begging vagrant. In ROMEO AND JULIET (1592) Shakespeare says that *palm to palm is holy palmers kiss*; Scott revived the word (out of use 150 years) in MARMION (1808). John Heywood in THE FOUR P'S (1569) presents a Palmer, a Pardoner, a Pothecary and a Pedlar in a contest—the pedlar the judge—as to which can tell the biggest lie. (A Pardoner is one licensed to sell papal pardons or indulgences. Also see *clyster*; *cp. chichevache.*) The Pardoner tells of a visit to hell, and how glad the devil was to let out the soul of Margery Coorson, so sharp-tongued a shrew that she was beyond even the devil's endurance. Whereupon the Palmer expresses his surprise: in all his travels he "never saw or never knew any woman out of patience"—and at once is awarded the prize for the biggest lie. The palmer took the palm.

paltripolitan. An insular city-dweller. Coined in scorn from *metropolitan* and *paltry.* Originally intended of a churchman; a *metropolis* was a cathedral city. "Martin Marprelate" in HAY ANY WORKE FOR COOPER (1589) threatened: *I will so thunderthump your paltripolitans . . .*

pam. See *loo.* French *pamphile* was the name of the card game, also of the knave (Jack) of clubs, the highest card in the game; hence *pam,* a winner, a winning trick. Thence the abbreviations, *pamphie, pawmie, pam.* Also *cp. lanterloo.* Hood in his STORM AT HASTINGS (1845) cried *A living Pam, omnipotent at loo!* (It was Wellington at Waterloo.) R. Estcourt used the word figuratively in THE FAIR EXAMPLE (1706): *Let me tell ye, Madam, scandal is the very pam in conversation.*

pamphagous. All-devouring; omnivorous. Greek *pan,* all + *phagos,* eating. Used in the 18th century.

pamphelet. A courtesan. Old French *pamphilet,* beloved by all; Greek *pan,* all + *philetos,* to be loved. Used (rarely) in the 16th century. Latin *Pamphilus, seu de Amore* (Old French *Pamphilet*) was the title of a short but very popular 13th century work, which gave its name—the English form is *pamphlet,* still current—to any brief printed work. Hence also *pamphil* (16th century), a memorandum, a note.

pampilion. A fur used in the 15th and 16th centuries, for the trimming of garments. Also the name of the animal—its identity now unknown—that bore this fur. In the 16th century, the word was also used for a rough, coarse woollen fabric. Also *pampaylyone, pawmpilyon, pampyllon, pampilioun, pampelyon,* and more.

pampination. The removing of shoots from vines; pruning. Latin *pampinus,* vine-tendril. Hence also *pampinary,* relating to vine-tendrils; *pampinose,* full of twigs and leaves, untrimmed. To *pampinate, pampine,* to prune; *pamping,* a tendril, young shoot; hence, a youth. Thomas Heywood in the Prologue to THE FAYRE MAYDE OF THE EXCHANGE (1607) said: *Meanewhile shore up your tender pamping twig That yet on humble ground doth lowely lie.* To *pampinulate,* on the other hand, was to adorn with curling threads; in R.D.'s translation (1592) of Columna's HYPNEROTOMACHIA; THE STRIFE OF LOVE IN A DREAM, we read of *her starrie forehead pampynulated with threds of gold.*

pan-. Greek *pas, pan,* all. *Cp. pant-.* For *pan,* bread, see *panary.* For the tin *pan,* see *pancheon.* Among the less remembered of the many English forms with *pan-* are: *pananthropism.* H. B. Forman in LIVING POETS (1871): *If Mr. Swinburne's creed is describable in one word, that word must be made for the occasion—pananthropism . . . he sees the spirit of man (which be it borne in mind he calls 'God') everywhere animating and informing the universe. panatom,* an atom of a supposed primary substance of which all elements are composed, an early reaching out toward the *electron. panclastic,* an explosive that smashes everything, an early dream of a super-H bomb. *pancrastical* (Greek *pagchrestes,* good for everything), like a panacea; *cp. panchrest. pandaedalian,* all of most skilful workmanship; see *daedal. pandiabolism,* pervasive influence of evil. *pannomy,* belief in the universal supremacy or supreme importance of reason. *pansciolism,* a universal smattering of knowledge, too nearly our current state. *panselene,* the full moon.

panache. A tuft or plume of feathers, especially as a head-dress or on a helmet. Via Italian from Latin *penna,* feather, whence also the *pen* with which I *pen* these words. Hence, a similar adornment, e.g. a tassel. Also *penache, panack, pannach, pinnach.* Hence *panached, pennached,* with varied stripes of colors like a plume, as *panached tulips.* Evelyn in his DIARY for 7 September, 1651, noted: *He had in his cap a pennach of heron.*

panada. A dish popular in the 17th century, still used in the 19th: bread boiled to a pulp, then served with sugar, currants, nutmeg, and other spices. Also *panado, panade; panatel, panadella, panadina; ponade.* Via the Romance languages from Latin *panem,* bread. Philemon Holland's translation (1603) of Plutarch's PHILOSOPHIE said: *They give pappes and panades unto their little babes.* John Phillips, in A SATYR AGAINST HYPOCRITES (1655): *It was no Christmas-dish with pruens made, Nor white-broath, nor capon-broth, nor sweet ponade.* The form *panade*—Old French *panart, penard,* poniard—was also used for a large knife; Chaucer in THE REEVE'S TALE (1386) says: *And by his belt he baar a long panade.* The food *panada* was used figuratively to mean pap, easily-swallowed nonsense, as when BLACKWOOD'S EDINBURGH MAGAZINE in 1822 spoke of persons that *swallow, without flinching, all the theological panada with which she may think fit to cram them.* It's all so much bread-pudding.

panade. See *panada.*

panarchy. Universal rule; universal realm —the converse of *anarchy* (*an,* not). *Cp. pant-.* Bailey in FESTUS (1839) speaks of *the starry panarchy of space.*

panaret. An all virtuous one. Greek *aretos,* virtuous. *Cp. pant-.*

panary. A storehouse for bread. Also *panatry,* whence *pantry;* Latin *panarium;*

pan, panem, bread; whence the sop to the masses, of the Roman emperors: *pan et circenses,* bread and circuses. *Cp. panification. Panary* was also used as an adjective, relating to bread. We find the noun in the translators' Preface to the 1611 (King James) BIBLE: *It is a panary of wholesome food, against fenowed traditions; a physician's shop (as St. Basil calls it) of preservatives against poysoned heresies; a pandect of profitable laws against rebellious spirits; a treasury of most costly jewels against beggarly elements; finally, a fountain of more pure water, springing up unto everlasting life.*

panbone. The cranium, skullbone. Used in the 16th century.

pancake bell. A bell rung on Shrove Tuesday about 11 A.M., to call the people to be shriven before Lent, but popularly associated with the frying of pancakes. It was the signal for the holiday to begin, as Dekker notes in THE SHOEMAKER'S HOLIDAY (1599): *Upon every Shrove-Tuesday, at the sound of the pancake bell, my fine dapper Assyrian lads shall clap up their shop windows, and away.* The eleven o'clock ringing, said the Water Poet (in JACKE-A-LENT; 1620) *by the helpe of a knavish sexton is commonly before nine.*

pancarpial. Consisting of all kinds of fruits. Greek *pan,* all + *karpos,* fruit. R.D., in his translation (1592) of Columna's HYPNEROTOMACHIA; THE STRIFE OF LOVE IN A DREAM told of nymphs *with pancarpiall garlands of all manner of flowers, upon their heades.*

pancheon. A large shallow bowl or vessel. Also *panshin, panshion, panchin,* and the like. Related to *pan* and *pankin* (a little *pan*); possibly Latin *patina* (*patna,* Medieval Latin *panna*); *puncheon, q.v.* By (humorous) extension, the paunch. The *pancheon* was used especially for holding milk, to let the cream separate.

panchrest. A universal remedy, a panacea. Also *panchreston, panchrestum*; the plural is *panchresta.* The adjective is *pancrastical*; see *pan-.*

pancratic. Universally accomplished. Also *pancratical.* This is a figurative development from the original sense. The *pancratium* (Greek *pancration*) was an athletic contest combining wrestling and boxing. Greek *pan,* all + *kratos,* bodily strength; *pagkrates,* all-powerful. *Epic poetry,* said THE EDINBURGH REVIEW in 1808, *has been considered by critics a sort of poetical pancratium.* Hence *pancratist, pancratiast,* contender (or victor) in the pancratium. The 19th century developed a *pancratic microscope,* one with many degrees of power. Hammond in a Sermon of 1660 spoke of *a spiritual height, a full pancratick habit* and Lowell in the BIGLOW PAPERS (1848) pressed *the advantages of a pancratic education.*

pandect. A treatise covering a subject exhaustively. Especially, *the pandects,* the compendium of Roman civil law, set down in 50 books by order of Emperor Justinian in the 6th century, the Justinian code, basis of modern law. Hence, the complete body of laws of a country.

pandemic. General; through all mankind. Greek *pan,* all + *demos,* people. This sense is still current, especially in connection with disease (opposed to *epidemic,* spread over a limited area). Also *pandemian,* especially in relation to love: sensual love; Greek *pandemos eros,* common love, opposed to *ouranious,* heavenly. Thus Peacock in RHODODAPHNE (1818) explained: *Uranian love . . . is the deity or genius of pure mental passion for the good and the beautiful; and pandemian* *love, of ordinary sexual attachment.* Thus Greek *pandemos Aphrodite* meant the earthly Venus. The PALL MALL GAZETTE of 8 September 1883 said: *It is the pandemic not the heavenly goddess whose praises he chants.*

panderize. To act as a go-between in amorous affairs; to work as a pander. Hence *pandership; panderism; pandaric, panderous. Calvin,* observed Jeremy Bentham in a TREATISE of 1656, *saith that mixt dancing of men and women together, are nothing else than panderships and provocations to whoredome.* From *Pandaros* (Boccaccio, Chaucer, Shakespeare), who procured for Troilus the favors of Chryseis. *Venus,* remarked Florio in his translation (1603) of Montaigne, *cunningly enhanced the market of her wares, by the brokerage or panderizing of the lawes.*

pandiculation. A stretching and yawning, as sometimes before or after sleep. Latin *pandere,* to spread out, + a diminutive ending.

pandoura. See *bandore.* Also *pandora, pandore, pandura, pandola, pandur* (*q.v.*). A three-stringed lute. A *pandurist,* according to Blount (1656), was one that played "on a musical instrument called a rebech, or on a violin."

pandur. A fierce and brutal soldier; originally, a Croatian guardsman. From Serbo-Croatian *pandur,* a mounted policeman or guard. Also *pandoor, pandour.* The name was first applied, in 1741, to private police organized by Baron Trenck on his Croatian estates, to repel robber bands along the Turkish frontier; later, as part of the Austrian army, the pandurs became notorious for their rapacity and brutality. The word *pandur* was earlier *bandur;* Medieval Latin *banderius,* one enrolled under somebody's *banner.*

pandy. A blow upon the outstretched palm, with a strap, stick, or ferule. From Latin *pande palmam!,* stretch out your open hand! Hence *palmy* was used in the same sense, especially in Scottish schools; *cp. palmer* (2). Kingsley in THE WATER-BABIES (1863) uses it as a verb: *she . . . pandied their hands with canes.* These were 19th century terms.

panguts. A huge, fat-bellied fellow (a term of contempt). The word is a derisive combination of Greek *pan,* all, and *guts.* A panguts keeps near to the cooking pans.

panification. A making into bread. Via French from Latin *panem,* bread; *cp. panary.* Hence *panifiable,* capable of being made into bread; *panifice,* the craft of making bread; also, a loaf of bread. The 18th century was concerned (France, 1781; England, 1779) with panifying potatoes; but FRASER'S MAGAZINE in 1854 fumed to *see the blessed idea of Christian communion degraded into a mere act of divine panification!*

panion. A 16th century shortening of *companion.* T. Wilson in his RHETORIQUE (1553) has: *Whether he be a gamester, an alehouse haunter, or a panion among ruffians.*

panisk. A little Pan, a deity attendant upon the god Pan. Also *panisc;* the feminine is *panisca.* Jonson in THE PENATES (1604) spoke of *the paniskes, and the silvanes rude;* Leitch in his translation (1847) of Müller's ANCIENT ART AND ITS REMAINS describes several works, e.g., *A panisca at the music of Apollo opens her mouth wide; A good natured panisc plucks a thorn from the foot of a satyr.*

panjandrum. A pompous pretender, a 'high-mucky-muck.' In the phrase *the Grand Panjandrum,* a mock title for a person of grand airs. From the nonsense passage invented by the playwright Foote to stump the actor Macklin, who boasted he could memorize any passage by reading it over once. Foote's test words, as quoted in THE QUARTERLY REVIEW (1775), were: *So she went into the garden to cut a cabbage-leaf to make an apple pie, and at the same time a great she-bear came running up the street and popped its head into the shop. "What! no soap?" So he died and she—very imprudently—married the barber. And there were present the Picninnies, the Joblillies, the Garyulies, and the Grand Panjandrum himself, with the little round button atop, and they all fell to playing the game of catch-as-catch-can till the gunpowder ran out at the heels of their boots.* Macklin also ran out.

pannage. The feeding of swine, cattle, etc., in a forest; the right to such pasturage; the payment for such a privilege. Hence, acorns, beech-mast, and other woodland fodder. Also *pownage, pannadge, paunage,* and the like; Old French *pasnage;* Latin *pastionem,* feeding; *pascere, pastum,* to feed, to pasture.

pannam. See *pedlers French.*

pannicle. A membrane; especially, a layer of muscular fibres beneath the skin, or the membranes of the brain. Also *pannikelle, pannycele, panicle,* and the like; via French from Latin *panniculus,* diminutive of *pannus,* cloth. Spenser used the word (incorrectly) to mean the panbone, skull, in THE FAËRIE QUEENE (1590): *He . . . Smote him so rudely on the pannikell That to the chin he clefte his head in twaine.*

pannikin. A small metal drinking vessel, a cannikin. Used in the 19th century, especially in Australia. Also *pannican, panakin, panikin.* Marryat in JACOB FAITHFUL (1834) pictured men *bringing out the bottle and tin pannikins, ready for the promised carouse.*

panomphean. Resounding with horrid or ominous sound. *The panomphaean Zeus* was the god considered as speaking oracles; Greek *pan,* all + *omphe,* voice of a god. Motteux in his translation (1694) of Rabelais continues Rabelais' humorous use: *Trinc is a panomphean word, that is, a word understood, used, and celebrated by all nations and signifies Drink.* Hence also *panomphic, panomphaic.* Peacock in MAID MARIAN (1822) speaks of *that very panomphic Pantagruelian saint, well known . . . as a female divinity, by the name of La Dive Bouteille* [the divine bottle]. Cockeram in 1623 mistranslated *panomphean* as 'all-hearing,' but he may not have known *la Dive Bouteille.*

panpharmacon. A remedy against all diseases and poisons; a panchrest (*q.v.*), a panacea. Greek *pan,* all + *pharmakon,* drug. Also *pampharmacon.* Hence *panpharmacal,* panacean. William Salmon in his translation (1694) of Bates DISPENSATORY said: *It is used by some as panpharmacon, but what diseases it will absolutely cure I think is scarcely determined.*

pan-pudding. A pudding baked in a pan. Explained (1736) as fritters; (1839) as 'pudding made of flour, with small bits of bacon in it.' It was a popular, a common dish, (1606) 'a good dish for a grosse stomack.' Hence it was used as a term of scorn, as in one of Nashe's letters, for which use see *impostume.* In the 17th century, *to stand to one's pan-pudding,* to stand firm, hold one's ground; Motteux' translation (1694) of Rabelais exclaimed: *How bravely did they stand to their pan-puddings!*

panse. To think, meditate; heed; attend to the sick, dress (a wound). Also *pans, pance, panch; pense.* Via French from Latin *pensare,* to weigh, consider; *pendere, pensum,* to hang, weigh, whence also *pendulum.* Hence *pensative, penseful, pensiful* (14th century into the 18th), thoughtful; supplanted by *pensive. Pensy* (15th century), pensive; *pensiness; pensily,* pensively, sadly—but *pensile* (17th century), hanging, suspended; steeply overhanging as in Shenstone's THE RUINED ABBEY (1750): *His azure stream, with pensile woods enclos'd.* The pansy, of course (French pensée, thought) is the flower of thoughtfulness. A. Hume in HYMNS (1594) urged: *Studie not nor panse not meikle* [much] *on the feeding of the flesh.*

pant-. A combining form from Greek *panto-,* all; *cp. pan-.* Thus *pantarchy,* a government by all the people; *cp. panarchy. pantarete,* all-virtuousness; *cp. panaret. pantagamy* (accent on the *tag*), a system whereunder all the men of a household or community are deemed married to all the women and vice versa, as among the 19th century Perfectionists at Oneida Creek in the U.S. *pantechnicon,* first, a bazaar for all kinds of artistic work, a building in Motcomb Street, Belgrave Square, London, 1830; the project failed and the building became a warehouse for storing furniture; hence *pantechnicon,* short for *pantechnicon van,* a moving van. *pantechnic,* relating to or including all the arts; Lowell in THE BIGLOW PAPERS (1848) perceived *the advantages of a pancratic* [*q.v.*] *or pantechnic education. pantisocracy,* a form of social organization without rank, all being equal; Dowden in his SHELLEY (1887) tells us that Southey and Coleridge *dreamed of pantisocracy on the banks of the Susquehanna*—hence, *pantisocrat. pantogelastic,* all-laughable. *pantomancer,* a diviner of universal skill; *pantomancy,* prophesying by any and all devices; *cp. aeromancy. pantomorph,* that which takes any and all shapes; *pantomorphic,* able to assume any shape, like fancy, like the old man of the sea. *pantophile,* a universal lover, a lover of the universe. *pantoglot,* one that speaks all languages; *pantoglottism. panurgic,* able or ready to do anything; Morley in his DIDEROT (1878) spoke of *no less panurgic and less encyclopaedic a critic than Diderot himself.* The noun *panurgy* (as in the late Greek *panourgia,* knavery) took an evil turn, meaning craftiness, complete guile; meddling in all matters.

pantagruelism. 'A sort of high spirits worked up in despite of accidents—ready to drink too, if you will'. Thus Rabelais, who drew the word from his character—whose name Rabelais also explains: *One Friday, when people were all at their prayers, great drops of water exuded from the ground like drops of sweat. When, however, they collected and drank this marvelous dew they found it naught but brine, worse and salter than seawater. Now as it came to pass that Pantagruel was born on this very day, his father gave him a corresponding name; for panta in Greek signifieth all, and gruel in Arabic means thirsty—wishing to suggest that on his birthday all the world was thirsty, and seeing, in the spirit of prophecy, that he would one day become the Lord of the Thirsty.* Thus *pantagruelism* came to mean (Donaldson, THE THEATRE OF THE GREEKS; 1860) Bacchanalian buffoonery as a cloak to cover some serious purpose. Hence, *pantagruelist,* a jolly tippler (17th and 18th centuries), a follower of Pantagruel; or a satirist, a follower of Rabelais. Adjectives include *pantagruelistic, pantagruelian, pantagruelical, pantagrueline.* Also note *pantagruelion,* a word Rabelais used for hemp, the material of the hangman's rope. Kingsley in TWO YEARS AGO (1857) spoke of *an immediate external application . . . of that famous herb pantagruelion, cure for all public ills and private woes.*

pantarbe. A precious stone that could attract gold as the magnet does iron; the stone of the sun. Good to carry in one's pocket.

pantler. Before the 12th century, this meant a baker; Latin *panem,* bread. In the 13th century it took on the meaning, one that worked in or had charge of, the pantry. Also *panter, paunter, pantyr, panterer. Pantler* was used from the 14th through the 17th century; Shakespeare has it several times (e.g., in CYMBELINE II, iii, 129). Its use lingered; Barham in THE INGOLDSBY LEGENDS (1842) related with gusto how *Pantler and servingman, henchman and page, Stand sniffing the duck-stuffing (onion and sage).*

pantomancy. See *pant-*; *cp. aeromancy.*

panurgy. See *pant-.*

papelard. A parasite, a sycophant; a hypocrite. Also as an adjective, hypocritical. Italian *pappare,* to eat + *lardo,* fat, *lard;* hence, a 'sponge,' a 'sucker.' Thus also *papelardry, papelardy*; Lydgate (1426) speaks of *papyllardie which is a manner of ypocrysie.* These are 14th and 15th century terms.

papelote. Porridge. Also *paplot, paplette.* Related to *pap,* the breast giving suck; also soft or semi-liquid food—the word being echoic of the sound of an infant's lips opening and closing. A 14th and 15th century word.

papengay. See *popinjay.*

paralogical. Unreasonable; characterized by false reasoning. Also *paralogic.* Greek *para,* beyond, beside + *logos,* reason. Also *paralogy,* false reasoning; *paralogism,* an instance thereof, a faulty syllogism. Also *paralogician, paralogist.* To *paralogize,* to reason falsely. Most of these terms developed in the 17th century.

parament. A decoration. Latin *parare,* to make ready, fit out, adorn. Also *paramento,* from the Italian. *A chamber of parament,* a richly decorated room, hung with tapestry; hence, a presence chamber, a state room. Chaucer, in THE LEGEND OF GOOD WOMEN (1385) has: *To daunsynge chaumberys full of paramentys . . . This Enyas is led.* The word was also used, as in THE KNIGHT'S TALE of Chaucer, to mean a richly decorated robe, a robe of state.

paranymph. The best man or the bridesmaid at a wedding. Greek *para,* beside + *nymphe,* bride. Used from the 17th century (Milton; Southey). THE QUARTERLY REVIEW of 1863 said of Mary Stuart: *The paranymphs of the bridal were to be the fiends of war.* By extension, one that woos or speaks for another ("Speak for yourself, John!"), an advocate, a spokesman. Urquhart's translation (1693) of Rabelais advances one *to supply the place of a paranymph, braul broker, proxenete or mediator.*

paraph. (1) A paragraph. (2) A mark, ¶, in the margin, to indicate a break. (3) A flourish after a signature, originally as a precaution against forgery. *Paraph* is a shortening (which occurred in the Medieval Latin form) of *paragraph,* from Greek *para,* by the side + *graphos,* written. In early manuscripts there were no breaks in the writing, but a mark was made—originally, a short horizontal stroke below the beginning of the line—to indicate a break in the thought.

parasynaxis. An unlawful meeting; a secret conventicle. Greek *para,* on the side + *syn,* together + *axis,* root *ag* (Latin *agere,* to move). This is one of the words dictionary-makers of the 17th and 18th centuries were fond of coining, without relation to any actual use. *Parasynaxis,* which indeed sounds conspiratory, is in Bailey (1751).

paration. The act of making ready. Latin *parare, paratum,* to make ready. A 17th century form, supplanted by *preparation.* In the 14th century, *pare* meant to get ready; to adorn; to put in shape; to trim. (The shifts in meaning took place in medieval French.) *It is synne,* said THE BOOK OF THE KNIGHT DE LA TOUR-LANDRY (1450), *to have so mani diverse clothes, and to do so moche cost to pare* [adorn] *the foule body.*

paratragediate. To write or speak in bombastic language, or (intentionally or unintentionally) in mock-tragic style. The accent, naturally, is on the *gee.* A 1659 attack upon a preacher queried: *How doth Mr. Pierce paratragoediate? How doth he tumble in his ugly tropes, and rowle himself in his rayling eloquence?* Also, *paratragoedia,* mock-tragedy, as in the comedies of Aristophanes.

paravail. Below or beneath; lowest. The opposite of *paramount.* A *tenant paravail* was one who held land from another tenant; in legal writers since the 16th century, the one that actually worked the land. From Old French *par,* through + *à val,* to the valley, used in the sense of down; *paramount* was *par* + *à mont* (Latin *ad montem*), to the hill. Blackstone in his legal COMMENTARIES (1766) explains: *The king therefore was styled lord paramount; A was both tenant and lord, or was a mesne lord; and B was called tenant paravail, or the lowest tenant.*

paravant. In front; before; hence, pre-eminently. From Old French *par,* through + *avant;* Latin *ab ante,* from before. Also *paravaunt.* Spenser uses the word several times in THE FAËRIE QUEENE, also in COLIN CLOUT (1595): *Yet that I may her honor paravant, And praise her worth, though far my wit above.*

paraventure. An old form of *peradventure, q.v.*

parbreak. See *per-*.

parcel. A small part, or portion. Also *parcelle, passell, parsyll;* Italian *particella,* Latin *particulum,* diminutive of *pars, partem,* part, whence also is *particular.* Chaucer in THE COMPLEYNTE UNTO PITE (1368) cries: *What nedeth to shewe parcel of my peyne?* Hence, *by parcels,* piecemeal. Used figuratively, usually in scorn, to mean an insignificant person; Jonson, in CYNTHIA'S REVELS (1599): *What parcel of man has thou lighted on for a master?*—or a group, or lot, as in *a parcel of lies.* Hence, *parcel-guilty,* somewhat to blame. Dekker, in THE GULS HORNBOOK (1609): *Their parcel-Greek, parcel-Latin gibberish.* In other combinations: *parcel-learned; parcel-jocose, parcel-stupid.* A common repetitive phrase was *part and parcel,* like *without let or hindrance; with bag and baggage.* Spenser in his HYMNE IN HONOUR OF BEAUTIE (1596) says that spiritual beauty *is heavenly borne, and can not die, Being a parcell of the purest* *skie . . . For of the soule the bodie forme doth take: For soule is forme, and doth the body make.* [Make here has dual sense: create, and match.]

parciloquy. Moderation in words, speaking little. Latin *parcus,* sparing + *loqui,* to speak. The habit or practice of being laconic. A 17th century word.

parcity. Sparingness, frugality; by extension, scantiness, littleness. Latin *parcus,* sparing. Largely replaced by *paucity,* smallness (of quantity or supply), from Latin *paucus,* small. Barclay in THE SHYP OF FOLYS (1509) wrote: *As nere as the parcyte of my wyt wyl suffer me.*

pardee. As a mild oath, By God! Hence, certainly, verily. Old French *par dé;* French *par dieu,* by God. Also *pardie, perdie, pardi, perdye, per dieu, pardieu, pardy,* and more. A very common exclamation, from the 13th century. Chaucer in THE CANTERBURY TALES (1386; Prologue) says: *And yet he hadde a thombe of gold, pardee;* this alludes to the proverb: An honest miller has a thumb of gold. Shakespeare says in HAMLET (1602): *For if the King like not the comedie, Why then belike he likes it not perdie.*

pardoner. See *palmer.*

paregal. Fully equal (in rank, power, value). Via Old French from Latin *per,* thoroughly + *aequilis,* equal. Also *peregal, paringale, peringall, perregal, paruyngal,* and more. Used since the 13th century; Watson in A DECACORDON OF TEN QUODLIBETICALL QUESTIONS (1602) spoke of *Our noble Elizabeth, prince peregall, paramount and paragon.* The word was also used as a noun; thus Langland in RICHARD THE REDELES (the heedless; 1399) lamented the loss *through partinge of youre powere to youre paragals.*

parergon. By-work; work other than one's main or usual employment; in painting, an ornamental adornment or subordinate element. Greek *para,* beside + *ergon,* work. Hence *parergal,* supplementary, also *paregetic. parergastical,* done as a by-work. *parergic,* relating to by-work. A *parergy* is something aside from the business or purpose in hand. Sir Thomas Browne in PSEUDODOXIA EPIDEMICA (1646) stated: *The Scriptures being serious, and commonly omitting such parergies, it will be unreasonable from hence to condemne all laughter.*

pareunia. Coitus. Greek *pareunaios; para,* beside + *eune,* lying, bed. The English word is listed in American dictionaries; O.E.D. shows it not. The adjective would be *pareuniac,* which makes the deed sound reprehensible.

paridigitate. Having an equal number of toes or fingers on each foot or hand, like most humans.

parlous. A shortened form of *perilous,* with the same meaning. Used from the 14th century. Being popular, it developed other senses: risky to deal with, ticklish; dangerously cunning; mischievous, wicked. Then, loosely, it was used to mean greatly, excessively, 'terribly,' and even 'preciously' as (1870) *She is parlous handsome*—though this contains an echo of the original sense. The word was used by—among many others—Shakespeare, Milton, Fielding, and Keats.

parmacety. An early variant of *spermaceti.* Also *parmacete, permacetty, parmasity,* and the like. Shakespeare in HENRY IV, PART ONE (1596) says that *the sov-eraign'st thing on earth was parmacity, for an inward bruise.*

parnel. A priest's mistress; by extension, a wanton young woman. Also *peronall,* *pernel*, and the like. From Old French *Peronel*; Latin *Petronilla* (feminine diminutive of *Petrus*, Peter), a woman's name (*Saint Petronilla*); hence, Peter's woman. Used from the 14th century. A ballad recorded in 1800 says: *Parnels march by two and three, Saying Sweetheart, come with me. Parnellism,* however, meant the doctrines of the Irish followers of Charles Stewart *Parnell,* who from 1880 to 1891 led the fight in the House of Commons for Home Rule in Ireland; THE SPECTATOR of 28 May, 1887, decried *the shameless and persistent obstruction of the Parnellite members.*

parsel. An early variant of *parsley*; used in recipes.

parti. (1) A (good or bad) match in matrimony. A 19th century use, from French *parti,* chosen. Byron in a letter to Moore in October 1814 said: *It is likely she will prove a considerable parti.* (2) In the phrase *parti pris,* mind made up, bias. Morely in his essay on Carlyle (1871) spoke of *that fatal spirit of parti pris which has led to the rooting of so much injustice, disorder, immobility and darkness in English intelligence.* (3) *parti-*, as a prefix, means part in one way, part in another, as *parti-colored*; *parti-named,* having various names. Shakespeare, in LOVE'S LABOURS LOST (1588) speaks of the *partie-coated presence of loose love.*

partlet. (1) A hen; hence, a woman. Originally a proper name, Old French *Pertelote* (*cp. parnel*), applied by Chaucer and others (Shakespeare in THE WINTER'S TALE, 1611, as *Dame Partlet*) to the hen. (2) A linen neckerchief or the like, worn from the 16th century into the 18th about the neck and shoulders of a woman. Originally *patlet*; a will of 1522 leaves a man *my velvett jacket, to make his childer patlettes and cuyffes.* Sidney in the ARCADIA (1586) tells of Parthenia's *tearing off her linnen sleeves and partlet to serve about his wounds.*

parvanimity. Littleness of spirit. Latin *parvus,* small + *animus,* spirit, mind: small-mindedness; the converse of *magnanimity.* De Quincey in 1830 wrote of *the meanness and parvanimity of Bonaparte.* Several English words have been formed with the prefix *parvi,* small; some are scientific. Others include *parvitude, parvity,* smallness; *parvipotent* (accent on the *vip*), of little power; *parviscient,* knowing little. The common quality of man is *parviscience.*

pascual. Relating to, or growing in, pastures. Also *pascuous.* Latin *pascuum,* pasture, grazing; *pascere, pastus,* to feed, whence also *pasture, pastor.* Also *pascage, pascuage,* the grazing of kine.

pash. (1) A head. So Shakespeare, in THE WINTER'S TALE (1611). (2) A smashing blow; hence, a heavy downpour, a swirling snowstorm. (3) The fragments left by a smashing blow; hence, debris; by extension, a great quantity of something. (4) A short form of *calipash*; *pee* for *calipee*: Foote in THE PATRON (1764) said: *Not the meanest member of my corporation but can distinguish the pash from the pee*; he was probably punning (*pash* for *passion*) on the two functions of the privy part. Also as a verb, *to pash,* to hurl, strike, smash. An echoic word, like *bash, smash, dash.* Shakespeare in TROILUS AND CRESSIDA says: *If I go to him, with my armed fist Ile pash him ore the face.*

pasha. See *bashaw.*

pasquil. See *pasquinader.*

pasquinader. A writer of lampoons, of satires. The forms *pasquil, pasquin, pas-*

quinade, were used both as noun and as verb, a lampoon (originally, one posted in a public place); to satirize, to lampoon. An ancient statue, mutilated, was unearthed in Rome, 1501, and set up by Cardinal Caraffa next his palace by the Piazza Navona. Annually on St. Mark's day this torso was decorated; at first eulogizing verses were affixed to it; later, these grew satiric. The figure was popularly known as *Pasquin* or *Pasquil,* probably from a schoolmaster near where it was found. The *pasquinade,* or satiric attack, was hung on this statue; answers might be hung on the statue of Marforio. Then the term spread, applied to any anonymous satirical writing. Prescott in THE CONQUEST OF MEXICO (1843) declares: *The white walls of the barracks were covered with epigrams and pasquinades levelled at Cortez.*

past. Also *paste.* See *frowze.*

pastiche. See *postiche.*

pastinate. To dig; to loosen the ground by digging. Also *pastine,* to dig; to plant in prepared soil. *Pastine,* as a noun, ground prepared for planting. From Latin *pastinare, pastinatus,* with the same meaning. *Pastinate* was also used in the 15th century to mean dug, prepared for planting. Hence *pastination,* digging.

pastry. In addition to the baked *pasties* this word denotes, it used also to mean (1) the place where the pasties are made. Shakespeare in ROMEO AND JULIET (1592) makes pleasing sound: *They call for dates and quinces in the pastrie.* (2) The art of the *pastry-cook.* Steele in THE SPECTATOR (No. 314; 1712) spoke of *the whole art of paistrey and preserving*; two years earlier, we learn: *To all young ladies at Edw. Kidder's Pastry School in Little Lincoln's Inn Fields, are taught all sorts of pastry and cookery.* And the SPORTING MAGAZINE of 1809 reported that *the sewing school, the pastry school, were then essential branches of female education.* Eheu fugaces!

patavinity. Provincialism in style; a provincial or dialect term. The word was first applied by the ancients (Latin *Patavinus,* of *Patavium,* now Padua) to the writings of Livy, as containing many local characteristics of his native city. Carew in his translation (1607) of Estienne's WORLD OF WONDERS said one could *find solecismes in Tullie, and I know not what patavinitie in Livie.* [*Tullie* was Marcus Tullius Cicero, accepted through the ages as a model of Latin style.]

patch. (1) A fool; a clown. T. Wilson (1553) said this is from the nickname, *Patch,* of Cardinal Wolsey's jester, but it may be from the clown's *patched* garb. Shakespeare makes three references to a *patched fool.* He also uses *patchery,* roguery. In RESPUBLICA (1553) we read: *usiree, perjuree, pitcherie, patcherie, pilferie, briberee, snatcherie, catcherie.* Shakespeare uses the word *patch* often: in LOVE'S LABOUR'S LOST (1594) he speaks of *a patch set on learning*; in MACBETH is the angry cry: *What soldiers, patch!* The term survives in the sense of an ill-natured person, especially a child, and in the compound form *crosspatch.* (2) Old meanings of *patch,* a piece of cloth: *not a patch on,* nowhere near, not fit to be compared to; Reade in THE CLOISTER AND THE HEARTH (1860): *He is not a patch on you for looks.* A tiny piece of black silk or courtplaster, often cut into an ingenious design, worn as a beauty-spot (especially in the 17th and 18th centuries). Hence, a *patch-box*: Pope in THE RAPE OF THE LOCK (1714): *Thrice from my trembling hand the patch-box fell.* Edmond Gosse in his essay THE

WHOLE DUTY OF WOMAN (1895) comments on THE LADIES' CALLING of the time of Charles II (1660); he quotes: *Any one of those baubles, the loosest appendage of the dress, a fan, a busk, perhaps a black patch, bears a price that would warm the empty bowels of a poor starving wretch*—and adds: *This was long before the days of very elaborate and expensive patches.* Yet Fletcher in THE ELDER BROTHER (1625) had observed: *Your black patches you wear variously, Some cut like stars, some in half moons, some lozenges.* Even earlier Marston in PASQUILL AND KATHERINE (1600) had cynically noted: *Blacke patches are worne, some for pride, some to stay the rhewme, and some to hide the scab.* Occasionally, even today, we may look upon *the patch that lent piquancy to the cheek of beauty.*

pathophobe. One that dreads disease. To be distinguished from a *hypochrondriac,* who finds the symptoms within himself, whereas the pathophobe flees them in others. He will run from however interesting a group, if one of its members sneezes. Hence, *pathophobia*; *cp. aeromancy.*

patibulary. Relating to the gallows. Hence, *patibulate,* to hang. Both terms were mainly in humorous use. Latin *patibulum,* a fork-shaped yoke placed on the neck of a criminal; *patere,* to lie open, to be exposed (as in the stocks). Hence *patible* was used in English (15th into the 18th century) to mean the horizontal bar of a cross; a gallows. Also in the 17th century, *patible* (from Latin *pati,* to suffer, whence also *patient,* long-suffering) was used to mean capable of suffering, enduring. SOCIETY of 11 June, 1881, spoke of *that distinguished burglar, after he had been duly patibulated.*

patrico. A hedge-priest, such a one as Touchstone sought (in Shakespeare's AS YOU LIKE IT). Also *paterco, patterco, patriarke co, patriarcho, patring cove.* Mentioned in Beaumont and Fletcher's THE BEGGAR'S BUSH (1622), Jonson's BARTHOLOMEW FAIR (1614), and other plays. Described in THE GENTLEMAN'S MAGAZINE of 1782: *stroling priests that marry under a hedge. The couple, standing on each side of a dead beast, were bid to live together till death them does part; and so shaking hands the wedding was ended. Cp. pedlers French.*

patruity. The relationship of an uncle. Latin *patruus,* father's brother; *pater, patrem,* father. In 17th century dictionaries we find *patruel,* nephew.

patten. A kind of shoe or overshoe. Perhaps from French *patte,* paw; perhaps related to French *patiner,* to skate. From the 14th century, the word *patten* was applied to (1) shoes the feet might be slipped into without fastening, like clogs or (2) the thick-soled shoe, chopine (*q.v.*), worn by women of fashion to increase their height. From the late 16th century, *patten* was applied to an overshoe that lifted one out of the mud or wet; especially (since the 17th century) of a wooden sole held on the foot by a leather loop, with an iron oval ring, or something of the sort, underneath. Pepys in his DIARY (24 January, 1660) spoke of his wife *exceedingly troubled with a pair of new pattens, and I vexed to go so slow.* Gay in TRIVIA described *good housewives* that *Safe thro' the wet on clinking pattens tread.* If the tongue *runs on pattens,* it keeps up a great clatter; thus in Udall's RALPH ROYSTER DOYSTER (1553) we read: *Your tongue can renne on patins as well as mine.* Greene and Lodge, in A LOOKING GLASSE FOR LONDON (1594), build a simile:

A womans eyes are like a pair of pattens, fit to save shoe-leather in summer, and to keep away the cold in winter. A pretty patten indeed!

pattens-and-clogs. A north-country name for the flower the *birdsfoot trefoil.* In the south, where leather was more plentiful and both Henry VIII and Elizabeth, with their courtiers, were often ajaunting, the same flower was called *boots-and-shoes.*

patulous. Open or opening widely; spreading, as the boughs of a tree. Latin *patere,* to be open, whence also *patulent,* open, expanded. THE BYSTANDER of 1790 pictured the bliss of reclining *under the umbrage of a patulous beech.*

pauciloquent. Speaking few words. Latin *paucus,* little, few + *loquentem,* speaking; *loqui, locutum,* to speak; whence also *elocution.* Hence *pauciloquy,* brevity in discourse. Beaumont in PSYCHE (1648) said: *Fear no discredit by pauciloquie.* To *paucify* is to lessen, to make few; Cowper in a letter of 26 December, 1792, said: *My opportunities of writing are paucified.*

pautener. (1) A vagabond, rascal. Also *pawtener, paytener*; sometimes misprinted *pantener.* MERLIN (1450) has: *A full fell pawtener is he that twies this day thus hath yow smyten to grounde.* (2) A small bag, wallet, purse. Used from the 14th into the 16th century.

pavan. A dance, grave and stately. The dancers were elaborately dressed. The dance, from Spain via France, came into England in the 16th century. Also *pavion, paven, pavin, pavane, pavine, pavaun.* Some suggest *pavan* is short for *Padovana,* from the city *Padua*; others, that it is from Spanish *pavo,* peacock, the stateliness and elaborate garb of the dancers suggesting the proud bird. Scott in THE MONASTERY (1820) says: *Your leg would make an indifferent good show in a pavin or a galliard.*

pavise. A shield large enough to protect the entire body, usually borne by a page in front of his knight, or an attendant in front of an archer. It was convex enough to shelter them both, and thus left free the hands of the active fighter. Also *pavis, pavais, pavois, pavache, pavice,* and the like; ultimately from *Pavia* in Italy, where such shields were originally manufactured. Used since the 14th century, obsolete (except historically) since the 17th. A *pavisade,* (*pavesade, pavisado*) was a screen of pavises set before a fighting line. Hence, a protection; More in 1534 speaks of man *clipped in on every syde with the pavice of God.*

pawnce. A variant form of *pansy* (French *pensée,* thought), the flower of meditation. Included in the bouquet in Spenser's April Eclogue of THE SHEPHERD'S CALENDAR (1579), a beautiful culling: *Bring hether the pincke and purple cullambine, With gelliflowres, Bring coronations, and sops in wine, Worne of paramoures. Strowe me the ground with daffadowndillies, And cowslips, and kingcups, and loved lillies: The pretie pawnce, And the chevisaunce Shall match with the fayre flowre delice.*

pax. (1) Peace; directly from the Latin *pax, pacem,* whence *pacify* and the *Pacific Ocean. Cp. peas.* Mainly in the churchly greeting *Pax vobiscum, pax vobis,* peace be with you. In schoolboy slang *Pax!* Peace! Keep quiet!, or (in a game) Truce!; also, a friend; *to be good pax,* to be good friends. (2) A ceremonial kiss; especially, to kiss *the pax*—which is (3) an osculatory, a tablet representing the Crucifixion or other religious subject, kissed by the priests and the congregation at Mass. In this sense, *pax* is sometimes confused with *pyx* (*pix*), *q.v.* Holinshed's CHRONICLE records the stealing of a pyx as the one outrage of the English on French soil; it is changed in Shakespeare's HENRY V (1599): *Fortune is Bardolph's foe, and frowns on him, For he hath stol'n a pax, and hang'd must be.*

paylaysward. See *palacious.*

paynim. The country or lands of the heathens, pagandom; also, a heathen, especially a Saracen, a Mohammedan. An early variant of *pagan,* via Old French from Latin *paganus,* of the countryside, rustic; *pagus,* a region, province, countryside. *Cp. pagany. Paynim* is a favorite word with historical novelists. Other forms for *pagandom* were *paynimy, paynimry.*

peagoose. Simpleton, ninny. This form is a shortening of *peakgoose.* The form *peak,* sometimes used alone to mean a fool, is also found in *hoddypeak* and *pekehoddie,* emphatic forms for the same meaning. We also find *hoddy-noddy, hoddy-doddy,* and *hoddypoll,* all meaning simpleton; the last two were also used to mean cuckold. *Peakgoose* is a favorite word with the playwrights of the 16th and 17th centuries; Crowne in THE MARRIED BEAU (1694) says *I'm a pe-goose with a Lady, but I'm the devil with a chamber-maid.* Harvey in 1586 observed: *He that would be thought a man, or seem anything worth, must be a great doer and a great speaker. He is a cipher, and but a peakgoose, that is neither of both: he that cannot be both, let him be one at least, if he mean to be accounted anybody. Or farewell all hope of value.*

peas. A variant form of *peace.* See *pease* (verb). Thus one of the poems in Tottel's MISCELLANY (1557) declares: *The cause of things I will not blame Lest I offend the prince of peas.*

pease. The former singular of *pea,* which came into being about 1600, because *pease* was thought to be the plural. The plural of *pease* was *peasen, peason, pesyn, pesen,* and the like, as in Tusser's HUNDREDTH GOOD POINTES OF HUSBANDRIE (1557), advising for February: *Sow peason and beanes in the wane of the moon; Who sowethe them sooner, he soweth too soon.* Washington Irving in SALMAGUNDI PAPERS (1807) spoke of *pease-blossom breeches;* one of the fairies in Shakespeare's A MIDSUMMER NIGHT'S DREAM (1590) is named *Pease-blossom.* And the *sweet-pease* has a beautiful delicate blossom. The word was often used to represent something trivial; More in A DIALOGUE OF COMFORT AGAINST TRIBULATION (1534) said: *All our penaunce without Christ's passion wer not worth a pease;* Thomas Bastard in CHRESTOLEROS (1598): *He learned logicke and arithmetique, yet neither brawls nor ciphers worth a peaze.* Some like it in the pot.—There was also (13th to 17th century) a verb *to pease,* to pacify, to grow calm, which was *peace* used as a word of action; it survives in the form *appease.* Sackville in A MIRROR FOR MAGISTRATES (1563), when the goddess leads him into hell, encounters Cereberus, *Foredinning the ayer with his horrible yel. Out of the diepe darke cave where he did dwell, The goddesse strayt he knewe, and by and by* [immediately] *He peaste and couched, while that we passed by.*

peason. Plural of *pease, q.v.* Surrey in his sonnet on THE FRAILTIE AND HURTFULNES OF BEAUTIE (1535) calls Beauty: *Tickell treasure abhorred of reason, Daungerous to deale with, vaine, of none availe; Costly in keping; past, not worth two peason; Slipper in sliding as is an eles taile; Harde to attaine; once gotten, not geason; Jewel of jeopardie . . .*

peat. An old form of *pet,* a darling. Also, a spoiled child; Shakespeare in THE TAMING OF THE SHREW (1596) has: *A pretty peate! It is best put finger in the eye, and she knew why*—the remainer of the passage implying a cry-baby. Being very common from 1570 to 1640, the word developed other uses: as a term of scorn for a woman, especially, *a proud peat.* Jonson in EVERY MAN OUT OF HIS HUMOUR (1599) described *Deliro's wife and idoll, a proud mincing peat, and as perverse as he is officious.* Also, a lawyer favored by a judge, referred to as his *peat.* Scott revived this use (in REDGAUNTLET; 1824); he also used *peat* (THE HEART OF MIDLOTHIAN; 1818) as a term of scorn for a man. Hence *peatry, peatship,* the character or behavior of a *peat.* A *peatery,* however, is a place where *peat* (chunks of decomposed and partly carbonized vegetable matter, used for fuel—the still current sense) is dug.

pebble-peeler. See *nipcheese.*

peccable. Liable to sin; sinning; sinful. Latin *peccare,* to sin; the negative *impeccable* has survived, showing that, among those educated enough to use the word, the sinless outnumber the sinners. *Cp. couth.* Also lapsed are *peccaminous,* full of sins; *peccancy* (not necessarily associated with *piquancy*); *peccant,* sinning; faulty; incorrect. Thus *peccavi,* I have sinned, was formerly more often than now used as a confession of guilt; *to cry peccavi,* to confess. Also *peccability,* susceptibility to sin; *finite intelligent beings,* said J. Clarke in AN ENQUIRY INTO THE CAUSE AND ORIGIN OF EVIL (1720), *necessarily suppose peccability.*

peccadill. A variant form of *peccadillo.* Spanish *pecadillo,* diminutive of *pecado,* sin; Latin *peccare, peccatum,* to miss, do amiss, sin; *cp. peccable.* The forms for sin were many: *peccadilian, peccadulian, peccaduliun, pecçadilia, peccadiglio, piccadillo, picadilio,* and more.

ped. A basket, a hamper with a lid. A *pedlar* (the noun occurs in the 14th century, long before the verb to *pedle, peddle*) was probably one that traveled around with his wares in a basket.

pedaile. A body of foot-soldiers; by extension, rabble. See *putage.*

pedaneous. Of low standing; petty. Latin *pedaneus,* relating to (or the size of) a foot; *pedem,* foot. Samuel Collins, in THE DEFENCE OF THE BISHOP OF ELIE (1617) exclaimed: *What pedaneous author have they not made a father of!* The word, though rare, is good.

pediluvium. A foot-bath; a washing of the feet. Latin *pedem,* foot + *luere,* to wash off. Also, by assimilation to *lave* (Latin *lavare,* to bathe), *pedilave.* These are 17th century forms; Landor in his IMAGINARY CONVERSATIONS (LEO XII), 1828, refers to the washing of the feet as a ritual: *After which holy function, go and prepare for the pediluvials.*

pedipulate. To work with the feet. Latin *pes, pedem,* foot. The word was coined in the 19th century, on the model of *manipulate* (Latin *manus,* hand). There were comments on *pedipulating snowshoes;* Oliver Onions in THE COMPLEAT BACHELOR (1900) said: *Bassishaw must have been as busy in his pedipulations as an organist.*

pedisequent. A footman; attendant, follower. Latin *pedem,* foot + *sequentem,* following; *sequi,* to follow, whence *obsequious, inconsequential.* Also *pedissequous* (an extra *s* has crept in), attendant upon. These are 17th century forms; Topsell in FOUR-FOOTED BEASTS (1607) spoke of a deer *forced to offer up his bloud and flesh to the rage of all the observant pedissequants of the hunting goddess Diana.*

pedlers French. The canting language, the special speech of the beggars, vagabonds, and thieves of Tudor times. It is used, to some extent, in plays of the period, and especially in the pamphlets and broadsides of the day. Both Harman in A CAVEAT OR WARENING FOR COMMON CURSETORS, VULGARELY CALLED VAGABONDES (1567) and Dekker in LANTHORNE AND CANDLE-LIGHT (Part Two of THE BELMAN OF LONDON; 1609) discuss it in detail. Some of its words are from Latin: *Togeman,* a cloak, from *toga; pannam,* bread, from *panis; cassan,* cheese, from *caseus.* Others of the words follow. *lightmans,* day; *darkmans,* night; *the harmans,* the stocks; *the harman beck,* the constable; *grannam,* corn; *ruffmans,* bushes, woods, hedges. *chete,* thing, in many compounds as *smelling-chete,* a nose, also an orchard or garden; *nab,* head; *nab-chete,* cap; *prattling chete,* tongue; *crashing chetes,* teeth; *fambles,* hands; *fambling chete,* a ring; *belly chete,* apron; *grunting chete,* pig. *prat,* a buttock (we still speak, in the circus, of a *pratfall*) ; *stampes,* legs; *stampers,* shoes. A *cove* (*cofe, co, cuffin*) was a man; a *mort* was a woman. Hence *patriarke co, patrico,* priest, especially a *hedge-priest; gentry cofe,* a nobleman; *kinchin co,* a boy, also *kitchen co. kinchin mort,* a girl; especially, the baby girl carried by a beggar woman to win pity and elicit pence; "she is brought at her full age to the *upright* to be broken, and so she is called a doxy until she come to the honor of an *altham.*" *autem,* altar, church; *autem* (*altham*) *mort,* married woman. *Rome mort,* queen; *Rome bowse,* wine; *Rome vile* (French *ville,* city), London. *ken,* house; *quier, queer, quyer,* evil; *quier ken,* prison; *quier cuffin,* justice of the peace. *bowsing ken,* tavern; *stauling ken,* place that will receive stolen goods. To *cut, cutte,* to say; to *cant,* to speak; to *towre,* to see, to *maunde,* ask; to *prig,* ride; to *nygle, niggle,* to have to do with a woman carnally. Chief among beggars was the *upright,* the master vagabond; his staff was called a *filtchman.* The *jarkeman* (*jackman*) could read and write; he provided (counterfeit) licenses, called *gybes;* the seals he affixed were called *jarkes.* The *frater* carried a *gybe* to beg for a hospital (*spittlehouse*). The *curtsey man* was a polite beggar with a piteous tale. The *verser* (*cp. gramercy*) was a thief's confederate, steering the victim (*verse,* to turn) into the snare. A *ruffler* was, or claimed to be, a veteran of the wars; a *whipjack,* an old mariner. These terms but scratch the surface of the Elizabethan underworld, yet in some measure I have —if I may quote Harman—*set before thee, good Reader, the leud lousey language of these leutering luskes and laysy lorels . . . an unknowen tounge onely but to these bold, beastly, bawdy beggers and vayne vacabonds.*

peel. See *pel.*

pegomancy. See *aeromancy.*

peirastic. Experimental; as an experiment; in experimental mood or wise. Greek *peirastikos; peiran,* to try. From the 17th century; Peacock in MELINCOURT (1817) speaks of *opening the subject peirastically.*

peize. Weight; burden; hence, weight of guilt and the like; a heavy blow or fall, as Spenser says of Ptolemy in THE FAËRIE QUEENE (1590) : *He with a peaze it brake.* The word was very common from the 14th to the 17th century; also as a verb, to weigh; to balance; to weigh in the mind, ponder; to press with weight, to force, to drive. Also *peise, payce, pese, peaze, peyse,* and the like. Old French *peis,* Latin *pensum,* something weighed; *pendere, pensum,* to weigh; also Latin *pensare,* to consider, whence English *pensive* and the rare *pensitate,* to ponder, to cogitate. In the 15th century, *peisage* (*pesage*) was a duty charged for weighing goods. Other forms are *peisant* (*pesant*), heavy, burdensome, oppressed; *peisy, peizie,* heavy; *peiser,* one who weighs or ponders; *peiseless,* without (much) weight; Sylvester in his version (1606) of Du Bartas has: *Like peizlesse plume born up by Boreas breath.*

pekehoddie. See *peagoose.*

pel. A stake, used in practicing swordcraft in the 14th century. Also, an early form for *pall, peel, pell.* Strutt, discussing the old use in SPORTS AND PASTIMES (1801), said: *The practitioner was then to assail the pel, armed with sword and shield, in the same manner as he would an adversary. Pel* is via French from Latin *palus,* stake, whence also *palisade, pale, pile, peel.* The noun *peel* has had several meanings beside the now current rind of fruit, often candied. (1) A pillow. (2) An equal, a peer. W. Hamilton, in WALLACE (1722): *In time of peace, he never had a peel, So courteous he was, and so genteel.* (3) A shovel; a baker's shovel. (4) Related to *pel*: a stake. Hence, a fence of stakes, a palisade (from the 13th to the 16th century); a small castle or tower; later, especially, one of the small towers or fortified dwellings built in the 16th century along the English-Scottish border, a *peel-house,* shortened to *peel.* Chaucer in THE HOUS OF FAME (1384) has: *I gan to romen til I fonde The castel gate on my ryght honde . . . Ther mette I cryinge many oon* [a one] *God save the lady of thys pel.*

pelf. Property pilfered or stolen, booty; property; money, wealth. Thus Shakespeare in the prologue to PERICLES (1608): *All perishen, of man, of pelfe, Ne ought escapende but himselfe.* This progression of meanings toward social acceptance altered, and the word came to mean money, disparagingly, "filthy lucre"; then trumpery, trash—Gosson in PLEASANT QUIPS FOR UPSTART NEWFANGLED GENTLEWOMEN (1595) decries *all this new pelfe now sold in shops, in value true not worth a louse.*

pell. A skin or hide; especially, a furred skin used for a cloak or its lining. From the 14th century; a little earlier was *pellet,* the skin of a sheep, which was replaced in the 15th century by *pelt.* Also *pellure, pelure* (from the 14th century), fur; especially for a garment or its lining. Latin *pellem,* skin. English *fell,* meaning hide, skin, is a common Teutonic form, related to Latin *pellem.* Hence, *pelured,* adorned with fur; *peltry* (in the 15th century; then again in 1701 in connection with the North American fur trade), pelts collectively; undressed skins; *peltier* (14th century *Guild of Peltyers*), a furrier. *peltage* (17th century), pelts collectively. Hence, *to pelt,* to skin; figuratively, to cheat, to fleece. A *pell* was also (from the 15th century) a skin, or roll of parchment; specifically, one of the two pells of the Exchequer: *pellis receptorum, pell of receipts,* and *pellis exituum, pell of disbursements.* Hence *Clerk* (*Master*) *of the Pells; the Pells,* the Office of the Exchequer. The word thus came to be used in general for accounts; loosely (humorously) for one's fortune, as in Canning's poem THE GRAND CONSULTATION (1802): *Our frugal doctor . . . Gives his pills to the public, the pells to his son.* A *pelisse, pelisson, pellycon,* was a garment of fur;

especially, a long mantle or cloak lined with fur. Caxton in his LIVES OF THE FATHERS (1491) pictures a priest with *his frocke, his pelycon and his Gospellis.* With this picture I am impelled to stop.

pellucidity. The quality of being very clear. Used from the 17th century, sometimes to mean physically transparent (Latin *per,* through + *lux, lucem,* light), sometimes of ideas and the mind. C. Lucas in 1756 observed that the Thames River *preserves her purity and pellucidity.* Of what river that washes a city can this still be said? Witness the already old jingle ending: "The River Rhone washes the city of Cologne . . . Who now will wash the River Rhone?"

pen. See *swan.*

pencel. See *banderol.*

penis. An old plural form of *penny; pennies.*

penistone. A coarse woollen cloth, used in the 16th and 17th centuries. From *Penistone,* a town in Yorkshire. Also *pennystone, penyston,* etc. An Act of Edward VI (1551) required that *clothes commonlye called pennystones or forest whites . . . shall conteyne in lengthe beinge wette betwixt twelve and thirtene yardes.*

pensative. See *panse.*

pensil. See *banderol.* Scott uses *pensil* in THE LAY OF THE LAST MINSTREL (1805).

pensitate. See *peize.*

penster. A literary hack, a puny wielder of the pen. Used, though rarely, from the 17th century. The ending is disparaging, as in *rhymster, punster, trickster,* or (16th century) *lewdster.* Meredith in HENRY RICHMOND (1871) cries *Oh! the poor penster!* 'Twere better if such did not make the pen stir.

pentice. The early form of *penthouse.* The word dropped its prefix, being via Old French *apentis, apendeis* from Late Latin *appenditium,* an appendage, applied to a chapel or other holy building architecturally dependent upon a church; Latin *ad,* to + *pendere,* to hang. (*Independent* means not hanging onto or from something else.) The word was early applied to a lean-to, a usually open-side shed with a sloping roof, attached to a larger building; hence by folk-etymology *pentice, pentis* by the 17th century became *penthouse.* Dickens (in BARNABY RUDGE, 1840) applies *penthouse* to a shed with a sloping roof, not attached to another building. The word was also used figuratively: Shakespeare in LOVE'S LABOUR'S LOST (1588) has: *With your hat penthouse-like oer the shop of your eyes;* Scott, in PEVERIL OF THE PEAK (1822): *His huge penthouse hat.* Tennyson, in VIVIEN (1859): *He dragg'd his eyebrow bushes down, and made A snowy penthouse for his hollow eyes.* Nowadays, a *penthouse* usually means a terraced apartment on the roof or top floor of a large building, such as Peter Sabbatino is neglecting for his Sabine farm.

peony. A plant, with beautiful globular flowers in shades of red and white. The roots, flowers, and seeds, were used as medicine, the seeds as spice. Medieval and Elizabethan soldiers went to war with a sprig of peony beneath their armor. It was the most ancient of healing plants; Pliny (70 A.D.) mentioned 20 diseases it could cure. Its origin is godly: *Paion,* physician to the gods, healed Pluto of a sore wound inflicted by Hercules. Aesculapius, Paion's master, jealous of this success, slew his rival, whereupon Pluto changed him into a flower, the *peony.* [Apollo took over the patronage of physicians, as Apollo *Paian*; the hymn to him, beginning *Io Paian,* gave us the word for an exultant song, a *paean.*] The peony —*piane, pyon, pyany, pionee, paeony,* and more—seems today less efficacious as a cure-all, but it survives as a beautiful flower.

per-. As a prefix *per* means through or thoroughly (*through* and *thorough* were originally the same word). Forgotten words with this prefix, most of them from the 16th century, include: *peragrate,* to travel through; *peramble, to* walk through or about (replaced since the 17th century by *perambulate*); *perbreak,* to burst through, to break asunder (14th-16th century), but also as a form of *parbreak,* to spue forth, to vomit; *percase* (from the 14th century), by chance; *percoct,* to heat or boil thoroughly; figuratively, overdone—Meredith in THE EGOIST (1879) urges us *to abstain from any employment of the obvious, the percoct . . . the overstrained*; *perduellion, perduellism,* treason, stark rebellion; *perempt,* to do away with, extinguish, to quash a case in court; this word survives in *peremptory*; *perendinate,* to put off till the day after tomorrow; especially, to keep putting off one's departure. There were rules against *perendination* in the medieval religious houses and in the colleges (even later), to help get rid of persisting guests; domiciliar hospitality finds this more of a problem. Also, *perflable,* that may be blown through, open to the winds; *periclitation,* the act of exposing or state of being exposed to great danger; *perissology,* redundance, using many more words than are needed (perish the thought!); *pernoctate,* to stay all night, to pass the night in study or prayer. A state of *perpotation* calls for Alcoholics Anonymous. Also *pervicacious,* extremely refractory, pig-headed; Richardson in CLARISSA HARLOWE (1748) speaks of *one of the most pervicacious young creatures that ever was heard of.* Let us persist no further.

peradventure. By chance. Old French *par aventure,* by chance; Latin *ad,* to + *venire, ventum,* to come. This word, in various forms—*paraventor, paraventure, per aunter, paraunter*—was very common from the 13th century; in the 16th, the form *peradventure* superseded the earlier forms. The phrase *out of* (*past, beyond*) *peradventure* means without doubt.

perdie. See *pardee.*

peregall. Equal. Also *peregal*; a variant of *paregal, q.v.* Spenser in THE SHEPHERD'S CALENDAR (1579; AUGUST) says *peregall to the best.*

peregrine. Foreign; imported; alien to the matter in hand; on a pilgrimage, traveling abroad. Also as a noun, a person residing in other than his native city or country; a pilgrim. Also *peregrin, perrygryne, perigrin.* Latin *peregrinus*; *per,* through + *ager,* field, country. It was first used in English as the name of the *peregrine falcon,* a favorite bird for hawking. A wandering swashbuckler who gives his name to a novel (1751) by Smollett is *Peregrine Pickle.* Another form of the word *peregrin,* which indeed has supplanted it, is *pilgrim. Peregrinage, peregrinancy,* are variant forms of *peregrination.*

perfit. An early variant of *perfect,* found in some of the first quarto and folio editions of Shakespeare. Also *perfitly.* For an instance of the use, see *term.*

perfuncturate. To do half-heartedly, to perform in a *perfunctory* way. Also *perfunctorize*; both in the 19th century. Latin *perfunctor* (which might well be used in English), one that acts in order to be done with a thing; *perfungi, perfunctum,* to perform, carry through, get rid of; *per,* through + *fungi,* to busy oneself, be engaged.

perhibit. To deem, consider, repute; to hold (someone or something) as . . . Latin *per,* through + *habere, habitum,* to hold, whence all our *habits.* Because of the smile on his face, the tall man was perhibited the perpetrator of the trick, and prohibited from further access to the premises.

perhiemate. To spend the winter. (Four syllables, accent on the *high.*) Latin *per,* through + *hiems,* winter. Many persons from the northern United States perhiemate in Florida. Do not confuse this with hibernation.

peri. A superhuman being, originally in Persian mythology; at first evil, but later pictured as benevolent and beautiful; hence, a fairy; a beautiful person. Persian *peri*; Zend *Pairika,* a female demon employed by Ahriman to cause eclipses, droughts, crop failures, and other misfortunes. Richardson in his PERSIAN DICTIONARY (1780) said *Perfume is the only food of peris.* Gilbert and Sullivan, after three great successes the titles of which begin with *P,* hesitated to risk a change; they fortified their next play, IOLANTHE (1882), by giving it two *P*'s in the subtitle: *The Peer and the Peri.*

periapt. A charm, an amulet. Sometimes the Greek form *periapton* was used in English; from *peri,* about + *haptos,* fastened; *haptein,* to fasten. Shakespeare in HENRY VI, PART ONE (1591) cries: *Now help, ye charming spells and periapts!* The word was also used (Chambers, 1741) of *a kind of medicine . . . which being tied about the neck, is supposed to prevent, or cure diseases.* Coleridge in 1816 said scornfully that *Superstition goes wandering . . . with its pack of amulets, bead-rolls, periapts . . .* but we hear in 1861 of *a spider having been sewn up in a rag and worn as a periapt about the neck to charm away the plague.* As Shakespeare said, a charming thought!

pericope. A short passage in or from a writing. Four syllables, accent on the *rick;* from Greek *peri,* around + *kope,* cutting. In classical literature, *pericope* meant a selection of verse that included strophe and antistrophe; in church usage, the portion of Scripture appointed for reading at service. The EDINBURGH REVIEW of January 1884 noted: *The pericope of 'the woman taken in adultery' is entirely omitted from this work.*

periculous. Full of danger. Used in the 16th and 17th centuries, as by Sir Thomas Browne; later, for humor. Supplanted by *perilous.* Also (19th century) *periculant,* in danger. Hogg in a poem of 1835 said: *'Tis really ridiculous To turn into frolic a case so periculous.*

peridrome. Something that 'runs' around, as a gallery or balcony on the four sides of a chamber or auditorium. Greek *peri,* around + *dromos,* running; a race or course. Thus a *hippodrome* is a place (Greek *hippos,* horse, as in *hippopotamus,* water horse) for horse races—as were indeed seen (charging steeds of cavalrymen) in the old melodramas of the New York Hippodrome.

periegesis. A description of a place or region; a journey through a countryside, a tour. Greek *peri,* around + *egesis,* leading (as might a guide). The word has five syllables, with the accent on the *gee.* Hence *periegetic,* describing places or objects of interest. Jonson called Drayton's POLY-OLBION (1622) a picture of the beauties of Albion, the white-cliffed isle of England [*Albion* means white land; but Drayton's title is *poly-,* many + *olbion,* blessed], *thy admired periegesis.*

perigenesis. The theory that reproduction results from rhythmical vibrations of protoplasmic molecules; "wave-generation." Edward Cope in THE ORIGIN OF THE FITTEST (1879) claimed: *The Dynamic Theory of reproduction I proposed in 1871, and it has since been adopted by Haeckel under the name of perigenesis.* Cope seems to have resented being Haeckeled.

perigord pie. A meat pie flavored with truffles, prized since the 17th century. The truffles were snouted in Périgord, in southwestern France. The term was later applied (also, *perigo pie*) to other highly seasoned meat pies.

perigraph. (1) An inscription around something, as one circling a coin. (2) A careless description, one that 'goes around' the subject. Greek *peri,* around + *graphe,* writing, line. Also *perigraphe.*

périhermenial. Relating to interpretation. Also (by error) *perihermiacal.* The term is derived from the title of Aristotle's treatise *Peri hermeneias,* Concerning Interpretation. Skelton in his REPLYCACION (1529) speaks of persons that *surmysed unsurely in their perihermeniall principles.* What are your perihermenial thoughts on that passage?

perileptic. Characterized by or relating to comprehension. Greek *perileptikos,* from *peri,* around + *lambanein,* to take, seize. A rare 17th century term, used by Ralph Cudworth in THE TRUE INTELLECTUAL SYSTEM OF THE UNIVERSE (1678): *The things in the world are not ádministered merely by spermatick reasons, but by perileptic (that is, comprehensive intellectual) reasons.*

perioeci. (Plural) Dwellers within the same parallel of latitude, but opposite meridians (east and west). The *antoeci* (pronounced *anteesee,* accent on the *tee*) are those living on opposite sides of the equator, but under the same meridian, at the same distance from the equator. The *antipodes* (formerly three syllables; now four, with a singular *antipos*), dwellers directly opposite on the globe, so that the soles of their feet (Greek *anti,* opposite + *pous, podes,* foot) are as it were planted against one another; also, opposite regions of the earth. The *antichthones* include the *antoeci* and the *antipodes.* Sir Thomas Browne, in CHRISTIAN MORALS (1682), used the terms figuratively: *Fools, which are antipodes unto the wise, conceive themselves to be but their perioeci, and in the same parallel with them.*

periscian. One that dwells within the polar circle. Greek *peri,* around + *skia,* shadow; as the earth revolves about the sun (in that pole's summer days), the periscian's shadow revolves about him. The accent is on the second syllable; for the plural the form *periscii* (*peri'-see-eye*) is also used. Sir Thomas Browne used the word figuratively (as an adjective) in his CHRISTIAN MORALS (1682): *In every clime we are in a periscian state, and with our light, our shadow and darkness walk about us.*

periwig. A wig; especially one worn by women, later (of another fashion) by men, as a fashionable adornment. French *perruque,* wig (a 15th century word, possibly—Spanish *peluca*—from Latin *pilus,* hair) became in English *perwyke* and then, by association with English *wig, periwig.* Also *periwinke*; and see *periwinkle.* The *periwig* was rather generally worn by men on formal occasions, from the 17th into the 19th century—George Washington wore one at his inaugural; in English courts of law, the practice lingered. Shakespeare in HAMLET (1602) protests *to see a robustious periwig-pated fellow tear a passion to tatters.* The word is also used figuratively to mean any covering or concealment; also as a verb; thus in 1825: *ginger-bread bakers periwig a few plum-buns with sugar-frost.*

periwinkle. In addition to being the name of some species of shell-fish (molluscs), and an old form of the word *periwig, q.v., periwinkle* is the name of a trailing evergreen plant with starry flowers. Other forms, from the year 1000, are *pervenke, pervink, pervincle*; *periwinkle* became the predominant form by 1600. The Latin form, *pervinca,* may be from *pervincere,* to conquer completely. This is what the flower seemed to do, for by the 14th century the word was applied to a person, meaning the peak (or flower) of perfection, as in THE ROMANCE OF SIR DEGREVANT (1400): *Courteous lady and wyse . . . thou art pervenk of pryse.* Later this pink of perfection lapsed, and the word was used playfully of a woman, as in the command to a chambermaid in Shirley's THE PRETTY FAIR ONE (1633): *Quick periwinkle to thy mistress now!*

perjink. Precise, minutely accurate; prim; particularly neat. Also *prejink, prejinct*; *perjinkety,* fussy. The word is a 19th century coinage, mainly Scotch; Barrie in A WINDOW IN THRUMS (1889) says: *He was looking unusually perjink.* Also, *on one's perjinks,* on one's good behavior.

perlegate. To read through. Latin *per,* through + *legere, lectum,* to direct, select; to read—whence also *election, selection, predilection*; *lectern.* Hence *perlection,* the act of reading through. [To *perligate* is to bind hard.] Burton in his translation (1885) of THE ARABIAN NIGHTS speaks of *perlections of the Koran.* The devout in many faiths undertake similar perlections; a good Christian perlegates the tales of the pearly gates. Note that *perligenous* means causing the formation of pearls; it is a perligenous disease that shifts the value of the oyster from esculence to opulence.

perligenous. See *perlegate.*

pernel. A variant form of *parnel, q.v.*

pernicious. Swift. Latin *per,* through, thoroughly + *niti, nixus,* to strive. Hence *pernicity,* speed, swiftness. The current *pernicious,* ruinous, fatal, is from Latin *per* + *nex, necem,* death; it was represented in English (16th and 17th centuries) also by *perniciable,* bringing destruction; *pernicion,* ruin; *perniciosity,* destructiveness. Kirby (1835) speaks of birds of *pernicious wing.*

perrie. Jewellry. Also *perree, perrey, perry, pierrye,* and the like. Via Old French *pierrie*; *pierre,* stone; ultimately from Latin *petra,* a stone, whence also *petrify* and the pun on which the Catholic church stands (Saint *Peter,* the rock of Christ). The word was used from the 14th century (Chaucer) to the 17th; Wyatt in a poem THE FAITHFUL LOVER GIVETH HIS MISTRESS HIS HEART (1541) wrote: *I cannot give broaches nor rings . . . Pierrie, nor pearl, orient and clear.* A *perrier* (15th to 18th century) was a cannon for firing stones; Hakluyt in his VOYAGES (1524) tells of *perriers of brasse, that shot a stone of three foote and a halfe.*

persand. See *barmkin.*

perscrute. To investigate thoroughly; to examine minutely. Also *perscrutate; perscrutation; perscrutator.* Latin *per,* through + *scrutari, scrutatum,* to examine; whence also *scrutiny* and the *inscrutable* ways of providence. Carlyle in PAST AND PRESENT (1843) exclaimed at *Such guessing, visioning, dim perscrutation of the momentous future!*

pert. See *apert.*

pertuse. To punch (a hole in), to bore. Latin *per,* through + *tundere, tusum,* to beat, hammer, whence also *contusion.* Also as an adjective, *pertuse, pertused,* full of little holes (as a dying leaf in autumn). Hence *pertusion,* the action of boring or punching (holes); a hole thus made.

perversiose. A 15th century variant of *perverse.* The morality MANKIND (1450) said *Thys perversyose ingratytude I can not rehers.* This and *perversionate* in the same play, are milder forms of *perverted.* In the same century *perverser* was used for *perverter,* corrupter. Until the mid-19th century the only meaning of *pervert* was one that turned from a doctrine accepted as true; his opposite was a *convert.*

pervestigate. To investigate diligently or thoroughly; to discover by research. Latin *per,* through + *vestigare, vestigatum,* to track, trace. Hence, *pervestigation.* Used in the 17th and 18th centuries.

pervial. Easily seen through; clear. Also *pervious, q.v. Perviable,* capable of being passed through, as (17th century) *perviable woods.* Latin *per,* through + *via,* way. Hence also *perviate,* to make one's way (or a way) through. *Pervial, pervially* may be used in the sense that "he who runs may read": Chapman in his translation (1611) of Homer's ILIAD said: *A man may pervially (or as he passeth) discerne all that is to be understood.* In OVID'S BANQUET Chapman said: *That poesie should be as pervial as oratory, and plainness her special ornament, were the plain way to barbarism.* Some modern poets have tried to avoid this barbarism by being especially obscure, *impervial.* A well-known twentieth century poet went into seclusion to create; on coming forth he read his poem to his wife and, if she understood it, he destroyed it. Most of his work is utterly impervial.

pervicacy. Obstinacy; wilfulness. (Accent on the first syllable.) From the 16th century; in the 17th, the form *pervicacity* was introduced, also *pervicacious,* pig-headed, refractory, very stubborn, Latin *pervicacem,* stubborn; *per,* completely + *vincere, vic-* to prevail against (whence also *convince, victory, invincible*). Hence, *pervicaciously.* Richardson in CLARISSA (1748) described *one of the most pervicacious young creatures that ever was heard of.* The cynic remarks that pervicacy consists in disagreement with me.

pervious. That can be passed through, permeable; open to the mind, intelligible; open to influence or argument, that can be persuaded. Hence *perviousness;* Latin *per,* through + *via,* way, whence also the surviving *impervious.* Stanley in THE HISTORY OF PHILOSOPHY (1659) said that *every country is pervious to a wise man; for the whole world is the country of a wise soul.* Emerson in MAY DAY (1867) observed that *The solid, solid universe Is pervious to love.*

pervulgate. To make public, make known. Latin *per,* thoroughly + *vulgare, vulgatum,* to make known *(vulgus, volgus,* the people, the mass); whence also *divulge. Vulgarization* was a 17th century term for popularizing; *vulgar* in the 15th and 16th centuries meant usual, common (as a noun, *the vulgar,* the common language, the vernacular; the common people); by the 16th century *vulgar* had come to mean uneducated; in the late 17th and 18th, not belonging to good society, coarsely commonplace, ill-bred. Hence *pervulgation,* the main purpose of American television. *In our olde vulgare,* said Elyot in THE BOKE NAMED THE GOVERNOUR (1531), *profite is called weale.*

pesame. Three syllables. A term of condolence, in the phrase *to give (receive) pesame.* Spanish *pesa me,* it grieves me. Lady Fanshawe recorded in her MEMOIRS (1676): *I waited upon the Queen to give her Majesty pesame of the King's death.*

pesen. See *pease.*

pess. A hassock; especially, one to rest the feet on or to kneel on, in church. In GAMMER GURTON'S NEEDLE (1575) we hear: *My gammer sat her down on her pes, and bad me reach thy breches.*

pessomancy. See *aeromancy.*

pestle. See *pestle-pie.*

pestle-pie. In the 18th century, "a large standing pye, which contains a whole gammon, and sometimes a neat's tongue also, together with a couple of fowls, and if a turkey not the worse." The word *pestle* is via French from Latin *pistillum,* diminutive of *pistrum,* from *pinsere, pistum,* to pound, crush. The *pestle and mortar,* for pounding and compounding drugs, came to be symbolic of the apothecary. From the bone-shape of the instrument, the word *pestle* came also to be applied to the leg; especially to the leg of an animal used for food. Hence, *the pestle of a lark,* something very small, a trifle. The word was occasionally applied to other objects of the same shape, or used for pounding, such as the policeman's club.

petard. A medieval instrument of war to breach a wall or blow in a gate; of bell-shaped metal, later of wood, filled with powder and laid against the target; fired by a fuse. Named from the loud noise. A *pet* was (echoic) an expulsion of anal wind; *petard,* a large *pet.* The word was later used of noisy rockets and firecrackers. Shakespeare in HAMLET (1604) says: *For tis the sport to have the enginer Hoist with his own petar.* The word was often used figuratively, as by Butler in HUDIBRAS (1678): *Eternal noise and scolding, The conjugal petard, that tears Down all portcullices of ears;* and Stevenson in THE INLAND VOYAGE (1878): *I never saw such a petard of a man* (though here the word may revert to its fundamental sense).

peter-see-me. A Spanish wine, popular in England in the 17th century, from a grape brought from Madeira (to the Rhineland, thence to Malaga) by one *Pedro Ximenes.* Also *Peter-sa-meene, Peter-semine.* Middleton and Rowley, in THE SPANISH GYPSY (1623): *Peter-see-me shall wash thy nowle.* Dekker in THE HONEST WHORE (PART TWO; 1630) called for *a pottle of Greeke wine, a pottle of Peter sa meene.*

petticoat tails. A sort of cake baked with butter, served (mainly in Scotland) with tea. Perhaps named from the shape, but more probably a corruption of French *petit gastel (gâteau),* little cake.

pettifactor. A lawyer that handles small cases. Also *petifactor.* A variant (both first used in the late 16th century) is *pettifogger.* By extension, a petty practitioner in any field; one that engages in sharp practices and chicanery. Thus *pettifoggery; to pettifog, to pettifogulize.*

pettilashery. A late 16th and early 17th century corruption of *petty larceny.* Also *pettilasserie, petulacerie.*

petulcous. Butting (like a ram); wantonly aggressive, offensively forward. Latin *petulcus,* butting, frisky; *petere,* to aim at. Hence also *petulcity* (accent on the *tull*), offensive forwardness. A 17th century term.

phaeacian. A glutton, a gourmand. (The first syllable is pronounced *fee.*) From *Phaeacia,* an island the inhabitants of which were infamous for their luxury. THE SPEAKER of 28 October, 1899: *He was a bon vivant, declined into a fat phaeacion . . . and latterly did nothing.*

phaeton. (1) A rash driver; one that by his rashness 'sets the world on fire.' From *Phaethon* (three syllables; the word means shining), the son of the sun—Helios and Clymene, in Greek mythology—who begged permission to drive the chariot of the sun just once, but could not control the horses, which plunged down until the earth was almost burned: Zeus saved it by hurling a thunderbolt that destroyed Phaethon. Thomas Watson in A BODY OF PRACTICAL DIVINITY (1692) said: *Sin is the Phaeton that sets the world on fire.* (2) A light four-wheeled open carriage, used in the 18th and 19th centuries; Felton in his book on CARRIAGES (1794) said: *The sizes and constructions of phaetons are more various than any other description of carriages.*

phalaric. A javelin wrapped in tow and pitch, hurled blazing (by catapult or hand) toward an enemy target to be set on fire. Latin *falarica*; Etruscan *fala,* a platform from which missiles were hurled. Sylvester's translation (1608) of Du Bartas has: *With brakes and slings and phalaricks they play, To fire their fortresse and their men to slay.* Note, however, that *phalarical, phalerical,* means inhumanly cruel, inhuman; *phalarism,* inhuman cruelty, delight in torture, supersadism. *Phalaris* was tyrant of Agrigentum in Sicily (570-554 B.C.). He roasted his enemies alive inside a brazen bull; the maker of the bull was its first victim; Phalaris, its last. The term *phalarism* has been replaced by *sadism,* from Comte Donatien Alphonse François de Sade (1740-1814) who called himself *Marquis de Sade.*

phantasiast. One that deals in phantasies. There was also a sect of heretics, of the Docetae, called *phantasiasts,* that held that the body of Christ was not material but a phantasm. In Smedley's book on the OCCULT SCIENCES (1855) there is mention of *Ben Jonson, who had some experience as a phantasiast.*

phantomnation. An illusion; the appearance of a spectre. The word itself was originally a phantomnation; it was first recorded in the dictionaries by a misreading. The original sense appears in Pope's translation (1725) of the ODYSSEY: *The phantome nations of the dead.*

pheeze. See *feeze.*

phil-. From the root *philein,* to love, *philos,* dear, the prefix *phil-, philo-* is used in many English words to mean lover, loving, love. Its converse, also frequent, is *mis-, q.v.* Among the forgotten words thus formed, are: *philadelphy,* brotherly love; *what in respect to others is called philanthropy* (love of man), said

Barrow in a sermon of 1677, with respect to Christians *is named philadelphy. philauty,* self-love, conceit (16th to 18th century). *philomythy,* love of talk. *philocalist,* lover of beauty. *philocomal,* relating to love of the hair, a fetishistical term overlooked by the psychoanalysts. *philocubist* (accent on the second syllable), a lover of play at dice—used by Aristophanes. *philoepiorcian,* fond of false oaths. *philogastric,* belly-loving, indulging the appetite; a *philopyg* is one especially fond of ham. *philogenitive,* fond of sexual activity. *philopogon* (accent on the second syllable), a lover of beards. *philopolemic,* fond of argument or strife. *philopornist* (accent on the third syllable), a lover of whores. Also *philodox,* a lover of his own opinion; hence, a dogmatic argufier. *philosophaster,* a shallow philosopher, a pretender to philosophy or wisdom; also *philosophist. philotimy,* love of honor, ambition. *philagathus* (accent on the second syllable; in Bailey, 1751, not in O.E.D.), a lover of the good, *philoxenist,* one who is hospitable to strangers.

philamot. See *filemot.*

philippic. A bitter attack, an invective. Originally applied to the orations (from 352 B.C.) of Demosthenes against Philip, king of Macedon, in defence of Athenian liberty. Burton (1864) spoke of *Lord North, sound asleep during one of Burke's philippics on him.* Hence *philippicize,* to deliver an invective.

philippize. To speak or write under bribery or corrupt influence. Also *philippizate* (17th century). The word was occasionally used by error for *philippicize*; see *philippic.* From the ancient belief (the charge was made by Demosthenes) that the (Pythian) priestess of Apollo was influenced to prophesy the things Philip of Macedon desired. Burke in his speech on THE FRENCH REVOLUTION (1790) said: The caballers *set him up as a sort of oracle; because, with the best intentions in the world, he naturally philippizes . . . in exact unison with their designs.*

philister. This is the German word for *Philistine,* borrowed by the English in the 19th century, for an unenlightened, uncultured person, a philistine. This use probably dates from a sermon preached by Pastor Götze in Jena in 1693, on the text *The Philistines be upon thee, Samson!* (*Philister über dir, Simson!*), at the funeral of a student killed by the townsmen in a quarrel between 'town and gown.' Hence, applied by students to townsmen, to all that are not students; hence, an unenlightened person. Also *philistee, philistian.*

philosopher's stone. A stone sought by the alchemists, capable of changing base into precious metals. Many identified it with the *elixir,* thus endowing it with the power of curing all wounds and diseases, thus prolonging life indefinitely. Thus Chaucer in THE CANON YEOMAN'S TALE (1386) says that *The philosophres stoon, Elixir clept, we sechen faste echoon* [we seek earnestly, each one]. For a report of its finding, see *whetstone. Cp. stone.*

phlegethontic. See *antiphlogistian.*

phlogiston. See *antiphlogistian.*

phthartic. Deadly, destructive. Greek *phthartikos,* destructive; *phtheirein,* to destroy. A 19th century word, at first applied (by doctors) to poisons. Also *phthora,* destruction (earlier; in Bailey, 1751). The early word for fluorine was *phthore,* because of the corrosive action of hydrofluoric acid. It will burn a hole in your suit, then your skin.

physiognomancy, phyznomancy. See *aeromancy.*

piacle. (Accent on the *pie.*) expiation; penance; an offering to wash away guilt; by transfer, an action that calls for expiation, a crime; guilt. Also *piaculum.* Latin *piaculum; piare,* to appease; *pius,* devout, conscientious. Hence, *piacularity,* the noun, in both senses; *piacular, piaculous, piaculary,* relating to atonement; sinful. Sir Thomas Browne in PSEUDODOXIA EPIDEMICA (1646) declared: *Piaculous it was unto the Romanes to pare their nayles upon the nundinae* [market-days; held in ancient Rome every ninth day] . . . *unto the ancient Britains it was piaculous to taste a goose. The Septuagint* (said G. Hickes in 1711) *called the scapegoat the piacular goat, because he was offered to be a piacle.*

pick-. A number of words, mainly naming types of person, have been formed from the verb *pick.* In addition to the still known *picklock* (which is also the name of the highest grade of wool) and *pickpocket,* there are the less familiar: *pickfault,* a petty fault-finder; Thomas Phaer in THE REGIMENT OF LIFE (1550), said: *I never intended nor yet do entend to satisfy the mindes of any such pikfaults. pickharness,* one who on the battle field steals the armor from the slain. *pickmote,* one who points out petty faults. *pickpenny,* a miser, a petty but greedy thief. *pickpurse* is well known, but in 1537 Latimer, and after him for a century other anti-Papists attacked the selling of indulgences and pardons as *purgatory pickpurse*: Olde in THE ANTICHRIST (1556): *That most gainful fornace of the Popes, pikepurse Purgatorie. pickquarrel,* a quarrelsome fellow. *pickshelf,* a pilferer of provisions. *pickstraw,* one who carps at trifles. *pickthank,* a stealer of 'thanks,' a sycophant, also used as a verb (17th century) as in a 1621 warning against giving credence to *pickthanking counsellors. Pickthank* is used by Shakespeare (HENRY IV, PART ONE; 1597) and Scott (THE ABBOTT; 1820). One should try to keep one's purse, if not one's mind, *pickfree* (safe from plundering).

pickedevant. A short pointed beard. Very popular in the late 16th and the early 17th century. Also *piquedevant, pickerdevaunt, peakedevant, pickenovant, pickitivant,* from French *pique devant,* peak in front. Hence, a man adorned with such a beard. The fashion grew out of style as the 17th century filled its course; Poole (PARNASSUS) in 1657 ridiculed a gallant: *A man consisting of a pickedevant and two mustachoes; to defeat him there needs but three clippes of a pair of cizzars,* and POOR ROBIN in 1709 could say: *Entreaties upon such an account are as ridiculous as pickedevant beards.*

pickeer. To maraud, pillage; to skirmish; reconnoitre; by extension, to skirmish amorously, flirt. Also *pickear, picquer, piquier, picqueer,* and more. Hence, a *pickeerer,* a skirmisher; one that picks a fight, a quarrelsome person. *pickeering,* skirmishing; wrangling, bickering; wordy or amorous interchange of advances. Used frequently in the 17th century, with relation to privateering, but roundabout from Late Latin *pecorare,* to carry off cattle; *pecora,* cattle (singular *pecus,* whence also *pecuniary*). Crowne in SIR COURTLY NICE (1685): *There was never such an open and general war made on virtue; young ones at thirteen will pickeere at it.*

pickle-herring. A buffoon, a merry-andrew. The word (from the preserved fish) was used in Germany in 1620 as the name of a character (*Pickelhering*) in a play;

a Dutch version used the name (*Pekelharingh*) in 1648; and Addison, in the first use of the word in English (THE SPECTATOR, No. 47, 1711) follows this: *A set of merry drolls . . . whom every nation calls by the name of that dish of meat which it loves best. In Holland, they are termed Pickled Herrings; in France, Jean Pottages; in Italy, Maccaronies; and in Great Britain, Jack Puddings.* Carlyle in SARTOR RESARTUS (1831) has: *Their high State Tragedy . . . becomes a pickle-herring farce to weep at, which is the worst kind of farce.*

pickwick. (1) An instrument for pulling up the wick of an oil lamp; used in the United States, 19th century. (2) A cheap cigar, in England, mid 19th century. Also *Pickwickian,* relating to *Mr. Pickwick,* in Dickens' POSTHUMOUS PAPERS OF THE PICKWICK CLUB (1837). Especially, *Pickwickian language*; *in a Pickwickian sense*: used to explain away an insult or liability: the words used, this phrase assures us, were spoken in a special sense that is completely without offence and harmless.

piepowder. (1) An itinerant; especially, a traveling pedlar. (2) Short for *piepowder court,* a court of summary justice, at fairs and markets (12th to 17th century), to handle vagabonds and administer justice among itinerant dealers and other non-residents. From French *pied poudreux,* dusty foot. Also called a *dustyfoot* (15th century). Jonson, in BARTHOLOMEW FAIR (1614): *Many are the yeerely enormities of this fayre, in whose courts of pye-pouldres I have had the honour during the three dayes sometimes to sit as judge.* Butler in HUDIBRAS (1664) uses it in a rhyme: *Have its proceedings disallow'd or Allow'd, at fancy of py-powder.*

piestrum. "An instrument to beat in pieces the bones of the head in drawing the child out of the womb." So in Bailey, 1751; this method of facilitating delivery seems to have lapsed from surgical practice, as the word is not in O.E.D. Bailey connects it with Greek *piestron,* which means pressing, squeezing, or an instrument for such action.

pignorate. See *impignorate.*

pigsney. Darling, sweetheart, pet. A term of endearment; literally *pig's eye,* that is, a tiny eye. In the same way *pinkeny, pinkany,* meaning literally tiny eye, was used (16th and 17th centuries) as a term of endearment. Thus Nashe in LENTEN STUFFE (1599) says of Hero: *She was a pretty pinckany and Venus Priest.* The earlier *pigsney*—also *pigsny, pygsnye, pigseie, pyggesnye,* and the like—was used from Chaucer's day into the 19th century, though in its later use it was often disparaging. Chaucer in THE MILLER'S TALE (1386) says: *She was a prymerole a piggesnye for any lord to leggen in his bedde.*

pilch. An outer garment of skin dressed with the hair. Chaucer gives as a proverb (1390): *After heet comethe colde, No man caste his pilchche away.* Old English *pylece, pelisse*; see *pell.* Also *pylche.* The verb *pilch* meant to pick, pluck; hence, to pilfer, rob. Hence *pilcher* was widely used in the 17th century, as a term of abuse, as in Jonson's THE POETASTER (1601): *you mungrels, you curres . . . you inhumane pilchers! Pilcher* was also used as a variant of *pilch,* and as meaning a scabbard—this in Shakespeare's ROMEO AND JULIET (1592): *Will you pluck your sword out of his pilcher by the ears?*

pilcrow. A paragraph. A 16th and 17th century term, apparently from *pilled* (*peeled*) *crow,* associated with that sound in common use, but corrupted (via earlier forms, *pilecrafte, pylcraft, parcraft,* from *paragraph.* Fletcher in THE NICE VALOUR (1625) plays on the term: *But why a peel-crow here? . . . A scarecrow had been better.* Samuel Sprigge in THE LIFE AND TIMES OF THOMAS WAKLEY (1897) wrote: *The leading article . . . calling attention to them with interjections . . . and all sorts of verbal pilcrows.*

pile. This old word had various meanings beyond those still current. From Latin *pilum,* earlier *pislum,* javelin, it was used in English from the 10th century to mean a dart, an arrowhead; a spike; the pointer of a sundial. In the 17th century it was brought back to the Latin sense, being used to translate *pilum,* the heavy javelin of the Roman infantry. Also, from the 14th century, a small castle or tower; also *peel, pel;* see *pel.* From the 15th century (Latin *pilus,* a hair), *pile* was used for hair, especially soft hair, down—still used in referring to carpets. Hence *piled* (1) heaped up; Milton in his sonnet ON SHAKESPEARE (1630): *What needs my Shakspear, for his honour'd bones, The labour of an age in piled stones?* (2) Pointed; Chapman in his translation (1611) of THE ODYSSEY: *Took to his hand his sharp-piled lance.* (3) Hairy; having a long nap, like velvet; Shakespeare in MEASURE FOR MEASURE (1603): *Thou'rt a three-pild piece I warrant thee.* Also *pileous* (*pie-lee-ous*), hairy; relating to hair.

pilgarlic. A bald head; a bald-headed man. Literally, a *pilled* (*peeled*) *garlic* head. Also *pyllyd garlick, pildgarlic, peelgarlic.* Often, in the 17th century, there was implication that the baldness came by disease, such as the pox. Also, in the 17th century, *pilgarlic* came to be used, in humor or mock pity, to mean poor fellow. In the phrase *poor pilgarlic,* it often referred to oneself, as when Swift in POLITE CONVERSATION (1738) said *They all went to the opera; and so poor Pilgarlick came home alone,* and Burns wrote in a letter (1793) to G. Thompson: *A ballad is my hobby-horse . . . sure to run poor pilgarlic, the bedlam jockey, quite beyond any useful point or post in the common race of men.*

pilledow. A tonsured priest. Literally, a *pilled* (*peeled,* i.e., bald) *daw;* the daw, being a black bird, brought to mind the black-garbed priest. Also *pilpate, pylpate,* short for *pilled pate* of the tonsured priest.

piller. See *complice.*

pillicock. (1) The penis. *Pill* and *cock* were used separately in this sense; *pill* also was figurative for testicle. The word *cock* took this meaning not directly from the barnyard animal, but from the *watercock,* supposedly representing a cock's head and comb—the tap of which suggested the penis. When Lear on the heath (Shakespeare, KING LEAR, 1605) says: *'Twas this flesh begot Those pelican daughters,* Edgar, disguised as a madman, sings the old song: *Pillicock sat on Pillicock Hill, Halloo, halloo, loo, loo!* [*pelican,* ungrateful, turning upon one's parents. The pelican mother supposedly fed her young on her own blood; the young thus gained strength, with which they tore her. Thus his daughters, with Lear.] (2) A term of endearment or compliment to a boy, like 'my pretty knave'; thus Urquhart in his translation (1653) of Rabelais cries: *By my faith, I cannot tell, my pillicock, but thou art more worth than gold.*

pilpate. See *pilledow.*

pilulous. The size of a pill; minute. Latin *pilula,* pill. Hence also *pilular,* relating to pills; *pilulist,* a dealer in pills. *piluliferous,* pill-producing; bearing round berries like pills.

piment. A drink of wine with honey and spices. Latin *pigmentum* meant *pigment,* paint; then the word was applied to a scented unguent, and in the Middle Ages to a scented and spiced drink. THE SQUIRE OF LOW DEGREE (1475) lists *wyne of Greek and muscadell, Both clare, pyment, and rochell.* Chaucer in his BOETHIUS (1374) pictures a sorry state: *They cowde make no pyment nor clarree.* (*Clare, clarree, clarry* are early forms of *claret.*) Chaucer also used *piment* as an adjective; see *mead.*

pinch. This common word has been used in several vivid compounds. Thus *pinchback,* a niggard (stingy of clothing, leaving the back bare). *pinchbelly,* stingy of food; also *pinch-commons, pinchcrust. pinchfart,* most miserly; Nashe in PIERCE PENILESSE (1592) refers to his *pinchfart penie-father*; also *pinchfist, pinchplum. pinchspotted,* discolored with pinch-marks; Shakespeare in THE TEMPEST (1611) cries: *Shorten up their sinewes With aged cramps, and more pinch-spotted make them then pard, or cat o' mountaine.* Even more common were *pinchpenny* and *pinchgut.* In the British Navy, if a ship were long at sea and provisions ran short, the sailors were paid extra; they called this *pinchgut pay, pinchgut money.* Hence *pinchgutted,* famished, as may you never be.

pinchbeck. An alloy (5 parts copper with 1 part zinc) that looks like gold, hence used for cheap jewelry; hence, spurious; imitation, sham. From Christopher *Pinchbeck* (died 1732) a watchmaker of Fleet Street, London, who invented the alloy; apparently his family name is a place-name; there is a village called *Pinchbeck* near Spalding. An advertisement in THE DAILY POST of 27 November, 1732, read: *The toys made of the late ingenious Mr. Pinchbeck's curious metal . . . are now sold only by his son and sole executor, Mr. Edward Pinchbeck.* Thackeray in THE VIRGINIAN (1859) said what is true of many a young woman this hundred years later: *Those golden locks were only pinchbeck.* Symonds in THE RENAISSANCE IN ITALY (1877) spoke of *a pinchbeck age of poetry.*

pinckany. See *pigsney.*

pind. To enclose; to dam up (as water); to put (animals) in a pound. In a farming book of 1641, Henry Best pictured a sorry state of lambs: *Theire excremente . . . berke together their tayles and hinder parts, and soe stoppe their fundament; the sheapheardes phrase is that such lambs are pinded, and that they must bee sette att liberty.* From the 9th century. Hence *pinder* (short *i*), an officer of the manor whose duty it was to impound stray beasts; in Nottingham in the 1760's there were two, "one for the fields and the other for the meadows." Also *pinfold,* a pound, a place for confining stray cattle, horses, sheep, etc. *In the ten provinces of Poland,* remarked A. White in 1899, *the Jews are confined as in a pinfold.*

pinguescent. Growing fat; causing to grow fat. Latin *pinguescere,* to grow fat; *pinguis,* fat. *pinguescence,* the process of growing fat. *pinguefy,* rarely *pinguedinize,* to make fat. *pinguefaction,* the act of fattening. Southey in 1797 pictured *a very brown looking man, of most pinguescent and fullmoon cheeks.* BLACKWOOD'S EDINBURGH MAGAZINE of 1825 more gruesomely pictured *buttocks pinguefying on their own steaks.*

pinionade. A comfit or conserve made with pine-nuts, enjoyed in the 14th and 15th centuries. Latin *pinea,* pine-nut. A 1390 recipe for *pynnonade* suggested: *Take almandes iblanched and draw them sumdeal thicke with goode broth . . . set on the fire and seethe it . . . Take pynes yfryed in oyle and therto white Powdour douce . . .*

pipient. Chirping like a young bird; hence, young, new-fledged. Collins in a sermon of 1607 spoke of *Anacreon's fonde doves, some perfect, some pipient, some hatcht, some half hatcht.* Thomas Adams in THE SPIRITUALL NAVIGATOR (1615) castigated *hypocrites, a pipient brood, cackling their own ripeness.*

pistle. Short for *epistle.* Also *pistel, pistol, pystol, pistelle, pystle,* and the like. Chaucer uses the word *pistel* to mean story. As a verb, to write an epistle on, to satirize; in PAPPE WITH A HATCHET (1589) we read: *Take heed, he will pistle thee.* A *pistoler* (*pystoler*) might be a letter-writer, or a church officer assigned to read the *Epistle*; Cardinal Wolsey had in his private chapel (said Cavendish in 1557) *a deane who was allwayes a great clarke and devyne; a subdeane, a repeter* [rehearser] *of the quyer; a gospeller; a pystoler; and xii syngyng prestes.*

pix. See *pyx.*

pizzle. The penis of an animal; especially that of a bull, which was (15th to 19th century) dried and used as a whip for flogging. Also *pissel, peezel, pizell,* and the like. In Shakespeare's HENRY IV, PART ONE (1597), when Prince Hal refers to Falstaff's weight—*this bed-presser, this horse-backbreaker, this huge hill of flesh* —Falstaff retorts with figures of the Princes' leanness: *You starveling, you elf skin, you dried neat's tongue, you bull's pizzle, you stockfish!* A *stockfish* is a dried and pressed codfish. Some editors have changed *elf skin* to *eel skin*; but it probably means snakeskin, which, as Oberon remarks in A MIDSUMMER NIGHT'S DREAM, is a *weed wide enough to wrap a fairy in.* Scott in a letter to Southey, of 17 June, 1814, spoke of *the wholesome discipline of a bull's pizzle and a straitjacket.*

placket. (1) A plan or map (16th century). (2) A piece of armour worn over the cuirass, or a leather jacket with steel strips. In this sense, also *placcate, placard, plaquet.* (3) A woman's petticoat; hence, a woman. Also, a pocket in a woman's skirt; but especially, the opening in a petticoat (to make it easy to take off), hence used with sexual implications, as in Shakespeare's KING LEAR (1605): *Keep thy foot out of brothels, thy hand out of plackets, thy pen from lender's books, and defy the foul fiend!*

plangent. Making the noise of waves breaking on the shore; loudsounding, used of a metallic or of a plaintive sound; hence *plangor,* loud lamentation; *plangorous.* Latin *plangere,* to strike noisily, beat the breast, bewail. Hence *plangiferous,* producing or accompanied by the sound of beating, like a lively plangiferous flagellation. *Plangency* might be either pleasant or unpleasant: Carlyle in FREDERICK THE GREAT (1858) says: *Friedrich Wilhelm's words, in high clangorous metallic plagency . . . fall hotter and hotter*; Stevenson in THE ARABIAN NIGHTS (1882) says: *Her voice had charm and plangency.*

planiloquent. Plain-speaking. Also *planiloquy,* plain speech. 17th and 18th century, after the Latin *planiloquus* of Plautus.

planiped. A barefoot person; also as an adjective, barefoot. Used by the Romans of an actor or gladiator that performed with naked feet.

planisphere. This word, combining two-dimensional *plane* with three-dimensional *sphere,* was used (from the 12th century) for a map of half the earth, or a projection of the "celestial sphere" as in one type of astrolabe. It sometimes found its way into poetry, as when Marvell in THE DEFINITION OF LOVE (published 1681) pictures himself and his beloved as poles apart, *Unless the giddy heaven fall . . . And, us to join, the world should all Be cramp'd into a planisphere.* The science-fiction writers who traverse light-years in a flash by "a wrinkle in space" should note this anticipation of their desires.

plash. (1) To interweave; see *pleach.* (2) A shallow pool; the sound a body makes on striking water, milder than a *splash.* (*Plash* and *splash* are both echoic words, in this sense.) Also as an adjective, a *plashed* bush or thicket. *The fresh fragrant flowers of divine Poesie,* said Richard Brathwait in 1638, *could not like to be removed nor transported to those thorny places and plashes of the Law.*

plastrography. Counterfeiting; forging another's handwriting. Greek *plastos,* moulded, forged (whence all the *plastics*) + *graphein,* to write. The word occurs only in 17th and 18th century dictionaries. A *plastograph* is an instance of such forgery.

platitudinarian. A dealer in platitudes. Also *platitudinizer.* THE PALL MALL GAZETTE in 1893 criticized an actor: *He moves platitudinising and attitudinising through a play.* THE STRAND MAGAZINE of August 1897 gave credit for the term overseas: *He has a rich gift of what an eminent American calls platitudinizing. The word . . . is most effective as indicating a constant ever-fed supply of pointless words, wrapped up in cotton-woolly sentences.*

plaudite. An appeal for applause at the end of a performance. (Three syllables: Latin *plaudite,* imperative of *plaudere,* to applaud.) Hence, applause. In this sense, shortened to *plaudit.* A *plauditor,* one that applauds. The forms *plaudiat* and *plause* were also used (16th century) for applause. The original meaning of *plausibility* was readiness to applaud or approve; the quality of deserving such approval, or an act of such desert. Also *plausive,* approving, applauding: *the plausive shouts.* In the LETTER-BOOK (1573) of Gabriel Harvey we read: *A plaudite and Deo gratias for so happy an event, And then to borrowe a nappe I shalbe contente.* GAMMER GURTON'S NEEDLE (1575) shows the conventional ending: *For Gammer Gurtons nedle sake, let us have a plaudytie.*

plaustrary. A wagoner. Latin *plaustrum,* a wagon, cart. The first syllable rhymes with *law.* Hence, *plaustral,* pertaining to a cart or wagon. Goldsmith in A CITIZEN OF THE WORLD (1762) observed: *Whether the grand jury, in council assembled, had gloriously combined to encourage plaustral merit, I cannot take upon me to determine.*

pleach. To intertwine stems and branches of young trees and bushes, to form a fence; to make a hedge in this wise; hence, to entwine, interlace. A variant form was *plash, q.v.,* from Old French *plaissier, plessier*; Old French *plesse,* hedge; Latin *plectere, plexus,* to weave, to tangle, whence *perplexed* and the *solar plexus.* A *pleacher* was a bough (as a quickthorn) woven to form a hedge, or a man making a hedge. Swinburne in AT ELEUSIS (POEMS AND BALLADS, 1865) describes: *Poppied hair of gold Persephone Sad-tressed and pleached low down about her brows.* Shakespeare used the word of folded arms, in ANTONY AND CLEOPATRA (1606): *Would'st thou . . . see Thy master thus with pleacht armes, bending down His corrigible neck?* Scott in THE FORTUNES OF NIGEL (1822) and others after him have spoken of *a pleached alley* or *pleached fences,* probably following Shakespeare, as in MUCH ADO ABOUT NOTHING (1599): *Bid her steale into the pleached bower Where hony-suckles ripened by the sunne Forbid the sunne to enter.*

pleonectic. Grasping, covetous, greedy. Greek *pleonektikos; pleonektes,* one that has or claims more than his share; *pleon,* more (as in *pleonasm,* use of more words than are needed) + *exein,* to have. Hence *pleonexia,* covetousness. THE PALL MALL GAZETTE of 15 September, 1882, somewhat pompously expressed a pious hope: *The pleonectic spirit which prompted this practice will no doubt be chastened into greater accordance with the principles of distributive justice.*

pleroma. See *anaplerosis.*

plethory. Over-fullness, superabundance; unhealthy excess. A 17th century form of *plethora* (probably fashioned after *plethoric,* as *historic—history,* etc.); Greek *plethore; plethein,* to become full. Other adjectives are *plethoretic, plethorical.* Into the mid-18th century *plethora* held the accent on the *thor;* since then, the preferred accent has been on the first syllable. Farrar in SEEKERS AFTER GOD (1868) complained—like many before and after—of *a plethora of words.* Burton in THE SCOT ABROAD (1864) spoke of *plethoric volumes which slumber in decorous old libraries.*

plight. As a noun. Peril, risk; sin; guilt. Hence, the undertaking of a risk or obligation: *trothplight,* pledge of betrothal; *plight-ring,* an engagement ring. This is a common Teutonic use; German *Pflicht,* duty. The form became merged with *plight (plait, pleat)*, via Old French from Latin *plicare,* to fold (whence also *complicate, complexion, implication, replica, reply,* and *multiplex* more). This second *plight* (14th century) meant a fold, then a state of being, a condition. At first neutral (good or bad condition), this came soon *(plyt of peril)* to imply danger, as to be *in a plight.* As a verb, similarly: to bring danger upon; also, to pledge. *I thee plight,* I assure you. Also, to fold (cloth); to fold in one's arms, embrace. Hence (14th century) *plightful,* dangerous, sinful; *plightless,* blameless. The Tudor writers often used the word in its neutral sense, meaning condition. Thus Vaux in his ballad THE AGED LOVER RENOUNCETH HIS LOVE (1550): *My muse doth not delight Me as she did before; My hand and pen are not in plight As they have bene of yore.* The Gravedigger in HAMLET sings three stanzas of this ballad; Goethe uses two stanzas of it in FAUST. Vaux also inquires: *What foodless beast can live long in good plight?*

pluck. As a noun. The act of plucking; that which is plucked; that with which something is plucked, tugged, pulled out —in various senses. *Cp. draught* (7). (1) a dung fork, two pronged. (2) Rejection or failure at a university. Mrs. Smythies in THE BRIDE ELECT (1852) declared: *Visions of a pluck danced before the weary eyes of tutor and pupil.* (3) The liver and lights of a fowl, animal, occasionally, human. In the late 18th century, *pluck* in this sense (from the physiological allocation of the emotions; the BIBLE says: *His bowels were loosed with fear*) began to be used, first in pugilistic slang, to mean courage. By the late 19th century, this meaning had become the most common; THE ILLUSTRATED LONDON NEWS of 1 November 1879 said: *Yes! The British word 'pluck' is the word to use. 'Courage', 'bravery', 'heroism' are all too feeble.* The meaning, liver, lungs, and heart was forgotten save in the countryside. Slang, however fresh it seeks to be in phraseology, is tenaciously conservative in source, rooted in folk beliefs; slang went right back to the viscera for its new coinage: *That guy's got guts!*

plumulaceous. Downy—like the best pillows before foam rubber. Etymologically the word means full of little feathers. A 19th century word, still effective for humor.

plungy. Rainy; bringing heavy showers. Chaucer in BOETHIUS (1374) speaks of *ploungy clowdes.*

pluriparous. Bearing two or more at a birth (as Mrs. Dionne); (less often), being the mother of two or more children. Latin *plus, plures,* more + *-parus,* bearing. From *plures* come also *plurifarious,* manifold, of divers fashions (17th century); *plurity,* the state of being more, a larger number, as when Thynne in his EPIGRAMS (1600) declared: *Pruritie of wemmen . . . seekes pluritie of men.*

plurity. See *pluriparous.*

pneumancy. See *aeromancy.*

pneumo-. A combining form from Greek *pneuma,* breath, wind, spirit. Also *pneumato-.* Found in many technical and scientific terms. Among the more general but less well remembered are: *pneumatophobia,* dread or dislike of the spiritual. *pneumatophony* (accent on the *toff*), speech by ghosts or other disembodied spirits, as Hamlet's father. *pneumatography;* spirit writing; an instance thereof is a *pneumatogram.* For *pneumatology,* see *minimifidian. pneumatomachy* (accent on the *tom*), battling against the spirit; *pneumatomachian* (accent on the *mayk*), an opponent of the Holy Spirit; especially one of a 4th century sect that denied the Holy Spirit; hence, a lover of the flesh. In scientific terms, *pneumo-* may be short for *pneumato-,* or for *pneumono-,* Greek *pneumon,* lung. Thus *pneumology* means (1) a discourse of spirits or (2) a treatise on, or the science of, the lungs. A book of 1613 was entitled: *The Admirable Historie of the Possession and Conversion of a Penitent Woman, Seduced by a Magician that Made Her to Become a Witch . . . whereunto is annexed a Pneumology, or Discourse of Spirits.*

pochette. A pocket fiddle, used in the 17th and the early 18th century. Also *pochette d'amore,* an early viola d'amore.

poculent. Fit for drinking; supplying drink. *poculari,* to frequent the cup; *poculum,* cup. Hence *poculation,* drinking. *poculary,* relating to drink; of the medieval church, a *poculary* was a pardon or indulgence for drinking. A translation (1537) of a sermon of Latimer's tells: *Some brought forth canonizations, some expectations, some pluralities and unions, some tot-quots and dispensations, some pardons, and these of wonderful variety, some stationaries, some jubilaries, some poculanes for drinkers, some manuaries for handlers of relicks, . . some oscularies for kissers.* Latin *pocillum,* a little cup, is a diminutive of *poculum;* hence *poculiform,* cup-shaped; *pocilliform,* shaped like a little cup. A *pocillator*

(17th century) was a cupbearer; *pocillation,* waiting upon or serving drinkers; filling the cup. A *pocill* was a small cup; hence, a draught, a potion; J. Jones in THE BATHES OF BUCKSTONE (1572) suggested that one *take in the morninge fastinge, in pocyll whay, made with ale, to purge choller.* Bacon in SYLVA (1626) observed that *some of those herbs, which are not esculent, are notwithstanding poculent; as hops, broom.* The root of *poculent* is *po,* to drink, whence also *potion, potation, hippopotami.* A reduplicated form of this root, *pipo,* became in classical Latin *bibo* and gave us *imbibe* and *bibulous. The art of poculation,* said THE NEW MONTHLY MAGAZINE in 1837, is *of the highest antiquity.*

podagra. See *corcousness.*

podalic. Relating to the feet. Also *podal.* The forms *pedal, pedestrian, impediment,* etc., are from Latin *pes, pedem,* foot; see *pedicle. Podalic* is from Greek *pous, pod-,* foot. *Podiatry* (accent on the *die*) is the treating of the feet. *Pediatry, pediatrics,* earlier *paedi-,* are from Greek *pais, paido-,* boy; *pedagogue,* a leader of boys; *pederast,* a lover of boys. Thus *paedocracy* is government by children, as in some families. A *paedonymic* is a name given to a person from the name of the person's child, as Althaea Meleagris was named from her son Meleager. [When Meleager was born, the Parcae put a log on the fire, saying the child would live till the log was burned. Althaea took it off and saved it; but when the grown Meleager killed her brothers, Althaea burned the log. When it was consumed and her son Meleager died, Althaea killed herself.]

poetaster. See *medicaster.* Also *poeticule,* a petty poet—the ending as in *animalcule; cp. critickin. poetling,* a young or beginning poet; also, *poet-sucker,* one that is still a babe, suckling at the breast of the muse. As Jonson puts it in THE STAPLE OF NEWS (1625): *What says my poet-sucker? He's chewing his muse's cud, I do see by him.* Also *poetastrical;* revived for slyly satiric use in Mainwaring's MURDER IN PASTICHE (1954): *Always in time—and just in time—Nappleby had managed to cut through the poetastrical frills and expose the truth.*

point-device. Perfectly correct; with extreme nicety. Especially in the phrase *at (by, to the) point device.* Chaucer in THE HOUS OF FAME (1384) *saw in dreme, at poynt devys, Helle and erthe and paradys.* Shakespeare uses the expression in TWELFTH NIGHT (II v) and in AS YOU LIKE IT (1600): *You are rather point device in your accoustrements.*

poke. In addition to being the name of several plants, one of which the North American Indians smoked like tobacco, another of which bears the poke-berry, and the name for a push or nudge or blow, *a poke in the nose, poke* was common from the 13th century, meaning a bag, smaller than a sack. It is probably of Gaelic origin, in various forms (*pough, poque*) being related to *pouch* and *pocket. To buy a pig in a poke* was to buy blind; too often when one opened to look, one let the cat out of the bag. Indeed the Scotch say *a cat in a poke;* the French, *chat en poche.* The *pocket* or *poke,* until the 17th century, was always a separate pouch, often on a belt, not a part of a garment. In the 15th century *poke* was also used to mean a wide sleeve (in those days the sleeve was a separate garment); they grew so extravagant—*Grete insolence of vesture,* we read in 1450: *gownes with long pokus, made in the maner of a bagpype*—that ultimately the wearing of pokes was forbidden. In the 19th century, *poke* was used of the stomach of a fish, especially when the hook is swallowed with the bait and catches in the stomach; thus Kipling in CAPTAINS COURAGEOUS (1897) cries: *Help us here, Harve. It's a big un. Poke-hooked, too.*

poking-stick. A rod used to stiffen the plaits of ruffs, in the 16th and 17th centuries. Some were of bone or wood; the best were of steel, to be applied hot. Autolycus in Shakespeare's THE WINTER'S TALE (1611) is peddling, among other items, *pins and poaking-stickes of steele.*

poleclipt. Hedged in by poles, as in Shakespeare's THE TEMPEST (1611): *Thy poleclipt vineyard, And thy sea-marge sterile.* Bailey (1751), assuming the first part of the word to be a variant of *poll, q.v.,* defined it as clipped in the head.

poll. A head. Used from the 13th century, still common in dialects, and in terms like *poll-tax* and *to take a poll,* to count heads. Also, the part of the head where the hair grows; a head of hair; Shakespeare in HAMLET (1602) has *His beard as white as snow, All flaxen was his pole.* Other forms were *poule, poil, pole, powle,* Scotch *pow.* Dutch *bol,* whence English *bolster.* Also, number of persons (like *head* of cattle) ascertained by counting; muster—as in Shakespeare's CORIOLANUS: *We are the greater pole, and in true feare They gave us our demands.* A *poll* or *poll man,* at Cambridge, 18th century (short for Greek *hoi polloi,* the multitude) a student working for or receiving a pass degree, i.e., one without honors. The verb *to poll* (from the 14th century) meant to clip, crop, shear, to cut off not the head (though occasionally that too) but the hair. Of an animal, to cut or cut off the horns. Hence, to despoil, to tax excessively, to plunder, fleece. *To poll and pill,* plunder and pillage; Cromwell, in his DECLARATION of January 1650: *whom you have fleeced and polled and peeled hitherto.* Hence *pollard,* a beast with its horns cut; beardless wheat, *cp. muticous;* a tree with trunk cut so as to form a rounded head, a thick close growth of young branches. Also (late 13th century) *pollard,* a base foreign coin (stamped with a head) circulated in England, worth about a penny; declared illegal in 1299.

pollard. See *poll.*

poly. A Greek word meaning much. Its plural is *polloi,* many, as in *hoi polloi,* the many; hence, the common people; by extension, the rabble. *Poly* has been used as a combining form in many English words, including: *polycracy* (accent on the *lick*), government by many rulers. *polyepic,* consisting of several words; Bentham in his treatise on LANGUAGE (1831) wrote: *This proposition will consist of one word only, or of divers words,—will be either monoepic or polyepic. polyergic,* working in many ways, having various functions. *polyethnic,* belonging to or embracing many races. *polyfenestral,* having many windows. *polylinguist. polyloquent,* speaking very much; *polylogy. polylychnous,* with many lamps or lights. *polymicrian* (*multum in parvo*), containing much in little space. *polyotical,* many-eared. *polyparous,* giving birth to many, also *multiparous; cp. pluriparous. polyponous,* busied with many tasks. *polyposist,* a hard drinker (accent on the *lip*). *polytopian,* a visitor to many places. *polytrophic,* highly nutritive (Greek *trephein,* to feed); *Hoggs flesh,* said Lovell in his HISTORY OF ANIMALS AND MINERALS (1661) *is of easie concoction . . . polytrophic, and of a thick and viscous juyce.*

polytropic, versatile, resourceful, capable of turning to many expedients; in Greek, *polytropos* might also mean much-traveled, *polytopic;* the word was applied to Ulysses in the ODYSSEY.

polyarchy. Government by many; the converse of *monarchy.* Hence, the *polyarch,* the people (pictured as rulers); *polyarchal, polyarchical.*

polycephalic. Many-headed. Literally, like Typhoeus, who had a hundred serpents' heads; or Scylla, whose six heads had each three rows of teeth, and who in later descriptions (Virgil) is endowed with a girdle of dogs' heads. A *polycephalist,* however, was a person that bowed to many heads or rulers.

polychete. One with very much hair. Also *polychaete* (pronounced *keet*); Greek *chaite,* mane.

polychrest. A medicine good for a number of ills. Also *polychreston, polychrestum.* Hence, more generally *polychrestic, polychrestical,* serving for various purposes; *polychresty,* capability of manifold service. Buck's HANDBOOK (1889) observes: *The same word may do duty in many different connections . . . Such words, useful in many ways, may be called polychrestic.*

polydipsia. Insatiable thirst. Also figurative, as in Hickeringill's JAMAICA (1660), speaking of some men's *poludipsie after gold.*

polygeneous. Of many kinds, *heterogeneous.* BLACKWOOD'S EDINBURGH MAGAZINE in 1818 spoke of *a patched, pyebald, and polygeneous affair.*

polyhistor. A man of deep and wide learning. Used in the 16th and 17th centuries. Also *polyhistorian. Polyhistory,* wide learning; *polyhistoric,* widely erudite. Also, with the same meanings, *polymath, polymathist; polymathy; polymathic.* Greek *manthanein,* to learn. Grote in his study of PLATO (1865) observed that Aristotle exhibited *much of that polymathy which he transmitted to the peripatetics generally.*

polylogize. To talk too much; to prate unendingly. See *poly* (*polylogy*).

polymite. Woven of different (colored) threads. Lydgate in THE LIFE OF OUR LADY (1410) pictured *Of yonge Josephe the cote polimite Wroughte by the power of all the Trinite.*

polymyth. A work that comprises many stories, like THE ARABIAN NIGHTS. Also *polymythy, polymythia.*

polyphagous. Eating very much; eating many kinds of food. Also *polyphagic, polyphagian.* A voracious eater: *a polyphagian, polyphage, polyphagist.* Hence *polyphagia, polyphagy,* excessive eating.

polyphonian. Many-voiced. Quarles in EMBLEMS (1635) pictures the air of the countryside: *Her shrill-mouthed choir sustain me with their flesh, And with their polyphonian notes delight me.* Also *polyphonic, polyphonous, polyphonical.* Note that *polyphonism* means the multiplication of a sound, as by echoes.

polypragmatist. A busybody. Also *polypragmist, polypragmon.* Greek *pragma,* thing done. Also *polypragmatic, polypragmatical, polypragmonic, polypragmonetic,* meddlesome; officious. Hence *polypragmony, polypragmaty, polypragmatism,* officious behavior, meddlesomeness. Used mainly in the 16th and 17th centuries, but THE SATURDAY REVIEW of 22 August, 1885, complained of *troublesome and polypragmatic operosity.* Harvey addressed a pamphlet, in 1597, *to the* *polypragmaticall . . . puppie, Thomas Nashe*; Dekker in the amusing picture of Tudor life, THE GULL'S HORNBOOK (1609) spoke of *good dry-brained polypragmonists.* It is well to mind one's own business.

pomander. (1) A mixture of aromatic substances, carried or worn as a safeguard against infection. Earlier *pomamber;* Old French *pome,* apple + *ambre,* amber. (2) A case for carrying this pungency, a hollow ball, often shaped like an apple or orange, of gold or other substance. Hence, anything scented or perfumed; Jonson in EVERY MAN OUT OF HIS HUMOUR (1599) says to a fop: *Away, good pomander; go.* In the same play he *walks all day hang'd in pomander chains.* By another extension (as a safeguard against evil) *pomander* was applied to a book of prayers or of magic prescriptions; a translation of 1650 was entitled *The Divine Pymander of Hermes Mercurius Trismegistus*: Thrice master of the pomander of alchemy. More devoutly, knowing that cleanliness is next to godliness, Robert Hill in THE PATHWAY TO PRAYER AND PIETIE (1610) said that we, *God's pomander, smell better by rubbing.*

pome. An apple, or a fruit of the apple kind. Via French *pome,* now *pomme,* from Latin *pomum*—at first the general word for fruit, then restricted to the apple. Other meanings rose from the shape: (1) the head of a cabbage, etc. *To pome* was (17th century) to form a head, as cabbage, lettuce, etc. (2) the golden apple, the ball that is a sign of dominion, borne before royalty or set on the top of a flagpole. (3) A metal ball filled with hot water and placed on the altar in cold weather, to keep the priest's hands warm and thus prevent accident to the chalice.

pomedorry. A 14th and 15th century dish, variously described. From *pome,* apple (the shape) + *dory* (French *doré*), gilded. It may be a ball of ground beef, or a mince of pork liver—in either case roasted and endored (gold coated) with a touch of flour and yolk of egg.

pomped. See *sloth.*

pompion. A large melon. The word later became *pompeon, pumpion, pumkin, pumpkin.* Used in derision, of a corpulent man, as by Shakespeare in THE MERRY WIVES OF WINDSOR (1598): *We'll use this unwholsome humidity, this grosse-watry pumpion.*

ponophobia. See *aeromancy.*

pooter. A *poting-stick,* poking-stick (*q.v.*), a rod used to stiffen the plaits of ruffs; at first of wood or bone; later of steel (applied hot). *To pote* (from the 10th century) meant to push, poke; hence, to form plaits or folds in cloth with a *potingstick.* For an instance of the use of *pooter,* see *bumrowl.*

popelot. A darling. Perhaps from Old French *poupelet,* little doll. Used by Chaucer in THE MILLER'S TALE (1386): *So gay a popelote or swiche a wenche.*

popeness. The quality of a pope, specifically, the sense of infallibility. As Archbishop Leighton perceived (and noted in THE PRACTICAL COMMENTARY. . . , 1684), *There is naturally this popeness in every man's mind, . . a kind of fancied infallibility in themselves.* Each of us speaks, fundamentally, *ex cathedra.*

poperin. See *medlar.*

popinjay. A parrot; then, the representation of a parrot: in tapestry; as an heraldic device; as the sign of an inn—*The Popin-*

jay in Norwich (1687); on a pole as a target. In the 14th and 15th centuries, applied to a person in praise of his beauty; in the 16th century and later, to a person contemptuously, as vain (in allusion to the bird's plumage as gaudy show) or as stupid (in allusion to the bird's mechanical repetition of words). Also *pape jay, papengay, popengiay,* etc. Ultimately from Arabic *babaghay,* imitative of the call of the bird.

poplet. A darling. By deterioration, a light woman, a wench. Also *poplolly,* a mistress. Perhaps related to *poppet, q.v.*; but Old French *poupelette,* darling, was the diminutive of *poupée*; Latin *pupa,* little girl, a Latin diminutive of which was *pupillus* (masculine), whence English *pupil.* Stanyhurst in his DESCRIPTION OF IRELAND (in Holinshed; 1577) wrote: *The prettie poplet his wife began to be a fresh occupieing giglot at home.*

poppet. This is the early form of *puppet*; but it was used in several senses that the later form did not carry on. It is via French from Latin *pupa,* a girl; the ending is a diminutive. (1) A small or dainty person; occasionally applied to a dwarf, but often (17th-19th centuries) as a term of endearment. (2) A doll; a tiny human figure used for witchcraft; hence, an idol. Chaucer has, in SIR THOMAS (1386): *This were a popet in an arm t'embrace For any woman smal and fair of face.* Beard in THE THEATRE OF GOD'S JUDGEMENT (1597) remarked that *as one of the three chapmen was employed . . . abroad, so the pretty poppet his wife began to play the harlot at home.* For another quotation, see *mob.*

porail. Poor people as a class. Rarely, poverty. Also *poraille, poveraille, poral, poorall,* and the like. Old French *povre,* poor + the collective ending (as in *canaille*). Used from the 13th to the 15th century.

porlockian. Unwelcomely intrusive; breaking in upon and forever breaking off a train of thought. With reference to the "gentleman from Porlock," who called while Coleridge was writing KUBLA KHAN and after whose departure the idea and inspiration for the poem never returned.

pornerastic. Given to harlotry. Greek *porne,* harlot + *erastes,* lover. Thus *pornography* was originally a writing about prostitutes, perhaps medical; the sense of 'obscene' came later. The *pornocracy* was government by (under the influence of) harlots; Ebersheim in his translation (1860) of Kurtz's HISTORY OF THE CHRISTIAN CHURCH speaks of the early 10th century, when *Theodora . . . and her equally infamous daughters . . . filled the See of Peter with their paramours, their sons, and grandsons . . . (the so-called pornocracy).* They filled the Tyrrhenian Sea with their enemies. Hence, a *pornocrat,* a member of a pornocracy. F. Harrison in THE CHOICE OF BOOKS (1870) said that in actual life *we hear nothing . . . of those pornerastic habits in high places, which are too often thrust before our eyes in fiction.*

porrect. To stretch out; hence, to proffer (a gift, a petition, a prayer); to tender for examination or correction (as in law or ecclesiastical courts). Also *porrectate.* From Latin *por, pro-,* forth + *regere,* to direct, to stretch. The noun *porrection,* a stretching out (as of a muscle), a proffering, is still used in religious references. In its literal sense, *porrect* is used mainly of parts of the body; Horatio Smith in THE TOR HILL (1826) speaks of *the Doctor again porrecting his forefingers.* Fielding in THE TRUE PATRIOT (1746) uses the word humorously: *Which I no sooner perceived than I porrected him a remembrance over the face.*

posnet. A small metal pot, with a handle and three feet, to stand over heat, for boiling. Used since the 14th century. Steele in THE TATLER (No. 245, 1710) speaks of *a silver posnet to butter eggs.*

posset. Curdled milk with wine or ale, with sugar and spice (and other things nice), frequent (15th to 18th century) as a delicacy, also taken for colds and given to bridegrooms. "It was anciently a custom," said Toone in his GLOSSARY of 1834, "to take a potation of this kind previous to retiring to rest for the night"; this custom is implicit in the remark in Shakespeare's MACBETH (1605): *The surfeted groomes doe mock their charge with snores. I have drugg'd their possets, That death and nature do contend about them.* In Hamlet *posset* is used as a verb, meaning to curdle. A SOBER DISCOURSE OF THE HONEST CAVALIER (1680) speaks of some who prefer *the possit basin before the hallowed font.*

postic. Hinder, *posterior.* Also *posticous* (used mainly in botany). Latin *posticus,* hinder; *post,* behind, after. Sir Thomas Browne in his PSEUDODOXIA EPIDEMICA (1646) noted *the postick and backward position of the feminine parts in quadrupedes.* Hence *posticum,* a rear entrance, back door. Before prohibition, the only access a woman had to a tavern or bar in the United States, was via the posticum. Note that *postify* meant (17th century) to nail or otherwise fasten to a post. Latin *postis,* post, is from *ponere, positus,* to put, set, place, whence *position, imposition, exposition* and other ways of keeping *posted; cp. postiche.*

postiche. Counterfeit; artificial. In sculpture, used of an ornament superadded to a completed work, especially if inappropriate. Also, as a noun, an imitation; counterfeiting, feigning. Via Italian *posticcio,* ultimately from Latin *postus, positus,* placed. English *pastiche, pasticcio* (Italian *pasticcio,* a pasty or pie; Romanic *pasta,* paste) is a mixture of various ingredients; a work or style made of selections from various artists (painters, writers, musicians, etc.) or periods; a work pieced together in imitation of another artist or style. Gosse in his LIFE OF DONNE (1899) said: *It was left to his Caroline disciples to introduce . . . a trick of pastiche, an alloy of literary pretence.* Ouida in THE WINTER CITY (1876) averred that *Fastidiousness, at any rate, is very good postiche for modesty.*

postjudice. A remaining bias, a bias that resisted removal. Hence also *postjudiced.* Coined, as the opposite of *prejudice,* in the 19th century. Used by Ruskin (PRAETERITA; 1886); Chesterton (R. BROWNING; 1905): *Prejudice is not so much the great intellectual sin as . . . postjudice, not the bias before the fair trial, but the bias that remains after.*

postknight. An arrant perjurer. Also, *knight of the post.* The Water Poet in his IN PRAISE OF HEMPSEED (1630) spoke of *a postknight, that for five groats gaine Would sweare, and for foure groats forsweare't againe.*

postliminy. The right to return home and resume one's former civic privileges, after banishment or imprisonment or capture. So in ancient Rome; in international law, applied to restoration of persons and things taken in war. Also *postliminium, postliminiage*; Latin, *post,* behind + *liminem,* threshold. Hence also *postliminary, postliminiary, postliminious. postliminiate,* to permit to return from banishment. Used in the 17th century. From the same source came another set of words, opposed to *preliminary;* Scott in WOODSTOCK (1826) notes: *The reresupper was a postliminary banquet . . . which made its appearance at ten or eleven.* Thus also *postliminous,* subsequent, as an appendix; *postliminate,* to place behind, to put subsequently.

postprandial. See *jentacular.*

posy. A short motto, at first a line or two of verse, to be inscribed in a ring, on a knife, etc. Also *posey, posie.* The word is a short form of *poesy,* which was often pronounced in two syllables. *Poesy* is a variant form of *poetry.* Hence, an emblem or emblematic device. Also, a bunch of flowers, a bouquet; hence, a bouquet of 'flowers' of poetry, an anthology (which is from Greek *anthos,* flower + *legein,* to gather). Hence *posy-waiscoat,* a flowered vest. Thackeray in THE VIRGINIAN (1859) has: *He has bought posey-rings at Tunbridge Fair.*

pot. The family of *pots* has grown through 800 years. The origin of *pot,* the deep, rounded vessel, is unknown, but it was early linked with the idea in words from Latin *potare, potatum,* to drink: *potable, potatory,* drinkable, pertaining to drink; *potability.* Also *potate,* liquid, drinkable; but also drunk (intoxicated), as also *potulent, potshotten, potshot* (in one sense); a *poter,* an habitual drinker of intoxicating liquids. And *potorious,* relating to drinking, drinking a lot; *potomania,* inability to stop drinking, *potomaniac,* a candidate for Alcoholics Anonymous. Among pot-proverbs: *The pot walks,* the liquor is passed from hand to hand (at a drinking bout). A 1680 translation of Boileau's LUTRIN reads: *Yet so, the fancy's richer, To end in pot, commence in pitcher!*—where the pitcher is the container of liquor, leading to the chamber-pot. *A little pot is soon hot* means that little men (being sensitive) anger quickly. Among compounds may be listed: *pot-ally, pot-companion, pot-mate, potpanion,* fellow drinker. *pot-bird,* an imitation of a bird (sound) in the theatre, formerly made by blowing a pipe in a pot of water. *potknight,* a drinker; there were many compounds relating to drink, of most of which the meaning is obvious, as *pot-quarrel, potman.* Also, *potboilery,* the practice of writing *to keep the pot aboiling. potcarrier,* a corrupt form of *poticary;* see *pottingar. potgallery,* a balcony projecting over a river (17th century); the law (1684) found such a structure an encroachment. A *pothead,* a stupid fellow; *potheaded.* A *pothunter* (1) a parasite, a sycophant (16th century); (2) a hunter taking *potshots,* i.e., interested only in filling his bag with game; a poor sport; (3) a man that competes for the sake of the 'pot' (loving-cup, prize; now, prize-money). *potwaller,* a would-be voter (before the Reform Act of 1832) who sought to qualify as a householder—one that had his own fireplace—by boiling a pot in the presence of witnesses at an open fire in the borough; also *pot-wabbler, pot-walloner, potwallader, potwalloper.* The last of these kept currency, and has been used for a dishwasher and a ship's cook, and as a term of scorn.

potamophilous. River-loving, as who in the springtide fails to be? *potamologist,* a student of rivers; *potamology; potamological.* Greek *potamos,* river; whence also *hippopotamus,* literally, river-horse. Also *potamic,* relating to rivers. Seeley in THE EXPANSION OF ENGLAND (1883) spoke of *three stages of civilization determined by geographical conditions, the potamic which clings to rivers, the thalassic which grows up around inland seas, and lastly the oceanic.*

potato-pie. The O.E.D. defines this as "a pie made with potatoes, containing meat, onions, etc." The Old English knew better; witness the TRUE GENTLEMAN'S DELIGHT (1676) : *A potato-pye for supper.—Take three pound of boiled and blanched potatoes, and three nutmegs, and half an ounce of cinamon beaten together, and three ounces of sugar, season your potatoes, and put them in your pie, then take the marrow of three bones rouled in yolks of eggs, and sliced lemon and large mace, and half a pound of butter, six dates quartered, put this into your pie, and let it stand an hour in the oven, then make a sharp caudle of butter, sugar, verjuice and white wine, put it in when you take your pie out of the oven.*

pote. See *pooter.* Also used as a noun: a stick for stirring or thrusting, a poker. A *potation* being a drink (Latin *potare, potatum,* to drink), the verb *potate* (used mainly as a participle: drunken) is sometimes shortened to *pote,* to drink. Motteux in his translation (1694) of Rabelais states: *Our means of life are pote, and cibe, and vest. Cibe* is food; Latin *cibare, cibatum,* to feed; *cibus,* food. Hence also *cibation,* feeding. *Cibation,* 'feeding the matter,' is the seventh process (gate) in alchemy, listed among the 'twelve gates' to the Philosopher's Stone in Fuller's WORTHIES OF ENGLAND (1662). *Vest* is clothing; Latin *vestem,* garment, whence also *investiture,* etc.

potews. A dish fit for a king, i.e., a comestible cooked in an earthen pot, which is broken off and thrown away when the food is ready to serve. (A glass in which the monarch's health was drunk was at once broken, so that it might not be defiled by meaner purpose.) Used in the 14th century.

pot-fury. A frenzy, or violence, induced by strong drink. *Cp. pot-valiant.* Bishop Hall referred to the *wondrous rablements of rimesters new* when in his third SATIRE (1597) he said: *With some pot-fury ravisht from their wit They sit and muse on some no-vulgar writ: As frozen dunghils in a winters morne That voyd of vapours seemed all beforne, Soone as the sun sends out his piercing beames Exhale out filthy smoke and stinking steames: So doth the base and the fore-barren brain Soone as the raging wine begins to raigne.*

potting. Drinking of liquor. From the *pot* which is refilled, with some idea of *potation; cp. pote.* Most uses in this sense spring from Shakespeare's in OTHELLO (1604) : *I learn'd it in England; where indeed they are most potent in potting.* Note *impotant,* not drinking.

pottingar. (1) An apothecary. The form is a 15th to 17th century corruption (revived by Scott in THE FAIR MAID OF PERTH, 1828) of *pothecar, pothecary.* Also *potingair, pottinger. Apothecary* is via Late Latin from Greek *apotheke,* storehouse; *pithenai,* to put. The form *pottinger* was also another word, related to *pottage* and *porringer,* meaning (2) a vessel for holding liquid food, a small basin. Used from the 15th century. Also (3) a *pottage* maker, a cook. This was, earlier, *potager.*

pottle. A measure, from the 14th century to the 17th equal to two quarts, half a gallon. A *pottle, potel,* is a little *pot.* Hazlitt in ENGLISH PROVERBS (1869) quotes: *Who'd keep a cow, when he may have a pottle of milk for a penny?* Hence, a container that holds this quantity (especially, 18th century, of liquor). Also, a small basket, especially a conical one for strawberries. Smollet in HUMPHREY CLINKER (1771; Letter of 2 June) writes: *She sent us a pottle of fine strawberries.* Disraeli in ENDYMION (1880) laments: *One never sees a pottle of strawberries now.* A *pottle-pot* was a two-quart tankard; hence, a heavy drinker, a drunkard.

pot-valiant. Courageous because of drink. *Cp. pot-fury.* Also *pot-valorous.* Hence *pot-valor, pot-valiance, pot-valiancy, pot-valiantry.*

poulter. A dealer in *poultry* and eggs. A *poult* was a young one of the domestic fowl and of game birds; it is now used of the young turkey. For *poulter's measure, see himpnes; appere. Poult* is a contraction of *pullet,* via French from Late Latin *pulla,* feminine of *pullus,* meaning a young animal. *Cp. pullaile.*

poultrycide. See *stillicide.* A writer in BLACKWOOD'S EDINBURGH MAGAZINE of 1841 *meditated all the varieties of poultrycide.*

pounce. A fine powder, especially pulverized cuttle-shell, sprinkled on an erasure or unsized paper to prevent the ink from running. Used from the 14th century. Colonel Hawker in his DIARY (1839) mentioned a *cuttlefish, which I never saw before (common as the shell is for pounce).* To *pounce,* in addition to the still current sense, to swoop upon and seize, meant to emboss metal, as a decoration, by striking it underneath so as to raise the surface; also, to scallop the edges of cloth, to cut ornamental holes or figures in cloth or metal; to pink. Chaucer in THE PARSON'S TALE (1386) says: *Ther is also the costlewe furrynge in hire gownes, so muche pownsonynge of chisel to maken holes.* Hence also a *pouncet-box,* a small perforated perfume-box; Shakespeare has, in HENRY IV, PART ONE (1596): *'Twixt his finger and his thumbe he held A pouncet-box: which ever and anon He gave his nose, and took't away againe.* Scott revived this in THE MONASTERY (1820) picturing *a silver pouncet-box containing a sponge dipped in the essence.* A *pounce-box,* however, is a powder-case.

pox. A name for various diseases characterized by *pocks* (which left tiny depressions sometimes called *o's*); in the 16th, 17th, and 18th centuries, syphilis. Often used as an exclamation of annoyance, or an imprecation: *A pox on it!* Also a verb, as in Arbuthnot's JOHN BULL (1712) wherein Jack *persuaded Peg that all mankind, besides himself, were poxed by that scarlet-faced whore.* Shakespeare, as often, puns (LOVE'S LABOUR'S LOST; 1588): *O that your face were not so full of O's!—A pox on that jest!*

Poysam. See *Charbon.*

prabble. A *brabble, q.v.,* a quarrel. The spelling represents the Welsh pronunciation of *brabble,* as by Fluellen in Shakespeare's HENRY V (1599): *I pray you to serve God, and keepe you out of prawles* [brawls] *and prabbles, and quarrels and dissentions. Cp. pribble.*

prado. A fashionable place—park, square, or avenue—for persons to display themselves. Latin *pratum,* meadow. The 17th century uses in English are in allusion to *the Prado,* a public park in Madrid, Spain; later, the word was used in the more general sense. Thus the SPORTING MAGAZINE in 1813 spoke of persons *taking their Sunday promenade upon the fashionable prado of White Conduit House.*

praefiscinal. A charm against witchcraft. Latin *prae,* in front of (*prevent* is, literally, to come before) + *fascinum,* witchcraft, charm. Used in the 17th century.

praemetial. Relating to, or given from, the first fruits, the earliest gathering. Latin *prae,* before + *metiri,* to measure, whence also the *thermometer* and the whole *metric* system. Bishop Hall in his dedication of his VARIOUS TREATISES (1621) to King James I, begged to *offer to your Majestie some praemetiall handfulls of that crop whereof you may challenge the whole harvest.*

prandial. See *jentacular.*

prat. (1) A trick; a prank, a frolic; a fraud; trickery. Used in Old English (10th and 11th centuries) and again from the late 15th century. As an adjective, cunning. (2) Usually in the plural, the buttocks. *Cp. pedlers French.* We speak of the circus clown's taking a *prat-fall.* Shakespeare in THE MERRY WIVES OF WINDSOR (1598) calls Falstaff disguised as a woman *Mother Prat*; Ford, beating Falstaff, cries *I'll prat her!*

pratincolous. Living in a meadow. (Accent on the *ink.*) A *pratincole* is a meadow-dwelling bird; Latin *pratum,* meadow + *incola,* inhabitant.

pravilege. A misused or an evil privilege. The word *privilege* (Latin *privilegium,* personal law) altered by association with *pravus,* perverse, evil; see *pravity.* The word *pravilege* was used from the 14th century (Wyclif) into the 17th; Purchas in his PILGRIMAGE (1613) speaks of *Priviledges and pravileges, whereby every John-a-Stile shall intercept the Church's due.*

pravity. Deformity, physical or moral; perversion, wickedness, evil. Now almost entirely replaced by *depravity,* another term for the same condition. Latin *pravitas,* from *pravus,* crooked, perverse, vicious. Hence also *prave,* wicked; Adlington in his translation (1566) of Apuleius speaks of *the prave opinion of men.* Another form (17th century) was *pravitous,* full of evil. Southey in SIR THOMAS MORE (1829) states: *The punishment . . . was proportioned to the apprehended and intended consequences of the offence, not to the pravity of the offender.* For another illustration, see *inescate.*

prawl. See *prabble.*

prease. A variant form of *press,* pressure. See *fraight.*

preconize. See *precony.*

precony. Public commendation, high praise. Latin *praeconium,* the office of a public crier, a proclaiming, laudation; *praeco, praeconem,* a herald; *prae,* before + *vocare,* to call. The word was used from the 14th to the 18th century, also in the Latin form, as in the translation (1653) of Bacon's NATURALL AND EXPERIMENTALL HISTORY OF WINDS: *It hath been abused both by false opinions and by false praeconiums.* Hence also *preconize,* to proclaim or to commend publicly; to call upon publicly, summon by name. The man who delivers the radio and television commercials is a *preconizer* (though few would recognize him by that name). *Preconize* has been used from the 15th century; preconizing is at its height in our publicity-ridden days.

precurrer. A forerunner; a *precursor* (which supplanted the other term; both are from Latin *pre,* before + *currere, cursum,* to run). Shakespeare, in THE PHOENIX AND THE TURTLE (1601) has *Thou shrieking harbinger, Foul precurrer of the fiend.* Also *precurse,* to forerun, to prognosticate; Shakespeare uses this as a noun, heralding, in HAMLET (1602): *And even the like precurse of fierce events.* Usually the events are dire, as though there were a pre-curse laid upon them. (*Curse,* of course, is of quite different origin, being deviously derived by Weekley, 1924, via French *coroz,* wrath, from Late Latin *corruptiare* "from *cor,* heart + *rumpere, rupt,* to break." The *cor* is more probably a form of *com,* altogether, a prefix with intensifying effect; but the O.E.D., 1933, says that *curse* has no parallel in Teutonic, Romanic, or Celtic, and is of origin unknown—though the thing itself is as old and as common as the common cold.) If your rival proves your precursor, you may curse after.

preen. A pin, a brooch. So used from the 10th century. By the 15th century, *preen* (*preyne, prine, pren, prin*) was used for anything of no consequence or value; Rolland in THE COURT OF VENUS (1560) said: *For sic storyis I cair thame not ane prene.* Hence, *preensworth,* the value of a pin; *preen-head, preen-point* were also used of things (persons) of no account. A *preencod, princod; preen-cushion*: a pin-cushion. Also the verb *to preen,* to sew; to pierce, transfix; to pin, fasten with a pin. Used from the 13th century; *preen* in the current sense of smoothing or adorning (probably a variant of *prune,* which originally also had this meaning) came into use at the end of the 14th century (Chaucer, in THE MERCHANT'S TALE; 1386). In the ANTURS OF ARTHUR (1400) we read: *Hur kerchefes were curiouse, with mony a proud prene.*

preeve. An early form of *proof, prove.*

prelal. Relating to printing; typographical. Latin *prelum,* a press. Fuller in THE APPEAL OF INJURED INNOCENCE (1659) wrote: *Prelial mistakes in defiance of all care will escape in the best corrected book;* later in the work: *There be some press faults in this my book, as for 'prelial' (wherever occurring) read 'prelal.'*

prelapsarian. Relating to the time or conditions before the fall of Man. Latin *pre,* before + *lapsus,* fall. M. D. Conway in DEMONOLOGY (1879) spoke of the *prelapsarian perfection symbolized by nudity.*

prelibatory. Relating to, or providing, a foretaste. Latin *prae,* before + *libare, libatum,* to take a little of, to taste—whence also *libation.* Thus *prelibate,* to taste beforehand; to give a foretaste; *prelibation.* Used from the 16th century; common in figurative use in the 17th, especially in religious writings, as when T. Adams in his EXPOSITION (1633) of the BIBLE: SECOND EPISTLE GENERAL OF PETER stated that *the wicked have a prelibation of that darkness they shall go unto hereafter.* Wordsworth makes poetic use of *prelibation* in THE PRELUDE (1805).

preludious. Introductory; relating to a *prelude.* Also *preludial, prelusive, prelusory;* Latin *prae,* before + *ludere, lusum,* to play (also, to play a game, to mock, whence *delusion, illusory*). Cleveland in THE SENSES' FESTIVAL (1651) observed: *Yet that's but a preludious bliss; Two souls pickearing in a kiss.*

premial. Relating to, or like, a reward. Also *premiant,* rewarding; to *premiate,* to reward. A *premie, premye,* a reward, a gift; later and still, a *premium.* And *premiable,* worthy of reward or prize; *premiability.* MANKIND (1450) said: *Your merytes were not premyabyll to the blys above.* Bale in his KING JOHAN (1550) remarked of the King that *the cytie of London, through his mere graunt and premye, Was first privyleged to have both mayer* *and shryve, Where before hys tyme it had but baylyves onlye.*

premorse. Bitten or broken off; abruptly truncate. Used from the 18th century.

prenarial. In front of the nostrils. Macaulay's schoolboy knows of the donkey whom a prenarial carrot led to work; hence, of any belly-lure.

prenostic. A 14th century form of *prognostic.* Used by Gower; Chaucer in FORTUNE (1398) : *Presnostik is thow wolt hir towr asayle.* Also *prenosticate; prenostication, prenosticature,* prognostication.

prentice. A short form of *apprentice,* used from the 14th century to the 18th. Later uses generally include an apostrophe, as Ruskin's in POLITICAL ECONOMY (1857): *Stupid tailor's 'prentices who are always stitching the sleeves in the wrong way upwards.* It was often used as an adjective—*prentice ear; prentice girl, prentice-work*—as when Burns in GREEN GROW THE RASHES (1784) says of Nature: *Her prentice han' she tried on man, An' then she made the lasses, O.*

preostend. To show or make manifest beforehand. Used in the 15th century, in THE MIROUR OF SALVACIOUN: *This delyvraunce of man also Godde preostendid When He patriarche Abraham from hurr of Chaldee delyvrid.*

prepense. To plan, meditate, or contrive in advance. Originally *purpense.* Also *prepend,* to weigh in advance, to premeditate. Both are from Latin *pre,* before + *pendere,* to weigh; *pensum,* thought; whence also *pensive.* The past participle *prepensed, prepenst* was used as an adjective, especially in the legal phrase *malice prepensed* (16th century) , now shortened to *malice prepense.* In Holinshed's CHRONICLES (1577) we read that Banquo *was slaine not by chancemedlie, as by the handling of the matter Makbeth woould have had it appeare, but even upon a prepensed devise.* Blackstone (1769) noted that "the benefit of clergy" was not extended to those that committed murder through *malice prepense.* Also *prepensive; prepensity.* Lord Berners' translation (1525) of Froissart spoke of *a thing prepensed by false traitoures to put the realme to trouble.*

prepollent. Predominating, prevailing. Also *to prepoll,* to excel. Latin *prae,* before + *pollere,* to be strong. Also *praepollence, praepollency; praepollent.* Used mainly in the 17th century, when the prepollency of good over evil was more often mooted.

prescind. To cut off prematurely or abruptly; to cut away suddenly; to cut off, detach; to abstract; to withdraw from, leave out of consideration. Latin *prae,* before + *scindere, scissum* (whence *scissors*) , to cut. Hence *prescission* (not to be confused with *precision*—the former ends with a *sh'n* sound; the latter, with *zh'n*) , the act of cutting off or abstracting. Berkeley in THE PRINCIPLES OF HUMAN KNOWLEDGE (1710) spoke of *an abstract idea of happiness, prescinded from all particular pleasure.*

president. A variant form of *precedent.* Used in the sense of pattern, model, by Spenser in the dedication of THE SHEPHERD'S CALENDAR (1579) : *Goe little book: they selfe present, As child whose parent is unkent, To him that is the president Of noblesse and of chevalree.*

prest. This was a common form, from the 13th century to the 17th. (1) As an adjective it meant ready, at hand, handy, alert. Drant, in his translation (1566) of

Horace, has: *Then cums this fox . . . with money preste in hand.* The word is via French from Latin *prae,* before, in front + *situ,* placed, *situated.* Dryden in his translation (1697) of Virgil's GEORGICS has: *The victim ox, that was for altars prest, Trim'd with white ribbons and with garlands drest.* (2) As a noun, from the 15th century, it meant a loan; especially one made to the king in an emergency; a forced loan or gift; hence, a tax; a deduction made from a payment; hence also, an advance payment; earnest-money on enlistment of a soldier or sailor. From the 16th century (3) *prest* was used as a verb, from the senses of the noun: to hire by an advance payment; to enlist—gradually this meaning merged with (and the word, seeming a past tense, was lost in) *press,* to draw into the king's service. Holland in his translation (1600) of Livy shows the transition: *So many as they thought able men of bodie to bear arms . . . to prest them for soldiours . . . otherwhiles levying and presting them to the seas to be gallieslaves.*

prestancy. Priority; pre-eminence. Latin, from *praestare,* to excel; *prae,* before + *stare,* to stand. Hence *prestantious,* outstanding, excellent. Thus Anthony Stafford's HEAVENLY DOGGE (1615) declares: *If then the prestancy of instructing be such, surely Diogenes . . . may in name but not in deed be a slave.*

prester. A burning or scorching whirlwind; also, a snake the bite of which was fabled to cause death by swelling. *Prester* was a Greek word, with the same meanings, from the root *pra-,* to burn, to blow. Topsell in his book on SERPENTS (1608) speaks of *the dipsas killing by thirst, and the prester by heat, as their very names do signify.* See *dipsas.* Emerson in his essay on SWEDENBORG (1847) says that philosophers are presters. The snake *prester* is not to be confused with the *prester* (from Greek *presbyter,* priest) in *Prester John,* a fabled Christian king supposed to have ruled in the Far East, first mentioned in the twelfth century, and later used as a symbol of high authority, as when Edward Guilpin in SKIALETHEIA (1598) said that *fooles do sit More honored than the Prester John of wit.*

preter-. (Latin *praeter,* beyond.) A number of English words have been formed with this prefix. We may mention *pretererogation,* action or performance beyond what is expected or required. *preterintentional,* beyond what was intended. *preterlethal,* occurring after death. *preternuptial,* outside the marriage relation. *preterscriptural,* beyond what is written. More frequent were: *pretergress,* to exceed the limits; to surpass; also *pretergression. preterlabent,* flowing past; H. A. Evans in his description of OXFORD AND THE COTSWOLDS (1905): *There is the old garden behind the house, with the stone steps descending thereunto, and the praeterlabent Coln. preterlapsed*; gone by, past. *preterlegal,* outside or not according to law.

preu. Brave, gallant; full of prowess. Also *prew, pru, preus.* Common in the 14th, 15th and early 16th centuries; reintroduced in the 18th century in the French form *preux,* especially in the phrase *preux chevalier.* Chaucer in THE MONK'S TALE (1386) says: *This king of kinges preu was and elate.*

prevent. The forgotten first meaning of *prevent* almost counters its present application. From Latin *pre,* before + *venire, ventum,* to come, *prevent* meant to come before, with the implication of helping or preparing the way. The BOOK

OF COMMON PRAYER (1549) calls out: *Prevent us, O Lord, in all our doings!* Shakespeare in JULIUS CAESAR (1601) uses the word in the sense of anticipate: *I do find it cowardly and vile, for fear of what might fall, so to prevent the time of life.* Milton, in the ODE ON THE MORNING OF CHRIST'S NATIVITY (1629) uses it in its literal sense, when, speaking of the "starled wizards" coming to the new-born Jesus, he cries: *O run, prevent them with thy humble ode And lay it lowly at His blessed feet.* In earthly affairs, however, the usual consequence of one person's *preventing* (coming before) another is that the first person takes what's good and keeps the second from getting it—which cold truth brought *prevent* to its present meaning.

pribble. A weak form of *prabble, q.v.* Used in *pribble and prabble*; *pribble-prabble,* to mean idle talk, chatter of discussion. Shakespeare in THE MERRY WIVES OF WINDSOR (1598) has the Welsh parson Sir Hugh Evans declare: *It were a goot motion, if we leave our pribbles and prabbles, and desire a marriage betweene Master Abraham and Mistris Anne Page.*

pricasour. A hunter; a speedy horseman. From the prick of the spurs. Chaucer in the Prologue to THE CANTERBURY TALES (1386) tells us: *A monk ther was . . . he was a prikasour aright Grehoundes he hadde as swift as fowel in flight.*

prick. Among the forgotten meanings of this many-pointed word may be found: A. Uses as a noun. (1) A minute part; a point of space, or a particle, in regard to its minuteness. Shakespeare in TROILUS AND CRESSIDA (1606) declares: *In such indexes, although small prickes To their subsequent volumes, there is seene The baby figure of the giant masse Of things to come at large. To the prick,* to the tiniest jot, with minute exactness. (2) A point in a progression; especially, *the prick,* the highest point. (3) A goad for oxen. Hence, *to work (spurn, kick) against the pricks.* Figuratively, a spur, an incentive; something that stimulates. THE MIROUR OF SALVACIOUN (1450) said: *His prikke specially is a womman gloosyng.* [*Gloosyng, glozing,* specious adornment.] (4) One of the marks on a dial or scale. Shakespeare makes bawdy pun upon this sense, in ROMEO AND JULIET: *The bawdy hand of the dyall is now upon the pricke of noone.* (5) A vulgar term of endearment. H. M., translating (1671) THE COLLOQUIES of Erasmus, observed: *One word alone hath troubled some, because the immodest maid, soothing the young man, calls him her prick . . . He who cannot away with this, instead of 'my prick,' let him say 'my sweetheart.'* (6) In the phrase *prick and praise* (*prize, prise, price*), praise for excellence. Medwall's NATURE (1500): *Nowforsoth I gyve the pryk and pryse, Thou art worth the weyght of gold.* Thornley's translation (1657) of Longus' DAPHNIS AND CHLOE: *The women gave him prick and praise for beauty.* B. Uses as a verb. (7) To detect a witch by pricking her until a spot was discovered that did not bleed. Pitcairn records (1661) in CRIMINAL TRIALS: *The magistrate and minister caused Johne Kinkaid, the common pricker, to prik her, and found two marks upon her, which he called the Devil his marks.* (8) To shoot at a *prick* (upright pole) or target; hence, to aim at (also figuratively). Harpsfield, in THE DIVORCE OF HENRY VIII (1555): *His authors roved far from the mark they should prick at.* (9) Of a hare: to make a track in running; hence, to track by the footprints. (10) To spur a horse on; hence, to ride fast, as in the first line of

Spenser's THE FAËRIE QUEENE (1590): *A gentle knight was pricking on the plaine.* Incidentally, this is the first instance in English narrative of a character in action at the start of a story, by now a commonplace of fictional technique. (11) *To prick fast upon,* to approach (a time or period) closely; *to prick new,* to approach closely in achievement or quality. Golding, in the Preface to Baret's ALVEARIE (1580) said that English *would pricke neere the learned tungs in strength.* (12) To jot down, to record in writing. (13) To mark on a list; hence, to choose, appoint. (14) To attire (at first, with garments fastened by bodkins and pins); hence, to attire elaborately. THE WORLDE AND THE CHYLDE (1500): *I am nat worthily wrapped nor went, But poorly pricked in poverty.*

prickmedaintie. One that is finical about dress; a dandy (of either sex). Also an adjective, affectedly nice in personal adornment. Also *pryckmedenty, prickmydante,* and the like. One meaning of *prick* was to pin somebody up; hence, to dress elaborately. Skelton in THE TUNNYNG OF ELYNOUR RUMMYNG (1529) said: *There was a pryckmedenty Sat lyke a seynty, And began to paynty* [pant] *As though she would faynty.*

prig. A tinker, a traveling mender of pots and pans; hence, a thief. A *prigman* (*prygman, pridgeman*) is one of the varieties of vagabond listed in the Elizabethan pamphlets; *cp. pedlers French.* Also a verb, *to prig,* to steal, to cheat. Shakespeare in THE WINTER'S TALE (1611) tells us a man *married a tinkers wife . . . and (having flowne over many knavish professions) he settled onely in rogue: some call him Autolycus.* Clowne: *Out upon him: prig, for my life, prig: he haunts wakes, faires, and beare-baitings.*

prill. To flow, spirt. A variant of *pirl, purl.* John Stow in A SURVEY OF LONDON (1598) describes an image *of Diana, and water convayd from the Thames prilling from her naked breast.*

primater. An error (of Holofernes, or the printer?) for *pia mater,* in early editions of Shakespeare's LOVE'S LABOUR'S LOST (1594): *This is a gift that I have, simple, simple; a foolish extravagant spirit, full of forms, figures, shapes, objects, ideas, apprehensions, motions, revolutions. These are begot in the ventricle of memory, nourished in the womb of primater, and delivered upon the mellowing of occasion.*

primerole. See *prymerole.*

princod. See *preen.*

princox. A pert, saucy boy; a youth affecting the manners of a man; a coxcomb. Usually spoken with a measure of contempt, as when old Capulet (in Shakespeare's ROMEO AND JULIET, 1592) dismisses the fiery Tybalt: *You are a princox; go!* Also *princock, primecock, princockes.* The etymology of the word is uncertain; it may be an alteration of *praecox,* early ripe, whence *precocious;* it may be *prime,* first + Latin *coquere, coxi, coctum,* to cook, to ripen; and certain sexual suggestions may have slipped in. But we may agree with Scott's exclamation, in KENILWORTH (1821): *God save us from all such misproud princoxes!* Coryat among his CRUDITIES (1611) speaks of *proud princocke scholars that are puffed up with the opinion of their learning.* Such have but sipped the Pierian spring.

priscan. Ancient, primitive. Latin *priscus,* old. Used in the 19th century, as in Rolleston's BRITISH BARROWS (1877): *A pack of wild dogs cooperating with priscan* *men in driving a herd of cattle . . . along a track in which a pitfall had been dug.*

Priscian. This is the name of a famous Roman grammarian, of about 520 A.D. Used in English in the phrase *to break (knock) Priscian's head,* to make an error in grammar. (The early references were, of course, to Latin grammar. English didn't count.) Shakespeare in LOVE'S LABOUR'S LOST (1594) speaks of *Priscian a little scratched,* meaning that a slight error (in Sir Nathaniel's Latin) has been made. Nowadays Priscian is quite o'er-thumped. English doesn't count.

prithee. An early variant of *I pray thee.* Also *prithy, prethy, preethee.* Used from the 16th century. Shakespeare in THE TEMPEST (1610) has: *Pre-thee no more: thou dost talke nothing to me.* Suckling in his play AGLAURA (1637) has a lively lyric, one stanza of which asks a shrewd question: *Why so dull and mute, young sinner? Prithee, why so mute? Will, when speaking well can't win her, Saying nothing do't? Prithee, why so mute?*

privado. An intimate; a ruler's favorite (male). Directly from the Spanish; used in English from about 1550. Steele's THE LYING LOVER (1704) shows the attitude: *What can I deny thee, my privado?*

probrosity. Scandal, infamy; railing. Hence *probrous,* infamous, defamatory. These are in 18th century dictionaries (Bailey, 1751); neither has won admittance to the O.E.D., which gives the noun *probre,* an insult, used in the 15th century. All are from Latin *probrum,* reproach, disgrace, from which we have kept *opprobrium.*

procacity. Pertness, sauciness; petulance. From Latin *procax, procacem,* petulant, insolent; *procare,* to demand. Hence also *procacious,* insolent; pert, forward. Burton in THE ANATOMY OF MELANCHOLY (1621) declares: *In vain are all your flatteries . . . Delights, deceits, procacities, Sighs, kisses, and conspiracies.*

procellosity. Tempestuousness. In Bailey, 1751; not in O.E.D., which does give the 15th century (Lydgate) *procelle,* a storm, and the 17th century *procellous,* stormy. All are from Latin *procella,* a storm; *pro,* before + the root *cel,* to drive, to strike —from which come also *celerity* and *gladiator.*

procerity. Height, tallness. Latin *procerus,* tall, lofty. Whence also (16th and 17th centuries) *procere, procerous,* tall, lofty—and *proceres,* nobles, head men, as in Bulwer-Lytton's HAROLD (1848): *In that chamber met the thegns* [thanes] *and proceres of his realm.* Johnson in THE LIFE OF THE KING OF PRUSSIA (1756) said: *When he met a tall woman, he immediately commanded one of his titanian retinue to marry her, that they might propagate procerity.*

procinct. Ready, prepared. Latin *procingere, procinctum,* to gird up. Also in the phrase *in procinct; procinctive,* girding itself for action; BLACKWOOD'S EDINBURGH MAGAZINE (1841) speaks of *the procinctive future. Procinct* is also a variant form of *precinct.* In the sense of ready, imminent, Milton says, in PARADISE LOST (1667): *Warr he perceav'd, warr in procinct.*

procrastinate. See *crastin.*

proculcate. To trample down; to despise, spurn. From the Latin *pro,* forward + *calcare,* to tread; *calcem,* heel. Thus to *inculcate* is to stamp into. Also *proculcation,* the act of trampling.

prodige. To squander. Also *prodege.* Latin *pro,* forth + *agere,* to drive. Hence also *prodigence,* a 17th century form for *prodigality.* The form *prodige* was also a variant, in the 15th to 17th century, for *prodigy,* which first meant something extraordinary that is an omen, and is from Latin *pro,* before + primitive Latin *agiom,* a thing said (*adiagium,* adage). Thus *prodigious* first meant ominous, portentous, as in Shakespeare's A MIDSUMMER NIGHT'S DREAM (1590): *Never mole, harelip, nor scar, Nor mark prodigious . . . Shall upon their children be.*

prodition. Betrayal, treachery. Latin *prodere, proditum,* to betray; *pro,* forth + *dare,* to give. Hence also *proditious, proditory, proditorious,* treacherous, traitorous. *Prodition* has been in use since the 15th century. Shakespeare in HENRY VI, PART ONE (1591) says: *Thou most usurping proditor, and not Protector of the king or realm.*

proface. 'May it do you good!'—a greeting, or a welcome before food. Sometimes used instead of a toast: Your health! From Old French *prou fasse!* short for *Bon prou vous fasse!* Latin *proficiat; pro,* in behalf of + *faciat,* may it do; *facere, factum.* Hence also *proficiat* (17th century), used as a friendly greeting; by deterioration, a payment to ensure a friendly reception. Urquhart in his translation (1653) of Rabelais declares: *These buzzards will have me to pay them here my welcom hither, and my proficiat.* Often used in connection with *preface,* as in the Water Poet's PRAISE OF HEMPSEED (WORKS; 1630) : *Preface; and proface, my masters, if your stomackes serve.* Shakespeare in HENRY IV, PART TWO (1597) says: *Master Page, good Master Page, sit. Proface! What you want* [lack] *in meat we'll have in drink.*

progress. A journeying; a journey; especially, a state journey by a royal or noble person. Elaborate celebration was provided by all the cities, lavish entertainment by all the feudal lords, en route. There are detailed and colorful records of many of the progresses of King Henry VIII and of his redheaded daughter. Indeed, Robert Laneham's one hold on history is *A letter whearin part of the entertainment untoo the Queenz majesty at Killingwoorth Castl in Warwick Sheer in this soomerz progress 1575 is signified, from a freend officer attendant in the coourt untoo hiz freend a citizen and merchaunt of London.*

prolabium. The outer part of the lip. The plural is *prolabia,* where the lipstick moves. Used in the 17th and 18th centuries; in anatomy still.

promethean. See *locofoco.*

prompture. Instigation, incitement. The word *prompt* was first used in English (14th century) as a verb, to incite. The forms are from Latin *promere,* to put or urge forth; *pro,* forth + *emere, emptum,* to buy, whence also *pre-empt* and *Caveat emptor.* Shakespeare in MEASURE FOR MEASURE (1603) says: *He hath falne by prompture of the blood.*

promulge. An early form of *promulgate* (15th century, but lingering into the 19th). The forms are from a Late Latin *promulgare,* to make public, shifted from *pro,* forth + *vulgare, vulgatum; vulgus,* the people; see *provulgate.*

pronephew. A great-grandson. Also *pronepot.* From Latin *pro,* before + *nepotem,* grandson, whence also *nepotism.* A *pronept, pronepte,* is a grand-niece, a *proniece.* The STATE PAPERS of England, after the death (1542) of Henry VIII, spoke of *the performance of the mariage betwene my Lord Princes Grace and the daughter of Scotland, the Kinges Majesties pronepce.* The words were rarely used after the 16th century.

propine. To offer or give to drink, as a cup of wine or (often in religious reference) 'a cup of affliction.' Hence, to offer, to present, to endow. From the Greek *pro,* toward + *pinein,* to drink. Used from the 14th into the 18th century, mainly in Scotland; Sir Walter Scott used it in IVANHOE (1819): *In expectation of the ample donation . . . which Cedric had propined.* Hence also *propination,* the offering of a drink, the drinking of one's health. In reference to 19th century Austrian Poland, *propination* means the monopoly of brewing and distilling and selling the products of such activity. George Gillespie, in A DISPUTE AGAINST THE ENGLISH-POPISH CEREMONIES (1637) said: *Whiles she propineth to the world the cup of her fornications.*

propoma. A drink made of wine and honey, usually taken before meals. Directly from the Greek *pro,* before + *poma,* drink. In English, also *propomate.* A 17th century term. See *mead.*

proreption. Slow advance; creeping forward. Latin *proripio, proreptum,* to drag forth, to creep forward; *pro,* forward + *rapere, repi, raptum* (whence also *rapt, rape*), to snatch, drag, hurry. On its course from Latin into English, the word slowed down.

prosilient. Prominent, outstanding. Latin *prosilientem,* leaping forth; *prosilire*; *pro,* forward + *salire, saltum,* whence also *salient, somersault* but not *table salt.* Also *prosiliate,* to stand out, be prominent; *prosiliency,* "leaping out" at one, prominence; *prosilition,* the act of leaping out. Gertrude Atherton in THE CONQUEROR (1902) declared that *Hamilton . . . not excepting Washington . . . was to Europeans the most prosilient of Americans.*

protervity. Waywardness, stubbornness; pertness; petulance. Latin *protervus,* pressing forward; impudent. Hence also English *proterve* (14th to 16th century), *protervous* (16th and 17th centuries), forword, stubborn, impudent. The noun, from the 15th century, lingered longer; Stevenson in 1882 said that in Hugo's *poems and plays there are the same unaccountable protervities.*

protocol. An original draft or note of a transaction or agreement; especially, of an agreement between powers; an original authority. A preamble. From Greek *proto,* first + *kolla,* glue; in the Middle Ages, Latin *protocollum,* Greek *protokollon,* a fly-leaf glued to a case, with a summary or account of the manuscript within. Hence *protocolic,* relating to *protocols*; to *protocolize,* to draw up *protocols,* to diplomatize; also to *protocol.*

protoplast. The first thing formed; the first men created, or first in a line; the original model. Greek *proto,* first + *plastos,* formed; *plassein,* to mould, fashion. From Greek *plastes,* the fashioner, *protoplast* was also used to mean the first fashioner, the creator; in this sense, also *protoplasmator*; Bieston in THE BAYTE AND SNARE OF FORTUNE (1550) wrote: *Thou knowest howe God the hygh prothoplasmator of erth formed man after hys owne ymage.* H. Busk in THE VESTRIAD (1819) exclaimed: *No more the protoplast of active beauty*; while MACMILLAN'S MAGAZINE for May, 1863, speculated *if Hebrew was the protoplast of speech.*

protreptic. Didactic; instructive. Also, a book or speech intended to teach. Greek *pro,* for + *trepein,* to turn, to direct the course of. Used from the 17th century. *Early proverbs,* said R. G. Moulton (PROVERBS; 1895) *are philosophical, not protreptical.*

provant. See *count palatine.*

provulgate. To make public; disseminate, propagate. Latin *provulgare, provulgatum*; *pro,* before + *vulgus,* the people, whence also *vulgar.* Hence *provulgation.* Also *provulge.* These forms shifted to *promulge* (*q.v.*) and *promulgate,* the latter of which survives. The earlier forms were used in the 16th century.

prow. Advantage, profit; good. Used from the 13th century. As an adjective, good, worthy, gallant. Also *preu* (*q.v.*), *proud, prod, pru.* Ultimately from Latin *prodise*; *prodesse,* to be useful, to do good. Chaucer in THE NUN'S PRIEST'S TALE (1386) declares: *I shal my self to herbes techen yow That shul been for your hele and for youre prow.* Also, in the 14th century, *to prow,* to be of advantage, beneficial; whence *prower,* one that helps, *purveyor,* provider of necessities. Pecock in THE REPRESSOR OF OVER MUCH BLAMING OF THE CLERGY (1449) says: *Crist which was . . . oure beest prower, ordeyned al that was best for us to have.*

proxenete. An agent; a go-between, especially a marriage broker. Greek *proxenein,* to be one's agent, *pro,* in behalf of + *xenos,* guest. For an illustration of its use, see *paranymph.*

pruinous. Frosty; relating to frost. Used in the 16th and 17th centuries; Latin *pruina,* hoar-frost. Hence also *pruinescence.* In the 19th century, *pruinate, pruinose* came into use in natural history, applied to fruit, etc., covered with a fine white powder like frost.

prunella. A strong material (originally silk, later worsted) used for students', clergymen's, and barristers' gowns and later for the tops of women's shoes. Pope used the word in his ESSAY ON MAN (1734): *Worth makes the man and want of it, the fellow; The rest is all but leather or prunella.* The word is also used as the name of a flower (the self-heal) and—by alteration from *brunella,* 'the browns'—was applied to a camp-fever prevalent among the German imperial troops in 1547 and 1566. The word was also used in the forms *prunelle, prunello. Prunello* is the Italian for *little prune*; Sir J. E. Smith in his MEMOIRS (1786) said that he *Dined at Brignolle, famous for the* Prunes de Brignolle, *which we have corrupted into Prunellas.* They were a noted product of Provence.

prymerole. A variant of *primerole,* an early spring flower; thence applied to a young and pretty woman. The word is a diminutive of *prime,* first (here referring to the season). It was frequent in the 14th, 15th and early 16th centuries, used by Gower, Chaucer, Lydgate; for an illustration of its use, see *pigsney.* It is probably a variation of *primrose.* Gower says in CONFESSIO AMANTIS (1390): *The frosti colde Janever . . . of his dole He gifth the ferste primerole.*

psaphonic. Planning (or securing) one's own elevation to fame or glory; like *Psapho.* Psapho was a Libyan who had a host of birds caught and taught to say "Psapho is a god." The birds were then released, whereafter the Africans worshiped Psapho. The story was first told by the Roman Aelianus Claudus, who died A.D. 140. From the Latin phrase

Psaphonis aves, the birds of Psapho, certain reference works [Brewer quotes the poet Moore; Benet follows Brewer] erroneously give the name as Psaphon. The phrase *Psapho's birds* has been applied to "puffers," flatterers, writers of blurbs, manipulators of 'public relations.'

psephomancy. See *aeromancy.*

pseudo. From Greek *pseudos,* falsity, *pseud-* and *pseudo-* have been used as prefixes meaning false, pretended, spurious. Many were coined for an occasion, and need no definition: *pseudo-Moses; pseudostatesman; pseudo-enthusiast; pseudopatroit; pseudobard* (Byron, 1809); *pseudoscience.* Also *pseudochronism,* an error in dating. *pseudodox,* holding a false opinion; *pseudodoxy. pseudograph,* a work attributed to one not its author, literary forgery; *pseudographer,* forger. *pseudologer,* habitual liar; *pseudology,* the art of lying. *pseudosoph* (accent on the first syllable), *pseudosopher* (accent on the second), one that pretends to wisdom, or falsely supposes himself wise; also *pseudosophical. pseudosophy.* Swinburne in THE QUARTERLY REVIEW of July 1902 exclaimed upon *so consummate and pseudosophical a quack.*

pseudomancy. Also *pseudomantis, pseudomantist,* a prophet (literally, a false prophet; but where is a true one, save in the lap of chance!) See *aeromancy.*

psychocorruptor. A device for speeding up the seduction of a soul. First employed (by this name) in Molnar's THE RED MILL (1923). It takes twenty years, we are told, to make devil's meat of the average New Yorker; the psychocorruptor is guaranteed to do it in an hour. Many feel that part of its secret has been incorporated in the "Crime Comics" books and other current forms of juvenile entertainment.

psychomachy. Also (17th century) *pseuchomachie.* A battle within the soul. Levin in THE OVERREACHER (1952), discussing Marlowe's DR. FAUSTUS, stated that *"Hell strives with grace" in a psychomachia.* A poem entitled *Psychomachia* was written by Prudentius about 400 A.D. It was the first European allegorical poem, and one of the most widely read works of the Middle Ages. From its picture of the battle of the soul grew the practice of giving the Seven Deadly Sins seven Vices as servants; in the drama, these Vices became part villain, part buffoon. Hence, by the 16th century, *the vice* meant the clown, the chief funmaker. This duality persisted in the character of Shylock, in Shakespeare's THE MERCHANT OF VENICE (1597), who was presented as a comic villain until the sympathetic portrait in Charles Macklin's performance at Drury Lane in 1741.

psychomancy. See *aeromancy.*

psychrolute. A 'polar bear,' one that bathes (swims) out of doors daily throughout the winter. Greek *psychros,* cold + *loutes,* bather; *louein,* to bathe. Contrariwise, *psychrophobia,* dread of cold; especially, of cold water.

psychurgy. Mental activity. Greek *psyche,* spirit, mind + *ergia,* working, whence also *energy.* A rarity still rarer in the Spring.

psycter. A jar for cooling wine. Greek *psykter; psychein,* to breathe, blow, cool; *psyche,* breath, spirit, soul.

psyctic. A refrigerant, especially, a medicine that cools. Greek *psyktikos,* cooling. Used from the 17th century.

psydracium. A lie-blister, a white blister on the tip of the tongue, said by old wives and the ancients to be caused by lying. Latin *psydracem* from Greek *psydros,* lying, false. Hence, *psydracious,* blistered from falsehood; deceitful.

psyllic. Relating to snake-charming, as the movements of the Indian that pipes a cobra. From Greek *Psylloi,* a race of Africa noted for their skill as snake-charmers. Gosse in THE ROMANCE OF NATURAL HISTORY (1860) observed that *fatal terminations of these exhibitions of the psyllic art now and then occur.*

pucelle. A maid. *La Pucelle,* the Maid of Orléans, Joan of Arc. Directly from the French, probably from Late Latin *puellicella,* diminutive of *puella,* girl. Also *pucell, pusel, pussle* and later (when the sense degenerated, and the word was used for a courtesan, a drab, a slut) *pusil, puzzel, puzzle*: (1607) *some filthy queans, especially our puzzles of Paris.* Sir Thomas More, in A DIALOGUE OF COMFORT AGAINST TRIBULATION (1534) says: *This girl is a metely good pussel in a house, never idle, but ever occupied and busy.* Shakespeare in HENRY VI PART ONE (1591) speaks of Joan of Arc as *pucelle or puzzel.*

pudding. This name of several delights has been used in various compounds. Note *pudding-filler,* a glutton, one that lives to eat. *pudding-head,* a stupid person, as Mark Twain's after all not so stupid *Pudd'nhead Wilson* (THE TRAGEDY OF—; 1894). *pudding-heart,* a coward. *pudding-time,* a lucky moment, the nick of time; *to come in pudding-time,* to arrive in time for dinner (which used to begin with pudding).

pudency. Modesty; susceptibility to shame. Latin *pudentem,* present participle of *pudere,* to make or be ashamed. *Cp. pudibund.* In Shakespeare's CYMBELINE (1611) Posthumus exclaims of his wife: *Me of my lawful pleasure she restrained And prayed me oft forbearance; did it with A pudency so rosy, the sweet view on't Might well have warmed old Saturn, that I thought her As chaste as unsunn'd snow.*

pudibund. Modest. This word pokes fun at the shamefast, as when Andrew Lang observed in BLACKWOOD'S EDINBURGH MAGAZINE of March 1900 that *English literature became the most pudibund . . . the world has ever known.* Earlier, it referred to things that were supposed to cause shame; thus Andrew Boorde in his COMPENDIOUS REGYMENT OF HELTH (1542) says: *If any man . . . doth burn in the pudibunde places . . .* There is also a noun form; the SATURDAY REVIEW of February 4, 1893, protested: *We cannot approve the editor's pudibundity in omitting a few 'indecent words.'* Also found are *pudic, pudique,* having a keen sense of shame; *pudicity,* modesty (with less scorn than *pudibundity*) ; *pudify,* to make ashamed, to cause to blush; and *pudor,* a proper modesty. They are all from Latin *pudere,* to make or to be ashamed; *cp. pudency.* Painter in THE PALACE OF PLEASURE (1566) wrote: *It is I that dooe purpose to marie this maide, who I doubt not is right honest and chaste, and also a pudique and pure virgin.*

pudor. See *pudibund.*

pug. As a noun: (1) The husks separated from seed in cleaning, the chaff of wheat or oats; the leavings of the cider-press, apple-pulp. Hence, *pug-drink,* thin cider, water cider. From the 15th century. (2) As a diminutive, of persons. A term of endearment, *my sweet pug.* Also *puglet, puggy.* Also: a courtesan, harlot, punk. *If,* suggested Sir Robert Cecil in a letter of 24 September, 1600, *you did remember the Lord Admyrall and the Lord Treasurer with a couple of pugges or some uscough* *baugh* [whisky] *or some such toyes, it would show that you do not neglect them, whoe, I protest, are to you wonderfull kynde.* Likewise, from the 16th century, a ship's boy; a bargeman, especially *western pug,* one who navigated a barge down the Thames to London. Lyly in ENDYMION (1591) speaks of *a western barge, when with a good winde and lustie pugges one may goe ten miles in two daies.* Just barging along! (3) Applied to anything small or stumpy: a dwarf; a lamb, hare, squirrel; a sprite or imp, such as Puck; hence, the *pug-dog; pug-nosed.* (4) Well pounded mud or clay, used for walls or in bricks (19th century). And (5), short for *pugilist;* see *pugillary.* Finally (borrowed in the 19th century from Hindi *pag,* footprint) there is (6) *pug,* print of a beast's foot. THE DAILY TELEGRAPH of 12 December, 1865, averred that *there are not many sensations worth getting up for so early . . . but to see the first pug of the tiger's track on the wet path is one of them.*

pugillary. A writing-tablet. The PHILOSOPHICAL TRANSACTIONS of 1758 listed; *Many pugillaries, styles, and stands with ink in them.* Also *pugil,* originally, a handful; since the 17th century, what can be picked up with the thumb and two fingers, a little handful. Latin *pugillus,* a handful. The root is *pug,* as in Latin *pugnus,* fist, whence *pugnacious;* also *pugilist, pugilism; pugilation* (17th and 18th centuries), boxing. Latin *pugnare, pugnatus,* to fight (originally, to box); hence also *pugnastics,* boxing exercises—a 19th century term modeled on *gymnastics; pugnatory* (17th century), *pugnatic* (19th century), related to fighting. Also *pugnant,* hostile, opposed; hence, hateful; replaced by *repugnant.* There is a term in botany, *pugioniform,* dagger-shaped; Latin *pugi-*[illegible] dagger, hand-knife. Also see *pug.*

pulicosity. The condition of being infested with fleas. Latin *pulicem,* flea; the ending *-osus* (English *-ous*) means full of; *cp. avidulous.* Hence also *pulicouse, pulicose,* full of fleas. Related to, or resembling, fleas: *pulicine, pulicarious, pulicary;* Ruskin in FORS CLAVIGERA (1872) inquires: *Has he multiplied himself into a host of pulicarious dragons?* From instances of pulicosity, spare us!

pullaile. Poultry. French *poule,* chicken; Latin *pullus,* the young of an animal, later, especially of the fowl; English *pullet; cp. poulter.* Also (15th century) *pullayle, pullayly,* (16th and 17th centuries) *pullery.* Hence *pullation,* a hatching of chickens. In the 17th century, the phrase *a pullarian auspicator* described an ancient practitioner of divination by a sacred chick. THE ROMANCE OF THE ROSE, Lydgate, Hoccleve, Caxton, all in the 15th century, use *pullaile.*

pullulate. To bud, sprout; spring up abundantly, teem. Latin *pullulare, pullulatum,* to sprout, grow, increase; *pullus,* young of an animal; see *pullaile.* THE TIMES of 6 October, 1890, spoke of *those lower forms of Christianity which pullulate so freely in the religious soil of the United States.* Hence *pullulant,* budding; *pullulation.* E. Johnson in THE RISE OF CHRISTENDOM (1890) said: *Virtues then fructify; in their pullulation, purity of heart is acquired.*

pulvil. A cosmetic or perfumed powder for the wig or person. Also *pulvilio, pulvillio;* Italian *polviglio,* fine powder, diminutive of *polve;* Latin *pulverem,* powder, whence *pulverize. To pulver* was a 17th century form of *pulverize; pulvering day* was Ash Wednesday; also, *to pulverate.* A number of forms from Latin *pulver* have been used; some of them survive in science, e.g., *pulveratricious,* rolling in the dust (of birds); *pulveratrix* (plural *pulveratrices,* also *pulveratores*) birds that habitually roll in the dust. Also, more general, *pulverescence,* tendency to become dusty or powdery; *pulverulent,* powdered, in the form of dust, powdery; *pulverulence.* Also *to pulvil,* to sprinkle or perfume with *pulvil; pulvilized,* so powdered and perfumed. Latin *pulvinus,* a cushion, had a diminutive *pulvinulus,* which gave us English *pulvillar,* cushion-like, pad-like, also *pulvinarian.* A *pulvinar* is still, in surgery, a small pad or cushion; also, the cushioned seat in the ancient Roman amphitheatre; a couch or cushioned seat of the gods. Hence *pulvinate,* pillowy, cushion-shaped; bulging. The powdered cosmetic (now called merely powder) was popular as *pulvil* from the 16th into the 19th century; Wycherley in THE COUNTRY WIFE (1675) said: *I have dressed you . . . and spent upon you ounces of essence and pulvillio*; Farquhar inquired, in THE CONSTANT COUPLE (1700): *How many pound of pulvil must the fellow use in sweetening himself from the smell of hops and tobacco?*

pulvinar. See *pulvil.*

pumie. An early form of *pumice* (stone); Latin *pumicem.* Also *pomys, pommes, pommice, pumis; pumysch, pomege;* the forms *pumy, pummy, pommie, pumey* and the like probably rose from the (oral) interpretation of *pumis stone* as *pumi stone.* Spenser in THE SHEPHERD'S CALENDAR (1579; March) says: *Pumie stones I threwe . . . From bough to bough he lepped light, And oft the pumies latched* [caught]. From the 10th century, pumice was used for polishing parchment and for removing stains. It was also used as a symbol of dryness, *as dry as a pumice*: Lyly exclaims in EUPHUES (1580): *If thou attempt againe to wring water out of the pommice*; Jonson, in EVERY MAN OUT OF HIS HUMOUR (1599) uses it of a man: *Could the pummise but hold up his eyes at other mens happiness, in any reasonable proportion: 'Slid, the slave were to be loved next heaven.*

pumpkinify. Literally, to make a pumpkin of, as in THE HEADLESS HORSEMAN of Washington Irving. Also *pumpkinize.* The words are used to mean to praise extravagantly, to glorify absurdly. Also *pumpkinification.* Thus *pumpkinism* is pompous behavior or language; absurdly exaggerate praise. The terms come from a travesty of the ritual transformation of Emperor Claudius Caesar into a god; attributed to Seneca, the travesty was called *Apokolokyntosis* (Greek, Transformation into a Pumpkin; *kolokynthe,* pumpkin). *The Senate,* said Merivale in his history of THE ROMAN EMPERORS (1856), *decreed his divinity, Seneca translated it into pumpkinity.*

pun. This far-from-forgotten word had less remembered forms: *punlet, punnigram; punnet; pundigrion, q.v.* It seems to be related to Latin *punctum,* point; though how, it is hard to see. *Punnology,* said THE EXAMINER in 1826, is of extreme antiquity.

punaise. A bed-bug. Via French (*putnais*) from Latin *putere,* to stink, whence also *putrefy, putrid, putrescent.* The forms *punayse, punese,* wrongly taken as a plural, gave us also *punee, punie, puny.* Holland in his translation (1601) of Pliny caught the perennial attitude: *punies or wall-lice, the most ill-favored and filthie vermin of all other, and which we loth and abhorre at the verie naming of them.* Strangely, Kirby and Spence in AN INTRODUCTION TO ENTOMOLOGY (1815) reported that *on dissecting the brain of a woman there were found in it abundance of vermicles and punaises.* Addison had better luck on dissecting a coquette's heart.

puncheon. (1) A short piercing instrument, a dagger, a bodkin. Used from the 14th century. Roundabout from Latin *puncta,* a point. Also *punchion, punson, punction* and the like. A *punchion-staff* (in North's translation, 1580, of Plutarch) is a sharp-pointed spear. (2) With the same variations in spelling, used since the 15th century, but its origin unknown, is another *puncheon* meaning a large cask. A beer *puncheon* held 72 gallons; a wine *puncheon,* 84; and a whisky *puncheon,* 180 gallons. The size of the wine *puncheon* was established by Parliament in the first year (1483) of the reign of Richard III. The puncheon was also used to hold fish, salt, prunes, and essences for perfume.

punctilionist. One that is particular about punctilios, a stickler over trifles. *Punctille,* a punctilio; a very minute matter was a *punctiuncle.*

pundigrion. A pun. Accent on the *dig.* Almost always used as the climax of a series of quibbling terms, as when Southey (OMNIANA, 1812) observes that many persons *will lose their friend rather than their jest, or their quibble, pun, punnet, or pundigrion.* As early as 1676 L'Estrange had mocked: *Quibble, pun, punnet, pundigrion, of which fifteen will not make up one single jest.* But earlier, the pun was taken more seriously. The Roman Catholic Church was founded on a pun, for which see *perrie.* The first two speeches of the Prince in Shakespeare's HAMLET (1601) are puns. Addison, speaking (in THE SPECTATOR, No. 61; 1711) of the sermons of Bishop Andrews, said that *the sinner was punned into repentance.* George Colman (the younger) in REMINISCENCES OF A FRESHMAN (BROAD GRINS, 1802) castigated *the intolerant pun-hater.*

punic. False, treacherous, especially in the phrase *Punic faith.* From *punicus,* earlier *poenicus, phoenicus,* a Phoenician, a Carthaginian. The *Punic apple* was the pomegranate; *punic* was also used (16th and 17th centuries) for a color, purple or 'yellow drawing to a red.' "Treacherous Carthage" was linked with "perfidious Albion" by Burke in a letter on the PROPOSALS FOR PEACE WITH THE REGICIDE DIRECTORY OF FRANCE (1796), in an *invective against the ministry of Great Britain, their habitual frauds, their proverbial punick perfidy.*

punk. A prostitute, harlot. From the late 16th century; Shakespeare in MEASURE FOR MEASURE (1603) says: *She may be a puncke; for many of them are neither maid, widow, nor wife.* Also *punque, pung.* Nares (1882) notes that *punk* was used by Butler and Dryden, but calls it 'a coarse term, which is deservedly growing obsolete.'

punnet. A round and usually shallow basket, for fruit or vegetables. Perhaps from *pun,* dialectal for *pound.* But see *pun.* The WESTMINSTER DAILY PRESS of 29 May, 1884, playing a frequent masculine game, declared that the new-fashion women's bonnets *suggest strawberry punnets turned upside down upon the head.*

purfle. A border; especially, a decorated border, an embroidered edge of a garment. Also as a verb, to border; to decorate, adorn. Used from the 13th century. Ultimately from Latin *per,* through + *filum,* thread. The phrase *in purfle* (as used, e.g., by Jonson in his masque of BLACKNESS, 1605) mean in profile; *profile* is from the same source as *purfle.* Milton in COMUS (1634) speaks of *Flowers of more mingled hew Than her purfl'd scarf can shew.* R. Ellis uses the word figuratively in his translation (1871) of Catullus: *the new, the dainty volume, Purfled glossily*—unless he intended a pun on the gloss.

purpur. A purple garment; especially as worn by royalty, *the purple.* From Latin *purpura,* the shell-fish that yielded the Tyrian dye; *purpur*—also *purpure, popere, pupre,* etc.—was an early (8th to 16th century) form of *purple.*

purslane. A plant, a succulent herb. It was used in salad, to keep the passions cool. In the 17th century, *to destroy warts, nothing is better than to rubbe them with purslaine.* The name comes from French *pourcelaine,* altered from Pliny's *porcillaca;* the more common Latin *portulaca* is still the scientific name of the plant. It had a soothing effect, like lettuce, *cp. sleepwort.* Spenser in MUIOPOTMOS (1590) speaks of *Fat colworts, and comforting perseline.*

putage. Harlotry. From the 15th century (the word, that is); in the 17th, *putanism.* Harlots collectively were called *putaile,* as in MERLIN (1450): *well x ml. of horsemen, without the putaile that ronne up and down and robbed the people*—though the O.E.D. thinks the word might mean foot-soldiers (*pedaile*) instead of camp-followers. A *putain* (directly from the French; in English 14th to 17th century) was a whore. Also *putaine,* whores collectively, whoredom; PASQUINE IN A TRAUNCE (1566) notes: *Putanies be those nuns we call the greene friers on strawbery banke.* The various forms are ultimately from Latin *putida; putris,* rotten, stinking, whence also *putrid; cp. punaise,* bed-bug—which brings us back to the whore.

putrescent. See *punaise.*

puzzle. See *pucelle.*

pygmachy. Boxing. Accent on the *pig;* Greek *pygme,* fist + *mache,* fight. A *pygmy* is a person big as a fist.

pyknic. Corpulent, fat. Not in O.E.D. Greek *pyknos,* dense, thick. A number of scientific terms, especially in zoology, are formed from this word; e.g., *pycnomorphic,* having a dense formation or structure. The tradition of the jolly fat man notwithstanding, being pyknic is seldom a picnic.

pylpate. See *pilledow.*

pyromancy. See *aeromancy.*

pyrrhic. At too great cost. Used especially in the phrase *pyrrhic victory,* from *Pyrrhus,* king of Epirus; he defeated the Romans at Asculum in Apulia (279 B.C.) but with so many of his own men slain that he remarked: "One more such victory and we are lost." In today's great wars all victories are pyrrhic.

pystoler. See *pistle.*

Pythian. Relating to Delphi, or the oracle or the priestess of Apollo there, or to the *Pythian games* held there (at first every eight years, then, like the Olympic games, every four). Hence also, ecstatic, frenzied, like the priestess when the god was in her. Also *Pythic.* Delphi was originally known as *Python,* perhaps from the legend that Apollo had slain the *python* (a monstrous snake) where his temple there was erected. Carlyle in THE FRENCH REVOLUTION (1837) said that the Count d'Aintrigues *rises into furor almost Pythic.* Hence also *python,* a spirit; one possessed by such a spirit, which speaks through the one possessed. Hence *pythoner, pythoness,* man, woman, with the power of divining, soothsayer. Chaucer in THE HOUS OF FAME (1384) speaks of *jugelours, magiciens and tregetours and phitonesses.*

pythoness. Also *pythonissa.* See *Pythian.* Hence *pythonic,* relating to divination, prophetic; *pythonism,* divination, communion with a spirit; *pythonist,* a soothsayer; *to pythonize,* to foretell.

pyx. A box or coffer. A small vase. Cp. *pax.* Also *pix*; *pyxis*; Greek *pyxis,* box; *pyxos,* box-tree. Especially (1) in church service, the vessel in which the consecrated bread of the sacrament is kept; (2) the box at the London mint where specimen new coins are kept to be tested; hence, *the trial of the pyx,* examination of the purity and weight of the coins; *pyx-feast, pyx-dinner,* meal of the jury of the Goldsmiths' Company, on the occasion of the trial of the pyx. (3) The mariner's compass.—We note in Smith's DICTIONARY OF GREEK AND ROMAN ANTIQUITIES (1842) that *Nero deposited his beard in a valuable pyxis, when he shaved for the first time.*

Q

quab. See *quop.*

quadrivial. See *trivial.*

quaestuary. Pertaining to profit, money-making. Latin *quaerere, quaestum* (*querere, questum,* whence *query, question*), to seek. In his FABLES (1694) R. L'Estrange refers to *the lawyers, the divines, and all quaestuary professions.*

quaff. To drink deeply, take a long draught; especially, to drain a cup at a draught. Used since the 16th century; Shakespeare says, in THE TAMING OF THE SHREW (1596): *quaft off the muscadell. Quaff up that bitter cup of affliction,* Bishop Hall (1633) urged himself; but Dekker in THE WHORE OF BABYLON (1607) more gaily exclaimed: *I quaffe full bowles of strong enchanting wines.*

quaint. I As an adjective. The earliest sense of *quaint* (*coint, coynte, qwaynt,* and more) was wise, ingenious; also, crafty, cunning. Then it was used to mean elegant, especially in speech; clever; also cleverly wrought, hence beautiful. It is via Old French *cointe* (*quointe, cuinte*) from Latin *cognitum,* known; *cognoscere,* to know; whence also *cognition; cp. coint.* Its use lapsed about 1650; it was revived about 1800, mainly in its present sense. II As a noun. (1) A woman's private parts. Chaucer sought no euphemism, in THE MILLER'S TALE (1386); he bluntly says: *Pryvely he caught her by the queynte.* The O.E.D. in Victorian innocence queries whether this is from the adjective, but it is a different word, being a variant form of the common English word, akin to Latin *cunnus;* Burton in his translation (1886) of THE ARABIAN NIGHTS spells it *coynte.* From the adjective, however, does come the sense, not in O.E.D., of (2) a clever trick; a cunning device. In HANDLYNG SYNNE (*cp. sigalder; slop*), the bishop, looking at the magic bag, commands the witch: *'Dame', seyd the bysshop, 'do thy quentyse, And late us se how hit shall ryse'. Thys wycche here charme began to sey, The slop ros up, and yede the weye.*

quair. An early (mainly Scotch) form of (1) *where.* (2) *quire.* This may be a variant of *choir,* as in Shakespeare's SONNET 73 (1592): *Bare ruin'd quires, where late the sweet birds sang* and in Milton's IL PENSOROSO (1632): *There let the pealing organ blow To the full-voiced quire below. Choir* is roundabout from Greek *choros,* company of singers or dancers. More often (from the 13th century) *quire, quair* (Old French *caier,* French *cahier;* Latin *quaterni,* set of four; *quattuor,* four) was a set of four sheets of parchment or paper, folded to form eight leaves; by extension, a pamphlet or booklet; then, a poem or prose piece short enough to fit in a quire. The best known work of this sort is *The Kingis Quair* (1423), by James I of Scotland.

quap. See *quop.*

quarrel. (1) An early form of *quarrer, quarry,* a place from which stone is obtained. Ultimately from Latin *quadrus,* square, four-sided; *quattuor,* four. From the same source came (2) *quarrel, quarry,* a short, square-headed arrow or bolt, used with the cross-bow and the arbalest. Also a square needle (15th century; for fishhooks); a square or diamond pane of glass (in lattice windows, 15th to 17th century); a four-sided tile; pavements in the 17th century might be *wrought checkerwise with small square quarels.* When persons seek to avoid a quarrel, the word is via Old French *quereler* from Latin *querela,* complaint, *queri,* to complain, whence both *querulous* and *quarrelsome*; *querulation, queruling,* the act of complaining; *querulist,* an habitual complainer; *querulental, querulential, querelous,* querulous, peevish; *querulity, querulosity,* a spirit of complaining. These should not be confused with forms from Latin *quaerere,* to ask, seek; *quaestio,* question, whence also *request, questionable.* In THE OBSERVER (No. 103; 1785), Cumberland spoke of a lady *rather captious and querulental.* Touchstone in THE TRIFLER (1788) averred: *I have carefully examined the various subjects of complaint . . . If my third fair querulist . . .*

quay. To subdue, daunt. Probably a variant of *quail.* Used by Spenser in THE FAËRIE QUEENE (1590): *Therewith his sturdie corage soon was quayd, And all his senses were with sudden dread dismayed.*

queach. A thicket, a dense growth of bushes. Also *queche.* Hence *queachy,* thickly grown—but also used (Peele, EDWARD I, 1593; Drayton, POLYOLBION, 1622) to mean swampy, sodden. MERLIN (1450) told that *thei rode so longe till thei com to a thikke queche in a depe valey.*

quean. A woman; but in early Middle English the word developed disreputable implications; it was very common in the 16th and 17th centuries, meaning a hussy, a strumpet. The Gothic *qino,* woman, is related to Zend *gena,* Greek *gyne,* whence *gynecology.* The well-known drinking song in Sheridan's THE SCHOOL FOR SCANDAL (1777) has the lines: *Here's to the flaunting extravagant quean And here's to the housewife that's thrifty.* Scott revived the innocent sense of the word, referring to a robust young woman, as in ROB ROY (1818): *It shows a kind heart . . . in sae young a quean; Mattie's a carefu' lass.* For further instances, see *bawdreaminy.*

qued. Evil, wicked. A most common word; also, *cwead, quead, kuead, cwed, queyd, quethe.* As a noun, a wicked or evil person; especially, the Devil. Hence, evil, harm. In PIERS PLOWMAN (1377), Langland said: *He shulde take the acquitance . . . and to the qued schewe it.* Also *quedhead, quedness, quedship,* evil.

queme. To please, gratify; to act so as to please; to be acceptable; to be suitable; to appease. Used from the 8th century; Palsgrave in 1530 says *I queme . . . This worde is now out of use.* Spenser, when in THE SHEPHERD'S CALENDAR (1579; MAY) he wrote *Such merimake holy saints doth queme,* felt it necessary to write 'please' in a gloss. The form in Middle High German was *bequaeme,* it is fitting; English *it becomes me,* as in *Mourning Becomes Electra* by Eugene O'Neill. We still say *becoming,* but we have forgotten *queme.* The word was also used as an adjective, meaning pleasing, agreeable; of pleasing appearance, beautiful, smooth (of the ocean); fit, fitting, convenient, handy; friendly, well disposed. THE DESTRUCTION

OF TROY (1400) urges: *Quit claym all querels, and be queme fryndes.* May all with you pass quemely!

quenelle. A ball of meat or fish, made into a paste, cooked, well seasoned. V. Stuart in EGYPT (1883) enjoyed *savoury quenelles of mutton enveloped in fennel leaves.*

quentyse. See *quaint.*

quern. A hand-mill; usually two circular stones, the upper one turned by hand. For grinding corn; also, *pepper-quern, mustard-quern.* From the 10th century; used by Chaucer (1374) and Shakespeare in A MIDSUMMER NIGHT'S DREAM (1596) when a fairy queries Puck: *Are you not he That frights the maidens of the villagery, Skim milk, and sometimes labor in the quern And bootless make the breathless housewife churn?* Sylvester uses the mill as an image for the teeth, in his translation (1591) of Du Bartas: *Two equall ranks of orient pearls . . . quern-like grinding small th' imperfect food.* There was also a *quern-chant, quern-song,* song of the miller.

quernal. Relating to the oak, oak-leaves, or acorns. Latin *quernus,* from *quercus,* oak. In his ANIMADVERSIONS (1599) Thynne refers to *the quernall crowne gyven to those which had saved a cytyzen.*

querulist. See *quarrel.*

quest. (1) A body of persons appointed to make an inquiry or *inquest,* a jury. Shakespeare uses this figuratively, in SONNET 46 (1600): *To side this title is impanelled A quest of thoughts, all tennant to the heart.* Hence, from the number in such a quest, twelve. AN ALMOND FOR A PARRAT (1589): *Ile have a spare fellowe shall make mee a whole quest of faces for three farthings.* A *questman,* a member of a *quest; questmonger* (disreputable), one that made a business of serving on a quest or of conducting inquests. *Quest* was frequently used as a short form for *inquest.* (2) The side of an oven. A pie was *quested* when its side was crushed against the oven or another pie, or so pressed as to be less well baked.

questionous. Full of *questions,* inquisitive. An apt term for a period attained by every normal child, when parents often complain "He does nothing but question us."

questrist. One that is seeking, goes in *quest* of. Shakespeare in KING LEAR (1605) tells that *thirty of his knights, Hot questrists after him, met him at gate.*

queth. To speak, declare. Also, a speech, a sound. Used from the 9th to the 16th century. Also *quethe, queythe.* The past of *queth* was *quoth,* sometimes still used to give an archaic effect (usually followed by the subject, *quoth the colonel*); *quotha* was short for *quoth he,* he said; also *quodha, catha.* Sometimes *quotha* was used in scorn, meaning forsooth! indeed! The phrase *alive and quething* meant alive and able to speak; when *quething* was forgotten, folk-practice changed the phrase to *alive and kicking.* In the 14th century, *quething* was used for *bequeathing;* a *quethe word* was a bequest, a *quething word* was a last farewell. I trust you will long be alive and quething.

queynt. See *quaint.*

quibble. As a noun. A play upon words. From this sense of *quibble* came the second sense, as still in the verb, to *quibble,* to indulge in purely verbal argument, to avoid the issue by a turn of phrases. A *quip* was originally a sharp or sarcastic remark; later, any clever turn of words, as in Milton's L'ALLEGRO (1632): *Quips and cranks and wanton wiles.* Both *quip* and *quibble* are probably from *quib,* which is a shortening of Latin *quibus,* 'from which things' (it can be seen, etc.). The word *quibus* occurred frequently in legal documents, hence came to be used of the verbal aspects of the legal mind. (In French, *quibus* was used to mean money, 'the wherewithal'; in Dutch, *kwibus,* a fool.) Johnson, in his Preface to Shakespeare (1765) said: *A quibble is to Shakespeare what luminous vapour is to the traveller; he follows it at all adventures; it is sure to lead him out of the way and sure to engulf him in the mire.*

quick. Living. Frequent in phrases: *quick cattle, quick beast*; also figuratively, as *the quick* (fertile) *earth*; Wyclif (The BIBLE; HEBREWS; 1382): *The word of God is quyk.* A *quick fence* is a hedge of living plants. Also *quick coals,* live, burning; *quick spring,* flowing; *quick steel,* brittle. It survives as a noun in *the quick and the dead* (The BIBLE: ACTS). *Cp. wizard.*

quiddany. A thick fruit jelly—*thicker than a syrup,* said a guide of 1616, *and not so thick nor stiff as marmalade.* Originally, a quince preserve (Latin *cydonia,* quince); also called *quindiniac; quiddanet, quidony; codinac, codigny,* a quince marmalade; *cotiniate,* a marmalade or confection of quinces. In the 18th century, *quiddany* was a general term for any fruit syrup or jelly. Hence *to quiddany,* to make into jelly, used figuratively in Ward's THE SIMPLE COBLER OF AGAWAM in America (1647): *He will . . . quidanye Christ with sugar and ratsbane.*

quiddity. (1) The essence of a thing. Formed with the ending *-ity* from *quid* (Latin, what), used also in English, meaning that which a thing is. (2) A thing intangible or nameless. (3) A subtlety in argument; subtlety in wit. The third meaning sprang from the frequency of scholastic arguments on *the quiddity* (essence) of things. Also *quiddit* and, by alteration, *quillity* and *quillet.* Shakespeare in LOVE'S LABOUR'S LOST (1588) speaks of *some tricks, some quillets, how to cheat the divell.* Also Urquhart has, in his translation (1653) of Rabelais: *One of them would call it . . . her staffe of love, her quillety.* Still another variant appeared in Guilpin's SKIALETHEIA (1598): *Then whats a wench but a quirke, quidlit case, Which makes a painters pallat of her face?* A line in W. S. Gilbert's PATIENCE (1881) runs: *To stuff his conversation full of quibble and of quiddity.* Also *quiddative, quidditative,* pertaining to the essence of a thing; full of equivocations; quirky.

quidnunc. (1) An inquisitive person; one that is constantly inquiring *Quid nunc?* (Latin: What now?) (2) A curiosity, someone or something to be talked about. Used from the 18th century, as by Steele in THE TATLER (1709); still occasionally employed in satire. Speaking of Pinero's THE IRONMASTER (1884) adapted from Ohnet's LE MAÎTRE DES FORGES of the year before, M. W. Disher in MELODRAMA (1954) said: *It was gloomy and that made it fashionable, for the new intellectual drama which quidnuncs talked about would of course be gloomy—the drama of ideas from "The Robbers" to "Leah" always had been because it had always come from the other side of the Rhine where brains worked solemnly.*

quier. A variant of *queer.* See *pedlers French.*

quillet. See *quiddity.*

quincunx. An arrangement of trees or other objects so that four mark the corners and one the center of a rectangle; an orchard may be a joined series of such quincunxes. Also *quincunce;* Latin *quinque,* five + *uncia,* ounce, one-twelfth; literally, five-twelfths; dots arranged in a quincunx signified five-twelfths of an as. [The original unit of currency at Rome, the *as,* was—with many later modifications—a bar of bronze weighing one Roman pound, twelve ounces.] Hence also *quincunxial,* more commonly *quincuncial.*

quintain. (1) A tilting post. Common in medieval knightly training, in 17th and 18th century country sports at weddings. Described in Toone's GLOSSARY (1834): "An upright post was fixed to the ground, having at the top a movable figure of a man, holding a shield . . . and at the other end a heavy sand bag; the player rode or run at full speed and attempted to strike the figure, which, if not done dexterously, he was struck and overthrown by a blow from the sandbag." Toone suggests that the word is from British *gwyntyn,* a vane. The O.E.D. traces it to Latin *quintus,* fifth, the grounds of the fifth division of the Roman legion being used for military exercises. Also *quintayne, qwaintan, quyntyne, quinten, quintan,* and the like. Also *quintal, quintel, quintil.* Shakespeare, in AS YOU LIKE IT (1600) says: *That which here stands up Is but a quintine, a meere liveless blocke.* (2) A variant of *quentin* or *quintin* (*St. Quentin* in Picardy; *Quintin,* in Brittany, France) a kind of linen or lawn. (3) A stanza of five lines, usually called a *cinquain.*

quip. See *quibble.*

quipu. The communications system or device of ancient Peru. Also *quipo, quippu, quippo;* Quichan *quipu,* knot. An arrangement of knotted and colored cords, that transmitted messages, and recorded such items as population, crops, number of workers, and tribute. Carlyle remarked (1830) that *history has been written with quipo-threads, with feather pictures, with wampum-belts.* The quipu system never attained the status of writing, unlike the neighboring hieroglyphics of the Maya—who also computed time accurately back some ninety million years, and set one date at 400 million years ago. They achieved this a thousand years before Archbishop Ussher (1581-1656) calculated that the creation of the world occurred 4004 B.C., which date for a long time after his determination was printed in the Authorized Version of the BIBLE.

quisquilious. Made up of rubbish. Also *quisquilian, quisquiliary.* From Latin *quisquiliae,* odds and ends; *quisque,* whatever it may be. Used since the 18th century. BLACKWOOD'S EDINBURGH MAGAZINE, in a travesty of Urquhart (1817), railed against *those shallow and fidimplicitary coxcombs, who fill our too credulous ears with their quisquiliary deblaterations.* FRASER'S MAGAZINE (1857) more soberly ventured into ornithology: *The jay's diet is sufficiently quisquilious.* Also see *nugacity.*

quisquous. Hard to handle, ticklish. Also *quisquose, quiscos, quiscoskos.* Used in Scotland in the 18th and 19th centuries; we read in TAIT'S MAGAZINE for 1836: *the ladies maybe a wee quiscoskos.*

quitrent. A sum paid in lieu of services due, as in feudal times. Often used figuratively, as by Cowper in TABLE TALK (1782): *The courtly laureate pays His quitrent ode, his peppercorn of praise.*

quiver. Nimble, quick. Shakespeare in HENRY IV, PART TWO (1597) says: *There was a little quiver fellow, and a' would manage his piece thus.* From the noun *quiver,* a case for arrows, came a verbal form, as in Milton's COMUS (1634): *Like a quiver'd nymph with arrows keen.* The form *quiverful* was often used figuratively, meaning many, echoing the BIBLE: PSALM 127: *As arrows in the hand of a mighty man, so are children of the youth. Happy is the man that hath his quiver full of them.*

quodlibetarian. (1) One who does as he pleases, or believes in doing as one pleases. (2) One who indulges in or discusses *quodlibets.* A *quodlibet* was a question (usually in philosophy or religion) posed as an exercise in argument; hence, *to do quodlibets,* to argue, to advance or present a thesis. Latin *quod,* what + *libet,* pleases. Also *quodlibetist, quodlibetary;* the latter term was applied either to the arguer or to the argument. To deal in such matters (i.e., to quibble) was, in the 18th century, to *quodlibetificate* (accent, naturally, on the *tiff*). Adjectives were *quodlibetal, quodlibetic, quodlibetical.*

quok. See *quooke.*

quondam. Former; that used to be. Directly from the Latin; in the 16th century, also *condam.* Often used in the 16th century, as by Latimer in his FOURTH SERMON BEFORE KING EDWARD VI (1549): *Make them quondammes, out with them, cast them out of ther office!* Hence *quondamship,* the condition of being out of office (also in Latimer's FOURTH SERMON). Shakespeare in LOVE'S LABOUR'S LOST (1588) says: *I did converse this quondam day with a companion of the king's.* Ruskin in FORS CLAVIGERA (1874) sighed over *the loquacious and speculative disposition . . . of all my quondam friends.*

quooke. An old variant of *quaked,* past tense of *to quake.* Chaucer used *quok, quoke;* Spenser in MUTABILITY (1596) tells that Jove *shooke His nectar-deawed locks, with which the skyes And all the earth beneath for terror quooke, And eft his burning levin-brond in hand he tooke.*

quop. To throb, quiver, palpitate. Also *quab, quag;* earlier *quap.* Chaucer in TROYLUS AND CRISEYDE (1374) has: *And lord how that his herte gan to quappe, Heryng her come.* Dryden (1679) also said *My heart quops.* As a noun *quab, quob* meant (1) a shapeless thing, as an ill-written work; Ford in THE LOVER'S MELANCHOLY (1628) spoke of *a trifle of mine own brain . . . a scholar's fancy, a quab; 'tis nothing else, a very quab.* (2) A *quagmire,* a marshy spot, also a *quag.* The verb *to quag,* to quiver, is used of flabby flesh "or a great dug."

quotha. See *queth.*

quotiety. Relative frequency, "howmanyness."

quysper. An early (Middle English) form of *whisper.*

qwalester. An early (Middle English) form of *chorister.*

qwaylle. An early (Middle English) form of *whale.*

qwysschewes. An early (Middle English) form of *cuisses;* see *cuish.*

R

rabato. See *rebato.* Old French *rabateau* has the same meaning.

rabblement. Also *rablement;* variant forms of *rabble;* used also (Spenser, THE FAËRIE QUEENE*;* 1590) of the tumult a rabble might cause. Shakespeare in JULIUS CAESAR (1601) pictures the proffering of the crown: *As hee refus'd it, the rabblement showted.* For another instance, see *pot-fury.*

rabiator. A violent, noisy person. Used in the 19th century, mainly in Scotland. Probably a variant (influenced by *rabid,* mad) of the earlier *rubiator,* a scoundrel.

rackrent. An excessive rent; a rent virtually equal to the value of the property. Also a verb; *It was a maxim with his family,* we read in Richardson's CLARISSA (1748) *never to rackrent old tenants or their descendants.* There is a current echo in TAIT'S EDINBURGH MAGAZINE of 1834: *Every year growing worse than the last in this rackrent country.* Pity the farmer, *the needy, hard-rackrented hinde,* of Sylvester's (1591) Du Bartas. James Mill in THE HISTORY OF BRITISH INDIA (1818) observed that *one third to the cultivator, and two thirds to the proprietor, would be accounted a rackrent in England.*

radknight. A tenant who in Old English times gave service on horseback in exchange for holding the land. Old English *rad,* riding, is related to *raid* and *road.* Also *radcnecht, radcniht;* in DOMESDAY BOOK, *radchenistre.*

ragery. Wantonness; a frolic. The Wife of Bath says in her Prologue (Chaucer, 1386): *I was yong and full of rageryе.*

ragman. (1) The devil. So used in the 14th and 15th centuries. (2) Earlier *raggeman, rageman* (three syllables, hard *g*), the name given to a statue of Edward I, appointing justices to hear complaints of injuries within 25 years. By extension, a list, a roll; also called *roll of ragman, ragman roll* (14th and 15th centuries). By further extension, a discourse; especially, a long, rambling, and partly meaningless discourse, *rigmarole. Rigmarole* is a variant form of *ragman roll,* superseding it in this sense by 1600. Also a game of chance, played with a written roll that contained various items with strings attached, each player to pull a string and discover his prize or penalty. There is a record of two men being fined in Durham, in 1377, for playing *ragman.* The roll for the game was supposed to be written by *King Ragman,* who was praised or blamed according to the draw. *Ragman's roll* is also the name of certain rolls recording instruments of homage to Edward I by Balliol of Scotland in 1296 (returned to the Scots by Edward III). Also *ragman('s) rew,* a book or catalogue (16th century); in this sense John Olde in his translation (1556) of Walter's ANTICHRIST speaks of *the noble ragge man rolls of those most holy fathers.*

ragmatical. Ill-behaved, riotous. Smollett has Tabitha Bramble exclaim, in HUMPH-

REY CLINKER (1771): *Roger gets this and Roger gets that; but I'd have you to know I won't be rogered at this rate by any ragmatical fellow in the kingdom.* See *roger.*

raik. The act of going; a journey; the ground over which animals usually move, pasture-land. From the 14th century; the word is an early form of *rake* (which had these and other meanings), which except in dialect and Scotch largely replaced *raik* by 1600. Also a verb, to go, walk, wander, walk through; Hogg in a poem of 1813 has: *to raike the lonely glen.* In another poem he uses the form as a noun: *The wolf and the kid their raike began.*

raines. See *rochet.*

rakehell. See *rakeshame.*

rakeshame. A dissolute fellow. The word was common in the 17th century. Coming earlier and outlasting *rakeshame* was the form *rakehell,* sometimes abbreviated to *rakel.* Spenser in THE FAËRIE QUEENE (1596) says: *Amid their rakehell bands They spide a lady.* Also *rakehellonian,* one of the tribe of *rakehells.* The noun *rake,* in the sense of a man of loose ways; especially, an idle dissipated man of fashion (18th and 19th centuries) is an abbreviation of *rakehell.* Some (e.g., Goldsmith in THE GIFT, 1777: *Cruel Iris, pretty rake, Dear mercenary beauty*) used *rake* of a woman.

ramage. Originally, the branches of a tree or grove (collectively); Late Latin *ramaticum,* Latin *ramus,* branch. Hence, the singing of birds in the trees, as in Drummond of Hawthornden's poem TO HIS LUTE (1616): *Birds their ramage did on thee bestow.* Hence also, applied as an adjective—*ramage hawk*—to untamed birds, fledglings, who flew from branch to branch; by extension from this use, the noun *ramage* was used in the sense of courage, wild spirit. Also, 14th into 16th century, *ramageous,* high-spirited. *Ramage* came to be a general term, applied to persons (shy) and to animals (untamed, wild) as in Chaucer's THE ROMAUNT OF THE ROSE (1366): *He is not wise ne sage No more than is a gote ramage.*

rame. (1) The bones or mere skeleton of a thing; dried stalks. J. Bell in his translation (1581) of Haddon's ANSWER TO OSORIUS said: *Natural fooles do destest the stinking rames . . . of that rebellious traytour.* (2) A branch of a tree. This use is from Latin *ramus,* branch, oar; English *ramuscle* (17th century), *ramuscule* (19th century) is a small branch. (3) A cry; a continuous repetition of the same sound —also a verb, to cry, to repeat, used since the 15th century.

ramekin. A small amount of cheese, with bread-crumbs, eggs, etc., baked and served in a special mold. Also *ramequin.* The word was sometimes used of the mold (1894, *little French china ramequin cases*) in which the mixture was baked; thus The Connoisseur (1754, No. 19) said: *Toasted cheese is already buried in rammelkins.* The word usually occurred in the plural—folks asked for more.

ramolade. A sauce for fish, of parsley, chibols, anchovies, capers, and other seasoning. Used in the 18th century. A *chibol* was a 'stone leek' or 'Welsh onion,' a sort of scallion midway between the onion and the leek, popular from the 14th to the 18th century.

ramous. Many-branched. Latin *ramus,* branch; see *rame.* A bush or a pedigree may be ramous.

ramp. See *rampike.* Middleton and Dekker in THE ROARING GIRL (1611): *The bouncing ramp, that roaring girl my mistress.*

rampallion. A raspscallion (*cp. scullion*), a ruffian scoundrel. Perhaps related to *ramp, q.v.* Nashe in his STRANGE NEWES (1593) advised: *Pocket not up this abuse at a rakehell rampalions hands.* For an instance in Shakespeare, used of a woman, see *catastrophe.*

rampike. A dead tree; especially, a spiky stump or stem of a tree. Hence *rampick,* decayed; bare. A glossary of 1881 spells the word *raunpick,* and explains it as "bare of bark or flesh, looking as if pecked by ravens"—as though *raun pick* were converted from *raven-peck.* A *ramp* (15th to 18th century) was a vulgar, brazen female; Gabriel Harvey in his LETTER-BOOK (1573) speaks of *An insatiable ramp Of Messalina's stamp*; the second syllable is probably *pike,* a pointed staff. A *rampallion* was (a male *ramp*), a ruffian, scoundrel. A man all skin and bones is rampick indeed.

random. This word was originally a noun, very common from the 13th to the 16th century. It was not used as an adjective (the use current today) until 1655, from the phrase *at random.* The earliest form was *randon*; also *randun, randoun, randowne*; *raundom, randome, randum.* The basic meaning of the word was impetuosity, speed, force, violence. (French *randir,* to gallop.) Hence, *with* (*in, on*) (*a*) *randon,* at great speed; also *a randon,* a headlong rush, a 'bee-line.' From the phrase *at random,* at great speed, developed the idea, without consideration, without control; hence, haphazard—from this sense came the use as an adjective. *The Frenchmen,* said Lord Berners in his translation of Froissart, *came on them with great randon, their speares in their restes.* The phrase *at random* was also used to mean free from control, hence at liberty, as in Spenser's THE FAËRIE QUEENE (1590): *The gentle lady, loose at randon lefte, the greenewood long did walk.*

randon. See *random.*

rap. To seize, to snatch; to carry off. An early (16th and 17th century) form of *rape, q.v.*; frequent in the phrase *rap and rend.* Also, to transport with joy, to rouse to *rapture*; apparently given this sense by back-formation from *rapt.* Shakespeare in CYMBELINE (1609) inquires: *What . . . thus raps you?*

rape. This word, still current as an act of violence or violation, as a rough file, a rasp, and as a vegetable (the turnip, etc.) had two uses now forgotten. In the DOMESDAY BOOK (1086) *rape* is used for a division of Sussex, which was divided into six *rapes,* each comprising several 'hundreds.' And in the 14th and 15th centuries, *rape* was used to mean haste, speed; especially in phrases: *to have rape*; *in* (*a*) *rape,* in haste, in a hurry. Thus Chaucer in TO HIS SCRIVENER (1374) blamed all errors upon the scribe: *All is thorugh thy necglygence and rape. Rape* was used through the same period as a verb, to hasten, to speed (someone) on. Thus Repentance, in Langland's PIERS PLOWMAN (1377) cries: *Awake! . . and rape thee to shrifte.*

rapey. A dish. Also *rapy, rapé*; French *raper,* to grate. Many ingredients, including meat or fish, were grated or ground; served with spices. Also *rapee,* a sauce for fish, described in a 15th century recipe: *Take the crustys of wyt bred and reysons, and bray hem wel in a morter; and after temper hem up with wyn, and wryng hem* *throw a cloth, and do thereto canel, that it be al colowryt of canel; and do thereto hole clowys, macys, and quibibz. The fysch schal be lucis other tenchis, fryid—or other maner fysch, so that yt be fresch, and wel yfryed—and do it in dischis, and that rap upon, and serve yt forth.*

raspis. A wine, belike made of *raspberries,* popular in the 15th and 16th centuries. Also *raspays, respice.* It was of 'a deepe redde enclining to blacke.' Said R. Mathew in 1662: *A very good friend of mine . . . was feasted . . . with respass wine. Raspis* was also an early name of the *raspisberry,* now *raspberry.*

rathe. Quick in action, speedy, prompt; soon; early. Hence also *rathely,* quickly. Also *rath, raith.* Used from the 10th century, common in the 14th and 15th centuries, surviving in the comparative degree, *rather,* sooner. *Rathe,* dying out in the 17th century (after Milton's *rathe primrose*), was revived in the 19th by Scott and other poets, as H. Coleridge (1833): *A rathe December blights my lagging May* and Swinburne (1880) *The labours, whence men reap Rathe fruit of hopes and fears.*

raught. An early form of *reached.* Also (Scotch) *raucht.* Shakespeare in ANTONY AND CLEOPATRA (1607) states: *The hand of death hath raught him.* Also an early past tense of *reek.* In the 16th century, *raught* was used as the present tense, to reach, to snatch (at, from). For another instance of its use, see *woolpack.*

raven. Also *ravenage,* ravenousness; *ravener,* plunderer, despoiler; *ravenry,* robbery, rapine. See *ravisable.*

ravin. See *ravisable.*

ravisable. Ravenous. French *ravir, raviss-,* to seize. Used, rarely, in the 15th century. *Ravenous* is from a form *raven, ravin,* meaning robbery, rapine; voracity, gluttony; plunder, prey. Used widely from 13th to 17th century, several times by Chaucer; Shakespeare uses it also as an adjective, in ALL'S WELL THAT ENDS WELL (1601): *I met the ravine lyon* (though this might be *raving,* raging). In the same general senses, *raven* (*ravyne, ravine, ravin*) was also widely used as a verb; Dryden in THE HIND AND THE PANTHER (1687) has: *The more they fed, they ravened still for more.*

raynecles. A medley with ground pork. Also *raynolls, raymolles.* In 15th century cook books: *Take swete porke, dates, figges, braied togeder, and put therto a fewe yolkes of eyren, and in the brayinge alay hit with a lytel brothe, and cast therto pouder of clowes, pouder of pepur, sugre, raisynges of corances, and colour hit with saffron, and medel al togeder; and then hille the stuffure in paste as men maken ruschewes* [see *rishews*]; *and then take the brothe of capons sothen* [seethed: boiled] *in herbes, and let hit boyle, and colour hit with saffron, and then put in therto the raynecles, and when thai byn boyled take hom up, and lay three of hom in a dissh, and pour brothe therto; and take grated chese medelet with pouder of ginger, and strewe above theron, and serve hit forthe.*

raynes. See *rochet.*

reaks. Pranks, wanton tricks, practical (i.e., mischievous) jokes. Spenser uses it in the form *rex.* In the phrase *to play rex,* this meant to play pranks; then by association with *rex,* king, *to play rex* came (by 1600) to mean to play the lord and master, to lord it over, to domineer. R. L'Estrange in his FABLES (1692) speaks of *throwing books at one another's heads* *and playing such reaks as if hell were broke loose.* The word was always used in the plural until its use died, about 1700; Scott revived it singularly, in ROB ROY (1818): *Mony a daft reik he has played.*

rearmouse. A bat; plural, *rearmice.* Also *reremice; hryremus, reremows,* and more. Shakespeare in A MIDSUMMER NIGHT'S DREAM (1590) says: *Some warre with reremise for their leathern wings.* The word was used in the 12th century and still survives in dialects; Browning in PARACELSUS (1835) queried: *Do the rearmice still Hang like a fretwork on the gate?* The German word for bat is *Fledermaus,* flitter-mouse; the French, *chauve souris,* bald mouse. The origin of the English word is not clear; the first syllable may be from Old English *hreran,* to move (flitter). *Rearmost,* of course, means last of all.

rease. See *roose.*

reave. See *reft.*

rebarbative. Unattractive, repellent. From (but none knows just how!) French *barbe,* Latin *barba,* beard. THE SATURDAY REVIEW of 12 November, 1892, said: *It is not very clear why Sir Robert Coke . . . bestows so much trouble and time on this very rebarbative lady.*

rebato. A stiff collar, worn by men and women from about 1580 to 1630, sometimes used to support a ruff. (The wire frame to support a ruff was also called a *rebato.*) Also *rebat, rebatu, rebato, rebater.* Margaret says to Hero, in Shakespeare's MUCH ADO ABOUT NOTHING (1599): *Troth, I think your other rebato were better.* The Water Poet (1630) gave his opinion of its purpose: *The tires, the periwigs, and the rebatoes Are made t'adorne ilshap'd inamoratoes.* The word was also used figuratively; Bishop Barlow (1601) protested against *men who have made scarfes and veiles and rebaters for sinnes;* Nashe in PIERCE PENNILESSE (1592): *Their lords authority is as a rebater to beare up the peacockes taile of their boasting.*

rebeck. (1) A medieval musical instrument, played into the 17th century, having three strings and played with a bow. The wooden top was often carved to represent a human head or other figure, usually grotesque. Also *ribibe, ribible, rubible, rebbec, rebec.* (2) A term of scorn for a woman. Chaucer has, in THE FRIAR'S TALE (1386), *Here woneth* [dwells] *an old rebekke;* in THE MILLER'S TALE, they *pleyen songes on a small rubible.*

reboation. A rebellowing echo. Latin *re,* again + *boare, boatum,* to bellow. Hence *reboant,* loudly re-echoing. Elizabeth Browning in A VISION OF POETS (1844) speaks of *Spiritual thunders . . . Crushing their echoes reboant With their own wheels.*

recche. To tell, narrate; explain; to go, make one's way. Also *reche, reccan, rechen, rachen,* and the like. A common Teuton form, in English until the 15th century. In FREEMASONRY (1430) we read of the Tower of Babel: *An angele smot hem so with dyveres speche, That never won wyste what other shuld reche.*

recumbentibus. A knock-down blow. A humorous application of Latin *recumbentibus,* the ablative plural of *recumbentem,* whence *recumbent; re,* back + *cumbentem,* lying, *cumbere, cubare,* to lie, whence also *incumbent, cubicle.* In the 17th century *recumbendibus* was also used; in 1681 Dryden coined *circumbendibus,* an invented humorous word for a roundabout way, a circumlocution. J. Heywood in one of his PROVERBS (1546) said:

Had you some husbande, and snapt at him thus, I wys he would geve you a recumbentibus.

recusant. This term is applied to a Roman Catholic (*Popish recusant*) who, especially between 1570 and 1791, risked fine and perhaps death by refusing to attend Church of England services. The earliest English form was the verb *recuse,* meaning to reject, from Latin *re-,* back + *causa,* cause. It might also be used as meaning to object to a judge as biased; thus King Henry VIII recorded in 1529 that the Queen *did protest at the said day, putting in libels recusatories of the judges.* The major use, however, was of religion, especially the denial by the Catholics of English church authority; thus Green's SHORT HISTORY OF THE ENGLISH PEOPLE (1874) declared that *heavy 'fines for recusancy' . . . became a constant source of supply to the Royal exchequer.*

red. There are even more *red* compound terms than *blue, q.v.,* especially of birds, animals, fishes, and minerals. Many more general ones have dropped from use. *red boots,* the feet (to above the ankles) stripped of the skin. A Tartar treatment of a foe: *Come here again, and I'll give you a pair of red boots to go home in. red box,* the case, covered with red leather, used by ministers of state to hold official documents; Thackeray in his MISCELLANY (1840) spoke of *solemn red box and tape men; red tape,* of course, is still prevalent. *red-breast,* a Bow Street runner: Dickens in a letter reported: *The Bow Street runners ceased out of the land soon after the introduction of the new police . . . They had no other uniform than a blue dress-coat, brass buttons . . . and a bright red cloth waistcoat . . . The slang name for them was Red-breasts. red button,* a Chinese mandarin of the first class, distinguished by a red button on his cap. Some substitute *red* for *round,* for the button of the panjandrum, *q.v. red cock,* as in *The red cock will crow in his house,* a fire deliberately set. *red-laced jacket,* the result of a flogging on the bare back. *red-lattice,* originally, a lattice painted red as sign of an alehouse; hence, an alehouse, tavern. Hence, *red-lattice phrases,* pot-house talk. Shakespeare in THE MERRY WIVES OF WINDSOR (1598): *You, rogue, will ensconce your rags, your cat-a-mountaine lookes, your red-lattice phrases, under the shelter of your honour. red rag,* the tongue; *red lane,* the throat. Gilbert, in DANIEL DRUCE (1876): *Stop that cursed red rag of yours, will you!* Also, from the phrase *a red rag to a bull,* a source of extreme annoyance; Saintsbury, in THE HISTORY OF ELIZABETHAN LITERATURE (1887): *Shakesperian clowns are believed to be red rags to some experienced playwrights;* this use is current.

redd. To save, free, rescue; to save from burning, put out (a fire); to free oneself, *to be or get redd (of);* to clear of debt, as Barclay in THE SHYP OF FOLYS (1509): *He that still borrows shall scant him quit or redde.* Also *hreddan, redde, red.* Also as a noun, *redd,* the act of clearing away; a clearance, arrangement; that which is cleared away, rubbish. Thus until the 15th century, when the word became confused with another *redd,* to clean up, clear; comb; separate (fighters); settle; *redd up,* put in order. Most of these senses, by the 19th century, had been given over to the form *rid.* Scott, of course, revived the older form, as in WAVERLEY (1814): *Fetch the chevalier to redd Mr. Wauverley and Vich Ian Vohr.* From this sense came *redder,* one that interferes, to make peace, in a quarrel, whence the old saying: *The redder gets aye the worst lick* *of the fray*—and *redding-straik,* a strike or blow received by a peacemaker; a very severe blow.

rede. Counsel, advice. *To give to rede,* to advise; *to take to rede,* to resolve, decide; *to be to rede,* to be an advisable course of action. Hence also, a plan, a course of action; an advantageous action, help, remedy. By further extension, taking counsel; deliberation. Also, a proverb, a story, a tale. In all these senses, the word was very frequent in Old English and until the 17th century; then it died away, to be revived by the poets of the 19th century, as Morris, in THE EARTHLY PARADISE (1870): *Therefore swift rede* [decision] *I take with all things here* and Browning in THE RING AND THE BOOK (1868) *All's a clear rede* [tale] *and no more riddle now. Rede* is a common Teutonic word; also *read, redd, reid, reyd;* past tense *radd, reorde, rade,* etc.—for it was also a verb as the action of the noun above. The verb, however, had some early meanings not carried into the noun: to govern, guide; in reference to God, to watch over, to save, deliver; to put in order (in this sense, *rede* is related to *ready*) to clear a way, to clean up, to comb the hair. Chaucer in THE HOUS OF FAME (1384) says: *Also wis God rede me.* So reid He all!

reduce. To bring back; to recall to mind; to recall the mind to (or from) a subject. Used from the 14th century; Latin *re,* back + *ducere, ductum,* to lead; whence also *induct, viaduct, aqueduct, duct,* and all sorts of *conduct.* Also, to lead a person back. *God,* said Caxton in his translation (1483) of THE GOLDEN LEGEND, *shal reduce and brynge you agayn unto the londe of your faders.* Especially, to lead back from error—thus, very common in the 17th century. Also, to bring back to a former state; to redress a wrong. Shakespeare in HENRY V (1599) says: *Which to reduce into our former favour You are assembled.* To bring into order; to put into practice; still occasionally used as in the phrase *to reduce to writing.* The sense of subdue, *reduce,* conquer, developed in the 15th century; *reduce,* diminish, dates from the mid 16th. Sackville in the Induction to A MIRROR FOR MAGISTRATES (1563) wrote, of the quick appearance of the stars at dusk: *The sodayne sight reduced to my minde The sundry chaunges that in earth we fynde.*

reechy. Smoky; dirty, squalid. Related to *reek.* Used from the 15th century; surviving in dialect. Shakespeare uses it in MUCH ADO ABOUT NOTHING (1599): *Like Pharaoes souldiours in the rechie painting* and in CORIOLANUS: *The kitchin malkin pinnes Her richest lockram 'bout her reechie necke.* Note that, in the early uses of *reek* there were often no disagreeable implications; it means rising like mist in Shakespeare's HENRY V, in reference to the valiant English that may die in France: *For there the sun shall greet them, And draw their honours reeking up to heaven;* SONNET 130, which claims the poet's *love as rare As any she belied with false compare,* speaks of *the breath that from my mistress reeks.*

refection. Refreshment. Originally either spiritual re-creation or physical recreation; later, mainly refreshing oneself with food and drink. Hence, an entertainment with food and drink; a repast. Latin *reficere, refectum; re,* again + *facere,* to make, whence also *factory, factotum, confection.* A *refectioner, refectorian, refectorer, refectorary,* was the person in a monastery in charge of the *refectory* and food supplies; the *refectory* was the dining hall, also *refectoire* (so in Pepys' DIARY, 23

January, 1667: *I was in the refectoire*). Also *refectionary,* relating to food supply; *refective,* refreshing, nourishing, tending to restore. To *refect* (from the 15th century), to refresh, to entertain with food and drink. *The knight and the friar,* said Peacock in MAID MARIAN (1822), *proceeded to refect themselves after their ride.* Burton in ZANZIBAR (1872) spoke of *the cocoanut, manioc, and broiled fish, offered by squatting negresses for their refection.* Braithwaite in THE ENGLISH GENTLEMAN (1630) declared: *The only sight of God is the true food and refection of our minds.*

refel. To disprove, prove to be false. Also *refell.* Common in the 16th and 17th centuries; later, supplanted by *refute.* Latin *refellere*; *re,* back + *fallere,* to deceive, whence also *fail, infallible.* Palsgrave (1530): *I can not refell your argument, it is so evydent*—a magnanimous admission few argufiers make.

refocillate. To refresh, reanimate, comfort. Used in the 17th and 18th centuries; the noun *refocillation* was used, though rarely, from the 16th into the 19th, e.g., by Coleridge. *Focillate* appears in 17th and 18th century dictionaries. The word meant literally to warm into life (*re,* again); Latin *focillare, focillatum* is from *focus,* hearth. Coryat in his CRUDITIES (1611) said: *The first view thereof did even refocillate my spirits and tickle my senses with inward joy*; Sterne in TRISTRAM SHANDY (1760) remarked: *The nose was comforted, nourish'd, plump'd up, refresh'd, refocillated, and set agrowing forever.*

reft. (A) As a noun. (1) Robbery. Used in the 14th and 15th centuries. (2) A fissure; a variant form of *rift.* (B) As an adjective (from the past participle of *reave,* reft; surviving in the forms *bereave, bereaved, bereft*). (1) Robbed. (2) Split, cleft. The verb *reave* likewise had the two meanings: to despoil, plunder, carry off, and to split, break into pieces. Hence *reaver,* plunderer, marauder; revived in the 19th century by Scott (REDGAUNTLET, 1824) in the Scotch forms *reiver, riever. Reavery* (13th to 15th century), robbery. Bulwer-Lytton in LUCRETIA (1846) says: *Through all this the reft tigress mourned her stolen whelp.*

regal. As a noun. (1) Royalty; royal authority; also, a kingdom, royal right or privilege; a ruler (Chaucer; 1385); a ring or a chalice used at a coronation. Latin *regalis*; *rex, regem,* king; whence also *royal* (via the French) and the adjective *regal.* The noun was in use from the 14th to the 17th century. *The regal of Scotland,* the coronation chair, placed on the stone of Scone. (2) A portable organ (usually plural, *regals*) common from 1550 to 1625, of reed pipes; played with keys by the right hand while the left hand worked a bellows. Also *rigalle, rigoll*; in French (Rabelais) *regualle.* (3) A groove, a slot, as in a battlement, or for a pulley or for joining boards. Used from the 15th century; also *regyll, riggle*; *raggle,* a groove in stone, as for fitting an edge of a roof.

regrate. (A) As a noun: (1) A variant (13th to 17th century) of *regret,* lamentation, sorrow. (2) Oppression. (3) Request. (B) As a verb: (1) to lament. (2) To buy (especially provisions) for resale at a profit—a practice long forbidden by English law (into the 17th century). (3) To repay, reward. (4) To grate upon, offend (the eye). A *regrater* was one that bought victuals for resale (at the same or a neighboring market); a wholesaler, a middleman.

reke. An old form for *rake, reach, reck, reek, rick.* Also (1) haste, noun and verb; hence, to make one's way, to go. (2) To drive, to thrust; past, *rack* (1275; *his spere he rack*). (3) To cover with earth or ashes; to bury. Chaucer, in THE REEVE'S PROLOGUE (1386): *Yet in our asshen olde is fyr yreke.*

rekels. Incense. Also *ricels, recles, rekliss, recheles, rychellys.* From Old English *recan,* to reek. A Trinity College HOMILY of 1200 spoke of *rechelis for his sweetnesse.*

religate. To bind together, to unite; to hold back, constrain. Latin *re,* back + *ligare, ligatum,* to bind, whence also *ligature.* Also *religation,* binding—both literally and figuratively, as in fellowship or communion with the Lord.

relume. To kindle again. Also *relumine*; short for *reillumine.* Hence, *relumination. Lumination* has been superseded by *illumination.* Latin *luminare, luminatum*; *lumen, luminem,* light. Shakespeare in OTHELLO (1604) declares: *I know not where is that Promethean heate That can thy light relume.* Often used figuratively, as in Campbell's THE PLEASURES OF HOPE (1799): *Lo, nature, life, and liberty relume The dim-eyed tenant of the dungeon gloom.*

remembrancer. Something that serves as a reminder: a register, a record; a memorandum book. Hawthorne in THE HOUSE OF THE SEVEN GABLES (1851) speaks of *freckles, friendly remembrancers of the April sun and breeze.* Also, a person trying to remember or recall. From the 14th century, the title of various English exchequer officials, e.g., *the King's (Queen's) Remembrancer,* the officer that collects debts due the crown. The post of *Remembrancer of the First Fruits* was abolished in Queen Victoria's day. Among the appellations Lamb finds for a poor relation (ESSAYS OF ELIA; 1823)—and, having been one, he should know—are: a *preposterous shadow, lengthening in the noontide of our prosperity,—an unwelcome remembrancer,—a drain on your purse,—a more intolerable dun upon your pride . . . Agathocles' pot,—A Mordecai in your gate,—a Lazarus at your door . . . the one thing not needful,—the hail in harvest,—the ounce of sour in a pound of sweet.*

remenant. Remainder. Used from the 13th through the 16th century; superseded by *remnant.* Chaucer has, in the Prologue, LEGEND OF GOOD WOMEN (1385): *Fyrst sat the god of love and thanne this queene . . . And sithyn al the remenant by and by.*

rementimutation. See *mentimutation.*

remora. A sucking-fish, little but believed to have the power to stop a ship. Spenser in his VISION OF THE WORLD'S VANITY (1591) says: *There clove unto her keele A little fish, that men call remora, Which stopt her course.* The accent is evidently on the *rem.* The word was common in the 17th and 18th centuries, in the general sense of an obstacle, of something that held one back. *That authoritie,* said Edmonds in his OBSERVATIONS (1604) to Caesar's COMMENTARIES, *was a remora to divers other nations of Gallia from shewing that defection by plaine and open revolt.*

renay. See *reny.*

renitency. Resistance, especially to constraint or compulsion. Also *renitence, renitation.* Latin *re,* back + *niti,* to struggle. Hence, to *renite,* to resist. *I dare say,* said Nathaniel Ward in THE SIMPLE COBLER OF AGAWAM (1647), *they that most* *renite will least repent.* Also *renitent,* recalcitrant; offering physical resistance, hard. THE EDINBURGH REVIEW of July 1882 noted: *The gaps left by renitent warriors were rapidly filled by intending plunderers*: the story of any war.

reny. To renounce; recant; refuse, say no. Also *renay,* related to *renegue* and to *deny;* Latin *renegare* (*denegare*); *re,* back, *de,* down + *negare, negatum,* to say no; *ne,* not + root *ag,* say—whence also *negative.* Thus (14th century) *renayrie, renoyrie,* apostasy; a *renay* (*reney, renye*), a *renegade,* apostate. Capgrave in the LIFE OF SAINT KATHERINE (1440) said: *We have heere a mayde whiche with obstinacye reneyeth oure lawes.* One of Shakespeare's songs in THE PASSIONATE PILGRIM (1597) runs: *My flocks feed not, My ewes breed not, My rams speed not; All is amiss. Love's denying, Faith's defying, Heart's renying, Causer of this. All my merry jigs are quite forgot, All my lady's love is lost, God wot.*

reose. To fall. In BEOWULF, and until the 13th century. Also *rese.*

reptitious. Creeping; "by privy means getting to high estate" (Blount, 1661). Also *reptant, reptatorial, reptatory,* creeping. Also creeping, but used of persons unable to rise to lofty ideas, is *repent* (accent on the *ree*); Evelyn in a letter to the other diarist, PEPYS, on 8 June, 1684, wrote: *He bravely enlarges the empire of our narrow speculations, and repent spirits, whose contemplations extend no further than their sense.* Latin *reptare,* frequentative of *repere, reptum,* to creep. Hence *reptation, reptility,* the act or habit of creeping. *Some serpents,* said C. Owen in his study of SERPENTS (1742) *are reptitious, creep on the belly; and some have feet.* Page Eve.

repugn. To oppose; to be contradictory; to offer resistance; to reject. Latin *re,* back + *pugnare, pugnatum,* to fight; whence also *impugn, pugnacious, pugilist;* Latin *pugna,* a battle. Hence, *repugnable,* that can be defeated or refuted. The root survives in *repugnance,* which meant (14th century) contradiction, then (15th century) opposition, resistance, before it reached, in the 17th century, the meaning of strong dislike it still carries. A 1457 Lichfield ordinance continues in effect *all other ordinaunces . . . which do not repugne to this ordinaunce.* Shakespeare in HAMLET (1601) uses *repugnant* to mean offering resistance; in HENRY VI, PART ONE: *My master's blushing cheeks When stubbornly he did repugn the truth.*

repumicate. To smooth, as with a pumicestone. Also *repumication;* Latin *pumicem,* pumice. R. Baron in THE CYPRIAN ACADEMY (1647) declared: *She that wanteth* [lacks] *a sleekestone to repumicate her linnen, will take a pibble.*

reremouse. See *rearmouse.*

rescous. An old form of *rescue* (14th to 17th century) both as noun and as verb. Bacon in THE ADVANCEMENT OF LEARNING (1605) speaks of *the ready rescussing of a mans selfe from scornes.*

resipiscence. Repentance; recognition of one's mistakes; turning to a better path or opinion. Latin *re,* again + *sapere,* to taste, to discern. Hence *resipiscent,* returning to a sound state of mind. Sir Thomas Browne in a letter of 1672 spoke of some one *so closely shut up within the holds of vice and iniquity, as not to find some escape by a postern of resipiscency.*

retchlessness. See *wretchlessness.*

rethe. Fierce, cruel; stern; strict; severe; terrible, dreadful. A common Old English word, used into the 15th century. Also *retheness,* fierceness, roughness; (in Scotland) eagerness. Often used of storms, and of the *rethe sea.*

rethor. An old variant of *rhetor,* a teacher of rhetoric; an orator; by extension, a windy speechifier. Also, a petty rhetorician or orator, a *rhetorculist* (17th century).

retiary. Pertaining to nets and webs; or to fighting with a net, like the Roman gladiatorial fighter with a net, the *retiarius.* Latin *rete,* a net. Used figuratively, as by Coleridge (see *illaqueate*) and Sir Thomas Browne in CHRISTIAN MORALS (1682): *Our inward antagonists, like retiary and laqueary combatants, with nets, frauds, and entanglements fall upon us.*

retromancy. See *aeromancy.*

revest. To clothe, to dress; applied especially (13th to 17th century) to ecclesiastics. Latin *re,* again (often merely emphatic) + *vestire,* to clothe. A common word, used also of things, as in a poem of Surrey's in Tottel's MISCELLANY (1547): *The pleasant plot revested green with warm.* Also, to *reinvest,* in the various senses of *invest.* From a mistaken notion that *revest* was the past participle (only), came a form *revesh, revess,* used from the late 14th into the 16th century; in 1555 it was said of a priest: *After he hath ravisshed himself in the vestry, he commeth forth to the aultare.*

revince. To refute, disprove. Latin *re,* back + *vincere,* to conquer. Hence also *revincible,* refutable. *The opinion of Copernicus,* said G. Watts in his translation (1640) of Bacon's DE AUGMENTIS SCIENTIARUM, *because it is not repugnant to the phenomena, cannot be revinced by astronomical principles.*

rex. See *reaks.*

rhabdomancy. See *aeromancy.*

rhapsody. Originally, an epic poem; especially, a book of the ILIAD or the ODYSSEY, which could be presented aloud at one time. In the 16th century, *rhapsody* came also to mean a miscellaneous collection, a confused gathering of things, or of poems, stories, etc.; a literary work of disconnected pieces; hence, any gathering, as when Sanderson in a sermon of 1647 spoke of *a cento and a rhapsody of uncircumcised nations.* Shakespeare in HAMLET (1601) speaks of a *rapsidie of words.* Addison in THE SPECTATOR (No. 46; 1711) remarked: *Thot would look like a rhapsody of nonsense to any body but myself.* The still current sense, of an exalted or exaggeratedly enthusiastic expression of feeling, came into wide use in the 18th century.

rhetorculist. See *rethor.*

rhinocerical. Heavy as a rhinoceros. Hence, heavy with money, rich. *Money,* says Shadwell in THE SQUIRE OF ALSATIA (1688), *the ready, the rhino. Thou shalt be rhinocerical, my lad.* The origin of *rhino,* slang for money from the 17th century, is unknown; it suffices to have it. *Rhinocerical* was used in THE TATLER (No. 260, 1710) to mean retroussé: *the little rhinocerical nose.* (*Rhinoceros* is from Greek *rhino,* nose + *keras,* horn. A *rhinobyon* is a nose-plug, as used by doctors and savages.)

rhonchisonant. Scoffing, mocking; making a sound like a snort. Greek *rhonchos,* a snore, a snort. The word *rhonchisonant* is found only in 17th and 18th century dictionaries; persons of the sort are more persistent.

rhopalic. Club-like. Greek *rhopalos,* a club. From the shape of the club—growing thicker toward one end—the word is applied to a line of poetry in which each word has one more syllable than its predecessor. Thus in MACMILLAN'S MAGAZINE of 15 November, 1862, we learn: *Taking this line . . . 'Goose, gather metrical monstrosities,' anyone who chooses may employ himself in searching for the instances of unconscious rhopalism in Shakespeare, Milton, or Wordsworth.*

rhyparography. The painting of mean or sordid subjects. From Greek *rhyparos,* filthy. *Rhyparography,* in Smith's DICTIONARY OF GREEK AND ROMAN ANTIQUITIES (1842) is linked with pornography; but sometimes it is synonymous with still-life or genre painting. Saintsbury in his NINETEENTH CENTURY LITERATURE (1896) uses it of descriptive writing: *The Lousiad (a perfect triumph of cleverness expended on what the Greeks called rhyparography).* Also *rhypography.* Hence *rhypographic; rhypographer, rhypographist,* a painter of mean subjects; Motteux in his translation (1694) of Rabelais speaks of the post of *puny riparographer, or riffraff-scribler of the sect of Pyrricus.* Greek *rhypos,* dirt, filth; but Greek *rhyptein,* to cleanse. Hence (17th and 18th centuries) *rhyptical,* cleansing; a *rhyptic,* a cleanser.

rhyptic. See *rhyparography.*

ribaudred. This word, called a "corrupt" reading in Shakespeare's ANTONY AND CLEOPATRA (for the passage, see *nag*), is probably a participle form coined from *ribaudery, ribaudrie,* variants of *ribaldry.* Thus it would mean bent upon ribaldry, rendered ribald, debauched.

ribibe. See *rebeck.*

ridibund. Easily stirred to laughter. Also *ridibundal;* Latin *ridere, risum,* to laugh, whence also *ridiculous, derision.* To *ridiculize* (17th century), to make ridiculous; *ridicle,* a 15th century form of *ridicule.* Urquhart in THE JEWEL (1652) said: *With no less impetuosity of ridibundal passion . . . she fell back in a swoon.*

riggish. Wanton, licentious. One meaning of *rig* (from the late 16th century) is a wanton woman; also *rigmutton; cp. lace. Nay fy on thee thou rampe, thou ryg,* we read in GAMMER GURTON'S NEEDLE (1575). Shakespeare in ANTONY AND CLEOPATRA (1606) has the Egyptian queen praised: *For vildest things Become themselves* [are seemly] *in her, that the holy priests Bless her, when she is riggish.* Also *riggite,* a mocker, one that makes game of others. Franklin in his AUTOBIOGRAPHY (1788) says: *My being esteemed a pretty good riggite, that is a jocular verbal satirist, supported my consequence in the society.*

rigmarole. Also *rig-my-role, riggmonrowle,* and the like. See *ragman.* Byron in DON JUAN (1818) declares: *His speech was a fine sample, on the whole, Of rhetoric, which the learn'd call rigmarole.* Hence *rigmarolery; rigmarolic, rigmarolish.*

rigol. A ring or circle. French *rigole,* water-course; hence gutter, groove. Also *riggal, regal.* Shakespeare in THE RAPE OF LUCRECE (1593) says: *About the mourning and congealed face Of that blacke bloud, a watrie rigoll goes, Which seems to weep upon the tainted place.*

rim. A membrane. (This is a different word from *rim,* edge, border.) Thus *rimside,* the flesh-side of a skin. Also, short for *rim of the belly,* the peritoneum. In the 16th century, *rim-burst, rymbirst, rumbursin,* a rupture. Shakespeare in HENRY V (1599) says: *I will fetch thy rymme out at thy throat, in droppes of crimson blood.* A gory thought!

ring. Used in various combinations. *ring-carrier,* a go-between. *ring-chopper,* a swindler that uses a worthless ring; also *ring-dropper, ring-faller.* The method was to drop a ring, pretend to find it (preferably, just as another also eyed it), then try to sell it as of great value. Hence also *ring-dropping.* The *ring-faller* is described in THE FRATERNITYE OF VACABONDES (1575). Southey in 1825 called ring-dropping stale, and in 1851 Mayhew (in LONDON LABOUR AND THE LONDON POOR) described a new technique. *ring-pigger* (16th century), a drunkard. *ring-time,* spring, the season when lovers dance in, and exchange, rings; Shakespeare in AS YOU LIKE IT (1600) has: *In the spring time, the onely pretty ring time, when birds do sing hey ding a ding ding.* What is so rare as a day in June?

ringo. See *eryngo.*

rishews. A dish of fruit. Also *ruschewes; cp. raynecles.* A recipe is in THE FORME OF CURY (1390): *Take fygges and raisons. Pyke hem, and waisshe hem in wyne. Grynde hem with apples and peeres ypared and ypiked clene; do thereto gode powdors, and hole spices. Make balles thereof. Frye in oyle, and serve hem forth.*

rivage. A bank, shore. Also *rive, ryve;* Old French *rive;* Latin *ripa,* bank; *rivus,* stream. Also (14th to 16th century) *rival, ryvaile, ryval,* a shore, a landing place. Persons living on opposite shores were *rivals;* they fished in the same stream, hence the current sense. An *arrival* (Latin *ar-, ad,* to) is a coming to the shore. Gower in the CONFESSIO AMANTIS (1390) wrote of *the hihe festes of Neptune Upon the stronde at the rivage.* Thus (17th century) *rival,* a small stream; *rivalet,* a rivulet.

rival. See *rivage.*

rixle. To reign, rulé; to prevail. Also *rixlan, rixlen, ryxle, ryxlie.* Old English *rixian,* to rule. The ANCREN REWLE (1225) observed: *Thus, lo! in everiche stat rixleth bitternesse.*

roat. See *rote.*

roborate. To ratify, confirm; to strengthen, invigorate; to harden. Latin *roborare, roboratum,* to strengthen; *robur, roboris (robustus),* hard (oak) wood; hence, strength. Hence *roborant,* strengthening, fortifying. Also (in 17th and 18th century dictionaries) *roborean, roboreous,* made of oak, or of the nature of oak or hard wood. *To what end served those false mirables of the magicians,* inquired John Gaule in THE MAGASTROMANCER (1651), *but to roborate or harden Pharaoh's heart?* From the same root come the more current *robust, robustious, robustic, robustful, robustous, robustuous.*

roc. An Eastern legendary bird, of enormous size and strength. Also *rock, roche, roque, ruc, ruch, rukh.* Arabic *rukh;* the bird is mentioned in Marco Polo's account of Madagascar, but is more familiar from the ARABIAN NIGHTS, in which—among other exploits—it carries off Sindbad the Sailor. The *roc's egg,* something unattainable; Thackeray in THE NEWCOMES (1855) says: *I might wish for the roc's egg.*

rocambole. Something that adds flavor of piquancy. Vanbrugh in THE FALSE FRIEND (1702) declared: *Difficulties are the rocombolle of love; I never valued an easy conquest.* Also *roccombo, rockenbole, rockanbowl, rocombole.* Literally, a kind of leek, Spanish garlic. A. Austey in THE NEW BATH GUIDE (1766) wrote of a man a woman must detest, who *puffs his vile* *rocambol breath in her face*; but Evelyn in ACETARIA, OR A DISCOURSE OF SALLETS [Salads] (1699) desired *a light touch on the dish, much better supplied by the gentler roccombo.*

roche. A rock; a cliff; a rocky height; a huge mass of stone. Old French *roche, rocque,* whence *rock.* Also *roch, roach*; *cp. roc.* Used from the 13th to the 17th century. Also (15th century) *roche,* a French wine, *Roche* being a common place-name in France. GENESIS AND EXODUS (1250) stated: *Jhesus was . . . biried in the roche cold;* the AGENBITE OF INWIT (1340) said figuratively: *The ilke roche is Jesu Crist him-zelf.*

rochet. An outer garment; especially, a bishop's linen surplice. Hence, *a rochet, a rocheter,* a bishop, a prelate. Also *rechet, rachet, ratchet, rotchet, rogett,* and more. Skelton in COLYN CLOUTE (WORKES; 1529) satirizes the luxury of the clergy: *In rotchettes of fine raynes, Whyte as morowes mylke Their tabertes* [tabards] *of fine silke, Their stirops of mixt gold begarred; There may no cost be spared. Their moyles* [mules] *golde doth eate; theyr neyghbours dye for meat. raynes* (*reines, raines*), a fine linen made at *Rennes,* Brittany. *morowes,* the morrow's, next morning's. *begarred,* variegated (?); French *bigarrer,* Scotch *begary,* to variegate.

rode. I As a verb. (1) To clear a dyke or stream of weeds (17th century, when from Dutch *roede,* a ten-foot measuring rod, *rode* was also used as a noun meaning a length of dyke or channel). (2) To fly at evening, as wild fowl toward land, or the woodcock in mating-time; Bensusan in his WILD LIFE STORIES (1907) said: *When a woodcock is roding, he must not vary his pace, his flight, or his song.* II As a noun. A variant form of (1) *read* (2) *road* (3) *rood* (4) *rud. Rud* (from the 10th to the 16th century; also *rudde, rode, rude*; related to *red*) meant ruddiness; thence, complexion. When the fair queen (*cp. levedi*; *urn*) was borne to her chamber, Orfeo exclaimed: *Allas! thy rode, that was so red, Is al wan as thou were ded.* Chaucer (1386) spelled it *rode*; Skelton (1529), *ruddys.*

roger. From the name came various other uses. (1) A begging vagabond claiming to be a poor scholar from Oxford or Cambridge. Apparently in this sense the *g* was hard; perhaps the word was related to *rogue.* In the following senses, the *g* was soft. (2) A phallus. So used in Urquhart's translation (1653) of Rabelais. Hence, *to roger,* to have intercourse; for an illustration of this use (which puns on the name *Roger*) see *ragmatical.* (3) In phrases. *The Jolly Roger,* the pirates' flag, a white skull with two crossed bones beneath, on a black field. *Roger's blast,* a whirling up of dust, somewhat as a water-spout, foreboding rain. In East Anglia, 19th century. Also, *a roger, a Sir Rodger. Roger de Coverley,* a country dance; also, *Sir Roger.* At first called *Roger of Coverley*; the name was changed under the influence of the popular *Sir Roger de Coverley* introduced by Addison in THE SPECTATOR (1711).

roin. See *roynish.*

rokelay. See *roquelaure.*

romage. An earlier form of *rummage, q.v.* Shakespeare has, in HAMLET (1601): *This, I take it, is . . . the chief head Of this post-hast and romage in the land.*

romal. A handkerchief, sometimes used as a headdress; specifically, the handkerchief used by the Indian thugs to strangle their victims. From Persian *rumal; ru,* face + *mal,* wiping. We are told by Sleeman in the RAMASEEANA (1836): *It was Fatima who invented the use of the roomal to strangle the great demon Rukut-beej-dana.*

ronyon. See *aroint.*

roorback. A false story circulated for political ends. Also *roorbach.* This term was used in the U.S. in the 19th century, after a story of 1844 pretending to be an extract from the *Travels of Baron Roorbach.* The BOSTON JOURNAL of 6 September, 1884, reported: *The Herald and the Globe abound in roorbacks which are designed to influence the vote in Maine.* And as Maine goes . . .

roose. Boasting, vainglory; a brag. So used from the 12th to the 15th century. In the 13th century it took on also the more moderate meaning, commendation, praise. Also *ros, rose, roos, royse, rowze; ruse; reouse, reeze, rease,* and more. Hence *to roose,* to boast; to praise; to flatter. A *rooser,* a braggart. A Towneley mystery of 1460 lists *the leg of a goys, With checkyns endorde, pork, partryk, to roys* (to boast, or to roast?). In the ballad of YOUNG ALLAN we read: *Some there reasd their hawk, their hawk, And some there reased their hound.* The Greek saying, Count no man happy until he is dead, has milder Saxon counterpart in the advice, *Ruse the fair day at night.*

ropery. Trickery, knavery. In Shakespeare's ROMEO AND JULIET (1592) the Nurse inquires: *I pray you sir, what sawcie merchant was this that was so full of his roperie?* In Fletcher's play THE CHANCES (1620) *ropery* in the first edition is replaced in the second folio by *roguery.*

roquelaure. A cloak of knee length worn by men in the 18th and early 19th centuries. Also *roccelo, rockalow,* and the like. Named from the French *Duke of Roquelaure* (1656-1738). Sterne in TRISTRAM SHANDY (1760) speaks of *wrapping myself up warm in my roquelaure, and paying a visit to this poor gentleman.* After the same duke, a short cloak worn by women was called a *rokelay.* Scott, in WAVERLEY (1814) has his heroine *put on her clean toy, rokelay, and scarlet plaid.*

rorid. Dewy; like dew. Latin *roridus; ros, rorem,* dew. Dekker in the SATIROMASTIX (1602) speaks of *rorid cloudes being suckt into the ayre.* Also *roscid,* dewy; *roscidating,* having a dewy or cooling effect. Hence also *roral,* dewy, *rorant,* falling like dew. Rawley, in his translation (1638) of Bacon's LIFE AND DEATH speaks of *refrigeratours which passe not by the stomach; drinkes roscidating, or engendering oyly juyces.*

rosasolis. A cordial of the juice of the sundew. Latin *rosa solis,* rose of the sun, originally *ros solis,* dew of the sun. Because of its medicinal use, the drink has also been called *rose of solace.* Later it was made not of the plant sundew, but of brandy, sugar, and spices. The drink was popular from the mid-16th to the mid-18th century.

roscid. See *rorid.*

rosee. A dish, flavored with rose-petals. Also, *rose, roseye.* In 14th and 15th century cookbooks are several inviting recipes. One is a spiced mixture of dates and nuts. Another says: *Take the flowris of rosys, and wasch hem wel in water, and after bray hem wel in a morter; and then tak almondys, and temper hem, and seth hem; and after take flesch of capons, or of hennys, and hac yt smale, and then bray hem wel in a morter, and than do yt in the rose, so that the flesch acorde* *wyth the mylk, and so that the mete be charchaunt; and after do yt to the fyre to boyle, and do thereto sugur and safron, that yt be wel ycolowrd, and rosy of levys and of the forseyde flowrys, and serve it forth.* Another recipe begins: *Take red roses, and grynd fayre in a morter with almaunde mylke.* Oh, the lost treats of Old England!

rote. (1) A medieval musical stringed instrument. The O.E.D. calls it "probably of the violin class"; Nares states that it is named *from the wheel (rota) which is turned to cause the vibration of the strings.* Spenser in THE FAËRIE QUEENE (1590) speaks of something as *worthy of great Phoebus' rote.* (2) Custom, habit; mechanical performance, surviving in the phrase *by rote,* by routine, by mere memory; also, by heart, with precision. For an illustration of this use, see *fescue.* (3) A squadron, company. (4) A wheel used as an instrument of torture. (5) The roaring of the sea. (6) A variant form of *rotten,* as in Chaucer's THE SECOND NUN'S TALE (1386) *Idilnesse is rote slogardye.* Shakespeare in CORIOLANUS (1607) uses the verbal form of sense (2): *Such words that are but roated in your memory.*

rother. An ox. Also *rother-beast; hryther, reother, ruther, rudder.* Hence, *rotheren,* relating or belonging to cattle; *rotherish,* resembling cattle. Used from the 9th to the early 17th century. Shakespeare in TIMON OF ATHENS (1605) says: *It is the pasture lards the rothers sides.*

rouk. (1) Mist, fog; steam. Also *roke* and *rook*; related to *reek.* (2) In the phrase *rouk and roun(d),* to talk privately. Hence *rouker,* a whisperer, tale-bearer. The RATIS RAVING (1500) declared that *a woman should . . . with no young men rouk na roune.* A *roun* is a mysterious saying, or a secret; a *rune*; 10th to 14th century, a writing (book or letter) or counsel, especially private or secret.

roun. See *rouk.*

rounce robble hobble. A representation of the tumult of thunder, in Stanyhurst's translation (1582) of the ÆNEIS: *A clapping fyerbolt (such as oft, with rownce robel hobble, Jove to the ground clatreth).* Later writers mockingly mimicked the roaring: Nashe, in Greene's MENAPHON (1589): *Then did he make heavens vault to rebounde, with rounce robble hobble of ruffe raffe roaring, and thwick thwack thurlery bouncing;* Jonson, in THE MASQUE OF QUEENES (1616): *Rouncy is over, robble is under, A flash of light and a clap of thunder.*

rouncival. Heroic (in size, volume); hence applied as noun or adjective to various large things. Also *rownseval, rownsifall, rounsefal, rouncifold, runsivill,* and the like. We are told that certain large bones of antediluvian animals were formerly taken to be bones of the heroes that fell with Roland at *Roncesvalles; hereof, I take it,* said Mandeville, *it comes that, seeing a great woman, we say she is a rouncival.* Blount in his 1674 wordbook suggests that the large 'marrowfat' *rouncival pea* is so called because it first came from *Roncesvalles* "at the foot of the Pyrenean Mountains." *Dost roare?* queried Dekker in SATIROMASTIX (1602); *th'ast a good rouncivall voice to cry Lanthorne and candle-light.* As a noun, the word was applied to (1) a heavy fall, a crash; (2) a kind of 'tumbling verse,' used for invective or flyting, not rhymed but alliterative; (3) a monster; (4) a large and boisterous or loose woman. Nashe in HAVE WITH YOU TO SAFFRON-WALDEN (1596) pictured *so fulsome a fat bonarobe and terrible rouncevall.*

rouncy. A horse, especially one for riding. A common medieval form, its origin unknown. In English 14th into the 16th century; revived in the 19th, as in Browning's ARISTOPHANES' APOLOGY (1875): *Race-horse sired, not rouncy born.* Also see *rounce robble hobble.*

rout. Besides the current sense of disorderly retreat of a defeated army, *rout* (via Old French from Latin *rupta,* a detachment; *rumpere, ruptum,* to break) had a range of meanings. A company, assemblage; Chaucer in THE KNIGHT'S TALE (1386) says: *To the palace rode there many a route of lordes.* A flock or pack of animals; a large number of things; Chaucer, in THE ROMAUNT OF THE ROSE (1366): *to pulle a rose of all that route to bere in my honde about.* Hence *in rout,* in order; *in a rout,* in a body, in a troop. The meaning of precipitate and disorderly retreat did not develop until the end of the 16th century (e.g., Shakespeare, CYMBELINE, 1611: *Then beganne . . . a rowt, confusion thicke: forthwith they flye*), but by the 13th century the word had developed unfavorable connotations. A disorderly or disreputable crowd. (By 14th century law) a gathering of three or more persons with criminal intent. The rabble; especially, *the common rowt* (Shakespeare, THE COMEDY OF ERRORS), *the vulgar rout.* Hence, a riot, disturbance, uproar. Also, a clamor, a fuss; especially (17th-19th century), *to make a rout about* something. Also, sway, influence; *to rule the rout, to bear the rout,* to have full control. And in the 18th and 19th centuries *rout* became (by humor, from the sense of disorderly crowd) a very common word for a fashionable gathering, a large evening party (Fielding, in AMELIA, 1742; Johnson, 1751; Smollett, 1771; Kinglsey, 1858; Ruskin, 1887). Hence such combinations as *rout-cake,* a rich cake for a reception or party; Thackeray in VANITY FAIR (1848) boasts: *He managed a couple of plates full of strawberries and cream, and twenty-four little rout cakes. Rout-seat, rout-chair,* benches or folding chairs brought in for the party; *rout-glasses, rout-china,* and the like. Little wonder Lady Lennox in her LIFE AND LETTERS (1767) sighed: *I own I am wore to death with routing.* As Hood remarks in MISS KILMANSEGG (1845): *For one of the pleasures of having a rout Is the pleasure of having it over.*

roynish. Scabby, covered with scurf; hence, coarse, base. Used since the 14th century; also, *roinish; roinous; roynyshe; runyous, roignous, royneous.* Chaucer uses the noun *roin,* a scab, in THE ROMAUNT OF THE ROSE (1366): *Hir nekke was of good fasoun . . . Withoute bleyne, scabbe, or royne.* The form *roin* was also used as a verb, 14th to 17th century, meaning (1) to clip, cut short; (2) to growl—so used by Spenser in THE FAËRIE QUEENE (1596; V ix 33). Shakespeare in AS YOU LIKE IT (1600) speaks of *the roynish clown, at whom so oft Your Grace was wont to laugh.*

rubetude. See *rubicund.*

rubiator. See *rabiator.* The form *rubiator* was fairly common in the 16th century.

rubible. See *rebeck.*

rubicund. Reddish, flushed; said especially of a highly colored countenance, the result of good living or good eating. *The attics,* said Bulwer-Lytton in PELHAM (1827), *were thronged with rubicund damsels.* There were many terms from Latin *ruber,* red, from pale pink to deep ruby. See *rubious.* Among them: *rube-*

facient, making one red, as a paint, an irritant, or a blush; *rubefacience, rubefaction. rubelet,* a small red gem. *rubent,* reddening. *rubescent,* turning red; blushing. *rubetude,* redness. *rubicundity,* redness of face from health and good living. *rubiferous,* reddish. *rubific,* producing redness; also *rubificative*; *to rubify.* Akin to these forms are those from Latin *rubigo, rubiginem,* rust: English *rubiginous, rubiginose,* rust-colored. *Rubiginy* is rustiness, but *rubigo* (16th century) is the organ of masculinity. Also *rubious,* ruby-colored. *rubor,* redness; *cp. rubric.* Shakespeare in PERICLES (1608) says that Marina is such a deft worker with the needle *that even her art sisters the natural roses; Her inkle, silke, twin with the rubied cherry.*

rubiginy. See *rubicund.*

rubious. See *rubicund.* Another word (16th and 17th centuries) for *ruby* is *rubine,* whence *rubineous,* of "the red splendour of the ruby." Shakespeare (followed by Keats and Meredith) uses *rubious,* in TWELFTH NIGHT (1601): *Dianas lip is not more smooth and rubious.*

rubric. Red earth or red ochre; thence, applied to various items usually marked or written in red; a heading of a chapter or other division of a book, hence any heading; a direction for the divine service in liturgical books; an entry on a church calendar, hence, a calendar of saints. Occasionally *rubric* was used as a verb, meaning to mark or print in red, instead of the more common *rubricate,* with the variant form *rubrish.* Hence also *rubrication*; *rubricator.* A *rubricist* is one that adheres to the letter of the (liturgical) *rubric.*

ruction. See *ruption.*

rud. See *rode.*

rudera. Ruins of a building, rubble, debris. Latin *rudus,* plural *rudera,* broken stone. The BRITISH CRITIC in 1798 gave *the author's reasons for asserting . . . though it does not appear in the rudera, that chimneys were common in the Roman houses.* Hence *ruderal,* growing in (or through) stone-rubble; *ruderary,* pertaining to rubble; *ruderous,* abounding in rubble. *To ruderate,* to cast upon rubble. Note that *ruderation,* however, is the making of a pavement, a wall, etc., with many rough pebbles in mortar.

rudesby. A rude person; one that is insolent or disorderly in his conduct. Drant in his translation (1567) of Horace's EPISTLES wrote: *To bearebaytinges or pricke playings our rudesbies must away.* Used in the 16th and 17th centuries, the word was renewed by Scott in THE MONASTERY (1820): *commoved by the speech of this rudesby.*

rudity. A late 16th and early 17th century form, meaning rudeness. In the 18th and 19th century, *rudish* was used to mean somewhat rude, as in Carlyle's REMINISCENCES (1881): *Nothing but rudish hands, rude though kind enough, being about.*

rue. The shrub grew tangled with the old Saxon word *rue,* sorrow, also a verb, *to rue,* to regret: *to rue the day.* Hence the rue symbolized bitterness, grief, repentance; later, pity, forgiveness. Under the name *herb of grace,* it was used to exorcise the devil or ward off the evil eye. Among the ancients, rue was used as a protection against poison; in 14th century England it was regarded as a cure-all. English law courts were strewn with rue, as a protection against contagion or vermin. In the 16th century, the bush was used to test the faithfulness of an absent lover, while chewing a leaf gave the beloved at home strength to resist temptation. Thus a punning 18th century proverb ran: *Rue in thyme should be a maiden's posie.*

ruff. Among the numerous meanings of this noun, we may note: (1) a *ruffle,* a circular frill on a sleeve (15th century); also, a fluted starched cloth worn stiff out around the neck, especially in the reigns of Elizabeth I and James I. Hence, *the wooden ruff,* the pillory. (2) a card game, also *ruff and honours,* in vogue 1590-1630; also, trumping, in a card game. (3) a roll on a drum. (4) a candle, candlewick. (5) a blockhead (17th century). (6) the highest degree of arousal or excitement: *in the ruff of . . .* In his FABLES (1692) L'Estrange exclaimed: *How many emperours and princes . . . in the ruff of all their glory have been taken down. In ruff, in (the) high ruff,* in fine spirits; *in a ruff,* in a passion. Hence, excitement, passion, vigor. Guilpin in SKIALETHEIA ("SHADOW OF TRUTH"; 1598) cried: *Hence with these fidlers, whose oyle-buttred lines Are panders unto lusts, and food to sinnes, Their whimpring sonnets, puling elegies, Slaunder the Muses, make the world despise Admired Poesie, marre resolutions ruffe, And melt true valour with lewd ballad stuffe.*

ruffler. Also *ruffeler.* See *pedlers French.*

rugose. Wrinkled. Also *rugous; rugosous* (with very many wrinkles); *rugate; rugulous, rugulose,* slightly wrinkled; with small wrinkles. Hence *rugosity.* Latin *ruga,* wrinkle (plural *rugae*) is also used in English; also *ruge.* The 17th century used a verb *to ruge,* to wrinkle.

rum. A number of compounds have developed from this word. I. From the sound (as of beating time). As a refrain, *rumbelow* (also *rumbolo, rumbillow, rumbylogh, rumbeloo,* etc.) used from the 14th to the 17th century, especially in sailor songs, to time their rowing and the like. Also *rumbelow* (14th and 15th centuries), a blow; (16th century) a resounding noise, a tumult; (17th century) a loose woman. The 19th century, as a refrain, favored such compounds as *rumptytumpty; rumptydum; rump-te-iddity.* Also *rumtum,* a prank, a practical joke. *rumgumption, rumblegumption,* common sense. *rumgumptious* (occasionally *rumgumshaws*), blunt and surly, speaking with a chip on one's shoulder. II. From *rum,* the strong drink made first in the West Indies, from sugar-cane. *rumbullion, rumbustion* (17th century) a potent rum drink, also called *kill-devil. rumbustious,* boisterous. *rumbo* (18th century) a strong rum punch. *rumbowling* (19th century), an inferior or adulterated drink; hence, anything inferior. Also in the 19th century, perhaps as a development from *rumbustion,* the drink *rumfustian* was popular, as a nightcap; its formula: the yolks of twelve eggs, a quart of strong (home-brewed) beer, a bottle of white wine, half a pint of gin, a grated nutmeg, the juice of a lemon-peel or orange-peel, a small quantity of cinnamon, and sugar to sweeten it.

rume. An old form of *room.* In the quotation at *wamble,* it stands for *rumor* or *rumble,* a noisy stir.

rummage. Originally, the stowing or arranging of casks in the hold of a vessel; the place of storage or stowage. By extension, miscellaneous articles; rubbish. Hence, *a rummage sale,* still current. Also bustle; turmoil. So used (in the form *romage, q.v.*) by Shakespeare. Also, a search; especially, a thorough search of a vessel by a customs officer. The verb (from the mid-15th century) had the same basic meanings: to arrange, as in the hold of a ship, to put in order; to search, *rummage through,* examine thoroughly; hence to disarrange, disorder; to rout out by searching; to turn or move about restlessly, as when Tennyson in a poem (WALK TO THE MAIL) of 1842 speaks of *a jolly ghost, that . . . tapt at doors, And rummaged like a rat.*

rumney. A sweet wine of Greece, popular in England in the 15th and 16th centuries. From *Romania,* used as the name of Greece.

rump. Used in several combinations: *rump-fed* (Shakespeare, MACBETH; 1606), probably means fed on rump (ham); but Nares (1882) suggested that it means fed or fattened in the rump. *rump-proud,* wanton; used in the late 16th century; *cp. callipygean. rump-roll,* a bustle on a dress; *cp. dress-improver.*

runagate. A variant, from the 16th century, of *renegate, renegade.* Also *runagade, runagado.* The change from *renegate* came by association with *run,* as in running away to the other side. *He is circumcised,* noted W. Davies in his TRAVELS (1614), *denying his Christian name, so that ever after he is called a runagado.*

runcation. Weeding. Evelyn in SYLVA (1664) gave suggestions *for the more commodious runcation, hawing, and dressing the trees.*

runnion. See *aroint.*

rupellary. Rocky. Latin *rupes,* rock. *rupestral, rupestrean, rupestrine,* relating to, growing or living among, or carved or written on rocks. Also *rupicoline, rupicolous,* dwelling among rocks. Evelyn in his DIARY of 27 February, 1700, noted: *In this rupellary nidary do the fowle lay eggs and breede.*

ruptile. Easily broken. Used in botany of parts that break irregularly, not along the lines of junction. Also *to rupt,* to break, to burst; to nullify. Latin *rumpere, ruptum,* to break, whence also *disrupt, eruption, rupture*; *ruption* (15th century), breach of the peace; not the synonymous *ruction,* of obscure origin; THE SPECTATOR of 27 December, 1891, spoke of *whisky, which produces motiveless ructions at fairs and social gatherings.*

rurigenous. Rustic; literally, born in the country. *Cp. montigenous.* Thus Edward Du Bois in A PIECE OF FAMILY BIOGRAPHY (1799) declares that *rurigenous cook-maids, and automatical bankers' clerks may take care of their autography.* Some 17th and 18th century dictionaries also give the form *rurigene,* born or abiding in the country.

ruse. See *roose.*

rushring. A ring made of *rushes,* made for a sweetheart, but deceitfully used for a wedding ring "by designing men." Quarles in THE SHEPHERDS ORACLES (1646) declared: *The lovesick swains Compose rushrings and myrtleberry chains*; Davenant in THE RIVALS (WORKS; 1668): *I'l crown thee with a garland of straw tnen, and I'le marry thee with a rush ring.*

ruskin. (1) A fur; used from the 13th to the mid-16th century. In A TREATYSE OF A GALAUNT (1550) we read: *Thou ruskyn galaunt, that poverte doth menace, For all thy warrocked hoode and thy proude araye.* (2) A container made of bark or roots; also, butter kept in such a vessel. Irish *rusg,* bark. D'Urfey in his PILLS TO PURGE MELANCHOLY (1719) said: *I have* *ruscan and cream joy, wherewith you may slabber you.* (3) A small *rusk,* a piece of crisp toasted bread. (4) In *Ruskin linen; Ruskin pottery, Ruskin ware*: after *John Ruskin* (1819-1900), who believed in combining utility and art.

ruth. See *couth.* This common Middle English word had many forms, among them *routhe, roth, reouth, rowith, rewth*; it is related to *rue.* Its first meaning (12th century) was compassion, pity, as in the phrase *to have ruth.* This sense is occasionally used in archaic diction, and survives in the form *ruthless*—apart from my most ruthful sister and the Biblical widow amid the alien corn. Later, *ruth* also meant repentance, remorse; then something to be sorry about; by extension, calamity, ruin, as when Nashe and Marlowe wrote in DIDO (1594): *Yet now I do repent me of his ruth, And wish that I had never wronged him so. ruthfulness,* sorrowfulness; *ruthness* compassion. *cp. wrouth. ruthful* meant either feeling or deserving pity; Shakespeare uses it in the latter sense in TITUS ANDRONICUS (1588): *Complots of mischief, treason, villainies ruthful to hear.*

ryke. Realm. German *Reich,* kingdom. Not in O.E.D. In the first SHEPHERDS' PLAY (TOWNELEY MYSTERIES, 1460) we read: 1st Shepherd: *I am ever alyke, wote I never what it gars, Is none in this ryke a shepherd fares wars* [worse]. 2d Shepherd: *Poore men are in the dyke And oft tyme mars; The world is slyke* [such like], *also helpars Is none here.* 1st Shepherd: *It is sayde fulle ryfe 'A man may not wyfe And also thryfe* [thrive] *And alle in a yere'.*

ryne. A 14th and 15th century contraction for *Rhenish wine.*

rynt. To give way; stand aside. Related to *aroint, q.v.* Also *rhint, roint, roynt.* Ray in 1674 recorded as proverbial *Rynt you, witch, quoth Besse Locket to her mother*; but *Rynt thee!* was the milkmaid's dismissal to a cow as she finished milking it.

ryptage. A Portuguese wine, imported into England in the 15th century.

S

Sabine. (1) A member of the Sabian race, who in ancient Italy occupied the central region of the Appenines; near the valley-folk, the Hernici, beyond whom on the next range of hills were the Volscians. Used in English especially in reference to the proverb *Sabini quod volunt somniant,* the Sabines dream what they will. (This by anticipation winks at Freud.) Holland used the idea figuratively, when in 1610 he spoke of the town *Grimsby, which our Sabins, following their own fancies, will have to be so called of one Grime a merchant.* (2) As an adjective, especially in the phrase *Sabine farm,* a gentleman's (recreational) farm, a pleasant retreat in the country. *Cp. pentice.* This is from the praises sung to his *Sabine farm* by the poet Horace (Quintus Horatius Flaccus, 65-8 B.C.), who received from the wealthy Maecenas the gift of a villa in the Sabine Hills. And there were, still earlier, the ravished *Sabine women* who gave sons to the founders of Rome.

sabulous. Sandy; consisting of or abounding in sand; growing in sandy places. Also *sabulose, sabuline.* Latin *sabulum,* also *saburra,* sand. Thence *saburration,* sand-bathing; *saburrate,* to bathe in sand, to ballast a ship (later, airship) with sandbags.

sack. See *sackbut.*

sackbut. (1) A musical instrument: a bass trumpet with a slide (like that of a trombone); used 15th to 18th century. Elyot in THE CASTEL OF HELTH (1533) recommends that *the entrayles . . . be exercised by blowyng, eyther by constraint, or playeng on shaulmes, or sackbottes.* The Geneva BIBLE (1560; DANIEL) translates Aramaic *sabbka* as *sackbut;* so also the King James (1611) and the Revised (1885) versions; the correct translation is *sambuca* (*q.v.*) as in the Septuagint and the Vulgate (Greek *sambuke*) versions. Also *sagbut, sagbout, shagbush, sackbutt.* With the same variety of forms, in the 17th century: (2) a butt of sack. A *butt* was a large cask (Late Latin *butta,* wineskin), of varying size; in the 15th century, 36 gallons; later, 108 to 140 gallons. Usually 108 gallons of ale, 126 of wine. Shakespeare in THE TEMPEST (1610) has: *I escaped upon a but of sacke, which the saylors heaved o'reboord. Sack* is a white wine, dry (French *vin sec,* dry wine). The two meanings were punned upon by playwrights, as in Fletcher's RULE A WIFE AND HAVE A WIFE (1624): *I' th' celler . . . he will make dainty music among the sackbutts.*

sackless. Secure, unmolested, unchallenged; hence, innocent (of); therefore harmless. Occasionally, by extension, feeble-minded; lacking energy. Also *sacklessly,* without just cause, innocently. Used from the 9th century. Douglas in the AENEIS (1513) spoke of a *citie sakles of batale, fre of all sic striffe.* Scott revived the word in IVANHOE (1819); BLACKWOOD'S

EDINBURGH MAGAZINE queried in 1831: *That you are sackless of this murder who shall testify?*

sad. The early uses of this word were quite different from its present sense of sorrowful, which first appeared in the late 14th century. The earliest meaning of *sad,* from the 10th century, was sated, full, weary (of): *sad of his company.* It is a common Teutonic word, Old Irish *satlech,* satiated, akin to Latin *satis,* enough; *satisfied.* By the early 14th century, other senses had developed: (1) Firm, strong; valiant; steadfast. Thus when Spenser in THE FAËRIE QUEENE (1590; III, 11) speaks of *sad lovers* he means constant ones. Milton in PARADISE LOST (1667) says: *Settl'd in his face I see Sad resolution and secure.* Fabyan in his CRONYCLE (1516) told the story of Prince Hal (which Shakespeare presents in HENRY IV); but when the Prince became Henry V, Fabyan continued, *sodainly he became a new man and tourned all that rage and wyldnes into sobernes and sadnes and the vyce into constant vertue.* Of things, *sad* meant firmly fixed; heavy (applied also to a blow, *a sad stroke*; to bread that hasn't risen properly; to a heavy rain and a fierce fire); dark in color; compact; solid (also as opposed to liquid; Wyclif in a Sermon of 1380 said: *Ther mete was ther bileve that thei hadden of sadde thingis, and ther drynke was ther bileve that thei hadden of moist thingis*). (2) Orderly; grave; trustworthy. Chaucer in THE MAN OF LAW'S TALE (1386) said: *In Surrey whilom dwelte a compaignye Of chapmen riche and therto sadde and trewe. Sad and wise, discreet,* or *true* made a frequent coupling; this may have helped form the line in Coleridge's THE ANCIENT MARINER (1798): *A sadder and a wiser man He rose the morrow morn.* (3) Dignified, grave in appearance. Chaucer in THE DETHE OF BLAUNCHE (1369) speaks of the *eyen my lady had, Debonayre, good, glad, and sad.* (4) Mature, serious; *in sad earnest* meant most seriously, as when one takes one's *solemn oath.* (5) Solidly learned; profound. The DESTRUCTION OF TROY (1400) spoke of *a philosoffer . . . In the syense full sad of the sevyn artes.* In the 17th century, from its sense of firm, solid, *sad* came to be used (6) as a term of emphasis, especially in a bad sense: wretched, abominably bad. Gay in THE BEGGAR'S OPERA (1727) says: *Our Polly is a sad slut.* As late as 1892 the London DAILY NEWS (January 25) called unpolished granite *a sad harbourer of soot and dust.* In this sense, application to a man in the phrase *a sad dog* was so frequent that the expression lost its force, especially if it was said with a smile. A *sadiron* was a solid iron, as opposed to a *box-iron.* In the 14th and 15th centuries, *to sad* meant to make solid or firm; to compress; to make steadfast; this was also the first application of *to sadden.* An agricultural work of 1600 stated that corn will grow better if *the ground be saddned a little in the bottom of every hole . . .* As they advised in the 14th century, Be sad to resist vice!

sadism. See *phalarism.*

St. Elmo's fire. See *corposant.*

St. Vitus' dance. A dancing mania, usually identified as chorea. Also St. Vitus's dance. *Cp. tarantism.*

sake. The original sense of this early and common Teuton word (also *sacu, sacke, sayck,* etc.) was a dispute, an offence; contention, crime. Hence a ground of accusation; *without sake,* without good reason. It was soon applied to a contention at law, a suit; and by the 13th century the expression *for the sake of . . .*, for the case (or cause) of . . . , had come to be used in the sense still current: *for her sake*. Hence also *for goodness' sake!* and the like.

salade. See *sallet*.

salamander. A lizard-like animal, supposedly immune to fire. (Benvenuto Cellini, 1500-1571, recorded that when he was a boy, his father boxed his ears, so that he would remember having seen one on his hearth.) Hence, a spirit living in the element fire; as the sylph, the air; the nymph, the water; the gnome, the earth —the four elements of medieval science. By extension, a firefighter, a soldier who braves fire in battle; a fire-eating performer; and in the 18th century, a woman that (so far as the world knows) resists temptations. Addison in THE SPECTATOR (1711; No. 198) observed: *A salamander is a kind of heroine in chastity, that treads upon fire . . .* Deloney in JACKE OF NEWBERIE (1597) uses the figure otherly: *Ile lay my life that as the salamander cannot live without the fire, so Jack cannot live without the smel of his dame's smock.*

salebrity. Ruggedness, unevenness. A shortened form (found only in 17th and 18th century dictionaries) of *salebrosity, salebrousness*. The adjective *salebrous*, rugged, was fairly frequent in the 17th century. Latin *salebrosus*; *salebra*, roughness, harshness; literally, a jolting place, from the root *sal*, leap. From the same root came *saliency*, leaping; *salience*, the quality of leaping forth, hence of standing out. Horatio Smith in THE MONEYED MAN (1841) said: *The great attenuation of the face . . . gave a singular saliency to the features.*

salep. See *saloop*.

salfay. The reward paid to one that finds and restores lost goods. Probably derived from *salvus*, saved. A 14th and 15th century word, worth restoring to the language.

saliency. See *salebrity*.

sallet. (1) An early form of *salad*. Also *selad, sallade, sallat, salette*, and more; Late Latin *salare, salatum*, to salt; *sal*, salt. Used figuratively to mean something mixed, usually with pleasant implications. Shakespeare in ALL'S WELL THAT ENDS WELL (1601) says: *She was the sweete margerom of the sallet, or rather the hearbe of grace*; and in HAMLET: *There was no sallets in the lines, to make the matter savoury*. By extension, *to pick a salad*, to do something trivial. *salad days*, days of green and inexperienced youth (Shakespeare, ANTONY AND CLEOPATRA). (2) A light globular helmet. Probably from Latin *caelata* (*galea*), ornamented (headpiece); *caelare, caelatum*, to engrave; *caelum*, a chisel. Shakespeare, in HENRY VI, PART TWO, says: *Many a time but for a sallet, my brainpan had bene cleft with a brown bill.* Heywood in EDWARD IV, PART ONE, uses it jestingly of a container: sack *sold by the sallet*. Also, by metonymy, the head; C. B. Stapylton in HERODIAN HIS IMPERIAL HISTORY (1652): *When wine was got into his drunken sallat*. The Spanish proverb has it, according to Abraham Hayward's THE ART OF DINING (1852) that it takes four persons to make a proper salad: a spendthrift for oil, a miser for vinegar, a counsellor for salt, and a madman to mix it. Then beware Gargantua!

Sally Lunn. A tea-cake or hot roll. Sold first at Bath about 1797 by Sally Lunn, who cried them through the town; then a baker named Dalmer bought her out;

he made a song for them that helped preserve the name. *Sally Lunns,* said the ENCYCLOPAEDIA OF COOKERY (1892), *should be cut open, well buttered, and served very hot.* Dickens smacks his lips over the Sally Lunn; Thackeray in PENDENNIS (1849) delights in *a meal of green tea, scandal, hot Sally-Lunn cakes, and a little novel-reading.*

salmagundy. A dish of fine-cut meat (or poultry), anchovies, eggs, onions, with spices and oil. Also *sallad-magundy, Solomon Gundy* (who, you remember, was born on Monday), *salmigundy.* Hence, any disorganized or haphazard mixture. T. Twining in RECREATIONS AND STUDIES (1761) inquired: *After all this salmagundis of quotation, can you bear another slice of Aristotle?* Washington Irving in 1807 wrote a book entitled *Salmagundi; or the Whim-whams and Opinions of L. Langstaff, Esq.*

saloop. A hot drink, of powdered *salep* (later of sassafras) with milk, ginger, and sugar, hawked in the London streets late at night and in the early morning. THE CENSOR of 1 December, 1803, remarked: *I was taking my pot of saloop, for I am not so extravagant as to drink coffee.* By 1851, Henry Mayhew observed in LONDON LABOUR AND THE LONDON POOR, *the saloop-stalls were superseded by the modern coffee-stalls.* Also *salop; a salop-house, Salopian-house,* where saloop was sold (used by Lamb in ESSAYS OF ELIA, 1822). The *salep* from which *saloop* was made, before native sassafras replaced it, was a meal made from ground tubers of orchidaceous plants. The word is from Arabic *thaleb,* the orchis, short for *khasyu'th-thalab,* fox's testicles, a folk name for the flower, as is the English *dogstones,* from the shape of the tuber. *Cp. stones. Orchis* is the Greek word for testicle; the diminutive is *orchidion. Saloop* was a favorite, inexpensive drink from the 17th century well into the 19th; the London street cry went: *Saloop! saloop! a hapenny a dish, hot saloop!*

salop. A variant form of *saloop, q.v.* The *salop houses* lasted in London into the 19th century, selling their drink made from the tuber of the early purple orchis, with milk, ginger, and sugar. It sounds like a delicious "soft" drink.

saltimbanco. See *exilient.*

sam. Together. From the 14th century; earlier *samen, samed,* both from the 9th century. Common Teuton forms, whence also *same.* Spenser in THE SHEPHERD'S CALENDAR (1579; MAY) asks: *What concord han light and darke sam?* There was also an early verb *sam,* to bring together, to join (in friendship, in marriage); to fasten together; to heap together, to collect. Also to coagulate, to curdle. Since the 15th century *sam* has been used only in dialect. *Cp. samded.*

samblind. See *sandblind.*

sambocade. A fritter, flavored with elder flowers. A culinary delight of the 14th and 15th centuries. Latin *sambucus,* the elder. Also *samakade, samace, semaka, samatard. Take and make a crust,* said a recipe of 1390, *and take a cruddes* [curds]; *do therto sugar . . . and somdel whyte of ayrene* [eggs], *and shake therin bloomes of elren . . .*

sambouse. A thin dough rolled around hashed meats. From the Near East; the English word is of the 17th century, but the pasty is still an Oriental delicacy.

sambuca. A musical instrument, triangular, stringed, with a high pitch. Also *sambuke, sambuque, sambuc.* It should not have been—but was—confused with the wind instrument, the *sackbut, q.v.* Ascham in TOXOPHILUS (1545) said: *This I am sure, that lutes, all maner of pypes, barbitons, sambukes . . . be condemned of Aristotle.*

samded. Half dead. Anglo-Saxon *sam,* Latin *semi,* half. In the 13th century Robert of Gloucester's CHRONICLE. See *sandblind.* Other words in which the prefix *sam-* occurs include *samhale,* half healthy, in poor health; *samripe; samsodden,* half cooked, hence 'half-baked,' stupid.

samfayle. Without fail; doubtless. French *sans* (*q.v.*), without. Also *saun-, san-, sain-, sanz-, sauns-, saunce- faile, -feil, -faille, -fail, -fale.* In Middle English *samfayle* was a common rhyming tag. Chaucer in THE HOUS OF FAME (1384) has: *And seyde he must unto Itayle As was hys destanye saunsfaille.* [Note the shift in *Italy,* making it two syllables for the rhyme.]

samhale. See *samded.*

samite. A silken fabric of medieval times, sometimes interwoven with gold; a garment or cushion of this material. The word is a favorite with poets, as (in the last century) Tennyson in IDYLS OF THE KING: *clothed in white samite, mystic, wonderful* and (in the present century) Graves in THE BARDS: *their many-shielded, samite-curtained Jewel-bright hall where twelve kings sit at chess.* (When kings are thus employed their people are safe.) The word *samite* comes roundabout from Greek *hexamiton; hexa-,* six + *mitos,* thread: the *samite* thread was made of six strands of silk or—as some suggest—in the weaving, the weft thread was looped at every sixth thread of the warp, making a loose but rich material, for royalty. Henry III of England had a robe of purple *samite;* but if *samite* was brought from the East by the Crusaders, Tennyson was a bit early in placing it upon the LADY OF THE LAKE in good King Arthur's golden days. Thackeray (1847) comments: *A surcoat of peach-coloured samite . . . bespoke him noble.* It is pleasant even in the twentieth century to think of a lady (1530) *vestured wyth samyte of grene.*

samsodden. See *samded.*

sandblind. See *cecity.* This is a corruption of *samblind,* semi-blind; *cp. samded.* The change is explained in Johnson's definition: 'having a defect in the eyes, by which small particles appear to fly before them.' Shakespeare plays on the size of 'sand particles' in THE MERCHANT OF VENICE (1596): *This is my true begotten father, who being more then sandblinde, high gravel blinde, knows me not. Cp. stone* (*stone blind*).

sanders. See *gaylede.*

sangrado. An ignorant physician. *Dr. Sangrado,* a character in Le Sage's GIL BLAS (1735), had only two remedies: bleeding and drinking hot water. Spanish *sangrador,* bleeder; Latin *sanguinem,* blood, whence also *sanguine* and *sanguinary.* Also, *sangrador.* In a letter of 1820, Scott wrote: *One is sadly off in France and Italy, where the sangrados are of such low reputation, that it were a shame even to be killed by them.*

sangrail. The Holy Grail, the platter Christ used at the Last Supper, used also by Joseph of Arimathea to catch Christ's blood at the Cross. Old French *Saint Graal;* Latin *gradalis,* perhaps from Latin *crater,* cup. The holy grail, *sangrail,* is often referred to as a cup. Also *sangrayle,* *sangreall.* Popular etymology has given the word other origins, as *sang real, sang roial,* royal blood; *sang real,* "being some of Christ's real blood." LE MORTE ARTHUR (1450) speaks of *The knights of the table round, The sangrayle when they had sought.* Meredith builds the word in a figure, in HENRY RICHMOND (1871): *They bear the veiled sun like a sangreal aloft to the wavy marble flooring of stainless cloud.*

sanguine. See *humour.* Chaucer in the Prologue to THE CANTERBURY TALES (1386) observes the physiological grouping: *Of his complexioun he was sangwyn.* Trevisa in his translation (1398) of Bartholomeus' DE PROPRIETATIBUS RERUM warned that *the use of pepyr is not proffitable to sangueyne men.*

sanguisuge. A leech; a bloodsucker (also figuratively). Latin *sanguis,* blood + *sugere, suctum,* to suck, whence also *suction.* Poe (1849) used the French form, *sangsue,* leech, as an English word. Of a human 'bloodsucker,' *sanguisorb* (Latin *sorbere, sorptum,* to *absorb*) has also been used. Hence *sanguisugous* (accent on the *syoo*), bloodthirsty, cruel; *sanguivorous,* feeding on blood. In Skelton's WORKS (1550) we read: *That blody judge And mighty sanguisuge; The Pope that is so huge, Is ever their refuge.* There are various references to the *sanguivorous vampire.*

sans. Without. Also *sance, saunce.* Borrowed from the French, in the 14th century. Used by Shakespeare in the "Seven ages of man" speech in AS YOU LIKE IT (1600): *Sans teeth, sans taste, sans eyes, sans everything.* Also in various combinations: *sans appel,* a person from whom there is no appeal, a final authority. *sans biding,* without delay. *sans dener,* a penniless person. *sans phrase,* with no more words (Sieyes voted for the death of Louis XVI: *la mort sans phrase*). *sans punie,* with no penalty, with impunity. *sans souci,* unconcern; also, a gay and free party. *sans fail,* doubtless; see *samfayle;* often used as a rhyming tag in Middle English verse, as in ARTHUR (1400): *Muchelnesse of men sainfayle Is nat victorie in batayle.*

santrel. A little saint. Old French *sainterel,* diminutive of *saint.* Urquhart in his translation (1653) of Rabelais dallies *with a thousand other jolly little sancts and santrels.*

santy. See *sonties.*

sapego. See *serpigo.*

sarcenet. A variant form of *sarsenet, q.v.*

sarculation. Hoeing. A *sarcle* was a hoe (18th century, translating Latin *sarculum; sarire,* to weed). Hence *sarcler,* a weeder. *Sarculation* is a rare 18th century word; 17th century dictionaries list *sarculate,* to hoe.

sark. A shirt or other garment worn next the skin; also, a surplice. Used from the 8th century (BEOWULF); Burns uses it in TAM O' SHANTER (1790): *Her cutty sark, o' Paisley harn, That while a lassie she had worn.* (*Cutty* means cut short, curtailed; occasionally it was used alone to mean a naughty, mischievous girl, or a cute one.) *Sark alone,* bare except for a shirt. An Aberdeen ruling of 1538 ordered one Bessie *to gang, sark alane, afore the procession.* The word is still used in Scotland. *A sarkful of sore bones,* a sore body.

sarsanet. A very fine and soft silk material; a garment made of this. Also *sarcenet, sarsnet, sarseynet, saircenett,* and more. Probably from the French *sarzin,*

Saracen; Medieval Latin *pannus Saracenicus,* Saracen cloth. Chaucer (THE ROMAUNT OF THE ROSE, 1366) uses the word in the form *sarsynysh, sarcenish. Sarsenet* was also used figuratively as an adjective, soft as silk—as in Shakespeare's HENRY IV, PART ONE (1596): *You swear like a comfit-makers wife . . . And givest such sarcenet suretie for thy oathes, As if thou never walks't further than Finsbury. Sweare me, Kate . . . a good mouth-filling oath.*

sassinous. Rocky. Italian *sasso*; Latin *saxum,* rock, whence also *saxatile,* stony; living or growing among rocks, also *saxicoline, saxicolous* (accents on the *sick*). *Cp. saxatile.*

satiability. Capability of being satiated. Latin *satiare, satiatus*; *satis,* enough. Note that *sateless,* that cannot be sated, insatiable, is from *sate,* earlier *sade,* to become weary, to be glutted, from the same root as *sad*—changed to *sate* by association with Latin *sat, satis,* enough, whence also *dissatisfied* [*Satisfied* is a "kangaroo word," containing a smaller synonym (*sated*) spelled within it; other such are *deceased, dead*; *recline, lie*; *precipitation, rain.*] And so on to satiety.

satinity. Smoothness (satin-like). *Satin* is probably from Late Latin *pannus setinus,* silken cloth; *seta,* silk. An inferior quality of *satin,* in the 17th century, was given a fancy Spanish ending and called *satinisco,* but scorned nonetheless; Overbury in his Characters (1615) speaks of a man who could afford only *mock-velvet or satinisco,* and Fuller in his WORTHIES (1661) scornfully lists stuffs called *perpetuano, satinisco, bombicino, Italiano . . .* A dandy, in the same century, from his shining garments, might be called a *satinist*—not to be confused though at times akin to a *Satanist.*

sation. Planting, sowing of seed. Latin *serere, satum,* to sow. Used from the 14th to the 18th century.

Saturn. Originally, the Italic god of agriculture (root *sa-,* to sow); later, identified with Greek *Cronos,* deposed as king of the gods by his son Zeus (Latin *Jupiter, q.v.*). The farthest from the sun of the seven planets known to antiquity. *Cp. Diana.* Because of its slow motion and remoteness, Saturn (in astrology) was deemed to make one cold, sluggish, gloomy; hence *saturnine.* As god of agriculture, however, the festival of Saturn, held in ancient times in mid-December, was a time of unrestrained revelry, even for the slaves; hence *saturnalia,* a period of general license and revelry (plural in form, but sometimes used as a singular).

satyrion. A kind of orchid; Greek *satyrion,* from *satyros,* satyr; so named because the plant was used as an aphrodisiac. The use was probably suggested by the testicular shape of the bulbs; various species of the plant are popularly known as *foolstones, dogstones, goatstones,* and more; *cp. stone.* The roots were at their highest potency if boiled in milk and eaten with white pepper. Such love-philtres, in ancient Rome, became so popular and so distracting from proper pursuits that they were forbidden by law.

saulee. Satisfaction of appetite; a good meal. *To saule,* to fill with food. Old French *saoul,* full of food or drink; Latin *satullus,* diminutive of *satur,* full; whence also English *saturity* (16th to 18th century), satisfaction, fullness. *Satiate* and *satisfy* are from Latin *satis,* enough. Note that a *saulie* (Scotland, 17th and 18th century) was a hired mourner at a funeral. —Langland in PIERS PLOWMAN (1377) said: *I wolde . . . forto have my fylle of that frute forsake al other saulee.*

saunderys. See *gaylede.*

saveloy. A highly seasoned sausage, cooked and dried. A corrupt form of *cervelat. Cervelat* was used in the 18th century for a short thick sausage, usually eaten cold. The word is from Old French *cervel,* Latin *cerebellum,* brain. From the shape of the *cervelat,* the word was also applied to a short reed musical instrument (also *cervalet,* as though with a diminutive ending) like the bassoon. The *saveloy* (three syllables) was enjoyed in the 19th century; Dickens mentions Solomon Pill *regaling himself* with an *Abernethy biscuit and a saveloy* in THE PICKWICK PAPERS (1837); and Smiles in LIFE AND LABOUR fifty years later mentions a *gastronomist* who *would stop at a stall in the Haymarket and luxuriate in eating a penny saveloy.*

sawgeat. A dish. It might seem related to a *sausage* (which is roundabout from Latin *salsum,* salted), but *sawgeat* is from *sawge, sauge,* now *sage.* A recipe from THE FORME OF CURY (1390): *Sawgeat. Take pork, and seeth it wel, and grinde it smale, and medle it with ayren and brede ygrated; do thereto powdor fort and safron, with pynes and salt. Take and close litulle balles in foiles of sawge. Wete it with a bator of ayren, and fry it, and serve it forth.*

saxatile. Stone-like. Latin *saxum,* rock. Hence *saxify,* to turn into stone, petrify. The plant *saxifrage* (break-stone) was so named because it grows in clefts of rock, but Pliny and many after him (Bailey, 1751) derive the name from the plant's (supposed) efficacy in breaking up stones in the human bladder. Hence *saxifragant, saxifragous* (accents on the second syllable), capable of dissolving such stones. *Cp. sassinous.*

saxhorn. See *barytone.*

say. See *sea.*

'sbodikins. A euphemistic variation of *God's bodikins,* God's little body. A common exclamation of the 17th and 18th centuries, as in DON QUIXOTE in English (1733): *'Sbodlikins! I find there's nothing in making love when a man's but once got well into't.*

scaberulous. See *scabredity.* Applied to writing, *scabrous* until Victorian days meant rough; Ben Jonson in DISCOVERIES (1637) said: *Lucretius is scabrous; Dryden* (1693) declared the verse of Persius *is scabrous and hobbling.*

scabredity. Roughness. Latin *scabrum,* rough, related to *scabere,* to scrape, scratch. Also *scabridity.* Hence *scabrid, scaberulous, scabriusculous,* somewhat *scabrous.* These words, from the Latin, should not be confused with the good old English *scab, scabby. Scabrous* first meant rough (as a rasp, or with tiny knobs); then, (of writing style) harsh, rough, unpolished; then (in the 19th century) risqué, obscene; THE ATHENAEUM of 3 March, 1894, was shocked that *Mr. Maude . . . has chosen to write about divorce and adultery . . . and many other scabrous topics.* Burton in THE ANATOMY OF MELANCHOLY (1624) lists among the *faults in physiognomie . . . inequalities, roughnesse, scabredity, palenesse, yellownes.*

scacchic. Relating to chess. Italian *scacchi,* chess. How quickly disuse destroys one's scacchic ability!

scaevity. Also *scevity.* Unluckiness. Latin *scaevus,* left-sided, awkward, unlucky. In 17th century dictionaries. Similarly *sinister* is from the Latin word for left-handed; *dexterity,* the Latin word for right-handed.

scaffolder. One of the gallery-gods; one that is in the gallery of a theatre (which until recently had no separate seats, but rows of long benches). Bishop Hall in his third SATIRE (1597) pictured a drink-inspired poet (*cp. pot-fury*): *There if he can with termes Italianate, Big-sounding sentences, and words of state, Faire patch me up his pure iambick verse, He ravishes the gazing scaffolders.*

scaldabanco. A hot disputant; a fiery preacher. Italian *scaldare,* to heat + *banco,* bench. A 17th century term, as in Bishop Hacket's sermon on Archbishop Williams (1670): *The Presbyterians, those scalda-banco's, or hot declamers, had wrought a great distast in the Commons at the King.* The similarly formed *mountebank* has survived; and *cp. bankrout.* (The mountebank and the strolling player formed the lowest legal class in the Middle Ages. In the tariff of damages for blows and other insults, for example, the graduated penalties an offended noble, merchant, peasant, etc. might exact, the mountebank in retaliation might cuff his assailant's shadow on a wall.)

scalpel. See *dentiscalp.*

scamble. Replaced later, in some senses, by *shamble* and *scramble.* To scatter money, fruit, sweetmeats, etc., for a crowd to scramble for; to struggle for such things; hence, to struggle indecorously and rapaciously. Thus Shakespeare has in KING JOHN (1595): *England now is left to tug and scamble and to part by th' teeth The un-owed interest of proud swelling state.* Also, to make one's way as best one can, to blunder along; to make shift (for a meal); to gather up as one can, to scrape together; to walk clumsily. Hence *scambling* (1) rapacious, as in Shakespeare's HENRY V (1599): *The scambling and unquiet time*; (2) makeshift, clumsily executed, slipshod; blundering; rambling. A *scambler* was a parasite, a sponger. In Lyly's SAPHO AND PHAO (1584), Molussus says: *I am in the deapth of my learning driven to a muse, how this Lent I shall scamble in the court, that was wont to fast so oft in the university,* and Criticus answers: *Thy belly is thy God.*

scandalum magnatum. See *scanmag.*

scandaroon. A swindler, a cheating pedlar. From the reputation (17th century) of *Iskanderun,* a seaport of Syria. There was an English trading post there, in the 18th and 19th century; when ships arrived, word of their safety was sent back to Aleppo by carrier pigeon; hence *scandaroon,* a kind of carrier pigeon.

scanmag. Scandal; malicious words against the highly placed. Humorous or satirical, as in Sheridan's THE CRITIC (1779): *The publisher . . . threateneing himself with the pillory, or absolutely indicting himself for scanmag.* The word is an abbreviation, *scan. mag.,* of Latin *scandalum magnatum,* scandal of magnates, made severely punishable in a statute of Richard II of England. The words, at first kept in the literal sense of malicious reports against persons in a position of dignity, were later used of anything scandalous. Thus Massinger, in THE CITY MADAM (1632): *'Tis more punishable in our house than scandalum magnatum.* The chief substance of many a "gossip-column" of today would once have been deemed scanmag.

scantle. To cut short, dole out; grow less; replaced by *to scant.* Also (16th century) *to scanten;* (17th century) *to scantelize.* As a noun, *scantle* (*skantell; scantlet; scantling*), a small piece. Shakespeare has, in HENRY IV, PART ONE (1596),

See how this river comes me cranking in, And cuts me from the best of all my land A huge halfe moon, a monstrous scantle out. The folio, however, has *cantle, q.v.*

scape. (1) Short for *escape.* Used in a passage in Randolph's THE MUSE'S LOOKING GLASS (1638; a defence of the theatres in the form of a play), which mentions all the London theatres then standing—as though a zealous Puritan wished them down: *That the Globe, Wherein, quoth he, reigns a whole world of vice, Had been consum'd: the Phoenix burnt to ashes: The Fortune whipt for a blind whore: Blackfryars, He wonders how it scap'd demolishing I' th' time of reformation: lastly, he wished The Bull might cross the Thames, to the Bear-Garden, And there be soundly baited.* The punning on the names did not scape Randolph's readers. *Escape* is from Latin *ex,* out + *cappa,* cloak; one leaves one's cloak in the pursuer's clutches, as in the BIBLE, MARK xiv. Among special meanings of *scape* were (a) a transgression through thoughtlessness; an inadvertent error, such as a slip of the tongue. (b) a cheating, a breaking from moral restraint; a serious sin, especially, a breach of chastity. (c) In the phrase *to let a scape,* to break wind. Chaloner in his translation (1547) of Erasmus' IN PRAISE OF FOLLY wrote: *I for my parte, through laughter, had almost let goe a scape, as Priapus did.* (2) The shaft of a column; the tongue of a balance. Also *scapus*; hence *escapement*; Greek *skapos,* related to *skeptron,* sceptre. (3) A view of scenery: short for *landscape, seascape, cloudscape,* and the like. The *scape* in these words is Old English *scipe,* ship, meaning state of, or quality, skill. The *ship* survives in such words as *hardship, partnership, scholarship, courtship.* Earlier words include *dolscipe,* folly; *gladship*; *drunkship*; *fiendship* (hostility; opposed to *friendship*). Also *beorscipe* (*beership,* feast); *eorlscipe,* manliness. This is still a live, usually humorous, combining form, as in *His Uglyship.* Beaumont and Fletcher said, in PHILASTER (1611): *I never lov'd his beyond-sea-ship.* In sense (1), cheating, Bishop Hall (SATIRE I, Book 3; 1597) said: *Was then no playning of the brewers scape, Nor greedy vintner mixed* [with water] *the strained grape.*

scapulimancy. See *aeromancy.*

scarlet. See *ciclatoun.* Originally *scarlet* meant a rich cloth, usually bright red, but sometimes of other colors (blue, green, brown). Other old meanings of *scarlet* include: a person that wears scarlet, a judge, a hunter (also, early 19th century, a *scarletite*); in the 18th century, a Mohock, an aristocrat street ruffian, as in J. Shebbeare's LYDIA (1755): *I expected to have seen her . . . encouraging the young bloods, bucks, and scarlets at a riot in Drury-lane.*

scatebrous. Bubbling out like water from a spring; abounding. Johnson (1755) defines it as 'abounding in springs.' Latin *scatere,* to gush, spring forth. Hence, *scatebrosity,* a gushing or bubbling out; used figuratively of 'gushy' conversation. In 17th and 18th century dictionaries.

scathe. One who wreaks harm, a wretch, a monster. So in BEOWULF (8th century). Hence, damage, harm. From the 10th century. Also a verb, to harm, to injure; to blast, to sear. *Scatheful, scathel,* harmful, dangerous. *Scathness,* harm. *Scathefire,* a fierce conflagration. Hence *scatheless,* unharmed; and the still current *scathing,* blasting, searing (of verbal attacks). Shakespeare says, in TITUS ANDRONICUS (1588): *And wherein Rome hath done you any* *scathe, Let him make treble satisfaction.* The negative form *unscathed* survives.

scatomancy. See *aeromancy.* The word is applied also to medical diagnosis by study of the feces. A dung-diviner is a *scatomanter.* Inspection of the feces, for such purposes, is *scatoscopy.* As a science, *scatology;* which is also used to mean *pornography,* as in Saintsbury's ELIZABETHAN LITERATURE (1887): *A large quantity of mere scatology and doggerel.*

Scavenger's daughter. See *duke. Scavenger,* here, is a folk-corruption of *Skevington.*

scenche. A cup. Also *schenche,* to pour out. These are 13th century forms; *cp. shenk.*

schoenobatic. Relating to rope-walking. Pronounced *skeenabatic,* accent on the *bat.* Greek *schoinos,* rope, *bainein,* to walk. Also *schoenobatist* (accent on the *no*), a rope-walker. Used of 19th century circus performers.

scholy. See *scolion.*

schoolpoint. A question for debate in the schools; a theoretical point; a fine point; a merely theoretical point, of no practical importance or concern. Used in the 16th and 17th centuries. *They stuff their sermons,* said Gouge in his COMMENTARY (1653; HEBREWS), *with obscure comparisons and curious schoolpoints.*

scialytic. Dispersing shadows; hence, figuratively, making one cheerful. *Cp. sciatheric.*

sciamachy. Shadow-boxing; a sham fight for exercise. Greek *skia,* shadow + *machesthai,* to fight. Pronounced *sigh-am'-a-ky. Cp. sciatheric.* Also used figuratively, as in THE CHRISTIAN'S REMEMBRANCER (1862): *As we have no taste for skiomachy, we leave the fuller exposure of this portentous mare's nest to other hands.*

sciapod. One of the *sciapodes* (four syllables, accent on the *sigh-ap'*), a race in Libya with feet so large the body could be sheltered under them. *Cp. monopode* (*mono-*).

sciatheric. Relating to, or to the study of, shadows. Also *scioterical, scioterique.* Greek *sciathericon,* a sundial (used rarely in English); literally, a shadow-catcher; *skia,* shadow + *theran,* to catch. The form *sciatherics* means the art or practice of making sundials. *Sciatherical,* relating to the shadows cast by the planets or (especially) the sun; *sciatherically,* after the manner of a sundial.

scibility. Ability to comprehend. Latin *scibilis; scire,* to know; *cp. sciolous.* The root is *sac, sec,* to split; divide, hence distinguish. The present participle of *scire* is *sciens, scientem,* whence all the *science* of the centuries.

sciolous. With a smattering of knowledge. Accent on the *sigh.* Also *sciolistic.* Late Latin *sciolus,* smatterer; diminutive of *scius,* knowing; *scire,* to know; *cp. scibility; scious.* Hence *sciolus, sciolist,* a pretender to knowledge, a conceited ignoramus. Also *sciolism.* Coleridge (1816) spoke of an *epidemic of a proud ignorance occasioned by a diffused sciolism.* A little knowledge is a dangerous thing. Farrar might have been looking forward or backward when he wrote, in 1876, of *the empty sciolism of much that calls itself criticism.* James Howell in DODONA'S GROVE, OR THE VOCALL FORREST (1640) said piously: *I could wish that these sciolous zelotists had more judgment joynd with their zeale.*

sciomancy. See *aeromancy.*

scioteric. See *sciatheric.*

scious. Possessing knowledge. Pronounced *sigh-s*; *cp. sciolous.* In the LITERARY REMAINS (1834) of Coleridge we find: *Brutes may be, and are, scious.* We find it nowhere else—except when con*scious.*

scirpean. Of or relating to bulrushes. Latin *scirpus,* bulrush. We think of the scirpean bank to which the infant Moses was entrusted.

sciscitation. Questioning; eagerness to know—a quality that, in many, lapses with childhood. Accent on the *siss.* Latin *sciscitari,* to ask, repetitive of *sciscere,* to seek to know, inceptive of *scire,* to know. *Cp. scibility.* A 17th century term; C. Nesse in THE HISTORY AND MYSTERY OF THE OLD AND THE NEW TESTAMENT (1690) said that Abraham *immediately departed without sciscitation or carnal reasonings.*

scoleye. To go to school; to be a scholar, to study. Old French *escole,* school. Also *scolay, scholey, skole-aye, schole heye.* Chaucer in the Prologue to THE CANTERBURY TALES (1386) tells us: *A clerk ther was of Oxenford also . . . But al that he mighte of his freendes hente, On bokes and on lerninge he it spente, and bisily gan for the soules prey Of hem that gaf him wher-with to scoleye.*

scolion. A song the parts of which were sung in succession, by various guests, at banquets in ancient Greece. Also *skolion, scolium*; plural, *scolia.* Sometimes played as a game, the first guest making up a line of verse, then passing a branch to any other he wished, who must make up and sing the next line. Although sometimes mispelled with *sch, scolium, scolia* should not be confused with *scholium, scholia,* an explanatory note (in the 16th century, also *scholy*)—from which there was a verb *to scholy,* to annotate, to comment. The scolion is said to have been invented by Terpander (7th century B.C.), who also, by increasing the lyre-strings from 4 to 7, invented the *heptachord.*

scollardical. A contemptuous term, as of an illiterate, for a man of learning. Whitlock in ZOOTOMIA (1654) exclaimed upon *these peevish scollardicall doctors (that will not let people believe lies quietly).*

scolopendra. A curious sea-fish that, when hooked, "casteth out his bowels, until he hath unloosed the hooke, and then swalloweth them up againe." Also *scolopender.* Spenser in THE FAËRIE QUEENE (1590) speaks of *Bright scolopendraes, arm'd with silver scales.* The word was also used (and still, in entomology) of a large, formidable centipede; by transfer, of an obnoxious woman, as in Shirley's THE GAMESTER (1633): *More wine, you varlets! And call your mistress up, you scolopendra.*

scomfit. To defeat, vanquish. A shortened form of *discomfit,* used in the 14th, 15th, and 16th centuries. Also as a noun; the STATE PAPERS of Henry VIII (1540) comment upon *the skumfite gyven upon O Neyle and O Donell at the laste insurreccion.* Also *to scomfish,* from *discomfish,* another variant of *discomfit.* Hence *scomfiter,* one that discomfits, a victor. *scomfiture,* defeat. Note also *scomm,* used in the 17th and 18th centuries to mean a scoff, jeer, flouting. This is from Greek *skomma*; *skoptein,* to jeer, scoff. Hence also *scommatism, scommatizing,* derision, scoffing; *scommatic, scommatical,* relating to or characterized by scoffs or derision. Henry More in MYSTERY OF INIQUITY (1664) said: *He that has been casting his angle a good part of the day into the* *river, and brings home no fish, may yet be rightly saluted Mr. Fisherman or Mr. Angler on his return, though not without some kind of scommatism at the bottom.*

scomm. See *scomfit.* Also *scomme, scom.* Note that *scom* is also an old variant of *scum.*

sconce. See *ensconce.*

scope. First used in the 16th century, this word meant a mark for shooting at; a goal; a desired object or person. Thus Spenser in THE FAËRIE QUEENE (1590) *cursed night, that reft from him so goodly scope. To scope,* to the purpose, as in Shakespeare's TIMON OF ATHENS (1607): *'Tis conceyv'd, to scope.*

scopiferous. Equipped with a dense brush of hair. Latin *scopae,* twigs; a broom or brush + *fer,* bearing. Hence also *scopiform,* broom-shaped; arranged in bundles; *scopulate,* brush-like, with brush-like hairs. Note that Latin *scopula,* brush, is diminutive of *scopa,* broom; but Latin *scopulus* means rock, *scopulosus,* craggy; hence English *scopulous* (*q.v.*), rocky; *scopulousness, scopulosity.*

scoptic. Mocking. Also *scoptical.* Greek *skoptikos; skoptein,* to jeer. Thus *scoptics,* satirical or mocking writings. Chapman commented (1611) on the ILIAD: *In this first and next verse, Homer* (*speaking scoptically*) *breakes open the fountaine of his ridiculous humor.*

scopulous. See *scopiferous.* Used in the 16th and 17th centuries; the words from the *brush* and *broom* forms came into English in the 18th century. *Cp. saxatile.*

scortatory. Relating to fornication or lewdness. Swedenborg wrote a book entitled (in English translation, 1794): *Delights of Wisdom concerning Conjugial Love: after which follow the Pleasures of Insanity concerning Scortatory Love. Cp. conjugial.* Latin *scortum,* an old hide, skin; hence, a harlot. Hence *scortator,* (Blount, 1656) "a whoremonger, a hunter of harlots"; *scortation,* fornication. John Rowland's translation (1658) of Muffet's THE THEATRE OF INSECTS said: *I see no reason why the modesty of the bee and of the drone, whereby they abandon publick scortation and venery, should debar them of the private use of copulation.*

scot. See *biscot.*

scour. See *skirr.*

scouse. See *lobscouse.*

scrabble. To make marks at random, scrawl; to scratch or scrape with the hands or feet; to scratch up (out, off), to gather up by scraping around. A frequentative form of *scrab,* to scratch, to claw; to snatch. A *scribble* is a mild *scrabble.* A *scrabble* is a scrawling or hastily made picture or piece of writing, as when Ruskin recorded, in the October 1881 NINETEENTH CENTURY: *Yesterday . . . came to me from the Fine Art Society, a series of twenty black and white scrabbles.* The 1537 BIBLE (1 SAMSON) pictured the captive Samson, who *raved in their handes and scrabled on the dores of the gate.* The word has been revived as the name of a game, a cross between cross-words and anagrams.

scrannel. Thin; harsh, unmelodious. Norwegian *skran,* lean, shriveled. Milton used the word first, in LYCIDAS (1637): *Their lean and flashy songs Grate on their scrannel pipes of wretched straw;* all other uses seem echoes of the first. Carlyle in SARTOR RESARTUS (1831) bemoans *a kind of infinite, unsufferable, Jew's-harping and scrannel-piping.* The word *scranny* was also used, in the 19th century, meaning thin, meagre (in dialects, crazy, silly), as when the rat speaks in Shelley's CLUB-FOOT THE TYRANT (1820): *Creeping thro' crevice, and chink, and cranny, With my snaky tail, and my sides so scranny.*

scribuncle. See *anonymuncle.*

scrine. A box for books and papers; a desk. Especially, a chest for sacred relics, a *shrine. Scrine* was used from the 13th to the 17th century, then replaced by the later form, *shrine.* Bailey in 1751 gives the original Latin form as also an English word: *scrinium,* a writing-desk, a chest. Hence *scrinerary, scriniary,* a keeper of the archives.

scripturient. Possessed of a powerful urge to write. Latin *scripturiri,* to desire to write; *scribere, scriptum,* to write, whence also *scribe, nondescript,* and all the *scriptures*; *cp. scrivener.* Hence also *scripturiency, a fault,* said Urquhart (1652; THE JEWEL) *in feeble pens.* Also known in hybrid (Greek and Latin) form, *cacoëthes scribendi,* itch to write.

scrivener. A professional penman; scribe, clerk, secretary. Earlier (13th to 15th century) *scrivein, scriveyn*; French *escrivain.* Hence *to scrive, to scriven.* Also *scrivenliche* (Chaucer), like a *scriver* or *scrivener.* Latin *scribere, scriptum,* to scratch, to write; *cp. scripturient.* From the Italian came 16th century English *scrivan, scrivano,* a clerk. Chaucer (1374) addressed a copyist: *Adam scryveyne if ever it thee byfalle Boece or Troylus for to wryten nuwe. Scrivener* was also used, with measure of contempt, to mean an author; Southey in SIR THOMAS MORE (1829) wrote: *A very little suffices for the stock in trade, upon which the scribes and scriveners of literature, who take upon themselves to direct the public, set up.*

scrochat. A sweetmeat popular from the 15th to the mid-17th century. The recipe is lost; but its favor may be judged from the many forms of the word, and the references to 56 of them, to 10 lb. of them: *scorzat, scorzatis, scorchet, scrottiszarttis, scrotchertis, schoiretts, schoters,* and other ways of wonder. It was a special favorite in Scotland.

scroyle. A scoundrel, wretch. A common word among 16th and 17th century dramatists; revived by Scott in KENILWORTH (1821). Shakespeare exclaims in KING JOHN (1595): *By heaven! these scroyles of Angiers flout you, kings!*

scrutable. That can be comprehended after scrutiny. *Cp. couth.* Latin *scrutari, scrutatum,* to ransack, search carefully; *scruta,* broken stuff, trash—the idea of the verb being apparently to hunt even amid the scraps. Hence also *scrute, scrutate, scrutinate, scrutine,* and the current *scrutinize.* Also *scrutation,* scrutiny; *scrutator, scrutineer*; *scrutinant, scrutinous,* occupied in investigating or examining; *scrutatory,* searching, examining.

scruto. A spring trap-door, flush with the floor of a stage, for a ghost to rise through, for sudden falls, and other effects. PUNCH in 1859 speaks of *gorgeous transformations, on which . . . scruto work, gas battens, and all the resources of 'sink and fly' have been lavished.*

scruze. To squeeze. In the 18th century often used in the form *scrouge* (pronounced *skroodge*) and in the 19th century used as a noun: a squeeze; a crowd. Perhaps a telescoping of *screw* and *squeeze.* Spenser has, in THE FAËRIE QUEENE (1590): *Having scruzed out of his carrion corse The lothfull life,* and again: *Whose sappy liquor, that with fulnesse sweld, Into her cup she scruzed with dainty* *breach Of her fine fingers.* The miserly villain of Dickens' A CHRISTMAS CAROL (1843) is named *Scrooge.*

scullion. One that performed menial duties in the kitchen, a kitchen-knave; hence often used as a term of scorn or abuse. For an instance of such use in Shakespeare, see *catastrophe.*

scur. See *skirr.*

scylid. An old form of *skilled,* skilful.

sea. An old variant of (1) *so;* (2) *say,* a cloth of fine texture, in the 16th century partly of silk, later all wool; the thread of which this cloth is woven; (3) the *see,* the papal seat. Roper in THE LIFE OF SYR THOMAS MORE (1557) recorded that when (1522) *the sea of Roome chaunced to be void* and Cardinal Wolsey (because of the intrigue of Emperor Charles V) was not chosen pope, the Cardinal *waxed so wood* [angry] *therwith that he studied to invent all waies of revengment of his grief gainst the Emperour.*

secern. (1) To separate; especially in thought, to divide into categories, to discriminate. Since the 17th century. Latin *se,* aside, apart + *cernere,* to sift, to separate, whence also *discern.* The SATURDAY REVIEW of 15 April, 1905, observed that *mimes cannot be utterly secerned from their life of mimicry.* (2) To separate from the blood; to secrete. Hence *secernent,* secreting; *secernment,* the act of secretion, also separating, as in THE YELLOW BOOK (1894): *With the universal use of cosmetics and the consequent secernment of soul and surface.*

secessive. Retired, private. Latin *se,* apart + *cedere, cessum,* to yield, to go. Hence *secess* (16th and 17th centuries), withdrawing, retirement (as to a monastery). The original sense of *secede* was to withdraw into retirement; then, the current use, to withdraw from fellowship, etc. Urquhart in his translation (1653) of Rabelais says: *Like dung-chewers and excrementitious eaters, they are cast into the privies and secessive places, that is the covents and abbeys.*

secre. An early form of *secret,* in all its uses. Accent on the second syllable, hence also spelled *secree.* From the 12th into the 15th century; used frequently by Chaucer.

secundate. To make lucky; to improve. Latin *secundare, secundatum,* to direct favorably; *secundus,* favorable. *Secundus* is the gerundive of *sequor, secutum,* to follow, meaning that which should follow. Hence *secundation,* the act of helping or favoring; prosperity. Found mainly in 17th and 18th century dictionaries.

seel. (1) To lurch suddenly on its side, as a ship in a storm. G. Sandys in his translation (1621) of Ovid's METAMORPHOSES wrote: *They plie their tasks: some seeling yards bestryd and take in sailes.* Also a noun, the heeling over of a ship. (2) *seele, cele, seill* (15th century), a canopy. Perhaps from French *ciel,* sky. (3) *sele, sil, seyll,* and many more forms, happiness, good fortune; opportune moment, favorable time; by extension, time of day, period of time. *To give the sele of the day,* to pass the time of day, greet pleasantly in passing. Hence also *seelihead, seeliness,* happiness. Chaucer said in BOETHIUS (1374): *Som man is wel and selily married.* It is from *seely,* happy; then, pious, holy, good; then, harmless, innocent, that there came (16th century) the still current sense of *silly.* (4) *seel,* to stitch the eyes of a bird; a falcon or hawk might be trained (16th and 17th centuries) by stitching its eyelids, tying the thread behind the bird's head. Hence, to hoodwink, to make blind. Thus Shakespeare in OTHELLO (1604) says: *Shee that so young could give out such a seeming To seele her fathers eyes up.* Also used figuratively as in Lyly's CAMPASPE (1584): *Al conscience is sealed at Athens*; Shakespeare in MACBETH: *Come, seeling night, skarfe up the tender eye of pittiful day.* This form, though at times spelled *seal,* is not related to *seal,* a mark or impression, which is via French from Latin *sigillum,* diminutive of *signum,* sign. It was earlier (12th century) *sile,* to sew up a bird's eyes; French *cil,* eyelash; Latin *cilium,* whence also *supercilious.* See *sile.* Shakespeare uses *seely,* silly, in RICHARD II: *Like seely beggars Who sitting in the stocks refuge* [excuse] *their shame, That many have and others must sit there.*

segnity. Slothfulness. Latin *segnitia*; *segnis,* slow, sluggish. Dictionary-makers of the 17th and 18th century were fond of fashioning words for future use. *Segnity* (in Cockeram, 1623; Blount, 1656; Bailey, 1721, 1751) has not yet had its day.

sejunge. To separate, disjoin. Also *sejugate, sejungate, sejoin.* From Latin *se-*, apart + *jungere, junctum,* to join or *jugare, jugatum,* to yoke. Hence also *sejunction, sejunctively*; *sejungible,* that may be separated. Bishop John Pearson in his EXPOSITION OF THE CREED (1659) stated: *The spawn and egge are sejungeable from the fish and fowl, and yet still retain the prolifick power of generation.*

selcouth. Unfamiliar, strange, marvellous; of different kinds. Old English *seldan,* seldom + *couth,* known. *What selcouth,* what wonder. *Me thinks selcouth, I have selcouth,* I wonder. Also used as a noun, a marvel; and as a verb, to make wonderful, to picture as marvelous. Used from the 9th into the 16th century; Spenser in THE FAËRIE QUEENE (1596) has: *She wondered much at his so selcouth case.* Scott revived the word in THE LORD OF THE ISLES (1814): *Deep import from that selcouth sign Did many a mountain seer divine.*

seld. (1) An early form of *seldom,* also used in compounds, as *seldseen*; *seldspeech,* taciturnity; *seld-showne* (Shakespeare in CORIOLANUS, 1607). (2) A seat, a throne; a shop (which may first have been but a bench); a stand for spectators. In this sense, *seld* is an early form of *settle.*

selenomancy. See *aeromancy.*

sellary. (1) A cellar. (2) An old spelling of *celery*; *We eat it like sellary,* said Swift in a letter of 1727 to Sheridan. (3) A male homosexual prostitute. The Latin form *sellarius* was coined by the Emperor Tiberius, from *sellaria,* a room with benches; *sella, selda,* a seat, *sedere,* to sit: hence *sellary,* 'one that practices lewdness on a settle.' *Cp. spintry.*

semble. A short form of the verb, used widely (13th through 17th century) for *assemble* and *resemble*; less often, for *dissemble.* Thus Dekker and Chettle in THE PATIENT GRISSIL (1603) wrote: *Hee does not flatter and semble, but tells his intentions.* The word *semble* is sometimes used, in legal and other formal phraseology (direct from the French) to mean, it seems. There was also a 15th and 16th century adjective *semble,* meaning similar, as in Hudson's translation (1584) of Du Bartas (JUDITH): *A tyrant vile Of name and deed that bare the semble stile That did this king.* Shakespeare in TWELFTH NIGHT (1601) used *semblative* to mean like, resembling: *Thy small pipe Is as the maidens organ, shrill, and sound,*

And all is semblative a womans part. Thus also *sembly* (14th into the 16th century) was used for *assembly.* Hence, *sembling,* representing, feigning; but used by 18th and 19th century entomologists to name the property certain moths possess of distinguishing and *assembling* the males from far away. A sort of telerotic attraction, semble.

semibousy. Half-drunk. *Bousy* has meant drunk since the 15th century, as in De Quincey's HERODOTUS (1842): *and every day* got *bousy as a piper.* The adjectives, also *bousyish,* are from the verb *bouse, bowse,* to drink to excess (in company). These forms were pronounced with a long *oo,* and have been supplanted by *booze.* See *bouse. Semibousy* occurs first in the 14th century, but the condition is perennial.

semiustulate. Half burnt. Latin *semi* + *ustulare*; *urere, ustum,* to burn. Hence also *ustulate.* Burton in THE ANATOMY OF MELANCHOLY (1621) states that: *Assation is a concoction of the inward moisture by heat; his opposite is a semiustulation.*

semivif. See *semyryfe.*

semyryfe. An error in Bailey's DICTIONARY (1751) for *semyvyf, semivif,* half dead. Latin *semi,* half + *vivus,* alive. The form *semivyf* (Langland, PIERS PLOWMAN, 1377) was used in the 14th century. *Cp. samded.*

sendal. (1) A rich material of fine silk; a garment thereof. Also *cendal, sandale, sendyll, sindall, syndale* and more. A common Romance word, used in English from the 13th century. In the 14th century, taken directly from Latin (and Greek) *sindon,* the word was also used in the classical sense, (2) fine linen, lawn; especially, a piece of such cloth used for a shroud or for dressing a wound. The first sense lingered in poetry, from Chaucer (Prologue to THE CANTERBURY TALES, 1386): *Lyned with taffata and with sendal* to Longfellow (BY THE SEASIDE, 1850): *Sails of silk and ropes of sendal, such as gleam in ancient lore.*

senek. See *seneschal.*

senesce. See *seneschal.*

seneschal. The official, in a king's or a lord's household, in charge of justice and all domestic administration, a majordomo. Also, an official in an English cathedral; by extension, a governor of a city or province; especially, of the English Channel Islands. The word is from Old Teutonic forms; *seni-,* old + *skalkoz,* servant. But note also Latin *senex,* old man (*senek* is used in 15th century English, for an elder), *senem,* old, *senior,* older, whence many common English words: *senile, senior, seniority. Senescent,* from Latin *senescere,* to grow old; less familiar is the English verb, as in a letter of Stevenson (1894): *My work will soon begin to senesce.* (Not yet, Robert!) The office of *seneschal,* or the seat of his administration, was *seneschalsy, seneschalty, seneschaunce, seneschausee.*

sennet. An early form of *signet,* sign, token, signal. Also, a set of notes on trumpet or cornet, as a signal, in Elizabethan stage-directions, Marlowe (FAUST; 1590): *sonnet;* Shakespeare (HENRY VI, PART THREE; 1590); *senet,* (HENRY VIII): *sennet*; Dekker, *sennate*; Marston, *synnet, signate.*

sennight. A week. Note that the French count the week differently, their term being *huit jours,* eight days. Similarly, where we say *fortnight* (fourteen nights), they say *quinze jours* (fifteen days). *Sennight day* is the same day in the following week.

senocular. Having six eyes. A convenient (though niggardly) word to be used by the B E M pensters of science fiction [B E M, bug-eyed monster]. Also *senoculate.*

sent. A shortened form of *assent,* used in the 14th and 15th centuries.

sepose. To set aside; to set apart, reserve; to brush aside, dismiss. Also *seposit, sepone,* to set apart. Latin *se,* aside + *ponere, positum,* to place, whence many English words: *pose, deposit, imposition,* etc. Hence *seposition,* a setting aside. These were all used in the 17th century. Thus Donne in a letter of 1609 remarked that *God seposed a seventh of our time for his exterior worship.*

sepult. To bury. Latin *sepelire, sepultum.* Hence also *sepelite, sepulture,* to bury. In 16th century wills (Surtees, 1544): *my body to be sepulted;* (Hulme, 1577): *my body to be sepilited.* Hence also *sepilible,* suited to burial; *sepelition,* burial. The various verb forms above were supplanted, about 1600, by *sepulchre.* Shakespeare (TWO GENTLEMEN OF VERONA, 1591) accents sepulchre on the second syllable; Jonson (in an EPIGRAM of 1616: *Where merit is not sepulcher'd alive*) and most since, on the first. The words were often used figuratively, burying other than corpses; thus Hall in his CHRONICLES (1548, of Henry IV) has: *An hundred more injuries, which he remitted and sepulted in oblivion.*

sequacious. Tending to follow the leadership or attitude or point of view of another; easily moulded. Latin *sequax,* follower (the plural *sequaces,* followers, was used in English, 16th and 17th centuries), *sequi, secutum,* to follow, whence *sequel, prosecute,* and *inconsequential* things. Of poetry and music, *sequacious* meant regular in metrical succession; of literature, maintaining one direction; De Quincey (RHETORIC; 1828) said that Milton moved *in paces too sequacious and processional.* Thomson in SUMMER (1746) wrote of *Those superstitious horrors that enslave The fond sequacious herd.*

sequent. In rare use as a noun, meaning a follower. Shakespeare in LOVE'S LABOUR'S LOST (1588) says: *And here he hath framed a letter to a sequent of the stranger queenes.* Also used in the 17th century, to mean *sequel. Elias de Trekingham was born,* said Fuller in his WORTHIES OF ENGLAND (1661), *at a village so called, as by the sequents will appear.* Especially in the phrase *logical sequent.*

sere. (1) Dry, withered. Common since the 9th century. Shakespeare in MACBETH (1605) says: *I have lived long enough; my way of life Is falne into the seare, the yellow leafe.* Also *sear, seer, seyr, seir.* Hence also *sere-souled,* withered of spirit; *the sere month,* August. (2) There is a noun *sere* (from Latin *sera,* bolt), meaning a claw, a talon, as in Chapman's translation (1618) of Hesiod: *The hawk once, having trust up in his seres The sweet-tuned nightingale.* (3) From still another background (Old Norse *ser,* for oneself) *sere* meant separate, single, distinct; various, sundry. Thus *sere-coloured,* parti-coloured; *(on) serewise,* in divers ways. In FLODDEN FIELD (1600) *sere* was used to mean 'all told': *The number did but mount To six and twenty thousand seere.*

serean. Pertaining to the Seres; related to silk. Also *serian, seric.* Latin *sericum,* which, via Anglo-Saxon *sioloc,* gave us English *silk.* Hence also *sericated,* clothed in silk; *sericeous,* silky, (in zoology and botany) covered with silky down. All from Greek *Seres* (two syllables), the inhabitants of Eastern Asia, whence silk came to the West. *The serian worm,* the silkworm; *the Seres' wool,* silk. Drummond of Hawthornden, in a poem of 1633, says, *Here are no serean fleeces.* And of course *the seric herb* is tea.

serendipity. The faculty of making happy finds. This is too good a word to have been wholly forgotten, for from Saul (who went to look for his father's asses and found a kingdom) to the most recent work of art, serendipity reigns. Horace Walpole, who coined the word, said in a letter of 28 January, 1754, that he took it from the title of a fairy-tale, *The Three Princes of Serendip*; the princes "were always making discoveries, by accidents and sagacity, of things they were not in quest of." *Serendip* was an early name of *Ceylon.* Any resemblance between *serendipity* and *heredipety* (*q.v.*) is purely coincidental. What Ogden Nash did with the word in THE PRIVATE DINING ROOM cannot be called serendipitous.

serenify. To grow serene. Also *serenize,* to make serene. The translation (1612) of Benvenuto's PASSENGER said: *It's now the faire, virmilion, pleasant spring, When meadowes laugh, and heaven serenifies.* Taft in ALBA (1598) wrote: *This my Icarian soaring ('bove my reach), Through beauty serenising falls my heart.* Note that *sereness* is a two-syllabled word, meaning the quality of being dry, withered, *sere. sereno,* the Spanish word for a nightwatchman, has been used in English stories of Spain. *serenitude* was a 17th century alternate for *serenity*; for *serene, serenous* (15th century); *serenissimous,* most serene, used by Jonson in THE NEW INNE, 1629. Thus *Serenissime, Serenissimo,* might be used before such titles as *Prince, Lord, Highness.*

sericated. See *serean.*

serinette. A bird organ. French *serin,* canary. The LONDON JOURNAL of 27 February, 1858, reported: *There are puppet-shows, and performances on the accordion, and the serinette in the subterranean passage.*

sermuncle. A short sermon (humorous —the word, not the lecture) ; also *sermonette.* These were both used in Victorian days, when a long sermon was expected, and usually delivered.

seron. A bale, especially of exotic products (almonds, cocoa, medicinal bark, etc.) wrapped in an animal's hide. A list of customs rates of 1545 includes *a cheste of sugar . . . a serone of soap . . . a barrell of pepper.*

serotine. Late in occurrence or appearance; toward or in the evening. Latin *sero,* late; in the 17th and 18th centuries, tardy pupils were marked *sero* (not *zero*). Also, *serotinous.* Longfellow in his translation (1868) of Dante's PURGATORIO says: *As far as ever eye could stretch Against the sunbeams serotine and lucent.*

serpent. (1) A deceitful or treacherous person. Shakespeare in A MIDSUMMER NIGHT'S DREAM (1590) has: *With doubler tongue Then thine (thou serpent) never adder stung.* (2) A kind of firework that burns with a serpentine motion. Pepys recorded in his DIARY for 6 June, 1666: *I made the women all fire some serpents.* (3) A 17th and 18th century bass wind instrument, of wood covered with leather, having three U-shaped turns. Similarly, other articles windingly shaped, as a spiral candle. A *serpentcleide* was an *ophicleide* of wood instead of brass. An *ophicleide* (Greek *ophis,* serpent + *kleid-,* key) was a development of the musical *serpent,* with a brass tube and with keys (usually eleven). It was played in the early 19th century, as the bass to the *key-bugle.*—It was a common belief regarding the snake, recorded in ancient Greek, also in Dryden's translation (1680) of OEDIPUS, that *a serpent ne'er becomes a flying dragon Till he has eat a serpent.*

serpenticide. See *stillicide.*

serpigo. A spreading skin disease; ringworm. Latin *serpere,* to creep; *serpentem,* creeping, whence *serpent.* The plural was *serpigoes* or (from the Latin) *serpigines.* Also *serpego, sarpego, sapego; surpeague, q.v.* Shakespeare in MEASURE FOR MEASURE (1603) lists *the gout, sapego, and the rheum.*

servage. Bondage, slavery; feudal service, homage. Also *servagery.* Chaucer uses the word in both senses: in THE CLERK'S TALE (1386): *It is greet shame . . . to been in servage To thee, that born art of a smal village;* and in THE DETHE OF BLAUNCHE (1369): *Al this I put in his servage As to my lorde, and dyd homage.*

sesame. Most children know *Open Sesame!* as the magic password to the cavern in the tale of ALI BABA AND THE FORTY THIEVES, for a long time before they learn that *sesame* is the name of an East Indian plant, especially known for its seeds, and for the oil pressed from them. Sesame seeds and honey make a delicious confection. Other names for the plant and the seed are *sesamum, sesamus, sesamine,* the last also used as an adjective, while *sesamoid, sesamoideal* mean shaped like a sesame seed. THE ARABIAN NIGHTS' ENTERTAINMENT (1785), telling the story, explained: *Sesame (which is a sort of corn).* Similarly, the Hebrew password used by Jephtha, *shibboleth, q.v.,* is explained in the Septuagint and the Vulgate as an ear of corn.

sesquipedalian. Of many syllables. Horace in THE ART OF POETRY (about 20 B.C.) spoke of *sesquipedalia verba,* words a foot and a half long; the 17th century seized upon the term, as in K.W.'s (1661) scorn of *noddle-puzzling sesquepedalian words.* Boswell (1791) applied the term, quite justly, to Johnson's Johnsonese. The term survives in pedantic humor. Hence, *sesquipedalianism, sesquipedalism, sesquipedality.* The terms are also transferred, to other sorts of great size, as in Sterne's TRISTRAM SHANDY (1759): *With a breadth of back, and a sesquipedality of belly, which might have done honour to a serjeant in the horse-guards.*

sew. As a noun. In Old English, juice, moisture. Later, broth, pottage; especially, onion broth. Then, a dish of minced meat stewed with onions. Thus *sewes,* dishes of meat. Chaucer uses *sewes* in THE SQUIRE'S TALE (1386), and Warner in ALBION'S ENGLAND (1586) liked *to have gud spiced sewe and roste, and plum-pies for a king.*

sewel. An old variant of *shewel,* scarecrow (in those times, usually scaredeer). Also *sewell; cp. aschewele.*

seynt. A girdle. Old French (also English) *ceint;* Latin *cingere, cinctus,* to bind, to gird. Also *ceynt, saynt, seinte, saint, sent.* A *seynture* (French *ceinture*), *centure,* a waist-belt. Used from the 13th into the 16th century. In Chaucer's Prologue to THE CANTERBURY TALES (1386) we read, of the Sergeant of the Law: *He rood but hoomly in a medlee cote, Girt with a ceint of silk with barres smale.*

shab. To get rid of; to put (a person) off; to slink or sneak away; to trick, deceive, or rob. *Shabaroon* (defined in 1700 as a ragamuffin, in 1847—*shabbaroon, shabroon*—as a mean shabby fellow, as though the form were derived from *shabby*), a disreputable fellow, a villain. THE LONDON SPY (E. Ward, 1703) speaks of *Poor loose shabroons in bawdy-houses bred.* The NEW MONTHLY MAGAZINE in 1838 noted that if *recognition from a coroneted carriage stamps you a lord . . . the notice of a shabaroon can be nothing less than a hint to your tailor to send in his bill.* J. P. Kennedy in ANNALS OF QUODLIBET (1840) said: *I hold the people in too much esteem to shab them off with anything of a secondary quality.* Hence also *shabrag,* the worse for wear; a down-at-the-heels, mean person. T. Bridges in HOMER TRAVESTIE (1762) wrote: *None of your Bromingham affairs, Nor any such like shabrag wares, But good new halfpence from the Mint, With honest George's face in print.*

shaffron. See *chamfrain.*

shamsheer. A variant of *scimitar,* more closely approximating the Persian form. The Anglo-Indian is *shumsheer.* Used in the 17th century.

Shandean. Whimsical; given to spurts of playfulness or nonsensicality, as in the novel TRISTRAM SHANDY (1759). The author, Laurence Sterne, described TRISTRAM SHANDY as a *civil, nonsensical, good-humoured Shandean book, which will do all your hearts good.* Sterne also said, in a letter of 9 July, 1762: *I had hired a chaise and horse . . . but, Shandeanlike, did not take notice that the horse was almost dead when I took him.* Jefferson, in his NOTES ON THE STATE OF VIRGINIA (1782) remarked: *His style is easy and familiar, except when he affects a Shandean fabrication of words.*

shandrydan. A carriage with a hood; a light cart. Also *shandry; shanderydan, shandaradan, shandradam, shatterydan, shattaradan.* Used in the early part of the 19th century; as Victoria's reign progressed and the carriages grew older, *shandrydan* was used, in humorous scorn, for an old rickety carriage.

shandy. Wild, boisterous; visionary, empty-headed. Also *shandy-pated.* Used mainly in the 18th and 19th centuries, possibly related to TRISTRAM SHANDY; see *Shandean. shandy* (19th century) might also be a shortening of *shandygaff, q.v.*

shandygaff. A mixture of beer and ginger-beer, popular in the 19th century. Hughes' TOM BROWN AT OXFORD (1861) pictures the pleasure: *With a large pewter, foaming with shandygaff, in each hand.* Christopher Morley was so struck with the drink that he wrote a book with title *Shandygaff* (1918).

shanks' mare. See *bayard.*

shard. A gap, a break. From the common Teutonic root *skar,* to separate; see *sharn.* Hence a gap in the land, or the dividing water; so used in Spenser's THE FAËRIE QUEENE (1590). By extension, a fragment of earthenware; *to break into shards (sherds),* to break beyond repair. Also used figuratively; Longfellow in EVANGELINE (1847) speaks of *the shards and thorns of existence.* Also *shard,* a patch of cow-dung; hence, *shard-born,* born in dung, as a beetle. Shakespeare in MACBETH (1605) says: *Ere to black Heccats summons The shard-borne beetle, with his drowsie hums, Hath rung nights yawning peale.* [Johnson, misinterpreting Shakespeare's *borne* as meaning carried, suggested in his DICTIONARY (1755): *Perhaps shard in Shakespeare may signify the the sheaths of the wings of insects.* Some writers have thence used *shard* to mean an insect's wing-case; Longfellow in HIAWATHA (1842); *The shining shards of* *beetles*; Earl Bulwer-Lytton in THE WANDERER (1857) wrote of *the advancing twilight's shard-born trumpeter.*] Hence *sharded,* broken into fragments (of the moon: crescent); living in dung; *shardy,* covered with dung; but also, having wing-cases, as the coleopterous insects. Shakespeare has *shards* in ANTONY AND CLEOPATRA; *sharded* in CYMBELINE.

sharn. Dung, especially of cattle. Also *scern, shearn, shairin, shurn,* and more. Old English *scearn,* root *skar,* to separate, whence also *shear* and *ploughshare. Cp. shard.* Hence *sharnbud, sharnbug,* dung-beetle. *sharny, sharny-faced,* bedaubed with dung. *The meat of frogges,* said Topsell in his book on SERPENTS (1608) *are greene hearbes, and humble-bees, or shorne-bugs.* Also, *sharn-penny,* the yearly payment per cow (especially, 12th and 13th centuries, to the Abbey of Bury St. Edmunds) in lieu of the dung the Abbey would have received from the manorial practice of having the tenant's cattle folded on the lord's land.

sharpshin. (1) Quick-witted, keen. Called 'proverbial' by Edwards, in WORDS, FACTS, AND PHRASES (1912), with its origin given German *scharf,* sharp + *Sinn,* wit. Not listed in O.E.D. (2) There is divergence of opinion here. The O.E.D. gives *sharpshin* "U.S. Probably a back-formation from *sharpshinned hawk*; ? in jocular allusion to the eagle on the coin. Apparently originally a name for some coin of very small value; later, used as a type of what has little value." Marryat in PETER SIMPLE (1834) said: *Four sharshins to a pictareen.* But A DICTIONARY OF AMERICANISMS (1951) says that a *sharpshin* (besides being short for the *sharpshinned hawk*) was an eighth of a coin: "one of the sharp-edged, wedge-shaped fragments of a coin cut to secure small change." Thus Mordecai in VIRGINIA IN BYGONE DAYS (1860) remarked: *Money is said to burn the pockets of some folks —sharpshins cut the pockets of all.*

shaveling. (1) A contemptuous term for a tonsured churchman. Common on Protestant lips in the 16th and 17th centuries; Tennyson speaks of a *turncoat shaveling* in his historical drama BECKET (1884). (2) A young fellow just able to shave. George J. Whyte Melville in GENERAL BOUNCE; OR, THE LADY AND THE LOCUSTS (1854) spoke of *the shavelings who aspire to dandyism.*

shaw. (1) A thicket, a small wood; especially, a strip of wood forming a border to a field. (2) The stalks and leaves of plants (potatoes, turnips) of which the edible parts are underground; the part that *shaws* (shows). Hence, *to shaw,* to cut off such tops. The playwright Shaw has given English the adjective *Shavian;* he was a Shaver of sham. Darwin (in F. Darwin, LIFE AND LETTERS, 1842) spoke of *a country . . . possessing a certain charm in the shaws, or straggling strips of wood, capping the chalky banks.* For a use of the word in Chaucer, see *galliard.*

shawm. A medieval wind instrument (of the oboe family), with a double reed in a globular mouthpiece. *Cp. bandore.* The word came via Middle English *schallemelle* and Old French *chalemel, chalemie,* from Latin *calamus,* reed. Walt Whitman uses *Calamus* for a group of his poems. *Shawm* appeared in many forms; Chaucer used *shalmyes, chalemyes, shalemeyes;* Caxton, *shalemuse;* Spenser, *shaumes.* Beaumont and Fletcher in THE KNIGHT OF THE BURNING PESTLE (1611) have the Citizen declare: *Ralph plays a stately part, And he must needs have shawns.* Tennyson and Swinburne use the word; the sun is so vivid to Francis Thompson that he cries, in his ODE TO THE SETTING SUN

(1888): *I* see *the crimson blaring of thy shawms!*

sheder. See *heder.*

sheltron. A phalanx; originally, a body of troops with their shields locked to form a roof and wall about them. Old English *scield,* shield + *truma,* troop. Also *scheltroun, schiltron, shultrum,* and the like; not used after the 15th century, except in historical references.

shench. See *shenk.*

shend. To disgrace; to blame, punish, revile, scold. This was a very common word, in many forms, from the 8th century; by the 15th it had dropped from use save in the participial form *shent,* bewildered, stupified, overcome with fatigue. *Cp. shent.* Thus in THE OUTLOOK of 11 February, 1905, we read *I stood utterly shent and powerless.* The word developed other meanings: to destroy, ruin; more mildly, to damage, spoil; defile, soil—Chaucer in THE PARSON'S TALE, 1386: *Whoso toucheth warm pitch, it shent his fingers*—to put to shame by one's superiority, as in Spenser's PROTHALAMIUM (1596): *These twain, that did excel The rest, so far, as Cynthia doth shend The lesser stars.* Also *shendfulness,* vileness; *shendlac,* infamy (13th century); *shendness,* (10th to 14th century); *shendship* (14th and 15th centuries), *shending* (13th to 16th century), disgrace, ignominy, ruin. A cynical proverb of 1400 has it that *Who saith truth is shent.*

shenk. To pour liquor, to give someone drink. Also *schench, scencan, shenche, shennkenn, senken, schenkyn. Cp. nuncheon. Shench,* a drink. Also, both verb and noun, *skink,* to pour out, serve, offer (mainly of drink); Chaucer, Douglas, Shirley, Dryden, Fletcher, Hobbes; Smollett in his translation (1755) of DON QUIXOTE: *Truce with your compliments and skink away!* The forms were used from the 8th to the 15th century. A 19th century form *shenkbeer,* from German *schenken,* to pour + *Bier,* beer, was used of a weak beer that had to be used quickly, lest it turn sour. Also *shenker,* a tavern keeper. Gower in CONFESSIO AMANTIS (1390) speaks of a pause at a *taverne forto schenche That drink which maketh the herte brenne.*

shent. The past participle of *shend, q.v.* Also (13th to 15th century) as a noun, disgrace; as an adjective, disgraced; ruined, stupefied; as a verb, to hesitate—*shenting for shame,* said THE DESTRUCTION OF TROY (1400). Shakespeare uses *shent,* meaning blamed, rebuked, in THE MERRY WIVES OF WINDSOR (1598); TWELFTH NIGHT; CORIOLANUS; HAMLET, where the Prince resolves to reproach his mother: *I will speak daggers to her, but use none. My tongue and soul in this be hypocrites, How in my words soever she be shent, To give them seals never, my soul, consent.*

sherd. See *shard.*

sherris. Wine of *Xeres* (a town in Andalusia, Spain). Shakespeare, in HENRY IV, PART TWO (1597), expert here also, declares that *The second property of your excellent sherris is, the warming of the blood.* Mistaken for a plural, *sherris* developed the still widely current *sherry.*

sherryvallies. Heavy trousers, buttoned on the outside of each leg, usually worn over other trousers, for rough journeys on horseback and the like. The word was used in the United States in the 18th and 19th centuries; it is ultimately from Arabic *sharawil,* Syriac *sharbala,* Persian *shalwar,* meaning that sort of garment. The form *sherwal* is still used for the loose trousers worn in parts of Asia.

sherwood. A greenwood, a pleasant forest. This came to be used as a general name, from the popularity of the story of Robin Hood in Sherwood Forest. Thus Phaer in his translation (1562) of the AENEID speaks of *the shirwood great where self defence and free resort Duke Romulus uptooke.*

shete. An early form of *sheet, shoot, shut.* A *sheter* was a shooter.

shevel. See *disannul.* To be *shevel-gabbit, shevel-mouthed,* is to have a wry mouth, from *shevel,* to distort or to become distorted. Thus *sheveled* and *disheveled* had the same meaning, though only the compound form (perhaps seeming the more emphatic) has survived.

shewel. See *aschewele.*

shibboleth. A pass-word, or a test-word, to check the identity or race of a person by his pronunciation. The Hebrew word *shibboleth* meant ear of corn or stream in flood; it was used, at the ford of the Jordan River, by Jephthah (in the BIBLE: JUDGES) to distinguish the fleeing Ephraimites (who pronounced not *sh* but *s*; see *sibboleth*) from his own Gileadite forces. The same shift has become fixed in the word *anti-Semitism*; the *Semites* are the descendants of *Shem.*

shidder. See *heder.*

ship. A variant form of *sheep,* still found in dialects. *Cp. lea.* Preserved in the old saying about *losing a ship for a hap'orth of tar.* Hot tar was used to brand sheep that grazed on the commons, to identify their ownership; not to buy a half-penny's worth of tar, to brand a sheep, might mean its loss. The phrase was applied to a man penny-wise, pound-foolish, one that failed in a great enterprise through a trifling lack.

ship-tire. A headdress resembling a ship, deemed a feminine adornment by some Elizabethans. See *tire.* Praised by Falstaff (Shakespeare wants us to sense his bad taste!) in THE MERRY WIVES OF WINDSOR (1598): *Thou hast the right arched beauty of the brow that becomes the ship-tire, the tire-valiant, or any tire of Venetian admittance.*

shog. To shake, jolt, jar. Also *shogge, shogke, shug,* and the like; echoic, like *jog;* in most senses supplanted by *shock.* Also, to shake a person in anger, or to wake him; hence, to annoy. By extension, to walk in a series of jerks, to *jog* along; later, to walk on and on; to continue steadily; to go away. Shakespeare in HENRY V (1599): *Will you shogge off?* Also *shoggle* (*shoogle, shuggle*), to shake; shake off; shake or settle down; walk unsteadily.

shoop. The fruit of the rose, the hip. Also *choop*; *showpe, shoup.* Used from the 15th century; a cook-book of 1721 tells *How to candy shoups.*

shootanker. A variant form of *sheet-anchor,* the large anchor used only in an emergency; hence, figuratively, a last resort or reliance. Thus Merygreeke, looking for a meal (in Udall's RALPH ROISTER DOISTER; 1553) says of Ralph: *For truely of all men he is my chiefe banker, Both for meate and money, and my chiefe shootanker.* Bishop Montague (1641) called Christ *the shootanker of salvation.*

shortheel. A prostitute. Also *shortheels.* A term of the late 16th and early 17th century, indicating lack of balance, aptness to fall. *Sue Shortheels, a whore* is one of the characters in Rowley's A MATCH AT MIDNIGHT (1633): Lyly in MIDAS (1592) describes such a woman: *High she was in the instep, but short in the heel; straight laced, but loose bodied.*

shot. See *biscot.*

shotclog. A person tolerated in the company because he pays the *shot* (see *shotfree*). Also *shotlog.* In Jonson's EVERY MAN OUT OF HIS HUMOUR (1599), when Fungoso, reforming, declares *I am out of those humours now,* Macilente retorts: *Well, if you be out, keep your distance, and be not made a shot-clog any more.* In the same play Carlo cries out: *Holla! Where be these shot-sharks!* meaning the drawers (the waiters) that wait to present the bill.

shote. A rush or rapid motion; especially, the flight of arrows. Hence, the arrows thus shot; the act of shooting with a bow. *All at one shote,* in a volley. A variant of *shoot* and *shot,* used in the 14th and 15th centuries.

shotfree. (1) Safe from shot, proof against missiles. Used from the 16th century; also figuratively as in W. Tooke's translation (1820) of Lucian, of a poor poet: *Why are the Muses invulnerable to you and shot-free?* (2) Free from payment of *shot* (charge at a tavern, etc., *cp. biscot*); by extension, unpunished, *scot-free;* also used of a meal that is gratis. Thus *shot-flagon,* a pot of ale given by the host when the customers have drunk more than a shilling's worth of ale. A *shot-pot,* one that spends enough to entitle him to a *shot-flagon.* Shakespeare in HENRY IV, PART ONE (1586) says with double pun: *Though I could scape shot-free at London, I fear the shot heere: here's no scoring, but upon the pate.*

shotshark. See *shotclog.*

shotten. The former past participle of *shoot.* Used from the 15th century of a fish that has spawned, has 'shot' its roe, hence is exhausted—especially, (figuratively) in the phrase *shotten herring,* applied to a useless, worn out, worthless person. Shakespeare in HENRY IV, PART ONE (1596) says: *If manhood, good manhood be not forgot upon the face of the earth, then I am a shotten herring.* Also, *shotten milk,* curdled milk. Hence, *shotten,* emaciated, worn; worthless. Sir Thomas More in a religious polemic about 1533 spoke of heretics that *have as much shame in their face as a shotten herring hath shrimps in her tail.*

shoulder. Used in many compounds, most of them self-explanatory. Among others: (1) *shoulder-clapper,* an officer assigned to arrest someone (as for debt), a bailiff, a sheriff's officer. Very common in Tudor times; also, *showlderclapped.* Dekker in LANTHORNE AND CANDLE-LIGHT (1609) speaks of bankrupts who revel after midnight, *and then march home again fearelesse of the blowes that any showlderclapper durst give them.* (2) *shoulder-stick,* a passenger on a stage-coach whose fare the driver did not turn in. In the 19th century, *to shoulder,* to cheat one's employer. (3) *shoulder-striker, shoulder-hitter,* one that gives a blow straight from the shoulder; by extension, a ruffian, a bully; Holmes in THE PROFESSOR AT THE BREAKFAST TABLE (1860) remarks that *no shoulder-striker hits out straighter than a child with its logic.*

shoup. An old variation of *shoop, q.v.*

showes. A variant form of *shoes.* Roper in THE LIFE OF SYR THOMAS MORE (1557) reported that Adrian VI, when he became Pope, *cominge on foote to Roome, before his entry into the Citye did put off his* *hosen and showes, barefoote and barlegged passing throwe the streates towards his pallacie.*

shrew. An evil or ill-disposed person; also, the devil, also, a malignant planet; hence, anything evil. Therefore, a scolding woman, especially, a bossy wife. Hence, to shrew, to curse, to *beshrew* (wish evil upon)—sometimes, as in Chaucer's THE NONNE PREESTES TALE (1386), with the *I*: *I shrewe us bothe two And first I shrewe myself both blood and bones If thou begyle me*—But often with the *I* omitted, as Shakespeare's CYMBELINE (1611): *Shrew me!* and THE WINTER'S TALE: *Shrew my heart!* Also *shreward,* a scoundrel; *shrewd,* wicked, evil, malignant; a *shrewd turn,* a malicious injury. Hence *shrewdhead, shrewdom, shrewdship, shrewhead, shrewishness,* wickedness, depravity, maliciousness. Only *shrewdness* (like *shrewd*) moved from the earlier meaning of wickedness to the current sense of sagacity, astuteness in practical affairs—still retaining, however, implication of ethical heedlessness. The insectivorous mammal, the *shrew* was thus named in England as early as the 7th century; an animal (such as the horse) paralyzed (supposedly) by being overrun by a shrew-mouse, was called *shrew-afflicted, shrew-run, shrew-struck,* the remedy being to lead or draw it through a briar growing (rooted) at both ends, and to bury the shrew alive in a hole bored in an ash tree (the *shrew-ash*).—The *shrew,* villain, wretch, gradually lost its force, and was used playfully, as by Stevenson in BLACK ARROW (1888): *Our poor shrew of a parson.* Swift in POLITE CONVERSATIONS (1738) used the word figuratively: *Marriage is honourable, but housekeeping is a shrew.*

shroud. Before this meant (late 16th century) a cloth for a corpse, it meant (from the 10th century) clothing in general, or an article of clothing. Foxe in his ACTES AND MONUMENTS (1563) spoke of Latymer's execution, but when he wrote *beyng stripped into his shroud,* Foxe by *shroud* meant undershirt. By extension (12th to 14th century), the vesture in which natural things are clothed; of the springtime Chaucer said, in THE ROMAUNT OF THE ROSE (1366), *And then bicometh the ground so proud That it wol have a newe shroud.* Incidentally, the shroud for burial was a white cloth, but association with the color of mourning has led to frequent references to *sable shroud;* Gilbert in RUDDIGORE (1887) speaks of *Inky clouds, Like funeral shrouds.*

shrow. An early form of *shrew, q.v.* In Shakespeare's LOVE'S LABOUR'S LOST (1594) Katharine exclaims: *A pox of that jest! And I beshrew all shrows!*

shunless. That cannot be avoided, inevitable. Shakespeare in CORIOLANUS (1607) speaks of *shunless destiny.*

shuttlecock. See *batler.*

shyderyd. A variant form of *shivered,* shattered. Skelton, when a gentlewoman sent him a skull (WORKES; 1529; *cp. brynnyng*) pictured the corpse *With sinnews wyderyd, With bonys shyderyd, With his worme etyn maw, And his gastly jaw Gasping asyde, Nakyd of hyde.*

sib. Kinship; hence, by extension, peace, amity, concord. This is a very common word from earliest English until the 16th century—even later as an adjective meaning related, akin. Also *sibness, sibred,* relationship; *sibsomeness,* peace, concord. *Sibman* and *sibling* were used until about 1450 to mean one close of kin; *sibling* has been revived in this century, in sociology, to mean a brother or sister. Gillespie, in A DISPUTE AGAINST THE ENGLISH-

POPISH CEREMONIES (1637) uses *sib* figuratively: *Nearer to sycophancy than to sincerity, and sibber to appeaching hostility than fraternal charity.* A *gossip* was originally a *god-sib,* relative by God, a sponsor at baptism, god-father or god-mother—from whose usual behavior came the current meaning of *gossip.*

sibboleth. To speak with a special pronunciation. See *shibboleth.* Sir Thomas Herbert, in A RELATION OF SOME YEARS TRAVAILE (1634), said that a place *is called Spawhawn (or as they sibboleth, Sphawhawn) and by most writers differently spelled.*

sibsomeness. See *sib.*

sibyl. A prophetess; a fortune-teller; a witch; a hag. Also *sibylla, sibille, sybil.* Greek *sibylla;* a woman possessed of powers of divination. There were supposedly ten of these in ancient times; Shakespeare in HENRY VI, PART ONE (1591) declares: *The spirit of deep prophecie she hath, Exceeding the nine sibyls of old Rome.* Hence also the *Sibylline books* of the *Sybilline oracles;* a *Sibyllianist* or *Sibyllist* was one, especially an early Christian, who accepted the Sibylline books as authentic. Sheridan in THE DUENNA (1775) exclaims: *Thou wanton sybil, thou amorous woman of Endor!* and again: *Handsome! Venus de Medicis was a sibyl to her.* In its more pleasant connotations, it is used as a girl's name, although my good friend, of Ilium, uses the form *Sybil.*

sic. An early form (later mainly Scotch) of *such.* The still earlier form was *swik, swilk.* Spenser in THE SHEPHERD'S CALENDAR says *Sike fancies weren foolerie.* Also *siccan,* such, such-like. The Latin word *sic,* so, thus, is still used, in parenthesis, to indicate an error or anything outlandish to which the writer wants to call attention, especially in something he is quoting—thus marking the other person's responsibility. *The modern reviewer's taste,* however, E. B. Box suggested in THE ETHICS OF SOCIALISM (1889), *is not really shocked by half the things he* sics *or otherwise castigates.*

sicarian. An assassin. Also, as an adjective, pertaining to or behaving like an assassin. Latin *sica,* dagger. Used rarely, but in the 15th, 17th, and 19th centuries. Also *sicarious;* W. Taylor remarked in THE MONTHLY REVIEW of 1811 that certain prejudices *may occasion Sicilian vespers, and expose to sicarious destruction every British resident.*

siccate. To dry, to make dry. Used in the 16th and 17th centuries; also *siccicate.* Latin *siccare, siccatum,* to dry; *siccus,* dry. Hence also *siccaneous, sicced,* dry; *siccative, siccific,* that has the property of absorbing moisture, of drying; *siccation,* the act of drying; *siccitude, siccity,* dryness.

sice. Six; especially, the throw of six at dice. Also *size, sysse, sys,* and the like; pronounced with long *i.* Chaucer in THE MONK'S TALE (1386) says: *Thy sys fortune hath turned into Aas.* Hence *sice cinque,* a throw of two dice with six and five turned up; similarly *sice quatre; sice trey; sice deuce; sice-ace, sizeace.*

sicer. Strong drink, intoxicating liquor. Used 13th to 17th century. The CURSOR MUNDI (1300) said: *He dranc never cisar ne wine.* Many other forms were used, such as *ciser, cisere, cysar, sychere;* from Late Latin *sicera* via Greek from Hebrew *shekar,* strong drink, whence the current dialectal *shiker* (short *i*), drunk. Via French from the same root came *cider.*

sicker. Safe, certain, dependable; firm, unshaken; stable; careful, cautious; indubitable; genuine; secure; fully convinced, assured, confident. A very common word up to 1500, thereafter northern and Scotch. Also *sicor, sycher, sycur, siker, sikkir, zykere, cykere, sekir, sekyre,* and the like. It was an early English formation from Latin *securus,* from which *secure* was first used in the 16th century. Also as a verb, *to sicker,* to secure, make safe, assure; to put trust in, to confirm by a surety; to betroth. Hence *sickerhead, sickerlaik, sickerness, sickerty,* certainty. Misyn in his translation (1435) of THE FIRE OF LOVE speaks of the *gostely fyer, in the whilk thay knawe thame-self sekyr.* Chaucer in THE LEGEND OF GOOD WOMEN (ARIADNE; 1384) said: *Now be we duchessis both I and ye And sekerede to the regalys* [royal house] *of Athenys.* A 15th century proverb said: *It is more sekyr a bird in your fist Than to have three in the sky a-bove.* Or two in the bush.

sideromancy. See *aeromancy.*

sigalder. A charm, incantation. Old English *sige,* victory + *galder. Galder* was used in BEOWULF to mean a charm, incantation; from *galan,* to sing, whence also the *nightingale.* Used from the 10th to the 13th century. Also *sigaldry, sygaldrye,* sorcery. Robert Manning of Brunne in HANDLYNG SYNNE (1303) used *sigalder* as a verb: *There was a wicche, and made a bagge, a bely of lethyr . . . she sigaldryd so thys bagge-bely That it yede and soke mennys ky* [that it went and sucked men's cattle].

sightsome. Delightful to behold. Also *sightly,* current in the alas more frequent *unsightly.*

sigil. (1) A small image; especially, one used as a charm. Also *sigillum.* (2) A seal or signet. (3) A sign or device: (a) initials to indicate words, or other abbreviations. In this sense, also *sigle* and (plural) *sigla: X is a known sigle for Jesus Christ.* (b) An occult symbol, especially in astrology, supposed to have or to indicate supernatural powers. Hence *sigillate,* to seal; *sigillated* (also *sigillate*), marked with a seal. *sigillary,* pertaining to a seal, subject to the influence of a seal or charm, thus Surtees in 1834: *That maiden kiss hath holy power O'er planet and sigillary hour. Sigilled,* wearing a seal or signet-ring. Pope in THE TEMPLE OF FAME (1711) said that they *Of talismans and sigils knew the power And careful watched the planetary hour.* From the inviolable seal of the Confessional came a special use of the form *sigilism,* as in THE ENGLISHMAN'S MAGAZINE for February, 1865: *The following appear to be the principle crimes against which the edicts of the Inquisition were fulminated: immorality in the confessional, sigilism (or revealing the secrets of the confessional).* Webb in his translation (1880) of Goethe's FAUST said: *A book with sevenfold sigil is the past!*

sike. (1) A small stream, which usually dried in the summer; a ditch or channel. Also *syke.* These are northern forms from Old English *sic;* the corresponding southern form was *sitch.* Scott revived the word, in a letter of 1818: *My lake is but a mill-pond, my brooks but sykes.* All over England the sike or sitch was used in marking property boundaries, and may be found in place-names through the land. (2) From Frisian *sike,* a breath, *sike* (13th to 15th century) was used to mean sigh, both noun and verb. The 9th century form of this word was *siche,* past tense *sight,* associated with *sigh.* Thus Chaucer, in TROYLUS AND CRISEYDE (1374): *With a sik she sorwfully answerde,* and in THE LEGEND OF GOOD WOMEN (1385), of Dido:

She siketh sore, and gan her selfe turmente.

siker. See *sicker.*

sile. (1) To move, glide; fall, subside; faint, *to sile away* (18th century), to faint away; to pour (as rain); to flow (as tears). (2) To strain or sieve; especially milk. Also *seil, soil.* Old farm and cook books advising one to *soil the milk* meant to cleanse it. Thus *sileclout,* cloth to strain milk through; *siledish.* (3) To cover the eyes; hence, to mislead, deceive; to conceal, hide. In this sense, more often (15th to 17th century) *seel, q.v.* Also, to sew up (the eyes of a hawk). Hudson in his translation (1584) of Du Bartas (JUDITH) wrote: *Thus siling human sight, it changed form: One while a rod, one while a creeping worm.*

sillabub. A drink made by milking a cow into sweetened and spiced cider. Sometimes the milk was mixed with spiced wine. Bailey (1751) quotes Minsheu's GUIDE INTO TONGUES (1617), saying the word is a contraction of *swilling bubbles.* The drink was a popular one from the 16th to the mid-19th century, and many forms of the word developed, including *sillub* (Scotch), *sillibouk, sylibewk, syllabud, solybubbe, selebube, sillybob.* Howell in a letter of 1645 urged: *Leave the smutty ayr of London and com hither . . . wher you may pluck a rose, and drink a cillibub.* By extension, *sillabub* was used of frothy, empty speech or writing; hence, anything insubstantial. THE DAILY NEWS of 11 May, 1889, wrote: *The new bonnets are the veriest trifles; mere syllabubs of frothed-up lace.* Thackeray used the form to mean a mixture; *Aunt Lambert,* he said in THE VIRGINIANS (1859), *was one great syllabub of human kindness.*

sillery. An excellent wine (especially *sillery sec*), from the village of Sillery, department of Marne, province of Champagne, France. The word has been extended to wine from the neighboring vineyards of Verzenay and Mailly. Also spelled *celery.* The Duke of Buckingham complained, in 1688: *As for French kickshaws, cellery and champain, in troth we 'ave none.* The wine was eagerly sought and gladly drunk in England from the 17th to the mid-19th century, especially for toasting royalty or celebrating great occasions.

silly. See *seel. Silly* is used by Coleridge (THE ANCIENT MARINER, 1798) to mean idle: *The silly buckets on the deck* were long without rainwater.

simarre. See *cymar.* Pope, translation (1720) of THE ILIAD: *The maids in soft simars of linen drest;* Scott, IVANHOE (1819): *a simarre of the richest Persian silk;* THE CENTURY MAGAZINE (August, 1893): *The dancing girl in soft simar.* As a bishop's robe (*chimer*) in the translation (1886) of Hugo's NOTRE DAME: *The simar had the worst of it in its collision with the cassock.*

simity. The state of being pug-nosed. Latin *simus,* Greek *sillus,* snub-nosed. Used in the 17th century, as in John Bulwer's ANTHROPOMETAMORPHOSIS (1650) where he notes that midwives *are wont to press the lateral parts of the nose, that this simity of children may be the sooner abolished.*

simkin. A simpleton. *Sim* is short for Simon. From *Simple Simon* of the nursery rhyme, probably also association with *simple* (shortened to *simp*) + the diminutive ending *kin,* comes the not unfriendly term *simkin,* also *simpkin.* Henry Mayhew in his LONDON LABOUR AND THE LON-

DON POOR (1861) says: *Pierrot is the simpkin of the ballet.*

simnel. A bun made of fine flour boiled, then baked. In particular, a rich currant bun, cooked for mid-Lent or Mothering Sunday—when it was customary to take presents (such as these cakes) to one's parents, or to visit one's parents and receive presents. C. S. Burne, in SHROPSHIRE FOLK LORE (1883) remarks that *Shrewsbury simnels are eaten by many who do not heed the pious habit of 'mothering' which they were intended to celebrate.* Herrick in HESPERIDES (TO DIANEME, 1648) says: *Ile to thee a simnel bring, 'Gainst thou go'st a Mothering.*

simony. The buying or selling of church offices or privileges; traffic in sacred things. Also *simonism.* From *Simon Magus* who (the BIBLE: ACTS viii) offered money to the Apostles. Hence *simonian, simoniac, simoniacle, simonient, simonier, simonist, simonite,* one that practices or upholds simony; *simonious,* relating to simony. Dekker in IF IT BE NOT GOOD (1612) declares: *None shall hold three or four church-livings (got by symonious gold).* Chaucer points out, in THE PARSON'S TALE (1386), that *both he that selleth and he that byeth thinges espirituels ben cleped symonyales.*

simpkin. See *simkin.*

simple. Among the less remembered uses is: a medicament of but one constituent; especially, an herb gathered for medicinal use. This sense was common, especially in the plural, from 1550 to 1750. Pope, in his translation (1725) of THE ODYSSEY, takes us *where prolific Nile With various simples clothes the fat'ned soil.* Hence, *to simple; simpling,* gathering herbs. Shakespeare in THE MERRY WIVES OF WINDSOR (1598) admires *These lisping-hawthorne buds, that . . . smell like bucklersberry in simple time.*

simpson. To dilute milk with water. Also, *to simpsonize.* Thus *simpson,* water used to dilute milk; *Mrs. Simpson,* the town or parish pump; a pump. Used from 1870, after a dairyman named *Simpson* was prosecuted for such augmentation of his product.

simular. A pretender. Thus Shakespeare has in KING LEAR (1606) *a simular of virtue.* He also uses it, in CYMBELINE, as an adjective, meaning having the appearance of: *with simular proof enough.*

sin. A word by many, if not forgotten, at least put aside. One errs as a result of environmental pressures; or one's neuroses are the consequence of inhibitions; obligations, responsibility, duty (*q.v.*) seem increasingly Victorian. Though the word *sin* may itself still be within recall, how many can name the seven deadly sins? These are *pride, sloth, envy, wrath, covetousness, lust, gluttony.* As the saints knew, the subtlest sin is pride. Among the old compounds with *sin* are: Sylvester, in his translation (1605) of Du Bartas: *Sucking the sin-bane of Assyrian ayre.* The title of a book by Egane (1673): *The Book of Rates now used in the Sin Custom-House of Rome.* Also *sin-boot* (*sin-bote, synbote*; 12th century), repentance. *sin-eater,* one hired to take on himself a dead person's sins, usually through food eaten beside the corpse; hence *sin-eating.* Murray's HANDBOOK OF SOUTH WALES in 1860 reported: *The superstition of the sin-eater is said to linger even now in the secluded vale of Cwm Amman. sin-rent,* an offering of money in expiation of sin; also *sin-money. sinflood,* the Deluge (used from the 16th century; actually a leap from German *sin-vlout,* general flood). *sin-*

wood, sinnewod (13th century), mad with sin. Nashe in 1593 spoke of *sin-gluttony*. Sin used to trouble folk a deal. And Charles Reade in THE CLOISTER AND THE HEARTH (1861) says: *The pair were driving a bargain in the sin-market.* At the booths of Vanity Fair.

sinapize. To sprinkle. Via Rabelais' French from Greek *sinapizein*; *sinapi*, mustard. A *sinapism* (from the 16th century) was a mustard plaster. Hence *sinapic*, relating to mustard; *sinapistic*, consisting of mustard. Looking at Paris in 1879 George Sala remarked: *In the majority of places of public entertainment the sinapistic condiment is simply vile.* Urquhart's translation (1653) of Rabelais says *he . . . took his head and into it synapised some powder of diamerdis.*

sincanter. A man (contemptuous); usually, an old decrepit man. Especially popular in the 16th and 17th centuries, the word took many forms; possibly from dicing (*cinque*, five; *quatre*, four) were *cinquanter, cinquecater, cincater, cenkanter*; also *sinkanter*; Blount's glossary of 1656 gives *succentor, he that singeth the base,* which suggests the origin of the forms *singcantor, sincantor.*

sindon. A fine thin fabric, linen, cambric, or muslin. Hence a garment or wrapper made thereof; specifically, the shroud in which the body of Jesus was wrapped. Also *syndon, sindony, sendony.* Hence *sindonless*, naked. *Many Papists,* said Cooke in POPE JOAN (1610), *are perswaded they have that syndon wherein Christs body was lapped.* A Coventry Mystery of 1450 said: *I gyf the this sindony than I have bowth* [bought], *To wynde the in whyl it is new.*

sin-eater. See *sin*.

singult. A sob. Latin *singultus*, talk broken by sobs; from the roots *sim*, together + *gvor, gul, glu*, to swallow—whence *voracious, omnivorous*, etc.; *gullet, gluttony*, and more. The form *singultus* is used in English to mean hiccuping, whence also *singultous, singultuous. Singultient*, sobbing; L. Morris in THE ODE OF LIFE (1879): *The great Universe wakes with a deep-drawn singultient breath.* Spenser uses the word *singult* (misprinted *singulf*) several times, e.g., in THE FAËRIE QUEENE (1590): *an huge heape of singultes did oppresse His strugling soule.*

sippet. A small piece of toasted or fried bread, for dipping into soup or gravy. *Sippet* is a diminutive of *sop*. Hence as a verb: *Sippet it and garnish the dish* (1681). By transference, a small piece of anything, a fragment: *This mumps,* say Beaumont and Fletcher in THE CAPTAIN (1612), *this lachrymae, this love in sippets.*

siquare. Point of time, moment. Usually in the phrase *in that siquare,* which occurs frequently in the Cotton manuscript (1300) of the CURSOR MUNDI.

siquis. A public notice or announcement, often posted, announcing something lost, or requesting information; later, especially a church notice asking if there is any reason why a certain candidate should not be granted ordination. From the first two words of the Latin notice: *Si quis,* If anyone—. Thus Jonson in EVERY MAN OUT OF HIS HUMOUR (1599): *Enter Cavalier Shift, with two siquisses in his hand.* Rarely used as a verb; thus, in THE GENTLEMAN INSTRUCTED (1713) *I must excuse my depart . . . otherwise, he may send hue and cry after me, and si quis me in the next Gazette.*

sirreverence. Originally this was an expression of respect, *save your reverence, sa' reverence, sir-reverence.* In the phrase *sir-reverence of,* it meant with all respect for, with apologies to; Massinger in THE VERY WOMAN (1634) said: *The beastliest man—sirreverence of this company—a rank whoremaster.* Then from the expression of apology, the word was transferred to that for which one apologized; Shakespeare shows the transition in THE COMEDY OF ERRORS (1590) when, speaking of a fat, greasy wench, he called her: *a very reverent body, ay, such a one, as a man may not speak of, without he say sir reverence.* Hence, a vent of anal wind; human excrement, or a lump thereof. In ROMEO AND JULIET Shakespeare says: *We'll draw thee from the mire of this sir-reverence love, wherein thou stick'st Up to the ears.* Smollett in HUMPHREY CLINKER (1771) said: *A plate of marmalade would improve a pan of sirreverence.* Head in THE ENGLISH ROGUE (1665) used it as a verb: *Another time sirreverencing in a paper, and running to the window with it.* "Cuthbert Cunny-Catcher," author of THE DEFENCE OF CONNY-CATCHING (1592) plays on the expression: *Sir reverence on your worship, had you such a moate in your eye that you could not see those fox-furd gentlemen, that hide under their gownes . . . more falshood then all the conny-catchers in England?*

siserary. A corruption of *(writ of) Certiorary.* Also *sessarary, sassarara, sassaray, sursurrara,* and the like. Hence, a severe tongue-lashing, a flood of abuse. *With a siserary,* with a vengeance, all of a sudden, violently. Smollett, in HUMPHREY CLINKER (1771): *I have gi'en the dirty slut a siserary.* Sterne, in TRISTRAM SHANDY (1765): *It was on Sunday in the afternoon, when I fell in love all at once with a sisserara.*

sist. To stop, stay, make stand; especially, by court or king's command. Also, to stop, to cease. Latin *sistere, stiti, statum;* to cause to stand; *stare,* to stand. Used in the 17th century; in the 18th, *sist* became a legal term, meaning to summon, to cause to appear before a court. Louthian in THE FORM OF PROCESS BEFORE THE COURT OF JUSTICIARY (1732) discussed *the manner of apprehending and sisting delinquents before the court.* Hence, *sistence,* stopping, pause. Howell in DODONA'S GROVE (1640) said: *Extraordinary must be the wisdome of him who floateth upon the streame of soveraigne favour, wherein there is seldom any sistence twixt sinking and swimming.* [In the 16th century, *sistence* was also used to mean help: a shortened form of *assistance.*] It is interesting to note (*cp. couth*) that, while simple forms of the past tenses of the Latin verb are used in English—*state, status, station, statue*—the present is represented in current English only by compounds: *assist, consist, desist, insist, persist, resist.* From the same root are *estate, obstinate, constituent, constitution, restitution, stability,* and even *justice.*

sitch. See *sike.* As marking boundaries, in Coventry, 1581: *A little way into the sitch there, called Sisley-hole . . . and under the bridge up the sitche to Hyndwell.*

sith. A shortened form of *sithen,* used in various senses of *then* and *since,* 9th to the 15th century.

sithe. (1) Used in the plural, *sithes,* chives. An alteration of *cive.* (2) A sieve, especially for straining milk. (3) A variation of *sigh.* (4) A going, a journey. In senses (2), (3), and (4), *sithe* was also used as a verb. The most frequent use (8th to 17th century) was in the sense of a journey, a path. This was common Teutonic, Gothic *sinths,* the causative form of which gave us English *send,* to cause to go. Other meanings of this *sithe* developed: fortune on a journey, hence, generally, fortune, luck; also misfortune, trouble (which often befell one on journeys); also, one's life-journey—thus in the CURSOR MUNDI (1300). Also *sithe,* time, occasion; used with numbers to express frequency, or multiplication, as one of the poems (1430) of Lydgate observes: *An hundred sithes better than they deserve.* Spenser in COLIN CLOUTS COME HOME AGAIN (1595) says: *The woods were heard to waile full many a sithe.* (time? or sigh?) In CURSOR MUNDI we also find the use as trouble: *In scorn and sithe to him and his.* May all your sithe be merry!

sithen. See *sith. Sithen* was also very frequent, 8th to 16th century. Also *sithence,* meaning *sith,* seeing that, since then. Chaucer has, in THE KNIGHT'S TALE (1386): *Never siththen that the world began . . .* Spenser, in THE FAËRIE QUEENE (1590): *Sithens silence lesseneth not my fire . . . I will reveal what ye so much desire.*

skainsmate. The O.E.D. says "Origin and exact meaning uncertain." The word occurs in Shakespeare's ROMEO AND JULIET (1592): *Scurvie knave, I am none of his flurt-gils, I am none of his skaines mates.* Partridge in SHAKESPEARE'S BAWDY (1948) defines it as ribald companion, and wonders (*skain* being an alternate spelling for *skein*) whether the word is not *skeinsmate,* one *amorously impleacht,* as Shakespeare phrases it in A LOVER'S COMPLAINT; *cp. impleach.*

skair. (1) A Scotch and northern dialect variant of *share,* both noun and verb. (2) To scatter, disperse; send in various directions. Used from the 12th to the 15th century. THE DESTRUCTION OF TROY (1400) said that the Greeks *skairen out skoutewacche for skeltyng of harme. To skelt* was to be diligent; also, to scatter.

skander. Slander. Noun and verb, of the 14th and 15th centuries. Also *skaunder.* The word sounds like a telescoping of *scandal* and *slander.* THE PASTON LETTERS in 1424 observed that one Walter *hath noysed and skaundered the seyd William.*

skaunce. A jest. A 15th century word, formed by false breaking up of *askanse.* Also *a skawnce.* Thus, in a Towneley Mystery of 1460: *Peace man, for godis payn! I said it for a skaunce.*

skeet. A long-handled scoop or shovel; especially, one for throwing water on the planks of a ship's sides in hot weather, or on the sails to make them the better hold a breeze. So used 15th to 19th century. Also (12th to 15th century; related to *shoot*) *skeet,* quickly, immediately; readily. Thus in a Towneley Mystery of 1460: *They were damned, soon and skete, unto the paine of hell.*

skelder. To beg; to live by begging, especially, by passing oneself off as a wounded soldier. Also, to swindle, to cheat. Thus Jonson in THE POETASTER (1601): *An honest decayed commander cannot skelder, cheat, nor be seene in a bawdie house, but he shall be straight in one of their wormewood comedies.* After the 17th century, the word was forgotten until reclaimed in the 19th century by Scott. Hence, *skeldering,* also used by Jonson (Dekker, Middleton), then Scott.

skellum. A rascal, scoundrel, villain. Jonson in the Introduction to Coryat's CRUDITIES (1611): *Going to steal 'em, He findeth soure graspes and gripes from a*

Dutch skelum. Burns, in TAM O' SHANTER (1790): *She tauld thee weel thou was a skellum, A blethering, blustering, drunken blellum.* In South Africa, in the 19th century, *skellum* was also used of animals, meaning a savage or brute beast.

skelt. See *skair.*

skew. As a noun. (1) The sky. *The skewes,* the heavens; clouds. Used until the 14th century. (2) A stone or slate for the gutter or gable of a roof. From the 13th century. (3) A sideglance. From the 17th century. Also, a slant; a deviation from a straight line; by extension, a slip, an error. *On the skew,* slantwise; so the current *askew.* Hence, as an adjective, *skew,* slanting, distorted, perverted. Survives as a term in mathematics, *skew lines; skew surface.* (4) A wooden dish; especially, a beggar's bowl (in the 16th and 17th centuries. As a verb. (1) To become overcast; to have the vision obscured by mist. (2) To escape, slip away (used from the 14th century); to move sideways; go obliquely; turn aside. Also, to look askance at, to look at suspiciously or condescendingly; hence, to cast aspersions upon. L'Estrange in his FABLES (1692) wisely observed: *'Tis dangerous skewing upon the errors of the age a man lives in.*

skink. See *shenk.* Also (1) a soup made with shin of beef. (2) A ham. (3) A variant form of *skunk.* The *skinking-pot* is the vessel from which wine was poured into a carafe.

skirm. See *skirr.*

skirr. To move rapidly or with great force (often implies a whirring sound); to run away; to ride rapidly (through, or in search of something). It shares these meanings with *scour.* The origin of the word is obscure. Toone in his GLOSSARY (1834) suggested that it is shortened from *skirmish,* which has a short form *skirm,* to engage in fight, to dart about, move rapidly. The O.E.D. looks hesitantly at Latin *excurrere,* to run out. It may be echoic of the whirring sound of speed. Shakespeare in MACBETH (1605) orders: *Send out moe horses, skirre the country round.* Beaumont and Fletcher in BONDUCA (1614) picture *the light shadows, That in a thought scur o'r the fields of corn.*

slade. A dingle or dell; a woodland glade; in some parts of England, a strip of greensward or of boggy land. Gower in CONFESSIO AMANTIS (1390) has: *He clymbeth up the banckes and falleth into slades depe.* Drayton uses it often in POLYOLBION (1622), e.g., of *satyrs, that in slades and gloomy dimbles dwell.* The *Gum Slade,* a beautiful clearing in a park at Sutton Coldfield in Warwickshire, is said to be the original of Shakespeare's woodland scenes in A MIDSUMMER NIGHT'S DREAM.

sleave. A filament of silk, obtained by separating the strands of a thicker thread. Hence, floss-silk. Also *sleeve.* Also *to sleave,* to divide silk; to separate, split, tear apart. Akin to *slive,* to split, divide; cut apart—whence, *sliver.* This verb was also used in the variants (past tense, *sleaved*) *sleided, sleded*; by Shakespeare in THE LOVER'S COMPLAINT (1597) and in PERICLES: *When they weavde the sleded silke With fingers long, small, white as milke.* Also *to slive,* to put on; to slide, slip, slip away; to loiter or to slip away. Shakespeare in MACBETH (1605) utters a heart-felt cry for *sleepe that knits up the ravel'd sleeve of Care.*

sleepwort. A plant, more familiar as *lettuce.* Also *sleepewort, slepwurt* (13th century); the first syllable indicates the narcotic property of the plant; *cp. purslane.* One might drink its milky juice; or boil the leaves in water and soak one's feet, binding some of the fresh leaves to one's temples to make sleep doubly sure.

sleeveless. Futile; bootless; leading to naught. Used very often from 1575 to 1700, in such phrases as *sleeveless word, sleeveless answer,—reason,—excuse.* Then, most frequently, *sleeveless errand.* This sometimes meant a journey that proves fruitless; sometimes, a pretended errand to get a person out of the way. Various writers have punned on the two senses of *sleeve,* including Shakespeare, who has Thersites say, in TROILUS AND CRESSIDA (1603): *I fain would see them meet, that that same young Trojan ass, that loves the whore there, might send that Greekish whoremasterly villain with the sleeve back to the dissembling luxurious drab, of a sleeveless errand.*

sleided. See *sleave.*

sleuthe. A variant form of *sloth,* one of the seven deadly sins. For a use of the form, see *vecordyous.* The seven deadly sins appear in Chaucer's THE PARSON'S TALE (1386); Gower's MIROUR DE L'OMME and CONFESSIO AMANTIS (1390); Lydgate's COURTE OF SAPYENCE (1430) and Hawes' THE PASSE TYME OF PLEASURE (1509) as well as in the popular morality play THE SEVEN DEADLY SINS, by Richard Tarlton (died 1588), the noted comic actor. This play was revived in 1590 and probably 1592, by the company Shakespeare joined in 1594. Hawes says of covetousness: *Whan erthe to erthe is nexte* [ready] *to reverte, And nature lowe in the laste aege, Of* [on] *erthely treasure earthe doth set his herte, Insacyatly upon covetyse to rage*—and of gluttony: *The pomped carkes* [pampered carcass] *with fode delycyous Erthe often fedeth with corrupte glotony And nothynge with werkes vertuous.*

slipper. An early form of *slippery,* in all its senses. Used from the 10th century; *slippery* first appeared in the 16th. Hence also *slipperous. slipperly,* insecurely. *slipperness, slipperiness.* Shakespeare in OTHELLO (1604) says: *A slipper and subtle knave, a finder of occasion.*

slive. See *sleave.*

slop. Among the many senses of this word may be noted: (1) A magic bag, used especially to steal milk from cows. *Cp. sigalder*: *Thys wycche here charme began to sey, the slop ros up . . . the sloppe lay stylle, as hyt ded wore.* (2) A loose outer garment, a mantle, a tunic; so used by Chaucer (THE PARSON'S TALE; 1386). (3) Most often (mainly in the plural), wide baggy hose or breeches, worn in the 16th and 17th centuries. Often applied to sailors' loose trousers; by extension, ready-made clothing from the ship's stores; hence, cheap garments. In the more elegant sense, Marston in THE SCOURGE OF VILLAINIE (SATIRE 10; 1599) inquires: *Faith say, what fashion are thou thinking on? A stitch't taffata cloake, a payre of slops Of Spanish leather?* (4) A mud-hole. This sense is related to *slip,* and survives in the slushy *slops* and the verb *to slop* (*over*). Guilpin in SKIALETHEIA (1598) pictures a youth *new printed to this fangled age; He weares a jerkin cudgeld with gold lace, A profound slop, a hat scarce pipkin high, a pair of dagge cases; his face, Furr'd with Cads-beard: his poynard on his thigh. He wallows in his walk his slop to grace.* [pipkin, a little pot; *dagge,* pistol; *Cads,* Cadiz, i.e., Spanish style].

sloth. See *sleuthe.*

slothound. A sleuth-hound; a sleuth. In addition to its current uses, *slot* meant the hoof-marks, hence the track, of a deer or other animal—sometimes used also of the scent. Hence, *to slot,* to track down. It was also used figuratively, by Milton (1645), Scott (1820) and in THE DAILY TELEGRAPH of 10 October, 1864: *The Emperor, who rarely quits the slot of an idea.* After the 16th century, Scott revived *slot-hound* in IVANHOE (1819), speaking of *the misfortunes which track my footsteps like slot-hounds.*

small beer. Inferior beer. Nashe, in FOUR LETTERS CONFUTED (1592) speaks of *poetry more spiritless than small beer.* Hence, persons or matters of no importance, trivialities. *To think no small beer of oneself,* to be bloated with self-importance; *Is it consistent,* asked PUNCH on 18 January, 1873, *for a teetotaller to think no small beer of himself?* Shakespeare has the line in OTHELLO (1604): *To suckle fooles, and chronicle small beer;* Thackeray (1844) and others have echoed the phrase. Addison in THE WHIG EXAMINER (1710; No. 4) declared: *As rational writings have been represented by wine, I shall represent those kinds of writings we are now speaking of, by small beer. Cp. Highgate.*

smell-. Several compounds of this common word have had wide currency. (1) *smellfeast.* A parasite, a greedy sponger; one who learns where a feast is being prepared, and comes uninvited. Very common 1550-1700; Browning in THE RING AND THE BOOK (1869) says: *The smellfeasts rouse them at the hint There's cookery in a certain dwelling-place.* (2) *smellfungus.* A faultfinder, a complaining person. This term was coined by Sterne as a nickname for Smollett, whose TRAVELS THROUGH FRANCE AND ITALY (1766) was a constant grumble. Washington Irving in SALMAGUNDI (1808) said: *Let the grumbling smellfungi . . . rail at the extravagance of the age.* (3) *smellsmock.* A licentious man. Heywood in A MAIDENHEAD WELL LOST (1634) declared: *I think you'll prove little better than a smellsmock, that can find out a pretty wench in such a corner.*

smerles. Ointment. Used from the 10th century; related to *smear.* Also *smyrels, smuriles, smirles,* and the like; in the 13th and 14th centuries *smerl, smerel,* mistaking the original form for a plural. The AYENBITE OF INWIT (1340) mentioned *the guode smel of the ilke smeriles.*

smilet. A light and little smile. Also *smylet.* Fraunce in COUNTESS PEMBROKE'S IVYCHURCH (1592) wrote that he *knew her face to be framing Now with a smylet's allure, and now to repell with a frowning.* Shakespeare, in KING LEAR (1605) speaks of *those happy smilets That play'd on her ripe lip.*

smock. From its use as the garment next a woman's skin, *smock* came to be used, especially among 16th and 17th century playwrights and often with double meaning, to refer to a woman herself. Shadwell in THE VOLUNTEERS (1692) said: *Thou wert a pretty fellow, to rebel all thy lifetime against princes, and trail a pike under a smock-rampant at last!* Shakespeare in ROMEO AND JULIET (1595) has the jesting Benvolio cry, when Peter and the Nurse come in: *Two, two—a shirt and a smock.* Hence, *to smock,* to dress in a smock; to make effeminate—Sylvester in BETHULIA'S RESCUE (1614): *no pomp . . . had ever power his manly mind to smock;* to make free with women—D'Urfey in PILLS TO PURGE MELANCHOLY (1719): *Then* *we all agree To . . . smock and knock it, Under the greenwood tree*; Swift in POLITE CONVERSATIONS (1738): *You don't smoke, I warrant you, but you smock. Cp. smoke.* In the 16th and 17th centuries, too, many compounds continued this double play: a *smock-agent, smock-officer,* a pander. *smock-fair,* happy hunting grounds for whores. *smock-employment. The smocktoy Paris.* Fletcher, in THE ELDER BROTHER (1625): *These smock-vermin, how eagerly they leap at old mens kisses.* Hickeringill, in PRIESTCRAFT (1705): *Great kindred, smock-simony, and whores, have advanced many a sot to the Holy Chair. smock-secrets* are such as women discuss among themselves. *smockage,* intercourse. A *smocker,* a woman's man; a lecher; THE GENTLEMAN'S MAGAZINE in 1756 said of a man whose nature fit its pages, that he *had formerly been a cocker, smocker, and foxhunter.* In the 18th and 19th centuries, a *smock-race* was a contest for females for which the prize was a smock; the Thomas Hughes that wrote TOM BROWN'S SCHOOL DAYS in his book THE SCOURING OF THE WHITE HORSE (1859) said: *I see, Sir, that 'smocks to be run for by ladies' is left out. smock-face;* pale and smooth or effeminate face; a male having such a face. Hence, *smock-faced,* effeminate. Vanbrugh in the Prologue to THE RELAPSE (1696) says: *Perhaps there's not a smock-face here today But's bold as Caesar to attack—a play.* A *smockster* was a go-between; Middleton in YOUR FIVE GALLANTS (1608) says: *You're a hired smockster; here's her letter, in which we are certified that you're a bawd.*

smoke. This common word (also *smeek; smook; smoca, smok, smoak, smoake, smokke*) developed various senses besides the persisting one. In the 19th century, when factories first multiplied, *the big smoke* was London. Our *out of the frying-pan into the fire* was earlier *out of the smoke into the fire*; Shakespeare in AS YOU LIKE IT (1600) has: *Thus must I from the smoake into the smother. To play smoke,* to deceive, misuse; WESTMINSTER MAGAZINE in 1774: *Their summum bonum lies in drinking themselves dead drunk . . . playing smoak with the girls.* [In those days *smoke* and *smock* (*smoke, smoake*) were pronounced alike; this is a pun; *cp. smock.*] *To sell smoke,* to swindle; a literal translation of Latin *fumum vendere. Smoke* is sometimes still used to mean tobacco, or a puffable portion thereof; Besant in ALL SORTS AND CONDITIONS OF MEN (1882) deprecated *the two-penny smoke, to which we cling, though it is made of medicated cabbage.* Also *Cape smoke,* an atrocious brandy notorious in 19th century South Africa; E.E. Napier mentioned *a young Hottentot* he came upon in 1849, *as fond of Cape smoke . . . as any of his tribe.* Shakespeare uses *to smoke* to mean to fumigate; to find, to unearth, *smoke him out*; *to smoke one's skin-coat* (KING JOHN), to thrash; *Some of you shall smoke for it,* have a hot time, suffer (TITUS ANDRONICUS). Also in combinations, as *smoke-box*; W. Barclay in NEPENTHES (1614), speaking of the use of tobacco: *Not as the English abusers do, which make a smoke-box of their skull.* Also *smokified,* blackened by smoke; BLACKWOOD'S EDINBURGH MAGAZINE in 1819 spoke of *scrawlings of chalk* on the *smokified wall.* R. Johnson's KINGDOM AND COMMONWEALTH (1630) pictured: *Their water brackish, their aire foggie and their fire smokish.* Not to mention the everlasting bonfire! No wonder Shakespeare uses *smoke* to mean 'a mist of words,' idle talk, in KING JOHN, TIMON OF ATHENS, LOVE'S LABOUR'S LOST: *Sweet smoke of rhetoric!*

and THE RAPE OF LUCRECE: *This helpless smoke of words.*

smotherlich. This word, used by Chaucer in THE REEVE'S TALE, to mean of dusky complexion, is related, in Toone's ETYMOLOGICAL DICTIONARY (1834) to *smother* and *smoke.* It is also spelled *smoterlich,* and is more probably related to *smut,* which is, however, a later word, from the Dutch *smodderen,* to *smut* or be *besmut.* There is no verb to *besmotre,* but *besmotered* occurs in Chaucer's Prologue (1386) to THE CANTERBURY TALES, which tells us that the Knight's gypon was *all bismotered with his habergeon.* Douglas in the AENEIS (1513) speaks of a *besmotterit face. Gypon* or *gipon,* from the Old French *jupon,* skirt, was a word for the tunic usually worn under the hauberk, or coat of mail. After Chaucer, *gipon* was frequent (also as *gepoun, gippon,* etc.) until the 17th century. It was revived by Sir Walter Scott in THE BRIDAL OF TRIERMAIN (1813): *With nought to fence his dauntless brest But the close gipon's under-vest. Hauberk,* related to the Norse *hals,* neck + *bergan,* to cover (whence also the sleeveless jacket of mail, the *habergeon, haberjoun*; *cp. acton*; and the heavy cloth *haberjet* or *hauberget,* which is named in MAGNA CARTA, 1215), was originally a piece of armor to protect the neck and shoulders; later the word was used of a long coat of armor, usually of chain mail.

smouch. (1) A portion of dried leaves of the ash tree, used to adulterate black tea. (2) A dirty mark or spot. A variant of *smutch, smudge.* (3) A hearty kiss, a buss. Whetstone, in THE RIGHT EXCELLENT HISTORYE OF PROMOS AND CASSANDRA (1578): *Come smack me, I long for a smouch.* (4) A Jew. In this sense, an alteration of *smouse,* with the same meaning. This is from Dutch *smous,* Jew, pedlar; Jewish *schmuoss,* Hebrew *shmuoth,* talk, tales, from 'the persuasive eloquence of the Jewish pedlars.' Scott in his JOURNAL for 1826 recorded: *I took lessons of oil painting . . . from a little Jew animalcule, a smouch called Burrell.* As a verb, *to smouch,* to pilfer, to deal unfairly or trickily, is still current. *To smouch* also (16th into the 19th century) meant to kiss. Gayton in PLEASANT NOTES UPON DON QUIXOT (1654) stated: *The Knights did so smouch them, that the lipfrolics were heard into the kitchin.* Lady Granville in a letter of 1811 complained: *The little hideous Duc de Berri smouches us all.* Hence *smoucher,* a fresh and frequent kisser.

snail-water. A dish of the 17th century, when snails were prized. *The Lady Honneywoods snaile-water. Take a quart of shell'd snailes, wash them in salt and water, then scalld them in boyling water; then distill them in a quart of milk upon white sugarcandy and a branch of speremint.*

snark. See *snirt.* But also, to find fault —a 19th century use. Beware of the boojum!

sneak-. Several compounds of this word have been used to indicate a mean, contemptible person. A *sneakaway,* a coward. A *sneakbill,* a starveling. Also *sneaksbill, sneaksby,* a mean-spirited person. Thus Dryden, in AMPHITRYON (1690): *There is no comparison between my master and thee, thou sneaksby.* A *sneaksman,* a sneak-thief. A *sneakup,* a cringing sneak, a shirk. Shakespeare, in HENRY IV, PART ONE: *The prince is a Jack, a sneakup. Sneakup* is also used (by Kingsley in WESTWARD HO!, 1855) for *snick up. Snick up,* go hang, was always used as an exclamation:

Let them go snick up! Let them go hang! *Cp. sneck.* Shakespeare has in TWELFTH NIGHT (1601): *We did keep time, sir, in our catches. Snecke up!* As a noun *snickup* (17th century) meant a hangman's rope; thus the Water Poet, IN PRAISE OF HEMP-SEED (1623) said: *A Tyburn hempen caudell well will cure you; . . . in Sparta it ycleped was snickup, which is in English gallows grass.*

sneaks. A mild, euphemistic oath, by God's *neaks.* Also *neagues, neakes, nigs;* thus *Snigs! well done!* Marston in ANTONIO AND MELLIDA (1602) has: *God's neakes they would have shone like my mystresse browe;* in ANTONIO'S REVENGE, the same year: *Sneaks, and I were worth but three hundred pound a year more, I could sweare richly. I'll go up and downe,* we find in Fletcher's THE KNIGHT OF MALTA (1619), *drinking small beere and swearing 'odds neagues.* It remains a matter of conjecture what are God's neaks (nicks, nail-holes?).

sneap. To nip or pinch (with fingers or frost); to reprove, chide. Also as a noun, a snub, a rebuke; so used in Shakespeare's HENRY IV, PART TWO (1597). Bishop Hall (WORKS, 1623) doubts *that we do hate our corruptions; when, at our sharpest, we but gently sneap them.* Shakespeare uses the verb in THE RAPE OF LUCRECE, and in LOVE'S LABOUR'S LOST: *Byron is like an envious sneaping frost That bites the first borne infants of the spring.*

sneb. To reprove, reprimand, rebuke; *to snub.* Also, *to snib.* Thus Chaucer in the Prologue to THE CANTERBURY TALES (1386) *Him wolde he snybben sharply for the nonys.* From the 14th to the 17th century, thereafter dialectal and Scotch. In the 19th century, a *snib* was also a catch or bolt for a door or window; hence *to snib,* to fasten; by extension, to shut in.

sneck. The latch of a door or gate. From the 14th century; in later use, dialectal or Scotch. Also *snek, snack, snake, snick.* The word sometimes referred only to the lever that raises the bar of the latch. *On the sneck,* latched; *off the sneck,* unlatched. *To draw a sneck* (16th century, also in Burns), to act stealthily. *A sneck posset,* a greeting that stops at the door, a cold reception. *A sneck-band,* a string fastened to the latch and passed through a hole to the outside of the door, so that the door can be opened from without. Scott in THE ANTIQUARY (1816) says: *The sneck was drawn and the Countess . . . entered my dwelling.* Hence, *to sneck,* to latch, to shut up. *Sneck-drawer,* a sneak thief, a sly or crafty fellow. Burns in his ADDRESS TO THE DEIL (1785) calls him *Ye auld, snickdrawing dog!* There was also a *sneck* (18th and 19th centuries), a sharp cut, a sharp clicking sound; a *snick*—and (as early as the 16th century) *to sneck,* to cut; to snatch. From the use of *sneck, sneck-band,* came the transferred use of *sneck,* a noose, a halter; also *snecket.* The imperative *Sneck up!* (*snick up, sneik up*) thus meant, Go hang! *Cp. sneak-.* Shakespeare in TWELFTH NIGHT (1600) has Sir Toby tell Malvolio *Sneck up!* . . *Dost think because thou art virtuous, there shall be no more cakes and ale?*

sned. To cut, to cut off. Also *snedde, snead, snad.* Used from the 8th into the 17th century; also figuratively. Gillespie, in his DISPUTE AGAINST THE ENGLISH-POPISH CEREMONIES (1637) observed: *They did in some sort snedde the reviving twigs of old superstition.* A number of words beginning *sn* have similar meanings, through the echoic quality of the *snick* or the *snip* of the scissors. Thus *sneck, q.v.,* a sharp clicking sound, also meant a sharp cut. Also *sneg.* To *snese* (13th century) was to run through with a weapon, to *spit. Cp. snickersnee. Sniters* are candle-snuffers. To *snithe* was a stronger word: to cut, to kill by cutting (especially 8th to 13th century). Also *snock,* a strong blow, a sharp *knock.* From *sned,* to cut, came *sned, snede,* a small piece, a morsel; and from the same source (Old English *snad*) with the same meaning, *snode.* THE AYENBITE OF INWIT (1341) spoke *of the lecherous that . . . vorzuelyth* [swallowed up] *the good snode wythoute chewynge.*

snib. See *sneb.*

snickersnee. This was originally the phrase *stick or snee, snick or snee,* to thrust or cut. It was from Dutch *steken,* to thrust + *snijen* (German *schneiden*), to cut. Hence *snick or snee, snick and snee,* to thrust and cut, to fight with knives—as was common among Dutch sailors, 16th to 18th centuries. Hence *snickasnee,* a combat with cut-and-thrust knives; a knife for such a combat. *Snick or snee* was altered in the 18th century into *snickersnee,* a knife-combat, or the knife; Irving used the word in FATHER KNICKERBOCKER'S HISTORY OF NEW YORK (1809); in THE MIKADO (1885) Gilbert has: *As I gnashed my teeth When from its sheath I drew my snickersnee.* The word *snick,* in addition to meaning to cut and to hit, a cut, a slight blow, also meant a sudden noise, a click, and was a variant form of *sneck, q.v.* A *snickle* was a noose, as was a *snick-up.* A *snick-snarl* was a knot, a tangle (17th century) in a thread or the thread of an argument.

snirt. To laugh in a suppressed manner, to *snicker.* 18th and 19th centuries. In the same period, *snirtle,* to laugh even more quietly (but mockingly), to *snigger.* All these words are echoic; also *sniff; snark; snork; snort; snur,* to snort; *snurt,* to snort, to sneer, to snore. *Snurt* was first written in the 15th century; a *snurter* was a snorer. Note that *snitch* first meant a slap on the nose; then, the nose; then it was used in the phrase *to turn snitch,* to turn informer; hence the verb, to *snitch* (*on*). Also *snite,* to wipe the nose; *snot,* to blow the nose. *Snot,* also *snat,* nasal mucus, was common (but not vulgar) from the 15th through the 17th century; earlier it meant the snuff of a candle, the burnt part of a candle wick. By 1800 *snottery* was being used as a term of contempt, meaning filthiness; Jonson in THE POETASTER (1601) says: *Teach thy incubus to poetize; And throw abroad thy spurious snotteries.* The O.E.D. defines *to snotter* with a sequence of echoic words: "to *snuffle, snore* or *snort . . .* to *snivel* or *snuffle* in weeping." Also *snoach* (14th century), *snotch* (long *o*; 19th century), to snuffle. Also *snoke,* to snuff or smell; to go snuffing (at); to sneak about, watching. Similary slang has said: Don't be so nosy!

snitch. See *snirt.*

snite. See *snirt.* Also, for *sniters,* see *sned.*

snithe. See *sned.*

snoach. See *snirt.*

snode. See *sned.*

snood. Used from the 8th century. See *coif.*

snork. See *snirt.*

snudge. A miser, a niggardly or sponging fellow. Also a covetous *snowge, snutch, snuch*; perhaps influential (with *scrouge, q.v.*) in Dickens' use of the name Scrooge ('putting on the screws') in THE CHRISTMAS CAROL. *To snudge* (*it*), to be miserly, to be stingy; also, to walk bent over, as though absorbed in concerns, *to snudge along*. Hence *snudgery*, miserliness; *cp. euclionism*. In the 17th century *snudge* was also used to mean to lie quiet, to nestle; Johnson in his DICTIONARY (1755) relates it to *snug*. Wilson in his RHETORIQUE (1553) says: *Some rich snudges, having great wealthe, goe with their hose out at heeles.* Dekker in OLD FORTUNATUS (1600) comments: *Snudges may well be called jailors: for if a wretch steal but into debt ten pounds, they lead him straight to execution.* In SUMMER'S LAST WILL AND TESTAMENT (1592) Nashe gnashes his teeth and cries: *I tell thee plain thou art a snudge!*

snurt. See *snirt*.

socage. Tenure of land by certain services other than knight-service, under the feudal system. Also *sokemanry*. Used by Spenser (1596) and historians; Coke UPON LITTLETON (1628) states that *every tenure which is not tenure in chivalrie is a tenure in socage. Soc, soke,* meant the right of local jurisdiction, or a district (shire or circuit) presided over by a person; such a man had the privilege of attendance at court. Hence *socman, sokeman,* a tenant holding land in socage.

soccus. See *buskin*.

sod. Boiled. Early past participle of *seethe*; also *sode, sodde, sodden.* Used literally of meat (13th to 17th century), hence as a noun (16th and 17th centuries) boiled meat; Elyot in 1548 spoke of *a simple feast, wherin is neither bake, roste, nor sodde.* Shakespeare used *sod* in THE RAPE OF LUCRECE (1594) to mean scalded, figuratively: *Her eyes, though sod in tears . . .* Of persons, *sod* was used in the 17th century to mean "pickled", soaked in liquor, *sod in sack. Twice sod,* unpalatable (all the flavor boiled away); Shakespeare in LOVE'S LABOUR'S LOST has Holofernes exclaim *Twice-sod simplicity!* Chapman in THE CONSPIRACIE OF CHARLES DUKE OF BYRON (1608) wrote: *You make all state before Utterly obsolete; all to come, twice sod.*

sodayne. A variant form of *sudden*. Also *sodeyn*; for an instance, see *agrise*. Miles Coverdale, in CERTAIN MOST GODLY, FRUITFUL, AND COMFORTABLE LETTERS (1564) presents a broadside ballad beginning *Some men for sodayne joye do wepe And some in sorow syng.* These two lines are spoken, slightly changed, by the Fool in Shakespeare's KING LEAR (I iv 191).

sodaynly. A variant form of *suddenly*. Sir Thomas More wrote the DIALOGUE OF COMFORT AGAINST TRIBULATION (1534) while in London Tower awaiting probable torture and certain death. Terror would come upon him *sodaynly*; he tried to counteract it by dwelling upon thoughts of the pain of torture; to advise otherwise, he wrote, had *as much reason as the medicine that I have heard for the toothache, to go thrice about a churchyard and never think on a fox tayle.* Even on the brink of death, More could smile at an old wives' tayle.

soil. See *assoil*.

soke. An old past tense of *suck*: *sucked.* For an instance of its use, see *sigalder*. The infinitive is spelled *to sugke* some ten lines later in the poem: *To sugke here* [their] *keyn in here pasture.*

Sol. The sun. The Latin word; Greek (Homeric) *Helios*. Often used (without an article, with a capital) to mean the sun. Thus Kyd in THE SPANISH TRAGEDY (1592): *Ere Sol had slept three nights in Thetis lap. Cp. Diana.*

sold. A sum of money; pay. Latin *solidum,* a whole amount, a sum. Also *sould, sowd, soud. To sold* (1) to solder; to fasten firmly; to close or heal (2) to pay; to engage the services of; to serve for pay. Also used figuratively, as by Chaucer in THE PRIORESS' TALE (1386): *O martyr soudit to virginitie.* From the same root, originally one that fights for pay, came *soldier.*

solein. Unique; alone; lonely; retiring, modest; solitary; averse to society, morose —in this sense replaced by the later spelling *sullen.* From Latin *solus,* alone. Chaucer in THE BOOK OF THE DUCHESS (1369) says: *Truly she was to mine eye The soleyn Phoenix of Arabye.* Gower in the CONFESSIO AMANTIS (1390) says *Thereof a solein tale I rede.* Spenser also spells the word *sollein;* he uses it seven times, e.g. in THE SHEPHERD'S CALENDAR (1579): *At last her solein silence she broke And gan his new budded beard to stroke.* As a noun, *solein* meant a single person, a solitary; also a portion of food or a meal for one person.

solicitudinous. See *sollicitudinous.* Latin *sollicitudinem* (also with one *l*), from *sollicitus,* English *solicitous,* also *solicitant.* Latin *sollus,* whole, entire + *ciere, citum,* to put in motion; hence, thoroughly moved, troubled; therefore, regardful, careful. The verb to *solicit* meant first to make anxious, fill with concern; to stir, rouse; hence, to entreat, urge—the current use. A woman urging or enticing men to immorality was (17th century) a *solicitress, solicitrix;* they had many tricks.

solivagant. Wandering alone. (Accent on the second syllable). Used from the 17th century; 'Monkshood' and Gamble in RUDYARD KIPLING (1902) have: *Dick walks out . . . and plays the solivagant for about ten years.*

sollar. An attic; an upper room or apartment; a garret used as a storeroom. Latin *solarium,* sun room; *sol,* sun. Also a chamber in a steeple or belfry. Payne in his translation (1886) of Boccaccio's DECAMERON pictured *a little uninhabited tower . . . that the shepherds climb . . . to a sollar at the top.* At opposite ends of a building are the sollar and the cellar.

sollevate. To raise in tumult or rebellion. Via Italian *sollevare,* from Latin *sub,* under + *levare, levatum,* to raise; *levis,* light. Hence *sollevation,* insurrection. J. Howell in LUSTRA LUDOVICI (LOUIS XIII OF FRANCE, 1646) said: *This dangerous sollevation was quashed by a high hand of royal power.*

sollicitudinous. Overflowing with care or consideration. Sir Thomas Browne in CHRISTIAN MORALS (1682) admonishes: *Move circumspectly, not meticulously, and rather carefully sollicitous than anxiously sollicitudinous.* Note that *meticulous* (from Latin *metus,* fear) originally meant fearful; hence the current meaning, over-regardful, over-careful about minute details. *Meticulosity,* in the 17th century, meant timorousness.

solonist. A wiseacre. Also, a *Solon,* applied ironically. Used from the 17th century, from *Solon* (638-559 B.C.), one of the "seven sages" of Greece. He was a great law-giver; the adjectives *Solonic, Solonian,* Solon-like, may refer to the standard of weights or of coinage he established, to his legislative program (which included a law against neutrality in times of sedition), or to his division of the population into four classes. They are more likely, however, in literary references, to stem from his famous remark "Count no man happy until he is dead" —which was in Shakespeare's mind when he wrote, in TITUS ANDRONICUS (1592): *But* *safer triumph is this funeral pomp That hath aspired to Solon's happiness And triumphs over chance in honour's bed.*

solp. See *sulp.* Thus *solping,* defilement.

solpuga. A poisonous ant or spider, mentioned in classical writings (Lucan; Pliny). Also *salpuga* and—described as inhabiting caverns or mines—*solifuge,* as though fleeing the sun (Latin *sol, solis,* sun + *fugere,* to flee, avoid). Holland in his translation (1601) of Pliny declared: *In Æthyopia . . . there is a great country . . . dispeopled at times by scorpions, and a kind of pismires called solpugae.*

solsecle. The marigold. A pleasant word; also *solsykelle, solsequy.* Strictly the name is *solsequium* (used in English in the 15th and 16th centuries), from *sol,* sun + *sequi,* to follow. There is the same meaning in the word *heliotrope,* from the Greek. A lyric poem of 1310 (in the Wright collection) said *Heo is solsecle of swetnesse.*

solsticke. See *sunstead.*

somewhen. See *anywhen.*

somne. To collect, assemble (from the 9th century). To summon (12th to 15th century); superseded by *summon.* Also *sumne, sompne.* Hence *somner* (*somenour, somenere*), *sompner, sompnour,* an official *summoner.* Also used figuratively, as in OF REPENTANCE (HOMILIES; 1563): *When the hyghest somner of all, whiche is death, shall come.* A *summoner* (14th to 18th century) was a petty officer who notified persons to appear in court; we still issue a *summons,* but the officer has been summoned to a higher court.

somniate. To dream (a thing); to make sleepy. Latin *somniare, somniatum; somnium,* dream. Hence also *somniation; somniatory, somnial,* relating to dreams; Urquhart in his translation (1693) of Rabelais speaks of *somnial divinations.* Note that in Latin *somnus* means sleep, as in the current *somnolent.* Less common words from *somnus* include *somniculous,* full of sleep, i.e., (1) drowsy, (2) inducing sleep, soporific but also, in this sense, *somnifying, somniferic, somniferous, somnific.* Thus *somniculosity,* sleepiness; *somnifery,* a place for sleep; *somnificator,* one that induces sleep: Southey in a letter of 1806 spoke of *the rector, a humdrum somnificator.* Per contra, a *somnifuge* is something or someone that drives away sleep. A *somnivolent* is one that eagerly (and often vainly) desires sleep. *Cp. sompnary.*

sompnary. See *oneiric.* Latin *somnus,* sleep, is responsible for many English words, including *somniloquacious, somniloquous, somniloquent,* talking, or given to talking, in one's sleep; hence *somniloquence, somniloquism, somniloquy; somniloquize.* For others, see *somniate.* Coleridge transferred the notion (LITERARY REMAINS; 1833): *How often the pen becomes the tongue of a systematic dream —a somniloquist!* Beshrew the gentleman from Porlock!

sompner. See *somne.*

sompter. A variant form of *sumpter, q.v.*

sonetist. A writer of sonnets; also *sonnetist, sonneteer, sonnetteer.* Usually these are terms of scorn, for one whose verses are disliked. Bishop Hall (8TH SATIRE; for the rest of the quotation, see *lightskirts*), poking fun at the over-adornment of pagan and Christian stories, exclaims: *Now good St. Peter weeps pure Helicon, Great Solomon sings in the English quire And is become a newfound sonetist . . .* The Bishop's SATIRES were burned in 1599, by order of the High

Commission, along with Marlowe's OVID and Marston's PYGMALION.

sonties. As a mild oath—Shakespeare in THE MERCHANT OF VENICE (1596): *By Gods sonties 'twill be a hard way to hit.* Also *santy, God's santy, God's sonties.* A corruption, either of *sanctity,* or of *saint* (Scotch and dialect *sont, sant, saunt, sauntie*; preserved in the Christmas *Santa Claus*).

soot. Thoughts of black smudge have accompanied this word since the 8th century; but side by side, until the 17th, came a far fairer notion. For *soot* (*sote, sout, soote* (*q.v.*), *sout, swote, swoot, swoote*) was an early form of *sweet,* in all its senses and its appeal to the senses. Thus Chaucer in THE ROMAUNT OF THE ROSE (1366) admires: *Thorough moisture of the welle wete Sprong up the sote grene gras.* Indeed "Here beginneth the Book of the Tales of Caunterbury"; *Whan that Aprille with his shoures sote The droghte of Marche hath perced to the rote . . . Than longen folk to goon on pilgrimages.* Davies in his ECLOGUES (1614) says: *As swoot as swans thy straines make Thames to ring. They dauncen deffly,* says Spenser in THE SHEPHERD'S CALENDAR (1579; APRIL), using the word as an adverb, *and singen soote.* And what is so rare as a day in the soot springtide?

soote. (1) A variant form of *suit.* (2) Sweet, in all its senses; see *soot. sootmeat* (17th century). [*sootless* and *sooty* refer, of course, to the *soot* removed by the *sootiman,* the chimneysweep.] Note Surrey's charming lines to Spring (1535) *wherein eche thing renewes, save onely the lover: The soote season, that bud and blome forth brings, With grene hath clad the hill, and eke the vale: The nightingale, with feathers new she sings; The turtle to her make hath tolde her tale.*

sooterkin. A sweetheart. From a Dutch diminutive form *soetekÿn; soet,* sweet. Hence, a person (in pleasant, familiar reference); a minor or imperfect literary work—as in an 1817 letter of Carlyle's: *After considerable flourishing, he ventured to produce this child of the Doctor's brain—and truly it seemed a very sooterkin. Good morrow,* said Betterton in THE REVENGE (1680); *my little sooterkin; how is't, my pretty life?*

sooth. Truth. Common (the word!) from the 8th to the 17th century; used later in poetry and in phrases *in sooth, my sooth, by my sooth, good sooth, sooth to say.* Shakespeare in A MIDSUMMER NIGHT'S DREAM (1590) exclaims: *Good troth you do me wrong—good sooth you do.* Also, the certainty of a matter; *soothsaying,* prognostication. By extension, flattery; smooth or plausible talk. Thus Shakespeare in RICHARD II (1593): *That ere this tongue of mine, that layd the sentence of dread banishment On yon proud man, should take it off again With words of sooth.* This use comes by association with *soothe; cp. soother. Sooth* also formed many compounds: *cp. forsooth; soothhead,* truth; *soothtell,* prophecy; *soothfast,* truthful, faithful, loyal; *soothness, soothfastness; soothful,* truthful; *soothless,* untruthful, false.

soother. A flatterer; a yes-man. So used in the 16th and 17th centuries. Used by Shakespeare in HENRY IV, PART ONE. What T. Wilson said in his RHETORIQUE (1553) —*This world . . . hath over many such as never honest man was, that is to saie, flatteres, fawners, and southers of mennes saiynges*—has little changed in 400 years. Note that the earliest meaning (10th century) of *to soothe* [see *sooth,* truth; whence *soothhead, soothship.* A *soothsayer* was one that tells the truth—then, one that claims to tell the truth about the future. *Soothsaw,* the act of speaking the truth, 10th to 15th century; *soothsay,* a true or wise saying, a proverb] was to verify, prove the truth; then, to maintain as true; then, to corroborate, support a person's statement; then, to blandish, cajole; flatter; gloss over—finally (17th century) the current meaning *to soothe,* to mollify, calm, set at ease.

sopheme. A variant of *sophism.* Chaucer in THE SQUIRE'S TALE (1386) said: *Ne couthe man by twenty thousand part Counterfete the sophemes of his art.*

sopie. A drink of spirits. Also *soupii.* Via Dutch (17th century); earlier English 10th century) *sope,* a draught, a drink; *a sip, a sup, a sop, a soup.* To *soupify,* to turn into soup; St. Nicholas (died 350) restored to life three children that had been soupified, hence is the patron saint of children. A *souper* (19th century Ireland) was a Protestant clergyman attempting to win Catholics as converts with soup or other charity; also, a person thus won to conversion. THE DAILY NEWS (20 January, 1896) reported: *They cannot believe in any Catholic honestly becoming a Protestant. The convert must be a souper.* Hence, *soupering; souperism.*—A volume of the year 1400 advises: *Drynke cler watir with a sope of vynegre.*

sopor. See *carus.*

sops-in-wine. The gillyflower, the clove-pink. Spenser in THE SHEPHERD'S CALENDAR (1579) rejoices *with hawthorne buds, and swete eglantine, And girlonds of roses and sopps in wine.* Also, a variety of apple; Burroughs in LOCUSTS AND WILD HONEY (1879) states that bees *will suck themselves tipsy upon varieties like the sops-of-wine.* This is hard to believe of the workaday bee; but I have seen lazy cows apple-tipsy.

sorbet. A 15th to 19th century variant of *sherbet.* From Turkish *shorbet,* perhaps associated with Italian *sorbire,* to imbibe. Described in 1613 (*sorbetta*) as a drink "made of water, suger, and juyce of lemons, mixed with amber and muske." In the mid-19th century, the term was used of a kind of sweetmeat or ice; Mabel Collins, in THE PRETTIEST WOMAN IN WARSAW (1885) says that *the sorbets are delicious sweets of almonds, pistachio, chocolate, or coffee.* More directly from Latin *sorbere,* to imbibe, came the rare *sorbillate,* to sip; *sorbicle,* a drink, a pleasant mixture that is to be drunk; *sorbile,* drinkable, liquid: *a sorbile egg,* advised a book of 1661, *clarifieth the voice.*

sorbillate. See *sorbet.*

sortance. Suitability, correspondence. Also *sortable,* accordant, suitable. Apparently *sortance* has been used only by Shakespeare, in HENRY IV, PART TWO (1597): *Here doth hee wish his person, with such powers As might hold sortance with his qualitie.*

sortes Virgilianae. See *aeromancy.*

sortilege. A casting of lots to determine an action, or to *forecast* the future; also *sortilege, sortiary* (17th century), *sortileger,* one that foretells by drawing lots (or other methods), a diviner. *Sortilegium, sortilegy,* divination, especially by lot; *sortilegic, sortilegious,* relating to or dependent upon divination or drawing lots. Latin *sortem,* lot + *legere,* to choose. From *sortem,* one's lot, came English *to sort,* to allot, *sort out, assort,* etc. The 16th and 17th century verb *to sort,* to sally out, is from French *sortir,* to go out (which the French trace from Latin *surgere, surrectum,* to rise, whence also *insurgent* and *resurrection*), whence also, a *sortie.* Scott in IVANHOE (1819) has *a woman infamous for sortileges and for witcheries.*

sotiltee. See *warner.*

soup maigre. A thin soup (also *soup meagre*), urged upon the English poor in the 18th century. THE CONNOISSEUR (1754, No. 19) protested in vain: *What, alas! are the weak endeavors of a few to oppose the daily inroads of fricasees and soup maigres?* The inundation is recorded in quotations set in Jesse's GEORGE SELWYN AND HIS CONTEMPORARIES (1844): Miss M. Townshend, 1766, *If you could persuade them of the wholesomeness of soup maigre and barley bread, it might be of great use to them;* the consequence, as seen by Warner, 1779: *Such a number of pinch-bellied, woebegone, skin-and-grief, lanthorn-jawed, soup-maigre subjects!* Thus is indicated the morient course of good cooking in England. Not long before, in THE GRUB STREET OPERA (which opened at the Haymarket in March 1737) Fielding sang the elegy of the major contribution of the English kitchen: *When mighty roast beef was the Englishman's food It ennobled our hearts and enriched our blood, Our soldiers were brave and our courtiers were good. Oh, the roast beef of Old England, And oh, for Old England's roast beef!*

soupify. See *sopie.*

souse. As a noun. (1) The parts of a pig or other animal usually pickled. From the 14th century; related to *sauce,* ultimately from Latin *sal,* salt. Also, an ear. *To sell souse,* to be in a surly mood. J. Russell in THE BABEES BOOK (1460) advised: *Salt, sowre, and sowse, alle suche thow set aside.* (2) A heavy blow or fall. *Souse for souse,* blow for blow. (3) Swooping down (as of a hawk) on a bird. *At souse,* on the rise, said of a bird on whom the hawk may swoop. (4) The French coin *sol, sou;* in 16th to 18th century English, *souse, sowse, sowce,* and the like. (5) The act of plunging into water, *a souse.* This, and the corresponding verb, survive. Each of the noun senses had a corresponding verb. GAMMER GURTON'S NEEDLE (1575): *Hoyse her, souce her, bounce her, trounce her.* Spenser in THE FAËRIE QUEENE (1590) *As when a gryfon . . . A dragon fiers encountreth in his flight . . . With hideous horror both together smight, And souce so sore that they the heavens affray.* Shakespeare in KING JOHN (1595): *The gallant monarch . . . like an eagle ore his ayerie towres, To sowse annoyance that comes neere his nest.* Pope in the Epilogue to his SATIRES (1738): *Come on then, Satire! gen'ral, unconfin'd, Spread thy broad wing, and souse on all the kind.* From the meaning, swoop, *souse* is used as an exclamatory adverb, meaning suddenly, in one swoop, like *plump! it fell;* somewhat as Shakespeare uses *jump* to mean exactly, in HAMLET: *jump at this dead hour.* Thus Farquhar in THE BEAUX' STRATAGEM (1706): *All our fair machine goes souse into the sea;* Browning in FIFINE AT THE FAIR (1872): *Foiled by the very effort, sowse, Underneath ducks the soul!* Carlyle was less metaphysical when he said (in FREDERICK THE GREAT; 1858): *Gundling comes souse upon the ice with his sitting-part.*

sovenance. Remembrance, memory. Also *souvenaunce, souvenance.* Via French *souvenir;* Latin *subvenire,* to come to help; *sub,* under + *venire,* to come. Used 15th into the 17th century. Spenser in

THE FAËRIE QUEENE (1590) tells: *Of his way he had no souvenaunce.*

sowel. A stout staff, cudgel. Especially, a stake sharpened at one end, used in making a hedge or fence, or for a hurdle. Used from the 9th century. Also *sahel, soul, sole*; and see *sowl.*

sowl. (1) Food eaten with bread (meat, cheese, etc.); food added to a broth or gravy, or the dish thus formed. Wyclif, speaking (1382) of Esau in GENESIS, wrote: *So bred takun and the sowil of potage ete and drunk.* Also *sowel, sowlle, suuel, sowvel, sole, soll, solwe* [the last three especially in sense (2)]. Hence, as a verb, *sowl,* to form or use as a relish. (2) *sowl,* to dirty, soil, make foul. Hence, *sowly,* unclean, foul. Perhaps by association with *sow,* the female pig. (3) *sowl,* to pull [by the ear(s)]. In CORIOLANUS (1607) Shakespeare reports: *Hee'l go, he sayes, and sole the porter of Rome Gates by th' eares.* He put his hand to his head to save his sowl.

spack. Quick, prompt, ready; used of persons. In 17th and 18th century dictionaries, *a spact lad or wench,* one apt to learn. Also *spake, spac.* Used mainly in the 13th and 14th centuries. Of birds and beasts, gentle, tame. In HANDLYNG SYNNE (1303) Brunne speaks of the spirit *so mylde and spake.*

spado. A eunuch. From the 15th century; Greek *spadon*; whence also *to spade, to spay, splay.* [Note that *spay* is not from *spadon,* but via Old French *espeer,* to cut with a sword; *espee,* sword; Latin *spatha,* Greek *spade,* wooden blade, paddle, sword; whence also *spatula* and the shoveling *spade.*] Sir Thomas Browne in PSEUDODOXIA EPIDEMICA (1646) said: *They live longest in every kinde that exercise it not at all, and this is true not only in eunuches by nature, but in spadoes by art!* A notion that Dr. Kinsey would dispute.

spae. A prediction; an omen. Also *to spae,* to prophesy. Used from the 13th century; frequent in Scott (GUY MANNERING; 1815). Also in various combinations: *spaedom, spaecraft, spaework,* prophecy, prophesying. *spaeman, spaewoman, spaewife,* fortune-teller; then witch; *spaewright, spaer.* The spaewoman often was, or pretended to be, dumb, as deprivation of this sense reputedly endowed one with second sight. The words, if not the beliefs, have persisted in Scotland.

spagyric. Alchemy. In its Latin form, the word was invented by Paracelsus (Theophrastus Bombastus von Hohenheim; 1493-1541), to name the science of chemistry in his day. Also *spagirique, spargerick,* and the like. An alchemist, a *spagyric, spagyrist, spagyrite.* Hence, the *spagyric, spagyrical* art. The terms were common in the 16th and 17th centuries. Though they could not solve the basic problem of transmutation, the *spagyrics* achieved many solutions; as J. Wright observed in his translation (1652) of Camus' NATURE's PARADOX: *The spagyrists in seeking the union of essences have . . . found out the dissolving of all naturall bodies.*

spancel. A fetter for hobbling cattle and horses; especially, a short rope for the hind legs of a cow while milking. Also the verb, *to spancel.* Used figuratively in a letter of 1844 by Sir Charles Napier: *Gough himself is all right, only spancelled by his staff; they wanted to tie my legs too, but I kicked the pail over, and spoiled the milking.* [Ten years later, Sir Charles was removed as commander of the Baltic fleet in the Crimean War, for his failure to storm Kronshtadt.]

spancounter. A game very popular in the early 17th century; also, *span-farthing.* Similar to *pitching pennies,* but instead of trying to toss nearest to a line, the first player tosses his coin, which the second player wins if his toss brings him within a span of it. Shakespeare in HENRY VI, PART TWO (1593) speaks of *Henry the fift (in whose time boyes went to span-counter for French crownes)*. Scott revived the word, speaking in GUY MANNERING (1815) of gamesters *rich enough to play at span-counter with moidores.*

spanker. Apart from its current meanings of one that metes out chastisement, a fore-and-aft sail, a fast walker, a fast horse, and a lively breeze, *spanker* has less remembered significance: (1) a gold coin; in the plural, money. Thus Cowley, in CUTTER OF COLEMAN STREET (1663): *Mean time, thou pretty little smith o' my good fortune, beat hard upon the anvil of your plot, I'll go and provide the spankers.* (2) Anything of exceptionally superior quality. Thus Smollett in PEREGRINE PICKLE (1751): *To turn me adrift in the dark with such a spanker!* Hence *spanking,* exceptionally good, unusually lively or smart; the 17th and 18th century knew there was something hearty, not in the least flagellant or—as we might say—sadistic, in *a spanking lass!*

spanner. A scoundrel, perhaps one that *spans* to both sides. The word appears in a title of 1653, quoted at *trepan.* From another source (related to *span,* to fasten, extend, draw tight, wind up) came *spanner,* the tool that wound the spring in a wheel-lock firearm, and the still surviving *spanner,* a sort of wrench. Howell in ENGLAND'S TEARS FOR THE PRESENT WARS (1644) laments: *My Prince his court is now full of nothing but buffcoats, spanners, and musket rests.*

sparable. A headless, wedge-shaped nail, used in the soles and heels of shoes. Also *sparibile, sperable, sparrable*; corrupted from *sparrow-bill,* named from the shape. Herrick in HESPERIDES (1648; EPIGRAM ON A COBBLER) wrote contemptuously: *His thumbnailes par'd afford him sperrables.*

sparple. To run in different directions; to scatter; to disperse. Also *disparple, tosparple*; *sparpil, sparpoil*; *sperple, spartle, sparfle, sparkle.* Used from the 14th to the 17th century. Also, to spread (rumours and the like); Udall (1548) translating Erasmus: *These sayinges were by secrete whisperinges sperpled abrode.*

spasmatomancy. See *aeromancy.*

spasmodism. The style of the *spasmodic (spasmic) school* of writers, painters, and composers, characterized by agitation, outbursts of excitement, and ups and downs of expression. Hence, *spasmodist,* one excelling in *spasmology,* a writer of that school. Reade in THE CLOISTER AND THE HEARTH (1861) wrote: *I would be prose laureate, or professor of the spasmodic, or something, in no time.* The school has become more familiar of recent years.

spatchcock. See *spitchcock.* Perhaps from the farmyard *cock,* but possibly short for *despatch cock.*

spate. A sudden flood, caused by heavy rains or melting snow; a sudden heavy downpour; a sudden outburst, flood of passion or words. The phrase *in spate* is used of streams in spring flood. Also *spait, spaight, speet, spyet,* and the like; a common word, 15th into the 19th century. Susan Ferrier, in MARRIAGE (1818) remarks that *A horse and cart were drowned at the ford last speat.* Mure in DIDO AND AENEAS (1614) tells of *death-bent Dido . . . Transported with a raging spait of* *ire.* Scott in his JOURNAL for 6 September, 1826, exclaimed: *Here is a fine spate of work!* And Rutherford, in a consoling letter of 1634, said: *God hath dried up one channel of your love by the removal of your husband. Let now that speat run upon Christ.* TAIT'S MAGAZINE of 1834 looked ahead and cried: *A foaming speat and blether of dictionary words!* It's time to stop.

spatiate. To wander, roam; range. Latin *spatiari, spatiatum; spatium,* space, whence the surviving *expatiate,* originally meaning to walk about, walk out. Bacon in SYLVA (1626) recommended *the fixing of the minde upon one object of cogitation, whereby it doth not spatiate and transcurre, as it useth.* BLACKWOOD'S EDINBURGH MAGAZINE in 1846 used the word literally: *Give him room and opportunity . . . to spatiate for the good of digestion.*

spatrify. To befoul. *To spat,* to spot, to defile; used from the 16th century. In the LIFE OF DR. FAUSTUS (1697), the innkeeper cried: *What! Have the rogues left my pots, and run away, without paying their reck'ning? I'll after them, cheating villains, rogues, cutpurses; rob a poor woman, cheat the spittle, and rob the King of his excise; a parcel of rustick, clownish, pedantical, high-shoo'd, low-minded, plowjobbing, cart-driving, pinchback'd, paralytic, fumbling, grumbling, bellowing, yellowing, peas-picking, hog-sticking, stinking, mangy, runagate, illbegotten, illcontrived, wry-mouth'd, spatrifying, dunghill-raking, costive, snorting, sweaty, farting whaw-drover dogs.*

spattania. An herb fabled to reach its full height and bloom at its first sprouting. Also *spattana, spattarmia, spatania.* Used figuratively, especially by late 16th century writers, as in Lodge's EUPHUES GOLDEN LEGACY (1590): *Love growes not like the hearb spattana to his perfection in one night.*

spectable. Presentable, worthy to be seen; within sight, visible. Latin *spectare,* to look, whence also *respective, respectable, inspection.* Also *spectabundal,* eager to see; Urquhart in THE JEWEL (1652) wrote: *By the inchanted transportation of the eyes and ears of its spectabundal auditorie.* Heywood in THE HIERARCHIE OF THE BLESSED ANGELS (1635) spoke of *that by which a woman is made more faire and spectable.*

speculum. A mirror, a reflector; a lens. Sir Thomas Browne in PSEUDODOXIA EPIDEMICA (1646) reminded his readers that *Archimedes burnt the ships of Marcellus with speculums of parabolical figures.* The word is current in surgery, as an instrument to widen bodily openings for inspection. It is from Latin *speculum,* a diminutive form from *specere, spectum,* whence also *inspect, respect, circumspect,* and all the *species.* A *specular* was a mirror of *specular stone,* a somewhat transparent substance (like mica) formerly used as glass or for ornamental purposes. Carew in a poem of 1640 wrote: *Give then no faith to the false specular stone, But let thy beauties by th' effects be knowne.* Several books have used *Speculum* as part of their title, e.g., *Speculum Meditantis* (Mirror of the Thoughtful; 1380) by Gower.

spelunk. A cave, a grotto. Used from the 14th century. In Sir Richard Guylforde's PYLGRYMAGE TO THE HOLY LAND (1511) we read: *Into the first of thyse two spelunkes entred the women.* Latin *spelunca;* Greek *spelugga;* Latin *specus,* cavern, den, pit; root *spec,* to see, to spy. The 19th century drew adjectives from the form:

speluncar (rarely *spelunceán*), relating to or resembling a cave, cavernous; *spelean, spelaean,* cave-dwelling, frequenting caverns. The scientific study of caves is *speleology.* In her travesty, MURDER IN PASTICHE (1954), Marion Mainwaring revived a form: *A light snapped on, dispelling Nappleby's speluncar revery.*

spence. A buttery, a pantry; a room where foods and drinks are kept; an eating-room; an inner room of a house, a parlor. Short for *dispense.* Also *spence,* a steward; short for *spencer,* short for *dispenser.* Used from the 13th century. In ST. CUTHBERT (1450) we read: *He bare the bordeclath to the spence.* The form *spencer* has also been used for (1) a kind of wig; in the 18th century, after Charles *Spencer,* third Earl of Sunderland (1674-1722); (2) a short double-breasted overcoat for men; late 18th and 19th century, after the second Earl *Spencer* (1758-1834); (3) a life belt, a life preserver; hence (slang), a glass of gin; after Knight *Spencer,* early 19th century.

sperate. Leaving room for hope; promising; especially of debts. The NEW JERSEY ARCHIVES of 1697 list: *A negro maid servant and debts sperate and desperate.* We know only *desperate* today. Latin *sperare,* to hope. Also *sperable,* with the same sense, as in a 1565 letter of the first Baron Burghley: *Wherin surely perceaving his own cause not sperable, he doth honorably and wisely . . . Speratory,* resting in hope, as in a 1629 Sermon of Donne, wherein Mammon offers *the present and possessory things of this world, God but the future and speratory things of the next.*

spermologer. (1) A gatherer of seeds. (2) A picker-up of trivia of current news, a gossip-monger; what we today would call a *columnist.* Also *spermologist.* Greek *sperma,* seed + *logos,* talker; used figuratively of a gossip in the Greek. Hence also *spermology,* (1) that branch of science which studies sperm or seeds; *spermatology.* (2) Trifling or babbling writing or talk, or an instance thereof; gossip. Our tabloid spermologists rush to record the pubic war skirmishes of those whom a vogue in the entertainment world has hoisted into headlines.

sperse. A shortened form of *disperse,* perhaps influenced by Italian *sperso; spergere,* to scatter. Used in the 16th and 17th centuries; by Spenser in his translation (1591) of Bellay's VISIONS and in THE FAËRIE QUEENE; by Dekker in THE WHORE OF BABYLON (1603): *Are those clowds sperst that strove to dimme our light?*

spheromancy. See *aeromancy.*

spherule. "A globose peridium, with a central opening through which sporidia are emitted." This is the current (scientific) meaning; but since the 17th century *spherule* has meant a little sphere. Thus M. Collins in SWEET AND TWENTY (1875) speaks of a fountain *throwing its showers of perennial spherules into the air untiringly.* A drop, a globule.

sphingeal. Relating to or resembling a sphinx. Also *sphyngeal, sphingal, sphingian, sphinxian.* From the subtlety of the *sphinx* (monster with head of a woman, wingèd body of a lion) and the mystery of its riddles, *sphingeal* was sometimes used to mean subtle, profound, enigmatic. From the ferocity of the *sphinx,* which devoured those that could not solve its riddle, *sphingeal* was used to mean cruel, fierce, devouring. The famous riddle of the *sphinx* (solved by Oedipus, whereupon the monster turned to stone, and stood near the pyramids of El-Gizeh in Egypt) asked: What is it that in the morning goes upon four legs; at noon, on two; in the evening, on three? Answer: man. Hence also *sphinxine,* mysterious; *sphinxineness,* obscurity.

sphyngeal. See *sphingeal.*

spicket. A variant form of *spigot,* used since the 15th century. A *spicket-wench* (17th century), a barmaid. Also, that which flows when the spigot is turned; the divine, John Day, in FESTIVALS (1615), spoke of men that *spend their birthright and patrimonies upon the spicket.*

spight. A variant form of *spite.* For an instance of its use, see *term.*

spikenard. An aromatic substance used in ancient times in the preparation of an ointment or oil; also, the plant yielding this. See *nard.* Also *spekenard, spyknard, spignard, spekenardy, spikanard*; in most forms, pronounced as two syllables. Wyclif in his BIBLE (MARK xiv; 1382) spoke of a woman *havynge a box of precious oynement spikanard.* Tennyson's IN MEMORIAM (1850) tells: *She bathes the Saviour's feet With costly spikenard and with tears.*

spincop. A spider. Also *spyncop, spincoppe.* Caxton in THE GAME AND PLAYE OF THE CHESSE (1474) said: *The lawes of somme ben like unto the nettis of spyncoppis.* The form *cop* was also used, in the 15th century, to mean spider; whence also *cobweb. Spincop* probably combined the idea of spinning with Old English *copp,* top, head. Myre in his INSTRUCTIONS FOR PARISH PRIESTS (1450) told them what to do *ef any flye, gnat, or coppe Down into the chalys droppe.*

spinee. A dish or dainty flavored with hawthorn flowers, a tasty of the 14th and 15th centuries. Also *spyneye, spynee, spine.* THE FORME OF CURY (1390) said, *for to make spynee: Nym the flowrys of the haw thorn clene gaderyd and bray hem al to dust; take and make gode thyk almand mylke, as tofore, and do therein of floer of hawthorn; and make it as a rose, and serve it forth.*

spinel. A precious stone, closely resembling the ruby. Also *spinnel, spynel, spinal,* and the like. Herbert in his book of TRAVELS (1665) mentioned *translucent stones which want neither beauty nor esteem; namely, topazes, amethysts, spinels . . .*

spinnel. See *spinel.* For an instance of its use, see *nonesopretty.*

spinther. A scintillation. The word is directly from the Greek; used in the 17th century. In the 19th, *spintherism* became the tehnical term for 'seeing stars' when the eye has been hit.

spintry. A male homosexual prostitute. Also, a place for his practices. From Latin *spintria,* from *sphincter* (muscle). Hence also *spintrian. Spintria* was also the term for the circle (arranged by the Emperor Tiberius) of thirteen joined homosexuals. The words were used in English in the 16th and 17th centuries. Thus Marvell in his STATE POEMS (1678) says that *Priapus . . . in the mimics of the spinstrian* [sic] *sport, outdoes Tiberius and his goatish court.* Jonson in SEJANUS (1603) speaks of men *ravish'd hence, like captives, and . . . dealt away unto his spintrics, sellaries, and slaves. Cp. sellary.*

spiracle. (1) Breath, spirit. Hence, a vent in a cave or other confined area, an airhole; a volcanic vent; an opening for breathing, especially in the lower animals; used figuratively by De Quincey (1854) of man: *The great phenomenon of war . . . keeps open in man a spiracle—an organ of respiration.* Also *spiraculum;* Latin *spiraculum,* a little breath; *spirare,* to breathe, whence also *expire; cp. spiration.* Hence *spiracular, spiraculiform,* shaped like (2) a little spire; a pinnacle. By extension (3) a lofty sentence, a fine conceit. Also, the blow-hole of a whale. Bullen in the CRUISE OF THE 'CACHALOT' noted that *A whale can no more force water through its spiracle than you or I through our nostrils.*

spiration. Breathing. Latin *spirare, spiratum,* to breathe; whence also *aspiration, inspiration, to expire,* etc. Note that while *spirate* also meant to breathe, *spirated* (Greek *speira,* coil) meant *spirally* twisted, like the horns of certain goats. The word *spirit* first meant breath (Latin *spiritus*); then, the breath of life, whence its current senses. *Spiration* was used specifically, beginning in the 16th century, for (1) the action of breathing as the life-giving act of God, and particularly for (2) the act of will that produced the Holy Ghost, "the eternal spiration of the Spirit."

spiss. Thick, dense, compact, close. Latin *spissus.* Used 16th into the 18th century. In his foreword To the Reader, Brerewood (1614) speaks of *this spisse and dense, yet polished, this copious, yet concise . . . treatise of the variety of languages.* Hence also *spiscious, spissous,* of thick consistency; *spissated, spissed,* thickened; *spissative,* tending or serving to thicken; *spissid, spissy,* thick, dense. Also *spissness, spissation, spissitude.* A *spissament* is a thickening substance, as flour in gravy.

spital. See *spittle.*

spitchcock. To cut up and cook; especially, to cut and broil or fry an eel, in bread-crumbs and chopped herbs. A form of *spatchcock,* originally *despatch cock,* a quickly cut and cooked fowl, as when guests arrive unexpectedly. Also a noun, a fowl thus prepared, or the method of preparing. Hence, to do anything on the spur of the moment; especially, to insert into, as General Buller reported in THE TIMES of 11 October, 1901: *I therefore spatchcocked into the middle of that telegram a sentence which . . .* which had results recorded in THE SPEAKER of 16 November, 1901: *Generals spatcock telegrams and receive dismissal.* Hence, to *spitcock,* to cut up, to deal with severely, as Lamb wrote in a letter of 1814: *If they catch me in their camps again let them spitchcock me!* Also used figuratively, as by W. Cartwright in THE ORDINARY (1634): *no mild words shall bury My spitted, spitchcock'd, rost'd fury.* W. King gave sound advice in his 1708 ART OF COOKERY: *No man lards salt pork with orange peel, Or garnishes his lamb with spitchcockt eel.*

spittle. A house for the indigent or diseased; a short form of *hospital.* Also *spittell, spyttell, spittaill,* and more. In the 16th century, *spittle* was used of a place meaner than a hospital; hence, a foul or loathsome place. In the 17th century, because of the other meaning of *spittle,* spit, the form was (except in compounds) largely replaced by *spital, spitall, spittal. To rob the spittle* (*spital*), to make profit in an especially mean fashion. In the other sense, there were the phrases *spittle of the sun* (16th and 17th centuries) gossamer; *spittle of the stars,* honey-dew. There was also an even earlier (12th to 17th century) *spittle,* also *spitter,* a small spade, related to the pointed *spit* for cooking. Thus, even in the 19th century, a *spitful* meant a spadeful; *spitish,* however, meant *spiteful; spitling,* refuse, rubbish (17th century). And (18th century) *spitpoison* was an appropriate name for a malicious or venomous person.

spleen. See *splenitive.*

splendidious. An early form of *splendid.* Used 15th to 17th century. Jonson in EVERY MAN OUT OF HIS HUMOUR (1599) inquires: *His lady? what, is shee faire? splendidious? and amiable?*

splenitive. Melancholy, or tending to produce such a state; irritable, ill-humored. Also *splenetive, splenative, spleenative* (HAMLET), *splenitic, splenetic, splenatic.* From the *spleen,* Greek *splen,* the supposed seat of melancholy, irritation—but also of gaiety and laughter. Gower indicates both in CONFESSIO AMANTIS (1390): *The splen is to malencolie assigned . . . the galle serveth to do wreche, The splen doth him to lawhe and plaie.* Shakespeare mentions the spleen as the seat of laughter in LOVE'S LABOUR'S LOST (1594) and in the Induction to THE TAMING OF THE SHREW: *Haply my presence May well abate the overmerrie spleene. On the spleen* (15th century), in jest. The sense of gaiety died out about 1700. Phineas Fletcher made a note in THE PURPLE ISLAND (1633): *Hence Stratonicus said, that in Crete dead men walked, because they were so splenitive and pale-coloured.*

spousebreach. Adultery; (rarely) an adulterer. Also, *spousebreak.* Other forms were *spowsebreche, spowsebrige,* and the like. The ANCREN REWLE (1225) said that David *forget him selven, so that he dude . . . on Bersabee spusbruche.* Warner, in ALBION'S ENGLAND (1589): *We severally are . . . arayned Of cuckoldie, of spousbreach, and of bastardy.* The common word for *adultery,* from the 12th into the 16th century; *cp. advowtrie.*

sprack. See *sprag.*

sprag. Smart, clever. Shakespeare, in THE MERRY WIVES OF WINDSOR, says: *He is a good sprag memory.* Also *sprack, spract,* smart, alert, in good health and spirits. The O.E.D. suggests that *sprag* (copied by Scott, Lamb, and others after Shakespeare) is a mispronunciation of *sprack;* but Shakespeare's form seems the earlier. Lady Granville, in a letter of 1817, said: *She gives life to society, and everything is more sprack.*

sprenge. An early form of *sprinkle.* Many forms of it were used, including *sprengan;* in the past tenses, *spreinde, sprent, spreyngde, spreynt, sprenct, sprant.* Chaucer once (in BOETHIUS, 1374) used: *The swetnesse of mannes welefulnesse is yspranid with manye bitternesses. Sprent* was used as a noun (from the 14th century) meaning a sprinkle; a spot (sprinkled on); a leap, a bound; a spring-trap or snare. As a verb, *to sprent,* to leap, to move with agility (common in the 15th century); to spurt out—Harding in a CHRONICLE of 1470, said *the blood . . . sprent out, all hot and new, Into his eyen*—as well as to sprinkle. Other forms of the verb *sprent* are *sprunt* (to move quickly or convulsively; to run) and the current *sprint.*

spreth. Used in the 14th century, meaning human, that is, frail, liable to sin.

springald. See *espringal.*

sprunt. See *sprenge.*

spurcidical. Bawdy in speech. Latin *spurcus,* foul + *dicere,* to speak. Hence *spurcitious,* foul, obscene; *spurcity,* foulness, obscenity. Thus Feltham in RESOLVES (1628): *Loose and unrinsed expressions are the purulent and spurcitious exhalations of a corrupted mind.*

spurgall. See *bum.*

squintifego. One that squints notably. Also *squintefuego.* Dryden in his translation (1693) of the SATIRES of Juvenal, said *The timbrel and the squintifego maid Of Isis awe thee, lest the gods for sin Should with a swelling dropsy stuff thy skin.*

squiny. To look sidelong or invitingly, as a prostitute on the prowl. Shakespeare has the mad Lear say to the blind Gloucester (KING LEAR; 1606); *I remember thine eyes well enough. Dost thou squiny at me? No, do thy worst, blind Cupid, I'll not love. Blind Cupid* was a common sign for a brothel, as was a bush for a tavern (though a *good wine needs no bush,* as Shakespeare says in the Epilogue to AS YOU LIKE IT; Publilius Syrus, about 40 B.C., said in Maxim 930: *You need not hang up the ivy-branch over the wine that will sell.*).

squitter-wit. See *squize.*

squize. A variant of *squeeze,* common from 1550 to 1650. Also *squiss.* These are echoic forms, as also *squish, squash, squirt, squitter,* and *spit, spatter, sputter, splutter* and the like. In the late 16th and into the 18th century, *squitter* was used meaning to void thin excrement; hence *squitter-book, squitter-pulp, squitter-wit,* a worthless writer, with diarrhoea of words but constipation of ideas. Also *squitter-breech(es),* one that soils his trousers.

staddle. A foundation. A very common Old English word, appearing also in such forms as *stathel, steddle, staidel, stavel;* Old English *stathol,* support, tree trunk. Hence, a support of any kind (a platform, a framework, a post); Spenser in THE FAËRIE QUEENE (1590): *His weake steps governing And aged limbs on cypress stadle stout.* Also, the mark left on anything by something lying on it. Also, especially, a young tree left when others are cut down, as the foundation of new growth. *To stadle,* to mark, leave an impression upon; *to staddle a wood,* to cut the woods leaving a sufficient number of young trees to replenish it.

stair-work. Casual activity on the stairway; used with sexual implications in Shakespeare's THE WINTER'S TALE (1611) when the Shepherd, finding the baby Perdita, declares: *This has beene some staire-worke, some trunke-worke, some behind-doore-worke: they were warmer that got this than the poor thing is here.* Note also, quite different in meaning though the figure is drawn by the same steps, *stairway wit,* discussed under *afterwit.*

staithe. Land bordering water, the shore. Also *steth, stath, stayth, stay,* and the like, from Old Teuton *stath,* root *sta-,* stand. Hence, an embankment; also, a landing-place; especially, a depot where coal is placed on board ships for delivery. The word was in use in the 9th century; as a loading-place for coal, since the 17th. A *staithman,* a man that checks the coal at the staithe.

stale. As a noun. (1) Theft; stealing; a variant of *steal,* used from the 10th to the 14th century. *By stale,* by stealth. (2) An upright side of a ladder; a long thin handle, as of a rake; a plant stalk; the shaft of an arrow or spear. (3) A decoy-bird; a living or imitation bird used to lure others of its kind, or birds of prey, into a net; hence, anything used as a lure to ensnare a person. Especially, an accomplice of a thief or sharper; a *common stale,* a prostitute used as a thief's decoy; hence, a term of contempt for a vulgar wanton or lewd woman. Shakespeare in MUCH ADO ABOUT NOTHING (1599) says: *Spare not to tell him that he hath* *wronged his honor in marrying the renowned Claudio . . . to a contaminated stale.* By extension, a tool, an unwitting cover for evil machination. Shakespeare plays on this sense and (4) *stale,* short for *stalemate* in chess, in THE TAMING OF THE SHREW: *I pray you, sir, is it your will To make a stale of me among these mates?* Note that, while a *stalemate* is now considered a drawn game, it was formerly a loss for the person inflicting it, as explained in Beale's translation (1656) of Biochimo's THE ROYAL GAME OF CHESS-PLAY: *A stale is given when one King hath lost all his men and hath but one place left to fly into; if then the adversary bar him of that place without checking him, so that he being now out of check cannot remove but into check, it is then a stale, and he that giveth it to the distressed King loseth the game.* Still another extension of sense (3) is a lover, mistress, or spouse, whose devotion is held up to ridicule for the amusement of a rival. Shakespeare in THE COMEDY OF ERRORS has the neglected wife Adriana complain: *But, too unruly deere, he breakes the pale And feedes from home; poore I am but his stale.* [In some of these senses there is an overtone of the adjective *stale,* no longer fresh; also, as in the quotation just given, of sense (6).] (5) A fixed position, or station; related to *stall.* Hence, a body of soldiers stationed for special service, as for an ambush, or to speed to any harassed part of the battlefield. *In stale,* in ambush; *flying stale,* a troop ready for emergency action. (6) Urine, especially of animals. Shakespeare in ANTONY AND CLEOPATRA (1606) has Octavius Caesar trying to recall Antony from his luxurious dallying with the serpent of the Nile; Caesar reminds him of campaigning days, when *Thou didst drinke The stale of horses and the gilded puddle Which beasts would cough at.*—Tofte in his translation (1608) of Ariosto's SATIRES wrote: *A wife that's more than faire is like a stale Or chanting whistle which brings birds to thrall.* Of language, as of the serpent of the Nile, it may be said: *Age cannot wither her, nor custom stale Her infinite variety.*

stalemate. See *stale.*

stalking-horse. A steed trained to walk slowly and as though grazing, so that the hunter, walking beside it, may approach game unnoticed, and shoot from under the horse's neck or belly. Hence, a light facsimile of a grazing horse, used in the same fashion. Hence, a person used as a "front"; an innocent or innocent-seeming individual that masks a sinister proceeding; any underhand expedient or pretext for accomplishing an evil design. Shakespeare uses the word of less sinister purposes, when in AS YOU LIKE IT (1600) the Duke says of Touchstone: *He uses his folly like a stalking-horse, and under the presentation of that he shoots his wit.*

stalworth. An early form of *stalwart. Stalwart,* appearing in the 14th century, was used mainly in Scotland until brought into English use by Scott. Scott also used the form *stalworth,* as in MARMION (1808): *He was a stalworth knight, and keen.*

stanhope. A light one-seated carriage, originally with two wheels, in the mid-19th century with four. Made for the Rev. Fitzroy *Stanhope* (1787-1864). Dickens spoke (THE PICKWICK PAPERS; 1837) of a vehicle *not exactly a gig, neither was it a stanhope.* The third Earl of Stanhope (1753-1816) was an inventor; after him were named the *Stanhope press,* a hand printing-press; the *Stanhope lens* used in a tube for magnifying; and the *Stanhoscope,* an improvement on the lens. Hence *stanhopian,* relating to one of the above; inventive.

stank. As a noun: A pond; a ditch of slow-moving water, a moat. Also, a dam to hold back water, a floodgate. Also used figuratively. CURSOR MUNDI in the 14th century said that Satan shall be cast into *a stinck and stanck of fire.* Fletcher in his version (1656) of Martial's EPIGRAMS spoke of *An inundation that orebears the banks And bounds of all religion; If some stancks Show their emergent heads? Like Seth's famed stone, Th'are monuments of thy devotion gone!* As a verb: hence, to dam, to strengthen the banks of a stream; to surround with a moat. Again Fletcher leans on Martial for a figurative use, saying I'll *stanck up the salt conducts of mine eyes To watch thy shame, and weep mine obsequies.* Both as a noun and verb this word appears also as *stanch, staunch;* also *stinch, stainch, staynche.* It is ultimately from Latin *stagnum,* pond, pool, whench also *stagnant, stagnate.* Italian *stancare,* to weary; from this sense, as an adjective, *stank* (*stanck, stanke*), weary, faint, exhausted. Spencer in THE SHEPHERD'S CALENDAR (1579) says: *I am so stiffe and so stanck.* By dropping the first letter we attained the word *tank.*

starky. Stiff, hard. Used from the 17th century, after the still current *stark.* Especially, *starky ground,* land that is dry (caked) and unworkable, as in heat after rain.

startup. (1) A boot worn by countrymen; usually in the plural. So in the 16th century. By the 17th century, gaiters or leggings; Sylvester in his rendering (1608) of Du Bartas' DECAY said: *Her neat, fit startups of green velvet be, flourisht with silver.* (2) A low-born person risen to prominence; supplanted by *upstart.* Shakespeare uses *upstart* only as an adjective, as Bolingbroke protests (RICHARD II; 1595): *Will you permit that I shall stand condemned A wandering vagabond, my rights and royalties Plucked from my arms perforce and given away To upstart unthrifts?* In MUCH ADO ABOUT NOTHING we find the other form: *That young start-up hath all the glory of my overthrow.*

starve. See *sterve.*

starve-lackey. A miserly pretentious gallant. Used as a name in Shakespeare's MEASURE FOR MEASURE (1603), as Pompey lists those in prison: . . . *Master Deep-vow, and Master Copper-spur, and Master Starve-lackey the rapier and dagger man* [i.e., bully], *and young Drop-heir* . . . Other combinations of *starve* are *starve-gutted,* famished (18th century); *starve-acre,* in Hardy's TESS OF THE D'URBERVILLES (1891): *'Tis a starve-acre place. Corn and swedes are all they grow.*

statuminate. To support, establish. Also *statumination.* Latin *statuminem,* a support; *statuere, statutum,* to set up, establish; *stare, statum,* to stand; whence also *status, state, statue, stature, statute; institute,* the *constitution,* and the *status quo.* Jonson in THE NEW INN (1631) says: *I will statuminate and underprop thee; If they scorn us, let us scorn them.*

stead. See *bested.*

stelled. Fixed, as the stars; formed into stars; studded with stars. Shakespeare in KING LEAR (1605) says that the sea *would have buoy'd up, And quench'd the stelled fires. Stelliferous, stelliferant, stelliferal,* bearing stars; *stellifer,* a knight hospitaler, whose shield bore a red star above a cross.

stellify. To deify, to set among the stars (literally, to make a star of. This activity, once a proud privilege of Zeus, is now the commonplace of any Hollywood publicity agent.). Hence, to extol, to praise to the sky. D'Urfey (OPERAS; 1721) pointed out: *This lady you have stellify'd, is my acquaintance.* Also, to compare to stars; to set or adorn (as) with stars; thus Drummond of Hawthorden in the sonnet THEN IS SHE GONE (1616) says *With roses here she stellified the ground.* The Water Poet (in THE DOG OF WAR, 1630) declared: *Thou shalt be stellified by me; I'le make the Dog Star wayte on thee, And in his room I'le seate thee.*

stellion. A lizard with star-like spots; Wyclif (1382) describes it as "a worm depeyntid as with sterris." Also *stellio,* which Bailey (1751) defines as "a spotted lizard that casts her skin (a sovereign remedy for the falling sickness) every half year, and commonly devours it." The term *stellion* was apparently applied (perhaps in ancient times) to a 'slippery customer,' a scoundrel; this use survives in two crimes: (1) *stellature* (Latin *stellatura*), fraud or graft by a Roman tribune in the supplying of provisions to soldiers. (2) *stellionate,* a general term for all frauds not distinguished by a separate name (18th century English law), but mainly, the granting of the same right (selling the same goods, etc.) to two different persons. The BIBLE (Douai version; 1609) declares: *The stellion stayeth on his handes, and tarieth in kings houses.*

stellionate. A fraud. See *stellion.*

stelliscript. The writing in the stars. Coined by Southey in THE DOCTOR (1835). Wherein is much food for thought.

stent. This form has been used from the 14th century, in various meanings. Also *steynte, stynt, stint*; related to *extent, extend, stend, stint.* (1) To assess, to tax; to levy; to determine the amount of an assessment. Also as a noun, the valuation of property, the amount assessed. This sense was used into the 17th century, later in Scotland. Burns in THE TWA DOGS (1786) says: *Our Laird gets in his racked rents, His coals, his kane, an' a' his stents.* (2) To extend, to stretch out (as a sail, a curtain, a tent, a person to torture). Also as a noun, a stake for stretching fishing-nets in a stream; the apparatus for setting up tents or stretching curtains was a *stenter*; later, influenced by *tent,* a *tenter*—whence also, the figure of keeping one *on tenterhooks,* stretched in anxiety. As an adjective *stent* (1) assessed, taxed, (2) distended; extended; taut. A *stentor* or *stentmaster* was a tax assessor, but also see *stentor.*

stentor. (1) A man with a loud voice. From a Greek warrior in the Trojan War, *Stentor,* with a voice as powerful as the voices of fifty men. Dickens in THE OLD CURIOSITY SHOP (1840) says *Laughing like a stentor, Kit gradually backed to the door, and roared himself out.* Hence *stentorial, stentorious, stentoronic,* and the current *stentorian.* A *stentorophonic horn* is a speaking trumpet (17th and 18th centuries). D'Urfey in HELL BEYOND HELL (1704) speaks of someone *bawling with stentorophonick might.* There is a verb, to *stent,* to assess, to tax; a *stentor* is (2) a *stentmaster,* a person assigned to set the amount of tax to be paid by a town or a parish, and its individual inhabitants. See *stent*; *cp. coss.*

stepony. Raisin wine, with lemon juice and sugar. A common 17th century drink. Also *stepney,* by association with a parish in East London; *stepany, stipone, stipony.* POOR ROBIN'S INTELLIGENCER of 1676 mentions *the faculty of spunging stiponie,* *and of enflaming the reckoning as occasion shall require.*

stercomancy. See *aeromancy.*

stercoraceous. Relating to faeces or dung. Latin *stercus, stercorem,* dung. Also *stercoral, stercorarious, stercorary, stercorean, stercoreous, stercorose, stercorous,* relating to, or full of, dung. *To stercorate,* to manure. *stercoration,* manuring; by extension, a disgusting remark. *stercoricolous* (accent on the *ick*), living in dung. *stercovorous,* feeding on dung. *stercory,* excrement; filth. A *stercorarian,* an old-fogy physician (whose favorite remedy was a purge). Also *stercorarian, stercorist, stercoranist, stercoranite,* (contemptuous), one that believes the "bread and wine" of the Eucharist are digested and evacuated; hence *stercoranism, stercorianism,* this belief. Swinburne in THE FORTNIGHTLY REVIEW (December, 1880) declared; *Unlike Dante, he never permitted the too fetid contact of their stercorous feculence to befoul the sandal of his Muse.* The REPORT of the London committee on Metropolitan Sewers, of 1834, noted that *pumping of stercoraceous filth is practised sometimes every night.* THE WESTMINSTER REVIEW (1832) used the word figuratively: *a sneaking stercoraceous policy.*

sternutation. The act of sneezing. Also *sternutament.* Used from the 16th century; in recent use, when not medical, the word is employed as pedantic humor. Latin *sternutare, sternutatum,* frequentative of *sternuere,* to sneeze. A *sternutatory* (*sternutory*) is a substance that causes sneezing; a powder, a dry errhine. Both these forms, and *sternutative,* are also used as adjectives, meaning causing sneezing. Thackeray in THE FITZ-BOODLE PAPERS (1842) mentions a man *seized with a violent fit of sneezing—sternutatory paroxysm he called it.*

sterquilinian. Of or appropriate to the dunghill. Also *sterquilinious.* Latin *stercus,* dung; *cp. stercoraceous.* Used in the 17th and 18th centuries; Howell in a letter of 1645 complained that *any sterquilinious rascal is licensed to throw dirt in the faces of Soveraign Princes in open printed language.*

sterve. This common Teutonic word (also *steorfan, staerfan, sterfen, storve, starve*) from the 10th to the 17th century meant to die. *Cp. asterve.* Thus Chaucer in TROYLUS AND CRISEYDE (1374) says that Christ *Upon a cros our soules for to beye* [buy] *First starf, and ros, and sit yn hevene above.* About the 15th century, *sterve* was used meaning to die a slow death, as from cold or hunger. Hence, to die of hunger; by the 17th century the form *starve* was predominant, and the extremity of death became less insistent. *To starve out,* to endure in extreme cold; Shakespeare in TROILUS AND CRESSIDA (1606): *Stand hoe, yet are we maisters of the field, Never goe home; here starve we out the night.* Shakespeare also used the word figuratively, as in THE COMEDY OF ERRORS: *His company must do his minions grace, Whilst I at home starve for a merrie looke.*

steven. (1) The voice; especially, a loud voice. *With one steven,* with one accord. Also speech, speaking, prayer; language. Chaucer in THE SQUIRE'S TALE (1386): *Ther is no fowl that fleeth under hevene That she ne shal wel understonde his stevene.* Hence also, sound, noise, outcry; report, fame. Hence also the verb *steven,* to shout, deafen with noise. (2) A time, occasion. *To change (by) stevens,* to take turns. *Unset steven,* without appointment, unexpectedly. Hence, a set time, a date fixed for a payment or a meeting; by transfer, a convened assembly. *To set a steven,* to appoint a time; *to break one's steven,* to fail to keep an appointment. Hence the verb *steven,* to appoint; to alternate, take turns. Perhaps this is the origin of *Even steven,* rhyming slang for equal turns or shares. (3) A summons, a command—also as a verb. (4) The stem of a ship; hence, *to steven,* to direct one's course; thus a Towneley Mystery of 1460 said that Jesus *raised hymself apon the thyrd day, And steven to heaven.* Note that *steven* used to rhyme with *heaven.* (5) In the 19th century, *steven* (still the short *e*) was slang (especially in sports) for money. The word, also occurring as *stevin, stevne, stevon,* is a common Teuton form; at least two earlier words fused in *steven.* Laneham in a letter of 1575 reported that *a doughty dwarf With steven full stout amids all the press, Said "Hail, syr King."*

stew. This word has several meanings not current. (1) A pond or tank in which fish are kept for the table. By extension, any pond; also, an artificial oyster-bed. This sense, from Old French *estui,* case, tub, was used from the 14th century into the 19th. Chaucer in the Prologue to THE CANTERBURY TALES (1386) says *Ful many a fat partrich hadde he in Muwe, And many a breem and many a luce in stuwe.* Also *stuy, stiewe, stywe, stue.* (2) A stove; a heated room. This is from Late Latin *stupa, stufa* (whence ultimately English *stove*), perhaps from *extufare*; Greek *tuphos,* vapor. From this developed various related senses. A vessel or caldron for boiling. So Spenser; and Shakespeare has, in MEASURE FOR MEASURE (1603): *Here in Vienna, Where I have seen corruption boil and bubble Till it o'er-run the stew.* A heated room; so Chaucer. Especially, a heated room used for hot air or vapor baths; hence, a hot bath. This was a most common use, into the 19th century. Hence, meat slowly boiled; usually mixed with vegetables, this is the current *stew.* Hence also, from frequent such use of the medieval public hot-air baths, a brothel. This also was a common use; Nashe cried out in CHRIST'S TEARES OVER JERUSALEM (1593): *London, what are thy suburbes but licensed stewes!* In this sense, both *stew* and *stews* were used as singular, though *stews* sometimes meant the 'red-light district'; also, the *stew-side.* Chaucer among his several uses in the sense of brothel, says, in THE FRIAR'S TALE (1386): *So been the women of the styves . . . yput out of my cure*—rhyming *styves* with *lyves.* This also appears as *stive.* Shakespeare has, in CYMBELINE (1611): *To mart as in a Romish stew.* A *stews* or a *stew,* by further extension, was used to mean a prostitute; in 1650 Weldon (COURT OF KING JAMES) declared: *Instead of that beauty he had a notorious stew sent him.* From the notion of boiling-up, finally, *stew* came to mean overheated, literally (bathed in perspiration) or figuratively, *in a stew,* in a state of great excitement or alarm. *To stew in one's own (water, grease) juice,* to be left to suffer the natural consequences of one's conduct. Shakespeare used the verb literally, bathed in perspiration: KING LEAR (1605): *Came there a reeking post, stew'd in his haste, half breathless, panting forth From Goneril his Mistris, salutations*—and with combined literal and figurative force in HAMLET: *In the rank sweat of an enseamed bed, stew'd in corruption.* Note that a *steward* was a keeper (*ward*) not of a *stew,* but of a *stiy,* which was related to *sty* (*pigsty*) but in Old English probably meant dwelling-place. Hence *stivy,* stuffy; Hewlett (BLACKWOOD'S EDINBURGH MAGA-

ZINE; February, 1899) said: *The sun of her smile was like a clean breath in the stivy den.* There are further complications, but it's better for them than for us to stew.

stichomancy. See *aeromancy.*

stickler. See *stightle.*

stightle. This word, with its variants, has moved along an entire pole of meanings. *Stightle* (13th to 15th century) is a frequentative of *stight,* to arrange, set in order, dispose. *Stightle*—after the 15th century, *stickle*—meant (1) to mediate, umpire; (2) to control, govern, ordain, dispose of; then with hostile indication (3) to dispose of, put down, defeat; (4) to fight, wrangle, dispute. So with *stightler* (15th and 16th centuries, *stiffler*) then *stickler,* a mediator, reconciler; a partisan; an instigator; a wrangler, meddler, busybody, down to the still current sense, *a stickler for,* one that insists upon a certain course or procedure. To compose a dispute: Drayton, in POLYOLBION (1612) *to the Muse refers The hearing of the cause, to stickle all these stirs.* To strive, take an active part: Dryden, in AMPHITRYON (1690): *Nay, the very goddesses would stickle in the cause of love.* To scruple, hesitate: Barholm in THE INGOLDSBY LEGENDS (1840) said that some persons *stickle not to aver that you are catercousin with Beelzebub himself. Stickler*—a factious contender, a wrangler. Penn in SOME FRUITS OF SOLITUDE (1693): *A devout man is one thing, a stickler is quite another.* An antagonist: Jackson in COMMENTARIES UPON THE APOSTLES CREED (1613): *Diomedes (who was one of the greatest sticklers against Troy).* A mediator, umpire: Shakespeare in TROILUS AND CRESSIDA (1606): *The dragon-wing of night ore-spreds the earth And stickler-like the Armies separates.*

still. I. As a verb—beyond the current senses of to lull, calm, stop—was a short form of *distil* (from which the noun, *a still,* widely survives). This first meant (14th century) to trickle down, fall in drops; thence, to extract the juice or essence of. Its most famous use is in that great sentence of Marlowe's TAMBURLAINE (1587): *If all the pens that ever poets held Had fed the feeling of their maisters thoughts, And every sweetnes that inspir'd their harts, Their minds, and muses on admyred theames; If all the heavenly quintessence they still From their immortall flowers of poesy, Wherein as in a myrrour we perceive The highest reaches of a humaine wit: If these had made one poems period And all combin'd in beauties worthiness, Yet should ther hover in their restless heads, One thought, one grace, one wonder at the least, Which into words no vertue can digest.* II. As an adverb: always, invariably. So used from the 13th century. Thus *still still,* on every occasion. *still as,* whenever. *still and anon, still an end,* every so often; Shakespeare in THE TWO GENTLEMEN FROM VERONA (1591) speaks of *A slave that still an end turnes me to shame.* Sir John Harington in his MOST ELEGANT AND WITTIE EPIGRAMS (1618) advised: *Lay down your stake at play, lay down your passion: A greedy gamester still hath some mishap. To chafe at luck proceeds of foolish fashion. No man throws still the dice in fortunes lap.* For another instance, see *stith.*

still-. Several compounds with this form have been used in English. (1) *stillroom.* A room in a house, with a *still* for the preparation of cordials and perfumes. Later, a room for keeping preserves, cakes, liqueurs, etc., and preparing tea, coffee, and the like. Having lost its first meaning, the word could give rise to such comment as this, in Harwood's LADY FLAVIA (1865): *There was babbling . . . in what are facetiously called the still-rooms of country mansions.* Hence, *stillroom maid.* (2) *still-sitting,* inactivity. (3) *still-stand.* Scott used this (THE LEGEND OF MONTROSE, 1819) to mean a truce; Shakespeare, to mean a standstill; HENRY IV, PART TWO (1597): *As with the tyde, swell'd up unto his height, That makes a still-stand, running neyther way.* (4) *stillworth.* Peaceful. A 13th century term (used by Layamon), apparently coined by analogy with *stalworth.* (5) *stillyard.* Used in the 18th century for *stillion,* a stand, or a framework on which a cask might stand, a gantry, *q.v. Stillified* (17th century) meant distilled, but *stilliform* meant drop-shaped, and *stillicidious, stillatitious,* produced by the falling of drops; see *stillatim, stillicide.* Thus *stillie* (16th century), sprinkled with drops.

stillatim. Drop by drop. From Latin *stilla,* drop. Suggesting the medieval torture, as when Evelyn in a letter of 1668 says: *cause abundance of cold fountain-water to be poured upon me stillatim, for a good half-hour together.* Stalactites are *stillatitious,* that is, produced by falling drops. This word may also mean issuing or falling in drops, as *the painful and stillatitious emission of urine.* See *stillicide.*

stillatory. See *stillitory.*

stillicide. The dripping of water. From Latin *stilla,* drop + *cidere,* to fall. Used in Scottish law for the dripping of rain-water from the eaves of a man's house upon another's land. Stevenson in AN APOLOGY FOR IDLERS (1888) says of school: *I am sure that it will not be the full, vivid, instructive hours of truancy that you regret . . . I have attended a good many lectures in my time. I still remember that the spinning of a top is a case of kinetic stability. I still remember that emphyteusis is not a disease, nor stillicide a crime.*

Cide, as a suffix from Latin *caedere,* to make fall, to slay, usually means the killing of, or the killer, destroyer. Thus *apricide,* of a boar. *avicide,* a bird. *bovicide,* an ox; humorously, a butcher. *brahminicide,* a brahmin. *cervicide,* a deer. *czaricide. deicide,* a god. *femicide,* a woman. *feticide, foeticide,* a foetus: an abortion. *fratricide,* a brother. *felicide,* a cat. *fungicide,* spores. *genocide,* a people (coined after World War II). *germicide. giganticide,* a giant. *hericide,* a lord or master. *herpecide,* a reptile. *hiricide,* a goat. *homicide,* a man. *infanticide. insecticide. larvicide. liberticide*: destroyer of liberty; used by Southey, Shelley, Carlyle. *lupicide,* a wolf. *macropicide,* a kangaroo. *matricide,* a mother. *microbicide. mundicide,* the world. *muricide,* a mouse. *nematocide,* worms. *nepoticide,* a favorite. *parasiticide. parenticide, parricide,* a parent. *patricide,* a father. *poultrycide. regicide,* a king. *serpenticide. sororicide,* a sister. *suicide,* oneself. *talpicide,* a mole. *tauricide,* a bull. *tomecide,* books. *vaticide,* a prophet. *verbicide,* the word: a liar, or a book-burner. *vermicide,* a worm. *vulpicide,* a fox.

A *lapicide* is a stone-cutter. A *Barmecide* is a person that offers imaginary benefits. In THE THOUSAND AND ONE NIGHTS (1450), *Barmecide* was a prince of Baghdad, who put a succession of empty dishes before a beggar, pretending they held a sumptuous feast. Hence Dickens in AMERICAN NOTES (1842) speaks of a *Barmecide feast.* And *barmecidal* means illusory, like hopes of relief of the world's woe by international homicide.

stillitory. A still, an alembic. Shakespeare uses the form *stillitorie;* from Chaucer's CANTERBURY TALES (1386) to the 18th century, *stillatory* was more frequent; but also *stillotorie, styllytory, stellatour, styllathre,* and more. Often used figuratively, as in Shakespeare's VENUS AND ADONIS (1592): *For from the stillitorie of thy face excelling Coms breath perfumd that breedeth love by smelling.*

stipony. See *stepony.*

stith. I. As a noun. An anvil; a variant of *stithy, q.v.* Both forms have been used from the 13th century. Also *steyth, stythe, stethe,* and the like. *Stithy* has been more often used figuratively. Surrey, in his elegy on Sir Thomas Wyatt (1542): *A head, where wisdom misteries did frame, Whose hammers bet still in that lively brain As on a stithe.* II. As an adjective. Unyielding; strong (*cp. stour*); formidable; firm; rigid (of the neck; also, in death); inflexible of purpose; stubborn. Also intense; violent (of a battle, storm, torrent); mighty. Used from BEOWULF to the 16th century, later in Scotland. Also used as an adverb, firmly, severely; and as a verb (14th century), to set firmly. Barbour in BRUCE (1375): *In battle so stith to stand;* ST. CUTHBERT (1450): *He was taken, and in to stithe fetters schakyn.*

stithy. An anvil; by extension, a forge, smithy. Used from the 13th century, in many forms, including *stethie, stythy, stethye, stythe;* in the north and Scotland, *stedy, stedee, steady, study, stoddy.* Related to Teutonic root *sta,* to stand. See *stith.* Often used figuratively; by Scott in KENILWORTH (1821); by Lowell in A FAMILIAR EPISTLE (1869): *Let whoso likes be beat, poor fool, On life's hard stithy to a tool.* Shakespeare in HAMLET (1602) has: *My imaginations are as foule As Vulcans stithy.*

stive. See *stew.*

stiver. (1) Something of small value; also, a tiny quantity. *Not a stiver,* nothing, not a bit. From Netherlands *stiver* (16th century) a coin worth about a penny. Also (2) *stiver, stivour,* a player on the bagpipe. Among the various meanings of *stive* (*q.v.*) was (13th century, Old French *estive*) bagpipe. (3) As a verb, *to stiver,* to stand stiff, bristle (especially of the hair); *stivery,* bristly, rough. This sense is related to *stiff.* Hence also *stiver cramped,* short of funds; *stiverless,* penniless. *The birds,* said a Devonshire PROVINCIAL REPORT of 1889, *look big in winter with their feathers all stivered out.* Browning in THE PIED PIPER OF HAMELIN (1842) has: *With him I proved no bargain-driver; With you, don't think I'll bate a stiver!*

stone. In various forms and combinations: *stone-ram,* a ram not castrated; so of other beasts; thus, *stone-priest, stone-puritan,* and the like, a lascivious priest, etc. *stone-buckle,* a buckle set with precious stones. *stone-eater,* a conjuror that pretends to eat stones. *stone-eyed,* with eyes motionless; also, blind; *stone blind,* wholly sightless; *cp. sandblind. stone's throw,* also *stone-cast. Cp. philosopher's stone; whetstone.* From the shape of their bulbs, varieties of the orchis (*cp. satyrion*) were popularly called *foolstones, goatstones, spotted dogstones, marsh dogstones, foxstones, sweetstones,* and the like. Shakespeare had one of these in mind when in HAMLET (1590) the chaste but mad Ophelia plucks *long-purples That liberal shepherds give a grosser name; But our cold maids do dead men's fingers call them.* Another name for the *long-purple* was *serapia stones,* from the god *Serapius,* worshipped at Canopus with gay fertility rites. Beaver stones were apparently a delicacy; Nashe in THE UNFORTUNATE TRAVELLER (1594) remembers Pliny's NATURAL HISTORY: *The hunter pursuing the beaver for his stones, hee bites them off and leaves them behinde for him to gather up, whereby he lives quiet.*

stonish. An early (15th to 18th century) variant of *astonish.* Also *stunys, stonis, stunnys, stonnyshe* (mainly Scotch). Hence *stonishment.* Shakespeare has, in VENUS AND ADONIS (1592): *Or stonisht, as night wandrers often are, Their light blowne out.*

stoopgallant. Something that humbles the great, that makes the *gallant* a mere man. Originally (early 16th century) a name for the 'sweating sickness,' a fever of swift fatality in the 15th and 16th centuries. Thus Hancock in 1560 remarked that *Ther were* [gallants] *dawncyng in the cowrte at 9 a' clocke that were deadd or aleven a' clocke.* Spenser in THE SHEPHERD'S CALENDAR (1579; FEBRUARY) says: *Youth is a bubble . . . Whose way is wildernesse, whose ynne penaunce, And stoopegallaunt age the hoste of greevaunce.* Nashe in HAVE WITH YOU TO SAFFRON-WALDEN (1596) promises a comedy that *shal bee called . . . 'Stoope Gallant; or, The Fall of Pride.'*

stooth. A variant form of *stud.* Also *stoth, stothe, stoith.* A will of 1530 mentioned *a gyrdell stothed with sylver.*

stor. Incense. Possibly from Latin *storax,* Greek *styrax*; both these forms have also been used in English for an aromatic gum. *Stor* was used from the 10th into the 14th century; *storax,* from the 14th; *styrax,* from the 16th century. Burton in THE ANATOMY OF MELANCHOLY (1621) lists *belzoin, ladanum, styrax, and such like gummes, which make a pleasant and acceptable perfume.* T. Green, in his UNIVERSAL HERBAL of 1820, distinguishes between dry *storax-in-the-lump* and liquid *storax-in-the-tear.*

storge. Natural love; especially, the feeling of parents for their children. Two syllables, *store-jee.* Greek *storge; stergein,* to love. Used from the 17th century; Thackeray in PENDENNIS (1850) admires *the maternal storge which . . . sanctifies the history of mankind.* S. Cox in his COMMENTARIES: JOB (1880) observed: *The ostrich resembles the stork . . . but lacks its pious, maternal storge.* What more appropriate bird?

storial. A variant (aphetic) of *historial,* historical. Chaucer in THE LEGEND OF GOOD WOMEN (1385) says: *And this is storyal soth, it is no fable.* In the 19th century, *storiation* was used to describe decoration (mainly in architecture) with designs representing historical or legendary subjects.

stot. As a noun: A horse; early, an inferior beast; hence, a clumsy person. Hence, as a term of contempt for a woman. Chaucer in THE FRIAR'S TALE (1386) says *Nay, olde stot, that is not myn entente.* Perhaps from the first meaning, *stot* was used, since the 16th century, to mean a quick jump back; a rebounding blow; a leap or swing (hence, the rhythm) of a dance. *To keep stot,* to keep time. The word was also used figuratively; Rutherford in a letter (1637) spoke of *a wrong step or a wrong stot in going out of this life.* As a verb, there seems to be a series. Thus *stot,* to rebound, bounce; jump, spring; to bound along but also to go unsteadily, lurch, stagger. And *stotay* (15th century), to totter, falter, come to a stop. But since the 14th century, *stote,* to stop, stand still. *Stoter,* to hit hard, to fell. And *stotter,* to stumble, to stagger.

These forms (as *stutter, totter,* etc.) are echoic. [Hence also the nouns *stoter,* a violent blow: Motteux' translation (1694) of Rabelais mentions *a swinging stoater with the pitchfork*—and the earlier (14th and 15th century) *stoteye,* hardihood in attack.]

stoth. See *stooth.*

stoun. To stun. To strike with amazement. A shortened form from Old French *estoner,* whence *astound, astonish,* also *astone,* to strike still as a stone. Used into the 17th century; replaced by *stun.* Spenser in THE FAËRIE QUEENE (1596) says: *So was he stound with stroke of her huge taile.* T. Heywood in THE BRAZEN AGE (1613) used it of softer powers: *My beauty, that charms gods, makes men amaz'd And stound with wonder.* Note that one form of *stoun* (*stowne, stown, stounne*) is *stound, q.v.*

stound. This common early form is a gathering of several roots and many meanings. It appears also as *stund, stond, stownd, stowned, stowunde,* and the like. As a noun: (1) A state of amazement; see *stoun.* (2) A wooden container for small beer. In this sense, a form of *stand;* used in the 17th and 18th centuries. (3) A moment, a short time. From the 10th century. This and its developments represent the most frequent use. In one of his ENTERTAINMENTS (1603), Jonson wrote: *Now they print it on the ground With their feete in figures round, Markes that will be ever found To remember this glad stound.* Hence *in a stound; in many stounds. By stounds,* from time to time; by turns. *Oft-stounds,* oftentimes. *That stounds,* at that moment. Hence, the propitious moment, an opportunity. THE LEGEND OF ST. KATHERINE (1225) exclaimed: *Nu is ower stunde!* [Now is our chance!] But also, a bad time, a time of trial or suffering; Chaucer in ANELIDA AND ARCITE (1374) cries *Alas! the harde stounde.* Hence, a pang, a shock, a sudden attack or sharp pain. May Jesus, says Spenser in THE SHEPHERD'S CALENDAR (1579; MAY) *keepe your corpse from the carefull stounds That in my carrion carcas abounds.* Variant developments of meaning include (4) station, place, position (at a given time); Drant in his translation (1566) of Horace's SATIRES wrote: *Stande still in stounde, kepe whishte (I say) whilst I do prove you mad.* (5) A fierce noise, roar. (From the 17th century; Drayton, Burton.) Carlyle in THE FRENCH REVOLUTION (1837) says: *One can fancy with what dolorous stound the noontide cannon . . . went off there.* As a verb, the action of the various noun meanings: (1) To stun as with a blow, *astound,* stupefy. (2) To remain, stay in one place or position (13th to 15th century). (3) To cause great pain to; to give a *stound* or shock; to be very painful, to smart. Also, as a verbal noun, *stounding;* a benumbing; a delay, lingering. *Stoundmeal,* at intervals, from time to time; gradually; Chaucer in TROYLUS AND CRISEYDE (1374) notices *this wynde that moore and moore thus stoundemele encresseth in my face.*

stoup. (1) A pail or bucket; a small cask; a drinking-vessel, of varying sizes. Especially, a container, a stone basin, of holy-water, in a church entrance-way. In common use from the 14th century. Pronounced *stoop.* It was written in many forms, including *stop, stowpe, stolp, stoope, stope, stoap.* Shakespeare, in TWELFTH NIGHT (1601): *Marian I say, a stoope of wine.* Blackmore, in LORNA DOONE (1869): *Parson took a stoop of cider.* THE PASTON LETTERS (1452): *Ye shul have a stope of bere to comforte yow.* Of the church, THE QUARTERLY REVIEW for April, 1899: *The famous alliance between the stoup and the sabre, which has reorganized the politics of France.* (2) A variant form of *stop.* Also *stoupaille* (15th century); *to make a stoupaille of,* to close, as with a plug. (3) A variant form of *stoop.* Davies' WITS BEDLAM, WHERE IS HAD WHIPPING-CHEER TO CURE THE MAD (1617) contains the epigram: *A flatterer (like a wrestler) stoupeth low To him he flatters; so, to overthrow: God blesse good princes from such stoupers; and Place such about them as doe upright stand.* So be it with all men!

stour. This was an early and common word. Also *stur, stowre, store, stower, stoor, storre, sture,* and the like. Pronounced *stoor.* As a noun. (1) An armed conflict, battle, fight; a struggle with adversity, pain, etc.; a death-struggle. (2) A time of turmoil and stress. Spenser uses this several times—e.g., THE FAËRIE QUEENE (1590): *I have beene trained up in warlike stowre*—and poets after him. Others, perhaps misinterpreting Spenser, have used *stour* to mean (3) occasion, place. Lodge, in ENGLAND'S HELICON (1600) wrote: *Oft from her lap at sundry stoures He leapt, and gathered sommer flowres.* The word in these senses is from Anglo-French *estur,* Old French *estour, estorn;* Teutonic root *sturmoz,* whence also *storm.* In the remaining uses as a noun, the sense was probably influenced by *stir.* (4) A tumult, roar, commotion. Thus Ramsay jested, in a MASQUE of 1730: *Minerva mim, for a' your mortal stoor, Ye shall with billy Bacchus fit the floor.* (5) A driving storm; hence, swirling or flying dust (or driving snow or scudding spray). Hence *like stour,* vigorously, swiftly; *to make (raise) a stour,* to raise a dust, make a fuss; *to blow (throw) stour in one's eyes,* to confuse, mislead, deceive. Thus as a verb: to whirl in a cloud of dust (or snow, etc.). As an adjective, *stoor* is a blending of two forms: Old English *stor,* great; and Middle English *stūr,* wild, vigorous, harsh. Hence its meanings: violent, fierce; grievous, severe; great (in quantity, size, or degree). Hence strong, stalwart; imposing (in bearing or speech); stubborn, stern, surly; harsh (of voice); coarse (of texture). In certain isles, said Maundeville in his TRAVELS (1400) *Are schepe as mykill* [large] *as oxen, bot the wool of them es grete and sture.* Chaucer in THE MERCHANT'S TALE (1386) inquires: *O stronge lady stoore, what dostow* [dost thou]? Herbert in THE TEMPLE avers that *Constancie knits the bones, and makes us stowre.* God gie ye good store! Spenser in THE FAËRIE QUEENE (MUTABILITY; 1596) pictures Spring all clad in *flowres (In which a thousand birds had built their bowres That sweetly sung, to call forth paramours): And in his hand a javelin he did beare, And on his head (as fit for warlike stoures) A guilt engraven morion he did weare; That as some did him love, so others did him feare.*

stover. A variant of *estover, q.v.* It developed other meanings: (1) Food essential for a journey. (2) Winter food for cattle; occasionally a specific type, as hay from clover. Iris says to Ceres in Shakespeare's THE TEMPEST (1610): *Thy turfy mountains, where live nibbling sheep, And flat meads thatch'd with stover, them to keep.*

stramineous. Relating to straw; by extension, worthless. Latin *stramen, straminem,* straw. Hence *stramage,* straw or rushes for spreading on a floor. From the Italian *stramazzone,* a knock-down blow (*stramazzo,* a straw mattress) comes the rapier stroke called *stramazon* (16th and

17th centuries; revived by Scott in WOODSTOCK, 1826). Saintsbury in his HISTORY OF CRITICISM (1900) wrote: *He not only seems to be dealing with men of straw, but answers them with, as Luther would say, a most stramineous argument.*

strappado. A medieval torture, often used to extort a confession: the victim's hands were tied behind his back and fastened to a pulley; by this he was hoist high and let fall part-way, with a jerk. Lea in THE HISTORY OF THE INQUISITION (1888) relates that *in some witch trials in Piedmont the oath to tell the truth was enforced with excommunication and 'tratti di corde,' or infliction of the torture known as the strappado.* The word was often used figuratively; Brathwait wrote a book (1615) entitled *A Strappado for the Divell.* The word is from Italian *strappata; strappare,* to pull, snatch; but because of the first syllable, it was sometimes mistakenly used as though it meant a beating, whipping; thus Bickerstaffe (PADLOCK; 1769): *He gave me the strappado on my shoulders, and the bastinado on the soles of my feet.* When Falstaff (in Shakespeare's HENRY IV, PART ONE; 1597) is asked for his reason, he retorts: *What, upon compulsion? Zounds, an I were at the strappado, or all the racks in the world, I would not tell you on compulsion. Give you a reason on compulsion! If reasons were as plentiful as blackberries, I would give no man a reason upon compulsion.* [For continuance of the conversation, see *pizzle.*]

stratopedarch. Commander of a camp. The accent goes on *top.* Used in histories written in the 19th century (Milman; Ramsay). Greek *stratos,* army + *pedon,* field, ground + *arches,* ruler.

stratuminate. To pave. Latin *stratum,* pavement (literally, a thing spread over, hence a bed cover, a horse cloth, etc.); *sternere, stratum,* to throw down, to spread out. In 17th and 18th century dictionaries; not in O.E.D.

stravagant. Aphetic for *extravagant,* in various senses: extraordinary, unsuitable; irrelevant. (The Italian, from Late Latin *extravagare,* also dropped the *e*: *stravagante.*) Also, a vagrant. The present participle of Latin *vagari, vagatum* (whence *divagate,* etc.) is *vagantem.* There was a 19th century Scottish verb to *stravaig,* to wander aimlessly. *Stravagant* was used in the 16th and early 17th century, as Chapman's MASK OF THE INNS OF COURT (1613): *The torch-bearers' habits were likewise of the Indian garb, but more stravagant than those of the maskers.*

streck. Straight, straightway; directly, immediately. Also *streke, strick, strek*; related to *stretch. Streck up,* in an upright position. Hampole in THE PRICKE OF CONSCIENCE (1340) wrote: *The synful soul than gos strik to helle.*

streek. An early variant of *stretch.* Also *streak, strek, streck. streek* developed also (14th century) the idea of moving along (quickly), or of urging along, as a donkey.

strepitation. A continuing or repeated noise; clattering. Latin *strepitare, strepitatum,* frequentative of *strepere,* to make a noise. Hence *strepent, streperous, strepitant, strepitous,* noisy. Neville, in PLATO REDIVIVUS (1681) bemoans *a poor gentleman who by means of the harangue of a strepitous lawyer, was found guilty of murder. Strepitate* (in 17th century dictionaries), to make a continual noise. The term *streperosity* was used in the 18th century, meaning high-sounding language. *Peace!* cried Shenstone in RURAL ELEGANCE (1750), *Peace to the strepent horn!* THE

NATION of 12 July, 1913, warned the world *to listen in the gathering darkness to the strepitation of Apollyon's wings.* A year later, their beating loosed all hell upon the world.

stridulous. Producing a shrill, grating sound. Latin *stridere,* to creak, whence also *strident; stridor,* a harsh, high-pitched sound. The frequentative form was *stridulare, stridulatum,* whence *stridulator* is used to mean an insect that emits *stridulation;* also the verb *stridulate* and the adjective *stridulant. Stridulatory, stridulent; stridulency* are used also in reference to persons. Rousseau, said Morley in his biography (1873), *sought new life away from the stridulous hum of men.* G. A. Lawrence in MAURICE DERING (1864) spoke of a *stridulous young person who . . . screams when she talks, and squalls when she sings.*

strobic. Spinning. Greek *strobos,* a twisting around. Thus *strobic circles,* a series of concentric circles, which appear to revolve when the surface on which they are marked is turned. The *stroboscope,* as a toy or scientific instrument, is also from Greek *strobos,* as is the *strobilus,* the pine-cone.

strole. A variant of *stroll.* It occurs in a burlesque Prologue to Shakespeare's KING JOHN, supposedly to be spoken before Colley Cibber's "amended" version of the play, and published in the WHITEHALL EVENING POST of 10 February, 1737: *And all our modern Muses, alias Misses, Still strole about the Temple, fond of kisses.* Cibber's version of Shakespeare's play was so savagely attacked—before it was read or seen—that Cibber went to a rehearsal, took his version from the prompter's desk, and walked out of the theatre. It was published in 1745—and deserved the attacks. Swift in 1720 said *So rotting* [rutting?] *Celia stroles the street, When sober folks are all abed.*

strooke. An old past form of *strike: stricken.* For an instance of its use, see *jar.*

stroud. A large but coarse blanket, manufactured (in Stroud, Gloucestershire?) to trade or sell to the American Indians. It was made from woollen rags. THE JOURNAL OF CAPTAIN TREAT (1752) contains the entry: *Be pleased to give to the son of the Piankasha king these two strowds to clothe him.*

stroy. Aphetic for *destroy,* but also used as a noun: in the 15th century, one who destroys; a waster, a *stroy-all, stroy-good;* in the 17th century, destruction. Bunyan has, in THE HOLY WAR (1692): *Nor did they partake or make stroy of any of the necessaries of Mansoul.*

stultiloquence. Foolish talk, babble. Latin *stultus,* foolish + *loquens,* talking. Also, *stultiloquy.* Hence *stultiloquent, stultiloquious.* Also *stulty* (14th century), *stultitious* (16th and 17th centuries), foolish. *Stultify, stultificate,* to render foolish or worthless; to reduce to absurdity. Urquhart, in his translation (1693) of Rabelais: *So great was the stultificating virtue of that . . . pulverized dose.* Swinburne in his STUDIES written in the year of my birth, speaks of *the blank and blatant jargon of epic or idyllic stultiloquence.*

stum. Unfermented or partly fermented grape-juice, must. Also *stoom.* From Dutch *stom,* dumb. The Germans call wine that has become flat *stummer Wein;* the French use the phrase *vin muet* for *stum.* Stum was often used, especially in the 17th and 18th centuries, for renewing vapid wines; hence, *stum* was applied to wine thus freshened, as by Butler in HUDIBRAS (1664):

I'll carve your name on barks of trees . . . Drink every letter on't in stum, And make it brisk champagne become. Shadwell in THE SQUIRE OF ALSATIA (1688) asked: *Is not rich generous wine better than hedge-wine stummed?* And in THE TRUE WIDOW (1679) Shadwell used the word figuratively: *'Tis the stum of love that makes it fret and fume.*

stupre. Violation of a woman. Latin *stuprum.* Wyclif's BIBLE (1382) speaks of *the sons of Jacob . . . waxing cruel for the stupre of the sister.* Hence *stuprous,* given to rape, adultery, whoredom. Also *stuprate;* Hall in his CHRONICLES (1548) said that Richard III *compassed all the means and waies that he could invent how to stuprate and carnally know his awne niece under the pretence of a cloaked matrimony.*

styrax. See *stor.*

styve. See *stew.*

suade. This 16th century form, from Latin *suadere* (whence also *suave*) was superseded by *persuade.* Also *suadible, suasible,* that is easily persuaded. Grimalde in Tottel's MISCELLANY (1557) advised: *Flee then ylswading pleasures, baits untrew.* The Roman goddess of persuasion was *Suada;* in English, *suada* was used to mean persuasive eloquence; Harvey (FOUR LETTERS; 1592) wrote: *How faine would I see . . . suadas hoony-bees in you rehiv'd.* Hence also *suasory, suasorian,* tending to persuade; *suasive; suasion; suasiveness.* The term *moral suasion* survives, although C. Nesse wrote in AN ANTIDOTE AGAINST ARMINIANISM (1700): *Moral suasion will never prove effectual to open the heart of man.*

suant. Following; working smoothly; suitable, agreeable. Via Old French *suiant* from Latin *sequi, secutum,* to follow, whence also *consecutive* and *inconsequential.* Hence *suantly,* evenly, smoothly, regularly. Used from the 15th century.

suaveolent. Sweet-smelling. Accent on the *vee.* Latin *suavis,* English *suave,* pleasing, sweet + *olens,* smelling, *olere,* to smell. Hence also *suaviloquence, suaviloquy,* pleasing speech; *suaviloquent, suaviloquious.* THE BANQUET in 1819 commented: *suaveolent, the viands valets bear.* A book was published in 1659 entitled: *A Collection of Authentic Arguments, Swaviloquent Speeches, and Prudent Reasons.*

suaviation. An amorous kissing. Not a duty peck, not a hearty buss, but the luscious labiation of mutually absorbed lovers. Latin *savium,* a love kiss, altered by association with *suavis,* sweet. *Meum savium* was a Roman pet phrase, meaning My Love. Hence also *suaviate,* to exchange such a kiss. The first *a* is pronounced *ah!*

suaviloquence. See *suaveolent.*

sub. Latin, under. Used in a number of Latin phrases once common in English. *sub dio* (16th-17th century), under the open sky. *sub* (now *in*) *forma pauperis* (16th-17th century), as a bankrupt, a pauper. *sub hasta,* under a spear, at auction (the Romans stood a spear as a sign of an auction sale). *sub Jove frigido* (19th century; Scott), under chilly Jupiter, in the open air. *sub judice* (from the 17th century), under judicial consideration, not yet settled. *sub modo,* with qualifications, under certain conditions. *sub pede sigilli* (from the 17th century), under the foot of the seal, under seal. *sub plumbo,* under lead, under the seal of the Pope. *sub poena* (14th century), under a penalty of; through its use as a threat if one ignores a summons, this became the current *subpoena*. *sub rosa,* under the rose, secretly. *sub sigillo,* under the seal (of confession), in utmost secrecy. *sub silentio,* in silence, with no notice being taken.

sub-. A host of words, mainly scientific, have been formed with the prefix *sub-*, under, close to, towards, somewhat, almost. Some of the forgotten ones are: *subact,* to work up (the ground in cultivating, dough in kneading, etc.); Jackson's COMMENTARIES UPON THE APOSTLES' CREED (1614): *Faith could not take root in them, unless first wrought and subacted by extraordinary signs and wonders. subagitate,* to have sexual intercourse; Urquhart's translation (1693) of Rabelais boasts of *this grand subagitatory achievement*; hence, *subagitation. subaquaneous,* underwater; more commonly *subaqueous, subaquatic. subarboreal,* under a forest of trees. *subarrhation,* betrothal or marriage by virtue of the man's giving a ring (or other pledge) to the woman: With this ring, I thee wed. *subaud,* to understand what is needed to complete a thought or construction; hence *subaudition*; *in a subauditur,* by implication, as in the CONTEMPORARY REVIEW of February 1880, which declares that modern fiction is *much occupied, though in a subauditur, with the skeleton in the cupboard of daily life. subbois,* underwood, underbrush. *subbosco* (humorous, 16th century), the hair on the lower part of the face. *subcineritious* (accent on the fourth syllable), baked under ashes. *subcingulum,* a broad belt or girdle worn beneath another, as by Anglo-Saxon bishops. *subcrustal,* lying under the crust of the earth. *subdial,* under the sky, in the open air (17th century). *subdichotomize,* subdivide; Noah Biggs, ON THE VANITY OF THE CRAFT OF PHYSIC (1651) says: *Subdichotomise it by the severe incision knife of rational argumentations. subdit,* under, subject (to). *subdititious,* placed under (also used of a suppository); also, by fraudulent substitution for the right thing. *subdolous* (accent on the first syllable), crafty, sly; D'Israeli in CHARLES I (1828): *The King was troubled, lest this subdolous and eloquent man should shake his resolution. subferulary* (from *ferule*), under school discipline, under strict control. *subfusc, subfuscous, subfusk,* of dusky or sombre hue. *subhastation,* auction, an auction sale (literally, placing under the spear; in ancient Rome a spear was set up as a sign of an auction). *subhumerate,* to take onto one's shoulder, to bear; *Nothing surer ties a friend,* said Feltham in RESOLVES (1628), *than freely to subhumerate the burthen which was his. subintellect,* to supply in thought, to understand; hence, *subintellection*; *cp. subaudition. subintelligence,* an implication; Browning in PARLEYINGS (1887) speaks of a *subintelligential nod and wink—Turning foes friends.* A *subintelligitur* is the unspoken, implied addition that completes a statement. *subite, subitane,* hasty, sudden, rash; *subitany, subitary, subitaneous,* hastily or suddenly made or done (Latin *subire,* to go stealthily; *sub + ire, itum,* to go, whence also *itinerary*). *subjugal,* under a yoke; under someone's dominion. *sublevaminous* (accent on third syllable), supporting, sustaining (Latin *levare,* raise): Feltham in RESOLVES speaks of God who governs all things *by His upholding and sublevaminous Providence. submonish,* to reprove gently, to admonish mildly (17th century); hence *submonition. submundane,* existing beneath the world. *subniveal, subnivean,* under the snow. *subnubilar,* below the clouds. *subpedaneous,* under or supporting the feet (as a footstool); used also of a mountain at the foot of another. *subreption,* suppressing the truth to obtain advancement, gifts, etc.; hence *subreptive, subreptitious*; *cp. ob* (5—*obreption*). *subrision,* the act of smiling; *subride*; *subrident, subrisive, subrisory. subsannate,* to mock, deride, also *subsanne*; hence, *subsannation*; *subsannator,* mocker. *subsella, subsellium,* a seat in a (Roman) amphitheatre; there were vaults running under the subsellia all around. *subsortition,* choice by lot of a substitute; *subsortitiously* (17th century). *substrati,* kneelers, members of a class of penitents in the early Christian church; a *substrator*; *substration,* their prostration, also the place where they knelt. *subsultation,* a hopping or skipping about; also to *subsult*; *subsultive, subsultory*; Cudworth in A TREATISE CONCERNING ETERNAL AND IMMUTABLE MORALITY (1688; imagine writing under that title today!) speaks of *fortuitous dancings or subsultations of the spirits. subtartarean,* below Tartarus, in the seventh hell. *subtectacle* (literally, under roof), protection, covering. *subtegulaneous,* under the eaves. *subtiliative,* rendering, or able to render, thin; dissolving. *subtrist,* melancholy. *subtrude,* to thrust under, to come stealthily; Hardy in WESSEX POEMS (1898): *I see the nightfall shades subtrude. subundane,* beneath the waves. *subvertise* (15th century), to subvert. *subvirate,* one less than a man.

subfumigation. A burning below, i.e., the generating of fumes or vapors, as of incense, especially in incantations, to offer sacrifice or summon spirits. Gower in CONFESSIO AMANTIS (1390) wrote: *With nigromance he wole assaile To make his incantacioun With hot subfumigacioun.* From the 16th century, the form *suffumigation* was used. Also *suffumige.* Hence *suffumigate*; *suffumigatious.*

subpedital. A shoe. Also *suppedital, suppeditary*; Latin *sub,* under + *pedem,* foot. A HUNDRED MERRY TALES (1526) shows that pedantic humor did not begin in the 19th century; instead of asking the cobbler to patch one's shoes, one asked: *Set me ii tryangyls and ii semy cercles uppon my subpedytals.* Lodge repeated this in 1596.

subtlety. See *warner.*

succade. Fruit preserved in (candied or syrup) sugar. Popular from the 15th century. *Succades,* sweetmeats, candied fruits or vegetables. Also *succate,* perhaps by association with *cate.* See *sucket. Succado,* a fruit syrup (16th century).

succarath. 'A monster-like beast,' reported in the 16th and 17th century as inhabiting the new world. Also *sucaratha.* When hunted, it was reputed to take its young on its back.

succedaneum. A substitute. In earlier use (17th century) the word was applied mainly to things; but Walpole in a letter of 1754 says: *In lieu of me, you will have a charming succedaneum, Lady Harriet Stanhope.* Also, *succedany, succedane.* Hence, *succedaneal, succedaneous.*

succlamation. Outcry; applause. In the first sense, the word has lapsed; in the second, it has been replaced by *acclamation*; *ad,* to; *sub,* under + *clamare, clamatus,* to call; whence also *proclaim*; *clamor.* Painter in THE PALACE OF PLEASURE, has Virginius tell how his daughter Virginia was ravished by Appius Claudius; *this succlamation and pitifull complainte so stirred the multitude that they promised all to helpe and relieve his sorrow.*

succubus. See *ephialtes.*

suckable. Used in the 19th century. (1) That can be sucked. M. Williams' SANSKRIT GRAMMAR (1846): *This division of food into four kinds, lickables, drinkables, chewables, and suckables, is not unusual in Indian writing.* (2) *A suckable,* a sweetmeat, liquid or candy. *Cp. sucket.*

suckeny. An outer garment; especially, a smock. Of Slavonic origin; Polish *suknia,* coat. Also *sukkenye, suckiney, surkney.* Chaucer says, in THE ROMAUNT OF THE ROSE (1366): *She hadde on a sukkenye. That not of hemp ne heerdis was.* [Heerdis is an old variant of *hards, hurds,* the coarser parts of hemp or flax. Thus Eden said in THE DECADES OF THE NEW WORLD (1555), of the coconut: *It is involved and covered with many webbes much like unto those hyrdes of towe which they use in Andalusia.*]

sucket. A variant of *succade, q.v.* Also *succate, soket, suckitte* (which many did), and other forms. From the verb *suck.* The delicacies called suckets varied in composition; there were wet suckets and dry suckets, suckets of pompion, suckets of citron, suckets of orange and orange rind, but in every form they were popular from the 15th to the 18th century, and still tickle the palate under another name. *Sucket* (*socket*) was also used (17th century) as a term of endearment, my sweet one; also figuratively, as in Cleveland's POEMS (1654): *Nature's confectioner, the bee, Whose suckets are moist alchimie.* Raleigh in THE PASSIONATE MANS PILGRIMAGE (1604) pictures the pilgrim, dying, *And then to tast those nectar suckets At the cleare wells Where sweetnes dwells, Drawne up by saints in christall buckets.*

suffibulum. A white rectangular veil, with purple border, worn by vestals (in ancient Rome) for the rites of sacrifice. Farrar, in DARKNESS AND DAWN (1891) has: *"Thanks, kindest of Vestals," said Titus, gratefully kissing the hem of her suffibulum.*

suffiment. A perfume or incense; especially, in the 17th century, one burned for medicinal purposes. Also, *suffite,* noun, and verb: to fumigate. Latin *suffire, suffitum,* fumigate.

suffisance. Sufficiency (of which this is an early form, much used by Chaucer); abundance; ability; satisfaction, also, a source of satisfaction. Hence, *suffisant, sufficient;* the earlier form dropped out of use in the 15th century. *Suffisantee,* property.

sufflaminate. To obstruct; balk. Wren in 1672 objected to long speeches, which *sufflaminate the progress of business.* THE ATHENAEUM of 27 July, 1907, noted *an advertisement of . . . 'the gas microscope' . . . which gave Sam Weller an occasion to sufflaminate Mr. Buzfuz.*

suffragan. Originally, a bishop considered as subordinate to the archbishop, who may summon him to a synod to give his *suffrage.* Also *soffragan, sofregann, suffrecan,* and many more; a common word from the 14th century. Apparently the early vote was *viva voce,* by acclamation; *suffrage* seems to be from Latin *sub,* under + *fragor,* uproar, akin to *frangere, fractum,* to break, whence English *fracture, infraction,* etc. By act of Henry VIII, extended under Queen Victoria, certain subordinate bishops were assigned to assist the bishop of a diocese; these were also called *suffragans.* Hence, by extension, an assistant, representative; a person or thing that helps. Richardson in CLARISSA HARLOWE (1748) speaks of a strumpet's *bedside, surrounded . . . by her* *suffragans and daughters.* Bulwer in CHIRONOMIA, OR THE ART OF MANUAL RHETORIC (1644) declared, of the hands: *These suffragans of speech by a lively sense afford that shadow which is the excellencie of the vocall pourtraicture.*

suffumigation. See *subfumigation.*

suggill. To beat black and blue. Also *sugill, suggilate.* Butler in HUDIBRAS rhymes: *Though we with blacks and blues are suggil'd Or, as the vulgar say, are cudgell'd.* Hence, to revile, defame. Archbishop Parker is quoted (1561) in Strype's LIFE, of the *flock that will not shrink to offer their blood for the defence of Christ's verity, if it be openly impugned, or secretly suggilled.* Hence *suggillation, sugillation*; beating black and blue; a black and blue mark, as from a blow or a sucking kiss; defamation, slander. The forms are roundabout from Latin *sugere, suctum,* to suck, whence also *suction*—which origin suggests the original sense of the terms.

sugke. See *soke.*

sugrative. Honeyed, sugary, sweet. Medieval Latin *suguratus*; Arabic *sukkar,* sugar. A 16th century Scotch form (poems of Douglas and Dunbar) was *sugurat,* sugared, sweet: *The sugurat sound of hir song.* Hawes in THE PASTIME OF PLEASURE (1509) wrote: *They were so wyse and so inventife, Theyr obscure reason, fayre and sugratife.*

suist. One that does as he pleases; one fit for Thelème. Two syllables; Latin *sui,* of oneself. Used in the 17th century, usually in scorn of a self-centred or self-opinionated person. In the 19th century appeared *suisection (sui + section*; Latin *secare, sectum,* to cut; whence also *sect*; *dissect,* to cut apart; *sex,* the division of male and female; and all the *insects*), self-analysis, which might have been more fruitful without Freud. Now everyone analyzes everyone else.

sulk. To plough: especially, of a boat through the seas. Stanyurst in his AENEIS (1582) told that *two serpents monsterus ouglye Plasht the water sulcking to the shore.* Latin *sulcus,* furrow. The current sense of *to sulk,* to be in sullen ill-humor, developed in the late 18th century, from the adjective *sulk,* hard to get rid of: Heywood in A CHALLENGE FOR BEAUTIE (1636) declared: *Never was thrifty trader more willing to put off a sulke commodity, than she was to truck for her maydenhead.* THE POOR KNIGHT'S PALACE (1579) pictured not sullen unwillingness but great activity in the statement that *saylers sulke upon the seas.*

sullen. A later form of *solein, q.v. Sullen* has meant—in addition to its current senses—flowing sluggishly (of water), so used by Scott (1814); by Shelley (1818) of milk; Milton (1628) speaks of *the sullen mole.* Also, of sombre hue or sound; gloomy, melancholy. Thus Shakespeare in ROMEO AND JULIET (1592) has: *Our solemn hymns to sullen dirges change,* and in RICHARD II: *The sullen passage of thy weary steps.* Young (1719) speaks of *sullen* (solemn) majesty; Hawthorne (1864) of a *sullen day.* May yours be sunny!

sulp. To pollute, defile. Also *solp.* Used in the 14th and 15th centuries; figuratively in POLITICAL POEMS (1412): *sulpid in synne derk as nyght.*

sultry. See *swelt.*

sumpter. Driver of a packhorse. Also, the horse; a beast of burden. *sompter, sumter, sometour, sumpture*; 15th and 16th century *sum,* the weight of a load; Romanic *sauma,* horse-load; Late Latin *sagma,* packsaddle. *sumptery,* baggage; also used as an adjective, relating to beasts of burden. *sumpter* was (rarely) used as a verb, meaning to put on one's back; to wear. In THE TRAGEDY OF RICHARD II (1590) we read: *For once Ile sumpter a gaudy wardropp.*

sumptify. To spend lavishly; to render sumptuous. (Latin *sumptus,* expense; *sumere, sumptum,* to take, lay hold of; assume: lay out, expend; from *sub+emere, emptum,* to buy, acquire; whence also *peremptory, consumption, caveat emptor, presume, resume,* and many *assumptions.* R. Hall (WORKS; 1560) spoke of: *His owne great sumpt and expenses in wearing of silke and other costly apparrell.*

sunstead. The time of the year (midway between the two equinoxes) when the sun is farthest from the equator and seems to stand still before returning; June 21 and December 22. Used in the 10th century; the early word for *solstice.* Note the several variants of *solstice*: *solstead; solsticke, solstist, solstacion, solsticion,· solsticy, solstitial* (which is also an adjective, along with *solstitian*), *solsticium, solstitium.* All these forms are from Latin *sol,* sun + *stare, steti, statum,* to stand still. *Sunstead* came into use again in the 17th century, as by Fitz-Geffrey (1636): *The season of the year wherein our Saviour was borne: namely in the winter sunstead.*

super-. Above, beyond. The opposite of *sub-, q.v.* Among forgotten words formed with this prefix are: *superact,* to actuate or impel from above. *superancy,* superiority, the quality of surpassing; *superate,* to rise above, to surpass, also (15th and 16th centuries) as an adjective, conquered. *superarrogate,* to behave with extreme arrogance; Gabriel Harvey in PIERCES SUPEREROGATION (1593) said *He hath builded towers of superarrogation in his owne head. superbiate,* to render haughty; to be proud; hence, *superbity, superbience,* pride; also 'proud' or luxuriant growth; *superbient, superbious,* insolent. *superbiloquence,* proud or arrogant speech; *superbiloquent. superbibe,* to drink excessively, or in addition to. *supercelestial, supercelical,* beyond the heavens. *superchery,* foul play; an attack at a disadvantage; trickery, deceit. *supercile, superciliosity,* superciliousness; *supercilian,* a supercilious person. *supercrescent,* growing over or on top of something. *supercritic,* a superior critic (fashioned after *superman*); THE WESTMINSTER GAZETTE (19 August, 1903) spoke of *the ideas which a superdramatist would convey to a supercritic. To superdevil,* to set the Devil over something; to give over to the devil; also, *supersatanize. superfidel,* believing too much, over-credulous. *superinenarrable,* supremely indescribable. *supernodical,* extremely silly; *supernodity. superosculation,* excessive or extremely amorous kissing (the word survives as a term in geometry). *superlation,* great exaggeration, extreme hyperbole. *superlucrate,* to make an extra profit; *superlucration*; *superlucrator. supernate,* to float on the surface; *supernatant,* floating on the surface (as a light liquid on a heavier one); *supernatation. superomnivalent,* supremely omnipotent. *superonerate,* to overload, to burden excessively. *supersaliency,* the leaping of the male (as the elephant) for copulation; *supersalient. superstit,* surviving; *superstitie,* power to survive. *superstitiate,* to regard superstitiously, to idolatrize; *superstitiosity,* credulous acceptance; *superstitiosities,* superstitious beliefs or observances. *supertelluric,* beyond the earth and its atmosphere, a word space-science will revive. *supervacaneal,* *supervacaneous, supervacuous,* superfluous, vainly added beyond what is necessary; Harpsfield in the papers on the DIVORCE OF HENRY VIII (1555) spoke of ideas *with long painted supervacaneall words exorned and set forth . . . For the avoiding of supervacaneous tediousness we will cut off all such endless matters.* Which sets us good example.

superable. That can be overcome or surmounted. Used from the 17th century; hence also *superability, superableness.* Johnson in The Rambler (no. 126; 1751) said that *antipathies are generally superable by a single effort.* Hobbes in his version (1629) of Thucydides was more personal: *If he be superable by money* . . . Much more frequent is the negative, *insuperable; cp. couth.*

supernaculum. A drinking that empties the glass to the last drop; also, a full cup. A liquor to be drunk to the last drop; hence, a wine of the best quality, by extension, anything of the highest excellence of its kind. Originally (16th century) and most frequently used as an adverb, *to drink supernaculum,* to empty and turn up the glass over one's left thumbnail, as a sign that the liquor has been completely consumed. The word —also *supernagulum, supernegulam*—is a modern Latin form of German *auf den Nagel (drinken)*, (to drink) on to the nail. Hence *supernacular* (of a drink), excellent. *Bacchus,* said Massinger and Dekker in THE VIRGIN MARTYR (1622), is the *grand patron of rob-pots, upsie-freesie tiplers, and supernaculum takers.* The word was also applied figuratively, as when Jonson in THE CASE IS ALTERED (1598) said: *I confesse Cupids carouse, he plaies supernegulum with my liquor of life.*

suppage. Relish, savoriness. A variation, influenced by *sup,* of Greek *opson,* relish. Hooker in ECCLESIASTICAL POLITY (1597) said that *for food they had bread, for suppage salt, and for sawce herbes.*

suppalpation. Coaxing, wheedling. Latin *sub,* under + *palpare, palpatum,* to stroke. Bishop Hall in ST. PAUL'S COMBAT (1625) urged: *Let neither buggs of fear, nor suppalpations of favour, weaken your hands from laying hold upon the beast of error.*

supparasitate. To fawn, flatter. Latin *sub,* under + *parasitari,* to play the parasite; Greek *parasitos,* that eats with another. Hence *supparasitation,* flattery. Bishop Hall in THE BEST BARGAINE (1623) observed: *At the last, a galling truth shall have more thanks than a smoothing supparasitation.*

suppeditate. (1) To furnish, supply. Cranmer in a letter to Cromwell in 1535 wrote: *There is not one article of those which I have drawn but would suppeditate sufficient occasion for a whole sermon.* Hence, *suppeditaments,* supplies; *suppeditator,* one that supplies. (2) To overthrow, subdue, stamp under foot; *cp. subpedital.* Also *suppedit.* Hall in his CHRONICLES (EDWARD IV; 1548) wrote of the attempt to *suppeditate high power and nobilitie.*

supplosion. To stamp with the feet, especially as a sign of disapproval. Latin *sup, sub,* under + *plaudere, plausum,* to applaud. Also, to *supplode.* A letter of Hugh Broughton (1599) says what is often true in the theatre: *It deserveth a supplosion or an hissing.* Today, however, a supplosion is usually a sign of impatience, when the entertainment is unduly late in starting.

surculation. Pruning; cutting off shoots for propagation. Latin *surculare, surcula-*

tum; surculus, surcle. A *surcle* is a small shoot or sprout of a plant. Hence *surculous,* like a shoot; *surculose,* full of, or producing, shoots or suckers.

surd. Stupid, senseless, irrational; also, insensible. So used in the 17th century; then forgotten. The same *surd* was used, however, in mathematics for an irrational number, and from this use, in the late 19th century, the word was again applied to humans as irrational, senseless. H. More in THE SONG OF THE SOUL (1642) had: *And foul blasphemous belch from their surd mouth resounds.*

surpeague. An anglicized form of *serpigo, q.v.* The first folio of Shakespeare's TROILUS AND CRESSIDA spells it *suppeago*: *The dry suppeago on the subject!,* A plague on't!

surprised. See *mistake.*

surquedry. Arrogance, presumption. Also *surquidry, surquidy, surquedy, surquidance, succudry, surcudry, cirquytrie,* and the like. Via French *surcuidier* from Late Latin *supercogitare; super-,* above + *cogitare,* to think (oneself). Hence *surquidant, surquidous, surquedous, surquedrous, surquidrous, succudrous,* haughty, arrogant. Used from the 14th century, common in the 17th. Marston in ANTONIO AND MELLIDA (1602) cries *O, had it eyes and eares and tongues, it might See sport, hear speech of most strange surquedries!* In the 16th and 17th centuries, *surquedry* was sometimes misused to mean excess, excessive indulgence, as in Marston's SATIRES (1598): *In strength of lust and Venus surquedry.* The word was revived by Scott in IVANHOE (1819): *Are ye yet aware what your surquedy and outrecuidance merit, for scoffing at the entertainment of a prince of the House of Anjou?*

surreined. Over-ridden; worn out (of a horse). Used by Shakespeare in HENRY V (1599): *A drench for sur-reyn'd jades.*

sursanure. Outward healing; the closing or superficial healing of a wound. Old French *sursanure;* Latin *super,* above + *sanus,* well. Chaucer warns, in THE FRANKLIN'S TALE (1386): *Well know ye that of a sursanure In surgerye is perilous the cure.*

suscitate. To rouse, to excite (as to a dispute or a rebellion); to stir to action; to quicken, vivify. Latin *sub* + *citare,* to excite; more familiar in the *resuscitation* of the drowning. Used from the 15th century. Donne in a sermon of 1631 said: *Such a joy a man must suscitate and awaken in himselfe.* Shelley (PROSE WORKS; 1811) wrote: *wildered by the suscitated energies of his soul almost to madness.*

suspectable. Liable to or deserving of suspicion. *Evermore,* said Richardson wisely in CLARISSA HARLOWE (1748), *is parade and obsequiousness suspectable.* The current *suspicious* now bears double burden: it means both the person suspecting, and the person or thing suspected. *Suspectable* might well be restored to the second of these duties. Or else, *suspectuous* (thus used in the 17th century) might be reclaimed for the first sense, the person full of suspicion.

sute. A variant form of *suit.* Also *soote, q.v.* Thomas Freeman, in RUBBE, AND A GREAT CAST (1614; the title from terms in bowling) satirized the extravagant footwear of the period: *What ordinary gallant now but goes On Spanish leather haltred with a rose; Circling with gold, or silver-spangled lace: 'Tis strange how times have altered the case. Lesse cost, then now's bestow'd on either foote, Did buy King William Rufus a whole sute.* (There is a pun in *case*: the circumstance; also, the cover of the foot.)

swad. A country bumpkin; widely used in the 16th and 17th centuries as a general term of abuse; R. Wilson in THE THREE LADIES OF LONDON (1584) cried: *Thou horson rascall swad avaunt!* Hence *swaddish,* loutish. Also, a squat, fat person; hence, a thick mass or bunch; a large quantity; a crowd. By extension, a soldier, especially one forced into service; also *swadgill, swadkin.* W. Vernon in BARDOLPH AND TRULLA (1757) wrote: *Trulla, while I thy love enjoy'd, Nor any of the swads beside With you might toy and kiss.*

swage. (1) Alleviation, relief. The noun was formed (in the 13th century) from the verb *swage,* to relieve, which is a shortened form of *assuage.* The shortening took place in the Romance tongues; thus Popular Latin *suaviare,* from *assuaviare, ad,* to + *suavis,* agreeable, whence also *suave.* (2) *swage,* also *swedge,* an ornamental groove, border, or mount on a candlestick, basin, or other vessel. Used from the 14th through the 17th century. Also, a curved depression on an anvil; a tool for shaping cold metal; hence, to *swage,* to shape.

swaid. A variant form of *swayed,* past tense of *to sway,* meaning to wield. Bishop Hall, in his first SATIRE of Book 3 (1597), wrote: *Time was, and that was term'd the time of gold, When world and time were yong, that now are old. When quiet Saturne swaid the mace of lead, and pride was yet unborne, and yet unbred.*

swan. Everyone knows the fair white bird, and the *swan-song,* from the legend that it sings only as it is dying. Also the American dialect *I swan,* I declare, as in the Constable's song: *Wal, I swan, I must be getting on.* There was also a *swan,* a variant of *swon,* an old word for a swineherd. Meredith used *swan* as a verb, applied to the calm swimming of the bird, in LORD ORMONT AND LADY AMINTA (1893): *The forest goddess of the Crescent, swanning it through a lake.* Few remember that, since Richard Coeur-de-Lion brought the swan into England from Cyprus, the male has been called the *cob,* the female, the *pen*; the little ones, *cygnets* (though these make beauty in the ballet).

swang. A 14th century form (present tense) of *swing.*

swash. Originally an echoic word, like *swish, crash*: the sound of a heavy blow. Especially, the clash of a sword on buckler (shield); hence, a *swasher, swashado, swashbuckler,* a noisy or swaggering bravo. *To swash,* to dash about, to beat; to strike sword on buckler or to make the noise of such clashing. Shakespeare has, in HENRY V (1599): *As young as I am, I have observ'd these three swashers. swasher* was used into the 17th century (Burton's THE ANATOMY OF MELANCHOLY; 1621), then revived by Scott in KENILWORTH (1821): *Known for a swasher and a desperate Dick. Swashbuckler,* though used in 1560 and by Nashe in 1593, does not occur in Shakespeare; it has, however, not only survived but along the way produced such forms as *swashbuckling, swashbucklering; swashbucklerdom, swashbucklerism, swashbucklery. Swash* and *swashing* were both used as adjectives, meaning swaggering, showy; S. Sewall in his DIARY (5 November, 1713) wrote: *I first see Col. Tho. Noyes in a swash flaxen wigg.* When Rosalind (in Shakespeare's AS YOU LIKE IT) is preparing to disguise herself as a man, she says: *We'll have a swashing and a martial outside As many other mannish cowards have*

That do outface it with their semblances. From the sound, *swash* came to be used (16th and 17th centuries) for a kind of drum. In 1609 Sir John Skene, in his translation of THE AULD LAWES AND CONSTITUTIONS OF SCOTLAND FAITHFULLIE COLLECTED, wrote: *After they heare the striak of the swesch* (*or the sound of the trumpet*). He meant the strike of the sword on shield, but some thought his parenthesis was not an alternative but an explanation. Thus Jameison's glossary in 1808 defines *swash* as trumpet, and several (Scotch) writers have used the word in that sense.—Milton in his HISTORY OF ENGLAND (1670) claims that *The Britans had a certain skill with their broad swashing swords and short bucklers.* Shakespeare's phrase *swashing blow* (in ROMEO AND JULIET) has been repeated by a foil of later writers.

swastika. See *fylfot.*

swelt. To die; to seem on the point of death from overpowering emotion; to faint. Hence, to be faint with heat; in this sense, the form *swelter* survives. By extension, to burn as with fever, to be hot with rage or other passion. Also, actively, to kill; to overheat, scorch; cause to rage. To *swelt one's heart,* to exert oneself to the utmost. Chaucer in TROYLUS AND CRISEYDE (1374) speaks of *His olde wo that made his herte to swelte.* Spenser has, in THE FAËRIE QUEENE (1590): *With huge impatience he inly swelt.* The old adjective *sweltry,* though still occasionally used, survives in the commoner *sultry.*

sweve. To sleep; to put to sleep (also to permanent sleep, death); to stupefy; to lull. Common from BEOWULF into the 13th century. Hence *swevet,* sleep, slumber. Also *sweven,* a dream, a vision; to dream; *swevener,* a dreamer. As a noun, *sweven* was used into the 17th century, and archaically later, as by Kingsley in his poem THE WEIRD LADY (1840): *Mary Mother she stooped from heaven; She wakened Earl Harold out of his sweven.*

swilk. An early form of *such.* Also *swilke, swilc, selke, suwilk, sylk, swyk,* and the like. A form most common, until the 15th century. Hampole set down a proverb in 1340: *Swilk als the tre es with bowes, Swilk es the fruyt that on it growes.* The SECRETA SECRETORUM (1400) mentioned the *chaterynge of bryddes* [birds] *and swylk lyk sounds.* For another use, see *ferly.*

swillbowl. A constant and heavy drinker, one that *swills the bowl.* Also *swielbolle, swylbowle, swibol. The swinish swillbowls make their gullet their god,* complained R. Younge in 1655; Holland (translating Pliny in 1601) was less disapproving of the *lustie tosse-pots and swill-bolls.* Deacon in TOBACCO TORTURED (1616) bemoaned: *Alas poore tobacco, my pretie tobacco; thou that hast bene hitherto accompted the aleknights armes, the beere-brewers badge, the swilbols swinetroffe, the tinkers trull.*

swink. To toil, work hard; to set to hard work, to overwork. A common Old English form from BEOWULF on, used into the 17th century and as an archaism later. Also *swinnkenn, suinc, zuynke, swynke,* and the like; in past tenses, *swank, swonke, iswonk, swinked.* Also a noun, *swink,* labor, toil; trouble; rarely, heavy drinking as in the proverb *After swink sleep* (also After liquor laziness). *swinked,* weary with toil; Milton in COMUS (1634) says *And the swink't hedger at his supper sate. swinker,* a laborer; *swinkhede, swinched* (to the 14th century), a state of toil. Also *swinkful,* troublesome, full of toil, irksome, distressing; *swinkless,* painless, free from toil and trouble. In Holmes' THE POET AT THE BREAKFAST TABLE (1872) it is wisely said: *We poor wives must swink for our masters.*

swith. Strongly, forcefully; very much; very fast; excessively. Also as an interjection, Quick! Get thee gone! A common Teutonic word, used in English into the 16th century, lingering in dialect. Also *swithly. swithness,* speed; Bullenden in the CHRONICLES OF SCOTLAND (1536) mentions a *herald namit for his gret swithnes, harefut.* Burns, in his poem TO A LOUSE, ON SEEING ONE ON A LADY'S BONNET AT CHURCH (1790), which contains the lines *O wad some Power the giftie gie us To see oursels as ithers see us!* also contains these words to the adventuresome pediculine pest: *Swith! in some beggar's haffet squattle; There ye may creep and sprawl and sprattle, Wi' ither kindred jumping cattle, In shoals and nations . . .* [*Haffet* (Old English *healfheafod, half-head,* the forepart of the head), the side of the head over and in front of the ears; by extension, the cheek. Scott in THE FAIR MAID OF PERTH (1828) says: *With the hair hanging down your haffets in that guise.*]

swithe. To burn, scorch; to be singed; to smart. Also to *swithen, swizzen*; past forms include *swath, swythe, swythyn, swithen.* The BESTIARY of 1220 said of the eagle: *The sunne switheth al his flight.* Also, in 19th century dialects, to *swither*; hence *swithering,* scorching, as when Crockett in THE MEN OF THE MOSS-HAGS (1895) spoke of *that day of swithering heat. Swither* had other uses. (1) From the 9th to the 13th century, the right (hand, side, and the like). (2) In the 18th and 19th centuries, mainly in Scotch and dialects, a state of excitement, a flurry; a state of perplexity, doubt; Ramsay, in his EPISTLE TO ARBUCKLE (1719) said he *stands some time in jumbled swither, To ride in this road, or that ither.* (3) From the 16th century, to be uncertain, to falter, to be undecided. Which somehow leaves one all in a swither.

swive. To copulate with (a woman). This is a special sense, in English, of a common Teuton word; meaning, in Old High German and Frisian, to sway, to make sudden movements. Also *swyfe, swiff*; the word is not, however, related to *wife, wive.* Chaucer, in THE MILLER'S TALE (1386) says: *Thus swyved was this Carpenters wyf; For all his keeping and his jalousye.* Dunbar in his POEMS (1520) exclaims *The Fiend me ryfe If I do ought but drynk and swyfe.*

swoopstake. As a noun, a variant of *sweepstake.* As an adverb, by sweeping the board—all the stakes at once; hence, indiscriminately. Shakespeare in HAMLET (1602) has the King, urging Laertes to the slaying of Hamlet, ask: *If you desire to know the certainty Of your dear father's death, is't writ in your revenge That, swoopstake, you will draw both friend and foe, Winner and loser?*

sworn at Highgate. See *Highgate.*

swound. An old form of *swoon*; it rhymes with *drowned.* Used in the 16th and 17th centuries. The past tense is *swounded.* Also *swow,* to swoon (13th and 14th centuries); whence *swowing,* swooning.

swounds. A common oath in the 16th and 17th centuries, being a euphemistic shortening of *By God's wounds.* Also *'sowns, 'swoundes, swones.* Nashe in AN ALMOND FOR THE PARRAT (1589) speaks of *some rufling courtier, that swears swoundes and blood.*

swych. A variant form of *such. Cp. swilk.*

sybarite. A person whose life turns upon his senses and his pleasures; an effeminate voluptuary. Originally, a citizen of Sybaris, a Greek city in Southern Italy, noted for its effeminate, luxurious ways. Also *sybaritan, sybarist.* Hence *sybarism, sybaritism; sybarital, sybaritic, sybaritical, sybaritish.* In THE FLOWRES OF SION (1623) Drummond of Hawthornden wrote: *Frail beauty to abuse, And (wanton sybarites) On past or present touch of sense to muse.* Jane West in THE MOTHER (1809) pictured *some feeble sybarite, Pain'd by a crumpled rose-leaf.*

sybil. See *sibyl.*

sybotic. Relating to a swineherd; engrossed in pigs. A pedantically humorous 19th century term, applied to persons that share Ho-ti's feeling for roast pig.

sycomancy. See *aeromancy.*

sye. This was a common Old English word, from the 7th to the 16th century. Its first meaning was to drip, to drop (as a liquid); hence, to pass through a strainer, to strain out; also, to fall, sink down. By extension: to collapse; to move from a source; to befall, happen; to depart—*to sye hethen* (here-thence), *to sye of life,* to die. Hence also *sye* as a noun, a drop; a spot or stain made by a drop; also, a strainer, especially one for milk. Chaucer has, in TROYLUS AND CRISEYDE (1374): *For when she gan here fader fer espye, Wel neigh down on here hors she gan to sye.*

syke. See *sike.*

syllabub. See *sillibub.* Because of the word *syllable,* from about 1700 the most frequent spelling has been *syllabub.*

sym-. A form of Greek *syn* (see *syn-*), with, together. Used as a prefix before *b, m, p.* We may mention: *symbol* (*bolos,* a throw), first used in English, after the Latin of Cyprian, Bishop of Carthage, 250 A.D., to mean the 'sign' of a Christian, i.e., the creed. Also, after Plautus (died 184 B.C.), a contribution, especially to a picnic or feast, one's share; Taylor in A SERMON FOR THE YEAR (1653): *He refused to pay his symbol;* Fuller in WORTHIES OF ENGLAND (1661), *Let me contribute my symbole on this subject. symbolatry, symbololatry,* excessive love of symbols. *symmelia,* see *symmelian. symmetrophobia,* dread of symmetry, avoidance of symmetry at all costs, as alleged in Egyptian temples, Japanese art, etc. *symmist,* a co-member of a secret society, a sharer in a mystery. *sympatetic,* a companion in a walk. *sympatric,* native to the same region; *sympatry. symphilism, symphily,* the act of living in common (in biology, when two different creatures live together in mutual benefit, *symbiosis*); *sympilious. symphrase,* a word made of several words run together, e.g., *he does many things, but Jack-of-all-tradesy. symphronistic,* of the same mind, as when understanding eyes meet; involving identity of thought. *sympneuma,* a companion spirit, spiritual spouse; *sympneumatic. sympolity,* an harmonious body of fellow citizens.

symmelian. A creature in which the hinder or lower limbs are fused. Greek *sym,* together + *melos,* limb. Also *symmelia.* A monster in actual life, but perhaps a basis for the belief in the mermaid, the most attractive of symmelians.

symposiast. One of a drinking-party, a banqueter. The original Greek of *symposium* meant a drinking together; hence, a convivial meeting for feasting and conversation. Also, a *symposiac.* Hence, *symposial, symposiacal, symposiastic. symposi-*

ast is still used for a member of a conference or contributor to a group-work.

syn-. Greek *syn,* together, with, used as an English prefix. Thus in *synallactic,* reconciliatory; *Retribution, as an end of punishment,* commented Whewell in GROTIUS (1853), *is properly what Aristotle refers to as synallactic justice. synallagmatic,* imposing mutual obligations, as a treaty or a contract. *synarchy,* joint government, cooperation in control. *syncretism,* a joining of two enemies against a common foe, as against a peacemaker in a street fight, or Russia and the West against Hitler; *syncretist; syncretic; syncretize. syndyasmian,* relating to a sexual union that is temporary or not exclusive; many in modern society are joined in syndyasmian couples. *synechthry,* living together in enmity, as an ill-matched but unseparated pair; the opposite of *symphilism, cp. sym-. synepigonic,* from a common ancestor. *synergy,* cooperation, working together; *synergetic, synergic. syngamical,* pertaining to sexual union; *syngamy. syngenesis,* the way we are conceived. *synoecism,* the joining of nearby towns and villages to form a city, as in the case of New York in 1898. *synomosy* (accent on the *no*), a body of men, as a political society, bound together by oath. *synorthography,* identical spelling of two words, as *bear,* the animal, and *bear,* endure; *synorthographic.*

synastry. Coincidence of the forces of the stars upon the lives of two persons. Greek *syn,* together + *astr-,* aster, star. Motley in THE HISTORY OF THE UNITED NETHERLANDS (1860) speculated, of the Earl of Leicester: *Born in the same day of the month and hour of the day with the Queen, but two years before her birth, the supposed synastry of their destinies might partly account, in that age of astrological superstition, for the influence which he perpetually exerted.*

synchysis. A confused arrangement; especially of words in a sentence, making the meaning obscure. Greek *syn,* together + *chein,* to pour. Hence, *synchytic,* confounding; prone to confuse.

synodite. A fellow-traveler. Greek *syn,* together + *hodites,* traveler; *hodos,* journey. H. L'Estrange, in CHARLES I (1654) said: *His council were his synodites.* The notion has fallen into a measure of disrepute.

sypar. A 16th century variation of *cypress* (tree). Also *syper, sypars, sypers.*

syrma. A long trailing robe, such as was worn by ancient tragic actors. Greek *syrma; syrein,* to drag along. *Cp. syrmaism; syrtes.* Hence *syrmatic,* in the tone or manner of a tragic actor.

syrmaism. The use of a purgative; the advocacy of or belief in such treatment. *syrmaea, surmaia,* a cathartic; especially, one passed through the body in preparation for (ancient Egyptian) embalming. Greek *syrmaia,* radish (used as a purge); *syrmos,* vomiting, purging; *syrein,* to drag along, sweep away, purge; *cp. syrma.*

syrtes. See *lotophagous.* Also *syrtis, syrt, sirt,* a quicksand; *syrtes* is the plural form; Greek *syrtis; syrein,* to drag away, sweep away; *cp. syrma.* THE MIRROR FOR MAGISTRATES (1575) said: *As doth the shipman well foresee the storm, And knowes what daunger lyes in syrtes of sande.* Young in THE OCEAN (1715) also knew the danger of *the syrt, the whirlpool, and the rock. Syrtis major* and *Surtis minor* were two large quicksands, of ancient times, in the Mediterranean Sea off Africa. Daniel used the word figuratively in an ECLOGUE of 1648: *The syrtes of my thought confounds my will.*

syssition. A meal eaten in common. Greek *syssitein,* to mess together; *syn* + *sitos,* food. Also *syssitia,* meals eaten in public; the practice of eating the main meal of the day at a general mess, as in ancient Sparta (instituted by Lycurgus, 9th century B.C.) and Crete. Symonds in SKETCHES OF ITALY AND GREECE (1874) wrote: *Necessity and the waiter drive them all to a sepulchral syssition.*

syte. Old form for *sight; site; cite; city,* and *syth, q.v.*

syth. Satisfaction; recompense. Short for *assyth.* Also *syith, site, syte.* Also as a verb, to give satisfaction to. *Sythment,* satisfaction; indemnification. Mainly Scotch; Douglas' AENEIS (1513): *I have gotten my heart's syte on him* (explained in the glossary: 'all the evil I wish'd him').

T

tabard. A coarse garment; especially, a loose outer shirt without sleeves, worn by peasants, foot-soldiers, monks. In the 16th and 17th centuries, the official dress of a herald. Common since the 13th century; hence, *The Tabard Inn,* in Southwark, where the pilgrims assembled in Chaucer's CANTERBURY TALES (1386). The inn stood until 1875; Toone, in his GLOSSARY of 1834, says it is *now corruptly called the Talbot. Cp. courtepy; rochet.*

tabefaction. Emaciation; wasting away. *tabefact,* wasted away; corrupted (15th century). *tabe, tabes,* gradual wasting away; consumption. Root *ta,* to run, melt, related to English *thaw.* Also *tabetic,* relating to emaciation; *a tabetic,* one afflicted with *tabes.*

tabellarious. Relating to letters, or a letter-carrier. Latin *tabellarius,* letter-carrier, courier; *tabella,* writing-tablet. Hence *tabellary,* a letter-carrier; a scrivener; also as an adjective, pertaining to such things; (of ancient practice) pertaining to voting tablets. A *tabellion* was a minor official clerk in the Roman Empire and until the Revolution in France; in England, 17th and 18th centuries.

tabor. A drum. Related to Persian *tabirah* and *taburak,* both meaning drum; possibly to Arabic *tanbur,* a kind of lyre. Also *tabour, taborn, tabron, tabberone, tawberne, talburn, tawbron,* and more. When the word *drum* was introduced, in the 16th century, *tabor* was used of a small drum. A *taborin* was one less wide but longer than the *tabor,* played with one drumstick, while the other hand manipulated a flute or fife. A *tabret* (*taberett, tabberet, tabarde, tabouret*) was also a small *tabor,* a *timbrel* (*q.v.*). Some of the Romance languages have the same word with an *m;* whence also, English *tambour,* drum, especially the large bass drum (also, a kind of embroidery or needlework made with the material stretched as on a drum-head). A *tamboura* was an oriental instrument of the lute family. A *tamborin, tambourin,* was a long narrow drum, especially of a type used in Provence. The French *tambour de basque,* on the other hand, is English *tambourine,* made familiar by the Salvation Army. From its drum-shape the low stool called *tabouret* drew its name; *privilege* (*honour*) *of the tabouret,* permission for a lady to sit in the Queen's presence. The tabor might also be the drummer, usually the *taborer.* Shakespeare in THE TEMPEST (1610) tells: *Then I beat my tabor, At which like unbackt colts they prickt their eares.*

tacenda. Things that should not be mentioned. Directly from the gerundive of Latin *tacere,* to be silent, whence also English *tacent,* silent. The imperative *tace* (pronounced *taý see*) is sometimes used as an admonition to silence; since the 17th century (Fielding in AMELIA, 1752; Scott in a letter of 1821), the sentence *Tace is Latin for a candle* has been used to let a person know he's to keep silent on a matter. BLACKWOOD'S EDINBURGH MAGAZINE of February 1883 referred to topics *regarded as tacenda by society.*

tache. I. As a noun. (1) A spot, blemish, physical or moral; a stain, stigma; a distinctive mark (good or bad). Caxton's THE GOLDEN LEGEND (1483): *She that never had tatche ne spot of corrupcion.* Related to *touch.* (2) A clasp, buckle, hook and eye, or other device for fastening. The same word as *tack.* (3) A flat pan for boiling maple sugar; also for drying tea-leaves. (4) Tinder. Also *teche, taich, tash,* and more. II. As a verb. (1) To stain or taint, especially morally; to stigmatize; to blemish. (2) To fasten, lay hold of (15th to 17th century, arrest). Replaced in this sense by *attach.* (3) To attack, to charge. Also *teccheless, tacheless,* stainless, without fault. In 1723 R. Hay wrote *A Vindication of Elizabeth More from the Imputation of being a Concubine; and her Children from the Tache of Bastardy.*

taille. Shape; especially, one's shape from shoulder to waist. From the French, used in the 17th century; in the 14th century, *tail* was used in the same sense. Pepys in his DIARY (13 July, 1663) said that Mrs. Stewart, *with her sweet eye, little Roman nose, and excellent taille, is now the greatest beauty I ever saw.*

take. Among the 91 major senses in which *take* has been used, we may note: *to take it on* (*one's honor, death,* etc.) to swear. Also, *to take one's death on it,* to stake one's life on it. Shakespeare in THE MERRY WIVES OF WINDSOR (1598) says: *I took't upon mine honour thou hadst it not. To take against,* to oppose, *to take for,* to favor. Foote in THE LAME LOVER (1770): *A wise man should well weigh which party to take for.* Also, *to take* (with the mind), to consider, to understand. Skelton in COLYN CLOUTE (WORKES; 1529): *For though my rime be ragged, Tattered and jagged, Rudely rayne beaten, Rusty and moothe eaten, If ye take well therewyth It hath in it some pith.* Steele in THE TATLER (1709; No. 1): *I take myself obliged in honour to go on. Take (it) with you,* bear (it) in mind; Lord Chesterfield in a letter of 1746: *Take this along with you, that the worst authors are always most partial to their own works. To take out,* to give vent to. Dryden, in the Preface of ALL FOR LOVE (1678): *He took out his laughter which he had stifled.* Also, *to take out,* to learn; Bishop Earle in his MICROCOSMOGRAPHIE (1628): *He hath taken out as many lessons of the world, as dayes. To take up,* to believe without examining, to take for granted; Bacon in SYLVA (1626): *It is strange how the ancients took up experiments upon credit, and yet did build great matters upon them. To take up for hawks,* to use (a worn-out horse) as food for hawks; hence, *taken up for hawks, tane up for hawks* (sometimes, just *taken up*), done for, ruined. Thus Udall in RALPH ROISTER DOISTER (1553 III iii); Brome turns the phrase in THE NORTHERN LASSE (1632): *Ile marrie out of the way: 'tis time I think: I shall be tane up for whores meat else.* Also, *to take up,* to take lodging; Pepys, in his DIARY for 14 October, 1662: *To Cambridge . . . and took up at the 'Beare'.* Also, *to take up,* to fill (a space, a time); Shakespeare in CORIOLANUS (1607): *schooleboys teares take up The glasses of my sight* [fill my eyes]. This sense survives when we *take up* someone's time. This shall take up no more.

taliation. A repayment of like for like. Latin *talis,* like. Used from the 15th into the 18th century; replaced by *retaliation.* Also *talio, talion.* Sometimes the Latin phrase *lex talionis,* the law of like, is used, for such principles as the Biblical "an eye for an eye, a tooth for a tooth"; also, for the infliction on an accuser that does not prove his case of the penalty that would have fallen upon the accused had he been found guilty. Also *talionic,* relating to such retaliation. Beaumont in PSYCHE (1648) observed: *Just Heav'n this taliation did decree, That treason treason's deadly scourge should be.*

talliate. To tax. Also, *to tallage, to tail. tallager,* tax-collector. Hence, *talliation,* levying a tax. As a noun, *tallage* was an arbitrary tax levied by early English kings upon crown towns and lands; they could also grant their feudal lords right to levy such a tax. Such *tallage* was abolished in 1340, the word being later applied to municipal taxes or customs duty or (especially) any arbitrary levy. The forms are via French *tailler* (whence English *tally* and *to tail,* to cut, *to tailor;* to cut in a specified way; to *entail;* to set a *tail* or tax upon) from Medieval Latin *talliare, taliare,* to tally, to cut; Latin *talea,* rod, cutting.

tallyman. (1) A man that sells in *tally-trade,* i.e., sells goods for payment on the instalment plan. He kept *tally* of the accounts, often grossly overcharging, as told in FOUR FOR A PENNY (1678; in the Harleian Miscellany): *The unconscionable tally-man . . . lets them have ten-shillings-worth of sorry commodities . . . on security given to pay him twenty shillings by twelve-pence a week.* (2) A clerk in charge of records; especially, one that checks a cargo. This sense is still current. (3) One that *lives tally,* i.e., cohabits without marriage; also, *to live on tally*: the implication being that the woman (by prostitution or otherwise) contributes to the couple's expense. Hence also, in each sense, *tallywoman. Mrs. Diana Trapes,* in Gay's THE BEGGAR'S OPERA, is called *the tallywoman*—perhaps combining senses (1) and (3).

talm. To tire, become exhausted; swoon. Also *taum, tawm.* Used from the 14th to the 17th century, later in dialects. Drant in THE WAILYNGS OF THE PROPHET HIEREMIAH (1566) wrote: *My babes dyd faynt, And sucklynges tawmed in the streetes.*

talma. A long, black, loosely draped cape or cloak. Named after François Joseph *Talma,* French tragedian (1763-1826). Hawthorne in THE MARBLE FAUN (1860) says: *If a lion's skin could have been substituted for his modern talma.* The talma is a traditional garment for the old-style tragedian of the 1890's.

talmouse. A 16th and 17th century dainty: a tart or sugared pastry, made with cheese, cream, and eggs; an early variety of cheesecake.

talpicide. Latin *talpa* (French *taupe*), a mole. See *stillicide.*

tambour. See *tabor.*

tampion. See *tompion.* The form *tampon,* directly from the French, is used in surgery, of a plug or 'tent' used to stop bleeding. The French verb *tamper* is a nasalized form of *taper,* to plug, which is ultimately echoic: *tap,* imitating the sound of tapping.

tanistry. A system of land-holding among the ancient Irish and Gaels, wherein the succession was established by vote, going supposedly to 'the eldest and worthiest' of the lord's survivors. The successor apparent (elected during the chief's life, to avoid violence and rebellion when he died) was called the *tanist,* also *tanister.* The election was usually held, legend tells, near large monoliths which, surviving today, are called *tanist stones.*

tank. See *stank.*

tanling. (A young) one tanned by the sun's rays. Shakespeare in CYMBELINE (1611) has the exiles pictured as *hot summer's tanlings and The shrinking slaves of winter.* Resort beaches (and sunlamps) have brought tanlings into style.

tanquam. A thing that only seems to exist. Latin *tanquam,* as if; as it were. In Cambridge University, in the 17th and 18th centuries (*tanquam socius,* as if a fellow), *a tanquam* was an associate or companion of a fellow of the University.

tantivy. Originally an adverb, meaning at full gallop, headlong. Perhaps the word is imitative, beating the rhythm of a galloping horse's feet; Bailey (1751) derives it from Latin *tanta vi,* with so great force. Then (17th century) a noun, a rapid gallop, a speedy flight. In 1681 a caricature was printed, showing High Church clergymen *riding tantivy* to Rome, behind the Duke of York; hence, during the Restoration, a High Churchman or a Tory was called a *tantivy.* By error (1785 on) *tantivy* was also used for the sound of a horn, especially during a chase. And in the late 17th century *to tantivy* was used, meaning to hurry away. Brome in THE JOVIAL CREW (1641) has: *Up at five a' clock in the morning . . . and tantivy all the country over, where hunting, hawking, or any sport is to be made.*

tantony. Related to Saint Anthony. Hence, used as an adjective of things associated with the saint: *tantony crutch, tantony pouch.* Also, as a noun, *tantony,* a hand-bell, a small church bell held in the hand (like the later schoolma'am's). Also, St. Anthony being the patron saint of swineherds, *tantony,* the smallest pig of a litter; hence, a person that follows another closely or obsequiously. Gauden in THE TEARS OF THE CHURCH OF ENGLAND (1659) says: *Some are such cossets and tantanies that they congratulate their oppressors and flatter their destroyers.*

tapester. A maker of *tapestry.* Via French from Late Latin *tapetium,* Greek *tapetion,* diminutive of *tapes,* cloth wrought with colored figures. *Tapissery* was the early form (14th-16th century) of *tapestry,* its weaving the most lucrative trade of the 15th century. Chaucer in the Prologue to THE CANTERBURY TALES (1386) lists *A webbe, a dyere, and a tapycer.* Also *tapister, tapicer, taphiser, tapecer, tapisser.* Chaucer also uses *tapester* as a form of *tapster,* a woman who tapped or drew ale in an inn; later, a bar-man, and in the 15th century one that sold retail, in small quantities.

tapet. A piece of figured cloth, for the wall, the table, and the like. Used from the 9th century; Greeek *tapes, tapeta.* The forms *tapis, tapissery* (*tappet, tapyte, tapit; tappes; tapecery, tapyssere, tappyssery, tapycerye,* and more), showing the popularity of the material, were introduced in the 15th century, followed then supplanted by *tapestry. Cp. tapester.* Sackville's Induction (1563) to A MIRROR FOR MAGISTRATES uses *tapets* figuratively, for foliage: winter had come and *The mantels rent, wherein enwrapped been The gladsom groves that nowe laye overthrowen, The tapets torne, and every tree downe blowen.* Chaucer used *tapet* as a verb in THE DETHE OF BLAUNCHE THE DUCHESSE (1369): *Hys hallys I wol do peynte with* *pure golde And tapite hem ful many folde.*

tapinage. Concealment, secrecy. Used 13th-15th century; listed in 17th and 18th century dictionaries. Thus *tapis, tapish,* to lie close to the ground, lurk, skulk. Warner in ALBION'S ENGLAND (1592) says *Now tappas closely, silly heart . . . the huntsmans-selfe is blind.* Scott revived the word, in PEVERIL OF THE PEAK (1823): *Your father . . . is only tappiced in some corner.*

tapinophoby. Hatred of the "low" in writing. A *tapinophobe* was a conscientious conservative (18th century), insisting that literature deal with lofty themes in worthy style. Greek *tapeinos,* low. There were riots of tapinophobes in the French theatre when Shakespeare's MACBETH was played (1819), at the 'low' word *mouchoir,* handkerchief; the Dublin riot at the opening of THE PLAYBOY OF THE WESTERN WORLD (1907) began when the decent girl mentioned her smock. Per contra, a great admirer of modern realistic books (e.g., FROM HERE TO ETERNITY) is a *tapinophile.*

taplash. The washings of the cask; very weak or stale beer. Used also figuratively, as when Colman in PROSE ON SEVERAL OCCASIONS (1769) accused a man of drawing *the taplash of another's brains.*

tar. To irritate, provoke; to wear out, fatigue (*terwyn, tary*). Also *tarre, tyrwian, terre; tarien, tarrie, tarye.* From the 9th to the 17th century. *tary,* annoyance. *terying,* provoking; *taryer, teryare,* a provoker; *tarring, terring, taryingness,* provocation. *tar and tig* (*tig and tar*), to act wantonly, to use violence (15th and 16th centuries). To *tar on,* to hound on, incite. Shakespeare uses *tarre on* in KING JOHN (1595), in TROILUS AND CRESSIDA: *Pride alone Must tarre the mastiffes on, as 'twere their bone,* and in HAMLET. The expression *tar on* was revived in the 19th century, as by Kingsley, and Carlyle (THE FRENCH REVOLUTION; 1837): *The cries, the squealings of children . . . and other assistants tarring them on, as the rabble does when dogs fight.*

taradiddle. A petty falsehood, a fib. Also, to tell fibs; to impose upon with fibs. Also *tarradiddle, tallydiddle.* Used from the 18th century; Gilbert makes the word part of a nonsensical refrain: *tarradiddle, tarradiddle, fol lol lay.* SOCIETY of 29 October, 1880, said: *Perhaps there is not a more facile . . . tarradiddler than the London correspondent of the provincial newspaper.*

tarantism. An hysterical affliction, being an irresistible impulse to dance. Epidemic in Apulia and regions of Italy nearby, from the 15th to the 17th century. Named from the town *Taranto* (Latin *Tarentum*); but by the peasants the disease was attributed to the sting of the *tarantula* (spider); hence, it was sometimes called *tarantulism.* Many thought that the dance was the cure for the disease; and the *tarantella* (a rapid whirling dance) has from the 15th century continued to be popular. The dance, prolonged until one fell from complete exhaustion, might cure one until the approach of warm weather the next year, when the victim might again prove susceptible. One that had the disease was a *tarantant* or *tarantato* (plural *tarantati*; feminine *tarantata,* plural *tarantate*). The great epidemics of chorea came somewhat later, in Swabia and other parts of Germany; supposedly cured by dancing before the shrine of St. Vitus. Cowley, in a note to his DAVIDIES (1638) indicated belief in the dancing treatment: *We should hardly be con-*

vinced of this physick, unless it be in the particular cure of the tarantism, the experiments of which are too notorious to be denyed or eluded.

tardigrade. Walking slowly, slowpaced; sluggish in thought, unprogressive. Latin *tardus,* slow + *gradus,* stepping. *Even in our tardigrade West Country,* said the PALL MALL GAZETTE of 28 December, 1883, *the farmer has begun to discover . . . that he, too, is an economical power.*

targe. A shield; especially, a light shield borne by foot-soldiers and archers. Possibly from Arabic *al-dargah,* the shield of wood and leather. Common from the 10th into the 16th century; Chaucer in the Prologue to THE CANTERBURY TALES (1386) pictures the Wife of Bath: *On hir heed an hat As brood as is a bokeler or a targe.* Milton in PARADISE LOST (1667) tells of Adam and Eve gathering fig-leaves *broad as Amazonian targe.* Scott revived the word; in THE LADY OF THE LAKE (1810): *Ill fared it then with Roderick Dhu, That on the field his targe he threw.*

tarn. A small mountain lake, with no large tributaries. From the Norse; used in England since the 13th century. Swinburne in W. COLLINS (1884) gives us *a picture of upland fell and tarnside copse in the curving hollow of a moor;* Burton in his translation (1886) of THE ARABIAN NIGHTS tells that *The sorceress took in hand some of the tarn-water.*

tarot. A kind of playing-card; the game played therewith. Also *taroc, tarok, tarock.* There were 22 figured tarot cards, all trumps; 21 were numbered, the other was *il Matto,* the fool—our joker. These cards were added to the regular pack (usually of 56, in four suits). Some games, however, used a different number; Gray in a letter of 1739 spoke of *taroc, a game with 72 cards all painted with suns and moons, devils and monks.* By the 19th century, good tarot packs were collectors' items; *a single pack of tarots, admirably painted about 1415 by Marziano,* W. Skeen reported in his EARLY TYPOGRAPHY (1872), *cost the enormous sum of 1500 golden crowns.* The tarot cards became especially popular for fortune-telling; THE PALL MALL GAZETTE of 18 August, 1900, declared: *As fall the tarot cards, so fell Each rose-page of the oracle.*

tarpeian. Relating to the *Tarpeius,* a rock on the Capitoline Hill at Rome, from which persons convicted of treason were hurled. Shakespeare has, in CORIOLANUS (1607): *Beare him to the rock tarpeian, and from thence Into destruction cast him . . . Let them pronounce the steepe tarpeian death.* Macaulay echoes, in HORATIUS (1843): *Now, from the rock Tarpeian . . .*

tarre. See *tar.*

tarriage. A 15th century form for *tarriance,* tarrying, delay; procrastination; also, sojourn, temporary stay. Shakespeare means expectant waiting, in THE PASSIONATE PILGRIM (1599), *When Cytherea, all in love forlorn, A longing tarriance for Adonis made Under an osier growing by a brook.* [For the remainder of the stanza, see *wistly.*]

tarry. A pleasant drink: (1) From the 16th century, the fermented sap of various palm trees, especially the date and the coconut. Also tingling *terry;* and *tarea, taree; tadie, taddy;* (most popular form in the 18th century) *toddey, toddie, toddy.* (2) *hot toddy* (since the 18th century), hot water, sugar, and brandy or rum or gin or whisky. Burns in THE HOLY FAIR (1786) wrote: *The lads and lasses,* *blythely bent To mind baith soul an' body, Sit round the table, weel content, An' steer about the toddy.* The Revenue Office in 1850 ruled that *The taree or juice of the palm tree is liable to duty, in its fermented or unfermented state.* A person may well wish to tarry with his toddy.

tary. See *tar.*

tassel. An old form of *tercel, q.v.* The *tercel-gentle* was the male of the peregrine falcon—used figuratively of a noble gentleman. In Shakespeare's ROMEO AND JULIET (1595), Romeo has just left the orchard beneath Juliet's window—*He jests at scars that never felt a wound. But soft! What light through yonder window breaks? It is the east, and Juliet is the sun!*—after their first wooing, when Juliet calls: *Hist, Romeo, hist!—Oh, for a falconer's voice, To lure this tassel-gentle back again!*

tate. (1) A tuft or lock of hair or wool; a handful of grass, hay, or the like. Hence, a small quantity, a little. Also, *tait, teat, tett.* Used from the 16th century; now Scotch. (2) Mainly in the forms *tath, tathe.* Cow dung, sheep dung, and the like, left lying for manure. Hence, grass growing on a field thus manured. In Scotland rank, luxuriant grass (18th and 19th centuries) if grown from heavy moisture was called *water tath*; if from dung, *nolt tath.* [*Nolt,* from the 15th century, a Scotch word for cattle; also *nowt.*] In the 17th and 18th centuries in certain parts of England (Norfolk, Suffolk) the lord of the manor had the right to pasture the tenants' sheep at night upon the manorial grounds, for the manure of the dung; this privilege was also called *tath.* (3) An Irish (17th century) measure of land, 60 Irish acres.

tath. See *tate.*

taurian. Relating to a bull. Also *taurean, tauric, taurine.* Latin *taurus,* bull. Hence also *taur,* a bull. *taurolatry,* worship of a bull (from the Golden Calf to 'John Bull'). *tauroboly,* the slaying of a bull, especially in sacrifice, as in the ancient rites for Cybele, which included a bath or baptism in the bull's blood. *tauromachy,* a bull-fight; *tauromachian, tauromachic. Immovable,* said M. Collins in FROM MIDNIGHT TO MIDNIGHT (1876), *as a taurine statue of Nineveh. Cp. taurus.*

tauricide. See *stillicide.* The first great tauricide was Theseus, who slew the Cretan Minotaur. Many a matador since has made claim, after the tauromachy. *Cp. taurian.*

taurus. The bull, second of the signs of the zodiac. Chaucer in THE ASTROLABE (1391) indicated: *Everiche of these 12 signes hath respecte to a certeyn parcel of the body of a man, and hath it in governaunce, as aries hath thin head, and taurus thy nekke and thy throte, gemyni thyn armholes and thin armes.* In Elizabeth's days, penny almanacs used to present the figure of a naked man, with the signs of the zodiac arrowed to the parts of the body under their governaunce. Shakespeare in TWELFTH NIGHT (1600) makes the tipsy Sir Andrew Aguecheek and Sir Toby Belch err, when Andrew suggests: *Shall we set about some revels?* Toby: *What shall we do else? Were we not born under Taurus?* Andrew: *Taurus! That's sides and heart.* Toby: *No sir, it is legs and thighs. Let me see thee caper. Ha! Higher. Ha ha! Excellent!*

tavel. To play at dice. From earliest Old English to the 13th century. Originally a noun, from Latin *tabula,* a table, a board for playing on. Used in Germanic before 400 A.D., *tavel,* a playing-table; also, a game of chance; and especially a die (*tavels,* dice) for the playing.

tead. Torch. See *tede.* Latin *taeda,* pine-torch. Spenser in his EPITHALAMION (1595) said of his bride: *Bid her awake; for Hymen is awake, And long since ready forth his maske* [merry procession] *to move, With his bright tead that flames with many a flake* [flash], *And many a bachelor to wait on him.*

tease. See *toze.*

tect. As a noun: a roof. Latin *tectum,* roof; *tegere, tectum,* to cover, whence also *protect.* Related to Greek *teknon,* product, whence the whole range of *technology* and the *technical.* Hence *tect-demolished,* with the roof destroyed, as in Lithgow's THE TOTALL DISCOURSE OF . . . 19 YEARS TRAVAYLES (1632): *tect-demolished churches, unpassable bridges*—and many remnants of cities bombed. As an adjective: *tect,* covered, hidden. Used from the 14th to the 17th century, as by Archbishop Parker in PSALMS (1557): *Why els no doubt, the heathen sect, Would say where is their god so tect?* Hence *tectly,* covertly; *tecture,* a covering, a canopy, a roof; *tectured,* covered. These forms were used in the 16th and 17th centuries; also figuratively, as in Bishop F. White's A REPLIE TO JESUIT FISHERS ANSWERE (1624): *Your . . . blandishments are but maskes and tectures of latent perfidiousnesse.*

tectonic. Relating to the arts of building. *Tectonics,* the arts of building, of houses and their equipment. Greek *tekton,* builder. Thus *tectonist,* a builder. William Wood in NEW ENGLANDS PROSPECT (1634) pitied the Indian squaws: *As is their husbands occasion these poor tectonists are often troubled, like snailes, to carrie their houses on their backs.*

ted. To spread (manure); see *tate* (*2*). To spread (new-mown grass) for drying. Hence, to scatter, to dissipate. Also *tedde, teede.* Used from the 15th century, still in dialects. Also figuratively. Lyly in EUPHUES (1580): *Then fall they to al disorder that may be, tedding that with a forke in one yeare, which was not gathered together with a rake, in twentie.* And J. Hamilton in MOSES (1870): *A day-dreamer gets hold of a beautiful thought, and teases and teds it, and tosses it out into a cloud fine and filmy.*

tede. A piece of pine (with resin) used as a torch. Used in the 16th and 17th centuries. Also *tead* (*q.v.*), *teade.* Spenser in MUIOPOTMOS (1590) has: *A burning teade about his head did move;* N. Whiting, in THE PLEASANT HISTORIE OF ALBINO AND BELLAMA (1637): *Bellama's bridall tede is lighted now.*

tedesco. Germanic; the Italian word, used especially in criticism, of a Teutonic influence in Italian art. Byron in his JOURNAL (20 February, 1814) referred to *the tedeschi dramatists.* C. C. Perkins (Italian Sculpture; 1883) spoke of *minute works in the 'semi-tedesco' style. Tedesco* is via Medieval Latin *theodiscus* from Gothic *thiudisk;* Middle High German *diutsch;* German *deutsch,* whence also *Dutch.* The word originally meant popular, national; Old High German *diota,* people, nation; used to translate Latin *vulgaris,* the vulgar tongue, the vernacular, it came to be applied to those that spoke it.

tediation. The act of wearying, or state of being wearied, as by an overlong discourse. Hence *tedify,* to weary, bore; T. Adams in THE SINNER'S PASSING-BELL (1613) warns of the long-winded speakers that *whiles they would intend to edify, do in* *event tedify.* Hence also *edification* is contrasted with *tedification.* The form that survives is *tedious.* [Note that *tediferous* (Latin *taeda,* torch + *ferre,* to bear, whence also *suffer*) means bearing a torch. See *tead, tede.*]

teen. Harm, damage; irritation, anger; ill-will; malice; affliction; trouble; trouble taken with something. By transfer, a cause of trouble, a vexatious matter. Common from the 10th to the 17th century. Chaucer in THE KNIGHT'S TALE (1386): *Nevere was ther no word hem bitwene Of jalousie of any oother tene.* Spenser in THE FAËRIE QUEENE (1590) : *Gainst that proud paynim king that works her teene.* Whetstone in his HEPTAMERON (1582), telling that Lord Promos will spare Andrugio if his sister Cassandra is kind, has Andrugio lament: *For wantyng his wyll in thee, he wyll wreake his teene on mee.* Also a verb, *to teen,* to vex, enrage; to harass; to harm; to cause grief; to grieve. THE WORLD AND THE CHILD (1522) said: *There is no emperor so keen, That dare me lightly tene.*

tele. Evil-speaking, calumny; blasphemy; blame. From Old English *tael,* also *tal,* whence the English form *tole.* The verb *to tele,* to speak evil of; to mock; also to deceive, entrap. Used from the 9th into the 15th century. In the last sense, a metrical homily of 1325 said that Christ *telid the fiend that telid our father Adam.*

temulent. Intoxicated, drunken. Latin *temetum,* intoxicating drink. Also *temulentious, temulentive.* Hence *temulence, temulency,* drunkenness. Urquhart in THE JEWEL (1652) declares that *the Spaniards are proud: the French inconstant . . . the Dutch temulencious.* Hence, *Dutch courage.*

tendance. Short form of *attendance.* Used from the 16th century to mean: attending to, taking care of; care (Milton); waiting in expectation (Spenser); attendants, retinue (Shakespeare; Scott; George Eliot). In TIMON OF ATHENS (1607): *His lobbies fill with tendance.*

tene. A variant form of *teen, q.v.*

tenebricose. Full of darkness; obscure; gloomy. Accent on the *neb.* Latin *tenebricus,* dark; the Latin ending *osus,* full of, usually became *ose* in words taken directly into English from the Latin, and *ous* in words taken via French; *cp. avidulous.* Peacock in MELINCOURT (1817) says: *He . . . has taken a very opaque and tenebricose view.* Also *tenebrificate* (accent on the *brif*), to darken, render obscure, obfuscate; hence *tenebrific, tenebrificous,* causing darkness or obscurity. *Tenebrio* (*tenebrion*), a night-prowler, a lurker in darkness; Urquhart in his translation (1693) of Rabelais declares: *The approach of the suns radiant beams expelleth goblins, bugbears . . . night-walking spirits, and tenebrions.* Also *tenebres* (accent on the *ten*), darkness; *tenebre, teneber, tenabur.* This is from Latin *tenebrae,* shades, darkness, and *tenebres* is sometimes used instead of *tenebrae* for the candle-extinguishing services during Holy Week. Other forms are *tenebrate,* darkened, dark; *tenebrose, tenebrous,* dark; *tenebrious,* pertaining to darkness; *tenebrity, tenebrosity,* darkness—all these may refer to physical, mental, or moral darkness. And *tenebrize,* to dwell in darkness. Young in NIGHT THOUGHTS (1742) queries: *Were moon, and stars, for villains only made? To guide, yet screen them, with tenebrious light?* The MEMOIRS OF ELIZABETH CARTER (1743) discussed an art with many unwitting practitioners: *The complete science of circumlocution, and* *the whole art of confounding, perplexing, puzzling, and tenebrificating a subject.*

teneritude. Softness, tenderness. Latin *tener,* tender. Also, *tenerity.* (*Tender* is via French from Latin *tener.*) Henry More in his SONG OF THE SOUL (1642) has: *Faithfulness, heart-struck teneritie; These be the lovely playmates of pure veritie.*

tenter. See *stent.*

tentiginous. Provoking lust, lascivious; roused to lust, lecherous. Latin *tentigo, tentiginem,* tenseness, rigidity; hence, lust. The form *tentigo* (long *i*) is used in English to mean a spell of priapism; lust. Jonson in THE DEVIL IS AN ASS (1616) queries: *Were you tentiginous? ha? would you be acting of the incubus?* And Nichols in the PROGRESS OF QUEEN ELIZABETH (1603) has: *If any be troubled with the tentigo* . . . May he find a helpful nurse!

tephramancy. See *aeromancy.* Also *tephromancy*; from Greek *tephra,* ashes. Urquhart's translation (1693) of Rabelais promises to disclose the truth by *tephromancy: thou wilt see the ashes thus aloft dispersed, exhibiting thy wife in a fine posture.*

teratical. Pertaining to monsters or prodigies. *Cp. teratoscopy.* Greek *terata,* marvels, which is also used in English of monstrous births. Hence also *teratism,* love of the marvellous or the prodigious. *teramorphous,* monstrous in appearance or form. Wollaston, in THE RELIGION OF NATURE DELINEATED (1722) pictures *Herodotus, possibly delighting in teratical stories.* Many playwrights picture a teratical aspect of nature on the brink of dire human events (as Shakespeare, before Julius Caesar's assassination).

teratoscopy. See *aeromancy*; *teratical.* J. Spencer in his study of PRODIGIES (1663) observed that *teratoscopy* (accent on the *tos*) *was anciently only a rational attendance to those . . . signs with which the Providence of Nature was noted to preface her works of greater note.*

tercel. The male of a hawk; especially, of the peregrine falcon and the goshawk. Also *tiercel, tarcel, tyercelle,* and many others. *Cp. tassel*; *gerfalcon.* Also *tercelet, tiercelet*; *tercellene.* Ultimately from popular Latin *tertiolus,* a little third; *tertius,* third. Some say it is thus named because it is a third smaller than the female; Sir Thomas Browne (TRACTS; 1682) suggests another reason: *When they lay three eggs . . . the first produceth a female and large hawk, the second of a midler sort, and the third a smaller bird, terecellene or tassel of the male sex.* In hunting days, *falcon* always meant the female. In the 16th and 17th centuries, *tercel* was sometimes applied figuratively to a person, as by Chapman in MAY DAY (1611): *Whose foole are you? Are not you the tassell of a gander?* Scott in THE ABBOT (1820) revived this application: *Marry, out upon thee, foul kite, that would fain be a tercel gentle!*

tere. A variant of *tor* (2), *q.v.*

teretism. Harsh, discordant speech or writing. Greek *teretisma,* twittering. Hence, *teretistical.* Bishop Hall in his SATIRES (IV i; 1598) spoke of *rough-hewn teretismes, writ in th'antique vain.*

tergiversation. Turning one's back on, deserting; abandoning a party or a cause. Latin *tergum,* the back + *vertere, versum,* to turn; whence also *conversant, vice versa,* etc. Hence *tergiverse, tergiversate,* to turn renegade; to use subterfuge or evasion. Also *tergiversant, tergiversator*; *tergiversatory* (accent on the *vers*), shifty. Occasionally *tergiversation* (accent on the *say*) is used of literal back-turning, as in the account (1660) of a proud king *allowing audience to none but on the knee, nor tergiversation in retiring.* J. Wilson in BLACKWOOD'S EDINBURGH MAGAZINE (1831) mocks: *'I am liberal in my politics,' says some twenty-times tergiversated turncoat.*

term. To set a *term* to; to *terminate* (which in this sense superseded *term*), to end. Robert Southwell, who died for his faith in 1595, in a poem anticipating the ODE TO THE SETTING SUN (1895) of his fellow-Catholic Francis Thompson, wrote: *God's spice I was, and pounding was my due . . . Some things more perfit are in their decaye, Like sparke that going out geeves clerest light; Such was my happe, whose dolefull dying day Begane my joye and termed fortune's spight.*

terra damnata. Worthless residue. The words are Latin, meaning condemned or forever rejected earth. Used for senses (2)and (3) of *caput mortuum, q.v.* Also used figuratively, as by Jonson in A TALE OF A TUB (1633): *She's such a vessel of faeces: all dried earth, terra damnata!*

terrae filius. A person of obscure parentage. Latin: a son of the earth. Used formerly at Oxford and other universities (Dublin) of an orator privileged to make humorous and satirical speeches. Hence, *terraefilial, terraefilian,* earthly, worldly (either sordid or sophisticated); Young in his NIGHT THOUGHTS (1742) commented that *Men of the world, the terraefilial breed, Welcome the modest stranger to their sphere.* Steele in THE GUARDIAN (1713) was reminiscent: *In my time . . . the terraefilius contented himself with being bitter upon the Pope, or chastising the Turk.* Later, the terraefilius ventured into scurrility or sideswipes at the University authorities, and the privilege was withdrawn. In 1721 Amherst, in his TERRAE FILIUS, OR THE SECRET HISTORY OF THE UNIVERSITY OF OXFORD, declared: *It is very uncertain when the terrae-filius will be able to regain his antient privileges.*

terreity. Earthiness; the essence of earth. French *terre;* Latin *terra,* earth (*terra firma,* the mainland; solid ground), whence also *territory.* Jonson in THE ALCHEMIST (1610) says; *The aqueitie, terreitie and sulphureitie Shall runne together againe, and all be annull'd.*

terremote. An earthquake. Latin *terrae motus,* movement of the earth. Hence *terremotive,* pertaining to an earthquake. The Latin root *ter-, ters-* originally meant parched; it may be the same root as in *terror, tremor,* which originally meant to quake. Certainly a terremote induces both tremor and terror. *Cp. terricole.* The noun *terremote* was used in the 14th and 15th centuries; the adjective *terremotive,* in the 19th. Gower in CONFESSIO AMANTIS (1390) has: *Wherof that al the halle quok, As it a terremote were.*

terricole. An earth-dweller. Something that lives on or in the earth. Latin *terra,* earth + *colere,* to inhabit. The word is also used as an adjective, earth-dwelling; so also *terricoline, terricolous* (which, however, shift the accent from the first to the second syllable). Note, however, that *terricrepant* (17th century) means frightening with sound, scolding to high heaven; *terriculament,* something that arouses terror; especially, a source of needless terror, a bugbear. Burton in THE ANATOMY OF MELANCHOLY (1621) urges his readers not to worry: *Such terriculaments may proceed from natural causes.* Fear comes easily to the terricole.

terriculament. See *terricole.*

terry. A trodden path. Especially, a ridge of earth between fields or used grounds. A 16th century homily (1563) complained: *They do wickedly which do turn up the ancient terries of the fields, that old men beforetime with great pains did tread out.*

tersion. The action of wiping. Latin *tergere, tersum,* to wipe, whence also *detergent,* something that wipes (dirt) away. Hence *tersive,* able to cleanse by wiping; Plot in THE NATURAL HISTORY OF OXFORDSHIRE (1677) pictures every young mother's hope: *Such a pleasant titillation as invites the patient* (the child) *to rub on the tersive water.*

tessaraglot. Pertaining to four languages; one that commands four languages. Greek *tessares, tesseres,* four + *glotta,* tongue. Hence *tessera,* in ancient times, a small quadrilateral tablet (wood, ivory, metal, bone) used as a tally or token. A *tessera of hospitality* was such a tablet broken between guest and host, as a sign of friendship, and kept as an identification. Hence (in English from the 16th century) a distinguishing token; a password. Calderwood, in DYING TESTIMONIES (1795): *exacts it from them as a tessera of their loyalty.* The plural, *tesserae,* was also used to mean dice; hence, *tesserarian, tesserarious,* relating to dice; the *tesserarian art;* dicing; *to tesserate,* to play at dice. A *tessel, tessella,* was a small *tessera;* especially, a lozenge (in medicine) or a mosaic, a tile. To *tessellate,* to form a mosaic (as a pavement) or mosaic design.

tessellate. See *tessaraglot.*

tesserate. See *tessaraglot.*

tester. A piece of armor for the head of a man or his horse. Old French *teste,* head; Latin *testa,* an earthen pot. In the 14th and 15th century *teste* was used in English to mean head. Also, 14th to 17th century *tester,* a canopy over a bed, hung from the ceiling or the bedposts. By transfer, a canopy carried over a person of high degree, or other such covering. Galt in LAWRIE TODD (1830) speaks of *a night under the starry tester of the heavens.* Chaucer lists, in THE KNIGHT'S TALE (1386): *The sheeldes brighte, testeres, and trappures, Gold hewen helmes, hauberkes.* In the 16th century, *tester* also meant sixpence; see *impeticos.*

testern. To give a *tester* to, to tip. See *impeticos.* In Shakespeare's THE TWO GENTLEMEN OF VERONA (1593) Speed complains: *To testify your bounty, I thank you, you have testerned me; in requital whereof, henceforth carry your letters yourself. And so, sir, I'll commend you to my master.* Proteus responds: *Go, go, be gone, to save your ship from wreck, Which cannot perish having thee aboard, Being destined to a drier death on shore.* Proteus is relying on the old saw: He that is born to hang will never drown.

testiculatory. Generative. Thus Urquhart in his translation (1693) of Rabelais speaks of Gargantua's *testiculatory ability.* Hence, *testiculose, testiculous,* of high generative power, (Bailey, 1751) 'that hath great cods.' In ancient times, a man gave *testimony* while placing his hands "between the thighs," as though swearing by his generative powers: Castrate me if I lie!

testril. Also *testrill; tester, teaster,* and the like. See *impeticos.*

tetragrammaton. A four-letter word. Plural, *tetragrammata.* Especially, the Hebrew word *YHVH,* vocalized as *Yahveh* or *Jehovah.* Others today are more frequent. Note the list of the divine tetragrammata among the sons of men: *Jeva, Deva, Isis, Jove, Theos, Zeus, Deus . . . Tien, Alla, Dios, Idio, Dieu, Lord.* Wither in his discussion (1665) of THE LORD'S PRAYER states: *Our English tongue as well as the Hebrew has a tetragrammaton, whereby God can be named; to wit, Good.*

tetrical. Harsh; austere; bitter; morose. Also *tetric.* Latin *tetricus,* harsh, forbidding; *taeter,* foul. Hence, *tetricity, tetritude, tetricality, tetricalness.* Gauden in HIERASPISTES (1653) declares: *It requires diligence to contend with younger ignorance, and elder obstinacy, and aged tetricalness.*

thalassiarch. A ruler of the sea; an admiral. Greek *thalassa,* the sea; noted in the rejoicing cry (recorded in Xenophon's ANABASIS, 400 B.C.) when the Greeks retreating in Armenia climbed Mt. Theches and beheld the sign of safety: *Thalassa! Thalassa!* Also *thalassian, thalassic,* pertaining to the sea; *cp. potamophilous. thalassical,* sea-green or sea-blue; *thalassarctine,* pertaining to the Polar Bear (constellation); *thalassocrat,* a master of the sea; *thalassophilous,* in love with the sea. There are also *thalassophobes;* because his wife was one, my old friend and classmate sold his yacht.

thalweg. A line tracing the lowest point of a valley; hence, the line along the deepest channel of a river or lake. German *Thal,* valley + *Weg,* way. The 1894 Agreement between Great Britain and the Congo State stipulated that the boundary *shall follow the thalweg of the Nile southwards to Lake Albert.*

Thanatopsis. See *athanasy.*

thankworthy. Deserving credit or thanks. Also *thankworth.* These words, pleasant in sound as in thought, were common from the 14th into the 17th century. They lingered later; Swinburne in BOTHWELL (1874) says: *And we that do it, we do it for all men's good, for the main people's love, thankworthily.*

tharborough. A variant of *thirdborough, q.v.*

thaumaturge. A wonder-worker, a magician. Greek *thaumat-,* wonder + *ergos,* working. Also *thaumaturgus, thaumaturgist. Cp. teratical.* Hence *thaumaturgy,* magic; *thumaturgize,* to work wonders. Carlyle in his essay (1825) on Schiller refers to *various thaumaturgic feats,* doubtless such as were seen by the folks in Mary Mitford's OUR VILLAGE (1824), performed by *Mr. Moon, the very pearl of all conjurors . . . with his wonderful exhibition of thaumaturgics.*

theandric. Relating to both God and man; partaking at once of the divine and the human. Greek *theos,* god + *andros, anthropos,* man. Hence also *theanthropic,* godmanly. From the Latin *deus,* god + *virilis,* manly, came the 17th century *deivirile,* meaning the same as *theandric.*

theangeline. A plant, Pliny said, that grew amid the cedars of high Libanus in Syria; it was an intoxicant herb, which gave the gift of prophecy.

theat. The ropes by which animals drew a carriage or a plough. Also, *theet. Out of theats, out of theet,* out of control, on the wrong course. A similar figure from the same field is *to kick over the traces.* About 1800 rope theats were replaced by iron traces.

theatro-. A combining form from Greek *theatron,* theatre. Among forgotten forms with *theatro-* are the following: *theatromania,* excessive fondness for theatregoing; *theatromaniac.* A milder theatre-lover is a *theatrophil (e)*; one who hates it is a *theatrophobe,* hence *theatrophobia.* In the 1890's, in Paris and London, there were experiments with an adaptation of the telephone, the *theatrophone,* transmitting plays from the stages of the various theatres. The PALL MALL GAZETTE of 6 December, 1891, reported that 'a preliminary trial has been made at the Savoy Hotel with complete success.' In 1897, Ouida in her novel THE MASSARENES spoke of *a modern woman of the world. As costly as an ironclad and as complicated as a theatrophone.* Today, even with television, too much is *theatrophony.*

thede. A people, nation; hence, the region occupied by a nation, a country. Used from the 9th century. SIR ORFEO (1320; *cp. levedi*) told that, when Orfeo found his wife, he *went him out of that thede, Right as he come the way he yede* [went]. Returning to his own land, disguised as a beggar, he was told *How her quen was stole oway Ten yer gon with fairy; And how her king en exile yede, But no man nist* [*na wist;* negative of *wist,* knew] *in wiche thede.*

thelemite. One who does as he pleases; a libertine. Greek *thelema,* will; but with allusion to the *Abbey of Thélème* in Rabelais, which had one rule: *Fay ce que vouldras,* Do what thou wilt. THE NATION of 24 October, 1908, however, did not agree with the definition 'libertine,' averring that the abbey's was a good rule *because, as its founder said, 'Men that are free, well-born, well-bred and conversant in honest companies have naturally an instinct and spur that prompts them unto virtuous actions.'* Also from the Greek, but without reference to Rabelais, comes the adjective *thelematic,* relating to the will; voluntary.

thelyphthoric. That corrupts or ruins women. Greek *thelys,* female + *phthora,* corruption. M. Madan in 1780 wrote a book entitled *Telyphthora; or, A Treatise on Female Ruin, in its Causes, Effects, Consequences, Prevention, and Remedy.* Fourteen years later Thomas Mathias inquired, in his poem THE PURSUITS OF LITERATURE: *Must I with Madan, bent on gospel truth, In telyphthoric lore instruct our youth?* The prefix *thely-,* female, is used in various scientific terms, such as *thelytokous, thelygenous,* producing only female offspring; hence *thelytoky*; *arrhenotoky, q.v.,* is the production only of males. Bailey in his DICTIONARY (1751) lists *thelygonum,* 'an herb which, when steeped in drink, is said to make a woman conceive a girl.' It is equally efficacious when drunk by the man.

then. A variant form of *than.* This use was very common until the 18th century; it occurs in many quotations in this volume. Another instance is in the epigram *Nullum stimulum ignavis* (Nothing can rouse the lazy) in Henry Parrot's THE MASTIVE, OR YOUNG WHELP OF THE OLDE DOGGE (1615): *Caecus awak't, was tolde the sunne appeared, Which had the darknes of the morning cleard: But Caecus sluggish thereto makes replie, 'The sunne hath further farre to goe then I'.*

theomagic, theomancy. See *aeromancy.*

theoric. As a noun. (1) Theory, as opposed to practice (Gower; 1390). (2) A theoretical writing or talk (Chaucer, THE ASTROLABE; 1391). (3) A mental survey. (4) An apparatus showing the principles of operation of a natural phenomenon. (5) A man devoted to contemplation or speculation about things. As an adjective. (1) *theorical, theoretic, theoretical,* contemplative; indulging in theory (as opposed to practice). (2) Relating to religious and other public spectacles, such as solemn embassies; the *theory* of Athens was a body of *theors,* officials sent to perform a solemn rite or duty. These forms (also *theorem,* etc.) are from Greek *theoria,* a viewing, *theoros, theaoros,* spectator; *theasthai,* to look on, contemplate. Chambers' CYCLOPAEDIA (1741) notes that, *by the law of Eubulus, it was made a capital crime to pervert the theoric money to any other use; even to employ it in the occasions of war.*

theriac. An antidote to poison; originally, to snake-bite. Also *theriacle* (accent on the *rye*); *treacle; treacle* was later expanded to mean a sovereign remedy, an *alexipharmac, q.v.,* also figuratively, as (More, DYALOGE; 1529) *the tryacle of holye scrypture. theriac* was also used figuratively, often with mention of the viper, the flesh of which was considered an essential ingredient in the antidote. Hence, *theriacal,* serving as or relating to an antidote.

therianthropic. Part beast, part man, like the sphinx and many ancient gods. Greek *therion,* diminutive of *ther,* wild beast + *anthropos,* man. *therianthropism,* representation or worship of such gods; *theriolatry,* worship of animal gods. *therimorphic,* shaped like a beast; relating to a god worshiped in the form of an animal. *theriomorphosis,* transformation into a beast or into the shape of a beast, as of Lucius, in THE GOLDEN ASS of Apuleius (155 A.D.)—which also contains the charming fable of Cupid and Psyche. Ford in his HANDBOOK OF SPAIN (1845) mentioned *portraits of theriomaniac Austrian royalty,* 'mad' about hunting wild beasts.

theriodic. Brutal, malignant. Greek *theriadia,* beastliness; *ther,* wild beast. In the 19th century applied, in medicine, to ulcers, etc.

theriomancy. See *aeromancy.*

therne. A girl, a maid, a young woman. Also *thorne; tharne.* Old Saxon *thiorna;* German *Dirne.* Often contrasted with *knave,* man, as in Brunne's HANDLYNG SYNNE (1303): *Two unweddyd . . . single knave and single tharne.*

thester. Dark. Also a verb, to grow dark; to make dark. Other forms were *thister, thestri* (the poem BODY AND SOUL, 1325, by Map: *In a thestri stude I stod*), *thostre, thiestre, thister, thestir,* and more. [*Stude* is a variant of *steed,* place—surviving in *homestead.*] This was a common word from BEOWULF into the 15th century, as in THE DESTRUCTION OF TROY (1400): *He throng into thicke wodes, thester within.* Hence *thesterness, thisterness,* darkness; Langland's PIERS PLOWMAN (1377) has *On a Thoresday in thesternesse thus was he taken.*

theurgy. White magic. First employed by the Egyptian Platonists to secure the aid of friendly spirits, to work miraculous benefit. Greek *theos,* god + *ergos,* working. Hence *theurgist; theurgical.* In the 16th and 17th centuries opposed to *goety, q.v.,* black magic. Bishop Lavington in 1751 declared: *In the Academy of Salamanca they taught both theurgy and goety in the publick schools.*

thew. This word (Old Saxon *thau,* custom, habit) has moved through a range of meanings. In the 8th and 9th centuries, it meant a custom, or general practice of a people or a class. Then, a custom or habit of an individual; hence a personal (mental or moral) quality—usually in the plural. Then a good quality or habit, a virtue; in the plural, good physical qualities; especially, the fair features of a woman. Then, the bodily powers of a man, as indicating strength. Shakespeare used the word in this sense, as in HENRY IV, PART TWO (1697): *Care I for the limbes, the thewes, the stature, bulke, and bigge assemblance of a man? Give mee the spirit.* So also in JULIUS CAESAR and HAMLET. Spenser uses it of moral quality in THE FAËRIE QUEENE (1590): *Helena . . . in all godly thewes and goodly prayse Did far excell.* The word was rarely used after the 16th century, until revived by Scott—ROB ROY, 1818: *My fellow-traveller, to judge by his thews and sinews, was a man who might have set danger at defiance*—in the physical sense, usually with *sinews;* since then *thews* has been synonymous with *muscles* or *tendons. To thew* (13th to 15th century), to instruct in morals; to discipline, to chastise; hence, *a thew* (13th to 16th century), an instrument (instead of the pillory, which was used for men) for punishing women; probably a form of cucking-stool, *q.v.*

thig. To receive, accept; to take food, to eat and drink. This common early English word came by 1300 to be limited to one special sense: to receive by begging, to beg. Also *thigger,* a beggar. Both these words, dying in the 17th century, were revived by Scott in the early 19th. Scott was fond of the phrase *thiggers and sorners; thigging and sorning,* which he explained as "a kind of genteel begging, or rather something between begging and robbing, by which the needy in Scotland used to extort cattle, or the means of subsistence, from those that had any to give." A MORAL FABLE (1470) of Henryson declared: *I eschame* [am ashamed] *to thig, I can not wirk.*

thilke. What was mentioned or indicated; that; this; these. Also *thilk, thylke, thulk, thelke, thik, thicky.* From *the* + *ilk,* same. Spenser in THE SHEPHERD'S CALENDAR (1579) moans: *I love thilke lasse (alas why doe I love?)*

thir. These (the plural of *this,* 14th to 16th century). Also, an old form of *their.*

third. A variant of *thrid, thread.* The original form of *third,* the numeral, was also *thrid;* Gothic *thridja;* Latin *tertius* but Greek *tritos;* Sanskrit *trtiyas.* Shakespeare may have meant *thread,* a constituent fibre, in THE TEMPEST (1611) when Prospero, accepting Ferdinand as betrothed to his daughter Miranda, says: *I have given you here a third of my own life, Or that for which I live.* In OTHELLO, Desdemona is called the half of her father Brabantio's soul; Prospero would hardly be setting much price on Miranda if we interpret *third* as the numeral.

thirdborough. A town constable. Also *thridborrow, tharborough, thredbearer.* Probably a corruption of Middle English *fridborgh, frithborh,* peace-pledge, peace-surety. The English, having lost the sense, formed various corruptions; the earliest printing of Shakespeare's TAMING OF THE SHREW (the Induction; 1586) says *headborough.* The tavern hostess speaks: *I know my remedy. I must go fetch the thirdborough.* Drunken Sly responds: *Third, fourth, or fift borough, Ile answere him by law*—and falls asleep. In LOVE'S LABOUR'S LOST: *I myselfe reprehend his owne person, for I am his graces tharborough.*

thirdendeal. A third part. Also *thirdel; thriddendel, thrydendeal, thurrendeale,* From the 10th century; also *halfendeal,* a half part; *farthingdeal,* a farthing's worth. As late as 1581 we are told that *a thyrdendeale of the Crowne of Thornes is shewed at Paris in the holy chappell* *there.* In the 16th and 17th centuries, a *thirdendeal* pot was one that held three pints of liquor.

thirl. (1) A hole, perforation, aperture. What we today call a *nostril* was originally a *nose-thirl.* Later, a door or a window; also, a small cavity or recess; a closet. (2) A bondsman; a variant of *thrill*; *thrall* (*cp. thrall*). Especially, *thirlage,* the obligation to take one's produce or work to a particular mill or forge (the landlord's) or to pay a fee instead. As a verb, (1) to pierce, penetrate, traverse—and the various literal and figurative senses of *thrill,* as when Ramsay in THE GENTLE SHEPHERD (1725) said: *His words they thirle like music through my heart.* (2) To reduce to bondage or hold in servitude; to limit a tenant to a particular mill; hence, to confine or restrict, as in Bryce's THE AMERICAN COMMONWEALTH (1888): *Great is their power, because they are deemed to be less thirled to a party or leader, because they speak from a moral standpoint.* (3) To hurl, or to fly, with a spinning motion. Frequent in the 16th century, possibly by fusion with *twirl* or *whirl.* Note that *thirlpool* was a name for the whale (15th to 17th century). Also *thirlepoll*; hence it might be from *thirl,* opening + *poll,* head; but other forms of the word were *whirlpool* (1522) and *hurlpool* (1556), so that there may be a connection with the tumult of the whale's blowing.—In the figurative sense, to pierce, Chaucer says in ANELIDA AND ARCITE (1374): *So thirllethe with the poynt of remember-aunce the sworde of sorowe.*

thisness. Used in the 17th century (again in the 19th); opposed to *thatness,* which is the quality of being something other than this. *This* had various forms: *thissen, thisne* (used by Bottom in Shakespeare's A MIDSUMMER NIGHT'S DREAM; 1596), in this manner. Also *thiskin, on thiskin wise, this gate, thishow* (after *somehow*) *this wise, on this wise,* in this manner, thus. *this half, a-this-half,* on this side. *thislike,* like this, in this way. *this while, this whiles,* during this time, meanwhile.

thisterness. This form occurs in the 13th century HAVELOCK THE DANE. See *thester.*

thole. In addition to the current use, as an oar-pin or rowlock, there are several forgotten uses of *thole.* (1) Forbearance, suffering, enduring; also, *tholing, tholance* (14th and 15th centuries). (2) *tholus,* a circular domed structure; especially (*thole*) the place in a temple or church where gifts are hung. Also, as a verb, *to thole,* to be subjected to, to suffer, endure; to put up with, to endure, to withstand. Hence *tholeburde, tholemode* (10th to 13th century), bearing patiently, submissive, meek. Chaucer in THE FRIAR'S TALE (1386) has: *So much wo as I have with you tholed.* Barrie is less patient, in A WINDOW IN THRUMS (1889): *I canna thole 'im.*

thonk. An old form for (1) thank, (2) thought (noun and verb). *thonkyng,* thought. In THE OWL AND THE NIGHTINGALE (13th century) *hire thonkes* means, with her will. Who'd a thonk it?

thorp. A hamlet; especially, in Middle English, an agricultural village. A Norse word, not common in Old English and appearing mainly (Langland, 1362; Chaucer, 1386) as *throp, throop. thorp* was seldom used in literary works after the 15th century, but survived through the countryside, and was restored to poetic use by Wordsworth (THE EXCURSION, 1814: *Welcome, wheresoe'er he came—Among the tenantry of thorpe and vill*) and Tennyson (THE BROOK, 1855: *I hurry down*

. . . *By twenty thorps;* ENOCH ARDEN, 1864).

thos. A beast of prey, of the dog family, named in Greek and Latin writers. Plural, *thoes.* Mentioned in 17th to 19th century English works, and variously identified; thus C. H. Smith in his book on DOGS (1839) says: *It may be, that one of the smaller thoes of Aristotle is the true jackal.*—Phillips in 1706 defined the *thos: A lynx, a creature resembling a wolf, but spotted like a leopard.* Apparently, one of the missing lynx!

thrall. One who is held in bondage; a slave, a captive. Also used to mean the condition of a thrall, *thraldom, thralship*; and as an adjective: *We now are captives that made others thrall*; and as a verb, *to thrall,* to enslave. *cp. thirl.* By the 17th century, the verb was largely replaced by *enthrall,* mainly with figurative application. *Thrall* was used both literally (often, *thrall of Satan*) and figuratively. Chaucer in THE ROMAUNT OF THE ROSE (1366) says *The God of Love . . . can wel these lordis thrallen.* Shakespeare refers to the King's guards, in MACBETH (1605), as *slaves of drink, and thralles of sleepe.*

thrasonical. Bragging; vainglorious. Also *thrasonic. A thraso, a thrasonist,* a swaggerer, a boaster. In Terence's play THE EUNUCH (161 B.C.) the *miles gloriosus,* the braggart soldier, is named *Thraso* (Greek *thrasys,* spirited). The popularity of the play in Tudor England brought the name into common use; *cp. gnathonical.* Hence also *thrasonism,* braggart behavior; *to thrasonize,* to play the daredevil, to brag. Shakespeare in AS YOU LIKE IT (1600) mentions that *Caesars thrasonical bragge of I came, saw, and overcame.*

threap. Originally, to rebuke, scold, blame. Common from the 9th to the 16th century, thereafter persisting in country speech; revived in the 19th century (Scott, C. Bronte, Bulwer-Lytton). Also *threpe, threep, threppe, threip, thraip,* and the like. Various meanings developed. To dispute, to inveigh (against), to haggle, to contend. Hence, as a noun, *threap,* quarreling, contention, contest. *To threap with kindness* was rarely used in the sense of to treat with kindness; more often, to attribute kindness to, to urge to the exercise of kindness. *To threap upon,* to impose upon, to try to press one's beliefs upon; to press (something) upon one, to urge one's acceptance or acquiescence. Failing that, *to threap down,* to beat down resistance, to silence by vehement or persistent assertion (this use might well be revived!), as R. W. Hamilton observed in NUGAE LITERARIAE (1841): *A man will say of a clamorous talker, he did not convince me, but he threaped me down.* The form *threapen,* in addition to these uses, borrowed the sense of *threaten* as well; *threapening,* threatening. Thence, *threap-land,* land of disputed ownership. In the sense of strongly affirming, persisting in a (challenged) point of view, Chaucer uses the word in the Prologue to THE CANON YEOMAN'S TALE (1386): *Sol gold is and Luna silver we threpe.* Thus also Scott in THE ANTIQUARY (1816): *He threeps the castle and lands are his ain as his mother's eldest son.* Beaumont in PSYCHE (1648) has the fair nymph cry: *Behold how gross a ly of ugliness They on my face have threaped!*

three-pile. With the loops of the pile-warp (that forms the nap—of carpetry, or velvet) formed of three threads, hence producing a trebly thick pile, of the finest quality. Hence, *three-piled,* of the highest quality; exquisite; by deterioration, over-fine, extreme. Elizabeth Barrett Browning in NATURE'S REMORSES (1861) has: *On three-piled carpet of compliments.* Shakespeare in LOVE'S LABOUR'S LOST (1588) speaks of the courtier's *Taffata phrases, silken tearmes precise, Three-pil'd hyperboles, spruce affectation.*

threne. A song of lamentation. Also *threnode, threnody* (Greek *ode,* song); *threnos.* Greek *threnos,* lament. Shakespeare uses the form *threnos* as a heading, in THE PHOENIX AND THE TURTLE (1601); in the body of the poem he uses *threne.* Stedman, in his VICTORIAN POETS (1876) calls Arnold's THYRSIS the best *threnode* since Shelley's ADONAIS; later he calls Tennyson's IN MEMORIAM *the great threnody of our language.* Other great ones are Milton's LYCIDAS and Swinburne's AVE ATQUE VALE, in memory of Baudelaire.

threpe. See *threap.*

thring. A very common Old English verb, with the basic meaning to press, to crowd; in this sense replaced by one of its forms, *throng.* By development, *thring* came to mean: to push forward, hasten; to press hard, oppress, repress; to press together, compress; to thrust with violence, to dash, knock, hurl (down)—also *downthring,* to press down, crush. Hence also, to press through, to pierce, penetrate, burst (out). A *thringer,* an overthrower. Also *thryng.* In the past tense, *thrang, thrange, thronge, throng, thrungen, thrung.* Of petty assemblages, Chaucer in THE ROMAUNT OF THE ROSE (1366) tells: *There was many a bird singing Throughout the yerde al thringing;* and Douglas in the AENEIS (1513): *The damecellis* [damsels] *fast to thar lady thringis.* In less pleasant fashion, from the same poem of Chaucer's: *In his sleve he gan to thringe A rasour sharpe and wel bitinge.* Rutherford in a letter of 14 March, 1637, exclaims: *There is no little thrusting and thringing to thrust in at Heaven's gates.* Luckily, it is entered by many a door as well as by many adored.

thro. Obstinacy in opposition; anger, wrath; struggle; trouble; also, eagerness, haste. Common in Old Norse; in English, 14th to 16th century. Also *thra.* Hence, as adjective, stubborn, angry; violent; fierce, bold in battle; (of a corpse) stiff, rigid. In the phrase *thriven and thro,* the word took on a favorable sense, very bold, hence, in general, excellent. This may have been influenced by the verb *to thro,* meaning to grow, to increase in size, to grow up. Also *throly, thraly,* eagerly; obstinately; furiously; Stewart in his CHRONICLE OF SCOTLAND (1535) said: *So thraly then togidder that they thrust, That speiris brake.* A Chester Mystery of 1500 said: *In this place, be you never so throe* [stubborn], *Shall you no longer dwell.*

throp. An early form of *thorp, q.v.*

thrum. (1) The end of a warp thread, unwoven and left on the loom when the web is cut off; hence, a tassel or fringe at the edge of a cloth. Also, the waste; *thrums,* scraps. Hence, *thread and thrum,* the good and the bad. A *thrum-cap,* one made of odds and ends; *thrum-chinned* (humorously), with a fringe of a beard. *To thrum caps* (or *buttons*), to spend time idly or on trivial matters (16th and 17th centuries, as in Nashe's THE UNFORTUNATE TRAVELER; 1594). Shakespeare in A MIDSUMMER NIGHT'S DREAM (1596) has Pyramus sing to the Fates, that weave the threads of human destiny: *O Fates, come, come, cut thread and thrum.* (2) *thrum, throm, throme, thrumme,* a company or crowd; a bundle (as of arrows); magnificence, splendor. Used from the 8th to the 15th century. ARTHUR AND MERLIN (1330) *Whiles thou were in our throme, No were we never overcome.*—The first *thrum* is from the Old Teutonic root *thrum;* Indo-European *trmo-;* Latin *term-,* Greek *terma,* end, whence also *interminable.* Before we terminate, we should mention that the second *thrum* is related to Old English *thrymm,* a multitude; Old Saxon *thrimman,* to swell.

thunderlight. Lightning. Originally *thunderlait, -layt, -leit, -leyt.* From Old English *ley,* flame, came *lait,* a flash of fire, as in Malory's MORTE D'ARTHUR (1485): *Ther felle a sodeyne tempest and thonder layte and rayne.* Chaucer uses *thunderlight* (in one manuscript *thonderleit*) several times; after him, the picturesque term was neglected until Leigh Hunt caught it up in his FEAST OF POETS (1815): *What shall move his placid might? Not the headlong thunderlight.*

thurifer. One who bears burning incense, especially as part of a ceremony or ritual. Also *thuribuler;* the vessel in which the burning incense is borne is a *thurible* (*thuribule, thoryble, turrible*). From the 14th century (now only in historical or technical writings), frankincense is *thus* (*th* as in *thin*). Latin *tus, thus, thurem;* Greek *thuos,* sacrifice, offering, incense; *thuein,* to sacrifice. Also *thurific, thuriferous,* incense-bearing; *thurificate, thurify,* to burn incense to; to perfume with incense. Nashe used the word in a lay sense when he remarked in LENTEN STUFFE (1599): *This herring . . . was sensed and thurified in the smoake.* Francis Thompson is more reverent in A CORYMBUS FOR AUTUMN (1888): *What is this feel of incense everywhere? Clings it round folds of the blanch-amiced clouds, Upwafted by the solemn thurifer, The mighty Spirit unknown, That swingeth the slow earth before the embannered Throne?*

thwite. To cut down, to pare away; to shape by paring. Used from the 9th century. Also in the popular phrase, used by More in a DYALOGE (1529): *to thwite a mill-post to a pudding-prick;* figuratively, to cut down the size of, to reduce (arrogance, complacency, etc.) to proper proportions, to 'take down a peg.' A diminutive of *to thwite* (also *thwyte, thwight,* etc.) was *to thwittle,* whence the variant and still current *whittle.* A *whit* —surviving in the expression *no whit the* (*worse,* etc.)—is a shaving, whittled off; hence, an insignificant bit.

thwittle. See *thwite.*

tib. Originally a pet-name for Isabel, *Tib, tib,* has shifted its sense. With a capital *T,* it was used (16th to the 18th century) as a representative name for a woman of the lower class—*Jack and Jill, Tib and Tom.* But with the capital withdrawn, one must judge from the particular context whether *tib* means a girl, or a sweetheart, or (as with Bailey, 1751) 'a poor sorry woman', or a woman of loose character, a strumpet (1589, *the bravest tipling tib that is within the towne;* 1618, *Where tinkers and their tibs doe oft repaire*). Also *tib,* or *tib of the buttery,* a goose; Brome in THE JOVIAL CREW (1641): *Here's Grunter and Bleater, with Tib of the buttry;* (1725) *on tibs thou shalt every day dine.* The phrase *On Tib's Eve, St. Tib's Eve,* meant never (like *the Greek Calends* and *Latter Lammas*). In the 19th century *to tibble,* or *to tib* (*out*) meant to slip out of school, to break bounds, as in Thackeray's THE NEWCOMES (1855): *I used what they call to tib out and run down to a public house.* A *tib-cat* or *tibby-cat* was a female cat; now called a *tabby-cat,* from the name *Tabitha.* Shakespeare in PERICLES (1608) has Marina say to the pander's servant: *Thou art the damned doorkeeper to every coistrel that comes enquiring for his tib.*

ticement. A 14th century shortening of *enticement.* Also *tice,* from the 13th to the 16th century (later as *'tice*), to *entice.* Bellenden translating (1533) Livy wrote: *He tyistit the young men of his ciete to his purpois.* Hence *ticer,* one that *entices.*

ticket-of-leave. A license to be at large after part of a prison term has been served; as in Australia, and in 19th century England of convicts released for good behavior. Hence, *ticket-of-leave man, ticket-of-leaver,* one thus released. THE TICKET-OF-LEAVE MAN, by Tom Taylor, in May, 1863, brought to the Olympic Theatre the first great detective in the drama. His removal of disguise and self-disclosure became traditionalized in three movements: Left hand removes cap—he says: "I." Right hand removes wig—he says "Hawkshaw." Left hand, holding cap, removes whiskers—he says: "the detective."

tickle. See *whilere.*

tiffany. Originally, though rarely in English, short for *Epiphany,* the Twelfth Day (January 6)—as in Shakespeare's TWELFTH NIGHT. *Tiffany* is really short (there were some forty variant forms in Old French) for *Theophany,* the manifestation of God. From the meaning of manifestation, revealing, the word was given English use as *tiffany,* short for *tiffany silk,* which cloths, said Holland in his translation (1601) of Pliny, 'instead of apparell to cover and hide, shew women naked through them.' Thus also Evelyn in his DIARY for June 1645: *shewing their naked arms through false sleeves of tiffany.* Hence, an article made of tiffany, such as a head-dress. Also used figuratively, as in Richard Franck's NORTHERN MEMOIRS (1658): *It's a tiffany plot; any man with half an eye may easily see through it.*

timbrel. A percussion instrument; often one like a tambourine, that can be held up in one hand. *Cp. tabor.* An earlier form was *timbre* (which survives in other senses), which by way of popular Latin *timbano* was used by Wyclif (1380) to translate Latin *tympanum* (Hebrew *toph*) in the 150TH PSALM. In later versions, and for similar Oriental instruments, *timbrel* was used. Also, a design shaped like a timbrel, as in Hall's CHRONICLES (HENRY VIII, 1548): *Of their hosen . . . the nether parts were of scarlet, poudred with tymbrelles of fyne golde.*

timpanize. See *tympany.*

tind. To light, to kindle; hence, to inflame, arouse; also, to catch fire, become ignited; to become inflamed or aroused. An early word, common in Old English and developing many forms, including *tend, tynd, tynne, tin, teyne, tinnd. tinder,* though surviving as a noun, was in the 13th century (also *tender*) used as a verb, to become inflamed, to glow. Herrick in HESPERIDES (1648, CANDLEMAS DAY) said: *Kindle the Christmas brand . . . Part must be kept wherewith to teend The Christmas log next year.* Dryden used the verb figuratively in THE DUKE OF GUISE (1682): *Shop-consciences . . . Preach'd up, and ready tined for a rebellion.*

tine. This survives as the technical term for the tooth or prong of a fork or pitchfork or other such pointed instrument; also, the pointed branches of a deer's horn. It was also used of a twig, and of the rung of a ladder. But there were other senses. (1) Loss (1320, Sir Tristram: *In winning and in tine . . . in joie and in pine*). Hence, affliction, trouble, sorrow. Spenser first, in THE FAËRIE QUEENE (1590): *To seek her out with labor and long tyne*; others have followed him. (2) A bit, a very little—always in the phrase *a little tine,* also as an adjective, very small, *tiny*. Shakespeare uses this in HENRY IV, PART TWO (1597): *A joynt of mutton, and any pretty little tine kickshawes,* and in KING LEAR. Also as a verb, *tine, tyne* (1) to shut; to enclose; to fence, hedge in; restrain. From the 7th century. (2) To lose, waste, spoil, ruin, bring to nought. From the 13th century. A Towneley Mytery of 1460 said: *Our joye is tynt.* A *tiner* (16th century) was a destroyer, a loser; Rolland in THE SEVIN SAGES (1560) exclaimed: *O subtell schrew . . . Tyner of treuth, with toung intoxicat.*

tintamar. A clamor, uproar, hubbub, racket—a great confused noise. The O.E.D. says it is of obscure origin; Bailey (1751) suggests Latin *tinnitus Martius,* a warlike jingling. [Note that Poe's *tintinnabulation of the bells,* while an echoic word, was not coined by him; Latin has *tintinnabulum,* a bell, a call-bell.] Also *tintamare, tintamarre, tintimar.* H. Greville in his DIARY for 21 November, 1834, said: *Such a tintamarre I never heard, but the audience were enthusiastic.* And THE ACADEMY of 28 December, 1901, complained: *The just praise he wishes to utter is forestalled by a tintamar of rash eulogy.*

tippet. Originally (13th century) a separate, long narrow slip of cloth, worn hanging from the hood, headdress, or sleeve. In the 15th century, also a scarf, or a short (wool or fur) cape. Especially, an ecclesiastical scarf (16th century on) worn around the neck, with the two ends hanging in front; hence, *tippet-captain, tippet-knight,* contemptuous terms for a priest; *tippet-scuffle,* ecclesiastical quarrel. Caxton in his translation (1481) of THE MIRROUR OF THE WORLD observed: *They be not alle clerkes that have short typettis.* The LONDON GAZETTEER in 1686 carried a notice: *Lost a sable tippet with scarlet and silver strings.*

tire. Besides the two major senses that survive—when you are *tired,* it is time to *retire*; when your car is not *tired,* it is time to *re-tire*—there were several now less remembered. (1) Apparatus, outfit, clothing; supplanted by *attire.* Hence, apparel; especially, a headdress. Hence, *tirement,* attire, *tirements,* garments. In combinations, *tirehouse,* wardrobe of a theatre; *tiring-house, tiring-room,* a dressing room, especially of a theatre. *tiremaid, tire-woman,* maid of the wardrobe; dressmaker. Pepys in his DIARY of 20 February, 1667, wrote: *To Mrs. Grotier's, the Queen's tire-woman, for a pair of locks for my wife* [hair, not chastity]. (2) A volley of shot. French *tir*; *tirer,* to shoot, to draw. Hence also (13th century) to pull, to tug; especially, as a hawk on flesh, to rend, to feed greedily. Hence, a *tire,* (3) a tough morsel given a hawk, to exercise its beak. Greene in MENAPHON (1589): *For all she hath let you flie like a hawk that hath lost her tyre.* Sir Robert Dallington in A METHOD FOR TRAVEL (1598) wrote: *The kitchin doctor gave his patient the necke and bones to tyre upon, and kept the wings himselfe.* Shakespeare uses this sense figuratively, meaning busily engaged—*Upon that were my thoughts tiring*—in TIMON OF ATHENS (1605). When he speaks in LOVE'S LABOUR'S LOST of *the tired horse,* he means, adorned with trappings. And he has in PERICLES: *I much marvaile that your lordship, Having rich tire about* *you, should at these early howers Shake off the golden slumber of repose.* For a glimpse of fancy headdress (Spenser, in THE FAËRIE QUEENE; 1590: *And on her head she wore a tyre of gold.* HISTRIOMASTIX; 1610: *My maisters, what tire wears your lady on her head?—Four squirrels tails tied in a true loves knot*), see *shiptire.*

tistytosty. See *tytetuste.*

titivil. A rascal, scoundrel; especially, a tattling or mischievous tell-tale; Cotgrave in 1611 has: *a tatling houswife, a titifill, a flebergebit.* Plautus once used the word *titivillitium,* apparently meaning a mere trifle. This may be the origin of *Titivil,* which was the name of the devil that gathered up the fragments of words dropped, skipped, or mumbled in the religious services, and took them to hell to be stored up against the offending one. From this, the name was used for a devil or demon in the Mystery Plays, then extended to persons. Also *tittifill, titifyl, titivillus.* In Hall's CHRONICLES (1548, EDWARD IV) we read: *Mistrusting lest her counsayl should by some titiville be published and opened to her adversaries.*

titubate. To stagger, reel, stumble; to stammer, stumble in speech. Latin *titubare, titubatum,* to stagger, to stammer, to hesitate. Also, *titubation.* S. Clarke in his ECCLESIASTICAL HISTORY (1650) has: *He went on without the least hesitation in his voice, or titubation of his tongue.* These two forms were used from the 17th century; in the 19th century, *titubant* and *titubancy* came into use, humorously or pedantically. Thus Peacock in THE MISFORTUNES OF ELPHIN (1829) admires *that amiable state of semi-intoxication which sets the tongue tripping, in the double sense of nimbleness and titubancy.*

to-. This is another of the English forms that mean their own opposite (see *avaunt*). (1) In the sense of motion toward or addition to. *to-cast,* to add. *tocome,* arrival (9th to 16th century); *tocome,* to befall, to approach, arrive (13th to 16th century). *to-draught,* a following, a retinue; a place that people are drawn to, a resort. *to-gainst,* toward with hostile intent; (1440) *Charelemaine's spear that togainst the Saracins he was want to bear. to-lay,* to put forward, allege. *to-neighe,* to approach. (2) Many more words were formed with *to-* in the sense of apart, asunder, in pieces, or other ideas of separation (equivalent to *zer* in German, Old Teuton *tiz,* Latin *dis*). *To-bear,* to carry in different directions; to take away; to separate persons (in feelings: make them enemies). *to-bell,* to swell exceedingly; to be swollen with pride or anger. *to-bent,* bent way over. *to-blow,* to puff up (with wind, or with an emotion); to blow away, scatter. *to-braid,* to wrench apart, pull to pieces; snatch away. *to-bray,* to beat to atoms. *to-break,* to demolish, scatter. *to-brenn,* to consume by fire. *tobune, to-bone,* to beat severely, thrash; also *to-bust. to-carve,* to cut to pieces. *tochew,* to chew to pieces. *to-chine,* to split apart. *to-clatter,* to knock to pieces (noisily). *to-crack,* to shatter. *to-cut,* to cut to bits: *The Cassydonyens* (1489) *were slayne and all to-cutt and cloven. to-dash,* to dash to pieces. *to-deal,* to divide into parts; to sever; to distribute. *to-do,* to sunder; to undo, open. *to-draw,* to pull apart, destroy by tearing to pieces. *todrese* (past, *to-drove*), to fall apart, decay. *to-drunk,* too drunk. *to-fare,* to disperse. *to-flap,* to knock to pieces. *to-fleet,* to float away, be carried away by current or tide. *to-frush,* to smash, drive violently into (as with an automobile. Most of these words had dropped out of use by the

16th century.). *to-gang,* to go away, to pass away. *to-gnide,* to crush to fragments. *to-go,* to go in different directions, pass away, disappear. *to-hale,* to drag apart; to pull about. *to-hene,* to mutilate by stoning. *to-hurt,* to knock asunder. *to-pull,* to pull to pieces. *to-race, to-rase,* to hack or tear to pieces. *to-rat,* to break up, to scatter. *to-reose,* to crumble, fall into ruins. *to-rush,* to disperse with force, to dash to pieces. *to-set,* distribute, divide. *to-shend,* to destroy utterly, ruin. *to-shoot,* to burst asunder. *to-skair,* to scatter, disperse. *to-spring,* to spring apart, burst asunder. *to-slive,* to cleave. *to-sned,* to cut to pieces. *to- sparple,* to scatter abroad. *to-squat,* to crush, squash. *to-stick,* to prick all over. *to-stink,* to smell abominably. *to-tight,* to stretch out, spread out. *to-torve,* to hurl about, to dash to pieces. *to-tose,* to tear to pieces. *to-twin,* to separate, divide. *to-whither,* to whirl to bits. *to-worth,* to come to naught; to perish. *to-wowe,* to scatter by blowing. *to-writhe,* to wrench or twist apart. *to-wry,* to twist about.

toaze. A variant of *toze, q.v.*

tocsin. An alarm, rung by a bell; also, the alarm bell. Provençal *tocar* (French *toucher,* originally an echoic word), to touch, strike + *senh* (Latin *signum* sign; later, bell), bell. Also used figuratively, as in A. Clarke's LIFE (1832): *He thought the seizure in my foot would turn to an attack of gout. This was a tocsin to me.*

tod. (1) A fox; hence, a crafty person. *Tod's birds, Tod's bairns,* persons of bad stock, an evil brood. Dunbar in a poem (1520) observed that *sum in ane lamb skin is ane tod.* (2) A measure of wool, 28 pounds; hence, any load, usually of a specified weight. Herrick in HESPERIDES (1648, CONJURATION TO ELECTRA) uses it figuratively, to mean clouds; *By those soft tods of wool With which the air is full.* (3) Short for *ivy-tod,* a bushy growth of ivy. (4) Short for *toddy,* whisky with hot water and sugar. *To tod,* to produce a tod of wool; Shakespeare inquires, in THE WINTER'S TALE (1611): *Let me see, every eleven wether toddes, every tod yeeldes pound and odde shilling; fifteen hundred shorne, what comes the wooll too?*

toddy. See *tarry.*

tofall. A smaller building with its roof sloping up to the wall of a main building, a lean-to. Hence, figuratively, a shelter; a dependent. Also, that which befalls. *The tofall of the day,* the end of the day; *the tofall of the night,* the beginning of the night. As a verb, *tofall* (see *to-*) meant collapse, to fall in pieces. Used from the 8th century; the noun survived the 15th century in Scotch and dialects. Thus Waddell in his rendering (1871) of THE PSALMS says: *The Lord my rock . . . and my to-fa'.*

tofore. An early form of *before.* Although a genuine, distinct word, from the 9th century, *tofore* (*toforen, toforn, tofor, toffore*) was sometimes treated as though it were short for *heretofore. Tofore God,* in the sight of God; CHAUCER'S DREME (1500) uses it to mean "by God!" *Madame, God tofore, ye shul be there.* Shakespeare in TITUS ANDRONICUS (1592) says: *Farewell, Lavinia, my noble sister, O that thou wert as thou tofore has been!*

toft. A homestead, the grounds for a house and its out-buildings. The frequent phrase *toft and croft* meant the entire holding, the homestead and the conjoined arable land. Used from the 10th century; in the 14th, *toft* was applied also to a knoll or hillock amid level lands; especially, one suited for a house or tower. Baring-Gould in ICELAND (1863) mentions *a farm named Tratharholt, crowning a toft which rises out of green meads and almost impossible swamps.* Bailey (1751) adds *toft* (*tuft,* French *touffe du bois*), a grove of trees; this seems to be an error repeated from Kersey's edition (1706) of Phillips' THE NEW WORLD OF ENGLISH WORDS.

tole. See *tele.*

tolter. To move unsteadily, to flounder; to stagger along; to toss and turn about. Also as an adjective, swaying, insecure, giddy. Henryson in ORPHEUS AND EURYDICE (1470) pictures Tantalus: *Before his face an apill hang also, Fast at his mouth, upon a tolter threid.*

tolutiloquence. Speech that moves briskly along, voluble discourse. The accent is on the *till* (till the speaker stops). Latin *tolutim,* at a trot; but Sir Thomas Browne discriminates, in PSEUDODOXIA EPIDEMICA OR ENQUIRIES INTO MANY RECEIVED TENENTS (1646), of horses' pacing: *Whether they move per latera, that is, two legs of one side together, which is tollutation or ambling; or per diametrum . . . which is succussation or trotting.* Properly *tolutation,* trotting; *tolutate,* to trot, to move smartly along. After the 17th century, used mainly for humor. R. L. Edgeworth in his LIFE (1796) said: *You compose in your chaise, and I on horseback, which . . . is the reason why your lines roll so smoothly, and mine partake so much of tolutation.*

tomblestere. See *tumbester.*

tomelet. A small volume. A *tome* is one volume of a literary work. Greek *tomos,* section (of a work); root *tom-,* cut, as also in *appendectomy* and the *atomic* age. There is a pun buried in Nashe's spelling of *tome,* in his Lenten Stuffe (1599): *To recount ab ovo, or from the church-booke, of his birth, howe the herring first came to be a fish, and then how he came to be king of fishes, and gradationately how from white to red he changed, would require as massie a toombe as Hollinshead.* [Raphael Holinshed was author of THE CHRONICLES OF ENGLAND, SCOTLANDE, AND IRELAND; 1577—source of much of Shakespeare's plot material.]

tompion. (1) A watch or clock of the sort made by *Thomas Tompion,* in the reign of good Queen Anne. For an instance of the use of the word, see *cosins.* (2) Another form of *tampion* (*q.v.*), a plug for stopping an aperture; especially, a bung for a cask, "a stopple of a great gun or mortar" (Bailey, 1751) "to keep out rain." Also *tomkin, tampoon, tampkin, tomking.*

tone. A contraction of *the one*; sometimes used for *one.* Pronounced *tun.* Similarly, *tother.* Thus Sir Thomas More in THE HISTORIE OF KING RYCHARDE THE THIRDE (1513) quoted the Lord Stanley: *"For while we," quoth he, "talke of one matter in the tone place, litle wote we wherof they talk in the tother place."* For another instance of its use, see *haut.*

toot. See *tut.*

tooth-fee. A gift to an infant when it cuts its first tooth. Also, *tooth-gift, tooth-money, tooth-piece.* Such gifts were a Viking custom. THE ACADEMY of 23 February, 1884, said: *What Sigmund gave his son was a sword, imon-lauk, a very fitting tooth-fee, or name-gift, to one who was to live and die in arms.* Thorpe, in his NORTHERN MYTHOLOGY (1851), of the god Frey, said: *Alfheim was given to him by the gods as tooth-money.*

toparch. The ruler of a petty state or small region. Greek *topos,* place + *arches,* ruler. Hence *toparchy,* the district thus ruled. Fuller in JOSEPH'S COAT (1640) explained: *By those many kings mentioned in the old Testament, thirty and one in the little land of Canaan . . . is meant onely toparchs, not great kings.*

topiarist. A landscape gardener; especially, one that trims and trains shrubs, trees, and hedges to grow in fanciful shapes. Greek *topia,* places, plural of *topion,* a little place; *topos,* a place. Also a *topiarius, topiary. Topiary* is more frequently an adjective (as also *topiarian*), relating to the art of shaping live plants into fanciful forms. The art itself was also called *topiary,* or *topiaria.* Thus R. Rinche in his translation (1599) of THE FOUNTAINE OF ANCIENT FICTION spoke of a statue *supported by foure images of Victoria hewen out . . . with inimitable skill of the art topiaria.* Holly, box, and yew were frequently used for such living figures, which were the delight of the Tudor gardeners, but which the late 17th century (Addison, Pope) denounced as a 'false wit' of the landscape. The fashion has returned; the LONDON MAGAZINE of June 1902 warned that *a topiary garden is by no means an inexpensive hobby to indulge in;* but THE NEW YORK TIMES of 1953 bore a headline *Topiary Art Revived on Maryland Farm* over an account of the estate of Harvey S. Ladew of Harford County, that ends: "The living growth is cut into likenesses of animals. Swans seem to swim across the top of one hedge. Along the walks, squirrels sit on their haunches and pheasants ruffle their tails. There are battlements of hemlock, and many of the hedges have windowlike openings so the stroller can enjoy the view." Scott in THE ANTIQUARIAN (1816) listed armchairs, towers, St. George and the dragon, as subjects of *topiarian* art, and Levens Hall, in Westmoreland, England, was named (in 1880) as having the most famous specimen of the work of the topiarist.

topomancy. See *aeromancy.*

tor. (1) As a noun: a high rock, or a rocky peak. Common from the 8th century; surviving in place names. Maxwell Anderson's play *High Tor* (1936) refers to a promontory on the Hudson River. (2) As an adjective: difficult, irksome, tedious; hard to conquer, hence sturdy. In this sense, also *tere.* In THE DESTRUCTION OF TROY (1400) the word is used several times, e.g., *Telemon, that is a tore king.*

toreutic. Relating to *toreutics,* the art of working in metal, ivory, etc.—embossing, chasing, working in relief, and the like. Pronounced *tor-you'-tic.* A *toreutes,* an artist in ivory or metal. These are 19th century terms (except for one use, by Evelyn, *toreutice,* in the 17th century). Thus THE ANTIQUITIES OF ATHENS (1837) called *the Minerva of the Parthenon, also by Phidias, wrought in ivory and gold, the noblest example of the toreutic art.*

torment. As a noun. An engine for hurling stones and other missiles at armies and fortress walls; worked by torsion. Latin *tormentum* is short for *torquementum; torquere, tortum,* to twist; whence also *torture,* of which *torment* (from the 13th century) meant an instrument. *Cp. tortive.* More mildly, an instrument of irritation or annoyance, a *tormentor,* applied to a sort of flea-trap (17th century). A book of CRIES OF LONDON includes: *Buy a trap, a mouse trap, A torment for the fleas; The hangman works but half the day; He lives too much at ease.* Often as *turment, tourmente* (directly from the French), a tempest, tornado, twister; a violent storm. R. Brunne chronicles in 1330: *Into the se of Spayn wer dryven in a torment.*

torous. Bulging; swollen; protuberant. Latin *torus,* swelling, bulge, muscle, earlier *storus;* the root is *ster, stra,* to strew, to spread (whence *consternation, constellation, location,* early Latin *stlocus; instrument, instruction,* and many more *constructions*: a very widespreading root). Hence also *torose,* big bulged; *torosity,* corpulence (in 17th and 18th century dictionaries).

torrent. See *burn.*

tortive. Twisting, twisted, *tortuous. Cp. torment.* Latin *torquere, torsi, tortum,* to twist, was prolific of English words. Among them are *torture,* twisting (on the rack); *torment; torsion; tortuous; tornado; tort,* an injury, a legal breach. Less common forms include *tortue, tortuose,* twisted; hence *tortuosity.* A *tortis* (*tortes, tortayes, tortyse*; 14th to 17th century) was a large wax candle, the wick being twisted; twisted tow dipped in pitch made a *torch.* Shakespeare says, in TROILUS AND CRESSIDA (1606): *Tortive and errant from his course of growth.*

torvity. Fierceness of aspect, grimness. From the 17th century. Also *torve, torvid, torvous,* grim, fierce-looking. *to torve,* to throw, cast (10th to 13th century). E. Ward in HUDIBRAS REDIVIVUS (1706) spoke of a man *Whose torvid aspect made him show so Like some revengeful Furioso.* (That rhyme should make one torve!)

tother. See *tone.*

totquot. (1) A dispensation to hold as many ecclesiastical benefices as one wishes to or can get; the holding of such; a person that holds them. *Totquots,* benefices held by one person. Hence generally (2) an indefinite or unlimited number. (3) A tax assessed in proportion to income (17th century). Latin *tot quot,* as much (as many) as . . . The word is frequent in anti-papal writings of the 16th and 17th centuries, as in Skelton's WHY NOT TO COURT? (1552): *We shall have a totquot from the Pope of Rome.*

totty. Unsteady, shaky, *tottery;* dizzy; fuddled. Formed after *totter, tottle.* Chaucer in THE REEVE'S TALE (1386) has: *Myn hed is toty of my swynk tonyght.* For another quotation, see *noll.* Used into the 17th century, the word was revived by Scott in the 19th, in IVANHOE (1819): *I was somewhat totty when I received the good knight's blow, or I had kept my ground.*

toune. An early variant of (1) *ton,* (2) *tone,* (3) *town,* (4) *tun,* (5) *tune.*

toupet. A curl, or artificial lock of hair atop the head, especially as peak adornment of a periwig. Also *toupee* (the current spelling, meaning a patch of false hair to cover a bald spot), *tupee, toppee.* For an illustration of this use, see *cosins.* From the first sense, *toupet* was used of a person of fashion, a gallant, a beau—who wore a toupet. Hence *toupet-coxcomb, toupet-man.* Richardson, in CLARISSA HARLOWE (1748): *A couple of brocaded or laced-waistcoated toupets, with sour screwed up half-cocked faces.* Again: *no mere toupet-man, but all manly.*

touse. See *toze.*

toute. The buttocks. Also *towte;* the Old English root *tut,* to stick out, project, related to *teat.* The verb *toot* (*tout*) meant to protrude, peep out; hence, to peer, to pry, to look at, to spy—from the 9th century to the 16th, surviving in dialects into the 19th. THE LAND OF COKAYNE (1305) says of the abbott: *He taketh maidin of the route And turnith up her white toute;* Chaucer uses the word in THE MILLER'S TALE (1386): and a Towneley Mystery of 1460 bids: *Come nar . . . and kys the dwillis* [devil's] *toute.* (This was a part of the Black Mass.)

tox. Short for intoxicate. In Thomas Heywood's PHILOCOTHONISTA; OR THE DRUNKARD OPENED, DISSECTED, AND ANATOMIZED (1635) we read: *When their more sober consciences can justifie against their toxed insolence*: the appeal from Philip drunk to Philip sober. *Intoxicate,* to put poison into; *to toxicate* is to poison. Note, however, that Greek *toxicon* had nothing to do with poison; it meant pertaining to the bow; Greek *toxa,* arrows, from *toxon,* bow. A poison for smearing on arrows was *toxicon pharmakon* (*pharmakon,* poison; drug, whence the whole *pharmacopoeia* —Greek *poein,* to make; a *poet* is a maker). Poisoned arrows were so common that the term for them was shortened to *toxicon*—whence *toxic* came to mean poisonous. But *toxology* means the study of archery; a *toxophile, toxophilist* is an ardent archer, as Ascham's treatise TOXOPHILUS (1545) attests.

toy. Many applications of the noun *toy* have passed from common use. (1) Amorous sport; a light caress. Spenser in THE FAËRIE QUEENE (1590): *A foe of folly and immodest toy.* Milton, of Adam, in PARADISE LOST (1667): *So said he, and forbore not glance or toy Of amorous intent, well understood Of Eve.* (2) A frisky movement, a bit of fun, an antic, a trick. (3) A trifling speech, a funny story; a pun; a light composition. Shakespeare in A MIDSUMMER NIGHT'S DREAM (1590): *I never may beleeve These anticke fables, nor these fairy toyes.* Scott, in KENILWORTH (1821): *Think of what that archknave Shakespeare says—a plague on him, his toys come into my head when I should think of other matters.* (4) A foolish fancy, an odd conceit; a whim, caprice. Especially, a foolish dislike. Hence, *to take (a) toy,* to take fright. Marlowe in HERO AND LEANDER (1593) said that to hear this *Made the well-spoken nymph take such a toy That down she sunk.* (5) A frivolous or lively tune. (6) A trifle, a foolish thing; *toys,* trumpery, worthless things. Shakespeare in MACBETH (1605): *From this instant, There's nothing serious in mortalitie: All is but toyes.* (7) A thing of little value kept as an ornament or curiosity, a trinket. Hence, anything small. (8) In thieves' slang, a watch. *Toy and tackle,* watch and chain. A *toy-getter,* a stealer of watches. (8) A person; used endearingly or contemptuously, or to indicate that the person is being used as a puppet or *toy.* Shakespeare, in THE MERRY WIVES OF WINDSOR: *Elves, list your names: Silence, you aiery toyes.* Dryden in THE SPANISH FRIAR (1681): *O vertue! vertue! . . That men should leave thee for that toy, a woman!* (9) A close-fitting linen or wool cap, with flaps descending to the shoulders, worn by women of the lower classes. Shakespeare, in THE WINTER'S TALE: *Any silke, any thred, any toyes for your head?* Later worn mainly in Scotland; *cp. coif.* Also, *toy-match.* Burns, in his poem TO A LOUSE: *I wad na be surpris'd to spy You on an auld wife's flainen* [flannel] *toy.*

toze. To comb or card (*tease*) wool. Also *toaze, tose, tooze;* related to *tease* and *touse.* Hence, *to toze, to tease out,* to search out, elicit. D. Rogers in his TREATISE ON THE SACRAMENTS (1633) urged: *Doe it more fully, toze your consciences.*

Shakespeare in THE WINTER'S TALE (1610) has: *Thinkest thou, for that I insinuate, or toaze from thee thy business, I am therefore no courtier?* Note also *tozy,* soft as teased wool; *toziness,* softness. Scott in ST. RONAN'S WELL (1824) said of a shawl: *I can tell it to be a real tozie. To tease* first (10th century) meant to pull the fibres apart, preparing for spinning; then, to tear to pieces; then, to persistently worry or annoy; finally (18th century, and still current), to bother slightly in mischief or sport. Also *teize, teaze, (cp. Lady Teazle), teez, tese. To touse* and its iterative form *to tousle* meant to tease wool; also, to pull about, handle roughly, *tussle.* It was also used figuratively, to fuss, stir around; Ford in HONOR TRIUMPHANT (1606) said: *I touze to gaine me fame and reputation.* Otway in THE SOULDIER'S FORTUNE (1681) smiled *to see a pretty wench and a young fellow touze and rouze and frouze and mouze.* Let us not tease this further.

tractatrix. A female shampooer. Latin *tractare, tractatus,* to handle, discuss; frequentative of *trahere, tractus,* to draw, drag. A *tract* or a *tractate* is a literary discussion; a *tractatule* is a short one. A *tractator* is one who handles or treats of a subject; but Martial (in Latin) used the feminine to refer to a person that handles a subject's head to wash the hair, and that sense came into English, as in M. and F. Collins' FRANCES (1874): *That stout Miss Cusanetta, with her shrill voice, and her hands of the tractatrix, is a strange creature.* The language offers us a strange tract o' tricks.

traditor. Traitor. Latin *tradere, traditum,* to hand over, deliver; *trans,* across + *dare,* give. *Traitor* is from the same source, via Old French. The Italian aphorism about literature, *traduttore, traditore,* translator, traitor, can almost be paralleled in English: *traductor, traditor.* But note that Latin *traditum,* handed over, also gave us English *tradition,* whence *traditive, traditious, traditory* are other forms for *traditional.* The verb *traduce* (Latin *traducere, traductum,* to lead across) has meant: to convey from one place to another; to translate; to pass on to offspring or posterity, hence, to transmit by propagation; also, to speak evil of and the other current senses. Davies on THE IMMORTALITY OF THE SOUL (1599) says of Nature: *For tho' from bodies she can bodies bring, yet could she never souls from souls traduce.* THE METROPOLIS (1819) declared: *To our sex, he is a very traditor, and . . . has planted thorns innumerable in the female breast.*

traductor. See *traditor.* Byron, in a note to DON JUAN (1823), commenting: *If there be any gem'man so ignorant as to require a traduction*—supplies one.

tralatitious. (1) Transferred; metaphorical, figurative. (2) Transferred from hand to hand, ordinary, commonplace. (3) Transferred from generation to generation, traditional; repeated by person after person. Latin *transferre, tralatum,* to bear across; whence also *transference* and many more *transfers.* Hence *tralation, tralatition,* metaphor, figurative use. Fuller in A PISGAH-SIGHT OF PALESTINE (1650) declared men *too often guilty of what may be termed tralatitious idolatry, when any thing . . . is loved or honoured above, or even with, God himself.* Holder in THE ELEMENTS OF SPEECH (1669), considering the etymology of the word *language,* said that 'language' properly refers to that of the tongue; *'written language' is tralatitiously so called.*

tranation. The act of swimming across; also, a crossing into another form, a metamorphosis. Latin *tranare, tranatum; trans,* across + *nare,* to swim. E. Gayton, in PLEASANT NOTES UPON DON QUIXOT (1654) states: *In his tranation he lookt about, and saw under him (though a farre off) his lord upon Rosinante, no bigger than a toad upon a ducking-stoole.*

tranect. A word occurring in Shakespeare's THE MERCHANT OF VENICE (1596): *Bring them, I pray thee, with imagin'd speed, Unto the tranect, to the common ferry Which trades in Venice.* The O.E.D. suggests this is an error, for *traject* (Latin *trans,* across + *jacere, jactum, to throw*). Nares, however, pictures the route from Padua: *There are four sluices leading from the Brenta into the Laguno of Venice, at the last of which there might be 'traino', or 'tranetto', a machine to draw the boat through the pass, and this might be rendered by some English writer 'tranect'.* No one since has used that method of reaching Venice.

translunary. Beyond the moon. The realm of El Dorado. In science, *translunary* is contrasted with *sublunary,* below the moon (that is, between moon and earth, or on the earth). Figuratively, *translunary* means fanciful, visionary. Thus Drayton, in 1627, declared that: *Neat Marlowe, bathèd in the Thespian springs, Had in him those brave translunary things That our first poets had: his raptures were All air and fire, which made his verses clear: For that fine madness still he did retain Which rightly should possess a poet's brain.* There is a hint here of the same linking as in Shakespeare's *The lunatic, the lover, and the poet Are of imagination all compact; lunatic* coming from *luna,* the moon, from the notion that mad folk are moon-struck.

transmew. A variant of *transmute* (from Latin *trans,* across + *mutare,* to change). Also *transmue.* Chaucer, in TROYLUS AND CRISEYDE (1375): *Thou must be first transmuwen in a stone.* Scott revived the form in THE MONASTERY (1820): *To cast my riding slough and transmew myself into some civil form.*

transumptive. Metaphorical, figurative. Latin *trans,* across + *sumere, sumptum,* to take; hence, also, to *assume, consume.* Also *transume,* to make an official copy of; to transfer, to convert, transmute. A *transumpt* was (legally) a copy of a record; hence, a reproduction of a work of art. Also *transumption;* a copying; a transfer; hence, a metaphor. *Metaphor* (Greek *meta,* across, beyond + *phor* from *pherein*) is the equivalent of *transfer, transume,* from the Latin. Lowell in AMONG MY BOOKS (1876) declares, speaking of Dante: *The form or mode of treatment, he says, is poetic, fictive, descriptive, digressive, transumptive.*

trape. To set down one's foot forcefully; hence, to tramp; to go about. Used from the 14th century; in the 17th century replaced by *trapes, traipse,* which is still current, *to go trapsing around. A trapse* was (17th into the 19th century; later in dialects) a gadabout; a slovenly woman. In 1749, Richardson wrote in a letter (4 August): *The lowest of all fellows, yet in love with a young creature who was traping after him.*

trattle. Idle talk, gossip, chatter. Also a verb. Used since the 14th century. Probably echoic, like *prattle; tattle.* The form *tattle,* which first meant to stammer, took over the sense of *trattle,* then replaced it. Thus *trittle-trattle* has been supplanted by *tittle-tattle,* which is still common, and usually commonplace. James I in his DEMONOLOGY (1597, when he was still but James VI of Scotland) spoke of *old womens trattles about the fire.* Further, discussing the false or *fourth kind of spirits, which by the Gentiles was called Diana and her wandering court, and amongst us was called the Phairy,* James said: *To speak of the many vain trattles founded upon that illusion: how there was a King and Queen of Phairy, of such a jolly court and train as they had . . . I think it liker Virgil's Campi Elysii nor anything that ought to be believed by Christians, except in general, that as I spake sundry times before, the Devil il-luded the senses of sundry simple creatures in making them believe that they saw and heard such things as were nothing so indeed.* There was a weaver in Shakespeare's A MIDSUMMER NIGHT'S DREAM (1594) that helped the fairy queen get to the bottom of the matter. Titania, the name of that queen, was used by Ovid as a title of Diana, who, as we note, is transformed from a goddess to a "phairy." The name *Titania* does not appear in Golding's translation, but Shakespeare, despite his "small Latin", found Titania for Oberon to tease with drops of love-in-idleness.

traulism. Stammering, especially at the beginning of a word. Greek *traulos,* mispronouncing, lisping. R. Harvey in PLAINE PERCEVALL THE PEACE-MAKER OF ENGLAND (1589) refers to the *so foorth following the traulila-lilismus, as farre as Will Solnes stuttring pronunciation may stumble over a breath.* THE WESTMINSTER GAZETTE (6 October, 1893) mentions *a professor of elocution who has caught a trick of stammering from those whom he has cured of traulism.*

travato. A twister, a sudden squall with swirling gusts of wind and rain. Also *travat.* Portuguese *travados,* whirlwind. Used from the 17th century.

traveler's joy. See *virgin's bower.* It would be.

tray-trip. See *treygobet.*

treacle. See *theriac.*

tread. As a noun. A footprint. A trodden way; a path; a way of life; Buckle in his essay on CIVILIZATION (1862) spoke of *conditions which determine the tread and destiny of nations.* Also, those that move on the routine paths of life; Chapman in his translation (1615) of the ODYSSEY: *the bread Which now he begg'd amongst the common tread.* Hence, a course or manner of behaving; custom; sometimes (16th and 17th centuries) used to mean trade, business. Also, the act of a male bird in intercourse; *a tread-fowl,* a male bird. Thus *the treadle,* the little membrane (chalaza) that holds the yolk of an egg in place; so called because it was thought to be the sperm; by extension, an egg. For this use, see *fraight; cp. tredefoule.*

treadfowl. See *tredefoule.*

treague. A truce. A form, via Medieval Latin *tragua, treuga,* from Gothic *triggwa;* see *treves.* This bears no relation to *intrigue,* which is via French from Latin *intricare, intricatum* (whence also English *intricate*) to entrap; *in* + *tricae,* tricks, traps (related to Latin *torquere,* to twist), whence also *extricate.* Spenser in THE FAËRIE QUEENE (1590) has: *Which to confirm, and fast to bind their league, After their weary sweat and bloody toile, She them besought, during their quiet treague, Into her lodging to repaire a while.*

trebuchet. (1) An engine of war, used in the middle ages for hurling heavy stones. Also *trabuch*; *trepejette, treybochet, trepeget, trebuke, trebuschet,* and the like. An early hybrid, of Latin *trans,* across + Old French *buc,* bulk, from West German *buh,* belly. (2) A trap to catch small birds and beasts. (3) An instrument for punishing women, a cucking-stool (*q.v.*), shaped like the catapult. (4) A tilting scale or balance for weighing. Southey in his JOAN OF ARC (1795) pictured a soldier *who kneeling by the trebuchet, Charged its long sling with death.*

tredefoule. A cock (tread a fowl). Listed by O.E.D. as *treadfowl.* Used by Chaucer in THE NUN'S PRIEST'S TALE (1386, *tredefoul*) and THE MONK'S TALE: *Thou wouldest han been a tredefowel aright.*

treen. Wooden; pertaining to or made from trees. Used from the year 1000. Spenser, in THE FAËRIE QUEENE (1590): *So left her, where she now is turned to treen mould.* (Spenser used the word as two-syllabled.) Evelyn in SYLVA (1670) declares *that a large tract of the world almost altogether subsist on these treen liquors; especially, that of the date.*

tregetry. Juggling; deception, trickery. Via Old French from a Latin form *trajectare* (whence *trajectory*); *trans,* across + *jactare,* to throw. Also *treget,* noun, and verb: to do juggling tricks; to deceive. Hence *tregetour, trygetour, tragetour, trigettur,* and many more (14th to 17th century), indicating the popularity of the juggler and mountebank. From its earliest use, the word was applied to a trickster, a deceiver. Scott revived the word in IVANHOE (1819); Bulwer-Lytton records in THE LAST OF THE BARONS (1843): *The more sombre tregetour . . . promised to cut off and refix the head of a sad-faced little boy.*

trelapser. See *trilapse.*

trencher. A knife or other cutting instrument (14th to 16th century). A flat piece of wood (later, also metal or earthenware) usually square or circular, on which meat was cut and served. The word is via Old French and popular Latin from Latin *truncare, truncatum,* to cut, lop off; *truncus,* the *trunk* of a tree. The word *trench* (from the 15th century) meant to cut; to cut into (Shakespeare, THE TWO GENTLEMEN OF VERONA, 1591: *This weake impress of love is as a figure Trench'd in ice*); to make (a cut) in (Shakespeare, VENUS AND ADONIS, 1592: *The wide wound, that the boar had trencht In his soft flank*). *To lick the trencher* (of someone), to toady. *A trencher-beard* is large and flat; *trencher-art,* that of the gourmet—or the glutton. *trencher-critic,* one who speaks fulsome praise (in return for which, he is made full at the table). *trencher-hero,* one valiant at the festive board; Peter Pindar, in THE CHURCHWARDEN (1792): *The trencher-heroes hate All obstacles that keep them from the plate;* also *trencher-knight* (Shakespeare, LOVE'S LABOUR'S LOST); and, in more democratic wise, *trencher-labourer,* and ultimately, *trencher-slave.* A *trencher-cap* (18th and early 19th century) was later called a *mortar-board:* the flat, square academic cap. *trencher-fly,* a parasite; also, *trencher-friend.* A *trencher-man,* in Sidney's ARCADIA (1586) was a cook; in Thackeray's PENDENNIS (1849), a dependent, hanger-on; usually it meant (with measure of admiration) a hearty eater, as in Shakespeare's MUCH ADO ABOUT NOTHING: *He's a very valiant trencher-man, he hath an excellent stomach.*

trencher-poetry. Rhymes to be traded for bread: verses written so as to secure the favors of a patron. For an instance of the use of the term, see *blowess.*

trepan. The current surgical *trepan,* from Greek *trepanon,* a borer, is unrelated to the 17th and 18th century *trepan,* of unknown origin, meaning to trick, to entrap; also, one who decoys persons to his advantage; a trick or trap. This meaning also uses the form *trapan, trappan;* it may be related to *trap.* A title of 1653 read: *The Total Rout, or a Brief Discovery of a Pack of Knaves and Drabs, intituled Pimps, Panders, Hectors, Trapans, Nappers, Mobs, and Spanners.*

tressilate. To thrill; to start with quick emotion, as surprise or joy. French *tressaillir,* to thrill, tremble; Laitn *trans,* across + *salire,* to jump. D. C. Murray in A DANGEROUS CATSPAW (1889) wrote: *The ladies tressilated deliciously. The crime began to take an air of romance.*

tretis. Well-proportioned, graceful. Via Old French from a popular Latin form *tracticius,* slender, from Latin *trahere, tractum,* to draw, draw out. Also *tretys, traytice, tretise, trety.* [Note that *tretys* is also an early variant of *treatise.*] Chaucer, in the Prologue to THE CANTERBURY TALES (1386), describes the Prioress: *Her nose tretys, her eyen greye as glas.*

treves. A 15th and 16th century form (Old English *trewes;* Gothic *triggwa,* covenant; *triggws,* true, sure. See *treague.*) of *truce.* Hence *trew,* to protect by a truce.

trew. A variant form of *true.* Spenser in THE FAËRIE QUEENE (1590) notes: *And there beside of marble stone was built An altare carv'd with cunning ymagery, On which trew Christians blood was often spilt. Cp. treves.*

trewage. A 13th to 16th century form of *tribute.* Also used of a toll-fee, or a payment for a privilege. Also *truage, truwage, trowage, triwage, trywage.* The word is via Old French from Latin *tribuere, tributum,* to assign, give, yield; ultimately from *tribus,* tribe, division of the people (originally, like all Gaul, divided into three parts); *tres* (*tribus,* dative), three. Hence, *trewager,* one expected to pay tribute.

treygobet. A dice game which starts with a throw of three; *trey go bet,* literally three go better. Played in the 15th and 16th centuries. *Trey* (*treye, trye, tray*) Old French *treis, trei*; French *trois.* Chaucer in THE PARDONER'S TALE (1386): *Sevene is my chaunce, and thyn is cynk* [*cinq,* five] *and treye.* In Shakespeare's LOVE'S LABOUR'S LOST (1594) Berowne and the Princess talk in rhyme. Berowne: *White-handed mistress, one sweet word with thee.* Princess: *Honey, and milk, and sugar—there is three.* Ber: *Nay then, two treyes, an if you grow so nice, Metheglin, wort, and malmsey. Well run, dice! There's half a dozen sweets.* Prin: *Seventh sweet, adieu.* Also *trey-trip* (*tray-trip; trei-trip, tretrip, tratrip*) a game in which a toss of *trey* won. In TWELFTH NIGHT Sir Toby Belch inquires: *Shall I play my freedom at tray-trip, and become thy bond-slave?*

triglot. A book in three languages. Also (as adjective) in, or competent in, three languages.

trigon. A triangle. Hence *trigonal,* triangular. Greek *tri,* three + *gonos,* cornered. Especially, in astrology, three signs of the zodiac 120 degrees apart, or a conjunction of three planets within one sign. In Shakespeare's HENRY IV, PART TWO (1598), when Falstaff kisses Doll Tearsheet, Prince Hal exclaims: *Saturn and Venus* *this year in conjunction! What says the almanac to that?* Poins: *And look whether the fiery trigon, his man, be not lisping to his master's old tables, his notebook, his counsel-keeper.* The *fiery trigon* was Aries, Leo, and Sagittarius; the *tables . . . notebook* mean Dame Quickly.

trilapse. A third fall into sin. Used as an adjective also, in the 16th and 17th century. J. Mill in his DIARY (1776) remarked: *This being a relapse to the woman and a trelapse to the man.* Latin *re,* again; *tri,* three + *lapsus,* fall, slip, lapse. Hence also *trilapser*; a church regulation of 1649 required that *trelapsers in fornication be brought before the Presbyterie.*

tripsome. Light-footed, nimble. A 19th century term; Catherine G. F. Gore in SKETCHES OF ENGLISH CHARACTER (1846) said: *He beholds the tripsome feet of Lady Clementina flit by him.* The verb *trip* first meant to tread lightly or nimbly; as Milton called in L'ALLEGRO (1632): *Come, and trip it as ye go On the light fantastic toe,* and a year later in ARCADES: *Nymphs and Shepherds dance no more . . . Trip no more in twilight ranks.* Hence *trip* is another word that means its own opposite: to step nimbly; to stumble; *cp. avaunt.*

tripudiation. The act of leaping or dancing for joy; exultation; although to J. Johnson in THE CLERGYMAN'S VADE MECUM (1709) came other thoughts: *The word implies tripudiation, or immodest dancing.* Also, a divination or prophesying from the behavior of fowl (especially the sacred chickens of the ancient Roman temples) when fed. Hence *tripudiary,* relating to such divination, or to dancing. *tripudial, tripudiant,* relating to dancing. Hence, a *tripudist.* Ultimately from Latin *tri,* three + Greek *pod,* foot, as when skipping or dancing. From the 17th into the 19th century, *tripudiate* meant to leap with excitement or joy; to stamp or trample (upon) in scorn or triumph. THE SATURDAY REVIEW of 5 May, 1888, observed: *On poor Colonel Slade . . . he tripudiates with all the chivalry of the 'varray perfit gentil knight' of controversy that he is.*

triquet. A set of verses arranged so that the outer edges of the lines form a triangle. Puttemham in THE ART OF ENGLISH POESIE (1589) tells: *A certain great Sultan of Persia called Ribuska entertaynes in love the Lady Selamour, sent her this triquet reverst pitiously bemoaning his estate, . . . To which Selamour, to make the match egall, and the figure entire, answered in a standing triquet.* A *triquet reversed* has the base on top; Selamour made "the figure entire" (the two poems forming a parallelogram) by a triangle with the point on top.

triquetrous. Triangular. Also *triquetral* (long *i*; accent on the *kwet*). Sir Thomas Browne in THE GARDEN OF CYRUS (1658) commented on the *figured pavements of the ancients, which consisted not all of square stones, but were divided into triquetrous segments.*

triskele. A figure consisting of three legs, or curved lines, joined, as though whirling. Greek *tri* + *skelos,* leg. Also *triskelion, triskelos*; *triskele* has two syllables. THE ATHENAEUM of 27 June, 1885, mentions *panels, on which were sculptured designs such as the 'sunsnake,' the swastika, and the triskele.*

trist. A 12th to 15th century form of *trust.* Also, an appointed waiting-place in the hunt; hence, a rendezvous. In the last sense, the word continued in the form *tryst,* with such phrases as *to make (set) tryst; to hold (keep) tryst; to break (crack) tryst. To bide tryst* is to wait for the other party to the meeting. *To trist,* to have confidence in, to trust, to believe; to hope. Wholly separate, via French from Latin *tristis,* sad, came another *trist,* sad, melancholy; also the noun *tristesse.* A York Mystery of 1440 called: *Hail! talker trystful* [trustworthy] *of trew tales!* Shakespeare in HAMLET (1602) says: *This solidity and compound mass, With tristfull visage as against the doome, Is thought-sicke at the act.* So too *tristily,* faithfully, surely (Chaucer)—later, sorrowfully.

tristiloquy. Mournful speech; a sad manner of speaking. Also *tristisonous,* of mournful sound. *Cp. trist.*

tritical. Trite, commonplace. (A good word, lost to the critical spirit.) Hence also *triticism,* a trite utterance or writing. Swift in 1709 wrote: *A Tritical Essay upon the Faculties of the Mind.* Disraeli in THE AMENITIES OF LITERATURE (1841) has: *To sermonise with a tedious homily or a tritical declamation.* Hence also *triticalness, triticality.* What some call a witticism a more discerning criticism might label as a triticism.

trittle-trattle. This reduplicative form of *trattle (q.v.),* idle talk (16th century), came later to be used of gewgaws, silly trifles, as when Crockett in THE GREY MAN (1896) spoke of the *buying of trittle-trattles at the lucky booths* of a fair.

trivet. A three-footed support, a tripod, Hence, a pot or other vessel with three 'feet' as supports. Via Old French from Latin *tri + pedem,* foot (the Greek form, *pod,* gives us *tripod*). Also *trefet, trevette, tryvett,* and the like. From the way it always stands firm on its own three feet came the expression *right as a trivet; cp. couth*—although Dryden in his translation (1700; BAUCIS) of Ovid's METAMORPHOSES recorded that *The trivet-table of a foot was lame.*

trivial. (1) Relating to the *trivium,* the lower division of the seven liberal arts studied in the medieval university: grammar, rhetoric, and logic. [The *quadrivium,* the higher division, comprised the mathematical sciences: arithmetic, geometry, astronomy, and music. Thus, the *quadrivial* arts. *Quadrivial* was also used of a point where four roads meet; *quadrivious,* going in four directions.] (2) Three-fold; triple. (3) Relating to a meeting of three roads. From this as a point where gossips also met, and news was exchanged, came the current senses of *trivial,* commonplace, inconsequential.

trochomancy. See *aeromancy.*

trophonian. Rendering forever sad. The temple of Apollo at Delphi was built by (the legendary) *Trophonios,* who after death was worshipped as a god. His oracle, in a cave in Boeotia, was so awe-inspiring that those that entered (like the King in the ballad) never smiled again. Thus Gosse in THE CONTEMPORARY REVIEW of January 1896 said: *His face had the solemn trophonian pallor.*

troth. An early and very common variant of *truth,* surviving in such expressions as *to plight one's troth; by my troth.* Also *trothful, trothless; troth-plight,* betrothal; a solemn engagement or promise.

troublable. An early variant for *troublesome;* Chaucer, in BOETHIUS (1374), speaks of the *trowblable ire that arayseth in hym.* Also *troublish, troublous, troubly; trouble* was an adjective as well as a noun, 14th and 15th centuries; again BOETHIUS; *The trouble wind that hight Auster.* Maundeville (1400) tells that *There is a well that iiij sithes* (times) *in the year chaungeth his colour: somtyme grene, somtyme red, somtyme cleer, & somtyme trouble.* Also *troublance, troubledness, troublement,* the act of troubling or state of being troubled. Although this volume may at times be abstruse, there is no trouble meant.

trow. (1) Faith, belief; pledged faith, covenant; fancy, supposition. (2) A boat or barge, a variant of *trough.* (3) Toll, *trewage, q.v.* (4) A variant of *troll,* a malevolent spirit; especially, the *sea-trow. To trow* is to trust, believe; the noun is *troth, q.v.* Hence *trowable,* credible. For *trowandise,* see *truandise.* The expression *I trow,* I believe, grew weak, and was often used to mean I suppose (I hope), or just to emphasize a question, as in Shakespeare's THE MERRY WIVES OF WINDSOR (1598): *Who's there, I troa?*

Troytown. A scene or sound of confusion. The name is taken from Troy in Asia Minor, to which it was more than confusion Helen brought. Also *Troy-fair;* sometimes just *Troy.* Otway in FRIENDSHIP IN FASHION (1678) said ironically: *And for the cittern, if ever Troy Town were a tune, he master'd it upon that instrument.* Also, a labyrinth, a maze. Wright (1859) explains the notion that *Troy was a town which had but one gate, and that it was necessary to go through every street to get to the market-place. They call a garden laid out spirally a city of Troy.*

truage. See *trewage.*

truandise. Idleness; begging; vagabondage; knavery. The definitions sound like a rogue's progress; page Hogarth. Also *trowandise, trewandyse, truantisse,* and the like. The earliest sense of *truant* was one that begs without need, an idle rogue. The word is related to Gaelic *truaghan,* wretched. The word truant (as any schoolboy knows) was often used as a loose term of abuse, as in Shakespeare's MUCH ADO ABOUT NOTHING (1599): *Hang him truant, there's no true drop of blood in him to be truly toucht with love.*

truchman. An interpreter. Via French *trucheman* and Medieval Latin *truchemannus* from the Arabic *turjaman; targama,* to translate; whence also the collection of Old Testament versions known as the *targum;* also *dragoman,* a current term in the Near East for a professional guide and interpreter. Hence also *truchwoman; truchmanry,* the function of an interpreter. The popularity of the word, in the 15th, 16th, and 17th centuries, is shown by its many forms, which include *tourcheman, truceman, trounchman, trunchman, treuchman, trudgeman.* Lord Berners in his translation (1525) of Froissart said: *They . . . toke a truchman that coulde speke Italyan, and commanded hym to go to the crysten host.* The word was also used figuratively; James I (1585) called poets *Dame Natures trunchmen;* Suckling in AGLAURA (1637) protested: *Our soules . . . will not need that duller truchman Flesh.*

trucidation. Savage slaughtering. Latin *trucidare,* for *trucicaedere; trucem,* ferocious + *caedere,* to cut down, to kill. See *stillicide.* In dictionaries from the 17th century; Stevenson, in a letter of 1883, uses it humorously: *I loathe the snails; but from loathing to actual butchery, trucidation of multitudes, there is still a step that I hesitate to take.* More grimly, one may wish there were less trucidation in the world.

truckle. Originally, a pulley wheel; a castor on furniture. Latin *trochlea,* Greek *trochilia; trochlea* is used in anatomy of a pulley-like structure, such as that at the elbow-joint. Hence, a *truckle-bed,* trundle-bed, a low bed on truckles; pushed under another, the "standing" bed, when not in use. Such a *truckle* was usually used for personal servants. Hence (17th century), *to truckle,* to sleep in such a bed; *to truckle under.* From this developed the meaning to be subservient, to submit, to act servilely, *to truckle to.* Shakespeare in THE MERRY WIVES OF WINDSOR (1598) says: *There's his chamber, his house, his castle, his standing-bed and truckle-bed.* Bishop Hall (SATIRE 6, Book 2; 1597) named conditions under which a 'trencher-chaplain' might be engaged to tutor a squire's sons: *First, that he lie upon the truckle-bed Whiles his yong maister lieth ore his hed. I should be a base truckler,* we read in George Eliot's MIDDLEMARCH (1872) *if I allowed any consideration of personal comfort to hinder me.*

truefast. Faithful. Used from the 10th century. In Lydgate's BALLAD OF OUR LADY (Thynne's edition of Chaucer; 1532) we read: *O trustie turtle truefastest of all true.*

trueful. Full of truth and loyalty. An early form for *truthful.*

truehead. Faithfulness.

true-love. A faithful lover. Sidney in ARCADIA (1586) knew the bond: *My true-love hath my heart, and I have his.* Hence, *true-love knot,* an ornamental bow, of two loops intertwined, used as a symbol of true love. Also, *true-love's knot, true lover's knot.*

true-lovers' knot. See *Hymen's torch.*

trueman. A faithful and trustworthy man. Obsolete since the 17th century.

truepenny. An honest fellow. Used in the 16th and 17th century. Shakespeare calls the ghost, in HAMLET (1602) *Art thou there, truepenny?* Occasionally used (probably as an echo of Shakespeare) in the 19th century, usually for a trusty old fellow: *Old Truepenny.*

trueship. Faithfulness (12th and 13th centuries).

truff. A cheating; later (15th to 17th century) a jest or idle tale. As a verb, to deceive; to obtain by deceit, to steal; to trifle with. Hence *truffery,* a mockery, a trifle. Caxton in THE GOLDEN LEGEND (1483) printed: *In the same errour Austyn fylle . . . and was brought to byleve the truffes and japes.* In the 17th century, *truff* was sometimes used for *truffle,* that delicacy celebrated by Pope in the DUNCIAD (1742): *Thy truffles, Perigord! thy hams, Bayonne!* Sparry in his translation (1591) of Cattan's GEOMANCY observed that *the topas and the truffle have power of chastity, and to subdue the flesh.* Methinks Cattan was truffing us.

trug. (1) A trull; prostitute. Also *truck; trugmallion, trugmullion.* Greene in A QUIP FOR AN UPSTART COURTIER (1592) said: *You, Tom tapster . . . have your trugges to draw men on to villainie.* Hence, *trugging-house,* a brothel. (2) A shallow pan for milk, used to let the cream separate. A shallow basket of wooden strips, with a handle across the top, for carrying fruit and vegetables. In the 14th century, a measure of wheat, two-thirds of a bushel. Hence *trug-corn, trug-wheat,* a measure of such grain as a tithe, to a vicar or local priest.

trusatile. Worked by pushing; like certain types of mill (such as blind Samson pushed). Latin *trusare, trusatum,* frequentative of *trudere, trusum,* whence also *intrude, intrusive, obtrude* and other thrustings.

trusion. In the 17th century, illegal entry; also, the action of pushing. Latin *trudere, trusum,* to push, whence also an unwelcome *intrusion* and an *abstruse* remark.

trutination. A weighing; consideration. Latin *trutinare, trutinatum; trutina,* from Greek *trutane,* balance. Hence also *trutinate,* to weigh (mentally), to consider. The words were rather common in the 16th and 17th centuries; in that period, too, astrologers said that the first way of rectifying a nativity was by *the trutine or scrutiny of Hermes.* Alas, as John Foxe pointed out in THE BOOK OF MARTYRS (1570), *human fragilitie suffereth not all thinges to bee pondered, trutinate, and weyed in just balance.*

truttaceous. Relating to the trout, like many anglers' tales . . . truttaceous broilings.

tryews. An old form of *truce.*

tryfellys. An old variant of *trifles,* plural of *trifle,* also *tryefull.*

tryst. See *trist.*

tuant. Killing; especially of language, biting, keen, cutting. Directly from the French in the 17th century: *tuant,* present participle of *tuer,* to kill; Latin root *tud,* to beat. Villiers, in THE REHEARSAL (1672): *Ay, I gad, but is not that tuant now, Ha? is it not tuant?* And Marvell, in THE REHEARSAL TRANSPROSED (1672): *Mr. Bayes is more civil than to say Villain and Caitiff, though these indeed are more tuant.*

tub. Used in various combinations or special senses: a covered carriage (19th century); also, *tub-gig, tub-cart. tub-fast,* abstinence during treatment in the *sweating tub, q.v.* below. *A tale of a tub,* a cock and bull story. *To throw out a tub to the whale,* to create a diversion in order to escape. *Every tub must stand on its own bottom.* Also, a *tub, sweating-tub, Doctors tub, cleansing tub, powdering-tub, Mother Cornelius' tub*: a tub in which a person afflicted with venereal disease sat lengthily, sweating and fasting. Since beef was also salted down, or powdered in a tub, writers played upon the two practices, as Shakespeare in MEASURE FOR MEASURE (1603): Lucio: *How doth my deere morsel, thy Mistris? Procures shee still? Ha?* Pompey: *Troth, sir, shee hath eaten up all her beefe, and she is her selfe in the tub.* And in TIMON OF ATHENS Shakespeare refers to both aspects of the treatment: *Season the slaves For tubs and baths; bring down rose-cheeked youth To the tub-fast and the diet.*

tubicination. The sounding of a trumpet. (Accent on the *neigh.*) Latin *tuba,* trumpet + *canere,* to sing, play. Hence, *tubicinate* (accent on the *bis*). No encores, please!

tubster. A contemptuous term for a preacher, especially a dissenting, peripatetic, exhortatory, and often hell-fire exponent of the Gospel. Also a *tubman, tub-preacher, tub-thumper.* All of these forms were common in the 17th century; thus T. Flatman in HERACLITUS RIDENS (1681; Heraclitus was 'the laughing philosopher') spoke of *a certain dissenting tubster, who told his audience he would . . . divide the observations he should make from his text, into forty-eight particulars.*

tucker. Originally (13th century) one that worked at fulling and dressing cloth.

Tucker's earth, fuller's earth. Other meanings came much later: (17th century), a piece of lace worn by women tucked in or around the top of the bodice; *Some of the girls have two clean tuckers in the week,* says Charlotte Brontë in JANE EYRE (1847); *the rules limit them to one.* Hence, *one's best bib and tucker*; see bib. Also, an instrument for tucking or plucking; a *pair of tuckers,* tweezers. *A tucker up* (to an old bachelor), a serving-maid who may well be a mistress. (19th century, colonial): daily rations taken along by a worker; *to earn one's tucker,* to earn about enough for one's keep.

tucket. A flourish or signal on a trumpet. Stage directions in Shakespeare's RICHARD II (1595); in HENRY V: *Then let the trumpets sound the tucket.* Also used figuratively; Meredith in ONE OF OUR CONQUERORS (1891) states: *A tucket of herald newspapers told the world of Victor's returning to his London.*

tugury. A hut; a (hermit's) cell. Latin *tugurium,* hut, shelter; root *teg,* cover. Also *tigurye, tygurie, tugurry.* Caxton's THE GOLDEN LEGEND (1483) exclaims: *O blessyd tygurie or lytyl hous!*

tumbester. A female tumbler or dancer, 13th to 15th century. Also *tumblester, tombester, tombistere.* From French *tomber,* to fall, probably of Norse origin; perhaps affected in some of its forms by *somersault,* which is via French from Latin *super,* above + *saltus,* leap. Chaucer has, in THE PARDONER'S TALE (1386): *And right anon thanne comen tomblesteres.* Herodias' daughter (Salomé), said a 15th century manuscript, *was a tumbestere, and tumblede byfore him and other grete lordes.*

tumbrel. (1) A medieval instrument for punishments, perhaps like a cucking-stool, *q.v.* Also *tumbril; tombrel, tumberell, tumrell, tumril, timbrell,* and more. (2) A cart built so that the body tilts back to dump its load; especially, a dung cart. Used (as in Dickens' A TALE OF TWO CITIES; 1859) of the carts that carried the condemned to the guillotine. (3) By transference, a person; especially, one full or drunk to vomiting. *Good lack!* in this sense cries Congreve in THE WAY OF THE WORLD (1700), *What shall I do with this beastly tumbril?* Fabyan in his CHRONICLES (1494) recorded: *myllers for stelyng of corne to be chastysed by ye tumbrell.*

tundish. A funnel; a shallow vessel with a tube at the bottom that fits into a bung-hole. Used in brewing, or in pouring liquids, gunshot, etc. The word was used figuratively, with sexual implications (from the funnel shape) of Claudio's arrest for lechery, in Shakespeare's MEASURE FOR MEASURE (1603). Duke: *Why should he die?* Lucio: *Why, for filling a bottle with a tundish.* A *tun* was a large cask or vat; the word is related to *tunnel.* A *tundish* is a *dish* equipped with a *funnel,* for filling a *tun.*

turb. A crowd; a heap; a troop; a clump of trees. Latin *turba,* crowd, which was likely to be *turbulent.* Latin *turbare,* to move in disorder, whirl; *disturb*; *cp. couth.* Hence also *turbine.* Watson in THE SHIP OF FOOLS (1509) said: *A great turbe of fools fleeth to our shyppe.*

turdefy. To turn into excrement. Old English *tord,* excrement; later *toord, torde, tourd, turd.* Hence *turdy,* befouled with ordure; relating to excrement. *Turd* was used from the 13th to the 17th century as a symbol of worthlessness; *Alle thingis,* said Wyclif (1382), *I deme as toordis, that I wynne Crist.* Note however that *turdiform* means looking like a thrush; Latin *turdus,* thrush.

turken. To alter for the worse, distort, pervert; then, more generally, to change, transform, refashion. Possibly through the French from Latin *torquere,* to twist; but more probably from *Turk,* as the Turks changed Christian temples into mosques, and Bible stories in Koran tales. Also *turkess, torcaese, turkeise, turkis, turkize, turcase.* Gascoigne in THE STEELE GLAS (1575) declared: *This poeticall license is a shrewde fellow . . . it maketh wordes longer, shorter, of mo sillables, of fewer; newer, older . . . and to conclude it turkeneth all things at pleasure.* Gabriel Harvey (MARGINALIA, 1577) mentioned *Eramus three cheafist paper bookes . . . his similes . . . apothegges . . . proverbs, newly turkissed.*

turmentise. An old variant of *torment.*

turtle. Short for the *turtle-dove.* The word *turtle* was probably originally echoic; Latin *turtur.* It was often used to symbolize marital tenderness and constancy, as by Shakespeare in THE WINTER'S TALE (1611; IV iv 154). Hence (Jonson, EVERY MAN IN HIS HUMOUR; 1598) *the happy state of turtle-billing lovers*; and affectionate lovers, as in Shakespeare's LOVE'S LABOUR'S LOST, were often amusedly called *turtles. cp. soote.* The best known literal use of the word is in THE SONG OF SOLOMON (BIBLE; King James' Version; 1611): *For lo! the winter is past, the rain is over and gone; the flowers appear on the earth; the time of the singing of birds is come, and the voice of the turtle is heard in our land.*

tussy. See *tuzzymuzzy.* John Done in his translation (1633) of Aristeas' AUNCIENT HISTORIE OF THE SEPTUAGINT recorded that *the master goldsmiths had laboured a girdle of flowers, and tussies of all fruits.*

tutament. A means of defence; a safeguard. Latin *tutamentum,* protection; *tutari,* to protect. Used in the 17th century.

tut-mouthed. With protruding lips; with a projecting lower jaw. Also *tute-mowitt.* From *toot,* one early meaning of which was to protrude (as lips do when tooting on a horn) + *mouth.* Dunbar in a poem of 1520 speaks of *my ladye with the mekle lippis . . . tute mowitt lyk an aip.*

tuzzymuzzy. A nosegay, a bunch of flowers. Hence, a silver or gold ornament shaped like flowers, leaves, or fruit, forming a buckle, a brooch, or the like. Also *tussy; tusmose, tussemose, tussie-mussie.* Golding in his translation (1587) of P. de Mornay's WOORKE CONCERNING THE TREWNESSE OF THE CHRISTIAN RELIGION told of Apollo's ordering *to remove the tuzzimuzzies of flowers from his feet.*

twank. See *twink.*

twiggen. Made of *twigs* or wickerwork. Also, arising from burning twigs and brushwood. Also *twiggy.* A *twiggen bottle,* one (as for much Chianti wine, today) covered with straw or wickerwork; Horatio Smith in TOR HILL (1826) exclaims: *What, neighbor Stiles, pawn thy wedding ring to fill the twiggen bottle!* Shakespeare had other filling in mind, in OTHELLO (1604): *Ile beat the knave into a twiggen bottle!* Morris in his translation (1875) of the AENEID pictures the moment *when with a mighty roar the twiggen flame goes up about the hollow side of brass.*

twigger. A prolific breeder; applied originally to a ewe. Hence, a lascivious person; especially, a strumpet. From the verb *twig,* to work vigorously. The word was common among late 16th and early 17th century playwrights: Marlowe and Nashe in THE TRAGEDY OF DIDO, QUEEN OF CARTH-

AGE (1594) say: *Go, you wag! You'll be a twigger when you come to age.*

twink. In addition to meaning to wink the eye, or to twinkle, or to tinkle, *twink* meant to chastise (by word or blow). Also *twank,* to spank. Both words seem echoic in origin. Elizabeth Carter ended a letter (1747): *I have been called away ten times, and shall be twinked if I do not leave you.* A year later, she *wrote a twinkation to Mr. Richardson about it, to which I received so civil an answer that I knew not how to be angry.*

twire. A glance, a leer. Also a verb, to peer, to peep. Also (both noun and verb) a variant of *twirl;* Burton in THE ANATOMY OF MELANCHOLY (1628) observes: *No sooner doth a young man see his sweetheart coming, but he . . . slickes his hair, twires his beard . . . Cp. twirk.* In SONNET 28, Shakespeare has: *When sparkling stars twire not thou guild'st th'eaven.* Steele, in THE CONSCIOUS LOVERS (1722) declares: *If I was rich, I could twire and loll as well as the best of them.*

twirk. A variant form of *twirl.* (The O.E.D. suggests that both *twire* and *twirk,* used in this sense, are misprints.) Breton, IN PRAISE OF VERTUOUS LADIES (1599): *If shee have her hand on the pette in her cheeke, he is twyrking of his mustachios.* The idea in *twirk* seems to be a combination of a *twirl* and a *tug.*

tympany. A swelling, as of pregnancy or pride. In NEWS FROM PURGATORY (1590) we read: *The maid fell sicke, and her disease was thought to be a timpany with two heels.* Burton in THE ANATOMY OF MELANCHOLY (1621): *Puffed with this timpany of self-conceit.* Addison extended the term to the effect of hoopskirts (SPECTATOR, No. 127; 1711), hoping *to unhoop the fair sex, and cure this fashionable tympany that is got among them.* Also used for *tympan, typanum,* a drum or similar instrument. Hence *timpanize, tympanize*: (1) to make swell (for an instance of this use, see *pagled*); (2) to beat on a drum; (3) to torture by stretching on the rack (as a skin on a drumhead). This is probably a misinterpretation of a passage in the BIBLE (HEBREWS 11, 35), which more probably means beaten to death (as with drumsticks). Hence *tympanism,* the state of being distended or swollen, as with pregnancy, pride, or gas; the beating to death with cudgels. In the 13th century, *timp,* a tambourine. Also *tympanous, tympanious,* swollen, inflated, bombastic; hollow, vain. Greek *tympanismos,* a beating of drums; *tympan* is probably echoic in origin, though without thought of Tin Pan Alley.

tyne. See *tine.*

tyromancy. See *aeromancy.* Greek *tyros,* cheese. Urquhart in his translation (1693) of Rabelais sought for the truth through *tyromancy, whereof we make some proof in a great Brehemont cheese.*

tytetuste. A posy, a *tuzzymuzzy, q.v.* This form was used in the 15th century. In the early 19th century *tistytosty* was also used of a nosegay; but apparently this word is related to *toss,* and the bunch of flowers was tossed to and fro in a sort of game, also called *tistytosty* (*teesty-tosty*). In the 16th century, however, *tistytosty* was used (1) as a refrain: *I shall be a lively lad, with hey tistye tosty.* (2) as a name for a bully, a blusterer.

U

uberate. To make fruitful or plentiful; to give suck, to nourish. Latin *uber,* udder. Hence *uberant,* abundant; A GAG FOR THE POPE (1624) has: *Like uberant springs to send forth flowing streams of truth into* the world. Also *uberous,* abundant, rich in milk (of breasts or udders); Robert Naunton in FRAGMENTA REGALIA (1635) declared: *My Lord . . . drew in too fast, like a child sucking on an over-uberous nurse.* Also, *uberousness, uberty,* fruitfulness, abundance. Evelyn in SYLVA (1706) speaks of *the uberous cloud.* Sir Thomas Herbert in A RELATION OF SOME YEARS TRAVAILE . . . INTO AFRIQUE AND THE GREATER ASIA (1634) reports that *the women give their infants suck as they hang at their backes, the uberous dugge stretched over her shoulder.*

ubiquarian. One that goes everywhere. The ANNUAL REGISTER of 1767 remarked: *The English being by their nature ubiquarians.* Latin *ubi,* place; *ubique,* everywhere. As an adjective, *ubiquarian,* that goes everywhere or is experienced or encountered everywhere: *the ubiquarian house sparrow.* Also, *ubication,* the fact of being in a place; *ubiation,* being in a (new) place. From 1600 to 1750 *ubi* was frequently used in English, meaning place, location; Sir Kenelm Digby in his treatise ON THE NATURE OF BODIES (1644) stated: *It is but assigning an ubi to such a spirit and he is presently* [immediately] *riveted to what place you please; and by multiplying the ubies . . .* Hence, *ubiety,* condition with respect to place; thus Bailey in THE MYSTIC (1855) spoke of *magic haschisch, which endows thought with ubiety.* Shakespeare used other powers to give to airy nothings ubiety—a local habitation and a name.

ughten. The dusk just before dawn. Also *ughtentide, ughtening,* the dawning. The *ughten-song, uhtsong,* was the religious service just before daybreak; matins. Lingard in his study of THE ANGLO-SAXON CHRONICLE (1844) stated that *the night-song . . . was frequently joined with the uhtsong;* Juliet protested it was the nightingale and not the lark.

ugsome. horrid, loathsome. Frequent almost to the 17th century; revived by Scott in THE ANTIQUARY (1816): *Like an auld dog that trails its useless ugsome carcass into some bush or bracken.* Then used by Bulwer-Lytton and Browning. Also *ugglesome; uglisome* (16th century); *cp. yglesome.* A stronger form of *ugly* (which Chaucer in THE CLERK'S TALE, 1386, spells *igly*).

uliginous. Moist, damp, slimy. Latin *uliginem,* moisture. Also *uliginose. Uliginal,* growing in moist ground. Used in the 16th and 17th centuries, though Smyth's SAILOR'S WORD-BOOK of 1867 lists *uliginous channels: those connecting the branches of rivers, by cuts through the soil.*

ullage. (1) The amount of wine (or other liquor) needed to fill the empty space in an almost full cask (because of loss by leakage or absorption). This is, more specifically, the *dry ullage.* Wine *on ullage* is wine in a cask not full. (2) The amount of wine in a partially filled cask; more specifically, this is the *wet ullage.* In the 19th century, the word was used for wine left in glasses or bottles; THE PALL MALL GAZETTE of 21 August, 1889, queried: *"Pray what is ullage?" "The washings out of casks," replied my friend.* The word has been in use since the 13th century.

ultion. Vengeance. Latin *ulcisci, ultus,* to punish, to avenge oneself on. Richard Tomlinson in his translation (1657) of Renodaeus' MEDICINAL DISPENSATORY, fairly enough declares that *a medicament . . . should leave in the mouth the ultion of the fault therein committed.* Sir Thomas Browne in CHRISTIAN MORALS (1682) reminds us that *to do good for evil is a soft and melting ultion, a method taught from Heaven to keep all smooth on earth.*

um-. Around. A number of verbs employed this prefix, from the 13th to the 16th century. Among them were *umgive, umgo, umlap, umlay, umlouk, umset*—all of which meant to surround, enclose, encompass. *Umgang,* the act of going around; hence, the distance thus covered, the circumference, circuit. A fuller form of the prefix was *umb-, umbe-,* as in: *umbcast,* to surround; *umbfold,* to embrace, *umblay,* to wrap around; *umbecast,* to surround, to meditate; *umbeclip,* to encircle; *umbethink,* to think about, to call to mind. There was a lot of encircling in those years; other verbs meaning to enclose, surround, included: *umbego, umbelap, umbelay, umbeset*; also, *umbefold, umbegang, umbegive, umbepitch, umbereach, umberun, umbestand, umbeswey, umbetigh, umbewalt. umbecarve, umbeshear,* to circumcise. *umbe* was also an adverb and a preposition, meaning around, about. In THE DESTRUCTION OF TROY (1400) we read that *umbe the sercle of the citie was sothely a playne.*

umbrage. See *couth*; *cp. patulous.* French *ombrage, ombre*; Latin *umbra,* shadow, whence also *umbrageous*—seldom used now save in humor, as when the sycophantic fox stood beneath the tree's umbrageous limb to seduce the gullible raven. Hence also *umbrosity* (17th century), the state of being shady; *umbrate, umbrous, umbrose. Umbratile* meant shady, shadowlike; living in retirement, 'in the shade'; hence, not public, secret. Also *umbratilous,* shadowy, faint; unreal. Doughty in ARABIA DESERTA (1888): *Many thus are umbratiles in the booths, and give themselves almost to a perpetual slumber.* Also *umbratic,* shadowy; foreshadowing; secluded; *umbratical,* remaining in seclusion; Jonson in DISCOVERIES (1636) said: *So I can see whole volumes dispatch'd by the umbraticall doctors on all sides.* Note that *umbrageous* meant not only abounding in shadow but (after the secondary sense of *umbrage,* from the 16th century) suspicious, quick to take offence. Thus Donne in a sermon of 1630 declared: *At the beginning some men were a little ombrageous, and startling at the name of the Fathers;* and George Digby exclaimed in ELVIRA (1667): *What power meer appearances have had . . . to destroy, With an umbragious nature, all that love Was ever able . . . To found and to establish.*

un-. Most of the words with the prefix *un-,* not, are easily understood. Note, however, *unhouseled,* not having had the last rites (the Eucharist) administered. Thus

Shakespeare in HAMLET; see *housel. unirrooted* (16th century), not eradicated. *unlede* (13th to 17th century), miserable, wicked; also, a vile or detestable person. *unleeful* (Chaucer), unlawful, illicit; also *unleesome. unlove,* to cease loving; Chaucer, in TROYLUS AND CRISEYDE (1374): *I ne kan . . . within myn herte fynde To unloven you. unlust,* distress; weariness, lack of appetite; slothfulness. *unnait,* useless, vain. *unparegal, unperegal* (Chaucer), unequal. *unpitous* (Chaucer), *unpiteous,* impious, wicked, merciless. *unpower,* helplessness. *unquert,* annoyance, trouble. *unraced* (Chaucer), not rooted up. *unscience* (Chaucer), ignorance, error. *unsele,* misery, misfortune, ill-luck; also as an adjective, wretched. *unshent,* unharmed, unspoiled. *unspeed,* poverty, misfortune (lack of *good speed*); *unspeedful,* of no avail; *unspeedy,* poor, unprofitable. *unspeered,* unasked. *untemed,* untamed. *untholemoodness,* impatience (Be not untholemood—accent on the *thole*—kind reader!). *untholing,* not to be borne, intolerable. *untimeous,* untimely. A *gentleman untrial,* one (not necessarily a gentleman by birth) brought up in an abbey. *untrist,* unbelieving; faithless; unreliable. *unwist* (Chaucer), without its being known; Spenser, in THE FAËRIE QUEENE (1590): *Of hurt unwist most danger doth redound. unwrast,* of little account, worthless; wicked. *unwrench,* an evil trick; a vice or sin. *unwry* (Chaucer: *unwre, onwrye*) to reveal; uncover, make naked; divulge. *unyeaned,* unborn (George Eliot, 1868: *blind only as unyeaned reason is*); not having given birth. *unzoned,* not limited to a region (*the unzoned gods*); not girt with a girdle; Sydney Dobell, in BALDER (1854): *One all unzoned in her deep haunts . . . Hastes not to hide her breast.*—Let me not be *undone* (brought to ruin; Caxton, Wyatt, Middleton, Fielding, Dickens)—though this, as most wordwork, is perforce *undone* (unfinished).

unaneled. Also *unnaneld, unanneald, unanealed.* See *anele.* Sterne in TRISTRAM SHANDY (1759) tells: *Obadiah had him led in as he was, unwiped, unappointed, unannealed.* For Shakespeare's use in HAMLET, which Sterne and most later users echo, see *housel.* [*Unaneled,* not anointed, is not to be confused with *unannealed,* the negative from *anneal,* to enamel or to burn colors into glass, eathenware, or metal. This is also spelled *aneal;* the forms but not the senses of the two words overlap.]

uncouth. See *couth.*

uncture. Ointment. A 15th century term.

uncuckold. To remove the stigma of cuckoldry, to unhorn. J. Moore in ZELUCO (1789) remarked, with perspicacity and probably regret: *I never yet heard of any method by which a man can be uncuckolded.* Also, *uncuckolded,* not yet horned. Shakespeare laments, in ANTONY AND CLEOPATRA (1606): *It is a deadly sorrow, to beholde a foule knave uncuckolded.*

uncular. Relating or belonging to an uncle. More often, *avuncular.* De Quincey in THE SPANISH MILITARY NUN (1847) remarked: *The grave Don clasped the hopeful young gentleman . . . to his uncular and rather angular breast.*

uncumber. See *cumber.*

uncunning. Ignorance. A common 14th and 15th century term. Also an adjective as in Chaucer's (1374) rendering of BOETHIUS: *any unkonnyng and unprofitable man.* Also *uncunninghead, uncunningship* (CURSOR MUNDI; AYENBITE OF INWIT, 14th century); *uncunningness,* ignorance, unskilfulness.

underfong. To receive, to accept; to come to possess; to admit to one's presence or friendship. By extension, to have understanding in; also, to take in hand, undertake. In all these senses, *underfo* was the common form from the 9th century until the end of the 12th century, when *underfong* largely replaced it, fading after the 16th. Past tense forms included *underfeng, underfangen, underfonge, underfynge.* Spenser used *underfong* to mean to take in, seduce, entrap; *Thou,* he says in THE SHEPHERD'S CALENDAR (1579; JUNE) *that by treacheree Didst underfong my lasse, to waxe so light.* The gloss explains this, 'deceive by false suggestion.' Similarly in THE FAËRIE QUEENE: *With his powre he . . . makes them subject to his mighty wrong, And some by sleight he eke doth underfong.*

undern. See *midovernoon.*

unear'd. Unploughed. From *ear,* to plough, of the same root as Greek *aroein,* Latin *arare,* to plough, till, whence English *arable.* Shakespeare's 2d SONNET asks: *For where is she so fair whose unear'd womb Disdains the tillage of thy husbandry?* The poem is urging young Southampton to marry; there is a pun in *husbandry.*

ungainly. See *gain.*

ungrayhair. As a verb, used by Fuller in THE HOLY WAR (1639): *Whilest his old wife plucked out his black hairs . . . his young one ungrayhaired him.* They left the platter clean!

unhouseled. See *housel; un-.*

universatility. The ability to turn effectively to many things. The word is a telescope of *universe* and *versatility.*

unkempt. See *compt.*

unnethes. A form of *unneath,* short for *underneath.* Used by Spenser in THE SHEPHERD'S CALENDAR (1579; JANUARY). Also *unneth, unneths.*

unready. Undressed; in deshabille. Also, *to unready,* to undress. Developed in the 16th century as the converse of *to ready,* to dress. In Shakespeare's HENRY VI, PART ONE (1591), when *the French leape ore the walles in their shirts,* they are hailed: *How now, my lords! What, all unreadie so?* Puttenham in THE ARTE OF ENGLISH POESIE (1589) tells of *a young gentlewoman who was in her chamber, making herself unready.*

unseminared. Deprived of virility; without seminal power. Used by Shakespeare in ANTONY AND CLEOPATRA (1606): *Tis well for thee, That being unseminar'd, thy freer thoughts May not flye forth of Egypt.* Cleopatra is talking to her eunuch, while she is aquiver for Antony in Rome.

untoun. Not suited to the town, rude, uncivil. In Wright's SPECIMENS OF LYRIC POETRY of the 13th century. This explanation is given in Herbert Coleridge's DICTIONARY OF THE OLDEST WORDS IN THE ENGLISH LANGUAGE (1863). More probably, *untoun* is a variant of *untowe, untowen,* Middle Low German *un(ge)togen,* uneducated; hence, untrained, unmannered, wanton. Also *untowe (n) ship,* wantonness. These forms are found from the 10th to the 15th century. Note also *untowned,* in Wolcot (Peter Pindar's) ODES TO THE ROYAL ACADEMICIANS (1783): *Find me in Sodom out . . . Ten gentlemen, the place shan't be untown'd.*

upas. A tree supposed to have existed in Java, so poisonous as to destroy all life within fifteen miles. Also, *upas tree.* From Malayan *upas pohun,* poison tree. The story of such a tree was told in the LONDON

MAGAZINE of 1783, and given credence and currency in Erasmus Darwin's THE LOVES OF PLANTS (1789): *Fierce in dread silence on the blasted heath Fell upas sits, the hydra-tree of death.* Hence, a deadly or destructive power; thus Byron in CHILD HAROLD'S PILGRIMAGE (1818): *This uneradicable taint of sin, This boundless upas, this all-blasting tree.*

upbray. A variant of *upbraid,* used by Spenser in THE FAËRIE QUEENE (1590); by Sidney, Marston, and others. The form is an error, from assuming that *upbraid* is the past tense.

upright. Also *upright man.* See *pedlers French.*

uranical. Pertaining to the heavens: astronomical; astrological. Greek *ouranos,* heaven. Also *uranic, ouranik, ouranic; uranian,* heavenly (but also, relating to the planet *Uranus.*)

uranomancy. See *aeromancy.*

urbacity. Excessive pride in one's city, or in dwelling in the city as opposed to a rustic environment.

urchin. A hedgehog. Also *urchun; nurchon, norchon; urchyn, urchion; hurcheon; irchin,* and more. Applied to (1) a fiend; *urchin of hell* (16th century); a goblin or elf, which might appear in the form of a hedgehog; (2) Cupid (18th century); (3) a person: a hunchback. an ugly woman, a hag (17th century). an ill-tempered or scheming girl; Goldsmith in THE GOODNATURED MAN (1768) said *You did indeed dissemble, you urchin you; but where's the girl that won't dissemble for a husband?* a mischievous youngster (feminine *urchiness*); a small child, an infant; usually with pity or scorn (this sense survives). As an adjective, *urchin,* mischievous; annoying; evil.

ure. Use, custom. Mainly in the phrases *in ure,* in use or practice; *out of ure,* out of use, disused. A very common word in the 15th and 16th centuries. Marston in THE SCOURGE OF VILLANIE (1598) calls damnation upon those that *dare to put in ure To make Jehova but a coverture To shade rank filth.* Wycherley in THE COUNTRY WIFE (1688) tells: *Yes, a man drinks often with a fool, as he tosses with a marker, only to keep his hand in ure.*

urimancy. See *aeromancy.*

urinator. A diver. Latin *urinari, urinatus,* to dive, swim under water. Hence also *urinate,* to dive; *urination,* diving. These senses were common from about 1650 to 1690. Beale in a letter (published in Boyle's WORKS; 1682) wrote that *His Majesty's urinator, Mr. Curtis, published in the Gazette how he had practised . . . Which minds me how easy it were . . . for our merchants, in all their voyages, to be furnished with such urinators.*

urisk. A supernatural denizen of the Scottish Highlands, akin to the English brownie. P. Graham informs us in THE SCENERY OF PERTHSHIRE (1806), that *the urisks were a sort of lubberly supernaturals, who . . . could be gained over by kind attentions, to perform the drudgery of the farm.*

urn. As a verb. (1) To put in a cinerary *urn;* to bury. (2) A variant form of *earn.* (3) To cause pain; to be in pain (15th and 16th centuries; mainly in Scotland). (4) A variant form of *run* or *ran.* Also *ourn.* When the fair queen of Sir Orfeo (*cp. levedi*) was stricken mad in her orchard, her maidens *ourn to the palace ful right And tolde bothe squier and knight That her quen awede* [go mad] *wold, And bad hem go and hir athold.*

Knightes urn, and levedis also, Damisels sexti and mo . . .

uryn. A variant form of *arain,* spider. Used in the 15th century.

usant. In the habit of, accustomed (to doing). Chaucer in THE PARSON'S TALE (1386) says: *He that is usant to this synne of glotonye.* Also, habitual; Parker in DIVES AND PAUPER (1470) keenly observed: *Comonly grete swerers and usant swerers ben full false.*

usquebaugh. Whisky. From the Gaelic *uisge,* water + *beatha,* life. Similarly, the Latin *aque vitae,* water of life. Very frequent in the 17th century; occasionally still used.

ustulation. Burning; (later) roasting. Also *ustion,* burning, searing; a surface that has been (or looks as though it has been) seared or cauterized. Hence, figuratively, burning desire, lust; Sanderson in a Sermon of 1624 reminded his hearers that marriage is *the sole allowed remedy against . . . burning lusts; by the apostle . . . commanded in case of ustion to all men.* Latin *urere, ustum,* to burn, whence also *combustion.* Hence also *ustulate,* scorched, or so brown as to seem scorched, as girls' backs back from Miami. *ustorious,* able to make things burn; *ustive,* caustic; good for a burn; a recipe book of 1599 states that *linteseede oyle is an excellent ustive oyntment.*

uxorium. A fine or tax paid by a male (Spartan, also Roman) citizen for not marrying. Latin *uxor,* wife; whence also *uxorious,* henpecked. The word *uxorium* is in Bailey (1751); not in O.E.D. Yet bachelors were taxed in England in 1695, to raise funds for the war against France; and since 1798 the British income tax has pressed more heavily upon the bachelor. Various communities in the United States have tried to impose a uxorium.

V

vaccimulgence. Milking of cows. Coleridge (BIOGRAPHIA LITERARIA, 1817) looked for a good servant, *scientific in vaccimulgence.* Latin *vacca,* cow; whence also *vaccarage, vaccary* (from the 15th century), a pasturage for cows; a dairy farm. For *vaccicide, cp. stillicide. Vaccine,* of course, was first associated with the cow: *variolae vaccinae,* cow pox, drawn from the hands of a milkmaid by Dr. Edward Jenner in 1796.

vacivity. Emptiness. A form in 18th century dictionaries; a variant for *vacuity. Vacuation* was also used (16th and 17th centuries) in this sense; but also as short for *evacuation.* Also *vacive,* vacuous. *Vacuefy* meant to create a vacuum, to make empty.

vade. (1) A variant of *ford* (*wade?*), a shallow place in a river. (2) An early form of *fade,* quite frequent from 1500 to 1650. Shakespeare, in RICHARD II (1593) declares: *One flourishing branch of his most royall roote . . . Is hackt downe, and his summer leafes all vaded.* Latin *vadere,* to go, whence also *invade, evade,* and also (3) *vade,* to go away, depart. Braithwait in BARNABEES JOURNAL (1638) warns: *Beauty feedeth, beauty fadeth; Beauty lost, her lover vadeth.* Hence also, *vading,* transitory, fleeting, passing away. *Vadosity,* the state of being fordable (17th century).

vade-mecum. Literally (Latin) go with me: a companion; a handbook; a guide. See *vadosity.* Often *Vade Mecum* was used as or in a book's title. The Odéon Theatre in 1797 planned a literary journal, said the MONTHLY MAGAZINE, *to be a valuable vade-mecum for such persons as are not in the habit of deciding on the merits of theatrical performances.* Each member of the audience was thus supplied with a pocket critic.

vadosity. The condition of being *vadable, vadeable,* fordable. Latin *vadosum; vadum,* a ford. A *vade, q.v.,* was (16th century) a shallow stretch of a river, across which one might *wade.* Old English *wadan, wade,* like Latin *vadere,* first meant to go, to walk, then to walk through water. From the Latin came *vade-mecum* (literally, go with me) used from the 17th century for a guide or handy reference book. Fielding in THE GRUB STREET OPERA (1731) recommended *the husband's vade-mecum . . . very necessary for all married men to have in their houses.* And Byron in DON JUAN (1818) called *Aristotle's rules The vade mecum of the true sublime Which makes so many poets, and some fools.*

vafrity. Craftiness. Listed in Bailey (1751), but not in O.E.D.—which does list *vafrous,* sly, crafty. Latin *vafrum,* cunning, crafty. Hall in his CHRONICLES (1548, HENRY VII) speaks of *the Englishmen, accordyng to their olde vaffrous varietie.*

vail. (1) To lower, in sign of submission or respect (one's eyes; a banner, a lance), or to take off (a hat, or other headdress). Also *vayle, vaill, veil.* Hence, to acknowledge surrender or defeat; to yield. Thus Kyd in his translation (1594) of CORNELIA has: *valing your christall eyes to your faire bosoms.* Coryat in his CRUDITIES (1611) gives instance of figurative use: *She will very near benumme and captivate thy senses, and make reason vale bonnet to affection.* (2) To have power, to *prevail;* to be of use. Via Old French from Latin *valoir,* to be of *value. Cp. vailable.*

vailable. Valuable; of advantage; effectual; legally valid. From *vail* (2); Latin *valoir,* to be of worth. Gower uses the word often; several times in CONFESSIO AMANTIS (1390), as when he observes that pity and justice *remuen alle vice, And ben of vertu most vailable To make a kinges regne stable.*

vair. A fur, very popular in the 13th and 14th centuries, used for trimming or lining garments, also for slippers. It was then the fur of a squirrel with gray back and white belly. Old French *vair;* Latin *varius,* parti-colored. The fur was later replaced by miniver and ermine; the word *vair* (though retained in heraldry, and revived in the 19th century by Scott, Swinburne, and more) dropped from the common speech. The same lapse occurred in French; hence, in the Cinderella story, the fairy slippers of Cinderella, made of *vair,* made sense to the people listening as *verre,* and became, in English translation, not fur but glass slippers.

valanche. Short for *avalanche.* The *a* was dropped in French, when folk usage turned *l'avalanche* into *la valanche; cp. napron.* Smollett in his TRAVELS IN FRANCE AND ITALY (1766) observed: *Scarce a year passes in which some mules and their drivers do not perish by the valanches.*

valetude. Here is a word that, especially in surviving forms, shifted until it came to mean its own opposite. Its first use in English was as meaning good health; from Latin *valetudo, valetudinem; valere,* to be well. Rolland in THE COURT OF VENUS (1560) declared: *There was worship with welth and valitude.* Then it came to mean, in general, the state of health; Cockeram in 1623 defines it: *valetude, health or sicknesse.* Then it moved on, to mean ill health; Tomlinson in his translation (1657) of Renodaeus' MEDICINAL DISPENSATORY reported *the valitude of many, and the death of more.* Hence *valetudinous, valetudinarious, valetudinary,* invalid, weakly; *valetudinarian* (still current); a *valetudinary* (17th century) was an infirmary, a hospital. Sheridan, in THE SCHOOL FOR SCANDAL, 1777, observes that *there are valetudinarians in reputation as well as constitution.*

vance-roof. See *vaunce.*

vapulation. Flogging. Latin *vapulare,* to be flogged, to receive a lashing—also, a tongue-lashing. Hence *vapulate,* to beat; to be flogged; there are blunders, said Samuel Parr in a letter of 1783, *for which a boy ought to vapulate.* Also *vapulary, vapulatory,* relating to flogging. E. Ward in THE LONDON SPY (1706) said: *Like an offender at a whipping-post . . . the more importunate he seems for their favorable usage, the severer vapulation they are to exercise upon him.* In the school and the Navy, as well as the vocabulary, *vapulation* has grown obsolete.

vardingale. A 16th and 17th century variant of *farthingale, q.v.* This form—also *verdugal; vardingard, verdyngale*—comes more directly from Spanish *verdugado; verdugo,* rod, stick. The Spanish *verdugo* also meant hangman; whence,

English *verdugo,* an executioner; also used as a term of abuse. Jonson in THE ALCHEMIST (1610) says of a Spaniard (who knows no English): *His great verdugoship has not a jot of language; so much the easier to be cozened, my Dolly!*

vasa. A 17th century variant of *vase.* Evelyn in a CHARACTER of 1651, stated: *One of their spurs engaged in a carpet . . . drew all to the ground, break the glass and the vasas in pieces.*

vastity. Emptiness, desolateness; later (17th century) vastness, immensity. Hence *vastitude,* laying waste; later, immensity. Also *vastation,* very common from 1600 to 1660, then supplanted by *devastation.* To *vast* (15th century), to lay waste, to destroy; *vastator,* destroyer. In all these forms *waste,* to lay *waste,* was the earlier meaning. Latin *vastus,* empty, void; hence the void of space, the *vast* reaches, therefore immense. Frequently *vast* was used as a noun, meaning space; Shakespeare in THE TEMPEST (1610) and in PERICLES: *Thou god of this great vast, rebuke these surges;* Milton, Blake, Keats, Tennyson. Shakespeare also uses *vastidity* (MEASURE FOR MEASURE), immensity. A use of *vast* that shows the shift in meaning, or rather a combining of immensity and waste, is in Shakespeare's HAMLET: *In the dead vast and middle of the night.*

vaticide. See *stillicide.*

vaticinate. To prophesy; to speak as a prophet. Latin *vaticinari, vaticinatum,* to forebode, prophesy; *vates,* prophet. In the 16th and 17th centuries, the Latin *vates* gave many English forms, including: *vatic, vatical,* relating to a prophet; inspired; also *vaticinal, vaticinatory, vaticinatric. vaticinant* (accent on the *tiss*), prophesying. A *vaticinar, vaticinator, vaticine,* prophet; feminine *vaticinatress, vaticinatrix. Vaticination, vaticine, vaticiny,* a prophecy. Latin *vates* was used in English to mean an inspired poet; also, those that tended the sacrificial rites among the ancient Druids. General P. Thompson exclaimed in 1829: *What if Humphrey has vaticinated? What if he has beaten all prognosticators since Nostradamus?* What indeed?

vaunce. A shortened form of *advance,* in its various senses; frequent in the 16th century. Also *vaunce-roof, vance-roof,* a garret. Thomas Raymond, in his AUTOBIOGRAPHY (1658) claimed that the "fayned names of your fellow Cavaliers" he was accused of having (at his trial for treason) *were only the names of such symples as I had caused to be gathered and hung up adrying in the vance-roof at my house.* The term was used figuratively by Gurnall in THE CHRISTIAN IN COMPLEAT ARMOUR; OR, A TREATISE OF THE SAINTS WAR AGAINST THE DEVIL (1655): *Canst thou hide any one sin in the vance-roof of thy heart?*

vavasour. A feudal tenant, ranking below a baron. From a medieval Latin form combined of *vassi vassorum,* vassals of vassals. A *vavasory* was an estate held by a *vavasour.* Also *favasour, vavyssour, valvasor,* and the like. Chaucer, in the Prologue to his CANTERBURY TALES (1386) says: *Was nowher such a worthy vavaser.* Anne Vavasour, lady-in-waiting of Queen Elizabeth I, and the mother of an illegitimate son of the 17th Earl of Oxford, is by some held to be the "Dark Lady" of the Shakespearean sonnets.

vaward. Short for *vamward,* which is a variant of *vantward,* later *vanguard.* Related to *forward,* the suffix *-ward* meaning in the direction of. Also *fauward, vawward* and the like. Shakespeare used the word figuratively in HENRY IV, PART TWO (1597): *We that are in the vaward of our youth;* Scott (in his JOURNAL, 1828) and others have echoed him.

vecordious. Full of folly; senseless; mad. Latin *vecordia,* madness; *ve,* not, without + *corda,* a harp-string (hence, harmony); influenced by *cor, cordem,* heart. Not in O.E.D., which lists *vecordy, vecord,* madness. The 1788 translation of Swedenborg's WISDOM OF THE ANGELS said: *Hence too the terms concord, discord, vecord (malicious madness), and other similar expressions.* Caxton in the PROHEMYE to his POLYCRONICON (1482) stated: *Historyes moeve and withdrawe emperours and kynges fro vycious tyrannye, fro vecordyous sleuthe* [sloth], *unto tryumphe and vyctorye in puyssaunt bataylles.*

vegete. Healthy, active, vigorous. Latin *vegere, vegetus,* to be active, lively; *vegetare, vegetatum,* to animate, enliven; hence, English *vegetate;* Latin *vegetabilis,* animating, vivifying; hence, English *vegetable.* Robert South in a Sermon of 1660 declared that *a well radicated habit, in a lively, vegete faculty, is like an apple of gold in a picture of silver.*

velitation. A slight engagement with an enemy, a skirmish; a verbal skirmish, a dispute. The second use was very common in the 17th century; revived by Scott in ST. RONAN'S WELL (1824): *While the ladies . . . were engaged in the light snappish velitation . . . which we have described.* The *velites* (three syllables) were light-armed soldiers in the Roman armies, used in skirmishes.

velleity. A wish or desire without any accompanying effort to realize it; the fact or quality of merely wishing for a thing. Latin *velle,* to wish. Hence also *to vell,* to desire without action toward realization of the desire; to daydream. Bishop Hall in his CONTEMPLATIONS UPON THE NEW TESTAMENT (1618) declared: *Thy word alone, thy beck alone, thy wish alone, yea, the least act of velleity from thee might have wrought this cure.* It is a characteristic of velleity, however, that it dreams and sighs, not acts. Lowell in his study of ROUSSEAU (1867) says: *He and all like him mistake emotion for conviction, velleity for resolve.*

vellication. A twitching or pulling; titillation, tickling. Urquhart in his translation (1693) of Rabelais inquires: *Is it not daily seen how schoolmasters . . . shake the heads of their disciples . . . that, by this erection, vellication, stretching and pulling their ears . . . they may stir them up? To vellicate,* to irritate; to pluck, nip, pinch, etc., with small sharp points; to tickle; to carp at, to criticize adversely. Latin *vellicare, vellicatum,* frequentative of *vellere,* to pull, pluck, twitch. Hence also *vellicative,* causing irritation or twitching; *vellicle,* something that nips and holds fast. A drama critic seems often a vellicating fellow.

velocious. Rapid. Used in the 17th and 18th century; the noun *velocity* has survived, as also the *velodrome,* a speed-palace. Latin *velox, velocis,* swift. The *velocipede* lingers in memory, but the *velociman,* a speedy traveling-machine worked by the hands, scarcely survived the 19th century. Charles Lutwidge Dodgson (better known in literature as Lewis Carroll) reported (in his LIFE by Collingwood; 1882): *Went out with Charsley, and did four miles on one of his velocimans, very pleasantly.* In 1819 there was advertised a *velocimanipede,* worked by hands and feet. The extremities, at least, were velocious. C. Nesse in A COMPLEAT AND COMPENDIOUS CHURCH HISTORY (1680) said: *Satan was seen to fall like lightning from heaven, to wit, viewably, violently, and velociously.*

vendible. Marketable, capable of being sold. Latin *vendibilis; vendere, ventum,* to sell, whence *inventory.* Hence also *vendibility.* As Shakespeare says in The Merchant of Venice (1595) *Silence is only commendable In a neat's tongue dri'd, and a maid not vendible.*

vendicate. To claim for oneself; to assert a claim; to claim ability. Latin *vendicatum,* from *vindicare, vindicatum,* to assert a claim, justify, *vindicate.* An Act of the reign of Henry VIII in 1544 declared that certain persons had *usurped and vendicated a fayned and an unlawfull power and jurisdiction within this realm.* John Lane in his CONTINUATION OF CHAUCER'S SQUIRE'S TALE (1616) declared: *We have two ladies which, with your trim pair, dare vendicate to sing.*

venditate. Originally, to put out for sale; hence, to display most favorably; to exhibit ostentatiously. Latin *venditare,* frequentative of *vendere; cp. vendible.* Hence *venditation,* favorable or ostentatious display. John Smith in SELECT DISCOURSES (1652) speaks of philosophers that *made their knowledge only matter of ostentation, to venditate and set off themselves.*

venery. (1) Hunting; the chase. Latin *venari,* to hunt. (2) The pursuit or enjoyment of sexual pleasure; also, a source of great enjoyment. Latin *Venus, Veneris,* goddess of love, desire. Hence, a *venerer* is a hunter; *venerial,* relating to the chase. *Venerilla,* a little *Venus,* applied familiarly to one's love, as in Burton's ANATOMY OF MELANCHOLY (1621): *She is his idol, lady, mistress, venerilla, queen, the quintessence of beauty. Venereous, venerious, venerous; venereal, venerial, veneral; venerian,* all are associated with sexual desire or intercourse; all may mean lustful. A *venerist,* a lustful person, a lecher. *venerean, venerian,* however, were often related to the planet *Venus,* as in Chaucer's Prologue to THE WIFE OF BATH'S TALE (1386): *For certes I am al Venerian In feelyng and myn herte is Marcian. venereal* is now associated with disease; hence, science fiction writers people the planet *Venus* with creatures they call *Venusians.* The adjective *venust* means beautiful, graceful; *venustity, venusty,* beauty. Hence *venustate,* to make beautiful, a self-applied process that much occupies the ladies.—These forms must not be confused with *venial,* pardonable, slight, from Latin *venia,* forgiveness. A *venial sin* is opposed to *a deadly sin, a mortal sin.* Shakespeare in OTHELLO (1604) says: *If they do nothing, 'tis a veniall slip.* Hence *venialia,* pardonable sins; *venialness, veniality,* the quality of being venial, a matter for divine or royal pardon or indulgence. In Middleton's A MAD WORLD, MY MASTERS (1608) Harebrain declares: *Your only deadly sin's adultery; All sins are venial but venereal.*

venefice. The use of poison or magic potions; sorcery through such use. Also *venefy,* to make such use. Latin *venenum,* poison + *-fic,* a combining form from *facere,* to make. Hence, *venefic,* dealing in poisoning; *venefical, veneficous* (accent on the second syllable); *veneficial, veneficious* (accent on third), dealing in or related to malignant sorcery and witchcraft. Jonson in THE MASQUE OF QUEENS (1609) speaks of witches that fetch *spindles, timbrels, rattles, or other venefical instruments.* Also *venenate,* to poison; to render poisonous; *venenation.* As an adjective, *venenate,* poisoned;

venene, poisonous, *venomous. Veneniferous,* laden with poison, as the *venenifluous* fangs of a rattlesnake. Wyclif (SELECT ENGLISH WORKS, 1380) stated that *The sixth work of lechery is venefice; that is then done when men usen experimentis to geten this work of lechery.*

ventose. (1) As a noun. a kind of cupping-glass, for blood-letting. Used in the 15th, 16th, and 17th centuries. (2) As a verb. to bleed someone with a cupping-glass, to practice cupping. (3) As an adjective. windy, flatulent; boastful, bragging. All are via the Romance languages from Latin *ventum,* wind + *-osus,* full of. J. Bigelow in BENCH AND BAR (1867) said: *The ventose orator was confounded, and put himself and the glass down together.* Also *ventositous,* full of wind; *ventoseness, ventosity,* windiness, flatulence, the state of being puffed up; pompous conceit; bombast. Washington Irving in SALMAGUNDI (1807) speaks of *a man of superlative ventosity, and comparable to nothing but a huge bladder of wind.*

Venus. The Roman goddess of love, especially sensual love; Greek *Aphrodite.* Hence, desire for sexual delights; see *venery.* Also beauty, charm; a beautiful woman; a quality that excites desire, a charm or grace; Middleton in YOUR FIVE GALLANTS (1608) pictures *a pretie, fat eyde wench, with a venus in her cheeke.* The second planet from the sun, between Mercury and Earth. *Cp. Diana.* The *girdle* (*zone*) *of Venus* made its possessor irresistible.

venust. See *venery.* Hence also *venustity, venustness, venusty.*

ver. Springtime. Also *vere.* Via French from Latin *ver,* spring, related to *viridis,* green, whence *verdant, verdure.* Chaucer in TROYLUS AND CRISEYDE (1374) glows with *The time of Aperil, when clothed is the mede With newe grene, of lusty veer the prime. Cp. vernaculous.* Also *vernant,* freshly green; *vernal,* flourishing in the spring. To *vernalize,* to render springlike, to freshen; *vernancy, vernation.* Also *vernality,* the lovely green quality of meadows in May; the springtime of one's spirit or one's days. Milton in PARADISE LOST (1667) says: *Else had the spring Perpetual smil'd on earth with vernant flours.*

verament. Truly, really. Also *veriment; verement, verrement;* Old French *voirement,* from *voir, veir;* Latin *verus,* true. Common 14th to 17th century, often (*in verament*) as a tag or rhyme-word. Chaucer in THE TALE OF SIR THOPAS (1386) invites us: *Liseneth, lordings, in good entent, And I wol tell you verament Of mirth and of solas* [solace].

verberate. To strike so as to make sound; to strike so as to cause pain, to flagellate. Latin *verberare, verberatum,* to beat; *verber,* a lash, scourge; a whipping. Hence also, *reverberate,* which is current. Shirley in LOVE TRICKS (1625) cries out: *You shall be verberated and reverberated, my exact piece of stolidity!* T. H. Croker, in his translation (1755) of ORLANDO FURIOSO uses it for Italian *tremolar,* to vibrate: *A fragrant breeze . . . Made the air trem'lous verberate around. Her mother,* said the PALL MALL GAZETTE of 1 August, 1866, *was a strict disciplinarian of the verberative school.*

verbicide. See *stillicide.* Holmes in THE AUTOCRAT AT THE BREAKFAST TABLE (1858) applied the term *verbicide* to punning, of which he was often guilty.

verbigerate. To keep on talking. Latin *verbi-,* word + *gerere,* to act, carry on. Hence, *verbigeration.* Listed in 17th and

18th century dictionaries. The words are now used for a psychopathological repetition of a word or phrase.

verdea. A white wine made from green grapes grown near Arcetri, near Florence, Italy. Also *verdeda, verde*; Italian *verde,* green. Especially popular in the 17th century. Fletcher and Massinger in THE ELDER BROTHER (1625) mention it as one of the treasures of Italy: *Say it had been at Rome, and seen the reliques, Drunk your verdea wine, and rid at Naples.* An essential part of the Grand Tour. Lewis Theobald (1688-1744), though it is for other reasons that Pope made him the main butt of THE DUNCIAD, invented a river *Verdé* to account for the name of this wine. His inventiveness was much more fruitful when he amended the report of Falstaff's death to *a' babbled of green fields.*

verderer. A judicial officer of the King's forest, charged with its preservation and maintenance, also against trespassers and poachers. A medieval post, though later for certain forests, notably New, Epping, and Dean. An extended form of *verder,* with the same meaning; via Old French *verd, vert,* from Latin *viridus,* green. The Medieval Latin name of the officer was *viridarius.* In English, also *verdour, viridary.* From the *veridarii* of the Bishop's Forest of Mendip, the term *verderer* came to be applied to a petty constable of a town; hence, certain towns and cities were divided into constabulary districts, each called a *verdery.* There were four *verderies,* e.g., in Wells. The form *viridary,* in addition to a *verderer,* might mean a *viridarium,* a pleasure garden, such as was attached to a villa of ancient Rome. Evelyn in his DIARY for 10 November, 1700, noted: *We went to see Prince Ludovisio's villa where was formerly the viridarium of the poet Sallust.*

verdugo. See *vardingale.*

vere. See *ver.*

verecund. Modest, shy. Latin *verecundus; vereri,* to *reverence,* stand in awe. Also, *verecundious, verecundous.* Hence, *verecundity, verecundness.* Used in the 17th and 18th centuries. Wotton (RELIQUIAE WOTTONIANAE, 1639) said: *Your brow proclameth much fidelity, a certain verecundious generosity graceth your eyes.*

verge. This word had a wide range of meanings, extending from the primal sense (Latin *virga*), a rod. Among these are: the organ of virility; a chariot-pole; a whip; a watch (short for a *verge-watch,* one with a rod-like spindle for the balance, used in the 18th century). But especially, the *verge* was a rod or wand carried (by the *Sergeant of the Verge*) as a sign of authority; also a rod held by a man swearing fealty to a lord, or becoming a lord's tenant. From these political uses, a whole new series of meanings arose. *Within the verge* meant within the authority of; the *verge* of the Lord High Steward (16th and 17th centuries) extended for twelve miles around the King's court. Queen Elizabeth I was within twelve miles of Deptford when Christopher Marlowe was killed there, 30 May, 1593; the fight thus occurred *within the verge,* hence it was a royal inquiry that exonerated Ingram Frizer, on grounds of self-defence. In the 18th century, *within the verge* usually meant the precincts of Whitehall as a place of sanctuary. Hence, *verge* came to mean: the bounds, limits, or precincts of a place; the rim, or edge; margin, brink, border; hence also the space within a boundary, room, scope: Dryden in DON SEBASTIAN

(1690) says: *Let fortune empty her whole quiver on me, I have a soul that like an ample shield Can take in all, and verge enough for more.* Shakespeare uses the word in several senses, also as a rim or circle, in RICHARD III (1594): *The inclusive verge Of golden metal, that must round my brow.* The word survives in the expression *on the verge of,* as in *They were on the verge of coming to blows.*

veriloquent. Truth-speaking. Also *veriloquous.* Latin *veri-,* truth (whence *verity*) + *loquentem,* speaking, *loqui,* to speak. Hence, *veriloquy* (accent in all of these, on the second syllable). Used in the 17th century, but rare—as it still seems to be. Also *veridic, veridical, veridicous.* The nouns *veridicality, veridicalness, veridity* were used in the 18th century; *verity,* used from the 14th, dropped largely out of use in the 18th, but in the 19th century verily superseded the other forms.

verjuice. The juice of unripe grapes, crab-apples and the like, used as a condiment or medicine. Old French *vert,* green + *jus,* juice. Also *veryose, vergus, vergws, vergious, werges, varges, vergesse* and more, because the liquor was very popular, from the 14th to the 18th century. Also used figuratively, as in Middleton's A GAME AT CHESS (1624): *This fat bishop hath . . . so squelch'd and squeez'd me, I've no verjuice left in me.* In THE HISTORIE OF THE TRYALL OF CHEVALRIE (1605) we read: *And that sowre crab do but leere at thee I shall squeeze him to vargis.* Often the word was used with the sense of sour, bitter: *verjuice countenance,* wit. Lowell in THE FABLE FOR CRITICS (1848) says: *His sermons with satire are plenteously verjuiced.* Thus Edward Guilpin, in SKIALETHEIA (1598): *Oh how the varges from his black pen wrung Would sauce the idiom of the English tongue!*

vermeil. A bright red. Also *vermil, vermeon, vermion.* Early and still poetic forms of *vermilion, vermillion.* From Latin *vermiculus,* a little worm, a major source of the coloring in early times. The word was used figuratively to mean a blush; blood; also, the dye or coloring to produce ruby lips and rosy cheeks. Moore in his renderings (1800) of Anacreon, speaks of *many vermil, honeyed kisses.* Barclay had earlier (THE SHIP OF FOOLS, 1509) advised: *Take not cold water instead of vermayll wine.*

vermiculation. Being eaten by, or infested with, worms; changing into little worms. Latin *vermiculus,* diminutive of *vermis, verminis,* worm, whence *vermin* and the *vermiform appendix.* Hence *vermiculate,* to become worm-eaten; *vermiculated* may mean worm-eaten, or so marked as to seem nibbled or crawled over by worms. Also *vermified,* infested with worms. Donne, in one of his LAST SERMONS (1630), fitly spoke of *putrefaction and vermiculation and incineration and dispersion in . . . the grave.*

vermiculist. A believer that generation is caused by *vermicules,* or tiny worms. Latin *vermiculus,* diminutive of *vermis, vermin-,* worm. In the 18th century the Italian scientist Spallanzani spoke of *the three principal systems respecting the generation of animals, the system of the ovarists, that of the vermiculists, and that founded upon the two liquors.*

vermion. See *vermeil.*

vermouth. See *wormwood.*

vernaculous. Low-bred; scurrilous. Latin *vernaculus,* domestic; *verna,* a home-born slave. [Not to be confused with *vernal,* relating to the spring; Latin *ver,* spring. See *ver.*] Hence the *vernacular* was the speech learned from the servants at home. *Vernaculary, vernacule, vernacular, vernaculous* are all adjectives referring to a native speech; the last had also the sense of slavish, or scurrilous, as in Jonson's VOLPONE (1605), speaking of men *subject to the petulancy of every vernaculous orator, that were wont to be the care of kings.* Also *vernile,* slavish, servile; *vernility,* servility. H. Clarke exclaimed in 1788: *Oh the stupidity and vernility of mankind, that there should be permitted such an abuse of power in the world, as either a public or a domestic gynecocracy!*

vernage. A strong sweet white Italian wine. Also *vernagelle.* Chaucer has, in THE MERCHANT'S TALE (1386): *He drinketh ypocras, clarre, and vernage, Of spices hote, to encrese his corrage.* For another instance of its use, see *bardolf.*

vernant. See *ver.*

vernicle. (1) The kerchief said to have belonged to *St. Veronica,* with which the face of Christ was wiped on his way to Calvary; His features became marked upon it. This cloth is still venerated as a relic; it is preserved at St. Peter's Cathedral in Rome. (2) Any similar cloth or vessel or ornament thus marked, used for devotion; especially, a token worn by pilgrims. Via Old French from the name *Veronica.* Also *vernycle; veronica, veronicle, veronique, verony.* Chaucer in the Prologue to THE CANTERBURY TALES (1386) describes the Pardoner: *A vernycle hadde he sowed up on his cappe.* Bishop Thomas Ken in his poem PSYCHE (1711) pleaded: *My soul, Lord, thy veronique make, That I may thy resemblance take.*

vernility. See *vernaculous.*

veronique. See *vernicle.*

verre. Glass; a vessel of glass. Chaucer in TROYLUS AND CRISEYDE (1374) bids him *that hath an head of verre Fro caste of stonys ware hym in the war.* French *verre,* Latin *vitrum,* glass. Used into the 16th century. *Cp. vair.*

verser. See *pedlers French.*

versute. Crafty, wily. Latin *versutum; vertere, versus,* to turn; whence also *vertex, vertigo, adversary* and many fields of *conversation.* Hence *versutiloquent, versutiloquous,* crafty or scheming in speech. Frequent since the 16th century; the word was not used earlier. Note that the *vertebrates* are those with a backbone that can turn. Also: *vertent year,* a cycle during which (according to Plato) the stars and planets complete a revolution of the heavens: 15,000 years. *vertible,* capable of turning or being turned; inconstant, mutable. *vertiginal, vertiginous,* giddy; also *vertigious.* One might lengthily discourse on the *vertiginal* and *versute* ways of those that plan television *advertising.*

vertsauce. A sauce made mainly with green herbs. Also *sauce verte, vergesauce.* Used in the 15th century.

vertuless. An old form (Chaucer) for *virtueless.*

vertumnal. Relating to the Springtime, vernal. Associated with *ver, q.v.,* but derived from *Vertumnus,* the Roman god of change, god of the seasons; *vertere (vortere), versum,* to turn, whence also *revert, convert, controvert, diversion, vice versa.* Hence *vertumnal,* changeable, fickle; but more often in the transferred sense of vernal, as when T. Adams says in EIRENOPOLIS (1622): *Her smiles are more reviving than the vertumnall sunneshine.*

verty. Alert, attentive; early. An aphetic form of *averty,* from Latin *ad,* to + *vertere,* to turn; *cp. versute.* Also *werty, vairtie.* Used in the 14th and 15th century, often coupled with *wise,* as by Barbour in THE BRUCE (1375): King Robert *. . . was wis in his deed and ek verty.*

vervain. A common plant, also called *verbena,* valued from earliest days for many virtues. The Persians bore it before the altars of the Sun. The Greeks called it "the sacred herb"; with it Zeus' banquet hall was purified. The Romans wore a sprig of it as a charm against sorcery. The Druids bore it in their processions; the stalks of it, infused with wine, were used to cure fevers and snakebites; its juices, smeared on the Druids' bodies, made them potent healers of all ills. They—like the Elizabethan country folk long after them—used vervain to establish and cement friendship, to win and hold true love. The Anglo-Saxons, calling it *ashthroat,* hung its dried roots about their necks to ward off sores. Not to be outdone, the Christians hailed it as the plant that grew at the foot of the Cross, hence had the power to heal and to bless. It was thrown, to bring good harvest and good fortune, on the great bonfires that blazed on Midsummer Night. (*cp. midsummer men.*) So great was its potency that other plants of magical virtue came to be known by its name: *verbenas, all kinds of sweet or sacred plants used for adorning altars, as bays, olive, rosemary, myrtle,* said Temple (1685) in his essay ON GARDENS. It remains a sweet, citron-scented plant of the gardens.

very. True, the real, genuine. Old French *verai*; Latin *verus,* true; whence also *verity.* From the 13th century. Fisher in the funeral sermon for the Countess of Richmond (1509) alluded to *all the lerned men of Englonde to whom she was a veray patronesse.* Timme in A PLAINE DISCOVERIE OF TEN ENGLISH LEPERS (1592) said: *They which are out of their wittes do not see the verie things, but the fantasies of their passion.* Rosalind in disguise (in Shakespeare's AS YOU LIKE IT; 1600) asks Orlando: *What would you say to me now, and I were your verie, verie Rosalind?* Also, true, faithful; lawful. Wycherley in THE PLAIN DEALER (1676) said: *Sir, Sir, your very servant; I was afraid you had forgotten me.*

vest. See *pote.*

vestigate. An early (16th and 17th century) form of *investigate.* Latin *vestigare, vestigatum,* to track; search; especially, to follow the trail of. Hence, *vestigating,* a footprint, as in Sir Thomas Herbert's A RELATION OF SOME YEARS TRAVAILE . . . INTO AFRIQUE AND THE GREATER ASIA (1634), wherein he states that the Cingalese claim *that Adam was there created and lived there; they believe it rather in regard his vestigatings are yet imprinted in the earth.* Hence also the still current *vestige,* a footprint, a remainder as a reminder.

vetanda. Things that should not be done. Literally (Latin), things that should be forbidden; Latin *vetare, vetatum,* to forbid. Hence also *vetation,* a forbidding (in 17th and 18th century dictionaries); *vetitive,* pertaining to the veto; having power to forbid. *Veto* means, literally, I forbid.

veterate. Of long standing, old, *inveterate* (which has replaced it); also, authoritative. 17th century dictionaries listed a verb *veterate,* to grow old. Latin *vetus, veteris,* old; whence also *veteran.* Hence, *veterescent,* growing old; *veteratorian* (noun: an old hand), crafty, subtle in deceit. [Note that *veterinarian* is from Latin *veterinae,* cattle.] Hence also, *vetust,* old, ancient; *vetusty* (accent on the first syllable), antiquity. John Halle, in AN HISTORICALL EXPOSTULATION AGAINST THE ABUSES OF CHYRURGERIE AND PHISICKE (1565) declared: *I have thought good to gather the councels and good documentes of dyvers good and veterate authors.*

vetitive. See *vetanda.*

viaggiatory. Frequently traveling. Via Italian *viaggiare,* to voyage, from Latin *via,* way. A *viadant* (17th century) was a wayfarer. Medwin in THE LIFE OF SHELLEY (1847) remarks upon *the viaggiatory English old maids, who scorn the Continent.* Hence also *viator,* traveler; *viatorial, viatorian, viatorious,* long-traveling; relating to travel. Also *viatic, viaticum,* a supply (money or provisions) for a journey; also, the Eucharist, administered to one about to set forth on the last journey. Used from the 16th century. T. Taylor in his translation (1822) of Apuleius said: *When a few days had elapsed, I rapidly collected my viatica in bundles.* The word is also used figuratively: *the grace of God is our viaticum,* or as in a letter of J. Jekyll (1775): *Bunbury's etchings and Sterne's Journey are almost as good viaticums in France as the post book.* The religious sense is exemplified in Kingsley's WESTWARD HO! (1855): *No absolution, no viaticum, nor anything! I die like a dog!*

viaticum. See *viaggiatory.*

vibratiunculation. The act of *vibrating* gently or slightly. A slight *vibration* is a *vibratiuncle.* The words were used in the 18th and 19th centuries, as in Thomas Reid's AN INQUIRY INTO THE HUMAN MIND (1764): *Our sensations arise from vibrations and our ideas from vibratiuncles.*

vice. See *psychomachy.*

victim. See *wizard.*

videnda. Things that ought to be seen. The gerundive plural of *videre,* to see. The same form appears in *agenda,* things that ought to be done. Sterne in TRISTRAM SHANDY (1760) states: *In my list, therefore, of videnda at Lyons this, tho' last, was not, as you see, least.* From the same source came the rare (16th century) English *vident,* a prophet, a seer.

viduity. Emptiness, the state of being destitute; hence, especially (though less often destitute), widowhood. Also, *viduation.* Latin *vidua,* widow; *viduus,* deprived, destitute, bereaved. Hence, in either sense, *vidual, viduate*; *viduous,* empty, unoccupied.

vilipend. (1) To regard as of little value, to despise; hence, to treat slightingly. Latin *vilis,* worthless, vile + *pendere,* to weigh, estimate, consider. This sense was very common in the 16th and 17th centuries, revived by Scott in WAVERLEY (1814): *a youth devoid of that petulant volatility which is impatient of, or vilipends, the conversation and advice of his seniors.* (2) Confused with this, especially in the 19th century, to *vilipend,* to vilify, to speak of with contempt, to represent as bad or worthless. Thackeray in VANITY FAIR (1848) says: *Menacing the youth with maledictions . . . and vilipending the poor innocent girl as the basest and most artful of vixens.* Also *vilipender*; *vilipenditory,* abusive; *vilipendious,* contemptible; *vilipendency,* the expression of contempt; *vilipension,* the act of despising.

vimineous. Pliable; made of pliable twigs or wickerwork. Latin *viminem,* osier, reed. Hence *viminal,* good for winding or binding (in 17th and 18th century dictionaries). Also *viminious.* Matthew Prior wrote, in ALMA (1717) *As in a hive's vimineous dome, Ten thousand bees enjoy their home.*

vinaceous. Wine-colored, a rosy red. In Pennant's BRITISH ZOOLOGY (1776) we read the description: *the rump a fine cinereous: breast and belly, pale chestnut dashed with a vinaceous cast.*

vince. While folk still argue as to who can screw the inscrutable, there is no doubt that the English once vinced the invincible, when with the help of God they destroyed The Invincible Armada of Philip II of Spain, July 21-29, 1588. As R. Adams said in 1590: *The English fleet . . . dispersed that invincible navy, and made it vincible.* The 18th century (Richardson) used the noun *vincibility. To vince* was a 16th century verb, meaning to defeat, to be victorious; from Latin *vincere, vici, victum,* as in Caesar's laconic report *Veni, vidi, vici,* I came, I saw, I conquered. The participle (Hail the conquering hero!) survives in the name *Vincent,* as of my cousin "the hunter". Strangely, the dupe in a game of bowls or other cheating play (16th century) was called the *vincent; Vincent's law,* the art of cheating—perhaps a cant perversion of *St. Vincent's law* of orthodoxy: "what everyone, everywhere, always believes". (*St. Vincent of Lerins,* died about 450 A.D.; whence, the *Vincentian* canon.) Universal credulousness marks the dupe.—in the 17th century *vincible* was applied especially to *vincible ignorance,* which, being superable, is not to be condoned; Donne in a Sermon of 1626 remarked: *God forgives none of that which is left undone, out of a wilfull and vincible ignorance.* Similarly, ignorance of the law, being vincible, is no excuse. A *vincetoxic* (17th century) was an antidote to poison. Note that both *evince* and *evict* are from *evincere, evictum,* to prove, from *vincere,* to conquer, to confute. *To evict* earlier meant to vanquish (in argument); to prove; to recover one's property, hence to remove another from one's property, the current sense.—Without being wholly invincible, some folk are hard to convince.

vindemiate. To harvest fruit, especially grapes; sometimes, (noun: *vindemy*) to take honey from the hive. Latin *vindemiare; vinum,* vine, wine + *demo; de,* away + *emo, emptus,* to take (whence *exemplary, example*), later, to buy (*Caveat emptor*). Hence *vindemial, vindemiatory,* relating to the gathering of grapes (or other fruit); *vindemiation.* The word *vindematrix,* a female vintager, is used as the name of a bright star in the constellation Virgo. In Isaac Todhunter's WILLIAM WHEWELL, D.D. (1831) a figurative use is quoted: *People will ask you to reckon your fruits: so vindemiate as fast as you can.*

vinipote. A wine-bibber. Latin *vinum,* wine + *potus,* having drunk; *potare,* to drink, whence *potation;* Greek *potas,* (drinkable, fresh) water; *potamos,* a river; whence *hippopotamus,* river-horse (*Philip —Philhippus*—lover of horses, as were Philip of Macedon and his son Alexander the Great.) One of our best American tellers of folktales is also a discriminating vinipote. He is also a *vinologist,* connoisseur in wines, although not given to *vinolency,* drunkenness. *Vinolent,* tending to make one drunk, fond of drinking, occurs several times in Chaucer. Urquhart in the THE JEWEL (1652) used *vinomadefied* (accent on the *mad*), soaked with wine.

vinolent. See *vinipote.*

vinomadefied. See *vinipote.*

vinum. See *metheglin.*

virelai. Also *virelay, verelai, verilay, vyrelay,* and more. See *virly.*

virginal. A popular musical instrument of the 16th and 17th centuries, with keys; like a *spinet* but without legs (hence virginal? or because favored by young ladies?). The *spinet* was triangular; the *virginal,* rectangular. Usually in the plural, *the virginals,* referring to one instrument; also *a pair of virginals*; there were also *double virginals,* the first in 1581. The *triangle* (*tryangle*) and the *harpsicon* were names for other varieties of the instrument, the *harpsicon* (also *harpsical*; an early *harpsichord*) being the largest. Pepys, ever gallant, on 16 March, 1663 (his DIARY tells) went *home by coach, buying at the Temple the printed virginall-book for her.* Pepys delighted in giving music lessons in his household; in the DIARY (19 June, 1666) he gives a teasing account of some delightful and perhaps virginal playing. The instrument was then as popular in England as the piano in pre-radio America; watching the loading of household effects into boats on the Thames during the great London fire (2 September, 1666) Pepys *observed that hardly one boat in three that had the goods of a house in, but there was a pair of virginalls in it.* The harpsichord, from its earliest days, was not only an instrument but a work of art, with paintings and jeweled inlay, a collector's item; Duke Alfonso II of Modena in 1598, for example, owed fifty-two harpsichords.

virgin's bower. The 'upright clamberer,' a climbing shrub (a variety of clematis), also known as traveler's joy. Mortimer's THE WHOLE ART OF HUSBANDRY in 1707 observed that *Double virgin's bower is a climbing tree, fit to cover some place of repose* (such as a virgin glade, belike). Keats mentions the shrub in ENDYMION (1818); Morris says, in THE EARTHLY PARADISE (1870): *And woodbine, and the odorous virgin's-bower, Hung in great heaps about that undyked tower.*

virgin's milk. A solution of benjamin (benzoin) in alcohol, with twenty parts of rose-water. Used in the 17th century as a cosmetic wash for the face and skin. A dandified gallant might boast that he bathed in virgin's milk. Also (German *Liebfraumilch*), a sweet white wine.

viridarium. See *verderer.*

viripotent. Possessing strength; (of a woman) physically fit for marriage. Latin *vir,* man, *vires,* strength + *potentem,* able. Hence, *viripotence, viripotency,* (accent on the *rip*) marriageability. Sir Edward Peyton in THE DIVINE CATASTROPHE OF THE KINGLY FAMILY OF THE HOUSE OF STUARTS (1652) noted that Mary Stuart, *when she attained to viripotency, was sought for a consort to the Dauphin of France.*

virl. A band or strip of metal, ivory, etc., placed along an edge or end of a piece of wood to keep it from wearing or splitting. Also *virlet,* a small *virl.* Used from the 15th century; related to *ferrule.* Thus Ramsay in THE GENTLE SHEPHERD (1725) speaks of *A winsome flute, o' plum-tree made, with ivory virles round.* Galt in SIR ANDREW WYLIE OF THAT ILK (1822) mentions *an ivory headed cane virled with gold.*

virly. A light dance, or dancing game, of the 14th and 15th centuries. Probably from *vireli,* an old French meaningless refrain. The form *vireli,* influenced by *lai* (English *lay*), song, became *virelai,* a short lyric poem or song. It developed in 14th century France; usually each stanza had two rhymes, the second in one stanza becoming the main rhyme in the next. Chaucer (1385), Gower, Lydgate used the word; Spenser (1579), Drayton; Dryden (THE FLOWER AND THE LEAF; 1700): *And then the band of flutes began to play, To which a lady sung a virelay.* The form, which became unfashionable about 1600, was revived by the light-verse writers of the late 19th century.

viron. A simple and earlier form of *environ.* As a noun, circuit, a circling course. As a verb, to go round, encircle. *In viron, in the viron of,* round about. Also *vironry,* environment. From Old French *viron; virer,* to turn; from Greek *gyros,* circle, whence *gyrate, gyroscope,* and the *autogyro,* now often seen in these environs.

visney. A liqueur: cherry brandy. Persian *wishneh,* cherry. An 18th century importation; Bailey in his HOUSEHOLD DICTIONARY (1736) gives a recipe: "Fill a large bottle or cask with morello cherries . . . and fill up the bottle or vessel with brandy . . ." Or you might buy Turkish visney in London—around 1700—at 20 shillings the gallon.

visnomy. See *viznomy.*

visor. See *bever.*

vitativity. Fondness of life; zest for living. Also *vitativeness,* used in phrenology. Hence *vitative,* fond of living.

vitilitigation. Quarrelsomeness; wrangling. Hence, *vitilitigious,* quarrelsome. Also *vitilitigate,* to backbite, to wrangle. H. Busk in THE VESTRIAD (1819), beginning the story of Paris and Helen, mentions the goddess *In heaven yclept Alecto . . . But discord called by mortals here on earth; A vitilitigating horrid girl,* who threw the apple. (Her Greek name was *Eris,* the opposite of *Eros.* There should be an adjective *eritic,* balancing *erotic.*) Nathaniel Ward in THE SIMPLE COBLER OF AGAWAM in America (1647) knew that *it is a most toylsome taske to runne the wild-goose chase after a well breath'd opinionist: they delight in vitilitigation.* If only it were witty litigation!

vizard. See *bever.*

viznomy. A variant of *visnomy* (*vysenamy, visenomy*), early forms of *physiognomy.* The form (from the 16th and early 17th centuries) was revived by Scott in THE BRIDE OF LAMMERMOOR (1818): *The loon has woodie written on his very visnomy,* and in KENILWORTH; Lamb and others continued its use.

vizor. See *bever.*

voidee. A parting dish; wine with spices or tidbits, at bedtime or before guests leave. From French *voidée, voider* (whence also *void, avoid*): emptying, as by departure. Used from the 14th century (Chaucer, TROILUS AND CRISEYDE; 1374) to the 17th. Sometimes the *voidee* was quite elaborate; Holinshed in his CHRONICLES (1587) mentioned *a voidee of spices with sixtie spice plates.*

voider. That which keeps things off or away, a screen, a piece of armor, especially a small piece over an unprotected portion of the body such as elbow or knee. Also a tray or basket into which things are put, to clear the table. A stage direction in Heywood's A WOMAN KILLED WITH KINDNESS (1607) reads: *Enter 3 or 4 servingmen, one with a voyder and a woodden knife to take away.* The word was also used figuratively, as in Dekker's THE GULL'S HORN-BOOK (1609):

Piers Ploughman layd the cloth, and Simplicity brought in the voyder. By extension, of a basket for dirty clothes, or of any receptacle for rubbish; some were indignant, said Purchas in his PILGRIMAGE (1613), *that our Britannia should make her Virginian lap to be the voider for her lewder and more disordered inhabitants.* From the sense of basket, *voider* came in the late 17th and early 18th century, to be used of an ornamented (wooden) basket for sweetmeats. Thus Lady Fanshawe relates in her MEMOIRS that, at Madrid: *Several times we saw the Feasts of Bulls and at them we had great voiders of dried sweetmeats brought us upon the King's account.* EVERYMAN (1520) made proffer: *A precious jewell I wyll gyve thee Called penaunce, voyder of adversyte.*

volage. Giddy; fickle, inconstant. Common from the 14th into the 16th century; reintroduced in the 18th century directly from the French *volage,* fickle, from Latin *volare,* to fly. Also *volageous; volage-brained.* Chaucer in THE ROMAUNT OF THE ROSE (1366) has: *She fulfilled of lustynesse, That was not yit twelve yeer of age, With herte wylde and thought volage.* And Ouida in STRATHMORE (1865) remarked upon *the volage, and somewhat indiscreet, Princesse de Lorine.*

volary. A large birdcage. The 17th and 18th century term for an aviary; also, the birds therein. Also *volarie, vollary, volery;* Latin *volare,* to fly. Also used figuratively, as in Jonson's THE NEW INNE (1629): *She now sits penitent and solitary, Like the forsaken turtle, in the volary Of the light heart, the cage she hath abused;* and in UNDERWOODS: *I thought thee then our Orpheus, that wouldst try, Like him, to make the air one volary.*

volpone. (Three syllables.) A cunning schemer or miser. From the character in Jonson's play VOLPONE (1606); Italian *volpe,* Latin *vulpis,* fox. The word was fairly frequent in the 17th and the early 18th centuries, as in a sermon of Sacheverell, 5 November, 1709: *In what . . . lively colours does the Holy Psalmist paint out the crafty insidiousness of such wilely volpones?*

voluper. A woman's headdress; especially, a kerchief wrapped about the head. [*Kerchief* comes from French *couvre-chef,* cover-head.] *Voluper* seems short for *enveloper;* Old French *envelopeur,* a kerchief. Chaucer in THE MILLER'S TALE (1386) says: *The tapes of her white voluper Were of the same suyte of hir coler.* Cranmer in the BIBLE (1539) translates one of the lines of THE SONG OF SONGS (BALLETTES OF SOLOMON): *Thy chekes are lyke a pece of a pomgranate within thy volupers.* He probably saw rosy English chekes on the Queen of Sheba.

vomitorium. A passageway from the seats, an exit, in the ancient theatre or amphitheatre. Also *vomitory.* Latin *vomitorium; vomere, vomitum,* to pour forth, vomit. This word, misunderstood, gave rise to the legend that at the Roman feasts a glutted one would rise, step out to the *vomitorium,* by a finger or feather in his mouth effect purgation and make room for more, and so back to the banquet table. There are always gross-gullets, but the Roman—like the Chinese at a many-coursed meal—would taste and test, nibbling at all but his special choice of the proffered viands. It was the theatre audience that 'vomited forth,' as Gibbon knew when he stated in THE DECLINE AND FALL OF THE ROMAN EMPIRE (1776): *Sixty-four vomitories (for by that name the doors were very aptly distinguished)* *poured forth the immense multitude.* The word was also used figuratively, as when John Wilson in NOCTES AMBROSIANAE (1826) described a man with *his tongue struck dumb in his cheek, and the vomitory of vociferation hermetically sealed.*

voraginous. Relating to or resembling a whirlpool or an abyss or chasm. Also *vorageous, voragious; vorage, vorago,* a whirlpool, a chasm; Latin *vorago; vorare,* to devour, whence also *voracious, voracity; vorant,* devouring; *vorax,* ravenous. Cokaine in DIANEA (1654) told of *a voraginous place, about the banks of which those men appeare that have perished by a violent death.* Reeve in GOD'S PLEA FOR NINEVEH, OR LONDONS PRECEDENT FOR MERCY (1657) used the word to mean with the swallowing capacity of an abyss, grieving *that we think to get our admission under God with voraginous paunches, and soaked gullets.*

vouchsafe. To bestow; grant, deign (to accept, to grant or to permit). Used from the 14th century, it developed many forms (as *votesafe, voutchafe, fochesafe, wetsaffe, wychsafe*); until the 16th century it was usually treated as two words, thus *vouching safe, wouch it safe.* Shakespeare in CYMBELINE (1611): *I have assayl'd her with musickes, but she vouchsafes no notice. You may see,* said Hakluyt in his VOYAGES (1599), *what gracious privileges and high prerogatives were by divers kings vouchsafed upon them.*

Vulcan's brow. A horned brow, the sign of the cuckold. The allusion is to the amours of Mars and Vulcan's wife, Venus. Rowlands, in his satire LOOKE TO IT: FOR ILE STABBE YE (1604), stabbed all sorts of sinners with his pen, among them the "huswife" always demanding money of her husband: *You that will have it, get it how he can, Or he shall weare a Vulcans brow, poore man. Ile stabbe thee.*

vulgarization. See *pervulgate.*

vulnerate. To wound. Latin *vulnerare, vulneratum; vulnerem (volnerem),* a wound. The adjective *vulnerable* survives. *vulneral, vulnerary,* helpful for wounds. *vulnerative,* likely to produce wounds; W. Taylor in THE MONTHLY REVIEW of 1818 wrote: *With a sort of hedgehog hostility, which points its vulnerative quills in every direction alike. vulnific, vulnifical,* causing wounds. *vulnerose,* full of wounds, badly wounded. *vulneration,* the act of wounding; the state of being wounded. In the 16th century, *vuln,* to wound, surviving in heraldry: *vulned,* represented as pierced by a weapon; *vulning,* wounding, used of the pelican, always shown wounding her own breast.

vulpicide. See *stillicide.*

vulpine. See *lupine.*

vyssare. Early (southern Middle English) form of *fisher.* Also *vysseth,* fishing.

vysycyon. Early (southern Middle English) form of *physician.*

W

wafery. See *chaundrye.*

waif. Goods (said Bailey, 1751) that a thief drops or leaves behind him, when overcharged or close pursued, which belong to the King or the Lord of the Manor, unless the owner convict the thief within a year and a day; if so, he shall have his goods again. Also *weif, wayve, wayff,* earlier *gwaif.* Used from the 13th century in Anglo-Latin, in English since 1375, often in the phrase *waif and straif* (*stray*). Often used figuratively as by Donne in DEVOTIONS (1624): *What a wayve and stray is that man that hath not Thy marks upon him!*—thus revived by Scott in PEVERIL OF THE PEAK (1823): *You are here a waif on Cupid's manor, and I must seize on you in name of the deity.* In the sense of a lost or homeless or neglected child, *waif* remains in use.

wain. An early (and now poetic) form of *wagon.* Old English *waen, waegen,* related to *way.* A *waner, wainman,* a wagoner. Also *wainful,* wagon-load, and other combinations. Thus *wainscot* meant originally a fine imported oak, from *wagon* + *schot,* load (?). A *wainwright* was a wagon builder.

waistcoateer. A prostitute. Women in the 16th and 17th centuries wore a *waistcoat,* a camisole or bodice, under their gown. The *waistcoateer* managed without the gown. A rebuke in Beaumont and Fletcher's WIT WITHOUT MONEY (1616) runs: *Doe you thinke you are here, sir, amongst your wastcoateers, your base wenches that scratch at such occasions? you're deluded.*

wait. As a noun: (1) a period of waiting; especially, in the theatre, intermission; also, an actor's time between appearances onstage. (2) A watchman, sentinel, spy; a body of guards. In particular, a watchman of the royal household that sounded the watch, on trumpet, fife, or other wind instrument. Hence, *the waits,* a group of wind instrumentalists maintained by a city. The word is related to Gothic *wahtwo,* English *watch*; Old French *wait, guait, guet,* watch, spy. Common since the 14th century. Mackyn in his DIARY (1553) said that the new Lord Mayor was attended by the *craftes of London, toward Westminster, with trumpets blohyng and the whets playing.* Hence, in general, wind instruments (hautboys, shawms, flutes). (3) By extension, a band of street singers and players of Christmas carols, in expectation of gifts. Thus *the sound of the waits,* says Irving in THE SKETCH BOOK (1820), *breaks upon the mid-watches of a winter night.* Whittier in THE PENNSYLVANIA PILGRIM (1872) tells how *On frosty Christmas eves He closed his eyes and listened to the sweet Old wait-songs sounding down his native street.*

waive. As a noun, "a woman," said Bailey (1751), "outlawed for contemptuously refusing to appear when sued in law. She is so called as being forsaken [*a* *waif, q.v.*] of the law, and not *an outlaw* as a man is, because women not being sworn in leets to the King, nor in courts as men are, cannot be outlawed." The earliest (13th century) meaning of the verb *waive* was to punish by depriving of the protection of the law. *Cp. leet.*

wale. In addition to current uses (to mark the flesh with *wales* or *weals,* etc.) *wale* was a verb, to choose (also with *out; to wale by,* to select and put aside); a noun, the act of choosing, the chosen, choice, the best; and an adjective, chosen, choice, excellent—from the 13th century. Common forms through the 16th century, they were renewed by Scott (GUY MANNERING, 1815: *The Bertrams were aye the wale o' the countryside!*) and others in the 19th. Thus De Quincey in his NOTES ON LANDOR (1847) states: *Our Arab friend, however, is no connoisseur in courts of law: small wale of courts in the desert.* The verb form of *wale* was used by Burns, Carlyle, Scott, and others. The adjectival use was not revived; it may be seen in THE DESTRUCTION OF TROY (1400): *She went up from that worthy into a wale chamber.*

wamble. To feel nausea; to twist about; to walk unsteadily; (of water, or blood) to seethe, to boil. While along one course the form *wamble* is related to Latin *vomere,* to vomit, the meanings may have come from different roots. In the first sense, the word was also used figuratively as when Lyly in ENDYMION (1591) spoke of *the rume of love that wambleth in his stomacke* and Middleton in A GAME AT CHESS (1624) declares that his soul *can digest a monster, without cruditie, A monster weightie as an elephant, And never wamble for it.*

wandsomely. Reluctantly. Used in the 14th and 15th centuries.

wanhope. Despair. Used since the 13th century; often in a religious sense, despair of salvation; then, in love poems using religious imagery. Thus Wyatt (in Tottel's MISCELLANY, 1542): *Renewyng with my suit my pain, My wanhope with your stedfastnesse.*

waniand. Used in the phrase *in the (wild) waniand*—short for *in the waniand* [waning] *moon,* supposed to be an unlucky period: an exclamatory term or imprecation, like "with a plague." Used in the 14th and 15th centuries; about 1550, replaced by *wanion (wannion, wenyon, wenian*); later, *with a (wild) wanion.* Shakespeare in PERICLES (1607) has: *Come away, or Ile fetch'th with a wanion. A (wild) wanion on, with a wanion to,* May a curse light upon—. Scott revived the phrases, as in WOODSTOCK (1826): *He would have battered the presbyterian spirit out of him with a wanion.*

wanlace. A circuit made by some of a hunting party, to intercept and head back the game. Hence: an appointed station in hunting; an intercepting movement, an ambush; a crafty device or plot. A hunting servant used for intercepting the game was called a *wanlasour, wandlessour.* Used into the 16th century.

wannion. See *waniand.*

wantroth. Unbelief. Also *wantruth.* In the 13th and 14th centuries.

wantrust. Lack of confidence. Used by Chaucer (TROYLUS AND CRISEYDE, 1374) and into the 15th century; a Coventry Mystery of 1450 avers: *Many a man with his wantruste hymsylf hathe slayn.*

wantsum. Poor, without—. An apt 12th and 13th century word.

wanweird. Misfortune, ill fate. Used in the 16th and 17th centuries. Mainly in Scotland; Douglas in the AENEIS (1513) wrote: *I tuik comfort heirof, thinkand but baid That hard wanwerd suld follow fortun glaid.*

wapentake. A subdivision of an English shire; a meeting (later, a court) of such a district. Also *wappentake, wapyntak,* and many more. The word is from Old Norse *vapnatak; vapn,* weapon + *tak,* taking. In Old Norse it meant a brandishing of weapons as a vote at an assembly or gathering of warriors; in Iceland, the picking up of weapons at the end of an assembly. Hence, an assembly meeting-place or district. The shires of England that have *wapentakes* have large Danish elements in their history: Yorkshire, Derbyshire, Notts, Lincolnshire, Northamptonshire, Leicestershire; Nottinghamshire (1846) was divided into six wapentakes. Other shire-divisions are the *hundreds.*

wapman. A human male. Used from the 10th to the 14th century, to distinguish a man from a woman. Also *waepman, weopmonne, wepenmon.* The word is from *weapon* + *man,* meaning the division of *man*kind that bears its own *weapon* (now familiarly referred to as *tool*).

wappened. Used by Shakespeare in TIMON OF ATHENS (1607): *This it is That makes the wappen'd widdow wed againe.* The meaning can only be guessed; some have suggested the word is a corruption of *wappered,* worn-out, but that hardly fits the sense. Among the meanings of the word *wap* are to throw, to envelop; these may afford suggestions.

wappenshawing. A muster of men under arms (into the 17th century) in a lordship or district. Also *wappenschawing, wappenshaw; wapinschawin, vaupynschauying,* and many more; sometimes modernized into *weaponshowing. Cp. wapentake.* Scott in THE FAIR MAID OF PERTH 1828) hails *the best wrestler . . . the king of the weapon-shawing—the breaker of mad horses.*

war. See *were.*

warish. To heal, to cure; to recover; by extension, to guard, protect, preserve; save, rescue. A common word from the 13th century; also *guarish; waris, warysche, warshe,* and the like. Chaucer says in THE BOOK OF THE DUCHESSE (1369): *I was warshed of al my sorwe.*

warison. Wealth, possessions. A variant (in Old French) of *guarison,* whence English *garrison* [originally meaning safety, then taking on the meaning of English *garnison, garnish,* to fit out, to supply, hence, means of defence. Chaucer in MELIBEUS (1386) says: *The gretteste and strongeste garnyson that a riche man may have, as wel to kepen his persone as his goodes, is that he be beloved among his subjetz and his neighebores.*] *To bring* (someone) *in* (or *to his*) *warison,* to make rich. Also, *to give in warison,* to give in marriage. Also figuratively, as in the PROVERBS OF HENDYNG (1325): *Wyt and wysdom is good warysoun;* Robert Manning of Brunne in HANDLYNG SINNE (1303) said: *Gyf thou ravysshe a mayden poore . . . thou has stole her warysun.* From treasure, *warison* came to mean the gift of a superior, a reward; then Chaucer (1366) used it to mean one's just due; reward or punishment. In THE BATTLE OF OTTERBOURNE occurs the line: *Mynstrels, playe up for your waryson* [reward, pay]; this poem was included in Percy's RELIQUES OF ANCIENT ENGLISH POETRY

(1765); Scott, probably mistaking the sense, used *warison* to mean the sounding call to attack: THE LAY OF THE LAST MINSTREL (1805): *Either receive within thy towers Two hundred of my master's powers Or straight they sound their warison And storm and spoil thy garrison.* Byron in DON JUAN (1824) follows: *As my friend Scott says, 'I sound my warison.'* Others have less wittingly continued Scott's mistake.

warlock. Originally, an oath-breaker, a traitor. From Old Saxon *war,* true (Pre-Teutonic root *wero,* Latin *verus*) + Old English *leogan,* to lie. It had many forms, including *werlau, warlaw, warlag, warelocke, warlike, warlok, warluck, warloghe, warlo.* From the 10th century (and in many uses in CURSOR MUNDI, 1300) *warlock* was used to mean the Devil. Hence, a devil, spirit of hell; damned soul in hell; a villain, a damnable soul; a monstrous creature—giant, cannibal, serpent, real or mythical creature hostile to man. By extension, one in league with the devil, a sorcerer, wizard, magician. From Scott's frequent use of *warlock* in this sense, the word grew again into currency. Dryden used the word to mean a man invulnerable (by certain metals); he spelled it (in his AENEIS, 1697) as though the word came from *war,* fighting + *luck,* fortune, saying of Aeneas: *It seems he was no warluck, as the Scots commonly call such men, who, they say, are iron-free, or lead-free.* The word was very common from the 9th to the 16th century. Goliath is referred to in these lines from CURSOR MUNDI: *Allas! quar sal we find a man that dar the fight, for mi sake, Again yon warlau undertake?* Burns used the word several times; in TAM O' SHANTER (1789) he has *Warlocks and witches in a dance* while auld Nick *screwed the pipes and gart them skirl.* Stevenson, though, would have disappointed the radio-TV give-away audience; in KIDNAPPED (1886) we read: *I'm nae warlock, to find a fortune for you in the bottom of a parritch* [porridge] *bowl.*

warnel. See *agnail.*

warner. A tart or cake built into an elaborate decoration, carried around before a course at a dinner. Used in the 16th century; from *to warn,* to announce. When Archbishop Warham was "inthroned" in 1505, the *warner* before the first course had eight towers, with flowers and battlements; atop each tower was a beadle in full costume. Often, although buttressed with wire and wood, and decorated with feathers, silk, and beads, the warner was eaten. A development of the same sort, wrought mainly of sugar, was the *subtlety,* from the meaning, an ingenious contrivance. It was often made in a form that alluded to the host's or the guest of honor's name or achievements. As early as 1390 (in THE FORM OF CURY) we read of *curious potages and meetes, and sotiltees.* They have varied in design from a nested pelican feeding her young to St. George slaying the dragon; their main modern counterpart is the wedding-cake.

warnish. (1) A variant (in the 14th century) of *garnish,* meaning to equip oneself; to furnish with supplies or guards. (2) An early form of *warn,* used several times, e.g., in CURSOR MUNDI (1300) as *Therof was wernist Moses.* Hence *warnison,* a supply of men and provisions, a garrison. Also *warnestore, warnstora, warmstore, warnystoor,* and the like, provender, *garniture. To warnestore* was to furnish with supplies; to fortify. Chaucer uses the word several times, as in

MELIBEUS (1386): *Ye sholde doon youre diligence to kepen youre persone and to warnestoor youre hous.*

warrok. To bind; also, a girth, a girdle. Also *warrock. warrick, warroke.* Langland in PIERS PLOWMAN (1362) said: *Sette my sadel uppon Soffre-til-I-seo-my-tyme, And loke thou warroke him well.* Also *cp. ruskin.*

warship. Caution, prudence; hence, sagacity. From *ware,* as in *beware,* be wary. Used from the 9th into the 13th century.

wase. A bundle of straw or reeds: used as a torch; used as a pad (in this sense, of cloth also) on the head to relieve it of pressure when a burden is borne upon it. Also *wayse, weize, weese,* and more. Used from the 14th century.

washway. A part of a road over which a shallow stream flows. Hence, a road deeper in the middle than at the sides. Also *washum* (Bailey, 1751). *To make washway of* (*with*), to make light of. Donne in a sermon of 1631 declared: *He that hath not been accustomed to a sin, but exercised in resisting it, will finde many tentations, but as a washway that he can trot through, and go forward religiously in his calling for all them.*

wastel. Bread made of the finest flour. Also *wastle, wastell, wastil.* Altered from Old French *guastel, gastel,* French *gâteau,* cake. Chaucer in the Prologue to THE CANTERBURY TALES (1386) says: *Of smale hounds hadde she that she fedde With rosted flessh or milk and wastel bredde.* For its use in a recipe, see *gaylede.*

wastethrift. An outrageous spendthrift. Used first by 17th century playwrights; Middleton, in A TRICK TO CATCH THE OLD ONE (1608): *Hee's a rioter, a wastthrift, a brothellmaister.* In 1868 H. Brandreth wrote a book entitled *Wastethrifts and Workmen. Of the mode of producing them, and their relative value to the community.*

water-. Among the many terms built upon *water,* some may be recalled. *water-ball,* a glass globe, filled with water, that collects and throws rays of light upon an object; also *hour water-ball,* a device that indicates the passing of time by means of a ball in water. *water-bed,* a bed on shipboard; a mattress with water inside, for an invalid. *water-break, water-breach,* an irruption of water, as through a dike; a stretch of broken water or rapids (Douglas, 1513; Wordsworth, 1806; Tennyson, THE BROOK, 1855). *water-bulge, water-bouge, water-bouget,* a skin or leather bag for bearing water; usually two on a pole across the shoulders of a man or the back of a beast. *watercaster,* one that diagnoses by examining the urine, a *uromantes;* in the 17th century, a quack; the Water Poet (1627): *the fare of quacksalvers, mountebanckes, ratcatching watercasters. water-cat, water-cracker,* kinds of fireworks. *waterfast* (16th century), watertight. *watergang* (13th century), a flood; an artificial water-course for drainage or irrigation; also (14th to 17th century), *watergate.* A *water-gate* (15th century) was a sluice or floodgate. *waterlade* (11th to 15th century), a channel, an aqueduct. *waterlag* (16th century), a scoundrel; probably short for *waterlagger, waterleader* (13th to 17th century) a carter of water for sale. *Waterloo,* a decisive contest: *to meet one's Waterloo,* to be finally defeated. Not from the almost ubiquitous fluid but from the village near Brussels where, on 18 June, 1815, Napoleon met his final defeat. Also *waterloo,* a bright blue color; Moore (1823): *Eyes of blue* (*Eyes of that bright, victorious tint Which English* *maids call 'Waterloo'*). Also *Waterloo cracker, Waterloo bang-up,* a kind of fireworks that makes a loud snap when the ends are pulled (often set by the dinner-plate at a celebration). *waterologer* (accent on the *ol*), a *watercaster* (contemptuous; 17th century); hence, *waterology. water-ordeal,* a medieval method of purging one bewitched, or of testing one's guilt: (1) hot water-ordeal (1701): *for the party accused to thrust his hands or feet into scalding water, on presumption that his innocence would receive no harm;* (2) cold water-ordeal: *for the defendant to be cast into a pond or river (as they now pretend to try witches) whether he would sink or swim. waterquake* (16th century, after *earthquake*), a tremor at sea. *water-rug* (Shakespeare, MACBETH; 1605), a shaggy type of dog. *waterscape* (17th century), escape from drowning. *watershoot, waterbough,* sucker or branch growing at the bottom of a tree. *watershot,* a sudden flood; as an adjective, with many streams (?): Kipling in KIM (1901) speaks of a *fruitful watershot valley,* but he might have had the other meaning in mind, as Golding's translation (1567) of Ovid's METAMORPHOSES said *deep valleyes have by watershotte been made of level ground. watersouchy,* perch (later, other fish) boiled and served in its own liquor; the recipe was brought from Holland in the 18th century; also *watersutchy, watersouchet, watersokey, waterzoutch.*

Waterloo. See *water-.*

wath. A ford; a fordable stream. Old English *waed, wado,* the sea, waves; Latin *vadum,* the sea; a shallow place, a ford, from the root *ba, va,* to go. A North Riding record of 1610 stated: *Forasmuch as Skipton bridge is likely to become ruinous by carriages of great burthen . . . a wath is there made passable.*

wayzgoose. An entertainment given by a master printer to his workmen, marking the beginning of work by candle-light; usually, "about Bartholomew-tide" (24 August). Later, it became an annual summer festivity of the printer's employees, with a dinner and a trip to the country. Bailey (1751) suggests that the word is from *wayz,* straw + *goose,* a stubble-goose, served at the feast. But there is no tradition that goose was served at these parties, and *wase* (*q.v.*), a wisp or bundle of straw, was never spelled *wayz* except by Bailey. In fact, before Bailey (and after him until people took his word for it), the form was *waygoose.* It is probably a folk change from an earlier, forgotten, word.

weanel. An animal newly weaned. Also *wennell, weynelle, weannel.* Used since the 15th century; by Spenser in THE SHEPHERD'S CALENDAR (1579). It was supplanted by *weanling,* which Bailey, however, (1751) defines as an animal ready to be weaned. In the 16th century, and later in dialects, *weanyer* (*wanyer, wayner, wenyer*) and in the 19th century *weaner* were also used for *weanling.*

webster. A weaver. Used from earliest times; after the 14th century, usually a man. Doughty, however, in ARABIA DESERTA (1888) with reference not to England remarks: *Good webster-wives weave in white borders made of their sheep's wool.*

ween. Opinion, belief; likelihood; doubt. *Withouten ween,* without doubt. A very common word, 9th through 15th century; still used in poetry as a verb: *I ween,* I think. Also to expect, to desire, to hope; Shakespeare in HENRY VI, PART ONE (1591) has: *Thy father . . . Levied an army, weening to redeem And have installed me in the diademe.* In the 14th and 15th centuries, there was an adjective *ween,* meaning beautiful: *weener than Guenevere,* said GAWAIN AND THE GREEN KNIGHT. But in the 17th century an *easy weener* meant an over-credulous person, one that believes too soon. *Weening,* supposing, as a noun, came also to mean insisting upon one's opinion; hence, self-conceit, *overweening.*

weet. A variant though popular form of *wit,* to know; the past tense forms were *wot, wist. Cp. wit.* Spenser uses *wetelesse* for meaningless: *That with fond termes and weetlesse words to blere myne eyes doest thinke* (THE SHEPHERD'S CALENDAR, 1579); later, it meant ignorant; *weetingly, wittingly,* knowingly. After about 1550, *weet* was for 150 years a poetic form, especially in such phrases as *I give you to weet.* In the 18th century, it was revived in imitation of Spenser, and given new forms: *I weet, he weets; weeted*—used so, e.g., by Shelley, Patmore, Swinburne. Shakespeare uses it but once, in ANTONY AND CLEOPATRA (1606):— *the world to weete We stand up peerlesse.*

weladay. See *wellaway.*

welk. To wilt, wither, fade; to diminish, shrink; to wane. Also, to *welken.* Gower, in CONFESSIO AMANTIS (1390) has: *The sea now ebbeth, now it floweth, The lond now welketh, now it groweth.* Also, to make fade, as in Spenser's THE SHEPHERD'S CALENDAR (1579): *But now sadde winter welked hath the day.*

welkin. (1) A cloud. From the 6th through the 12th century: Beowulf. (2) The vault of heaven, the sky. Very common; but after the 15th century, mainly in dialects or in poetry. Also in phrases; *by the welkin;* Ben Jonson in THE POETASTER (1601): *This villainous poetry will undo you, by the welkin.* Also, *to the welkin.* Of loud sounds: *to rend the welkin, to make the welkin ring;* Marlowe in TAMBURLANE, PART ONE (1587): *As when a fiery exhalation Wrapt in the bowels of a freezing cloude, Fighting for passage, makes the welkin cracke;* Shakespeare makes *the welkin answer* in the Induction to THE TAMING OF THE SHREW (1596). Also, *out of my welkin,* beyond my ken, out of my sphere, as in Shakespeare's TWELFTH NIGHT (1601): *Who you are, and what you would, are out of my welkin.*

wellaway. Alas! As an exclamation of sorrow, this dates back at least to Alfred (9th century) and was heard—in many forms—for a thousand years. Its earliest form was probably *wellawo (wail a woe),* Old English *wa la wa,* woe, lo!, woe. It was used as a refrain, *Sing wellaway; my song is wellaway.* Chaucer in THE BOOK OF THE DUCHESS (1369) tells: *Phyllis also for Demophon Henge* [hanged] *hirselfe, so weylaway.* Spenser in THE FAËRIE QUEENE (1596) echoing Gower (1390) has: *Ah woe is me and wellaway, quoth hee . . . that ever I this dismall day did see.* Other similar exclamations of sorrow—formed as variants of these—were *welladay, wellanear;* in Scotland *wellawins.* All of these had many spelling variants; *wellaway* has 70 listed in O.E.D. They might be spelled with one *l,* or with hyphens, or as three words, e.g., *well y weye.* The word was sometimes used to mean a lament, as in Shakespeare's PERICLES (1608): *His daughter's woe and heavie welladay.* If this went on, I might echo Coleridge's ANCIENT MARINER (1798): *Ah wel-a-day! what evil looks Had I from old and young!*

well-thewed. Virtuous, well-mannered. Gower; Spenser (THE SHEPHERD'S CALENDAR; 1579); Skelton in WHY NOT TO COURT?: *Thy tongue is not wel thewde.*

well-willy. Benevolent, generous. Also *good-willy.* Chaucer, in TROYLUS AND CRISEYDE (1374) has: *Venus mene I, the welwilly planet.*

wem. To disfigure, mutilate, impair; to desecrate, to harm; to stain (with sin), to defile; to stain (with spots). Widely used from the 9th to the 14th century; also as a noun, stain (of sin), blemish. Often in the phrase *without (en) wem, wemless,* immaculate; thus the Lord foretells, in a Towneley mystery (1460): *My son shall in a madyn light . . . wythouten wem, as sun through glass.* Layamon (1275) tells, of a man, *that through his wrath his wit was iwemmid.* Also, *wemod,* (Old English *wea,* trouble, malice + *mod,* mood), angry, passionate.

wench. A girl, young woman; a maidservant; used as a familiar term to a sweetheart, wife, daughter, trusted maidservant; a disreputable or wanton woman, a mistress, a prostitute. Also *weynche, winch.* From the 9th to the 14th century, *wenchel (wencel, wince),* a child (of either sex); a slave, a servant; a common woman. To *wench,* to *wench out (time),* to frequent prostitutes. Shakespeare uses the forms often: *the wenching rogues* (TROILUS AND CRESSIDA, 1606); *beeing too wenchlesse* (PERICLES); and (CYMBELINE) *Do not play in wench-like words with that Which is so serious.*

were. I. As a noun. (1) A man, a male. (Sanskrit *vira,* Latin *vir,* whence *virility.*) Hence (probably) *a werewolf, werwolf,* a human changed or able to change into a wolf. (2) A husband. From this sense *wer,* short for *wergeld,* (3) man-money: a price set on a man according to his rank, paid as a fine in cases of homicide or other crime, instead of other punishment. Common in 11th to 15th century; revived in historical novels. Taylor in EDWIN THE FAIR (1842) quotes a law: *He that within the palace draws his sword Doth forfeit an Earl's were.* (4) Danger, trouble, perplexity; apprehension, dread; mental trouble, doubt, uncertainty. *In were of,* in danger of. This sense is from Middle English *werre,* whence also *war,* which at first meant perplexity, confusion, and has always meant trouble. *To have no were,* to be in no doubt. (5) A protector, defender (13th century). II. As a verb. (1) To check, restrain; repel; defend, guard; to ward off. Used in this sense in HANDLYNG SYNNE (1303): *Frost ne snogh, haile ne reyne, Of colde ne hete felte they no peyne; Heere* [hair] *ne nailes never grewe Ne solowed* [soiled] *clothes ne turned hewe; Thundyr ne lightning did hem no dere, Goddys mercy ded hit from hem were.* (2) To support (a cause), to maintain (an opinion). (3) To have, possess. A common Teutonic word into the 15th century, later in Scotland. Also *wered,* a band, troop, company; *wereful,* doubtful; *werewall,* a rampart, a bulwark, also figuratively as in Sir Richard Holland's THE BUKE OF THE HOWLAT (1450): *The armes of the Douglass . . . Of Scotland the werewall.*

wergeld. Man-money; a price set on a man in proportion to his rank, to be paid if he is killed, in lieu of other punishment. Old English *wer,* man; *cp. were* + *geld, gield,* yield (not to be confused with German *Gelt,* gold). Also *wergild, weregeheld, wargeld, weregild.*

wermod. A variant form of *wormwood, q.v.* Used from the 8th to the 15th century; also, *wermot, wermode, weremod, wormode.*

Wertherian. Morbidly sentimental. Like *Werther,* in THE SORROWS OF YOUNG

WERTHER (1774) by Goethe, which initiated an outburst of suicides. Also *Werterian; Wertherism.*

werwolf. See *were.*

whate. (1) Quickly. Used in the 12th, 13th, and 14th centuries. (2) Divination; augury; fortune, fate, luck. Also *hwat, quate, wate*; Old English *hwata,* augur. So used, 10th to 15th century, as in St. Gregory (14th century): *This is a child of goode whate.* In the sense of good luck, it appears in FLORICE AND BLANCHEFLOUR (1330): *And be hit erly and be hit late To thi wille thou shalt have whate.*

wherret. A sharp blow, as a box on the ear. A *wherret-stopper,* however (18th century), was a bumper or other device on a boat in case of collision. *Wherret* was also a verb, to strike, often figurative, as in Swift's JOURNAL TO STELLA (30 September, 1711): *The Whigs are in a rage about the peace, but we'll wherret them, I warrant.*

whethen. Whence; from whatever place. *Cp. whyne.* Used 12th to 15th century.

whetstone. Figuratively, something that sharpens the wits. Randolph (WORKS; 1635) had a pedlar at Cambridge bring out a whetstone, and descant: *Leaving my brains, I come to a more profitable commodity; for, considering how dull half the wits of this university be, I thought it not the worst traffic to sell whetstones. This whetstone will set such an edge upon your inventions, that it will make your rusty iron brains purer metal than your brazen faces. Whet but the knife of your capacities on this whetstone, and you may presume to dine at the Muses' Ordinarie, or sup at the Oracle of Apollo.* Nares states that *to give the whetstone* "was a standing jest among our ancestors, as a satirical premium to him who told the greatest lie," and quotes TOO GOOD TO BE TRUE (1580) to show there were "jocular games" with the whetstone given as the greatest liar's prize. The passage is, however, obviously satiric, and the O.E.D. states that a whetstone was hung about the neck of a liar, as an actual punishment (London, 1418): *He, as a fals lyere . . . shal stonde . . . upon the pillorye . . . with a westone aboute his necke.* Thence, of course, many phrases attack such persons as *lie for the whetstone,* i.e., deserve it for their lies. Mrs. Centlivre in THE BUSIE BODY (1709) said: *If you be not as errant a cuckold as ere drove bargain upon the Exchange, I am a son of a whetstone.* When Sir Kenelm Digby, boasting that on his travels he had seen the philosopher's stone, was asked to describe it, he hesitated, and Francis Bacon interjected: *"Perhaps it was a whetstone."*

whiffler. (1) A smoker of tobacco; usually contemptuous. Used from the 17th to the 19th century; so also (2) a trifler; an insignificant—or a shifty and evasive—person. In LADY ALIMONY (1659) we read: *Such whifflers are below my scorn, and beneath my spite.* (3) One of a body of advance guards, armed with javelin, battle-ax, sword, or staff, and wearing a chain, whose duty it is to keep the way clear for a procession or public spectacle. Since the 16th century; continued well into the 19th, when they were replaced by regular soldiers, constabulary, or police. By extension, a swaggerer, a bully. The earlier spelling was *wiffler, wifler,* from *wifle,* a javelin; Sanskrit *vip,* shaft of an arrow, rod; Indo-European *wip,* to wave, shake. Addison in THE SPECTATOR (No. 536; 1712) said: *Our fine young ladies . . . retain in their service . . . as great a number as they can of supernumerary fellows,* *which they use like whifflers.* Shakespeare uses the word figuratively, in HENRY V (1599): *The deep-mouth'd sea, Which like a mighty whiffler 'fore the king, Seems to prepare his way.*

whilere. Some time ago; recently. Also *whyleare; erewhile.* Used by Chaucer (1386), Shakespeare (THE TEMPEST III ii 127; 1610), and Milton (1630); revived in MARMION (1808) by Scott. Spenser used the word several times, in THE FAËRIE QUEENE (1590), as in the first stanza of Canto VIII: *When I bethinke me on that speech whyleare Of Mutability, and well it way: Me seemes, that though she all unworthy were Of the heavens' rule, yet very sooth to say, In all things else she beares the greatest sway. Which makes me loath this state of life so tickle And love of things so vaine to cast away, Whose flowring pride, so fading and so fickle Short Time shall soon cut down with his consuming sickle.* [*Tickle,* from the 14th century, meant uncertain, unreliable; hence insecure, dangerous. Also, in the 15th century, fastidious, squeamish; in the 16th, difficult to deal with. Some of these senses have been taken over by *ticklish,* as when one finds oneself in *a ticklish situation.*]

whilom. An early form of *while, whiles.* Also *whilome, hwilum, whylome, whilhom, whilene, whillon,* and more. It was used also as an adverb, meaning at times; once upon a time; in times to come. As an adjective, meaning the former, the late. A common word from early times; used by Chaucer, as in THE KNIGHT'S TALE (1386): *Whilom as olde stories tellen us Ther was a duc that highte Theseus.* Used also by Spenser, Dryden, Fielding, Scott.

whimwham. A fantastic object or idea; a trifle of adornment, dress, speech, or fancy. Reduplicated in the same period (16th century) as *flimflam, jimjam,* and the like, all used for trivial or frivolous objects or concerns. Skelton in THE TUNNYNG OF ELYNOUR RUMMYNG (1529) pictures a fancy hat *After the Sarasyns gyse, With a whym wham, Knyt with a trim tram Upon her brayne pan.* Shirley and Fletcher declare in THE NIGHT WALKER (1625): *They'll pull ye all to pieces, for your whim-whams, your garters and your gloves.* In the 18th century, *whimwham* was also used for a fancy flourish after one's signature. The word was also used, as a euphemism or double entendre, with sexual intent; thus, by the Water Poet (1641): *He caus'd some formes of flowers . . . 'twixt the beast legges to be painted To hide his whimwham;* and by Sterne in TRISTRAM SHANDY (1759): *coaxed many of the oldlicensed matrons . . . to open their faculties afresh, in order to have this whimwham of his inserted.* Also, more playfully, *whimsy-whamsy.* Both *whim* and *whimsy* may be shortenings of these forms, originally mock-echoic.

whindle. To whimper. A diminutive of *whine.* Also *whinnel, whinil.* Also as a noun, a whine or a whining person. Jonson in THE SILENT WOMAN (1609) speaks of *a whiniling dastard.*

whinid. See *finew.*

whipjack. See *pedlers French.*

whipping-boy. A boy educated along with a young noble, and flogged whenever the princeling did something adjudged to merit flogging, or roused his tutor's ire. Bishop Gilbert Burnet in his HISTORY OF HIS OWN TIME (1715) mentioned *William Murray of the bed-chamber, that had been whipping-boy to King Charles the First.* Shakespeare uses *whipping-cheer* to mean 'a banquet of lashes' in HENRY IV, PART TWO (1598); the Beadle that has arrested Doll Tearsheet says: *The constables have delivered her over to me, and she shall have whipping cheer enough, I warrant her.* Convicted whores were then publicly whipped, often on a *whipping-bench* or in the *whipping-stocks,* or tied to the *whipping-pole* (*-post*). It is no wonder that Doll and Hostess Quickly vehemently protest.

whipster. A term of reproach, with various shades of meaning: a lively, violent fellow (such as might swing a mean whip); a lascivious or licentious one. Shakespeare used the term of an insignificant, contemptible fellow, and others (as Dickens, Thackeray, Stevenson) have followed him —OTHELLO (1604): *I am not valiant neither: But every punie whipster gets my sword.* Also *whipstart*; largely replaced, in the last sense, by *whippersnapper.*

whist. Silent, hushed; free from noise or disturbance. Also a verb, to be silent; to hush. Used by Chaucer (1400), Milton (1629), Bridges (1890; SHORTER POEMS). Shakespeare uses it in one of his most delightful songs (THE TEMPEST; 1611): *Come unto these yellow sands And then take hands. Curtsied when you have, and kist The wild waves whist, Foot it featly here and there And, sweet sprites, the burden bear.* Also *whister,* to whisper; *whisterer,* a whisperer. The card game *whist* is said to have come from the demand for silence; but at first (17th century) the game was called *whisk;* from *to whisk,* to move lightly and rapidly, as with a *whiskbroom.* Hence *whisker,* a *whist-player.* Lady Bristol wrote in a letter of 1723: *The wiskers have promised me some diversion.*

whit. See *thwite.*

white. In special forms and combinations: *white acre,* see *black acre. white boy* (*white son; white-headed boy; white hen's chick*), a favorite or a fortunate person (man). *whitecap,* one that, in the U.S. in the 1890's, attacked supposed offenders against the public morals; a sort of Junior Ku Klux Klan. *whitechapel,* low, vulgar; from the *Whitechapel* district of London; also used in special phrases: *whitechapel portion,* two torn smocks and what nature gave; *whitechapel beau,* one that dresses with a needle and thread, and undresses with a knife; *a whitechapel shave,* whitening (powder) spread on the jaws with the hand. *whitefoot,* a member of a violent Irish secret society, flourishing about 1832. *whitefriars,* relating to the Whitefriars district of London (once a sanctuary, hence a resort of those liable to arrest), hence, profligate, loosemoral'd. *white-livered,* cowardly, showing *the white feather*: the true game breed of fighting cock has no white feathers; hence, *to show the white feather,* to be cowardly, to manifest fear. *whiteness,* nakedness; Chapman in THE REVENGE FOR HONOUR (1654) said: *'Twas a rape Upon my honour, more then on her whiteness.* (The O.E.D. inclines to include such examples under the meaning, purity.) *white mouse,* a mean, despicable person (not so obnoxious as a *rat*; note that since the days of 'guinea pig' experimentation the *white mouse* has tended to become a pet). *white night* (French, *nuit blanche*), a sleepless night. *whitesmith,* a worker in "white iron," a tinsmith; also, one that finishes or polishes metal goods, as distinguished from one, the *blacksmith,* that forges them; used from the 14th century. *white wing,* a member of the street-cleaning force of an American city, in the days before automobiles; Philip Barry pictures their departure in his play *White Wings* (1926).

white witch, one that practices *white magic,* i.e., uses witchcraft for beneficent purposes. Similarly, a *white lie* is one told to help, or to avoid hurting, somebody. Among phrases: *to hit the white* (i.e., the center of a target), to be correct, to do or say the right thing. *to mark with a white stone,* to consider fortunate or especially happy (the ancients used a white stone to memorialize good fortune). *white woman,* a 'female' ingredient; a term in alchemy, as in Jonson's THE ALCHEMIST (1610): *Your red man, and your white woman, With all your broths, your menstrues, and materialls.*

whor. An old form of *where.*

whorage. Company of whores. Also *whorism, whoredom.* Hardy, in TESS OF THE D'URBERVILLES (1891) has: *If I had known you was of that sort, I wouldn't have so let myself down as to come with such a whorage as this is!* From the root of *whore,* Indo-European *qar-,* came also Latin *carus,* dear; Old Irish *cara,* friend, *caraim,* I love. Until the 16th century, it was spelled without the *w*: *hore, hoor, howre, heore,* and more. Shakespeare uses *whoremasterly* to mean lecherous, in TROILUS AND CRESSIDA (1606): *That Greekish whoremaisterly villaine.* The defiance in JULIUS CAESAR—*The fault, dear Brutus, is not in our stars, But in ourselves, that we are underlings*—becomes ironic observation in KING LEAR: *An admirable evasion of whoremaster-man, to lay his goatish disposition to the charge of a star.*

whyne. Whence. A contraction of *whethen*; also *quein, qwyne, quhene, wheyn.* Used 13th to 16th century.

widdershins. In the direction opposite to the usual; counterclockwise; against the apparent movement of the sun, hence unlucky. To *stand (start) widdershins,* (of the hair) to stand on end. Used since the 16th century; also *withershins, widdersins, wodsyns, weddirshynnis,* and many more; Middle High German *widersinnen,* to return; *wieder,* back, again + *sind,* direction, way. Alexander Montgomery, in THE FLYTING BETWIXT MONTGOMERY AND POLWART (1585) said that *Thir venerabill virginis quhom ye wald call witches . . . nine times, wirdersones, about the thorne raid.* It was the ritual procedure of black magic to do all things widdershins.

widgeon. A wild duck; hence, a fool, a simpleton. Also *wigeon.* So used in the 17th and 18th centuries, as by Butler in the wordplayful HUDIBRAS (1663): *Th' apostles of this fierce religion, Like Mahomet's, were ass and widgeon.* The goose, the gull, and the coney (rabbit) have also been slandered in this fashion.

wifkin. Womankind. It corresponded to *mankin,* which was replaced by *mankind.* The first meaning of *wife* was woman; this survives in such expressions as *fish wife; an old wives' tale.* Also *wifman,* woman.

wiggery. (1) Wigs collectively, or the practice of wearing them. (2) From the law-court wigs, *wiggery* was used by Carlyle to mean empty formality or 'red tape,' as in PAST AND PRESENT (1843): *Some wisdom among such mountains of wiggery.*

wight. I. As a noun. A living being; then, a preternatural or unearthly being; then, a human being, gradually with pity or contempt implied. Also used of inanimate things personified, as by Chaucer in his poem (1399) *To yow, my purse, and to noon other wight Complayn I, for ye be my lady dere. Aught* and *naught* are derived from *awiht, e'er a wight* and *nawiht, ne'er a wight.* The form was common from the 8th century. Shakespeare in OTHELLO (1604) has: *She was a wight (if ever such wights were) . . . To suckle fooles, and chronicle small beer.* II. As an adjective. Strong, valiant; powerful, mighty; violent, of powerful effect; powerful to resist force, strongly built; agile, nimble, swift. Used until the 16th century, by Shakespeare in LOVE'S LABOUR'S LOST; revived by Scott, as in THE LAY OF THE LAST MINSTREL (1805): *Mount thee on the wightest steed.* Also *wightlayke, whitling,* a brave man, a warrior.

wil. A variant form of *will.* The faculty of conscious and intentional action; the power or exercise of deliberate choice in action. Often in the expression *free will,* but without freedom *will* is, in this sense, an empty word. Freud and modern mechanism have done much to discredit the power, and indeed the very notion, of the will; *free-willer* (a believer in the will) is a term of contempt. Sir Philip Sidney in THE DEFENCE OF POESIE (1595) made a shrewd distinction between man's *erected wit,* which enables him to envision the perfect way, and his *infected wil,* which cannot attain it: our reason suffices, but our *combersome servant passion* too often proves not servant but master of our will. So true is this, that *will* came even to mean lust, carnal desire, as in Shakespeare's THE RAPE OF LUCRECE (1593): *'My will is strong, past reason's weak removing' . . . Thus graceless holds he disputation 'Tweene frozen conscience and hot-burning will.* Will might be viewed as life's helmsman; reason sets the course; but emotion turns askew the eyes bent on the chart, jiggles the magnetic needle, and sweeps up a storm that leaves the helmsman helpless at the wheel. Rare is the man who is master of helmsmanship . . . Only the minister and the lawyer now have great concern for the will.

willesful. An early form of *wilful,* used in the 13th and 14th centuries. Thus a legend of 1290 spoke of a *maiden that beeth willesful, follie for to do.*

will-gill. An effeminate man. Also *will-jill. Hermaphrodite* is a telescope of the god *Hermes* and the goddess *Aphrodite;* hence English *will-gill* (*William-Gillian*), used since the mid-17th century.

will-he, nill-he. Whether he desires or not. Latin *nolens volens.* Thus also *will-she, nill-she; will-ye, nill-ye;* finally shaping as *willy-nilly,* regardless of one's wishes.

willy. (1) A basket; a fish-trap; (from 1780, also *twilly* or *willow*), a machine that revolves, with spikes inside that open and clean wool, cotton, flax. (2) As an adjective: willing; well-disposed. Lydgate in THE TEMPLE OF GLAS (1403) cries *Willi planet, O Esperus so bright, that woful hertes can appese.* Chaucer calls Venus *well-willy, q.v.* (3) See preceding entry.

wimble. (1) A gimlet; an auger. From the 13th century. White in THE NATURAL HISTORY OF SELBORNE (1789) said that a fieldmouse *nibbles a hole with his teeth so regular as if drilled with a wimble.* Hence, *to wimble,* to bore, to pierce; figuratively, to insinuate oneself into; W. Leigh in THE CHRISTIAN'S WATCH said he did not know *how this spirit hath entred and wimbled into your souls.* (2) As an adjective: quick, nimble. Used 16th to 18th century; Spenser in THE SHEPHERD'S CALENDAR (1579; MARCH) says of Cupid: *He was so wimble.*

wimple. A veil; especially, a cloth folded to cover the head, chin, cheeks, and neck, formerly worn in general by women, now by nuns. Hence, a fold, a wrinkle, a rippling in a stream. Hence, a crafty turn or trick; Scott in THE HEART OF MIDLOTHIAN (1818) says: *There is aye a wimple in a lawyer's clew.* As a verb, *to wimple*: to veil (sometimes, to take the veil); to cover; to fall in folds—Spenser in THE FAËRIE QUEENE (1590) speaks of *a veil, that wimpled was full low*; to ripple, to wind, meander, as *a wimpling brook.* Old French *guimple,* whence also *guimp, gimp.* Chaucer used the word often, as in TROYLUS AND CRISEYDE (1374): *Do away youre wimpil and shew youre face bare. Wimpled,* rippled, falling in folds like a wimple, enveloped in a wimple—hence (rarely) blindfolded, as in Shakespeare's LOVE'S LABOUR'S LOST (1588), of Cupid: *This wimpled, whyning, purblind, wayward boy.*

Winchester goose. A venereal swelling. The public brothels of the late 16th and early 17th century, at Bankside in Southwark, were under the jurisdiction of the Bishop of Winchester. Shakespeare uses the term in HENRY VI, PART ONE (1591) and alludes to it in TROILUS AND CRESSIDA: *It should be now, but that my fear is this, Some galled goose of Winchester would hiss.* Hence, also, a prostitute; THE ENGLISH GAZETTEER of 1778 records in its discussion of Southwark: *In the times of popery here were no less than* 18 *houses on the Bankside, licensed by the Bishops of Winchester to keep whores, who were, therefore, commonly called Winchester geese.* Sometimes, in both senses, the term was shortened to *goose.*

windlass. In addition to the contrivance familiar for weighing anchor on a ship, *windlass* (16th and 17th centuries) was a variant of *wanlace, q.v.* Also *winless, windlace, windelase, windlatch*; and used as a verb: *to windlass,* to act craftily; to decoy, ensnare. *My young mind,* said Sidney in ASTROPHEL AND STELLA (1586), *whom love doth windlas so. To fetch a windlass,* to circle round. Hence *windlass,* a roundabout course of action, a crafty device. Hamlet, in Shakespeare's play (1602) declares: *And thus do we of wisdom and of reach, With windlasses and with assays of bias, By indirections find directions out.*

windore. An altered form of *window,* from the belief that the word originated as a *door* to the *wind.* Actually, *window* is from Old Norse *vindauga; vindr,* wind + *auga,* eye. It replaced the Old English *eyethurl. Windore* was used from the 16th through the 18th century.

wis. See *wit.*

wiseacreish. Like a *wiseacre*; of a fool that has an air of wisdom. There was an Old English word *witie* (9th to 14th century), meaning a prophet; prophetic; and to prophesy. This was confused with *wise,* and combined with *seggher,* sayer, taking the forms *wiseaker, wiseacre.* Hence also *wiseacreism, wiseacrery, wiseacredom, wiseacredness.* In the 17th century, the *acre* was occasionally interpreted as referring to land (hence, also, *a wiseacres,* as a singular), as though meaning a landed fool, or one that would pass for wise because he is wealthy—like a dogmatic millionaire. A particularly annoying brand of wiseacre is that which displays what Saintsbury in his CORRECTED IMPRESSIONS (1895) calls *ex post facto wiseacreishness.*

wist. See *wit.*

wistly. Silently; eagerly. Supplanted by *wistfully,* which was influenced in meaning by *wishful.* In Shakespeare, RICHARD II (1595) and THE PASSIONATE PILGRIM (see *tarriage*); Venus is waiting by *A brook* *where Adon used to cool his spleen. Hot was the day, she hotter that did look For his approach, that often there had been. Anon he comes, and throws his mantle by, And stood stark naked on the brook's green brim. The sun looked on the world with glorious eye, Yet not so wistly as this queen on him. He, spying her, bounced in wheras he stood. "O Jove," quoth she, "why was I not a flood!"*

wit. To know. A very common Teuton form. Its inflections included *I wat,* I know, *God wot,* God knows; *I wist,* I knew; *he had wist.* But *wis* was also an early and common verb, meaning to make known, hence to show the way, guide, lead; manage, control, instruct, order. *He that this world began,* said a Towneley Mystery of 1460, *wysh us the way!* There was also an early and common adjective and adverb *iwis, ywis,* Old English *gewis,* certain, certainly. There was also an early and common verb *iwite, ywite* (Old English *gewitan,* to look at, to know) which meant to learn, to understand; also (from the idea of looking at the place you intended to go to), to go away, depart; and by extension, to die. *Iwis* and *iwite* were often written as two words, *i wis; i wite.* From all this arose certain confusions. Thus *i wis,* certain, was taken as a verb, I know, and on the assumption that it was the present of the past form *wist,* to some extent replaced *I wot* (*wat*). Thus Shakespeare (HENRY VI, PART ONE; 1591) says *If I wish, he did;* Lyly (EUPHUES, 1606): *You gall me more with those tearmes than you wisse;* so also, e.g., Milton and Mrs. Browning. Also, *i wis* being sometimes written *i wist,* about 1550 *wist* came to be used as a verb in the present: *wist,* to know, with a past tense form *wisted.* One edition of EUPHUES has *wist* in the passage just quoted; Buckle (THE INFLUENCE OF WOMEN IN THE PROGRESS OF KNOWLEDGE, 1858) said of Hamlet *Though he wists not of this, he is moved . . . takes up a skull, and his speculative faculties begin to work.* The verb *to wit* was used in many phrases, to wit (earlier *that is to wit*): *Ye shall wit, please it you to wit,* let me tell you. *do* (*to*) *wit, give to wit, let wit,* to inform, to reveal, to show. Also *it is to wit* (*witting*), it is to be noted; *it were to wit,* it calls for investigation, one ought to find out. A *witword* was a testament, last will; hence *to wit,* to bequeath; *witting,* bequest. The form *wite* (as *iwite,* above) was also a verb, meaning to go away; to die. But from Old English, meaning to know, to observe, the verb *wite* (*wyte*) developed the sense to censure, to blame, to accuse—but also, from the sense to observe, it came to mean to take care, to guard, defend, preserve. In all these senses, *wite* was very common from the 8th to the 14th century. *Witless,* without knowledge; *witeless,* without guilt, blameless. However, a *wite* was a wise man (also, one of the *witan,* the members of the Anglo-Saxon council, the *witenagemot*). Chaucer, in the Prologue to THE CANTERBURY TALES (1386) used a variant form: *For aught I woot, he was of Dertemouthe.* Spenser in THE FAËRIE QUEENE (1590): *The peril of this place I better wot than you.* Whitney (SIGHTS AND INSIGHTS, 1876): *We wit well of many things we would never prove.* Elizabeth Barrett Browning, in GREEK CHRISTIAN POETS (1842): *If by chance an Attic voice be wist.*—Which is enough of *wit.* As Tennyson says in the SECOND SONG OF THE OWL (1830): *Thy tuwhits are lull'd, I wot.* —Hence also *witne,* to testify (used until the 15th century) and *witness* (Old English *gewitnes, witnes*), which first meant knowledge, understanding. Chaucer (BOE-

THIUS, 1374) meaning evidently, plainly, says: *In this wise more clerely and more witnesfully.—The five wits* was sometimes merely another term for *the five senses*; but Shakespeare in SONNET 141 says: *But my five wits nor my five senses can Dissuade one foolish heart from serving thee,* and Hawes in THE PASTIME OF PLEASURE (1509) lists *the five wits* as *common wit, imagination, fantasy, estimation* [judgment], *and memory.* As the Greeks observed, Memory is the mother of the Muses.

witcracker. See *witsnapper.*

wite. See *wit.*

witenagemot. See *wit.* Old English *witena,* wise men + *gemot,* assembly. Browning (1855) rhymes *witanagemot* with *bag 'em hot.* The word is sometimes used of any assembly, as by Sir Michael Foster in his Presidential Address to the British Association (1899) : *the first select witenagemote of the science of the world.*

withers. The highest part of a horse's back, between the shoulderblades. Also *wither, weather.* Lyly in EUPHUES (1580) said: *Wring not a horse on the withers, with a false saddle.* Nashe and others echoed the phrase, figuratively, then Shakespeare in HAMLET (1602): *Let the gall'd jade winch: our withers are unwrung.* The idea is that something pinches in a sensitive spot. Others after Shakespeare have used the phrase, on to Symonds in THE RENAISSANCE IN ITALY (1886): *There is not a city of Italy which Tassoni did not wring in the withers of its self-conceit.*

withershins. See *widdershins.*

witie. See *wiseacreish.*

witnesfully. See *wit.*

witsnapper. One that makes witty or caustic remarks, as though snapping a whip of words. Also, *witcracker*; more mildly, *witwright.* Shakespeare in MUCH ADO ABOUT NOTHING (1599) says: *A colledge of witte-crackers cannot flout mee out of my humour; dost thou think I care for a satyre or an epigram?*—and in the MERCHANT OF VENICE exclaims: *What a witte-snapper are you!*

wittol. A man aware of and not objecting to (perhaps encouraging) the unfaithfulness of his wife; a contented *cuckold, q.v.* Middle English *wetewold* (*cp. wit,* to know), like *cokewold,* cuckold. Also *wital, wittall, whittoll.* Weekley (ETYMOLOGICAL DICTIONARY, 1921) says *wittol* is "apparently" from *witewal, woodwale,* the green woodpecker—"a simple and amiable bird," says Partridge, in SHAKESPEARE'S BAWDY, 1948—which (legend has it) hatched the cuckoo's eggs and reared the young. Weekley suggests a pun on *wit* (Anglo-Saxon *witol,* knowledge), the complaisant husband being a *wit-all,* one that knows all. [*Woodwale* may be from *wood* + *wail,* cry, or *wood* + *wale,* foreign, akin to *Welsh*; from Anglo-Saxon *waelisc,* foreign; *wealh,* foreigner, slave: note this linkage.] Bishop Hall in a sermon of 1597 cried out upon *Fond witwal that wouldst load thy witless head with timely horns.* Shakespeare uses the word in THE MERRY WIVES OF WINDSOR (1598), also a compound: *They say the jealous wittolly-knave hath masses of money.* Ford in his HANDBOOK to Spain (1845) informed prospective tourists: *Most of this finger talk, wittoly wit, as well as the figs, is confined to the lower classes.* 'Wittoly wit' by finger talk would be making the sign of horns on the head; the O.E.D. explains *the figs* as 'A fig to you!' digitally represented: hand outthrust with thumb between the next two fingers. *Wittolry,* complaisant cuckoldry; by extension, extreme folly. A *wittee* (17th century), a woman whose adultery was urged or forced upon her by her husband. In Shakespeare's LOVE'S LABOUR'S LOST (1594) when we hearken to those *that have been at a great feast of languages, and stolen the scraps,* after being served *Priscian a little scratched* and the longest word in the Latin language, *honorificabilitudinitatibus,* we hear a sample of *true wit* in Moth's pun *Offered by a child to an old man, which is wit-old.* Holofernes: *What is the figure? What is the figure?* Moth: *Horns.* [*Wit-old,* feeble of mind; but the sequent *Horns* pricks home the pun on *wittol.*]

witword. A last will, testament. See *wit.*

wizard. See *pad.* Originally a wise man (*wise* + *ard*); later used in scorn; then used for the male *witch. Witch* was probably first used as a verb, more common as *to bewitch,* allied to German *weihen,* to consecrate; Latin *victima,* victim, originally a sacrificial beast, from root *veg, vig,* wake, vigor: *victima* is *vig* with the superlative ending, the most vigorous, choicest, hence selected for sacrifice. Though naturally associated with them, *victim* is thus of different origin from *victor, victory,* from Latin root *vic,* conquer: *vincere, victum.* There is another root *viv, vig,* live (earlier *gvig,* whence English *quick*) whence *vital, victuals* and the general *vitality* of the wizard.

wlat. Nausea; disgust, loathing. Also *wlating, wlatness.* As an adjective, *wlat, wlath, wlatful, wlatsome, wlatsum, wlathsum,* loathsome, disgusting. *To wlate,* to feel disgust; to loathe. Used from the 10th to the 15th century. Wyclif in his rendering (1382) of the BIBLE: ECCLESIASTES wrote: *I wlatede all my bisynesse.*

wlite. Beauty, splendor; face, countenance. Also *wliti,* beautiful. Used from the 9th to the 13th century. In THE OWL AND THE NIGHTINGALE (1250) we read: *The lilie mid hire faire wlite Welcumeth me.*

wlonk. Rich, splendid, magnificent. Used from Old English into the 15th century, becoming a conventional epithet in alliterative verse. Also a noun, a beautiful woman; Dunbar in TWA MARIIT WEMEN (1508) said: *The wedow to the tothir wlonk warpit* [spoke] *ther wordis.* By extension, *wlonk,* proud, haughty; so used in BEOWULF; *wlonkhede, wlonkness,* pride.

wod. A variant of *wood, q.v.*

wodehouse. See *woodwose.*

woe worth. May evil befall! A curse upon! Used especially in the 16th and 17th centuries; especially in such phrases as *Woe worth the day!* THE MIRROR FOR MAGISTRATES (1563) ran on: *Woe worth the ground where grew the tow'ring mast, Whose sailes did beare us through the waters' rore: Woe worth the winde that blew the banefull blast, Woe worth the wave, whose surge so swiftlie bore My tragicke barke to England's fatal shore. Woe worth the mast, the sailes, winde, waves and all That causelesse did conspire poore Alfredes fall.*

wold. See *old.*

won. See *wone.* In addition to being the past form of *win, won* was also a variant form of *one, wan, when,* and the past participle of *wind.* Thus also *wonce* (16th century), once. The form *wont,* past of *wone,* became in itself a noun: custom, habit, *It is my wont*—recorded by Jonson (1755) as 'out of use'; and a verb, *to wont,* to make (someone) accustomed; to use habitually; to be accustomed. Hence the past tense *wonted.* The GOODLY PRIMER of 1535 besought the Lord: *Wont me to Thy paths.* Shakespeare in HENRY VI, PART ONE (1591) says: *Talbot is taken, whom we wont to fear.* Nashe in PIERCE PENNILESSE HIS SUPPLICATION TO THE DEVIL (1592) tells of one who resolved *to poyson the stream where this jolly forester wonted to drink.* Some persons enjoy a certain type of story, but not she of Chaucer's THE CLERK'S TALE (1386): *She never was to swiche gestes woned.*

wone. (1) Habit, custom. *In wone,* customarily. *To have in wone, to be in wone, to have wone,* to be accustomed. (2) Staying in a place, remaining, hence *without wone,* without delay. Hence also *wone,* a dwelling place; figuratively, this world. (3) A palace; apartments or chambers; occasionally, a city, as in THE DESTRUCTION OF TROY (1400): *Yonder won* [Troy] *for to wyn.* (*with*) *in one's wone,* in one's possession. Also *worthy in wone,* distinguished in the world. *In wone, within wones,* everywhere, anywhere, often used as a tag, to end a line in verse, or a stanza. (4) Hope of a favorable outcome; recourse, expedient, course of action. *To have, know, see, no other* (*better*) *wone.* Hence (5) resources, abundance; (*full*) *good* (*great*), *wone,* a goodly number, a great quantity; *in wone,* abundance. Hence also (6) fortune, wealth, possessions. There was a verb *wone,* related to *woe,* meaning to bewail, lament, mourn. In the senses above, the more common verb form was *won,* very common from the 8th century, used into the 19th, and still poetically in the past form *wont; to be wont,* to be accustomed. See *won.* Milton uses the word literally in PARADISE LOST (1667), where the creatures of the Lord's Sixth Day *out of the ground up rose As from his laire the wilde beast where he wonns In forest wilde;* Spenser uses it figuratively in THE FAËRIE QUEENE (1590): *Wastefull wayes, Where daungers dwelt, and perils most did wonne;* Holland in his translation (1610) of William Camden's BRITANNIA uses it punningly: *Wheresoever the Roman winneth, there he wonneth.* Reginald Pecock in THE REPRESSOR OF OVER MUCH BLAMING OF THE CLERGY (1449) applies it to one of the hardest things for many to grow accustomed to: *wone thee not to love money.* He that, while living, did not achieve this, now, as THE XI PAINS OF HELL (1275) would have it, *woneth and groneth day and nyht.*

wont. See *wone; won. Wonted* (accustomed; sometimes used alone, to mean acclimatized) is a fresh past form developed (in the 14th century) when *wont* was used as a separate verb in the present tense. *Wontedness,* habituation, the state of being accustomed; *wonting,* making (someone) accustomed. Also *wontless* (*q.v.*), unaccustomed; unusual. Southey in JOAN OF ARC (1795) has: *He . . . all astonish'd at their force And wontless valour, rages round the field.* The *wonting-penny,* wages paid a herdsman to guard beasts in a place until they were used to it and would stay of their own accord, after which the owner wouldn't be wanting him any more.

wontless. Unaccustomed. Spenser in his HYMN (1596) to Beauty, to that *great goddesse, queene of beauty, Mother of love, and of all worlds delight,* exclaimed: *Ah whither, Love, wilt thou now carrie mee? What wontlesse fury dost thou now inspire Into my feeble breast, too full of thee?*

wood. Insane, mad. Thence, vehemently excited, uncontrolled; ferocious, furious.

Also *wod, wode, wyd, void, wodde,* and more. Used from the 8th through the 16th century. A *woodman,* a lunatic; *to wood* (14th and 15th centuries), to go mad; to rave. Spenser in THE FAËRIE QUEENE (1590) speaks of one *Through unadvised rashness woxen wood.* Shakespeare plays on the word in A MIDSUMMER NIGHT'S DREAM (1590): *Heerė am I, and wood within this wood, Because I cannot meet my Hermia.* For another instance of its use, see *sea.*

woodcock. A gull, simpleton, 'easy mark.' So used (from the 15th century) because of the ease with which the bird, the *woodcock,* is ensnared. Gosson in THE SCHOOL OF ABUSE (1579) wrote that *Cupide sets upp a springe for woodcockes, which are entangled ere they descrie the line.* Shakespeare puts the same figure in Polonius' mouth, in HAMLET (1602); in TWELFTH NIGHT, when Malvolio picks up the letter written to trap him, Fabian whispers: *Now is the woodcocke neere the gin.*

woodhouse. See *woodwose.*

woodwale. See *wittol.*

woodwose. A wild man of the woods; a savage; a satyr. Used from the 11th century. Also, a representation of such a person, as in a pageant or in wood-carving. Also, *wodwos, woodwyss, woodose, wodehouse,* and the like. T. Wilson in his RHETORIQUE (1553) declared: *Some wente naked, some romed lyke woodoses, none did anye thing by reason.*

wooingly. Like a wooer, with amorous words. Used by Wyclif (1382 rendering of the BIBLE: PROVERBS) to mean impudently, wantonly; by Shakespeare, to mean alluringly, in MACBETH (1605): *The heavens breath Smells wooingly here.*

woolpack. (1) Used figuratively of things resembling a pack of wool, as a spread of white water, a fleecy cloud. Thus in Nashe's LENTEN STUFFE (1599) we read that when Hero bent over to kiss the drowned Leander, *boystrous woolpacks of ridged tides came rowling in and raught him from her.* One is reminded of Hugo's line: *The fleece of the sinister sheep of the sea.* (2) Same as *woolsack*; especially as the seat, a bag of wool, of the Lord Chancellor in the House of Lords; hence, *the woolsack,* the Lord Chancellorship. Note that Shakespeare (HENRY IV, PART ONE; 1597) refers to fat Falstaff as a *woolsack.*

woosel. See *ousel.*

woot. (1) Old present tense of *wit, q.v.* (2) Short for *Wilt thou?* Used by Shakespeare in ANTONY AND CLEOPATRA and HAMLET (1602), where Hamlet cries to Laertes, in Ophelia's grave: *Woot weep? Woot fight? Woot fast? Woot tear thyself? Woot drink up eisel? Eat a crocodile? I'll do't . . . Be buried quick with her, and so will I.*

wormwood. A plant (artemisia absinthium), proverbial for its bitter taste. The name is altered from the earlier *wermod*; the French form gives us *vermouth,* the liquor made by steeping wormwood in white wine. (So, for that matter, was *absinthe.*) The word is used as a symbol of bitter and grievous things, as when Shakespeare in LOVE'S LABOUR'S LOST (1588) wants *To weed this wormwood from your fruitfull braine.* Wormwood also was used for its medicinal and magical virtues. Wormwood roots under your pillow brought your lover to you in your dreams —true dreams, issuing from the unpretentious gate of horn, not the illusory dreams from the falsely alluring gate of ivory. As

Dian's bud (*cp. Diana*), wormwood cured one of the madness of love; indeed, *wood, q.v.*, was an early word for mad; *wormwood*: it cleared your body of worms and your mind of maggots.

wort. A general name for plants used for food or medicine; a pot-herb. Old English *wyrt,* root, plant. Used until the mid-17th century. It survives as the last syllable of many plants once thus used, as *colewort, liverwort.* Chaucer in THE CLERK'S TALE (1386) says: *Whan she homward cam she wolde brynge Wortes or othere herbes tymes ofte.* Chaucer uses the two words as synonymous; Verstegan in 1605 noted: *Woortes, for which wee now use the French name of herbes.*

worthy. (As a noun): A distinguished or eminent person; especially, a man of noble character. Also, a hero of antiquity. Used lightly, of any person, as by Scott in KENILWORTH (1821): *The two worthies left the apartment together.* Also applied, figuratively, to things of value, as in Shakespeare's LOVE'S LABOUR'S LOST (1588): *In her faire cheeke, Where several worthies make one dignity. The nine worthies* (of the world): three Jews, Joshua, David, and Judas Maccabeus; three heathens (said Bailey, 1751; 'Gentiles,' says O.E.D.), Hector, Alexander, and Julius Caesar; and three Christians, Arthur, Charlemagne, and Godfrey of Bouillon. There is a burlesque *Pageant of the Nine Worthies* in Shakespeare's LOVE'S LABOUR'S LOST. Sir John Ferne in THE BLAZON OF GENTRIE (1586) declared that Semiramis *is one of the nine worthies of that sex.* What man will venture to select the other eight? Hence, *nine-worthiness,* excellence equal to that of the nine worthies; Butler in HUDIBRAS (1663) said: *The foe, for dread Of your nine-worthiness, is fled.*

wot. See *wit.*

wough. See *wowe.* Also *woh, woch, woghe, wothe, wow,* and more. *Wough* also meant a wall (of a house), a partition—from the 9th century. *In the castell,* said THE DESTRUCTION OF TROY (1400), *all was bare as a bast, to the bigge wcghes.* In DIVES AND PAUPER (1470): *God lykeneth flaterers to theym that playstren and paynten walles and wowes without.*

wowe. An early form of (1) *woe,* (2) *woo,* (3) *wough,* wrong, injury, harm. *Wough* was common from the 9th to the 16th century; it was also an adjective, meaning first bent, crooked, hence evil, wicked, wrong (like *Richard Crookback*). *To do* (*work*) *wough,* to do wrong or evil (to). *To have wough,* to be in the wrong; *without(en) wough,* truly. In SIR TRISTRAM (1320) we read: *They seiyen he hadde the right, The steward hadde the wough.*

wrack. (1) A variant form of *wreak, q.v.* Hence, *wrackful,* vengeful, angry; *wracksome,* destructive. (2) An error for *rack,* as in *rack and ruin.* Hence, the *wracking of criminals;* thus also Shakespeare in HENRY VI, PART ONE (1591): *like a man new haled from the wrack; wracking whirlwinds* (Milton, PARADISE LOST, 1663). (3) A variant form of *wreck. Wreck* is from a common Norse form, *wrekan,* to drive; originally, *wreck* meant to cast on shore, or anything (not necessarily goods from a ship) cast upon the shore; the North Riding records of 1666 report *a warrant against 11 Britton men for riotously taking a whale and other wreck.*

wrake. A variant form of *wreak, q.v.,* both as noun and as verb. Hence *wrakeful,* vengeful.

wreak. Earlier *wrecche,* to rouse; *wreche,* vengeance. Thus, *to do* (*have, make,* *nim, seek, take*) *wreche.* A very common word. Also *wrecheful, wracchful,* vengeful. *To wreak,* to drive, press (7th to 11th century); to give vent to (anger and the like) *in, on, against, upon* someone. To punish; to avenge; to harm; in the form *to wreak vengeance on,* still used. Also as a noun, *wreak*: vengeance; an act of retribution; repayment; harm, injury. Jonson in EVERY MAN OUT OF HIS HUMOUR (1599) cries: *Would to heaven (In wreak of my misfortunes) I were turn'd To some faire water-nymph.*

wreck. See *wrack.*

wretchlessness. Recklessness; heedlessness; neglect. Originally an erroneous form (in Raleigh's HISTORY OF THE WORLD; 1634) of *retchlessness,* an old variant of *recklessness.* Thus also *wretchless* (16th to 18th century), heedless, imprudent; neglectful.

wrethe. See *wroath.* Used from the 9th into the 16th century. Also as a verb, *to wrethe,* to anger, irritate; to become angry. Also to feel anger toward; a poem of 1500 queried: *Quhy wrethis thou me?* Hence *wrethful, wrethfulness* (later *wrathful, wrath*); Yonge in 1422 (translating SECRETA SECRETORUM; THE GOVERNAUNCE OF PRYNCES) warned: *He that hath a sharpe nose and smale, he is wrethful.* There was another Old English verb, *to wrethe* (9th to 13th century), to prop or hold up; to lean upon for support, to depend upon—used figuratively of the Lord as man's prop.

wright. A constructor; especially, a carpenter or joiner. Sometimes (8th to 14th century) applied to the Lord. Also as a verb, to build. Also *wright-garth,* a joiner's yard; *wright-craft,* and more. There was also a noun *wright,* shortened from Old English *gewyrht* (whence also *iwurht*), what one deserves; hence praise, also blame, fault. Hence *wrightful,* having deserved something; *wrightlesslike,* undeservedly (13th century). *Wright,* as a handicraftsman, has survived as a suffix, in such words as *millwright, shipwright, wainwright*; by extension, *playwright.*

writhled. Wrinkled. As though from a frequentative form of *writhe.* Shakespeare in HENRY VI, PART ONE (1591) has the French Countess exclaim in scorn, when first she sees Lord Talbot: *It cannot be this weak and writhled shrimp Should strike such terror to his enemies.* She soon discovers her mistake.

writrix. A female writer. The word belittles the ability of the woman in the field of letters. Thomas Nugent in his translation (1772) of Isla's HISTORY OF . . . FRIAR GERUND DE CAMPAZAS asks: *Why should it not be said, she was not a common woman, but a geniusess, and an elegant writrix?*

wroath. Distress; disaster. A variant of *ruth, q.v.* Also *wroth* (not to be confused with *wroth,* great anger, earlier *wrethe,* and in the 17th century replaced by *wrath. Wroth* as an adjective, very angry, *wrathful,* has lasted longer. These words are from the same source as *writhe*). Shakespeare in THE MERCHANT OF VENICE (1596) has Aragon, after choosing the wrong casket, say: *Sweet, adieu. Ile keepe my oath, Patiently to bear my wroath.*

wry. (1) To cover, spread a cover over, as a fire or a table, or a horse. To cover with armor or clothing, to attire. To cover so as warm, protect, or conceal; to cover up, to hide; thus Chaucer in TROYLUS AND CRISEYDE (1374) speaks of *God, to whom ther nys no cause ywrye.* (2) To go on one's way; to turn, bend;

to incline, deviate; to twist. Audelay (POEMS; 1426) spoke of a man that *wrys away fro Godys word to his wyckydnes.* As youngsters often seek to imitate important figures, copying the cough of genius, so Hoby records in his translation (1561) of Castiglione's THE COURTIER a man *that thought he resembled much Kyng Ferdinande the yonger of Aragon, and regarded not to resemble hym in anye other poynt but in the often lyftyng up hys head, wrying therewythall a part of hys mouth, the whych custome the king had gotten by infyrmitye.*

wust. A variant form of *wist,* past of *wit, q.v.*

wynd. A narrow lane or cross-street. The *wynd head,* the higher end of a narrow street. For its use as a verb, in Scotland, see *hap.*

X

xenia. Gifts, says Bailey (1751) "bestowed upon friends, guests, and strangers, for the renewing of friendship." The singular is *xenium,* such a gift. Also, one made by subjects to their prince when he passes through their estates (usually traditional, often compulsory). Greek *xenos,* guest, stranger. Also *xenagogue,* one who conducts strangers, a guide; *xenagogy,* a guide-book; *xenelasy,* the expulsion of foreigners; historically, a law that could be invoked at Sparta to achieve that end. Hence *xenial,* of the relation of host and guest; used of such a friendly relation between two persons of different countries. The *xenian Zeus,* the god Zeus as protector of the rights of hospitality. A *xenophile* is one friendly to foreigners or foreign things; the opposite, a *xenophobe.* Thus *xenodochy* means the entertainment of strangers; *xenodochium* (*xenodochy*), a house of reception for strangers (pilgrims), a guest-house; in the Dark Ages, often attached to a monastery.

xenomancy. See *aeromancy.*

Y

y-. A prefix (Old English and German *ge-*, earlier *gi-*; Teutonic *ga*). It had various uses, the most frequent of which was to form the past tense of verbs. Most of these died in the 15th century. From the mid-16th century poets attempting archaic effects added the prefix *y*, often without adding any meaning; thus *yshrilled* (Spenser); *ysprout, ysteer; star-ypointing* (Milton). The most common of the forms, still lingering in poetic use, is *yclept*, named; see *clepe*. Often the *y* was changed to *i*, as in *iclosed, igranted, ipassed*. The form is common in Chaucer and Lydgate, but almost completely unused by Gower. Among favorites of later poets are *ybent, ybound, ybrought, yclad, ydamned, ydight, ydrad, ywrought*. Also *yblent*, (1) blinded; (2) mingled, confused, blurred. *ybrent*, burned. *ycore*, chosen, hence choice, comely. *ycoroned, ycronet*, crowned. *ycorven*, carved. *ydodded*, shorn. *ydought*, grown strong. *ydreght*, drawn. *yfere* (noun) a companion; (adverb) in company, together—used frequently as a tag in verse, as in Spenser's THE FAËRIE QUEENE (1590): *O goodly golden chaine, wherewith yfere The virtues linked are in lovely wise. yfet*, brought, fetched, acquired. *yflawe*, flayed. *yflemed*, put to flight; exiled. *yfong*, taken, seized; received. *ygilt*, sinned; gilded; Nashe (in MARTIN'S MONTHS MINDE, 1589): *My hope once was my old shoes should be stitcht, My thumbs ygilt, they were before bepitcht. yglent*, made radiant. *ygyved*, fettered. *yhabited*, clothed. *yhaded, yhoded*, consecrated, ordained. *yhald*, yielded. *yheedid*, headed. *yheled*, (1) healed; (2) covered, concealed; (3) also *yeled*, anointed. *yhevid*, grieved. *yhillid*, flayed. *yholpe(n)*, helped. *yhonge*, hanged. *yhote (n)*, called, etc. (from *hight*). *ykremyd*, crumbled. *ykitt, ykyt*, cut. *yleof*, mutually beloved; hence, a pair of lovers. *ylogged*, lodged. *ymered*, purified. *ymet*, dreamt; met. *ynem(p)ned*, named. *ynome (n)*, *ynume*, taken. *ypitte*, put. *yrerd*, raised. *yschad*, shed. *ysesid, yseysed*, seized. *ysessed*, ceased. *ysinwed*, sinned. *yso (c) ht*, sought. *yteyd*, tied. *ythrungin*, hurled. *ytwynned*, separated. *yvenkessyd, yvenquyst*, vanquished. *ywaged*, hired. *ywhyngged*, winged. *ywived*, married. *yworewid*, worried. *ywroken*, avenged; punished. There are many more, but most are readily recognized by dropping the *y*. I have omitted them, and that is why.

yahoo. A degraded or bestial person. From the name invented by Swift in GULLIVER'S TRAVELS (1726), for a species of brute in the form of a man, slaves of the noble race of *houyhnhnm*, an intelligent tribe of the horse. Used frequently since; also as a verb; Yates in THE ROCK AHEAD (1868) spoke of *a dam low-bred lot, yahooin' all over the place.*

yale. A fabulous beast with horns and tusks. Used from the 15th century; a figure in heraldry. Also *gaill, gale, jall,* *jail, yeale, eale. Yale* was also an old form of *ale.*

yam. A rest-house on a post route. From the Russian; used from the 16th century. The ASIATIC ANNUAL REGISTER of 1800 said: *Each night they reached a yam, and each week a city.* Hence *yamstchik* (*yamshik, yamsheek*), a driver of a post-horse.

yap. Clever, nimble; eager; hungry. A Northern and Scotch form of *yepe, q.v.*

yard. The still current *yard* meaning enclosure is Old Saxon *gard* (whence also *garden*), as in *vineyard* and *orchard;* Latin *hortus,* garden; related to *court.* There was another *yard,* probably related to Latin *hasta,* spear, meaning a stick, a slender shoot of a tree. This survives in *sailyard,* and the reduplicating *yardstick.* Other senses this *yard* had include: a twig; hence, a trifle, a thing of no value. A means of punishment; hence, punishment, the rod. From the use of a rod in measuring land, *a yard,* an area of a quarter of an acre; a measure of length: (9th to 15th century) 16½ feet; (14th century and now standard) 3 feet. By optimistic transfer, the phallus (as also Latin *virga,* rod); Shakespeare in LOVE'S LABOUR'S LOST (1588) has one of his frequent puns: Armado: *I do adore thy sweet Grace's slipper.* Boyet (aside to Dumain): *Loves her by the foot.* Dumain (aside to Boyet): *He may not by the yard.*

yare. Ready, prepared. Also as an adverb, quickly, nimbly. The adverb was sometimes used as an exclamation, as in Shakespeare's ANTONY AND CLEOPATRA (1606) and THE TEMPEST, or (*full yare*) as a rhyming tag—thus in the ballad of GUY WARWICK (1400): *And wyth hys fyst he smote me sore: Sythen he flew awey full yore.* The adjective was common from BEOWULF into the 19th century, especially as a sea term, meaning responding readily to the helm, easily manageable; thus Shakespeare (also in ANTONY AND CLEOPATRA): *Their shippes are yare, yours heavy.*

yark. To make ready, prepare. A verbal form of *yare, q.v.* Also, to put in position. To *yark to,* shut; *yark up,* open. By extension, to ordain, appoint; grant, bestow.

yaspen. See *yepsen.*

yate. To bestow, to grant; to acknowledge, to confess; to provide, to give, to offer. Used from the 12th to the 15th century. Also *yeitt, yete, yatte;* hence *nait,* to refuse.

yaud. A mare, especially an old, worn-out mare. Also *yawde, yode, yade;* related to *jade.* Hence, a strumpet—thus *yaudson, yaldson,* son of a whore, a 15th and 16th century term of abuse. Also *yaudswiver* (16th century), one that carnally knows a mare.

yclad. See *y-.* Spenser has, in THE SHEPHERD'S CALENDAR (1579; APRIL), the charming line to "faire Elisa": *yclad in scarlet, like a maiden queene.*

yclept. See *clepe.*

ydromancy. A variant (used by Maundeville, 1400, etc.) of *hydromancy.* See *aeromancy.*

yedding. A song; discourse. By extension, a gest, a verse romance. Used from the 10th to the 15th century; Chaucer in the Prologue to THE CANTERBURY TALES (1386) in one of his best portraits, of the frere, the *worthy limitour cleped Huberd,* says: *Wel coude he singe and pleyen on a rote, Of yeddinges he bar utterly the prys.*

yede. See *yode.*

yeme. To care for, take notice of, consider; look attentively (upon); to take care of, guard, protect; to have charge of, govern, manage, control; to observe (a command, a holiday). Also the noun *yeme,* care. Hence *in yeme,* in one's care. To *nim yeme, take yeme,* take note, give heed, etc. Hence *yemeless,* careless, negligent; *yemelest,* negligence; *yemelich,* full of care, anxious; *yemer,* a keeper, guardian, ruler. The forms were common from the 8th to the 15th century. Dunbar in a poem of 1520 speaks of a guardian *dispoilit of the tresur that he yemit.* There was also a form *yensel* (*yhemsale, yemseill*), care, custody, used from the 12th to the 15th century.

yene. An old plural form of *eye* (*eyes, eien, yen*).

yeoman. Originally, a servant of superior rank, in a royal or noble household. Also *yeman, ymnan,* probably related to *youngman,* the youth of a noble house trained as a page or a *yeoman.* Hence, to do *yeoman service,* to do excellent and faithful work (often with implication that the assignment was onerous). The body-guard of the ruler of England (first archers, appointed when Henry VII was crowned; 1485) consists of *The Yeomen of the Guard;* these survived in London and the title of a Gilbert and Sullivan play (1888). By extension (15th to 17th century), a landholder under the rank of a gentleman; hence, in general, a sturdy and respected commoner. Skelton in MAGNYFYCENCE (1520) pictured life's vicissitudes: *To day hote, to morowe outragyous colde; to day a yoman, to morowe made a page.*

yepe. Cunning, crafty; shrewd; astute, wise, sagacious, prudent; active, nimble, alert; bold, daring. Old English *geap,* open, curved, crooked, crafty; Teuton root, *gaup;* Old Norse, *gaupn,* hollow made by the cupped hands; see *yepsen.* Hence *yephede, yepship,* cunning, sagacity. Also *yeply,* craftily. Layamon's BRUT (1205) said: *Julius Caesar he was yep.*

yepsen. The cupping of the hands; also, as much as the cupped hands will hold. Also *yaspen, ipson, yespe, espin,* and the like. Used from the 14th century, lingering beyond the 16th in dialects. Old English *geap,* open, spacious, curved; the Old Teuton root is *gaup,* Old Norse *gaupn,* hollow of the cupped hands, whence also English *gowpen,* with the same meaning as *yepsen.*

yerk. (1) To draw stitches tight; to bind tightly. Revived by Scott in THE LAY OF THE LAST MINSTREL (1805) and THE HEART OF MIDLOTHIAN (1818): *His hands and feet are yerked as tight as cords can be drawn.* Hence, to crack a whip; to strike, to beat; hence, to rouse, to excite. Skelton; Spenser; Shakespeare (OTHELLO, 1604): *Nine, or ten times I had thought t'have yerk'd him here under the ribbes.* BLACKWOOD'S EDINBURGH MAGAZINE in 1833 declared: *We should yerk the yokel of a Yankee with the knout.* Hence also, to jerk; to carp (at); to jerk (out) words, strike up a song; to compose rapidly, *yerk up* a book; to go at something eagerly, pitch into. The word was first used (1450) as a term in bootmaking, of the twitch (jerk) at the end of drawing through the thread; naturally it is used in Dekker's THE SHOEMAKER'S HOLIDAY (1600). Shakespeare used it (again) in HENRY V (1599) of wounded steeds that *with wild rage Yerke out their armed heeles at their dead masters.*

yern. To run (to which it is related). Also as an adjective: *yern,* hearty; eager; covetous, greedy; earnestly occupied; swift, nimble, active. The adverb form was *yernly* or *yerne,* eagerly, heartily, gladly; swiftly, immediately, soon. A *yerner* was a runner. The words were in common use from the 9th through the 14th century. Chaucer says in THE MILLER'S TALE (1386): *But of hir song, it was as loude and yerne As any swalwe sittynge on a berne.*

yestreen. Yesterday evening. Corrupted into such forms as *the strene, the straine, ystrewine, yhistrewyn, yistrevyn.* The ballad FAIR ELLEN (in Child's collection, 1800) has: *I dreamed a dream san the straine.* Scott revived *yestreen,* which had never been wholly abandoned by nostalgic poets.

yesty. A variant of *yeasty,* in the sense of frothy, insubstantial; or foamy, like troubled waters. Shakespeare uses it in HAMLET (V ii 199) and in MACBETH 1605): *Though the yesty waves Confound and swallow navigation up.*

yfere. See *y-*. Note that *yferre* was also a 17th century pseudo-archaism for *afar.* For an instance of its use, see *depeint.*

yglesome. Ugly. An early opposite to handsome. Not in the O.E.D. *Cp. ugsome.* Hoby in his translation (1561) of Castiglione's THE COURTIER said that *Beawtie is a face pleasant, meerie, comelye, and to be desired for goodnesse, and Foulness a face dark, yglesome, unpleasant, and to be shonned for yll.*

ylome. Frequently. Related to *loom.* Used often in the phrase *oft and ylome;* from the 10th to the 14th century.

ynkehorne. See *inkhorn. Emong al other lessons,* said Wilson in THE ARTE OF RHETORIQUE (1553), *this should first be learned, that we never affect any straunge ynkehorne termes, but so speak as is commonly received, neither sekyng to be over fine, nor yet livyng over carelesse.*

yode. Went. The old past tense of *go.* Also *yead, yede. Cp. sigalder.* The word was mistakenly used as a present—*yode, yede,* to go, in the 16th century. Scott revived the form, in MARMION (1808): *In other pace than forth he yode, Returned Lord Marmion.*

yomer. Sorrowful; wretched; grievous. Used from BEOWULF to the 14th century. Also as a verb, to murmur; to complain; to lament; to mourn. THE DESTRUCTION OF TROY (1400) said that the Greeks *us to grefe broght . . . And to you and also yours yomeryng for ever.*

yong. Going; gait; journey; course. Also *yeong, yoing, iong.* Also a verb, to go. Used from the 10th century; Myrc in his INSTRUCTIONS FOR PARISH PRIESTS (1450) said: *Make thy clerk before the yynge, To bere lyght, and belle rynge.*

yoni. See *lingam.*

younghede. Youth. Used in the 13th and 14th centuries. Chaucer, in THE ROMAUNT OF THE ROSE (1366) speaks of a woman *that shorter was a foot, ywis, That she was wont in her yonghede.*

ypocras. See *hippocras.*

ysope. An old variant of *hyssop.* Also *ysoop.* For an instance of its use, see *bouce-Jane.*

ywis. See *wit.*

yys. An old form of (1) *yes,* (2) *eyes.*

Z

zibeline. Sable, the animal and its fur. Also, a woollen cloth with a somewhat furry surface, used for women's dresses. THE POPULAR SCIENCE MONTHLY of May 1889 averred: *In 1188 or thereabout no person was allowed to wear garments of vair, gray, zibeline, or scarlet color.*

zimme. A gem. The word, which Bulwer-Lytton uses twice, is an error; he misunderstood the Old English symbol for *dg* which looks like a *z,* thus reading *zimm* for *gimm,* gem. Thus in HAROLD (1848): *Taking from his own neck a collar of zimmes . . . of great price.*

zitella. A girl; a maiden. From the Italian; plural, *zitelle.* Mrs. Behn in THE FEIGN'D CURTIZANS (1679) exclaimed: *A curtizan! and a zitella too? a pretty contradiction!*

zither. See *cithern.*

zonulet. A little *zone,* a *zonelet;* especially, a girdle or belt (for a maiden's waist). Herrick says in HESPERIDES (1648), of his JULIA'S RIBAND: *'Tis that zonulet of love Wherein all pleasures of the world are wove.*

zoophobia. See *aeromancy.*

zounds. A euphemistic shortening of *By God's wounds,* as a mild oath. Also *zwounds; zoones, zauns, zownds, zons, dzowns.* Shakespeare exclaimed in KING JOHN (1623)—and the present reader well may echo him: *Zounds, I was never so bethumpt with words!*

zygomancy. See *aeromancy.*

zykere. A variant form of *sicker, q.v.*

zymurgy. The art of fermentation, as in the making of wine. Greek *zyme,* leaven + *ourgia,* working. For centuries, monks have been among the most skilled *zymurgists.* With them, we take our leaven.

Mnemosyne

Mnemosyne—Memory—is the mother of the Muses. Memory not only amuses but amazes, though sometimes she leads us into a mazè. Fortunate the man that combines a good memory with a good "forgettery," the ability to organize relative knowledge for recall, while relegating ephemera and trivia to that mental refuse heap which used to be called oblivion but today is known as the subconscious. The working of the "subconscious mind" is implicit in the late Brander Matthews' remark that a gentleman need not know Latin, but he should at least have forgotten it . . . Who won the pennant in 1942?

There must have been a beginning, and in the beginning was the word. Shortly after the prime cosmetic week of October 18, 4004 B.C. (according to the chronology that tempted Newton before the apple), the Lord brought every beast of the field and every fowl of the air unto Adam, and what he called each one, that was its name. Adam did not linger in the Garden long enough, apparently, to label all the plants. What the Lord provided and Lucifer protracted was taken over by Prometheus, whose name means the Forethinker. Whatever could then be brought to mind, his wards the Greeks had a word for it. They had, for example, some dozen words for as many kinds of pestle, to pound cosmetics and condiments, for the two chief sources of human delight. Their verbal ingenuity was such that scientists have continued to use their forms, and those of their Roman followers, as endings (dacr*on,* pluton*ium*) or as full words (*nitrogen, pyrex*) in the creation of new terms for new discoveries, developments, and inventions.

So fine were the classical distinctions, indeed, that in the course of coarser days many were forgotten. In addition to those discussed in the body of this book, English forms are appended here of a sampling of such words, which may prove serviceable to those still in quest of discrimination.

abatic, untrodden, inaccessible
ablautic, without slippers, barefoot
abyrtaca, a salad of leeks, cresses, and sour sauce
acacy, guilelessness, innocence
acalypse. an unveiling
accinct, well-girded; properly equipped
acetary, a salad with vinegar and oil
achenic, mute with surprise
achrestous, entirely useless
acmaic, in top form; in full bloom; prime
acroamatic. relating to entertainment

acroatic, intended only to be heard, as a radio program
acrobate, to walk on tiptoe
acrotous, unapplauding; receiving with disapproval
adapanetous, inexhaustible
adelic, obscure; unknown
adia, freedom from fear
adoxic, unorthodox; disreputable
aeiparthenous, forever virgin
aganacticous, irritable, peevish
agasthenic, endowed with great strength
agathophrontic, good-natured
agrote, a rustic, a greenhorn
agyniac, one that has no wife; wifeless
alastic, not forgetting; desiring revenge
alazonic, roguily boastful
aliped, wingfooted; one that has winged (speedy) feet
alipile, a slave, at baths, that plucks the hair from the armpits
aluta, a soft leather shoe
amblothridian, an abortive child (used of an adult as a term of contempt)
amburbial, around the city
ameletic, unworthy of care
amelic, negligent, careless
amicacous, not half-bad
amphesic, two-edged
amphithoazic, hurrying aimlessly; relating to rushing around
ampotic, relating to the ebb of the tide; on the downgrade
anandrous, without a husband
ananetous, never relaxed
anaphalautic, with high bare forehead
anaptous, invincible
anarrhopic, slanting upwards
anatolic, relating to the east; eastern
ancistron, a fishhook
andromanic, lusting after men
anebous, unable to grow a beard
anecbatous, without exit; dead-end
anemoliotic, full of windy arrogance; boastfully loquacious
anenious, provokingly insolent
aniatic, incurable; hopeless
anicula, a little old woman (used as an endearment)
anilastic, merciless, pitiless
antefict, an ornament or design for a roof-front or a forehead
anteric, relating to or seeking vengeance for slighted love
anymphous, without a bride
aphadic, displeasing
aphanite, destroyer
aphanous, invisible; secret (converse of *diaphanous*)
aphebic, past one's youth
aphilous, without a friend
aphrasia, folly
aphrodiasm, quick desire
aphthartous, undecaying, imperishable
aplestous, insatiable
apocrote, a snap of the fingers
apocroustic, with power to repel
apoglutic, with tiny rump
apograph, a census-taker
apomaxy, a cleansing
apomosia, denial under oath
apoplymatic, persistently filthy
apotmic, unlucky
aquilifer, a standard bearer (literally, eagle carrier)
arator, a plowman
arbyle, a half-boot
arcary, one in charge of the money
arenate, to strew with sand; to mix with sand; to grind into sand
aretological, relating to or full of talk about virtue
arietate, to butt like a ram
aristodination, the bearing of fine children
arrhatic, relating to a promise, pledge, or pawning
arrhenopiper, one that looks lewdly at men
arter, a felt shoe
arthmotic, relating to a league or union

artigamous, newly wed
artiphrontic, of sound mind
aserous, disdainful; irksome
askera, a fur-lined shoe
aspasian, gladly welcoming
astytic, incapable of erection
asymbatic, irreconcilable
asyretic, relating to lifting one's clothes and exposing one's body; an exhibitionist of this type
atalous, delicate, tender
athanic, not subject to death
athesphatic, great beyond words
athrous, gathered in a crowd; full of mob spirit
aucupate, to hunt or snare birds
axitious, working harmoniously together
azytic, unyoked; unmarried

babacious, chattering; prone to idle talk
banausic, relating to handicraft; made by hand
bastern, a sedan chair
bausic, prudish; priggish
baxa, a wooden shoe
bdolotic, prone to break wind
biastic, one that uses force; relating to the use of force
bisulcate, with two furrows or wrinkles
blichanotic, with running nose
bomolochus, a lickspittle
brabeutic, relating to an umpire
brimage, to snort with indignation
bromation, a light repast
bucranic, bullheaded
bumastous, large-breasted
busycon, a large fig

cacomorphous, ugly in form
cacosmic, relating to a world of evil
caculor, an attendant on a soldier
caecigene, (one) born blind
calendary, an account-book (The *Kalends* were the days for paying bills.)
callonymic, (relating to) a beautiful name
calobate, a walker on stilts; to walk on stilts
calyptic, hidden
candytale, a clothespress
caperate, full of wrinkles
carbatine, a shoe of undressed leather
carica, a dried fig
carnifex, the executioner
carotic, stupefying; strongly soporific
casabund, on the verge of falling
catarrhopic, slanting downwards
cathalic, full of salt; witty
catosopher, a false reasoner; a trickster
catulition, desire for the male
cenocranic, emptyheaded
cesticil, a ring placed on the head to balance and spread the weight of a burden
cestrous, with a rough tongue
cetharion, a dice-box
cethidon, a ballot-box
charoptic, glad-eyed
chasmin, a yawn
chelomatic, marked with knotches
chiromactron, a hand-towel
chironomy, pantomime; gesticulation
chloe, the first green sprouting of the spring
chrysocomic, golden-haired
clanculary, secret; anonymous; one to whom a secret is entrusted
clavicary, a key-maker, a decipherer
closmatic, relating to thread; providing a clue
clunal, relating to the hind parts
cnisa, fumes of cooking fat
colator, an attendant on a priest
colax, a fawning flatterer
coleatic, relating to the penis
columbiate, to bill and coo, to kiss like doves
colythron, a ripe fig
comedonious, given to overeating
compastes, a braggart
compas, a noisy brag

conamence, great effort
conarotic, well-fed; plump
concacation, defilement with dung or feces
concinnity, state of being skilfully put together
concubium, the period of the first sleep at night
confossate, pierced full of holes
coniate, plastered
copelatic, relating to oars
copist, an habitual quarreler; a liar
copriate, to tell obscene stories
copriot, a teller of obscene stories
cornupate, to pierce with horns; to gore; to cuckold
cosmarion, a decoration on a dress
crastinate, to postpone till the morrow
crissate, to ripple the haunches; hence, *crissation*
crustulary, a pastry maker
cuppedous, fond of delicacies

dagma, a bite
dagmatic, biting
damartic, relating to a tamed one, to a wife (*adam,* Greek, untamable; *adam,* Hebrew, man)
danistic, relating to money-lending
degluption, peeling off of skin or shell
deipnetic, relating to mealtime; enjoying one's meals; one that is fond of eating
delema, mischief; damage
demeaculum, an underground passage
dentiscalp, a toothpick
dercunic, sleeping with one's eyes open
dergmatic, relating to or taking a clear view
desipid, out of one's mind
deta, to be sure, naturally
dicrotous, applauding enthusiastically
dmoa, a slave won in war
dolop, one that lays an ambush
dorimachy, a battle with long spears
dormitate, to fall asleep
drupetic, ripened on the tree; ready to fall
dysalotic, hard to take or catch
dysergetic, hard to waken

ecclitic, avoiding work
ecletic, (relating to) forgiving and forgetting
edormiant, sleeping it off
elelichthontic, earth-shaking
elixate, to boil thoroughly; to extract the essence of
emansor, a soldier that overstays his leave, A W O L
emicate, to spring out, to appear suddenly
emosyne, skill in hurling
encratic, having mastery or firm hold; in secure command
enolmon, a three-legged stool
enophile, a lover of wine
entaticous, stimulating; invigorating; aphrodisiac
eoan, relating to the dawn
eolous, shifting, changeable
epacmic, mature; at the highest peak
epaulion, the day after the wedding
ephemerolog, a recorder of trifles
epholly, something dragged along; an extra burden
epicaustic, burnt at the end
epulator, a feaster
epulone, a guest at a banquet
epulonic, relating to carousing
eranist, a contributor to a fund
erannous, lovely
erygmatic, given to belching
erygmelous, loud-bellowing; roaring horrendously
eubrotic, good to eat
euclunious, with pretty buttocks
eucrene, well watered
eucrepit, well shod
euesic, well-pointed (dagger or epigram)
eumorphous, beautifully shaped
euporous, well-provided
eupory, ample resources
eurhine, keen of smell

eurhopic, easily sliding; pleasantly inclined, like the descent to Avernus
euthemonic, well arranged; well managed; neat
euthenctic, beautiful-sounding
evancalous, pleasant to embrace

farciment, a mixture (meat, etc.) for stuffing
forable, susceptible to perforation; (figurative) easily bored
forule, a bookcase
furacious, given to thievery
furuncle, a petty thief

gallinaceous, relating to or full of poultry
gambrinous, relating to or full of beer
gamelial, relating to the nuptials
geitonic, relating to a neighborhood
gemebund, continuously moaning or groaning
geniculate, to bend the knee; with or relating to the bent knee
goneus, a begetter (male)
grasontic, smelling like a goat
gromphadic, relating to or like an old sow
gryptopolist, a dealer in trifles or gewgaws
gynnic, effeminate
gynopiper, one that looks lewdly at women

habra, a favorite slave
halotic, easy to take or catch
hamaxiac, big as a wagonload
hebetate, dulled, blunted; to dull
hebetic, youthful; in early prime
hednon, a wedding present
hedolion, a theatre bench
heliocaustic, relating to sunburn
hemicacous, half bad
hemion, half-ass
hestic, agreeable, pleasing
himeric, yearning for, desiring
himeroomany, sexual intercourse
himertic, yearned for; desired; desirable
hippocome, an attendant on a horseman
hippomanic, lusting after horses
holcade, a ship being towed
homelic, of the same age
homorous, sharing a border
hyphalic, in Davy Jones's locker; that cannot be plumbed
hypocephalian, relating to things under the head (as a cushion)
hypocephalion, something to put under the head
hypopion, a black eye
hythlotic, relating to or characterized by idle talk or nonsense

icuncula, a small image or icon
illacrimable, unmoved by tears, pitiless
illecebrose, seductively attractive
illicitator, a conniving bidder at an auction, to induce higher bids
illitate, to besmear; to overdecorate the (feminine) face
impastuous, unfed; famished
inenodable, that cannot be disentangled; inexplicable
infandous, unspeakable; abominable
infrenate, unbridled
ionthadykin, a shaggy dog
iphigenic, born strong
ipsedixitism, dogmatic assertion; the assumption that one's word establishes the fact

killotic, ass-colored
kinebic, mean with money, niggardly
klobion, a birdcage
knestron, a scraper; a backscratcher
kyma, a pregnant woman
kyphon, a rogue that has been or is in the pillory

lacismatic, all tattered and torn
laicast, a man fond of women, a gynophile
laiscarpotic, extremely lustful
lasanon, a closestool
lathetic, likely to escape notice

lecka, a woman that has just given birth
legulian, an ambulance chaser
leptesic, fine-pointed
leviped, lightfooted
lestic, relating to robbery
lingulacca, a chatterbox
logomachy, a war of words
longomachy, a battle with javelins
lutose, covered with or full of mud

macellary, relating to the food market
manticulator, a purse-snatcher
manticule, a handbag
mantissa, a worthless addition or contribution
medea, the genitals
memnon, jet black (from *Memnon,* King of the Ethiopians)
meraculous, somewhat pure; only slightly soiled or defiled
merulator, a wine-bibber
messonic, relating to boundaries
microlipet, (one that is) annoyed at trifles
microloger, one that collects trifles
micromatic, small-eyed
microthymic, narrow-minded
molobrous, greedy
moreta, a salad with garlic
murial, relating to brine
myron, a sweet juice used as an ointment

namatious, full of springs
nelipot, one that goes barefoot
neophrontic, childish in thoughts
nimeity, overmuchness; superfluity
novendial, lasting nine days, as a wonder or the Roman rites upon a shower of meteorites
nundinate, to go to market to trade
nycterent, one that hunts by night
nygma, a sting; a tiny hole
nystatic, drowsy; relating to drowsiness

oarotic, talkative (Greek *oar* means wife)
ocellate, spotted; with little eyes
ociped, swift of foot
oculeous, full of eyes; "all eyes"
oestrous, always in heat
olbious, full of happiness
olesiptolic, city-destroying
onomasticon, a wordbook; a list of names
opipeuter, a Peeping Tom
opsigon, one late-born
orectic, relating to the appetite
orestian, a mountaineer; relating to mountains
orgiophant, a teacher or revealer of secret rites
orinda, bread made of rice meal
orphny, the utter black of night
orygmadotic, very noisy; relating to uproar
osphrantic, of pleasant odor
oxalm, a sour sauce
oxydersic, sharp-sighted
oxythymous, quick to anger
ozote, many-branched

paigmatic, playful as a child
palaimolops, one that cannot be taught new tricks; a veteran at roguery
pallaptern, round-heeled; a woman of easy virtue
pamphagite, one that eats everything
pannychous, lasting all night
paratiltra, a slave that depilates her mistress
parectate, to reach or attain a marriageable condition; ripe for marriage
paregory, consolation
parra, a bird of ill omen
parthenon, a maiden's room
pauliped, small-footed; one that has little feet
paupercule, a person somewhat poor, one in hard straits
penirate, equipped with a tail or penis
percite, to rouse thoroughly, to excite greatly
peridine, a rover, a pirate

peripole, a streetwalker
peron, a rawhide boot
pervicacious, extremely stubborn
philalethe, one that loves to forget
philalethes, one that loves the truth
phlyarotic, relating to or consisting of silly talk
pholcous, bowlegged
pholeter, a lurker in holes
phorine, thick-skinned
phraster, an expounder; a speaker of empty words
phtheirotic, relating to or infested with lice
plagiger, one that bears the marks of a lashing
plebicole, one that seeks the favor of the common man
plorable, lamentable, deplorable
plysma, water in which something has been washed
pogonology, the study of beards
pollicitator, one that makes promises
polypragmatic, busy with many things
pomerium, a space kept clear, both sides of the wall of a castle or town
popinal, relating to a restaurant
popinary, a lunchroom cook, an egg scrambler
poppizate, to cluck with the tongue and lips
pordy, a noisome noisy annoying breaking of wind
potiuncle, a little drink
prochnial, relating to submission or bending the knee
pronoia, foreseeing, foresight
prosumia, a boat used for scouting or spying
pseudothyron, a secret door or entrance
psexy, a rub down, currying
psocic, infested with book-lice; with an itch for reading
psychrophile, a lover of the cold
ptarmic, that makes one sneeze; relating to sneezing
ptochocracy, government by the poor
ptomatis, a cup that must be emptied before being set down, as it will not stand open-end-up
pulicose, full of fleas
pulifugous, that drives fleas away
pygmic, big as a fist
pyralis, an insect that lives in fire
pyrate, to take a hot or steam bath
pyria, a steam bath
pysmatic, relating to interrogation; always asking questions

quodlibetarian, one that argues impractical or trivial questions; a self-satisfied disputatious person

resex, the stub left on a pruned branch
rhadion, a comfortable shoe
rhanter, a sprinkler (person or instrument)
rhapismatic, relating to spanking or striking with the hand
rhastic, not at all complicated or difficult
rhochthodic, relating to the roaring of the sea
rimator, one that lays open, discloses; an investigator

scaphis, a cup shaped like a boat
scaurous, with large ankles
schalide, a forked stick used as a prop
scommatic, relating to or consisting of jeers or mockery
screator, one that hems and haws
sedularium, a cushion to sit on; the seat of a car
selma, a rowers' bench
sequacious, following; subservient
serotine, happening late
sessile, sitting; relating to sitting
sicary, a dagger man; an assassin
siculary, a stiletto man
sigalous, not saying a word

silenic, bearded but bald
simpule, a small ladle
sirotic, scorching
sophrontic, with a keen mind
speluncate, cavernous; marked with caves or cavities
stalix, a stake for fastening nets
stephanic, relating to a crown or wreath
stigon, one branded or tattooed
stips, a contribution
strophist, one that seeks to wriggle out; a shrewd self-exculpator
stytic, causing erection
sudorium, a sweat-bath; a steamroom
sugillate, to bruise; make black and blue
synchlytic, strewn together; mixed haphazard

talionic, relating to an eye for an eye
talla, onion skin
tamian, one that gives out money
telephanous, visible afar
telkin, one of spiteful nature
tergilla, pigskin
ternate, coming in threes; relating to three
thanatic, very dangerous; death-dealing
thanatous, on the brink of death
thaptomic, relating to funeral rites (of a distinguished person)
thelymachy, a war of women
thelyphantic, manifestly effeminate
theriac, relating to wild animals
thersigenic, race-destroying; genocidic
thetic, relating to menials or service
thriobole, a pebble-tosser; a fortune-teller
thrion, the postlapsarian garb of Adam and Eve (a fig leaf)
titivillity, a thing of little account
tragulary, a hurler of javelins or darts; a scoffer
trestate, a runaway; a coward
triodite, a lounger at meetingplaces; a loafer
triorchid, extremely lascivious
trochadon, a running-shoe
trogalion, a sweet bit to munch
trygotic, relating to dregs
tuburcinate, to eat greedily
typhedan, a dummox
tyrophagous, cheese-eating

uberous, abundant
umbratilous, in the shade; in retirement; private

vanidictor, one that takes the truth in vain
verna, a slave born in the home (hence *vernacular*)
vervagate, to plow a fallow field
vinolent, drunk on wine
vitabund, that should be shunned

xenial, hospitable; friendly to strangers
xiphomachy, a battle with sabers
xyresic, razor-sharp

zacotic, very angry; prone to fits of fury
zatrikion, chess
zogrion, a menagerie

Words from the Latin are even more numerous than those from the Greek, as I shall illustrate with a listing merely of some that employ the prefix *inter*. *Inter* may be used as an intensive; it may mean between; it may indicate mutual activity or relationship. Many of the compounds formed with this prefix are still current (e.g., *interest, interdenominational, intervene*). Of the less remembered, some are self-evident and just listed below, some are briefly defined.

interamnian, situate between two rivers

interarboration, the overlapping of branches of two or more trees

interaulic, between royal courts, as *interaulic politics*

interbastate, to quilt, to sew between cotton or other material so as to hold in place. Also *interbaste*

interbrace, to embrace mutually

interchaff, to exchange jests

interchase, to adorn or decorate between

intercide, to interrupt; to fall through (literally and figuratively)

interclassis, an intermediate bookcase in a library, as between two larger ones, or two windows

intercolline, between hills

intercome

intercommonage, the practice of sharing with others, especially used of pasture, of "the commons". Hence, *intercommoner*

intercrural, between the legs. Urquhart in his translation (1693) of Rabelais, speaks of *my intercrural pudding*

interdespise

interdigitate, to lock together the fingers of the hand

interduct, a space between sentences, in printing or writing (17th century)

interemption, slaughter

interenjoy

interess, early form of *interest*

interficient, destroying; hence *interfector,* used in 17th century astrology of a baleful planet

interfrication, rubbing together

interfulgent, shining between

intergenital, between the genital parts

intergential, international, between races

intergerine, like a partition-wall

intergern, to snarl back

interination, ratification, confirmation

interition, a perishing, going to ruin

interknow, to know mutually; *interknowledge,* shared knowledge

interlaqueate, entangled

interlucent, shining between; *interlucidation* (between, or mutual)

interluency, a flowing between

interlunation, the period between the old and the new moon; hence, a blank interval. Also *interlune*

intermealary, between meals. Also *intermealiary*

intermeate, to pass through (replaced by *permeate*); to flow between

intermell, to intermingle; also a noun, used of hand-to-hand combat

intermess, something served between courses at a banquet; also used figuratively. Earlier, *entremess*

intermundial, between two worlds

internecion, slaughter, massacre

internecive, a 19th century form of *internecine.* That helpful house-organ of the *New York Times, "Winners and Sinners",* has reminded its readers that *internecine* originally meant very destructive: *internecine* war, war of extermination. Butler used it in this sense in HUDIBRAS (1663): *Th'Egyptians worshipp'd dogs and for Their faith made internecine war.* (The edition of 1674 has *fierce and zealous war.*) Johnson in his *Dictionary* of 1755, misunderstanding this passage, defined *internecine, endeavouring mutual destruction,* and the notion of mutual slaughter has been common in the word since.

internect, to interconnect; *internexion,* mutual connection

interorbital, between the eyes, as an *interorbital fist*

interosculate, to be or form a go-between, a connecting link; to interpenetrate

interplicate, to fold between or together

interpolity, mutual citizenship; used by Bulwer-Lytton in THE CAXTONS (1849)

interpretament, used by Milton (1645) for *interpretation*

interprice, a 16th century variant of *enterprise*

interpoint, to mark with points ("periods") between words and clauses; also figuratively, as *words interpointed with sighs.* Also *interpunct*

interrogue, interrogate

interscapular, between the shoulderblades, as a back-slapping

intersilient, appearing suddenly in the midst of something; leaping between

intersomnial, within a dream

intersomnious, "between sleeping and waking"

interturb, to disturb by interrupting. *Don't interturb me!* Also *interturbation; interturber*

intervigilate, to watch intermittently. Hence, *intervigilation;* an *intervigilant.* Also an adjective, *intervigilant,* likely to lose one's liberty

interwish, to make a joint or mutual wish; also a noun